Matthew Helmke
Andrew Hudson
Paul Hudson

Ubuntu

UNLEASHED

2011 Edition

SAMS | 800 East 96th Street, Indianapolis, Indiana 46240 USA

Ubuntu Unleashed 2011 Edition:
Covering 10.10 and 11.04

ISBN-13: 978-0-672-33344-6

ISBN-10: 0-672-33344-9

Library of Congress Cataloging-in-Publication Data

Helmke, Matthew.

Ubuntu unleashed : covering 10.10 and 11.04 / Matthew Helmke, Andrew Hudson, Paul Hudson. – 6th ed.

p. cm.

Rev. ed. of: Ubuntu unleashed : covering 9.10 and 10.4 / Andrew Hudson ... [et al.]. 2010.

ISBN 978-0-672-33344-6 (pbk. : alk. paper)

1. Ubuntu (Electronic resource) 2. Linux. 3. Operating systems (Computers) I. Hudson, Andrew, 1978- II. Hudson, Paul, 1979- III. Title.

QA76.76.063U36 2010

005.4'32–dc22

2010043436

Library of Congress Cataloging-in-Publication data is on file.

Printed in the United States of America

First Printing December 2010

Trademarks

Warning and Disclaimer

Bulk Sales

Pearson offers excellent discounts on this book when ordered in quantity for bulk purchases or special sales. For more information, please contact:

U.S. Corporate and Government Sales
1-800-382-3419
corpsales@pearsontechgroup.com

For sales outside of the U.S., please contact:

International Sales
+1-317-581-3793
international@pearsontechgroup.com

Acquisitions Editor
Debra Williams Cauley

Development Editor
Michael Thurston

Managing Editor
Sandra Schroeder

Project Editor
Mandie Frank

Copy Editor
Barbara Hacha

Indexer
Brad Herriman

Proofreader
Jennifer Gallant

Technical Editor
Dallas Releford

Publishing Coordinator
Kim Boedigheimer

Multimedia Developer
Dan Scherf

Cover and Interior Designer
Gary Adair

Composition
Mark Shirar

Contents at a Glance

Table of Contents

About the Authors

Matthew Helmke is an active member of the Ubuntu community. He is an administrator for the Ubuntu Forums (www.ubuntuforums.org) and chairman of the Ubuntu Forums Council. He coauthored the most recent editions of The Official Ubuntu Book. Matthew first used UNIX in 1987 while studying LISP on a Vax in a summer program at Northern Arizona University. He has run a business using only free and open-source software, has consulted, and is currently working on a master's degree in Information Resources and Library Science at the University of Arizona while working as the Senior Technical Documentation Specialist for iPlant Collaborative (www.iplantcollaborative.org). The iPlant Collaborative project, among other things, is creating an advanced bioinformatics cyberinfrastructure to help biologists solve grand challenges in the plant sciences. You can find out more about Matthew at matthewhelmke.com or drop him a line with errata or suggestions at matthew@matthewhelmke.com.

Andrew Hudson is a freelance journalist who specializes in writing about Linux. He has significant experience in Red Hat and Debian-based Linux distributions and deployments and can often be found sitting at his keyboard tweaking various settings and config files just for the hell of it. He lives in Wiltshire, which is a county of England, along with his wife, Bernice, and their son, John. Andrew does not like Emacs. He can be reached at andy.hudson@gmail.com.

Paul Hudson is a recognized expert in open-source technologies. He is also a professional developer and full-time journalist for *Future Publishing*. His articles have appeared in *Mac Format, PC Answers, PC Format, PC Plus,* and *Linux Format*. Paul is passionate about free software in all its forms and uses a mix of Linux and BSD to power his desktops and servers. Paul likes Emacs. Paul can be contacted through http://hudzilla.org.

Dedication

To Heather, Saralyn, Sedona, and Philip—the most amazing family a guy could hope for, to my grandfather for always believing in me and teaching me to believe in myself, and to my friends in the Ubuntu community, especially those with whom I work most closely in the Ubuntu Forums.

—Matthew Helmke

Acknowledgments

I am solely responsible for this edition of Ubuntu Unleashed, but freely acknowledge that I am standing on the shoulders of giants. I want to express my gratitude to Andrew Hudson and Paul Hudson for the solid foundation that past editions of the book (up to *Ubuntu Unleashed 2008*) provided to this update. Thanks to Ryan Troy for helping with the 2010 edition. Thank you to the many people who helped with technical edits and advice, especially Andrew Lenards, Robert Day, John Wregglesworth, Jeremy Foshee, and several developers who wanted to remain anonymous. A huge debt of gratitude is owed to the Ubuntu community, Canonical, and Mark Shuttleworth for inviting me to participate in the community, including my role in the forums, a turn on the EMEA membership board, and two Ubuntu Developer Summits. Thanks to the Ubuntu All Stars for the chance to jam with you on guitar. Thank you to the entire Ubuntu community for your labor of love to create this wonderful operating system. Finally, thanks to my colleagues at Pearson, especially Debra Williams Cauley, for the trust placed in me and the opportunity to collaborate on projects like this one.

—Matthew Helmke

We Want to Hear from You!

As the reader of this book, *you* are our most important critic and commentator. We value your opinion and want to know what we're doing right, what we could do better, what areas you'd like to see us publish in, and any other words of wisdom you're willing to pass our way.

You can email directly to let us know what you did or didn't like about this book—as well as what we can do to make our books stronger.

Please note that we cannot help you with technical problems related to the topic of this book, and that due to the volume of mail we received, we might not be able to reply to every message.

When you write, please be sure to include this book's title and author as well as your name and email address. We will carefully review your comments and share them with the author and editors who worked on the book.

Email: opensource@samspublishing.com

Mail: Debra Williams Cauley
Sams Publishing
800 East 96th Street
Indianapolis, IN 46240 USA

Reader Services

Visit our website and register this book at informit.com/register for convenient access to any updates, downloads, or errata that might be available for this book.

Introduction

We are pleased to present the *2011 edition* of *Ubuntu Unleashed.* Ubuntu is a Linux-based computer operating system that has taken the world by storm. From its humble beginning in 2004, Ubuntu has risen to be the vanguard of desktop Linux, as well as a popular choice for servers.

Ubuntu descends from one of the oldest and most revered Linux distributions, Debian. Debian is assembled by a team of talented volunteers, is one of the most stable and customizable distributions of Linux, and is well respected for its quality and technological prowess. It is, however, an operating system for geeks; the bar for entry into the Debian realm is set high, and its user base tends to be highly proficient and expects new users to learn the ropes before joining in. That is both appropriate and okay.

What Ubuntu has done is leverage the quality of Debian to create an operating system that ordinary people can use. That doesn't mean that Ubuntu users are not technologically proficient, just that they do not have to be. In fact, many talented and respected software developers love Ubuntu because it allows them to concentrate on their specific interests instead of the details of the operating system. This book is for these people and for those who aspire to joining their ranks.

If you are new to Linux, you have made a great decision by choosing this book. Sams Publishing's *Unleashed* books offer an in-depth look at their subjects, taking in both beginner and advanced users and moving them to a new level of knowledge and expertise. Ubuntu is a fast-changing distribution that has an updated release twice a year. We have tracked the development of Ubuntu from early on to make sure that the information in this book mirrors closely the development of the distribution. A full copy of Ubuntu is included on the enclosed disc, and it is possible for you to install Ubuntu from that disc in less than an hour!

Do not let the reputation of Linux discourage you, however. Many people who have heard of Linux think that it is found only on servers, looking after websites and email. Nothing could be further from the truth. Distributions like Ubuntu are making huge inroads in to the desktop market. Corporations are realizing the benefits of running a stable and powerful operating system that is easy to maintain and easy to secure. The best part is that as Linux distributions make improvements, the majority of those improvements are shared freely, allowing you to benefit from the additions and refinements made by one distribution, such as Red Hat, while continuing to use a different distribution, such as Ubuntu, which also shares its improvements. You can put Ubuntu to work today and be assured of a great user experience. Feel free to make as many copies of the software as you want; Ubuntu is freely and legally distributable all over the world—no copyright lawyers are going to pound on your door.

We would like to take a moment to introduce a concept called *"The Three Levels of Listening"* from Alistair Cockburn's *Agile Software Development*, published by Addison Wesley. These describe how a person learns and masters a technique. We all start at the first stage and progress from there. Few reach the last stage, but those who do are incredibly effective and efficient. People aiming for this stage are the very ones for whom we intend this book.

- **Following**—The stage where the learner looks for one very detailed process that works and sticks to it to accomplish a task.
- **Detaching**—The stage where the learner feels comfortable with one method and begins to learn other ways to accomplish the same task.
- **Fluent**—The stage where the learner has experience with or understanding of many methods and doesn't think of any of them in particular while doing a task.

A myriad of books focus on the first set of users. This is not one of them. It is our goal in *Ubuntu Unleashed* to write just enough to be sufficient to get you from where you are to where you want or need to be. This is not a book for newcomers who want or need every step outlined in detail, although we do that occasionally. Ubuntu Unleashed is intended for intermediate and advanced users, or those who wish to become one. Our goal is to give you a nudge in the right direction, to help you enter the higher stages by exposing you to as many different tools and ideas as possible; we want to give you some thoughts and methods to consider, and spur you on to seek out more.

Licensing

Software licensing is an important issue for all computer users and can entail moral, legal, and financial considerations. Many consumers think that purchasing a copy of a commercial or proprietary operating system, productivity application, utility, or game conveys ownership, but this is not true. In the majority of cases, the *end user license agreement*

(EULA) included with a commercial software package states that you have paid only for the right to use the software according to specific terms. This generally means you may not examine, make copies, share, resell, or transfer ownership of the software package. More onerous software licenses enforce terms that preclude you from distributing or publishing comparative performance reviews of the software. Even more insidious licensing schemes (and supporting legislation, especially in the United States) contain provisions allowing onsite auditing of the software's use!

This is not the case with the software included with this book. You are entirely free to make copies, share copies, and install the software on as many computers as you want—we encourage you to purchase additional copies of this book to give as gifts, however. Be sure to read the README file on the disc included with this book for important information regarding the included software and disk contents. After you install Ubuntu, go to www.gnu.org/licenses/gpl.html to find a copy of the GNU GPL. You will see that the GPL provides unrestricted freedom to use, duplicate, share, study, modify, improve, and even sell the software.

You can put your copy of Ubuntu to work right away in your home or at your place of business without worrying about software licensing, per-seat workstation or client licenses, software auditing, royalty payments, or any other type of payments to third parties. However, be aware that although much of the software included with Ubuntu is licensed under the GPL, some packages on this book's disc are licensed under other terms. There is a variety of related software licenses, and many software packages fall under a broad definition known as *open source*. Some of these include the Artistic License, the BSD License, the Mozilla Public License, and the Q Public License.

For additional information about the various GNU software licenses, browse to www.gnu.org/. For a definition of open-source and licensing guidelines, along with links to the terms of nearly three dozen open-source licenses, browse to www.opensource.org/.

Who This Book Is For

This book is for anyone who wants to go beyond basic beginner uses for Ubuntu. Although the contents are aimed at intermediate to advanced users, new users who pay attention will benefit from the advice, tips, tricks, traps, and techniques presented in each chapter. Pointers to more detailed or related information are also provided at the end of each chapter.

If you are new to Linux, you might need to learn some new computer skills, such as how to research your computer's hardware, how to partition a hard drive, and (occasionally) how to use a command line. This book helps you learn these skills and shows you how to learn more about your computer, Linux, and the software included with Ubuntu. Most important, it will help you overcome your fear of the system by learning more about what it is and how it works.

What This Book Contains

Ubuntu Unleashed is organized into seven parts, covering installation and configuration, Ubuntu on the desktop, system administration, programming and housekeeping, and a reference section. A disc containing the entire distribution is included so that you have everything you need to get started. This book starts by covering the initial and essential tasks required to get Ubuntu installed and running on a target system.

If you are new to Ubuntu, read the chapters in Part I, "Installation and Configuration" first. You will learn the following:

- Detailed steps that walk you through installation
- How to configure Ubuntu to suit your tastes
- Foundational knowledge that enables you to understand Ubuntu

Part II, "Desktop Ubuntu," is aimed at users who want to use Ubuntu on desktop systems. You will learn the following:

- How to access the Internet in traditional and unique ways
- The productivity applications that are included and some others that are available
- How to enjoy multimedia in Ubuntu
- Other options for desktop software
- An introduction to games in Ubuntu

Part III, "System Administration," covers

- Managing users and groups
- Automating tasks and using shell scripts
- Monitoring system resources and availability
- Backup strategies and software
- Networking
- Remote access

Part IV, "Ubuntu as a Server" gives you the information you need to start building your own file, web, and other servers for use in your home or office.

- File and print servers
- Web servers
- Using FTP for serving files across the Internet and local networks
- Building and deploying email servers

- Proxying
- Database creation, management, and manipulation
- Using LDAP for storing information on users and security
- The basics of LTSP
- Using Ubuntu with cloud computing

Part V, "Programming Linux," provides a great introduction to how you can extend Ubuntu capabilities even further using the development tools supplied with it. We introduce

- Opportunistic developments
- Helping with testing Ubuntu releases
- Programming in Perl, Python, PHP, C, C++ and Mono

Part VI, "Ubuntu Housekeeping," looks at some of the more advanced skills you need to keep your system running in perfect condition, including the following:

- Managing software on your computer
- Securing your machine against attack from outsiders and viruses
- Performance tuning
- Kernel and module management

The references in Part VII, "Appendixes," give you scope to explore in even more depth some of the topics covered in this book as well as historical context to Ubuntu and installation resources.

Conventions Used in This Book

A lot of documentation is included with every Linux distribution, and Ubuntu is certainly no exception. It is impossible to cover every option of every command included in the distribution and, going with our intent to help you become fluent, we focus on teaching you how to find information you need while giving a quality overview worthy of the intermediate or advanced user. However, this book offers numerous tables of various options, commands, and keystrokes to help condense, organize, and present information about a variety of subjects.

This edition is also packed full of screenshots to illustrate Ubuntu-specific graphical utilities—especially those related to system administration or the configuration and administration of various system and network services.

To help you better understand code listing examples and sample command lines, several formatting techniques are used to show input and ownership. For example, if the command or code listing example shows typed input, the input is formatted in boldface, as follows:

```
$ ls
```

If typed input is required, as in response to a prompt, the sample typed input also is in boldface, like so:

```
Delete files? [Y/n] y
```

All statements, variables, and text that should appear on your display use the same boldface formatting. In addition, command lines that require root or super-user access are prefaced with the `sudo` command, as follows:

```
$ sudo printtool &
```

Command-line examples that any user can run are prefaced with a dollar sign ($), like so:

```
$ ls
```

The following elements provide you with useful tidbits of information that relate to the discussion of the text:

NOTE

A note provides additional information you might find useful as you are working. Notes augment a discussion with ancillary details or point you to an article, a whitepaper, or another online reference for more information about a specific topic.

TIP

A tip contains a special insight or a timesaving technique, as well as information about items of particular interest to you that you might not find elsewhere.

CAUTION

A caution warns you about pitfalls or problems before you run a command, edit a configuration file, or choose a setting when administering your system.

SIDEBARS CAN BE GOLDMINES

Just because it is in a sidebar does not mean that you will not find something new here. Be sure to watch for these elements that bring in outside content that is an aside to the discussion in the text. You will read about other technologies, Linux-based hardware, and special procedures to make your system more robust and efficient.

Other formatting techniques include the use of italics for placeholders in computer command syntax. Computer terms or concepts are also italicized upon first introduction in text.

Finally, you should know that all text, sample code, and screenshots in *Ubuntu Unleashed* were developed using Ubuntu and open-source tools.

Read on to start learning about and using the latest version of Ubuntu. Experienced users will want to consider the new information in this edition when planning or considering upgrades. There are many Linux distributions from different vendors, but many derive from, or closely mimic, the Debian distribution.

CHAPTER 1

Installing Ubuntu

IN THIS CHAPTER

- Before You Begin the Installation
- Step-by-Step Installation
- Reference

Not that long ago, the mere mention of installing Linux struck fear into the hearts of mortal men. Thanks to a campaign of fear, uncertainty, and doubt (commonly referred to as FUD), Linux garnered a reputation as something of an elitist operating system that could be installed, configured, and used only by extreme computer geeks and professionals. Nowadays, it is a different story entirely, and Ubuntu is one of the easiest distros to install. In this chapter, we cover how to get started with the install disc, including booting into Ubuntu Live CD to test your system. Then we cover the actual installation of Ubuntu, looking at the various options available. The whole process is pain free with Ubuntu, as you are about to learn.

Before You Begin the Installation

Installing a new operating system is a major event, and you should make sure that you have properly thought through what is going to take place. The first thing to consider is how the hardware will be affected by the software that you propose to install. Although Ubuntu will run well on a wide variety of hardware, it is worth while checking your hardware components because there may be a banana skin waiting for you to slip on. This section provides some areas for you to investigate and think about, and may even save you hours of frustration when something goes wrong. Problems are becoming less frequent, but they still crop up occasionally.

You start by researching and documenting your hardware. This information will prove helpful later on during the installation.

Researching Your Hardware Specifications

At the absolute minimum, you should know the basics of your system, such as how much RAM you have installed and what type of mouse, keyboard, and monitor you have. Knowing the storage capacity and type of hard drive you have is important because it will help you plan how you will divide it up for Ubuntu and troubleshoot if problems occur. A small detail, such as whether your mouse uses the USB or PS/2 interface, will ensure proper pointer configuration—something that should happen without any problem, but you will be glad you knew in case something does go wrong! The more information you have, the better prepared you will be for any problems.

You can make an inventory or at least a quick list of some basic features of your system. Again, the items you most want to know include the amount of installed memory, the size of your hard drive, the type of mouse, the capabilities of the display monitor (such as maximum resolution), and the number of installed network interfaces (if any).

Installation Options

Ubuntu is made available in three main forms: the Desktop CD, the Server install CD, and the Alternate install CD (we are not including derivative distributions like Kubuntu or Ubuntu Netbook edition in this list). For most people, the Desktop CD will be what you want; the alternate is mainly used for upgrading existing Ubuntu users to the latest version, as well as allowing installation on either low-powered systems or in places where fine-tuned, custom requirements exist. The Server install CD can get a LAMP server up and running in about 20 minutes (Linux, Apache, MySQL, and PHP), but as you will learn in this book, all these components are available to the Ubuntu default distribution.

Planning Partition Strategies

Partitioning is a topic that can make novice Linux users nervous. Coming from a Microsoft world, where you might be used to having just one hard drive, it can seem a bit strange to use an operating system that makes partitioning a hard drive possible or even preferable and common.

Depending on your needs, you can opt to have a single large partition to contain everything, or you may prefer to segment your installation across several partitions to match your individual needs.

If you are installing Ubuntu in a corporate or business environment, the needs of the business should be a primary concern. Be careful to ensure that you build in an adequate upgrade path that allows you to extend the life of the system and add any additional storage or memory.

Knowing how software is placed on your hard drive for Linux involves knowing how Ubuntu organizes its file system. This knowledge will help you make the most out of hard drive space. In some instances, such as when you're planning to have user directories mounted via NFS or other means, this information can help head off data loss, increase security, and accommodate future needs. Create a great system, and you'll be the hero of information services. The Linux file system is covered along with commands to manipulate files and directories in Chapter 4, "Command Line Quickstart."

To plan the best partitioning scheme, research and know the answers to these questions:

- How much disk space does your system require?
- Do you expect your disk space needs to grow significantly in the future?
- Will the system boot only Ubuntu, or do you need a dual-boot system?
- How much data will require backup, and what backup system will work best? (See Chapter 13, "Backing Up" for more information on backing up your system.)

DVD INSTALLATION JUMP START

To install Ubuntu Desktop from the disc included with this book, you must have at least a 1GHz Pentium 4 CPU, 5GB of hard drive space, and 512MB RAM. A monitor with a display resolution of 1024 x 768 is strongly recommended.

The Boot Loader

During installation, Ubuntu automatically installs GRUB2 (Grand Unified Boot Loader) to the Master Boot Record (MBR) of your hard drive. Handily enough, it also detects any other operating systems, such as Windows, and adds entries in GRUB2 as appropriate. If you have a specific requirement not to install GRUB2 to the MBR, you need to install using the Alternate disc, which will allow you to specify the install location for GRUB2.

Installing from CD or DVD

The BIOS of most PCs support booting directly from a CD or DVD drive and enable you to set a specific order of devices (such as floppy, hard drive, CD-ROM, or USB) to search for bootable software. Turn on your PC and set its BIOS if required (usually accessed by pressing a Function or the Del key after powering on); then insert your Ubuntu install media and boot to install Ubuntu.

Step-by-Step Installation

This section provides a basic step-by-step installation of Ubuntu from the install disc. The install process itself is fairly straightforward, and you should not encounter any real problems.

It is useful to have your computer ready to connect to the Internet so that you can download updates as soon as you have finished the installation. Although it's typically recommended to not have your computer connected up, Ubuntu's unique security configuration means that it effectively blocks all incoming network ports, so it is fairly secure until you start opening these ports.

Installing

To get started, insert the DVD into your drive and reboot your computer. The initial screen offers a variety of languages for you to use during installation (see Figure 1.1) and two options. Try Ubuntu boots and runs Ubuntu from the CD without making any changes to your system so that when you remove the CD and reboot, everything will be as it was before. Install Ubuntu will install Ubuntu alongside or instead of your current operating system. Select Install Ubuntu to begin.

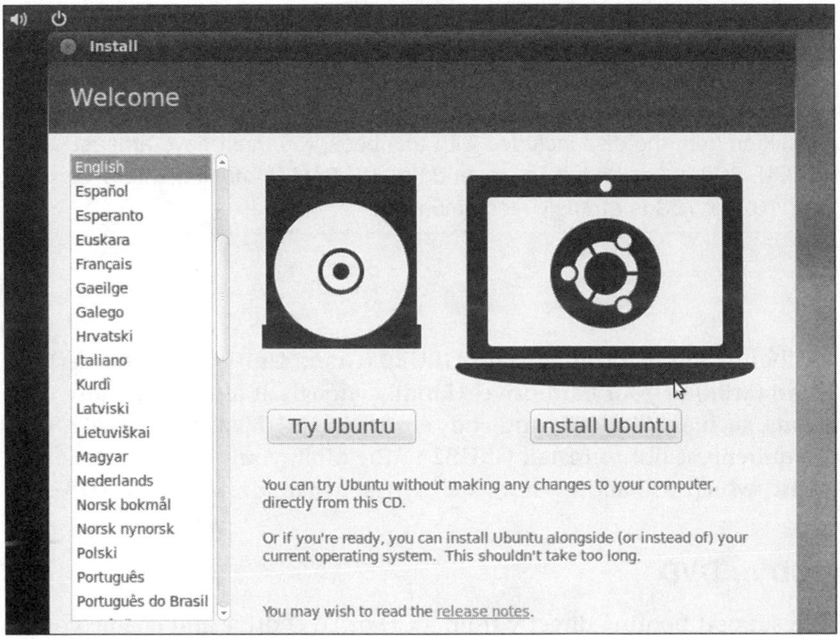

FIGURE 1.1 Choose a language for the installation in this opening screen.

Figure 1.2 shows the Preparing to Install Ubuntu screen. If you select the two check boxes at the bottom, Ubuntu downloads extra software, such as multimedia codecs and any software updates that have been released since the disk was created, and includes them in the installation. Doing so is recommended.

If other operating systems are found on your system, you will be given the option to install Ubuntu alongside them or to erase them and use the whole disk for Ubuntu.

Next, you have the option to either erase and use the entire hard disk for your installation (recommended for people who are new to Linux and are nervous about partitioning a hard drive) or specifying partitions manually, which is not as difficult as it sounds, as shown in Figure 1.3.

Because this is a book for people who want a deeper understanding of their system, we recommend a simple partitioning scheme here and give some reasons for our choices.

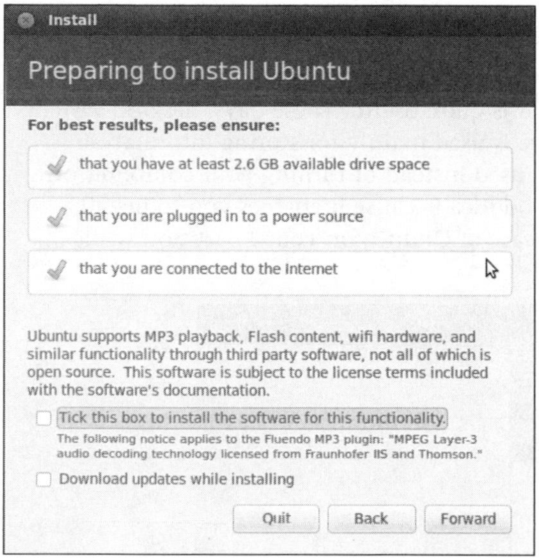

FIGURE 1.2 Before proceeding, double-check that your system meets the requirements shown.

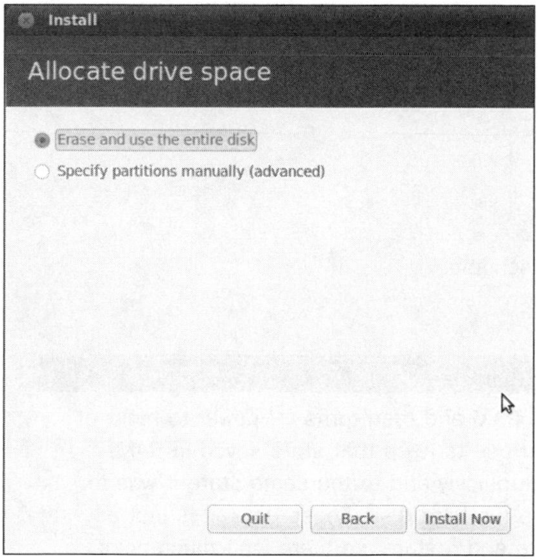

FIGURE 1.3 What do you want to do with your hard drive?

Your needs may vary, so we give some principles to consider so that you may adjust our recommendations to your situation.

Most users will benefit from three simple partitions, shown in Figure 1.4. Here we have a swap partition, a root partition (denoted by /), and a home partition where data for each user on the system will be stored. The swap partition was previously used for those times when there was not enough memory for running processes, so the Linux kernel could move stored information from RAM to the hard drive and use that swap space as extra RAM. This is slow, but there are times when it is quite useful. These days, desktop systems come with more memory, and the swap space is used mainly for storing information during suspend and hibernate, which can be used instead of turning your computer off. Having /home on a separate partition is a good idea because it enables you to install a different Linux distribution or a different release of Ubuntu on your / partition while retaining your user data.

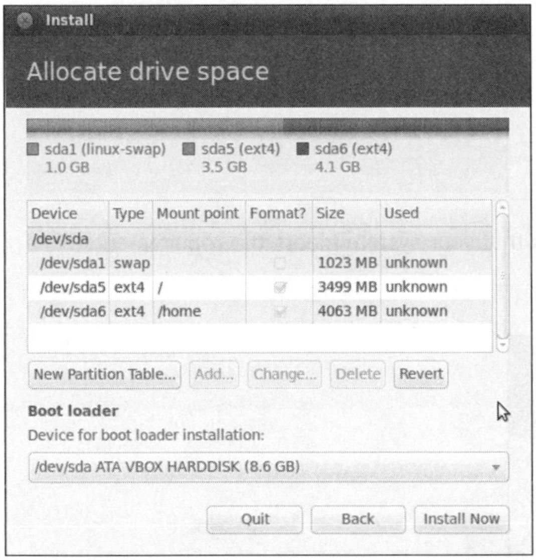

FIGURE 1.4 A simple, but useful partitioning scheme.

NOTE

Suspend saves your current system state to RAM and then turns off power to most of the system, but maintains just enough power use to keep that state saved in RAM. When you restart your system, it comes back quickly and to the same state it was in. Hibernate saves your current system state to the hard disk. These days, it is just as fast to boot from scratch as it is to hibernate and restore, so there isn't much point in using it.

We recommend a / partition of at least 3GB, a swap partition that is about 1.5 to 2 times the size of your installed RAM, and then using the rest of the disk for /home. More complex systems, such as servers, may find more complex partitioning schemes useful, especially when multiple hard drives are available. Read Chapter 4 for a quick discussion of the parts of the Linux file system to get an idea of parts of the file system that could benefit from residing on their own (or even multiple!) partitions or disks.

After you have made your partitioning selections, installation continues by asking about your current location; it helps you select the most appropriate keyboard layout for your system based on that location and the most common language used there, and asks you to enter your name, a username that you will use to login to the system, and a password. You can even choose to encrypt your /home folder during the process.

CAUTION

When you set your password, be sure to remember what you entered! If you forget it, you will not be able to do much with your new system because you will not be able to log on to it.

When setting a password, make sure that it has a mixture of letters and numbers to make it more secure. For instance, a good example of a password is T1a5c0p. Although this may seem like garbage at first glance, the easy way to remember it is by remembering the phrase This Is A Good Choice Of Password, shortened to Tiagcop, and finally substituting some of the letters with similar-looking numbers. Experiment with some phrases to see what you can come up with.

While you are doing this, the Ubuntu install has already begun to copy files to your hard drive. This makes the process even faster than it used to be. Now that all necessary information has been input, you will be shown a series of information screens while the installation is completed. These are filled with interesting content about Ubuntu and are worth reading while you wait.

When the process is complete, you will be prompted to restart the computer. Do so, and remove the install media when it is ejected. Then log in when the reboot is complete. That's it!

In previous editions of this book, this chapter was longer and described a process that was sometimes confusing and fraught with peril. The Ubuntu developers deserve high praise for making this so incredibly easy and fast. The Linux kernel supports more hardware than ever, and the Ubuntu kernel gurus (who make the decisions about what hardware modules to enable, among other things) do a great job so that most hardware works out of the box.

If you do run into trouble, go to ubuntuforums.org as a great first resource, give a list of your hardware (you did make that list we suggested, right?) and any error messages you have received, and you should either find someone who can help you or get some direction to another source of assistance.

First Update

It used to be that the first thing that you needed to do with your new system was update it to the latest package versions. You do this mainly to ensure that you have the latest security updates available. Remember that first installation step where we recommended checking the box to have software updates downloaded during the installation process? That means these updates were acquired during the installation and that your system should be up-to-the-minute current.

If you want to double-check that you have all the current versions of software and security updates installed, see Chapter 32, "Managing Software," for assistance.

Wubi—The Easy Installer for Windows

Also included on the Ubuntu CD is Wubi, which allows you to install an Ubuntu system within Windows. In effect, Wubi creates a large file to hold all the Ubuntu information and provides a way, using the Windows bootloader, to boot into Ubuntu without having to do any partitioning at all. What's more, it's almost as fast as the real thing and much faster than a Live CD. To get started with Wubi, you need to insert the Ubuntu disc into your CD drive while Windows is booted. You'll see a screen similar to Figure 1.5.

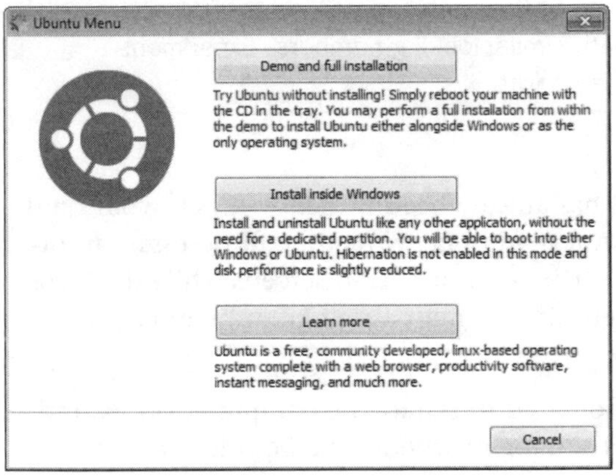

FIGURE 1.5 The auto-start menu gives you a gateway to Ubuntu. Click Install inside Windows to start the Wubi installation.

Click the option to Install inside Windows to be taken to the next screen; there you can choose some basic configuration options using the drop-down menus, as shown in Figure 1.6.

Wubi creates an image file on your hard drive and modifies the Windows bootloader to allow you to boot into Ubuntu or Windows. Don't worry, though; your hard disk hasn't actually been modified, but a rather large file has been created to hold Ubuntu. When you restart your system you'll see the Ubuntu option, so press the down-arrow key and press Enter to begin booting into your new Ubuntu system.

The first time you start up a Wubi Ubuntu installation, it does some post-installation configuration before loading the GNOME desktop. You now have a fully functional Ubuntu system.

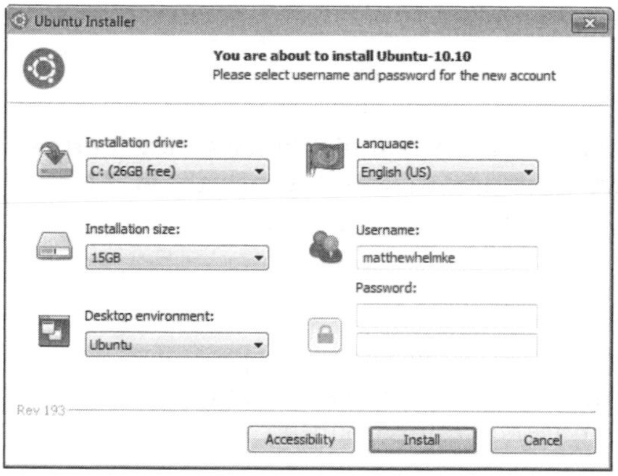

FIGURE 1.6 You can select some configuration options before you start the installation.

If you decide that you want to do a proper installation, you'll need to remove Ubuntu and Wubi. Fortunately, as part of the Wubi installation, an entry is added to the Add/Remove Programs tool in Windows allowing you to quickly and easily remove Wubi and the associated Ubuntu installation. Just remember to back up any files that you want to keep!

Shutting Down

At some point, you are going to want to shut down your computer. As with most things in Linux, there are different ways to do it. You can use the power icon located in the upper-right corner of your screen and its drop-down menu, as in Figure 1.7. From there you can also choose to hibernate (saves a copy of the running state to disk and shuts down) or suspend (saves the current running state to memory).

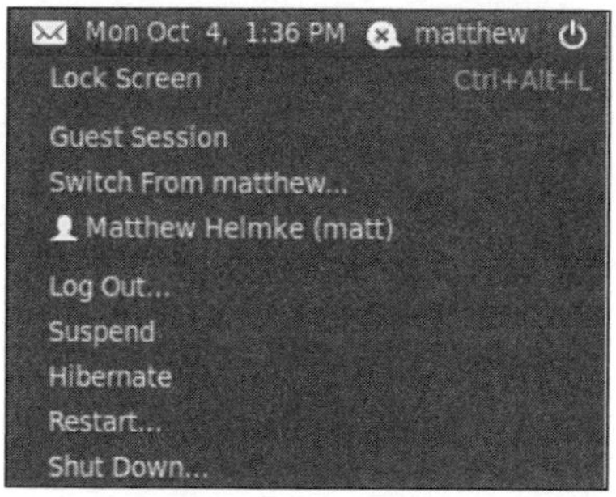

FIGURE 1.7 You have several options in the power icon menu.

If you are working at the command line, you can immediately shut down your system by using the `shutdown` command like this:

```
$ sudo shutdown -h now
```

You can also use the shutdown command to restart your computer, as follows:

```
$ sudo shutdown -r now
```

For new users, installing Ubuntu is the beginning of a new and highly rewarding journey on the path to learning Linux. For Ubuntu system administrators, the task ahead is to fine-tune the installation and to customize the server or user environment.

Reference

- www.ubuntu.com—The place to start when looking for news, information, and documentation about installing, configuring, and using Ubuntu.
- www.ubuntu.com/desktop/get-ubuntu/download—This page has specific information and links for downloading, burning, and installing the current release of the Ubuntu desktop edition. There are comparable links available from the main page for Ubuntu Netbook and Server editions and other projects.
- www.nwc.com/columnists/1101colron.html—How to use Intel's Pre-execution Environment (PXE) protocol to remote boot workstations.
- www.gnu.org/software/grub/—Home page for the GRUB boot loader.

CHAPTER 2

Post-Installation Configuration

IN THIS CHAPTER

Now that the primary task of installing Ubuntu has been completed, you can begin to customize your new operating system. By default, Ubuntu presents you with a pretty blank canvas with which to personalize your experience. Some people choose to stick with the default look and feel, whereas others go for a full makeover.

In this chapter, we'll take a look at getting up and running with Ubuntu, including a quick tour around the desktop. We will also take a look at some of the ways in which you can customize your Ubuntu installation and show you how to do some basic administration tasks. By the end of this chapter, you should feel comfortable enough to move on through the rest of the book.

NOTE

Throughout this chapter, we introduce you to several key applications relevant also to other chapters of this book. We include them here because they are essential to getting your system to work as you intend. You will find it worthwhile to refer back to this chapter as you work your way through the book.

Troubleshooting Post-Installation Configuration Problems

A lot of work has gone into Ubuntu to make it as versatile as possible, but sometimes you may come across a piece of hardware that Ubuntu is not sure about. Knowing what to do in these situations is important, especially when you are working with Ubuntu for the first time.

Because Ubuntu (and Linux in general) is built on a resilient UNIX foundation, it is much more stable than some operating systems. However, even though things might seem to be working fine, Ubuntu could have a problem that might not affect the appearance of the system. In this section, you learn how to examine some of Ubuntu's built-in error logs to help you discover or diagnose unseen problems. Ubuntu has a command that responds with detailed messages that are output directly by the operating system: the `dmesg` command. This command is commonly used with the `grep` command to filter output. The `dmesg` command takes its output directly from the `/var/log/messages` file, so you can choose to either run `dmesg` or to read the file directly by typing `less /var/log/messages`. The output is fairly detailed, so be prepared for an initial shock when you see how much information is generated. You might find it easier to generate a file with the `dmesg` output by using the following command:

```
matthew@seymour:~$ dmesg > dmesg.txt
```

This takes the output from the `dmesg` command and stores it in a new text file called `dmesg.txt`. You can then browse it at your leisure using your choice of text editor, such as `vi` or `emacs`. You can even use the `less` command, like so:

```
matthew@seymour:~$ less dmesg.txt
```

The messages are generated by the kernel, by other software run by `/etc/init.d`, and by Ubuntu's runlevel scripts. You might find what appear to be errors at first glance, but some errors are not really problems (for example, if a piece of hardware is configured but not present on your system).

Thanks to Google, troubleshooting is no longer the slow process it used to be. You can copy and paste error messages into Google's search bar to bring up a whole selection of results similar to the problem you face. Remember, Google is your friend, especially www.google.com/linux, which provides a specialized search engine for Linux. You can also try http://marc.info, which browses newsgroup and mailing list archives. Either way, you are likely to come across people who have had the same problem as you.

It is important to work on finding and testing only one solution to one problem at a time; otherwise, you may end up getting no work done whatsoever. You should also get into the habit of making backup copies of all files that you modify, just in case you make a bad situation worse. Use the copy command like this:

```
matthew@seymour:~$ cp file file.backup20101010
```

You should not use a .bak extension on your backup file because this could get overwritten by another automatic process and will leave you frustrated when you try to restore the original file. I like to use backupYYYYMMDD, as in the preceding code where I used the release date for Ubuntu 10.10: 2010(year)10(month)10(day).

If something breaks as a result of your changing the original file, you can always copy the original back into place using the command like this:

```
matthew@seymour:~$ cp file.backup20101010 file
```

(Something as simple as this can really save your bacon, especially when you are under pressure because you've changed something you shouldn't have changed on a production system. It is better not to make sweeping changes on a production system!)

The sudo Command

You will find as you work through this book that Ubuntu relies on the `sudo` command while working at the command line. This command is used in front of other commands to tell Ubuntu that you want to run the specified command with super-user powers. This sounds really special, and it actually is. When you work using the `sudo` command, you can make wide-ranging changes to your system that impact the way it runs. Be extra careful when running any command prefixed with `sudo`, however; a wrong option or incorrect command can have devastating consequences.

The use of `sudo` is straightforward. All you have to do is enter it like this:

```
matthew@seymour:~$ sudo command commandoptions
```

Just replace the word *command* with the command that you want to run, along with any options. For example, the following command opens your `xorg.conf` file in vi and enables you to make any changes as the super-user before being able to save it:

```
matthew@seymour:~$ sudo vi /etc/X11/xorg.conf
```

Whenever you execute a command using sudo, you are prompted for your password. This is the same password that you use to log in to Ubuntu, so it is important that you remember it.

Sometimes, however, you may want to work with a classic root prompt instead of having to type `sudo` in front of every command (perhaps if you have to work with lots of commands at the command line that require super-user access, for example). `sudo` enables you to do this by using the `sudo -i` command. Again, you are prompted for your password, which you should enter, after which Ubuntu gives you the standard root prompt, as follows:

```
matthew@seymour:~#
```

From here, you can execute any command without having to keep entering `sudo`.

Software Update

This topic is covered in greater detail in Chapter 32, "Managing Software," but it is worthy of a quick mention now so that from the start you can benefit from any available security and bug fixes. The easiest way to check for updates is Update Manager, which is really a GUI wrapper for the command `apt-get`. Open Update Manager from the menu at System, Administration, Update Manager. When the window opens, click Check and enter your password. Update Manager then checks the Ubuntu software repositories to determine whether any updates are available. When it detects that new versions of installed software

are available, they will appear in the window. Each one has a check box that you can uncheck if you don't want to install a particular software update. Then click Install Updates to complete the process (Figure 2.1). Software repositories are discussed later in this chapter.

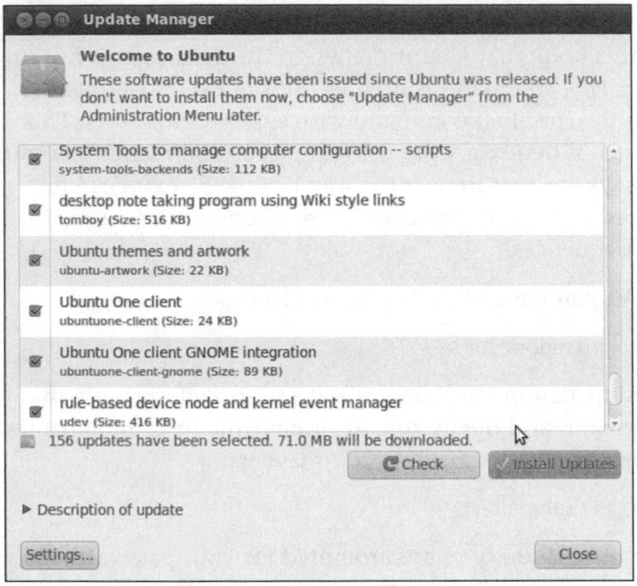

FIGURE 2.1 Update Manager showing available software updates.

Another way of updating your system is to use the command line. This is vital on servers that do not have a GUI installed, and it is sometimes quicker than using Update Manager on a desktop computer. I like to use the command line to manage all the computers on my home network because I can use SSH to connect to each from a terminal and perform updates from another room in the house, and anyone using that computer is left undisturbed. You will learn how to connect like this later in the book; I just want to whet your appetite for now.

To use the command line, go to the Applications, Accessories menu and select Terminal. This is the command line (commonly referred to as the *terminal*) and is one of the most powerful features of Linux. It is covered in more detail in Chapter 4, "Command Line Quickstart," and Chapter 35, "Command Line Masterclass," so we won't delve too deeply here.

You are greeted with a prompt similar to the one here:

```
matthew@seymour:~$
```

A blinking cursor also displays. Ubuntu is awaiting your first command. Here we want to issue the following command:

```
matthew@seymour:~$ sudo apt-get update
```

This command tells the package management utility apt-get to check the Ubuntu repositories and look for any updates to your installed software. In a matter of seconds, Ubuntu completes all of this, and your screen should look something like this:

```
matthew@seymour:~$ sudo apt-get update
[sudo] password for matt:
Hit http://security.ubuntu.com maverick-security Release.gpg
Ign http://security.ubuntu.com/ubuntu/ maverick-security/main Translation-en
Hit http://us.archive.ubuntu.com maverick Release.gpg
Ign http://us.archive.ubuntu.com/ubuntu/ maverick/main Translation-en
Ign http://us.archive.ubuntu.com/ubuntu/ maverick/main Translation-en_US
Ign http://security.ubuntu.com/ubuntu/ maverick-security/main Translation-en_US
Ign http://security.ubuntu.com/ubuntu/ maverick-security/multiverse Translation-en
Ign http://security.ubuntu.com/ubuntu/ maverick-security/multiverse Translation-en_US
Ign http://security.ubuntu.com/ubuntu/ maverick-security/restricted Translation-en
Ign http://security.ubuntu.com/ubuntu/ maverick-security/restricted Translation-en_US
Ign http://security.ubuntu.com/ubuntu/ maverick-security/universe Translation-en
Ign http://security.ubuntu.com/ubuntu/ maverick-security/universe Translation-en_US
Ign http://us.archive.ubuntu.com/ubuntu/ maverick/multiverse Translation-en
Ign http://us.archive.ubuntu.com/ubuntu/ maverick/multiverse Translation-en_US
Ign http://us.archive.ubuntu.com/ubuntu/ maverick/restricted Translation-en
Ign http://us.archive.ubuntu.com/ubuntu/ maverick/restricted Translation-en_US
Ign http://us.archive.ubuntu.com/ubuntu/ maverick/universe Translation-en
Ign http://us.archive.ubuntu.com/ubuntu/ maverick/universe Translation-en_US
Hit http://us.archive.ubuntu.com maverick-updates Release.gpg
Hit http://security.ubuntu.com maverick-security Release
Ign http://us.archive.ubuntu.com/ubuntu/ maverick-updates/main Translation-en
Ign http://us.archive.ubuntu.com/ubuntu/ maverick-updates/main Translation-en_US
Ign http://us.archive.ubuntu.com/ubuntu/ maverick-updates/multiverse Translation-en
Ign http://us.archive.ubuntu.com/ubuntu/ maverick-updates/multiverse Translation-
en_US
Ign http://us.archive.ubuntu.com/ubuntu/ maverick-updates/restricted Translation-en
Ign http://us.archive.ubuntu.com/ubuntu/ maverick-updates/restricted Translation-en_US
Ign http://us.archive.ubuntu.com/ubuntu/ maverick-updates/universe Translation-en
Ign http://us.archive.ubuntu.com/ubuntu/ maverick-updates/universe Translation-en_US
Hit http://security.ubuntu.com maverick-security/main Sources
Hit http://us.archive.ubuntu.com maverick Release
Hit http://us.archive.ubuntu.com maverick-updates Release
Hit http://security.ubuntu.com maverick-security/restricted Sources
Hit http://security.ubuntu.com maverick-security/universe Sources
Hit http://security.ubuntu.com maverick-security/multiverse Sources
Hit http://security.ubuntu.com maverick-security/main i386 Packages
Hit http://security.ubuntu.com maverick-security/restricted i386 Packages
Hit http://us.archive.ubuntu.com maverick/main Sources
Hit http://security.ubuntu.com maverick-security/universe i386 Packages
Hit http://security.ubuntu.com maverick-security/multiverse i386 Packages
```

```
Hit http://us.archive.ubuntu.com maverick/restricted Sources
Hit http://us.archive.ubuntu.com maverick/universe Sources
Hit http://us.archive.ubuntu.com maverick/multiverse Sources
Hit http://us.archive.ubuntu.com maverick/main i386 Packages
Hit http://us.archive.ubuntu.com maverick/restricted i386 Packages
Hit http://us.archive.ubuntu.com maverick/universe i386 Packages
Hit http://us.archive.ubuntu.com maverick/multiverse i386 Packages
Hit http://us.archive.ubuntu.com maverick-updates/main Sources
Hit http://us.archive.ubuntu.com maverick-updates/restricted Sources
Hit http://us.archive.ubuntu.com maverick-updates/universe Sources
Hit http://us.archive.ubuntu.com maverick-updates/multiverse Sources
Hit http://us.archive.ubuntu.com maverick-updates/main i386 Packages
Hit http://us.archive.ubuntu.com maverick-updates/restricted i386 Packages
Hit http://us.archive.ubuntu.com maverick-updates/universe i386 Packages
Hit http://us.archive.ubuntu.com maverick-updates/multiverse i386 Packages
Reading package lists... Done
```

```
matthew@seymour:~$
```

Upgrade your software by entering:

```
matthew@seymour:~$ apt-get dist-upgrade
```

Because you have already checked for updates, Ubuntu automatically knows to download and install only the packages it needs. The `dist-upgrade` option works intelligently to ensure that any dependencies that are needed can be satisfied and will be installed, even if major changes are needed. You can also use the option upgrade. Upgrade it isn't as smart as `dist-upgrade`, but may be a better choice on a production server. Upgrade will not make major changes to software installations, but only those necessary for security and simple package updates. This allows the systems administrator more flexibility to keep up to date with security but keep running setups otherwise unchanged.

COMMAND LINE APT-GET ALTERNATIVES

Ubuntu has an alternative to `apt-get` called `aptitude`. It works in pretty much the same way as `apt-get` with the exception that `aptitude` also includes any recommended packages on top of the requested packages when installing or upgrading. You use `aptitude` mostly the same as you use `apt-get`; for instance, you could issue the command `aptitude update` and it would update the repository information. To upgrade, the options are `aptitude safe-upgrade` and `aptitude full-upgrade`. You can also issue the command `aptitude` without any options, which brings up a text-based package manager that you can use to select packages.

Configuring Software Repositories

Ubuntu uses software repositories to get information about available software that can be installed on your system. Ubuntu is based on a much older Linux distribution called Debian. Debian has access to tens of thousands of different packages, which means that

Ubuntu has access to these packages, too. The Debian packages are made available in Ubuntu's Universe repository. A set of volunteers called Masters of the Universe (MOTUs) are well trained and follow strict guidelines to package software and make even more packages available to Ubuntu users in Universe. The Universe repository is filled with optional and often useful or fun software and is enabled by default, along with other official repositories containing software necessary for Ubuntu to be installed and run in all its various official forms, security updates, and software updates.

You can adjust which repositories are enabled using the Software Sources GUI tool, available in Update Manager by clicking Settings. On the first tab (Ubuntu Software), you have five options to choose from. The default settings are shown in Figure 2.2. It is entirely up to you which options you check, but make sure that as a minimum the first check box is checked to allow you access to Canonical-supported Open Source software, which includes all the packages necessary for a basic Ubuntu installation and a few more that are commonly used. The more boxes you check, the wider your selection of software. It's also a good idea to make sure that the Proprietary Drivers for Devices box is checked in order to benefit from drivers that could enhance your system's performance.

FIGURE 2.2 You can find or add other options under the Updates and Other Software tabs.

OPEN SOURCE VERSUS PROPRIETARY

You may hear some arguments about using proprietary drivers or other software in Ubuntu. Some people feel that it goes against what Open Source stands for because the program code that is used for the drivers or software cannot be viewed and modified by the wider community but only by the original developers or company that owns it. There is also a strong argument that says users should have to undergo the least amount of work for a fully functional system.

Ubuntu takes a middle-of-the-road stance on this and leaves it up to the user to decide. Open source software is installed by default, but options are given to allow proprietary software to be installed easily.

After you are happy with your selections, switch to the Updates tab to configure Ubuntu's behavior when updates are available (see Figure 2.3). By default, both the important security updates and recommended updates are checked to ensure that you have the latest bug fixes and patches. You can also choose to receive proposed updates and *backports* (software that is released for a newer version of Ubuntu but re-programmed to be compatible with the current release), but we'd recommend this only if you are happy to carry out testing for the community, because any updated software from these repositories can have an adverse effect on your system.

FIGURE 2.3 Configure which updates you want, and you want them to be handled in the Updates tab of Software Sources.

Ubuntu also allows you to configure how often it checks for updates, as well as how they are installed. By default, Ubuntu checks daily for updates and, if any are available, will notify you. However, you can change the frequency and the actions Ubuntu carries out when it finds available updates. We recommend keeping the notification-only option because this allows you to see what updates are available prior to them being installed. If you want to save time, choose Download All Updates in the Background to configure Ubuntu to silently download the updates before giving you the option to install them.

CAUTION

We don't recommend selecting the option that automatically installs security updates. It's important that you have the option of choosing to install updates, because there is always the chance that an update may cause problems. The last thing you want is for your system to suddenly stop working because an update was installed that has broken something without your knowledge.

Part of the magic of Ubuntu is the ease in which you can upgrade from major version to major version, such as moving from 10.04 to 10.10. Some Ubuntu releases are called LTS, for Long Term Support, and are intended for those who do not want to upgrade their operating system as often. It is possible to do this. By ensuring that the release upgrade option is set to Long Term Supported releases only, you'll be prompted to upgrade your version of Ubuntu only to what will be the next Long Term Supported version, which is scheduled to be 12.04, to be released in April of 2012.

The Other Software tab lets you add other repositories. It comes by default with everything you need to connect to and use Canonical's partner repository, with non-free (usually in the licensing sense, but occasionally for payment) software from companies that have an agreement with Canonical to make it easily available to interested users. This repository is disabled by default and you must enable it by checking a box next to its entry in the Other Software tab if you want to use it.

Installing Graphics Drivers

Ubuntu is extremely good at detecting and configuring graphics cards. You can check whether you have a video card or some other piece of hardware that could benefit from using a proprietary driver with the Additional Drivers Manager. When you open it, it scans your system, and then you can choose to enable or disable any proprietary drivers found, depending on your personal preference. (See the "Open-Source Versus Proprietary" note earlier in this chapter.)

You can find the Additional Drivers Manager under the System, Administration menu, which is shown in Figure 2.4.

If you elect to use a listed proprietary driver, Ubuntu will first confirm that you are happy to proceed and then automatically download and install the driver. This may require you to log out and back in again for the driver to take effect.

For the most part, Ubuntu will detect and configure the majority of graphics cards from the start, and even if it has problems, it will attempt to give you a display of some sort. This feature is known as BulletProof X, and it allows you access to tools that may help you fix your problem by trying different combinations of graphics cards and monitors.

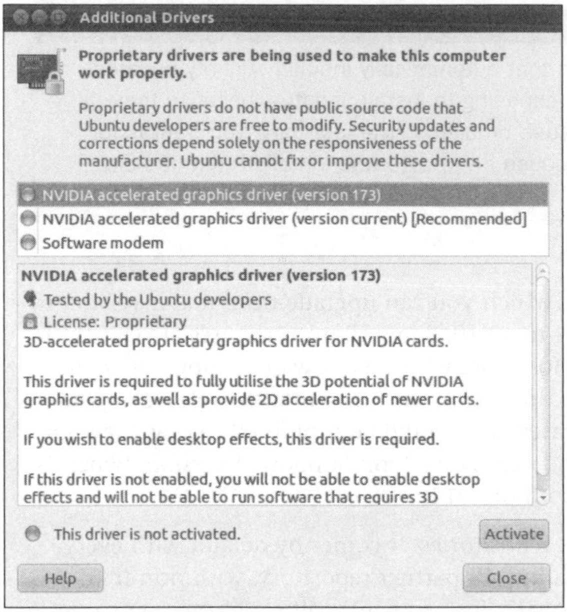

FIGURE 2.4 Toggle the usage of proprietary and other drivers with a simple point-and-click interface.

Changing Ubuntu's Look and Feel

GNOME, the default window manager for Ubuntu, has a number of options to change how it looks and feels. The default theme is Human; this takes a blend of the GNOME Clearlooks theme, mixes it with icons from the Tango Project, and adds a little spice direct from Ubuntu. However, it is not to everyone's taste, so in this section we look at changing the visual style of Ubuntu.

Changing the Desktop Background

Perhaps the easiest and most dramatic change you can make is to change the default desktop background. It is as simple as right-clicking on the desktop and selecting the option to Change Desktop Background to see the dialog box shown in Figure 2.5. Ubuntu comes with a small selection of wallpaper to start with, but you can add others. One favorite source is http://art.gnome.org/backgrounds/, where you can find a great selection of desktop wallpaper and which is linked from Get More Backgrounds Online.

As you click a wallpaper, Ubuntu automatically applies it so that you can quickly see whether you like it. When you are happy with your selection, keep the dialog box open so we can change other aspects of the desktop.

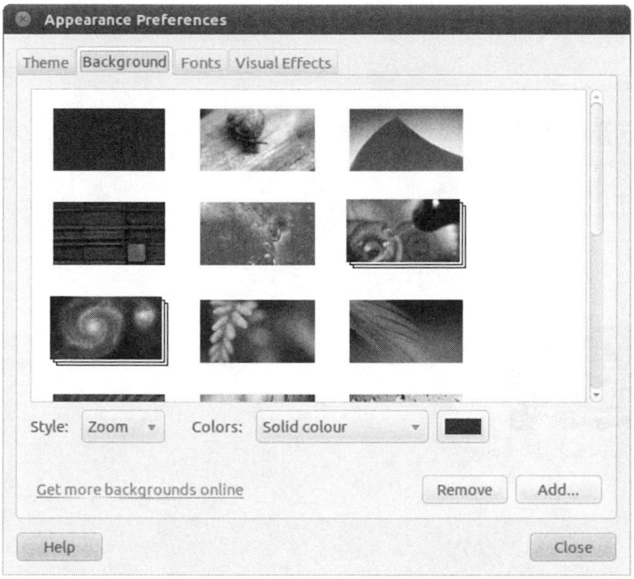

FIGURE 2.5 Choose one of the default wallpapers, or use the Add option to select your own image file.

Changing Colors

Next up are the colors that Ubuntu defaults to. When Ubuntu was originally launched in October 2004, it came with a predominantly brown theme, which over time turned to caramel color, and later to orange. Ubuntu 10.04 introduced a new color scheme using aubergine (purple) and orange and a new overall theme. The theme may be changed as well as the colors it uses. Select System, Preferences, Appearance from the menu. Or if you've kept the dialog box open from the previous section, click the Theme tab. You will see a list of predefined themes that you can choose from (see Figure 2.6).

Alternatively, you can click the Customize button to mix up your own look and feel, as shown in Figure 2.7. You can choose to change the window decorations (title bar, minimize, maximize buttons, and so on), the general color scheme, and the icon theme. As you select an option, Ubuntu automatically applies it to the desktop so you can get an idea of how it will look. When you're happy with your selections, click Close to return to the main Theme dialog box and move on to the next section.

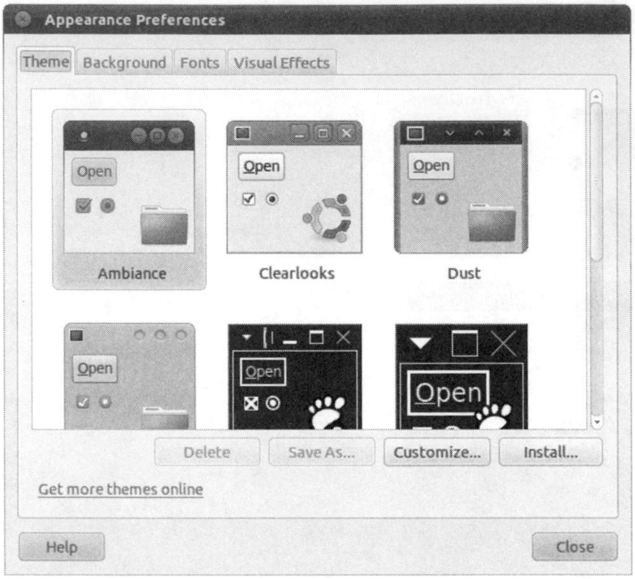

FIGURE 2.6 Either use the default themes or mix and match elements of them to match your specifications.

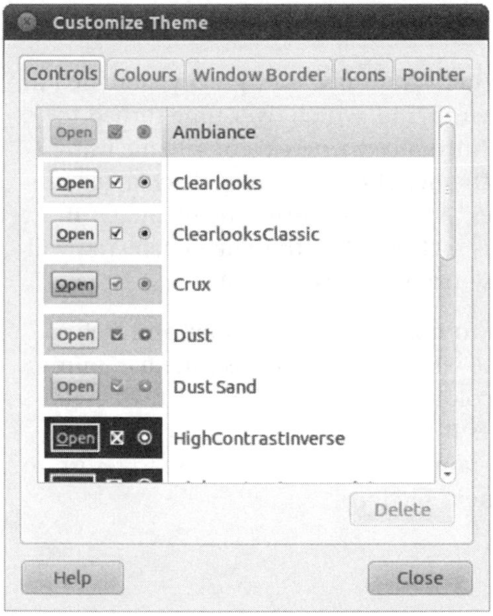

FIGURE 2.7 Use any number of combinations of icons, colors, and window decorations to give you a truly personalized look and feel.

Modifying System Fonts

GNOME also enables you to change the fonts used throughout Ubuntu. If you have difficulty reading one font, just exchange it for another.

In the Appearance dialog box you will see a tab called Fonts. Click this tab to see the options available for changing system fonts, which are shown in Figure 2.8. Click each font name to customize the font used for that function.

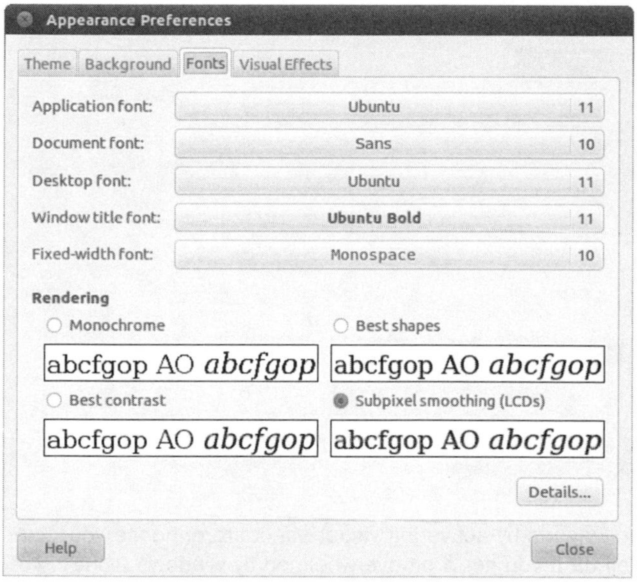

FIGURE 2.8 Keep your fonts relatively simple for ease of use, or if you prefer, indulge your love of calligraphic fonts!

For instance, you may prefer your Window Title Font to be italicized, so click the font name and select the Italic option. Clicking OK immediately applies the change, again giving you a good idea of whether it works. Sometimes a font can look good within the Font Preferences screen, but when it comes to using it, you wonder why on earth you chose it. Choose your fonts wisely!

Visual Effects

Perhaps the most exciting part of Ubuntu is that it comes by default with some snazzy visual effects to enhance the look and feel of your desktop. Click the Visual Effects tab to see the options available for configuring the level of effects, shown in Figure 2.9. In keeping with Ubuntu's philosophy of keeping things simple, there are three options to choose, from which you can elect to turn off all visual effects, use a basic set of effects, or use a lot of visual effects. If you choose this last option you will need to have a relatively fast computer with plenty of memory (at least 1GB) and a decent video card to ensure that the computer doesn't grind to a halt while rendering effects.

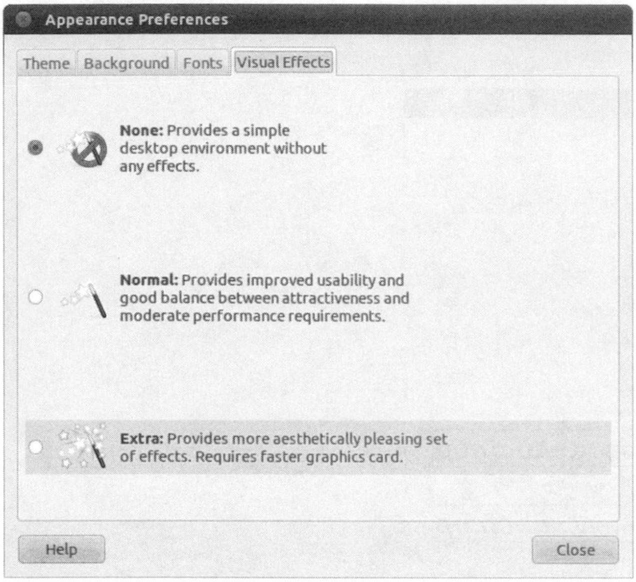

FIGURE 2.9 Wow your friends and colleagues by activating visual effects to enhance your user experience. Alternatively, switch them all off if you get a bit overwhelmed by windows flying everywhere!

Preferred Behaviors

Ubuntu can detect and adapt to certain events. Sometimes you may want Ubuntu to open one application rather than another, or sometimes to not do anything at all. This is called Ubuntu's behavior, and you can modify it to work as you want it to. From the System, Preferences menu, select Preferred Applications.

Preferred applications are the applications that Ubuntu calls on when it wants to open an Internet site, an email, or a terminal (see Figure 2.10). Ubuntu makes it easy for you by automatically detecting the available options. Alternatively, if you want to specify your own particular application that may not appear in the list by default, select the Custom option within the application type and enter the command used to launch the application into the field along with any options, arguments, or switches that you want to use.

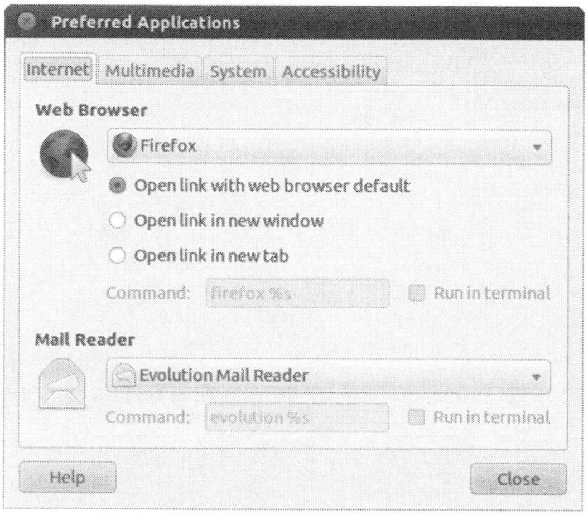

FIGURE 2.10 Setting preferred Internet applications.

Input Devices

The primary interface between you and your computer is your keyboard and mouse. Both of these are essential to the correct usage of your computer, so it is important that they are configured correctly. Windows users will be familiar with the basic options, so it could come as somewhat of a shock to learn that you can do a few more nifty things with a keyboard and mouse in Ubuntu.

Keyboard Shortcuts

If you have used a computer for more than a few years, you probably use keyboard shortcuts for popular commands. Ubuntu allows you to set your own keyboard shortcuts for a variety of system commands. The easy-to-use Keyboard Shortcuts option under System, Preferences lists a lot of actions that you can program shortcuts for (see Figure 2.11).

If you have one of those multimedia keyboards with lots of extra keys, this is the place to configure their use. Just click the shortcut next to the action you want to configure and press the key that you want to map to this action. Repeat this until you have exhausted all the combinations that you want to configure. Then click Close to finish.

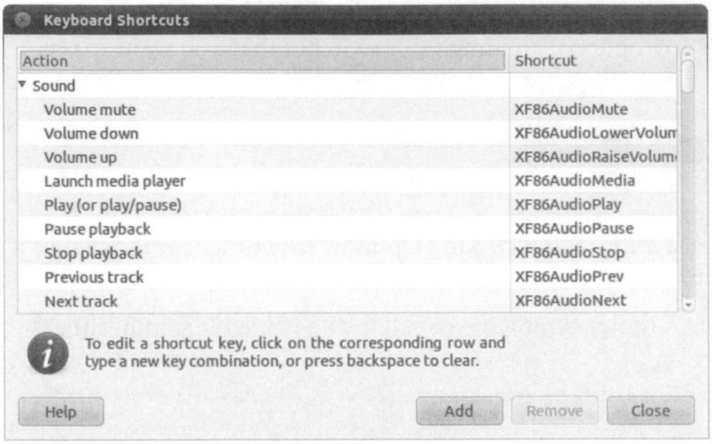

FIGURE 2.11 Make your life easier and your work go more quickly by configuring useful keyboard shortcuts.

Keyboard Layout

Getting the layout of your keyboard right can make a huge difference in how you work. When you installed Ubuntu (see Chapter 1), you specified the default keyboard layout to use. However, there may be times when you need to switch layouts, which you can do using the Keyboard option in the System, Preferences menu (see Figure 2.12).

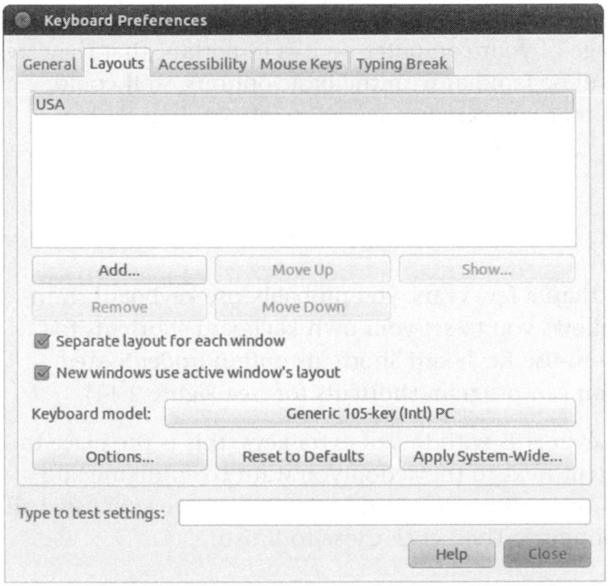

FIGURE 2.12 Use the Keyboard Layout tool to ensure that you have your keyboard settings configured correctly.

I often use this because I also install support for other languages and occasionally type using those languages. This is also valuable for people who prefer to type using Dvorak or other keyboard layout variations within a language group, such as those who prefer either the U.S. or UK variant of the English keyboard (which have different locations for some of the symbols).

You can also use the Keyboard Layout tool to configure special key behaviors. For instance, some people prefer to swap the Caps Lock and left Ctrl key around. You can set this option and others in the Layouts tab by clicking Options. Experiment with what is available here; you may come up with some customization ideas that are useful to you.

Ubuntu can also configure and enforce typing breaks, all in the name of good health. Simply set the length of working time, the duration of the break, and whether you want to be able to postpone. When this is activated at the end of the first length of working time, Ubuntu locks the computer and will not let you log back in until the break duration has passed. However, if you are in the middle of something important, setting the Postpone option may prove useful.

Mouse

There's not much to configuring a mouse. Ubuntu does a great job of detecting most mice. The most useful option from System, Preferences, Mouse is the Locate Pointer option, which highlights the mouse pointer when you press the Ctrl key. If you are left-handed, you can also swap the mouse buttons over, but this is a matter of personal preference.

Detecting and Configuring a Printer

Setting up a printer in Linux used to be so difficult that previous editions of this book included an entire chapter filled with command-line magic and scary looking configuration files. This is no longer the case most of the time. Ubuntu includes drivers for many printers, and it is usually easier to install and use a printer in Ubuntu than in other operating systems. This is not an absolute rule, though. Some printer manufacturers will not write and release drivers for Linux and for some printers, no open source driver exists. It is still a very good idea to spend some time on the Internet searching for printers that are well known to work with Linux before buying. One great resource is the Open Printing database from The Linux Foundation at www.openprinting.org/printers.

If you choose wisely, all you need to do is plug your printer into the computer and turn it on. In many cases, Ubuntu will find the printer and add the driver automatically. Within a couple of minutes, you should be able to use it. You can go to System, Administration, Printing to see all installed and configured printers and change their settings. From here you can choose to enable printer sharing on a network, set options for default print quality, print a test page, and more.

Configuring Power Management in Ubuntu

System, Preferences, Power Management gives you control of how Ubuntu will handle power-saving features in specific situations (Figure 2.13). You can have the display dim the backlight to use less power when on battery, put the display to sleep after a certain amount of inactivity, spin down your hard disks (kind of like turning them off, but not completely; this just makes them stop moving until a request is made from them, saving power in the interim) and set your computer to suspend, hibernate, or turn off when the battery reaches a certain level.

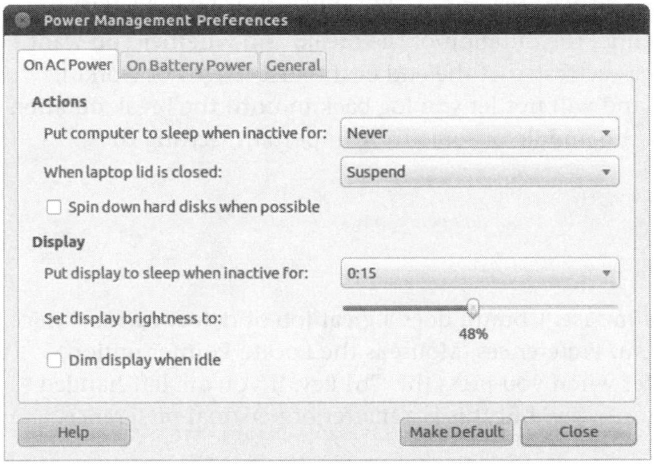

FIGURE 2.13 Configure specific power-related actions with Power Management Preferences.

Ubuntu provides good support for suspend and hibernate. Suspend means that your computer writes its current state to memory and goes into a low-power mode, whereas Hibernate writes the current state of the system to disk and powers off the computer. Either way, your computer will start much faster the next time you use it.

Setting the Date and Time

Linux provides a system date and time; your computer hardware provides a hardware clock-based time. In many cases, it is possible for the two times to drift apart. Linux system time is based on the number of seconds elapsed since January 1, 1970. Your computer's hardware time depends on the type of clock chips installed on your PC's motherboard, and many motherboard chipsets are notoriously subject to drift.

Keeping accurate time is important on a single workstation, but it is critically important in a network environment. Backups, scheduled downtimes, and other networkwide actions need to be accurately coordinated.

The Ubuntu installer *sets the date and time during the installation process when it asks for your location.* If you move or just want to change the settings, for example, to have your computer automatically synchronize its clock with official time servers on the Internet, you can do so.

Ubuntu provides several date and time utilities you can use at the command line or during a GUI session, including these:

- `time-admin`—Ubuntu's graphical date, time, and network time configuration tool
- `date`—Used to display, set, or adjust the system date and time from the command line
- `hwclock`—A root command to display, set, adjust, and synchronize hardware and system clocks

Changing the Time and Date

Ubuntu's graphical tool is the simplest way to set your system date and time and the most obvious for a desktop user. The client is found in System, Administration, Time & Date.

To make any changes to this tool, you need to unlock it by clicking the Unlock button. Only a user who has administrator privileges may use this tool, and you will need to enter your password to authenticate. After you've done this, you are able to change any of the options.

Manually set the date and time in the GUI (Figure 2.14), or have your computer obtain updated date and time information via the Internet by changing the Configuration setting and selecting Keep Synchronized with Internet Servers. To do this, you need to have `ntpd` time daemon support installed. If it is not present, Ubuntu asks whether you want to retrieve it, and then installs it so that you can proceed. After it has been installed, you will be able to select specific Internet time servers to synchronize with (Figure 2.15). You should choose servers close to your location.

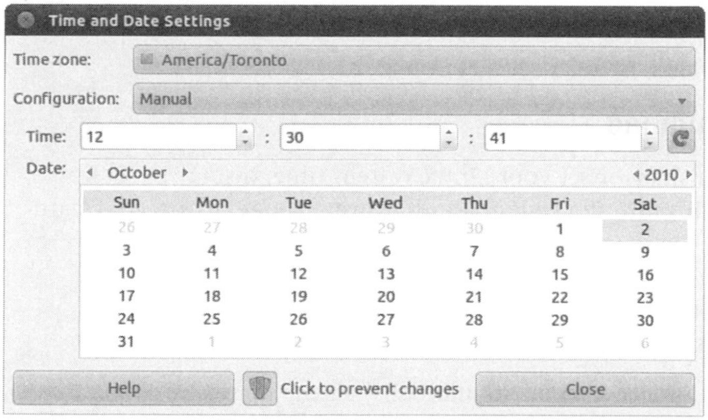

FIGURE 2.14 You can manually set your system date and time.

FIGURE 2.15 Select specific Internet time servers close to your location.

Using the `date` Command

Use the `date` command to display or set your Linux system time. This command requires you to use a specific sequence of numbers to represent the desired date and time. To see your Linux system's idea of the current date and time, use the `date` command like this:

```
matthew@seymour:~$ date
Sat Sep  4 10:20:51 MST 2010
```

To adjust your system's time (for example, to September 4, 2010 at 10:33 a.m.), use a command line with the month, day, hour, minute, and year, like so:

```
matthew@seymour:~$ sudo date 090410332010
Sat Sep  4 10:33:00 MST 2010
```

Using the `hwclock` Command

Use the `hwclock` command to display or set your Linux system time, display or set your PC's hardware clock, or to synchronize the system and hardware times. To see your hardware date and time, use `hwclock` with its `—show` option, like so:

```
matthew@seymour:~$ sudo hwclock —show
Sat 04 Sep 2010 05:25:17 PM MST  -0.806770 seconds
```

Use `hwclock` with its `—set` and `—date` options to manually set the hardware clock, like so:

```
matthew@seymour:~$ sudo hwclock —set —date "09/04/10 10:33:00"
matthew@seymour:~$ hwclock —show
Sat 04 Sep 2010 10:33:09 AM MST  -0.904668 seconds
```

In these examples, the hardware clock has been set using `hwclock`, which is then used again to verify the new hardware date and time. You can also use `hwclock` to set the Linux system date and time using your hardware clock's values with the Linux system date and time.

For example, to set the system time from your PC's hardware clock, use the `—hctosys` option, like so:

```
matthew@seymour:~$ sudo hwclock —hctosys
```

To set your hardware clock using the system time, use the `—systohc` option, like so:

```
matthew@seymour:~$ sudo hwclock —systohc
```

Configuring Wireless Networks

Wireless networking used to be a bear to configure for Linux, requiring a lot of complicated steps to connect to a wireless network. That has become a much easier task, and Ubuntu includes a great utility called Network Manager that makes connecting to and managing wireless networks extremely easy.

When you log in to Ubuntu, you should see the Network Manager applet appear in the top panel (see Figure 2.16). This is the applet that handles and monitors network connections.

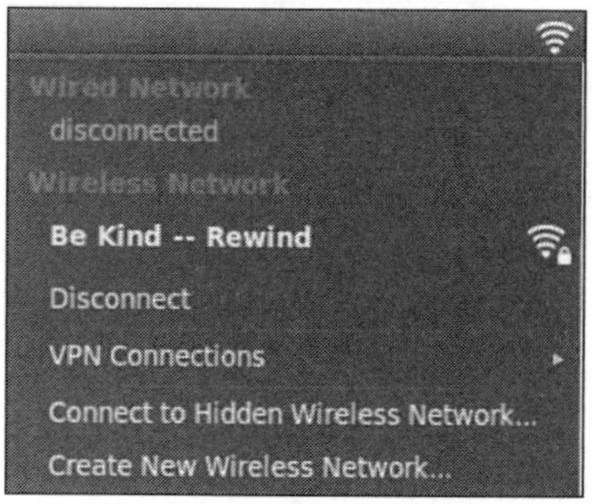

FIGURE 2.16 The Network Manager notification applet, shown here already connected to a wireless network.

Click the applet icon in the toolbar to connect to a wireless network. If your wireless access point broadcasts its SSID, it should appear in the list under wireless networks (similar to Figure 2.16). Click the desired network, and Network Manager will detect what encryption (if any) is in use and ask you for the passkey. Enter this and Network Manager will start the wireless connection. The passkey is then stored in the default keyring, a secure area that is unique to your login. From now on, whenever you log in to Ubuntu and are in range of this network, Network Manager will start the connection automatically.

If for some reason your wireless network does not appear (you might have your SSID hidden), you must use the Connect to Other Wireless Network option, in which you will enter the network name, wireless security type, and when needed, the password for the connection.

Network Manager can handle WEP and WPA Personal encryption. You are advised to use WPA encryption because it is the stronger of the two. WEP encryption is easily broken.

Network Manager can also connect to Cisco VPN connections, using the `vpnc` software. Install this using `synaptic` and you will be able to specify connection settings as appropriate or if you have access to a predefined configuration (`.pcf` file), you can import it directly into Network Manager.

Reference

- www.x.org/—The X.Org Foundation.
- https://help.ubuntu.com/community/InstallingSoftware—Ubuntu Community help documentation for installing software in Ubuntu.
- https://help.ubuntu.com/community/Repositories/Ubuntu—Ubuntu community help documentation defining and describing software repositories.
- https://help.ubuntu.com/community/Printers—Ubuntu Community help for finding printers that work and troubleshooting specific printers.
- https://help.ubuntu.com/community/WifiDocs/WirelessTroubleShootingGuide—Ubuntu Community help for troubleshooting wireless networking.

CHAPTER 3

Working with GNOME

IN THIS CHAPTER

Imagine a world of black screens with white text, or for those of you who remember, dark green screens with light green text. That used to be the primary interface for users to access computers. Computing has moved on significantly and has adopted the graphical user interface, or GUI, as standard on most desktop and workstation platforms.

Ubuntu has a beautiful GUI based on a window manager called GNOME (the Gnu Network Object Model Environment). Based on the ethos of simplicity and elegance, GNOME offers a rich and full interface that you can easily use to be productive. The principal design objective is an intuitive system with sane default settings, meaning that it should be easy to pick up and use, and it also has good localization/internationalization support and accessibility.

GNOME uses the X Window System, the graphical networking interface found on many Linux distributions that provides the foundation for a wide range of graphical tools and window managers. More commonly known as just X, it can also be referred to as X11R7 and X11 (as found on Mac OS X). Coming from the world-renowned Massachusetts Institute of Technology, X has gone through several versions, each of which has extended and enhanced the technology. The open source implementation is managed by the X.Org foundation, whose board includes several key figures from the open source world.

The best way to think about how X works is to see it as a client/server system. The X server provides services to programs that have been developed to make the most of the graphical and networking capabilities that are available under the server and in the supported libraries. X.Org provides versions for many platforms, including Linux and Mac OS X. Originally implemented as XFree86, X.Org was forked when a row broke out over certain restrictions that were going to be included in the XFree86 license. Taking a snapshot of code that was licensed under the previous version of the license, X.Org drove forward with its own implementation based on the code. Almost in unison, most Linux distributions turned away from XFree86 and switched their development and efforts to X.Org.

A desktop environment for X provides one or more window managers and a suite of clients that conform to a standard graphical interface based on a common set of software libraries. When they are used to develop associated clients, these libraries provide graphical consistency for the client windows, menus, buttons, and other onscreen components, along with some common keyboard controls and client dialogs. In this chapter you will learn how to work with GNOME and learn something about the version of X that is included with Ubuntu. If you want to learn more about some of the other desktop environments that are available to use with Ubuntu, including KDE and Xfce, take a look at Chapter 8, "Other Ubuntu Desktops."

THE UBUNTU FAMILY

When people talk about Ubuntu, they generally mean the standard distribution, which uses the GNOME window manager. However, a number of derivatives of Ubuntu use other window managers, and they are freely available for you to download and use. For instance, Kubuntu uses the KDE window manager, whereas Xubuntu uses Xfce. Despite their very visual differences, all three rely on the same core system. It is easy for you to add that window manager to your existing system by using one of the *-desktop meta-packages. These packages are designed to install all the base applications that are linked to that version of Ubuntu, so installing the kubuntu-desktop package would automatically install all the software needed for Kubuntu while retaining your existing desktop environment.

The GNOME Desktop Environment

The GNOME project, which was started in 1997, is the brainchild of programmer whiz Miguel de Icaza. GNOME provides a complete set of software libraries and clients. GNOME depends on a window manager that is GNOME-aware. This means that to provide a graphical desktop with GNOME elements, the window manager must be written to recognize and use GNOME. Some compliant window managers that are GNOME-aware include `Compiz` (the default GNOME window manager in Ubuntu), Metacity (the fallback if the hardware being used is not powerful enough for Compiz), Enlightenment, Window Maker, and IceWM.

Ubuntu uses GNOME's user-friendly suite of clients to provide a consistent and user-friendly desktop. GNOME clients are found under the `/usr/bin` directory, and GNOME configuration files are stored under the `/etc/gnome` and `/usr/share/gnome` directories, with user settings stored in the home directory under `.gnome` and `.gnome2`.

The standard Ubuntu desktop is shown in Figure 3.1.

FIGURE 3.1 Ubuntu's GNOME desktop.

You can configure your desktop in various ways and by using different menu items under the Preferences menu, which can be found as part of the main Desktop menu. The myriad of configuration options allow you to tailor every aspect of your system's look and feel, as discussed in Chapter 2, "Post-Installation Configuration."

Eye Candy for the Masses

Recent development work carried out on X has allowed the introduction of a number of hardware-accelerated effects within Ubuntu and its window managers. No longer do you have to drool at your Mac OS X-using colleagues when they work; now Ubuntu has a whole load of "wow" effects designed to add that professional touch to Linux. In fact, you colleagues will probably be drooling over your setup. If your graphics card is powerful enough, the desktop effects will be available out of the box.

Ubuntu uses the Compiz window manager, which to most end users will not appear any different from Metacity, the standard window manager in use by Ubuntu. You should already have the latest graphics card driver for your system installed. To check, see System, Administration, Additional Drivers. Check out Chapter 2 for more information on this tool.

After you have verified you have the best graphic driver installed, look at the menu option under System, Preferences called Appearance (see Figure 3.2). Open it up and select the Visual Effects tab. By default this is set to None, but try setting it to Normal or Extra to see what happens. After a couple of seconds you may see your window decorations (title bar, minimize and maximize buttons) disappear and then reappear. It may seem that nothing has happened, but grab hold of the window title bar and move it around. If everything has gone according to plan, it should wobble! Click Close to save the settings, and welcome to a world of fancy effects.

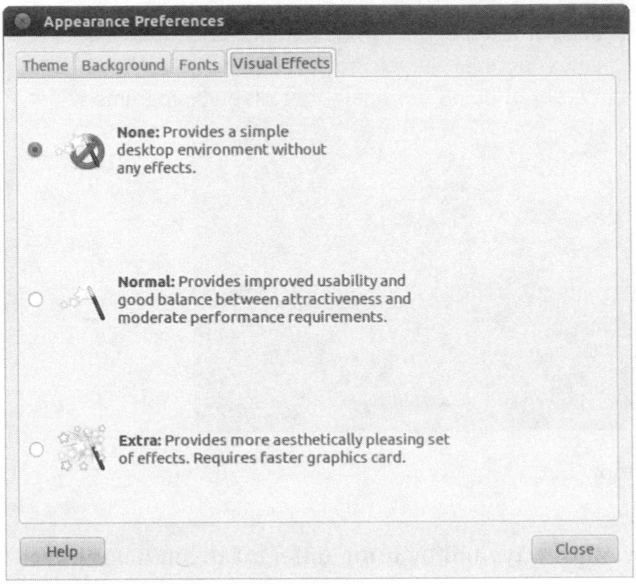

FIGURE 3.2 Use the Visual Effects tool to set the scene for some snazzy 3D effects.

The most obvious effect is that of "wobbly windows," which provide a fluid effect when you move your windows around the desktop area. Have fun exploring the new options and toys you have available. Try installing simple-ccsm from the Ubuntu repositories and playing with the new menu item at System, Preferences, Simple Compiz Config Settings Manager for more control over the flashy fun.

Basic X Concepts

The underlying engine of X11 is the X protocol, which provides a system of managing displays on local and remote desktops. The protocol uses a client/server model that allows an abstraction of the drawing of client windows and other decorations locally and over a network. An X server draws client windows, dialog boxes, and buttons that are specific to the local hardware and in response to client requests. The client, however, does not have to be specific to the local hardware. This means that system administrators can set up a network with a large server and clients and enable users to view and use those clients on workstations with totally different CPUs and graphics displays.

Because X offers users a form of distributed processing, Ubuntu can be used as a very cheap desktop platform for clients that connect to a powerful X server. The more powerful the X server, the larger the number of X-based clients that can be accommodated. This functionality can breathe new life into older hardware, pushing most of the graphical processing on to the server. A fast network is a must if you intend to run many X clients because X can become bandwidth hungry.

NOTE

A great way to demonstrate the capability of X to handle remote clients is Edubuntu's use of LTSP, covered in Chapter 23, "Linux Terminal Server Project (LTSP)." It is designed to set up a main server and a set of dumb terminals that display programs that are being run on the server.

X is hugely popular in the UNIX and Linux world for a variety of reasons. That it supports nearly every hardware graphics system is a strong point. This and strong multiplatform programming standards give it a solid foundation of developers committed to X. Another key benefit of X is its networking capability, which plays a central point in administration of many desktops and can also assist in the deployment of a thin-client computing environment. Being able to launch applications on remote desktops and also standardize installations highlight the versatility of this powerful application.

More recent versions of X have also included support for shaped windows (that is, nonrectangular), graphical login managers (also known as *display managers*), and compressed fonts. Each release of X brings more features designed to enhance the user experience, including being able to customize how X client applications appear, right down to buttons and windows. Most office and home environments run Linux and X on their local machines. The more-enlightened companies and users harness the power of the networking features of X, enabling thin-client environments and allowing the use of customized desktops designed specifically for that company. Having applications launch from a single location makes the lives of system administrators a lot easier because they have to work on only one machine, rather than several.

Using X

X.Org 7.5 is the X server that is used with Ubuntu. The base `Xorg` distribution consists of many packages (well over 100MB) including the server, support and development libraries, fonts, various clients, and documentation. An additional 1,000 or more X clients, fonts, and documentation are also available in the Ubuntu repositories.

The `/usr` directory and its subdirectories contain the majority of `Xorg's` software. Some important subdirectories are

- `/usr/bin`—This is the location of the X server and various X clients. (Note that not all X clients require active X sessions.)
- `/usr/include`—This is the path to the files necessary for developing X clients and graphics such as icons.

- `/usr/lib`—This directory contains required software libraries to support the X server and clients.
- `/usr/lib/X11`—This directory contains fonts, default client resources, system resources, documentation, and other files that are used during X sessions and for various X clients. You will also find a symbolic link to this directory, named `X11`, under the `/usr/lib` directory.
- `/usr/lib/modules`—This path to drivers and the X server modules used by the X server enables use of various graphics cards.

The main components required for an active local X session are installed on your system if you choose to use a graphical desktop. These components are the X server, miscellaneous fonts, a *terminal client* (that is, a program that provides access to a shell prompt), and a client known as a *window manager.* Window managers administer onscreen displays, including overlapping and tiling windows, command buttons, title bars, and other onscreen decorations and features.

Elements of the `xorg.conf` File

Traditionally, the most important file for `Xorg` has been the `xorg.conf` configuration file. This file contained configuration information that was vital for X to function correctly and was usually created during the installation of Ubuntu.

BULLET PROOF X

Ubuntu now comes with a useful feature called Bullet Proof X. In short, it is designed to work no matter what may happen, so in the event of some cataclysmic event that destroys your main X system, you will still have some graphical way of getting yourself back into a fully functional X-based system.

Modern versions of `Xorg` do not create an `xorg.conf` file by default. Instead, various files ending in *.conf reside in the `/usr/share/X11/xorg.conf.d` directory and are automatically loaded by X at boot, prior to reading any `xorg.conf`. These files can each contain one or more sections in the same format used by `xorg.conf`. Users can create the file and continue making custom configurations in `/etc/xorg.conf` as has been traditionally done, but the file is not created by default. What is included in the previously mentioned individual files should not be changed, but you may override those settings by creating your own xorg.conf file.

NOTE

We will refer to using an `xorg.conf` file from here on, but keep the preceding information in mind to prevent confusion.

Let's take a look at the potential contents of `xorg.conf` so that you can get an idea of what X is looking for. The components, or sections, of the `xorg.conf` file specify the X session or *server layout,* along with pathnames for files that are used by the server, any options relating directly to the server, any optional support modules needed, information relating to the mouse and keyboard attached to the system, the graphics card installed, the monitor in use, and the resolution and color depth that Ubuntu uses. These are the essential components:

- `ServerLayout`—Defines the display, defines one or more screen layouts, and names input devices.
- `Files`—Defines the location of colors, fonts, or port number of the font server.
- `Module`—Tells the X server what graphics display support code modules to load.
- `InputDevice`—Defines the input devices, such as the keyboard and mouse; multiple devices can be used.
- `Monitor`—Defines the capabilities of any attached display; multiple monitors can be used.
- `Device`—Defines one or more graphics cards and specifies what optional features (if any) to enable or disable.
- `Screen`—Defines one or more resolutions, color depths, perhaps a default color depth, and other settings.

The following sections provide short descriptions of these elements; the `xorg.conf` man page contains full documentation of all the options and other keywords you can use to customize your desktop settings.

The `ServerLayout` Section

As noted previously, the `ServerLayout` section of the `xorg.conf` file defines the display and screen layouts, and it names the input devices. A typical `ServerLayout` section from an automatically configured `xorg.conf` file might look like this:

```
Section "ServerLayout"
        Identifier     "single head configuration"
        Screen      0  "Screen0" 0 0
        InputDevice    "Mouse0" "CorePointer"
        InputDevice    "Keyboard0" "CoreKeyboard"
        InputDevice    "DevInputMice" "AlwaysCore"
EndSection
```

In this example, a single display is used (the numbers designate the position of a screen), and two default input devices, Mouse0 and Keyboard0, are used for the session.

The `Files` Section

The `Files` section of the `xorg.conf` file might look like this:

```
Section "Files"
    RgbPath     "/usr/lib/X11/rgb"
    FontPath   "unix/:7100"
EndSection
```

This section lists available session colors (by name, in the text file `rgb.txt`) and the port number to the X font server. The font server, `xfs`, is started at boot and does not require an active X session. If a font server is not used, the `FontPath` entry could instead list each font directory under the `/usr/lib/X11/fonts` directory, as in this example:

```
FontPath "/usr/lib/X11/fonts/100dpi"
FontPath "/usr/lib/X11/fonts/misc"
FontPath "/usr/lib/X11/fonts/75dpi"
FontPath "/usr/lib/X11/fonts/type1"
FontPath "/usr/lib/X11/fonts/Speedo"
...
```

These directories contain the default compressed fonts that are available for use during the X session. The font server is configured by using the file named `config` under the `/etc/X11/fs` directory. This file contains a listing, or catalog, of fonts for use by the font server. By adding an `alternate-server` entry in this file and restarting the font server, you can specify remote font servers for use during X sessions. This can help centralize font support and reduce local storage requirements (even though only 25MB is required for the almost 5,000 fonts installed with Ubuntu and X).

The `Module` Section

The `Module` section of the `xorg.conf` file specifies loadable modules or drivers to load for the X session. This section might look like this:

```
Section "Module"
        Load  "dbe"
        Load  "extmod"
        Load  "fbdevhw"
        Load "glx"
        Load "record"
        Load  "freetype"
        Load  "type1"
        Load  "dri"

EndSection
```

These modules can range from special video card support to font rasterizers. The modules are located in subdirectories under the `/usr/lib/modules` directory.

The `InputDevice` Section

The `InputDevice` section configures a specific device, such as a keyboard or mouse, as in this example:

```
Section "InputDevice"
        Identifier  "Keyboard0"
        Driver      "kbd"

        Option  "XkbModel"      "pc105"
        Option  "XkbLayout"     "us"
EndSection
Section "InputDevice"
        Identifier  "Mouse0"
        Driver      "mouse"
        Option      "Protocol" "IMPS/2"
        Option      "Device" "/dev/input/mice"
        Option      "ZAxisMapping" "4 5"
        Option      "Emulate3Buttons" "yes"
EndSection
```

You can configure multiple devices, and multiple `InputDevice` sections might exist. The preceding example specifies a basic keyboard and a two-button PS/2 mouse (actually, a Dell touchpad pointer). An `InputDevice` section that specifies use of a USB device could be used at the same time (to enable mousing with PS/2 and USB pointers) and might look like this:

```
Section "InputDevice"
        Identifier  "Mouse0"
        Driver      "mouse"
        Option      "Device" "/dev/input/mice"
        Option      "Protocol" "IMPS/2"
        Option      "Emulate3Buttons" "off"
        Option      "ZAxisMapping" "4 5"
EndSection
```

The `Monitor` Section

The `Monitor` section configures the designated display device as declared in the `ServerLayout` section, as shown in this example:

```
Section "Monitor"
        Identifier   "Monitor0"
        VendorName   "Monitor Vendor"
        ModelName    "Monitor Model"
        DisplaySize  300     220
```

```
        HorizSync    31.5-48.5
        VertRefresh 50-70
        Option "dpms"
EndSection
```

Note that the X server automatically determines the best video timings according to the horizontal and vertical sync and refresh values in this section. If required, old-style modeline entries (used by distributions and servers prior to XFree86 4.0) might still be used. If the monitor is automatically detected when you configure X (see the "Configuring X" section, later in this chapter), its definition and capabilities are inserted in your `xorg.conf` file from the `MonitorsDB` database. This database contains more than 600 monitors and is located in the `/usr/share/hwdata` directory.

The Device Section

The `Device` section provides details about the video graphics chipset used by the computer, as in this example:

```
Section "Device"
        Identifier      "Intel Corporation Mobile 945GM/GMS,\943/940GML Express
Integrated Graphics Controller"
        Driver          "intel"
        BusID           "PCI:0:2:0"
EndSection
```

This example identifies an installed video card as using an integrated Intel 945 graphics chipset. The `Driver` entry tells the `Xorg` server to load the `intel` kernel module. Different chipsets have different options. For example, here's the entry for a NeoMagic video chipset:

```
Section "Device"
        Identifier    "NeoMagic (laptop/notebook)"
        Driver        "neomagic"
        VendorName    "NeoMagic (laptop/notebook)"
        BoardName      "NeoMagic (laptop/notebook)"
    Option     "externDisp"
    Option     "internDisp"
EndSection
```

In this example, the Device section specifies the driver for the graphics card (`neomagic_drv.o`) and enables two chipset options (`externDisp` and `internDisp`) to allow display on the laptop's LCD screen and an attached monitor.

The `Xorg` server supports hundreds of different video chipsets. If you configure X11 but subsequently change the installed video card, you need to edit the existing `Device` section or generate a new `xorg.conf` file, using one of the X configuration tools discussed in this chapter, to reflect the new card's capabilities. You can find details about options for some chipsets in a companion man page. You should look at these sources for hints about optimizations and troubleshooting.

The Screen Section

The Screen section ties together the information from the previous sections (using the Screen0, Device, and Monitor Identifier entries). It can also specify one or more color depths and resolutions for the session. Here's an example:

```
Section "Screen"
        Identifier "Screen0"
        Device     "Videocard0"
        Monitor    "Monitor0"
        DefaultDepth     24
        SubSection "Display"
                Viewport   0 0
                Depth     16
                Modes     "1024x768" "800x600" "640x480"
        EndSubSection

EndSection
```

In this example, a color depth of thousands of colors and a resolution of 1024768 is the default, with optional resolutions of 800x600 and 64x480. Multiple Display subsection entries with different color depths and resolutions (with settings such as Depth 24 for millions of colors) can be used if supported by the graphics card and monitor combination. You can also use a DefaultDepth entry (which is 24, or thousands of colors, in the example), along with a specific color depth to standardize display depths in installations.

You can also specify a desktop resolution larger than that supported by the hardware in your monitor or notebook display. This setting is known as a *virtual* resolution in the Display subsection. This allows, for example, an 800 X 600 display to pan (that is, slide around inside) a virtual window of 1024 X 768.

NOTE

If your monitor and graphics card support multiple resolutions and the settings are properly configured, you can use the key combination of Ctrl+Alt+Keypad+ or Ctrl+Alt+Keypad- to change resolutions on-the-fly during your X session.

Configuring X

Ubuntu usually does a good job of detecting your graphics card and monitor, although sometimes problems can arise if the PC's video card is not recognized. If your display is not configured correctly, Ubuntu provides some tools to help you make changes to the way your display is set up.

You can use the gnome-display-properties client to configure your displays. Start in the menu at System, Preference, Monitors. You will see a window similar to Figure 3.3, but with information for your specific hardware.

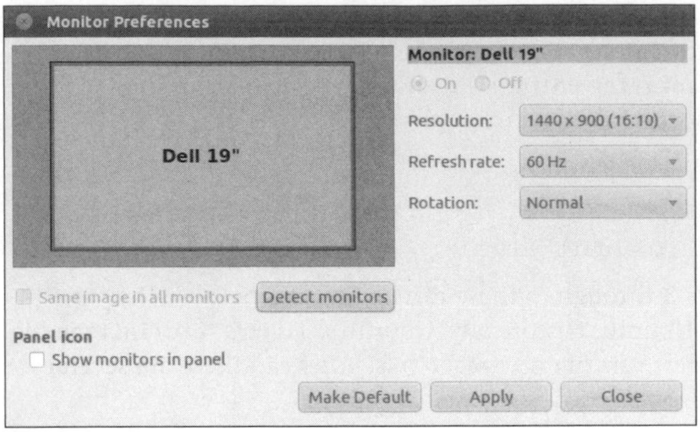

FIGURE 3.3 The gnome-display-properties client provides a graphical configuration interface for adjusting display settings.

The Monitor Preferences window shows the current selected screen, along with details of the model, resolutions available, the refresh rate, and orientation. In the event that you are using two screens (dual- or multi-head displays, or when a projector is attached) you have the ability to select whether it is the primary or secondary screen, and the physical location of it. Click Detect Monitors if a second monitor does not appear or if you have just plugged in a projector. Select Same Image in all monitors if you want to mirror your display. Click Apply when you are satisfied with your settings.

Starting X

You can start X sessions in a variety of ways. The Ubuntu installer sets up the system to have Linux boot directly to an X session using a display manager called GDM, for GNOME Display Manager. This is an X client that provides a graphical login. After you log in, you use a local session (running on your computer) or, if the system is configured to do so, an X session running on a remote computer on the network.

Logging in via a display manager requires you to enter a username and password. You can also start X sessions from the command line. The following sections describe these two methods.

NOTE

If you have used the Server install, your system will boot to a text login—see Chapter 4, "Command Line Quickstart," for more details on what to do here.

Using a Display Manager

An X display manager presents a graphical login that requires a username and password to be entered before access is granted to the X desktop. It also allows you to choose a different desktop for your X session. Whether an X display manager is presented after you boot

Linux is controlled by a *runlevel*—a system state entry in /etc/event.d/. The following runlevels as handled by Ubuntu are as follows:

- 0 - halt (Do NOT set initdefault to this.)
- 1 - Multiuser text mode
- 2 - X – graphical multiuser mode
- 6 - reboot (Do NOT set initdefault to this.)

You may see mention of Runlevels 3 through 5; these can be ignored because they are treated the same as Runlevel 2 in Ubuntu. Historically, Ubuntu used the /etc/inittab file to handle runlevels, but with Upstart this file no longer exists. Instead there are several files under the /etc/events.d/ directory, including an individual file for each of the virtual consoles (accessible by pressing Ctrl+Alt+F1 to F7). However, you are still able to create an inittab file, if you want to override any defaults held by Ubuntu. Make sure you create the inittab file as root and include at least one line similar to the following:

```
id:1:initdefault:
```

This will force your system to start up in text mode.

Configuring Your Login Screen

The gdm display manager is part of the GNOME library and client distribution included with Ubuntu and provides a graphical login when a system boots directly to X. Its login hosts menus of window managers, languages, and system options for shutting down (halting) or rebooting the workstation. Although you can edit (as root) gdm.conf under the /etc/gdm directory to configure gdm, a much better way to configure GNOME's display manager is to use the convenient GUI client.

You launch this client from the System Menu, under Administration, Login Screen. Click Unlock and you will be prompted for your password. Next, you see the Login Screen Settings window, as shown in Figure 3.4.

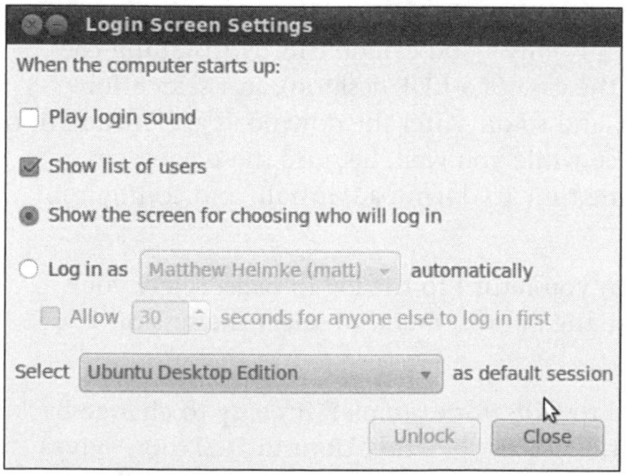

FIGURE 3.4 Configuring GDM.

Here you can decide whether to play a login sound, show a list of users, show the screen for choosing who will log in, whether to allow a specific user to be logged in automatically at startup, and if so, whether to do so only after a delay of a specific number of seconds to allow someone else to log in, and what Ubuntu edition or desktop environment to use as the default session if you have more than one installed.

It is generally a good idea not to log anyone in automatically, but rather to require a user and password for log in, because you do not always know who will turn the machine on. I have a specific exception in my house on a computer set up for my kids to use. It automatically logs in to a very limited account filled with educational games, but no administrative access after a short ten second delay in case I am starting the computer and want to log in with my account and password to perform system maintenance.

CAUTION

We strongly recommend that you never set either of these two options unless you have an unimportant system containing no private or important data. It's the equivalent of leaving your car unlocked, with the windows rolled down and signs around it reading "Steal Me." Only if you fit a very special case should you use this, such as if you are creating a system that is designed to be used in a public access area, like as a kiosk, where it would not be unusual for some dimwit to turn the computer off every so often! In this scenario, you may not be available to log on to the system and may prefer it to default to the locked-down account that you created.

Changing Window Managers

Ubuntu makes it fairly painless to switch to another window manager or desktop environment. By *desktop environment,* we refer to not only the window manager but also the suite of related applications, such as productivity or configuration tools.

First, you need to ensure that you have the relevant desktop environment installed on your system; the easiest way to do this is by installing the relevant *-desktop package (as described earlier in the sidebar "The Ubuntu Family." You can do this by installing the package kubuntu-desktop, for example (in the case of a KDE desktop); just search for desktop and look for Xubuntu or Kubuntu, and so on. After the download and installation is complete (you might want to grab a coffee while you wait, because these packages include a ton of dependencies and take some time to download, install, and configure), you are all set to change environments.

Next, you need to log out of Ubuntu. When you return to the log in page, select your name (as shown in Figure 3.5) and then use the bottom menu to select the session you want to use.

Here you can choose to switch your session to KDE (for example). It's easy to change back should you not like your new environment. Chapter 8, "Other Ubuntu Desktops," gives you a brief introduction to some of the desktop environments other than GNOME that are available from the Ubuntu repositories.

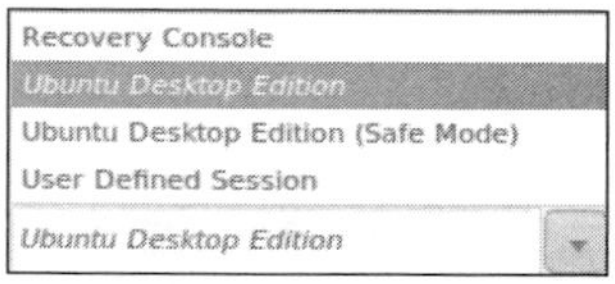

FIGURE 3.5 Use the Select Session option to select the desktop environment of your choice before you log in.

Reference

- www.gnome.org/—The launch point for more information about GNOME, links to new clients, and GNOME development projects.
- www.x.org/—Curators of the X Window System.
- www.x.org/Downloads_mirror.html—Want to download the source to the latest revision of X? Start at this list of mirror sites.
- www.xfree86.org/—Home of The XFree86 Project, Inc., which provided a graphical interface for Linux for nearly 10 years.
- https://wiki.ubuntu.com/X—The place to get started when learning about X and Ubuntu.
- https://wiki.ubuntu.com/X/Config—Great information about configuring X on Ubuntu.

CHAPTER 4

Command Line Quickstart

IN THIS CHAPTER

The Linux command line, sometimes called the terminal, is one of the most powerful tools available for computer system administration and maintenance. It is an efficient way to perform complex tasks accurately and much more easily than it would seem at a first glance. Knowledge of the commands available to you and also how to string them together will make using Ubuntu even easier for many tasks. Many of the commands were created by the GNU Project as free software analogs to previously existing proprietary UNIX commands. If you are interested, you can learn more about the GNU Project at www.gnu.org/gnu/thegnuproject.html.

This chapter looks at some of the basic commands that you need to know to be productive at the command line. You will find out how to get to the command line, and learn some of the commands used to navigate the file system. Later in the book we present a Command Line Masterclass (Chapter 30), which explores the subject in greater depth. The skills you learn in this chapter will help you get started using the command line with confidence.

What Is the Command Line?

If you spend any amount of time with experienced Linux users, you will hear them mention the command line. Some, especially those who have begun their journey in the Linux world using distributions, like Ubuntu, that make it easy to complete many tasks using a graphical user interface (GUI), may speak with trepidation about the mysteries of the text interface. Others will either praise its power or comment about doing something via the command line as if it is the most natural and obvious way to complete a task.

It is not necessary for you to embrace either extreme. You may develop an affinity for the command line when performing some tasks and prefer the GUI for others. This is where most users end up today. Some may say that you will never need to access the command line because Ubuntu offers a slew of graphical tools that enable you to configure most things on your system. There are some good reasons to acquire a fundamental level of comfort with the command line that you should consider before embracing that view.

Sometimes things go wrong, and you may not have the luxury of a graphical interface to work with. In these situations, a fundamental understanding of the command line and its uses can be a real lifesaver. Also, some tasks end up being far easier and faster to accomplish from the command line.

NOTE

Don't be tempted to skip over this chapter as irrelevant. You should take the time to work through the chapter and ensure that you are comfortable with the command line before moving on. Doing so will benefit you greatly for years to come.

Initially, some may be tempted to think of the command line as the product of some sort of black and arcane art, and in some ways it can appear to be extremely difficult and complicated to use. However, with a little perseverance, by the end of this chapter you will start to feel comfortable using the command line and you'll be ready to move on to Chapter 35, "Command Line Masterclass."

More importantly, though, you will be able to make your way around a command line–based system, which you are likely to encounter if you ever work with a Linux server since many Linux servers have no GUI and all administration is done using a command line interface via SSH.

This chapter introduces you to commands that enable you to do the following:

- **Perform routine tasks**—Logging in and out, changing passwords, listing and navigating file directories
- **Implement basic file management**—Creating files and folders, copying or moving them around the file system, renaming and deleting them
- **Execute basic system management**—Shutting down or rebooting, using text-based tools to edit system configuration files, and reading man pages, which are entries for commands included as files already on your computer in a standardized manual format

The information in this chapter is valuable for individual users or system administrators who are new to Linux and are learning to use the command line for the first time.

TIP

Those of you who have used a computer for many years will probably have come into contact with MS-DOS, in which case being presented with a black screen will fill you with a sense of nostalgia. Don't get too comfy; the command line in Linux is different from (and actually more powerful than) its distant MS-DOS cousin. Even cooler is that, whereas MS-DOS skills are transferable only to other MS-DOS environments, the skills that you learn at the Linux command line can be transferred easily to other UNIX and UNIX-like operating systems, such as Solaris, OpenBSD, FreeBSD, and even Mac OS X, which provides access to the terminal.

USER ACCOUNTS

A good place to start is with the concept of user-based security. For the most part, only two types of people will access the system as users (although there will be other accounts that run programs and processes, here we are talking about accounts that represent human beings rather than something like an account created for a web server process). Most people have a regular user account. These users can change anything that is specific to their account, such as the wallpaper on the desktop, their personal preferences, the configuration for a program when it is run by them using their account, and so on. Note that the emphasis is on anything that is specific to them. This type of user is not able to make systemwide changes that could affect other users.

To make systemwide changes, you need to use super-user privileges, such as the account you created when you started Ubuntu for the first time (see Chapter 1, "Installing Ubuntu"). With super-user privileges you have access to the entire system and can carry out any task, even destructive ones! To help prevent this from happening, this user does not run with these powers enabled at all times, but instead spends most of the time with the look and feel of a regular user.

To use your super-user privileges from the command line you need to preface the command you want to execute with another command, `sudo`, followed by a space and the command you want to run. As a mnemonic device, some think of this as "super-user do." When you press Enter (after typing the remaining command) you will be prompted for your password, which you should type in followed by the Enter key. As usual on any UNIX-based system, the password will not appear on the screen while you are typing it as a security measure, in case someone is watching over your shoulder. Ubuntu will then carry out the command, but with super-user privileges.

An example of the destructive nature of working as the super-user can be found in the age-old example, `sudo rm -rf /`, which erases everything on your hard drive. If you enter a command using `sudo` as a regular user who does not have an account with super-user privileges, an error message will appear and nothing will happen because the command will not run. We recommend that you don't try this particular command as a test, though. If you enter this command using an account with super-user privileges, you will soon find yourself starting over with a fresh installation and hoping you have a current backup of all of your data. You need to be especially careful when using your super-user privileges; otherwise, you may do irreparable damage to your system.

However, the ability to work as the super-user is fundamental to a healthy Linux system and should not be feared, but rather respected and used only with focused attention. Without this ability you would not be able to install new software, edit system configuration files, or do a large number of important administration tasks. By the end of this chapter you will feel comfortable working with your super-user privileges and be able to adequately administer your system from the command line. By the way, you have already been performing operations with super-user privileges from the GUI if you have ever been asked to enter your password to complete a specific task, such as installing software updates. The difference is that most graphical interfaces limit the options that users have and make it a little more difficult to do some of the big, disruptive tasks, even the ones that are incredibly useful.

Ubuntu works slightly differently from many other Linux distributions. If you study some other Linux distros, especially older or more traditional ones, you will hear about a specific user account called `root`, which is a super-user account. In those distros, instead of typing in `sudo` before a command while using a regular user account with super-user privileges, you log in to the `root` account and simply issue the command without entering a password. In those cases, you can tell when you are using the root account at the command line because you will see a pound sign (#) in the command line prompt in the place of the dollar sign ($).

For example, `matthew@seymour:~# vs the usual matthew@seymour:~$`.

In Ubuntu the `root` account is disabled by default because forcing regular users with super-user privileges to type a specific command every time they want to execute a command as a super-user should have the benefit of making them carefully consider what they are doing when they use that power. It is easy to forget to log out of a root account, and entering a powerful command while logged in to `root` can be catastrophic. However, if you are more experienced and comfortable with the more traditional method of using super-user privileges and want to enable the root account, you can use the command `sudo passwd`. When prompted, enter your user password to confirm that your user account has super-user privileges. You will then be asked for a new UNIX password, which will be the password for the root account, so make sure and remember it. You will also be prompted to repeat the password, in case you've made any mistakes. After you've typed it in and pressed Enter, the `root` account will be active. You'll find out how to switch to `root` later on.

An alternative way of getting a root prompt, without having to enable the root account, is to issue the command `sudo -i`. After entering your password you will find yourself at a root prompt (#). Do what you need to do and when you are finished, type `exit` and press Enter to return to your usual prompt. You can learn more about `sudo` and `root` from an Ubuntu perspective at https://help.ubuntu.com/community/RootSudo.

Ubuntu offers a number of ways to access the command line. One way is to press the key combination Ctrl+Alt+F1, after which Ubuntu will switch to a black screen and a login prompt like this:

```
Ubuntu 10.10 maverick seymour ttyl
seymour login:
```


TIP

This is one of six virtual consoles that Ubuntu provides. After you have accessed a virtual console, you can use the Ctrl+Alt + any of F1 through F6 to switch to a different console. If you want to get back to the graphical interface, press Ctrl+Alt+ F7. You can also switch between consoles by holding the Alt key and pressing either the left or the right cursor key to move down or up a console, such as tty1 to tty2.

At the login prompt enter your username and press the Enter key. You will be asked for your password, which you should enter. Note that Ubuntu does not show any characters while you are typing your password in. This is a good thing because it prevents any shoulder surfers from seeing what you've typed or the length of the password.

Pressing the Enter key drops you to a shell prompt, signified by the dollar sign:

```
matthew@seymour:~$
```

This particular prompt tells me that I am logged in as the user `matthew` on the system `seymour` and I am currently in my home directory; Linux uses the tilde (~) as shorthand for the home directory, which would usually be something like `/home/matthew`.

TIP

Navigating through the system at the command line can get confusing at times, especially when a directory name occurs in several places. Fortunately, Linux includes a simple command that tells you exactly where you are in the file system. It's easy to remember because the command is just an abbreviation of present working directory, so type **pwd** at any point to get the full path of your location. For example, typing **pwd** after following these instructions shows `/home/yourusername`, meaning that you are currently in your home directory.

Using the pwd command can save you a lot of frustration when you have changed directory half a dozen times and have lost track.

Another way to quickly access the terminal is to use the desktop menu option Applications, Accessories, Terminal. This opens up `gnome-terminal`, which allows you to access the terminal while remaining in a GUI environment. This time, the terminal appears as white text on an aubergine (dark purple) background. This is the most common method for most desktop users, but both are useful.

Regardless of which way you access the terminal, using the virtual tty consoles accessible at Ctrl + Alt + F1-6 or via the windowed version atop your GUI desktop, you will find the rest of the usage details that we cover work the same. As you continue to learn and experiment beyond the contents of this book, you may start to discover some subtle differences between the two and develop a preference. For our purposes, either method will work quite well.

With that, let's begin.

Navigating Through the File System

Use the `cd` command to navigate the file system. This command is generally used with a specific directory location or pathname, like this:

```
matthew@seymour:~$ cd /etc/apt/
```

The `cd` command can also be used with several shortcuts. For example, to quickly move up to the *parent* directory, the one above the one you are currently in, use the cd command like this:

```
matthew@seymour:~$ cd ..
```

To return to your home directory from anywhere in the Linux file system, use the cd command like this:

```
matthew@seymour:~$ cd
```

You can also use the `$HOME` shell environment variable to accomplish the same thing. Type this command and press Enter to return to your home directory:

```
matthew@seymour:~$ cd $HOME
```

You can accomplish the same thing by using the tilde (~) like this:

```
matthew@seymour:~$ cd ~
```

Don't forget you can always use `pwd` to remind you where you are within the file system!

The `ls` command lists the contents of the current directory. It's commonly used by itself, but a number of options (also known as switches) are available for `ls` and give you more information. For instance, the following command returns a listing of all the files and directories within the current directory, including any hidden files (denoted by a `.` prefix) as well as a full listing, so it will include details such as the permissions, owner and group, size, and last modified time and date:

```
matthew@seymour:~$ ls -la
```

You can also issue the command

```
matthew@seymour:~$ ls -R
```

This command scans and lists all the contents of the subdirectories of the current directory. This might be a lot of information, so you may want to redirect the output to a text file so you can browse through it at your leisure by using the following:

```
matthew@seymour:~$ ls -laR > listing.txt
```

TIP

The previous command sends the output of `ls -laR` to a file called `listing.txt` and demonstrates part of the power of the Linux command line. At the command line you are able to use files as inputs to commands, or generate files as outputs as shown. For more information about combining commands, see Chapter 30. In the meantime, note that you can read the contents of that text file using the command `less listing.txt`, which will let you read the file bit by bit using the arrow keys to navigate in the file (or `Enter` to move to the next line), the spacebar to move to the next page, and q to exit when done.

Table 4.1 shows some of the top-level directories that are part of a standard Linux distro.

TABLE 4.1 Basic Linux Directories

Name	Description
`/`	The root directory
`/bin`	Essential commands
`/boot`	Boot loader files, Linux kernel
`/dev`	Device files
`/etc`	System configuration files
`/home`	User home directories
`/lib`	Shared libraries, kernel modules
`/lost+found`	Directory for recovered files (if found after a file system check)
`/media`	Mount point for removable media, such as DVDs and floppy disks
`/mnt`	Usual mount point for local, remote file systems
`/opt`	Add-on software packages
`/proc`	Kernel information, process control
`/root`	Super-user (root) home
`/sbin`	System commands (mostly root only)

TABLE 4.1 Continued

Name	Description
`/srv`	Holds information relating to services that run on your system
`/sys`	Real-time information on devices used by the kernel
`/tmp`	Temporary files
`/usr`	Software not essential for system operation, such as applications
`/var`	Variable data (such as logs); spooled files

Knowing these directories can help you find files when you need them. This knowledge can even help you partition hard drives when you install new systems by letting you choose to put certain directories on their own distinct partition, which can be useful for things like isolating directories from one another, such as a server security case like putting a directory like /boot that doesn't change often on its own partition and making it read-only and unchangeable without specific operations being done by a super-user during a maintenance cycle. Desktop users probably won't need to think about that, but the directory tree is still quite useful to know when you want to find the configuration file for a specific program and set some program options systemwide to affect all users.

Some of the important directories in Table 4.1, such as those containing user and root commands or system configuration files, are discussed in the following sections. You may use and edit files under these directories when you use Ubuntu.

Linux also includes a number of commands you can use to search the file system. These include the following:

- `whereis` *command*—Returns the location of the command (e.g. /bin, /sbin, or /usr/bin/command) and its man page, which is an entry for the command included as a file already on your computer in a standardized manual format.
- `whatis` *command*—Returns a one-line synopsis from the command's man page.
- `locate` *`file`*—Returns locations of all matching file(s); an extremely fast method of searching your system because `locate` searches a database containing an index of all files on your system. However, this database (which is several MB in size and named `mlocate.db`, under the `/var/lib/mlocate` directory) is built daily at 6:25 a.m. by default, and does not contain pathnames to files created during the workday or in the evening. If you do not keep your machine on constantly, you can run the `updatedb` command with super-user privileges to manually start the building of the database. More advanced users can change the time the database is updated by changing a `cron` job that calls the command. There is a script in `/etc/cron.daily` called `mlocate` that does this as part of the daily maintenance for the database. You would need to either remove that script from `/etc/cron.daily` and put it the root `crontab` or change when the daily tasks are run. If you don't know how to do this right now, you should wait until you have read and understand Chapter 11,

"Automating Tasks," and its discussion of cron, after which the preceding description will be clear.

- apropos *subject*—Returns a list of commands related to subject.
- type *name*—Returns how a name would be interpreted if used as a command. This generally shows options or the location of the binary that will be used. For example, type ls returns ls is aliased to `` `ls -color=auto' ``.

Managing Files with the Shell

Managing files in your home directory involves using one or more easily remembered commands. Basic file management operations include paging (reading), moving, renaming, copying, searching, and deleting files and directories. Here are some commands to do these tasks:

4

- cat *filename*—Outputs contents of filename to display
- less *filename*—Allows scrolling while reading contents of filename
- mv *file1 file2*—Renames *file1* to file2 and may be used with full pathnames to move the file to a new directory at the same time
- mv *file dir*—Moves file to specified directory
- cp *file1 file2*—*Copies file1* and creates file2
- rm *file*—Deletes file
- rmdir *dir*—Deletes directory (if empty)
- grep *string file(s)*—Searches through files(s) and displays lines containing matching string (a string is a series of characters like letters, numbers, and symbols, such as a word)

Note that each of these commands can be used with pattern-matching strings known as *wildcards* or *expressions*. For example, to delete all files in the current directory beginning with the letters abc, you can use an expression beginning with the first three letters of the desired filenames. An asterisk (*) is then appended to match all these files. Use a command line with the rm command like this:

```
matthew@seymour:~$ rm abc*
```

Linux shells recognize many types of filenaming wildcards, but this is different from the capabilities of Linux commands supporting the use of more complex expressions. You learn more about using wildcards in Chapter 11, "Automating Tasks."

NOTE

You can also learn more about using expressions by reading the grep manual pages (man grep).

Working with Compressed Files

Another file management operation is compression and decompression of files, or the creation, listing, and expansion of file and directory archives. Linux distributions usually include several compression utilities you can use to create, compress, expand, or list the contents of compressed files and archives. These commands include:

- `bunzip2`—Expands a compressed file
- `bzip2`—Compresses or expands files and directories
- `gunzip`—Expands a compressed file
- `gzip`—Compresses or expands files and directories
- `tar`—Creates, expands, or lists the contents of compressed or uncompressed file or directory archives known as *tape archives* or *tarballs*

Most of these commands are easy to use. However, the `tar` command, which is the most commonly used of the bunch, has a somewhat complex set of command-line options and syntax. This flexibility and power are part of its popularity; you can quickly learn to use `tar` by remembering a few of the simple command line options. For example, to create a compressed archive of a directory, use `tar`'s `czf` options like this:

```
matthew@seymour:~$ tar czf dirname.tgz dirname
```

The result is a compressed archive (a file ending in `.tgz`) of the specified directory (and all files and directories under it). Add the letter `v` to the preceding options to view the list of files added during compression and archiving while the archive is being created. To list the contents of the compressed archive, substitute the c option with the letter `t`, like this:

```
matthew@seymour:~$ tar tzf archive
```

However, if many files are in the archive, a better invocation (to easily read or scroll through the output) is

```
matthew@seymour:~$ tar tzf archive | less
```

TIP

In the previous code example, we used a pipe character (|). Each pipe sends the output of the first command to the next command. This is another of the benefits of the command line under Linux—you can string several commands together to get the desired results.

To expand the contents of a compressed archive, use `tar`'s `zxf` options, like so:

```
matthew@seymour:~$ tar zxf archive
```

The `tar` utility decompresses the specified archive and extracts the contents in the current directory.

Essential Commands from the /bin and /sbin Directories

The `/bin` directory contains essential commands used by the system for running and booting the system. In general, only the root operator uses the commands in the `/sbin` directory. The software in both locations is essential to the system; they make the system what it is, and if they are changed or removed, it could cause instability or a complete system failure. Often, the commands in these two directories are *statically* linked, which means that the commands do not depend on software libraries residing under the `/lib` or `/usr/lib` directories. Nearly all the other applications on your system are *dynamically* linked—meaning that they require the use of external software libraries (also known as *shared* libraries) to run. This is a feature for both sets of software.

The commands in `/bin` and `/sbin` are kept stable to maintain foundational system integrity and do not need to be updated often, if at all. For the security of the system, these commands are kept in a separate location and isolated where changes are more difficult and where it will be more obvious to the system administrator if unauthorized changes are attempted or made.

Application software changes more frequently, and applications often use the same functions that other pieces of application software use. This was the genesis of shared libraries. When a security update is needed for something that is used by more than one program, it has to be updated in only one location, a specific software library. This enables easy and quick security updates that will affect several pieces of non-system-essential software at the same time by updating one shared library, contained in one file on the computer.

Using and Editing Files in the /etc Directory

System configuration files and directories reside under the `/etc` directory. Some major software packages, such as Apache, OpenSSH, and `xinetd`, have their own subdirectories in `/etc` filled with configuration files. Others like crontab or fstab use one file. Some examples of system-related configuration files in `/etc` include the following:

- `fstab`—The file system table is a text file listing each hard drive, CD-ROM, floppy, or other storage device attached to your PC. The table indexes each device's partition information with a place in your Linux file system (directory layout) and lists other options for each device when used with Linux (see Chapter 36, "Kernel and Module Management"). Nearly all entries in `fstab` can be manipulated by root using the `mount` command.
- `modprobe.d/`—This folder holds all the instructions to load kernel modules that are required as part of the system startup.

- passwd—The list of users for the system, including special-purpose nonhuman users like syslog and couchdb, along with user account information.
- sudoers—A list of users or user groups with super-user access.

Protecting the Contents of User Directories—/home

The most important data on a Linux system resides in the user's directories, found under the /home directory. Segregating the system and user data can be helpful in preventing data loss and making the process of backing up easier. For example, having user data reside on a separate file system or mounted from a remote computer on the network might help shield users from data loss in the event of a system hardware failure. For a laptop or desktop computer at home, you might place /home on a separate partition from the rest of the file system, so that if the operating system is upgraded, damaged, or reinstalled, /home would be more likely to survive the event intact.

Using the Contents of the /proc Directory to Interact with the Kernel

The content of the /proc directory is created from memory and exists only while Linux is running. This directory contains special files that either extract information from or send information to the kernel. Many Linux utilities extract information from dynamically created directories and files under this directory, also known as a *virtual file system*. For example, the free command obtains its information from a file named **meminfo:**

```
matthew@seymour:~$ free

         total     used      free      shared   buffers     cached
Mem:     4055680   2725684   1329996   0        188996      1551464
-/+ buffers/cache: 985224    3070456
Swap:    8787512   0         8787512
```

This information constantly changes as the system is used. You can get the same information by using the cat command to see the contents of the meminfo file:

```
matthew@seymour:~$ cat /proc/meminfo
MemTotal:                4055680 KB
MemFree:                 1329692 KB
Buffers:                  189208 KB
Cached:                  1551488 KB
SwapCached:                    0 KB
Active:                  1222172 KB
Inactive:                1192244 KB
Active(anon):             684092 KB
Inactive(anon):               16 KB
Active(file):             538080 KB
Inactive(file):          1192228 KB
Unevictable:                  48 KB
Mlocked:                      48 KB
SwapTotal:               8787512 KB
```

```
SwapFree:                8787512 KB
Dirty:                       136 KB
Writeback:                     0 KB
AnonPages:                673760 KB
Mapped:                   202308 KB
Shmem:                     10396 KB
Slab:                     129248 KB
SReclaimable:             107356 KB
SUnreclaim:                21892 KB
KernelStack:                2592 KB
PageTables:                30108 KB
NFS_Unstable:                  0 KB
Bounce:                        0 KB
WritebackTmp:                  0 KB
CommitLimit:            10815352 KB
Committed_AS:            1553172 KB
VmallocTotal:        34359738367 KB
VmallocUsed:              342300 KB
VmallocChunk:        34359387644 KB
HardwareCorrupted:             0 KB
HugePages_Total:               0
HugePages_Free:                0
HugePages_Rsvd:                0
HugePages_Surp:                0
Hugepagesize:               2048 KB
DirectMap4k:               38912 KB
DirectMap2M:             4153344 KB
```

The `/proc` directory can also be used to dynamically alter the behavior of a running Linux kernel by "echoing" numerical values to specific files under the `/proc/sys` directory. For example, to "turn on" kernel protection against one type of denial of service (DOS) attack known as *SYN flooding*, use the echo command to send the number 1 (one) to the following `/proc` path:

```
matthew@seymour:~$ $ sudo echo 1 >/proc/sys/net/ipv4/tcp_syncookies
```

Other ways to use the /proc directory include the following:

- Getting CPU information, such as the family, type, and speed from `/proc/cpuinfo`.
- Viewing important networking information under `/proc/net`, such as active interfaces information under `/proc/net/dev`, routing information in `/proc/net/route`, and network statistics in `/proc/net/netstat`.
- Retrieving file system information.
- Reporting media mount point information via USB; for example, the Linux kernel reports what device to use to access files (such as `/dev/sda`) if a USB camera or hard drive is detected on the system. You can use the `dmesg` command to see this information.

4

- Getting the kernel version in /proc/version, performance information such as uptime in /proc/uptime, or other statistics such as CPU load, swap file usage, and processes in /proc/stat.

Working with Shared Data in the /usr Directory

The /usr directory contains software applications, libraries, and other types of shared data for use by anyone on the system. Many Linux system administrators give /usr its own partition. A number of subdirectories under /usr contain manual pages (/usr/share/man), software package shared files (/usr/share/*name_of_package, such as /usr/share/emacs*), additional application or software package documentation (/usr/share/doc), and an entire subdirectory tree of locally built and installed software, /usr/local.

Temporary File Storage in the /tmp Directory

As its name implies, the /tmp directory is used for temporary file storage; as you use Linux, various programs create files in this directory.

Accessing Variable Data Files in the /var Directory

The /var directory contains subdirectories used by various system services for spooling and logging. Many of these variable data files, such as print spooler queues, are temporary, whereas others, such as system and kernel logs, are renamed and rotated in use. Incoming electronic mail is usually directed to files under /var/spool/mail.

Linux also uses /var for other important system services. These include the top-most File Transfer Protocol (FTP) directory under /var/ftp (see Chapter 18, "Remote File Serving with FTP"), and the Apache web server's initial home page directory for the system, /var/www/html. (See Chapter 17, "Apache Web Server Management," for more information on using Apache.)

NOTE

There is a recent trend to move data that is served from /var/www and /var/ftp to /srv, but this is not universal.

Logging In to and Working with Linux

You can access and use a Linux system in a number of ways. One way is at the console with a monitor, keyboard, and mouse attached to the PC. Another way is via a serial console, either by dial-up via a modem or a PC running a terminal emulator and connected to the Linux PC via a null modem cable. You can also connect to your system through a wired or wireless network, using the telnet or ssh commands. The information in this section shows you how to access and use the Linux system, using physical and remote text-based logins.

NOTE

This chapter focuses on text-based logins and use of Linux. Graphical logins and using a graphical desktop are described in Chapter 3, "Working with GNOME."

Text-Based Console Login

If you sit down at your PC and log in to a Linux system that has not been booted to a graphical login, you see a prompt similar to this one:

```
Ubuntu 10.10 maverick seymour ttyl
seymour login:
```

Your prompt might vary, depending on the version of Ubuntu you are using and the method you are using to connect. In any event, at this prompt, type in your username and press Enter. When you are prompted for your password, type it in and press Enter.

NOTE

Your password is not echoed back to you, which is a good idea. Why is it a good idea? Well, people are prevented from looking over your shoulder and seeing your screen input. It is not difficult to guess that a five-letter password might correspond to the user's spouse's first name!

Logging Out

Use the `exit` or `logout` command or Ctrl+D to exit your session. You are then returned to the login prompt. If you use virtual consoles, remember to exit each console before leaving your PC. (Otherwise, someone could easily sit down and use your account.)

Logging In and Out from a Remote Computer

Although you can happily log in on your computer, an act known as a *local* login, you can also log in to your computer via a network connection from a remote computer. Linux-based operating systems provide a number of remote access commands you can use to log in to other computers on your local area network (LAN), wide area network (WAN), or the Internet. Note that not only must you have an account on the remote computer, but the remote computer must be configured to support remote logins—otherwise, you won't be able to log in.

NOTE

See Chapter 14, "Networking," to see how to set up network interfaces with Linux to support remote network logins and Chapter 11 to see how to start remote access services (such as `sshd`).

The best and most secure way to log in to a remote Linux computer is to use `ssh`, the Secure Shell client. Your login and session are encrypted while you work on the remote computer. The `ssh` client features many command-line options, but can be simply used with the name or IP address of the remote computer, like this:

```
matthew@seymour:~$ ssh 192.168.0.41
The authenticity of host '192.168.0.41 (192.168.0.41)' can't be established.
RSA key fingerprint is e1:db:6c:da:3f:fc:56:1b:52:f9:94:e0:d1:1d:31:50.
Are you sure you want to continue connecting (yes/no)?
```

yes

The first time you connect with a remote computer using `ssh`, Linux displays the remote computer's encrypted identity key and asks you to verify the connection. After you type `yes` and press Enter, you are warned that the remote computer's identity (key) has been entered in a file named `known_hosts` under the `.ssh` directory in your home directory. You are also prompted to enter your password:

```
Warning: Permanently added '192.168.0.41' (RSA) \
to the list of known hosts.
matthew@192.168.0.41's password:
matthew@babbage~$
```

After entering your password, you can work on the remote computer, which you can confirm by noticing the changed prompt that now uses the name of the remote computer on which you are working. Again, because you are using `ssh`, everything you enter on the keyboard in communication with the remote computer is encrypted. When you log out, you will return to the shell on your computer.

```
matthew@babbage~$ logout
matthew@seymour:~$
```

Using Environment Variables

A number of in-memory variables are assigned and loaded by default when you log in. These variables are known as shell *environment variables and* can be used by various commands to get information about your environment, such as the type of system you are running, your home directory, and the shell in use. Environment variables are used to help tailor the computing environment of your system and include helpful specifications and setup, such as default locations of executable files and software libraries. If you begin writing shell scripts, you might use environment variables in your scripts. Until then, you need to be aware only of what environment variables are and do.

The following list includes a number of environment variables, along with descriptions of how the shell uses them:

- `PWD`—provides the full path to your current working directory, used by the `pwd` command, such as `/home/matthew/Documents`

- USER—declares the user's name, such as matthew
- LANG—sets the default language, such as English
- SHELL—declares the name and location of the current shell, such as /bin/bash
- PATH—sets the default location(s) of executable files, such as /bin, /usr/bin, and so on
- TERM—sets the type of terminal in use, such as vt100, which can be important when using screen-oriented programs, such as text editors
- You can print the current value of any environment variable using echo $VARIABLE-NAME, like this:

```
matthew@seymour:~$ echo $USER
matthew
matthew@seymour:~$
```


NOTE

Each shell can have its own feature set and language syntax, as well as a unique set of default environment variables. See Chapter 15, "Remote Access for SSH and Telnet," for more information about using the different shells included with Ubuntu.

You can use the env or printenv command to display all environment variables, like so:

```
matthew@seymour:~$ env
ORBIT_SOCKETDIR=/tmp/orbit-matthew
SSH_AGENT_PID=1729
TERM=xterm
SHELL=/bin/bash
WINDOWID=71303173
GNOME_KEYRING_CONTROL=/tmp/keyring-qTEFTw
GTK_MODULES=canberra-gtk-module
USER=matt
hew
SSH_AUTH_SOCK=/tmp/keyring-qTEFTw/ssh
DEFAULTS_PATH=/usr/share/gconf/gnome.default.path
SESSION_MANAGER=local/seymour:/tmp/.ICE-unix/1695
USERNAME=matthew
XDG_CONFIG_DIRS=/etc/xdg/xdg-gnome:/etc/xdg
DESKTOP_SESSION=gnome
PATH=/usr/local/sbin:/usr/local/bin:/usr/sbin:/usr/bin:/sbin:/bin:/usr/games
PWD=/home/matt
hew
GDM_KEYBOARD_LAYOUT=us
LANG=en_US.utf8
```

```
GNOME_KEYRING_PID=1677
MANDATORY_PATH=/usr/share/gconf/gnome.mandatory.path
GDM_LANG=en_US.utf8
GDMSESSION=gnome
HISTCONTROL=ignoreboth
SPEECHD_PORT=7560
SHLVL=1
HOME=/home/matt
hew
LOGNAME=matt
hew
LESSOPEN=¦ /usr/bin/lesspipe %s
DISPLAY=:0.0
LESSCLOSE=/usr/bin/lesspipe %s %s
XAUTHORITY=/var/run/gdm/auth-for-matthew-PzcGqF/database
COLORTERM=gnome-terminal
OLDPWD=/var/lib/mlocate
_=/usr/bin/env
```

This abbreviated list shows some of the common variables. These variables are set by configuration or *resource* files contained in the /etc, /etc/skel, or user /home directory. You can find default settings for bash, for example, in /etc/profile and /etc/bashrc as well as .bashrc or .bash_profile files in your home directory. Read the man page for bash for details about using these configuration files.

One of the most important environment variables is $PATH, which defines the location of executable files. For example, if, as a regular user, you try to use a command that is not located in your $PATH (such as the imaginary command command), you will see something like this:

```
matthew@seymour:~$ command
-bash: command: command not found
```

If the command that you're trying to execute exists in the Ubuntu software repositories, but is not yet installed on your system, Ubuntu will respond with the correct command to install the command.

```
matthew@seymour:~$ command


The program 'command' is currently not installed. You can install it by typing:

sudo apt-get install command
```

However, you might know that command is definitely installed on your system, and you can verify this by using the whereis command, like so:

```
$ whereis command
command: /sbin/command
```

You can also run the command by typing its full pathname or complete directory specification, like this:

```
$ /sbin/command
```

As you can see in this example, the command `command` is indeed installed. What happened is that by default, the `/sbin` directory is not in your $PATH. One of the reasons for this is that commands under the `/sbin` directory are normally intended to be run only by root. You can add /sbin to your $PATH by editing the file `.bash_profile` in your home directory (if you use the bash shell by default, like most Linux users). Look for the following line:

```
PATH=$PATH:$HOME/bin
```

You can then edit this file, perhaps using the `vi` editor (discussed later in this chapter), to add the `/sbin` directory like so:

```
PATH=$PATH:/sbin$HOME/bin
```


Save the file. The next time you log in, the /sbin directory is in your $PATH. One way to use this change right away is to read in the new settings in .bash_profile by using the bash shell's source command like so:

```
$ source .bash_profile
```

You can now run commands located in the `/sbin` directory without the need to explicitly type the full pathname.

Some Linux commands also use environment variables, for example, to acquire configuration information (such as a communications program looking for a variable such as `BAUD_RATE`, which might denote a default modem speed).

To experiment with the environment variables, you can modify the `PS1` variable to manipulate the appearance of your shell prompt. If you are working with `bash`, you can use its built-in `export` command to change the shell prompt. For example, if your default shell prompt looks like this:

```
matthew@seymour:~$
```

You can change its appearance by using the PS1 variable like this:

```
$ PS1='$OSTYPE r00lz ->'
```

After you press Enter, you see

```
linux-gnu r00lz ->
```

NOTES

See the `bash` man page for other variables you can use for prompt settings.

Using the Text Editors

Linux distributions include a number of applications known as *text editors* that you can use to create text files or edit system configuration files. Text editors are similar to word processing programs, but generally have fewer features, work only with text files, and might or might not support spell checking or formatting. Text editors range in features and ease of use and are found on nearly every Linux distribution. The number of editors installed on your system depends on what software packages you've installed on the system.

Some of the more popular console-based text editors include:

- `emacs`—The comprehensive GNU `emacs` editing environment, which is much more than an editor; see the section "Working with `emacs`" later in this chapter.
- `joe`—Joe's Own Editor, a text editor, which can be used to emulate other editors.
- `nano`—A simple text editor similar to the `pico` text editor included with the `pine` email program.
- `vim`—An improved, compatible version of the `vi` text editor (which we call `vi` in the rest of this chapter because it has a symbolic link named `vi` and a symbolically linked manual page).

Note that not all text editors are *screen oriented,* meaning designed for use from a terminal. Some of the text editors are designed to run from a graphical desktop and which provide a graphical interface with menu bars, buttons, scrollbars, and so on, are:

- `gedit`—A GUI text editor for GNOME
- `kate`—A simple KDE text editor
- `kedit`—Another simple KDE text editor

A good reason to learn how to use a text-based editor, such as `vi or nano`, is that system maintenance and recovery operations almost never take place during X Window sessions, negating the use of a GUI editor. Many larger, more complex and capable editors do not work when Linux is booted to its single-user or maintenance mode. If anything does go wrong with your system and you can't log into the X Window system and its graphical user interface, knowledge and experience of using both the command line and text editors will turn out to be very important. Make a point of opening some of the editors and playing around with them; you never know—you might just thank me someday!

Another reason to learn how to use a text-based editor under the Linux console mode is so that you can edit text files through remote shell sessions, because many servers will not host graphical desktops.

Working with `vi`

The one editor found on nearly every UNIX and Linux system is the `vi` editor, originally written by Bill Joy. This simple-to-use but incredibly capable editor features a somewhat cryptic command set, but you can put it to use with only a few commands. Although many experienced UNIX and Linux users use `vi` extensively during computing sessions, many users who do only quick and simple editing might not need all its power and may prefer an easier-to-use text editor such as `pico` or GNU `nano`. Diehard GNU fans and programmers definitely use `emacs`.

However, learning how to use `vi` is a good idea. You might need to edit files on a Linux system with a minimal install, or a remote server without a more extensive offering of installed text editors. Chances are nearly 100 percent that `vi` will be available.

You can start an editing session by using the `vi` command like this:

```
matthew@seymour:~$ vi file.txt
```

The vi command works by using an insert (or editing) mode, and a viewing (or command) mode.

When you first start editing, you are in the viewing mode. You can use your arrow or other navigation keys (as shown later) to scroll through the text. To start editing, press the `i` key to insert text or the `a` key to append text. When you're finished, use the Esc key to toggle out of the insert or append modes and into the viewing (or command) mode. To enter a command, type a colon (`:`), followed by the command, such as `w` to write the file, and press Enter.

Although `vi` supports many complex editing operations and numerous commands, you can accomplish work by using a few basic commands. These basic `vi` commands are

- **Cursor movement**—`h, j, k, l` (left, down, up, and right)
- **Delete character**—`x`
- **Delete line**—`dd`
- **Mode toggle**—`Esc`, `Insert` (or `i`)
- **Quit**—`:q`
- **Quit without saving**—`:q!`
- **Run a shell command**—`:sh` (use `'exit'` to return)
- **Save file**—`:w`
- **Text search**—`/`

NOTE

Use the `vimtutor` command to quickly learn how to use `vi`'s keyboard commands. The tutorial takes less than 30 minutes, and it teaches new users how to start or stop the editor, navigate files, insert and delete text, and perform search, replace, and insert operations.

Working with `emacs`

Richard M. Stallman's GNU `emacs` editor, like `vi`, is included with Ubuntu and nearly every other Linux distribution. Unlike other UNIX and Linux text editors, `emacs` is much more than a simple text editor—it is an editing environment and can be used to compile and build programs and act as an electronic diary, appointment book, and calendar; use it to compose and send electronic mail, read Usenet news, and even play games. The reason for this capability is that `emacs` contains a built-in language interpreter that uses the Elisp (`emacs` LISP) programming language. `emacs` is not installed in Ubuntu by default. To use emacs, the package you need to install is called `emacs`. See Chapter 32, "Managing Software."

You can start an `emacs` editing session like this:

```
matthew@seymour:~$ emacs file.txt
```

TIP

If you start `emacs` when using X11, the editor launches in its own floating window. To force `emacs` to display inside a terminal window instead of its own window (which can be useful if the window is a login at a remote computer), use the `-nw` command-line option like this: `emacs -nw file.txt`.

The `emacs` editor uses an extensive set of keystroke and named commands, but you can work with it by using a basic command subset. Many of these basic commands require you to hold down the Ctrl key, or to first press a *meta* key (generally mapped to the Alt key). The basic commands are listed in Table 4.2.

TABLE 4.2 Emacs Editing Commands

Action	Command
Abort	Ctrl+G
Cursor left	Ctrl+B
Cursor down	Ctrl+N
Cursor right	Ctrl+F
Cursor up	Ctrl+P
Delete character	Ctrl+D
Delete line	Ctrl+K
Go to start of line	Ctrl+A
Go to end of line	Ctrl+E
Help	Ctrl+H
Quit	Ctrl+X, Ctrl+C
Save As	Ctrl+X, Ctrl+W
Save file	Ctrl+X, Ctrl+S

TABLE 4.2 Continued

Action	Command
Search backward	Ctrl+R
Search forward	Ctrl+S
Start tutorial	Ctrl+H, T
Undo	Ctrl+X, U

TIP

One of the best reasons to learn how to use `emacs` is that you can use nearly all the same keystrokes to edit commands on the `bash` shell command line. Another reason is that like `vi`, `emacs` is universally available for installation on nearly every UNIX and Linux system, including Apple's Mac OS X.

Working with Permissions

Under Linux (and UNIX), everything in the file system, including directories and devices, is a file. And every file on your system has an accompanying set of permissions based on ownership. These permissions provide data security by giving specific permission settings to every single item denoting who may read, write, and/or execute the file. These permissions are set individually for the file's owner, for members of the group the file belongs to, and for all others on the system.

You can examine the default permissions for a file you create by using the `umask` command, which lists default permissions using the number system explained next, or by using the `touch` command and then the `ls` command's long-format listing like this:

```
matthew@seymour:~$ touch file
matthew@seymour:~$ ls -l file
-rw-r--r-- 1 matthew matthew 0 2010-06-30 13:06 file
```

In this example, the touch command is used to quickly create a file. The ls command then reports on the file, displaying the following (from left to right):

- **The type of file created**—Common indicators of the type of file are in the leading letter in the output. A blank (which is represented by a dash, as in the preceding example) designates a plain file, `d` designates a directory, `c` designates a character device (such as `/dev/ttyS0`), and `b` is used for a block device (such as `/dev/sda`).
- **Permissions**—Read, write, and execute permissions for the owner, group, and all others on the system. (You learn more about these permissions later in this section.)
- **Number of links to the file**—The number one (`1`) designates that there is only one file, whereas any other number indicates that there might be one or more hard-linked

files. Links are created with the `ln` command. A hard-linked file is an exact copy of the file, but it might be located elsewhere on the system. Symbolic links of directories can also be created, but only the root operator can create a hard link of a directory.

- **The owner**—The account that owns the file; this is originally the file creator, but you can change this designation using the `chown` command.
- **The group**—The group of users allowed to access the file; this is originally the file creator's main group, but you can change this designation using the `chgrp` command.
- **File size and creation/modification date**—The last two elements indicate the size of the file in bytes and the date the file was created or last modified.

Assigning Permissions

Under Linux, permissions are grouped by owner, group, and others, with read, write, and execute permission assigned to each, like so:

```
Owner    Group    Others
Rwx      rwx      rxw
```

Permissions can be indicated by mnemonic or octal characters. Mnemonic characters are

- `r` indicates permission for an owner, member of the owner's group, or others to open and read the file.
- `w` indicates permission for an owner, member of the owner's group, or others to open and write to the file.
- `x` indicates permission for an owner, member of the owner's group, or others to execute the file (or read a directory).

In the previous example for the file named `file`, the owner, `matthew`, has read and write permission. Any member of the group named `matthew` may only read the file. All other users may only read the file. Also note that default permissions for files created by the root operator (while using sudo or a root account) will be different because of `umask` settings assigned by the shell.

Many users prefer to use numeric codes, based on octal (base 8) values, to represent permissions. Here's what these values mean:

- `4` indicates read permission.
- `2` indicates write permission.
- `1` indicates execute permission.

In octal notation, the previous example file has a permission setting of `664` (read + write or `4 + 2`, read + write or `4 + 2`, read-only or `4`). Although you can use either form of permissions notation, octal is easy to use quickly after you visualize and understand how permissions are numbered.

NOTE

In Linux, you can create groups to assign a number of users access to common directories and files, based on permissions. You might assign everyone in accounting to a group named `accounting` and allow that group access to accounts payable files while disallowing access by other departments. Defined groups are maintained by the root operator, but you can use the `newgrp` command to temporarily join other groups to access files (as long as the root operator has added you to the other groups). You can also allow or deny other groups' access to your files by modifying the group permissions of your files.

Directory Permissions

Directories are also files under Linux. For example, again use the `ls` command to show permissions like this:

```
matthew@seymour:~$ mkdir directory
matthew@seymour:~$ ls -ld directory
drwxr-xr-x                      2 matthew  matthew  4096 2010-06-30 13:23 directory
```

In this example, the `mkdir` command is used to create a directory. The `ls` command and its `-ld` option is used to show the permissions and other information about the directory (not its contents). Here you can see that the directory has permission values of `755` (read + write + execute or `4 + 2 + 1`, read + execute or `4 + 1`, and read + execute or `4 + 1`).

This shows that the owner can read and write to the directory and, because of execute permission, also list the directory's contents. Group members and all other users can list only the directory contents. Note that directories require execute permission for anyone to be able to view their contents.

You should also notice that the `ls` command's output shows a leading `d` in the permissions field. This letter specifies that this file is a directory; normal files have a blank field in its place. Other files, such as those specifying a block or character device, have a different letter.

For example, if you examine the device file for a Linux serial port, you will see:

```
matthew@seymour:~$ ls -l /dev/ttyS0
crw-rw---- 1 root dialout 4, 64 2010-06-30 08:13 /dev/ttyS0
```

Here, `/dev/ttyS0` is a character device (such as a serial communications port and designated by a c) owned by root and available to anyone in the `dialout` group. The device has permissions of `660` (read + write, read + write, no permission).

On the other hand, if you examine the device file for an IDE hard drive, you see:

```
matthew@seymour:~$ ls -l /dev/sda
brw-rw---- 1 root disk 8, 0 2010-06-30 08:13 /dev/sda
```

In this example, b designates a block device (a device that transfers and caches data in blocks) with similar permissions. Other device entries you will run across on your Linux system include symbolic links, designated by s.

You can use the chmod command to alter a file's permissions. This command uses various forms of command syntax, including octal or a mnemonic form (such as u, g, o, or a and rwx, and so on) to specify a desired change. The chmod command can be used to add, remove, or modify file or directory permissions to protect, hide, or open up access to a file by other users (except for the root account or a user with super-user permission and using sudo, either of which can access any file or directory on a Linux system).

The mnemonic forms of chmod's options are (when used with a plus character, +, to add, or a minus sign, -, to remove):

- u—Adds or removes user (owner) read, write, or execute permission
- g—Adds or removes group read, write, or execute permission
- o—Adds or removes read, write, or execute permission for others not in a file's group
- a—Adds or removes read, write, or execute permission for all users
- r—Adds or removes read permission
- w—Adds or removes write permission
- x—Adds or removes execution permission

For example, if you create a file, such as a readme.txt, the file will have default permissions (set by the umask setting in /etc/bashrc) of

```
-rw-r--r-- 1 matthew matthew 0 2010-06-30 13:33 readme.txt
```

As you can see, you can read and write the file. Anyone else can only read the file (and only if it is outside your home directory, which will have read, write, and execute permission set only for you, the owner). You can remove all write permission for anyone by using chmod, the minus sign, and aw like so:

```
matthew@seymour:~$ chmod a-w readme.txt
matthew@seymour:~$ ls -l readme.txt
-r--r--r-- 1 matthew matthew 0 2010-06-30 13:33 readme.txt
```

Now, no one can write to the file (except you, if the file is in your home or /tmp directory because of directory permissions). To restore read and write permission for only you as the owner, use the plus sign and the u and rw options like so:

```
matthew@seymour:~$ chmod u+rw readme.txt
matthew@seymour:~$ ls -l readme.txt
-rw-r--r-- 1 matthew matthew 0 2010-06-30 13:33 readme.txt
```

You can also use the octal form of the chmod command, for example, to modify a file's permissions so that only you, the owner, can read and write a file. Use the chmod command and a file permission of 600, like this:

```
matthew@seymour:~$ chmod 600 readme.txt
matthew@seymour:~$ ls -l readme.txt
-rw------- 1 matthew matthew 0 2010-06-30 13:33 readme.txt
```

If you take away execution permission for a directory, files might be hidden inside and may not be listed or accessed by anyone else (except the root operator, of course, who has access to any file on your system). By using various combinations of permission settings, you can quickly and easily set up a more secure environment, even as a normal user in your home directory.

Understanding Set User ID and Set Group ID Permissions

Two more types of permission are "set user ID", known as *suid*, and "set group ID," or *sgid*, permissions. These settings, when used in a program, enable any user running that program to have program owner or group owner permissions for that program. These settings enable the program to be run effectively by anyone, without requiring that each user's permissions be altered to include specific permissions for that program.

One commonly used program with suid permissions is the passwd command:

```
matthew@seymour:~$ ls -l /usr/bin/passwd
-rwsr-xr-x 1 root root 42856 2010-01-26 10:09 /usr/bin/passwd
```

This setting allows normal users to execute the command (as root) to make changes to a root-only accessible file, /etc/passwd.

You also can assign similar permission with the chfn command. This command allows users to update or change finger information in /etc/passwd. You accomplish this permission modification by using a leading 4 (or the mnemonic s) in front of the three octal values.

NOTE

Other files that might have suid or guid permissions include at, rcp, rlogin, rsh, chage, chsh, ssh, crontab, sudo, sendmail, ping, mount, and several UNIX-to-UNIX Copy (UUCP) utilities. Many programs (such as games) might also have this type of permission to access a sound device.

Files or programs that have suid or guid permissions can sometimes present security holes because they bypass normal permissions. This problem is compounded if the permission extends to an executable binary (a command) with an inherent security flaw because it could lead to any system user or intruder gaining root access. In past exploits, this typically happened when a user fed a vulnerable command with unexpected input (such as a long pathname or option); the command would fail, and the user would be presented a root prompt. Although Linux developers are constantly on the lookout for poor programming practices, new exploits are found all the time, and can crop up unexpectedly, especially in newer software packages that haven't had the benefit of peer developer review.

Savvy Linux system administrators keep the number of suid or guid files present on a system to a minimum. The `find` command can be used to display all such files on your system:

```
matthew@seymour:~$ sudo find / -type f -perm /6000 -exec ls -l {} \;
```

NOTE

The `find` command is quite helpful and can be used for many purposes, such as before or during backup operations. See the section "Using Backup Software" in Chapter 13, "Backing Up."

Note that the programs do not necessarily have to be removed from your system. If your users really do not need to use the program, you can remove the programs execute permission for anyone. You have to decide, as the root operator, whether your users are allowed, for example, to mount and unmount CD-ROMs or other media on your system. Although Linux-based operating systems can be set up to accommodate ease of use and convenience, allowing programs such as `mount` to be suid might not be the best security policy. Other candidates for suid permission change could include the `chsh`, `at`, or chage commands.

Working as Root

The root, or super-user account, is a special account and user on UNIX and Linux systems. Super-user permissions are required in part because of the restrictive file permissions assigned to important system configuration files. You must have root permission to edit these files or to access or modify certain devices (such as hard drives). When logged in as root, you have total control over your system, which can be dangerous.

When you work in root, you can destroy a running system with a simple invocation of the `rm` command like this:

```
matthew@seymour:~$ sudo rm -rf /
```

This command line not only deletes files and directories, but also could wipe out file systems on other partitions and even remote computers. This alone is reason enough to take precautions when using root access.

The only time you should run Linux as the super-user is when you are configuring the file system, for example, or to repair or maintain the system. Logging in and using Linux as the root operator isn't a good idea because it defeats the entire concept of file permissions.

Knowing how to run commands as the super-user (root) without logging in as root can help avoid serious missteps when configuring your system. In Ubuntu, you can use `sudo` to allow you to execute single commands as root and then quickly return to normal user status. For example, if you would like to edit your system's file system table (a simple text file that describes local or remote storage devices, their type, and location), you can use `sudo` like this:

```
matthew@seymour:~$ sudo nano -w /etc/fstab
Password:
```

After you press Enter, you are prompted for a password that gives you access to root. This extra step can also help you "think before you leap" into the command. Enter the root password, and you are then editing `/etc/fstab`, using the nano editor with line wrapping disabled (thanks to the -w).

CAUTION

Before editing any important system or software service configuration file, make a backup copy. Then make sure to launch your text editor with line wrapping disabled. If you edit a configuration file without disabling line wrapping, you could insert spurious carriage returns and line feeds into its contents, causing the configured service to fail when restarting. By convention, nearly all configuration files are formatted for 80-character text width, but this is not always the case. By default, the `vi` and `emacs` editors don't use line wrap.

Creating Users

When a Linux system administrator creates a user, an entry in `/etc/passwd` for the user is created. The system also creates a directory, labeled with the user's username, in the `/home` directory. For example, if you create a user named `heather`, the user's home directory is `/home/heather`.

NOTE

In this chapter, you learn how to manage users from the command line. See Chapter 10, "Managing Users," for more information on user administration with Ubuntu using graphical administration utilities, such as the graphical `users-admin` client found in the menu at System, Administration, Users and Groups.

Use the `useradd` command, along with a user's name, to quickly create a user:

```
matthew@seymour:~$ sudo useradd ryan
```

After creating the user, you must also create the user's initial password with the passwd command:

```
matthew@seymour:~$ sudo passwd ryan


Changing password for user ryan.
New password:
Retype new password:
passwd: all authentication tokens updated successfully.
```

Enter the new password twice. If you do not create an initial password for a new user, the user cannot log in.

You can view useradd's default new user settings by using the command and its -D option, like this:

```
matthew@seymour:~$ useradd -D
GROUP=100
HOME=/home
INACTIVE=-1
EXPIRE=
SHELL=/bin/sh
SKEL=/etc/skel
CREATE_MAIL_SPOOL=no
```

These options display the default group ID, home directory, account and password policy (active forever with no password expiration), the default shell, and the directory containing defaults for the shell.

The useradd command has many command-line options. The command can be used to set policies and dates for the new user's password, assign a login shell, assign group membership, and other aspects of a user's account. See man useradd for more info.

Deleting Users

Use the userdel command to delete users from your system. This command removes a user's entry in the system's /etc/passwd file. You should also use the command's -r option to remove all the user's files and directories (such as the user's mail spool file under /var/spool/mail):

```
matthew@seymour:~$ sudo userdel -r andrew
```

If you do not use the -r option, you have to manually delete the user's directory under /home, along with the user's /var/spool/mail queue.

Shutting Down the System

Use the `shutdown` command to shut down your system. The `shutdown` command has a number of different command-line options (such as shutting down at a predetermined time), but the fastest way to cleanly shut down Linux is to use the `-h` or halt option, followed by the word `now` or the numeral zero (`0`), like this:

```
matthew@seymour:~$ sudo shutdown -h now
```

or

```
matthew@seymour:~$ sudo shutdown -h 0
```

To incorporate a timed shutdown and a pertinent message to all active users, use shutdown's time and message options, like so:

```
matthew@seymour:~$ sudo shutdown -h 18:30 "System is going down for maintenance this
evening at 6:30 p.m. Please make sure you have saved your work and logged out by
then or you may lose data."
```

This example shuts down your system and provides a warning to all active users 15 minutes before the shutdown (or reboot). Shutting down a running server can be considered drastic, especially if there are active users or exchanges of important data occurring (such as a backup in progress). One good approach is to warn users ahead of time. This can be done by editing the system Message of the Day (MOTD) `motd` file, which displays a message to users when they login using the command line interface, as is common on multi-user systems.

It used to be that to create a custom MOTD you only had to use a text editor and change the contents of `/etc/motd`. However, this has changed in Ubuntu as the developers have added a way to automatically and regularly update some useful information contained in MOTD using cron. To modify how the MOTD is updated, you should install update-motd and read the man page.

You can also make downtimes part of a regular schedule, perhaps to coincide with security audits, software updates, or hardware maintenance.

You should shut down Ubuntu for only a few very specific reasons:

- You are not using the computer, no other users are logged in or expected to need or use the system, such as your personal desktop or laptop computer, and you want to conserve electrical power.
- You need to perform system maintenance that requires any or all system services to be stopped.
- You want to replace integral hardware.

TIP

Do not shut down your computer if you suspect that one or more intruders has infiltrated your system; instead, disconnect the machine from any or all networks and make a backup copy of your hard drives. You might want to also keep the machine running to examine the contents of memory and to examine system logs. Exceptions to this are when the system contains only trivial data files and non-essential services, such as a personal computer that is only used to run a web browser, and when you have no intention of trying to track down what an intruder may have changed, either to repair the damage or to try to catch them using computer forensics, but rather plan to merely wipe everything clean and rebuild or reinstall the system from scratch.

Rebooting the System

You should also use the `shutdown` command to reboot your system. The fastest way to cleanly reboot Linux is to use the `-r` option, and the word `now` or the numeral zero (`0`):

```
matthew@seymour:~$ sudo shutdown -r now
```

or

```
matthew@seymour:~$ sudo shutdown -r 0
```

Both rebooting and shutting down can have dire consequences if performed at the wrong time (such as during backups or critical file transfers, which arouses the ire of your system's users). However, Linux-based operating systems are designed to properly stop active system services in an orderly fashion. Other commands you can use to shut down and reboot Linux are the halt and reboot commands, but the shutdown command is more flexible.

Reading Documentation

Although you learn the basics of using Ubuntu in this book, you need time and practice to master and troubleshoot more complex aspects of the Linux operating system and your distribution. As with any operating system, you can expect to encounter some problems or perplexing questions as you continue to work with Linux. The first place to turn for help with these issues is the documentation included with your system; if you cannot find the information you need there, check Ubuntu's website.

Using Apropros

Linux, like UNIX, is a self-documenting system, with man pages accessible through the `man` command. Linux offers many other helpful commands for accessing its documentation. You can use the `apropos` command—for example, with a keyword such as `partition`—to find commands related to partitioning, like this:

```
matthew@seymour:~$ apropos partition
addpart         (8)     - Simple wrapper around the "add partition" ioctl
all-swaps       (7)     - Event signaling that all swap partitions have been ac...
```

```
cfdisk        (8)   - Curses/slang based disk partition table manipulator fo...
delpart       (8)   - Simple wrapper around the "del partition" ioctl
fdisk         (8)   - Partition table manipulator for Linux
gparted       (8)   - Gnome partition editor for manipulating disk partitions.
Mpartition    (1)   - Partition an MSDOS hard disk
Partprobe     (8)   - Inform the OS of partition table changes
Partx         (8)   - Telling the kernel about presence and numbering of on-...
Pvcreate      (8)   - Initialize a disk or partition for use by LVM
Pvresize      (8)   - Resize a disk or partition in use by LVM2
Sfdisk        (8)   - Partition table manipulator for Linux
```

To find a command and its documentation, you can use the `whereis` command. For example, if you are looking for the `fdisk` command, you can do this:

```
$ whereis fdisk
fdisk: /sbin/fdisk /usr/share/man/man8/fdisk.8.gz
```


Using Man Pages

To learn more about a command or program, use the `man` command, followed by the name of the command. Man pages are stored in places like `/usr/share/man` and `/usr/local/share/man`, but you don't need to know that. To read a man page, such as the one for the `rm` command, use the `man` command like this:

```
matthew@seymour:~$ man rm
```

After you press Enter, the less command (a Linux command known as a *pager*) displays the man page. The less command is a text browser you can use to scroll forward and backward (even sideways) through the document to learn more about the command. Type the letter `h` to get help, use the forward slash to enter a search string, or press `q` to quit.

NOTE

Nearly all the hundreds of commands included with Linux each have a man page; however, some do not or may only have simple pages. You may also use the `info` command to read more detailed information about some commands or as a replacement for others. For example, to learn even more about `info` (which has a rather extensive manual page), use the `info` command like this:

```
$ info info
```

Use the arrow keys to navigate through the document and press `q` to quit reading.

The following programs and built-in shell commands are commonly used when working at the command line. These commands are organized by category to help you understand the command's purpose. If you need to find full information for using the command, you can find that information under the command's man page.

- **Managing users and groups**—chage, chfn, chsh, edquota, gpasswd, groupadd, groupdel, groupmod, groups, mkpasswd, newgrp, newusers, passwd, umask, useradd, userdel, usermod
- **Managing files and file systems**—cat, cd, chattr, chmod, chown, compress, cp, dd, fdisk, find, gzip, ln, mkdir, mksfs, mount, mv, rm, rmdir, rpm, sort, swapon, swapoff, tar, touch, umount, uncompress, uniq, unzip, zip
- **Managing running programs**—bg, fg, kill, killall, nice, ps, pstree, renice, top, watch
- **Getting information**—apropos, cal, cat, cmp, date, diff, df, dir, dmesg, du, env, file, free, grep, head, info, last, less, locate, ls, lsattr, man, more, pinfo, ps, pwd, stat, strings, tac, tail, top, uname, uptime, vdir, vmstat, w, wc, whatis, whereis, which, who, whoami
- **Console text editors**—ed, jed, joe, mcedit, nano, red, sed, vim
- **Console Internet and network commands**—bing, elm, ftp, host, hostname, ifconfig, links, lynx, mail, mutt, ncftp, netconfig, netstat, pine, ping, pump, rdate, route, scp, sftp, ssh, tcpdump, traceroute, whois, wire-test

Reference

- https://help.ubuntu.com/community/UsingTheTerminal—The Ubuntu community help page for using the terminal.
- https://help.ubuntu.com/community/LinuxFilesystemTreeOverview—The Ubuntu community help page for and overview of the Linux file system tree.
- https://help.ubuntu.com/community/RootSudo—An Ubuntu community page explaining sudo, the philosophy behind using it by default, and how to use it.
- www.vim.org/—Home page for the `vim` (`vi` clone) editor included with Linux distributions. Check here for updates, bug fixes, and news about this editor.
- www.gnu.org/software/emacs/emacs.html—Home page for the FSF's GNU `emacs` editing environment; you can find additional documentation and links to the source code for the latest version here.
- www.nano-editor.org/—Home page for the GNU `nano` editor environment.

CHAPTER 5

On the Internet

IN THIS CHAPTER

The Internet is everywhere. From cell phones to offices, from game consoles to iPads, we are surrounded by multiple access routes to online information and communication. Ubuntu is no outsider when it comes to accessing information through the Internet; it comes equipped with all the tools you need to connect to other people across the globe.

In this chapter we'll take a look at some of the popular Internet applications that are available with Ubuntu. You'll find out about Firefox and the new option, Google Chrome. We'll also investigate some of the email clients available. Other topics include RSS feed readers, Instant Messaging (through IRC and other networks), and reading newsgroups.

A BRIEF INTRODUCTION TO THE INTERNET

The Internet itself was first brought to life by the U.S. Department of Defense in 1969. It was called ARPANET after the Department of Defense's Advanced Research Projects Agency. Designed to build a network that would withstand major catastrophe (this was the peak of the Cold War), it soon grew to encompass more and more networks to build the Internet. Then, in 1991, Tim Berners-Lee of CERN developed the idea of the World Wide Web, including Hypertext Transfer Protocol (HTTP) and Hypertext Markup Language (HTML). This gave us what we now know to be the Internet.

Getting Started with Firefox

One of the most popular web browsers, and in fact the default web browser in Ubuntu, is Mozilla Firefox (see Figure 5.1). Built on a solid code base that is derived from the Mozilla Suite, Firefox offers an open source and more secure alternative to surfing the Internet using Internet Explorer, regardless of your operating system.

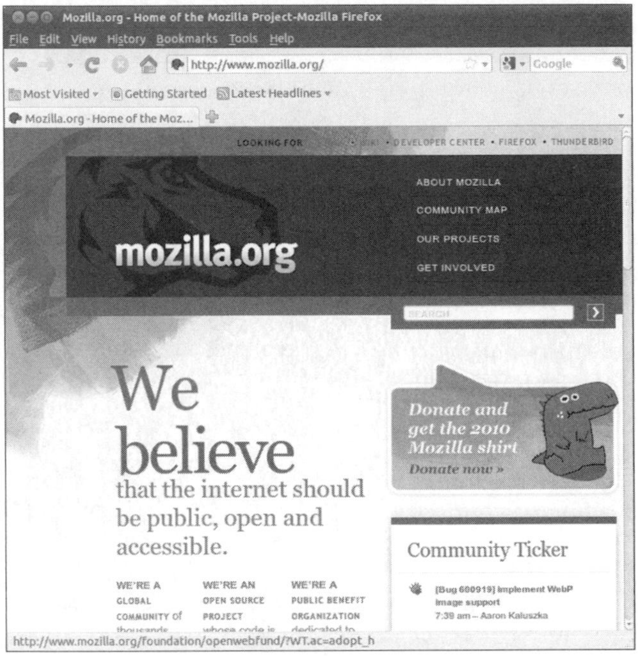

FIGURE 5.1 Mozilla Firefox—rediscover the Web. Firefox enables you to add on numerous extensions, further enhancing your experience.

In Ubuntu you can find Firefox in the menu at Applications, Internet. An even simpler way to start Firefox is to click the small Firefox icon in the top panel next to the System menu. Either way, Firefox opens.

Beyond the basic program are a wealth of plug-ins and extensions that can increase the capabilities of Firefox beyond simple web browsing. Plug-ins such as Shockwave, Flash, and Java are available for installation instantly, offered to you when first needed, as are multimedia codecs for viewing video content. Extensions provide useful additions to the browsing experience. For example, ForecastFox is an extension that gives you your local weather conditions, and Bandwidth Tester is a tool that calculates your current bandwidth. As Firefox grows, there will be more and more extensions and plug-ins that you can use to enhance your browsing pleasure.

You can find and obtain these plug-ins and extensions easily because Mozilla developers have created a site dedicated to helping you get more from Firefox. You don't have to search to find the site as there is a link in the Firefox menu at Tools, Add-ons, Get Add-ons that takes you directly to it. Particular favorites are the Adblock Plus and the StumbleUpon plug-ins. Adblock Plus allows you to nuke all those annoying banners and animations that take up so much bandwidth while you are browsing. StumbleUpon is a neat plug-in that takes you to web pages based on your preferences. Be warned, though, that StumbleUpon can be quite addictive, and you will end up wasting away many hours clicking the stumble button!

FLASH

You can easily enable Flash in your browser by installing the `flashplugin-installer` package or better yet, you can deal with the whole issue of codecs and functionality for your entire operating system right off by installing `ubuntu-restricted-extras`. Either way, Ubuntu will download the official package from Adobe and install it on your system. A browser restart is required before you try to access any Flash-enabled content.

To make things even easier, if you have not yet installed this package and visit a web page that requires flash, a pop up window will appear with information and a link to help you install it easily.

Another plug-in that we make a lot of use of is Xmarks. If, like us, you work across multiple computers and operating systems, you will no doubt have had to re-create bookmarks at every different computer and try to keep them the same. Xmarks makes this whole process much easier by allowing you to synchronize your bookmarks to multiple browsers (for example, Firefox and Google Chrome) running on different operating systems (Windows, Mac OS X, Linux).

Checking Out Google Chrome and Chromium

Anyone who has been paying attention to tech news over the last year has heard about the explosive appearance of Google Chrome (Figure 5.2). This new browser is fast, secure, expandable with extensions, and the hottest new toy on geek desktops. It is based on WebKit and other technologies, and it downloads and renders quickly while being standards compliant. You can learn more about the easy installation of Google Chrome at www.google.com/chrome?platform=linux.

Chrome is not a completely open source, but the main foundational parts are made available as Google Chromium, shown in Figure 5.3, which has most of the functionality of Chrome, but it is missing the Google branding, automatic updates, and is used as the test and development foundation for Chrome releases. As a point of interest, chromium is the metal from which chrome is made, hence the names.

You can learn more about Chromium at http://code.google.com/chromium/. It used to be necessary to install Chromium from the Google website or from the Personal Package Archive of the Google Chromium developers. Now, you may simply install chromium-browser from the Ubuntu repositories.

FIGURE 5.2 Google Chrome running in Ubuntu.

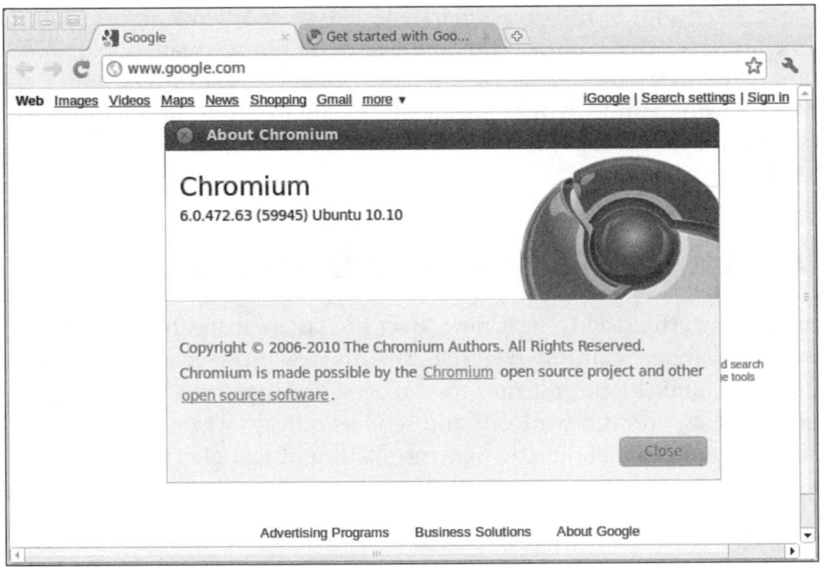

FIGURE 5.3 Chromium is the source from which Chrome is made, and it works very well.

Choosing an Email Client

Back in the earlier days of UNIX there were various text-based email clients such as elm and pine (Pine Is Not Elm). Although they looked basic, they allowed the average user to interact with email, both for composing and reading correspondence, and had some sophisticated and useful features that might not have been expected. Still, when computing became mainstream, there was a realization that people wanted friendly GUI interfaces. Soon there came a flood of email clients, some of them even cross-platform and compatible among Linux, Windows, and Mac OS X, and even traditional UNIX.

Evolution

Evolution is the standard email client that comes with Ubuntu, although to call it simply an email client is to sincerely underrate its usefulness as an application. Not only does it handle email, but it can also look after contacts and calendars and help you manage your tasks (see Figure 5.4).

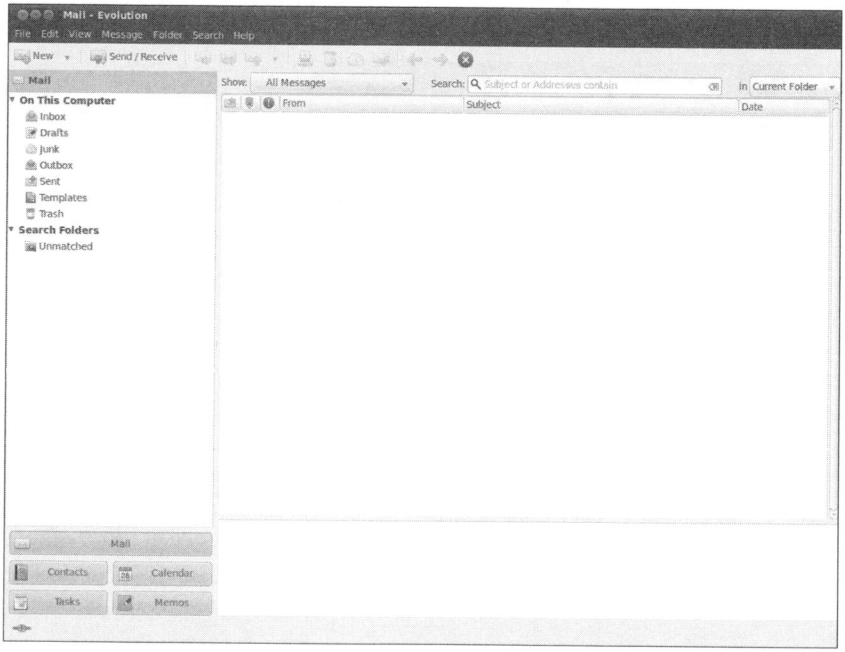

FIGURE 5.4 With Evolution you can handle all your email and contacts, as well as make appointments and track tasks.

You need to have the following information to successfully configure Evolution (or any email client):

- Your email address
- Your incoming email server name and type (that is, pop.email.com, POP, and IMAP)
- Your username and password for the incoming mail server
- Your outgoing mail server name (that is, smtp.email.com)

As many people are moving to web-based mail options like Google's Gmail or Yahoo! Mail, email programs have started to decline in popularity. One thing that sets Evolution apart is that you can still use it for the other features and disable the email portion of the program by selecting "none" as your mail transfer agent instead of POP, IMAP, and so on. In addition, Evolution can interact with an existing web calendar program if it uses one of the common formats, such as CalDAV. This allows you to use your calendar remotely as you are used to, but also permits the Ubuntu desktop to have access to your events and embed them into your desktop panel (which it does by default using Evolution).

Mozilla Thunderbird

Mozilla Thunderbird (see Figure 5.5) is the sister program to Firefox. Whereas Firefox is designed to browse the Web, Thunderbird's specialty is communication. It can handle email, network news (see later in this chapter), and RSS feeds.

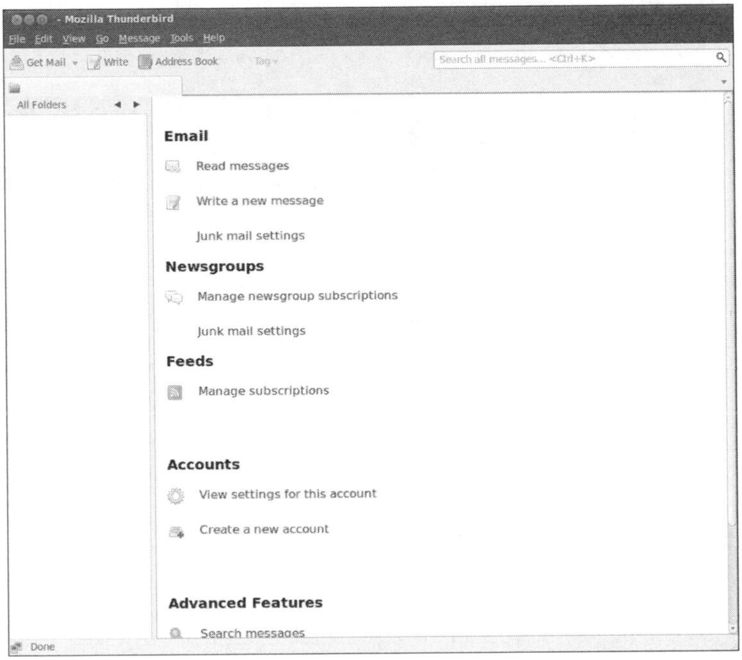

FIGURE 5.5 The natural companion to Firefox, Mozilla's lightweight email client, Thunderbird, can be found in use all over the world.

Thunderbird is not installed by default with Ubuntu, but you can install it from the Ubuntu repositories. The package is called thunderbird. As with Firefox, there are many plug-ins and extensions to enhance your email. You can also use Thunderbird for Usenet news reading.

Other Mail Clients

The mail clients that we've covered are only a few of those available. Claws is very popular because it offers spell check while typing and is well suited for use in large network environments in which network overhead and RAM usage are important considerations. Mutt is an older text-based email program that is still beloved by sysadmins for its configurability and feature set, including the easy use of GPG keys for signing email. Alpine is another text-based program based on the classic Pine, with a few upgrades. Kmail is commonly used by lovers of the KDE desktop that is commonly run as a part of many Linux-based operating systems. All of these and more are available for installation from the Ubuntu software repositories.

RSS Readers

RSS is one of the protocols of Web 2.0, the current generation of Internet content. RSS has really taken off, thanks to adoption by a large number of websites and portals.

The key advantage of RSS is that you can quickly read news from your choice of websites at a time that suits you and from one location, meaning you don't have to go to each site to view their content. Some services offer just the articles' headlines, whereas others offer full articles for you to view. RSS feeds can be accessed in various ways, even through your web browser!

Firefox

Firefox implements RSS feeds as what it calls Live Bookmarks (shown in Figure 5.6), which are essentially bookmarks with sub-bookmarks, each linking to a new page from your chosen website. Some people like to have several news sites grouped together in a folder called News in the Firefox toolbar, because this allows them to quickly browse through a collection of sites and pick out articles of interest.

FIGURE 5.6 Live Bookmarks for Firefox, making all your news fixes just a mouse click away.

Liferea

Of course, not everyone wants to read RSS feeds with the browser. The main problem with reading RSS feeds with Firefox is that you get to see only the headline, rather than any actual text. This is where a dedicated RSS reader comes in handy, and Liferea (see Figure 5.7) is one of the best.

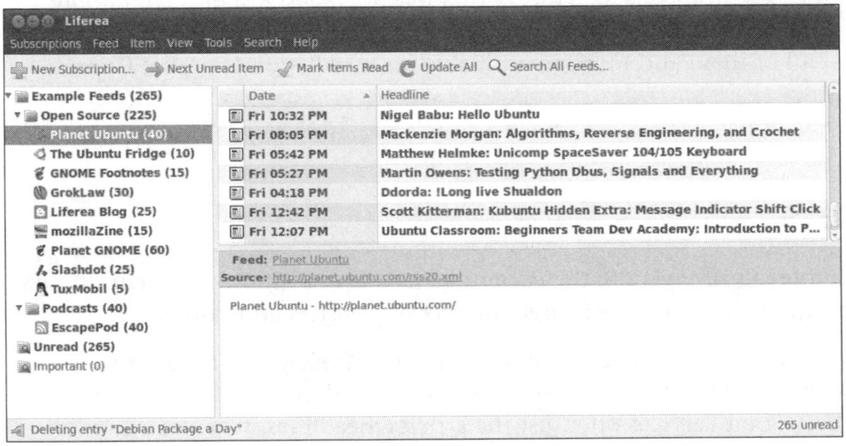

FIGURE 5.7 Read your daily news feeds with Liferea, a fantastic and easy-to-use RSS feed reader.

It is not installed by default but Liferea is available from the repositories under the name liferea. After it is installed, you can find it in the menu at Applications, Internet, Liferea.

By default, Liferea offers a number of RSS feeds, including Planet Debian, Groklaw, and Slashdot. Adding a new feed is straightforward. You select New Subscription under the Feeds menu and paste the URL of the RSS feed into the box. Liferea then retrieves all the current items available through that field, and displays the feed name on the left side for you to select and start reading.

Instant Messaging and Video Conferencing with Empathy

Instant Messaging is one of the biggest ways for people to interact over the Web. AOL was the primary force behind this, especially in America, but other networks and systems soon came onto the market, providing users with a wealth of choice.

No longer just a consumer tool, instant messaging is now a part of the corporate world, with many companies deploying internal instant messaging software for collaboration.

Empathy is the default messaging program in Ubuntu; it can be found in the menu at Applications, Internet, Empathy and can be seen in Figure 5.8. It supports text, voice, and video chat as well as file transfers using common protocols like Google Talk, AIM, and more. All you have to do is know your account information with a specific service and enter it in to Empathy—and the rest is easy.

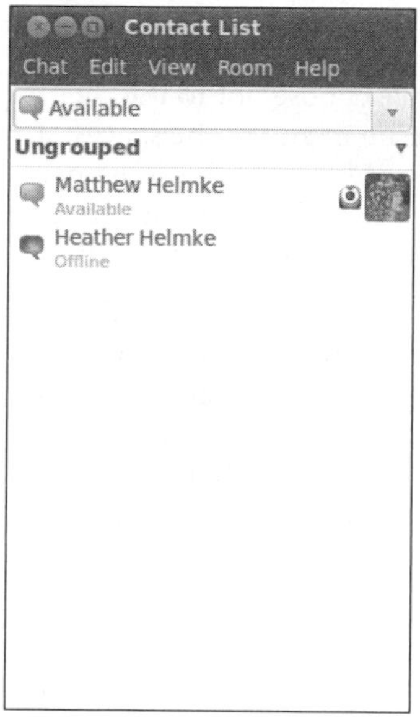

FIGURE 5.8 Empathy is easy to set up and use for great collaboration.

You can learn more about Empathy at https://help.ubuntu.com/community/Empathy.

Internet Relay Chat

As documented in RFC 2812 and RFC 2813, the IRC protocol is used for text conferencing. Like mail and news, IRC uses a client/server model. Although it is rare for an individual to set up and run an IRC server, it can be done. Most people use public IRC servers and access them with IRC clients. IRC is also the favorite and most common form of quick communication among developers in the Ubuntu community, so if that interests you, then you will certainly want to learn to use this tool.

Ubuntu provides a number of graphical IRC clients in the repositories, including XChat, Pidgin, and Quassel. You can even use Empathy, although other products are better suited for this specific task. Ubuntu also makes the console clients epic and irssi available in the repositories for those who eschew X and a graphical interface. Don't laugh, there are actually many who do this, and not just server admins, especially because they can be run on a remote server and accessed over SSH using Byobu or Screen allowing them to be left running 24/7 on that remote server. For more about Byobu and Screen, see Chapter 35, "Command Line Masterclass." If you don't already have a favorite IRC client, you should try them all.

XChat is a very popular IRC client, and the most common recommendation for IRC newcomers using Ubuntu, so we will use it as an example. After you install the program, the documentation for XChat is available in `/usr/share/docs/xchat`. It is a good idea to read them before you begin because they include an introduction and cover some of the basics of IRC.

The XChat application enables you to assign yourself up to three nicknames. You can also specify your real name and your username. Because many people choose not to use their real names in IRC chat, you are free to enter any names you desire in any of the spaces provided. You can select multiple nicknames; you might be banned from an IRC channel under one name, and you could then rejoin using another. If this seems slightly juvenile to you, you are beginning to get an idea of the type of behavior on many IRC channels (but not the ones where serious developer and Ubuntu community interactions take place).

When you open the main XChat screen, a list of IRC servers appears, as shown in Figure 5.9. After you choose a server by double-clicking it, you can view a list of channels available on that server by choosing Window, Channel List. The XChat Channel List window appears. In that window, you can choose to join channels featuring topics that interest you. To join a channel, you double-click it. Ubuntu uses irc.freenode.net for the server and the primary support channel is #ubuntu.

FIGURE 5.9 The main XChat screen presents a list of available public servers from which to select.

THE WILD SIDE OF IRC

Do not be surprised at the number of lewd topics and the use of crude language on public IRC servers. For a humorous look at the topic of IRC cursing, see www.irc.org/fun_docs/nocuss.html. This site also offers some tips for maintaining IRC etiquette, which is essential if you do not want to be the object of any of that profanity! Here are some of the most important IRC etiquette rules:

- Do not use colored text, all-capitalized text, blinking text, or "bells" (beeps caused by sending ^G to a terminal).
- Show respect for others.
- Ignore people who act inappropriately.

After you select a channel, you can join in the conversation, which appears as onscreen text. The messages scroll down the screen as new messages appear. For an example, see Figure 5.10. You can continue learning about IRC at https://help.ubuntu.com/community/InternetRelayChat.

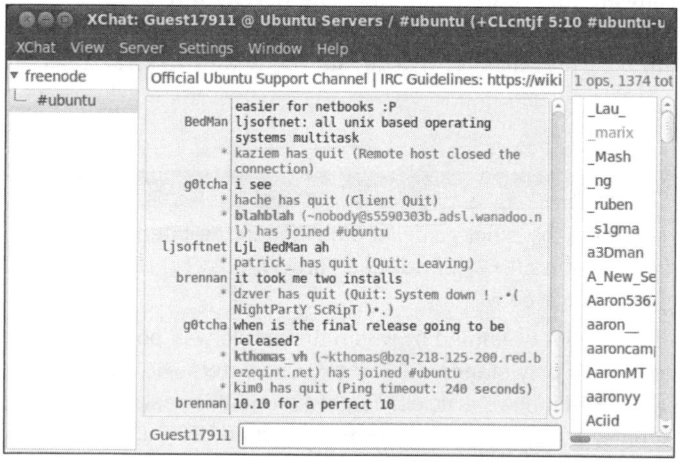

FIGURE 5.10 Join in an online chatroom about your favorite distro, with XChat.

TIP

You can establish your own IRC server even though Ubuntu does not provide one. Setting up a server is not a task for anyone who is not well versed in Linux or IRC.

A popular server is IRCd, which you can obtain from ftp://ftp.irc.org/irc/server/. Before you download IRCd, you should look at the README file to determine what files you need to download, and read the information at http://www.irchelp.org/irchelp/ircd/.

Usenet Newsgroups

The concept of newsgroups revolutionized the way information was exchanged between people across a network. The Usenet network news system created a method for people to electronically communicate with large groups of people with similar interests. As you will see, many of the concepts of Usenet news are embodied in other forms of collaborative communication.

Usenet newsgroups act as a form of public bulletin board system. Any user can subscribe to individual newsgroups and send (or post) messages (called articles) to the newsgroup so that all the other subscribers of the newsgroup can read them. Some newsgroups include an administrator, who must approve each message before it is posted. These are called moderated newsgroups. Other newsgroups are open, allowing any subscribed member to post a message. When an article is posted to the newsgroup, it is transferred to all the other hosts in the news network.

Usenet newsgroups are divided into a hierarchy to make it easier to find individual newsgroups. The hierarchy levels are based on topics, such as computers, science, recreation, and social issues. Each newsgroup is named as a subset of the higher-level topic. For example, the newsgroup `comp` relates to all computer topics. The newsgroup `comp.laptops` relates to laptop computer issues. Often the hierarchy goes several layers deep. For example, the newsgroup `comp.databases.oracle.server` relates to Oracle server database issues.

NOTE

The format of newsgroup articles follows the strict guidelines defined in the Internet standards document Request for Comments (RFC) 1036. Each article must contain two distinct parts: header lines and a message body.

The header lines identify information about when and by whom the article was posted. The body of the message should contain only standard ASCII text characters. No binary characters or files should be posted within news articles. To get around this restriction, binary files are converted to text data, through use of either the standard UNIX uuencode program or the newer Multipurpose Internet Mail Extensions (MIME) protocol. The resulting text file is then posted to the newsgroup. Newsgroup readers can then decode the posted text file back into its original binary form.

A collection of articles posted in response to a common topic is called a thread. A thread can contain many articles as users post messages in response to other posted messages. Some newsreader programs allow users to track articles based on the threads to which they belong. This helps simplify the organization of articles in the newsgroup.

TIP

The free news server, `news.gmane.org` makes the Red Hat and Ubuntu mail lists available via newsgroups. The beta list is available as `gmane.linux. redhat.rhl.beta`. It is a handy way to read threaded discussions and some prefer it to using the Ubuntu mail list archives.

The protocol used to transfer newsgroup articles from one host to another is Network News Transfer Protocol (NNTP), defined in RFC 975. (You can search RFCs at ftp://metalab.unc.edu/pub/docs/rfc/; look at the file `rfc-index.txt`.) NNTP was designed as a simple client/server protocol that enables two hosts to exchange newsgroup articles in an efficient manner.

Whether or not your Ubuntu machine is set up as a news server, you can use a newsreader program to read newsgroup articles. The newsreader programs require just a connection to a news server. It does not matter whether the news server is on the same machine or is a remote news server on the other side of the world.

Several programs are available to connect to news servers to read and post articles in newsgroups. If you are interested in Usenet, you might want to check out a program from the Ubuntu repositories called Pan. Pan is a graphical newsreader client that has the capability to download and display all the newsgroups available on a server and display posted news articles. However, Usenet is an old system that predates the creation of the World Wide Web. It was the place to be in the early days and the source of many great memories, but today is little better than a ghost town with wind-blown tumbleweeds, spam, and illegal exchanges of pirated content. Most Internet service providers used to run free Usenet servers, and connecting was easy and common, but most of the free ones are gone now and traffic has dwindled. Feel free to experiment or try to relive the glory days, but Usenet is, alas, well past its prime.

Ubuntu One Cloud Storage

Anyone who has installed Ubuntu has access to a free online cloud storage application called Ubuntu One. The service is built in to the Ubuntu desktop, and the best place to begin is from the menu at System, Preferences, Ubuntu One. By signing up you will receive 2GB of space to use to store anything you would like and make it available to multiple computers with access from Ubuntu desktops (with plans to expand to other Linux distributions and even other operating systems in the future) as well as via a web interface. If that isn't enough space, larger accounts are available for a fee, which in turn helps support future Ubuntu development. An Ubuntu One account is also needed to purchase music from the Ubuntu One Music Store, covered in Chapter 7, "Multimedia Applications."

Reference

- www.novell.com/products/desktop/features/evolution.html—The home of Evolution, the standard email client for Ubuntu.
- www.mozilla.com/—The home page for Mozilla Firefox, Thunderbird, and the Mozilla Suite.
- www.spreadfirefox.com/—The Firefox advocacy home page is useful for converting those Internet Explorer types.
- https://one.ubuntu.com/—The website for Ubuntu One.
- http://en.wikipedia.org/wiki/Usenet—For a history of Usenet.

CHAPTER 6

Productivity Applications

IN THIS CHAPTER

- Introducing OpenOffice.org
- Office Suites for Ubuntu
- Productivity Applications Written for Microsoft Windows
- Reference

Many businesses have already found a way to benefit from open source software, such as office productivity suites like OpenOffice.org and its commercial counterpart, StarOffice, recently renamed Oracle Open Office. These have the cost benefits of not having to pay license fees or support costs. However, more applications beyond these are available in Ubuntu. In this chapter we will explore some of them.

NOTE

It's important to understand that even though OpenOffice.org does very well most of the time, especially with less-complex documents, it is not 100 percent compatible with Microsoft Office. Why is this? Microsoft is notoriously secretive about its proprietary file formats, and the only way that OpenOffice.org could ensure compatibility would be to reverse-engineer each file format, an exercise akin to taking apart a telephone to see how it works. This reverse-engineering is difficult to do in a legal way and is rarely perfect. However, OpenOffice.org manages to maintain a very high standard of importing and exporting, so you should not experience too many problems except with documents of great complexity. As an example, this book was primarily written using OpenOffice.org, whereas the post-production at the publisher uses Microsoft tools.

A productivity suite is defined as two or more applications bundled together and used for creating documents, presentations, spreadsheets, and databases. Other applications that may be included in the bundle are email clients, calculators/formula editors, illustration or drawing software, and more. Commonly, they are all tied together by a default look and feel, which makes sticking to one particular suite much easier. Because Ubuntu uses OpenOffice.org as its standard office suite, we will introduce you to Writer and Calc, the two most popular OpenOffice.org components. We will also take a brief look at some of the other Linux-based office suites.

WORKING WITH OPENOFFICE.ORG

For the majority of users of productivity suites, OpenOffice.org should fulfill most, if not all, of your requirements. However, the first hurdle is not whether it can do what you require of it, but rather whether it can successfully import and export to proprietary Microsoft formats at a standard that is acceptable to your needs. In the main, OpenOffice.org should import and export with minimal hassle, perhaps getting a bit stuck with some of the more esoteric Microsoft Office formatting. Given that most users do not go much beyond tabs, columns, and tables, this level of compatibility should suffice.

However, you are strongly advised to round up a selection of documents and spreadsheets that seem the most likely to be difficult for the import/export filter and test them thoroughly (of course, keeping a backup of the originals!). There is nothing worse for a system administrator who has deployed a new productivity suite than to suddenly get users complaining that they cannot read their files. This would quickly destroy any benefits gained from the other useful functions within OpenOffice.org, and could even mark the return of proprietary formats and expensive office suites.

On the positive side, OpenOffice.org supports a huge array of file formats and is capable of exporting to nearly 70 types of documents. Such a variety of file formats means that you should be able to successfully use OpenOffice.org in nearly any environment, including formats no longer used by currently produced and maintained software, so it may be able to open some old files and documents you had once given up for lost.

Introducing OpenOffice.org

OpenOffice.org contains a number of productivity applications for use in creating text documents, preparing spreadsheets, organizing presentations, managing projects, and so on. The following components of the OpenOffice.org package are included with Ubuntu:

- **Writer**—This word processing program enables you to compose, format, and organize text documents. If you are accustomed to using Microsoft Word, the functionality of OpenOffice.org Writer will be familiar to you. You will learn how to get up and running with Writer later on in this chapter.
- **Calc**—This spreadsheet program enables you to manipulate numbers in a spreadsheet format. Support for all but the most esoteric Microsoft Excel functions means that trading spreadsheets with Excel users should be successful. Calc offers some limited compatibility with Excel macros, but those macros generally have to be

rewritten. We walk through setting up a basic spreadsheet with some formulas and show you how to build a basic Data Pilot later on in this chapter.

- **Impress**—This presentation program is similar to Microsoft PowerPoint and enables you to create slide show presentations that include graphs, diagrams, and other graphics. Impress also works well with PowerPoint files.

NOTE

The following five applications are not included by default with Ubuntu, but are quite useful. All but Dia are a part of the OpenOffice.org project and add features to the suite that are not used as often as those Ubuntu installs by default. You will need to install them from the Ubuntu repositories if you desire or require their functionality.

- **Math**—This math formula editor enables you to write mathematical formulas with a number of math fonts and symbols for inclusion in a word processing document. Such symbols are highly specialized and not easily included in the basic functionality of a word processor. This is of interest primarily to math and science writers, but Math can be useful to anyone who needs to include a complex formula in text.
- **Base**—This is a fully functional database application.
- **Draw**—This graphics application allows you to create images for inclusion in the documents produced with OpenOffice.org. It saves files only in OpenOffice.org format, but it can import most common image formats.
- **Dia**—This technical drawing editor from the GNOME Office suite enables you to create measured drawings, such as those used by architects and engineers. Its functionality is similar to that of Microsoft Visio. When installed, it is found in the menu under Applications, Graphics, Dia Diagram Editor.
- **Planner**—You can use this project management application for project planning, scheduling, and tracking; this application is similar to, but not compatible with, Microsoft Project. It is found in the Office menu as the Project Management item.

A BRIEF HISTORY OF OPENOFFICE.ORG

The OpenOffice.org office suite is based on a commercial suite called StarOffice. Originally developed by a German company, StarOffice was purchased by Sun Microsystems in the United States. One of the biggest complaints about the old StarOffice was that all the component applications were integrated under a StarOffice "desktop" that looked very much like a Microsoft Windows desktop, including a Start button and menus. This meant that to edit a simple document, unneeded applications had to be loaded, making the office suite slow to load, slow to run, and quite demanding on system resources.

After the purchase of StarOffice, Sun Microsystems released a large part of the StarOffice code under the GNU Public License, and development began on what has become OpenOffice.org, which is freely available under the GPL. Sun also continued development on StarOffice. The significant differences between the free and commercial versions of the software are that StarOffice provides more fonts and even more import/export file filters than OpenOffice.org (these filters cannot be provided in the GPL version because of licensing restrictions), and StarOffice provides its own relational database, Software AGs Adabas D database.

Recently, Sun was bought by Oracle. Although no announcements have been made, there is some question as to what will happen with OpenOffice.org under the new owners. To make things more interesting, IBM has imported the GPL-licensed OpenOffice codebase and released its own free-as-in-cost office suite based on it called Lotus Symphony, which also has some proprietary additions.

Configuring OpenOffice.org

The installation of OpenOffice.org is done on a systemwide basis, meaning that all users have access to it. However, users may configure OpenOffice.org for their individual needs. This initial configuration happens the first time each user loads any one of the OpenOffice.org components, and might mean the application takes a little longer to load that first time.

TIP

OpenOffice.org is constantly improving its productivity applications. You can check the OpenOffice.org website (http://www.openoffice.org/) for the latest version. The website provides a link to download the source or a precompiled version of the most current working installation files. A more current version might offer file format support that you need. Should you need a Windows-compatible version, you will also find it at the website.

Figure 6.1 shows the Office menu, which is found under Applications. You can see the entries for Presentation (Impress), Spreadsheet (Calc), and Word Processor (Writer).

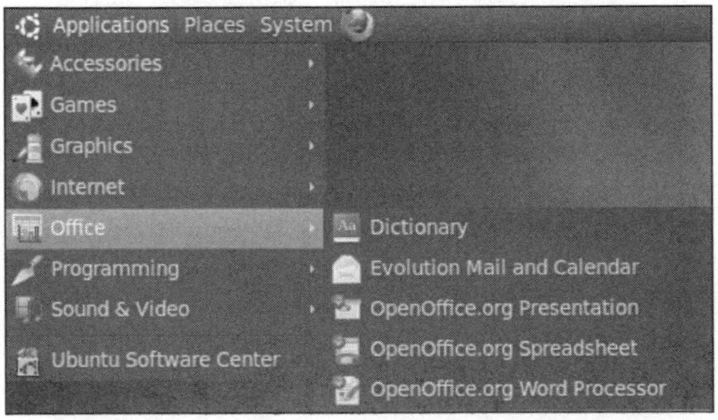

FIGURE 6.1 The OpenOffice.org suite provided by Ubuntu is simple to configure and use.

As is the case with many Linux applications, you may be somewhat overwhelmed by the sheer number of configuration options available to you in OpenOffice.org. Mercifully, a lot of thought has gone into organizing these options, which are available if you click the Tools menu and select Options. It does not matter which program you use to get to this dialog box; it appears the same if summoned from Writer, Impress, or Calc. It acts as a central configuration management tool for all OpenOffice.org applications. You can use it to set global options for all OpenOffice.org applications, or specific options for each individual component. For instance, in the dialog shown in Figure 6.2, you can change the user details and information, and this is reflected across all OpenOffice.org applications.

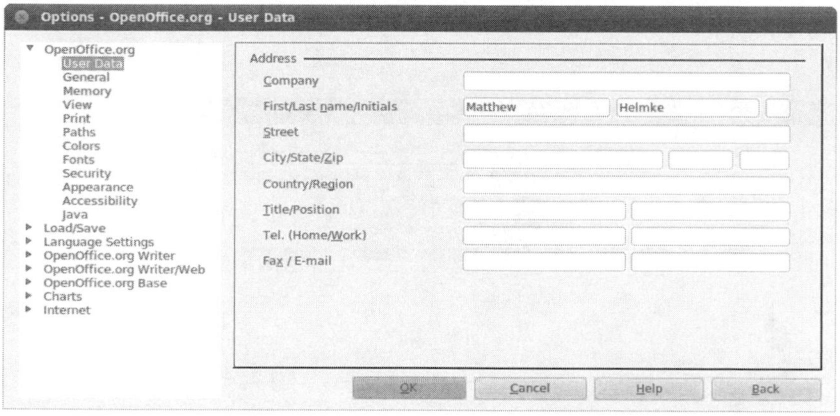

FIGURE 6.2 You can set user details for all OpenOffice.org applications from this dialog.

OpenOffice.org is a constant work in progress, but the current release is on par with the Sun version of StarOffice 8. You can browse to the OpenOffice.org website to get documentation and answers to frequently asked questions and to offer feedback.

Working with OpenOffice.org Writer

Of all the applications that make up OpenOffice.org, the one that you are most likely to use regularly is Writer, the OpenOffice.org word processor. With a visual style very similar to Microsoft's Word, Writer has a number of strengths over its commercial and vastly more expensive rival. In this section you will learn how to get started with Writer and make use of some of its powerful formatting and layout tools.

NOTE

You may be interested to know that Writer was the primary word processor chosen to write and edit this book.

Getting Started with Writer

You can access Writer from the menu at Applications, Office, selecting OpenOffice.org Word Processor. After a few seconds Writer opens up with a blank document and a blinking cursor awaiting your command. It can be tempting to just dive in and start typing your document, but it can be worthwhile to do some initial configuration before you start work.

First, make sure that the options are set to your requirements. Click the Tools menu and select Options to bring up the Options dialog box, as shown in Figure 6.2. The initial screen allows you to personalize OpenOffice.org with your name, address, and contact details, but there are options to configure features that you might also want to alter. Check that your default paths are correct by clicking the Paths option. You may prefer to alter the My Documents path, as shown in Figure 6.3, to something a little more specific than just the Documents directory.

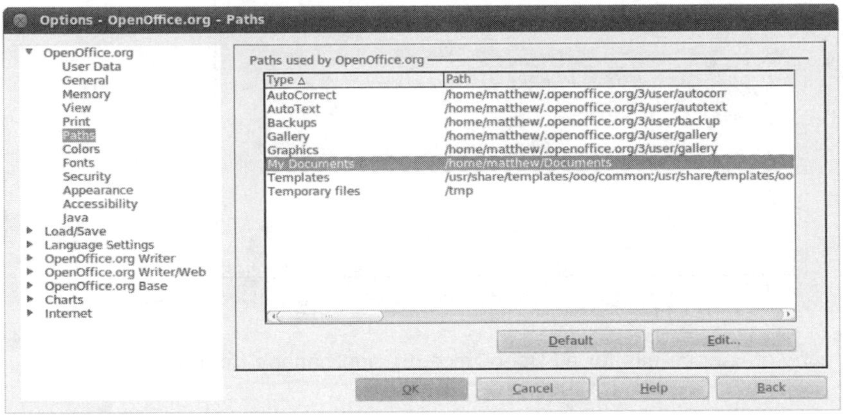

FIGURE 6.3 Click the Edit button to choose your default documents directory.

You can set OpenOffice.org to save in Microsoft Word format by default, should you so require. This can be done under the Load/Save General options shown in Figure 6.4, and it is a good idea if you value your work to change the Autorecovery settings so that it saves every couple of minutes.

Also shown in Figure 6.4 are a number of options that are specific to Writer. A little bit of time working through these options can give you a highly personalized and extremely productive environment.

Working with Styles and Formatting

One of the significant benefits of using Writer is the ability to easily apply formatting and styles to extremely complex documents. Depending on the types of documents you work with, you might want to consider creating your own styles beyond the 20 included by default. You can access styles through either the Style drop-down box in the toolbar or the Styles and Formatting window shown in Figure 6.5. If you cannot see the window, press the F11 key to display it.

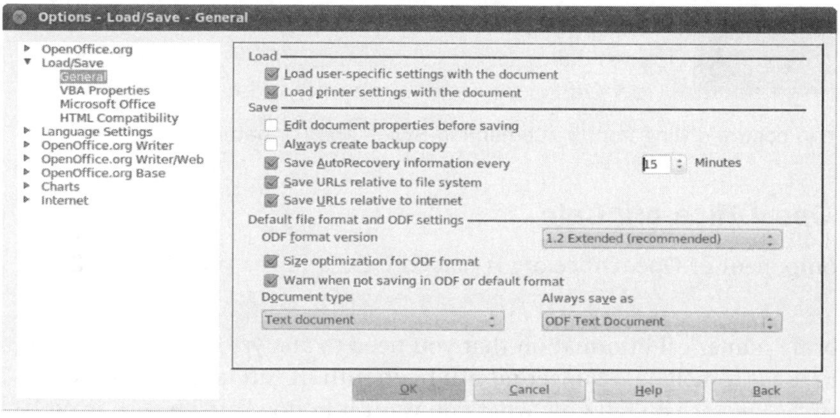

FIGURE 6.4 Make sure that you are working with most appropriate file formats.

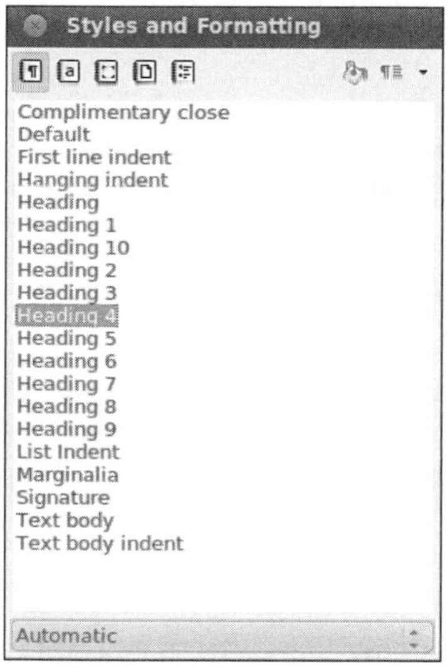

FIGURE 6.5 Writer's quick and easy-to-use Styles and Formatting tool.

The easiest way to work with the Styles and Formatting tool is to highlight the text you want to style and double-click the required style in the window. There are quite a few to choose from, but you might find them restrictive if you have more specialized needs. To start defining your own styles, click the button shown in Figure 6.6 to bring up options to add, modify, and load styles for pages, paragraphs, lists, characters, and frames.

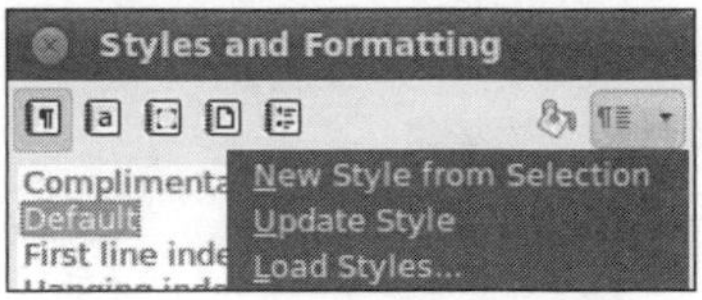

FIGURE 6.6 You can control styling from a submenu in Styles and Formatting.

Working with OpenOffice.org Calc

The spreadsheet component of OpenOffice.org is named Calc, and is a very capable Excel alternative.

Calc is used for storing numerical information that you need to analyze in some way. For instance, you could use it to help you budget month by month. It can take care of the calculations for you, as long as you tell Calc what you want it to do. Anyone with experience in Excel will feel right at home with Calc.

In this section, we will show you how to get started with Calc, including entering formulas and formatting. We will also take a look at some of the more advanced features of Calc, including the Data Pilot feature, which allows you to easily summarize information.

Getting Started with Calc

You can either click the shortcut icon that is located on the top GNOME panel, or select Spreadsheet from the Office menu under the Applications main menu. Whichever route you take, the result is the same and Calc starts to load.

By default, Calc loads with a blank spreadsheet ready for you to enter information into it, as in Figure 6.7.

Calc's layout makes it easy to organize information into rows and columns. As you can see in the example, we have salespeople listed in the left column, customers in the second column, Invoice Date in the third column, and finally Revenue in the fourth column. At the moment, there are no formulas entered to help you interpret the data. Clicking the E30 cell selects it and enables you to enter a formula in the top formula bar. If you begin with the equal sign, Calc knows that you are entering a formula and works accordingly.

In this example, we want to know the total revenue brought in up to now, so the formula to enter is =sum(E4:E29), followed by Return. Calc automatically enters the result into cell E43 for you to see. Now you want to see what the average order value was. To do this, you have to obtain the number of orders made. For this you can use the counta function to count the number of entries in a given list. This is usually used when you need to find out how many entries are in a text list. So, in cell B30, enter =counta(B4:B29) and press Enter. Calc now counts the number of entries in the range and returns the total in B43. Then you need to divide the total revenue by the number of orders to find the average order value. So, in cell E31, enter the formula =E30/B30 to get the average order value.

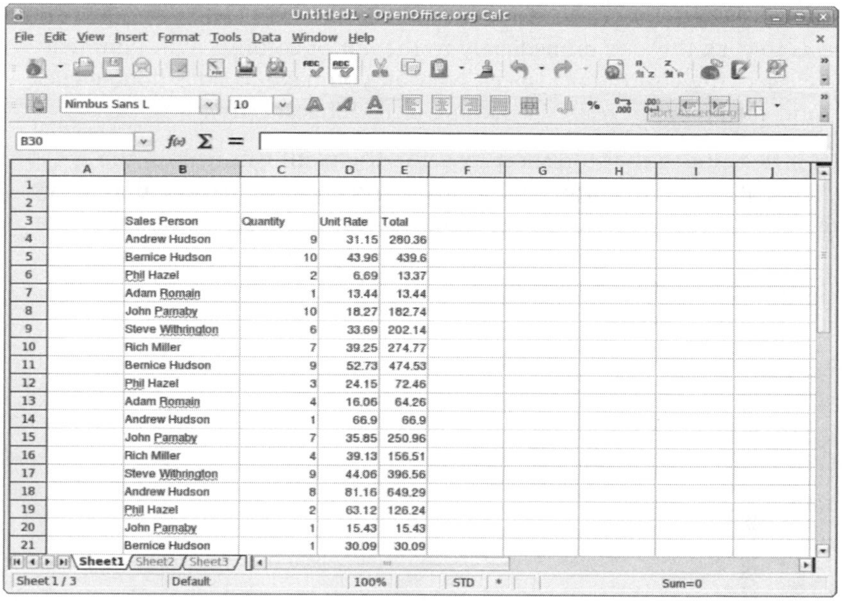

FIGURE 6.7 Use Calc to store numerical and statistical information.

TIP

Calc offers some nifty little features that you can use quickly. The handiest one in our opinion is the capability to select multiple cells and see straight away the total and average of the range. You will find these figures in the bottom-right status bar. This has saved us numerous times when we have needed to get this information quickly!

Formatting Spreadsheets

Getting back to our example, it looks a little basic at the moment because no formatting is involved. For instance, what's the billing currency? You can also see that some of the cells have text that does not fit, which is highlighted by a small right arrow in the cell. We should also add some labels and titles to our spreadsheet to make it a bit more visually appealing.

To start, all the revenue figures can be changed into currency figures. To do this, select all the cells containing revenue information and click the small coin icon shown in Figure 6.8. This immediately formats the cells so that they display the dollar sign and also puts in a thousands separator to make the numbers easier to read.

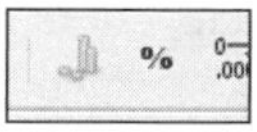

FIGURE 6.8 Make numbers more meaningful with the currency and percentage icons.

Now you need to space all the cells so that you can read all the information. A quick and easy way to do this is to click the area immediately to the left of column A and immediately above row 1 to select the entire spreadsheet. Now all you have to do is double-click the dividing lines, and each column resizes according to its longest entry.

Next you can add a little color to the worksheet by using the paint can icon in the toolbar. Select the range B2 to E2 with the mouse cursor and click the background color icon to bring up the color window shown in Figure 6.9. Select the color you want to use and Calc fills the cells with that color. You can also change the font color by using the icon immediately to the right in the same way.

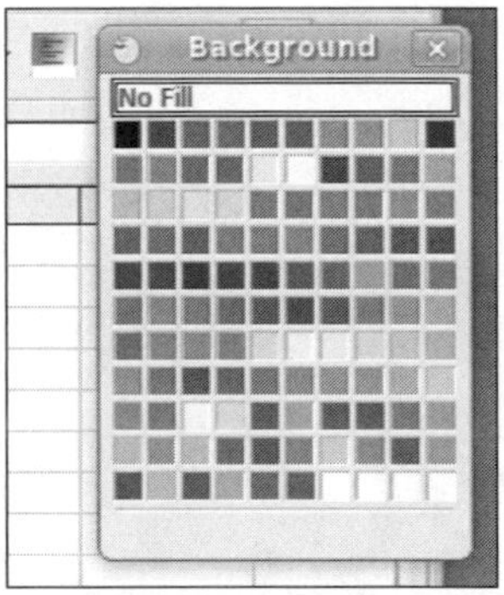

FIGURE 6.9 Add a touch of color to an otherwise dull spreadsheet with the fill background icon.

Finally, you need a couple more finishing touches. The first is to enlarge the font for the column headers. Select the range B2 to E2 again and click the font size in the toolbar to change it to something a little larger. You might also want to use the bold and italic options to further emphasize the headers and the totals.

If you have followed the steps as described, you should end up with a spreadsheet similar to the one in Figure 6.10.

Summarizing Data with Calc

Calc includes a powerful tool that lets you summarize large groups of data to help you when you need to carry out any analysis. This tool is called a *data pilot*, and you can use it to quickly summarize data that might normally take a long time if you did the calculations manually. Using the sample spreadsheet from earlier, we will take you through how to build a simple data pilot and show you how to analyze and manipulate long lists of data.

The previous section featured a spreadsheet that showed salespeople, customers, date of invoice, and revenue. At the foot of the spreadsheet were a couple of formulas that enabled you to quickly see the total revenue earned and the average order value.

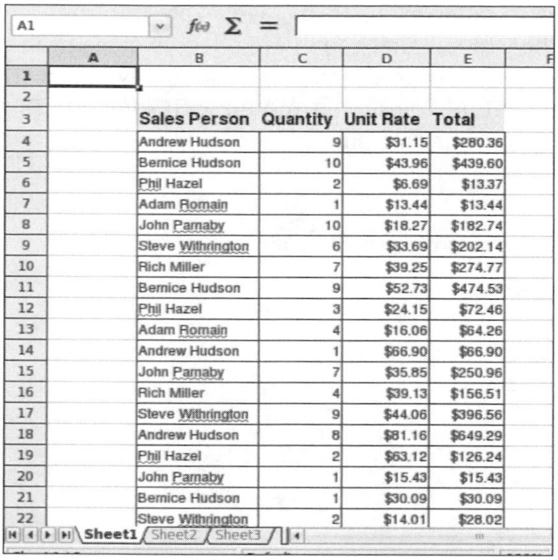

FIGURE 6.10 The finished spreadsheet, looking a lot better than before!

Now you want to find out how much salespeople have earned individually. You could add this up manually with a calculator, but that would defeat the point of using Calc. So, you need to create a data pilot to summarize the information.

First, you need to select all the cells from B2 to E42 because they contain the data you want to analyze. After these are selected, click the Data menu and select Data Pilot, Start to open the Data Pilot Wizard. The first screen is shown in Figure 6.11 and is defaulted to Current Selection. Make sure that you choose this one to use the data in the selected range, and click OK to continue.

FIGURE 6.11 Use either the current selection or an external data source to provide the data pilot with information.

The next screen enables you to lay out your data pilot as you want it. In this example you want to have the Sales Person in the left column marked Row Fields, so click and drag the Sales Person option from the list on the right and drop it onto the Row Fields area. You're also interested in the average unit rate for each salesperson, so drag Unit Rate into the Data Fields section and double-click it. In the window that comes up, select Average from the list and click the OK button. Finally, drag Revenue to the Data Field area so you can see how much revenue each salesperson brought in. You should end up with something like Figure 6.12; you are almost ready to display your data pilot.

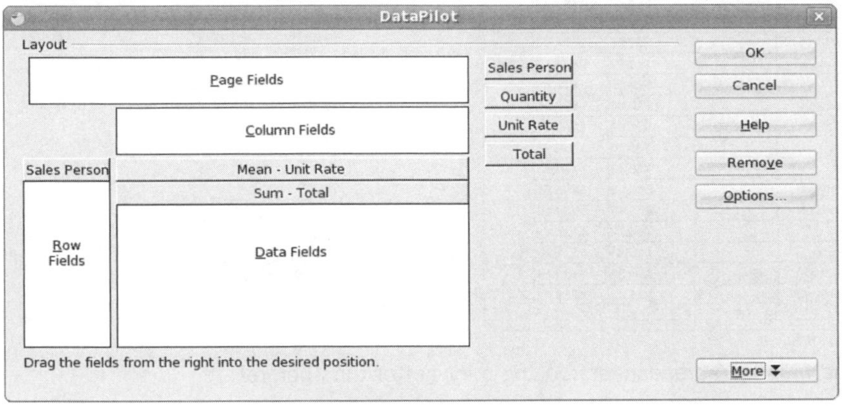

FIGURE 6.12 Lay out your data pilot as you want it.

The final piece in the puzzle is to tell Calc where you want to place the finished data pilot. To do this, click the More button to drop down some extra options and select the box Send Results To to choose a new sheet. When you click OK now, Calc builds the data pilot and displays it on a new sheet in your workbook. The new data pilot is shown in Figure 6.13.

Office Suites for Ubuntu

As we have mentioned earlier, OpenOffice.org is the default application suite for Ubuntu. However, as is common in the open source world, there are plenty of alternatives should you find that OpenOffice.org does not meet your specific requirements. These include the popular Gnome Office and also KOffice, the default KDE productivity suite. You are more likely to hear more about OpenOffice.org, especially as more and more people realize that it is generally compatible with Microsoft Office file formats. Interestingly, the state of Massachusetts not long ago elected to standardize on two file formats for use in government: the Adobe Acrobat PDF format and the OASIS OpenDocument format, both of which are supported natively in OpenOffice.org.

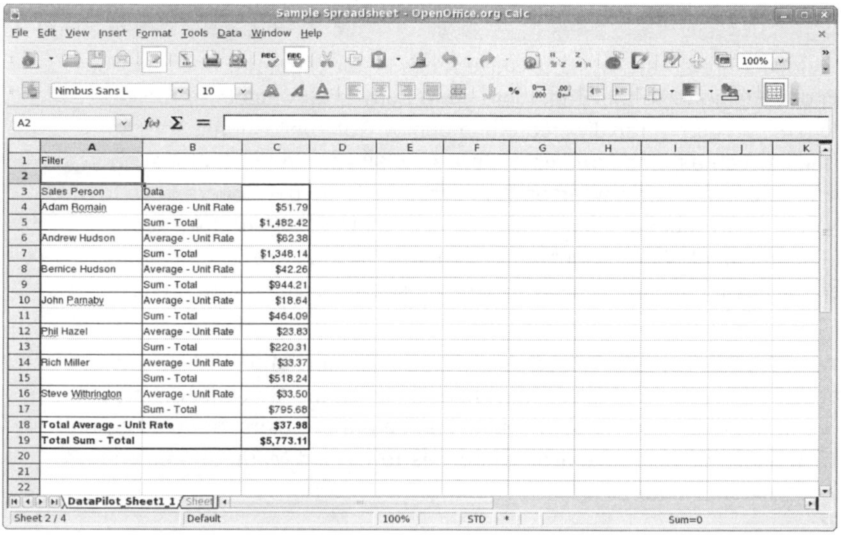

FIGURE 6.13 Summarize large volumes of numerical data with ease, using Calc's Data Pilot function.

NOTE

The decision by the state of Massachusetts to standardize on PDF and OpenDocument has huge ramifications for the open source world. It is the first time that OpenDocument, an open standard, has been specified in this way. It means that anyone who wants to do business with the state government must use OpenDocument-based file formats, and not the proprietary formats in use by Microsoft. Unfortunately for Microsoft, it does not have support for OpenDocument in any of its applications, making them useless to anyone wanting to work with the state government. This is despite Microsoft being a founding member of OASIS, who developed and ratified the OpenDocument standard.

Working with Gnome Office

The other office suite available for GNOME is Gnome Office, which is a collection of individual applications. Unlike OpenOffice.org, Gnome Office does not have a coherent suite of applications, meaning that you have to get used to using a word processor that offers no integration with a spreadsheet and cannot work directly with a presentation package. However, if you need only one or two components, it is worthwhile investigating Gnome Office.

THE GTK WIDGET SET

Open Source developers are always trying to make it easier for people to build applications and help in development. To this end, there are a number of widgets or toolkits that other developers can use to rapidly create and deploy GUI applications. These widgets control things such as drop-down lists, Save As dialogs, window buttons, and general look and feel. Unfortunately, whereas Windows and Apple developers have to worry about only one set of widgets each, Linux has a plethora of different widgets, including GTK+, QT, and Motif. What is worse is that these widgets are incompatible with one another, making it difficult to easily move a finished application from one widget set to another.

GTK is an acronym for GIMP Tool Kit. GIMP, the GNU Image Manipulation Program, is a graphics application very similar to Adobe Photoshop. By using the GTK-based jargon, we save ourselves several hundred words of typing and help move along our discussion of GNOME Office. You might also see similar references to QT and Motif, as well as other widget sets, in these chapters.

Here are some of the primary components of the Gnome Office suite that are available in Ubuntu:

- **AbiWord**—This word processing program enables you to compose, format, and organize text documents and has some compatibility with the Microsoft Word file format. It uses plug-ins (programs that add functionality such as language translation) to enhance its functionality.
- **Gnumeric**—This spreadsheet program enables you to manipulate numbers in a spreadsheet format. Support for all but the most esoteric Microsoft Excel functions means that users should have little trouble trading spreadsheets with Excel users.
- **GIMP**—This graphics application allows you to create images for general use. It can import and export all common graphic file formats. GIMP is similar to Adobe's Photoshop application and is described in Chapter 7, "Multimedia Applications."
- **Evolution**—Evolution is a mail client with an interface similar to Microsoft Outlook, providing email, scheduling, and calendaring. It is described in Chapter 5, "On the Internet."

The loose association of applications known as Gnome Office includes several additional applications that duplicate the functionality of applications already provided by Ubuntu. Those extra GNOME applications are not included in a default installation of Ubuntu to eliminate redundancy. They are all available from the Gnome Office website, at www.gnome.org/gnome-office/. Evolution is available with Ubuntu by default. You have to install the remaining components using the Ubuntu repositories.

Ubuntu provides the AbiWord editor, shown in Figure 6.14, as part of its Extras. AbiWord can import XML, Microsoft Word, RTF, UTF8, plain text, WordPerfect, KWord, and a few other formats. AbiWord is notable for its use of plug-ins, or integrated helper applications, that extend its capabilities. These plug-ins add language translation, HTML editing, a thesaurus, a Linux command shell, and an online dictionary, among other functions and features. If you need a simple yet powerful word processing application, you should examine AbiWord.

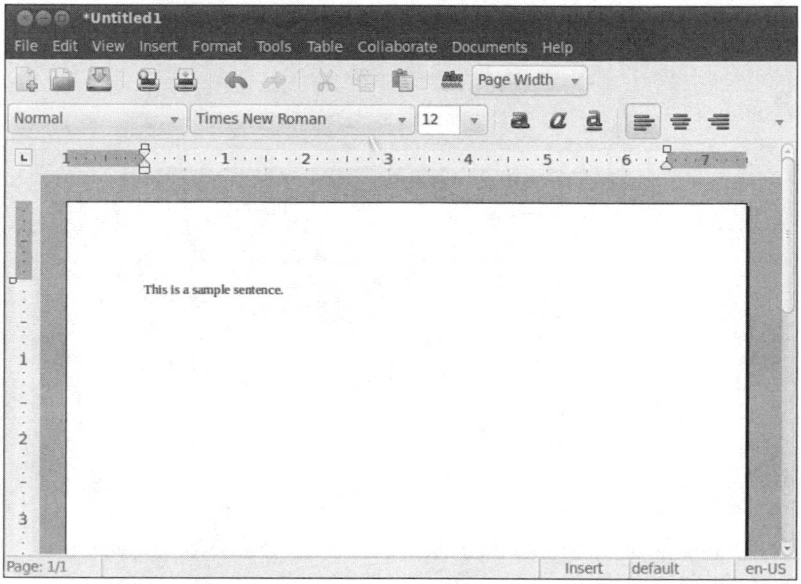

FIGURE 6.14 AbiWord is a word processing program for Ubuntu, GNOME, and X11. It handles some formats that OpenOffice.org cannot, but does not yet do well with Microsoft Word formats.

AbiWord is not installed by default in Ubuntu, so you'll need to install it either using `apt-get` or `synaptic`. The package is simply called `abiword`, although you might want to install the meta-package `gnome-office`, which will include the other Gnome Office applications.

After you've installed Abiword, it becomes available in the Applications menu, under the Office submenu. Simply click the icon to launch the application.

If you are familiar with Microsoft Works, the AbiWord interface will be familiar to you because its designers based the interface on Works.

You can use the Gnumeric spreadsheet application to perform financial calculations and to graph data, as shown in Figure 6.15. It can import comma- or tab-separated files, text, or files in the Gnumeric XML format, saving files only as XML or text. You need to install Gnumeric using either `apt-get` or `synaptic` in the same way as Abiword. If you have already installed the `gnome-office` package, Gnumeric will be available under Applications, Office as Gnumeric Spreadsheet.

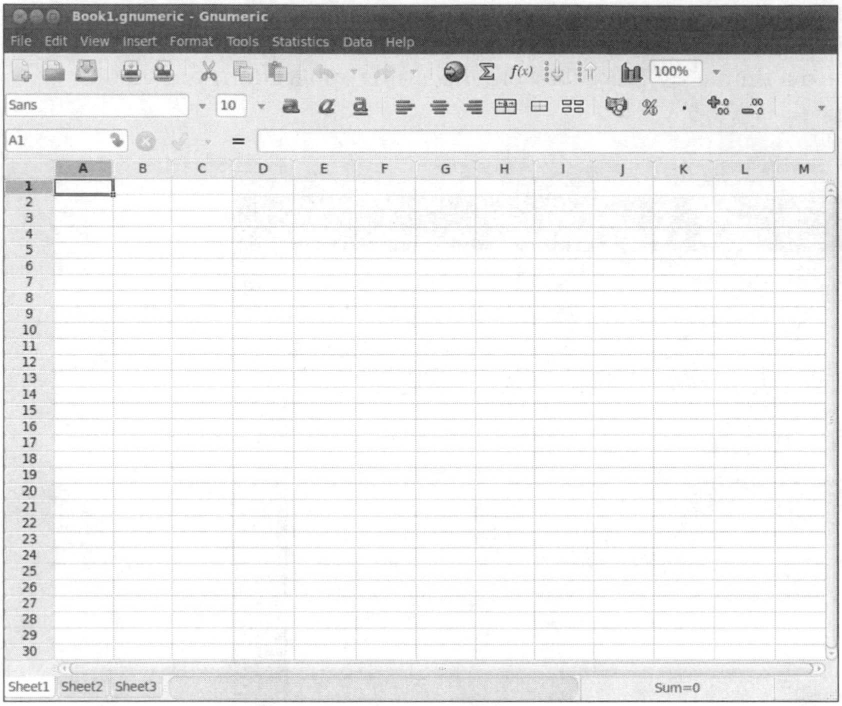

FIGURE 6.15 GNOME's Gnumeric is a capable financial data editor—here working with the same spreadsheet used earlier. OpenOffice.org also provides a spreadsheet application, as does KOffice.

After you press Enter, the main Gnumeric window appears. You enter data in the spreadsheet by clicking a cell and then typing in the text box. To create a graph, you click and drag over the spreadsheet cells to highlight the desired data, and then you click the Graph Wizard icon in Gnumeric's toolbar. Gnumeric's graphing component launches, and you are guided through a series of dialogs to create a graph. When you are finished, you can click and drag a blank area of your spreadsheet, and the graph appears.

The Project Planner application is useful for tracking the progress of projects, much like its Windows counterpart, Microsoft Project. When the main window is displayed, you can start a new project or import an existing project. The application provides three views: Resources, Gantt Charts, and Tasks.

Working with KOffice

The KDE office suite KOffice was developed to provide tight integration with the KDE desktop. Integration enables objects in one application to be inserted in other applications via drag-and-drop, and all the applications can communicate with each other, so a change in an object is instantly communicated to other applications. The application integration provided by KDE is a significant enhancement to productivity. (Some GNOME desktop applications share a similar communication facility with each other.) If you use the KDE desktop instead of the default GNOME desktop, you can enjoy the benefits of this integration, along with the Konqueror web and file browser.

The word processor for KOffice is KWord. KWord is a frames-based word processor, meaning that document pages can be formatted in framesets that hold text, graphics, and objects in enclosed areas. Framesets can be used to format text on a page that includes text and images within columns that the text needs to flow around, making KWord an excellent choice for creating documents other than standard business letters, such as newsletters and brochures.

KWord and other components of KOffice are still under development and lack all the polished features of OpenOffice.org and AbiWord. However, it does have the capability to work with the OpenDocument format found in OpenOffice.org, as well as limited compatibility with Microsoft file formats.

You can access the KOffice components from the Office menu.

KWord asks you to select a document for your session. The KWord client, shown in Figure 6.16, offers sophisticated editing capabilities, including desktop publishing.

FIGURE 6.16 The KOffice KWord word processing component is a sophisticated frames-based WYSIWYG editor that is suitable for light desktop publishing, supporting several formats, including WordPerfect.

The KOffice KSpread client is a functional spreadsheet program that offers graphing capabilities. Like KWord, KSpread can be accessed from the Office menu.

KDE includes other productivity clients in its collection of KOffice and related applications. These clients include an address book, time tracker, calculator, notepad, and scheduler. One popular client is Kontact, which provides daily, weekly, work week, and monthly views of tasks, to-do lists, and scheduled appointments with background alarms. A journal, or diary, function is also supported within it, and you can synchronize information with your Palm Pilot. You can launch this client from the Office menu.

A typical Kontact window is shown in Figure 6.17.

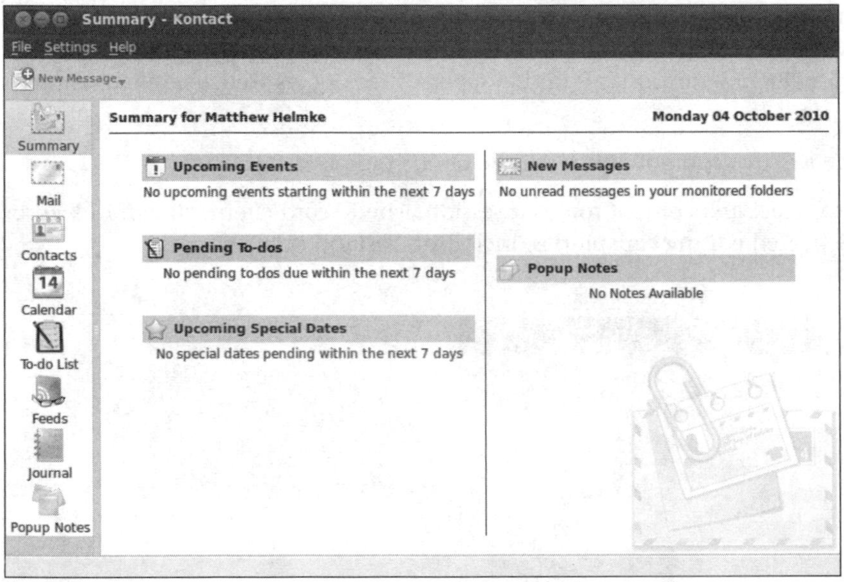

FIGURE 6.17 KDE's Kontact client supports editing of tasks and schedules that you can sync with your PDA. Shown here is the address book.

Productivity Applications Written for Microsoft Windows

Microsoft Windows is fundamentally different from Linux, yet you can install and run some Microsoft Windows applications in Linux by using an application named Wine. Wine enables you to use Microsoft Windows and DOS programs on Unix-based systems. Wine includes a program loader that you can use to execute a Windows binary, along with a `.dll` library that implements Windows command calls, translating them to the equivalent Unix and X11 command calls. Because of frequent updates to the Wine code base, Wine is not included with Ubuntu. Download a current version of Wine from www.winehq.org/. To see whether your favorite application is supported by Wine, you can look at the Wine application database at http://appdb.winehq.org/appbrowse.php.

Other solutions, primarily CodeWeavers' CrossOver Office, enable use of Microsoft productivity applications. If you are after a painless way of running not only Microsoft

Office, but also Apple iTunes and other software, you should investigate CodeWeavers. CrossOver Office is one of the simplest programs you can use to get Windows-based programs to work. Check out www.codeweavers.com to download a trial version of the latest software. It requires registration, but do not worry—the guys at CodeWeavers are great and will not misuse your details. The big plus is that you get a whole month to play around with the trial before you decide whether to buy it. Of course, you might get to the end of the 30 days and realize that Linux does what you want it to do and you don't want to go back to Windows. Do not be afraid; take the plunge!

RELEVANT UBUNTU COMMANDS

The following commands give you access to productivity applications, tools, and processes in Ubuntu if you want or need to start them from the command line:

- `oowriter`—OpenOffice.org's Writer
- `oocalc`—OpenOffice.org's Calc
- `ooimpress`—OpenOffice.org's Impress
- `koshell`—KDE's KOffice office suite shell
- `kspread`—KDE's KSpread spreadsheet
- `gimp`—The GIMP (GNU Image Manipulation Package)
- `gnumeric`—A spreadsheet editor for GNOME
- `planner`—A project management client for GNOME
- `abiword`—A graphical word processor for GNOME

Reference

- www.openoffice.org—The home page for the OpenOffice.org office suite.
- www.oracle.com/us/products/applications/open-office/index.html—The home page for Oracle Open Office, a paid version of the office suite with proprietary upgrades.
- www.gnome.org/gnome-office/—The GNOME Office site.
- www.koffice.org/—The home page for the KOffice suite.
- www.codeweavers.com/—Website of the hugely popular CrossOver Office from CodeWeavers that allows you to run Windows programs under Linux.

CHAPTER 7

Multimedia Applications

IN THIS CHAPTER

- Sound and Music
- Graphics Manipulation
- Using Digital Cameras with Ubuntu
- Burning CDs and DVDs in Ubuntu
- Viewing Video
- Reference

The twenty-first century has become the century of the digital lifestyle, with millions of computer users around the world embracing new technologies, such as digital cameras, MP3 players, and other assorted multimedia gadgets. Whereas ten years ago you might have had a small collection of WAV files scattered about your Windows installation, today you are more likely to have hundreds, if not thousands, of MP3 files scattered across various computers. Along with video clips, animations, and other graphics, the demand for organizing and maintaining these vast libraries is driving development of applications. Popular proprietary applications such as iTunes and Google's Picasa are coveted by Linux users, but open source applications are appearing that provide real alternatives, and for some people these the final reasons they need to move to Linux full time.

This chapter provides an overview of some of the basic multimedia tools included with Ubuntu. You will see how to create your own CDs, watch TV, rip audio CDs into the open source Ogg audio format for playback, as well as manage your media library. You will also learn about how Ubuntu handles graphics and pictures and more.

Sound and Music

Linux had a reputation of lacking good support for sound and multimedia applications in general. However, great strides have been made in recent years to correct this, and support is now a lot better than it used to be. (It might make you smile to know that Microsoft no longer supports the Microsoft Sound Card, but Linux users still enjoy support for it, no doubt just to annoy the folks in

Redmond.) UNIX, however, has always had good multimedia support as David Taylor, UNIX author and guru, points out:

> The original graphics work for computers was done by Evans & Sutherland on UNIX systems. The innovations at MIT's Media Lab were done on UNIX workstations. In 1985, we at HP Labs were creating sophisticated multimedia immersive work environments on UNIX workstations, so maybe UNIX is more multimedia than suggested. Limitations in Linux support doesn't mean UNIX had the same limitations. I think it was more a matter of logistics, with hundreds of sound cards and thousands of different possible PC configurations.

That last sentence sums it up quite well. UNIX had a limited range of hardware to support; Linux has hundreds of sound cards. Sound card device driver support has been long lacking from manufacturers, and there is still no single standard for the sound subsystem in Linux.

In this section, you learn about sound cards, sound file formats, and the sound applications provided with Ubuntu.

Sound Cards

Ubuntu supports a wide variety of sound hardware and software. Two models of sound card drivers compete for prominence in today's market:

- ALSA, the Advanced Linux Sound Architecture, which is entirely open source
- OSS, the Open Sound System, which offers free and commercial drivers

Ubuntu uses ALSA because ALSA is the sound architecture for the 2.6 series kernels. OSS may still be found here and there, but it is no longer is widespread use and should be considered deprecated.

ALSA supports a long list of sound cards. You can review the list at www.alsa-project.org/main/index.php/Main_Page if you are interested, but Ubuntu detects most sound cards during the original installation and should detect any new additions to the system during boot up. To configure the sound card at any other time, use the `sound preferences` graphical tool found in the menu at System, Preferences, Sound.

In addition, Ubuntu uses an additional layer of software called PulseAudio. PulseAudio is a sound server and acts as a mediator between the various multimedia programs that have sound output and the ALSA kernel drivers. Over the years there have been many different sound servers used in Linux, each with different strengths, usability issues, and levels of documentation. These various sound servers have often been forced to run side by side on the same computer causing all sorts of confusion and issues. PulseAudio aims to replace all of them and work as a single handler to accept output from applications which use the APIs for any of the major sound servers already in use such as ESD, OSS, Gstreamer, and aRts and route the various output streams together through one handler. This gives several advantages, including the ability to control the output volume of various programs individually.

PulseAudio is still quite young and its full potential has not yet been realized; however, it has already had great improvements in the intervening releases and is better and more powerful than ever in 10.10. Although there were stability issues and complaints in the first release that included PulseAudio, those don't seem to be a problem anymore except in unusual hardware combinations and special cases and more and more features have been implemented. For more information about PulseAudio, please see www.pulseaudio.org/.

Adjusting Volume

Ubuntu offers a handy utility that you can use to control the volumes for various outputs from your computer. For a simple master volume control, just left click the speaker icon in the top-right corner of the screen and move the slider left or right, as shown in Figure 7.1.

FIGURE 7.1 Control the master volume level with the volume slider.

Alternatively you can control all the output volumes for the system to make sure that you have set everything to your taste, as shown in Figure 7.2. To access the volume control, left-click the speaker icon and select Sound Preferences.

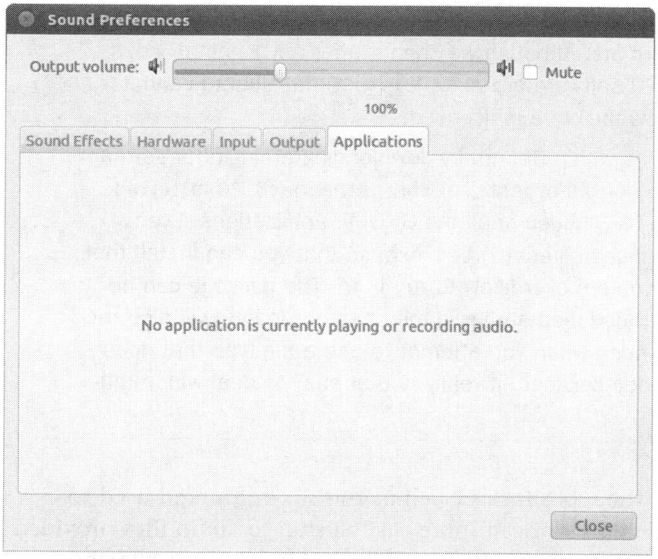

FIGURE 7.2 Use the volume control to manage volume settings for all your sound output devices.

Sound Formats

A number of formats exist for storing sound recordings. Some of these formats are associated with specific technologies, and others are used strictly for proprietary reasons. Ubuntu supports several of the most popular sound formats, including:

- raw (`.raw`)—More properly known as ***headerless format***, audio files using this format contain an amorphous variety of specific settings and encodings. All other sound files contain a short section of code at the beginning—a header—that identifies the format type.
- MP3 (`.mp3`)—A popular, but commercially licensed, format for the digital encoding used by many Linux and Windows applications. MP3 is not supported by any software included with Ubuntu by default but may be easily installed later. In fact, the first time you try to play an MP3 file, Ubuntu will ask if you want to install the codec needed and will help you through the whole, simple process.
- WAV (`.wav`)—The popular uncompressed Windows audio-visual sound format. It is often used as an intermediate file format when encoding audio.
- Ogg-Vorbis (`.ogg`)—Ubuntu's preferred audio encoding format. You enjoy better compression and audio playback, and freedom from lawsuits when you use this open-source encoding format for your audio files.
- FLAC (`.flac`)—This is a lossless format popular with audiophiles. The name stands for Free Lossless Audio Format and it is a compressed format, like MP3, but does not suffer from any loss of quality.

NOTE

Because of patent and licensing issues, Ubuntu does not by default support the MPEG, MPEG2, and MPEG3 (MP3) file formats. Although we cannot offer any legal advice, it appears that individuals using MP3 software are okay; it is just that Ubuntu cannot distribute the code because of how the code is licensed.

You can also enable the MP3 codec within Ubuntu by downloading a plugin for gstreamer, the GNOME audio system. You do this by installing the `gstreamer0.10-plugins-ugly` package, which enables the MP3 codec in all the GNOME applications. Even better, there is a package called `ubuntu-restricted-extras` that you can install that will enable all the major formats you are ever likely to run in to. The package can be found in the repositories, and as mentioned earlier in the chapter, Ubuntu will also recommend specific packages as needed when you attempt to use a file type that does not currently have an installed codec package. It really is that easy to deal with multimedia formats in Ubuntu.

Ubuntu even includes software in the repositories (such as the `sox` command used to convert between sound formats) so that you can more easily listen to audio files provided in a wide variety of formats, such as AU (from NeXT and Sun), AIFF (from Apple and SGI), IFF (originally from Commodore's Amiga), RA (from Real Audio), and VOC (from Creative Labs).

TIP

For an introduction to audio formats, check out the list of audio file formats at www.file-info.com/filetypes/audio with links to detailed information for each.

Ubuntu also offers several utilities for converting sound files from one format to another. Conversion utilities come in handy when you want to use a sound in a format not accepted by your current application of choice. The easiest one to use is also the easiest to install. Install the `soundconverter` package and then look for the application in the menu at Applications, Sound & Video, Sound Converter. It has a clear graphical interface and easy to understand configuration options.

Listening to Music

If you're anything like we are, you might be a huge music fan. One of the downsides of having a fairly large music collection is the physical problem of having to store so many CDs. Wouldn't it be great if you could pack them all away somewhere, yet still have access to all the music when you want it? Some manufacturers experimented with rather bulky jukeboxes that stored 250 CDs at once. The main downside with that was that finding a particular piece of music could take hours, having to cycle through each CD in the hope that it would match your mood.

Fortunately for you and me, Ubuntu is fantastic at working with CDs, even allowing you to rip all your CD collection into a vast searchable music library, letting you quickly create playlists and even giving you the ability to create your own customized CDs. Getting started couldn't be easier, mainly because Ubuntu comes preconfigured with everything you need to get started.

Rhythmbox

Rhythmbox is a useful application that will play CDs if you insert an audio CD into your computer. It will also attempt to obtain information about the CD from the Internet. If it's successful, you'll see the name of the CD appear in Rhythmbox, as shown in Figure 7.3.

When you're ready to play your CD, simply click the name of the CD under the devices section and click the Play button. You can also define whether the CD should just repeat itself until stopped, or whether you want to shuffle the music (randomize the playlist).

Of course, just listening to your CDs doesn't really change anything; Rhythmbox acts just like a regular CD player, allowing you to listen to specific tracks and define how you want to listen to your music by using playlists or sorting it by artists. The real fun starts when you click the Copy to Library button in your toolbar. Rhythmbox then starts to extract, or rip, the audio from your CD and store it within the Music directory that is found under your home directory.

Depending on the speed of your optical drive and the power of your computer, the ripping process can take up to 15 minutes to complete a full CD. As it goes along, Rhythmbox automatically adds the files to your media library, which you can access by clicking the Music button on the left side of the Rhythmbox screen, as you can see in Figure 7.4.

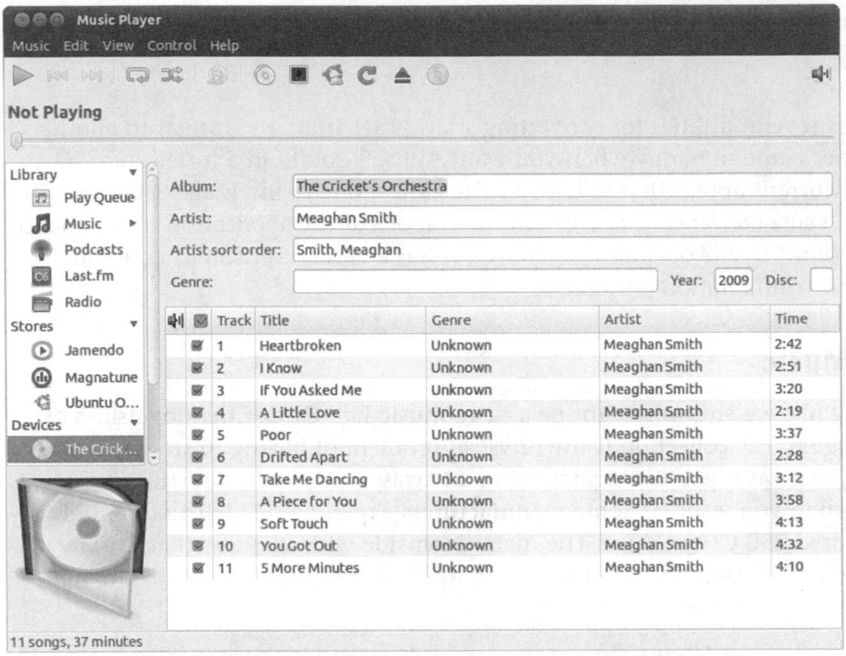

FIGURE 7.3 Rhythmbox automatically downloads information about your CD, if it's available.

Within the Rhythmbox interface you can easily browse through the list of artist names or album titles, which affects the track listing that appears at the bottom of the screen. The numbers after each artist and album tell you how many tracks are assigned to that specific entry, giving you a heads up before you click them. Double-clicking any entry automatically starts the music playing, so for example, double-clicking an artist's name causes the music tracks associated with that artist to start playing. When a track starts to play, Rhythmbox automatically attempts to retrieve the CD artwork, which it then displays in the bottom-left corner of the screen.

There's a lot more that you can do with Rhythmbox, including download and listen to podcasts. A good place to start is the Ubuntu UK podcast at http://podcast.ubuntu-uk.org/. All you have to do is click an RSS link for the feed on that page, copy the link URL, and go to Rhythmbox. There, press Ctrl+P, or go to Music, New Podcast Feed, paste the link into the field, and click the Add button. Rhythmbox then contacts the server and attempts to download the most recent episodes of your chosen podcast, which you can see happening in Figure 7.5.

Banshee

Of course, other programs are available for listening to music within Ubuntu. A particular favorite for many is Banshee, another music application that can handle ripping and playing back music, download cover art, sync with portable players, and can even play

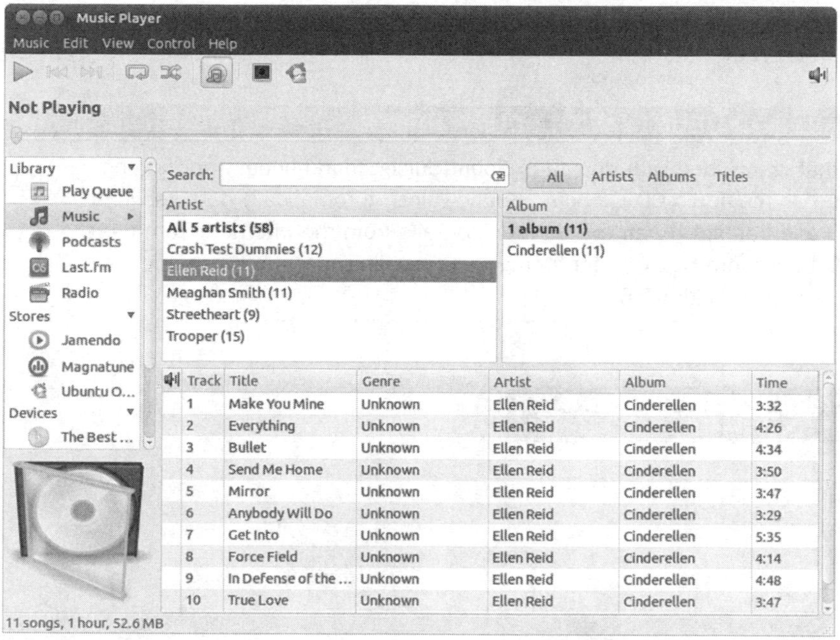

FIGURE 7.4 Rhythmbox gives you a neat interface to browse through your music collection.

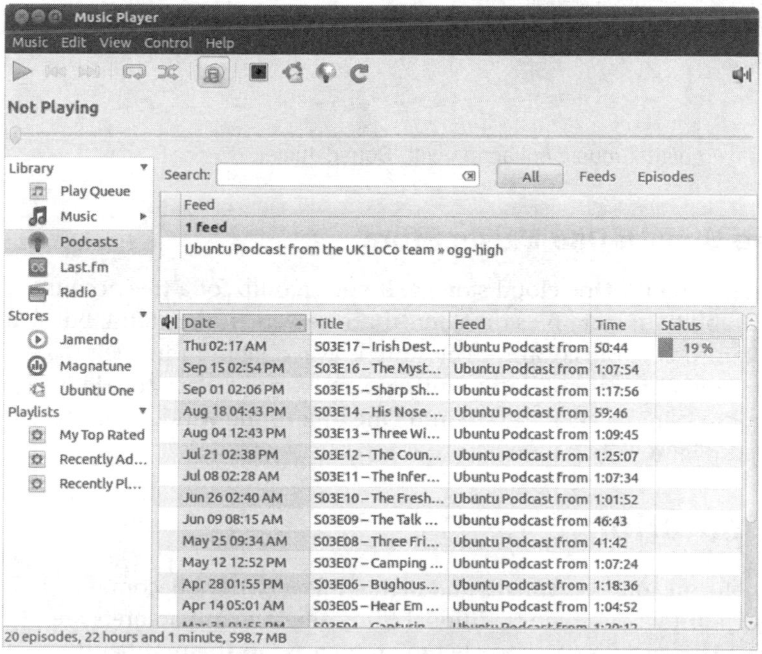

FIGURE 7.5 Manage your podcasts using Rhythmbox and never miss an episode again.

video. Banshee is not installed by default with Ubuntu, so you'll need to download and install it. The package name in the Ubuntu repositories is banshee.

GETTING MUSIC INTO UBUNTU WITH SOUND JUICER

A handy utility that is included with Ubuntu is Sound Juicer, found under Applications, Sound and Video as the Audio CD Extractor. Sound Juicer automatically detects when you install a CD and attempt to retrieve the track details from the Internet. From there it will rip the CD tracks into Ogg files for storage on your filesystem. You can see Sound Juicer in action in Figure 7.6

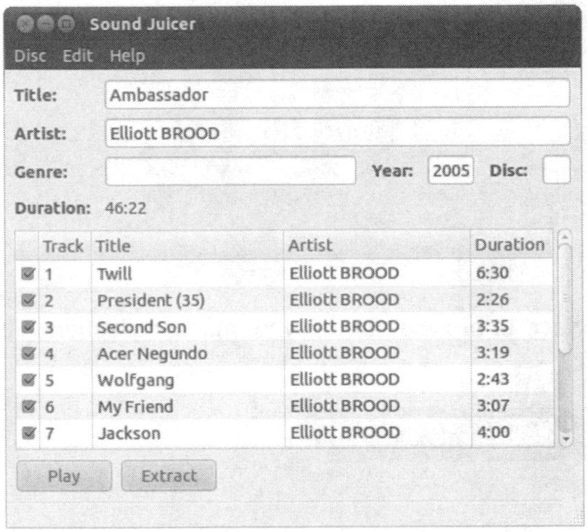

FIGURE 7.6 Create your own digital music collection with Sound Juicer.

Buying Music in the Ubuntu One Music Store

In Chapter 5 we mentioned Ubuntu One cloud storage. If you sign up for a free account, not only do you have the ability to store files on Ubuntu-run servers in the cloud, but you also gain access to the Ubuntu One Music Store. The store is available right inside Rhythmbox Music Player (and at the time of this writing plans were in place to add it to Banshee also). In Rhythmbox, simply click the Ubuntu One link in the window on the left of the screen to get started (Figure 7.7).

Graphics Manipulation

Over a very short period of time, digital cameras and digital imagery have become extremely popular, to the point where some traditional film camera manufacturers are switching solely to digital. This meteoric rise has led to an increase in the number of applications that can handle digital imagery. Linux, thanks to its rapid pace of development, is now highly regarded as a multimedia platform for editing digital images.

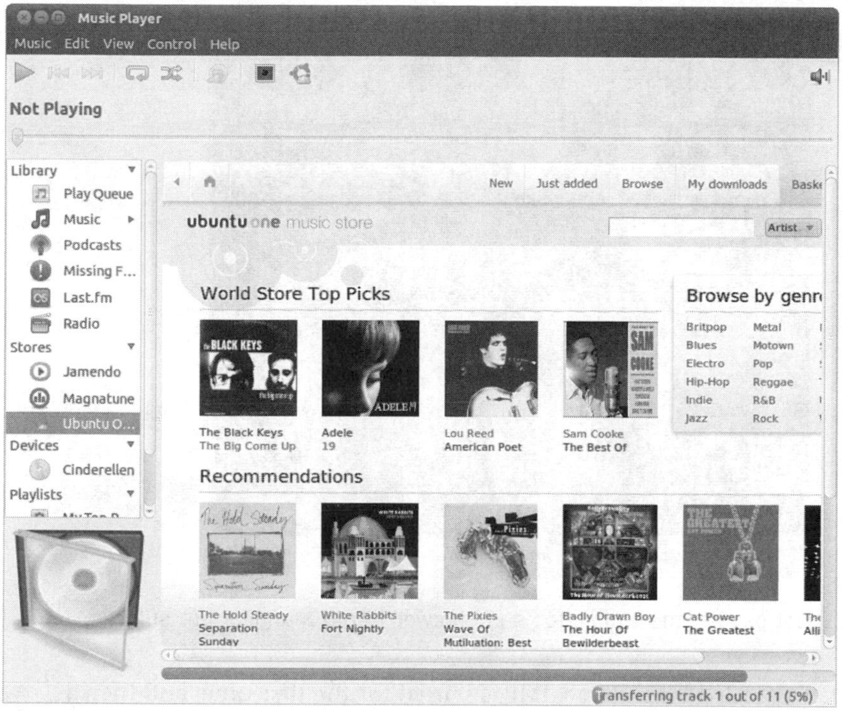

FIGURE 7.7 Ubuntu One Music Store.

By default Ubuntu installs the very useful Shotwell Photo Manager (Figure 7.8) in Applications, Graphics, Shotwell Photo Manager. This application is very similar to other photo managers like iPhoto and includes simple tools that are adequate for many users such as red eye reduction, cropping, and color adjustment as well as the ability to interact with online photo hosts such as Facebook, Flickr, and Picasa.

The rest of this section discusses GIMP, a powerful graphics manipulation tool that intermediate and advanced users are likely to enjoy. You also learn about graphic file formats supported by Ubuntu, as well as some tools you can use to convert them if the application you want to use requires a different format.

The GNU Image Manipulation Program

One of the best graphics clients available is GIMP. GIMP is a free, GPL-licensed image editor with sophisticated capabilities that can import and export more than 30 different graphics formats, including files created with Adobe Photoshop. It is often compared with Photoshop, and GIMP represents one of the GNU Projects' first significant successes. Many images in Linux were prepared with GIMP.

GIMP is not installed by default, but after you install it from the repositories it can be found in the menu at Applications, Graphics, GIMP Image Editor.

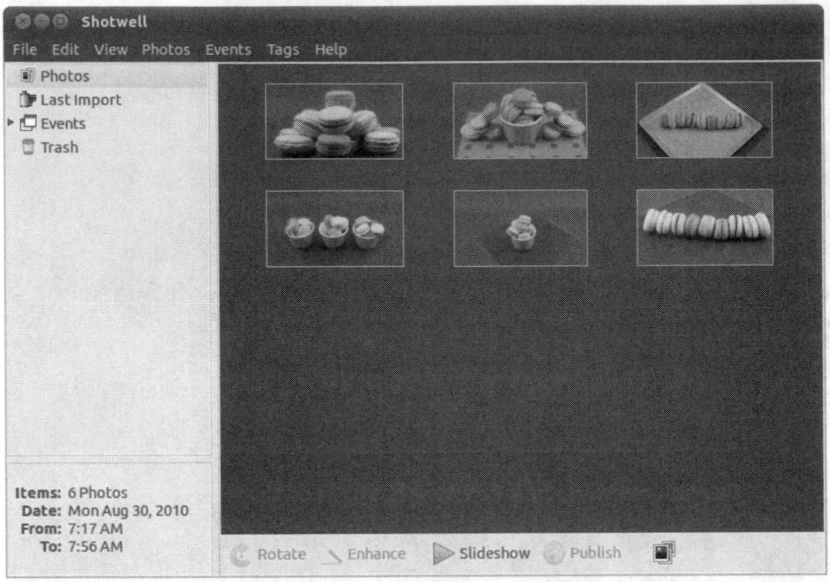

FIGURE 7.8 For most people, the simple tools in Shotwell Photo Manager are sufficient.

You see an installation dialog box when GIMP is started for the first time, and then a series of dialog boxes that display information regarding the creation and contents of a local GIMP directory. This directory can contain personal settings, preferences, external application resource files, temporary files, and symbolic links to external software tools used by the editor.

WHAT DOES PHOTOSHOP HAVE THAT GIMP DOES NOT?

Although GIMP is powerful, it does lack two features Adobe Photoshop offers that are important to some graphics professionals.

The first of these is the capability to generate color separations for commercial press printers (CMYK for the colors cyan, magenta, yellow, and key [or black]). GIMP uses RGB (red, green, and blue), which is great for video display, but not so great for printing presses. The second feature GIMP lacks is the use of Pantone colors (a patented color specification) to ensure accurate color matching. These deficiencies might not last long. A CMYK plug-in is in the works (an early version is available from cue.yellow-magic.info/softwares/separate-plus/index.html), and the Pantone issues are likely to be addressed in the near future as well.

If these features are unimportant to you, GIMP is an excellent tool. If you must use Adobe Photoshop, you may want to explore using Wine or Codeweavers because there have been consistent reports of success running Photoshop on Linux with these tools. Bear in mind, though, that both Ubuntu and Photoshop release regularly, so check www.winehq.org/ and www.codeweavers.com/ for the current info before assuming it will work.

After the initial configuration has finished, GIMPs main windows and toolboxes appear (Figure 7.9). GIMPs main window contains tools used for selecting, drawing, moving, view enlarging or reducing, airbrushing, painting, smudging, copying, filling, and selecting color.

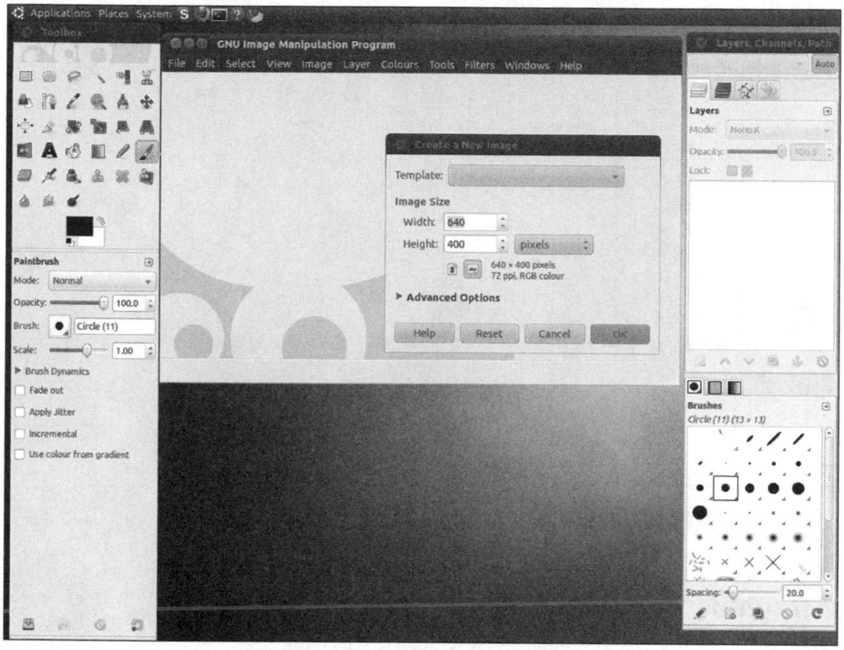

FIGURE 7.9 Right-click an image window to access GIMPs cascading menus.

Using Scanners in Ubuntu

With the rise of digital photography, there has been an equal decline in the need for image scanners. However, there are still times that you want to use a scanner, and Ubuntu makes it easy with a program installed by default in the menu at Applications, Graphics, Simple Scan. Simple Scan (Figure 7.10) is designed to do one thing, scan photos or documents easily. It has few settings or options but does all the things most people would want or need.

You can also use many types of image scanners with GIMP, which is likely to be the choice of people who like to tinker with settings and options or who need greater flexibility than is offered by Simple Scan. If it wasn't installed when you installed GIMP, install the `xsane` package. Then, when you scan from GIMP you will have an abundance of settings and options that you can use. You will also be able to use `XSane` by itself, finding it in the menu at Applications, Graphics, XSane Image Scanner.

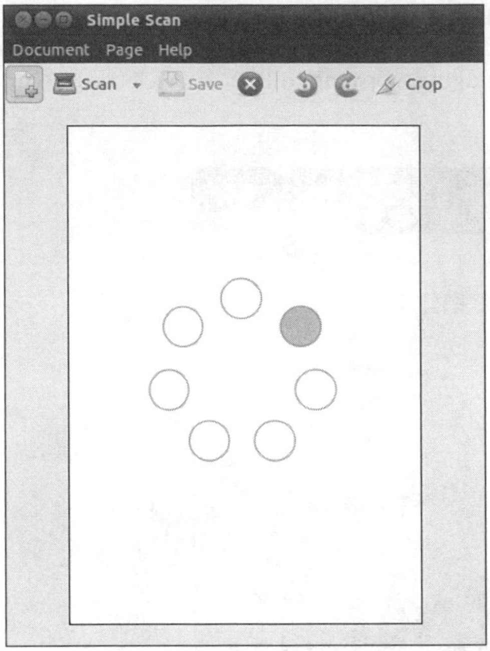

FIGURE 7.10 Simple Scan makes scanning easy.

Working with Graphics Formats

Image file formats are developed to serve a specific technical purpose (lossless compression, for example, where the file size is reduced without sacrificing image quality) or to meet a need for a proprietary format for competitive reasons. Many file formats are covered by one or more patents. For example, the GIF format had fallen into disfavor with the open-source crowd because the patent holder waited a while before deciding to enforce his patent rights rather than being upfront with requests for patent royalties.

If you want to view or manipulate an image, you need to identify the file format to choose the proper tool for working with the image. The file's extension is your first indicator of the file's format. The graphics image formats supported by the applications included with Ubuntu include:

- `.bmp`—Bitmapped graphics, commonly used in Microsoft Windows
- `.gif`—CompuServe Graphics Interchange Format
- `.jpg`—Joint Photographic Experts Group
- `.pcx`—IBM Paintbrush
- `.png`—Portable Network Graphics
- `.svg`—Scalable Vector Graphics
- `.tif`—Tagged Image File format

An extensive list of image file extensions can be found in the `man` page for ImageMagick, an excellent application included with Ubuntu, which you learn more about in upcoming sections of this chapter.

TIP

Ubuntu includes dozens of graphics conversion programs in its software repositories that are accessible through the command line as well as from a GUI, and there are few, if any, graphics file formats that cannot be manipulated when using Linux. These programs can be called in Perl scripts, shell scripts, or command-line pipes to support many types of complex format conversion and image manipulation tasks. See the man pages for the `ppm`, `pbm`, `pnm`, and `pgm` families of commands. Also see the man page for the `convert` command, which is part of a suite of extremely capable programs included with the ImageMagick suite.

Sometimes, a file you want to manipulate in some way is in a format that cannot be used by either your graphics application or the final application. The solution is to convert the image file—sometimes through several formats. The `convert` utility from ImageMagick is useful, as is the `netpbm` family of utilities. If it is not already installed, ImageMagick can be installed easily from the Ubuntu repositories; the `netpbm` tools are always installed by default. Convert is super simple to use from the command line. Here is an example:

```
matthew@seymour~:$ convert image.gif image.png
```

The `convert` utility converts between image formats recognized by ImageMagick. Color depth and size also can be manipulated during the conversion process. You can use ImageMagick to append images, surround them with borders, add labels, rotate and shade them, and perform other manipulations well suited to scripting. Other commands associated with ImageMagick include `display`, `animate`, `identify`, and `import`. The application supports more than 130 different image formats—(all listed in the man page for ImageMagick).

The `netpbm` tools are installed by default because they compose the underpinnings of graphics format manipulation. The man page for each image format lists related conversion utilities; the number of those utilities gives you some indication of the way that format is used and shows how one is built on another:

- The man page for `ppm`, the *portable pixmap* file format, lists 47 conversion utilities related to `ppm`. This makes sense because `ppm`, or *portable pixmap*, is considered the lowest common denominator for color image files. It is therefore often used as an intermediate format.
- The man page for `pgm`, the portable graymap file format, lists 22 conversion utilities. This makes sense because `pgm` is the lowest common denominator for grayscale image files.
- The man page for `pnm`, the portable anymap file format, lists 31 conversion utilities related to it. However, there is no format associated with PNM because it operates in concert with `ppm`, `pgm`, and `pbm`.

- An examination of the man page for `pbm`, the portable bitmap file format, reveals no conversion utilities. It's a monochrome format and serves as the foundation of the other related formats.
- The easiest way to resize or rotate image files is to install the `nautilus-image-converter` package from the repositories. This lets you right click an image when you are viewing files in the File Browser (for example, from Places > Pictures) and choose menu options to resize or rotate one or multiple images without opening another program.

Capturing Screen Images

You can use graphics manipulation tools to capture images that are displayed on your computer screen. Although this technique was used for the production of this book, it has broader uses; there is truth to the cliché that a picture is worth a thousand words. Sometimes it is easier to show an example than it is to describe it.

A captured screen image (also called a screen grab or a screenshot) can be used to illustrate an error in the display of an application (a font problem, for example) or an error dialog that is too complex to copy down by hand. You might just want to share an image of your beautifully crafted custom desktop configuration with your friends or illustrate your written documents.

When using the default GNOME desktop, you can take advantage of the built-in screenshot mechanism (`gnome-panel-screenshot`). You can use this tool by pressing the Print Screen key. (Alt+Print Screen takes a screenshot of only the window that has focus on a desktop.) Captured images are saved in `.png` format. You can also find the tool in the menu at Applications, Accessories, Take Screenshot.

Using Digital Cameras with Ubuntu

Most digital cameras used with Ubuntu fall into one of two categories: webcams (small, low-resolution cameras connected to the computer's interface) or handheld digital cameras that record image data on disks or memory cards for downloading and viewing on a PC. Ubuntu supports both types. Other types of cameras, such as surveillance cameras that connect directly to a network via wired or wireless connections, need no special support (other than a network connection and viewing software) to be used with a Linux computer.

Ubuntu supports hundreds of different digital cameras, from early parallel-port (CPiA chipset-based) cameras to today's USB-based cameras. You can even use Intel's QX3 USB microscope with Ubuntu. The following sections describe some of the more commonly used types of still camera hardware and software supported by Ubuntu.

Handheld Digital Cameras

Because of the good development carried out in the Linux world, you are able to plug almost any digital camera in to your computer through a USB interface, and Ubuntu automatically recognizes the camera as a USB mass storage device. You can even set

Ubuntu to recognize when a camera is plugged in so that it automatically imports your photographs for you.

Using Shotwell Photo Manager

Ubuntu comes by default with a pretty good photo manager called Shotwell Photo Manager (Figure 7.11) that includes simple adjustment tools. You can import your photos into Shotwell, assign tags to them, sort and arrange them, and even upload them to your favorite Internet photo hosting sites such as Facebook, Flickr, and Picasa.

FIGURE 7.11 Browse your photo collection and correct minor problems with Shotwell Photo Manager.

Burning CDs and DVDs in Ubuntu

Linux is generally distributed via the Internet as disc images called ISOs that are ready to be written to CDs or DVDs. Therefore learning how to burn discs is essential if you have to download and install a Linux distribution. You can use CDs and DVDs to:

- Record and store multimedia data, such as backup files, graphics images, and music.
- Rip audio tracks from music CDs (*ripping* refers to extracting music tracks from a music CD) and compile your own music CDs for your personal use.
- Although USB storage devices such as thumb drives are making CDs and DVDs almost as rare as floppy disks, they aren't quite gone, and many people still find them useful. As long as that remains true, we want to make sure this information is available.

7

Creating CDs and DVDs with Brasero

Although adequate for quick burns and use in shell scripting, the command-line technique for burning CDs and DVDs is an awkward choice for many people (but we are still going to cover doing so later in this chapter, because others find it useful and desirable). Fortunately, Ubuntu provides several graphical clients; the most useful is Brasero.

Brasero is an easy-to-use graphical CD and DVD burning application that is installed by default. You can find it in the menu at Applications, Sound & Video, Brasero Disc Burner.

Brasero takes a project-based approach to disc burning, opening up with a wizard that allows you to select from four different tasks that you'll commonly want to do. You can see the opening screen in Figure 7.12. Brasero also remembers previous "projects," allowing you to quickly create several copies of a disc, which is ideal if you're planning sto pass on copies of Ubuntu to your friends and family.

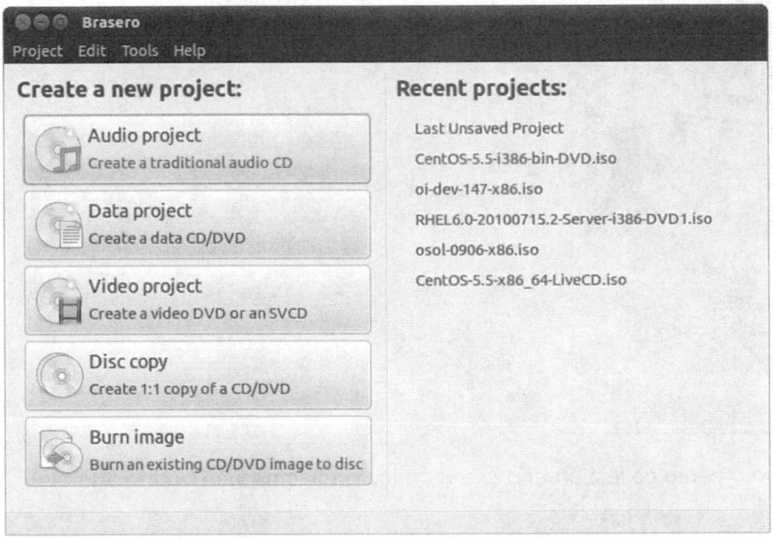

FIGURE 7.12 Brasero gives you an intuitive way to create data and audio CDs and DVDs.

Burning a Data CD or DVD is as easy as selecting the option in the opening screen and dragging and dropping the files you want to include from the directory tree on the left to the drop area on the right. If you insert a blank CD or DVD in your writer, Brasero keeps an eye on the disc size, and tells you when you reach or exceed the limits. It will also create iso files, which are disc images that contain everything that would exist on the medium if you burned a real CD or DVD in one file that can be mounted by computer file systems, which is useful if you want to create multiple copies of the same disc or if you want to share a disc image, perhaps using a USB thumb drive or over the Internet.

Finally, click the Burn button, input a label for the disc, and Brasero will start creating your new CD or DVD or image file. How long it takes to create a CD or DVD depends on the amount of data you are writing and the speed of your drive.

Creating CDs from the Command Line

In Linux, creating a CD at the command line is a two-step process. You first create the `iso9660`-formatted image, and you then burn or write the image onto the CD. The `iso9660` is the default file system for CD-ROMs.

Use the `mkisofs` command to create the ISO image. The `mkisofs` command has many options (see the man page for a full listing), but use the following for quick burns:

```
matthew@seymour~:$ mkisofs -r -v -J -l -o /tmp/our_special_cd.iso /source_directory
```

The options used in this example are:

- `-r`—Sets the permission of the files to more useful values. `UID` and `GID` (individual and group user ID requirements) are set to zero, all files are globally readable and searchable, and all files are set as executable (for Windows systems).
- `-v`—Displays verbose messages (rather than terse messages) so that you can see what is occurring during the process; these messages can help you resolve problems if they occur.
- `-J`—Uses the Joliet extensions to `ISO9660` so that your Windows-using buddies can more easily read the CD. The Joliet (for Windows), Rock Ridge (for UNIX), and HSF (for Mac) extensions to the `iso9660` standard are used to accommodate long filenames rather than the eight-character DOS filenames that the `iso9660` standard supports.
- `-l`—Allows 31-character filenames; DOS does not like it, but everyone else does.
- `-o`—Defines the directory where the image will be written (that is, the output) and its name. The `/tmp` directory is convenient for this purpose, but the image could go anywhere you have write permissions.
- `/source_directory`—Indicates the path to the source directory; that is, the directory containing the files you want to include. There are ways to append additional paths and exclude directories (and files) under the specified path—it is all explained in the man page, if you need that level of complexity. The simple solution is to construct a new directory tree and populate it with the files you want to copy, and then make the image using that directory as the source.

Many more options are available, including options to make the CD bootable.

After you have created the ISO image, you can write it to the CD with the `cdrecord` command:

```
matthew@seymour~:$ cdrecord -eject -v speed=12 dev=0,0,0 /tmp/our_special_cd.iso
```

The options used in this example are:

- `-eject`—Ejects the CD when the write operation is finished.
- `-v`—Displays verbose messages.
- `speed=`—Sets the speed; the rate depends on the individual drive's capabilities. If the drive or the recordable medium is poor, you can use lower speeds to get a good burn.

- dev=—Specifies the device number of the CD writer (the number I told you to write down earlier).

NOTE

You can also use the blank= option with the cdrecord command to erase CD-RW disks. The cdrecord command has fewer options than mkisofs does, but it offers the -multi option, which enables you to make multisession CDs. A multisession CD enables you to write a data track, quit, and then add more data to the CD later. A single-session CD can be written to only once; any leftover CD capacity is wasted. Read about other options in the cdrecord man page.

Current capacity for CD media is 700MB of data or 80 minutes of music. (There are 800MB/90 minute CDs, but they are rare.) Some CDs can be overburned; that is, recorded to a capacity in excess of the standard. The cdrecord command and some graphical programs are capable of overburning if your CD-RW drive supports it. You can learn more about overburning CDs at www.cdmediaworld.com/hardware/cdrom/cd_oversize.shtml/.

Creating DVDs from the Command Line

There are several competing formats for DVD. The formats are:

- DVD+R
- DVD-R
- DVD+RW
- DVD-RW

Differences in the + and – formats have mostly to do with how the data is modulated onto the DVD itself, with the + format having an edge in buffer underrun recovery. How this is achieved impacts the playability of the newly created DVD on any DVD player. The DVD+ format also has some advantages in recording on scratched or dirty media. Most drives support the DVD+ format. As with any technology, your mileage may vary.

We focus on the DVD+RW drives because most drives support that standard. The software supplied with Ubuntu has support for writing to DVD-R/W (rewritable) media as well. It will be useful for you to review the DVD+RW/+R/-R[W] for Linux HOWTO at http://fy.chalmers.se/~appro/linux/DVD+RW/ before you attempt to use dvd+rw-tools, which you need to install to enable DVD creation (also known as mastering) as well as the cdrtools package. You can ignore the discussion in the HOWTO about kernel patches and compiling the tools.

TIP

The 4.7GB size of DVD media is measured as 1000 megabytes per gigabyte, instead of the more traditionally used, but not entirely accurate, 1024 megabytes per gigabyte (more appropriately written GiB), so do not be surprised when the actual formatted capacity, about 4.4GB, is less than you anticipated. A good explanation of the difference and the need for the correction is available at http://en.wikipedia.org/wiki/Gibibyte. Most hard drive manufacturers have also made the switch. `dvd+rw-tools` does not allow you to exceed the capacity of the disk.

You need to have the `dvd+rw-tools` package installed (as well as the `cdrtools` package). The `dvd+rw-tools` package contains the `growisofs` application (that acts as a front end to `mkisofs`) as well as the DVD formatting utility.

You can use DVD media to record data in two ways. The first way is much the same as that used to record CDs in a session, and the second way is to record the data as a true file system, using packet writing.

Session Writing

To record data in a session, you use a two-phase process:

1. Format the disk with `dvd+rw-format /dev/scd0` (only necessary the first time you use a disk, where `/dev/scd0` is the device name for your drive).
2. Write your data to the disk with `growisofs -Z /dev/scd0 -R -J` */your_files*.

The `growisofs` command simply streams the data to the disk. For subsequent sessions, use the `-M` argument instead of `-Z`. The `-Z` argument is used only for the initial session recording; if you use the `-Z` argument on an already used disk, it erases the existing files.

CAUTION

Some DVDs come preformatted; formatting them again when you use them for the first time can make the DVD useless. Always be sure to carefully read the packaging your DVD comes in to ensure that you are not about to create another coaster!

TIP

Writing a first session of at least 1GB helps maintain compatibility of your recorded data with other optical drives. DVD players calibrate themselves by attempting to read from specific locations on the disk; you need data there for the drive to read it and calibrate itself.

Also, because of limitations to the ISO9660 file system in Linux, do not start new sessions of a multisession DVD that would create a directory past the 4GB boundary. If you do so, it causes the offsets used to point to the files to "wrap around" and point to the wrong files.

Packet Writing

Packet writing treats the CD or DVD disk like a hard drive in which you create a file system (like ext3) and format the disk, and then write to it randomly as you would to a conventional hard drive. This method, although commonly available on Windows-based computers, was long considered experimental for Linux and was never used much anyway as USB thumb drives became common before the use of CD or DVD-RWs had the opportunity. We do not cover this in detail here, but a quick overview is appropriate.

TIP

DVD+RW media are capable of only about 1,000 writes, so it is very useful to mount them with the `noatime` option to eliminate any writing to update their inodes or simply mount them read-only when it's not necessary to write to them.

It is possible to pipe data to the `growisofs` command:

```
matthew@seymour~:$ sudo your_application ¦ growisofs -Z /dev/scd0=/dev/fd/0
```

It is also possible to burn from an existing image (or file, named pipe, or device):

```
matthew@seymour~:$ sudo growisofs -Z /dev/scd0=image
```

The `dvd+rw-tools` documentation, found at `/usr/share/doc/dvd+rw-tools/index.html`, is required reading before your first use of the program. We also suggest that you experiment with DVD-RW (rewritable) media first, as if you make mistakes then you will still be able to reuse the disk, rather than creating several new coasters for your coffee mug.

Viewing Video

You can use Ubuntu tools and applications to view movies and other video presentations on your PC. This section presents some TV and motion picture video software tools included with the Ubuntu distribution you received with this book.

TV and Video Hardware

To watch TV and video content on your PC, you must install a supported TV card or have a video/TV combo card installed. A current list of TV and video cards supported in Linux can be found at www.exploits.org/v4l/.

Freely available Linux support for TV display from video cards that have a TV-out jack is improved over a couple of years ago, but still rather poor. That support must come from the X driver, not from a video device that Video4Linux supports with a device driver. Some of the combo TV-tuner/video display cards have support, including the Matrox

Marvel, the Matrox Rainbow Runner G-Series, and the RivaTV cards. Many other combo cards lack support, although an independent developer might have hacked something together to support his own card. Your best course of action is to perform a thorough Internet search with Google.

Many of the TV-only PCI cards are supported. In Linux, however, they are supported by the video chipset they use, and not by the name some manufacturer has slapped on a generic board (the same board is typically sold by different manufacturers under different names). The most common chipset is the Brooktree `Bt***` series of chips; they are supported by the `bttv` device driver.

If you have a supported card in your computer, it should be detected during installation. If you add it later, the hardware detection utility should detect it and configure it. It is possible to try to configure it by hand, but because the Ubuntu kernel czars try to compile every hardware option available as a module and make it available, doing so isn't likely to be of much use. Even so, this is what you would do:

First, to determine what chipset your card has, use the `lspci` command to list the PCI device information, find the TV card listing, and look for the chipset that the card uses. For example, the `lspci` output for one computer shows

```
matthew@seymour~:$ lspci
00:00.0 Host bridge: Advanced Micro Devices [AMD] AMD-760 [IGD4-1P] System Con-
troller (rev 13)
00:01.0 PCI bridge: Advanced Micro Devices [AMD] AMD-760 [IGD4-1P] AGP Bridge
00:07.0 ISA bridge: VIA Technologies, Inc. VT82C686 [Apollo Super South] (rev 40)
00:07.1 IDE interface: VIA Technologies, Inc. VT82C586B PIPC Bus Master IDE (rev 06)
00:07.2 USB Controller: VIA Technologies, Inc. USB (rev 1a)
00:07.3 USB Controller: VIA Technologies, Inc. USB (rev 1a)
00:07.4 SMBus: VIA Technologies, Inc. VT82C686 [Apollo Super ACPI] (rev 40)
00:09.0 Multimedia audio controller: Ensoniq 5880 AudioPCI (rev 02)
00:0b.0 Multimedia video controller: Brooktree Corporation Bt878 Video Capture (rev
02)
00:0b.1 Multimedia controller: Brooktree Corporation Bt878 Audio Capture (rev 02)
00:0d.0 Ethernet controller: Realtek Semiconductor Co., Ltd. RTL-8029(AS)
00:0f.0 FireWire (IEEE 1394): Texas Instruments TSB12LV23 IEEE-1394 Controller
00:11.0 Network controller: Standard Microsystems Corp [SMC] SMC2602W EZConnect
01:05.0 VGA compatible controller: nVidia Corporation NV15 [GeForce2 Ti] (rev a4)
```

Here, the lines listing the multimedia video controller and multimedia controller say that this TV board uses a Brooktree `Bt878` Video Capture chip and a Brooktree `Bt878` Audio Capture chip. This card uses the `Bt878` chipset. Your results will be different, depending on what card and chipset your computer has. This card happened to be an ATI All-in-Wonder VE (also known as ATI TV-Wonder). (The VE means *Value Edition*; hence, there is no TV-out connector and no radio chip on the card; what a value!).

Then you would figure out what module was needed, probably using Google to search for "Bt878 linux" or "Bt878 Ubuntu," and start reading documentation. You would want to look for official pages first rather than blog posts. Finally, you would then need to enter some information into /etc/modules.conf. This file does not exist anymore in a default Ubuntu installation, but may be created as needed and will be read at boot time. Then, you would calculate the module and kernel dependencies with `sudo depmod -a` and `sudo modprobe <module name>` to load the module. Again, this is not necessary in Ubuntu as the people doing kernel configuration create a module for everything that exists, so if it is available to them, they will make it available to you with no extra work on your part, and the system scans to see what should be loaded at boot and pulls in what is needed then.

Video Formats

Ubuntu recognizes a variety of video formats. The formats created by the MPEG group, Apple, and Microsoft dominate, however. At the heart of video formats are the *codecs*—the encoders and decoders of the video and audio information. These codecs are typically proprietary, but free codecs do exist. Here is a list of the most common video formats and their associated file extensions:

- `.mpeg`—The MPEG video format; also known as `.mpg`
- `.qt`—The QuickTime video format from Apple
- `.mov`—Another QuickTime video format
- `.avi`—The Windows audio visual format

Viewing Video in Linux

Out of the box, Ubuntu does not support any of the proprietary video codecs due to licensing restrictions. However this functionality can be acquired if you install the `ubuntu-restricted-extras` package from the Ubuntu software repositories. You can learn more about this at https://help.ubuntu.com/community/RestrictedFormats.

You can watch video files and video DVDs with Totem Movie Player (Figure 7.13), which is installed by default and may be found in the menu at Applications, Sound & Video, Movie Player. This may also be used with several other file formats and for both video and audio and is especially well suited for almost anything you are likely to want to use after the ubuntu-restricted-extras package is installed.

ADOBE FLASH

The Adobe Flash plug-in for the Firefox browser is a commercial multimedia application that isn't provided with Ubuntu out of the box, but many people find it useful. Adobe Flash enables you to view Flash content at websites that support it. The easiest way of getting hold of the official version of Flash is to install the `ubuntu-restricted-extras` package. After you've done this, any flash animations will play quite happily within any Firefox-based browsers.

Another interesting video viewer application is VLC (Figure 7.14), which is available in the software repositories. VLC uses its own set of audio and video codecs and supports a wider range of video formats than any other media player we have encountered. If VLC can't play it, it probably can't be played.

FIGURE 7.13 Totem Movie Player works with most common video and audio formats.

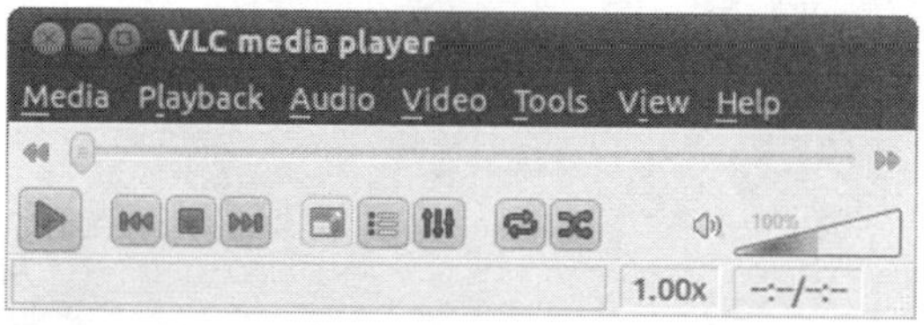

FIGURE 7.14 VLC is a powerful and capable media player.

Personal Video Recorders

The best reason to attach a television antenna to your computer, however, is to use the video card and the computer as a personal video recorder.

The commercial personal video recorder, TiVo, started a new trend by using Linux running on a PowerPC processor to record television programming with a variety of customizations. You can turn your computer into a personal digital video recorder with Myth TV from www.mythtv.org/, a Linux-based digital video recorder software project, made even easier for Ubuntu users by the Mythbuntu project at www.mythbuntu.org/. Everything you need is available in the Ubuntu repositories and may be installed and configured easily thanks to the people involved in these projects.

Video Editing

You can now create and edit video in Ubuntu using PiTiVi (Figure 7.15), installed by default and found in the menu at Applications, Sound & Video, PiTiVi Video Editor. You may import any video clip in any format that is supported by GStreamer, the main multimedia framework used in Ubuntu. This should include the files created by your digital camera, which should mount in Ubuntu as a storage device, making the transfer of the files from the camera to your computer quick and easy. PiTiVi lets you move scenes around, cut things, add your own soundtrack, and more.

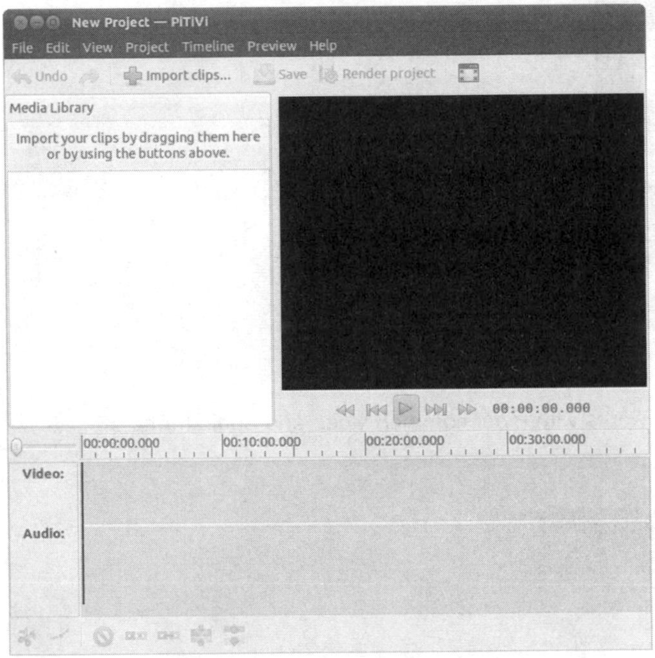

FIGURE 7.15 PiTiVi Video Editor.

Reference

- www.videolan.org/—A VideoLAN project with good documentation.
- http://fy.chalmers.se/~appro/linux/DVD+RW/—The DVD+RW/+R/-R[W] for Linux, a HOWTO for creating DVDs under Linux.
- www.gimp.org—Home page of The GIMP (Gnu Image Manipulation Program).
- http://f-spot.org—Home page of the F-Spot project.
- www.sane-project.org—Home page of the SANE (Scanner Access Now Easy) project.
- www.imagemagick.org—Home page for ImageMagick.
- http://gimp.net/tutorials/—Official tutorials for The GIMP.

CHAPTER 8

Other Ubuntu Desktops

IN THIS CHAPTER

When you install Ubuntu, by default you will use the GNOME desktop, discussed in Chapter 3. The GNOME desktop has specific strengths that appeal to many users. However, some of us have unique requirements or just like to tinker. This chapter will discuss some of the alternatives to GNOME, their strengths and weaknesses, and how to install them. This is not a complete listing of all the options available, but rather a brief survey of some of the more popular options to consider helping you get your feet wet in the realm of Linux desktop software.

GNOME IS NOT THE ONLY OPTION

When you install Ubuntu, you also install the GNOME desktop. However, this is neither your only option nor are you limited to only one desktop installed at a time. Each of the desktops we discuss in this chapter may be installed alongside GNOME in standard Ubuntu and you will be allowed to choose which one to use each time you log in as well as which one to use by default. This makes testing a new option less risky, because switching back to what you already know is simple.

Desktop Environment

A desktop environment is a graphical user interface for computers, specifically an interface that uses the idea of a physical office desk as a metaphor to make interacting with the computer simple to comprehend. As in a real-world office, a computer desktop environment will use files to contain documents which contain information that is necessary for office tasks to be done. Computer systems take the metaphor further by adding applications, programs that allow users to create, manipulate and delete those documents as needed, much as might be done in the real world, but with greater efficiency and often with greater power.

A computer desktop will include a windowing system, another metaphoric way to deal with information that makes conceptualizing the complexity occurring behind the scenes in the digital realm easier. Files, folders (or directories), and applications open in a graphic display that may be moved around the user's desktop just as paper documents and file folders may be moved to different locations on a physical desktop for convenience and efficiency. This windowing system will include the graphical bits (called widgets) needed to draw the windows on the screen as well as all the program code needed to perform the actions desired behind the scenes while displaying those actions using the pretty metaphor. For example, moving a document from one folder to another on a desktop involves little more than a mouse click followed by a drag and drop. Behind the scenes, the desktop environment is listening to the window manager's instructions to move a file from one directory to another and then telling the window manager to draw the event on the screen as it is accomplished.

The Ubuntu software repositories include all the popular desktop environments available for Linux and make installing and trying them out easy to do. It is also possible for an adventurous person to find other desktop environments that will work on Ubuntu and download and install them. We don't cover that process here.

It is also possible to use one desktop environment while substituting a different window manager into that environment instead of using the one that comes with the desktop environment by default. For example, the standard GNOME window manager is called Metacity. It is stable and works quite well. However, Ubuntu uses a different window manager called Compiz if the installation process detects the presence of video hardware capable of taking advantage of the extra flashy features it provides (otherwise the installer configures Ubuntu to use Metacity). To make matters more interesting, you can replace either of those with other window managers such as Enlightment (Figure 8.1), which does things in a unique and interesting manner.

In this chapter, we focus on complete desktop environments using the default window manager. In addition, because this is an Ubuntu-focused book, we focus on Ubuntu refined versions of environments such as KDE and Xfce rather than their default versions, although the default versions are also available in the Ubuntu repositories if you want to seek them out.

KDE and Kubuntu

The KDE project began back in 1996 with the goal of creating a quality desktop environment for the Linux desktop that was free, worked well, and which was well-integrated, meaning that programs and interfaces would have a consistent look and feel where all the parts fit together seamlessly, rather than looking like a jumbled compilation of a bunch of assorted bits.

FIGURE 8.1 Enlightment is a very unique and interesting desktop environment option.

The project has always been focused on end users rather than creating a simple GUI for the systems administrator. This is an important point, because from the beginning, the intent has been to make any computer user comfortable and able to do what they want to do without necessarily requiring a full grasp of what is happening behind the scenes. This focus continues today and is shared by other desktop environments, notably GNOME, which was started in 1997 by people once involved in the KDE project who left after a dispute over software licensing.

The cause of that dispute no longer exists as the licenses today are equivalently free, but the projects diverged a bit in their focus: GNOME seeking a desktop of zenlike simplicity with simple and elegant defaults and use while KDE pursues more flash and configuration options. Honestly, they are each great desktop environments that are well-integrated with a high degree of professionalism and quality and are easily the top two in the Linux world—try them both and see which you prefer.

Kubuntu is a project that started in the Ubuntu community very early on with the simple goal of allowing users to install and use KDE in Ubuntu. To make this even easier for people who already know they prefer KDE over GNOME, you can download an install disk for Kubuntu, which is Ubuntu minus GNOME plus KDE plus a few Kubuntu-specific enhancements. You may also install Kubuntu in standard Ubuntu and alongside GNOME by installing the `kubuntu-desktop` package from the Ubuntu software repositories.

Kubuntu (Figure 8.2) uses a different set of default programs for most tasks: web browsing, email, and so on. Most were written specifically for the KDE desktop environment, making KDE one of the most closely integrated and consistent Linux desktops available.

FIGURE 8.2 The Kubuntu desktop.

Xfce and Xubuntu

Xfce is a lighter desktop environment that requires less memory and processing power than either GNOME or KDE and is therefore often suggested for use on older machines. It does not deserve to be relegated to that role because it also works great on current hardware and is often a quality choice for a different reason. Xfce has been developed using the traditional UNIX philosophy of software: do one thing, do it well, and play well with others.

Each part of the Xfce desktop environment is modular, you may add or remove bits at will, substitute other programs that perform the same function, and everything created by or included in Xfce is expected to work according to simple standards that allow other programs to interact with it easily.

On one hand this sometimes means that people look at Xfce and think it isn't as seamlessly integrated and smooth as the two main desktop environments. On the other hand, it means that if you prefer the GNOME file manager (Nautilus) over the one included with Xfce (Thunar), then just install Nautilus and use it, either side by side with Thunar or remove Thunar completely. This is a huge part of what makes Xfce so lightweight, it has very few dependency requirements and is highly flexible.

Originally, Xubuntu (Figure 8.3) was designed to create a lighter weight version of Ubuntu that would run well on older hardware because of the lighter code dependencies of Xfce. Over time, some people discovered they liked the desktop environment for other reasons and the older hardware use case became less of a focus. It was the modularity of Xfce combined with a smoothness of operation that won people over and the distribution began to take some of the favored bits from Ubuntu's customized version of GNOME and added them to Xfce to replace some of its defaults. What we have today is a very nice amalgamation of Ubuntu GNOME bits, Xfce bits, and a few other things not included by default in either.

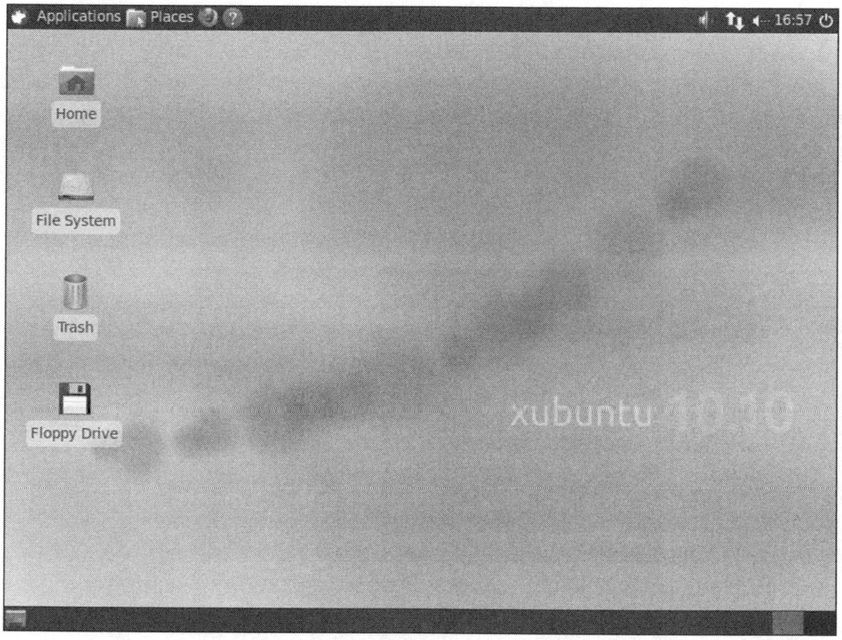

FIGURE 8.3 The Xubuntu desktop.

Xubuntu still uses less memory and fewer CPU cycles than a standard Ubuntu or Kubuntu install; however, thinking of it only in those terms doesn't do it justice. To install Xubuntu with the Xfce desktop environment, install the `xubuntu-desktop` package.

Ubuntu Netbook Edition

Although Ubuntu Netbook Edition (UNE) is specifically focused on creating a version of Ubuntu ready to install and run well on small, low-powered devices, some have found its interface to be preferable to any standard desktop. For that reason, we don't want to limit your thinking and lead you to believe it is suitable only for those devices.

UNE comes with most of the same programs included that are in the standard Ubuntu installation. The main difference is that in UNE the graphical interface has been modified to save space on small screens, making this a far better option for users with small monitors.

The UNE interface is smooth and pretty, but looks different than a traditional window management system with overlapping windows of content or open programs. Here all programs open full-screen by default. There is only a top panel on the screen from which you can switch from window to window. It isn't designed for you to drag and drop from window to another (although you can just as easily cut and paste, so real functionality is not lost), but rather to maximize the screen real estate for whatever you are using at a particular moment.

When you have no windows open or they are all minimized, UNE uses a unique menu system (Figure 8.4) that makes finding what you need easy and uses nice, large icons that are easy to view on a small screen. Most people using a netbook prefer using this interface on their computer over the standard GNOME interface. We have also met several laptop and even desktop users who use it simply because they find it more interesting, enjoyable, or beautiful.

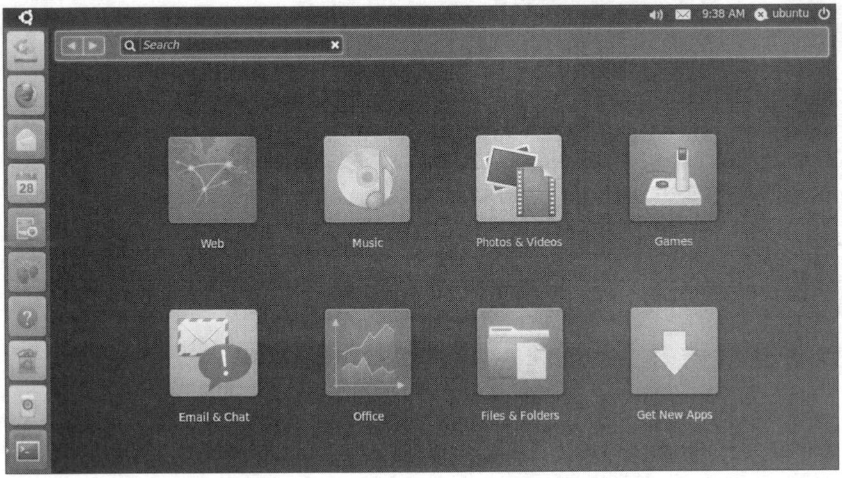

FIGURE 8.4 Ubuntu Netbook Edition uses a unique and beautiful menu system.

You can install Ubuntu Netbook Edition with the `ubuntu-netbook` package from the software repositories. If you want to do a fresh installation on a netbook, you can download it and follow the easy instructions for creating a bootable USB thumb drive (because netbooks do not include CD or DVD drives) at www.ubuntu.com/netbook/get-ubuntu/download.

LXDE and Lubuntu

The previously discussed desktop environments are all officially recognized derivatives of Ubuntu, acknowledged by the developer community and well-represented within it. This section discusses a project that is hoping to achieve that same status, but which is still quite new and experimental, Lubuntu. Lubuntu is based on LXDE.

LXDE is an extremely fast desktop environment that uses less memory and fewer CPU cycles than any of the others discussed. It is being developed specifically with lower powered computers such as netbooks in mind, but that isn't the sole use case. For example, Knoppix, which is a Linux distribution that runs from a live, bootable CD or DVD, now uses LXDE. Knoppix is a longtime favorite of sysadmins for emergency repairs of unbootable systems as well as for its portability. It recently switched from KDE to LXDE to benefit from this lightness because running an operating system from a CD or DVD is generally much slower than when it is installed on a hard drive.

As the focus in Xubuntu turned from speed and lightness to enjoying the flexibility of Xfce, a gap was created. Users and developers interested in less-expensive hardware, such as mobile Internet devices and ARM or Mips-processor based computers, wanted to find a way to run a distribution of Linux that shared the community of Ubuntu, a beautiful and useful desktop, and that did not get bogged down on slower machines. LXDE is quite new and its development philosophy fits quite well with the hopes and dreams of these users, so it seems a perfect fit.

The Lubuntu (Figure 8.5) distribution is still very new and is not yet recommended for use as a primary desktop. The developers are working within the Ubuntu community and making consistent progress, and if you are inclined, they are also appealing for interested people to join the development team and help out. You may install `lubuntu-desktop` from the Ubuntu repositories to check out the current progress. Who knows? Maybe you will discover it is already both stable and useful enough for your needs. Even if it isn't ready, it may excite or interest you so much that you decide to jump in and help out.

FIGURE 8.5 The Lubuntu desktop is quite attractive.

Reference

- www.gnome.org/—The official site for the GNOME desktop.
- http://blogs.gnome.org/metacity/2007/12/23/start-reading-here/ - Metacity does not have an official home page, as this post on the official Metacity blog explains.
- www.compiz.org/—The official site of Compiz.
- www.enlightenment.org/—The official site of Enlightment.
- www.kde.org/—The official site for the KDE desktop.
- www.kubuntu.org/—The official Kubuntu site.
- www.xfce.org/—The official site for the Xfce desktop.
- www.xubuntu.org/—The official Xubuntu site.
- www.ubuntu.com/netbook—The official Ubuntu Netbook Edition site.
- www.lxde.org/—The official site for the LXDE desktop.
- http://lubuntu.net/—The official Lubuntu site.
- www.knoppix.net/—The site for the live CD/DVD Linux distribution, Knoppix.

- http://xwinman.org/—A nice discussion of many of the different window managers and desktop environments available for Linux and UNIX systems. Much of the discussion on this site is dated, but the links are generally valid and useful and the site gives a good overview of the many options available.
- http://en.wikipedia.org/wiki/Desktop_environment—A detailed definition of a desktop environment, how they work, why they exist, and so on.
- http://en.wikipedia.org/wiki/Comparison_of_X_Window_System_desktop_environments—An amazing list of available desktop environments complete with a comparison of features.

CHAPTER 9

Games

IN THIS CHAPTER

Playing games is a fun part of computing. For some of us, games are a big part of the appeal of any operating system, at least for uses beyond the business or corporate environment. From the humble card games that entertain millions during their coffee breaks, to the heavily involved first-person shooters that involve players dotted around the globe, Linux offers a quality gaming platform that may surprise you.

In this chapter we'll explore some of the common games available for you to download and install easily in Ubuntu.

Ubuntu Gaming

A small number of games come installed by default with standard desktop Ubuntu, mostly simple things to divert your attention for a few minutes between tasks, games such as solitaire or sudoku (Figure 9.1). These are easy to try out and learn, and you may find them enjoyable.

Most of us who enjoy games will want to find something more. Thankfully, games for Linux do not stop there—several popular games have native Linux support. We will discuss a small number of our favorites here.

Emulators

In addition, there are even emulators available that enable you to play classic games, such as the LucasArts ScummVM games like Secret of Monkey Island, natively under Linux. There are emulators for DOS, NES, SNES and many more. If you are interested in them, do a search online for

Dgen/SDL, DosBox, xtrs, FCEUltra, GnGeo, SDLMama, ScummVM, and Stella. The documentation for emulators is hit or miss, but if you are lucky you may be able to play your favorite old games for consoles or operating systems that no longer exist or which current OS versions do not support.

FIGURE 9.1 The default games as listed in the Applications, Games menu.

Installing Proprietary Video Drivers

A major gripe of Linux users has been the difficulty involved in getting modern 3D graphics cards to work. Thankfully, both AMD (owner of the now-defunct ATI brand) and Nvidia support Linux, albeit by using closed-source drivers. This means that Ubuntu does not ship with native 3D drivers activated for either graphics card, but they are easily installed, often during or just after the operating system is installed. These drivers are needed for most of the more visually spectacular games.

Both Nvidia and AMD produce proprietary drivers, meaning that the source code is not open or available for outside developers to read or modify. Because of this it is hard for some Linux distros to include them as part of their standard installation. The Ubuntu community has taken a pragmatic approach of including both Nvidia and AMD drivers within the main Ubuntu distro, but disabled by default. That way anyone who has Nvidia or AMD hardware and wants to do so can activate those drivers to take advantage of their features.

NOTE

If you think that proprietary drivers are the only way on Linux, we should mention that there is a lot of development going into providing totally free and open source drivers for slightly older graphics cards. Ubuntu will automatically select the best "free" driver for your system and allow you to switch the proprietary driver should you want to. Although the open source drivers will provide 3D acceleration, this support doesn't always extend to a full feature set or to the more recent graphics cards.

It's very easy to activate the proprietary driver if you need to; from the menu select System, Administration, and Hardware Drivers.

Installing a different hardware driver requires super-user privileges, so a confirmation check will be run to see if you are permitted and then you will be asked for your password. After the Hardware Drivers dialog window has opened, read the descriptions and look for the recommended entry for your hardware, highlight it, and click Activate at the lower right. Ubuntu will confirm that you want to use the proprietary driver and, if you agree, will automatically download and configure the relevant driver. If you want to revert to the open driver, do the same thing, but select the activated driver and click Remove at the lower right, as shown in Figure 9.2, in the same place where the earlier Activate button was.

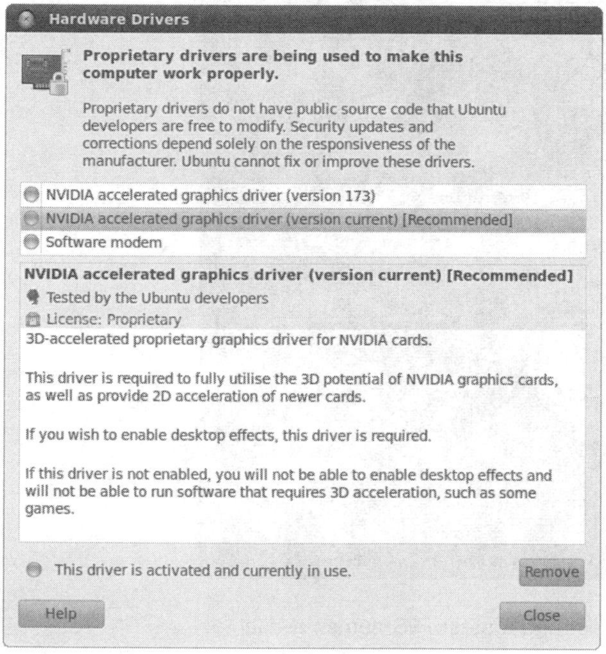

FIGURE 9.2 Use the Hardware Drivers Manager to activate or deactivate the appropriate proprietary graphics driver for your graphics card.

Installing Games in Ubuntu

In this section we'll take a look at how to install some of the more popular games for Ubuntu, all of which may be easily installed using Ubuntu Software Center, along with hundreds more listed in under Games. Alongside the usual shoot-'em-up games, you'll also find one or two strategy-focused titles.

Warsow

Warsow is a free and very fast-paced first-person shooter (FPS) game that is available on Windows, Mac OS X, and Linux. Members of the Ubuntu community have packaged the game and make it available directly and easily for Ubuntu users from the software repositories. The game involves quick movements, grabbing power ups and weapons before your enemies do, and trying to plant a bomb and steal your enemy's flag without anyone seeing you. You can jump, dash, dodge, and even wall jump your way through out the colorful 3D environment. Figure 9.3 shows a game just getting started with lots of weapons, platforms and ramps, and power-ups in sight.

FIGURE 9.3 Warsow is one of the newest and fastest FPS games available.

Scorched 3D

Scorched 3D is based on an old DOS game called Scorched Earth. The object and game play are similar: there are multiple players and you enter targeting details to try to destroy the other players using a variety of missile-like weapons. You earn points for each win and can buy new weapons at the end of each round. This time around, there is an amazing array of weapons available and the game play is completely in stunning 3D as seen in Figure 9.4.

Scorched 3D is based on turns. Each player shoots once, then all other players take a shot before the first player shoots again. The game allows you to have more than 20 players at the same time, including both human and computer controlled players. You may play a local game, over a LAN, or even over the Internet. Scorched 3D also runs on Windows, Mac OS X and Linux, so you may play with your friends regardless of what platform their computer uses.

FIGURE 9.4 Scorched 3D in action.

Frozen Bubble

Frozen Bubble is an amusing little game with sharp graphics, nice music, and easy game play. You may play alone or against another player. The goal is to use your colored marbles to knock down the ones above you within a certain amount of time. You have to hit at least two at a time that are the same color as the one you shoot for anything to fall; otherwise, your shot joins the menagerie above and brings your demise somewhat more quickly, as illustrated in Figure 9.5. There is a lot more to Frozen Bubble, but even with the details it is easy enough for a child to play and interesting enough to hold the interest of most adults.

SuperTux

Many of us grew up in the era when game play was more important than graphics. Even so, we still liked flashy and pretty looking games. SuperTux is a throwback to the Mario era. It is a 2D side scroller in which you jump, run, and occasionally shoot something if you have the appropriate power-up. This time, your hero is Tux, the Linux penguin. There are more than 25 levels available, as well as a level editor for you to create your own. If you enjoy running, jumping, hitting your head to get money, and jumping on your enemies, this game is for you. Figure 9.6 gives you the basic look and feel.

FIGURE 9.5 Move left or right to aim, press up to fire.

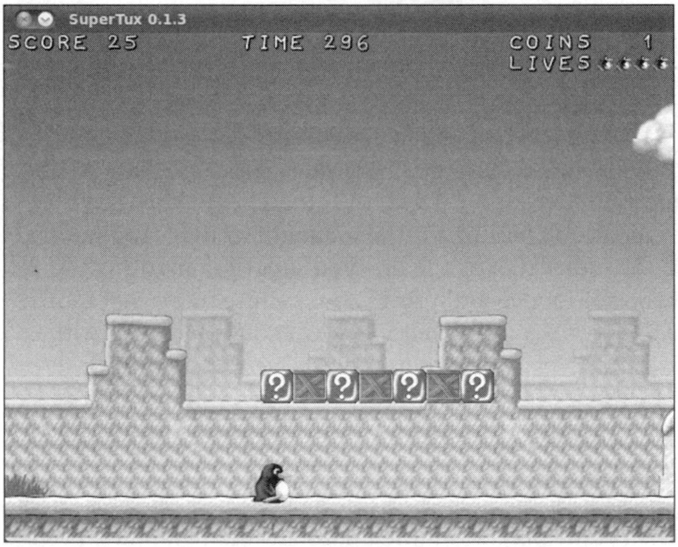

FIGURE 9.6 Although the look and feel of this game takes me back to my childhood, it is far from dull or boring.

Battle for Wesnoth

One of the most popular games currently available for Linux is Battle for Wesnoth (see Figure 9.7), a strategy game featuring both single and multiplayer options. Based in a fantasy land, you are responsible for building armies to wage war against your foes who are attacking you. Game play may be based on scenarios, such as in single player mode where some scenarios are preinstalled and others may be easily downloaded, or based on trying to better your friends at a LAN party or online.

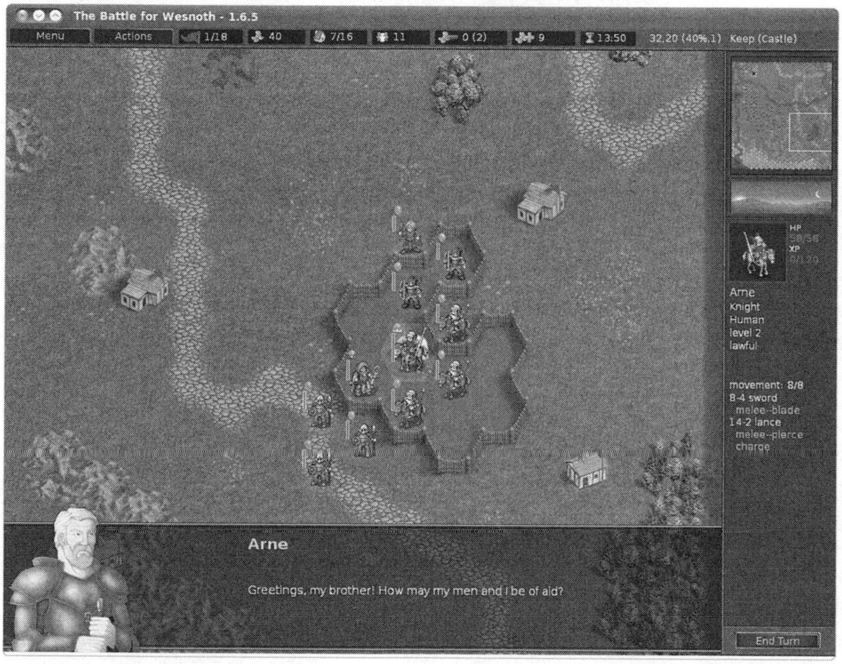

FIGURE 9.7 Flex your strategic brain by playing Battle for Wesnoth—a rich and full land of fantasy of adventure.

Battle for Wesnoth also comes with a map editor that lets you create your own scenarios. There is an active community that shares their work and welcomes new contributions. You will find the URL for the website in the Reference section of this chapter.

Games for Kids

Kids, both young and old, are not left out. Check out game packages such as gCompris, Childsplay, and TuxPaint to get started. Some of these are educational, some teach computer skills such as using a mouse or a keyboard, and others are just for amusement.

Many developers are also parents who have placed a high priority on making quality software for their children to enjoy on their favorite platform. You can search for children's games in the Ubuntu Software Center and find lots of great things to try.

Playing Windows Games

Ubuntu is primarily aimed at desktop computer users who want a system that is stable, powerful, and easy to use. It is not primarily a gaming platform. In fact, compared to Windows, there are not nearly as many games available or being developed (although the number is growing and has improved) This doesn't mean hard-core gamers need to feel left out, though. There are two projects that exist to help game lovers play most Windows-based games on Linux.

A project called Wine uses application interfaces to make Windows programs believe they are running on a Windows platform and not a Linux platform. Bear in mind that Wine stands for *wine is not an emulator*, so do not start thinking of it as such—the community can get quite touchy about it!

Wine is a compatibility layer (not an emulator) that aims to make Windows software believe it is running on Windows even when it is running on Linux. Although the open-source, free software project won't run everything, it does run a very large number of Windows programs, including many games.

Cedega is a fork of the Wine project that adds some proprietary touches and a focus on games and, for a fee, allows you to download and use their compatibility layer.

TIP

The keys to successful gaming in Linux are to always read the documentation thoroughly, always investigate the Internet resources thoroughly, and always understand your system. Installing games is a great way to learn about your system because the reward of success is so much fun.

Reference

- www.linuxgames.com/—A good source of up-to-date information about the state of Linux gaming.
- www.warsow.net/—The official site of Warsow.
- www.scorched3d.co.uk/—The official site of Scorched 3D.
- www.frozen-bubble.org/—The official site of Frozen Bubble.
- http://supertux.lethargik.org/—The official site of SuperTux.
- http://wesnoth.org/—The official site of Battle for Wesnoth.
- http://gcompris.net/—The official site of gCompris.

- http://childsplay.sourceforge.net/index.php—The official site of Childsplay.
- www.tuxpaint.org/—The official site of TuxPaint.
- www.nvnews.net/vbulletin/forumdisplay.php?f=14—The Official Nvidia Linux driver support forum.
- www.nvidia.com/object/unix.html—Home page for the Nvidia Unix/Linux drivers.
- http://support.amd.com/us/gpudownload/Pages/index.aspx—Home page for the ATI Linux drivers, including drivers for Linux.
- https://help.ubuntu.com/community/Wine—Ubuntu community documentation for Wine.
- www.winehq.org/—The official site of Wine, which includes good information about software that is known to work with the current version in an application database subsite at http://appdb.winehq.org/.
- https://help.ubuntu.com/community/Cedega—Ubuntu community documentation for Cedega.
- www.transgaming.com/—The official TransGaming Technologies website provides details of games that are directly supported under Cedega.

CHAPTER 10
Managing Users

IN THIS CHAPTER

System administrators would have a boring, but much easier life without users. In reality, it's impossible to have a system with absolutely no users, so it is important that you learn how to effectively manage and administer your users as they work with your system. Whether you are creating a single user account or modifying a group that holds hundreds of user accounts, the fundamentals of user administration are the same.

User management and administration includes allocating and managing home directories, putting in place good password policies, and applying an effective security policy that includes things such as disk quotas and file and directory access permissions. We will take a look at all these areas within this chapter as well as some of the different types of users that you are likely to find on a typical Linux system.

User Accounts

You normally find three types of users on Linux systems: the super-user, the day-to-day user, and the system user. Each type is essential to the smooth running of your system. Learning the differences between the three is essential if you are to work efficiently and safely within your Linux environment.

All users who access your system must have accounts on the system. Ubuntu uses the `/etc/passwd` file to store information on the user accounts that are present on the system. All users, regardless of their type, have a one line entry in this file which contains their username (typically used for logging in to the system), an encrypted field for the password (which contains an x to denote that a password is present), a User ID (commonly referred to as the UID) and a Group ID (commonly referred to as the GID). The last two fields show the location of the home directory (usually `/home/username`) and the default shell for the user (`/bin/bash` is the default for new users). There is also a field called GECOS that uses a comma delimited list to record information about the account or the user, most often when this is used it will record the user's full name and contact information.

NOTE

Although the password field contains an x, this doesn't mean that what you read here is the actual password! All passwords are stored in `/etc/shadow` in an encrypted format for safe keeping. Ubuntu automatically refers to this file whenever a password is required.

In keeping with long-standing tradition in UNIX-style operating systems, Ubuntu make use of the well-established UNIX file ownership and permission system. To start with, everything in these systems is treated as a file and all files (which can include directories and devices) can be assigned one or more of read, write and execute permissions. These three 'flags' can also be assigned as desired to each of three categories: the owner of the file, a member of a group, or anyone else on the system. The security for a file is drawn from these permissions and from file ownership. As the system administrator (also commonly referred to as the super-user) it is your responsibility to manage these settings effectively and ensure that the users have proper UIDs and GIDs. Perhaps most importantly the system administrator has the ability to lock away sensitive files from users who should not have access to them through these file permissions.

The Super-User/Root User

No matter how many system administrators there are for a system, there can only be one super-user account. The super-user account, more commonly referred to as the root user, has total and complete control over all aspects of the system. They can access any part of the file system, read, change, or delete any file, grant and revoke access to files and directories, and can carry out any operation on the system, including destroying it if they so wish. The root user is unique in that it has a UID of 0 and GID of 0.

In other words, the root user has supreme power over your system. With this in mind, it's important that you do not work as root all the time as you may inadvertently cause serious damage to your system, perhaps even making it totally unusable. Instead, you should rely on root only when you need to make specific changes to your system that require root privileges. As soon as you've finished your work you can switch back to your normal user account to carry on working.

In Ubuntu you execute a command with root, or super-user, privileges using the `sudo` command like this:

```
matthew@seymour:~$ sudo apt-get update
```

You will then be prompted for your password, which will not show on the screen as you enter it, and press `Enter`. Ubuntu will then carry out the command (in this case updating information about available software) as if you were running it as root.

THE ROOT USER

If you've used other Linux distros then you may be a little puzzled by the use of the sudo command as not all distros use it. In short, Ubuntu allows the first user on the system access to full root privileges using the `sudo` command. It also disables the root account so no one can actually login with the username root.

In other Linux distros you change to the root user by issuing the command `su -` and then entering the root password when prompted. This lands you at the root prompt, which is shown as a pound sign (#). From here you are able to execute any command you wish. To get to a root prompt in Ubuntu you need to execute the command `sudo -i` which, after you enter your password, will give you the prompt so familiar to other Linux distros. When you've finished working as root just type `exit` and hit `Enter` to get back to a normal user prompt ($).

A regular user is someone who logs on to the system to use it for nonadministrative tasks such as word processing or email. These users do not need to make system wide changes or manage other users. However, they might want to be able to change settings specific to their account (for instance, a desktop background). Depending on how much control the system administrator (the root or super-user) likes to wield, regular users might not even be able to do that!

The super-user grants privileges to regular users using file and directory permissions (as covered in Chapter 4, "Command Line Quickstart"). For example, if the super-user does not want you to change your settings in `~/.profile` (the ~ is a shell shortcut representing your home directory), root can alter the permissions so that you may read from, but not write to, that file.

CAUTION

Because of the potential for making a catastrophic error as the super-user, always use your system as a regular user and only use your super-user powers temporarily to do specific administration tasks. This is easier to remember in Ubuntu where the use of sudo is default and the root account is initially disabled. If you work on a multiuser system, consider this advice an absolute rule; if root were to delete the wrong file or kill the wrong process, the results could be disastrous for the system (and likely the business that owns and operates it). On your home system, you can do as you please. Running as root makes many things easier, but much less safe, and we still do not recommend doing so. In any setting, however, the risks of running as root are significant and we cannot stress how important it is to be careful when working as root.

The third type of user is the system user. The system user is not a person, but rather an administrative account that the system uses during day-to-day runnings of various services. For example, the system user named `www-data` owns the Apache web server and all the associated files. Only that user and root can have access to these files—no one else can access or make changes to these files. System users do not have a home directory or password, nor do they permit access to the system through a login prompt.

You will find a list of all the users on a system in the `/etc/passwd` file.

User IDs and Group IDs

A computer is, by its very nature, a number-oriented machine. It identifies users and groups by numbers known as the *user ID (UID)* and *group ID (GID)*. The alphabetic names display on your screen just for ease of use.

As previously mentioned, the root user is UID 0. Numbers from 1 through 499 and number 65,534 are the system, sometimes called logical or psuedo users. Regular users have UIDs beginning with 1,000; Ubuntu assigns them sequentially beginning with this number.

With only a few exceptions, the GID is the same as the UID.

Ubuntu creates a private GID for every UID of 1,000 and greater. The system administrator can add other users to a GID or create a totally new group and add users to it. Unlike Windows NT and some UNIX variants, a group cannot be a member of another group in Ubuntu (or any Linux distribution).

File Permissions

As you learned in Chapter 4, there are three types of permissions: read, write, and execute (r, w, x). For any file or directory, permissions are assigned to three categories: user, group, and other. In this section, we will focus on group permissions. Before we do, we want to highlight three commands used to change the group, user, or access permissions of a file or directory:

- `chgrp`—Changes the group ownership of a file or directory
- `chown`—Changes the owner of a file or directory
- `chmod`—Changes the access permissions of a file or directory

These commands can be used to reproduce organizational structures and permissions in the real world in your Ubuntu system (see the next section, "Managing Groups"). For example, a human resources department can share health-benefit memos to all company employees by making the files readable (but not writable) by anyone in an accessible directory. On the other hand, programmers in the company's research and development section, although able to access each other's source code files, would not have read or write access to HR pay scale or personnel files (and certainly would not want HR or marketing poking around R&D).

These commands are used to easily manage group and file ownerships and permissions from the command line. It is essential that you know these commands because there are times when you are likely to have only a command-line interface to work with; such as when a well-meaning but fat-fingered system administrator set incorrect permissions on X11 rendering the system incapable of working with a graphical interface (No, we won't tell that story, but if you press them, most systems administrators have similar tales of woe).

USER STEREOTYPES

As is the case in many professions, exaggerated stereotypes have emerged for users and system administrators. Many stereotypes contain elements of truth mixed with generous amounts of hyperbole and humor and serve to assist us in understanding the characteristics of and differences in the stereotyped subjects. The stereotypes of the *luser* and the *BOFH* (not-so-nice terms for users and administrators, respectively) serve as cautionary tales describing what behavior is acceptable and unacceptable in the computing community.

Understanding these stereotypes allows you to better define the appropriate and inappropriate roles of system administrators, users, and others. You can find a description of each on Wikipedia at: http://en.wikipedia.org/wiki/BOFH and http://en.wikipedia.org/wiki/Luser.

Managing Groups

Groups can make managing users a lot easier. Instead of having to assign individual permissions to every user, you can use groups to grant or revoke permissions to a large number of users quickly and easily. Setting group permissions allows you to set up workspaces for collaborative working and to control what devices can be used, such as external drives or DVD writers. This approach also represents a secure method of limiting access to system resources to only those users who need them. As an example, the system administrator could put the users `matthew`, `ryan`, `heather`, `holly`, `debra`, and `mark` in a new group named `unleashed`. Those users could each create files intended for their group work and `chgrp` those files to `unleashed`.

Now, everyone in the `unleashed` group—but no one else except root—can work with those files. The system administrator would probably create a directory owned by that group so that its members could have an easily accessed place to store those files. The system administrator could also add other users such as `sonya` and `nicole` to the group and remove existing users when their part of the work is done. The system administrator could make the user `matthew` the group administrator so that `matthew` could decide how group membership should be changed. You could also put restrictions on the DVD writer so that only `matthew` could burn DVDs, thus protecting sensitive material from falling into the wrong hands.

Group Listing

Different UNIX operating systems implement the group concept in various ways. Ubuntu uses a scheme called *UPG (user private group)* where by default all users are assigned to a group with their own name. (The user's username and group name are identical.) All the groups on a system are listed in /etc/group file.

Here is a example of a portion of the /etc/group file:

```
matthew@seymour:~$ cat /etc/group
root:x:0:
daemon:x:1:
bin:x:2:
sys:x:3:
adm:x:4:matthew
tty:x:5:
disk:x:6:
mail:x:8:
news:x:9:
fax:x:21:matthew
voice:x:22:
cdrom:x:24:matthew
floppy:x:25:matthew
tape:x:26:matthew
www-data:x:33:
crontab:x:107:
ssh:x:109:
admin:x:115:matthew
saned:x:116:
gdm:x:119:
matthew:x:1000:
ntp:x:122:
```

In this sample you see a number of groups, mostly for services (mail, news, and so on) and devices (floppy, disk, and so on). As previously mentioned, the system services groups allow those services to have ownership and control of their files. For example, adding postfix to the mail group, as shown previously, enables the postfix application to access mail's files in the manner that mail would decide for group access to its file. Adding a regular user to a device's group permits the regular user to use the device with permissions granted by the group owner. Adding user `matthew` to the group cdrom, for example, allows `matthew` to use the optical drive device. You learn how to add and remove users from groups in the next section.

Group Management Tools

Ubuntu provides several command-line tools for managing groups, but also provides graphical tools for doing so. Most experienced system administrators prefer the command-line tools because they are quick and easy to use, are always available even when there is no graphic user interface, and because they can be included in scripts she may write if the system administrator wants to write a quick program to perform a repetitive task.

Here are the most commonly used group management command-line tools:

- `groupadd`—This command creates and adds a new group.
- `groupdel`—This command removes an existing group.
- `groupmod`—This command creates a group name or GIDs but doesn't add or delete members from a group.
- `gpasswd`—This command creates a group password. Every group can have a group password and an administrator. Use the `-A` argument to assign a user as group administrator.
- `useradd -G`—The `-G` argument adds a user to a group during the initial user creation. (More arguments are used to create a user.)
- `usermod -G`—This command allows you to add a user to a group so long as the user is not logged in at the time.
- `grpck`—This command checks the `/etc/group` file for typos.

Let's say there is a DVD-RW device (`/dev/scd0`) on our computer that the system administrator wants a regular user named `ryan` to have permission to access. This is the process to grant `ryan` that access:

1. Add a new group with the groupadd command:

```
matthew@seymour:~$ sudo groupadd dvdrw
```

2. Change the group ownership of the device to the new group with the chgrp command:

```
matthew@seymour:~$ sudo chgrp dvdrw /dev/scd0
```

3. Add the approved user to the group with the usermod command:

```
matthew@seymour:~$ sudo usermod -G dvdrw ryan
```

4. Make user ryan the group administrator with the gpasswd command so that he can add new users to the group:

```
matthew@seymour:~$ sudo gpasswd -A ryan
```

Now `ryan` has permission to use the DVD-RW drive, as would anyone else added to the group by either the super-user or ryan because he is now also a group administrator and can add users to the group.

The system administrator can also use the graphical interface that Ubuntu provides, as shown in Figure 10.1. It is accessed from the menu at System, Administration, Users and Groups.

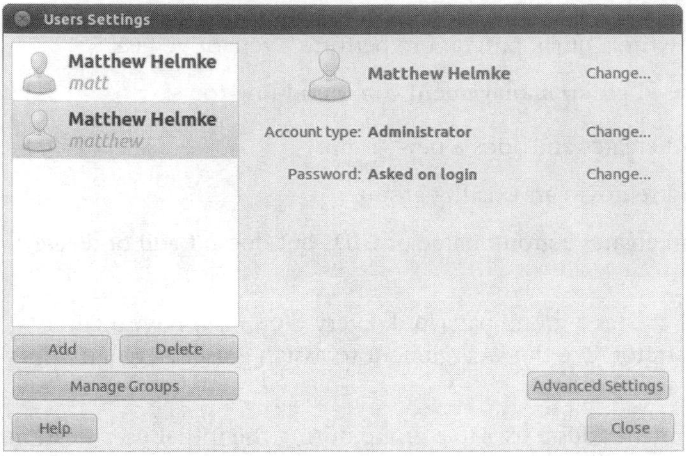

FIGURE 10.1 Use Manage Groups to assign users to groups.

Note that the full set of group commands and options are not available from the graphical interface. This limits the usefulness of the GUI to a subset of the most frequently used commands. You learn more about using the Ubuntu User Manager GUI in the next section of this chapter.

Managing Users

Users must be created, assigned a UID, provided a home directory, provided an initial set of files for their home directory, and assigned to groups so that they can use the system resources securely and efficiently. The system administrator in some situations might want or need to not only restrict a user's access to specific files and folders, but also the amount of disk space an account may use.

User Management Tools

As with groups, Ubuntu provides several command-line tools for managing users, but also provides graphical tools for doing so. Most experienced system administrators prefer the command-line tools because they are quick and easy to use, are always available even when there is no graphic user interface, and because they can be included in scripts she may write if the system administrator wants to write a quick program to perform a repetitive task. Here are the most common commands to manage users:

- `useradd`—This command adds a new user account to the system. Its options permit the system administrator to specify the user's home directory and initial group or to create the user with the default home directory and group assignments (based on the new account's username).

- `useradd -D`—This command sets the system defaults for creating the user's home directory, account expiration date, default group, and command shell. See the specific options in `man useradd`. Used without any arguments, it displays the defaults for the system. The default set of files for a user are found in `/etc/skel`.

NOTE

The set of files initially used to populate a new user's home directory are kept in `/etc/skel`. This is convenient for the system administrator because any special files, links, or directories that need to be universally applied can be placed in `/etc/skel` and will be duplicated automatically with appropriate permissions for each new user.

```
matthew@seymour:~$ ls -la /etc/skel

total 32

drwxr-xr-x   2 root root  4096 2010-04-25 12:14 .

drwxr-xr-x 154 root root 12288 2010-07-01 16:30 ..

-rw-r--r--   1 root root   220 2009-09-13 22:08 .bash_logout

-rw-r--r--   1 root root  3103 2010-04-18 19:15 .bashrc

-rw-r--r--   1 root root   179 2010-03-26 05:31 examples.desktop

-rw-r--r--   1 root root   675 2009-09-13 22:08 .profile
```

Each line provides the file permissions, the number of files housed under that file or directory name, the file owner, the file group, the file size, the creation date, and the filename.

As you can see, root owns every file here. The `useradd` command copies everything in `/etc/skel` to the new home directory and resets file ownership and permissions to the new user.

Certain user files might exist that the system administrator doesn't want the user to change; the permissions for those files in `/home/username` can be reset so that the user can read them but can't write to them.

- `userdel`—This command completely removes a user's account (thereby eliminating that user's home directory and all files it contains).

- passwd—This command updates the "authentication tokens" used by the password management system.

TIP

To lock a user out of his account, use the following command:

```
matthew@seymour:~$ sudo passwd -l username
```

This prepends an ! (exclamation point, also called a bang) to the user's encrypted password; the command to reverse the process uses the -u option.

- usermod—This command changes several user attributes. The most commonly used arguments are -s to change the shell and -u to change the UID. No changes can be made while the user is logged in or running a process.
- chsh—This command changes the user's default shell. For Ubuntu, the default shell is /bin/bash, known as the Bash, or Bourne Again Shell.

Adding New Users

The command-line approach to adding a user is quite simple and can be accomplished on a single line. In our example below, the system administrator uses the useradd command to add the new user heather. The command adduser (a variant found on some UNIX systems) is a symbolic link to useradd, so both commands work the same. In this example, we use the -p option to set the password the user requested; we use the -s to set her special shell (in place of the default bash shell), and the -u option to specify her UID. (If we create a user with the default settings, we do not need to use these options.) All we want to do can be accomplished on one line:

```
matthew@seymour:~$ sudo useradd heather -p c00kieZ4ME -s /bin/zsh -u 1042
```

The system administrator can also use the graphical interface that Ubuntu provides. You will find this in the menu at System, Administration, Users and Groups. Here, the system administrator is adding a new user to the system where user heather uses the bash command shell.

These are the steps we used to add the same account as shown in the preceding command, but using the graphical User Manager interface:

1. Launch the Ubuntu User Manager graphical interface from the menu at System, Administration, Users and Groups.
2. Click the Add User button to bring up the Add User dialog window (again, refer back to Figure 10.1).

3. Fill in the form with the new user's name and desired username (Figure 10.2).

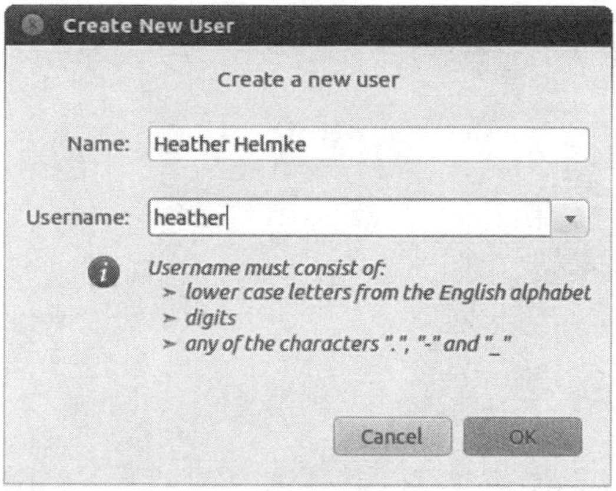

FIGURE 10.2 Adding a new user is simple. The GUI provides a set of options for user management spread over several screens as shown here.

4. Assign a good password (Figure 10.3).

FIGURE 10.3 Change User Password.

5. Highlight the new user in the list and click Advanced Settings (Figure 10.4).

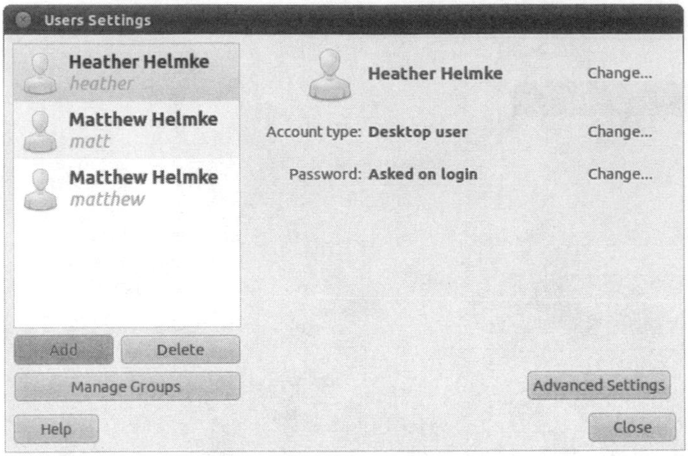

FIGURE 10.4 Look for the Advanced Settings button.

6. You may change User Privilege settings here as you like, then click the Advanced tab (Figure 10.5).

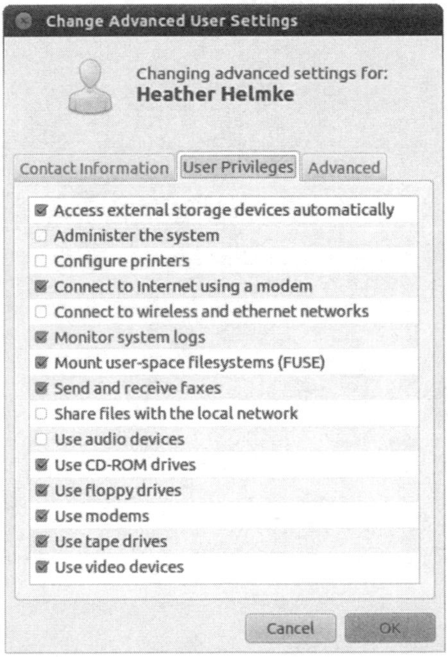

FIGURE 10.5 Change Advanced User Settings, User Privileges.

7. Open the drop down shell menu to select the desired shell (Figure 10.6).

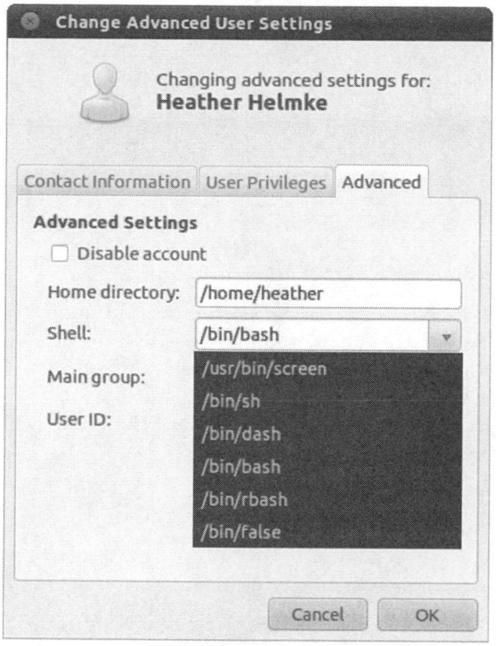

FIGURE 10.6 Change Advanced User Settings, Advanced, Shell.

8. Either use the arrows to the right of the User ID box to adjust the UID up or down, or assign a number greater than 1000 by entering it directly in the box. The system will prevent you from assigning a number already in use by another user account (Figure 10.7).
9. Click OK to save the settings.

   Note that the user is being manually assigned the UID of 1042 because that is her UID on another machine that will be connected to this machine. Systems keep track of users by UID numbers and not by names. Even though the accounts would have the same usernames, the two machines would not recognize `heather` as the same user if two different UIDs were assigned.

NOTE

A Linux username can be any alphanumeric combination that does not begin with a special character reserved for shell script use (see Chapter 11, "Automating Tasks," for disallowed characters, mostly <space> and punctuation characters). Usernames are often the user's first name plus the first initial of her last name or the first initial of the user's first name and his entire last name. These are common practices on larger systems with many users because it makes life simpler for the system administrator, but neither is a rule nor a requirement.

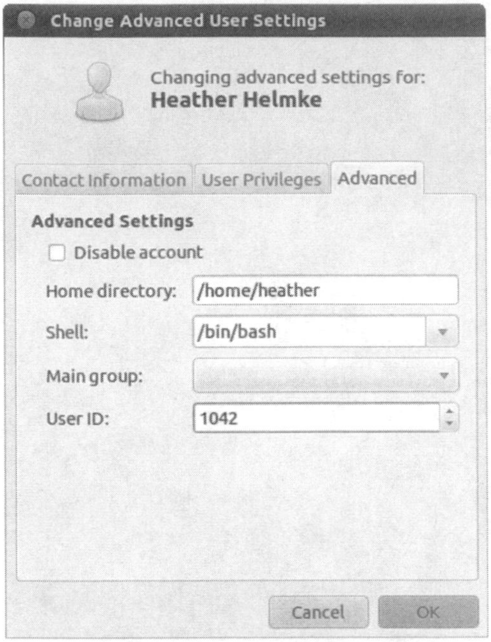

FIGURE 10.7 Change Advanced User Settings, Advanced, UID.

Monitoring User Activity on the System

Monitoring user activity is part of the system administrator's duties and an essential task in tracking how system resources are being used. The `w` command tells the system administrator who is logged in, where he is logged in, and what he is doing. No one can hide from the super-user. The `w` command can be followed by a specific user's name to show only that user.

The `ac` command provides information about the total connect time of a user measured in hours. It accesses the `/var/log/wtmp file` for the source of its information. The ac command proves most useful in shell scripts to generate reports on operating system usage for management review. Note that to use the `ac` command you will have to install the acct package from the Ubuntu repositories.

TIP

Interestingly, a phenomenon known as *timewarp* can occur where an entry in the `wtmp` files jumps back into the past and `ac` shows unusual amounts of time accounted for users. Although this can be attributed to some innocuous factors having to do with the system clock, it is worthy of investigation by the system administrator because it can also be the result of a security breach.

The last command searches through the `/var/log/wtmp` file and lists all the users logged in and out since that file was first created. The user reboot exists so that you might know who has logged in since the last reboot. A companion to `last` is the command `lastb`, which shows all failed, or bad, logins. It is useful for determining whether a legitimate user is having trouble or a hacker is attempting access.

NOTE

The accounting system on your computer keeps track of usage user statistics and is kept in the current `/var/log/wtmp` file. That file is managed by the `init` and `login` processes. If you want to explore the depths of the accounting system, use the GNU info system: `info accounting`.

Managing Passwords

Passwords are an integral part of Linux security, and they are the most visible part to the user. In this section, you learn how to establish a minimal password policy for your system, where the passwords are stored, and how to manage passwords for your users.

System Password Policy

An effective password policy is a fundamental part of a good system administration plan. The policy should cover the following:

- Allowed and forbidden passwords
- Frequency of mandated password changes
- Retrieval or replacement of lost or forgotten passwords
- Password handling by users

The Password File

The password file is `/etc/passwd`, and it is the database file for all users on the system. The format of each line is as follows:

```
username:password:uid:gid:gecos:homedir:shell
```

The fields are self-explanatory except for the `gecos` field. This field is for miscellaneous information about the user, such as the user's full name, office location, office and home phone numbers, and possibly a brief text message. For security and privacy reasons, this field is little used today, but the system administrator should be aware of its existence because the `gecos` field is used by traditional UNIX programs such as `finger` and `mail`. For that reason, it is commonly referred to as the *finger information field*. The data in this field will be comma delimited; the `gecos` field can be changed with the `chfn` (change `finger`) command.

Note that a colon separates all fields in the `/etc/passwd` file. If no information is available for a field, that field is empty, but all the colons remain.

If an asterisk appears in the password field, that user will not be permitted to log on. Why does this feature exist? So that a user can be easily disabled and (possibly) reinstated later without having to be created all over again. The traditional UNIX way of accomplishing this task is for the system administrator to manually edit this field. Ubuntu provides a more elegant method with the `passwd -l` command mentioned earlier in this chapter.

Several services run as pseudo-users, usually with `root` permissions. These are the system, or logical, users mentioned previously. You would not want these accounts available for general login for security reasons, so they are assigned `/sbin/nologin` or `/bin/false` as their shell, which prohibits any logins from these accounts.

A list of `/etc/passwd` reveals the following (abridged for brevity):

```
matthew@seymour:~$ cat /etc/passwd
root:x:0:0:root:/root:/bin/bash
bin:x:2:2:bin:/bin:/bin/sh
sys:x:3:3:sys:/dev:/bin/sh
games:x:5:60:games:/usr/games:/bin/sh
man:x:6:12:man:/var/cache/man:/bin/sh
mail:x:8:8:mail:/var/mail:/bin/sh
news:x:9:9:news:/var/spool/news:/bin/sh
uucp:x:10:10:uucp:/var/spool/uucp:/bin/sh
www-data:x:33:33:www-data:/var/www:/bin/sh
gnats:x:41:41:Gnats Bug-Reporting System (admin):/var/lib/gnats:/bin/sh
nobody:x:65534:65534:nobody:/nonexistent:/bin/sh
messagebus:x:102:106::/var/run/dbus:/bin/false
avahi:x:105:111:Avahi mDNS daemon,,,:/var/run/avahi-daemon:/bin/false
couchdb:x:106:113:CouchDB Administrator,,,:/var/lib/couchdb:/bin/bash
haldaemon:x:107:114:Hardware abstraction layer,,,:/var/run/hald:/bin/false
kernoops:x:109:65534:Kernel Oops Tracking Daemon,,,:/:/bin/false
gdm:x:112:119:Gnome Display Manager:/var/lib/gdm:/bin/false
matthew:x:1000:1000:Matthew Helmke,,,,:/home/matthew:/bin/bash
sshd:x:114:65534::/var/run/sshd:/usr/sbin/nologin
ntp:x:115:122::/home/ntp:/bin/false
pulse:x:111:117:PulseAudio daemon,,,:/var/run/pulse:/bin/false
```

Note that none of the password fields show a password, but rather contain an `x`. This is because they are shadow passwords, a useful security enhancement to Linux.

Shadow Passwords

It is considered a security risk to keep passwords in `/etc/passwd` because anyone with read access could run a cracking program on the file and obtain the passwords with little trouble. To avoid this risk, *shadow passwords* are used so that only an `x` appears in the password field of `/etc/passwd`; the real passwords are kept in `/etc/shadow`, a file that can only be read by the system administrator (and *PAM*, the *Pluggable Authentication Modules* authentication manager; see the “PAM Explained” sidebar for an explanation of PAM).

Special versions of the traditional `password` and `login` programs must be used to enable shadow passwords. Shadow passwords are automatically enabled during installation of Ubuntu.

Let's examine an abbreviated listing of the shadow companion to `/etc/passwd`, the `/etc/shadow` file:

```
matthew@seymour:~$ sudo cat /etc/shadow
root:!:14547:0:99999:7:::
daemon:*:14544:0:99999:7:::
bin:*:14544:0:99999:7:::
sys:*:14544:0:99999:7:::
games:*:14544:0:99999:7:::
man:*:14544:0:99999:7:::
mail:*:14544:0:99999:7:::
www-data:*:14544:0:99999:7:::
irc:*:14544:0:99999:7:::
nobody:*:14544:0:99999:7:::
libuuid:!:14544:0:99999:7:::
syslog:*:14544:0:99999:7:::
messagebus:*:14544:0:99999:7:::
kernoops:*:14544:0:99999:7:::
gdm:*:14544:0:99999:7:::
matthew:$6$wtML.mV4$.I5WeTp9tgGkIjJM4uLR5p6TVUqPrSvJ0N2W/t//0jVBrWQrOySEEDvXsA/sKSEl
QsfmNmfPJYxVrjZ21/Ir70:14564:0:99999:7:::
sshd:*:14547:0:99999:7:::
ntp:*:14548:0:99999:7:::
usbmux:*:14724:0:99999:7:::
pulse:*:14725:0:99999:7:::
```

The fields are separated by colons and are, in order:

- The user's login name.
- The encrypted password for the user.
- The day of which the last password change occurred, measured in the number of days since January 1, 1970. This date is known in UNIX circles as the epoch. Just so you know, the billionth second since the epoch occurred was in September 2001; that was the UNIX version of Y2K—as with the real Y2K, nothing much happened.
- The number of days before the password can be changed (prevents changing a password and then changing it back to the old password right away—a dangerous security practice).
- The number of days after which the password must be changed. This can be set to force the change of a newly issued password known to the system administrator.
- The number of days before the password expiration that the user is warned it will expire.

- The number of days after the password expires that the account is disabled (for security).
- Similar to the password change date, although this is the number of days since January 1, 1970 that the account has been disabled.
- The final field is a "reserved" field and is not currently allocated for any use.

Note that password expiration dates and warnings are disabled by default in Ubuntu. These features are not often used on home systems and usually not even used for small offices. It is the system administrator's responsibility to establish and enforce password expiration policies if they are to exist.

The permissions on the `/etc/shadow` file should be set so that it is not writable or readable by regular users: The permissions should be **600**.

PAM EXPLAINED

Pluggable Authentication Modules (PAM) is a system of libraries that handle the tasks of authentication on your computer. It uses four management groups: account management, authentication management, password management, and session management. This allows the system administrator to choose how individual applications will authenticate users. Ubuntu has preinstalled and preconfigured all the necessary PAM files for you.

The configuration files in Ubuntu are found in `/etc/pam.d`. These files are named for the service they control, and the format is as follows:

```
type control module-path module-arguments
```

The type field is the management group that the rule corresponds to. The control field tells PAM what to do if authentication fails. The final two items deal with the PAM module used and any arguments it needs. Programs that use PAM typically come packaged with appropriate entries for the **`/etc/pam.d` directory.** To achieve greater security, the system administrator can modify the default entries. Misconfiguration can have unpredictable results, so back up the configuration files before you modify them. The defaults provided by Ubuntu are adequate for home and small office users.

An example of a PAM configuration file with the formatted entries as described previously is shown next. Here are the contents of `/etc/pam.d/gdm`:

```
#%PAM-1.0
auth    requisite       pam_nologin.so
auth    required        pam_env.so readenv=1
auth    required        pam_env.so readenv=1 envfile=/etc/default/locale
auth    sufficient       pam_succeed_if.so user ingroup nopasswdlogin
@include common-auth
auth    optional        pam_gnome_keyring.so
@include common-account
```

```
session [success=ok ignore=ignore module_unknown=ignore default=bad]
pam_selinux.so open
session required        pam_limits.so
@include common-session
session [success=ok ignore=ignore module_unknown=ignore default=bad]
pam_selinux.so close
session optional        pam_gnome_keyring.so auto_start
@include common-password
```

Amusingly, even the PAM documents state that you do not really need (or want) to know a lot about PAM to use it effectively.

You will likely need only the PAM system administrator's guide. You can find it at www.kernel.org/pub/linux/libs/pam/Linux-PAM-html/Linux-PAM_SAG.html.

Managing Password Security for Users

Selecting appropriate user passwords is always an exercise in trade-offs. A password such as *password* (do not laugh, it has been used too often in the real world and with devastating consequences) is just too easy to guess by an intruder. So are simple words or number combinations (the numbers from a street address or date of birth, for example). You would be surprised how many people use easily guessed passwords such as 123456, iloveyou, Qwerty, or abc123.

On the other hand, a password such as `2a56u'"F($84u&#^Hiu44Ik%$([#EJD` is sure to present great difficulty to an intruder (or an auditor). However, that password is so difficult to remember that it would be likely that the password owner would write that password down on a sticky note attached to his monitor.

The system administrator has control, with settings in the `/etc/shadow` file, over how often the password must be changed. The settings can be changed by the super-user using a text editor, or the `chage` command (see `man shadow` and `man chage` for details).

Changing Passwords in a Batch

On a large system, there might be times when a large number of users and their passwords need some attention. The super-user can change passwords in a batch by using the `chpasswd` command, which accepts input as a name/password pair per line in the following form:

```
matthew@seymour:~$ sudo chpasswd username:password
```

Passwords can be changed *en masse* by redirecting a list of name and password pairs to the command. An appropriate shell script can be constructed with the information gleaned from Chapter 11.

However, Ubuntu also provides the `newusers` command to add users in a batch from a text file. This command also allows a user to be added to a group, and a new directory can be added for the user, too.

10

Granting System Administrator Privileges to Regular Users

On occasion, it may be necessary for a regular user to run a command as if they were the root user. They usually do not need these powers, but a user might on a special occasion—for example, to temporarily access certain devices or run a command for testing purposes.

There are two ways to run commands with root privileges. The first way is useful if you are the owner of both the super-user account (an enabled root account) and a regular user; the second way is useful if you are not a regular user but are not privileged to access all super-user functions (this might happen on a large, multiuser network with senior and junior administrators as well as regular users). Let's look at each.

Temporarily Changing User Identity with the `su` Command

This first scenario requires the existence of a root account, which is not enabled by default on Ubuntu systems and is not generally recommended in the Ubuntu community. However, there are times when it makes sense. Discussing that is beyond the scope of this chapter, but for the sake of argument, for the scenario and details in this section assume we are operating in one of those special cases and that a root account has been enabled.

What if you have access to an enabled root account as a super-user, but are logged on as a regular user because you are performing nonadministrative tasks, and you find you need to do something that only the super-user can do? The `su` command is available for this purpose.

NOTE

A popular misconception is that the `su` command is short for *super-user*; it really just means *substitute user*. An important but often overlooked distinction is that between `su` and `su -`. In the former instance, you become that user but keep your own environmental variables (such as paths). In the latter, you inherit the environment of that user. This is most noticeable when you use `su` to become the super-user, root. Without appending the `-`, you do not inherit the path variable that includes `/bin` or `/sbin`, so you must always enter the full path to those commands when you just `su` to `root`.

Don't forget that on a standard Ubuntu system, the first created user is classed as root, whilst the true root account is disabled. To enable the root account you would enter the command `sudo passwd` at the command line and enter your password and a new root password. After this has been completed, you can `su` to root. We suggest you read this before doing so to ensure you understand the reason the root account is not enabled by default: https://help.ubuntu.com/community/RootSudo.

Because almost all Linux file system security revolves around file permissions, it can be useful to occasionally become a different user with permission to access files belonging to other users or groups or to access special files (such as the communications port /dev/ttyS0 when using a modem or the sound device /dev/audio when playing a game). You can use the su command to temporarily switch to another user identity, and then switch back.

The su command spawns a new shell, changing both the UID and GID of the existing user and automatically changes the environmental variables associated with that user, known as *inheriting the environment*. Refer to Chapter 4 for more information on environment variables.

The syntax for the su command is as follows:

```
matthew@seymour:~$ su option username arguments
```

The man page for su gives more details, but some highlights of the su command are here:

```
-c, --command COMMAND
      pass a single COMMAND to the shell with -c

-m, --preserve-environment
      do not reset environment variables

-l   a full login simulation for the substituted user,
     the same as specifying the dash alone
```

You can invoke the su command in different ways that yield diverse results. By using su alone, you can become root, but you keep your regular user environment. This can be verified by using the printenv command before and after the change. Note that the working directory (you can execute pwd as a command line to print the current working directory) has not changed. By executing the following, you become root and inherit root's environment:

```
matthew@seymour:~$ su -
```

By executing the following, you become that user and inherit the super-user's environment—a pretty handy tool. (Remember: Inheriting the environment comes from using the dash in the command; omit that, and you keep your "old" environment.) To become another user, specify a different user's name on the command line:

```
matthew@seymour:~$ su - other_user
```

When leaving an identity to return to your usual user identity, use the exit command. For example, while logged on as a regular user,

```
matthew@seymour:~$ su - root
```

the system prompts for a password:

```
Password:
```

When the password is entered correctly, the root user's prompt appears:

```
root~#
```

To return to the regular user's identity, just type:

```
root~# exit
```

This takes you to the regular user's prompt:

```
matthew@seymour:~$
```

If you need to allow other users access to certain commands with root privileges, you must give them the password for the root account (often referred to as the root password) so that they can use `su`—that definitely is not a secure solution. The next section describes a more flexible and secure method of allowing normal users to perform selected root tasks and the preferred method for sharing and using super-user privileges in Ubuntu.

Granting Root Privileges on Occasion—The `sudo` Command

It is often necessary to delegate some of the authority that root wields on a system. For a large system, this makes sense because no single individual will always be available to perform super-user functions. The problem is that UNIX permissions come with an all-or-nothing authority. Enter sudo, an application that permits the assignment of one, several, or all the root-only system commands.

> **NOTE**
>
> As mentioned earlier, the `sudo` command is pervasive in Ubuntu, because it is used by default. If you want to get to a root shell, thereby removing the need to type **sudo** for every command, just enter `sudo -i` to get the root prompt. To return to a normal user prompt, enter `exit` and press `Return`. Again, this is a bit dangerous because if you are not paying attention and forget to exit root, you could cause severe damage to the system. It is usually better to choose one method or the other and use it consistently, and the Ubuntu community consistently uses and recommends using `sudo` for each command, even if it gets tedious, because it is a good reminder to think about what you are doing.

After it is configured, using `sudo` is simple. An authorized user merely precedes a super-user authority-needed command with `sudo`, like this:

```
matthew@seymour:~$ sudo command
```

When the command is entered, `sudo` checks the `/etc/sudoers` file to see whether the user is authorized to wield super-user privileges; if so, `sudo` use is authorized for a specific length of time. The user is then prompted for her password (to preserve accountability and provide some measure of security), and then the command is run as if root had issued it. During the time allotted, which is 15 minutes by default in Ubuntu, `sudo` can be used again once or multiple times without a password. If an unauthorized user attempts to execute a `sudo` command, a record of the unauthorized attempt is kept in the system log and a mail message is sent to the super-user.

Three man pages are associated with `sudo`: `sudo`, `sudoers`, and `visudo`. The first covers the command itself, the second the format of the `/etc/sudoers` file, and the third the use of the special editor for `/etc/sudoers`. You should use the special editing command because it checks the file for parse errors and locks the file to prevent others from editing it at the same time. The `visudo` command uses the `vi` editor, so you might need a quick review of the vi editing commands found in Chapter 4, "Command Line Quickstart," in the section "Working with vi." You begin the editing by executing the visudo command with this:

```
matthew@seymour:~$ sudo visudo
```

The default /etc/sudoers file looks like this:

```
# /etc/sudoers
#
# This file MUST be edited with the 'visudo' command as root.
#
# See the man page for details on how to write a sudoers file.
#
Defaults      env_reset

# Host alias specification

# User alias specification

# Cmnd alias specification

# User privilege specification
root    ALL=(ALL) ALL

# Uncomment to allow members of group sudo to not need a password
# (Note that later entries override this, so you might need to move
# it further down)
# %sudo ALL=NOPASSWD: ALL

# Members of the admin group may gain root privileges
%admin ALL=(ALL) ALL
```

The basic format of a sudoers line in the file is as follows:

```
user host_computer=command
```

The user can be an individual user or a group (a % in front identifies a name as a group). The host_computer is normally ALL for all hosts on the network and localhost for the local machine, but the host computer can referenced as a subnet or any specific host. The command in the sudoers line can be ALL, a list of specific commands, or a restriction on specific commands (formed by prepending a ! to the command). A number of options are available for use with the sudoers line, and aliases can be used to simplify the assignment of privileges. Again, the sudoers man page will give the details, but here are a few examples:

If we add the line

```
%wheel        ALL=(ALL)        NOPASSWD: ALL
```

any user we add to the wheel group can execute any command without a password.

10

Suppose that we want to give a user `john` permission across the network to be able to add users with the graphical interface. We would add the line:

```
john ALL=/users-admin
```

or perhaps grant permission only on her local computer:

```
john 192.168.1.87=/usr/bin/users-admin
```

If we want to give the editor group system wide permission with no password required to delete files:

```
%editors ALL=NOPASSWD: /bin/rm
```

If we want to give every user permission with no password required to mount the CD drive on the localhost:

```
ALL localhost=NOPASSWD:/sbin/mount /dev/scd0 /mnt/cdrom /sbin/umount /mnt/cdrom
```

It is also possible to use wildcards in the construction of the sudoers file. Aliases can be used, too, to make it easier to define users and groups. Although the man page for sudoers contains some examples, www.komar.org/pres/sudo/toc.html provides illustrative notes and comments of sudo use at a large mythical, example company. The sudo home page at www.sudo.ws/ is also a useful resource for additional explanations and examples.

The following command presents users with a list of the commands they are entitled to use:

```
matthew@seymour:~$ sudo -l
```

ADDING EXTRA `SUDO` USERS

As mentioned earlier, by default Ubuntu grants the first created user full root access through the `sudo` command. If you need to add this capability for other users, you can do this easily by adding each user to the `admin` group or by using the User Manager tool to allow them to administer the System, which can be found in the User Privileges tab when you edit the properties for a user.

Disk Quotas

On large systems with many users, you often need to control the amount of disk space a user can use. Disk quotas are designed specifically for this purpose. Quotas, managed per each partition, can be set for both individual users as well as groups; quotas for the group need not be as large as the aggregate quotas for the individuals in the groups.

When files are created, both a user and a group own them; ownership of the files is always part of the metadata about the files. This makes quotas based on both users and groups easy to manage.

NOTE

Disk quota management is not really useful or needed on a home system and rarely, if ever, on a small office system. It is unlikely you will see or implement this in either circumstance.

To manage disk quotas, you must have the `quota` and `quotatool` packages installed on your system. Quota management with Ubuntu is not enabled by default and has traditionally been enabled and configured manually by system administrators. System administrators use the family of quota commands, such as `quotacheck` to initialize the quota database files, `edquota` to set and edit user quotas, `setquota` to configure disk quotas, and `quotaon` or `quotaoff` to control the service. (Other utilities include `warnquota` for automatically sending mail to users over their disk space usage limit.)

Implementing Quotas

Quotas are not be enabled by default, even if the quota software package is installed on your Ubuntu system. When quotas are installed and enabled, you can see which partitions have either user quotas, group quotas, or both by looking at the fourth field in the `/etc/fstab` file. For example, one line in `/etc/fstab` shows that quotas are enabled for the `/home` partition:

```
/dev/hda5      /home     ext3         defaults,usrquota,grpquota 1 1
```

The root of the partition with quotas enabled will have the files quota.user or quota.group in them (or both files, if both types of quotas are enabled), and the files will contain the actual quotas. The permissions of these files should be **600** so that users cannot read or write to them. (Otherwise, users would change them to allow ample space for their music files and Internet art collections.) To initialize disk quotas, the partitions must be remounted. This is easily accomplished with the following:

```
matthew@seymour:~$ sudo mount -o ro,remount partition_to_be_remounted
mount_point
```

The underlying console tools (complete with man pages) are:

- `quotaon`, `quotaoff`—Toggles quotas on a partition
- `repquota`—A summary status report on users and groups

10

- `quotacheck`—Updates the status of quotas (compares new and old tables of disk usage); it is run after fsck
- `edquota`—A basic quota management command

Manually Configuring Quotas

Manual configuration of quotas involves changing entries in your system's file system table, `/etc/fstab`, to add the `usrquota` mount option to the desired portion of your file system. As an example in a simple file system, quota management can be enabled like this:

```
LABEL=/          /                ext3    defaults,usrquota        1 1
```

Group-level quotas can also be enabled by using the `grpquota` option. As the root operator, you must then create a file (using our example of creating user quotas) named quota.user in the designated portion of the file system, like so:

```
matthew@seymour:~$ sudo touch /quota.user
```

You should then turn on the use of quotas using the `quotaon` command:

```
matthew@seymour:~$ sudo quotaon -av
```

You can then edit user quotas with the `edquota` command to set hard and soft limits on file system use. The default system editor (`vi` unless you change your `EDITOR` environment variable) will be launched when editing a user's quota.

Any user can find out what their quotas are with:

```
matthew@seymour:~$ quota -v
```

NOTE

Ubuntu does not support any graphical tools that enable you to configure disk quotas. A Quota mini-HOWTO is maintained at www.tldp.org/HOWTO/Quota.html.

RELATED UBUNTU COMMANDS

You will use these commands to manage user accounts in Ubuntu:

- `ac`—A user account-statistics command
- `change`—Sets or modifies user password expiration policies
- `chfn`—Creates or modifies user finger information in `/etc/passwd`
- `chgrp`—Modifies group memberships
- `chmod`—Changes file permissions
- `chown`—Changes file ownerships
- `chpasswd`—Batch command to modify user passwords
- `chsh`—Modifies a user's shell
- `groups`—Displays existing group memberships
- `logname`—Displays a user's login name
- `newusers`—Batches user management command

- `passwd`—Creates or modifies user passwords
- `su`—Executes shell or command as another user
- `sudo`—Manages selected user execution permissions
- `useradd`—Creates, modifies, or manages users
- `usermod`—Edits a user's login profile

Reference

- http://tldp.org/HOWTO/User-Authentication-HOWTO/—The User-Authentication HOWTO describes how user and group information is stored and used for authentication.
- http://tldp.org/HOWTO/Shadow-Password-HOWTO.html—The Shadow-Password HOWTO delves into the murky depths of shadow passwords and even discusses why you might not want to use them.
- http://tldp.org/HOWTO/Security-HOWTO/—A must-read HOWTO, the Security HOWTO is a good overview of security issues. Especially applicable to this chapter are sections on creating accounts, file permissions, and password security.
- http://tldp.org/LDP/sag/html/index.html—A general guide, the Linux System Administrator's Security Guide has interesting sections on limiting and monitoring users.
- http://www.kernel.org/pub/linux/libs/pam/index.html—The Pluggable Authentication Modules suite contains complex and highly useful applications that provide additional security and logging for passwords. PAM is installed by default in Ubuntu. It isn't necessary to understand the intricacies of PAM to use it effectively.

CHAPTER 11

Automating Tasks

IN THIS CHAPTER

- Running Services at Bootup
- Beginning the Boot Loading Process
- Starting and Stopping Services Manually
- Using Upstart
- Scheduling Tasks
- Basic Shell Control
- Writing and Executing a Shell Script
- Reference

In this chapter you learn about the five ways to automate tasks on your system: making tasks into services that run as your system starts, making them services you start and stop by hand, scheduling them to run at specific times, connecting multiple commands together on the shell, and writing custom scripts that group everything under one command.

After you turn on the power switch, the boot process begins with the computer executing code stored in a chip called the BIOS; this process occurs no matter what operating system you have installed. The Linux boot process begins when the code known as the boot loader starts loading the Linux kernel and ends only when the login prompt appears.

As a system administrator, you will use the skills you learn in this chapter to control your system's services and manage runlevels on your computer. Understanding the management of the system services and states is essential to understanding how Linux works (especially in a multi-user environment) and will help untangle the mysteries of a few of your Ubuntu system's configuration files. Furthermore, a good knowledge of the `cron` daemon that handles task scheduling is essential for administrators at all skill levels.

This chapter is also an introduction to the basics of creating *shell scripts*, or executable text files written to conform to shell syntax. Shell scripts run like any other command under Linux and can contain complex logic or a simple series of Linux command-line instructions. You can also run other shell scripts from within a shell program. The features and functions for several Linux shells are discussed in this chapter after a short introduction to working from the shell command line. You learn how to write and execute a simple shell program using `bash`, one of the most popular Linux shells and the default shell in Ubuntu and most other distributions.

Running Services at Bootup

Although most people consider a computer to be either on or off, in Ubuntu there are a number of states in between. Known as *runlevels*, they define what system services are started upon bootup. These services are simply applications running in the background that provide some needed function to your system, such as getting information from your mouse and sending it to the display; or a service could monitor the partitions to see whether they have enough free space left on them. Services are typically loaded and run (also referred to as being started) during the boot process, in the same way as Microsoft Windows services are. Internally, Ubuntu uses a system known as Upstart instead of the classic and venerable SysVinit, but Upstart has a special backward compatibility layer that can use runlevels in the way that Linux veterans are accustomed to doing for services not otherwise handled by Upstart. There will be more on Upstart later in the chapter.

You can manage nearly every aspect of your computer and how it behaves after booting via configuring and ordering boot scripts, as well as by using various system administration utilities included with Ubuntu. In this chapter, you learn how to work with these boot scripts and system administration utilities. This chapter also offers advice for troubleshooting and fixing problems that might arise with software configuration or the introduction or removal of various types of hardware from your system.

Beginning the Boot Loading Process

Although the actual boot loading mechanism for Linux varies on different hardware platforms (such as the SPARC, Alpha, or PowerPC systems), Intel-based PCs running Ubuntu most often use the same mechanism throughout product lines. This process is accomplished through a basic input/output system, or BIOS. The BIOS is an application stored in a chip on the motherboard that initializes the hardware on the motherboard (and often the hardware that's attached to the motherboard). The BIOS gets the system ready to load and run the software that we recognize as the operating system.

As a last step, the BIOS code looks for a special program known as the boot loader or boot code. The instructions in this little bit of code tell the BIOS where the Linux kernel is located, how it should be loaded into memory, and how it should be started.

If all goes well, the BIOS looks for a bootable volume such as a floppy disk, CD-ROM, hard drive, RAM disk, USB drive, or other media. The bootable volume contains a special hexadecimal value written to the volume by the boot loader application (such as Ubuntu's default GRUB2 since Ubuntu 9.10 or GRUB in older releases, or even LILO, which some older distributions used, although LILO has never been shipped by default by Ubuntu) when the boot loader code was first installed in the system's drives. The BIOS searches volumes in the order established by the BIOS settings (for example, USB first, followed by a DVD-ROM, and then a hard drive) and then boots from the first bootable volume it finds. Modern BIOSs allow considerable flexibility in choosing the device used for booting the system.

NOTE

If the BIOS detects a hardware problem, the boot process will fail and the BIOS will generate a few beeps from the system speaker. These "beep codes" indicate the nature of the problem the BIOS has encountered. The codes vary among manufacturers, and the diagnosis of problems occurring during this phase of the boot process is beyond the scope of this book and does not involve Linux. If you encounter a problem, you should consult the motherboard manual or contact the manufacturer of the motherboard.

Next, the BIOS looks on the bootable volume for boot code in the partition boot sector also known as the Master Boot Record (MBR) of the first hard disk. The MBR contains the boot loader code and the partition table—think of it like an index for a book, plus a few comments on how to start reading the book. If the BIOS finds a boot loader, it loads the boot loader code into memory. At that point, the BIOSs job is completed, and it passes control of the system to the boot loader.

The boot loader locates the Linux kernel on the disk and loads it into memory. After that task is completed, the boot loader passes control of the system to the Linux kernel. You can see how one process builds on another in an approach that enables many different operating systems to work with the same hardware.

NOTE

Linux is very flexible and can be booted from multiple images on a CD-ROM, over a network using PXE (pronounced "pixie") or NetBoot, or on a headless server with the console display sent over a serial or network connection. Work is even underway to create a special Linux BIOS at www.coreboot.org/ that will expedite the boot process because Linux does not need many of the services offered by the typical BIOS.

This kind of flexibility enables Linux to be used in a variety of ways, such as remote servers or diskless workstations, which are not generally seen in personal home use.

Loading the Linux Kernel

In a general sense, the kernel manages the system resources. As the user, you do not often interact with the kernel, but instead you interact with the applications that you are using. Linux refers to each application as a process, and the kernel assigns each process a number called a *process ID (PID)*. Traditionally, the Linux kernel loads and runs a process named `init`, which is also known as the "ancestor of all processes" because it starts every subsequent process. Ubuntu has replaced `init` with Upstart, which is being written by Ubuntu developers and made available for any distribution to use, but we will walk through the traditional method first because Upstart allows for backward compatibility for those services it is not yet configured to handle. We will discuss Upstart shortly.

This next step of the boot process traditionally begins with a message that the Linux kernel is loading, and a series of messages that are printed to the screen, giving you the status of each command. A failure should display an error message. The `quiet` option may be passed to the kernel at boot time to suppress many of these messages. Ubuntu does not display these messages by default, but instead uses a boot process created by the Fedora/Red Hat developers called Plymouth that is fast and incorporates a beautiful boot screen.

If the boot process were halted at this point, the system would just sit idle and the screen would be blank. To make the system useful for users, we need to start the system services. Those services are some of the applications that allow us to interact with the system.

System Services and Runlevels

The `init` command traditionally boots a Linux system to a specific system state, commonly referred to as its runlevel.

Runlevels determine which of the many available system services are started, as well as in which order they start. A special runlevel is used to stop the system, and a special runlevel is used for system maintenance. As you will see, there are other runlevels for special purposes.

You traditionally use runlevels to manage the system services running on a Linux computer. All these special files and scripts are set up during installation but you can change and control them manually.

Runlevel Definitions

The runlevels are defined in a traditional Linux system in `/etc/init.d`. Some distributions use the traditional /etc/inittab file to manage boot services. Ubuntu has not used this for several years since Upstart has been created and is used in the boot process, so by default the file does not exist. However, if you have used one in the past and want to create one in Ubuntu, it will be read and honored. Since it is not standard in Ubuntu, we are not going to cover /etc/inittab.

Each runlevel tells the `init` command what services to start or stop. Although runlevels might all have custom definitions, Ubuntu has adopted some standards for runlevels:

- **Runlevel 0**—Known as "halt," this runlevel is used to shut down the system.
- **Runlevel 1**—This is a special runlevel, defined as "single," which boots Ubuntu to a root access shell prompt where only the root user may log in. It has networking, X, and multi-user access turned off. This is the maintenance or rescue mode. It allows the system administrator to perform work on the system, make backups, or repair configuration or other files.
- **Runlevel 2**—This is the default runlevel for Ubuntu.
- **Runlevels 3–5**—These runlevels aren't used in Ubuntu but are often used in other Linux distributions.
- **Runlevel 6**—This runlevel is used to reboot the system.

Runlevel 1 (also known as single-user mode or maintenance mode) is most commonly used to repair file systems and change the root password on a system when the password has been forgotten. Trespassers with physical access to the machine can also use runlevel 1 to access your system.

CAUTION

Never forget that uncontrolled physical access is virtually a guarantee of access to your data by an intruder.

Booting into the Default Runlevel

Ubuntu boots into runlevel 2 by default, which means it starts the system as normal and leaves you inside the X Window System looking at the Gnome login prompt. It knows what runlevel 2 needs to load by looking in the `rc*.d` directories in `/etc`. Ubuntu contains directories for rc0.d through to rc5.d and rcS.d.

Assuming that the value is `1`, the `rc` script then executes all the scripts under the `/etc/rc.1` directory and then launches the graphical login.

If Ubuntu is booted to runlevel 1, for example, scripts beginning with the letter K followed by scripts beginning with the letter S under the `/etc/rc1.d` directory are then executed:

```
matthew@seymour:~$ ls /etc/rc1.d/
K10jackd         K20rsync              K20vboxdrv   K80cups      S70pppd-dns
K15pulseaudio    K20saned              K20winbind   README       S90single
K20acpi-support  K20saslauthd          K74bluetooth S30killprocs
K20kerneloops    K20speech-dispatcher  K77ntp       S70dns-clean
```

These scripts, as with all scripts in the `rc*.d` directories, are actually symbolic links to system service scripts that reside in the `/etc/init.d` directory.

The `rc1.d` links are prefaced with a letter and number, such as K15 or S10. The (K) or (S) in these prefixes indicate whether or not a particular service should be killed (K) or started (S) and pass a value of stop or start to the appropriate `/etc/init.d` script. The number in the prefix executes the specific `/etc/init.d` script in a particular order. The symlinks have numbers to delineate the order in which they are started. Nothing is sacred about a specific number, but some services need to be running before others are started. You would not want your Ubuntu system to attempt, for example, to mount a remote Network File System (NFS) volume without first starting networking and NFS services.

Understanding `init` Scripts and the Final Stage of Initialization

Each `/etc/init.d` script, or `init` script, contains logic that determines what to do when receiving a start or stop value. The logic might be a simple switch statement for execution, as in this example:

```
case "$1" in
```

```
  start)
        start
        ;;
  stop)
        stop
        ;;
  restart)
        restart
        ;;
  reload)
        reload
        ;;
  status)
        rhstatus
        ;;
  condrestart)
        [ -f /var/lock/subsys/smb ] && restart ¦¦ :
        ;;
  *)
        echo $"Usage: $0 {start¦stop¦restart¦status¦condrestart}"
        exit 1
esac
```

Although the scripts can be used to customize the way that the system runs from power-on, absent the replacement of the kernel, this script approach also means that the system does not have to be halted in total to start, stop, upgrade, or install new services.

Note that not all scripts will use this approach, and that other messages might be passed to the service script, such as restart, reload, or status. Also, not all scripts will respond to the same set of messages (with the exception of start and stop, which they all have to accept by convention) because each service might require special commands.

After all the system scripts have been run, your system is configured and all the necessary system services have been started. If you are using a runlevel other than 5, the final act of the `init` process is to launch the user shell—`bash`, `tcsh`, `zsh`, or any of the many command shells available. The shell launches and you see a login prompt on the screen.

Controlling Services at Boot with Administrative Tools

You can configure what services run at startup from the menus at System, Preferences, Startup Applications (shown in Figure 11.1). Here Ubuntu lists all the services that you can have automatically start at boot time. They are usually all enabled by default, but you can uncheck the ones you don't want and click OK. It is not recommended that you disable services randomly "to make things go faster." Some services might be vital for the continuing operation of your computer, such as the graphical login manager and the system communication bus.

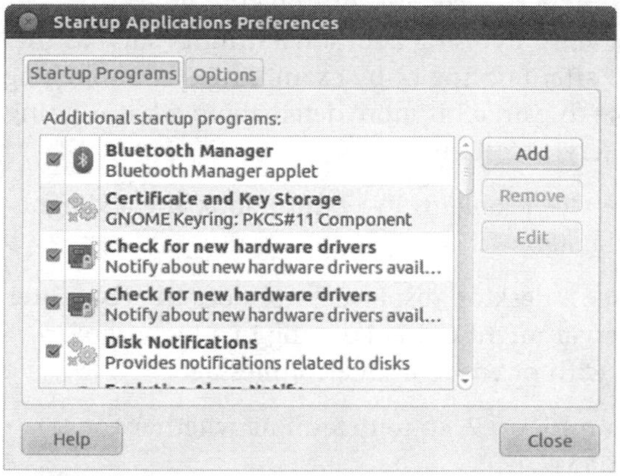

FIGURE 11.1 You can enable and disable Ubuntu's bootup services by toggling the check boxes in the Services dialog.

Changing Runlevels

After making changes to system services and runlevels, you can use the `telinit` command to change runlevels on-the-fly on a running Ubuntu system. Changing runlevels this way allows system administrators to alter selected parts of a running system to make changes to the services or to put changes into effect that have already been made (such as reassignment of network addresses for a networking interface).

For example, a system administrator can quickly change the system to maintenance or single-user mode by using the `telinit` command with its `S` option like this:

```
matthew@seymour:~$ sudo telinit S
```

The telinit command uses the init command to change runlevels and shut down currently running services.

After booting to single-user mode, you can then return to multi-user mode, like this:

```
matthew@seymour:~$ sudo telinit 2
```

TIP

Linux is full of shortcuts: If you exit the single-user shell by typing `exit` at the prompt, you will go back to the default runlevel without worrying about using `telinit`.

Troubleshooting Runlevel Problems

Reordering or changing system services during a particular runlevel is rarely necessary when using Ubuntu unless some disaster occurs. But system administrators should have a basic understanding of how Linux boots and how services are controlled in order to perform troubleshooting or to diagnose problems. By using additional utilities such as the dmesg | less command to read kernel output after booting or by examining system logging with cat /var/log/messages | less, it is possible to gain a bit more detail about what is going on when faced with troublesome drivers or service failure.

To better understand how to troubleshoot service problems in Ubuntu, look at the diagnosis and resolution of a typical service-related issue.

In this example, `X` will not start: You don't see a desktop displayed, nor does the computer seem to respond to keyboard input. The `X` server might either be hung in a loop, repeatedly failing, or might exit to a shell prompt with or without an error message.

The `X` server only attempts to restart itself in runlevel 2, so to determine whether the `X` server is hung in a loop, try switching to runlevel 1.

> **TIP**
>
> If you are working on a multi-user system and might inadvertently interrupt the work of other users, first ask them to save their current work, then change to a safer runlevel, such as single user mode.

Change to runlevel 1 by running the command **`telinit 1`. This switch to runlevel 1 will stop the `X`** server from attempting to restart itself.

Now you can easily examine the error and attempt to fix it.

First, try to start the `X` server "naked" (without also launching the window manager). If you are successful, you will get a gray screen with a large `X` in the middle. If so, kill `X` with the Ctrl+Alt+Backspace key combination, and look at your window manager configuration. (This configuration varies according to which window manager you have chosen.)

Let us assume that `X` won't run "naked." If we look at the log file for Xorg (it's clearly identified in the `/var/log` directory), we'll pay attention to any line that begins with `(EE)`, the special error code. We can also examine the error log file, `.xsessions-error`, in our home directory if such a file exists.

If we find an error line, the cause of the error might or might not be apparent to us. The nice thing about the Linux community is that it is very unlikely that you are the first person to experience that error. Enter the error message (or better, a unique part of it) into www.google.com/linux and discover what others have had to say about the problem. You might need to adjust your search to yield usable results, but that level of detail is beyond the scope of this chapter. Make adjustments and retest as before until you achieve success.

Fix the `X` configuration and start `X` with **`startx`. Repeat as necessary.**

CAUTION

Before making any changes to any configuration file, always make a backup copy of the original, unmodified file. Our practice is to append the extension `.original` to the copy because that is a unique and unambiguous identifier.

If you need to restore the original configuration file, do not rename it, but copy it back to its original name.

Starting and Stopping Services Manually

If you change a configuration file for a system service, it is usually necessary to stop and restart the service to make it read the new configuration. If you are reconfiguring the `X` server, it is often convenient to change from runlevel 2 to runlevel 1 to make testing easier and then switch back to runlevel 2 to re-enable the graphical login. If a service is improperly configured, it is easier to stop and restart it until you have it configured correctly than it is to reboot the entire machine.

The traditional way to manage a service (as root) is to call the service's `/etc/init.d` name on the command line with an appropriate keyword, such as `start`, `status`, or `stop`. For example, to start the Apache web server, call the `/etc/init.d/apache2` script like this:

```
sudo /etc/init.d/apache2 start
Starting apache 2.2 web server                                      [  OK  ]
```

The script will execute the proper program(s) and report the status of it. Stopping services is equally easy, using the stop keyword.

Using Upstart

Upstart was originally developed for Ubuntu. It is currently in use by a growing number of distributions including Fedora (9 and later), Nokia's Maemo platform, and Google's Chrome OS. Upstart is an event based replacement for the `/sbin/init` daemon and System-V init system. It handles starting of tasks and services during boot and stops them during shutdown. It also supervises them while the system is running and is intended to become a way to have tasks and services start or stop automatically based on specific events that happen rather than having to call a script manually to start or stop them. This is a big change and a big deal because it will make the overall system much more flexible, configurable, and responsive to conditions.

Basically, in Upstart, tasks and services are started and stopped by events. Events are generated as other tasks and services are started and stopped and may be received from any other process on the system. Services may be respawned if they die unexpectedly and communication with the init daemon occurs over D-Bus. Planned features that have not yet been implemented include the ability for events to be created at timed intervals or at scheduled times or as files or directories are changed and the creation of user services that users can start and stop themselves. This means that eventually Upstart jobs could even replace the venerable `cron` as well as do things previously impossible on any UNIX or Linux version!

For now, Upstart is being used for boot and shutdown and not all services have Upstart jobs written. Those that exist reside as expected in `/etc/init` and are easily accessible in the same basic manner as init jobs. If an Upstart job exists and you try to manage it using the traditional method, you will get a message like this:

```
matthew@seymour:~$ sudo /etc/init.d/ufw stop
```

Rather than invoking init scripts through /etc/init.d, use the service(8) utility, e.g. service ufw stop. Because the script you are attempting to invoke has been converted to an Upstart job, you may also use the stop(8) utility, e.g. stop ufw.

In this case, to start or stop Ubuntu's Uncomplicated Firewall (UFW), you just enter `sudo start ufw` or `sudo stop ufw`. Simple.

Upstart is still quite new and in heavy development. Not much documentation exists and this is on purpose. Processes and features are not yet set in stone, so while the foundation is being extended the development team felt it best to keep the details a bit muddy to keep information that is changing quickly from propagating and requiring a ton of work or making it impossible to fix or replace incorrect or changed information later in the public knowledgebase. If you want to learn more about Upstart, start with http://upstart.ubuntu.com/. More details are expected to be released as development continues, but if you are the impatient type who loves to play with the latest shiny toy and aren't afraid of getting your hands dirty, then with some digging you should be able to find what you want or need using the website and the examples already installed on your computer.

Scheduling Tasks

There are three ways to schedule commands in Ubuntu, all of which work in different ways. The first is the `at` command, which specifies a command to run at a specific time and date relative to today. The second is the `batch` command, which is actually a script that redirects you to the `at` command with some extra options set so your command runs when the system is quiet. The last option is the `cron` daemon, which is the Linux way of executing tasks at a given time.

Using `at` and `batch` to Schedule Tasks for Later

If there is a time-intensive task you want to run, but you do not want to do it while you are still logged in, you can tell Ubuntu to run it later with the `at` command. To use `at`, you need to tell it the time at which you want to run and then press Enter. You will then see a new prompt that starts with `at>`, and everything you type there until you press `Ctrl+D` will be the commands you want `at` to run.

When the designated time arrives, at will perform each action individually and in order, which means later commands can rely on the results of earlier commands. In this next example, run at just after 5 p.m., at is used to download and extract the latest Linux kernel at a time when the network should be quiet:

```
matthew@seymour:~$ at now + 7 hours
at> wget http://www.kernel.org/pub/linux/kernel/v2.6/linux-2.6.10.tar.bz2
at> tar xvfjp linux-2.6.10.tar.bz2
at> <EOT>
job 2 at 2010-07-08 20:01
```

Specifying `now + 7 hours` as the time does what you would expect: `at` was run at 8 p.m., so the command will run just after 3 a.m.

If you have a more complex job, you can use the `-f` parameter to have `at` read its commands from a file, like this:

```
echo wget http://www.kernel.org/pub/linux/kernel/v2.6/linux-2.6.10.tar.bz2\;
tar xvfjp linux-2.6.10.tar.bz2 > myjob.job
at -f myjob.job tomorrow
```

As you can see, at is flexible about the time format it takes; you can specify it in three ways:

- Using the `now` parameter, you can specify how many minutes, hours, days, or weeks relative to the current time—for example, `now + 4 weeks` would run the command one month from today.
- You can also specify several special times, including `tomorrow`, `midnight`, `noon`, or `teatime` (4 p.m.). If you do not specify a time with `tomorrow`, your job is set for precisely 24 hours from the current time.
- You can specify an exact date and time using `HH:MM MM/DD/YY` format—for example, 16:40 22/12/10 for 4:40 p.m. on the 22nd of December 2010.

When your job is submitted, `at` will report the job number, date, and time that the job will be executed; the queue identifier; plus the job owner (you). It will also capture all your environment variables and store them along with the job so that, when your job runs, it can restore the variables, preserving your execution environment.

The job number and job queue identifier are both important. When you schedule a job using `at`, it is placed into queue "a" by default, which means it runs at your specified time and takes up a normal amount of resources.

There is an alternative command, `batch`, which is really just a shell script that calls `at` with a few extra options. These options (`-q b -m now`, if you were interested) set `at` to run on queue b (`-q b`), mailing the user on completion (`-m`), and running immediately (`now`). The queue part is what is important: Jobs scheduled on queue b will only be executed when system load falls below 0.8—that is, when the system is not running at full load.

Furthermore, it will run with a lower niceness, meaning a queue jobs usually have a niceness of 2, whereas b queue jobs have a niceness of 4.

Because `batch` always specifies `now` as its time, you need not specify your own time; it will simply run as soon as the system is quiet. Having a default niceness of 4 means that batched commands will get less system resources than a queue job's (`at`'s default) and less system resources than most other programs. You can optionally specify other queues using `at`. Queue c runs at niceness 6, queue d runs at niceness 8, and so on. However, it is important to note that the system load is only checked before the command is run. If the load is lower than 0.8, your batch job will be run. If the system load subsequently rises beyond 0.8, your batch job will continue to run, albeit in the background, thanks to its niceness value.

When you submit a job for execution, you will also be returned a job number. If you forget this or just want to see a list of other jobs you have scheduled to run later, use the `atq` command with no parameters. If you run this as a normal user, it will print only your jobs; running it as a super-user will print everyone's jobs. The output is in the same format as when you submit a job, so you get the ID number, execution time, queue ID, and owner of each job.

If you want to delete a job, use the `atrm` command followed by the ID number of the job you want to delete. This next example shows `atq` and `atrm` being used to list jobs and delete one:

```
matthew@seymour:~$ atq
14      2010-01-20 23:33 a matthew
16      2010-02-03 22:34 a matthew
17      2010-01-25 22:34 a matthew
15      2010-01-22 04:34 a matthew
18      2010-01-22 01:35 b matthew
matthew@seymour:~$ atrm 16
matthew@seymour:~$ atq
14      2010-01-20 23:33 a matthew
17      2010-01-25 22:34 a matthew
15      2010-01-22 04:34 a matthew
18      2010-01-22 01:35 b matthew
```

In that example, job 16 is deleted using `atrm`, and so it does not show up in the second call to `atq`.

The default configuration for `at` and `batch` is to allow everyone to use it, which is not always the desired behavior. Access is controlled through two files: `/etc/at.allow` and `/etc/at.deny`. By default, `at.deny` exists but is empty, which allows everyone to use `at` and `batch`. You can enter usernames into `at.deny`, one per line, to stop those users scheduling jobs.

Alternatively, you can use the `at.allow` file; this does not exist by default. If you have a blank `at.allow` file, no one except root is allowed to schedule jobs. As with `at.deny`, you can add usernames to `at.allow` one per line, and those users will be able to schedule jobs. You should use either `at.deny` or `at.allow`: When someone tries to run `at` or `batch`,

Ubuntu checks for her username in `at.allow`. If it is in there, or if `at.allow` does not exist, Ubuntu checks for her username in `at.deny`. If her username is in `at.deny` or `at.deny` does not exist, she is not allowed to schedule jobs.

Using `cron` to Run Jobs Repeatedly

The `at` and `batch` commands work well if you just want to execute a single task at a later date, but they are less useful if you want to run a task frequently. Instead, the `crond` daemon exists for running tasks repeatedly based upon system—and user—requests. Cron has a similar permissions system to `at`: Users listed in the `cron.deny` file are not allowed to use Cron, and users listed in the `cron.allow` file are. An empty `cron.deny` file—the default—means everyone can set jobs. An empty `cron.allow` file means that no one (except root) can set jobs.

There are two types of jobs: system jobs and user jobs. Only root can edit *system* jobs, whereas any user whose name appears in `cron.allow` or does not appear in `cron.deny` can run *user* jobs. System jobs are controlled through the `/etc/crontab` file, which by default looks like this:

```
SHELL=/bin/sh
PATH=/usr/local/sbin:/usr/local/bin:/sbin:/bin:/usr/sbin:/usr/bin

# m h dom mon dow user   command
17 *    * * *   root    cd / && run-parts —report /etc/cron.hourly
25 6    * * *   root    test -x /usr/sbin/anacron || ( cd / && run-parts —report
/etc/cron.daily )
47 6    * * 7   root    test -x /usr/sbin/anacron || ( cd / && run-parts —report
/etc/cron.weekly )
52 6    1 * *   root    test -x /usr/sbin/anacron || ( cd / && run-parts —report
/etc/cron.monthly )
```

The first two lines specify which shell should be used to execute the job (defaults to the shell of the user who owns the `crontab` file, usually `/bin/bash`), and the search path for executables that will be used. It's important that you avoid using environment variables in this path statement, because they may not be set when the job runs.

The next line starts with a pound sign (#) and so is treated as a comment and ignored. The next four lines are the important parts: They are the jobs themselves.

Each job is specified in seven fields that define the time to run, owner, and command. The first five commands specify the execution time in quite a quirky order: minute (0–59), hour (0–23), day of the month (1–31), month of the year (1–12), and day of the week (0–7). For day of the week, both 0 and 7 are Sunday, which means that 1 is Monday, 3 is Wednesday, and so on. If you want to specify "all values" (that is, every minute, every hour, every day, and so on), use an asterisk, `*`.

The next field specifies the username of the owner of the job. When a job is executed, it uses the username specified here. The last field is the command to execute.

So, the first job runs at minute 17, every hour of every day of every month and executes the command `run-parts /etc/cron.hourly`. The `run-parts` command is a simple script that runs all programs inside a given directory—in this case, `/etc/cron.hourly`. So, in this case, the job will execute at 00:17 (17 minutes past midnight), 01:17, 02:17, 03:17, and so on, and will use all the programs listed in the `cron.hourly` directory.

The next job runs at minute 25 and hour 6 of every day of every month, running `run-parts /etc/cron.daily`. Because of the hour limitation, this script will run only once per day, at 6:25 a.m. Note that it uses minute 25 rather than minute 17 so that daily jobs do not clash with hourly jobs. You should be able to guess what the next two jobs do, simply by looking at the commands they run!

Inside each of those four directories (`cron.hourly`, `cron.daily`, `cron.weekly`, and `cron.monthly`) are a collection of shell scripts that will be run by `run-parts`. For example, in `cron.daily` you will have scripts like `logrotate`, which handles backing up of log files, and `makewhatis`, which updates the `whatis` database. You can add other system tasks to these directories if you want to, but you should be careful to ensure your scripts are correct.

CAUTION

The `cron` daemon reads all the system `crontab` files and all user `crontab` files once a minute (on the minute, i.e. at 6:00:00, 6:01:00, and so on) to check for changes. However, any new jobs it finds will not be executed until at least 1 minute has passed.

For example, if it is 6:01:49 (that is, 49 seconds past 1 minute past 6 a.m.) and you set a `cron` job to run at 6:02, it will not execute. At 6:02, the `cron` daemon will reread its configuration files and see the new job, but it will not be able to execute it. If you set the job to run at 6:02 a.m. every day, it will be executed the following morning and every subsequent morning.

This same situation exists when deleting jobs. If it is 6:01:49 and you have a job scheduled to run at 6:02, deleting it will make no difference: `cron` will run it before it rereads the `crontab` files for changes. However, after it has reread the `crontab` file and noticed the job is no longer there, it will not be executed in subsequent days.

There are alternative ways of specifying dates. For example, you can use sets of dates and times by using hyphens of commas, such as hours 9–15 would execute at 9, 10, 11, 12, 13, 14, and 15 (from 9 a.m. to 3 p.m.), whereas 9, 11, 13, 15 would miss out at the even hours. Note that it is important you do not put spaces into these sets because the `cron` daemon will interpret them as the next field. You can define a step value with a slash (/) to show time division: `*/4` for hours means "every four hours all day," and `0-12/3` means "every three hours from midnight to noon." You can also specify day and month names rather than numbers, using three-character abbreviations: Sun, Mon, Tue, Fri, Sat for days, or Jan, Feb, Mar, Oct, Nov, Dec for months.

As well as system jobs, there are also user jobs for those users who have the correct permissions. User jobs are stored in the `/var/spool/cron` directory, with each user having his own file in his named after his username—for instance, `/var/spool/cron/matthew` or

/var/spool/cron/root. The contents of these files contain the jobs the user wants to run and take roughly the same format as the /etc/crontab file, with the exception that the owner of the job should not be specified because it will always be the same as the filename.

To edit your own crontab file, type crontab -e. This brings up a text editor (vim by default, but you can set the EDITOR environment variable to change that) where you can enter your entries. The format of this file is a little different from the format for the main crontab because this time there is no need to specify the owner of the job—it is always you.

So, this time each line is made up of six fields: minute (0–59), hour (0–23), day of the month (1–31), month of the year (1–12), day of the week (0–7), and then the command to run. If you are using vim and are new to it, press i to enter insert mode to edit your text; then press Esc to exit insert mode. To save and quit, type a colon followed by wq and press Enter.

When programming, we tend to use a sandbox subdirectory in our home directory where we keep all sorts of temporary files that we were just playing around with. We can use a personal job to empty that directory every morning at 6 a.m. so that we get a fresh start each morning. Here is how that would look in our crontab file:

```
0 6 * * * rm -rf /home/matthew/sandbox/*
```

If you are not allowed to schedule jobs, you will be stopped from editing your crontab file.

After your jobs are placed, you can use the command crontab -l to list your jobs. This just prints the contents of your crontab file, so its output will be the same as the line you just entered.

If you want to remove just one job, the easiest thing to do is type crontab -e to edit your crontab file in vim; then, after having moved the cursor to the job you want to delete, type dd (two *d*s) to delete that line. If you want to delete all your jobs, you can use crontab -r to delete your crontab file.

Basic Shell Control

Ubuntu includes a rich assortment of capable, flexible, and powerful shells. Each shell is different but has numerous built-in commands and configurable command-line prompts and might include features such as command-line history, the ability to recall and use a previous command line, and command-line editing. As an example, the bash shell is so powerful that it is possible to write a minimal web server entirely in bash's language using 114 lines of script (see the link at the end of this chapter).

Although there are many shells to choose from, most people stick with the default, bash. This is because bash does everything most people need to do, and more. Only change your shell if you really need to.

Table 11.1 lists each shell, along with its description and location, in your Ubuntu file system.

TABLE 11.1 Shells with Ubuntu

Name	Description	Location
bash	The Bourne Again SHell	/bin/bash
ksh	The Korn shell	/bin/ksh, /usr/bin/ksh
pdksh	A symbolic link to ksh	/usr/bin/pdksh
rsh	The restricted shell (for network operation)	/usr/bin/rsh
sh	A symbolic link to bash	/bin/sh
tcsh	A csh-compatible shell	/bin/tcsh
zsh	A compatible csh, ksh, and sh shell	/bin/zsh

LEARNING MORE ABOUT YOUR SHELL

All the shells listed in Table 11.1 have accompanying `man` pages, along with other documentation under the `/usr/share/doc` directory. Some of the documentation can be quite lengthy, but it is generally much better to have too much documentation than too little! The `bash` shell includes more than 100 pages in its manual, and the `zsh` shell documentation is so extensive that it includes the `zshall` meta `man` page (use `man zshall` to read this overview)!

The Shell Command Line

Having a basic understanding of the capabilities of the shell command line can help you write better shell scripts. If, after you have finished reading this short introduction, you want to learn more about the command line, check out Chapter 35, "Command Line Masterclass." You can use the shell command line to perform a number of different tasks, including:

- Searching files or directories with programs using pattern-matching, or expressions; these commands include the GNU `gawk` (linked as `awk`) and the `grep` family of commands, including `egrep` and `fgrep`.
- Getting data from and sending data to a file or command, known as *input* and *output redirection*.
- Feeding or filtering a program's output to another command (called using *pipes*).

A shell can also have built-in *job-control* commands to launch the command line as a background process, suspend a running program, selectively retrieve or kill running or suspended programs, and perform other types of process control.

Multiple commands can be run on a single command line using a semicolon to separate commands:

```
matthew@seymour:~$ w ; free ; df
 18:14:13 up  4:35,  2 users,  load average: 0.97, 0.99, 1.04
USER     TTY      FROM              LOGIN@   IDLE   JCPU   PCPU WHAT
matthew    tty7     :0                13:39    4:35m 24:34  0.32s gnome-session
matthew    pts/0    :0.0              17:24    0.00s  1.19s  4.98s gnome-terminal
             total       used       free     shared    buffers     cached
Mem:       4055692    1801104    2254588          0     134096     757532
-/+ buffers/cache:     909476    3146216
Swap:      8787512          0    8787512
Filesystem           1K-blocks      Used Available Use% Mounted on
/dev/sda1             14421344   6509276   7179508  48% /
none                   2020136       336   2019800   1% /dev
none                   2027844      3004   2024840   1% /dev/shm
none                   2027844       224   2027620   1% /var/run
none                   2027844         0   2027844   0% /var/lock
none                   2027844         0   2027844   0% /lib/init/rw
/dev/sda6            284593052 144336704 125799860  54% /home
```

This example displays the output of the `w`, `free`, and `df` commands. Long shell command lines can be extended inside shell scripts or at the command line by using the backslash character (\). For example,

```
matthow@coymour: $ ooho "thio io a long \
> command line and" ; echo "shows that multiple commands \
> may be strung out."
this is a long command line and
shows that multiple commands may be strung out.
```

The first three lines of this example are a single command line. In that single line are two instances of the echo command. Note that when you use the backslash as a line-continuation character, it must be the last character on the command line (or in your shell script, as you will see later on in this chapter).

Using the basic features of the shell command line is easy, but mastering use of all features can be difficult. Entire books have been devoted to using shells, writing shell scripts, and using pattern-matching expressions. The following sections provide an overview of some features of the shell command line relating to writing scripts.

GROKKING GREP

If you plan to develop shell scripts to expand the capabilities of pattern-matching commands such as `grep`, you will benefit from learning more about using expressions. One of the definitive guides to using the pattern-matching capabilities of UNIX and Linux commands is *Mastering Regular Expressions* by Jeffrey E. F. Freidl (O'Reilly), ISBN: 0-596-52812-4.

Shell Pattern-Matching Support

The shell command line allows you to use strings of specially constructed character patterns for wildcard matches. This is a different simpler capability than that supported by GNU utilities such as `grep`, which can use more complex patterns, known as *expressions*, to search through files or directories or to filter data input to or out of commands.

The shell's pattern strings can be simple or complex, but even using a small subset of the available characters in simple wildcards can yield constructive results at the command line. Some common characters used for shell pattern matching are:

- *—Matches any character. For example, to find all files in the current directory ending in `.txt`, you could use

  ```
  matthew@seymour:~$ ls *.txt
  ```

- ?—Matches a single character. For example, to find all files in the current directory ending in the extension `.d?c` (where ? could be 0–9, a–z, or A–Z), you could use

  ```
  matthew@seymour:~$ ls *.d?c
  ```

- `[xxx]` or `[x-x]`—Matches a range of characters. For example, to list all files in a directory with names containing numbers, you could use

  ```
  matthew@seymour:~$ ls *[0-9]*
  ```

- `\x`—Matches or escapes a character such as `?` or a tab character. For example, to create a file with a name containing question mark, you could use

```
matthew~$ touch foo\?
```

Note that the shell might not interpret some characters or regular expressions in the same manner as a Linux command, and mixing wildcards and regular expressions in shell scripts can lead to problems unless you're careful. For example, finding patterns in text is best left to regular expressions used with commands such as `grep`; simple wildcards should be used for filtering or matching filenames on the command line. And although both Linux command expressions and shell scripts can recognize the backslash as an escape character in patterns, the dollar sign ($) will have two wildly different meanings (single-character pattern matching in expressions and variable assignment in scripts).

CAUTION

Make sure you read your command carefully when using wildcards; an all-too-common error is to type something like `rm -rf * .txt` with a space between the `*` and the `.txt`. By the time you wonder why the command is taking so long, Bash will already have deleted most of your files. The problem is that it will treat the `*` and the `.txt` separately. `*` will match everything, so Bash will delete all your files.

Redirecting Input and Output

You can create, overwrite, and append data to files at the command line, using a process called *input* and *output redirection*. The shell recognizes several special characters for this process, such as >, <, or >>.

In this example, the output of the `ls` command is redirected to create a file named `textfiles.listing`:

```
matthew@seymour:~$ ls *.txt >textfiles.listing
```

Use output redirection with care because it is possible to overwrite existing files. For example, specifying a different directory but using the same output filename will overwrite the existing `textfiles.listing`:

```
matthew@seymour:~$ ls /usr/share/doc/mutt-1.4/*.txt >textfiles.listing
```

Fortunately, most shells are smart enough to recognize when you might do something foolish. Here, the bash shell warns that the command is attempting to redirect output to a directory:

```
matthew@seymour:~$ mkdir foo
matthew@seymour:~$ ls >foo
bash: foo: Is a directory
```

Output can be appended to a file without overwriting existing content by using the append operator, >>. In this example, the directory listing will be appended to the end of `textfiles.listing` instead of overwriting its contents:

```
matthew@seymour:~$ ls /usr/share/doc/mutt-1.4/*.txt >>textfiles.listing
```

You can use *input redirection* to feed data into a command by using the < like this:

```
matthew@seymour:~$ cat < textfiles.listing
```

You can use the shell *here* operator, <<, to specify the end of input on the shell command line:

```
matthew@seymour:~$ cat >simple_script <<DONE
> echo ""this is a simple script""
> DONE
$ cat simple_script
echo ""this is a simple script""
```

In this example, the shell will feed the cat command you are typing (input) until the pattern `DONE` is recognized. The output file `simple_script` is then saved and its contents verified. This same technique can be used in scripts to create content based on the output of various commands and define an end-of-input or delimiter.

Piping Data

Many Linux commands can be used in concert in a single, connected command line to transform data from one form to another. Stringing Linux commands together in this fashion is known as using or creating *pipes*. Pipes are created on the command line with the bar operator (¦). For example, a pipe can be used to perform a complex task from a single command line like this:

```
matthew@seymour:~$ find /d2 -name '*.txt' -print ¦ xargs cat ¦ \
tr ' ' '\n' ¦  sort ¦ uniq >output.txt
```

This example takes the output of the find command to feed the cat command (`via xargs`) the name all text files under the `/d2` command. The content of all matching files is then fed through the `tr` command to change each space in the data stream into a carriage return. The stream of words is then sorted, and identical adjacent lines are removed using the `uniq` command. The output, a raw list of words, is then saved in the file named `output.txt`.

Background Processing

The shell allows you to start a command and then launch it into the background as a process by using an ampersand (`&`) at the end of a command line. This technique is often used at the command line of an X terminal window to start a client and return to the command line. For example, to launch another terminal window using the `xterm` client,

```
matthew@seymour:~$ xterm &
[3] 1437
```

The numbers echoed back show a number (3 in this example), which is a *job* number, or reference number for a shell process, and a *Process ID* number, or PID (1437 in this example). The `xterm` window session can be killed by using the shell's built-in `kill` command, along with the job number like this:

```
matthew@seymour:~$ kill %3
```

Or the process can be killed by using the kill command, along with the PID, like so:

```
matthew@seymour:~$ kill 1437
```

Background processing can be used in shell scripts to start commands that take a long time, such as backups:

```
matthew@seymour:~$ tar -czf /backup/home.tgz /home &
```

Writing and Executing a Shell Script

Why should you write and use shell scripts? Shell scripts can save you time and typing, especially if you routinely use the same command lines multiple times every day. Although you could also use the history function (press the Up or Down keys while using `bash` or use the `history` command), a shell script can add flexibility with command-line argument substitution and built-in help.

Although a shell script won't execute faster than a program written in a computer language such as C, a shell program can be smaller in size than a compiled program. The shell program does not require any additional library support other than the shell or, if used, existing commands installed on your system. The process of creating and testing shell scripts is also generally simpler and faster than the development process for equivalent C language commands.

NOTE

Hundreds of commands included with Ubuntu are actually shell scripts, and many other good shell script examples are available over the Internet—a quick search will yield numerous links to online tutorials and scripting guides from fellow Linux users and developers. For example, the `startx` command, used to start an X Window session from the text console, is a shell script used every day by most users. To learn more about shell scripting with `bash`, see the Advanced Bash-Scripting Guide, listed in the "Reference" section at the end of this chapter. You'll also find *Sams Teach Yourself Shell Programming in 24 Hours* a helpful guide to learning more about using the shell to build your own commands.

When you are learning to write and execute your first shell scripts, start with scripts for simple, but useful tasks. Begin with short examples, and then expand the scripts as you build on your experience and knowledge. Make liberal use of comments (lines preceded with a pound # sign) to document each section of your script. Include an author statement and overview of the script as additional help, along with a creation date or version number. Write shell scripts using a text editor such as `vi` because it does not automatically wrap lines of text. Line wrapping can break script syntax and cause problems. If you use the `nano` editor, include its `-w` flag to disable line wrap.

In this section, you learn how to write a simple shell script to set up a number of *aliases* (command synonyms) whenever you log on. Instead of typing all the aliases every time you log on, you can put them in a file by using a text editor, such as `vi`, and then execute the file. Normally these changes are saved in systemwide shell configuration files under the `/etc` directory to make the changes active for all users or in your `.bashrc`, `.cshrc` (if you use `tcsh`), or `.bash_profile` files in your home directory.

Here is what is contained in `myenv`, a sample shell script created for this purpose (for `bash`):

```
#!/bin/sh
alias ll='ls -l'
alias ldir='ls -aF'
alias copy='cp'
```

This simple script creates command *aliases*, or convenient shorthand forms of commands, for the `ls` and `cp` commands. The `ll alias` provides a long directory listing: The `ldir` alias is the `ls` command, but prints indicators (for directories or executable files) in listings. The `copy` alias is the same as the `cp` command. You can experiment and add your own options or create aliases of other commands with options you frequently use.

You can execute `myenv` in a variety of ways under Linux. As shown in this example, you can make `myenv` executable by using the `chmod` command and then execute it as you would any other native Linux command:

```
matthew@seymour:~$ chmod +x myenv
```

This line turns on the executable permission of `myenv`, which can be checked with the `ls` command and its `-l` option like this:

```
matthew@seymour:~$ ls -l myenv
-rwxr-xr-x    1 matthew matthew  0 2010-07-08 18:19 myenv
```

Running the New Shell Program

You can run your new shell program in several ways. Each method will produce the same results, which is a testament to the flexibility of using the shell with Linux. One way to run your shell program is to execute the file `myenv` from the command line as if it were a Linux command:

```
matthew@seymour:~$ ./myenv
```

A second way to execute `myenv` under a particular shell, such as `pdksh`, is as follows:

```
matthew@seymour:~$ pdksh myenv
```

This invokes a new `pdksh` shell and passes the filename `myenv` as a parameter to execute the file. A third way will require you to create a directory named `bin` in your home directory, and to then copy the new shell program into this directory. You can then run the program without the need to specify a specific location or to use a shell. You do this like so:

```
matthew@seymour:~$ mkdir bin
matthew@seymour:~$ mv myenv bin
matthew@seymour:~$ myenv
```

This works because Ubuntu is set up by default to include the executable path `$HOME/bin` in your shell's environment. You can view this environment variable, named `PATH`, by piping the output of the `env` command through `fgrep` like so:

```
matthew@seymour:~$ env ¦ fgrep PATH
/usr/kerberos/bin:/usr/local/bin:/bin:/usr/bin: \
/usr/X11R6/bin:/sbin:/home/matthew/bin
```

As you can see, the user (`matthew` in this example) can use the new `bin` directory to hold executable files. Another way to bring up an environment variable is to use the `echo` command along with the variable name (in this case, `$PATH`):

```
matthew@seymour:~$ echo $PATH
/usr/kerberos/bin:/usr/local/bin:/usr/bin:/bin:/usr/X11R6/bin:/home/bball/bin
```

CAUTION

Never put `.` in your `$PATH` to execute files or a command in the current directory—this presents a serious security risk, especially for the root operator, and even more so if `.` is first in your `$PATH` search order. Trojan scripts placed by crackers in directories such as `/tmp` can be used for malicious purposes, and will be executed immediately if the current working directory is part of your `$PATH`.

Storing Shell Scripts for Systemwide Access

After you execute the command myenv, you should be able to use ldir from the command line to get a list of files under the current directory and ll to get a list of files with attributes displayed. However, the best way to use the new commands in myenv is to put them into your shell's login or profile file. For Ubuntu, and nearly all Linux users, the default shell is bash, so you can make these commands available for everyone on your system by putting them in the /etc/bashrc file. Systemwide aliases for tcsh are contained in files with the extension .csh under the /etc/profile.d directory. The pdksh shell can use these command aliases as well.

NOTE

To use a shell other than bash after logging in, use the chsh command from the command line or the system-config-users client during an X session. You'll be asked for your password (or the root password if using system-config-users), as well as the location and name of the new shell (see Table 11.1). The new shell will become your default shell, but only if its name is in the list of acceptable system shells in /etc/shells.

Interpreting Shell Scripts Through Specific Shells

The majority of shell scripts use a *shebang line* (#!) at the beginning to control the type of shell used to run the script; this bang line calls for an sh-incantation of bash:

```
#!/bin/sh
```

A shebang line (it is short for "sharp" and "bang", two names for # and !) tells the Linux kernel that a specific command (a shell, or in the case of other scripts, perhaps awk or Perl) is to be used to interpret the contents of the file. Using a shebang line is common practice for all shell scripting. For example, if you write a shell script using bash, but want the script to execute as if run by the Bourne shell, sh, the first line of your script will contain #!/bin/sh, which is a link to the bash shell. Running bash as sh will cause bash to act as a Bourne shell. This is the reason for the symbolic link sh, which points to bash.

THE SHEBANG LINE

The shebang line is a magic number, as defined in /usr/share/magic—a text database of magic numbers for the Linux file command. Magic numbers are used by many different Linux commands to quickly identify a type of file, and the database format is documented in the section five manual page named magic (read by using man 5 magic). For example, magic numbers can be used by the Linux file command to display the identity of a script (no matter what filename is used) as a shell script using a specific shell or other interpreter such as awk or Perl.

You might also find different or new environment variables available to your scripts by using different shells. For example, if you launch `csh` from the `bash` command line, you will find several new variables or variables with slightly different definitions, such as:

```
matthew@seymour:~$ env
...
VENDOR=intel
MACHTYPE=i386
HOSTTYPE=i386-linux
HOST=thinkpad.home.org
On the other hand, bash might provide these variables or variables of the same name
with a slightly different definition, such as
$ env
...
HOSTTYPE=i386
HOSTNAME=thinkpad.home.org
```

Although the behavior of a shebang line is not defined by POSIX, variations of its use can be helpful when you are writing shell scripts. For example, as described in the `wish` man page, you can use a shell to help execute programs called within a shell script without needing to hard code pathnames of programs. The `wish` command is a windowing Tool Control Language (`tcl`) interpreter that can be used to write graphical clients. Avoiding the use of specific pathnames to programs increases shell script portability because not every UNIX or Linux system has programs in the same location.

For example, if you want to use the `wish` command, your first inclination might be to write

```
#!/usr/local/bin/wish
```

Although this will work on many other operating systems, the script will fail under Linux because `wish` is located under the `/usr/bin` directory. However, if you write the command line this way,

```
#!/bin/sh
exec wish "$@"
```

you can use the `wish` command (as a binary or a shell script itself); your first inclination might be to write in Linux.

Using Variables in Shell Scripts

When writing shell scripts for Linux, you work with three types of variables:

- **Environment variables**—Part of the system environment, you can use them in your shell program. New variables can be defined, and some of them, such as `PATH`, can also be modified within a shell program.
- **Built-in variables**—Variables such as options used on the command (interpreted by the shell as a *positional argument*) are provided by Linux. Unlike environment variables, you cannot modify them.

- **User variables**—Variables defined within a script when you write a shell script. You can use and modify them at will within the shell script but are not available to be used outside of the script.

A major difference between shell programming and other programming languages is that in shell programming, variables are not *typed*—that is, you do not have to specify whether a variable is a number or a string, and so on.

Assigning a Value to a Variable

Say that you want to use a variable called `lcount` to count the number of iterations in a loop within a shell program. You can declare and initialize this variable as follows:

Command	Environment
`lcount=0`	`pdksh and bash`
`set lcount=0`	`tcsh`

NOTE

Under pdksh and bash, you must ensure that the equal sign (`=`) does not have spaces before and after it.

To store a string in a variable, you can use the following:

Command	Environment
`myname=Sanjiv`	`pdksh and bash`
`set myname=San-jiv`	`tcsh`

Use the preceding variable form if the string doesn't have embedded spaces. If a string has embedded spaces, you can do the assignment as follows:

Command	Environment
`myname="Sanjiv Guha"`	`pdksh and bash`
`set myname="Sanjiv Guha"`	`tcsh`

Accessing Variable Values

You can access the value of a variable by prefixing the variable name with a $ (dollar sign). That is, if the variable name is `var`, you can access the variable by using `$var`.

If you want to assign the value of `var` to the variable `lcount`, you can do so as follows:

Command	Environment
`lcount=$var`	`pdksh and bash`
`set` `lcount=$var`	`tcsh`

Positional Parameters

It is possible to pass options from the command line or from another shell script to your shell program.

These options are supplied to the shell program by Linux as *positional parameters*, which have special names provided by the system. The first parameter is stored in a variable called `1` (number 1) and can be accessed by using `$1` within the program. The second parameter is stored in a variable called `2` and can be accessed by using `$2` within the program, and so on. One or more of the higher numbered positional parameters can be omitted while you're invoking a shell program.

Understanding how to use these positional parameters and how to access and use variables retrieved from the command line is necessary when developing more advanced shell programs.

A Simple Example of a Positional Parameter

For example, if a shell program `mypgm` expects two parameters—such as a first name and a last name—you can invoke the shell program with only one parameter, the first name. However, you cannot invoke it with only the second parameter, the last name.

Here is a shell program called `mypgm1`, which takes only one parameter (a name) and displays it on the screen:

```
#!/bin/sh
#Name display program
if [ $# -eq 0 ]
then
   echo "Name not provided"
else
   echo "Your name is "$1
fi
```

If you execute mypgm1, as follows,

```
$ bash  mypgm1
```

you get the following output:

```
Name not provided
```

However, if you execute mypgm1, as follows,

```
$ bash  mypgm1 Sanjiv
```

you get the following output:

```
Your name is Sanjiv
```

The shell program mypgm1 also illustrates another aspect of shell programming: the built-in variables provided to the shell by the Linux kernel. In mypgm1, the built-in variable $# provides the number of positional parameters passed to the shell program. You learn more about working with built-in variables in the next major section of this chapter.

Using Positional Parameters to Access and Retrieve Variables from the Command Line

Using positional parameters in scripts can be helpful if you need to use command lines with piped commands requiring complex arguments. Shell programs containing positional parameters can be even more convenient if the commands are infrequently used. For example, if you use your Ubuntu system with an attached voice modem as an answering machine, you can write a script to issue a command that retrieves and plays the voice messages. The following lines convert a saved sound file (in .rmd or voice-phone format) and pipe the result to your system's audio device:

```
#!/bin/sh
# play voice message in /var/spool/voice/incoming
rmdtopvf /var/spool/voice/incoming/$1 ¦ pvfspeed -s 8000 ¦ \
pvftobasic >/dev/audio
```

A voice message can then easily be played back using this script (perhaps named pmm):

```
$ pmm name_of_message
```

Shell scripts that contain positional parameters are often used for automating routine and mundane jobs, such as system log report generation, file system checks, user resource accounting, printer use accounting, and other system, network, or security administration tasks.

Using a Simple Script to Automate Tasks

You could use a simple script, for example, to examine your system log for certain keywords. If the script is run via your system's scheduling table, /etc/crontab, it can help automate security monitoring. By combining the output capabilities of existing Linux commands with the language facilities of the shell, you can quickly build a useful script to perform a task normally requiring a number of command lines. For example, you can create a short script, named greplog, like this:

```
#!/bin/sh
#    name:  greplog
#      use:  mail grep of designated log using keyword
# version:  v.01 08aug02
#
#  author: bb
#
# usage: greplog [keyword] [logpathname]
#
#  bugs: does not check for correct number of arguments

# build report name using keyword search and date
log_report=/tmp/$1.logreport.`date '+%m%d%y'`

# build report header with system type, hostname, date and time
echo "==============================================================" \
      >$log_report
echo "           S Y S T E M   M O N I T O R   L O G" >>$log_report
echo uname -a >>$log_report
echo "Log report for" `hostname -f` "on" `date '+%c'`      >>$log_report
echo "==============================================================" \
      >>$log_report ; echo "" >>$log_report

# record log search start
echo "Search for->" $1 "starting" `date '+%r'` >>$log_report
echo "" >>$log_report

# get and save grep results of keyword ($1) from logfile ($2)
grep -i $1 $2 >>$log_report

# build report footer with time
echo "" >>$log_report
echo "End of" $log_report at `date '+%r'` >>$log_report

# mail report to root
mail -s "Log Analysis for $1" root <$log_report
```

```
# clean up and remove report
rm $log_report
exit 0
```

In this example, the script creates the variable `$log_report`, which will be the filename of the temporary report. The keyword ($1) and first argument on the command line is used as part of the filename, along with the current date (with perhaps a better approach to use $$ instead of the date, which will append the script's PID as a file extension). Next, the report header containing some formatted text, the output of the `uname` command, and the hostname and date is added to the report. The start of the search is then recorded, and any matches of the keyword in the log are added to the report. A footer containing the name of the report and the time is then added. The report is mailed to root with the search term as the subject of the message, and the temporary file is deleted.

You can test the script by running it manually and feeding it a keyword and a pathname to the system log, `/var/log/messages`, like this:

```
# greplog FAILED /var/log/messages
```

Note that your system should be running the `syslogd` daemon. If any login failures have occurred on your system, the root operator might get an email message that looks like this:

```
Date: Thu, 23 Oct 2003 16:23:24 -0400
From: root <root@stinkpad.home.org>
To: root@stinkpad.home.org
Subject: FAILED

=============================================================
          S Y S T E M   M O N I T O R   L O G
Linux stinky 2.4.22-1.2088.nptl #1 Thu Oct 9 20:21:24 EDT 2003 i686 i686 i386
+GNU/Linux
Log report for stinkpad.home.org on Thu 23 Oct 2003 04:23:24 PM EDT
=============================================================

Search for-> FAILED starting 04:23:24 PM

Oct 23 16:23:04 stinkpad login[1769]: FAILED LOGIN 3 FROM (null) FOR bball,
+Authentication failure

End of /tmp/FAILED.logreport.102303 at 04:23:24 PM
```

To further automate the process, you can include command lines using the script in another script to generate a series of searches and reports.

Built-In Variables

Built-in variables are special variables provided to shell by Linux that can be used to make decisions within a shell program. You cannot modify the values of these variables within the shell program.

Some of these variables are:

- `$#`—Number of positional parameters passed to the shell program
- `$?`—Completion code of the last command or shell program executed within the shell program (returned value)
- `$0`—The name of the shell program
- `$*`—A single string of all arguments passed at the time of invocation of the shell program

To show these built-in variables in use, here is a sample program called `mypgm2`:

```
#!/bin/sh
#my test program
echo "Number of parameters is $#"
echo "Program name is $0"
echo "Parameters as a single string is $*"
```

If you execute `mypgm2` from the command line in `pdksh` and `bash` as follows,

```
$ bash mypgm2 Sanjiv Guha
```

you get the following result:

```
Number of parameters is 2
Program name is mypgm2
Parameters as a single string is Sanjiv Guha
```

Special Characters

Some characters have special meaning to Linux shells; these characters represent commands, denote specific use for surrounding text, or provide search parameters. Special characters provide a sort of shorthand by incorporating these rather complex meanings into a simple character. Some special characters are shown in Table 11.2.

TABLE 11.2 Special Shell Characters

Character	Explanation
$	Indicates the beginning of a shell variable name
¦	Pipes standard output to next command
#	Starts a comment
&	Executes a process in the background
?	Matches one character
*	Matches one or more characters
>	Output redirection operator
<	Input redirection operator
`	Command substitution (the backquote or backtick—the key above the Tab key on most keyboards)
>>	Output redirection operator (to append to a file)
<<	Wait until following end-of-input string (HERE operator)
[ ]	Range of characters
[a-z]	All characters a through z
[a,z] or [az]	Characters a or z
Space	Delimiter between two words

Special characters are very useful to you when you're creating shell scripts, but if you inadvertently use a special character as part of variable names or strings, your program will behave incorrectly. As you learn in later parts of this section, you can use one of the special characters in a string if you precede it with an *escape character* (/, or backslash) to indicate that it isn't being used as a special character and shouldn't be treated as such by the program.

A few special characters deserve special note. They are the double quotes ("), the single quotes ('), the backslash (\), and the backtick (`)—all discussed in the following sections.

Using Double Quotes to Resolve Variables in Strings with Embedded Spaces

If a string contains embedded spaces, you can enclose the string in double quotes (") so that the shell interprets the whole string as one entity instead of more than one.

For example, if you assigned the value of `abc def` (`abc` followed by one space, followed by `def`) to a variable called `x` in a shell program as follows, you would get an error because the shell would try to execute `def` as a separate command:

Command	Environment
`x="abc def"`	`pdksh and bash`
`set x = "adb` `def"`	`tcsh`

The shell will execute the string as a single command if you surround the string in double quotes as follows:

Command	Environment
`x=abc def`	`pdksh and bash`
`set x=abc` `def`	`tcsh`

The double quotes resolve all variables within the string. Here is an example for `pdksh` and `bash`:

```
var="test string"
newvar="Value of var is $var"
echo $newvar
```

Here is the same example for `tcsh`:

```
set var="test string"
set newvar="Value of var is $var"
echo $newvar
```

If you execute a shell program containing the preceding three lines, you get the following result:

```
Value of var is test string
```

Using Single Quotes to Maintain Unexpanded Variables

You can surround a string with single quotes (`'`) to stop the shell from expanding variables and interpreting special characters. When used for the latter purpose, the single quote is an *escape character*, similar to the backslash, which you learn about in the next section. Here, you learn how to use the single quote to avoid expanding a variable in a shell script. An unexpanded variable maintains its original form in the output.

In the following examples, the double quotes in the preceding examples have been changed to single quotes.

```
pdksh and bash:
var='test string'
newvar='Value of var is $var'
echo $newvar
tcsh:
set var = 'test string'
set newvar = 'Value of var is $var'
echo $newvar
```

If you execute a shell program containing these three lines, you get the following result:

```
Value of var is $var
```

As you can see, the variable `var` maintains its original format in the results, rather than having been expanded.

Using the Backslash as an Escape Character

As you learned earlier, the backslash (\) serves as an escape character that stops the shell from interpreting the succeeding character as a special character. Say that you want to assign a value of `$test` to a variable called `var`. If you use the following command, the shell reads the special character $ and interprets `$test` as the value of the variable `test`. No value has been assigned to `test`; a null value is stored in `var` as follows:

Command	Environment
`var=$test`	`pdksh and bash`
`set` `var=$test`	`tcsh`

Unfortunately, this assignment may work for `bash` and `pdksh`, but it returns an error of "undefined variable" if you use it with `tcsh`. Use the following commands to correctly store `$test` in `var`:

Command	Environment
``var=`wc -l test.txt` ``	`pdksh and bash`
``set var = `wc -l test.txt` ``	`tcsh`

The backslash before the dollar sign (\$) signals the shell to interpret the $ as any other ordinary character an*d not to associate any sp*ecial meaning to it. You could also use single quotes (') around the $test variable to get the same result.

Using the Backtick to Replace a String with Output

You can use the backtick (`) character to signal the shell to replace a string with its output when executed. This is called command substitution. This special character can be used in shell programs when you want the result of the execution of a command to be stored in a variable. For example, if you want to count the number of lines in a file called `test.txt` in the current directory and store the result in a variable called `var`, you can use the following command:

Command	Environment
`var=\$test`	pdksh and bash
`set var = \$test`	tcsh

Comparison of Expressions in pdksh and bash

Comparing values or evaluating the differences between similar bits of data—such as file information, character strings, or numbers—is a task known as *comparison of expressions*. Comparison of expressions is an integral part of using logic in shell programs to accomplish tasks. The way the logical comparison of two operators (numeric or string) is done varies slightly in different shells. In `pdksh` and `bash`, a command called `test` can be used to achieve comparisons of expressions. In `tcsh`, you can write an expression to accomplish the same thing.

This section covers comparison operations using the `pdksh` or `bash` shells. Later in the chapter, you learn how to compare expressions in the `tcsh` shell.

The `pdksh` and `bash` shell syntax provide a command named `test` to compare strings, numbers, and files. The syntax of the `test` command is as follows:

```
test expression
or
[ expression ]
```

Both forms of the `test` commands are processed the same way by `pdksh` and `bash`. The `test` commands support the following types of comparisons:

- String comparison
- Numeric comparison
- File operators
- Logical operators

String Comparison

The following operators can be used to compare two string expressions:

- `=`—To compare whether two strings are equal
- `!=`—To compare whether two strings are not equal
- `-n`—To evaluate whether the string length is greater than zero
- `-z`—To evaluate whether the string length is equal to zero

Next are some examples using these operators when comparing two strings, `string1` and `string2`, in a shell program called `compare1`:

```
#!/bin/sh
string1="abc"
string2="abd"
if [ $string1 = $string2 ]; then
   echo "string1 equal to string2"
else
   echo "string1 not equal to string2"
fi

if [ $string2 != string1 ]; then
   echo "string2 not equal to string1"
else
   echo "string2 equal to string2"
fi

if [ $string1 ]; then
   echo "string1 is not empty"
else
   echo "string1 is empty"
fi

if [ -n $string2 ]; then
   echo "string2 has a length greater than zero"
else
   echo "string2 has length equal to zero"
fi

if [ -z $string1 ]; then
   echo "string1 has a length equal to zero"
else
  echo "string1 has a length greater than zero"
fi
```

If you execute compare1, you get the following result:

```
string1 not equal to string2
string2 not equal to string1
string1 is not empty
string2 has a length greater than zero
string1 has a length greater than zero
```

If two strings are not equal in size, the system pads out the shorter string with trailing spaces for comparison. That is, if the value of `string1` is `abc` and that of `string2` is `ab`, string2 will be padded with a trailing space for comparison purposes—it will have a value of ab.

Number Comparison The following operators can be used to compare two numbers:

- -eq—To compare whether two numbers are equal
- -ge—To compare whether one number is greater than or equal to the other number
- -le—To compare whether one number is less than or equal to the other number
- -ne—To compare whether two numbers are not equal
- -gt—To compare whether one number is greater than the other number
- -lt—To compare whether one number is less than the other number

The following shell program compares three numbers, number1, number2, and number3:

```
#!/bin/sh
number1=5
number2=10
number3=5

if [ $number1 -eq $number3 ]; then
   echo "number1 is equal to number3"
else
   echo "number1 is not equal to number3"
fi

if [ $number1 -ne $number2 ]; then
   echo "number1 is not equal to number2"
else
   echo "number1 is equal to number2"
fi

if [ $number1 -gt $number2 ]; then
   echo "number1 is greater than number2"
else
   echo "number1 is not greater than number2"
fi

if [ $number1 -ge $number3 ]; then
   echo "number1 is greater than or equal to number3"
else
   echo "number1 is not greater than or equal to number3"
fi

if [ $number1 -lt $number2 ]; then
```

```
   echo "number1 is less than number2"
else
   echo "number1 is not less than number2"
fi

if [ $number1 -le $number3 ]; then
   echo "number1 is less than or equal to number3"
else
   echo "number1 is not less than or equal to number3"
fi
```

When you execute the shell program, you get the following results:

```
number1 is equal to number3
number1 is not equal to number2
number1 is not greater than number2
number1 is greater than or equal to number3
number1 is less than number2
number1 is less than or equal to number3
```

File Operators

The following operators can be used as file comparison operators:

- `-d`—To ascertain whether a file is a directory
- `-f`—To ascertain whether a file is a regular file
- `-r`—To ascertain whether read permission is set for a file
- `-s`—To ascertain whether a file exists and has a length greater than zero
- `-w`—To ascertain whether write permission is set for a file
- `-x`—To ascertain whether execute permission is set for a file

Assume that a shell program called `compare3` is in a directory with a file called `file1` and a subdirectory `dir1` under the current directory. Assume that `file1` has a permission of `r-x` (read and execute permission) and `dir1` has a permission of `rwx` (read, write, and execute permission). The code for the shell program would look like this:

```
#!/bin/sh
if [ -d $dir1 ]; then
   echo "dir1 is a directory"
else
   echo "dir1 is not a directory"
fi

if [ -f $dir1 ]; then
   echo "dir1 is a regular file"
else
```

```
   echo "dir1 is not a regular file"
fi

if [ -r $file1 ]; then
   echo "file1 has read permission"
else
   echo "file1 does not have read permission"
fi

if [ -w $file1 ]; then
   echo "file1 has write permission"
else
   echo "file1 does not have write permission"
fi

if [ -x $dir1 ]; then
   echo "dir1 has execute permission"
else
   echo "dir1 does not have execute permission"
fi
```

If you execute the shell program, you get the following results:

```
dir1 is a directory
file1 is a regular file
file1 has read permission
file1 does not have write permission
dir1 has execute permission
```

Logical Operators

Logical operators are used to compare expressions using Boolean logic, which compares values using characters representing `NOT`, `AND`, and `OR`.

- `!`—To negate a logical expression
- `-a`—To logically `AND` two logical expressions
- `-o`—To logically `OR` two logical expressions

This example named `logic` uses the file and directory mentioned in the previous `compare3` example.

```
#!/bin/sh
if [ -x file1 -a -x dir1 ]; then
   echo file1 and dir1 are executable
else
   echo at least one of file1 or dir1 are not executable
fi
```

```
if [ -w file1 -o -w dir1 ]; then
   echo file1 or dir1 are writable
else
   echo neither file1 or dir1 are executable
fi

if [ ! -w file1 ]; then
   echo file1 is not writable
else
   echo file1 is writable
fi
If you execute logic, it will yield the following result:
file1 and dir1 are executable
file1 or dir1 are writable
file1 is not writable
```

Comparing Expressions with `tcsh`

As stated earlier, the method for comparing expressions in `tcsh` is different from the method used under `pdksh` and `bash`. The comparison of expression demonstrated in this section uses the syntax necessary for the `tcsh` shell environment.

String Comparison

The following operators can be used to compare two string expressions:

- `==`—To compare whether two strings are equal
- `!=`—To compare whether two strings are not equal

The following examples compare two strings, `string1` and `string2`, in the shell program `compare1`:

```
#!/bin/tcsh
set string1 = "abc"
set string2 = "abd"

if  (string1 == string2)  then
   echo "string1 equal to string2"
else
   echo "string1 not equal to string2"
endif

if  (string2 != string1)  then
   echo "string2 not equal to string1"
else
   echo "string2 equal to string1"
endif
```

If you execute compare1, you get the following results:

```
string1 not equal to string2
string2 not equal to string1
```

Number Comparison

These operators can be used to compare two numbers:

- >=—To compare whether one number is greater than or equal to the other number
- <=—To compare whether one number is less than or equal to the other number
- >—To compare whether one number is greater than the other number
- <—To compare whether one number is less than the other number

The next examples compare two numbers, number1 and number2, in a shell program called compare2:

```
#!/bin/tcsh
set number1=5
set number2=10
set number3=5

if  ($number1 > $number2)  then
   echo "number1 is greater than number2"
else
   echo "number1 is not greater than number2"
endif

if  ($number1 >= $number3) then
   echo "number1 is greater than or equal to number3"
else
   echo "number1 is not greater than or equal to number3"
endif

if  ($number1 < $number2)  then
   echo "number1 is less than number2"
else
   echo "number1 is not less than number2"
endif

if  ($number1 <= $number3) then
   echo "number1 is less than or equal to number3"
else
   echo "number1 is not less than or equal to number3"
endif
```

When executing the shell program compare2, you get the following results:

```
number1 is not greater than number2
number1 is greater than or equal to number3
number1 is less than number2
number1 is less than or equal to number3
```

File Operators

These operators can be used as file comparison operators:

- -d—To ascertain whether a file is a directory
- -e—To ascertain whether a file exists
- -f—To ascertain whether a file is a regular file
- -o—To ascertain whether a user is the owner of a file
- -r—To ascertain whether read permission is set for a file
- -w—To ascertain whether write permission is set for a file
- -x—To ascertain whether execute permission is set for a file
- -z—To ascertain whether the file size is zero

The following examples are based on a shell program called compare3, which is in a directory with a file called file1 and a subdirectory dir1 under the current directory. Assume that file1 has a permission of r-x (read and execute permission) and dir1 has a permission of rwx (read, write, and execute permission).

The following is the code for the compare3 shell program:

```
#!/bin/tcsh
if  (-d dir1) then
   echo "dir1 is a directory"
else
   echo "dir1 is not a directory"
endif

if (-f dir1)  then
   echo "file1 is a regular file"
else
   echo "file1 is not a regular file"
endif

if (-r file1) then
   echo "file1 has read permission"
else
   echo "file1 does not have read permission"
```

```
endif

if (-w file1) then
   echo "file1 has write permission"
else
   echo "file1 does not have write permission"
endif

if (-x dir1) then
   echo "dir1 has execute permission"
else
   echo "dir1 does not have execute permission"
endif

if (-z file1) then
   echo "file1 has zero length"
else
   echo "file1 has greater than zero length"
endif
```

If you execute the file `compare3`, you get the following results:

```
dir1 is a directory
file1 is a regular file
file1 has read permission
file1 does not have write permission
dir1 has execute permission
file1 has greater than zero length
```

Logical Operators

Logical operators are used with conditional statements. These operators are used to negate a logical expression or to perform logical ANDs and ORs:

- `!`—To negate a logical expression
- `&&`—To logically `AND` two logical expressions
- `||`—To logically `OR` two logical expressions

This example named `logic` uses the file and directory mentioned in the previous `compare3` example.

```
#!/bin/tcsh
if ( -x file1 && -x dir1 ) then
   echo file1 and dir1 are executable
else
   echo at least one of file1 or dir1 are not executable
endif
```

```
if ( -w file1 || -w dir1 ) then
   echo file1 or dir1 are writable
else
   echo neither file1 or dir1 are executable
endif

if ( ! -w file1 ) then
   echo file1 is not writable
else
   echo file1 is writable
endif
```

If you execute `logic`, it will yield the following result:

```
file1 and dir1 are executable
file1 or dir1 are writable
file1 is not writable
```

The `for` Statement

The `for` statement is used to execute a set of commands once each time a specified condition is true. The `for` statement has a number of formats. The first format used by `pdksh` and `bash` is as follows:

```
for curvar in list
do
    statements
done
```

This form should be used if you want to execute `statements` once for each value in `list`. For each iteration, the current value of the list is assigned to `vcurvar`. `list` can be a variable containing a number of items or a list of values separated by spaces. The second format is as follows:

```
for curvar
do
    statements
done
```

In this form, the `statements` are executed once for each of the positional parameters passed to the shell program. For each iteration, the current value of the positional parameter is assigned to the variable `curvar`.

This form can also be written as follows:

```
for curvar in $
do
```

```
    statements
done
```

Remember that `$@` gives you a list of positional parameters passed to the shell program, quoted in a manner consistent with the way the user originally invoked the command.

Under `tcsh`, the `for` statement is called `foreach`. The format is as follows:

```
foreach curvar (list)
    statements
end
```

In this form, `statements` are executed once for each value in `list`, and, for each iteration, the current value of `list` is assigned to `curvar`.

Suppose that you want to create a backup version of each file in a directory to a subdirectory called `backup`. You can do the following in `pdksh` and `bash`:

```
#!/bin/sh
for filename in *
do
   cp $filename backup/$filename
   if [ $? -ne 0 ]; then
      echo "copy for $filename failed"
   fi
done
```

In the preceding example, a backup copy of each file is created. If the copy fails, a message is generated.

The same example in `tcsh` is as follows:

```
#!/bin/tcsh
foreach filename (`/bin/ls`)
   cp $filename backup/$filename
   if ($? != 0) then
      echo "copy for $filename failed"
   endif
end
```

The while Statement

The `while` statement can be used to execute a series of commands while a specified condition is true. The loop terminates as soon as the specified condition evaluates to false. It is possible that the loop will not execute at all if the specified condition initially evaluates to false. You should be careful with the `while` command because the loop will never terminate if the specified condition never evaluates to false.

ENDLESS LOOPS HAVE THEIR PLACE IN SHELL PROGRAMS

Endless loops can sometimes be useful. For example, you can easily construct a simple command that constantly monitors the 802.11b link quality of a network interface by using a few lines of script:

```
#!/bin/sh
while :
 do
   /sbin/iwconfig eth0 ¦  grep Link ¦ tr '\n' '\r'
 done
```

The script outputs the search, and then the `tr` command formats the output. The result is a simple animation of a constantly updated single line of information:

Link Quality:92/92 Signal level:-11 dBm Noise level:-102 dBm

This technique can also be used to create a graphical monitoring client for X that outputs traffic information and activity about a network interface:

```
#!/bin/sh
xterm -geometry 75x2 -e \
bash -c \
 "while :; do \
     /sbin/ifconfig eth0 ¦ \
     grep 'TX bytes' ¦
      tr '\n' '\r' ; \
done"
```

The simple example uses a bash command-line script (enabled by -c) to execute a command line repeatedly. The command line pipes the output of the `ifconfig` command through `grep`, which searches `ifconfig`'s output and then pipes a line containing the string `"TX bytes"` to the `tr` command. The `tr` command then removes the carriage return at the end of the line to display the information inside an `/xterm` X11 terminal window, automatically sized by the `-geometry` option:

```
RX bytes:4117594780 (3926.8 Mb)  TX bytes:452230967 (431.2 Mb)
```

Endless loops can be so useful that Linux includes a command that will repeatedly execute a given command line. For example, you can get a quick report about a system's hardware health by using the sensors command. But instead of using a shell script to loop the output endlessly, you can use the `watch` command to repeat the information and provide simple animation:

```
$ watch "sensors -f ¦ cut -c 1-20"
```

In pdksh and bash, the following format is used for the while flow control construct:

```
while expression
do
    statements
done
In tcsh, the following format is used:
while (expression)
    Statements
end
```

If you want to add the first five even numbers, you can use the following shell program in pdksh and bash:

```
#!/bin/bash
loopcount=0
result=0
while [ $loopcount -lt 5 ]
do
   loopcount=`expr $loopcount + 1`
   increment=`expr $loopcount \* 2`
   result=`expr $result + $increment`
done

echo "result is $result"
```

In tcsh, this program can be written as follows:

```
#!/bin/tcsh
set loopcount = 0
set result = 0
while ($loopcount < 5)
   set loopcount = `expr $loopcount + 1`
   set increment = `expr $loopcount \* 2`
   set result = `expr $result + $increment`

end

echo "result is $result"
```

The until Statement

The until statement can be used to execute a series of commands until a specified condition is true.

The loop terminates as soon as the specified condition evaluates to True.

In pdksh and bash, the following format is used:

```
until expression
do
    statements
done
```

As you can see, the format of the until statement is similar to that of the while statement, but the logic is different: In a while loop, you execute until an expression is False, but in an until loop, you loop until the expression is True.

If you want to add the first five even numbers, you can use the following shell program in pdksh and bash:

```
#!/bin/bash
loopcount=0
result=0
until [ $loopcount -ge 5 ]
do
   loopcount=`expr $loopcount + 1`
   increment=`expr $loopcount \* 2`
   result=`expr $result + $increment`
done

echo "result is $result"
```

The example here is identical to the example for the while statement, except that the condition being tested is just the opposite of the condition specified in the while statement.

The tcsh shell does not support the until statement.

The repeat Statement (tcsh)

The repeat statement is used to execute only one command a fixed number of times.

If you want to print a hyphen (-) 80 times with one hyphen per line on the screen, you can use the following command:

```
repeat  80 echo '-'
```

The select Statement (pdksh)

The select statement is used to generate a menu list if you are writing a shell program that expects input from the user online. The format of the select statement is as follows:

```
select  item in itemlist
do
    Statements
```

```
done
```

itemlist is optional. If it isn't provided, the system iterates through the item entries one at a time. If itemlist is provided, however, the system iterates for each entry in itemlist and the current value of itemlist is assigned to item for each iteration, which then can be used as part of the statements being executed.

If you want to write a menu that gives the user a choice of picking a Continue or a Finish, you can write the following shell program:

```
#!/bin/ksh
select  item in Continue Finish
do
   if [ $item = "Finish" ]; then
      break
   fi
done
```

When the select command is executed, the system displays a menu with numeric choices to the user—in this case, 1 for Continue and 2 for Finish. If the user chooses 1, the variable item contains a value of Continue; if the user chooses 2, the variable item contains a value of Finish. When the user chooses 2, the if statement is executed and the loop terminates.

The shift Statement

The shift statement is used to process the positional parameters, one at a time, from left to right. As you'll remember, the positional parameters are identified as $1, $2, $3, and so on. The effect of the shift command is that each positional parameter is moved one position to the left and the current $1 parameter is lost.

The shift statement is useful when you are writing shell programs in which a user can pass various options. Depending on the specified option, the parameters that follow can mean different things or might not be there at all.

The format of the shift command is as follows:

```
shift  number
```

The parameter number is the number of places to be shifted and is optional. If not specified, the default is 1; that is, the parameters are shifted one position to the left. If specified, the parameters are shifted number positions to the left.

The if Statement

The if statement evaluates a logical expression to make a decision. An if condition has the following format in pdksh and bash:

```
if [ expression ]; then
    Statements
```

```
elif [ expression ]; then
    Statements
else
    Statements
fi
```

The if conditions can be nested. That is, an if condition can contain another if condition within it. It isn't necessary for an if condition to have an elif or else part. The else part is executed if none of the expressions that are specified in the if statement and are optional if subsequent elif statements are true. The word fi is used to indicate the end of the if statements, which is very useful if you have nested if conditions. In such a case, you should be able to match fi to if to ensure that all if statements are properly coded.

In the following example for bash or pdksh, a variable var can have either of two values: Yes or No. Any other value is invalid. This can be coded as follows:

```
if [ $var = "Yes" ]; then
   echo "Value is Yes"
elif [ $var = "No" ]; then
   echo "Value is No"
else
   echo "Invalid value"
fi
```

In tcsh, the if statement has two forms. The first form, similar to the one for pdksh and bash, is as follows:

```
if (expression) then
    Statements
else if (expression) then
    Statements
else
    Statements
endif
```

The if conditions can be nested—that is, an if condition can contain another if condition within it. It isn't necessary for an if condition to have an else part. The else part is executed if none of the expressions specified in any of the if statements are true. The optional if part of the statement (else if (expression) then) is executed if the condition following it is true and the previous if statement is not true. The word endif is used to indicate the end of the if statements, which is very useful if you have nested if conditions. In such a case, you should be able to match endif to if to ensure that all if statements are properly coded.

Using the example of the variable var having only two values, Yes and No, here is how it would be coded with tcsh:

```
if ($var == "Yes") then
```

```
   echo "Value is Yes"
else if ($var == "No" ) then
   echo "Value is No"
else
   echo "Invalid value"
endif
```

The second form of the `if` condition for `tcsh` is as follows:

```
if (expression) command
```

In this format, only a single command can be executed if the expression evaluates to true.

The case Statement

The `case` statement is used to execute statements depending on a discrete value or a range of values matching the specified variable. In most cases, you can use a `case` statement instead of an `if` statement if you have a large number of conditions.

The format of a `case` statement for `pdksh` and `bash` is as follows:

```
case str in
   str1 | str2)
      Statements;;
   str3|str4)
      Statements;;
   *)
      Statements;;
esac
```

You can specify a number of discrete values—such as `str1`, `str2`, and so on—for each condition, or you can specify a value with a wildcard. The last condition should be `*` (asterisk) and is executed if none of the other conditions are met. For each of the specified conditions, all the associated statements until the double semicolon (;;) are executed.

You can write a script that will echo the name of the month if you provide the month number as a parameter. If you provide a number that isn't between 1 and 12, you will get an error message. The script is as follows:

```
#!/bin/sh


case $1 in
   01 | 1) echo "Month is January";;
   02 | 2) echo "Month is February";;
   03 | 3) echo "Month is March";;
   04 | 4) echo "Month is April";;
   05 | 5) echo "Month is May";;
   06 | 6) echo "Month is June";;
```

```
    07|7) echo "Month is July";;
    08|8) echo "Month is August";;
    09|9) echo "Month is September";;
    10) echo "Month is October";;
    11) echo "Month is November";;
    12) echo "Month is December";;
    *) echo "Invalid parameter";;
esac
```

You need to end the statements under each condition with a double semicolon (;;). If you do not, the statements under the next condition will also be executed.

The format for a case statement for tcsh is as follows:

```
switch (str)
   case str1|str2:
      Statements
      breaksw
   case str3|str4:
      Statements
      breaksw
   default:
      Statements
      breaksw
endsw
```

You can specify a number of discrete values—such as str1, str2, and so on—for each condition, or you can specify a value with a wildcard. The last condition should be default and is executed if none of the other conditions are met. For each of the specified conditions, all the associated statements until breaksw are executed.

The example that echoes the month when a number is given, shown earlier for pdksh and bash, can be written in tcsh as follows:

```
#!/bin/tcsh


set month = 5
switch  ( $month )
   case 1: echo "Month is January" ;  breaksw
   case 2: echo "Month is February" ;  breaksw
   case 3: echo "Month is March" ;  breaksw
   case 4: echo "Month is April" ;  breaksw
   case 5: echo "Month is May" ;  breaksw
   case 6: echo "Month is June" ;  breaksw
   case 7: echo "Month is July" ;  breaksw
   case 8: echo "Month is August"  ;  breaksw
   case 9: echo "Month is September" ;  breaksw
```

```
   case 10: echo "Month is October" ;  breaksw
   case 11: echo "Month is November" ;  breaksw
   case 12: echo "Month is December" ;  breaksw
   default: echo "Oops! Month is Octember!" ;  breaksw
endsw
```

You need to end the statements under each condition with `breaksw`. If you do not, the statements under the next condition will also be executed.

The `break` and `exit` Statements

You should be aware of two other statements: the `break` statement and the `exit` statement.

The `break` statement can be used to terminate an iteration loop, such as a `for`, `until`, or `repeat` command.

`exit` statements can be used to exit a shell program. You can optionally use a number after `exit`. If the current shell program has been called by another shell program, the calling program can check for the code (the `$?` or `$status` variable, depending on shell) and make a decision accordingly.

Using Functions in Shell Scripts

As with other programming languages, shell programs also support functions. A function is a piece of a shell program that performs a particular process; you can reuse the same function multiple times within the shell program. Functions help eliminate the need for duplicating code as you write shell programs.

The following is the format of a function in `pdksh` and `bash`:

```
func(){
   Statements
}
```

You can call a function as follows:

```
func param1 param2 param3
```

The parameters `param1`, `param2`, and so on are optional. You can also pass the parameters as a single string—for example, `$@`. A function can parse the parameters as if they were positional parameters passed to a shell program from the command line as command-line arguments, but instead use values passed inside the script. For example, the following script uses a function named `Displaymonth()` that displays the name of the month or an error message if you pass a month number out of the range 1 to 12. This example works with `pdksh` and `bash`:

```
#!/bin/sh
Displaymonth() {
   case $1 in
      01 | 1) echo "Month is January";;
```

```
      02 ¦ 2) echo "Month is February";;
      03 ¦ 3) echo "Month is March";;
      04 ¦ 4) echo "Month is April";;
      05 ¦ 5) echo "Month is May";;
      06 ¦ 6) echo "Month is June";;
      07 ¦ 7) echo "Month is July";;
      08 ¦ 8) echo "Month is August";;
      09 ¦ 9) echo "Month is September";;
      10) echo "Month is October";;
      11) echo "Month is November";;
      12) echo "Month is December";;
      *) echo "Invalid parameter";;
   esac
}
Displaymonth 8
```

The preceding program displays the following output:

```
Month is August
```

RELATED UBUNTU AND LINUX COMMANDS

You can use these commands and tools when using the shell or writing shell scripts:

- `chsh`—Command used to change one's login shell
- `kibitz`—Allows two-person interaction with a single shell
- `mc`—A visual shell named the GNU Midnight Commander
- `nano`—An easy-to-use text editor for the console
- `shar`—Command used to create shell archives
- `vi`—The `vi` (actually `vim`) text editor

Reference

- `/usr/src/linux/init/main.c`—The best place to learn about how Linux boots. Fascinating reading, really. Get it from the source! You need to have the kernel source installed to read this.
- https://help.ubuntu.com/community/Grub2—Ubuntu community documentation for GRUB2.
- www.ibm.com/developerworks/linux/library/l-grub2/index.html—An IBM guide for migrating to GRUB2.The still yet-to-be-completed manual can be found at www.gnu.org/software/grub/manual/.
- www.gnu.org/software/bash/bash.html—The `bash` home page at the GNU Software Project.

- www.tldp.org/LDP/abs/html/—Mendel Cooper's "Advanced Bash-Scripting Guide."
- www.freeos.com/guides/lsst/—Linux shell scripting tutorial.
- http://kornshell.com/—The Korn Shell website.
- http://web.cs.mun.ca/~michael/pdksh/—The `pdksh` home page.
- www.tcsh.org/—Find out more about `tcsh` here.
- www.zsh.org/—Examine `zsh` in more detail here.

CHAPTER 12

System-Monitoring Tools

IN THIS CHAPTER

- Console-Based Monitoring
- Graphical Process and System Management Tools
- KDE Process- and System-Monitoring Tools
- Reference

To keep your system in optimum shape, you need to be able to monitor it closely. This is imperative in a corporate environment where uptime is vital and any system failures and downtime can be quite expensive. Whether it is checking processes for errant daemons, or keeping a close eye on CPU and memory usage, Ubuntu provides a wealth of utilities designed to give you as little or as much feedback as you want. This chapter looks at some of the basic monitoring tools, along with some tactics designed to keep your system up longer. Some of the monitoring tools cover network connectivity, memory, and hard drive usage, and you will learn how to manipulate active system processes, using a mixture of graphical and command-line tools.

Console-Based Monitoring

Those familiar with UNIX system administration already know the `ps`, or process display, command commonly found on most flavors of UNIX. Because of the close relationship between Linux and UNIX, it also includes this command, which allows you to see the current processes running on the system, as well as who owns them and how resource-hungry they are.

Although the Linux kernel has its own distinct architecture and memory management, it also benefits from enhanced use of the `/proc` file system, the virtual file system found on many UNIX flavors. Through the `/proc` file system you can communicate directly with the kernel to get a deep view of what is currently happening. Developers tend to use the `/proc` file system as a way of extracting information from the kernel and for their programs to manipulate that information into more human readable formats. A full discussion of the /proc file system is beyond the scope of this book. To get a better idea of what it contains you can take a look at http://en.tldp.org/LDP/Linux-Filesystem-Hierarchy/html/proc.html for an excellent and in-depth guide.

Processes can also be controlled at the command line, which is important because you might sometimes have only a command-line interface. Whenever an application or command is launched, either from the command line or a clicked icon, the process that comes from the kernel is assigned an identification number called a *process ID* or *PID* for short. This number is shown in the shell if the program is launched via the command line.

```
matthew@seymour:~$ gedit &

[1] 9649
```

In this example, gedit has been launched in the background, and the (bash) shell reported a shell job number ([1] in this case). A job number or job control is a shell-specific feature that allows a different form of process control, such as sending or suspending programs to the background and retrieving background jobs to the foreground (see your shell's man pages for more information if you are not using bash).

The second number displayed (9649 in this example) represents the process ID. You can get a quick list of your processes by using the ps command like this:

```
matthew@seymour:~$ ps
  PID TTY          TIME CMD

 9595 pts/0    00:00:00 bash

 9656 pts/0    00:00:00 gedit

 9657 pts/0    00:00:00 ps
```

As you can see, the output includes the process ID, abbreviated as PID, along with other information, such as the name of the running program. As with any UNIX command, many options are available; the proc man page has a full list. One useful option is -e, which lists all processes running on the system. Another is aux, which provides a more detailed list of all the processes. You should also know that ps works not by polling memory, but through the interrogation of the Linux /proc or process file system.

The /proc directory contains many files—some of which include constantly updated hardware information (such as battery power levels, and so on). Linux administrators often pipe the output of ps through grep to display information about a specific program, like this:

```
matthew@seymour:~$ ps aux | grep bash
matthew       9656  0.0  0.1  21660  4460 pts/0    Ss   11:39   0:00 bash
```

This example returns the owner (the user who launched the program) and the PID, along with other information, such as the percentage of CPU and memory usage, size of the command (code, data, and stack), time (or date) the command was launched, and name of the command. Processes can also be queried by PID like this:

```
matthew@seymour:~$ ps 9656
  PID TTY      STAT   TIME COMMAND
 9656 pts/0    S      0:00 gedit
```

You can use the PID to stop a running process by using the shell's built-in `kill` command. This command asks the kernel to stop a running process and reclaim system memory. For example, to stop `gedit` in the example, use the `kill` command like this:

```
matthew@seymour:~$ kill 9656
```

After you press Enter, then press Enter again, the shell reports

```
[1]+  Terminated              gedit
```

Note that users can `kill` only their own processes, but `root` can kill them all. Controlling any other running process requires root permission, which should be used judiciously (especially when forcing a `kill` by using the `-9` option); by inadvertently killing the wrong process through a typo in the command, you could bring down an active system.

Using the `kill` Command to Control Processes

The `kill` command is a basic UNIX system command. You can communicate with a running process by entering a command into its interface, such as when you type into a text editor. But some processes (usually system processes rather than application processes) run without such an interface, and you need a way to communicate with them as well, so we use a system of signals. The `kill` system accomplishes that by sending a signal to a process, and you can use it to communicate with any process. The general format of the `kill` command is

```
matthew@seymour:~$ kill option PID
```

Note that if you are using `kill` on a process you do not own, you need to have super-user privileges and preface the `kill` command with `sudo`.

A number of signal options can be sent as words or numbers, but most are of interest only to programmers. One of the most common is the one we used previously to kill gedit:

```
matthew@seymour:~$ kill PID
```

This tells the process with PID to stop; you supply the actual PID. However, without a signal option, there is no guarantee that a process will be killed, because programs can catch, block, or ignore some terminate signals (and this is a good thing, by design).

```
matthew@seymour:~$ kill -9 PID
```

This includes a signal for `kill` that cannot be caught (9 is the number of the SIGKILL signal); you can use this combination when the plain `kill` shown previously does not work. Be careful, though. Using this does not allow a process to shut down gracefully, and shutting down gracefully is usually preferred because it closes things out that the process may have been using and ensures that things such as logs are written before the process disappears.

```
matthew@seymour:~$ kill -1 PID
```

This is the signal to "hang up"—stop—and then clean up all associated processes as well (1 is the number of the `SIGHUP` signal).

As you become proficient at process control and job control, you will learn the utility of a number of `kill` options. A full list of `signal` options can be found in the `kill` man page.

Using Priority Scheduling and Control

No process can make use of the system's resources (CPU, memory, disk access, and so on) as it pleases. After all, the kernel's primary function is to manage the system resources equitably. It does this by assigning a priority to each process so that some processes get better access to system resources and some processes might have to wait longer until their turn arrives. Priority scheduling can be an important tool in managing a system supporting critical applications or in a situation in which CPU and RAM usage must be reserved or allocated for a specific task. Two useful applications included with Ubuntu include the `nice` and `renice` commands. (`nice` is part of the GNU `Coreutils` package, whereas `renice` is inherited from BSD UNIX.)

The `nice` command is used with its `-n` option, along with an argument in the range of `-20` to `19`, in order from highest to lowest priority (the lower the number, the higher the priority). For example, to run the `conky` client with a low priority, use the `nice` command like this (more on conky later in this chapter):

```
matthew@seymour:~$ nice -n 12 conky &
```

The `nice` command is typically used for disk- or CPU-intensive tasks that might be obtrusive or cause system slowdown. The `renice` command can be used to reset the priority of running processes or control the priority and scheduling of all processes owned by a user. Regular users can only numerically increase process priorities (that is, make tasks less important) with this command, but a user with super-user privileges can use `sudo` to access the full nice range of scheduling (`-20` to `19`).

System administrators can also use the `time` command to get an idea of how much time and what proportion of a system's resources are required for a task, such as a shell script. (Here, `time` is used to measure the duration of elapsed time; the command that deals with civil and sidereal time is the `date` command.) This command is used with the name of another command (or script) as an argument like this:

```
matthew@seymour:~$ sudo time -p find / -name conky
/home/matthew/conky
/etc/conky
/usr/lib/conky

/usr/bin/conky
real 30.19
user 1.09
sys 2.77
```

Output of the command displays the time from start to finish, along with the user and system time required. Other factors you can query include memory, CPU usage, and file system input/output (I/O) statistics. See the `time` command's man page for more details.

Nearly all graphical process-monitoring tools include some form of process control or management. Many of the early tools ported to Linux were clones of legacy UNIX utilities. One familiar monitoring (and control) program is `top`. Based on the `ps` command, the `top` command provides a text-based display of constantly updated console-based output showing the most CPU-intensive processes currently running. It can be started like this:

```
matthew@seymour:~$ top
```

After you press Enter, you see a display as shown in Figure 12.1. The `top` command has a few interactive commands: Pressing **h displays the help screen; pressing k prompts you to enter the pid** of a process to kill; pressing **n prompts you to enter the pid** of a process to change its nice value. The top man page describes other commands and includes a detailed description of what all the columns of information `top` can display actually represent; have a look at top's well-written `man` page.

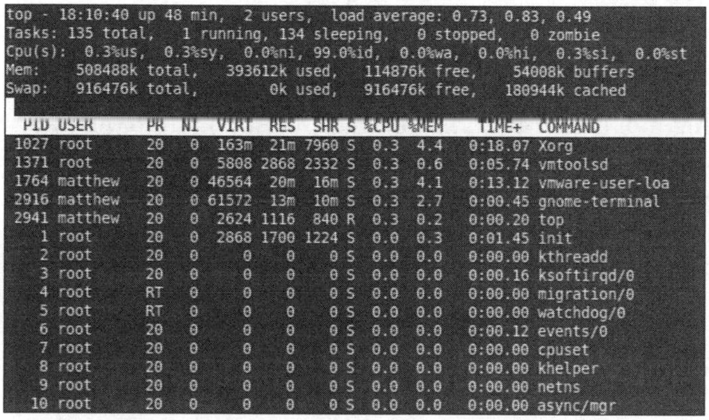

FIGURE 12.1 The **top** command can be used to monitor and control processes.

The `top` command displays quite a bit of information about your system. Processes can be sorted by PID, age, CPU or memory usage, time, or user. This command also provides process management, and system administrators can use its `k` and `r` keypress commands to kill and reschedule running tasks, respectively.

The `top` command uses a fair amount of memory, so you want to be judicious in its use and not leave it running all the time. When you've finished with it, simply press **q to quit top**.

12

Displaying Free and Used Memory with `free`

Although `top` includes some memory information, the `free` utility displays the amount of free and used memory in the system in kilobytes (the `-m` switch displays in megabytes). On one system, the output looks like this:

```
matthew@seymour:~$ free
             total       used       free     shared    buffers     cached
Mem:       4055680    3327764     727916          0     280944    2097568
-/+ buffers/cache:     949252    3106428
Swap:      8787512          0    8787512
```

This output describes a machine with 4GB of RAM memory and a swap partition of 8GB. Note that none of the swap is being used, and that the machine is not heavily loaded. Linux is very good at memory management and "grabs" all the memory it can in anticipation of future work.

TIP

A useful trick is to employ the `watch` command; it repeatedly reruns a command every two seconds by default. If you use

```
matthew@seymour:~$  watch free
```

you can see the output of the free command updated every two seconds. Use Ctrl-C to quit.

Another useful system-monitoring tool is `vmstat` (*virtual memory statistics*). This command reports on processes, memory, I/O, and CPU, typically providing an average since the last reboot; or you can make it report usage for a current period by telling it the time interval in seconds and the number of iterations you desire, like this:

```
matthew@seymour:~$ vmstat 5 10
```

This runs `vmstat` every five seconds for 10 iterations.

Use the `uptime` command to see how long it has been since the last reboot and to get an idea of what the load average has been; higher numbers mean higher loads.

Disk Space

Along with system load it is important to keep an eye on the amount of free hard drive space that your computer has remaining.

It's very easy to do this, mainly by using the `df` command, like this:

```
matthew@seymour:~$ df
```

Just using the command alone returns this output:

```
Filesystem           1K-blocks      Used Available Use% Mounted on
/dev/sda1             14421344   6584528   7104256  49% /
none                   2020124       348   2019776   1% /dev
none                   2027840      2456   2025384   1% /dev/shm
```

```
none                    2027840       220   2027620    1% /var/run
none                    2027840         0   2027840    0% /var/lock
none                    2027840         0   2027840    0% /lib/init/rw
/dev/sda6             284593052 147323812 122812752   55% /home
```

Here you can see each drive as mounted on your system, as well as the used space, the available space, the percentage of the total usage of the disk, and finally where it is mounted on your system.

Unless you are good at doing math in your head, you may find it difficult to work out exactly what the figures mean in megabytes and gigabytes, so it's recommended that you use the `-h` switch to make the output human readable, like this:

```
matthew@seymour:~$ df -h
Filesystem            Size  Used Avail Use% Mounted on
/dev/sda1              14G  6.3G  6.8G  49% /
none                  2.0G  348K  2.0G   1% /dev
none                  2.0G  2.4M  2.0G   1% /dev/shm
none                  2.0G  220K  2.0G   1% /var/run
none                  2.0G     0  2.0G   0% /var/lock
none                  2.0G     0  2.0G   0% /lib/init/rw
/dev/sda6             272G  141G  118G  55% /home
```

Disk Quotas

Disk quotas are a way to restrict the usage of disk space either by user or by groups. Although rarely—if ever—used on a local or standalone workstation, quotas are definitely a way of life at the enterprise level of computing. Usage limits on disk space not only conserve resources, but also provide a measure of operational safety by limiting the amount of disk space any user can consume.

Disk quotas are more fully covered in Chapter 10, "Managing Users."

Graphical Process and System Management Tools

The GNOME and KDE desktop environments offer a rich set of network and system-monitoring tools. Graphical interface elements, such as menus and buttons, and graphical output, including metering and real-time load charts, make these tools easy to use. These clients, which require an active X session and (in some cases) root permission, are included with Ubuntu.

If you view the graphical tools locally while they are being run on a server, you must have X properly installed and configured on your local machine. Although some tools can be used to remotely monitor systems or locally mounted remote file systems, you have to properly configure pertinent X11 environment variables, such as `$DISPLAY`, to use the software or use the `ssh` client's `-X` option when connecting to the remote host.

System Monitor

The first place to look in the standard Ubuntu desktop for a graphical monitoring tool is in the menu at System, Administration, System Monitor. This tool is informative, easy to use and understand, and very useful. It has tabs for information about your system configuration, running processes, available resources, and local file systems (Figures 12.2 to 12.5).

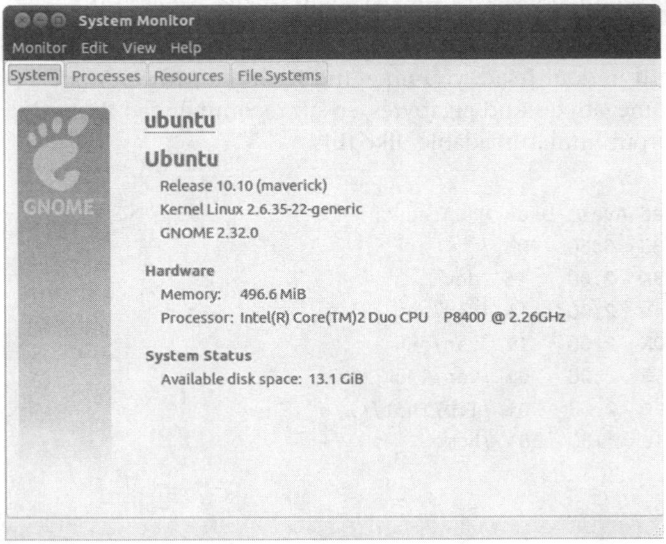

FIGURE 12.2 The System tab in System Monitor.

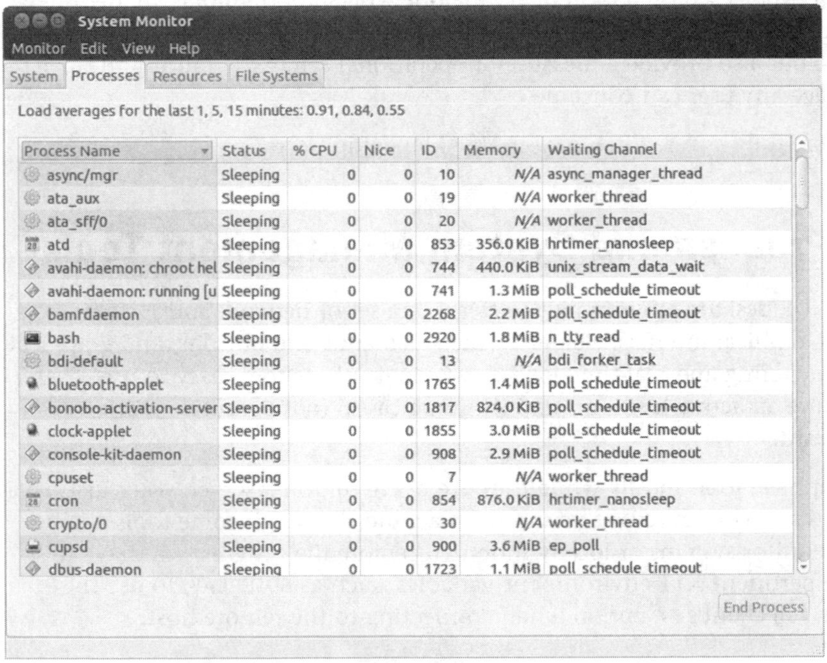

FIGURE 12.3 The Processes tab in System Monitor.

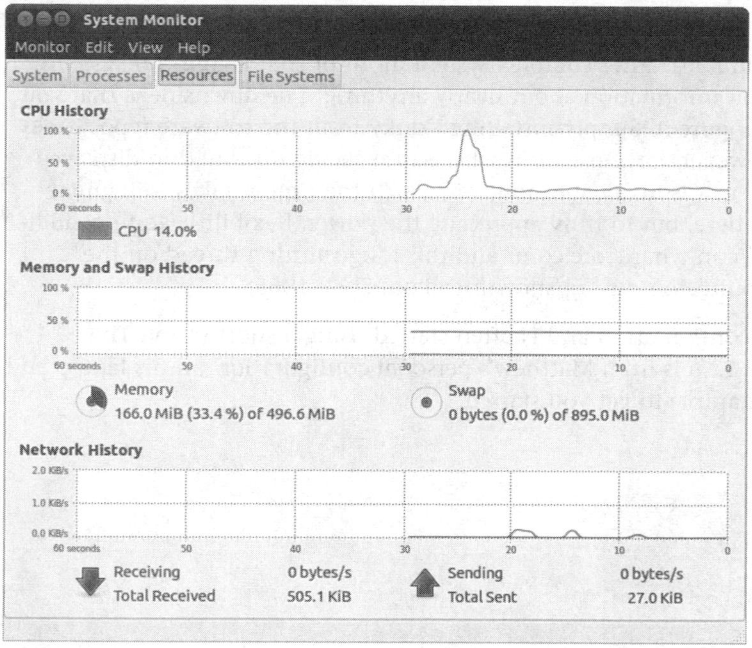

FIGURE 12.4 The Resources tab in System Monitor.

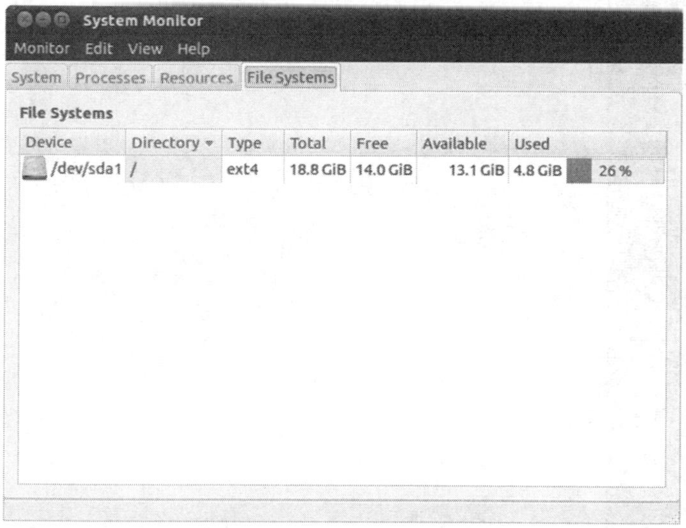

FIGURE 12.5 The File Systems tab in System Monitor.

Conky

Conky is a highly configurable, rather complex system monitor that is light on system resources and can give you information about nearly anything. The downside is that you need to learn how to configure it. Simply installing Conky from the software repositories only gets you started. However, for those of us who want specific information displayed on our desktop at all times, it is invaluable and well worth the time it takes to figure it out. We give an example here, but to truly appreciate the power, flexibility, and possibilities of Conky, visit http://conkyhardcore.com/ and this long-running thread on the Ubuntu Forums http://ubuntuforums.org/showthread.php?t=281865.

Conky uses text files for configuration and is often started using a short script. The example shown in Figure 12.6 is from Matthew's personal configuration on his laptop and is intended as a simple example to get you started.

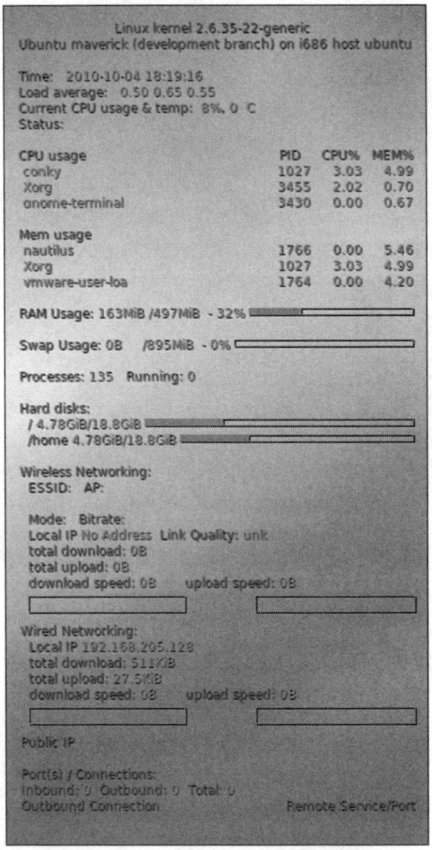

FIGURE 12.6 Conky can be configured to give up to the moment information about anything.

In this example, Conky gives information about the kernel, the operating system, the hostname of the system, and the current time and date. It continually updates with information on load averages, CPU usage and temperature, battery status, RAM and disk usage. In addition, it shows networking details, including the internal network IP address and the IP address assigned to the outside-facing router the network uses to connect to the wider world and current inbound and outbound network connections. (The IP address is assigned by the ISP, and it changes, so if you try to attack Matthew's home network using it, you will find that the IP address is being used by someone else now). That is a lot of information in a small space. This setup isn't as pretty as some you will see at the previous links, nearly all of which have their setup details made freely available by the person who wrote the configurations.

In this example, Matthew is using two files to run Conky. The first is called conkyrc and is a text file that includes the configuration details for what you see in Figure 12.6:

```
# Use Xft?
use_xft yes


# Xft font when Xft is enabled
xftfont InconsolataSSi:size=9


# gap is the number of pixels from the starting point under alignment
#minimum_size 10 10
gap_x 13
gap_y 45


# Text alignment, other possible values are commented#alignment top_left
alignment top_right
#alignment bottom_left
#alignment bottom_right


# Add spaces to keep things from moving about?  This only affects certain objects.
use_spacer right

# Subtract file system buffers from used memory?
no_buffers yes

# Use double buffering (reduces flicker, may not work for everyone)
double_buffer yes

# Allows icons to appear, window to be moved, and transparency
own_window yes
```

```
own_window_type override
own_window_transparent yes
#own_window_hints undecorated,below,skip_taskbar

# set to yes if you want Conky to be forked in the background
background yes

# Update interval in seconds
update_interval 1

cpu_avg_samples 1
net_avg_samples 1

# -- start display config --

TEXT
${alignc}${color #DA9347}$sysname kernel $kernel
${alignc}${color #DA9347}${exec cat /etc/issue.net} on $machine host $nodename

${color #DA9347}Time:${color #E7E7E7}   $time
${color #DA9347}Load average:${color #E7E7E7}   $loadavg
${color #DA9347}Current CPU usage & temp:${color #E7E7E7}  ${cpu}%${color #DA9347},
${color #E7E7E7}${acpitemp}C
${color #DA9347}Status:${color #E7E7E7}   ${battery BAT0}


${color #DA9347}CPU usage         ${alignr}PID     CPU%   MEM%
${color #E7E7E7} ${top name 1}${alignr}${top pid 1}   ${top cpu 1}   ${top mem 1}
${color #E7E7E7} ${top name 2}${alignr}${top pid 2}   ${top cpu 2}   ${top mem 2}
${color #E7E7E7} ${top name 3}${alignr}${top pid 3}   ${top cpu 3}   ${top mem 3}


${color #DA9347}Mem usage
${color #E7E7E7} ${top_mem name 1}${alignr}${top_mem pid 1}   ${top_mem cpu 1}
${top_mem mem 1}
${color #E7E7E7} ${top_mem name 2}${alignr}${top_mem pid 2}   ${top_mem cpu 2}
${top_mem mem 2}
${color #E7E7E7} ${top_mem name 3}${alignr}${top_mem pid 3}   ${top_mem cpu 3}
${top_mem mem 3}


${color #DA9347}RAM Usage:${color #E7E7E7} $mem/$memmax - $memperc% $membar


${color #DA9347}Swap Usage:${color #E7E7E7} $swap/$swapmax - $swapperc% ${swapbar}
```

```
${color #DA9347}Processes:${color #E7E7E7} $processes  ${color
#DA9347}Running:${color #E7E7E7} $running_processes ${color #DA9347}


${color #DA9347}Hard disks:
  / ${color #E7E7E7}${fs_used /}/${fs_size /} ${fs_bar /}
  ${color #DA9347}/home ${color #E7E7E7}${fs_used /home}/${fs_size /home} ${fs_bar
/home}


${color #DA9347}Wireless Networking:
  ${color #DA9347}ESSID: ${color #E7E7E7}${wireless_essid wlan0}  ${color
#DA9347}AP: ${color #E7E7E7}${wireless_ap wlan0}
 ${color #DA9347}${exec iwconfig wlan0 ¦ grep "Frequency" ¦ cut -c 24-44}
  ${color #DA9347}Mode: ${color #E7E7E7}${wireless_mode wlan0}  ${color
#DA9347}Bitrate: ${color #E7E7E7}${wireless_bitrate wlan0}
  ${color #DA9347}Local IP ${color #E7E7E7}${addr wlan0}  ${color #DA9347}Link
Quality: ${color #E7E7E7}${wireless_link_qual_perc wlan0}
  ${color #DA9347}total download: ${color #E7E7E7}${totaldown wlan0}
  ${color #DA9347}total upload: ${color #E7E7E7}${totalup wlan0}
  ${color #DA9347}download speed: ${color #E7E7E7}${downspeed wlan0}${color #E7E7E7}
${color #DA9347} upload speed: ${color #E7E7E7}${upspeed wlan0}
  ${color #E7E7E7}${downspeedgraph wlan0 15,150 ff0000 0000ff} $alignr${color
#E7E7E7}${upspeedgraph wlan0 15,150 0000ff ff0000}


${color #DA9347}Wired Networking:
  ${color #DA9347}Local IP ${color #E7E7E7}${addr eth0} ${color #DA9347}
  ${color #DA9347}total download: ${color #E7E7E7}${totaldown eth0}
  ${color #DA9347}total upload: ${color #E7E7E7}${totalup eth0}
  ${color #DA9347}download speed: ${color #E7E7E7}${downspeed eth0}${color #E7E7E7}
${color #DA9347} upload speed: ${color #E7E7E7}${upspeed eth0}
  ${color #E7E7E7}${downspeedgraph eth0 15,150 ff0000 0000ff} $alignr${color
#E7E7E7}${upspeedgraph eth0 15,150 0000ff ff0000}


${color #DA9347}Public IP ${color #E7E7E7}${execi 5 curl 'http://***a-website-that-
returns-your-ip-address—see below***'}


${color #DA9347}Port(s) / Connections:
${color #DA9347}Inbound: ${color #E7E7E7}${tcp_portmon 1 32767 count}  ${color
#DA9347}Outbound: ${color #E7E7E7}${tcp_portmon 32768 61000 count}  ${color
#DA9347}Total: ${color #E7E7E7}${tcp_portmon 1 65535 count}
${color #DA9347}Outbound Connection ${alignr} Remote Service/Port${color #E7E7E7}
```

12

```
${tcp_portmon 1 65535 rhost 0} ${alignr} ${tcp_portmon 1 65535 rservice 0}
${tcp_portmon 1 65535 rhost 1} ${alignr} ${tcp_portmon 1 65535 rservice 1}
${tcp_portmon 1 65535 rhost 2} ${alignr} ${tcp_portmon 1 65535 rservice 2}
${tcp_portmon 1 65535 rhost 3} ${alignr} ${tcp_portmon 1 65535 rservice 3}
${tcp_portmon 1 65535 rhost 4} ${alignr} ${tcp_portmon 1 65535 rservice 4}
${tcp_portmon 1 65535 rhost 5} ${alignr} ${tcp_portmon 1 65535 rservice 5}
```

Most of these details are clear, but one is particularly interesting. There are commercial and other sites that, if you visit them, will return your IP address. This is easily accomplished several ways. Matthew chose to put the following PHP in a file on a server he owns and he calls it directly. Doing so can help you not to feel guilty about constantly hitting someone else's server for this information.

```
<?
 $remote = $_SERVER["REMOTE_ADDR"];
   echo $remote;
 ?>
```

Finally, although you can run conky from the command line at any time after it is set up, to make it more convenient many people choose to keep their config files in their /home directory somewhere and then write a script with the custom location. If you add a pause to the beginning of the script, then you can add the script to System, Preferences, Startup Applications and have it come up after all your other desktop processes are up and running. Here is a simple example:

```
#!/bin/bash
sleep 45 &&
exec conky -d -c ~/conky/conkyrc &
# sleep 50 &&
# exec conky -d -c ~/conky/conkyrc_weather &

exit
```

Save it in /home/username/conky along with all your conky config files, make it executable, then have the startup applications process call it at boot. Notice that this way you can also run more than one instance of Conky at a time, perhaps having your regular instance in the upper right of the screen and a weather instance or something else in a different location. The possibilities are vast.

Other

Some of the graphical system- and process-monitoring tools that come with Ubuntu include the following:

- `vncviewer`—AT&T's open source remote session manager (part of the `Xvnc` package), which can be used to view and run a remote desktop session locally. This software (discussed in more detail in Chapter 15, "Remote Access with SSH and Telnet") requires an active, background, X session on the remote computer.

- `gnome-nettool`—A GNOME-developed tool that enables system administrators to carry out a wide range of diagnostics on network interfaces, including port scanning and route tracing.
- `ethereal`—This graphical network protocol analyzer can be used to save or display packet data in real time and has intelligent filtering to recognize data signatures or patterns from a variety of hardware and data captures from third-party data capture programs, including compressed files. Some protocols include AppleTalk, Andrew File System (AFS), AOL's Instant Messenger, various Cisco protocols, and many more.

KDE Process- and System-Monitoring Tools

KDE provides several process- and system-monitoring clients. Integrate the KDE graphical clients into the desktop taskbar by right-clicking the taskbar and following the menus.

These KDE monitoring clients include the following:

- `kdf`—A graphical interface to your system's file system table that displays free disk space and enables you to mount and unmount file systems with a pointing device.
- `ksysguard`—Another panel applet that provides CPU load and memory use information in animated graphs.

Enterprise Server Monitoring

Servers used in enterprise situations require extreme uptime. It is beyond the scope of this book to discuss topics such as redundancy, fail-safe and fail-over safeguards, and so on. However, there are a couple of tools we wanted to mention to help an enterprise sysadmin get started.

Landscape

Canonical, the company that finances much of the Ubuntu development, has a monitoring service incorporated into its systems administration tool, Landscape. Landscape has a special dashboard that gives monitoring information and creates an interface for managing multiple Ubuntu systems easily including Ubuntu Enterprise Cloud and Amazon EC2 installations. For more information, see www.canonical.com/enterprise-services/landscape.

Other

There are a myriad of quality monitoring tools available. We have only touched on one of the more basic options. For more information about other enterprise server monitoring options, such as Zenoss and Nagios, take a look at https://help.ubuntu.com/community/Servers#Monitoring.

Reference

- http://and.sourceforge.net/—Home page of the auto nice daemon (AND), which can be used to prioritize and reschedule processes automatically.
- http://sourceforge.net/projects/schedutils/—Home page for various projects offering scheduling utilities for real-time scheduling.
- www.ethereal.com/—Home page for the Ethereal client.
- https://help.ubuntu.com/community/VNC—Setting up Virtual Network Computing (VNC) remote desktop software on Ubuntu.

CHAPTER 13

Backing Up

IN THIS CHAPTER

This chapter examines the practice of safeguarding data by creating backup copies, restoring that same data if necessary, and recovering data in case of a catastrophic hardware or software failure. The chapter gives you a full understanding of the reasons for sound backup practices. You can use the information here to make intelligent choices about which strategies are best for you. The chapter also shows you how to perform some types of data recovery and system restoration on your own and gives guidance on when to seek professional assistance.

Choosing a Backup Strategy

Backups are always trade-offs. Any backup will consume time, money, and effort on an ongoing basis; backups must be monitored, validated, indexed, stored, and new media continuously purchased. Sound expensive? The cost of not having backups is the loss of your critical data. Re-creating the data from scratch will cost time and money, and if the cost of doing it all again is greater than the cost associated with backing up, you should be performing backups. At the foundation, backups are nothing more than insurance against financial loss for you or your business.

Your first step in formulating and learning to use an effective backup strategy is to choose the strategy that is right for you. First, you must understand some of the most common (and not so common) causes of data loss so that you are better able to understand the threats your system faces. Then, you need to assess your own system, how it is used and by whom, your available hardware and software resources, and your budget constraints. The following sections look at each of these issues in detail, as well as offering some sample backup systems and discussing their use.

Why Data Loss Occurs

Files disappear for any number of reasons: They can be lost because the hardware fails and causes data loss; your attention might wander and you accidentally delete or overwrite a file. Some data loss occurs as a result of natural disasters, and other circumstances beyond your control. A tornado, flood, or earthquake could strike, the water pipes could burst, or the building could catch on fire. Your data, as well as the hardware, would likely be destroyed in such a disaster. A disgruntled employee might destroy files or hardware in an attempt at retribution. And any equipment might fail, and it all will fail at some time—most likely when it is extremely important for it not to fail.

A CASE IN POINT

A recent Harris poll of Fortune 500 executives found that roughly two-thirds of them had problems with their backups and disaster-recovery plans. How about you?

Data can also be lost because of malfunctions that corrupt the data as it attempts to write to the disk. Other applications, utilities, and drivers might be poorly written, buggy (the phrase most often heard today is "still beta quality"), or might suffer some corruption and fail to correctly write that all-important data you have just created. If that happened, the contents of your data file would be indecipherable garbage of no use to anyone.

All these accidents and disasters offer important reasons for having a good backup strategy; however, the most frequent cause of data loss is human error. Who among us has not overwritten a new file with an older version or unintentionally deleted a needed file? This applies not only to data files, but also to configuration files and binaries. While perusing the mail lists, Usenet newsgroup postings, or online forums, stories about deleting entire directories such as `/home`, `/usr`, or `/lib` seem all too common. On a stable server that is not frequently modified or updated, you can choose to mount `/usr` read-only to prevent writing over or deleting anything in it. Incorrectly changing a configuration file and not saving the original in case it has to be restored (which happens more often than not because the person reconfigured it incorrectly) is another common error.

TIP

To make a backup of a configuration file you are about to edit, use the cp command:

```
matthew@seymour:~$ cp filename filename.original
```

And to restore it:

```
matthew@seymour:~$ cp filename.original filename
```

Never edit or move the `*.original file`, or the original copy will be lost. You can change the file's mode to be unwritable, so that if you try to delete it, you will prevent and will receive a warning.

Proper backups can help you recover from these problems with a minimum of hassle, but you have to put in the effort to keep backups current, verify they are intact, and practice restoring the data in different disaster scenarios.

Assessing Your Backup Needs and Resources

By now you have realized that some kind of plan is needed to safeguard your data, and, like most people, you are overwhelmed by the prospect. Entire books, as well as countless articles and whitepapers, have been written on the subject of backing up and restoring data. What makes the topic so complex is that each solution is truly individual.

Yet, the proper approach to making the decision is very straightforward. You start the process by asking:

- What data must be safeguarded?
- How often does the data change?

The answers to these two questions determine how important the data is, determine the volume of the data, and determine the frequency of the backups. This in turn will determine the backup medium. Only then can the software be selected that will accommodate all these considerations. (You learn about choosing backup software, hardware, and media later in this chapter.)

Available resources are another important consideration when selecting a backup strategy. Backups require time, money, and personnel. Begin your planning activities by determining what limitations you face for all these resources. Then, construct your plan to fit those limitations, or be prepared to justify the need for more resources with a careful assessment of both backup needs and costs.

TIP

If you are not willing or capable of assessing your backup needs and choosing a backup solution, there are legions of consultants, hardware vendors, and software vendors who would love to assist you. The best way to choose one in your area is to ask other UNIX and Linux system administrators (located through user groups, discussion groups, or mail lists) who are willing to share their experiences and make recommendations. If you cannot get a referral, ask the consultant for references and check them out.

Many people also fail to consider the element of time when formulating their plan. Some backup devices are faster than others, and some recovery methods are faster than others. You need to consider that when making choices.

To formulate your backup plan, you need to determine the frequency of backups. The necessary frequency of backups should be determined by how quickly the important data on your system changes. On a home system, most files never change, a few change daily, and some change weekly. No elaborate strategy needs to be created to deal with that. A good strategy for home use is to back up (to any kind of removable media) critical data frequently and back up configuration and other files weekly.

At the enterprise level on a larger system with multiple users, a different approach is called for. Some critical data is changing constantly, and it could be expensive to re-create; this typically involves elaborate and expensive solutions. Most of us exist somewhere in between these extremes. Assess your system and its use to determine where you fall in this spectrum.

Backup schemes and hardware can be elaborate or simple, but they all require a workable plan and faithful follow-through. Even the best backup plan is useless if the process is not carried out, data is not verified, and data restoration is not practiced on a regular basis. Whatever backup scheme you choose, be sure to incorporate in it these three principles:

- **Have a plan**—Design a plan that is right for your needs and have equipment appropriate to the task. This involves assessing all the factors that affect the data you are backing up. We will get into more detail later in the chapter.
- **Follow the plan**—Faithfully complete each part of your backup strategy, and then verify the data stored in the backups. Backups with corrupt data are of no use to anyone. Even backup operations can go wrong.
- **Practice your skills**—Practice restoring data from your backup systems from time to time, so when disaster strikes, you are ready (and able) to benefit from the strength of your backup plan. (For restoring data, see the section, "Using Backup Software.") Keep in mind that it is entirely possible that the flaws in your backup plan will only become apparent when you try restoring!

SOUND PRACTICES

You have to create your own best-backup plan, but here are some building blocks that go into the foundation of any sound backup program:

- Maintain more than one copy of critical data.
- Label the backups.
- Store the backups in a climate-controlled and secure area.
- Use secure, offsite storage of critical data. Many companies choose bank vaults for their offsite storage, and this is highly recommended.
- Establish a backup policy that makes sense and can be followed religiously. Try to back up your data when the system is consistent (that is, no data is being written), which is usually overnight.
- Keep track of who has access to your backup media, and keep the total number of people as low as possible. If you can, allow only trusted personnel near your backups.
- Routinely verify backups and practice restoring data from them.
- Routinely inspect backup media for defects and regularly replace them (after destroying the data on them if it is sensitive).

Evaluating Backup Strategies

Now that you are convinced you need backups, you need a strategy. It is difficult to be specific about an ideal strategy because each user or administrator's strategy will be highly individualized, but here are a few general examples:

- **Home user**—At home, the user has the Ubuntu installation DVD that takes less than an hour to reinstall, so the time issue is not a major concern. The home user will want to back up any configuration files that have altered, keep an archive of any files that have been downloaded, and keep an archive of any data files created while using any applications. Unless the home user has a special project in which constant backups are useful, a weekly backup is probably adequate. The home user will likely use a DVD-RW, external hard drive or other removable media for backups.
- **Small office**—Many small offices tend to use the same strategy as the home user, but are more likely to back up critical data daily and use manually changed tape drives. If they have a tape drive with adequate storage, they will likely have a full system backup as well because restoring from the tape is quicker than reinstalling from the CDs. They also might be using a CD-RW or DVD writers for backups. Although they will use scripts to automate backups, most of it is probably done by hand.
- **Small enterprise**—Here is where backups begin to require higher-end equipment such as autoloading tape drives with fully automated backups. Commercial backup software usually makes an introduction at this level, but a skillful system administrator on a budget can use one of the basic applications discussed in this chapter. Backups are highly structured and supervised by a dedicated system administrator.
- **Large enterprise**—These are the most likely setting for the use of expensive, proprietary, highly automated backup solutions. At this level, data means money, lost data means lost money, and delays in restoring data means money lost as well. These system administrators know that backups are necessary insurance and plan accordingly.

Does all this mean that enterprise-level backups are better than those done by a home user? Not at all. The "little guy" with Ubuntu can do just as well as the enterprise operation at the expense of investing more time in the process. By examining the higher-end strategies, we can apply useful concepts across the board.

NOTE

If you are a new sysadmin, you might be inheriting an existing backup strategy. Take some time to examine it and see if it meets the current needs of the organization. Think about what backup protection your organization really needs, and determine if the current strategy meets that need. If it does not, change the strategy. Consider whether the current policy is being practiced by the users, and, if not, why it is not.

BACKUP LEVELS

UNIX uses the concept of backup levels as a shorthand way of referring to how much data is backed up in relation to a previous backup. It works this way:

A level 0 backup is a full backup. The next backup level would be 1.

Backups at the other numbered levels will back up everything that has changed since the last backup at that level or a numerically higher level (the `dump` command, for example, offers 10 different backup levels). For example, a level 3 followed by a level 4 will generate an incremental backup from the full backup, whereas a level 4 followed by a level 3 will generate a differential backup between the two.

The following sections examine a few of the many strategies in use today. Many strategies are based on these sample schemes; one of them can serve as a foundation for the strategy you construct for your own system.

Simple Strategy

If you need to back up just a few configuration files and some small data files, copy them to a USB stick, engage the write-protect tab, and keep it someplace safe. If you need just a bit more backup storage capacity, you can copy the important files to a CD-RW disk (up to 700MB in size), or a DVD-RW disk (up to 8GB for data). Many users have switched to using an external hard drive for backups because they are becoming less and less expensive and hold a great amount of data.

In addition to configuration and data files, you should archive each user's home directory, as well as the entire `/etc` directory. Between the two, that backup would contain most of the important files for a small system. Then, you can easily restore this data from the backup media device you have chosen, after a complete reinstall of Ubuntu, if necessary.

Experts used to say that if you have more data than can fit on a floppy disk, you really need a formal backup strategy. Because a floppy disk only held a little over 1MB (and is now incredibly obsolete), perhaps we should change that to "if you have more data than can fit on a cheap USB stick." In any case, some formal backup strategies are discussed in the following sections. We use a tape media backup as an example for convenience because they have been incredibly popular and standard in the past and are still quite common, even as people move to new options such as portable hard drives and cloud storage.

Full Backup on a Periodic Basis

This backup strategy involves a backup of the complete file system on a weekly, bi-weekly, or other periodic basis. The frequency of the backup depends on the amount of data being backed up, the frequency of changes to the data, and the cost of losing those changes.

This backup strategy is not complicated to perform, and it can be accomplished with the swappable disk drives discussed later in the chapter. If you are connected to a network, it is possible to mirror the data on another machine (preferably offsite); the `rsync` tool is particularly well suited to this task. Recognize that this does not address the need for archives of the recent state of files; it only presents a snapshot of the system at the time the update is done.

Full Backups with Incremental Backups

This scheme involves performing a full backup of the entire system once a week, along with a daily incremental backup of only those files that have changed in the previous day, and it begins to resemble what a sysadmin of a medium to large system would traditionally use.

This backup scheme can be advanced in two ways. In one way, each incremental backup can be made with reference to the original full backup. In other words, a level 0 backup is followed by a series of level 1 backups. The benefit of this backup scheme is that a restoration requires only two tapes (the full backup and the most recent incremental backup). But because it references the full backup, each incremental backup might be large (and grow ever larger) on a heavily used system.

Alternatively, each incremental backup could reference the previous incremental backup. This would be a level 0 backup followed by a level 1, followed by a level 2, and so on. Incremental backups are quicker (less data each time), but require every tape to restore a full system. Again, it is a classic trade-off decision.

Modern commercial backup applications such as Amanda or BRU assist in organizing the process of managing complex backup schedules and tracking backup media. Doing it yourself using the classic dump or employing shell scripts to run `tar` requires that the system administrator handle all the organization herself. For this reason, complex backup situations are typically handled with commercial software and specialized hardware that are packaged, sold, and supported by vendors.

Mirroring Data or RAID Arrays

Given adequate (and often expensive) hardware resources, you can always mirror the data somewhere else, essentially maintaining a real-time copy of your data on hand. This is often a cheap, workable solution if no large amounts of data are involved. The use of RAID arrays (in some of their incarnations) provides for a recovery if a disk fails.

Note that RAID arrays and mirroring systems will just as happily write corrupt data as valid data. Moreover, if a file is deleted, a RAID array will not save it. RAID arrays are best suited for protecting the current state of a running system, not for backup needs.

Making the Choice

Only you can decide what is best for your situation. After reading about the backup options in this book, put together some sample backup plans; run through a few likely scenarios and assess the effectiveness of your choice.

In addition to all the other information you have learned about backup strategies, here are a couple of good rules of thumb to remember when making your choice:

- If the backup strategy and policy is too complicated (and this holds true for most security issues), it will eventually be disregarded and fall into disuse.
- The best scheme is often a combination of strategies; use what works.

Choosing Backup Hardware and Media

Any device that can store data can be used to back it up, but that is like saying that anything with wheels can take you on a cross-country trip. Trying to fit ten gigabytes worth of data on a big stack of CD-RWs is an exercise in frustration, and using an expensive automated tape device to save a single copy of an email is a waste of resources.

Many people use what hardware they already have for their backup operations. Many consumer-grade workstations have a DVD-RW drive, but they typically do not have the abundant free disk space necessary for performing and storing multiple full backups.

In this section, you learn about some of the most common backup hardware available and how to evaluate its appropriateness for your backup needs. With large storage devices becoming increasingly affordable (2terabyte hard drives can now be had for around $100), decisions about backup hardware for the small business and home users have become more interesting.

Removable Storage Media

Choosing the right media isn't as easy as it used to be back when floppy drives were the only choice. Today, most machines have DVD-ROM drives that can read but not write DVDs, which rules them out for backup purposes. Instead, USB hard drives and solid-state "pen" drives have taken over the niche previously held by floppy drives: you can get a 4GB drive for under $10.00, and you can even get capacities up to 128GB for good prices if you shop around. Both USB hard drives and solid-state drives are highly portable. Support for these drives under Ubuntu is very good and the storage space is rising although prices are falling constantly. A 1TB USB external hard drive will cost about $50.00. The biggest benefits of USB drives are data transfer speed and portability.

CD-RW and DVD+RW/-RW Drives

Compared to floppy drives and some removable drives, CD-RW drives and their cousins, DVD+RW/-RW drives, can store large amounts of data and are useful for a home or small business. CD writers and media that were once very expensive are at commodity prices today, although automated CD changing machines, necessary for automatically backing up large amounts of data, are still quite costly. A benefit of CD and DVD storage over tape devices is that the archived uncompressed file system can be mounted and its files accessed randomly just like a hard drive (you do this when you create a data CD, see Chapter 7, "Multimedia Applications"), making the recovery of individual files easier.

Each CD-RW disk can hold 650MB–700MB of data (the media comes in both capacities at roughly the same cost); larger chunks of data can be split to fit on multiple disks. Some backup programs support this method of storage. After they are burned and verified, the shelf life for the media is at least a decade or longer.

DVD+RW/-RW is similar to CD-RW, but it is more expensive and can store up to 8GB of uncompressed data per disk.

Honestly, though, these are an old technology and, although they haven't completely died off, the use of either CDs or DVDs for backup has dropped off considerably. It won't be long before they become almost as rare as floppy disks and drives.

Network Storage

For network backup storage, remote arrays of hard drives provide one solution to data storage. With the declining cost of mass storage devices and the increasing need for larger storage space, network storage (NAS or Network Attached Storage) is available and supported in Linux. These are cabinets full of hard drives and their associated controlling circuitry, as well as special software to manage all of it. These NAS systems are connected to the network and act as a huge (and expensive) mass storage device.

More modest and simple network storage can be done on a remote desktop-style machine that has adequate storage space (up to eight 1TB drives is a lot of storage space, easily accomplished with off-the-shelf parts), but then that machine (and the local system administrator) has to deal with all the problems of backing up, preserving, and restoring its own data, doesn't it? Several hardware vendors offer such products in varying sizes.

Tape Drive Backup

Tape drives have been used in the computer industry from the beginning. Tape drive storage has been so prevalent in the industry that the `tar` command (the most commonly used command for archiving) is derived from the words Tape ARchive. Capacities and durability of tapes vary from type to type and range from a few gigabytes to hundreds of gigabytes with commensurate increases in cost for the equipment and media. Autoloading tape-drive systems can accommodate archives that exceed the capacity of the file systems.

TIP

Older tape equipment is often available in the used equipment market and might be useful for smaller operations that have outgrown more limited backup device options.

Tape equipment is well supported in Linux and, when properly maintained, is extremely reliable. The tapes themselves are inexpensive, given their storage capacity and the ability to reuse them. Be aware, however, that tapes do deteriorate over time and, being mechanical, tape drives can and will fail.

CAUTION

Neglecting to clean, align, and maintain tape drives puts your data at risk. The tapes themselves are also susceptible to mechanical wear and degradation. Hardware maintenance is part of a good backup policy. Do not ever forget that it is a question of when—not if—hardware will fail.

Cloud Storage

Services such as Amazon's AWS and S3 or Canonical's Ubuntu One offer a way to create and store backups offsite. Larger companies may create their own offsite, online storage options as well. In each of these and similar cases, data is copied and stored remotely on a file server set aside specifically for that purpose. The data backups may be scheduled with great flexibility and according to the plans and desires of the customer. These are generally more expensive options than the average home user may need, but not always as shown by Ubuntu One's offer of up to 2GB of free storage that is easily kept in sync with your Ubuntu desktop with an option to increase the space for a fee.

Cloud storage is a backup solution that is recent and growing in popularity, but it is also a technology that is changing rapidly. To learn more about the options mentioned here, take a look at https://one.ubuntu.com/ and http://aws.amazon.com/s3/. Although these are not the only services of the kind available, they offer a good introduction to the concept. If you like to roll your own, you definitely want to take a look at Ubuntu Enterprise Cloud at www.ubuntu.com/cloud.

Using Backup Software

Because there are thousands of unique situations requiring as many unique backup solutions, it comes as no surprise that Linux offers many backup tools. Along with command-line tools such as `tar` and `dd`, Ubuntu also provides a graphical archiving tool, File Roller, that can create and extract files from archives. Ubuntu also provides support for the Amanda backup application—a sophisticated backup application that works well over network connections and can be configured to automatically back up all the computers on your network. Amanda works with drives as well as tapes.

NOTE

The software in a backup system must support the hardware, and this relationship can determine which hardware or software choices you make. Many sysadmins choose particular backup software not because they prefer it to other options, but because it supports the hardware they own.

The price seems right for free backup tools, but consider the software's ease of use and automation when assessing costs. If you must spend several hours implementing, debugging, documenting, and otherwise dealing with overly elaborate automation scripts, the real costs go up.

`tar`: The Most Basic Backup Tool

The `tar` tool, the bewhiskered old man of archiving utilities, is installed by default. It is an excellent tool for saving entire directories full of files. For example, here is the command used to back up the `/etc` directory:

```
matthew@seymour:~$ sudo tar cvf etc.tar /etc
```

Here, the options use tar to create an archive, be verbose in the message output, and use the filename etc.tar as the archive name for the contents of the directory /etc.

Alternatively, if the output of tar is sent to the standard output and redirected to a file, the command appears as follows:

```
matthew@seymour:~$ sudo tar cv /etc > etc.tar
```

and the result is the same.

All files in the /etc directory will be saved to a file named etc.tar. With an impressive array of options (see the man page), tar is quite flexible and powerful in combination with shell scripts. With the -z option, it can even create and restore gzip compressed archives while the -j option works with bzipped files.

Creating Full and Incremental Backups with tar

If you want to create a full backup, the following will create a bzip2 compressed tarball (the j option) of the entire system:

```
matthew@seymour:~$ sudo tar cjvf fullbackup.tar.bz2 /
```

To perform an incremental backup, you must locate all the files that have been changed since the last backup. For simplicity, assume that you do incremental backups on a daily basis. To locate the files, use the find command:

```
matthew@seymour:~$ sudo find / -newer name_of_last_backup_file ! -a -type f
-print
```

When run alone, find will generate a list of files system wide and print it to the screen. The ! -a -type eliminates everything but regular files from the list; otherwise, the entire directory would be sent to tar even if the contents were not all changed.

Pipe the output of our find command to tar as follows:

```
matthew@seymour:~$ sudo find / -newer name_of_last_backup_file ! -type d -print ¦\
 tar czT - backup_file_name_or_device_name
```

Here, the T - option gets the filenames from a buffer (where the - is the shorthand name for the buffer).

NOTE

The tar command can back up to a raw device (one with no file system) as well as a formatted partition. For example,

```
matthew@seymour:~$ sudo tar cvzf /dev/hdd  /boot  /etc /home
```

backs up those directories to device /dev/hdd (not /dev/hda1, but to the unformatted device itself).

The tar command can also back up over multiple floppy disks:

```
matthew@seymour:~$ sudo tar czvMf /dev/fd0 /home
```

This will back up the contents of `/home` and spread the file out over multiple floppies, prompting you with this message:

```
Prepare volume #2 for '/dev/fd0' and hit return:
```

Restoring Files from an Archive with `tar`

The `xp` option in tar will restore the files from a backup and preserve the file attributes as well, and `tar` will create any subdirectories it needs. Be careful when using this option because the backups might have been created with either relative or absolute paths. You should use the `tvf` option with `tar` to list the files in the archive before extracting them so that you will know where they will be placed.

For example, to restore a `tar` archive compressed with `bzip2`,

```
matthew@seymour:~$ sudo tar xjvf ubuntutest.tar.bz2
```

To list the contents of a tar archive compressed with `bzip2`,

```
matthew@seymour:~$ sudo tar tjvf ubuntutest.tar.bz2
tar: Record size = 8 blocks

drwxr-xr-x matthew/matthew        0 2010-07-08 14:58 other/

-rwxr-xr-x matthew/matthew     1856 2010-04-29 14:37 other/matthew helmke public.asc

-rwxr-xr-x matthew/matthew      170 2010-05-28 18:11 backup.sh

-rwxr-xr-x matthew/matthew     1593 2009-10-11 10:38 backup method
```

Note that because the pathnames do not start with a backslash, they are relative pathnames and will install in your current working directory. If they were absolute pathnames, they would install exactly where the paths state.

The GNOME File Roller

The GNOME desktop file archiving graphical application File Roller (`file-roller`) will view, extract, and create archive files using `tar`, `gzip`, `bzip`, `compress`, `zip`, `rar`, `lha`, and several other compression formats. Note that File Roller is only a front-end to the command-line utilities that actually provide these compression formats; if they are not installed, File Roller cannot use that format.

CAUTION

File Roller will not complain if you select a compression format that is not supported by installed software until after you attempt to create the archive. Install any needed compression utilities first.

File Roller is well-integrated with the GNOME desktop environment to provide convenient drag-and-drop functionality with the Nautilus file manager. To create a new archive, select Archive, New to open the New Archive dialog box, and navigate to the directory where you want the archive to be kept. Type your archive's name in the Selection: /root text box at the bottom of the New Archive dialog box. Use the Archive type drop-down menu to select a compression method. Now, drag the files that you want to be included from Nautilus into the empty space of the File Roller window, and the animated icons will show that files are being included in the new archive. When you are done, a list of files will be shown in the previously blank File Roller window. To save the archive, simply select Archive, Close. Opening an archive is as easy as using the Archive, Open dialog to select the appropriate archive file. You can learn more at https://help.ubuntu.com/community/File%20Roller.

Ubuntu also offer the KDE `ark` and `kdat` GUI tools for backups; they are installed only if you select the KDE desktop during installation, but you can search through Synaptic to find them. Archiving has traditionally been a function of the system administrator and not seen as a task for the individual user, so no elaborate GUI was believed necessary. Backing up has also been seen as a script driven, automated task in which a GUI is not as useful. Although that's true for sysadmins, home users usually want something a little more attractive and easier to use, and that's the gap `ark` was created to fill.

The KDE `ark` Archiving Tool

You launch `ark` by launching it from the command line. It is integrated with the KDE desktop (such as File Roller is with GNOME), so it might be a better choice if you use KDE. This application provides a graphical interface to viewing, creating, adding to, and extracting from archived files. Several configuration options are available with `ark` to ensure its compatibility with MS Windows. You can drag and drop from the KDE desktop or Konqueror file browser to add or extract files, or you can use the `ark` menus.

As long as the associated command-line programs are installed, `ark` can work with `tar`, `gzip`, `bzip2`, `zip`, and `lha` files (the latter four being compression methods used to save space by compaction of the archived files).

Existing archives are opened after launching the application itself. You can add files and directories to the archive or delete them from the archive. After opening the archive, you can extract all of its contents or individual files. You can also perform searches using patterns (all `*.jpg` files, for example) to select files.

Choosing New from the File menu creates new archives. You then type the name of the archive, providing the appropriate extension (`.tar`, `.gz`, and so on), and then proceed to add files and directories as you desire.

Using the Amanda Backup Application

Provided with Ubuntu, Amanda is a powerful, network backup application created by the University of Maryland at College Park. Amanda is a robust backup and restore application best suited to unattended backups with an autoloading tape drive of adequate capacity. It benefits from good user support and documentation.

Amanda's features include compression and encryption. It is intended for use with high-capacity tape drives, floptical, CD-R, and CD-RW devices.

Amanda uses GNU `tar` and `dump`; it is intended for unattended, automated tape backups, and is not well suited for interactive or ad hoc backups. The support for tape devices in Amanda is robust, and file restoration is relatively simple. Although Amanda does not support older Macintosh clients, it will use Samba to back up Microsoft Windows clients, as well as any UNIX client that can use GNU tools (which includes Mac OS X). Because Amanda runs on top of standard GNU tools, file restoration can be made using those tools on a recovery disk even if the Amanda server is not available. File compression can be done on either the client or server, thus lightening the computational load on less powerful machines that need backing up.

CAUTION

Amanda does not support dump images larger than a single tape and requires a new tape for each run. If you forget to change a tape, Amanda continues to attempt backups until you insert a new tape, but those backups will not capture the data as you intended them to. Do not use too small a tape or forget to change a tape, or you will not be happy with the results.

There is no GUI interface for Amanda. Configuration is done in the time-honored UNIX tradition of editing text configuration files located in /etc/amanda. The default installation in Ubuntu includes a sample `cron` file because it is expected that you will be using `cron` to run Amanda regularly. The client utilities are installed with the package `amanda-client`; the Amanda server is called `amanda-server`. Install both. As far as backup schemes are concerned, Amanda calculates an optimal scheme on-the-fly and schedules it accordingly. It can be forced to adhere to a traditional scheme, but other tools are possibly better suited for that job.

The `man` page for Amanda (the client is `amdump`) is well written and useful, explaining both the configuration of Amanda as well as detailing the several programs that actually make up Amanda. The configuration files found in `/etc/amanda` are well commented; they provide a number of examples to assist you in configuration.

The program's home page is www.amanda.org. There, you will find information on subscribing to the mail list, as well as links to Amanda-related projects and a FAQ.

Alternative Backup Software

Commercial and other freeware backup products do exist; BRU and Veritas are good examples of effective commercial backup products. Here are some useful free software backup tools that are not installed with Ubuntu:

- `flexbackup`—This backup tool is a large file of Perl scripts that makes `dump` and `restore` easier to use. `flexbackup's` command syntax can be found by using the command with the `-help` argument. It also can use `afio`, `cpio`, and `tar` to create and restore archives locally or over a network using `rsh` or `ssh` if security is a concern. Its home page is www.edwinh.org/flexbackup/. Note that it has not received any updates or changes in a very long time.

- `afio`—This tool creates `cpio` formatted archives, but handles input data corruption better than `cpio` (which does not handle data input corruption very well at all). It supports multi-volume archives during interactive operation and can make compressed archives. If you feel the need to use `cpio`, you might want to check out `afio` at http://freshmeat.net/projects/afio/.

Many other alternative backup tools exist, but covering all of them is beyond the scope of this book. Two good places to look for free backup software are Freshmeat (www.freshmeat.net) and Google (www.google.com/linux).

Copying Files

Often, when you have only a few files that you need to protect from loss or corruption, it might make better sense to simply copy the individual files to another storage medium rather than to create an archive of them. You can use the `tar`, `cp`, `rsync`, or even the `cpio` commands to do this, as well as a handy file management tool known as `mc`. Using `tar` is the traditional choice because older versions of `cp` did not handle symbolic links and permissions well at times, causing those attributes (characteristics of the file) to be lost; `tar` handled those file attributes in a better manner. `cp` has been improved to fix those problems, but `tar` is still more widely used. `rsync` has recently been added to Ubuntu and is an excellent choice for mirroring sets of files, especially when done over a network.

To illustrate how to use file copying as a backup technique, the examples here show how to copy (not archive) a directory tree. This tree includes symbolic links and files that have special file permissions we need to keep intact.

Copying Files Using `tar`

One choice for copying files into another location would be to use the `tar` command where you would create a `tar` file that would be piped to tar to be uncompressed in the new location. To accomplish this, first change to the source directory. Then, the entire command resembles

```
matthew@seymour:~$ tar cvf files | (cd target_directory ; tar xpf)
```

In this command *files* are the filenames you want to include; use `*` to include the entire current directory.

Here is how the command shown works: You have already changed to the source directory and executed tar with the `cvf` arguments that tell tar to

- c—Create an archive.
- v—Verbose; lists the files processed so we can see that it is working.

- f—The filename of the archive will be what follows. (In this case, it is -.)

The following tar commands can be useful for creating file copies for backup purposes:

- l—Stay in the local file system (so you do not include remote volumes).
- atime-preserve—Do not change access times on files, even though you are accessing them now, to preserve the old access information for archival purposes.

The contents of the tar file (held for us temporarily in the buffer, which is named -) are then piped to the second expression, which will extract the files to the target directory. In shell programming (refer to Chapter 11, "Automating Tasks"), enclosing an expression in parentheses causes it to operate in a subshell and be executed first.

First we change to the target directory, and then

- x—Extract files from a tar archive.
- p—Preserve permissions.
- f—The filename will be -, the temporary buffer that holds the tared files.

Compressing, Encrypting, and Sending tar Streams

The file copy techniques using the tar command in the previous section can also be used to quickly and securely copy a directory structure across a LAN or the Internet (using the ssh command). One way to make use of these techniques is to use the following command line to first compress the contents of a designated directory, and then decompress the compressed and encrypted archive stream into a designated directory on a remote host:

```
matthew@seymour:~$ tar cvzf - data_folder ¦ ssh remote_host '( cd
~/mybackup_dir; tar xvzf - )'
```

The tar command is used to create, list, and compress the files in the directory named data_folder. The output is piped through the ssh (secure shell) command and sent to the remote computer named remote_host. On the remote computer, the stream is then extracted and saved in the directory named /mybackup_dir. You will be prompted for a password to send the stream.

Copying Files Using cp

To copy files, we could use the cp command. The general format of the command when used for simple copying is

```
matthew@seymour:~$ cp -a source_directory target_directory
```

The -a argument is the same as giving -dpR, which would be

- -d—Preserves symbolic links (by not dereferencing them) and copies the files that they point to instead of copying the links.
- -p—Preserves all file attributes if possible. (File ownership might interfere.)
- -R—Copies directories recursively.

The cp command can also be used to quickly replicate directories and retain permissions by using the -avR command-line options. Using these options preserves file and directory permissions, gives verbose output, and recursively copies and re-creates subdirectories. A log of the backup can also be created during the backup by redirecting the standard output like this:

```
matthew@seymour:~$ sudo cp -avR directory_to_backup destination_vol_or_dir 1 >
/root/backup_log.txt
```

or

```
matthew@seymour:~$ sudo cp -avR ubuntu /test2 1 > /root/backup_log.txt
```

This example makes an exact copy of the directory named /ubuntu on the volume named /test2, and saves a backup report named backup_log.txt under /root.

Copying Files Using mc

The Midnight Commander (available in the Universe repository, under the package "mc"; see Chapter 32, "Managing Software" for how to enable the Universe and Multiverse repositories) is a command-line file manager that is useful for copying, moving, and archiving files and directories. The Midnight Commander has a look and feel similar to the Norton Commander of DOS fame. By executing mc at a shell prompt, a dual-pane view of the files is displayed. It contains drop-down menu choices and function keys to manipulate files. It also uses its own virtual file system, enabling it to mount FTP directories and display the contents of tar files, gzipped tar files (.tar.gz or .tgz), bzip files, DEB files, and RPM files, as well as extract individual files from them. As if that was not enough, mc contains a File Undelete virtual file system for ext2/3 partitions. By using cd to "change directories" to an FTP server's URL, you can transfer files using the FTP protocol. The default font chosen for Ubuntu makes the display of mc ugly when used in a tty console (as opposed to an xterm), but does not affect its performance.

In the interface, pressing the F9 key drops down the menu, and pressing F1 displays the Help file. A "feature" in the default GNOME terminal intercepts the F10 key used to exit mc, so use F9 instead to access the menu item to quit, or simply click the menu bar at the bottom with your mouse. The configuration files are well documented, and it would appear easy to extend the functionality of mc for your system if you understand shell scripting and regular expressions. It is an excellent choice for file management on servers not running X.

Using rsync

An old favorite for backing up is rsync. One big reason for this is because rsync allows you to only copy those files that have changed since the last backup, so although the initial backup may take a long time, subsequent backups are much faster. It is also highly configurable, can be used with removable media such as USB hard drives or over a network. Here is an example of one way you could use rsync.

First, create an empty file and call it backup.sh:

```
matthew@seymour:~$ sudo touch backup.sh
```

Then, using your favorite text editor, enter the following command into the file and save it:

```
sudo rsync --force --ignore-errors --delete --delete-excluded --exclude-
from=/home/matthew-exclude.txt --backup --backup-dir=`date +%Y-%m-%d` -av /
/media/externaldrive/backup/seymour
```

Make the file executable:

```
matthew@seymour:~$ sudo chmod +x backup.sh
```

This command uses several options with rsync and puts them in a script that is quick and easy to remember and run. The script can be run at the command line using sudo sh ./backup.sh or as an automated cron job.

Here is a rundown of what is going on in the command. Basically, rsync is told to copy all new and changed files (what to backup) and delete from any existing backup any files that have been deleted on the source (and back them up in a special directory, just to be safe). It is told where to place the backup copy, and is given details on how to deal with specific issues in the process. Read man rsync for more options and to customize to your needs.

Following are the options used here:

- `--force`—Forces deletion of directories in the target location that are deleted in the source, even if the directories in the destination are not empty
- `--ignore-errors`—Tells `--delete` to go ahead and delete files even when there are I/O errors
- `--delete`—Deletes extraneous files from destination directories
- `--delete-excluded`—Also deletes excluded files from destination directories
- `--exclude-from=/home/matt-exclude.txt`—Prevents backing up files or directories listed in this file (it is a simple list with each excluded directory on its own line)
- `--backup`—Creates backups of files before deleting them from a currently existing backup
- ``--backup-dir=`date +%Y-%m-%d` ``—Creates a backup directory for the previously mentioned files which will look like this: 2010-07-08
- `-av`--Tells rsync to use archive mode and verbose mode

- /—Denotes the directory to back up. In this case, it is the root directory of the source, so everything in the filesystem is being backed up. You could put /home here to backup all user directories, or make a nice list of directories to exclude in the filesystem
- `/media/externaldrive/backup/seymour`—Sets the destination for the backup as the /backup/seymour directory on an external hard drive mounted at /mount/externaldrive

To restore from this backup to the same original location, you reverse some of the details and may omit others. Something like this would work nicely:

```
matthew@seymour:~$ sudo rsync --force --ignore-errors --delete --delete-excluded
/media/externaldrive/backup/seymour /
```


System Rescue

There will come a time when you need to engage in system rescue efforts. This need arises when the system will not even start Linux so that you can recover any files. This problem is most frequently associated with the boot loader program or partition table, but it could be that critical system files have been inadvertently deleted or corrupted. If you have been making backups properly, these kinds of system failures are easily, though not quickly, recoverable through a full restore. Still, valuable current data might not have been backed up since the last scheduled backup, and the backup archives are found to be corrupt, incomplete, or missing. A full restore also takes time you might not have. If the problem causing the system failure is simply a damaged boot loader, a damaged partition table, a missing library, or misconfiguration, a quick fix can get the system up and running and the data can then be easily retrieved.

In this section, we will give you a couple quick things you can try when your system fails to boot to restore a broken boot loader or recover your data.

The Ubuntu Rescue Disc

The Ubuntu installation DVD works quite well as a live DVD. To use it, insert the disc and reboot the computer, booting from the DVD just as you did when you installed Ubuntu originally and ran it from the DVD.

Restoring the GRUB2 Boot Loader

The easiest way to restore a broken system's GRUB2 files is simply to replace them. This will only work with Ubuntu 9.10 or later and only if the system uses GRUB2 (which it will if it was originally installed using 9.10 or later, but might not if Ubuntu was originally installed using an older Ubuntu release and upgraded as GRUB2 is not automatically installed during release upgrades).

To get started, boot using the live DVD and open a terminal from the menu at Applications, Accessories, Terminal. Then you need to determine which of the hard drive's partitions holds the Ubuntu installation, which you can discover using

```
matthew@seymour:~$ sudo fdisk -l
```

Unless you customized your installation, in which case you probably already know your partitioning scheme and the location of your Ubuntu installation, the partition will probably be on a drive called sda on the first partition, which you can mount now using

```
matthew@seymour:~$ sudo mount /dev/sda1 /mnt
```

This will mount the drive in the current filesystem (running from the live DVD) at /mnt, where it will be accessible to you for reading and modifying as needed. Next, you will reinstall GRUB2 on this device:

```
matthew@seymour:~$ sudo grub-install -root-directory=/mnt/ /dev/sda
```

At this point, you should reboot (using your hard drive and not the live DVD) and all should be well. After the reboot is complete, enter

```
matthew@seymour:~$ sudo update-grub
```

This will refresh the GRUB2 menu and complete the restoration. A lot of great information about GRUB2 is available at https://help.ubuntu.com/community/Grub2.

Saving Files from a Non-Booting Hard Drive

If restoring the GRUB2 boot loader fails and you are still unable to boot from the hard drive, you can try to use the live DVD to recover your data. Boot and mount the hard drive as shown previously, then attach an external storage device such as a USB thumb drive or an external hard drive. Then, copy the files you want to save from the mounted drive to the external drive.

If you are unable to mount the drive at all, your options become more limited and possibly more expensive. It is likely that either the hardware has failed or the files system has become badly corrupted. In either case, recovery is either impossible or more difficult and best left to experts if the data is important to you. But, the good news is that you have been making regular backups, right? So, you probably only lost a day or maybe a week of work and can buy a new drive, install it, and start from scratch, putting the data from your backup on your new Ubuntu installation on the new hardware.

Every experienced system administrator has had this happen because no hardware is infallible. We expect occasional hardware failures and that's why we have good backup and recovery schemes in place for data. There are two types of sysadmins: those who lose data when this happens and those who have good schemes in place. Be forewarned and be wise.

If you didn't have a backup, which happens to most sysadmins only once in their lives because they learn from the mistake, stop messing with the hard drive immediately. Your best bet to recover the data will be very expensive, but you should look for a company that specializes in the task and pay them to do it. If your data is not worth the expense for recovery and you want to try to recover it yourself, you can try, but this isn't a task for the faint of heart and more often than not, the data is simply lost. Again, the moral of the story is backup regularly, check your backups to be sure they are valid, and repeat. Practice restoring from backups before you need to do it, perhaps with a test system that is not vital and won't hurt anything if you make a mistake.

Reference

- https://help.ubuntu.com/community/BackupYourSystem—An excellent place to start for learning and examining backup methods in Ubuntu.
- www.tldp.org/—The Linux Documentation Project offers several useful HOWTO documents that discuss backups and disk recovery.

CHAPTER 14
Networking

IN THIS CHAPTER

- Laying the Foundation: The **`localhost`** Interface
- Networking with TCP/IP
- Network Organization
- Hardware Devices for Networking
- Using Network Configuration Tools
- Dynamic Host Configuration Protocol
- Wireless Networking
- Beyond the Network and onto the Internet
- Common Configuration Information
- Configuring Digital Subscriber Line Access
- Configuring Dial-Up Internet Access
- Troubleshooting Connection Problems
- Reference

One of the benefits of open source technology in general and Linux is particular is that it can be used effortlessly across several networking environments as well as the Internet. With strong support for the standard Internet protocol TCP/IP, Linux can talk to all the UNIX flavors, including Mac OS X, Windows (with the help of Samba), NetWare (IPX), and even older protocols such as DECNET and Banyan Vines. Many organizations use Linux as an Internet gateway, allowing many different clients to access the Internet through Linux, as well as communicate via email and instant messaging. Most important is its built-in support for IPv6, which should start to see a significant uptake very soon. It's safe to say that whatever networking protocol you'll come across, Linux will be able to work with it in some way.

This chapter covers network and Internet connectivity, as most networks invariably end up connected to the Internet in some shape or form. You will learn about how to get the basics right, including configuration and management of network cards (*NICs*) and other network services with Ubuntu. You will also find out how to manage network services from the command line—again an important lesson in case you are ever confined to a command prompt. We will also look at connectivity options, both for inbound and outbound network traffic and the importance of PPP (*Point to Point Protocol*).

We will focus on the use of text interfaces and manual configurations in this chapter. We also include an overview of basic graphical network management in Ubuntu, which is becoming more and more popular. The GUI option has become much more stable, useful and easy-to-comprehend, to the point that this will be the way most desktop users now interact with networking. However, this is a book for power users who want to learn about the guts of their system, so let's roll up our sleeves and prepare to get our hands dirty.

Laying the Foundation: The `localhost` Interface

The first thing that needs to be in place before you can successfully connect to a network or even to the Internet is a `localhost` interface, sometimes called a *loopback interface*, but more commonly referenced as `lo`. The TCP/IP protocol (see "Networking with TCP/IP" later on in this chapter) uses this interface to assign an IP address to your computer and is needed for Ubuntu to establish a PPP interface.

Checking for the Availability of the Loopback Interface

You should not normally have to manually create a loopback interface because Ubuntu creates one automatically for you during installation. To check that one is set up, you can use the `ifconfig` command, which will list all networking interfaces available, including the lo interface if it exists, like this:

```
matthew@seymour:~$ ifconfig

lo        Link encap:Local Loopback
          inet addr:127.0.0.1  Mask:255.0.0.0
          inet6 addr: ::1/128 Scope:Host
          UP LOOPBACK RUNNING  MTU:16436  Metric:1
          RX packets:270 errors:0 dropped:0 overruns:0 frame:0
          TX packets:270 errors:0 dropped:0 overruns:0 carrier:0
          collisions:0 txqueuelen:0
          RX bytes:20748 (20.7 KB)  TX bytes:20748 (20.7 KB)
```

What you see in this example is evidence that the loopback interface is present and active. The `inet addr` is the IP number assigned to the `localhost`, typically `127.0.0.1` along with the broadcast mask of `255.0.0.0` and that there has been little activity on this interface (RX = receive and TX = transmit). If your output does not look like the one shown previously, you must hand-configure the `localhost` interface after you finish the rest of this section. You can also see the Ipv6 address that is assigned to `lo`, which is `::1/128`, referred to as the `inet6 addr`.

Configuring the Loopback Interface Manually

The `localhost` interface's IP address is specified in a text configuration file that is used by Ubuntu to keep record of various network wide IP addresses. The file is called `/etc/hosts` and usually exists on a system, even if it is empty. The file is used by the Linux kernel and other networking tools to enable them to access local IP addresses and hostnames. If you have not configured any other networking interfaces then you may find that the file looks something like this:

```
127.0.0.1      localhost
127.0.1.1      seymour



# The following lines are desirable for IPv6 capable hosts

::1     localhost ip6-localhost ip6-loopback

fe00::0 ip6-localnet

ff00::0 ip6-mcastprefix

ff02::1 ip6-allnodes

ff02::2 ip6-allrouters

ff02::3 ip6-allhosts127.0.0.1       localhost
```


The first line defines the special `localhost` interface and assigns it an IP address of 127.0.0.1. You might hear or read about terms such as *`localhost`*, *loopback*, and *dummy interface;* all these terms refer to the use of the IP address `127.0.0.1`. The term *loopback interface* is used to describe how to Linux networking drivers, it looks as though the machine is talking to a network that consists of only one machine; the kernel sends network traffic to and from itself on the same computer. This is sometimes referred to as a "dummy interface" because the interface doesn't really exist; it is not a real address as far as the outside world is concerned; it exists only for the local machine, to trick the kernel into thinking that it and any network aware programs running that require a network interface to operate have one available without them actually being aware that the connection is a connection to the same machine. It is a dummy, not in the sense of stupid or silent, but in the sense that it is a mock up or substitute for something real.

Each networked Ubuntu machine on a LAN will use this same IP address for its `localhost`. If for some reason you discover that an Ubuntu computer does not have this interface, perhaps because some well-meaning person deleted it without understanding it was needed, you can edit the `/etc/hosts` file to add the `localhost` entry as you saw previously, and then use the `ifconfig` and `route` commands using your sudo permissions to create the interface like this:

```
matthew@seymour:~$ sudo /sbin/ifconfig lo 127.0.0.1
matthew@seymour:~$ sudo /sbin/route add 127.0.0.1 lo
```

These commands will create the `localhost` interface in memory (all interfaces, such as `eth0` or `ppp0`, are created in memory when using Linux), and will then add the IP address `127.0.0.1` to an internal (in-memory) table so that the Linux kernel's networking code can keep track of routes to different addresses.

Use the `ifconfig` command as shown previously to test the interface.

You should now be able to use `ping` to check that the interface is responding properly like this (using either `localhost` or its IP address):

```
matthew@seymour:~$ ping -c 3 localhost
PING localhost (127.0.0.1) 56(84) bytes of data.

64 bytes from localhost (127.0.0.1): icmp_seq=1 ttl=64 time=0.154 ms

64 bytes from localhost (127.0.0.1): icmp_seq=2 ttl=64 time=0.159 ms

64 bytes from localhost (127.0.0.1): icmp_seq=3 ttl=64 time=0.153 ms



--- localhost ping statistics ---

3 packets transmitted, 3 received, 0% packet loss, time 1998ms

rtt min/avg/max/mdev = 0.153/0.155/0.159/0.010 ms
```

The `-c` option is used to set the number of pings, and the command, if successful (as it was here), returns information regarding the round-trip speed of sending a test packet to the specified host.

The second line in the `/etc/hosts` file uses the actual hostname of the computer and assigns it to a similar private IP address that is unique to that computer. In the earlier code example, you can see that `127.0.1.1` is assigned to seymour, which is the computer on which that `hosts` file resides.

The remaining lines are used for IPv6 and can be ignored with the exception of the line that begins `::1`—this is used to define the localhost connection for IPv6, which you can text with the `ping6` command at the terminal like this:

```
matthew@seymour:~$ ping6 -c 3 ::1

PING ::1(::1) 56 data bytes

64 bytes from ::1: icmp_seq=1 ttl=64 time=0.102 ms

64 bytes from ::1: icmp_seq=2 ttl=64 time=0.140 ms

64 bytes from ::1: icmp_seq=3 ttl=64 time=0.140 ms

--- ::1 ping statistics ---
```

```
3 packets transmitted, 3 received, 0% packet loss, time 1998ms

rtt min/avg/max/mdev = 0.102/0.127/0.140/0.020 ms
```

Networking with TCP/IP

The basic building block for any network based on UNIX hosts is the Transport Control Protocol/Internet Protocol (*TCP/IP*) suite, which includes three protocols even though only two get to be in the abbreviation. The suite consists of the Internet Protocol (*IP*), Transport Control Protocol (*TCP*), and Universal Datagram Protocol (*UDP*). IP is the base protocol. The TCP/IP suite is *packet*-based, which means that data is broken into little chunks on the transmit end for transmission to the receiving end. Breaking data up into manageable packets allows for faster and more accurate transfers. In TCP/IP, all data travels via IP packets, which is why addresses are referred to as IP addresses. It is the lowest level of the suite.

TCP is also a connection-based protocol. Before data is transmitted between two machines, a connection is established between them. When a connection is made, a stream of data is sent to the IP to be broken into the packets that are then transmitted. At the receiving end, the packets are put back in order and sent to the proper application port. TCP/IP forms the basis of the Internet; without it the Internet would be a very different place indeed, if it even existed!

On the other hand, UDP is a connectionless protocol. Applications using this protocol just choose their destination and start sending. UDP is normally used for small amounts of data or on fast and reliable networks. If you are interested in the internals of TCP/IP, see the "Reference" section at the end of this chapter for places to look for more information.

UBUNTU AND NETWORKING

Chances are that your network card was configured during the installation of Ubuntu. You can use the ifconfig command or Ubuntu's graphical network configuration tools to edit your system's network device information or to add or remove network devices on your system. Hundreds of networking commands and utilities are included with Ubuntu—far too many to cover in this chapter and more than enough for coverage in two or three volumes.

Nearly all ethernet cards can be used with Linux, along with many PCMCIA wired and wireless network cards. The great news is that many USB wireless networking devices also work just fine with Linux, and more are supported with each new version of the Linux kernel. You can check the Linux USB Project at www.linux-usb.org/ for the latest developments or to verify support for your device.

After reading this chapter, you might want to learn more about other graphical network clients for use with Linux. The GNOME `ethereal` client (more at www.ethereal.com/), for example, can be used to monitor all traffic on your LAN or specific types of traffic. Another client, Nmap, can be used to scan a specific host for open ports and other running services (more at http://nmap.org/).

TCP/IP Addressing

To understand networking with Linux, you need to know the basics of TCP/IP addressing. Internet IP addresses (also known as *public* IP addresses) are different from those used internally on a local area network, or *LAN*. Internet IP addresses are assigned (for the United States and some other hosts) by the American Registry for Internet Numbers, available at www.arin.net/. Entities that need an Internet address apply to this agency to be assigned an address. The agency assigns Internet service providers (*ISPs*) one or more blocks of IP addresses, which the ISPs can then assign to their subscribers.

You will quickly recognize the current form of TCP/IP addressing, known as IPv4 (IP Version 4). In this method, a TCP/IP address is expressed of a series of four decimal numbers—a 32-bit value expressed in a format known as dotted decimal format, such as `192.168.0.1`. Each set of numbers is known as an *octet* (eight ones and zeros, such as `10000000` to represent `128`) and ranges from zero to 255.

The first octet usually determines what *class* the network belongs to. There are three classes of networks:

- **Class A**—Consists of networks with the first octet ranging from 1 to 126. There are only 126 Class A networks—each composed of up to 16,777,214 hosts. (If you are doing the math, there are potentially 16,777,216 addresses, but no host portion of an address can be all zeros or 255s.) The "10." network is reserved for local network use, and the "127." network is reserved for the loopback address of 127.0.0.1. Loopback addressing is used by TCP/IP to enable Linux network-related client and server programs to communicate on the same host. This address will not appear and is not accessible on your LAN.

NOTE

Notice that zero is not included in Class A. The zero address is used for network-to-network broadcasts. Also, note that there are two other classes of networks, Classes D and E. Class D networks are reserved for multicast addresses and not for use by network hosts. Class E addresses are deemed experimental, and thus are not open for public addressing.

- **Class B**—Consists of networks defined by the first two octets with the first ranging from 128 to 191. The "128." network is also reserved for local network use. There are 16,382 Class B networks—each with 65,534 possible hosts.

- **Class C**—Consists of a network defined by the first three octets with the first ranging from 192 to 223. The "192." network is another that is reserved for local network use. There are a possible 2,097,150 Class C networks of up to 254 hosts each.

No host portion of an IP address can be all zeros or 255s. These addresses are reserved for broadcast addresses. IP addresses with all zeros in the host portion are reserved for network-to-network broadcast addresses. IP addresses with all 255s in the host portion are reserved for local network broadcasts. Broadcast messages are not typically seen by users.

These classes are the standard, but a *netmask* also determines what class your network is in. The netmask determines what part of an IP address represents the network and what part represents the host. Common netmasks for the different classes are:

- **Class A**—255.0.0.0
- **Class B**—255.255.0.0
- **Class C**—255.255.255.0

Because of the allocation of IP addresses for Internet hosts, it is now impossible to get a Class A network. It is also nearly impossible to get a Class B network (all the addresses have been given out, but some companies are said to be willing to sell theirs), and Class C network availability is dropping rapidly with the continued growth of Internet use worldwide.

LIMITS OF CURRENT IP ADDRESSING

The current IPv4 address scheme is based on 32-bit numbering and limits the number of available IP addresses to about 4.1 billion. Many companies and organizations (particularly in the United States) were assigned very large blocks of IP addresses in the early stages of the growth of the Internet, which has left a shortage of "open" addresses. Even with careful allocation of Internet-connected host IP addresses and the use of `network address translation` (NAT) to provide communication to and from machines behind an Internet-connected computer, the Internet might run out of available addresses.

To solve this problem, a newer scheme named IPv6 (IP version 6) is being implemented. It uses a much larger addressing solution that is based on 128-bit addresses, with enough room to include much more information about a specific host or device, such as global positioning server (GPS) or serial numbering. Although the specific details about the entire contents of the an IPv6 address have yet to be finalized, all Internet-related organizations appear to agree that something must be done to provide more addresses.

You can get a good overview of the differences between IPv4 and IPv6 policies regarding IP address assignments, and the registration process of obtaining IP addresses at https://www.arin.net/knowledge/v4-v6.html and https://www.arin.net/resources/request.html.

Ubuntu supports the use of IPv6 and includes a number of networking tools conforming to IPv6 addressing.

Migration to IPv6 is slow in coming, however, because the majority of computer operating systems, software, hardware, firmware, and users are still in the IPv4 mindset. Supporting IPv6 requires rewriting many networking utilities, portions of operating systems currently in use, and firmware in routing and firewall hardware.

Using IP Masquerading in Ubuntu

Three blocks of IP addresses are reserved for use on internal networks and hosts not directly connected to the Internet. The address ranges are from 10.0.0.0 to 10.255.255.255, or 1 Class A network; from 172.16.0.0 to 172.31.255.255, or 16 Class B networks; and from 192.168.0.0 to 192.168.255.255, or 256 Class C networks. Use these IP addresses when building a LAN for your business or home. Which class you choose can depend on the number of hosts on your network.

Internet access for your internal network can be provided by a PC running Ubuntu or a router. The host or device is connected to the Internet and is used as an Internet gateway to forward information to and from your LAN. The host should also be used as a firewall to protect your network from malicious data and users while functioning as an Internet gateway.

A PC used in this fashion typically has at least two network interfaces. One is connected to the Internet and the other connected to the computers on the LAN (via a hub or switch). Some broadband devices also incorporate four or more switching network interfaces. Data is then passed between the LAN and the Internet using *network address translation*, or *NAT*, sometimes known in Linux circles as *IP masquerading*.

NOTE

Do not rely on a single point of protection for your LAN, especially if you use wireless networking, provide dial-in services, or allow mobile (laptop or PDA) users internal or external access to your network. Companies, institutions, and individuals relying on a "moat mentality" have often discovered to their dismay that such an approach to security is easily breached. Make sure that your network operation is accompanied by a security policy that stresses multiple levels of secure access, with protection built into every server and workstation—something easily accomplished when using Linux.

Ports

Most servers on your network have more than one task. For example, web servers often have to serve both standard and secure pages. You might also be running an FTP server on the same host. For this reason, applications are provided *ports* to use to make "direct" connections for specific software services. These ports help TCP/IP distinguish services so that data can get to the correct application. If you check the file `/etc/services`, you will see the common ports and their usage. For example, for FTP, HTTP, and Post Office Protocol (email retrieval server), you will see:

```
ftp     21/tcp
http    80/tcp     http     # WorldWideWeb HTTP
pop3    110/tcp    pop-3    # POP version 3
```

The ports defined in `/etc/services` in this example are 21 for FTP, 80 for HTTP, and 110 for POP3. Some other common port assignments are 25 for *simple mail transport protocol (SMTP)* and 22 for *secure shell (SSH)* remote login. Note that these ports are not set in stone, and you can set up your server to respond to different ports. For example, although port 22 is listed in `/etc/services` as a common default for SSH, the sshd server can be configured to listen on a different port by editing its configuration file `/etc/ssh/sshd_config`. The default setting (commented out with a pound sign) looks like this:

```
#Port 22
```

Edit the entry to use a different port, making sure to select an unused port number, such as

```
Port 2224
```


Save your changes, and then restart the sshd server. (Refer to Chapter 11, "Automating Tasks," to see how to restart a service.) Remote users must now access the host through port `2224`, which can be done using `ssh`'s `-p` (port) option like this:

```
$ ssh -p 2224 remote_host_name_or_IP
```

Network Organization

Properly organizing your network addressing process grows more difficult as the size of your network grows. Setting up network addressing for a Class C network with fewer than 254 devices is simple. Setting up addressing for a large, worldwide company with a Class A network and many different users can be extremely complex. If your company has fewer than 254 *hosts* (meaning any device that requires an IP address, including computers, printers, routers, switches, and other devices) and all your workgroups can share information, a single Class C network will be sufficient.

Subnetting

Within Class A and B networks, there can be separate networks called *subnets*. Subnets are considered part of the host portion of an address for network class definitions. For example, in the 128. Class B network, you can have one computer with an address of 128.10.10.10 and another with an address of 128.10.200.20; these computers are on the same network (128.10.), but they have different subnets (128.10.10. and 128.10.200.). Because of this, communication between the two computers requires either a router or a switch. Subnets can be helpful for separating workgroups within your company.

Often subnets can be used to separate workgroups that have no real need to interact with or to shield from other groups' information passing among members of a specific workgroup. For example, if your company is large enough to have its own HR department and payroll section, you could put those departments' hosts on their own subnet and use your router configuration to limit the hosts that can connect to this subnet. This configuration prevents networked workers who are not members of the designated departments from being able to view some of the confidential information the HR and payroll personnel work with.

Subnet use also enables your network to grow beyond 254 hosts and share IP addresses. With proper routing configuration, users might not even know they are on a different subnet from their co-workers. Another common use for subnetting is with networks that cover a wide geographic area. It is not practical for a company with offices in Chicago and London to have both offices on the same subnet, so using a separate subnet for each office is the best solution.

Subnet Masks

Subnet masks are used by TCP/IP to show which part of an IP address is the network portion and which part is the host. Subnet masks are usually referred to as *netmasks*. For a pure Class A network, the netmask would be 255.0.0.0; for a Class B network, the netmask would be 255.255.0.0; and for a Class C network, the netmask would be 255.255.255.0. Netmasks can also be used to deviate from the standard classes.

By using customized netmasks, you can subnet your network to fit your needs. For example, your network has a single Class C address. You have a need to subnet your network. Although this is not possible with a normal Class C subnet mask, you can change the mask to break your network into subnets. By changing the last octet to a number greater than zero, you can break the network into as many subnets as you need.

For more information on how to create customized subnet masks, see Day 6, "The Art of Subnet Masking," in *Sams Teach Yourself TCP/IP Network Administration in 21 Days*. That chapter goes into great detail on how to create custom netmasks and explains how to create an addressing cheat sheet for hosts on each subnet. The Linux Network Administrator's Guide also has good information about how to create subnets at www.tldp.org/LDP/nag2/index.html.

Broadcast, Unicast, and Multicast Addressing

Information can get to systems through three types of addresses: unicast, multicast, and broadcast. Each type of address is used according to the purpose of the information being sent, as explained here:

- **Unicast**—Sends information to one specific host. Unicast addresses are used for Telnet, FTP, SSH, or any other information that needs to be shared in a one-to-one exchange of information. Although it is possible that any host on the subnet/network can see the information being passed, only one host is the intended recipient and will take action on the information being received.
- **Multicasting**—Broadcasts information to groups of computers sharing an application, such as a video conferencing client or online gaming application. All the machines participating in the conference or game require the same information at precisely the same time to be effective.

- **Broadcasting**—Transmits information to all the hosts on a network or subnet. *Dynamic Host Configuration Protocol (DHCP)* uses broadcast messages when the DHCP client looks for a DHCP server to get its network settings, and *Reverse Address Resolution Protocol (RARP)* uses broadcast messages for hardware address to IP address resolution. Broadcast messages use .255 in all the host octets of the network IP address. (10.2.255.255 will broadcast to every host in your Class B network.)

Hardware Devices for Networking

As stated at the beginning of this chapter, networking is one of the strong points of the Linux operating system. This section covers the classes of devices used for basic networking. Note that this section talks about hardware devices, and not Linux networking devices, which are discussed in the section, "Using Network Configuration Tools."

Network Interface Cards

A computer must have a *network interface card (NIC)* to connect to a network. Currently, there are several topologies (ways of connecting computers) for network connections. These topologies range from the old and mostly outdated 10BASE-2 to the much newer and popular wireless Wi-Fi or 802.11 networking.

Each NIC has a unique address (the hardware address, known as *media access control*, or MAC), which identifies that NIC. This address is six pairs of hexadecimal bits separated by colons (:). A MAC address looks similar to this: 00:60:08:8F:5A:D9. The hardware address is used by DHCP (see "Dynamic Host Configuration Protocol" later in this chapter) to identify a specific host. It is also used by the *Address Resolution Protocol (ARP)* and *Reverse Address Resolution Protocol (RARP)* to map hosts to IP addresses.

This section covers some of the different types of NIC used to connect to your network.

Token Ring

Token ring networking was developed by IBM. As the name implies, the network is set up in a ring. A single "token" is passed from host to host, indicating the receiving host's permission to transmit data.

Token ring has a maximum transfer rate of 16Mbps (16 million bits per second). Unlike 10BASE-2 and 10BASE-5, token ring uses what is called *unshielded twisted pair (UTP)* cable. This cable looks a lot like the cable that connects your phone to the wall. Almost all token ring NICs are recognized by Linux.

10BASE-T

10BASE-T was the standard for a long time. A large number of networks still use it. 10BASE-T also uses UTP cable. Instead of being configured in a ring, 10BASE-T mostly uses a star architecture. In this architecture, the hosts all connect to a central location (usually a hub, which you learn about later in the section titled "Hubs and Switches"). All the data is sent to all hosts, but only the destination host takes action on individual packets. 10BASE-T has a transfer rate of 10Mbps.

10BASE-T has a maximum segment length of 100 meters. There are many manufacturers of 10BASE-T NICs, and most are recognized by Ubuntu.

100BASE-T

100BASE-T was popular around the turn of the millennium, keeping the same ease of administration as 10BASE-T while increasing the speed by a factor of 10. For most networks, the step from 10BASE-T to 100BASE-T is as simple as replacing NICs and hubs. Most 100BASE-T NICs and hubs can also handle 10BASE-T and can automatically detect which is in use. This allows for a gradual network upgrade and usually does not require rewiring your whole network. Nearly every known 100BASE-T NIC and most generic NICs are compatible with Linux. 100BASE-T requires category 5 unshielded twisted pair cabling.

1000BASE-T

1000BASE-T—usually referred to as *gigabit ethernet*—is the accepted standard in enterprise networking, with most NICs being detected and configured correctly by Ubuntu. Like 100BASE-T NICs, gigabit NICs automatically downgrade if they are plugged in to a slower network. Also like 100BASE-T, gigabit NICs require category 5 unshielded twisted pair cabling; however, many institutions are now deploying category 6 cables because they have much longer range and so are often worth the extra cost. You will find that most newer computers are sold with gigabit NICs.

Fiber Optic and Gigabit Ethernet

Fiber optic is more commonly used in newer and high-end installations because the cost of upgrading can be prohibitive for older sites.

Fiber optics were originally used on *fiber distributed data interface (FDDI)* networks, similar to token ring in structure except that there are two rings—one is primary and the other is secondary. The primary ring is used exclusively, and the secondary sits idle until there is a break in the primary ring. That is when the secondary ring takes over, keeping the network alive. FDDI has a speed of 100Mbps and has a maximum ring length of 62 miles. FDDI uses several tokens at the same time that, along with the faster speed of fiber optics, account for the drastic increase in network speed.

As stated, switching to a fiber optic network can be very costly. To make the upgrade, the whole network has to be rewired, and all NICs must be replaced at the same time. Most FDDI NICs are recognized by Linux.

Fiber-related gigabit is termed 1000BASE-X, whereas 1000BASE-T gigabit ethernet uses twisted-pair (see the "Unshielded Twisted Pair" section, later in this chapter).

Wireless Network Interfaces

Wireless networking, as the name states, works without network cables and is an extremely popular option, particularly for those whose spouses do not like wires trailing everywhere! Upgrading is as easy as replacing network cards and equipment, such as routers and switches. Wireless networking equipment can also work along with the traditional wired networking using existing equipment.

It might not be practical to upgrade a desktop or large server to wireless just yet if the wiring is already in place. Wireless networking is still generally slower than a traditional wired network. However, this situation is changing with wider adoption of newer protocols, such as 802.11n (alongside the older 802.11b and the still current and common 802.11g), along with the introduction of more compliant and inexpensive wireless NICs. Some 802.11g NICs work at up to 108Mbps, which appears faster than 100BASE-T wired networking on the surface. However, in practice, it is a great deal slower: Unless your networking environment has paper-thin walls, you can usually halve the reported speed of Wi-Fi network devices, so 108Mbps works about to be about half the speed of 100BASE-T. The newer 802.11n promises to be up to seven times faster than 802.11g, but adoption of and standardization within implementations of 802.11n is going slowly.

With each new Linux kernel release, more and more wireless NICs are compatible. That said, it is usually better to get brand name wireless NICs, because you have a better chance of compatibility. Wireless networking is discussed more later in this chapter.

Network Cable

Currently, three types of network cable exist: coaxial, unshielded twisted pair (UTP), and fiber. Coaxial cable (rarely used today) looks a lot like the coaxial cable used to connect your television to the cable jack or antenna. UTP looks a lot like the cable that runs from your phone to the wall jack (the jacks are a bit wider). Fiber cable looks sort of like the RCA cables used on your stereo or like the cable used on your electrical appliances in your house (two separate segments connected together). The following sections discuss UTP and fiber network cable in more detail.

Unshielded Twisted Pair

Unshielded twisted pair (UTP) uses color-coded pairs of thin copper wire to transmit data. Six categories of UTP exist—each serving a different purpose:

- **Category 1 (Cat1)**—Used for voice transmissions such as your phone. Only one pair is used per line—one wire to transmit and one to receive. An RJ-11 plug is used to connect the cable to your phone and the wall.
- **Category 2 (Cat2)**—Used in early token ring networks. Has a transmission rate of 4Mbps (million bits per second) and has the slowest data transfer rate. An RJ-11 plug is also used for cable connections.
- **Category 3 (Cat3)**—Used for 10BASE-T networks. It has a transmission rate of 10Mbps. Three pairs of cables are used to send and receive signals. RJ-11 or RJ-45 plugs can be used for Cat3 cables, usually deferring to the smaller RJ-11. RJ-45 plugs are similar in design to RJ-11, but are larger to handle up to four pairs of wire and are used more commonly on Cat5 cables.
- **Category 4 (Cat4)**—Used in modern token ring networks. It has a transmission rate of 16Mbps and is less and less common because companies are switching to better alternatives. RJ-45 plugs are used for cable connections.
- **Category 5 (Cat5)**—The fastest of the UTP categories with a transmission rate of up to 1000Mbps. It is used in both 100BASE-T and 1000BASE-T networks and uses four pairs of wire. Cat5 cable came out just as 10BASE-T networks were becoming popular

and isn't much more expensive than Cat3 cable. As a result, most 10BASE-T networks use Cat5 UTP instead of Cat3. Cat5 cable uses RJ-45 plugs.

- **Category 6 (Cat6)**—Also rated at 1000Mbps, this cable is available in two forms: stranded for short runs (25-meter) and solid for up to 100-meter runs, but which should not be flexed.

Fiber Optic Cable

Fiber optic cable (fiber) is usually orange or red in color. The transmission rate is 100Mbps and has a maximum length of 62 miles. Fiber uses a two-pronged plug to connect to devices. A couple of advantages to fiber are that because it uses light instead of electricity to transmit its signal, it is free from the possibility of electromagnetic interference and is also more difficult to tap into and eavesdrop.

Hubs and Switches

Hubs and switches are used to connect several hosts together on a star architecture network. They can have any number of connections; the common sizes are 4, 8, 16, 24, and 48 connections (ports)—each port has a light that comes on when a network connection is made (link light). Their use enables you to expand your network easily; you can just add new hubs or switches when you need to add new connections. Each unit can connect to the other hubs or switches on the network, typically, through a port on the hub or switch called an *uplink* port. This enables two hubs or switches, connected by their uplink ports, to act as one hub or switch. Having a central location where all the hosts on your network can connect allows for easier troubleshooting of problems. If one host goes down, none of the other hosts are affected (depending on the purpose of the downed host). Because hubs and switches are not directly involved with the Linux operating system, compatibility is not an issue.

If you are constructing a small to mid-size network, it is important to consider whether you intend to use either hubs or switches. Hubs and switches are visually the same in that they have rows of network ports. However, under the hood, the difference is quite important. Data is sent as packets of information across the network; with a hub the data is transmitted simultaneously to all the network ports, irrespective of which port the destination computer is attached to.

Switches, however, are more intelligent because they can direct packets of information to the correct network port that leads to the destination computer. They do this by "learning" the MAC addresses of each computer that is attached to them. In short, using switches minimizes excess packets being sent across the network, thus increasing network bandwidth available. In a small network with a handful of computers, the use of hubs might be perfectly acceptable and you will find that hubs are generally cheaper than switches. However, for larger networks of 15 computers or more, you should consider implementing a switched network.

TIP

Troubleshooting network connections can be a challenge, especially on large networks. If a user complains that he has lost his network connection, the hub or switch is a good place to start. If the link light for the user's port is lit, chances are the problem is with the user's network configuration. If the link light is not on, the host's NIC is bad, the cable is not inserted properly, or the cable has gone bad for some reason.

Routers and Bridges

Routers and bridges are used to connect different networks to your network and to connect different subnets within your network. Routers and bridges both serve the same purpose of connecting networks and subnets, but they do so with different techniques. The information in the following sections will help you choose the connection method that best suits your needs.

Bridges

Bridges are used within a network to connect different subnets. A bridge blindly relays all information from one subnet to another without any filtering and is often referred to as a *dumb gateway*. This can be helpful if one subnet in your network is becoming overburdened and you need to lighten the load. A bridge is not very good for connecting to the Internet, however, because it lacks filtering. You really do not want all traffic traveling the Internet to be able to get through to your network.

Routers

Routers can pass data from one network to another, and they allow for filtering of data. Routers are best suited to connect your network to an outside network, such as the Internet. If you have a web server for an internal intranet that you do not want people to access from the Internet, for example, you can use a router's filter to block port 80 from your network. These filters can be used to block specific hosts from accessing the Internet as well. For these reasons, routers are also called *smart gateways*.

Routers range in complexity and price from an enterprise-grade Cisco brand router that can cost thousands of dollars to consumer brands designed for home or small office use that can be less than a hundred dollars.

Initializing New Network Hardware

All the initial network configuration and hardware initialization for Ubuntu is normally done during installation. At times, however, you could have to reconfigure networking on your system, such as when a host needs to be moved to a different subnet or a different network, or if you replace any of your computer's networking hardware.

Linux creates network interfaces in memory when the kernel recognizes that a NIC or other network device is attached to the system. These interfaces are unlike other Linux interfaces, such as serial communications ports, and do not have a corresponding device file in the /dev directory. Unless support for a particular NIC is built in to your kernel, Linux must be told to load a specific kernel module to support your NIC. More than 100 such modules are located in the /lib/modules/2.6.XX-XX/kernel/net directory (where XX-XX is your version of the kernel).

You can initialize a NIC in several ways when using Linux. When you first install Ubuntu, automatic hardware probing detects and configures your system to use any installed NICs. If you remove the original NIC and replace it with a different make and model, your system will not automatically detect and initialize the device unless you configure Ubuntu to use automatic hardware detection when booting. Ubuntu should detect the absence of the old NIC and the presence of the new NIC at boot time.

If you do not use automatic hardware detection and configuration, you can initialize network hardware by:

- Manually editing the /etc/modprobe.conf file to prompt the system to recognize and support the new hardware upon reboot
- Manually loading or unloading the new device's kernel module with the modprobe command

The following sections explain these methods in greater detail.

Editing the /etc/modprobe.conf File

This file may not be present when you first look for it, so you may need to create a blank file in a text editor. You can manually edit the /etc/modprobe.conf file to add a module dependency entry (also known as a *directive*) to support a new NIC or other network device. This entry includes the device's name and its corresponding kernel module. After you add this entry, the Linux kernel recognizes your new networking hardware upon reboot. Ubuntu runs a module dependency check upon booting.

For example, if your system uses a RealTek NIC, you could use an entry like this:

```
alias eth0 8139too
```

The example entry tells the Linux kernel to load the 8139too.o kernel module to support the eth0 network device. On the other hand, if you have an Intel Ethernet Pro NIC installed, you would use an entry like this:

```
alias eth0 eepro100
```

Other parameters can be passed to a kernel module using one or more option entries, if need be, to properly configure your NIC. See the modprobe.conf man page for more information on using entries. For more specifics regarding NIC kernel modules, examine the module's source code because no man pages exist (a good opportunity for anyone willing to write the documentation).

Using modprobe to Manually Load Kernel Modules

You do not have to use an /etc/modprobe.conf entry to initialize kernel support for your new network device. As root (using sudo), you can manually load or unload the device's kernel module using the modprobe command, along with the module's name. For example, use the following command line to enable the example RealTek NIC:

```
matthew@seymour:~$ sudo modprobe 8139too
```

After you press Enter, you will see this device reported from the kernel's ring buffer messages, which can be displayed by the dmesg command. Here's a portion of that command's output:

```
matthew@seymour:~$ dmesg
...
eth0: RealTek RTL8139 Fast Ethernet at 0xce8ee000, 00:30:1b:0b:07:0d, IRQ 11
eth0: Identified 8139 chip type 'RTL-8139C'
eth0: Setting half-duplex based on auto-negotiated partner ability 0000.
...
```

Note that at this point, an IP address or other settings have not been assigned to the device. Linux can use multiple ethernet interfaces, and the first ethernet device will be numbered eth0, the second eth1, and so on. Each different ethernet device recognized by the kernel might have additional or different information reported, depending on its kernel module. For example,

```
matthew@seymour:~$ dmesg
...
eepro100.c:v1.09j-t 9/29/99 Donald Becker http://cesdis.gsfc.nasa.gov/linux/drive
rs/eepro100.html
eepro100.c: $Revision: 1.36 $ 2000/11/17 Modified by Andrey V. Savochkin
&#x194;<saw@saw.sw.com.sg> and others
PCI: Found IRQ 10 for device 00:0d.0
eth0: Intel Corporation 82557 [Ethernet Pro 100], 00:90:27:91:92:B5, IRQ 10.
 Board assembly 721383-007, Physical connectors present: RJ45
 Primary interface chip i82555 PHY #1.
 General self-test: passed.
 Serial sub-system self-test: passed.
 Internal registers self-test: passed.
 ROM checksum self-test: passed (0x04f4518b).
...
```

In this example, an Intel Ethernet Pro 100 NIC has been recognized. To disable support for a NIC, the kernel module can be unloaded, but usually only after the device is no longer in use. Read the next section to learn how to configure a NIC after it has been recognized by the Linux kernel and how to control its behavior.

Using Network Configuration Tools

If you add or replace networking hardware after your initial installation, you must configure the new hardware. You can do so using either the command line or the graphical configuration tools. To configure a network client host using the command line, you can use a combination of commands or edit specific files under the `/etc` directory. To configure the hardware through a graphical interface, you can use Ubuntu's graphical tool for X called `nm-connection-editor`, found at System, Preferences, Network Connections. This section introduces command-line and graphical software tools you can use to configure a network interface and network settings on your Ubuntu system. You'll see how to control your NIC and manage how your system interacts with your network.

Using the command-line configuration tools can seem difficult if you are new to Linux. For anyone new to networking, the `nm-connection-editor` graphical tool is the way to go. Both manual and graphical methods require super user privileges to work. You should not edit any scripts or settings files used by graphical network administration tools on your system. Your changes will be lost the next time the tool is run! Either use a manual approach all the time and write your own network setup script, or stick to using graphical configuration utilities. Don't switch back and forth between the two methods.

Command-Line Network Interface Configuration

You can configure a network interface from the command line using the basic Linux networking utilities. You configure your network client hosts either with commands to change your current settings or by editing a number of system files. Two commands, `ifconfig` and `route`, are used for network configuration. The `netstat` command displays information about the network connections.

/sbin/ifconfig

`ifconfig` is used to configure your network interface. You can use it to:

- Activate or deactivate your NIC or change your NIC's mode
- Change your machine's IP address, netmask, or broadcast address
- Create an IP alias to allow more than one IP address on your NIC
- Set a destination address for a point-to-point connection

You can change as many or as few of these options as you'd like with a single command. The basic structure for the command is:

```
ifconfig [network device] options
```

Table 14.1 shows a subset of ifconfig options and examples of their uses.

TABLE 14.1 **ifconfig** Options

Use	Option	Example
Create alias	`[network device]`	`ifconfig eth0:0_:[number]`
		`10.10.10.10`
Change IP address		`ifconfig eth0 10.10.10.12`

TABLE 14.1 Continued

Use	Option	Example
Change the netmask	`netmask [netmask]`	`fconfig eth0 netmask 255.255.255.0`
Change the broadcast	`broadcast [address]`	`ifconfig eth0 broadcast 10.10.10.255`
Take interface down	`down`	`ifconfig eth0 down`
Bring interface up	`up (add IP address)`	`ifconfig eth0 up (ifconfig eth0 10.10.10.10)`
Set NIC promiscuous	`[-]promisc`	`ifconfig eth0` promisc mode on [off]
	`[ifconfig eth0 -promisc]`	
Set multicasting mode	`[-]allmulti`	`eth0_on` [off] `allmulti [ifconfig eth0 -allmulti]`
Enable [disable]	`[-]pointopoint [address] oth0_pointopoint`	`ifconfig_`point-to-point address `10.10.10.20 [ifconfig eth0 pointopoint_10.10.10.20]`

The `ifconfig` man page shows other options that enable your machine to interface with a number of network types such as AppleTalk, Novell, IPv6, and others. Again, read the man page for details on these network types.

NOTE

Promiscuous mode causes the NIC to receive all packets on the network. It is often used to sniff a network. Multicasting mode enables the NIC to receive all multicast traffic on the network.

If no argument is given, `ifconfig` displays the status of active interfaces. For example, the output of `ifconfig`, without arguments and one active and configured NIC, looks similar to this:

```
matthew@seymour:~$ ifconfig
eth0      Link encap:Ethernet  HWaddr 00:90:f5:8e:52:b5
          UP BROADCAST MULTICAST  MTU:1500  Metric:1
          RX packets:0 errors:0 dropped:0 overruns:0 frame:0
          TX packets:0 errors:0 dropped:0 overruns:0 carrier:0
```

```
          collisions:0 txqueuelen:1000
          RX bytes:0 (0.0 B)  TX bytes:0 (0.0 B)
          Interrupt:30 Base address:0xc000
lo        Link encap:Local Loopback
          inet addr:127.0.0.1  Mask:255.0.0.0
          inet6 addr: ::1/128 Scope:Host
          UP LOOPBACK RUNNING  MTU:16436  Metric:1
          RX packets:314 errors:0 dropped:0 overruns:0 frame:0
          TX packets:314 errors:0 dropped:0 overruns:0 carrier:0
          collisions:0 txqueuelen:0
          RX bytes:25204 (25.2 KB)  TX bytes:25204 (25.2 KB)

wlan0     Link encap:Ethernet  HWaddr 00:16:ea:d4:58:88
          inet addr:192.168.1.106  Bcast:192.168.1.255  Mask:255.255.255.0
          inet6 addr: fe80::216:eaff:fed4:5888/64 Scope:Link
          UP BROADCAST RUNNING MULTICAST  MTU:1500  Metric:1
          RX packets:325832 errors:0 dropped:0 overruns:0 frame:0
          TX packets:302754 errors:0 dropped:0 overruns:0 carrier:0
          collisions:0 txqueuelen:1000
          RX bytes:207381807 (207.3 MB)  TX bytes:40442735 (40.4 MB)
```

The output is easily understood. The `inet` entry displays the IP address for the interface. UP signifies that the interface is ready for use, `BROADCAST` denotes that the interface is connected to a network that supports broadcast messaging (`ethernet`), `RUNNING` means that the interface is operating, and `LOOPBACK` shows which device (`lo`) is the loopback address. The *maximum transmission unit (MTU)* on `eth0` is 1500 bytes. This determines the size of the largest packet that can be transmitted over this interface (and is sometimes "tuned" to other values for performance enhancement). `Metric` is a number from 0 to 3 that relates to how much information from the interface is placed in the routing table. The lower the number, the smaller the amount of information.

The `ifconfig` command can be used to display information about or control a specific interface using commands that are listed in Table 14.1. For example, to deactivate the first Ethernet device on a host, use the `ifconfig` command, the interface name, and the command `down` like this:

```
matthew@seymour:~$ sudo ifconfig eth0 down
```

You can also configure and activate the device by specifying a hostname or IP address and network information. For example to configure and activate ("bring up") the `eth0` interface with a specific IP address, use the `ifconfig` command like this:

```
matthew@seymour:~$ sudo ifconfig eth0 192.168.2.9 netmask 255.255.255.0 up
```

If you have a host defined in your system's `/etc/hosts` file (see the section "Network Configuration Files" later in this chapter), you can configure and activate the interface according to the defined hostname like this:

```
matthew@seymour:~$ sudo ifconfig eth0 dogdog.hudson.com up
```

Read the next section to see how to configure your system to work with your LAN.

/sbin/route

The second command used to configure your network is the `route` command. `route` is used to build the routing tables (in memory) implemented for routing packets as well as displaying the routing information. It is used after `ifconfig` has initialized the interface. `route` is normally used to set up static routes to other networks via the gateway or to other hosts. The command configuration is like this:

```
route [options] [commands] [parameters]
```

To display the routing table, use the `route` command with no options. The display will look similar to this:

```
matthew@seymour:~$ route
Kernel IP routing table
Destination   Gateway            Genmask          Flags  Metric  Ref  Use  Iface

192.168.1.0   *                  255.255.255.0    U      2       0    0    wlan0

link-local    *                  255.255.0.0      U      1000    0    0    wlan0

default       WirelessAccessPt   0.0.0.0          UG     0       0    0    wlan0
```

In the first column, `Destination` is the IP address (or, if the host is in `/etc/hosts` or `/etc/networks`, the hostname) of the receiving host. The default entry is the `default` gateway for this machine. The `Gateway` column lists the gateway that the packets must go through to reach their destination. An asterisk (*) means that packets go directly to the host. `Genmask` is the netmask. The `Flags` column can have several possible entries. In our example, `U` verifies that the route is enabled and `G` specifies that `Destination` requires the use of a gateway. The `Metric` column displays the distance to the `Destination`. Some daemons use this to figure the easiest route to the `Destination`. The `Ref` column is used by some UNIX flavors to convey the references to the route. It isn't used by Linux. The Use column indicates the number of times this entry has been looked up. Finally, the `Iface` column is the name of the interface for the corresponding entry.

Using the `-n` option to the route command will give the same information, substituting IP addresses for names and asterisks (*), and looks like this:

```
matthew@seymour:~$ /sbin/route -n

Kernel IP routing table

Destination   Gateway       Genmask          Flags  Metric  Ref  Use  Iface

192.168.1.0   0.0.0.0       255.255.255.0    U      2       0    0    wlan0

link-local    0.0.0.0       255.255.0.0      U      1000    0    0    wlan0

0.0.0.0       192.168.1.0   0.0.0.0          UG     0       0    0    wlan0
```

14

The `route` command can add to the table using the `add` option. With the `add` option, you can specify a host (`-host`) or a network (`-net`) as the destination. If no option is used, the `route` command assumes that you are configuring the host issuing the command. The most common uses for the `route` command are to add the default gateway for a host, for a host that has lost its routing table, or if the gateway address has changed. For example, to add a gateway with a specific IP address, you could use the following:

```
matthew@seymour:~$ sudo route add default gw 149.112.50.65
```

Note that you could use a hostname instead of an IP address if desired. Another common use is to add the network to the routing table right after using the `ifconfig` command to configure the interface. Assuming that the `208.59.243.0` entry from the previous examples was missing, replace it using the following command:

```
matthew@seymour:~$ sudo route add -net 208.59.243.0 netmask 255.255.255.0 dev eth0
```

You also can use route to configure a specific host for a direct (point-to-point) connection. For example, say that you have a home network of two computers. One of the computers has a modem through which it connects to your business network. You typically work at the other computer. You can use the route command to establish a connection through specific hosts using the following command:

```
matthew@seymour:~$ sudo route add -host 198.135.62.25 gw 149.112.50.65
```

The preceding example makes the computer with the modem the gateway for the computer you are using. This type of command line is useful if you have a gateway or firewall connected to the Internet. There are many additional uses for the route command, such as manipulating the default packet size. See the man page for those uses.

/bin/netstat

The `netstat` command is used to display the status of your network. It has several parameters that can display as much or as little information as you prefer. The services are listed by *sockets* (application-to-application connections between two computers). You can use `netstat` to display the information in Table 14.2.

TABLE 14.2 **netstat** Options

Option	Output
`-g`	Displays the multicast groups configured
`-i`	Displays the interfaces configured by `ifconfig`
`-s`	Lists a summary of activity for each protocol
`-v`	Gives verbose output, listing both active and inactive sockets
`-c`	Updates output every second (good for testing and troubleshooting)
`-e`	Gives verbose output for active connections only
`-C`	Displays information from the route cache and is good for looking at past connections

Several other options are available for this command, but they are used less often. As with the route command, the man page can give you details about all options and parameters.

Network Configuration Files

As previously stated, five network configuration files can be modified to make changes to basic network interaction of your system:

- /etc/hosts—A listing of addresses, hostnames, and aliases
- /etc/services—Network service and port connections
- /etc/nsswitch.conf—Linux network information service configuration
- /etc/resolv.conf—Domain name service domain (search) settings
- /etc/host.conf—Network information search order (by default, /etc/hosts and then DNS)

After these files are modified, the changes are active. As with most configuration files, comments can be added with a hash mark (#) preceding the comment. All these files have a man page written about them for more information.

Adding Hosts to /etc/hosts

The /etc/hosts file is a map of IP to hostnames. If you are not using DNS or another naming service, and you are connected to a large network, this file can get quite large and can be a real headache to manage. A small /etc/hosts file can look something like this:

```
127.0.0.1       localhost
127.0.1.1       optimus

# The following lines are desirable for IPv6 capable hosts
::1     ip6-localhost ip6-loopback
fe00::0 ip6-localnet
ff00::0 ip6-mcastprefix
ff02::1 ip6-allnodes
ff02::2 ip6-allrouters
ff02::3 ip6-allhosts
```

The first entry is for the loopback entry. The second is for the name of the machine. If no naming service is in use on the network, the only host that `myhost` will recognize by name is `yourhost`. (IP addresses on the network can still be used.)

Service Settings in /etc/services

The `/etc/services` file maps port numbers to services. The first few lines look similar to this (the `/etc/services` file can be quite long, more than 500 lines):

```
# Each line describes one service, and is of the form:
#
# service-name port/protocol [aliases ...]  [# comment]

tcpmux      1/tcp                # TCP port service multiplexer
tcpmux      1/udp                # TCP port service multiplexer
rje         5/tcp                # Remote Job Entry
rje         5/udp                # Remote Job Entry
echo        7/tcp
echo        7/udp
discard     9/tcp       sink null
discard     9/udp       sink null
systat      11/tcp      users
```

Typically, there are two entries for each service because most services can use either TCP or UDP for their transmissions. Usually after `/etc/services` is initially configured, you will not need to change it.

Using /etc/nsswitch.conf After Changing Naming Services

This file was initially developed by Sun Microsystems to specify the order in which services are accessed on the system. A number of services are listed in the `/etc/nsswitch.conf` file, but the most commonly modified entry is the `hosts` entry. A portion of the file can look like this:

```
passwd:         compat
group:          compat
shadow:         compat

hosts:          files dns mdns
networks:       files

protocols:      db files
services:       db files
ethers:         db files
rpc:            db files

netgroup:       nis
```

This tells services that they should consult standard UNIX/Linux files for `passwd`, `shadow`, and `group` (`/etc/passwd`, `/etc/shadow`, `/etc/group`, respectively) lookups. For host lookups, the system checks `/etc/hosts` and if there is no entry, it checks DNS. The commented `hosts` entry lists the possible values for `hosts`. Edit this file only if your naming service has changed.

Setting a Name Server with /etc/resolv.conf

`/etc/resolv.conf` is used by DNS, the domain name service. The following is an example of `resolv.conf`:

```
nameserver 192.172.3.8
nameserver 192.172.3.9
search mydomain.com
```

This sets the nameservers and the order of domains for DNS to use. The contents of this file will be set automatically if you use Dynamic Host Configuration Protocol, or DHCP (see the section on "Dynamic Host Configuration Protocol" later in this chapter).

Setting DNS Search Order with /etc/host.conf

The `/etc/host.conf` file lists the order in which your machine will search for hostname resolution. The following is the default `/etc/host.conf` file:

```
order hosts, bind
```

In this example, the host checks the `/etc/hosts` file first and then performs a DNS lookup. A couple more options control how the name service is used. The only reason to modify this file is if you use NIS for your name service or you want one of the optional services. The `nospoof` option can be a good option for system security. It compares a standard DNS lookup to a reverse lookup (host-to-IP then IP-to-host) and fails if the two don't match. The drawback is that often when proxy services are used, the lookup fails, so you want to use this with caution.

Using Graphical Configuration Tools

Ubuntu has made some big improvements to how desktop users may configure networking using graphical configuration tools. For most people, all you will need to know is contained in Chapter 2, "Post-Installation Configuration," in the section about Network Manager. For others, you may configure your network connections by right clicking the networking icon on your top panel and choosing "Edit Connections." from the menu as shown in Figure 14.1. From the Network Connections window that opens, you may select from various types of connections to configure, including Wired, Wireless, Mobile Broadband, VPN and DSL as shown in Figure 14.2. By default, each is set to auto configure and most users will never need to change the settings available here. For those who require doing so, choosing the appropriate tab and clicking the "Add" button will give the opportunity to configure and fine tune settings as needed, such as in the wireless connection example in Figure 14.3.

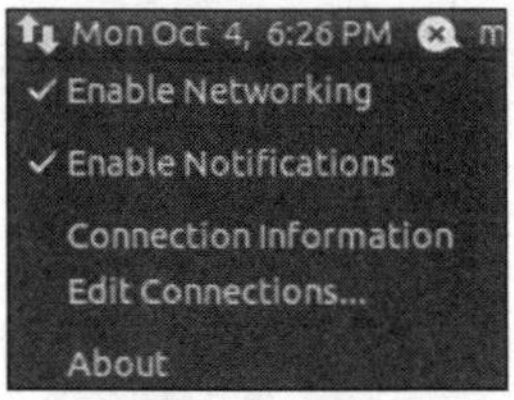

FIGURE 14.1 Use nm-connection-editor to configure your network devices.

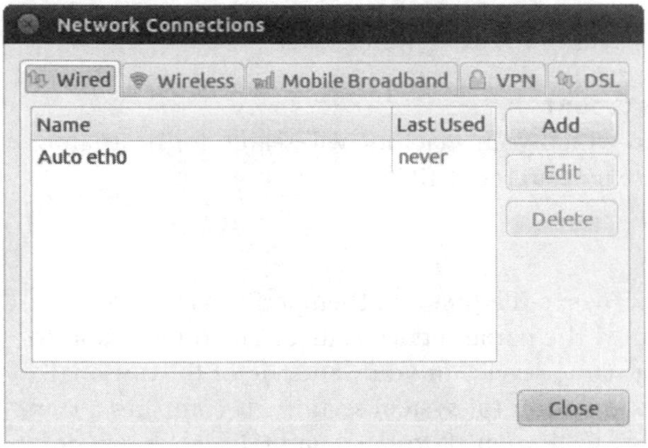

FIGURE 14.2 Choose the connection type to configure from the tabs in Network Connections.

Dynamic Host Configuration Protocol

As its name implies, *Dynamic Host Configuration Protocol (DHCP)* configures hosts for connection to your network. DHCP allows a network administrator to configure all TCP/IP parameters for each host as he connects to the network after activation of a NIC. These parameters include automatically assigning an IP address to a NIC, setting name server entries in `/etc/resolv.conf`, and configuring default routing and gateway information for a host. This section first describes how to use DHCP to obtain IP address assignment for your NIC, and then how to quickly set up and start a DHCP server using Ubuntu.

NOTE

You can learn more about DHCP by reading RFC2131 "Dynamic Host Configuration Protocol" from www.ietf.org/rfc/rfc2131.txt.

FIGURE 14.3 Assign a static IP address to a network interface.

How DHCP Works

DHCP provides persistent storage of network parameters by holding identifying information for each network client that might connect to the network. The three most common pairs of identifying information are:

- **Network subnet/host address**—Used by hosts to connect to the network at will
- **Subnet/hostname**—Enables the specified host to connect to the subnet
- **Subnet/hardware address**—Enables a specific client to connect to the network after getting the hostname from DHCP

DHCP also allocates to client's temporary or permanent network (IP) addresses. When a temporary assignment, known as a *lease*, elapses, the client can request to have the lease extended, or, if the address is no longer needed, the client can relinquish the address. For hosts that will be permanently connected to a network with adequate addresses available, DHCP allocates infinite leases.

DHCP offers your network some advantages. First, it shifts responsibility for assigning IP addresses from the network administrator (who can accidentally assign duplicate IP addresses) to the DHCP server. Second, DHCP makes better use of limited IP addresses. If a user is away from the office for whatever reason, the user's host can release its IP address for use by other hosts.

Like most things in life, DHCP is not perfect. Servers cannot be configured through DHCP alone because DNS does not know what addresses that DHCP assigns to a host. This means that DNS lookups are not possible on machines configured through DHCP alone; therefore, services cannot be provided. However, DHCP can make assignments based on DNS entries when using subnet/hostname or subnet/hardware address identifiers.

NOTE

The problem of using DHCP to configure servers using registered hostnames is being addressed by Dynamic DNS which, when fully developed, will enable DHCP to register IP addresses with DNS. This will allow you, for example, to register a domain name (such as matthewhelmke.com) and be able to easily access that domain's web server without needing to use static IP addressing of a specific host. The largest hurdle to overcome is the security implication of enabling each host connecting to the system to update DNS. A few companies, such as www.dyndns.org/, are already offering Dynamic DNS services and have clients for Linux.

Activating DHCP at Installation and Boot Time

Ubuntu automatically defaults your network interfaces to using DHCP, because it is the simplest way of setting up a network interface. With *dynamic*, or DHCP-assigned IP addressing schemes for your NIC, the broadcast address is set at `255.255.255.255` because `dhclient`, the DHCP client used for IP configuration, is initially unaware of where the DHCP server is located, so the request must travel every network until a server replies.

The instruction to use DHCP for your NIC can be found under `/etc/network/interfaces`, with a line that says `dhcp`.

Other settings specific to obtaining DHCP settings are saved in the file named `dhclient.conf` under the `/etc/dhcp3/dhclient.conf` directory and are documented in the `dhclient.conf` main page. More than 100 options are also documented in the `dhcp-options` main page.

However, using DHCP is not that complicated. If you want to use DHCP and know that there is a server on your network, you can quickly configure your NIC by using the `dhclient` like this:

```
matthew@seymour:~$ sudo dhclient
Internet Systems Consortium DHCP Client V3.1.3
Copyright 2004-2009 Internet Systems Consortium.
All rights reserved.
For info, please visit https://www.isc.org/software/dhcp/

Listening on LPF/eth0/00:90:f5:8e:52:b5
Sending on   LPF/eth0/00:90:f5:8e:52:b5
Listening on LPF/virbr0/ee:1a:62:7e:e2:a2
Sending on   LPF/virbr0/ee:1a:62:7e:e2:a2
Listening on LPF/wlan0/00:16:ea:d4:58:88
Sending on   LPF/wlan0/00:16:ea:d4:58:88
Sending on   Socket/fallback
```

```
DHCPDISCOVER on eth0 to 255.255.255.255 port 67 interval 7
DHCPDISCOVER on wlan0 to 255.255.255.255 port 67 interval 3
DHCPOFFER of 192.168.1.106 from 192.168.1.1
DHCPREQUEST of 192.168.1.106 on wlan0 to 255.255.255.255 port 67
DHCPACK of 192.168.1.106 from 192.168.1.1
bound to 192.168.1.106 — renewal in 35959 seconds.
```

In this example, the first ethernet device, `eth0`, has been assigned an IP address of 192.168.1.106 from a DHCP server at 192.168.1.1. The renewal will take place in 35959 seconds, or about 10 hours (cool tip: Google will convert this for you if you search for 35959 seconds in hours).

DHCP Software Installation and Configuration

Installation of the DHCP client and server is fairly straightforward, mainly because Ubuntu already includes `dhclient` in a default installation, but also because installing software is easy using `synaptic` or `apt-get`.

DHCP dhclient

DHCP is automatically enabled when you install Ubuntu, so you don't need to worry about having to enable it. The DHCP client, `dhclient`, sends a broadcast message that the DHCP server replies to with networking information for your host. After it has this, you're done!

You can however, fine-tune how `dhclient` works, and where and how it obtains or looks for DHCP information. You probably will not need to take this additional effort; but if you do, you can create and edit a file named `dhclient.conf`, and save it in the `/etc` directory with your settings.

CAUTION

You shouldn't just go ahead and overwrite your `dhclient.conf` with any old file, because it could lead you to painful networking problems. Instead, copy the file like this:

```
matthew@seymour:~$ sudo cp /etc/dhcp3/dhclient.conf/
etc/dhcp3/dhclient.conf.backup
```

That way, if anything goes wrong, you can then use the backup to restore the original settings by copying it back to its original location in place of the modified file.

A few of the `dhclient.conf` options include:

- `timeout time ;`—How long to wait before giving up trying (60 seconds is the default)
- `retry time ;`—How long to wait before retrying (five minutes is the default)
- `select-timeout time ;`—How long to wait before selecting a DHCP offer (zero seconds is the default)
- `reboot time ;`—How long to wait before trying to get a previously set IP (10 seconds is the default)

- `renew date ;`—When to renew an IP lease, where `date` is in the form of <weekday> <year>/<month>/<day> <hour>:<minute>:<second>, such as 3 `2010/7/7 22:01:01` for Wednesday, July 7, 2010 at 10:01 p.m.

See the `dhclient.conf` man page for more information on additional settings.

DHCP Server

Again, the easiest way to install the DHCP server on your computer is to use either `synaptic` or `apt-get` to retrieve the dchp3-server package. If you are so inclined, you can go to the Internet Software Consortium (ISC) website and download and build the source code yourself (www.isc.org/). However, we recommend you stay with the package in the Ubuntu repositories because it will be very easy to update if there are security updates.

If you decide to install from a source downloaded from the ISC website, the installation is very straightforward. Just unpack your `tar` file, run `./configure` from the root of the source directory, run `make`, and finally, if there are no errors, run `make install`. This puts all the files used by the DHCP daemon in the correct places. If you have the disk space, it is best to leave the source files in place until you are sure that DHCP is running correctly; otherwise, you can delete the source tree.

NOTE

For whichever installation method you choose, be sure that a file called `/etc/dhcp3/dhcpd.leases` is created. The file can be empty, but it does need to exist for `dhcpd` to start properly.

Using DHCP to Configure Network Hosts

Configuring your network with DHCP can look difficult, but is actually easy if your needs are simple. The server configuration can take a bit more work if your network is more complex and depending on how much you want DHCP to do.

Configuring the server takes some thought and a little bit of work. Luckily, the work involves editing only a single configuration file, `/etc/dhcp3/dhcpd.conf`. To start the server at boot time, use the `service`, or `ntsysv` commands.

The `/etc/dhcp3/dhcpd.conf` file contains all the information needed to run `dhcpd`. Ubuntu includes a sample `dhcpd.conf` in `/usr/share/doc/dhcp*/dhcpd.conf.sample`. The DHCP server source files also contain a sample `dhcpd.conf` file.

The `/etc/dhcp3/dhcpd.conf` file can be looked at as a three-part file. The first part contains configurations for DHCP itself. The configurations include:

- **Setting the domain name**—`option domain-name "example.org".`
- **Setting DNS servers**—`option domain-name-servers ns1.example.org, ns2.example.org` (IP addresses can be substituted.)
- **Setting the default and maximum lease times**—`default-lease-time 3600` and `max-lease-time 14400.`

Other settings in the first part include whether the server is the primary (authoritative) server and what type of logging DHCP should use. These settings are considered defaults and can be overridden by the subnet and host portion of the configuration in more complex situations.

NOTE

The `dhcpd.conf` file requires semicolons (`;`) after each command statement. If your configuration file has errors or runs improperly, check for this.

The next part of the `dhcpd.conf` deals with the different subnets that your DHCP server serves; this section is quite straightforward. Each subnet is defined separately and can look like this:


```
subnet 10.5.5.0 netmask 255.255.255.224 {
 range 10.5.5.26 10.5.5.30;
 option domain-name-servers ns1.internal.example.org;
 option domain-name "internal.example.org";
 option routers 10.5.5.1;
 option broadcast-address 10.5.5.31;
 default-lease-time 600;
 max-lease-time 7200;
}
```

This defines the IP addressing for the `10.5.5.0` subnet. It defines the IP address ranging from `10.5.5.26` through `10.5.5.30` to be dynamically assigned to hosts that reside on that subnet. This example shows that any TCP/IP option can be set from the subnet portion of the configuration file. It shows which DNS server the subnet will connect to, which can be good for DNS server load balancing, or which can be used to limit the hosts that can be reached through DNS. It defines the domain name, so you can have more than one domain on your network. It can also change the default and maximum lease time.

If you want your server to ignore a specific subnet, the following entry can be used to accomplish this:

```
subnet 10.152.187.0 netmask 255.255.255.0 {
}
```

This defines no options for the `10.152.187.0` subnet; therefore, the DHCP server ignores it.

The last part of your `dhcp.conf` is for defining hosts. This can be good if you want a computer on your network to have a specific IP address or other information specific to that host. The key to completing the host section is to know the hardware address of the host. As you learned in "Hardware Devices for Networking," earlier in this chapter, the hardware address is used to differentiate the host for configuration. Your hardware address can be obtained by using the `ifconfig` command as described previously. The hardware address is on the `eth0` line labeled `"Hwaddr"`.

```
host hopper {
  hardware ethernet 08:00:07:26:c0:a5;
  fixed-address hopper.matthewhelmke.com;
}
```

This example takes the host with the hardware address `08:00:07:26:c0:a5` and does a DNS lookup to assign the IP address for hopper.matthewhelmke.com to the host.

DHCP can also define and configure booting for diskless clients like this:

```
host bumblebee {
  hardware ethernet 0:0:c0:5d:bd:95;
  filename "vmunix.bumblebee";
  server-name "kernigan.matthewhelmke.com";
}
```

The diskless host bumblebee will get its boot information from server `kernigan.matthewhelmke.com` and use `vmunix.bumblebee` kernel. All other TCP/IP configuration can also be included.

CAUTION

Remember, only one DHCP server should exist on a local network to avoid problems. Your DHCP might not work correctly on a LAN with hosts running outdated legacy operating systems. Often Windows NT servers will have the Windows DHCP server installed by default. Because there is no configuration file for NT to sort through, that DHCP server configures your host before the Linux server if both machines are on the same LAN. Check your NT servers for this situation and disable DHCP on the NT server; afterward, your other DHCP-enabled hosts should configure correctly. Also, check to make sure that there are no conflicts if you use a cable or DSL modem, wireless access point (WAP), or other intelligent router on your LAN that can provide DHCP.

Other Uses for DHCP

A whole host of options can be used in `dhcpd.conf`: Entire books are dedicated to DHCP. The most comprehensive book is *The DHCP Handbook*, available at www.dhcp-handbook.com/. You can define NIS domains, configure NETBIOS, set subnet masks, and define time servers, or many other types of servers—to name a few of the DHCP options you can use. The preceding example will get your DHCP server and client up and running.

The DHCP server distribution contains an example of the `dhcpd.conf` file that you can use as a template for your network. The file shows a basic configuration that can get you started with explanations for the options used.

Wireless Networking

Linux has had support for wireless networking since the first standards were developed in the early 1990s. With computers getting smaller and smaller, the uses for wireless networking increased; meanwhile, the transmission speeds are increasing all the time. There are several ways to create a wireless network. The following sections introduce you to several Linux commands you can use to initialize, configure, and manage wireless networking on your Ubuntu system.

Support for Wireless Networking in Ubuntu

The Linux kernel that ships with Ubuntu provides extensive support for wireless networking. Related wireless tools for configuring, managing, or displaying information about a wireless connection include:

- `iwconfig`—Sets the network name, encryption, transmission rate, and other features of a wireless network interface
- `iwlist`—Displays information about a wireless interface, such as rate, power level, or frequency used
- `iwpriv`—Uses `i` to set optional features, such as roaming, of a wireless network interface
- `iwspy`—Shows wireless statistics of a number of nodes

Support varies for wireless devices, but most modern (that is, post-2005) wireless devices should work with Ubuntu. In general, Linux wireless device software (usually in the form of a kernel module) support the creation of an ethernet device that can be managed by traditional interface tools such as `ifconfig`—with wireless features of the device managed by the various wireless software tools.

For example, when a wireless networking device is first recognized and initialized for use, the driver will most likely report a new device:

```
zd1211rw 5-4:1.0: firmware version 4725


zd1211rw 5-4:1.0: zd1211b chip 050d:705c v4810 \
high 00-17-3f AL2230_RF pa0 g—NS

zd1211rw 5-4:1.0: eth2

usbcore: registered new interface driver zd1211rw
```

This output (from the `dmesg` command) shows that the `eth2` device has been reported. If DHCP is in use, the device should automatically join the nearest wireless subnet and be automatically assigned an IP address. If not, the next step is to use a wireless tool such as iwconfig to set various parameters of the wireless device. The iwconfig command, along with the device name (eth2 in this example), will show the status:

```
matthew@seymour:~$ iwconfig eth2
eth2      IEEE 802.11b/g  ESSID:"SKY35120"  Nickname:"zd1211"
          Mode:Managed  Frequency:2.462 GHz  \
Access Point: 00:18:4D:06:8E:2A
          Bit Rate=24 Mb/s
          Encryption key:0EFD-C1AF-5C8D-B2C6-7A89-3790-07A7-AC64-0AB5\
-C36E-D1E9-A230-1DB9-D227-2EB6-D6C8   Security mode:open
          Link Quality=100/100  Signal level=82/100
          Rx invalid nwid:0  Rx invalid crypt:0  Rx invalid frag:0
          Tx excessive retries:0  Invalid misc:0   Missed beacon:0
```

This example shows a 24Mbps connection to a network named SKY35120. To change a parameter, such as the transmission rate, use a command-line option with the iwconfig command like this:

```
matthew@seymour:~$ sudo iwconfig eth0 rate 11M
```

Other options supported by the iwconfig command include essid, used to set the NIC to connect to a specific network by named; mode, used to enable the NIC to automatically retrieve settings from an access point or connect to another wireless host; or freq, to set a frequency to use for communication. Additional options include channel, frag, enc (for encryption), power, and txpower. Details and examples of these options are in the iwconfig manual page.

You can then use the ifconfig command or perhaps a graphical Ubuntu tool to set the device networking parameters, and the interface will work as on a hardwired LAN. One handy output of the iwconfig command is the link quality output, which can be used in shell scripts or other graphical utilities for signal monitoring purposes.

Advantages of Wireless Networking

Advantages of wireless networking are its mobility and potential range. If you have a large enough antenna network, your network can stretch many miles. This would be an expensive network, but one that would easily break out of the brick and mortar confines of the office.

Wireless networking would also be a great advantage to college campuses to eliminate the need to tear through walls to install cabling because more and more students expect to have a network connection in their dorm rooms. Wireless networking cards are very reasonable in price and can easily be issued to each student as he requires them.

Home networkers can also benefit from wireless networking. For those who cannot do wired network modifications to their homes, wireless networking removes the unsightly wires running along baseboards and ceilings that are required to connect computers in different rooms. With a wireless home network, you are not even confined to inside the house. Depending on the transmit power of your router, you can sit out in your backyard and watch clouds drifting by as you type away.

Choosing the right types of wireless devices is an important decision. The next sections discuss some of the basic differences between current protocols used for wireless networking.

Choosing from Among Available Wireless Protocols

The Institute of Electrical and Electronics Engineers (IEEE) started to look seriously at wireless networking in 1990. This is when the 802.11 Standard was first introduced by the Wireless Local Area Networks Standards Working Group. The group based the standard roughly around the architecture used in cellular phone networks. The wireless network is controlled by a base station, which can be just a transmitter attached to the network or, more commonly these days, a router.

Larger networks can use more than one base station. Networks with more than one base station are usually referred to as *distribution systems*. A distribution system can be used to increase coverage area and support roaming of wireless hosts. You can also employ external omnidirectional antennas to increase coverage area, or if required, use point-to-point, or directional antennas to connect distant computers or networks. Right now, the least expensive wireless Linux networks are built using devices (such as access points or NICs) supporting 802.11b, although the faster 802.11g devices tend to get more shelf space. Devices are available marketed as N or Pre-N, meaning that they implement a draft standard, while the IEEE carry on debating the full N standard. Significantly more power throughput and range are promised by hardware that supports N, but this specification has yet to be formally agreed upon and so implementations are not necessarily standard.

An early standard, 802.11a, offers greater transmission rates than 802.11b, and a number of 802.11a wireless NICs are available (some products provide up to 72Mbps, but will not work with 802.11b devices). Wireless networking devices based on 802.11g, which has the speed improvement of 802.11a and is compatible with 802.11b, are very common. Other wireless protocols include Bluetooth, which provides up to 720Kbps data transfers. Bluetooth is intended for short-range device communications (such as for a printer) and supports a typical range of only 10 meters. Bluetooth is unlike IrDA, which requires line-of-sight (devices that are aimed at each other). Bluetooth use conflicts with 802.11 networks because it also uses the 2.4GHz band. You can find out more at www.bluetooth.com/.

The 802.11 standard specifies that wireless devices use a frequency range of 2400–2483.5MHz. This is the standard used in North America and Europe. In Japan, however, wireless networks are limited to a frequency range of 2471MHz–2479MHz because of Japanese regulations. Within these ranges, each network is given up to 79 non-overlapping frequency channels to use. This reduces the chance of two closely located wireless networks using the same channel at the same time. It also allows for channel hopping, which can be used for security.

Beyond the Network and onto the Internet

Ubuntu supports Internet connections and the use of Internet resources in many different ways. You will find a wealth of Internet-related software included with this book's version of Ubuntu, and you can download hundreds of additional free utilities from a variety of sources. To use them, you must have a working Internet connection.

In this section, you learn how to set up an Internet connection in Ubuntu using a modem and Point-to-Point Protocol (PPP) as well as other connection methods, including Digital Subscriber Line (DSL) and cable modem services. Just a few years ago, getting a dial-up connection working was difficult—hence, an entire chapter of this book was devoted to it. Today, as long as you have a hardware modem, dial-up configuration is simple. The Ubuntu developers and the wider Linux community have made great progress in making connectivity easier.

Although many experienced Linux users continue to use manual scripts to establish their Internet connectivity, new users and experienced system administrators alike will find Ubuntu's graphical network configuration interface much easier to use. You learn how to use the Internet Connection Wizard in this chapter, as well as how to configure Ubuntu to provide dial-in PPP support. The chapter also describes how to use Roaring Penguin's DSL utilities for managing connectivity through a cable modem connection.

Common Configuration Information

Although Ubuntu enables great flexibility in configuring Internet connections, that flexibility comes at the price of an increase in complexity. To configure Internet connectivity in Ubuntu, you must know more about the details of the connection process than you can learn from the information typically provided by your Internet service provider (ISP). In this section of the chapter, you learn what to ask about and how to use the information.

Some ISPs are unaware of Linux or unwilling to support its use with their service. Fortunately, that attitude is rapidly changing, and the majority of ISPs offer services using standard protocols that are compatible with Linux, even if they (or their technical support people) aren't aware that their own ISPs are Linux-friendly. You just need to press a little for the information you require.

If you are one of the few remaining people using a dial-up modem account (referred to in Linux as *PPP* for the Point-to-Point Protocol it uses), your ISP will provide your computer with a static or dynamic IP (Internet Protocol) address. A dynamic IP address changes each time you dial in, whereas a static IP address remains the same. The ISP also might automatically provide your computer with the names of the domain name service (dns) servers. You need to know the telephone number that your computer will dial in to for making the connection; your ISP supplies that number, too. You will also need a working modem and need to know the device name of the modem (usually `/dev/modem`).

NOTE

Most IP addresses are dynamically assigned by ISPs; ISPs have a pool of addresses, and you get whatever address is available. From the ISP's viewpoint, a small number of addresses can serve a large number of people because not everyone will be online at the same time. For most Internet services, a dynamic IP works well because it is the ISP's job to route that information to you, and it sits in the middle—between you and the service you want to use. But a dynamic IP address changes, and if someone needs to find you at the same address (if you run a website or a file transfer site, for example), an IP that changes every time you log on will not work well. For that, you need a static IP. Because your ISP cannot reuse that IP with its other customers, it will likely charge you more for a static IP than a dynamic IP. The average consumer doesn't need the benefit of a static IP, so he is happy paying less for a dynamically assigned IP. Also, the DNS information can be provided automatically by the ISP by the Dynamic Host Configuration Protocol, or DHCP.

If you are using DSL access or a cable modem, you might have a dynamic IP provided through DHCP, or you might be assigned a static IP. You might automatically be provided with the names of the DNS servers if you use DHCP, or you might have to set up DNS manually (in which case, you have to know the IP addresses of the DNS servers).

In all cases, you have to know your username, your password, and for the configuration of other services, the names of the mail servers and the news server. This information can be obtained from your ISP if you specifically ask for it.

NOTE

The information in this book will help you understand and avoid many connection issues, but you might experience connection problems. Keep the telephone number of the technical help service for your ISP on hand in case you are not able to establish a connection. But be aware that few ISPs offer Linux support, and you might need to seek help from a Linux-savvy friend or a Linux user's group if your special circumstances cannot be handled from the knowledge you gain from this book. Of course, the best place to look is on the Internet. Use Google's Linux page (www.google.com/linux/) to research the problem and see if any other users have found fixes or workarounds.

Configuring Digital Subscriber Line Access

Ubuntu also supports the use of a digital subscriber line (DSL) service. Although it refers to the different types of DSL available as xDSL, that name includes ADSL, IDSL, SDSL, and other flavors of DSL service; they can all be configured using the Internet Connection Wizard. DSL service generally provides 256Kbps to 24Mbps transfer speeds and transmits data over copper telephone lines from a central office to individual subscriber sites (such as your home). Many DSL services provide asymmetric speeds with download speeds greater than upload speeds.

NOTE

DSL service is an "always-on" type of Internet service, although you can turn off the connection under Ubuntu using the network configuration tool found under System, Administration, Network. An always-on connection exposes your computer to malicious abuse from crackers who trawl the Internet attempting to gain access to other computer systems. In addition to the capability to turn off such connections, Ubuntu is also preconfigured to not listen on any network ports, which means that any attempts to gain access to your computer will fail because Ubuntu will reject the request. This is the Ubuntu equivalent of putting up a 12-foot steel fence surrounding your computer.

A DSL connection requires that you have an ethernet network interface card (sometimes a USB interface that is not easily supported in Linux) in your computer or notebook. Many users also configure a gateway, firewall, or other computer with at least two network interface cards to share a connection with a LAN. We looked at the hardware and protocol issues earlier on in this chapter. Advanced configuration of a firewall or router, other than what was addressed during your initial installation of Ubuntu, is beyond the scope of this book.

Understanding Point-to-Point Protocol over Ethernet

Establishing a DSL connection with an ISP providing a static IP address is easy. Unfortunately, many DSL providers use a type of PPP protocol named Point-to-Point Protocol over Ethernet (*PPPoE*) that provides dynamic IP address assignment and authentication by encapsulating PPP information inside ethernet frames. Roaring Penguin's `rp-pppoe` clients are available from the Roaring Penguin site (www.roaringpenguin.com/penguin/pppoe/rp-pppoe-3.8.tar.gz), and these clients make the difficult-to-configure PPPoE connection much easier to deal with. You can download and install newer versions (see the Roaring Penguin link in the "Reference" section at the end of this chapter).

NOTE

ADSL modems were frequently supplied by ISPs when they originally started to roll out ADSL services. Today however, in much of the world these modems are optional, which is a good thing because many people choose to purchase a router with an in-built modem to create a dedicated connection. In the United States, these devices are very rare, but you can usually replace the supplied modem with an aftermarket modem if you want to spend the money. Either way, using a router can save many headaches and will allow you to easily connect more than one computer to an Internet connection. Note that if you are using a cable connection then they usually come with an ethernet cable, in which case you just need a router (which is pretty much how all Internet access works in the United States, because combination modem/router devices are very rare in the U.S.). Check with your ISP before buying to ensure that whatever router you do end up with can be supported by them. You might find that your ISP even supplies a router as part of the package!

Configuring a PPPoE Connection Manually

You should only need to use these steps if you are using a modem supplied by your ISP, and not a router. The basic steps involved in manually setting up a DSL connection using Ubuntu involve connecting the proper hardware, and then running a simple configuration script if you use `rp-pppoe` from Roaring Penguin.

First, connect your DSL modem to your telephone line, and then plug in your ethernet cable from the modem to your computer's network interface card. If you plan to share your DSL connection with the rest of your LAN, you need at least two network cards—designated `eth0` (for your LAN) and `eth1` (for the DSL connection).

The following example assumes that you have more than one computer and will share your DSL connection on a LAN.

First, log in as `root`, and ensure that your first `eth0` device is enabled and up (perhaps using the `ifconfig` command). Next, bring up the other interface, but assign a null IP address like this:

```
matthew@seymour:~$ sudo /sbin/ifconfig eth1 0.0.0.0 up
```

Now use the `adsl-setup` command to set up your system. Type the command like this:

```
matthew@seymour:~$ sudo /sbin/adsl-setup
```

You will be presented with a text script and be asked to enter your username and the Ethernet interface used for the connection (such as `eth1`). You will then be asked to use "on demand" service or have the connection stay up all the time (until brought down by the root operator). You can also set a timeout in seconds, if desired. You'll then be asked to enter the IP addresses of your ISP's DNS servers if you haven't configured the system's `/etc/resolv.conf` file.

After that, you will be prompted to enter your password two times, and have to choose the type of firewall and IP masquerading to use. (You learned about IP masquerading in the "Using IP Masquerading in Ubuntu" section, earlier in this chapter.) The actual configuration is done automatically. Using a firewall is essential today, so you should choose this option unless you intend to craft your own set of firewall rules—a discussion of which is beyond the scope of this book. After you have chosen your firewall and IP masquerading setup, you will be asked to confirm, save, and implement your settings. You are also given a choice to allow users to manage the connection, a handy option for home users.

Changes will be made to your system's `/etc/sysconfig/network-scripts/ifcfg-ppp0`, `/etc/resolv.conf`, `/etc/ppp/pap-secrets`, and `/etc/ppp/chap-secrets` files.

After configuration has finished, use the `adsl-start` command to start a connection and DSL session, like this:

```
matthew@seymour:~$ sudo /sbin/adsl-start
```

The DSL connection should be nearly instantaneous, but if problems occur, check to make sure that your DSL modem is communicating with the phone company's central office by examining the status LEDs on the modem. Because this varies from modem to modem, consult your modem user's manual.

Make sure all cables are properly attached, that your interfaces are properly configured, and that you have entered the correct information to the setup script.

If IP masquerading is enabled, other computers on your LAN on the same subnet address (such as `192.168.0.XXX`) can use the Internet, but must have the same `/etc/resolv.conf` name server entries and a routing entry with the DSL-connected computer as a gateway. For example, if the host computer with the DSL connection has an IP address of `192.168.0.1`, and other computers on your LAN use addresses in the `192.168.0.XXX` range, use the `route` command on each computer like this:

```
matthew@seymour:~$ sudo /sbin/route add default gw 192.168.0.1
```

Note that you can also use a hostname instead if each computer has an `/etc/hosts` file with hostname and IP address entries for your LAN. To stop your connection, use the `adsl-stop` command like this:

```
matthew@seymour:~$ sudo /sbin/adsl-stop
```

Configuring Dial-Up Internet Access

Most ISPs provide dial-up connections supporting PPP because it is a fast and efficient protocol for using TCP/IP over serial lines. PPP is designed for two-way networking; TCP/IP provides the transport protocol for data. One hurdle faced by new Ubuntu users is how to set up PPP and connect to the Internet. It is not necessary to understand the details of the PPP protocol to use it, and setting up a PPP connection is easy. You can configure the PPP connections manually using the command line or graphically during an X session using Ubuntu's Network Configuration Tool. Each approach produces the same results.

PPP uses several components on your system. The first is a daemon called `pppd`, which controls the use of PPP. The second is a driver called the high-level data link control (*HDLC*), which controls the flow of information between two machines. A third component of PPP is a routine called `chat` that dials the other end of the connection for you when you want it to. Although PPP has many "tunable" parameters, the default settings work well for most people.

Ubuntu includes some useful utilities to get your dial-up connection up and running. In this section we will take a look at two options that will have you on the Internet in no time.

The first way is to configure a connection using `pppconfig`, a command line utility to help you to configure specific dial-up connection settings.

Enter the following command:

```
matthew@seymour:~$ sudo pppconfig
```

Before you connect for the first time you need to add yourself to both the dip and dialout groups by using the commands:

```
matthew@seymour:~$ sudo adduser YOURNAMEHERE dip
matthew@seymour:~$ sudo adduser YOURNAMEHERE dialout
```

After this has been done it is just a simple matter of issuing the `pon` command to connect, and the `poff` command to disconnect. You can create as many different profiles as you need, and can launch specific ones by using the command `pon profilename`, again using the `poff` command to disconnect.

CAUTION

Many software modems will not work with Linux because the manufacturers will not release programming information about them or provide Linux drivers. An external serial port modem or ISA bus modem will almost always work; USB and PCI modems are still problematic. It is suggested that you do a thorough Google search using your modem's name and model number to see how others have solved problems with that particular modem. Links to software modem compatibility sites appear at the end of this chapter.

Troubleshooting Connection Problems

The Linux Documentation Project at www.tldp.org/ offers many in-depth resources for configuring and troubleshooting these connections. The Internet search engine Google is also an invaluable tool for dealing with specific questions about these connections. For many other useful references, see the "Reference" section at the end of this chapter.

Here are a few troubleshooting tips culled from many years of experience:

- If your modem connects and then hangs up, you are probably using the wrong password or dialing the wrong number. If the password and phone number are correct, it is likely an authentication protocol problem.
- If you get connected but cannot reach websites, it is likely a domain name resolver problem, meaning that DNS is not working. If it worked yesterday and you haven't "adjusted" the associated files, it is probably a problem at the ISP's end. Call and ask.
- Always make certain that everything is plugged in. Check again—and again.
- If the modem works in Windows, but not in Linux no matter what you do, it is probably a software modem no matter what it said on the box.
- If everything just stops working (and you do not see smoke), it is probably a glitch at the ISP or the telephone company. Take a break and give them some time to fix it.
- Never configure a network connection when you have had too little sleep or too much caffeine; you will just have to redo it tomorrow.

RELATED UBUNTU AND LINUX COMMANDS

You will use these commands when managing network connectivity in your Ubuntu system:

- `dhclient`—Automatically acquire, and then set IP info for a NIC
- `ethereal`—GNOME graphical network scanner
- `firestarter`—Ubuntu's basic graphical firewalling tool for X

- `ifconfig`—Displays and manages Linux networking devices
- `iwconfig`—Displays and sets wireless network device parameters
- `route`—Displays and manages Linux kernel routing table
- `ssh`—The OpenSSH remote-login client and preferred replacement for `telnet`
- `nm-connection-editor`—Ubuntu's GUI for configuring network connections

Reference

The following websites and books are great resources for more information on the topics covered in this chapter. Networking is complex. The more you take the time to learn, the easier setting up and maintaining your network will be.

Websites

- https://help.ubuntu.com/10.04/serverguide/C/network-configuration.html—Official networking help for Ubuntu.
- www.ietf.org/rfc.html—Go here to search for, or get a list of, Request for Comments (RFC).
- www.oth.net/dyndns.html—For a list of Dynamic DNS service providers, go to this site.
- www.isc.org/products/DHCP/dhcpv3-README.html—The DHCP README is available at this site.
- www.ieee.org—The Institute of Electrical and Electronics Engineers (IEEE) website.

Books

- Joe Casad, *Sams Teach Yourself TCP/IP Network Administration in 21 Days*, Sams Publishing, ISBN: 0-672-31250-6
- Craig Hunt and Gigi Estabrook, *TCP/IP Network Administration*, O'Reilly Publishing, ISBN: 1-56592-322-7
- Frank J. Derfler, Frank Derfler, and Jeff Koch, *Practical Networking*, Que Publishing, ISBN: 0-7897-2252-6
- Steve Litt, *Samba Unleashed*, Sams Publishing, ISBN: 0-672-31862-8
- Ralph Droms and Ted Lemon, *The DHCP Handbook*, Sams Publishing, ISBN: 0-672-32327-3

CHAPTER 15

Remote Access with SSH and Telnet

IN THIS CHAPTER

- Setting Up a Telnet Server
- Telnet Versus SSH
- Setting Up an SSH Server
- The SSH Tools
- Remote X
- Reference

Controlling your system remotely is one of the cooler things you can do with Ubuntu—with just a bit of configuration, you can connect from any Linux box to another computer in a variety of ways. If you just want to check something quickly or if you have limited bandwidth, you have the option of using only the command line, but you can also connect directly to the X server and get full graphical control.

Understanding the selection of tools available is largely a history lesson. For example, Telnet was an earlier way of connecting to another computer through the command line, but that has since been superseded by SSH. That is not to say that you should ignore Telnet; you need to know how to use it so you have it as a fallback. However, SSH is preferred because it is more secure. We cover both in this chapter.

Setting Up a Telnet Server

Telnet is an older service. The client is part of the default installation, but is not activated by default. The server is not part of the default installation. This is because everything Telnet transmits and receives is in plain text, including passwords and other sensitive information. Telnet is generally not a good choice for communication. However, you may want to install Telnet for certain situations, such as connecting to piece of equipment that doesn't have SSH available, such as embedded systems where having a small OS footprint is important and more secure methods of communication are not available. In addition, sometimes Telnet is the quickest and easiest way to test newly installed services during configuration, such as a Postfix mail server. You might also want to install Telnet to learn about it and test it, simply because you may run across moments in the real world where no other option exists.

If you decide to install Telnet, use Synaptic or apt to install `telnetd`. This will install the server.

Start by configuring your firewall to allow connections through port 23. If this port is blocked, you will not be able to use Telnet. See Chapter 33, "Securing Your Machines," for help doing this.

After that is configured, type **`telnet <your IP>`**. This will test to confirm both the client and server are installed and working by connecting from your terminal using the client back to the server running on your own computer. You are prompted to enter your username and password. The whole conversation should look something like this:

```
matthew@seymour:~$ telnet 192.168.1.102
Trying 192.168.1.102...
Connected to 192.168.1.102 (192.168.1.102)
Escape character is '^]'.

Welcome to babbage
Ubuntu 10.04 LTS

* All access is logged *

login: matthew
Password:
Last login: Sun Jul  4 10:08:34 2010 from seymour
matthew@babbage~$
```

TIP

The server responds with `Welcome to babbage, Ubuntu 10.04 LTS`, which is a customized message. Your machine will respond similarly. This may be insecure: giving away version numbers is never a smart move on a machine that may be accessed from outside of a secure network. In fact, even saying `Ubuntu` is questionable. In those instances, you can edit the `issue` and `issue.net` files in your `/etc` directory to change the message displayed.

To use Telnet to connect to a different computer, use that computer's IP address on the network instead of using your own. You can use Telnet on local networks as well as across the internet to connect to any computer running the server on an open port.

Telnet uses port 23, but you can use it with other ports by adding the port to the IP address like in this example where we use it to connect to port 110 to test a POP3 connection/server:

```
matthew@seymour:~$ telnet 192.168.1.102 110
```

Telnet Versus SSH

Although Telnet is worth keeping around as a fail-safe, last resort option, SSH is superior in virtually every way. Telnet is fast but also insecure. As stated earlier, it sends all your text, including your password, in plain text that can be read by anyone with the right tools. SSH, on the other hand, encrypts all your communication and so is more resource-intensive but secure—even a government security agency sniffing your packets for some reason would still have a hard time cracking the encryption.

Andy Green, posting to the `fedora-list` mailing list, summed up the Telnet situation perfectly when he said, "As Telnet is universally acknowledged to encourage evil, the service `telnetd` is not enabled by default." It is worthwhile taking the hint: Use Telnet as a last resort only.

Setting Up an SSH Server

If not installed already, the OpenSSH server can be installed through Synaptic by adding the openssh-server package. As you might have guessed, `sshd` is the name for the SSH server daemon.

Start by configuring your firewall to allow connections through port 22. If this port is blocked, you will not be able to use SSH. See Chapter 33for help doing this.

Two different versions of SSH exist, SSH1 and SSH2. The latter is newer, more secure, comes with more features, and is the default in Ubuntu. Support for SSH1 clients is best left disabled so older clients can not connect. This is done by default in the `/etc/ssh/sshd_config` file on this line:

```
Protocol 2
```

If you have no other option and absolutely have to allow an older client to connect, add a new line:

```
Protocol 1
```

SSH Tools

To the surprise of many, OpenSSH actually comprises a suite of tools. We have already seen `ssh`, the secure shell command that connects to other machines, and `sshd`, the SSH server daemon that accepts incoming SSH connections. However, there is also `sftp`, a replacement for `ftp`, `scp`, and `rcp`.

You should already be familiar with the `ftp` command because it is the lowest-common-denominator system for handling FTP file transfers. Like Telnet, though, `ftp` is insecure: It sends your data in plain text across the network and anyone can sniff your packets to pick out a username and password. The SSH replacement, `sftp`, puts FTP traffic over an SSH link, thus securing it.

The `rcp` command might be new to you, largely because it is not used much anymore. Back in its day, `rcp` was the primary way of copying a single file to another server. As with `ftp`, `scp` replaces `rcp` by simply channeling the data over a secure SSH connection. The difference between `sftp` and `scp` is that the former allows you to queue and copy many files at once, whereas the latter is usually used to just send one, although `scp` can be used with the -r option to send an entire directory at once. See the man page for details.

Using `scp` to Copy Individual Files Between Machines

The most basic use of the `scp` command is to copy a file from your current machine to a remote machine. You can do that with the following command:

```
scp test.txt 192.168.1.102:
```

The first parameter is the name of the file you want to send, and the second is the server to which you want to send it. Note that there is a colon at the end of the IP address. This is where you can specify an exact location for the file to be copied. If you have nothing after the colon, as in the previous example, `scp` copies the file to your home directory. As with SSH, `scp` prompts you for your password before copying takes place.

You can rewrite the previous command so you copy `test.txt` from the local machine and save it as `newtest.txt` on the server:

```
scp test.txt 192.168.1.102:newtest.txt
```

Alternatively, if there is a directory where you want the file to be saved, you can specify it like this:

```
scp test.txt 192.168.1.102:subdir/stuff/newtest.txt
```

The three commands so far have all assumed that your username on your local machine is the same as your username on the remote machine. If this is not the case, you need to specify your username before the remote address, like this:

```
scp test.txt usernamenewtest.txt
```

You can use `scp` to copy remote files locally, simply by specifying the remote file as the source and the current directory (`.`) as the destination:

```
scp 192.168.1.102:remote.txt .
```

If you want to copy files from one remote machine to another remote machine using `scp`, the best method is to first `ssh` to one of the remote machines and then use `scp` from that location.

Using `sftp` to Copy Many Files Between Machines

`sftp` is a mix between `ftp` and `scp`. Connecting to the server uses the same syntax as `scp`—you can just specify an IP address to connect using your current username, or you can specify a username using *`username@ipaddress`. You can optionally add a colon and a directory, as with `scp`*. After you are connected, the commands are the same as `ftp`: `cd`, `put`, `mput`, `get`, `quit`, and so on.

In one of the `scp` examples, we copied a remote file locally. You can do the same thing with `sftp` with the following conversation:

```
matthew@seymour:~$ sftp 192.168.1.102
Connecting to 192.168.1.102...
matthew@192.168.1.102's password:
sftp> get remote.txt
Fetching /home/matthew/remote.txt to remote.txt
/home/matthew/remote.txt        100%  23    0.0KB/s    00:00
sftp> quit
matthew@seymour:~$
```

Although FTP remains prominent because of the number of systems that do not have support for SSH, SFTP is gaining in popularity. Apart from the fact that it secures all communications between client and server, SFTP is popular because the initial connection between the client and server is made over port 22 through the `sshd` daemon. Someone using SFTP connects to the standard `sshd` daemon, verifies himself, and then is handed over to the SFTP server. The advantage to this is that it reduces the attack vectors because the SFTP server cannot be contacted directly and so cannot be attacked as long as the `sshd` daemon is secure.

Using `ssh-keygen` to Enable Key-Based Logins

There is a weak link in the SSH system, and, inevitably, it lies with users. No matter what lengths system administrators go to in training users to be careful with their passwords, monitors around the world have Post-it notes attached to them with "pAssw0rd" written on them. Sure, it has a mix of letters and numbers, but it can be cracked in less than a second by any brute-force method. *Brute-forcing* is the method of trying every password possibility, starting with likely words (such as *password* and variants, or *god*) and then just trying random letters (for example, *a*, *aa*, *ab*, *ac*, and so on).

Even very strong passwords are no more than about 16 characters; such passwords take a long time to brute-force but can still be cracked. The solution is to use key-based logins, which generate a unique, 1024-bit private and public key pair for your machine. These keys take even the fastest computers a lifetime to crack, and you can back them up with a password to stop others from using them.

Creating an SSH key is done through the `ssh-keygen` command, like this:

```
matthew@seymour:~$ ssh-keygen –t dsa
```

Press Enter when it prompts you where to save your key, and enter a passphrase when it asks you to. This passphrase is just a password used to protect the key—you can leave it blank if you want to, but doing so would allow other people to use your account to connect to remote machines if they manage to log in as you.

After the key is generated, change the directory to `.ssh` (`cd ~/.ssh`), which is a hidden directory where your key is stored and also where it keeps a list of safe SSH hosts. Assuming you use the default options, here you will see the files `id_dsa` and `id_dsa.pub`. The first is your private key and should never be given out. The second is your public key, which is safe for distribution. You need to copy the public key to each server you want to connect to via key-based SSH.

Using `scp`, you can copy the public key over to your server, like this:

```
matthew@seymour:~$ scp id_dsa.pub 192.186.1.102:
```

This places `id_dsa.pub` in your home directory (for an account that uses the same user-name as your local account) on `192.186.1.102`. The next step is to SSH into `192.186.1.102` normally and set up that key as an authorized key. So, you can SSH in as yourself:

```
matthew@seymour:~$ ssh 192.168.1.102
```

After logging in normally, type:

```
matthew@babbage:~$ cat id_dsa.pub >> .ssh/authorized_keys
matthew@babbage:~$ chmod 400 .ssh/authorized_keys
```

The touch command creates the authorized_keys file (if it does not exist already); then you use `cat` to append the contents of `id_dsa.pub` to the list of already authorized keys. Finally, `chmod` is used to make authorized_keys read-only.

With that done, you can type `exit` to disconnect from the remote machine and return to your local machine. Then you can try running `ssh` again. If you are prompted for your passphrase, you have successfully configured key-based authentication.

That is the current machine secured, but what about every other machine? It is still possible to log in from another machine using only a password, which means your remote machine is still vulnerable.

The solution to this is to edit the `/etc/ssh/sshd_config` file. This will require super-user privileges. Look for the PasswordAuthentication line and make sure it reads no (and that it is not commented out with a #). Save the file, and run `kill -HUP 'cat /var/run/sshd.pid'` to have `sshd` reread its configuration files. With that done, `sshd` accepts only connections from clients with authorized keys, which stops crackers from brute-forcing their way in.

TIP

For extra security, you are strongly encouraged to set `PermitRootLogin` to no in `/etc/ssh/sshd_config`. When this is set, it becomes impossible to SSH into your machine using the root account—you must connect with a normal user account and then use `su` or `sudo` to switch to root. This is advantageous because most brute-force attempts take place on the root account because it is the only account that is guaranteed to exist on a server.

Also, even if a cracker knows your user account, she has to guess both your user password and your root password to take control of your system.

Of course, if you don't have a root account enabled on your box, this isn't an issue because it is already impossible to log in directly as root. Hooray for slightly more secure defaults in Ubuntu!

Virtual Network Computing (VNC)

Everything we have looked at so far has been about remote access using the command-line, with no mention so far of how to bring up a graphical user interface. There are several ways of doing this in Ubuntu, some of which are linked in the "Reference" section later in this chapter. Here we will discuss the most popular and the most preferred by the Ubuntu community, which is also the best supported by the developers: Virtual Network Computing (VNC).

VNC is a system for controlling a computer remotely and sharing desktops over a network using a graphical interface. It was created at the Olivetti & Oracle Research Lab, which was acquired by AT&T in 1999 and closed down in 2001. Since then, several of the members of the development team got together to create a free and open source version of the code (using the GPL), and from that base many different version have appeared. VNC is widespread in the Linux world and, to a lesser extent, in the Windows world. Its main advantage is its widespread nature: nearly all Linux distros bundle VNC, and clients are available for a wide selection of platforms.

Start by configuring your firewall to allow connections through port 5900. If this port is blocked, you will not be able to use VNC. See Chapter 33, "Securing Your Machines," for help doing this.

To set up VNC on your Ubuntu computer to allow others to access your desktop, you only need to tell Ubuntu who should be allowed to connect to your session. This is done from the menu at System, Preferences, Remote Desktop. By default, your desktop is not shared. Check Allow other users to view your desktop to Share It. Most likely, you also want to check Allow other users to control your desktop; otherwise, people will be able to see what you are doing but not interact with the desktop—which is not very helpful. If you are using this as a remote way to connect to your own desktop or one that is running unattended when you will need access, uncheck You must confirm each access to this machine. If this is not done, when you try to connect from your remote location, Ubuntu will pop up a message box on the local machine asking Should This Person Be Allowed to Connect? Because you are not there to click Yes, the connection will fail. If you want to let someone else remotely connect to your system, keep this box enabled so you know when people are connecting. You should always enter a password, no matter who it is that will connect. The options suggested are shown in Figure 15.1.

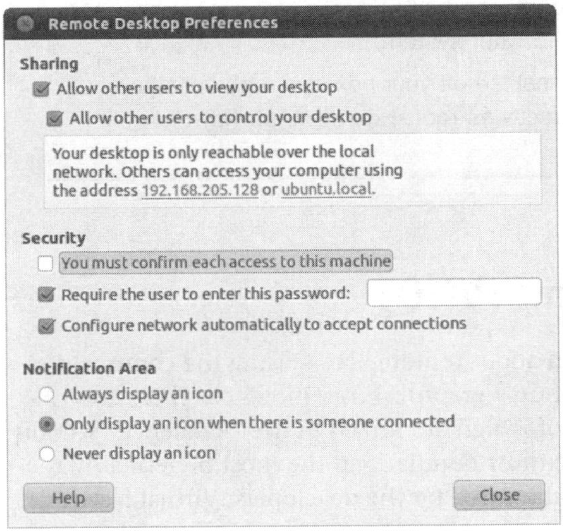

FIGURE 15.1 Remote Desktop Preferences.

To access a computer that is running VNC from your Ubuntu desktop, in the menu click Applications, Internet, Remote Desktop Viewer. The program starts by searching the local network for shared desktops. If any are found, they will be listed. In Figure 15.2, Heather's computer is shown.

From the screen in Figure 15.2, click Connect. You will then be allowed to select one of the hosts shown in the previous list from a drop box, find others on the network, or enter an IP address of your choosing that correlates to a computer you have already set up somewhere to be accessed using VNC as in Figure 15.3. Then choose your other options and click Connect to begin.

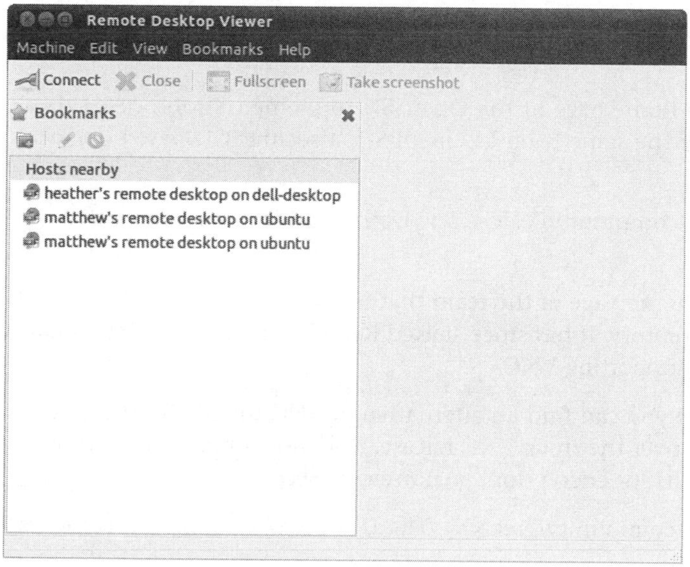

FIGURE 15.2 Remote Desktop Viewer.

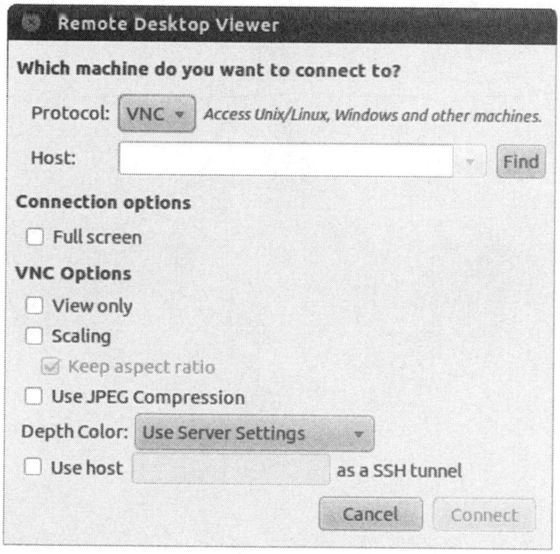

FIGURE 15.3 Choose the machine to which you want to connect.

When you are finished, click Close.

VNC should not be considered secure over the Internet or on untrusted internal networks.

Reference

- www.telnet.org—Telnet's home page.
- https://help.ubuntu.com/community/SSH—The Ubuntu community documentation for SSH.
- www.openssh.com—The home page of the OpenSSH implementation of SSH that Ubuntu uses. It is run by the same team as OpenBSD, a secure BSD-based operating system.
- https://help.ubuntu.com/community/VNC—The Ubuntu community documentation for VNC.
- www.realvnc.com—The home page of the team that made VNC at AT&T's Cambridge Research Laboratory. It has since started RealVNC Ltd., a company dedicated to developing and supporting VNC.
- www.tightvnc.com—Here you can find an alternative to VNC called TightVNC that has several key advances over the stock VNC release. The most important feature is that TightVNC can use SSH for encryption, guaranteeing security.
- https://help.ubuntu.com/community/FreeNX—The Ubuntu community documentation for FreeNX.
- www.nomachine.com/—Another alternative to VNC is in the pipeline, called NX. The free implementation, FreeNX, is under heavy development at the time of writing but promises to work much faster than VNC.

CHAPTER 16

File and Print

IN THIS CHAPTER

- Using the Network File System
- Putting Samba to Work
- Network and Remote Printing with Ubuntu
- Creating Network Printers
- Using the Common UNIX Printing System GUI
- Avoiding Printer Support Problems
- Reference

In the early days of computing, file and printer sharing was pretty much impossible because of the lack of good networking standards and interoperability. If you wanted to use a printer connected to another computer, you had to save the file to a floppy disk and walk over. Sometimes people do the same thing today using a USB thumb drive or emailing the file. However, there are better ways.

Both file and printer sharing are important because it is not unusual for someone to own more than one computer. Whether you want to share photographs among various computers or have a central repository available for collaboration, file sharing is an important part of our information age. Alongside this is the need to be able to share printers; after all, people do not want to have to plug and unplug a computer to a printer just so they can print out a quick letter.

Whatever your reasons for needing to share files and printers across a network, you find out how to do both in this chapter. We look at how you can share files using the popular UNIX NFS protocol and the more Windows-friendly Samba system. You also find out how to configure network-attached printers with interfaces such as JetDirect. We look at both graphical and command-line tools, so you should find something to suit the way you work.

CAUTION

By default, Ubuntu ships with all its network ports blocked. That is, it does not listen to any requests on any network ports when it is first installed. To configure the firewall, use UFW as described in Chapter 33, "Securing Your Machines".

Using the Network File System

Network File System (NFS) is the protocol developed by Sun Microsystems that allows computers to use a remote file system as if it were a real part of the local machine. A common use of NFS is to allow users' home directories to appear on every local machine they use, thus eliminating the need to have physical home directories. This opens up hot desking and other flexible working arrangements, especially because no matter where the users are, their home directory follows them around.

Another popular use for NFS is to share binary files between similar computers. If you have a new version of a package that you want all machines to have, you have to the upgrade only on the NFS server, and all hosts running the same version of Ubuntu will have the same upgraded package.

Installing and Starting or Stopping NFS

NFS is not installed by default on Ubuntu, so you need to install the `nfs-kernel-server` package. NFS itself consists of several programs that work together. One is `portmap`, which maps NFS requests to the correct daemon. Two others are `nfsd`, which is the NFS daemon, and `mountd`, which controls the mounting and unmounting of file systems.

Ubuntu automatically adds NFS to the system startup scripts, so it will always be available after you have configured it. To check this, use the command `sudo /etc/init.d/nfs-kernel-server status` and it will show you that the service is running. If you need to manually start the NFS server, use the following command:

```
matthew@seymour:~$ sudo /etc/init.d/nfs-kernel-server start
 * Exporting directories for NFS kernel daemon:  [ OK ]
Starting NFS kernel daemon:                          [ OK ]
```

In this example, NFS has been started. Use stop to stop the service, or restart to restart the server. This approach to controlling NFS proves handy, especially after configuration changes have been made. See the next section on how to configure NFS support on your Ubuntu system.

NFS Server Configuration

You can configure the NFS server by editing the `/etc/exports` file. This file is similar to the `/etc/fstab` file in that it is used to set the permissions for the file systems being exported. The entries look like this:

```
/file/system yourhost(options) *.yourdomain.com(options) 192.168.0.0/24(options)
```

This shows three common clients to which to share /file/system. The first, `yourhost`, shares `/file/system` to just one host. The second, `.yourdomain.com`, uses the asterisk (*) as a wildcard to enable all hosts in yourdomain.com to access `/file/system`. The third share enables all hosts of the Class C network, 192.168.0.0, to access `/file/share`. For security, it is best not to use shares, such as the last two across the Internet, because all data will be readable by any network the data passes by.

Table 16.1 shows some common options.

TABLE 16.1 **/etc/fstab** Options

Option	Purpose
`rw`	Gives read and write access
`ro`	Gives read-only access
`async`	Writes data when the server, not the client, feels the need
`sync`	Writes data as it is received

The following is an example of an `/etc/exports` file:

```
# /etc/exports: the access control list for filesystems which may be exported
#               to NFS clients.  See exports(5).
/home/matthew 192.168.0.0/24(rw,no root squash)
```

This file exports (makes available) `/home/matthew` to any host in 192.168.0.* and allows users to read from and write to `/home/matthew`.

After you have finished with the `/etc/exports` file, the following command exports all the file systems in the `/etc/exports` file to a list named xtab under the `/var/lib/nfs` directory, which is used as a guide for mounting when a remote computer asks for a directory to be exported:

```
matthew@seymour:~$ sudo exportfs -a
```

The `-r` option stands for reexport and tells the command to rereads the entire `/etc/exports` file and (re)mount all the entries. You can also use the `exportfs` command to export specific files temporarily. Here's an example using `exportfs` to export a file system:

```
matthew@seymour:~$ /usr/sbin/exportfs -o async yourhost:/usr/tmp
```

This command exports `/usr/tmp to yourhost` with the `async` option.

Be sure to restart the NFS server after making any changes to `/etc/exports`. If you prefer, you can use Ubuntu's `shares-admin` graphical client to set up NFS while using the X Window System. Start the client by clicking the System menu and then selecting the Shared Folders menu item from the Administration menu.

After you press Enter, you are prompted for your password. Type in the password and click OK; the main window will then display. Click the Add button to open the Add Share dialog box.

In the Path drop-down box, choose the directory that you want to share; in the Share drop-down box, choose NFS. Click the Add Host button that appears to specify which hosts, IP addresses, or networks are allowed access to the directory. By default, a directory is exported as read/write, but you can choose read-only by ticking the Read-Only option. When finished, click the OK button, click the Apply button, and then use the File menu to quit.

NFS Client Configuration

To configure your host as an NFS client (to acquire remote files or directories), you need to ensure that you have the nfs-common package installed, to be able to access NFS shares. After you've installed this, edit the `/etc/fstab` file as you would to mount any local file system. However, instead of using a device name to be mounted (such as `/dev/sda1`), enter the remote hostname and the desired file system to be imported. For example, one entry might look like this:

```
# Device              Mount Point  Type  Options       Freq Pass
yourhost:/home/share  /export/share   none   nfs  0    0
```

NOTE

If you use `autofs` on your system, you need to use proper `autofs` entries for your remote NFS mounts. See the `section 5` man page for `autofs`.

You can also use the `mount` command, as root, to quickly attach a remote directory to a local file system by using a remote host's name and exported directory. For example:

```
matthew@seymour:~$ sudo mount -t nfs 192.168.2.67:/music /music
```

After you press Enter, the entire remote directory appears on your file system. You can verify the imported file system using the `df` command, as follows:

```
matthew@seymour:~$ df
Filesystem            1k-blocks      Used Available Use% Mounted on
/dev/hda2              18714368   9642600   8121124  55% /
/dev/hda1                 46636     13247     30981  30% /boot
none                     120016         0    120016   0% /dev/shm
192.168.2.67:/music    36875376  20895920  14106280  60% /music
```

Make sure that the desired mount point exists before using the mount command. When finished using the directory (perhaps for copying backups), you can use the `umount` command to remove the remote file system. Note that if you specify the root directory (/) as a mount point, you cannot unmount the NFS directory until you reboot (because Linux complains that the file system is in use).

Putting Samba to Work

Samba uses the *Session Message Block (SMB)* protocol to enable the Windows operating system (or any operating system) to access Linux files. Using Samba, you can make your Ubuntu machine look just like a Windows computer to other Windows computers on your network. You do not need to install Windows on your PC.

Samba is a complex program—the Samba man page (when converted to text) for just the configuration file is 330KB and 7,226 lines long. Although Samba is complex, setting it up and using it does not have to be difficult. There are many options, which accounts for some of Samba's complexity. Depending on what you want, Samba's use can be as easy or as difficult as you would like it to be.

Fortunately, Ubuntu includes a very easy way to access files on a Windows network share by default. To start, click Places, Network from the menu. You will see a Windows Network icon that, when double-clicked, will show you all Windows domains or workgroups found on your network. Simply double-click any computer icon there to access shares and files.

To share from your Ubuntu desktop, simply right-click a folder you own while using the file browser, most likely one in your `/home/username` directory, and select Sharing Options. You will be given a chance to confirm your desire to share the folder and give it a name. Sharing gives others the permission to view, but not necessarily to create or delete files, although those permissions are also available from this menu. If you don't have the Windows sharing service already installed on your computer, Ubuntu will prompt you for permission to install it.

NOTE

Most Ubuntu users will not need the information contained in the rest of this section because installing the sharing service also takes care of the configuration and as a result, everything should just work.

The *Samba Web Administration Tool (SWAT)* can be used to configure Samba from a web browser. SWAT provides an easy way to start and stop the Samba server; set up printing services; define remote access permissions; and create Samba usernames, passwords, and shared directories. This section delves into the basics of configuring Samba, and you should first read how to manually configure Samba to get an understanding of how the software works. At the end of this section, you will see how to enable, start, and use SWAT to set up simple file sharing.

Like most of the software that comes with Ubuntu, Samba is licensed under the GPL and is free. Installation is straightforward and the software is in the Ubuntu repositories. Regardless of which route you take, you should snag the `samba` and `swat` packages.

Installing from source code can be more time-consuming. If you do not want to install using Ubuntu's default locations, however, installing from the source code is a more configurable method. Just download the source from www.samba.org/ and unpack the files. Change into the source directory and, as root, run the command, `./configure` along with any changes from the defaults. Then run `make`, `make test` (if you want), followed by `make install` to install Samba in the specified locations.

NOTE

If you haven't done so, you might need to install a meta-package (a single package that provides several related packages) called `build-essential`. This package automatically installs all the `make` tools, plus other development utilities that you will need to compile software from source code.

When you install Samba, it is a good idea to also install the `samba-doc` and `samba-doc-pdf` packages because they contain extensive documentation in text, PDF, and HTML format. After you install it, you can find this documentation in `/usr/share/doc/samba*/doc`. If you install Samba using your Ubuntu disc, you can find a large amount of documentation in the directory tree starting at `/usr/share/doc/samba-doc` or `/usr/share/doc/samba-doc-pdf` in several formats, including PDF, HTML, and text, among others. Altogether, almost 3MB of documentation is included with the source code.

After installing Samba, you can either create the file `/etc/samba/smb.conf` or use the `smb.conf` file supplied with Samba, which is located by default under the /etc/samba directory with Ubuntu. You can find nearly a dozen sample configuration files under the `/usr/share/doc/samba*/examples` directory.

NOTE

Depending on your needs, `smb.conf` can be a simple file of fewer than 20 lines or a huge file spanning many pages of text. If your needs are complex, I suggest you browse through The Official Samba Howto and Reference Guide, or TOSHARG. This helpful guide can be found at http://samba.org/samba/docs/man/Samba3-HOWTO/.

Manually Configuring Samba with `/etc/samba/smb.conf`

The `/etc/samba/smb.conf` file is broken into sections. Each section is a description of the resource shared (share) and should be titled appropriately. The three special sections are as follows:

- `[global]`—Establishes the global configuration settings (defined in detail in the `smb.conf` man page and Samba documentation, found under the `/usr/share/doc/samba/docs` directory)
- `[homes]`—Shares users' home directories and specifies directory paths and permissions
- `[printers]`—Handles printing by defining shared printers and printer access

Each section in your `/etc/samba/smb.conf` configuration file should be named for the resource being shared. For example, if the resource `/usr/local/programs` is being shared, you could call the section [programs]. When Windows sees the share, it is called by whatever you name the section (programs in this example). The easiest and fastest way to set up this share is with the following example from smb.conf:

```
[programs]
path = /usr/local/programs
writeable = true
```

This bit shares the /usr/local/programs directory with any valid user who asks for it and makes that directory writable. It is the most basic share because it sets no limits on the directory.

Here are some parameters you can set in the sections:

- Requiring a user to enter a password before accessing a shared directory
- Limiting the hosts allowed to access the shared directory
- Altering permissions users are allowed to have on the directory
- Limiting the time of day during which the directory is accessible

The possibilities are almost endless. Any parameters set in the individual sections override the parameters set in the [global] section. The following section adds a few restrictions to the [programs] section:

```
[programs]
path = /usr/local/programs
writeable = true
valid users = mhelmke
browseable = yes
create mode = 0700
```

The valid users entry limits userid to just mhelmke. All other users can browse the directory because of the browseable = yes entry, but only mhelmke can write to the directory. Any files created by ahudson in the directory give ahudson full permissions, but no one else will have access to the file. This is the same as setting permissions with the chmod command. Again, there are numerous options, so you can be as creative as you want to when developing sections.

Setting Global Samba Behavior with the [global] Section

The [global] section set parameters establishes configuration settings for all of Samba. If a given parameter is not specifically set in another section, Samba uses the default setting in the [global] section. The [global] section also sets the general security configuration for Samba. The [global] section is the only section that does not require the name in brackets.

Samba assumes that anything before the first bracketed section not labeled [global] is part of the global configuration. (Using bracketed headings in /etc/samba/smb.conf makes your configuration file more readable.) The following sections discuss common Samba settings to share directories and printers. You will then see how to test your Samba configuration.

Sharing Home Directories Using the [homes] Section

The `[homes]` section shares out Ubuntu home directories for the users. The home directory is shared automatically when a user's Windows computer connects to the Linux server holding the home directory. The one problem with using the default configuration is that the users see all the configuration files (such as `.profile` and others with a leading period in the filename) that they normally wouldn't see when logging on through Linux. One quick way to avoid this is to include a path option in the `[homes]` section. To use this solution, any users who require a Samba share of their home directory need a separate "home directory" to act as their Windows home directory.

For example, this pseudo home directory could be a directory named `share` in each user's home directory on your Ubuntu system. You can specify the path option when using SWAT by using the `%u` option when specifying a path for the default `homes` shares (see the section, "Configuring Samba Using SWAT" later in this chapter). The complete path setting would be this:

```
/home/%u/share
```

This setting specifies that the directory named share under each user's directory is the shared Samba directory. The corresponding manual `smb.conf` setting to provide a separate "home directory" looks like this:

```
[homes]
        comment = Home Directories
        path = /home/%u/share
        valid users = %S
        read only = No
        create mask = 0664
        directory mask = 0775
        browseable = No
```

If you have a default `[homes]` section, the share shows up in the user's Network Neighborhood as the user's name. When the user connects, Samba scans the existing sections in `smb.conf` for a specific instance of the user's home directory. If there is not one, Samba looks up the username in `/etc/passwd`. If the correct username and password have been given, the home directory listed in `/etc/passwd` is shared out at the user's home directory. Typically, the `[homes]` section looks like this (the `browseable = no entry` prevents other users from being able to browse your home directory and is a good security practice):

```
[homes]
browseable = no
writable = yes
```

This example shares out the home directory and makes it writable to the user. Here's how you specify a separate Windows home directory for each user:

```
[homes]
browseable = no
writable = yes
path = /path/to/windows/directories
```

Sharing Printers by Editing the `[printers]` Section

The `[printers]` section works much like the `[homes]` section but defines shared printers for use on your network. If the section exists, users have access to any printer listed in your Ubuntu `/etc/printcap` file.

Like the `[homes]` section, when a print request is received, all the sections are scanned for the printer. If no share is found (with careful naming, there should not be unless you create a section for a specific printer), the `/etc/printcap` file is scanned for the printer name that is then used to send the print request.

For printing to work properly, you must correctly set up printing services on your Ubuntu computer. A typical `[printers]` section looks like the following:

```
[printers]
comment = Ubuntu Printers
browseable = no
printable = yes
path = /var/spool/samba
```

The `/var/spool/samba` is a spool path set just for Samba printing.

Testing Samba with the `testparm` Command

After you have created your `/etc/smb.conf` file, you can check it for correctness by using the `testparm` command. This command parses through your `/etc/smb.conf` file and checks for any syntax errors. If none are found, your configuration file will probably work correctly. It does not, however, guarantee that the services specified in the file will work. It is merely making sure that the file is correctly written.

As with all configuration files, if you are modifying an existing, working file, it is always prudent to copy the working file to a different location and modify that file. Then, you can check the file with the `testparm` utility. The command syntax is as follows:

```
matthew@seymour:~$ sudo testparm /path/to/smb.conf.back-up
Load smb config files from smb.conf.back-up
Processing section "[homes]"
```

```
Processing section "[printers]"
Loaded services file OK.
```

This output shows that the Samba configuration file is correct, and, as long as all the services are running correctly on your Ubuntu machine, Samba should be working correctly. Now copy your old `smb.conf` file to a new location, put the new one in its place, and restart Samba with the command `/etc/init.d/smbd restart`. Your new or modified Samba configuration should now be in place.

Starting, Stopping, and Restarting the smbd Daemon

Once your `smb.conf` file is correctly configured, you may want to start, stop, or restart your Samba server daemon. This can be done with the `/usr/sbin/smbd` command, which (with no options) starts the Samba server with all the defaults. The most common option you will change in this command is the location of the `smb.conf` file; you change this option if you don't want to use the default location `/etc/smb/smb.conf`. The `-s` option allows you to change the `smb.conf` file Samba uses; this option is also useful for testing whether a new `smb.conf` file actually works. Another useful option is the `-l` option, which specifies the log file Samba uses to store information.

To start, stop, or restart Samba from the command line, use the `/etc/init.d/samba` script with a proper keyword, such as `start`, like this:

```
matthew@seymour:~$ sudo /etc/init.d/samba start
```

Using the smbstatus Command

The `smbstatus` command reports on the current status of your Samba connections. The syntax is as follows:

```
/usr/bin/smbstatus [options]
```

Table 16.2 shows some of the available options.

TABLE 16.2 **mbstatus** Options

Option	Result
`-b`	Brief output
`-d`	Verbose output
`-s /path/to/config`	Used if the configuration file used at startup is not the standard one
`-u username`	Shows the status of a specific user's connection
`-p`	Lists current `smb` processes, which can prove useful in scripts

Connecting with the smbclient Command

The `smbclient` command allows users on other Linux hosts to access your `smb` shares. You cannot mount the share on your host, but you can use it in a way that is similar to an FTP client. Several options can be used with the `smbclient` command. The most frequently used is `-I` followed by the IP address of the computer to which you are connecting. The `smbclient` command does not require root access to run:

```
matthew@seymour:~$ smbclient -I 10.10.10.20 -Uusername%password
```

This gives you the following prompt:

```
smb: <current directory on share>
```

From here, the commands are almost identical to the standard UNIX/Linux FTP commands. Note that you can omit a password on the `smbclient` command line. You are then prompted to enter the Samba share password.

Mounting Samba Shares

There are two ways to mount Samba shares to your Linux host. Mounting a share is the same as mounting an available media partition or remote NFS directory except that the Samba share is accessed using SMB. The first method uses the standard Linux `mount` command:

```
matthew@seymour:~$ sudo mount -t smbfs //10.10.10.20/homes /mount/point -o
username=heather,dmask=777,\
 fmask=777
```


NOTE

You can substitute the IP address for hostname if your name service is running or the host is in your `/etc/hosts` file.

This command mounts `heather`'s home directory on your host and gives all users full permissions to the mount. The permissions are equal to the permissions on the `chmod` command.

The second method produces the same results using the `smbmount` command, as follows:

```
matthew@seymour:~$ sudo smbmount //10.10.10.20/homes /mount/point -o
username=heather,dmask-777,\ fmask=777
```

To unmount the share, use the following standard command:

```
matthew@seymour:~$ sudo umount /mount/point
```

You can also use these mount commands to mount true Windows client shares to your Ubuntu host. Using Samba, you can configure your server to provide any service Windows can serve, and no one but you will ever know.

Configuring Samba Using SWAT

The Samba team of developers has made administering Samba much easier with the Samba Web Administration Tool (SWAT). SWAT is a web-based configuration and maintenance interface that gets as close to a point-and-click Samba environment as possible. This section provides a simple example of how to use SWAT to set up SMB access to a user's home directory and how to share a directory.

NOTE

You need to enable the root account by giving it a password by using the command `sudo passwd root`. Not enabling the root account prevents you from using SWAT effectively.

You need to perform a few steps before you can start using SWAT. First, make sure you have the Samba and the `swat` packages installed. You then enable SWAT access to your system by editing the `/etc/inetd.conf` file by changing the following lines to remove the `#<off>#` comments if present:

```
#<off># swat  stream  tcp  nowait.400  root\
  /usr/sbin/tcpd  /isr/sbin/swat
```

Save the file, and then restart the `openbsd_inetd` daemon using the following command:

```
matthew@seymour:~$ sudo /etc/init.d/openbsd-inetd restart
```

Next, start an X session, launch Firefox, and browse to the http://localhost:901 *uniform resource locator (URL)*. You are presented a login prompt. Enter the root username and password, and then click the OK button. The screen clears, and you see the main SWAT page, as shown in Figure 16.1.

TIP

You can also configure Samba using Ubuntu's `shares-admin` client. Launch the client from the command line of an X terminal window or select the System, Administration, Shared Folders menu item.

First, click the Globals icon in SWAT's main page. You see a page similar to the one shown in Figure 16.2. Many options are in the window, but you can quickly set up access for hosts from your LAN by simply entering one or more IP addresses or a subnet address (such as 192.168.0.—note the trailing period, which allows access for all hosts; in this example, on the 192.168.0 subnet) in the Hosts Allow field under the Security Options section. If you need help on how to format the entry, click the Help link to the left of the field. A new web page appears with the pertinent information.

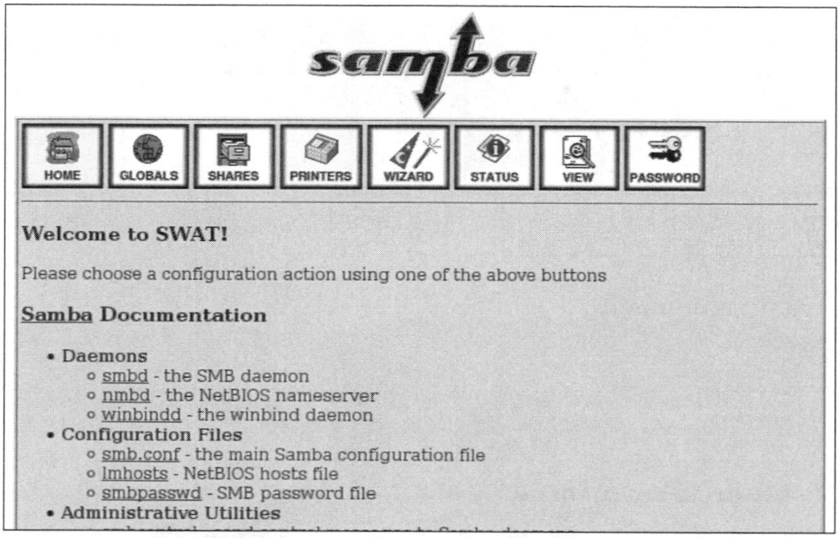

FIGURE 16.1 You can use SWAT to easily configure and administer Samba on your system.

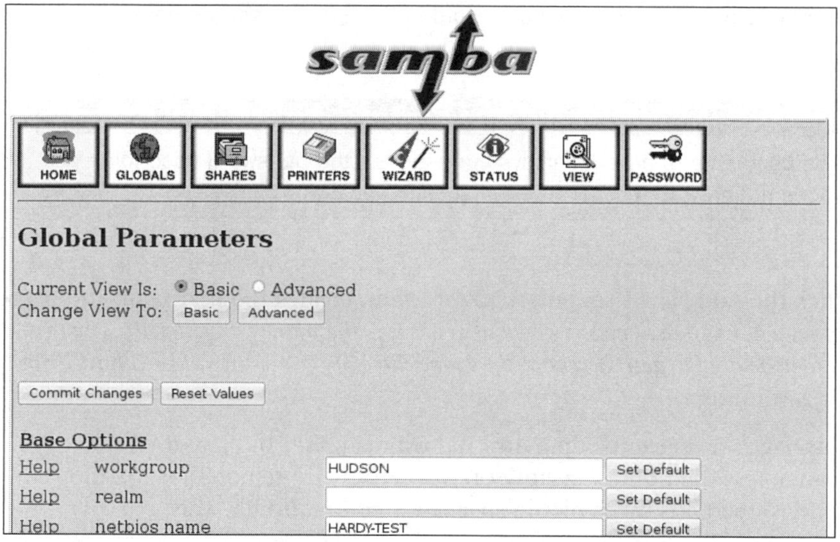

FIGURE 16.2 Configure Samba to allow access from specific hosts or subnets on your LAN.

When finished, click the Commit Changes button to save the global access settings. The next step is to create a Samba user and set the user's password. Click the Password icon on the main SWAT page (refer to Figure 16.1). The Server Password Management page opens, as shown in Figure 16.3. Type a new username in the User Name field; then type a password in the New Password and Retype New Password fields.

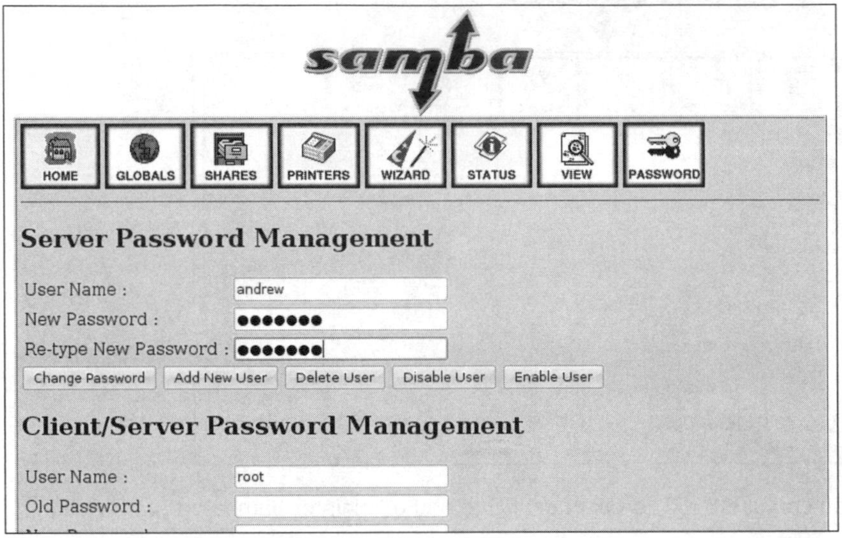

FIGURE 16.3 Enter a Samba username and password in the SWAT Password page.

NOTE

You must supply a username of an existing system user, but the password used for Samba access does not have to match the existing user's password.

When finished, click the Add New User button. SWAT then creates the username and password and displays `Added user` *`username`* *(where* `username` *is the name you entered). The new Samba user should now be able to gain access to the home directory from any allowed host if the Samba (*`smb`*)* server is running.

For example, if you have set up Samba on a host named `mini` that has a user named `andrew`, the user can access the home directory on `mini` from any remote host (if allowed by the Globals settings), perhaps by using the `smbclient` command like this:

```
matthew@seymour:~$  smbclient //mini/andrew -U andrew
added interface ip=192.168.0.68 bcast=192.168.0.255 nmask=255.255.255.0
Password:
Domain=[MYGROUP] OS=[Unix] Server=[Samba 3.0.28]
smb: \> pwd
Current directory is \\mini\andrew\
smb: \> quit
```

Click the Status icon to view Samba's status or to start, stop, or restart the server. You can use various buttons on the resulting web page to control the server and view periodic or continuous status updates.

You can also use SWAT to share a Linux directory. First, click the Shares icon in the toolbar at the top of the main Samba page. Then, type a share name in the Create Shares field, and click the Create Shares button. The SWAT Shares page displays the detailed configuration information in a dialog box, as shown in Figure 16.4, providing access to detailed configuration for the new Samba share.

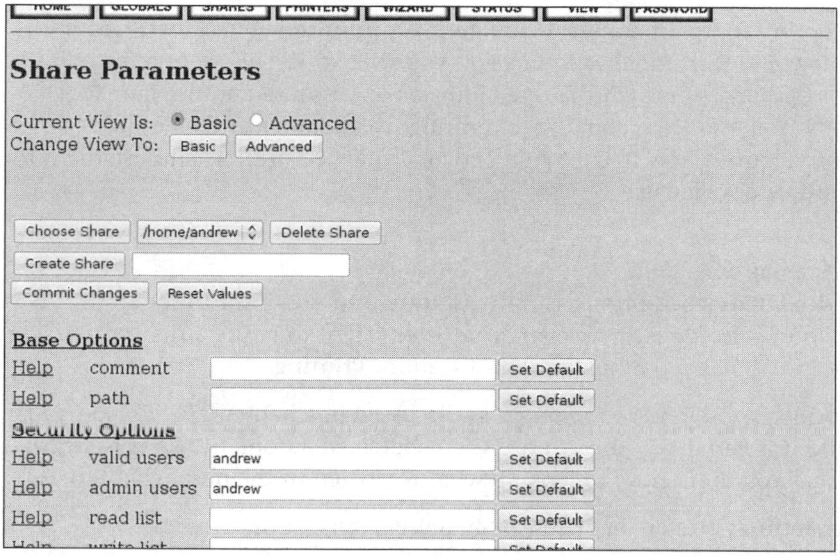

FIGURE 16.4 Use the SWAT Shares page to set up sharing of a portion of your Linux file system.

Type the directory name (such as `/music`) you want to share in the Path field under the Base options. Select No or Yes in the Read-Only field under Security options to allow or deny read and write access. Select Yes in the Guest OK option to allow access from other users and specify a hostname, IP address, or subnet in the Hosts Allow field to allow access. Click the Commit Changes button when finished. Remote users can then access the shared volume. This is how a Linux server running Samba can easily mimic shared volumes in a mixed computing environment!

Alternatively, use the `shares-admin` client (from the command line or the Server Settings Samba Server menu item on the System Settings menu). Unlock the tool by clicking the Unlock button, use the Add button to create new shares, and use the Properties button to edit the share's access options.

Network and Remote Printing with Ubuntu

Chapter 2, "Post-Installation Configuration," discussed how to set up and configure local printers and the associated print services. This section covers configuring printers for sharing and access across a network.

Offices all over the world benefit from using print servers and shared printers. It is a simple thing to do and can bring real productivity benefits, even in small settings.

Creating Network Printers

Setting up remote printing service involves configuring a print server and then creating a remote printer entry on one or more computers on your network. This section introduces a quick method of enabling printing from one Linux workstation to another Linux computer on a LAN. You also learn about SMB printing using Samba and its utilities. Finally, this section discusses how to configure network-attached printers and use them to print single or multiple documents.

Enabling Network Printing on a LAN

If the computer with an attached printer is using Ubuntu and you want to set up the system for print serving, use the `system-config-printer` client to create a new printer, which is available in the menu at System, Administration, Printing.

First, install any printers you have to the server as discussed in Chapter 2 (Click Add and wait a moment and it is very likely the printer will be detected automatically; it is probably easy enough that you don't have to look up what is written in the other chapter).

Next, open Server,Settings and enable Publish Shared Printers Connected to This System. Click OK.

Then, right-click any printer's icon and select Share. That's it. Most users will not need the information in the rest of this section, even to enable access to CUPS via the web interface.

To enable sharing manually, edit your `/etc/cups/cupsd.conf` file. Look for the section that begins with `<Location />` and modify it so that it reads as follows:

```
<Location />
Order Deny,Allow
Deny From All
Allow From 127.0.0.1
Allow From 192.168.0.*
</Location>
```

This tells CUPS to share your printers across the network 192.168.0.*, for example. Make sure to change this to match your own network settings.

Next you need to look in the same file for the section that starts:

```
Listen localhost:631
```

Modify it to show this:

```
Listen 631
```

This tells CUPS to listen on port 631 for any printer requests.

Session Message Block Printing

Printing to an SMB printer requires Samba, along with its utilities such as the `smbclient` and associated `smbprint` printing filter. You can use the Samba software included with Ubuntu to print to a shared printer on a Windows network or set up a printer attached to your system as an SMB printer. This section describes how to create a local printer entry to print to a remote shared printer using SMB.

Setting up an SMB or shared printer is usually accomplished under Windows operating systems through configuration settings using the Control Panel's Network device. After enabling print sharing, reboot the computer. In the My Computer, Printers folder, right-click the name or icon of the printer you want to share and select Sharing from the pop-up menu. Set the Shared As item, and then enter a descriptive shared name, such as **`HP2100`, and a password.**

You must enter a shared name and password to configure the printer when running Linux. You also need to know the printer's workgroup name, IP address, and printer name and have the username and password on hand. To find this information, select Start, Settings, Printers; then right-click the shared printer's listing in the Printers window and select Properties from the pop-up window.

You can use CUPS to configure Samba to use your printers by editing the `smb.conf` file.

In the global section enter the following lines, if they are not already there:

```
...
load printers = yes
printing = cups
printcap name = cups
```

This tells Samba to use CUPS to provide printing services. Next you need to create a new section in the `smb.conf` file at the end of the file, as follows:

```
[printers]
comment = Use this for All Printers
path = /var/spool/samba
browseable = no
public = yes
guest ok = yes
writable = no
printable = yes
printer admin = root, andrew
```

This publishes your printers to the network and allows others to connect to them via Windows clients.

Make sure you restart the Samba service using the command shown earlier to make Samba pick up the changes to the configuration file.

Using the Common UNIX Printing System GUI

You can use CUPS to create printer queues, get print server information, and manage queues by launching a browser (such as Firefox) and browsing to http://localhost:631. CUPS provide a web-based administration interface, as shown in Figure 16.5.

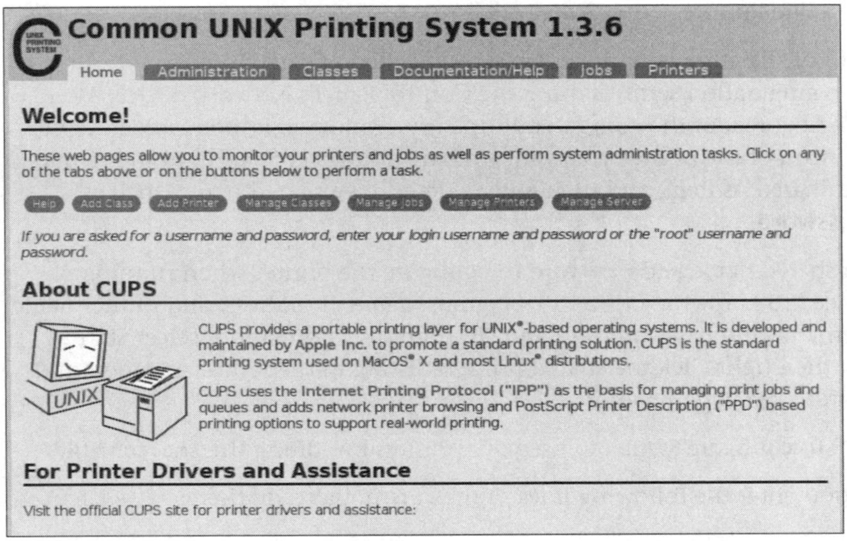

FIGURE 16.5 Use the web-based CUPS administrative interface to configure and manage printing.

If you click the Administration tab in the browser page, you can start configuring your printers, as shown in Figure 16.6.

Creating a CUPS Printer Entry

This section provides a short example of creating a Linux printer entry using CUPS's web-based interface. Use the CUPS interface to create a printer and device queue type (such as local, remote, serial port, or Internet); then you enter a device *uniform resource identifier (URI)*, such as `lpd://192.168.2.35/lp`, which represents the IP address of a remote UNIX print server and the name of the remote print queue on the server. You also need to specify the model or make of printer and its driver. A Printers page link allows you to print a test page, stop the printing service, manage the local print queue, modify the printer entry, or add another printer.

In the Admin page, click the Add Printer button and then enter a printer name in the Name field (such as `lp`), a physical location of the printer in the Location field, and a short note about the printer (such as its type) in the Description field. Figure 16.7 shows a sample entry for an HP 2100 LaserJet.

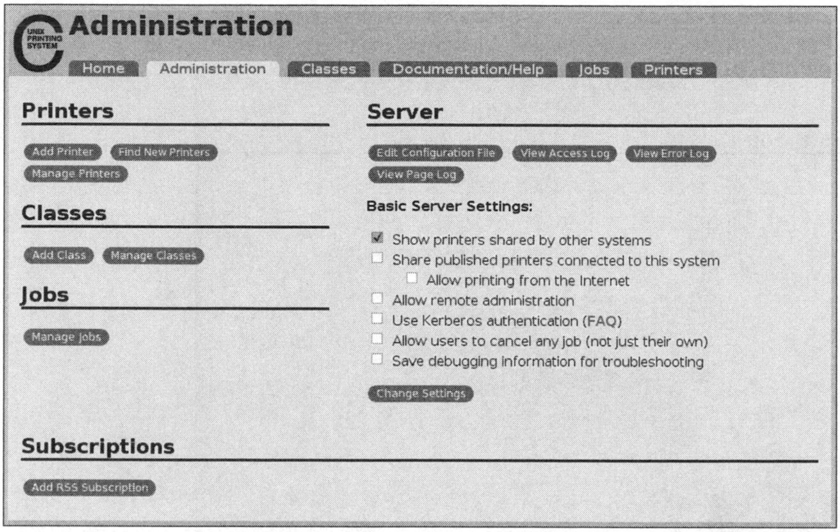

FIGURE 16.6 Enter the root password to perform printer administration with CUPS.

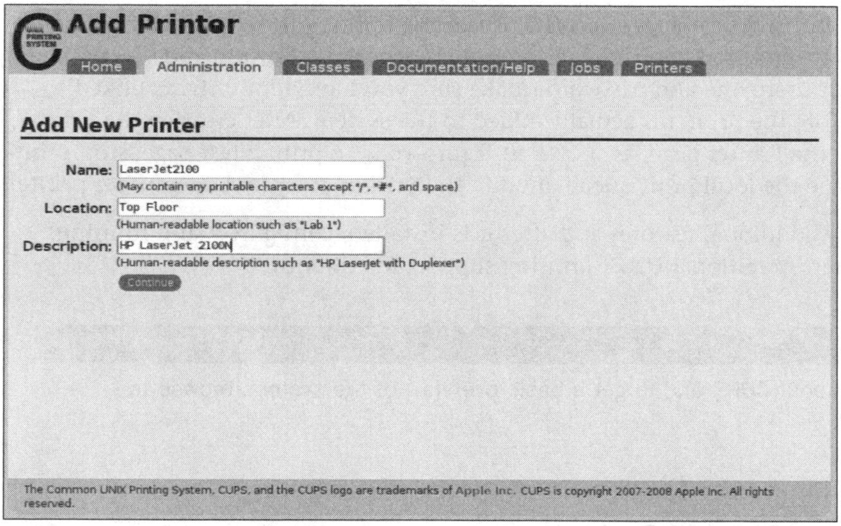

FIGURE 16.7 Use CUPS to create a new printer queue.

Click the Continue button. You can then select the type of printer access (local, remote, serial port, or Internet) in the Device page. For example, to configure printing to a local printer, select LPT1 or, for a remote printer, select the LPD/LPR Host or Printer entry.

Again click Continue and select a printer make as requested in the dialog box shown in Figure 16.8.

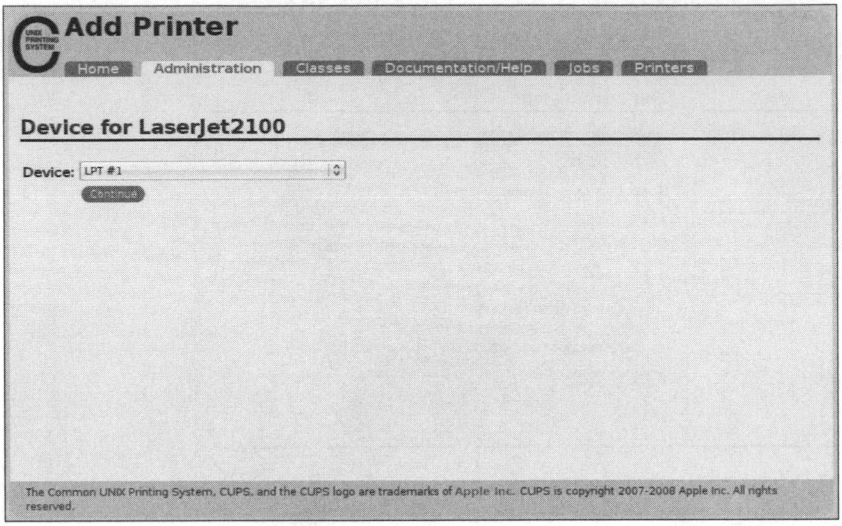

FIGURE 16.8 Select a printer make when creating a new queue.

After you click Continue, you then select the driver by choosing the exact model of your printer from the list provided. Finish by clicking the Add Printer button, and you will be prompted for your username and password (make sure you have admin rights linked to your account) before the printer is actually added to the system. After creating the printer, you can then use the Printer page, as shown in Figure 16.9, to print a test page, stop printing service, manage the local print queue, modify the printer entry, or add another printer.

CUPS offers many additional features and after it is installed, configured, and running, provides transparent traditional UNIX printing support for Ubuntu.

NOTE

To learn more about CUPS and to get a basic overview of the system, browse to www.cups.org/.

Avoiding Printer Support Problems

Troubleshooting printer problems can prove frustrating, especially if you find that your new printer is not working properly with Linux. Keep in mind, however, that nearly all printers on the market today work with Linux. However, some vendors have higher batting averages in the game of supporting Linux. If you care to see a scorecard, browse to www.linuxprinting.org/vendors.html.

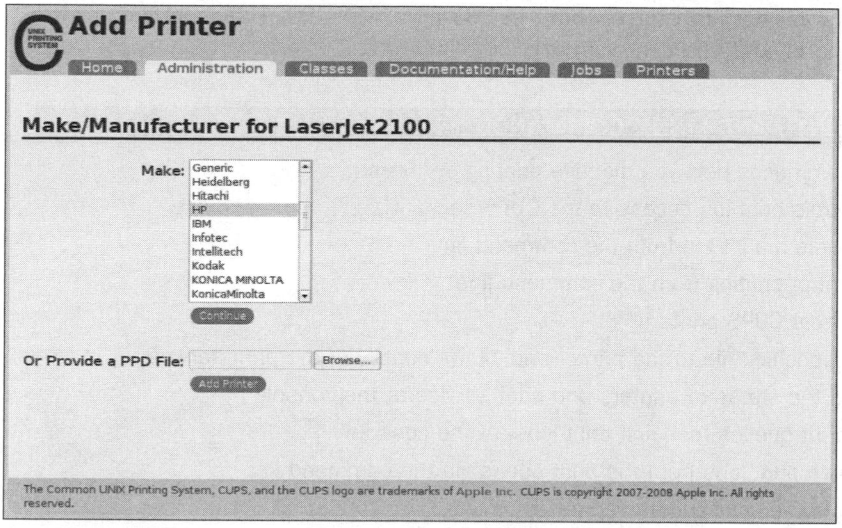

FIGURE 16.9 Manage printers easily using the CUPS Printer page.

All-in-One (Print/Fax/Scan) Devices

Problematic printers, or printing devices that might or might not work with Ubuntu, include multifunction (or *all-in-one*) printers that combine scanning, faxing, and printing services. You should research any planned purchase and avoid any vendor unwilling to support Linux with drivers or development information.

One shining star in the field of Linux support for multifunction printers is the HP support of the HP OfficeJet Linux driver project at http://hpoj.sourceforge.net/. Printing and scanning are supported on many models, with fax support in development.

Using USB and Legacy Printers

Other problems can arise because of a lack of a printer's USB vendor and device ID information—a problem shared by some USB scanners under Linux. For information regarding USB printer support, check with the Linux printing folks (at the URL in the start of this section) or with the Linux USB project at www.linux-usb.org/.

Although many newer printers require a *universal serial bus (USB)* port, excellent support still exists for legacy parallel-port (IEEE-1284) printers with Linux, enabling sites to continue to use older hardware. You can take advantage of Linux workarounds to set up printing even if the host computer does not have a traditional parallel printer port or if you want to use a newer USB printer on an older computer.

For example, to host a parallel-port-based printer on a USB-only computer, attach the printer to the computer using an inexpensive USB-to-parallel converter. USB-to-parallel converters typically provide a Centronics connector; one end of that connector is plugged in to the older printer, and the other end is plugged in to a USB connector. The USB connector is then plugged in to your hub, desktop, or notebook USB port. On the other hand, you can use an add-on PCI card to add USB support for printing (and other devices) if the legacy computer does not have a built-in USB port. Most PCI USB interface cards add at least two ports, and you can chain devices via a hub.

RELATED UBUNTU AND LINUX COMMANDS

The following commands help you manage printing services:

- `accept`—Controls print job access to the CUPS server via the command line
- `cancel`—Cancels a print job from the command line
- `disable`—Control printing from the command line
- `enable`—Controls CUPS printers
- `lp`—Sends a specified file to the printer and allows control of the print service
- `lpc`—Displays the status of printers and print service at the console
- `lpq`—Views print queues (pending print jobs) at the console
- `lprm`—Removes print jobs from the print queue via the command line
- `lpstat`—Displays printer and server status

Reference

- https://help.ubuntu.com/community/SettingUpNFSHowTo—Ubuntu community documentation for setting up NFS.
- https://help.ubuntu.com/community/SettingUpSamba—Ubuntu community documentation for setting up Samba.
- https://help.ubuntu.com/community/Swat—Ubuntu community documentation for SWAT.
- www.samba.org/—Base entry point for getting more information about Samba and using the SMB protocol with Linux, UNIX, Mac OS, and other operating systems.
- www.samba.org/samba/docs/man/Samba-HOWTO-Collection/SWAT.html—Official Samba documentation for using SWAT.
- www.linuxprinting.org/—Browse here for specific drivers and information about USB and other types of printers.
- www.cups.org/—A comprehensive repository of CUPS software and information.
- www.pwg.org/ipp/—Home page for the Internet Printing Protocol standards.
- www.cs.wisc.edu/~ghost/—Home page for the Ghostscript interpreter.

CHAPTER 17

Apache Web Server Management

IN THIS CHAPTER

- About the Apache Web Server
- Installing the Apache Server
- Starting and Stopping Apache
- Runtime Server Configuration Settings
- File System Authentication and Access Control
- Apache Modules
- Virtual Hosting
- Logging
- Other Web Servers for Use with Ubuntu
- Reference

This chapter covers the configuration and management of the Apache web server and includes an overview of some of the major components of the server and discussions of text-based and graphical server configuration. You will see how to start, stop, and restart Apache using the command line. The chapter begins with some introductory information and then shows you how to install, configure, and use Apache.

About the Apache Web Server

Apache is the most widely used web server on the Internet today, according to a Netcraft survey of active websites in July 2010, which is shown in Table 17.1 (from http://news.netcraft.com/archives/2010/08/11/august-2010-web-server-survey-4.html).

Note that these statistics do not reflect use on internal networks, known as *intranets*.

The name *Apache* appeared during the early development of the software because it was "a patchy" server, made up of patches for the freely available source code of the NCSA HTTPd web server. For a while after the NCSA HTTPd project was discontinued, a number of people wrote a variety of patches for the code, to either fix bugs or add features they wanted. A lot of this code was floating around and people were freely sharing it, but it was completely unmanaged.

After a while, Brian Behlendorf and Cliff Skolnick set up a centralized repository of these patches, and the Apache project was born. The project is still composed of a small core group of programmers, but anyone is welcome to submit patches to the group for possible inclusion in the code.

TABLE 17.1 Netcraft Survey Results (August 2010)

Server	Number	Percent share
Apache	119,664,128	56.06%
Microsoft	53,434,586	25.03%
Google	15,526,781	7.27%
nginx	11,713,607	5.49%
lighttpd	1,821,824	0.85%

There has been a surge of interest in the Apache project over the past several years, partially buoyed by a new interest in open source on the part of enterprise-level information services. It's also due in part to crippling security flaws found in Microsoft's Internet Information Services (IIS); the existence of malicious web task exploits; and operating system and networking vulnerabilities to the now-infamous Code Red, Blaster, and Nimda worms. IBM made an early commitment to support and use Apache as the basis for its web offerings and has dedicated substantial resources to the project because it makes more sense to use an established, proven web server.

In mid-1999, The Apache Software Foundation was incorporated as a nonprofit company. A board of directors, who are elected on an annual basis by the ASF members, oversees the company. This company provides a foundation for several open-source software development projects, including the Apache Web Server project.

TIP

You'll find an overview of Apache in its frequently asked questions (FAQs) at http://httpd.apache.org/docs/2.2/faq/. In addition to extensive online documentation, you'll also find the complete documentation for Apache in the HTML directory of your Apache server. If you have Apache running on your system, you can access this documentation by looking at http://localhost/manual/index.html.

To determine the precise version of Apache included with your system, use the web server's `-V` command-line option like this:

```
matthew@seymour:~$ /usr/sbin/apache2 -V
```

The output displays the version number, build date and time, platform, and various options used during the build. You can use the `-v` option to see abbreviated version information.

Installing the Apache Server

You can install Apache through APT or build it yourself from source code. The Apache source builds on just about any UNIX-like operating system and on Win32.

If you are about to install a new version of Apache, you should shut down the old server. Even if it's unlikely that the old server will interfere with the installation procedure, shutting it down ensures that there will be no problems. If you do not know how to stop Apache, see the "Starting and Stopping Apache" section later in this chapter.

Installing from the Ubuntu repositories

You can install the `apache2` package from the Ubuntu software repositories. Updated packages usually contain important bug and security fixes. When an updated version is released, install it as quickly as possible to keep your system secure.

NOTE

Check the Apache site for security reports. Browse to http://httpd.apache.org/security_report.html for links to security vulnerabilities for Apache 1.3, 2.0, and 2.2. Subscribe to a support list or browse through up-to-date archives of all Apache mailing lists at http://httpd.apache.org/mail/ (for various articles) or http://httpd.apache.org/lists.html (for comprehensive and organized archives).

CAUTION

You should be wary of installing experimental packages, and never install them on production servers (that is, servers used in "real life"). Very carefully test the packages beforehand on a host that is not connected to a network!

For more information on installing software from the Ubuntu repositories, see chapter 32, "Managing Software."

The Apache package installs files in the following directories:

- `/etc/apache2`—This directory contains the Apache configuration file, `apache2.conf`.
- `/etc/init.d/`—The tree under this directory contains the system startup scripts. The Apache package installs a startup script named `apache2` for the web server under the `/etc/init.d` directory. This script, which you can use to start and stop the server from the command line, also automatically starts and stops the server when the computer is halted, started, or rebooted.
- `/var/www`—The package installs the default server icons, Common Gateway Interface (CGI) programs, and HTML files in this location. If you want to keep web content elsewhere, you can do so by making the appropriate changes in the server configuration files.

- `/usr/share`—If you've installed the `apache2-doc` package, you'll find a copy of the Apache documentation in HTML format here. You can access it with a web browser by going to http://localhost/manual/.
- `/usr/share/man`—Ubuntu's Apache package also contains manual pages, which are placed underneath this directory. For example, the `apache2` man page is in Section 8 of the `man` directory.
- `/usr/sbin`—The executable programs are placed in this directory. This includes the server executable itself, as well as various utilities.
- `/usr/bin`—Some of the utilities from the Apache package are placed here—for example, the `htpasswd` program, which is used for generating authentication password files.

`/var/log/apache2`—The server log files are placed in this directory. By default, there are two important log files (among several others): `access_log and error_log`. However, you can define any number of custom logs containing a variety of information. See the section "Logging," later in this chapter, for more detail.

When Apache is being run, it also creates the file `apache2.pid`, containing the process ID of Apache's parent process in the `/var/run/` directory.

NOTE

If you are upgrading to a newer version of Apache, APT does not write over your current configuration files.

Building the Source Yourself

You can download the source directly from www.apache.org/. The latest version at the time of this writing (2.2.16) is a 6MB compressed tape archive, and the latest pre-2.0 version of Apache is 1.3.42. Although many sites continue to use the older version (for script and other compatibility reasons), most sites are migrating to or are starting out using the latest stable version.

After you have the `tar` file, you must unroll it in a temporary directory, such as `/tmp`. Unrolling this `tar` file creates a directory called `apache_version_number`, *where* `version_number` *is the version you have downloaded (for example,* `apache_1.3.34`).

There are two ways to compile the source—the old, familiar way (at least, to those of us who have been using Apache for many years) by editing Makefile templates, and the new, easy way using a `configure` script. You will first see how to build Apache from source the easy way. The `configure` script offers a way to have the source software automatically configured according to your system. However, manually editing the configuration files before building and installing Apache provides more control over where the software is installed and which capabilities or features are built in to Apache.

TIP

As with many software packages distributed in source code form for Linux and other UNIX-like operating systems, extracting the source code results in a directory that contains a `README` and an `INSTALL` file. Be sure to peruse the `INSTALL` file before attempting to build and install the software.

Using `./configure` to Build Apache

To build Apache the easy way, run the `./configure` script in the directory just created. You can provide it with a `—prefix` argument to install it in a directory other than the default, which is `/usr/local/apache/`. Use this command:

```
matthew~/usr/src/apache2$ sudo ./configure —prefix=/preferred/directory/
```

This generates the Makefile that is used to compile the server code.

Next, type **`make`** to compile the server code. After the compilation is complete, type **`make install`** as root to install the server. You can now configure the server via the configuration files. See the "Runtime Server Configuration Settings" section for more information.

TIP

A safer way to install a new version of Apache from source is to use the `ln` command to create symbolic links of the existing file locations (listed in the "Installing with APT" section earlier in this chapter) to the new locations of the files. This method is safer because the default install locations are different from those used when the package installs the files. Failure to use this installation method could result in your web server process not being started automatically at system startup.

Another safe way to install a new version of Apache is to first back up any important configuration directories and files (such as `/etc/apache2`) and then use the `apt-get` command to remove the server. You can then install and test your new version and, if needed, easily restore your original server and settings.

It is strongly recommended that you use Ubuntu's version of Apache until you really know what happens at system startup. No "uninstall" option is available when installing Apache from source!

Apache File Locations After a Build and Install

Files are placed in various subdirectories of `/usr/local/apache` (or whatever directory you specified with the `—prefix` parameter) if you build the server from source.

The following is a list of the directories used by Apache, as well as brief comments on their usage:

- /usr/local/apache/conf—This contains several subdirectories and the Apache configuration file, httpd.conf. Debian-based systems such as Ubuntu often rename this to apache2.conf, so your mileage may vary. See the section "Editing apache2.conf" later in this chapter to learn more about configuration files.
- /usr/local/apache—The cgi-bin, icons, and htdocs subdirectories contain the CGI programs, standard icons, and default HTML documents, respectively.
- /usr/local/apache/bin—The executable programs are placed in this directory.
- /usr/local/apache/logs—The server log files are placed in this directory. By default, there are two log files—access_log and error_log—but you can define any number of custom logs containing a variety of information (see the "Logging" section later in this chapter). The default location for Apache's logs as installed by Ubuntu is /var/log/apache2.

A QUICK GUIDE TO GETTING STARTED WITH APACHE

Setting up, testing a web page, and starting Apache using Ubuntu can be accomplished in just a few steps. First, make sure that Apache is installed on your system. Either select it during installation or install the server, and related package files (see Chapter 32if you need to install the server software).

Next, set up a home page for your system by editing (as root) the file named index.html under the /var/ www directory on your system. Make a backup copy of the original page or www directory before you begin so you can restore your web server to its default state if necessary.

```
Start Apache through the Services window (under System, Administration from the
menu bar), making sure to enable "Web Server".
```

You can also use the apache2 script under the /etc/init.d/ directory, like this:

```
matthew@seymour:~$ sudo /etc/init.d/apache2 start
```

You can then check your home page by running a favorite browser and using localhost, your system's hostname, or its Internet Protocol (IP) address in the URL. For example, with the links text browser, use a command line like this:

```
matthew@seymour:~$ links http://localhost/
```

For security reasons, you should not start and run Apache as root if your host is connected to the Internet or a company intranet. Fortunately, Apache is set to run as the user and group www-data no matter how it is started (by the User and Group settings in /etc/apache2/apache2.conf). Despite this safe default, Apache should be started and managed by the user named www-data, defined in /etc/passwd as:

```
www-data:x:33:33:www-data:/var/www:/bin/sh
```

After you are satisfied with your website, use the Services configuration dialog to ensure that Apache is started.

Starting and Stopping Apache

At this point, you have installed your Apache server with its default configuration. Ubuntu provides a default home page named `index.html` as a test under the `/var/www/` directory. The proper way to run Apache is to set system initialization to have the server run after booting, network configuration, and any firewall configuration. See Chapter 11, "Automating Tasks," for more information about how Ubuntu boots.

It is time to start it up for the first time. The following sections show how to either start and stop Apache or configure Ubuntu to start or not start Apache when booting.

Starting the Apache Server Manually

You can start Apache from the command line of a text-based console or X terminal window, and you must have root permission to do so. The server daemon, `apache2`, recognizes several command-line options you can use to set some defaults, such as specifying where `apache2` reads its configuration directives. The Apache `apache2` executable also understands other options that enable you to selectively use parts of its configuration file, specify a different location of the actual server and supporting files, use a different configuration file (perhaps for testing), and save startup errors to a specific log. The `-v` option causes Apache to print its development version and quit. The `-V` option shows all the settings that were in effect when the server was compiled.

The `-h` option prints the following usage information for the server:

```
matthew@seymour:~$ apache2 -h
Usage: apache2 [-D name] [-d directory] [-f file]
              [-C "directive"] [-c "directive"]
              [-k start|restart|graceful|stop]
              [-v] [-V] [-h] [-l] [-L] [-t]
Options:
  -D name            : define a name for use in <IfDefine name> directives
  -d directory       : specify an alternate initial ServerRoot
  -f file            : specify an alternate ServerConfigFile
  -C "directive"     : process directive before reading config files
  -c "directive"     : process directive after reading config files
  -e level           : show startup errors of level (see LogLevel)
  -E file            : log startup errors to file
  -v                 : show version number
  -V                 : show compile settings
  -h                 : list available command line options (this page)
  -l                 : list compiled in modules
  -L                 : list available configuration directives
  -t -D DUMP_VHOSTS : show parsed settings (currently only vhost settings)
-t                 : run syntax check for config files
```

Other options include listing Apache's *static modules*, or special, built-in independent parts of the server, along with options that can be used with the modules. These options are called *configuration directives* and are commands that control how a static module works. Note that Apache also includes nearly 50 *dynamic modules*, or software portions of the server that can be optionally loaded and used while the server is running.

The `-t` option is used to check your configuration files. It's a good idea to run this check before restarting your server, especially if you've made changes to your configuration files. Such tests are important because a configuration file error can result in your server shutting down when you try to restart it. There is a bug in the internal username settings for Apache2 in Ubuntu that gives you this error if you enter:

```
matthew@seymour:~$ sudo apache2 -t
apache2: bad user name ${APACHE_RUN_USER}
```

If this happens to you, enter the command this way to force the command to use the expected username settings and you will get the proper output:

```
matthew@seymour:~$ sudo APACHE_RUN_USER=www-data APACHE_RUN_GROUP=www-data
apache2 -t
```

NOTE

When you build and install Apache from source, start the server manually from the command line through `sudo` (such as when testing). You do this for two reasons:

- The standalone server uses the default HTTP port (port 80), and only the super-user can bind to Internet ports that are lower than 1024.
- Only processes owned by root can change their UID and GID as specified by Apache's User and Group directives. If you start the server under another UID, it runs with the permissions of the user starting the process.

Note that although some of the following examples show how to start the server through `sudo`, you should do so only for testing after building and installing Apache.

Using `/etc/init.d/apache2`

Ubuntu uses the scripts in the `/etc/init.d` directory to control the startup and shutdown of various services, including the Apache web server. The main script installed for the Apache web server is `/etc/init.d/apache2`, although the actual work is done by the `apache2ctl` shell script included with Apache.

NOTE

`/etc/init.d/apache2` is a shell script and is not the same as the Apache server located in `/usr/sbin`. That is, `/usr/sbin/apache2` is the program executable file (the server); `/etc/init.d/apache2` is a shell script that uses another shell script, `apache2ctl`, to control the server. See Chapter 11, "Automating Tasks," for a description of some service scripts under `/etc/init.d` and how the scripts are used to manage services such as `apache2`.

You can use the `/etc/init.d/apache2` script to control the web server. Here are some of the most common options to include with the command:

- `start`—The system uses this option to start the web server during bootup. You, through sudo, can also use this script to start the server.
- `stop`—The system uses this option to stop the server gracefully. You should use this script, rather than the `kill` command, to stop the server.
- `reload`—You can use this option to send the `HUP` signal to the `apache2` server to have it reread the configuration files after modification.
- `restart`—This option is a convenient way to stop and then immediately start the web server. If the `apache2` server isn't running, it is started.
- `status`—This option indicates whether the server is running; if it is, it provides the PID for each instance of the server.

For example, to check on the status of your server, use the command

```
matthew@seymour:~$ sudo /etc/init.d/apache2 status
```

This prints the following on my machine. Your PID(s) will be different:

```
apache2 (pid 4743) is running...
```

This indicates that the web server is running.

In addition to the previous options, the `apache2` script also offers these features:

- `help`—Prints a list of valid options to the `apache2` script (which are passed onto the server as if called from the command line).
- `force-reload`—Restarts the server while forcing it to reload configuration files.

17

TIP

Use the `force-reload` option if you are making many changes to the various server configuration files. This saves time when you are stopping and starting the server by having the system simply reread the configuration files.

Runtime Server Configuration Settings

At this point, the Apache server will run, but perhaps you want to change a behavior, such as the default location of your website's files. This section talks about the basics of configuring the server to work the way you want it to work.

Runtime configurations are stored in just one file—`apache2.conf`, which is found under the `/etc/apache2` directory. This configuration file can be used to control the default behavior of Apache, such as the web server's base configuration directory (`/etc/apache2`), the name of the server's process identification (PID) file (`/var/run/apache2.pid`), or its response timeout (300 seconds). Apache reads the data from the configuration file when started (or restarted). You can also cause Apache to reload configuration information with the command `/etc/init.d/apache2 reload`, which is necessary after making changes to its configuration file. (You learned how to accomplish this in the earlier section, "Starting and Stopping Apache.")

Runtime Configuration Directives

You perform runtime configuration of your server with configuration directives, which are commands that set options for the `apache2` daemon. The directives are used to tell the server about various options you want to enable, such as the location of files important to the server configuration and operation. Apache supports nearly 300 configuration directives using the following syntax:

```
directive option option...
```

Each directive is specified on a single line. See the following sections for some sample directives and how to use them. Some directives only set a value such as a filename, whereas others enable you to specify various options. Some special directives, called sections, look like HTML tags. Section directives are surrounded by angle brackets, such as `<directive>`. Sections usually enclose a group of directives that apply only to the directory specified in the section:

```
<Directory somedir/in/your/tree>
  directive option option
  directive option option
</Directory>
```

All sections are closed with a matching section tag that looks like this: `</directive>`. Note that section tags, like any other directives, are specified one per line.

TIP

Apache is configured with an alias that lets you view the documentation installed in /usr/share/doc using your web browser at localhost/manual. After installing and starting Apache, you'll find an index of directives at http://localhost/manual/mod/directives.html.

Editing `apache2.conf`

Most of the default settings in the config file are okay to keep, particularly if you've installed the server in a default location and aren't doing anything unusual on your server. In general, if you do not understand what a particular directive is for, you should leave it set to the default value.

The following sections describe some of the configuration file settings you *might* want to change concerning operation of your server.

ServerRoot

The ServerRoot directive sets the absolute path to your server directory. This directive tells the server where to find all the resources and configuration files. Many of these resources are specified in the configuration files relative to the ServerRoot directory.

Your ServerRoot directive should be set to /etc/apache2 if you installed the Ubuntu package or /usr/local/apache (or whatever directory you chose when you compiled Apache) if you installed from the source. This is commented out in the file, but apache2 -V shows that this default has been compiled into the package.

Listen

The Listen directive is actually in a file called ports.conf that is included from apache2.conf and indicates on which port you want your server to run. By default, this is set to 80, which is the standard HTTP port number. You might want to run your server on another port—for example, when running a test server that you don't want people to find by accident. Do not confuse this with real security! See the "File System Authentication and Access Control" section for more information about how to secure parts of your web server.

User and Group

The User and Group directives should be set to the UID and group ID (GID) the server will use to process requests.

In Ubuntu, set these configurations to a user with few or no privileges. In this case, they're set to user www-data and group www-data—a user defined specifically to run Apache. If you want to use a different UID or GID, be aware that the server will run with the permissions of the user and group set here. That means in the event of a security breach, whether on the server or (more likely) in your own CGI programs, those programs will run with the assigned UID. If the server runs as root or some other privileged user, someone can exploit the security holes and do nasty things to your site. Always think in terms of the specified user running a command such as rm -rf / because that would wipe all files from your system. That should convince you that leaving apache as a user with no privileges is probably a good thing.

Instead of specifying the User and Group directives using names, you can specify them using the UID and GID numbers. If you use numbers, be sure that the numbers you specify correspond to the user and group you want and that they're preceded by the pound (#) symbol.

Here's how these directives look if specified by name:

```
User apache
Group apache
```

Here's the same specification by UID and GID:

```
User #48
Group #48
```

17

TIP

If you find a user on your system (other than root) with a UID and GID of `0`, your system has been compromised by a malicious user.

ServerAdmin

The `ServerAdmin` directive should be set to the address of the webmaster managing the server. This address should be a valid email address or alias, such as `webmaster@gnulix.org`, because this address is returned to a visitor when a problem occurs on the server.

ServerName

The `ServerName` directive sets the hostname the server will return. Set it to a fully qualified domain name (FQDN). For example, set it to `www.your.domain` *rather than simply* www. This is particularly important if this machine will be accessible from the Internet rather than just on your local network.

You don't need to set this unless you want a name other than the machine's canonical name returned. If this value isn't set, the server will figure out the name by itself and set it to its canonical name. However, you might want the server to return a friendlier address, such as `www.your.domain`. *Whatever you do,* `ServerName` should be a real domain name service (DNS) name for your network. If you're administering your own DNS, remember to add an alias for your host. If someone else manages the DNS for you, ask that person to set this name for you.

DocumentRoot

Set this directive to the absolute path of your document tree, which is the top directory from which Apache will serve files. By default, it's set to `/var/www/`. If you built the source code yourself, `DocumentRoot` is set to `/usr/local/apache/htdocs` (if you did not choose another directory when you compiled Apache).

UserDir

The `UserDir` directive disables or enables and defines the directory (relative to a local user's home directory) where that user can put public HTML documents. It is relative because each user has her own HTML directory. This setting is disabled by default but can be enabled to store user web content under any directory.

The default setting for this directive, if enabled, is `public_html`. Each user can create a directory called `public_html` under her home directory, and HTML documents placed in that directory are available as `http://servername/~username`, *where* `username` *is the username of the particular user.*

DirectoryIndex

The `DirectoryIndex` directive indicates which file should be served as the index for a directory, such as which file should be served if the URL `http://servername/_SomeDirectory/` is requested.

It is often useful to put a list of files here so that if `index.html` (the default value) isn't found, another file can be served instead. The most useful application of this is to have a CGI program run as the default action in a directory. If you have users who make their web pages on Windows, you might want to add `index.htm` as well. In that case, the directive would look like `DirectoryIndex index.html index.cgi index.htm`.

Apache Multiprocessing Modules

Apache Version 2.0 and greater now uses a new internal architecture supporting multiprocessing modules (MPMs). These modules are used by the server for a variety of tasks, such as network and process management, and are compiled into Apache. MPMs enable Apache to work much better on a wider variety of computer platforms, and they can help improve server stability, compatibility, and scalability.

Apache can use only one MPM at any time. These modules are different from the base set included with Apache (see the "Apache Modules" section later in this chapter) but are used to implement settings, limits, or other server actions. Each module in turn supports numerous additional settings, called *directives*, which further refine server operation.

The internal MPM modules relevant for Linux include:

- `mpm_common`—A set of 20 directives common to all MPM modules
- `prefork`—A nonthreaded, preforking web server that works similar to earlier (1.3) versions of Apache
- `worker`—Provides a hybrid multiprocess multithreaded server

MPM enables Apache to be used on equipment with fewer resources yet still handle massive numbers of hits and provide stable service. The `worker` module provides directives to control how many simultaneous connections your server can handle.

NOTE

Other MPMs are available for Apache related to other platforms, such as `mpm_netware` for NetWare hosts and `mpm_winnt` for NT platforms. An MPM named `perchild`, which provides user ID assignment to selected daemon processes, is under development. For more information, browse to the Apache Software Foundation's home page at www.apache.org.

Using `.htaccess` Configuration Files

Apache also supports special configuration files, known as `.htaccess` files. Almost any directive that appears in `apache2.conf` can appear in an `.htaccess` file. This file, specified in the `AccessFileName` directive in `apache2.conf` sets configurations on a per-directory (usually in a user directory) basis. As the system administrator, you can specify both the name of this file and which of the server configurations can be overridden by the contents of this file. This is especially useful for sites in which there are multiple content providers and you want to control what these people can do with their space.

To limit which server configurations the `.htaccess` files can override, use the `AllowOverride` directive. `AllowOverride` can be set globally or per directory. For example, in your `apache2.conf` file, you could use the following:

```
# Each directory to which Apache has access can be configured with respect
# to which services and features are allowed and/or disabled in that
# directory (and its subdirectories).
#
# First, we configure the "default" to be a very restrictive set of
# permissions.
#
<Directory />
    Options FollowSymLinks
    AllowOverride None
</Directory>
```

Options Directives

To configure which configuration options are available to Apache by default, you must use the `Options` directive. `Options` can be `None`; `All`; or any combination of `Indexes`, `Includes`, `FollowSymLinks`, `ExecCGI`, and `MultiViews`. `MultiViews` are not included in `All` and must be specified explicitly. These options are explained in Table 17.2.

TABLE 17.2 Switches Used by the **Options** Directive

Switch	Description
`None`	None of the available options are enabled for this directory.
`Indexes`	In the absence of an `index.html` file or another `DirectoryIndex file`, a listing of the files in the directory is generated as an HTML page for display to the user.
`Includes`	Server-side includes (SSIs) are permitted in this directory. This can also be written as `IncludesNoExec` if you want to allow includes but don't want to allow the `exec` option in them. For security reasons, this is usually a good idea in directories over which you don't have complete control, such as `UserDir` directories.
`FollowSymLinks`	Allows access to directories that are symbolically linked to a document directory. You should never set this globally for the whole server and only rarely for individual directories. This option is a potential security risk because it allows web users to escape from the document directory and could potentially allow them access to portions of your file system where you really don't want people poking around.
`ExecCGI`	CGI programs are permitted in this directory, even if it is not a directory defined in the `ScriptAlias` directive.

TABLE 17.2 Continued

Switch	Description
`MultiViews`	This is part of the `mod_negotiation` module. When a client requests a document that can't be found, the server tries to figure out which document best suits the client's requirements. See `http://localhost/manuals/mod/_mod_negotiation.html` for your local copy of the Apache documentation.

NOTE

These directives also affect all subdirectories of the specified directory.

`AllowOverrides` Directives

The `AllowOverrides` directives specify which configuration options `.htaccess` files can override. You can set this directive individually for each directory. For example, you can have different standards about what can be overridden in the main document `root` and in `UserDir` directories.

This capability is particularly useful for user directories, where the user does not have access to the main server configuration files.

`AllowOverrides` can be set to `All` or any combination of `Options`, `FileInfo`, `AuthConfig`, and `Limit`. These options are explained in Table 17.3.

TABLE 17.3 Switches Used by the **`AllowOverrides`** Directive

Switch	Description
`Options`	The `.htaccess` file can add options not listed in the `Options` directive for this directory.
`FileInfo`	The `.htaccess` file can include directives for modifying document type information.
`AuthConfig`	The `.htaccess` file might contain authorization directives.
`Limit`	The `.htaccess` file might contain `allow`, `deny`, and `order` directives.

File System Authentication and Access Control

You're likely to include material on your website that isn't supposed to be available to the public. You must be able to lock out this material from public access and provide designated users with the means to unlock the material. Apache provides two methods for accomplishing this type of access: authentication and authorization. You can use different criteria to control access to sections of your website, including checking the client's IP address or hostname, or requiring a username and password. This section briefly covers some of these methods.

CAUTION

Allowing individual users to put web content on your server poses several important security risks. If you're operating a web server on the Internet rather than on a private network, you should read the WWW Security FAQ at www.w3.org/Security/Faq/www-security-faq.html.

Restricting Access with `allow` and `deny`

One of the simplest ways to limit access to website material is to restrict access to a specific group of users, based on IP addresses or hostnames. Apache uses the `allow` and `deny` directives to accomplish this.

Both directives take an address expression as a parameter. The following list provides the possible values and use of the address expression:

- All can be used to affect all hosts.
- A hostname or domain name, which can either be a partially or a fully qualified domain name; for example, `test.gnulix.org` or `gnulix.org`.
- An IP address, which can be either full or partial; for example, `212.85.67` or `212.85.67.66`.
- A network/netmask pair, such as `212.85.67.0/255.255.255.0`.
- A network address specified in classless inter-domain routing (CIDR) format; for example, `212.85.67.0/24`. This is the CIDR notation for the same network and netmask that were used in the previous example.

If you have the choice, it is preferable to base your access control on IP addresses rather than hostnames. Doing so results in faster performance because no name lookup is necessary—the IP address of the client is included with each request.

You also can use `allow` and `deny` to provide or deny access to website material based on the presence or absence of a specific environment variable. For example, the following statement denies access to a request with a context that contains an environment variable named `NOACCESS`:

```
deny from env=NOACCESS
```

The default behavior of Apache is to apply all the deny directives first and then check the allow directives. If you want to change this order, you can use the `order` statement. Apache might interpret this statement in three different ways:

- `Order deny,allow`—The deny directives are evaluated before the `allow` directives. If a host is not specifically denied access, it is allowed to access the resource. This is the default ordering if nothing else is specified.
- `Order allow,deny`—All `allow` directives are evaluated before `deny` directives. If a host is not specifically allowed access, it is denied access to the resource.

- Order mutual-failure—Only hosts that are specified in an allow directive and at the same time do not appear in a deny directive are allowed access. If a host does not appear in either directive, it is not granted access.

Consider this example. Suppose you want to allow only persons from within your own domain to access the `server-status` resource on your web. If your domain were named `gnulix.org`, you could add these lines to your configuration file:

```
<Location /server-status>
    SetHandler server-status
    Order deny,allow
    Deny from all
    Allow from gnulix.org
</Location>
```

Authentication

Authentication is the process of ensuring that visitors really are who they claim to be. You can configure Apache to allow access to specific areas of web content only to clients who can authenticate their identity. There are several methods of authentication in Apache; Basic Authentication is the most common (and the method discussed in this chapter).

Under Basic Authentication, Apache requires a user to supply a username and a password to access the protected resources. Apache then verifies that the user is allowed to access the resource in question. If the username is acceptable, Apache verifies the password. If the password also checks out, the user is authorized and Apache serves the request.

HTTP is a stateless protocol; each request sent to the server and each response is handled individually, and not in an intelligent fashion. Therefore, the authentication information must be included with each request. That means each request to a password-protected area is larger and therefore somewhat slower. To avoid unnecessary system use and delays, protect only those areas of your website that absolutely need protection.

To use Basic Authentication, you need a file that lists which users are allowed to access the resources. This file is composed of a plain text list containing name and password pairs. It looks very much like the `/etc/passwd` user file of your Linux system.

CAUTION

Do not use `/etc/passwd` as a user list for authentication. When you're using Basic Authentication, passwords and usernames are sent as base64-encoded text from the client to the server—which is just as readable as plain text. The username and password are included in each request that is sent to the server. So, anyone who might be snooping on Net traffic would be able to get this information!

To create a user file for Apache, use the `htpasswd` command. This is included with the Apache package. If you installed using the packages, it is in `/usr/bin`. Running `htpasswd` without any options produces the following output:

```
Usage:
        htpasswd [-cmdps] passwordfile username
        htpasswd -b[cmdps] passwordfile username password

        htpasswd -n[mdps] username
        htpasswd -nb[mdps] username password
 -c  Create a new file.
 -n  Don't update file; display results on stdout.
 -m  Force MD5 encryption of the password.
 -d  Force CRYPT encryption of the password (default).
 -p  Do not encrypt the password (plaintext).
 -s  Force SHA encryption of the password.
 -b  Use the password from the command line rather than prompting for it.
 -D  Delete the specified user.
On Windows, TPF and NetWare systems the '-m' flag is used by default.
On all other systems, the '-p' flag will probably not work.
```

As you can see, it isn't a very difficult command to use. For example, to create a new user file named `gnulixusers` with a user named `wsb`, you need to do something like this:

```
sudo htpasswd -c gnulixusers wsb
```

You would then be prompted for a password for the user. To add more users, you would repeat the same procedure, only omitting the `-c` flag.

You can also create user group files. The format of these files is similar to that of `/etc/groups`. On each line, enter the group name, followed by a colon, and then list all users, with each user separated by spaces. For example, an entry in a user group file might look like this:

```
gnulixusers: wsb pgj jp ajje nadia rkr hak
```

Now that you know how to create a user file, it's time to look at how Apache might use this to protect web resources.

To point Apache to the user file, use the `AuthUserFile` directive. `AuthUserFile` takes the file path to the user file as its parameter. If the file path is not absolute—that is, beginning with a `/`—it is assumed that the path is relative to the `ServerRoot`. Using the `AuthGroupFile` directive, you can specify a group file in the same manner.

Next, use the `AuthType` directive to set the type of authentication to be used for this resource. Here, the type is set to `Basic`.

Now you need to decide to which realm the resource will belong. Realms are used to group different resources that will share the same users for authorization. A realm can consist of just about any string. The realm is shown in the Authentication dialog box on the user's web browser. Therefore, you should set the realm string to something informative. The realm is defined with the AuthName directive.

Finally, state which type of user is authorized to use the resource. You do this with the require directive. The three ways to use this directive are as follows:

- If you specify valid-user as an option, any user in the user file is allowed to access the resource (that is, provided she also enters the correct password).
- You can specify a list of users who are allowed access with the users option.
- You can specify a list of groups with the group option. Entries in the group list, as well as the user list, are separated by a space.

Returning to the server-status example you saw earlier, instead of letting users access the server-status resource based on hostname, you can require the users to be authenticated to access the resource. You can do so with the following entry in the configuration file:

```
<Location /server-status>
    SetHandler server-status
    AuthType Basic
    AuthName "Server status"
    AuthUserFile "gnulixusers"
    Require valid-user
</Location>
```

Final Words on Access Control

If you have host-based as well as user-based access protection on a resource, the default behavior of Apache is to require the requester to satisfy both controls. But assume that you want to mix host-based and user-based protection and allow access to a resource if either method succeeds. You can do so using the satisfy directive. You can set the satisfy directive to All (this is the default) or Any. When set to All, all access control methods must be satisfied before the resource is served. If satisfy is set to Any, the resource is served if any access condition is met.

Here's another access control example, again using the previous server-status example. This time, you combine access methods so all users from the Gnulix domain are allowed access and those from outside the domain must identify themselves before gaining access. You can do so with the following:

```
<Location /server-status>
    SetHandler server-status
    Order deny,allow
    Deny from all
    Allow from gnulix.org
    AuthType Basic
    AuthName "Server status"
```

```
    AuthUserFile "gnulixusers"
    Require valid-user
    Satisfy Any
</Location>
```

There are more ways to protect material on your web server, but the methods discussed here should get you started and will probably be more than adequate for most circumstances. Look to Apache's online documentation for more examples of how to secure areas of your site.

Apache Modules

The Apache core does relatively little; Apache gains its functionality from modules. Each module solves a well-defined problem by adding necessary features. By adding or removing modules to supply the functionality you want Apache to have, you can tailor Apache server to suit your exact needs.

Nearly 70 core modules are included with the basic Apache server. Many more are available from other developers. The Apache Module Registry is a repository for add-on modules for Apache, and it can be found at http://modules.apache.org/. The modules are stored in the `/usr/lib/apache2/modules` directory (your list might look different):

```
httpd.exp                 mod_cgi.so            mod_mime_magic.so
mod_actions.so            mod_charset_lite.so   mod_mime.so
mod_alias.so              mod_dav_fs.so         mod_negotiation.so
mod_asis.so               mod_dav_lock.so       mod_proxy_ajp.so
mod_auth_basic.so         mod_dav.so            mod_proxy_balancer.so
mod_auth_digest.so        mod_dbd.so            mod_proxy_connect.so
mod_authn_alias.so        mod_deflate.so        mod_proxy_ftp.so
mod_authn_anon.so         mod_dir.so            mod_proxy_http.so
mod_authn_dbd.so          mod_disk_cache.so     mod_proxy_scgi.so
mod_authn_dbm.so          mod_dumpio.so         mod_proxy.so
mod_authn_default.so      mod_env.so            mod_reqtimeout.so
mod_authn_file.so         mod_expires.so        mod_rewrite.so
mod_authnz_ldap.so        mod_ext_filter.so     mod_setenvif.so
mod_authz_dbm.so          mod_file_cache.so     mod_speling.so
mod_authz_default.so      mod_filter.so         mod_ssl.so
mod_authz_groupfile.so    mod_headers.so        mod_status.so
mod_authz_host.so         mod_ident.so          mod_substitute.so
mod_authz_owner.so        mod_imagemap.so       mod_suexec.so
mod_authz_user.so         mod_include.so        mod_unique_id.so
mod_autoindex.so          mod_info.so           mod_userdir.so
mod_cache.so              mod_ldap.so           mod_usertrack.so
```

```
mod_cern_meta.so        mod_log_forensic.so  mod_version.so
mod_cgid.so             mod_mem_cache.so     mod_vhost_alias.so
```

Each module adds new directives that can be used in your configuration files. As you might guess, there are far too many extra commands, switches, and options to describe them all in this chapter. The following sections briefly describe a subset of those modules available with Ubuntu's Apache installation.

To enable a module, use this command:

```
matthew@seymour:~$ sudo a2enmod module_name
```

To disable a module, use this:

```
matthew@seymour:~$ sudo a2dismod module_name
```

Note that these want the actual name of the module, not the filename, for example mod_version.so is the filename, but version is the name of the module. You have to know the name of the module to use either command, but in most cases it is as simple as the difference in this example. Also, once you run either command, you need to restart Apache2 to activate the new configuration:

```
matthew@seymour:~$ sudo /etc/init.d/apache2 restart
```

mod_access

`mod_access` controls access to areas on your web server based on IP addresses, hostnames, or environment variables. For example, you might want to allow anyone from within your own domain to access certain areas of your web. See the "File System Authentication and Access Control" section for more information.

mod_alias

`mod_alias` manipulates the URLs of incoming HTTP requests, such as redirecting a client request to another URL. It also can map a part of the file system into your web hierarchy. For example, the following fetches contents from the `/home/wsb/graphics` directory for any URL that starts with /images/:

```
Alias /images/ /home/wsb/graphics/
```

This is done without the client knowing anything about it. If you use a redirection, the client is instructed to go to another URL to find the requested content. More advanced URL manipulation can be accomplished with `mod_rewrite`.

mod_asis

`mod_asis` is used to specify, in fine detail, all the information to be included in a response. This completely bypasses any headers Apache might have otherwise added to the response. All files with an `.asis` extension are sent straight to the client without any changes.

As a short example of the use of mod_asis, assume you've moved content from one location to another on your site. Now you must inform people who try to access this resource that it has moved, as well as automatically redirect them to the new location. To provide this information and redirection, you can add the following code to a file with a .asis extension:

```
Status: 301 No more old stuff!
Location: http://gnulix.org/newstuff/
Content-type: text/html

<HTML>
 <HEAD>
  <TITLE>We've moved...</TITLE>
 </HEAD>
 <BODY>
   <P>We've moved the old stuff and now you'll find it at:</P>
   <A HREF="http://gnulix.org/newstuff/">New stuff</A>!.
 </BODY>
</HTML>
```

mod_auth

mod_auth uses a simple user authentication scheme, referred to as Basic Authentication, which is based on storing usernames and encrypted passwords in a text file. This file looks very much like UNIX's /etc/passwd file and is created with the htpasswd command. See the "File System Authentication and Access Control" section earlier in this chapter for more information about this subject.

mod_auth_anon

The mod_auth_anon module provides anonymous authentication similar to that of anonymous FTP. The module enables you to define user IDs of those who are to be handled as guest users. When such a user tries to log on, he is prompted to enter his email address as his password. You can have Apache check the password to ensure that it's a (more or less) proper email address. Basically, it ensures that the password contains an @ character and at least one . character.

mod_auth_dbm

mod_auth_dbm uses Berkeley DB files instead of text for user authentication files.

mod_auth_digest

An extension of the basic mod_auth module, instead of sending the user information in plain text, mod_auth_digestis sent via the MD5 Digest Authentication process. This authentication scheme is defined in RFC 2617. Compared to using Basic Authentication, this is a much more secure way of sending user data over the Internet. Unfortunately, not all web browsers support this authentication scheme.

To create password files for use with mod_auth_dbm, you must use the htdigest utility. It has more or less the same functionality as the htpasswd utility. See the man page of htdigest for further information.

mod_autoindex

The mod_autoindex module dynamically creates a file list for directory indexing. The list is rendered in a user-friendly manner similar to those lists provided by FTP's built-in ls command.

mod_cgi

mod_cgi allows execution of CGI programs on your server. CGI programs are executable files residing in the /var/www/cgi-bin directory and are used to dynamically generate data (usually HTML) for the remote browser when requested.

mod_dir and mod_env

The mod_dir module is used to determine which files are returned automatically when a user tries to access a directory. The default is index.html. If you have users who create web pages on Windows systems, you should also include index.htm, like this:

```
DirectoryIndex index.html index.htm
```

mod_env controls how environment variables are passed to CGI and SSI scripts.

mod_expires

mod_expires is used to add an expiration date to content on your site by adding an Expires header to the HTTP response. Web browsers or cache servers won't cache expired content.

mod_headers

mod_headers is used to manipulate the HTTP headers of your server's responses. You can replace, add, merge, or delete headers as you see fit. The module supplies a Header directive for this. Ordering of the Header directive is important. A set followed by an unset for the same HTTP header removes the header altogether. You can place Header directives almost anywhere within your configuration files. These directives are processed in the following order:

1. Core server
2. Virtual host
3. <Directory> and .htaccess files

```
<Location>
<Files>
```

mod_include

mod_include enables the use of server-side includes on your server, which were quite popular before PHP took over this part of the market.

mod_info and mod_log_config

mod_info provides comprehensive information about your server's configuration. For example, it displays all the installed modules, as well as all the directives used in its configuration files.

mod_log_config defines how your log files should look. See the "Logging" section for further information about this subject.

mod_mime and mod_mime_magic

The mod_mime module tries to determine the MIME type of files from their extensions.

The mod_mime_magic module tries to determine the MIME type of files by examining portions of their content.

mod_negotiation

Using the mod_negotiation module, you can select one of several document versions that best suits the client's capabilities. There are several options to select which criteria to use in the negotiation process. You can, for example, choose among different languages, graphics file formats, and compression methods.

mod_proxy

mod_proxy implements proxy and caching capabilities for an Apache server. It can proxy and cache FTP, CONNECT, HTTP/0.9, and HTTP/1.0 requests. This isn't an ideal solution for sites that have a large number of users and therefore have high proxy and cache requirements. However, it's more than adequate for a small number of users.

mod_rewrite

mod_rewrite is the Swiss army knife of URL manipulation. It enables you to perform any imaginable manipulation of URLs using powerful regular expressions. It provides rewrites, redirection, proxying, and so on. There is very little that you can't accomplish using this module.

TIP

See http://localhost/manual/misc/rewriteguide.html for a cookbook that gives you an in-depth explanation of what the mod_rewrite module is capable of.

mod_setenvif

mod_setenvif allows manipulation of environment variables. Using small snippets of text-matching code known as *regular expressions*, you can conditionally change the content of environment variables. The order in which SetEnvIf directives appear in the configuration files is important. Each SetEnvIf directive can reset an earlier SetEnvIf directive when used on the same environment variable. Be sure to keep that in mind when using the directives from this module.

mod_speling

mod_speling is used to enable correction of minor typos in URLs. If no file matches the requested URL, this module builds a list of the files in the requested directory and extracts those files that are the closest matches. It tries to correct only one spelling mistake.

mod_status

You can use mod_status to create a web page containing a plethora of information about a running Apache server. The page contains information about the internal status as well as statistics about the running Apache processes. This can be a great aid when you're trying to configure your server for maximum performance. It's also a good indicator of when something's amiss with your Apache server.

mod_ssl

mod_ssl provides Secure Sockets Layer (Versions 2 and 3) and transport layer security (Version 1) support for Apache. At least 30 directives exist that deal with options for encryption and client authorization and that can be used with this module.

mod_unique_id

mod_unique_id generates a unique request identifier for every incoming request. This ID is put into the UNIQUE_ID environment variable.

mod_userdir

The mod_userdir module enables mapping of a subdirectory in each user's home directory into your web tree. The module provides several ways to accomplish this.

mod_usertrack

mod_usertrack is used to generate a cookie for each user session. This can be used to track the user's click stream within your web tree. You must enable a custom log that logs this cookie into a log file.

mod_vhost_alias

mod_vhost_alias supports dynamically configured mass virtual hosting, which is useful for Internet service providers (ISPs) with many virtual hosts. However, for the average user, Apache's ordinary virtual hosting support should be more than sufficient.

There are two ways to host virtual hosts on an Apache server. You can have one IP address with multiple CNAMEs, or you can have multiple IP addresses with one name per address. Apache has different sets of directives to handle each of these options. (You learn more about virtual hosting in Apache in the next section of this chapter.)

Again, the available options and features for Apache modules are too numerous to describe completely in this chapter. You can find complete information about the Apache modules in the online documentation for the server included with Ubuntu or at the Apache Group's website.

Virtual Hosting

One of the more popular services to provide with a web server is to host a virtual domain. Also known as a *virtual host*, a virtual domain is a complete website with its own domain name, as if it was a standalone machine, but it's hosted on the same machine as other websites. Apache implements this capability in a simple way with directives in the `apache2.conf` configuration file.

Apache now can dynamically host virtual servers by using the `mod_vhost_alias` module you read about in the preceding section of the chapter. The module is primarily intended for ISPs and similar large sites that host a large number of virtual sites. This module is for more advanced users and, as such, it is outside the scope of this introductory chapter. Instead, this section concentrates on the traditional ways of hosting virtual servers.

Address-Based Virtual Hosts

After you've configured your Linux machine with multiple IP addresses, setting up Apache to serve them as different websites is simple. You need only put a `VirtualHost` directive in your `apache2.conf` file for each of the addresses you want to make an independent website:

```
<VirtualHost 212.85.67.67>
ServerName gnulix.org
DocumentRoot /home/virtual/gnulix/public_html
TransferLog /home/virtual/gnulix/logs/access_log
ErrorLog /home/virtual/gnulix/logs/error_log
</VirtualHost>
```

Use the IP address, rather than the hostname, in the VirtualHost tag.

You can specify any configuration directives within the `<VirtualHost>` tags. For example, you might want to set `AllowOverrides` directives differently for virtual hosts than you do for your main server. Any directives that aren't specified default to the settings for the main server.

Name-Based Virtual Hosts

Name-based virtual hosts enable you to run more than one host on the same IP address. You must add the names to your DNS as CNAMEs of the machine in question. When an HTTP client (web browser) requests a document from your server, it sends with the request a variable indicating the server name from which it's requesting the document. Based on this variable, the server determines from which of the virtual hosts it should serve content.

NOTE

Some older browsers are unable to see name-based virtual hosts because this is a feature of HTTP 1.1 and the older browsers are strictly HTTP 1.0–compliant. However, many other older browsers are partially HTTP 1.1–compliant, and this is one of the parts of HTTP 1.1 that most browsers have supported for a while.

Name-based virtual hosts require just one step more than IP address-based virtual hosts. You must first indicate which IP address has the multiple DNS names on it. This is done with the `NameVirtualHost` directive:

```
NameVirtualHost 212.85.67.67
```

You must then have a section for each name on that address, setting the configuration for that name. As with IP-based virtual hosts, you need to set only those configurations that must be different for the host. You must set the `ServerName` directive because it's the only thing that distinguishes one host from another:

```
<VirtualHost 212.85.67.67>
ServerName bugserver.gnulix.org
ServerAlias bugserver
DocumentRoot /home/bugserver/htdocs
ScriptAlias /home/bugserver/cgi-bin
TransferLog /home/bugserver/logs/access_log
</VirtualHost>

<VirtualHost 212.85.67.67>
ServerName pts.gnulix.org
ServerAlias pts
DocumentRoot /home/pts/htdocs
ScriptAlias /home/pts/cgi-bin
TransferLog /home/pts/logs/access_log
ErrorLog /home/pts/logs/error_log
</VirtualHost>
```

TIP

If you are hosting websites on an intranet or internal network, users will likely use the shortened name of the machine rather than the FQDN. For example, users might type http://bugserver/index.html in their browser location field rather than http://bugserver.gnulix.org/index.html. In that case, Apache would not recognize that those two addresses should go to the same virtual host. You could get around this by setting up `VirtualHost` directives for both `bugserver` and `bugserver.gnulix.org`, but the easy way around it is to use the `ServerAlias` directive, which lists all valid aliases for the machine:

```
ServerAlias bugserver
```

For more information about `VirtualHost`, refer to the help system on http://localhost/_manual.

Logging

Apache provides logging for just about any web access information you might be interested in. Logging can help with:

- System resource management, by tracking usage
- Intrusion detection, by documenting bad HTTP requests
- Diagnostics, by recording errors in processing requests

Two standard log files are generated when you run your Apache server: `access_log` and `error_log`. They are found under the `/var/log/apache2` directory. (Others include the SSL logs `ssl_access_log`, `ssl_error_log` and `ssl_request_log`.) All logs except for the `error_log` (by default, this is just the `access_log`) are generated in a format specified by the `CustomLog` and `LogFormat` directives. These directives appear in your `apache2.conf` file.

A new log format can be defined with the `LogFormat` directive:

```
LogFormat "%h %l %u %t \"%r\" %>s %b" common
```

The `common` log format is a good starting place for creating your own custom log formats. Note that most of the available log analysis tools assume you're using the `common` log format or the `combined` log format—both of which are defined in the default configuration files.

The following variables are available for `LogFormat` statements:

- `%a` Remote IP address.
- `%A` Local IP address.
- `%b` Bytes sent, excluding HTTP headers. This is shown in Apache's Combined Log Format (CLF). For a request without any data content, a `-` is shown instead of `0`.

- %B Bytes sent, excluding HTTP headers.
- %{VARIABLE}e The contents of the environment variable VARIABLE.
- %f The filename of the output log.
- %h Remote host.
- %H Request protocol.
- %{HEADER}i The contents of HEADER; header line(s) in the request sent to the server.
- %l Remote log name (from identd, if supplied).
- %m Request method.
- %{NOTE}n The contents of note NOTE from another module.
- %{HEADER}o The contents of HEADER; header line(s) in the reply.
- %p The canonical port of the server serving the request.
- %P The process ID of the child that serviced the request.
- %q The contents of the query string, prepended with a ? character. If there's no query string, this evaluates to an empty string.
- %r The first line of request.
- %s Status. For requests that were internally redirected, this is the status of the original request—%>s for the last.
- %t The time, in common log time format.
- %{format}t The time, in the form given by format, which should be in strftime(3) format. See the section "Basic SSI Directives" later in this chapter for a complete list of available formatting options.
- %T The seconds taken to serve the request.
- %u Remote user from auth; this might be bogus if the return status (%s) is 401.
- %U The URL path requested.
- %V The server name according to the UseCanonicalName directive.
- %v The canonical ServerName of the server serving the request.

You can put a conditional in front of each variable to determine whether the variable is displayed. If the variable isn't displayed, - is displayed instead. These conditionals are in the form of a list of numerical return values. For example, %!401u displays the value of REMOTE_USER unless the return code is 401.

You can then specify the location and format of a log file using the `CustomLog` directive:

```
CustomLog logs/access_log common
```

If it is not specified as an absolute path, the location of the log file is assumed to be relative to the `ServerRoot`.

Other Web Servers for Use with Ubuntu

To determine the best web server for your use, consider the needs of the website you manage. Does it need heavy security (for e-commerce), multimedia (music, video, and pictures), or the capability to download files easily? How much are you willing to spend for the software? Do you need software that is easy to maintain and troubleshoot or that includes tech support? The answers to these questions might steer you to something other than Apache.

The following sections list some of the more popular alternatives to using Apache as your web server.

Sun ONE Web Server

There is evidence that the Sun Java System Web Server (formerly known as the iPlanet Web Server, and subsequently Sun ONE Web Server) might be even more popular than Apache in strictly corporate arenas. The server got its start as the Netscape Enterprise Server—one of the first powerful web servers ever to hit the market. Sun ONE Web Server comes in many flavors, and all of them are big. In addition to the enterprise-level web server that can be run on Ubuntu, the software features application, messaging, calendar, and directory servers—just to name a few.

Sun ONE Web Server is great for handling big web needs, and it comes with an appropriately big price tag. It's definitely not something to run the school website—unless your school happens to be a major state university with several regional campuses. For more information on Sun Java System Web Server, you can visit its website (wwws.sun.com/software/products/web_srvr/home_web_srvr.html). Since Oracle bought Sun, the future of this project is unknown, however at the time of this writing the website is still up and the product is still being sold.

Nginx

Pronounced "engine-x", this is a lightweight and extremely fast web server. It is free and open source and is known for stability, high performance, and low resource use. It powers many well-known websites like Wordpress, Hulu, and SourceForge. It is not as configurable as Apache, nor as well documented in English since it originates from Russia, but for specific use cases it is an excellent option and is quite easy to set up and use. Take a closer look at http://nginx.org/en/ and http://wiki.nginx.org/Main.

Zope

Zope is another open-source web server making strong inroads in the web server market. What makes Zope different is that it is managed completely through a web-based graphic interface. This has broad appeal for those who are not enthused about a command-line–only interface.

Zope is a product of the Zope Corporation (formerly Digital Creations), the same firm that made the Python programming language. And, like all things open source, it is free. Information on Zope can be found at both www.zope.com (for the commercial version) and www.zope.org (for the open-source version).

lighttpd

Another speedy open-source lightweight server is lighttpd, or "lighty." Like Nginx, lighttpd is designed for high-performance and low resource use. YouTube, Wikipedia and others are using lighttpd for its scalability and quickness. It is worth checking out at www.lighttpd.net.

Reference

- http://news.netcraft.com/archives/web_server_survey.html—A statistical graph of web server usage by millions of servers. The research points out that Apache is by far the most widely used server for Internet sites.
- www.apache.org/—Extensive documentation and information about Apache are available at The Apache Project website.
- http://modules.apache.org/—Available add-on modules for Apache can be found at The Apache Module Registry website.

CHAPTER 18

Remote File Serving with FTP

IN THIS CHAPTER

- Choosing an FTP Server
- Installing FTP Software
- The FTP User
- Configuring the Very Secure FTP Server
- Using the **ftphosts** to Allow or Deny FTP Server Connection
- Reference

File Transfer Protocol (FTP) was once considered the primary method used to transfer files over a network from computer to computer. FTP is still heavily used today, although many graphical FTP clients now supplement the original text-based interface command. As computers have evolved, so has FTP, and Ubuntu includes many ways with which to use a graphical interface to transfer files over FTP.

This chapter contains an overview of the available FTP software included with Ubuntu, along with some details concerning initial setup, configuration, and use of FTP-specific clients. Ubuntu also includes an FTP server software package named `vsftpd`, the Very Secure FTP Daemon, and a number of associated programs you can use to serve and transfer files with the FTP protocol.

Choosing an FTP Server

FTP uses a client/server model. As a client, FTP accesses a server, and as a server, FTP provides access to files or storage. Just about every computer platform available has software written to enable a computer to act as an FTP server, but Ubuntu provides the average user with the capability to do this without paying hefty licensing fees and without regard for client usage limitations.

There are two types of FTP servers and access: anonymous and standard. A *standard* FTP server requires an account name and password from anyone trying to access the server. *Anonymous* servers allow anyone to connect to the server to retrieve files. Anonymous servers provide the most flexibility, but they can also present a security risk.

Fortunately, as you will read in this chapter, Ubuntu is set up to use proper file and directory permissions and common-sense default configuration, such as disallowing root to perform an FTP login.

NOTE

Many Linux users now use OpenSSH and its suite of clients, such as the `sftp` command, for a more secure solution when transferring files. The OpenSSH suite provides the `sshd` daemon and enables encrypted remote logins (see Chapter 15, "Remote Access with SSH and Telnet," for more information).

Choosing an Authenticated or Anonymous Server

When you are preparing to set up your FTP server, you must first make the decision to install either the authenticated or anonymous service. *Authenticated* service requires the entry of a valid username and password for access. As previously mentioned, *anonymous* service allows the use of the username `anonymous` and an email address as a password for access.

Authenticated FTP servers are used to provide some measure of secure data transfer for remote users, but will require maintenance of user accounts as usernames and passwords are used. Anonymous FTP servers are used when user authentication is not needed or necessary, and can be helpful in providing an easily accessible platform for customer support or public distribution of documents, software, or other data.

If you use an anonymous FTP server in your home or business Linux system, it is vital that you properly install and configure it to retain a relatively secure environment. Generally, sites that host anonymous FTP servers place them outside the firewall on a dedicated machine. The dedicated machine contains only the FTP server and should not contain data that cannot be restored quickly. This dedicated-machine setup prevents malicious users who compromise the server from obtaining critical or sensitive data. For an additional, but by no means more secure setup, the FTP portion of the file system can be mounted read-only from a separate hard drive partition or volume, or mounted from read-only media, such as CD-ROM, DVD, or other optical storage.

Ubuntu FTP Server Packages

The Very Secure `vsftpd` server is licensed under the GNU GPL. The server can be used for personal or business purposes and is the FTP server covered in the remainder of this chapter.

Other FTP Servers

One alternative server is NcFTPd, available from www.ncftp.com. This server provides its own optimized daemon. Additionally, NcFTPd has the capability to cache directory listings of the FTP server in memory, thereby increasing the speed at which users can obtain a list of available files and directories. Although NcFTPd has many advantages over some other FTP servers, NcFTPd is not GPL-licensed software, and its licensing fees vary according to the maximum number of simultaneous server connections ($199 for 51 or more concurrent users and $129 for up to 50 concurrent users, but free to education institutions with a compliant domain name).

NOTE

Do not confuse the `ncftp` client with `ncftpd`. The `ncftp-3.1` package included with Ubuntu is the client software, a replacement for `ftp-0.17`, and includes the `ncftpget` and `ncftpput` commands for transferring files via the command line or by using a remote file uniform resource locator (URL) address. `ncftpd` is the FTP server, which can be downloaded from www.ncftpd.com.

Another FTP server package for Linux is ProFTPD, licensed under the GNU GPL. This server works well with most Linux distributions and has been used by a number of Linux sites, including ftp.kernel.org and ftp.sourceforge.net. ProFTPD is actively maintained and updated for bug fixes and security enhancements. Its developers recommend that you use the latest release (1.2.10 at the time of this writing) to avoid exposure to exploits and vulnerabilities. Browse to www.proftpd.org to download a copy.

Yet another FTP server package is `Bsdftpd-ssl`, which is based on the BSD `ftpd` (and distributed under the BSD license). `Bsdftpd-ssl` offers simultaneous standard and secure access using security extensions; secure access requires a special client. For more details, browse to http://bsdftpd-ssl.sc.ru.

Previously, this book covered an FTP server called wu-ftp. We had some concerns about it, such as the fact that when testing it to update this chapter we discover it runs as root by default and therefore presents a significant security risk. For that reason, and the fact that the package seems to be abandoned and no longer maintained by its authors, we are not covering it in this edition.

Finally, another alternative is to use Apache (and the HTTP protocol) for serving files. Using a web server to provide data downloads can reduce the need to monitor and maintain a separate software service (or directories) on your server. This approach to serving files also reduces system resource requirements and gives remote users a bit more flexibility when downloading (such as enabling them to download multiple files at once). See Chapter 17, "Apache Web Server Management," for more information about using Apache.

Installing FTP Software

As part of the standard installation, the client software for FTP is already installed. You can verify that some FTP-related software is installed on your system by using `dpkg`, `grep`, and `sort` commands in this query:

```
matthew@seymour:~$ dpkg –get-selections ¦ grep ftp ¦ sort
ftp                          install
lftp                          install
```

Above is the output from a fresh installation of Ubuntu 10.10 and what you see are basic FTP clients. These allow you to use FTP to connect to other computers to interact with remote files. You need an FTP server to allow other systems to interact with files on your computer. In this chapter we will discuss one FTP server application, vsftpd.

If vsftpd is not installed, install the package `vsftpd` from the Ubuntu repositories. For more information about installing packages, see chapter 32, "Managing Software."

NOTE

If you host an FTP server connected to the Internet, make it a habit to always install security updates and bug fixes for your server software.

The FTP User

Instead of files being uploaded or managed by a current user when anonymous connections are made to your FTP server, an FTP user is created when vsftp is installed. This user is not a normal user per se, but a name for anonymous FTP users. The FTP user entry in `/etc/passwd` looks like this:

```
ftp:x:116:124:ftp daemon,,,:/srv/ftp:/bin/false
```

The numbers will differ on each system because they depend on the number of configured users on the system, but the rest of the information will be the same.

NOTE

The FTP user, as discussed here, applies to anonymous FTP configurations and server setup. Our FTP user is configured to use /srv/ftp as the default directory. Other Linux distributions may use a different default directory, such as `/usr/local/ftp`, for FTP files and anonymous users.

This entry follows the standard `/etc/passwd` entry: username, password, User ID, Group ID, comment field, home directory, and shell. To learn more about `/etc/password`, see the section "Configuring Your Firewall" in Chapter 33, "Securing Your Machines."

Each of the items in this entry is separated by colons. In the preceding example, you can see that the Ubuntu system hosting the server uses `shadowed password` because an `x` is present in the traditional password field. The shadow password system is important because it adds an additional level of security to Ubuntu; the shadow password system is normally installed during the Ubuntu installation.

The FTP server software uses this user account to assign permissions to users connecting to the server. By using a default shell of `/bin/false` for anonymous FTP users versus `/bin/bash` or some other standard, interactive shell, an anonymous FTP user, will be unable to log in as a regular user. `/bin/false` is not a shell, but a program usually assigned to an account that has been locked. As root inspection of the `/etc/shadow` file shows (see Listing 18.1), it is not possible to log in to this account, denoted by the * as the password.

LISTING 18.1 Shadow Password File **ftp** User Entry

```
# cat /etc/shadow
bin:*:11899:0:99999:7:::
daemon:*:11899:0:99999:7:::
adm:*:11899:0:99999:7:::
lp:*:11899:0:99999:7:::
...
ftp:*:12276:0:99999:7:::
...
```

The shadow file (only a portion of which is shown in Listing 18.1) contains additional information not found in the standard /etc/passwd file, such as account expiration, password expiration, whether the account is locked, and the encrypted password. The * in the password field indicates that the account is not a standard login account; thus, it does not have a password.

Although shadow passwords are in use on the system, passwords are not transmitted in a secure manner when using FTP. Because FTP was written before the necessity of encryption and security, it does not provide the mechanics necessary to send encrypted passwords. Account information is sent in plain text on FTP servers; anyone with enough technical knowledge and a network sniffer can find the password for the account you connect to on the server. Many sites use an anonymous-only FTP server specifically to prevent normal account passwords from being transmitted over the Internet.

Figure 18.1 shows a portion of a Wireshark capture of an FTP session. The wireshark client is a graphical browser used to display network traffic in real time, and it can be used to watch packet data, such as an FTP login on a LAN.

QUICK AND DIRTY FTP SERVICE

Conscientious Linux administrators will take the time to carefully install, set up, and configure a production FTP server before offering public service or opening up for business on the Internet. However, you can set up a server very quickly on a secure LAN by following a few simple steps:

1. Ensure that the FTP server package is installed, networking is enabled, and firewall rules on the server allow FTP access. See Chapter 14, "Networking," to learn about firewalling.
2. If anonymous access to server files is desired, create and populate the /srv/ftp/public directory. Do this by mounting or copying your content, such as directories and files, under this directory. You don't want to use symlinks, however, because a clever anonymous user could easily use that against you to access other parts of your file system. If you are new to this, copy your content into the directory.
3. Edit and then save the appropriate configuration file (such as `/etc.vsftpd.conf for vsftpd`) to enable access.
4. You must then start or restart the FTP server like this: `sudo service vsftpd restart`.

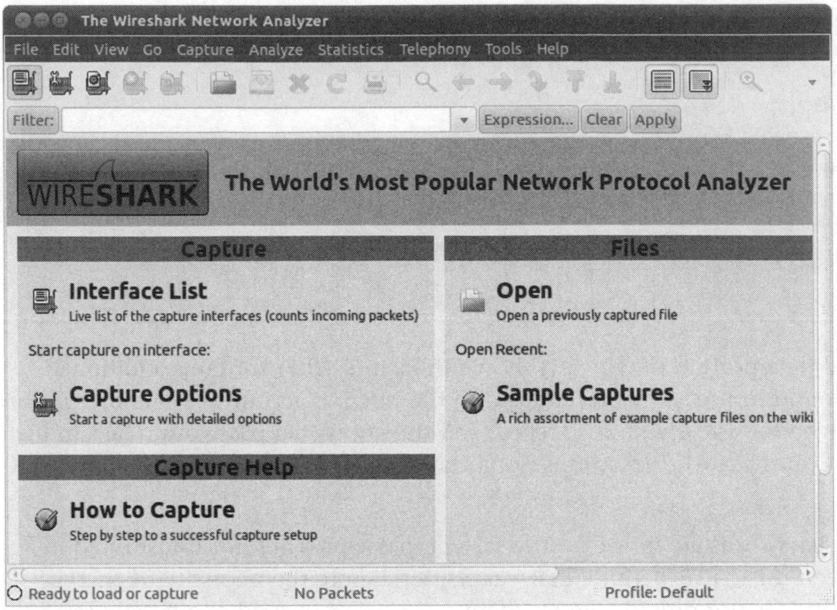

FIGURE 18.1 The Wireshark client can filter and sniff FTP sessions to capture usernames and passwords.

You can use the service to start, stop, restart, and query the `vsftpd` server. You must have root permission to use the `vsftpd` script to control the server, but any user can query the server (to see if it is running and to see its process ID number) using the `status` keyword, like this:

```
matthew@seymour:~$ sudo service vsftpd status
```

You can also use a shorter version just for finding the status of the FTP daemon like this:

```
matthew@seymour:~$ status vsftpd
```

Administrator permissions are not required to use the `status` command, so we do not need to use sudo.

Configuring the Very Secure FTP Server

`The server` offers simplicity, security, and speed. It has been used by a number of sites, such as ftp.debian.org, ftp.gnu.org, rpmfind.net, and ftp.gimp.org. Note that despite its name, the Very Secure FTP server does not enable use of encrypted usernames or passwords.

Its main configuration file is `vsftpd.conf`, which resides under the `/etc` directory. The server has a number of features and default policies, but these can be overridden by changing the installed configuration file.

By default, anonymous logins are disnabled. Users are not allowed to download or upload files, create new directories, or delete or rename files. The configuration file installed by

Ubuntu allows local users (that is, users with a login and shell account) to log in and then access their home directory. This configuration presents potential security risks because usernames and passwords are passed without encryption over a network. The best policy is to deny your users access to the server from their user accounts. To change these and other settings, edit the well-commented config file at /etc/vsftp.conf. For example, to change these two settings, edit the following lines:

```
# Allow anonymous FTP? (Disabled by default)
anonymous_enable=NO
#
# Uncomment this to allow local users to log in.
local_enable=YES
```

If you want to allow anonymous use of your FTP server, change NO to YES in the first couplet. As you can see in the second couplet, in Ubuntu 10.10, the local user setting was changed by Ubuntu from the default setting that did not allow local users to log in. We suggest commenting the line back out by placing a # at the front if you are going to run an anonymous FTP server. The default settings here work great if you are only allowing one user FTP access on the back end of a web server, for example, which is becoming the more common use for FTP, at least until we can convince the world to move to using SSH. See the "Telnet vs. SSH" discussion in Chapter 15and replace "Telnet" with "FTP" for an idea of why this would be a good move.

Controlling Anonymous Access

Toggling anonymous access features for your FTP server is done by editing the `vsftpd.conf` file and changing related entries to `YES` or `NO` in the file. Settings to control how the server works for anonymous logins include the following:

- `anonymous_enable`—Disabled by default. Use a setting of `YES`, and then restart the server to turn on anonymous access.
- `anon_mkdir_write_enable`—Allows or disallows creating of new directories.
- `anon_other_write_enable`—Allows or disallows deleting or renaming of files and directories.
- `anon_upload_enable`—Controls whether anonymous users can upload files (also depends on the global `write_enable` setting). This is a potential security and liability hazard and should rarely be used; if enabled, consistently monitor any designated upload directory.
- `anon_world_readable_only`—Allows only anonymous users to download files with world-readable (444) permission.

After making any changes to your FTP server configuration file, make sure to restart the server; this forces `vsftpd` to reread its settings.

Other vsftpd Server Configuration Files

You can edit `vsftpd.conf` to enable, disable, and configure many features and settings of the `vsftpd` server, such as user access, filtering of bogus passwords, and access logging. Some features might require the creation and configuration of other files, such as the following:

- `/etc/vsftpd.user_list`—Used by the `userlist_enable` and the `userlist_deny` options; the file contains a list of usernames to be denied access to the server.
- `/etc/vsftpd.chroot_list`—Used by the `chroot_list_enable` and `chroot_local_user` options, this file contains a list of users who are either allowed or denied access to a home directory. An alternate file can be specified by using the `chroot_list_file` option.
- `/etc/vsftpd.banned_emails`—A list of anonymous password entries used to deny access if the `deny_email_enable` setting is enabled. An alternative file can be specified by using the `banned_email` option.
- `/var/log/vsftpd.log`—Data transfer information is captured to this file if logging is enabled using the `xferlog_enable` setting.

TIP

Whenever editing the FTP server files, make a backup file first. Also, it is always a good idea to comment out (using a pound sign at the beginning of a line) what is changed instead of deleting or overwriting entries. Follow these comments with a brief description explaining why the change was made. This leaves a nice audit trail of what was done, by whom, when, and why. If you have any problems with the configuration, these comments and details can help you troubleshoot and return to valid entries if necessary. You can use the `dpkg` command or other Linux tools (such as mc) to extract a fresh copy of a configuration file from the software's package archive. Be aware, however, that the extracted version will replace the current version and overwrite your configuration changes.

Default vsftpd Behaviors

The contents of a file named `.message` (if it exists in the current directory) are displayed when a user enters the directory. This feature is enabled in the configuration file. FTP users are not allowed to perform recursive directory listings, which helps reduce bandwidth.

Other default settings are that specific user login controls are not set, but you can configure the controls to deny access to one or more users.

The data transfer rate for anonymous client access is unlimited, but you can set a maximum rate (in bytes per second) by using the `anon_max_rate` setting in `vsftpd.conf`. This can be useful for throttling bandwidth use during periods of heavy access, but waiting until heavy use occurs to change the setting could cause problems because you would kill any current connections when you restart the FTP server daemon. If you anticipate heavy FTP usage, change this setting before it happens or during a scheduled maintenance cycle. Another default is that remote clients will be logged out after five minutes of idle activity or a stalled data transfer. You can set idle and stalled connection timeouts by uncommenting idle_session_timeout and setting the time in seconds before idle sessions are disconnected.

Other settings that might be important for managing your system's resources (networking bandwidth or memory) when offering FTP access include:

- dirlist_enable—Toggles directory listings on or off.
- `dirmessage_enable`—Toggles display of a message when the user enters a directory. A related setting is `ls_recurse_enable`, which can be used to disallow recursive directory listings.
- `download_enable`—Toggles downloading on or off.
- `max_clients`—Sets a limit on the maximum number of connections.
- max_per_ip—Sets a limit on the number of connections from the same IP address.

Using the `ftphosts` File to Allow or Deny FTP Server Connection

You can create a file in `/etc` called `ftphosts` to allow or deny specific users or addresses from connecting to the FTP server. The format of the file is the word `allow` or `deny`, optionally followed by a username, followed by an IP or a DNS address.

```
allow username address
deny username address
```

Listing 18.2 shows a sample configuration of this file.

LISTING 18.2 **`ftphosts`** Configuration File for Allowing or Denying Users

```
# Example host access file
#
# Everything after a '#' is treated as comment,
# empty lines are ignored
allow fatima 208.164.186.1 208.164.186.2 208.164.186.4
deny richard 208.164.186.5
allow jane ubuntuforums.org
deny john naughtysite.net
allow ahmed 192.168.101.*
allow ahmed *.ubuntu.com
allow ahmed *.matthewhelmke.net
deny anonymous 201.*
```

The * is a wildcard that matches any combination of that address. For example, allow ahmed `*.matthewhelmke.net` allows the user `ahmed` to log in to the FTP server from any address that contains the domain name matthewhelmke.net. Similarly, the anonymous user is not allowed to access the FTP if the user is coming from a 201 public class C IP address. You should set the permissions on this file to 600.

Changes made to your system's FTP server configuration files only become active after you restart `inetd` because configuration files are only parsed at startup. To restart `inetd` as root, issue the command `/etc/init.d/inetutils-inetd restart`. This makes a call to the same shell script that is called at system startup and shutdown for any runlevel to start or stop the `inet` daemon. `inetd` should report its status as

```
# /etc/init.d/inetutils-inetd restart
Stopping internet superserver inetd:                                        [  OK  ]
Starting internet superserver inetd:                                        [  OK  ]
```

After it is restarted, the FTP server is accessible to all incoming requests.

Reference

- www.cert.org/—Computer Emergency Response Team.
- www.openssh.com/—The OpenSSH home page and source for the latest version of OpenSSH and its component clients, such as sftp.
- http://vsftpd.beasts.org/—Home page for the `vsftd` FTP server.
- https://help.ubuntu.com/community/FtpServer—Ubuntu community documentation for setting up and using an FTP server.
- https://help.ubuntu.com/10.04/serverguide/C/ftp-server.html—Official Ubuntu documentation for setting up and using vsftp.

CHAPTER 19

Handling Email

IN THIS CHAPTER

- ▶ How Email Is Sent and Received
- ▶ Basic Postfix Configuration and Operation
- ▶ Using Fetchmail to Retrieve Mail
- ▶ Choosing a Mail Delivery Agent
- ▶ Mail Daemons
- ▶ Alternatives to Microsoft Exchange Server
- ▶ Reference

Email is still the dominant form of communication over the Internet. It is fast, free, and easy to use. However, much of what goes on behind the scenes is extremely complicated and would appear scary to anyone who does not know much about how email is handled. Ubuntu comes equipped with a number of powerful applications that will help you build anything from a small email server, right through to large servers able to handle thousands of messages.

This chapter shows you how to configure Ubuntu to act as an email server. We look at the options available in Ubuntu and examine the pros and cons of each one. You will also learn how mail is handled in Linux, and to a lesser extent, UNIX.

How Email Is Sent and Received

Email is transmitted as plain text across networks around the world using the *Simple Mail Transfer Protocol* protocol (*SMTP*). As the name implies, the protocol itself is fairly basic, and it has been extended to add further authentication and error reporting/messaging to satisfy the growing demands of modern email. Mail *transfer agents*, or MTAs, work in the background transferring email from server to server, allowing emails to be sent all over the world. You may have come across such MTA software such as Sendmail, Postfix, Fetchmail, Exim, or Qmail.

SMTP allows each computer that the email passes through to forward it in the right direction to the final destination. When you consider the millions of email servers across the world, you have to marvel at how simple it all seems.

Here is a simplified example of how email is successfully processed and sent to its destination:

1. matthew@seymourcray.net composes and sends an email message to heather@gracehopper.net.
2. The MTA at seymourcray.net receives Matthew's email message and queues it for delivery behind any other messages that are also waiting to go out.
3. The MTA at seymourcray.net contacts the MTA at gracehopper.net on port 24. After gracehopper.net acknowledges the connection, the MTA at seymourcray.net sends the mail message. After gracehopper.net accepts and acknowledges receipt of the message, the connection is closed.
4. The MTA at gracehopper.net places the mail message into Heather's incoming mailbox; Heather is notified that she has new mail the next time she logs on.

However, several things can go wrong during this process. Here are a few examples:

What if Heather does not exist at gracehopper.net? In this case, the MTA at gracehopper.net will reject the email and notify the MTA at seymourcray.net of what the problem is. The MTA at seymourcray.net will then generate an email message and send it to matthew@seymourcray.net, informing him that no Heather exists at gracehopper.net (or perhaps just silently discard the message and give the sender no indication of the problem, depending on how the email server is configured).

What happens if gracehopper.net doesn't respond to seymourcray.net's connection attempts? (Perhaps the server is down for maintenance.) The MTA at seymourcray.net notifies the sender that the initial delivery attempt has failed. Further attempts will be made at intervals decided by the server administrator until the deadline is reached, and the sender will be notified that the mail is undeliverable.

The Mail Transport Agent

Several MTAs are available for Ubuntu, each with its pros and cons. Normally they are hidden under the skin of Ubuntu, silently moving mail between servers all over the world with need for little or no maintenance. Some MTAs are extremely powerful, being able to cope with hundreds of thousands of messages each day, whereas some are geared more toward smaller installations. Other MTAs are perhaps not as powerful, but are packed full with features. In the next section, we take a look at some of the more popular MTAs available for Ubuntu.

Sendmail

Sendmail handles the overwhelming majority of emails transmitted over the Internet today. It is extremely popular across the Linux/UNIX/BSD world and is well supported. A commercial version is available that has a GUI interface for ease of configuration.

As well as being popular, Sendmail is particularly powerful compared to some of the other MTAs. However, it is not without its downsides, and you will find that other MTAs can handle more email per second in a larger environment. The other issue with Sendmail is that it can be extremely complicated to set it up exactly as you want it. A few books are available specifically for Sendmail, but the most popular one has more than a thousand pages, reflecting the complex nature of Sendmail configuration.

We can be thankful, however, that the default configuration for Sendmail works fine for most basic installations out of the box, making further configurations unnecessary. Even if you want to use it as a basic email server, you only need to do some minor tweaks. The level of complexity associated with Sendmail often leads to system administrators replacing it with one of the other alternatives that is easier to configure.

Postfix

Postfix has its origins as the IBM Secure Mailer, but was released to the community by IBM. Compared to Sendmail, it is much easier to administer and has a number of speed advantages. Postfix offers a pain-free replacement for Sendmail, and you are able to literally replace Sendmail with Postfix without the system breaking a sweat. In fact, the applications that rely on Sendmail will automatically use Postfix instead and carry on working correctly (because Postfix uses a Sendmail wrapper, which deceives other programs into thinking that Postfix is Sendmail). This wrapper, or more correctly interface, makes switching to Postfix extremely easy if you are already running Sendmail. Postfix also happens to be the MTA of choice for Ubuntu, so it is this one that we spend more time on later in this chapter.

For enhanced security, many Postfix processes used to use the `chroot` facility (which restricts access to only specific parts of the file system) for improved security, and there are no `setuid` components in Postfix. With the current release of Ubuntu, a `chroot` configuration is *no longer used* and is, in fact, discouraged by the Postfix author. You can manually reconfigure Postfix to a `chroot` configuration, but that is no longer supported by Ubuntu.

If you are starting from scratch, Postfix is considered a better choice than Sendmail.

Qmail and Exim

Qmail is a direct competitor to Postfix but is not provided with Ubuntu. Qmail is designed to be easier to use than Sendmail, as well as faster and more secure. However, Qmail isn't a drop-in replacement for Sendmail, so migrating an existing Sendmail installation to Qmail is not quite as simple as migrating from Sendmail to Postfix. Qmail is relatively easy to administer, and it integrates with a number of software add-ons, including web mail systems and POP3 servers. Qmail is available from www.qmail.org/.

Exim is yet another MTA, and it is available at www.exim.org/. Exim is considered faster and more secure that Sendmail or Postfix, but is much different to configure that either of those. Exim and Qmail use the `maildir` format rather than `mbox`, so both are considered "NFS safe" (see the following sidebar).

19

MDIR VERSUS MAILBOX

Qmail also introduced `maildir`, which is an alternative to the standard UNIX method of storing incoming mail. `maildir` is a more versatile system of handling incoming email, but it requires your email clients to be reconfigured, and it is not compatible with the traditional UNIX way of storing incoming mail. You will need to use mail programs that recognize the `maildir` format. (The modern programs do.)

The traditional `mbox` format keeps all mail assigned to a folder concatenated as a single file and maintains an index of individual emails. With `maildir`, each mail folder has three subfolders: `/cur`, `/new`, and `/tmp`. Each email is kept in a separate, unique file. If you are running a mail server for a large number of people, you should select a file system that can efficiently handle a large number of small files.

`mbox` does offer one major disadvantage. While you are accessing the monolithic `mbox` file that contains all your email, suppose that some type of corruption occurs, either to the file itself or to the index. Recovery from this problem can prove difficult. The `mbox` files are especially prone to problems if the files are being accessed over a network and can result in file corruption; one should avoid accessing `mbox` mail mounted over NFS, the Network File System, because file corruption can occur.

Depending on how you access your mail, `maildir` does permit the simultaneous access of `maildir` files by multiple applications; `mbox` does not.

The choice of a *mail user agent (MUA)*, or email client, also affects your choice of mail directory format. For example, the `pine` program does not cache any directory information and must reread the mail directory any time it accesses it. If you are using `pine`, `maildir` is a poor choice. More-advanced email clients perform caching, so `maildir` might be a good choice, although the email client cache can get out of synchronization. It seems that no perfect choice exists.

Ubuntu provides you with mail alternatives that have both strong and weak points. Be aware of the differences among the alternatives and frequently reevaluate your selection to make certain that it is the best one for your circumstances.

Choosing an MTA

Other MTAs are available for use with Ubuntu, but those discussed in the previous sections are the most popular. Which one should you choose? That depends on what you need to do. Postfix's main strengths is that it scales well and can handle large volumes of email at high speeds, not to mention that it is much easier to configure than the more cryptic Sendmail. However, you may find that there are specific things that you need that only Sendmail can provide. It is easy to switch between MTAs when you need to.

The Mail Delivery Agent

SMTP is a server-to-server protocol that was designed to deliver mail to systems that are always connected to the Internet. Dial-up systems connect only at the user's command; they connect for specific operations, and are frequently disconnected. To accommodate this difference, many mail systems also include a *mail delivery agent*, or MDA. The MDA transfers mail to systems without permanent Internet connections. The MDA is similar to an MTA (see the following note), but does not handle deliveries between systems and does not provide an interface to the user.

NOTE

Procmail or Spamassassin are examples of MTAs; both provide filtering services to the MTA while they store messages locally and then make them available to the MUA or email client for reading by the user.

The MDA uses the POP3 or IMAP protocols for this process. In a manner similar to a post office box at the post office, POP3 and IMAP implement a "store and forward" process that alleviates the need to maintain a local mail server if all you want to do is read your mail. For example, dial-up Internet users can intermittently connect to their ISP's mail server to retrieve mail using Fetchmail—the MDA recommended by Ubuntu (see the section "Using Fetchmail to Retrieve Mail" later in this chapter).

The Mail User Agent

The *mail user agent*, or *MUA*, is another necessary part of the email system. The MUA is a mail client, or mail reader, that allows the user to read and compose email and provides the user interface. (It is the email application itself that most users are familiar with as "email.") Some popular UNIX command-line MUAs are `elm`, `pine`, and `mutt`. Ubuntu also provides modern GUI MUAs: Evolution, Thunderbird, Mozilla Mail, Balsa, Sylpheed, and KMail. For comparison, common non-UNIX MUAs are Microsoft Outlook, Outlook Express, Pegasus Mail, and Apple Inc.'s Mail.

The Microsoft Windows and Macintosh MUAs often include some MTA functionality; UNIX does not. For example, Microsoft Outlook can connect to your Internet provider's mail server to send messages. On the other hand, UNIX MUAs generally rely on an external MTA such as Sendmail. This might seem like a needlessly complicated way to do things, and it is if used to connect a single user to her ISP. For any other situation, however, using an external MTA allows you much greater flexibility because you can use any number of external programs to handle and process your email functions and customize the service. Having the process handled by different applications gives you great control over how you provide email service to users on your network, as well as to individual and *small office/home office* (SOHO) users.

For example, you could do the following:

- Use Evolution to read and compose mail.
- Use Sendmail to send your mail.
- Use `xbiff` to notify you when you have new mail.
- Use Fetchmail to retrieve your mail from a remote mail server.
- Use Procmail to automatically sort your incoming mail based on sender, subject, or many other variables.
- Use Spamassassin to eliminate the unwanted messages before you read them.

Basic Postfix Configuration and Operation

Because Postfix is the Ubuntu-recommended MTA, the following sections provide a brief explanation and examples for configuring and operating your email system. As mentioned earlier, however, Postfix is an extremely complex program with many configuration options. As such, this chapter only covers some of the basics.

Postfix is not installed by default. To use it, install the `postfix` package from the Ubuntu software repositories. During installation you will be asked a series of questions to help configure Postfix immediately. You should research the settings for your situation before you start; some are merely preferential, but others are based on your hardware, network, and use case. You will be asked:

```
General type of mail configuration: Internet Site


System mail name: mail.matthewhelmke.com
Root and postmaster mail recipient: <admin_user_name>
Other destinations for mail: mail.example.com, example.com, localhost.example.com,
localhost
Force synchronous updates on mail queue?: No
Local networks: 127.0.0.0/8

Mailbox size limit (bytes): 0
Local address extension character: +
Internet protocols to use: all
```

If you make a mistake and answer a configuration question incorrectly, you can go back through the process again by entering this from the command line:

```
matthew@seymour:~$ sudo dpkg-reconfigure postfix
```

Postfix configuration is maintained in files in the `/etc/postfix` directory with much of the configuration being handled by the file `main.cf`. You don't have to use the command above to change these settings, but may do so by editing the appropriate file(s). The syntax of the configuration file, `main.cf`, is fairly easy to read (see the following example):

```
# See /usr/share/postfix/main.cf.dist for a commented, more complete version
# Debian specific:  Specifying a file name will cause the first
# line of that file to be used as the name.  The Debian default
# is /etc/mailname.
#myorigin = /etc/mailname

smtpd_banner = $myhostname ESMTP $mail_name (Ubuntu)
biff = no

# appending .domain is the MUA's job.
```

```
append_dot_mydomain = no

# Uncomment the next line to generate "delayed mail" warnings
#delay_warning_time = 4h

# TLS parameters
smtpd_tls_cert_file=/etc/ssl/certs/ssl-cert-snakeoil.pem
smtpd_tls_key_file=/etc/ssl/private/ssl-cert-snakeoil.key
smtpd_use_tls=yes
smtpd_tls_session_cache_database = btree:${queue_directory}/smtpd_scache
smtp_tls_session_cache_database = btree:${queue_directory}/smtp_scache

# See /usr/share/doc/postfix/TLS_README.gz in the postfix-doc package for
# information on enabling SSL in the smtp client.

myhostname = optimus
alias_maps = hash:/etc/aliases
alias_database = hash:/etc/aliases
mydestination = optimus, localhost.localdomain, , localhost
relayhost =
mynetworks = 127.0.0.0/8
mailbox_size_limit = 0
recipient_delimiter = +
inet_interfaces = all
```

A useful command for configuring Postfix is postconf. It allows you to display and change many configuration settings without editing and saving configuration files. The command's syntax is rather complex, but once learned it becomes a faster way to quickly adjust settings. For example, the following command sets the `myhostname` parameter:

```
matthew@seymour:~$ sudo postconf -e
myhostname=mail.matthewhelmke.com
```

You can learn more about postconf from the man page.

You start, stop, and restart Postfix using this command, using the appropriate one of those three action words:

```
matthew@seymour:~$ sudo /etc/init.d/postfix start
```

Complicated email server setup is beyond the scope of this book, and we would point you in the direction of *Postfix: The Definitive Guide,* by Kyle Dent. This is a great reference, and rather unusual because it is a complete and useful reference in only 250 pages or so. However, if you want to know something specific about Postfix, this is the book to read.

However, the following five sections address some commonly used advanced options. For more information on Postfix, as well as other MTAs, see the "Reference" section at the end of this chapter.

Configuring Masquerading

Sometimes you might want to have Postfix masquerade as a host other than the actual hostname of your system. Such a situation could occur if you have a dial-up connection to the Internet and your ISP handles all your mail for you. In this case, you will want Postfix to masquerade as the domain name of your ISP. For example, the following will strip any messages that come from `matthew.gracehopper.net` to just `gracehopper.net`:

```
masquerade_domains = gracehopper.net
```

Using Smart Hosts

If you do not have a full-time connection to the Internet, you will probably want to have Postfix send your messages to your ISPs mail server and let it handle delivery for you. Without a full-time Internet connection, you could find it difficult to deliver messages to some locations (such as some underdeveloped areas of the world where email services are unreliable and sporadic). In those situations, you can configure Postfix to function as a smart host by passing email on to another sender instead of attempting to deliver the email directly. You can use a line such as the following in the `main.cf` file to enable a smart host:

```
relayhost = mail.isp.net
```

This line causes Postfix to pass any mail it receives to the server `mail.isp.net` rather than attempt to deliver it directly. Smart hosting will not work for you if your ISP, like many others, blocks any mail relaying. Some ISPs block relaying because it is frequently used to disseminate spam.

Setting Message Delivery Intervals

As mentioned earlier, Postfix typically attempts to deliver messages as soon as it receives them, and again at regular intervals after that. If you have only periodic connections to the Internet, as with a dial-up connection, you likely would prefer Sendmail to hold all messages in the queue and attempt to deliver them whenever you connect to your ISP.

As dialup connections have become the exception rather than the rule and are now quite rare, Ubuntu does not configure them by default and does not include the pppd daemon in the default installation. If you need this, install pppd from the Ubuntu software repositories. You can then configure Postfix to hold messages for later delivery by adding the following line to `/etc/ppp/peers/ppp0`:

```
/usr/sbin/sendmail -q
```

This line causes Postifix to automatically send all mail when connecting to your ISP.

However, Postfix will still attempt to send mail regardless of whether the computer is on or off line, meaning that your computer may dial out just to send email. To disable this, you need to enter the following line into `mail.cf`:

```
defer_transports = smtp
```

This stops any unwanted telephone calls from being placed!

TIP

If you use networking over a modem, there is a configuration file for `pppd` called `ppp0`, which is located in `/etc/ppp/peers`. Any commands in this file automatically run each time the PPP daemon is started. You can add the line `sendmail -q` to this file to have your mail queue automatically processed each time you dial up your Internet connection.

Mail Relaying

By default, Postfix will not relay mail that did not originate from the local domain. This means that if a Postfix installation running at gracehopper.net receives mail intended for seymourcray.net, and that mail did not originate from gracehopper.net, the mail will be rejected and will not be relayed. If you want to allow selected domains to relay through you, add an entry for the domain to the `main.cf` file like this:

```
mynetworks = 192.168.2.0/24, 10.0.0.2/24, 127.0.0.0/8
```

The IP address needs to be specified in CIDR format. For a handy calculator, head on over to www.subnet-calculator.com/cidr.php. You must restart Postfix for this change to take effect.

CAUTION

You need a good reason to relay mail; otherwise, do not do it. Allowing all domains to relay through you will make you a magnet for spammers who will use your mail server to send spam. This can lead to your site being blacklisted by many other sites, which then will not accept any mail from you or your site's users—even if the mail is legitimate!

Forwarding Email with Aliases

Aliases allow you to have an infinite number of valid recipient addresses on your system, without having to worry about creating accounts or other support files for each address. For example, most systems have "postmaster" defined as a valid recipient, but do not have an actual login account named "postmaster." Aliases are configured in the file `/etc/aliases`. Here is an example of an alias entry:

```
postmaster: root
```

This entry forwards any mail received for "postmaster" to the root user. By default, almost all the aliases listed in the `/etc/aliases` file forward to root.

CAUTION

Reading email as root is a security hazard; a malicious email message can exploit an email client and cause it to execute arbitrary code as the user running the client. To avoid this danger, you can forward all of root's mail to another account and read it from there. You can choose one of two ways for doing this.

You can add an entry to the `/etc/aliases` file that sends root's mail to a different account. For example, `root: foobar` would forward all mail intended for root to the account foobar.

The other way is to create a file named `.forward` in root's home directory that contains the address that the mail should forward to.

Anytime you make a change to the `/etc/aliases` file, you will need to rebuild the aliases database before that change will take effect. This is done with the following:

```
$ sudo newaliases
```

Using Fetchmail to Retrieve Mail

SMTP is designed to work with systems that have a full-time connection to the Internet. What if you are on a dial-up account? What if you have another system store your email for you and then you log in to pick it up once in a while? (Most users who are not setting up servers will be in this situation.) In this case, you cannot easily receive email using SMTP, and you need to use a protocol, such as POP3 or IMAP, instead.

NOTE

Remember when we said that some mail clients can include some MTA functionality? Microsoft Outlook and Outlook Express can be configured to use SMTP and, if you use a dial-up connection, will offer to start the connection and then use SMTP to send your mail, so a type of MTA functionality is included in those mail clients.

Unfortunately, many MUAs do not know anything about POP3 or IMAP. To eliminate that problem, you can use a program called Fetchmail to contact mail servers using POP3 or IMAP, download mail off the servers, and then inject those messages into the local MTA just as if they had come from a standard SMTP server. The following sections explain how to install, configure, and use the Fetchmail program.

Installing Fetchmail

Similar to other packages, Fetchmail can be installed using either `synaptic` or `apt-get`.

You can get the latest version of Fetchmail at www.catb.org/~esr/fetchmail.

Configuring Fetchmail

After you have installed Fetchmail, you must create the file `.fetchmailrc` in your home directory, which provides the configuration for the Fetchmail program.

You can create and subsequently edit the `.fetchmailrc` file by using any text editor. The configuration file is straightforward and quite easy to create; the following sections explain the manual method for creating and editing the file. The information presented in the following sections does not discuss all the options available in the `.fetchmailrc` file, but covers the most common ones needed to get a basic Fetchmail installation up and running. You must use a text editor to create the file to include entries like the ones shown as examples—modified for your personal information, of course. For advanced configuration, see the man page for Fetchmail. The man page is well written and documents all the configuration options in detail.

CAUTION

The `.fetchmailrc` file is divided into three sections: global options, mail server options, and user options. It is important that these sections appear in the order listed. Do not add options to the wrong section. Putting options in the wrong place is one of the most common problems that new users make with Fetchmail configuration files.

Configuring Global Options

The first section of `.fetchmailrc` contains the global options. These options affect all the mail servers and user accounts that you list later in the configuration file. Some of these global options can be overridden with local configuration options, as you learn later in this section. Here is an example of the options that might appear in the global section of the `.fetchmailrc` file:

```
set daemon 600
set postmaster foobar
set logfile ./.fetchmail.log
```

The first line in this example tells Fetchmail that it should start in daemon mode and check the mail servers for new mail every 600 seconds, or 10 minutes. Daemon mode means that after Fetchmail starts, it will move itself into the background and continue running. Without this line, Fetchmail would check for mail once when it started and would then terminate and never check again.

The second option tells Fetchmail to use the local account foobar as a last-resort address. In other words, any email that it receives and cannot deliver to a specified account should be sent to foobar.

The third line tells Fetchmail to log its activity to the file `./.fetchmail.log`. Alternatively, you can use the line `set syslog`—in which case, Fetchmail will log through the syslog facility.

Configuring Mail Server Options

The second section of the `.fetchmailrc` file contains information on each of the mail servers that should be checked for new mail. Here is an example of what the mail section might look like:

```
poll mail.samplenet.org
proto pop3
no dns
```

The first line tells Fetchmail that it should check the mail server mail.samplenet.org at each poll interval that was set in the global options section (which was 600 seconds in our example). Alternatively, the first line can begin with skip. If a mail server line begins with `skip`, it will not be polled as the poll interval, but will only be polled when it is specifically specified on the Fetchmail command line.

The second line specifies the protocol that should be used when contacting the mail server. In this case, we are using the POP3 protocol. Other legal options are IMAP, APOP, and KPOP. You can also use

AUTO here—in which case, Fetchmail will attempt to automatically determine the correct protocol to use with the mail server.

The third line tells Fetchmail that it should not attempt to do a *Dynamic Name Server (DNS)* lookup. You will probably want to include this option if you are running over a dial-up connection.

Configuring User Accounts

The third and final section of `.fetchmailrc` contains information about the user account on the server specified in the previous section. Here is an example:

```
user foobar
pass secretword
fetchall
no flush
```

The first line, of course, simply specifies the username that is used to log in to the email server, and the second line specifies the password for that user. Many security conscious people cringe at the thought of putting clear-text passwords in a configuration file, and they should if it is group or world readable. The only protection for this information is to make certain that the file is readable only by the owner; that is, with file permissions of **600**.

The third line tells Fetchmail that it should fetch all messages from the server, even if they have already been read.

The fourth line tells Fetchmail that it should delete the messages from the mail server after it has completed downloading them. This is the default, so we would not really have to specify this option. If you want to delete the messages from the server after downloading them, use the option `flush`.

The configuration options you just inserted configured the entire `.fetchmailrc` file to look like this:

```
set daemon 600
set postmaster foobar
set logfile ./.fetchmail.log

poll mail.samplenet.org
proto pop3
no dns

user foobar
pass secretword
fetchall
flush
```

This file tells Fetchmail to do the following:

- Check the POP3 server mail.samplenet.org for new mail every 600 seconds.
- Log in using the username foobar and the password secretword.
- Download all messages off the server.
- Delete the messages from the server after it has finished downloading them.
- Send any mail it receives that cannot be delivered to a local user to the account foobar.

As mentioned before, many more options can be included in the `.fetchmailrc` file than are listed here. However, these options will get you up and running with a basic configuration.

For additional flexibility, you can define multiple `.fetchmailrc` files to retrieve mail from different remote mail servers while using the same Linux user account. For example, you can define settings for your most often used account and save them in the default `.fetchmailrc` file. Mail can then quickly be retrieved like this:

```
$ fetchmail -a
1 message for matthew at mail.matthewhelmke.com (1108 octets).
reading message 1 of 1 (1108 octets) . flushed
```

By using Fetchmail's `-f` option, you can specify an alternative resource file and then easily retrieve mail from another server, as follows:

```
$ fetchmail -f .myothermailrc
2 messages for matthew at matthew.helmke.com (5407 octets).
reading message 1 of 2 (3440 octets) ... flushed
reading message 2 of 2 (1967 octets) . flushed
You have new mail in /var/spool/mail/matthew
```

By using the -d option, along with a time interval (in seconds), you can use Fetchmail in its daemon, or background mode. The command will launch as a background process and retrieve mail from a designated remote server at a specified interval. For more-advanced options, see the Fetchmail man page, which is well written and documents all options in detail.

CAUTION

Because the `.fetchmailrc` file contains your mail server password, it should be readable only by you. This means that it should be owned by you and should have permissions no greater than `600`. Fetchmail will complain and refuse to start if the `.fetchmailrc` file has permissions greater than this.

Choosing a Mail Delivery Agent

Because of the modular nature of mail handling, it is possible to use multiple applications to process mail and accomplish more than simply deliver it. Getting mail from the storage area and displaying it to the user is the purpose of the MDA. MDA functionality can be found in some of the mail clients (MUAs), which can cause some confusion to those still unfamiliar with the concept of UNIX mail. As an example, the Procmail MDA provides filtering based on rulesets; KMail and Evolution, both MUAs, provide filtering, but the MUAs `pine`, `mutt`, and Balsa do not. Some MDAs perform simple sorting, and other MDAs are designed to eliminate unwanted emails, such as spam and viruses.

You would choose an MDA based on what you want to do with your mail. We will look at five MDAs that offer functions you might find useful in your particular situation. If you have simple needs (just organizing mail by rules), one of the MUAs that offers filtering might be better for your needs. Ubuntu provides the Evolution MUA as the default selection (and it contains some MDA functionality as previously noted), so try that first and see whether it meets your needs. If not, investigate one of the following MDAs provided by Ubuntu.

Unless otherwise noted, all the MDA software is provided in the Ubuntu repositories. Chapter 32, "Managing Software," details the general installation of any software.

Procmail

As a tool for advanced users, the Procmail application acts as a filter for email, as it is retrieved from a mail server. It uses rulesets (known as *recipes*) as it reads each email message. No default configuration is provided; you must manually create a `~/.procmail` file for each user, or users can create their own.

There is no systemwide default configuration file. The creation of the rulesets is not trivial and requires an understanding of the use of regular expressions that is beyond the scope of this chapter. Ubuntu does provide three examples of the files in `/usr/share/doc/procmail/examples`, as well as a fully commented example in the `/usr/share/doc/procmail` directory, which also contains a `README` and `FAQ`. Details for the rulesets can be found in the man page for Procmail as well as the man pages for `procmailrc`, `procmailsc`, and `procmailex`, which contain examples of Procmail recipes.

Spamassassin

If you have used email for any length of time, you have likely been subjected to spam—unwanted email sent to thousands of people at the same time. Ubuntu provides an MDA named Spamassassin to assist you in reducing and eliminating unwanted emails. Easily integrated with Procmail and Sendmail, it can be configured for both system wide and individual use. It uses a combination of rule sets and blacklists (Internet domains known to mail spam).

Enabling Spamassassin is simple. You must first have installed and configured Procmail. The `README` file found in `/usr/share/doc/spamassasin` provides details on configuring the `.procmail` file to process mail through Spamassassin. It will tag probable spam with a unique header; you can then have Procmail filter the mail in any manner you choose. One interesting use of Spamassasin is to use it to tag email received at special email accounts established solely for the purpose of attracting spam. This information is then shared with the Spamassassin site where these "spam trap" generated hits help the authors fine-tune the rulesets.

Squirrelmail

Perhaps you do not want to read your mail in an MUA. If you use your web browser often, it might make sense to read and send your mail via a web interface, such as the one used by Hotmail or Yahoo! Mail. Ubuntu provides Squirrelmail for just that purpose. Squirrelmail is written in PHP and supports IMAP and SMTP. It supports MIME attachments, as well as an address book and folders for segregating email.

You must configure your web server to work with PHP 4. Detailed installation instructions can be found in `/usr/share/doc/squirrelmail/INSTALL`. After it is configured, point your web browser to the default install location, www.yourdomain.com/squirelmail/, to read and send email.

Virus Scanners

Although the currently held belief is that Linux is immune to email viruses targeted at Microsoft Outlook users, it certainly makes no sense for UNIX mail servers to permit infected email to be sent through them. Although Ubuntu does not provide a virus scanner by default, some of the more popular scanners are available in the Ubuntu repositories. Take a look at ClamAV as the most popular example.

Autoresponders

Autoresponders automatically generate replies to received messages; they are commonly used to notify others that the recipient is out of the office. Mercifully, Ubuntu does not include one by default, but you can find and install an autoresponder like `vacation` or `gnarwl` from the Ubuntu software repositories. If you are subscribed to a mailing list, be aware that automatic responses from your account can be very annoying to others on the list. Please unsubscribe from mail lists before you leave the office with your autoresponder activated.

Alternatives to Microsoft Exchange Server

One of the last areas in which a Microsoft product has yet to be usurped by open-source software is a replacement for Microsoft Exchange Server. Many businesses use Microsoft Outlook and Microsoft Exchange Server to access email, as well as to provide calendaring, notes, file sharing, and other collaborative functions. General industry complaints about Exchange Server center around scalability, administration (backup and restore in particular), and licensing fees.

A "drop-in" alternative needs to have compatibility with Microsoft Outlook because it's intended to replace Exchange Server in an environment in which there are Microsoft desktops in existence using Outlook. A "work-alike" alternative provides similar features to Exchange Server, but does not offer compatibility with the Microsoft Outlook client itself; the latter is typical of many of the open-source alternatives.

Several "drop-in" alternatives exist, none of which are fully open source because some type of proprietary connector is needed to provide the services to Microsoft Outlook clients (or provide Exchange services to the Linux Evolution client). For Outlook compatibility, the key seems to be the realization of a full, open implementation of *MAPI*, the Microsoft *Messaging Application Program Interface*. That goal is going to be difficult to achieve because MAPI is a poorly documented Microsoft protocol. For Linux-only solutions, the missing ingredient for many alternatives is a usable group calendaring/scheduling system similar in function to that provided by Exchange Server/Outlook.

Of course, independent applications for these functions abound in the open-source world, but one characteristic of "groupware" is its central administration; another is that all components can share information.

The following sections examine several of the available servers, beginning with Microsoft Exchange Server itself and moving toward those applications that have increasing incompatibility with it. None of these servers are provided with Ubuntu.

Microsoft Exchange Server/Outlook Client

Exchange Server and Outlook seem to be the industry benchmark because of their widespread deployment. They offer a proprietary server providing email, contacts, scheduling, public folders, task lists, journaling, and notes using Microsoft Outlook as the client and MAPI as the API. If you consider what Microsoft Exchange offers as the "full" set of features, no other replacement offers 100 percent of the features exactly as provided by Microsoft Exchange Server—even those considered "drop-in" replacements. The home page for the Microsoft Exchange server is www.microsoft.com/exchange/.

CommuniGate Pro

CommuniGate Pro is a proprietary, drop-in alternative to Microsoft Exchange Server, providing, email, webmail, LDAP directories, a web server, file server, contacts, calendaring (third party), Voice over IP, and a list server. The CommuniGate Pro MAPI Connector provides access to the server from Microsoft Outlook and other MAPI-enabled clients. The home page for this server is www.stalker.com/.

Oracle Beehive

Oracle Beehive is probably the closest that you will get to an Exchange replacement, allowing you to collaborate by instant messaging, email, sharing files (workspaces), calendaring, and other tools. Beehive is available for Linux platforms and its homepage is www.oracle.com/us/products/middleware/beehive/index.html.

Bynari

Bynari provides a proprietary group of servers to act as a drop-in replacement for Microsoft Exchange Server for email, calendaring, public folders, scheduling, address book, webmail, and contacts. Although it runs on Linux, it offers no Linux clients although it can be used with Evolution and Thunderbird, and the connector provides services to Microsoft Outlook only. The home page is www.bynari.net/.

Open-Xchange

Open-Xchange has a great pedigree having been owned and developed by Novell/SUSE until being spun off by itself into its own company. Working with open standards, it provides a number of collaboration options and is firmly based on Linux. It can work with a wide variety of protocols, making it one of the best connected suites available. You can get the open source version at www.open-xchange.com.

phpgroupware

phpgroupware is an open-source application written in PHP (and used with MySQL or postgresql plus a web server and an IMAP mail server). phpgroupware provides a web-based calendar, task list, address book, email, news headlines, and a file manager. Its modular nature enables you to plug in various components (around 50 at the last count) as you need them. The home page is www.phpgroupware.org/.

PHProjekt

PHProjekt is open-source software written in PHP (used with MySQL, postgresql, Oracle, Informix, or MS-sql). PHProjekt provides calendaring, contact manager, time card system, project management, online chat, threaded discussion forum, trouble ticket system, email, public files, notes bookmarks, voting system, task lists, reminders, site search, and integration with the PostNuke news site application. It provides no Exchange/Outlook compatibility whatsoever. The home page is www.PHProjekt.com/.

Horde

Horde is a PHP-based application framework. When combined with an HTTP server (Apache, Microsoft IIS, Netscape) and MySQL database, IMP/Horde offers modules that provide webmail, contact manager, calendar, CVS viewer, file manager, time tracking, email filter rules manager, notes, tasks, chat, newsgroups, forms, bug tracking, FAQ repository, and presentations. The home page is www.horde.org/.

Reference

Websites

- www.sendmail.org/—This is the Sendmail home page. Here you will find configuration information and FAQs regarding the Sendmail MTA.
- www.postfix.org/—This is the Postfix home page. If you are using the Postfix MTA, you can find documentation and sample configurations at this site.
- help.ubuntu.com/community/Postfix—Ubuntu community documentation for Postfix.www.qmail.org/—This is the home page for the Qmail MTA. It contains documentation and links to other resources on Qmail.
- https://help.ubuntu.com/community/ClamAV – Ubuntu comunity documentation for ClamAV.
- www.rfc-editor.org/—A repository of RFCs—Request for Comments—that define the technical “rules” of modern computer usage.
- www.procmail.org/—The Procmail home page.

Books

- *Sendmail* (O'Reilly Publishing)—This is the de facto standard guide for everything Sendmail. It is loaded with more than 1,000 pages, which gives you an idea of how complicated Sendmail really is.
- *Postfix* (Sams Publishing)—An excellent book from Sams Publishing that covers the Postfix MTA.
- *Postfix: The Definitive Guide* (O'Reilly Publishing)—Another excellent resource for Postfix.
- *Running Qmail* (Sams Publishing)—This is similar to the Postfix book from Sams Publishing except that it covers the Qmail MTA.

CHAPTER 20

Proxying and Reverse Proxying

IN THIS CHAPTER

You can never have enough of two things in this world: time and bandwidth. Ubuntu comes with a proxy server—Squid—that enables you to cache web traffic on your server so that websites load faster and users consume less bandwidth.

What Is a Proxy Server?

A *proxy server* lies between client machines—the desktops in your company—and the Internet. As clients request websites, they do not connect directly to the web and send the HTTP request. Instead, they connect to the local proxy server. The proxy then forwards their request on to the web, retrieves the result, and hands it back to the client. At its simplest, a proxy server really is just an extra layer between client and server, so why bother?

The three main reasons for deploying a proxy server are as follows:

- **Content control**—You want to stop people whiling away their work hours reading celebrity news or downloading MP3s.
- **Speed**—You want to cache common sites to make the most of your bandwidth.
- **Security**—You want to monitor what people are doing.

Squid is capable of all of these and more.

Installing Squid

Squid is easily installed the usual way from the Ubuntu software repositories where it is called squid. After Squid is installed, it is automatically enabled for each bootup. You can check this by running `ps aux | grep squid` when the machine boots. If for some reason you see nothing there, run `/etc/init.d/squid start`.

Configuring Clients

Before you configure your new Squid server, set up the local web browser to use it for its web access. Doing so enables you to test your rules as you are working with the configuration file.

To configure Firefox, select Preferences from the Edit menu. From the dialog that appears, select the Advanced settings using the icon in the top row, and within Advanced, select the Network tab. Then click the Settings button next to Configure how Firefox connects to the Internet and select the Manual Proxy Configuration option. Check the box beneath it labeled Use the Same Proxy for All Protocols. Enter `127.0.0.1` as the IP address and `3128` as the port number. See Figure 20.1 for how this should look. If you are configuring a remote client, specify the IP address of the Squid server rather than 127.0.0.1.

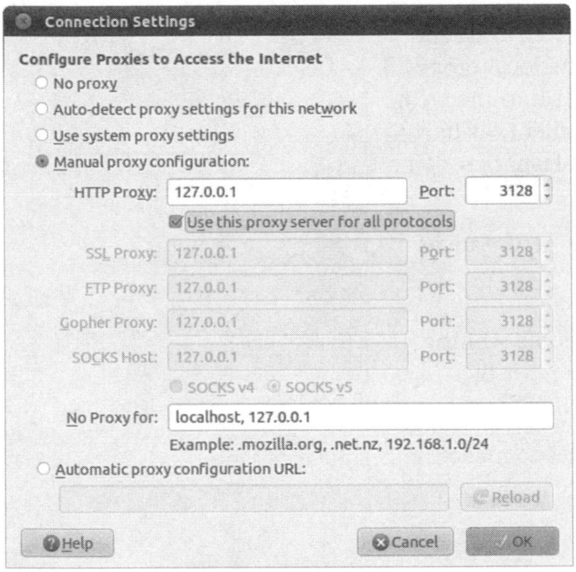

FIGURE 20.1 Setting up Firefox to use 127.0.0.1 routes all its web requests through Squid.

Other web browsers such as Google Chrome, Opera, and so on can be configured similarly. The difference will be the labels used and menu locations for the options, so a little digging may be needed to discover where this may be adjusted in a specific browser's settings.

Access Control Lists

The main Squid configuration file is `/etc/squid/squid.conf`, and the default Ubuntu configuration file is full of comments to help guide you. The default configuration file allows full access to the local machine but denies the rest of your network. This is a secure place to start; we recommend you try all the rules on yourself (`localhost`) before rolling them out to other machines.

Before you start, open two terminal windows. In the first, change to the directory `/var/log/squid` and run this command:

```
sudo tail -f access.log cache.log
```

That reads the last few lines from both files and (thanks to the `-f` flag) follows them so that any changes appear in there. This allows you to watch what Squid is doing as people access it. We refer to this window as the "log window," so keep it open. In the other window (again, with sudo), bring up the file `/etc/squid/squid.conf` in your favorite editor. We refer to this window as the "config editor," and you should keep it open, too.

To get started, search for the string `acl all`—this brings you to the access control section, which is where most of the work needs to be done. You can configure a lot elsewhere, but unless you have unusual requirements, you can leave the defaults in place.

NOTE

The default port for Squid is 3128, but you can change that by editing the `http port` line. Alternatively, you can have Squid listen on multiple ports by having multiple `http_port` lines: `80`, `8000`, and `8080` are all popular ports for proxy servers.

The `acl` lines make up your *access control lists (ACLs)*. The first 16 or so define the minimum recommended configuration that set up ports to listen to, and so on. You can safely ignore these. If you scroll down further (past another short block of comments), you come to the `http_access` lines, which are combined with the `acl` lines to dictate who can do what. You can (and should) mix and match acl and http_access lines to keep your configuration file easy to read.

Just below the first block of `http_access` lines is a comment like `# INSERT YOUR OWN RULE(S) HERE TO ALLOW ACCESS FROM YOUR CLIENTS`. This is just what we are going to do. First, though, scroll just a few lines further; you should see these two lines:

```
http_access allow localhost
http_access deny all
```

They are self-explanatory: The first says, "Allow HTTP access to the local computer, but deny everyone else." This is the default rule, as mentioned earlier. Leave that in place for now, and run `service squid start` to start the server with the default settings. If you have not yet configured the local web browser to use your Squid server, do so now so that you can test the default rules.

In your web browser (Firefox is assumed from here on, because it is the default in a standard Ubuntu install, but it makes little difference), go to the URL www.ubuntulinux.org. You should see it appear as normal in the browser, but in the log window you should see a lot of messages scroll by as Squid downloads the site for you and stores it in its cache. This is all allowed because the default configuration allows access to the `localhost`.

Go back to the config editor window and add this before the last two `http_access` lines:

```
http_access deny localhost
```

So, the last three lines should look like this:

```
http_access deny localhost
http_access allow localhost
http_access deny all
```

Save the file and quit your editor. Then, run this command:

```
kill -SIGHUP 'cat /var/run/squid.pid'
```

That looks for the *process ID (PID)* of the Squid daemon and then sends the `SIGHUP` signal to it, which forces it to reread its configuration file while running. You should see a string of messages in the log window as Squid rereads its configuration files. If you now go back to Firefox and enter a new URL, you should see the Squid error page informing you that you do not have access to the requested site.

The reason you are now blocked from the proxy is because Squid reads its ACL lines in sequence, from top to bottom. If it finds a line that conclusively allows or denies a request, it stops reading and takes the appropriate action. So, in the previous lines, `localhost` is being denied in the first line and then allowed in the second. When Squid sees `localhost` asking for a site, it reads the `deny` line first and immediately sends the error page—it does not even get to the `allow` line. Having a `deny all` line at the bottom is highly recommended so that only those you explicitly allow are able to use the proxy.

Go back to editing the configuration file and remove the `deny localhost` and `allow localhost` lines. This leaves only deny all, which blocks everyone (including the `localhost`) from accessing the proxy. Now we are going to add some conditional allow statements: We want to allow `localhost` only if it fits certain criteria.

Defining access criteria is done with the `acl` lines, so above the `deny all` line, add this:

```
acl newssites dstdomain news.bbc.co.uk slashdot.org
http_access allow newssites
```

The first line defines an access category called `newssites`, which contains a list of domains (`dstdomain`). The domains are news.bbc.co.uk and slashdot.org, so the full line reads, "Create a new access category called newssites that should filter on domain, and contain the two domains listed." It does *not* say whether access should be granted or denied to that category; that comes in the next line. The line `http_access allow newssites` means,

"Allow access to the category `newssites` with no further restrictions." It is not limited to `localhost`, which means that applies to every computer connecting to the proxy server.

Save the configuration file and rerun the `kill -SIGHUP` line from before to restart Squid; then go back to Firefox and try loading www.ubuntu.com. You should see the same error as before because that was not in our `newssites` category. Now try http://news.bbc.co.uk, and it should work. However, if you try www.slashdot.org, it will *not* work, and you might also have noticed that the images did not appear on the BBC News website either. The problem here is that specifying slashdot.org as the website is specific: It means that http://slashdot.org will work, whereas www.slashdot.org will not. The BBC News site stores its images on the site http://newsimg.bbc.co.uk, which is why they do not appear.

Go back to the configuration file, and edit the `newssites` ACL to this:

```
acl newssites dstdomain .bbc.co.uk .slashdot.org
```

Putting the period in front of the domains (and in the BBC's case, taking the news off, too) means that Squid will allow any subdomain of the site to work, which is usually what you will want. If you want even more vagueness, you can just specify `.com` to match `*.com` addresses.

Moving on, you can also use time conditions for sites. For example, if you want to allow access to the news sites in the evenings, you can set up a time category using this line:

```
acl freetime time MTWHFAS 18:00-23:59
```

This time, the category is called freetime and the condition is `time`, which means we need to specify what time the category should contain. The seven characters following that are the days of the week: Monday, Tuesday, Wednesday, tHursday, Friday, sAturday, and Sunday. Thursday and Saturday use capital *H* and *A* so they do not clash with Tuesday and Sunday.

With that category defined, you can change the `http_access` line to include it, like this:

```
http_access allow newssites freetime
```

For Squid to allow access now, it must match both conditions—the request must be for either *.bbc.co.uk or slashdot.org, and during the time specified. If either condition does not match, the line is not matched and Squid continues looking for other matching rules beneath it. The times you specify here are inclusive on both sides, which means users in the `freetime` category will be able to surf from 18:00:00 until 23:59:59.

You can add as many rules as you like, although you should be careful to try to order them so that they make sense. Keep in mind that all conditions in a line must be matched for the line to be matched. Here is a more complex example:

- You want a category `newssites` that contains serious websites people need for their work.

20

- You want a category `playsites` that contains websites people do not need for their work.
- You want a category `worktime` that stretches from 09:00 to 18:00.
- You want a category `freetime` that stretches from 18:00 to 20:00, when the office closes.
- You want people to be able to access the news sites, but not the play sites, during working hours.
- You want people to be able to access both the news sites and the play sites during the free time hours.

To do that, you need the following rules:

```
acl newssites dstdomain .bbc.co.uk .slashdot.org
acl playsites dstdomain .tomshardware.com ubuntulinux.org
acl worktime time MTWHF 9:00-18:00
acl freetime time MTWHF 18:00-20:00
http_access allow newssites worktime
http_access allow newssites freetime
http_access allow playsites freetime
```

NOTE

The letter D is equivalent to MTWHF in meaning, "All the days of the working week."

Notice that there are two `http_access` lines for the `newssites` category: one for `worktime` and one for `freetime`. This is because all the conditions must be matched for a line to be matched. Alternatively, you can write this:

```
http_access allow newssites worktime freetime
```

However, if you do that and someone visits news.bbc.co.uk at 2:30 p.m. (14:30) on a Tuesday, Squid will work like this:

- Is the site in the `newssites` category? Yes, continue.
- Is the time within the `worktime` category? Yes, continue.
- Is the time within the `freetime` category? No; do not match rule, and continue searching for rules.

It is because of this that two lines are needed for the `worktime` category.

One particularly powerful way to filter requests is with the `url_regex` ACL line. This allows you to specify a regular expression that is checked against each request: If the expression matches the request, the condition matches.

For example, if you want to stop people downloading Windows executable files, you would use this line:

```
acl noexes url_regex -i exe$
```

The dollar sign means "end of URL," which means it would match www.somesite.com/virus.exe but not www.executable.com/innocent.html. The `-i` part means "not case-sensitive," so the rule will match `.exe`, `.Exe`, `.EXE`, and so on. You can use the caret sign (^) for "start of URL."

For example, you could stop some pornography sites using this ACL:

```
acl noporn url_regex -i sex
```

Do not forget to run the `kill -SIGHUP` command each time you make changes to Squid; otherwise, it will not reread your changes. You can have Squid check your configuration files for errors by running `squid -k parse` as root. If you see no errors, it means your configuration is fine.

NOTE

It is critical that you run the command kill -SIGHUP and provide it the PID of your Squid daemon each time you change the configuration; without this, Squid will not reread its configuration files.

Specifying Client IP Addresses

The configuration options so far have been basic, and you can use many more to enhance the proxying system you want.

After you are past deciding which rules work for you locally, it is time to spread them out to other machines. You do so by specifying IP ranges that should be allowed or disallowed access, and you enter these into Squid using more ACL lines.

If you want to, you can specify all the IP addresses on your network, one per line. However, for networks of more than about 20 people or using *Dynamic Host Control Protocol (DHCP)*, that is more work than necessary. A better solution is to use *classless inter-domain routing (CIDR)* notation, which allows you to specify addresses like this:

```
192.0.0.0/8
192.168.0.0/16
192.168.0.0/24
```


Each line has an IP address, followed by a slash and then a number. That last number defines the range of addresses you want covered and refers to the number of bits in an IP address. An IP address is a 32-bit number, but we are used to seeing it in dotted-quad notation: A.B.C.D. Each of those quads can be between 0 and 255 (although in practice some of these are reserved for special purposes), and each is stored as an 8-bit number.

The first line in the previous code covers IP addresses starting from 192.0.0.0; the /8 part means that the first 8 bits (the first quad, 192) is fixed and the rest is flexible. So, Squid treats that as addresses 192.0.0.0, 192.0.0.1, through to 192.0.0.255, then 192.0.1.0, 192.0.1.1, all the way through to 192.255.255.255.

The second line uses `/16`, which means Squid will allow IP addresses from 192.168.0.0 to 192.168.255.255. The last line has `/24`, which allows from 192.168.0.0 to 192.168.0.255.

These addresses are placed into Squid using the `src` ACL line, as follows:

```
acl internal_network src 10.0.0.0/24
```

That line creates a category of addresses from 10.0.0.0 to 10.0.0.255. You can combine multiple address groups together, like this:

```
acl internal_network src 10.0.0.0/24 10.0.3.0/24 10.0.5.0/24 192.168.0.1
```

That example allows 10.0.0.0 through 10.0.0.255, then 10.0.3.0 through 10.0.3.255, and finally the single address 192.168.0.1.

Keep in mind that if you are using the local machine and you have the web browser configured to use the proxy at 127.0.0.1, the client IP address will be 127.0.0.1, too. So, make sure you have rules in place for `localhost`.

As with other ACL lines, you need to enable them with appropriate `http_access allow` and `http_access deny` lines.

Example Configurations

To help you fully understand how Squid access control works, and to give you a head start developing your own rules, the following are some ACL lines you can try. Each line is preceded with one or more comment lines (starting with a #) explaining what it does:

```
# include the domains news.bbc.co.uk and slashdot.org
# and not newsimg.bbc.co.uk or www.slashdot.org.
acl newssites dstdomain news.bbc.co.uk slashdot.org

# include any subdomains or bbc.co.uk or slashdot.org
acl newssites dstdomain .bbc.co.uk .slashdot.org

# only include sites located in Canada
acl canadasites dstdomain .ca

# only include working hours
acl workhours time MTWHF 9:00-18:00

# only include lunchtimes
acl lunchtimes time MTWHF 13:00-14:00
```

```
# only include weekends
acl weekends time AS 00:00-23:59

# include URLs ending in ".zip". Note: the \ is important,
# because "." has a special meaning otherwise
acl zipfiles url_regex -i \.zip$

# include URLs starting with https
acl httpsurls url_regex -i ^https

# include all URLs that match "hotmail"
url_regex hotmail url_regex -i hotmail

# include three specific IP addresses
acl directors src 10.0.0.14 10.0.0.28 10.0.0.31

# include all IPs from 192.168.0.0 to 192.168.0.255
acl internal src 192.168.0.0/24

# include all IPs from 192.168.0.0 to 192.168.0.255
# and all IPs from 10.0.0.0 to 10.255.255.255
acl internal src 192.168.0.0/24 10.0.0.0/8
```

When you have your ACL lines in place, you can put together appropriate `http_access` lines. For example, you might want to use a multilayered access system so that certain users (for example, company directors) have full access, whereas others are filtered. For example:

```
http_access allow directors
http_access deny hotmail
http_access deny zipfiles
http_access allow internal lunchtimes
http_access deny all
```

Because Squid matches those in order, directors will have full, unfiltered access to the web. If the client IP address is not in the directors list, the two deny lines are processed so that the user cannot download `.zip` files or read online mail at Hotmail. After blocking those two types of requests, the `allow` on line four allows internal users to access the web, as long as they do so only at lunchtime. The last line (which is highly recommended) blocks all other users from the proxy.

20

Reference

- www.squid-cache.org/—The home page of the Squid web proxy cache.
- www.deckle.co.za/squid-users-guide/—The home page of *Squid: A User's Guide*, a free online book about Squid.

- https://help.ubuntu.com/community/Squid—Ubuntu community documentation for setting up Squid.
- There are two excellent books on the topic of web caching. The first is *Squid: The Definitive Guide* (O'Reilly) by Duane Wessels, ISBN: 0-596-00162-2. The second is *Web Caching* (O'Reilly) also by Duane Wessels, ISBN: 1-56592-536-X.

Of the two, the former is more practical and covers the Squid server in depth. The latter is more theoretical, discussing how caching is implemented. Wessels is one of the leading developers on Squid, so both books are of impeccable technical accuracy.

CHAPTER 21

Administering Database Services

IN THIS CHAPTER

This chapter is an introduction to MySQL and PostgreSQL, two database systems that are available in the Ubuntu repositories. You will learn what these systems do, how the two programs compare, and how to consider their advantages and disadvantages. This information can help you choose and deploy which one to use for your organization's database needs.

The database administrator (DBA) for an organization has several responsibilities, which vary according to the size and operations of the organization, supporting staff, and so on. Depending on the particular organization's structure, if you are the organization's DBA, your responsibilities might include the following:

- **Installing and maintaining database servers**—You might install and maintain the database software. Maintenance can involve installing patches as well as upgrading the software at the appropriate times. As DBA, you need to have root access to your system and know how to manage software (see Chapter 32, "Managing Software"). You also need to be aware of kernel, file system, and other security issues.
- **Installing and maintaining database clients**—The database client is the program used to access the database (you'll learn more on that later in this chapter, in the section "Database Clients"), either locally or remotely over a network. Your responsibilities might include installing and maintaining these client programs on users' systems. This chapter discusses

how to install and work with the clients from both the Linux command line and through its graphical interface database tools.

- **Managing accounts and users**—Account and user management include adding and deleting users from the database, assigning and administering passwords, and so on. In this chapter, you will learn how to grant and revoke user privileges and passwords for MySQL and PostgreSQL.
- **Ensuring database security**—To ensure database security, you need to be concerned with things like access control, which ensures that only authorized people can access the database, and permissions, which ensure that people who can access the database cannot do things they should not do. In this chapter, you will learn how to manage Secure Shell (SSH), web, and local GUI client access to the database. Planning and overseeing the regular backup of an organization's database and restoring data from those backups is another critical component of securing the database.
- **Ensuring data integrity**—Of all the information stored on a server's hard disk storage, chances are the information in the database is the most critical. Ensuring data integrity involves planning for multiple-user access and ensuring that changes are not lost or duplicated when more than one user is making changes to the database at the same time.

A Brief Review of Database Basics

Database services under Linux that use the software discussed in this chapter are based on a *client/server* model. Database clients are often used to input data and to query or display query results from the server. You can use the command line or a graphical client to access a running server. Databases generally come in two forms: flat file and relational. A *flat file* database can be as simple as a text file with a space, tab, or some other character delimiting different parts of the information. One example of a simple flat file database is the `/etc/passwd` file. Another example could be a simple address book that might look something like this:

```
Doe~John~505 Some Street~Anytown~NY~12345~555-555-1212
```

You can use standard UNIX tools such as grep, awk, and perl to search for and extract information from this primitive database. Although this might work well for a small database such as an address book that only one person uses, flat file databases of this type have several limitations:

- **They do not scale well**—Flat file databases cannot perform random access on data. They can only perform sequential access. This means they have to scan each line in the file, one by one, to look for specific information. As the size of the database grows, access times increase and performance decreases.
- **Flat file databases are unsuitable for multi-user environments**—Depending on how the database is set up, it either enables only one user to access it at a time or

allows two users to make changes simultaneously, and the changes could end up overwriting each other and cause data loss.

These limitations obviously make the flat file database unsuitable for any kind of serious work in even a small business—much less in an enterprise environment. Relational databases, or relational database management systems (RDBMSs) to give them their full name, are good at finding the relationships between individual pieces of data. An RDBMS stores data in tables with fields much like those in spreadsheets, making the data searchable, and sortable. RDBMSs are the focus of this chapter.

NOSQL

There is an exception to what was just said. A fairly new category of databases is now in use, usually referred to as "NoSQL" in casual conversation. Unlike typical flat file databases, NoSQL databases are a form of structured storage that is suitable for large and high traffic uses. These databases have been written and put into use in places where flat files are unsuitable but where relational databases are slower than desired. It is important to note that while NoSQL databases work great when scalability and speed are desirable, you can not be certain with all NoSQL databases that data is replicated and available instantly across a large installation. It generally is, but there is no guarantee of up-to-the-moment data. This is okay for some applications (web search), but would be disastrous for others (like a financial institution).

There are many forms of NoSQL databases each with different intents and applications. Some are created and used by big names you will recognize such as Google's BigTable and Apache's Cassandra. Ubuntu uses Apache's CouchDB for several applications. Other common ones include MongoDB and BerkleyDB. For this chapter, we will concentrate on the more traditional relational databases that are used for most applications, but we urge you to keep an eye on what is happening in the NoSQL world.

Oracle, DB2, Microsoft SQL Server, and the freely available PostgreSQL and MySQL are all examples of RDBMSs. The following sections discuss how relational databases work and provide a closer look at some of the basic processes involved in administering and using databases. You will also learn about SQL, the standard language used to store, retrieve, and manipulate database data.

How Relational Databases Work

An RDBMS stores data in tables, which you can visualize as spreadsheets. Each column in the table is a field; for example, a column might contain a name or an address. Each row in the table is an individual record. The table itself has a name you use to refer to that table when you want to get data out of it or put data into it. Figure 21.1 shows an example of a simple relational database that stores name and address information.

last_name	first_name	address	city	state	zip	phone
Doe	John	501 Somestreet	Anytown	NY	55011	555-555-1212
Doe	Jane	501 Somestreet	Anytown	NY	55011	555-555-1212
Palmer	John	205 Anystreet	Sometown	NY	55055	123-456-7890
Johnson	Robert	100 Easystreet	Easytown	CT	12345	111-222-3333

FIGURE 21.1 In this visualization of how an RDBMS stores data, the database stores four records (rows) that include name and address information, divided into seven fields (columns) of data.

In the example shown in Figure 21.1, the database contains only a single table. Most RDBMS setups are much more complex than this, with a single database containing multiple tables. Figure 21.2 shows an example of a database named `sample_database` that contains two tables.

phonebook

last_name	first_name	phone
Doe	John	555-555-1212
Doe	Jane	555-555-1212
Palmer	John	555-123-4567
Johnson	Richard	555-111-4321

cd_collection

id	title	artist	year	rating
1	Mindbomb	The The	1989	4
2	For All You've Done	Hillsong	2004	
3	Trouser Jazz	Mr Scruff	2002	5
4	Natural Elements	Acoustic Alchemy	1988	3
5	Combat Rock	The Clash	1982	4
6	Life for Rent	Dido	2003	5
7	Adiemus 4	Karl Jenkins	2000	4
8	The Two Towers	Howard Shore	2002	5

FIGURE 21.2 A single database can contain two tables—in this case, phonebook and `cd_collection`.

In the `sample_database` example, the phonebook table contains four records (rows) and each record hold three fields (columns) of data. The `cd_collection` table holds eight records, divided into five fields of data.

If you are thinking that there is no logical relationship between the `phonebook` table and the `cd_collection` table in the `sample_database` example, you are correct. In a relational database, users can store multiple tables of data in a single database—even if the data in one table is unrelated to the data in others.

For example, suppose you run a small company that sells widgets and you have a computerized database of customers. In addition to storing each customer's name, address, and phone number, you want to be able to look up outstanding order and invoice information for any of your customers. You could use three related tables in an RDBMS to store and organize customer data for just those purposes. Figure 21.3 shows an example of such a database.

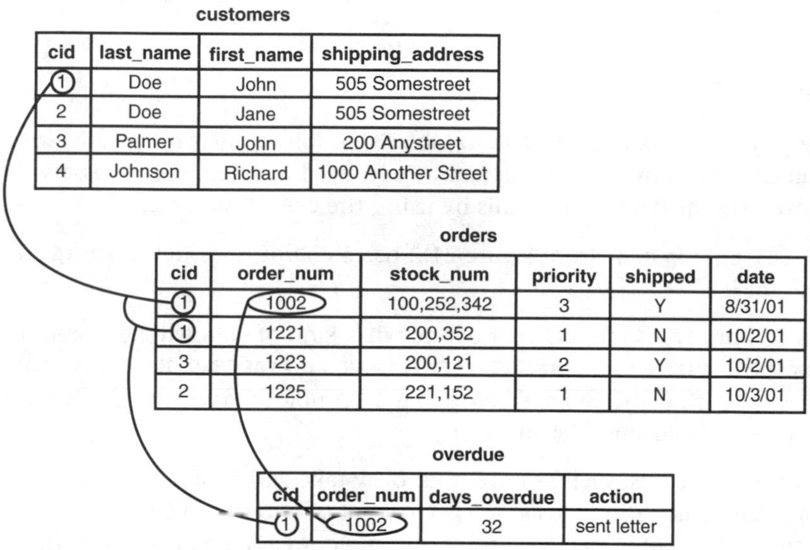

customers

cid	last_name	first_name	shipping_address
1	Doe	John	505 Somestreet
2	Doe	Jane	505 Somestreet
3	Palmer	John	200 Anystreet
4	Johnson	Richard	1000 Another Street

orders

cid	order_num	stock_num	priority	shipped	date
1	1002	100,252,342	3	Y	8/31/01
1	1221	200,352	1	N	10/2/01
3	1223	200,121	2	Y	10/2/01
2	1225	221,152	1	N	10/3/01

overdue

cid	order_num	days_overdue	action
1	1002	32	sent letter

FIGURE 21.3 You can use three related tables to track customers, orders, and outstanding invoices.

In the example in Figure 21.3, we have added a customer ID field to each customer record. This field holds a customer ID number that is the unique piece of information that can be used to link all other information for each customer to track orders and invoices. Each customer is given an ID unique to him; two customers might have the same data in their name fields, but their ID field values will never be the same. The Customer ID field data in the Orders and Overdue tables replaces the Last Name, First Name, and Shipping Address field information from the `Customers` table. Now, when you want to run a search for any customer's order and invoice data, you can search based on one key rather than multiple keys. You get more accurate results in faster, easier-to-conduct data searches.

Now that you have an idea of how data is stored in an RDBMS and how the RDBMS structure enables you to work with that data, you are ready to learn how to input and output data from the database. This is where SQL comes in.

Understanding SQL Basics

SQL (pronounced "S-Q-L" or "sequel" depending on who is talking) is a database query language understood by virtually all RDBMSs available today. You use SQL statements to get data into and retrieve data from a database. As with statements in any language, SQL statements have a defined structure that determines their meanings and functions.

As a DBA, you should understand the basics of SQL, even if you will not be doing any of the actual programming yourself. Fortunately, SQL is similar to standard English, so learning the basics is simple.

Creating Tables

As mentioned previously, an RDBMS stores data in tables that look similar to spreadsheets. Of course, before you can store any data in a database, you need to create the necessary tables and columns to store the data. You do this by using the `CREATE` statement.

For example, the `cd_collection` table from Figure 21.2 has 5 columns, or fields: `id`, `title`, `artist`, `year`, and `rating`.

SQL provides several column types for data that define what kind of data will be stored in the column. Some of the available types are `INT`, `FLOAT`, `CHAR`, and `VARCHAR`. Both `CHAR` and `VARCHAR` hold text strings, with the difference being that `CHAR` holds a fixed-length string, whereas `VARCHAR` holds a variable-length string.

There are also special column types, such as `DATE`, that only take data in a date format, and `ENUM`s (enumerations), which can be used to specify that only certain values are allowed. If, for example, you wanted to record the genre of your CDs, you could use an `ENUM` column that accepts only the values `POP`, `ROCK`, `EASY_LISTENING`, and so on. You will learn more about `ENUM` later in this chapter.

Looking at the `cd_collection` table, you can see that three of the columns hold numerical data and the other two hold string data. In addition, the character strings are of variable length. Based on this information, you can discern that the best type to use for the text columns is type `VARCHAR`, and the best `type to use for the others is INT`. You should notice something else about the `cd_collection` table: One of the CDs is missing a rating, perhaps because we have not listened to it yet. This value, therefore, is optional; it starts empty and can be filled in later.

You are now ready to create a table. As mentioned before, you do this by using the `CREATE` statement, which uses the following syntax:

```
CREATE TABLE table_name (column_name column_type(parameters) options, ...);
```

You should know the following about the `CREATE` statement:

- **SQL commands are not case sensitive**—For example, CREATE TABLE, create table, and Create Table are all valid.
- **Whitespace is generally ignored**—This means you should use it to make your SQL commands clearer.

The following example shows how to create the table for the `cd_collection` database:

```
CREATE TABLE cd_collection
(
id INT NOT NULL,
title VARCHAR(50) NOT NULL,
artist VARCHAR(50) NOT NULL,
year VARCHAR(50) NOT NULL,
rating VARCHAR(50) NULL
);
```

Notice that the statement terminates with a semicolon. This is how SQL knows you are finished with all the entries in the statement. In some cases, the semicolon can be omitted, and we will point out these cases when they arise.

TIP

SQL has a number of reserved keywords that cannot be used in table names or field names. For example, if you keep track of CDs you want to take with you on vacation, you would not be able to use the field name `select` because that is a reserved keyword. Instead, you should either choose a different name (`selected`?) or just prefix the field name with an `f`, such as `fselect`.

Inserting Data into Tables

After you create the tables, you can put data into them. You can insert data manually with the `INSERT` statement, which uses the following syntax:

```
INSERT INTO table_name VALUES('value1', 'value2', 'value3', ...);
```

This statement inserts `value1`, `value2`, and so on into the table `table_name`. The values that are inserted constitute one row, or *record*, in the database. Unless specified otherwise, values are inserted in the order in which the columns are listed in the database table. If, for some reason, you want to insert values in a different order (or if you want to insert only a few values and they are not in sequential order), you can specify which columns you want the data to go in by using the following syntax:

```
INSERT INTO table_name (column1,column4) VALUES('value1', 'value2');
```

You can also fill multiple rows with a single `INSERT` statement, using syntax such as the following:

```
INSERT INTO table_name VALUES('value1', 'value2'),('value3', 'value4');
```

In this statement, `value1` and `value2` are inserted into the first row and `value3` and `value4` are inserted into the second row.

The following example shows how you would insert the Nevermind entry into the cd_collection table:

```
INSERT INTO cd_collection VALUES(9, 'Nevermind', ''Nirvana', '1991,
''NULL);
```

MySQL requires the NULL value for the last column (rating) if you do not want to include a rating. PostgreSQL, on the other hand, lets you get away with just omitting the last column. Of course, if you had columns in the middle that were null, you would need to explicitly state NULL in the INSERT statement.

Normally, INSERT statements are coded into a front-end program so users adding data to the database do not have to worry about the SQL statements involved.

Retrieving Data from a Database

Of course, the main reason for storing data in a database is so you can later look up, sort, and generate reports on that data. Basic data retrieval is done with the SELECT statement, which has the following syntax:

```
SELECT column1, column2, column3 FROM table_name WHERE search_criteria;
```

The first two parts of the statement—the SELECT and FROM parts—are required. The WHERE portion of the statement is optional. If it is omitted, all rows in the table table_name are returned.

The *column1, column2, column3 indicates the name of the columns you want to see. If you want to see all columns, you can also use the wildcard* * to show all the columns that match the search criteria. For example, the following statement displays all columns from the cd_collection table:

```
SELECT * FROM cd_collection;
```

If you wanted to see only the titles of all the CDs in the table, you would use a statement such as the following:

```
SELECT title FROM cd_collection;
```

To select the title and year of a CD, you would use the following:

```
SELECT title, year FROM cd_collection;
```

If you wanted something a little fancier, you can use SQL to print the CD title followed by the year in parentheses, as is the convention. Both MySQL and PostgreSQL provide string concatenation functions to handle problems such as this. However, the syntax is different in the two systems.

In MySQL, you can use the `CONCAT()` function to combine the `title` and `year` columns into one output column, along with parentheses. The following statement is an example:

```
SELECT CONCAT(title," (",year, ")") AS TitleYear FROM cd_collection;
```

That statement lists both the title and year under one column that has the label `TitleYear`. Note that there are two strings in the `CONCAT()` function along with the fields—these add whitespace and the parentheses.

In PostgreSQL, the string concatenation function is simply a double pipe (`¦¦`). The following command is the PostgreSQL equivalent of the preceding MySQL command:

```
SELECT (genus¦¦'' ('¦¦species¦¦')') AS TitleYear FROM cd_collection;
```

Note that the parentheses are optional, but they make the statement easier to read. Once again, the strings in the middle and at the end (note the space between the quotes) are used to insert spacing and parentheses between the title and year.

Of course, more often than not, you do not want a list of every single row in the database. Rather, you only want to find rows that match certain characteristics. For this, you add the `WHERE` statement to the `SELECT` statement. For example, suppose you want to find all the CDs in the `cd_collection` table that have a rating of 5. You would use a statement like the following:

```
SELECT * FROM cd_collection WHERE rating = 5;
```

Using the table from Figure 21.2, you can see that this query would return the rows for *Trouser Jazz*, *Life for Rent*, and *The Two Towers*. This is a simple query, and SQL is capable of handling queries much more complex than this. Complex queries can be written using logical AND and logical OR statements. For example, suppose you want to refine the query so it lists only those CDs that were not released in 2003. You would use a query like the following:

```
SELECT * FROM cd_collection WHERE rating = 5 AND year != 2003;
```

In SQL, != means "is not equal to." So once again looking at the table from Figure 21.2, you can see that this query returns the rows for *Trouser Jazz* and *The Two Towers* but does not return the row for *Life for Rent* because it was released in 2003.

So, what if you want to list all the CDs that have a rating of 3 or 4 except those released in the year 2000? This time, you combine logical `AND` and logical `OR` statements:

```
SELECT * FROM cd_collection WHERE rating = 3 OR rating = 4 AND year != 2000;
```

This query would return entries for *Mind Bomb*, *Natural Elements*, and *Combat Rock*. However, it wouldn't return entries for *Adiemus 4* because it was released in 2000.

TIP

One of the most common errors among new database programmers is confusing logical AND and logical OR. For example, in everyday speech, you might say, "Find me all CDs released in 2003 and 2004." At first glance, you might think that if you fed this statement to the database in SQL format, it would return the rows for *For All You've Done* and *Life for Rent*. In fact, it would return no rows at all. This is because the database interprets the statement as, "Find all rows in which the CD was released in 2003 and was released in 2004." It is, of course, impossible for the same CD to be released twice without requiring a new ISBN and therefore a new database entry, so this statement would never return any rows, no matter how many CDs were stored in the table. The correct way to form this statement is with an OR statement instead of an AND statement.

SQL is capable of far more than is demonstrated here. But as mentioned before, this section is not intended to teach you all there is to know about SQL programming; rather, it teaches you the basics so you can be a more effective DBA.

Choosing a Database: MySQL Versus PostgreSQL

If you are just starting out and learning about using a database with Linux, the first logical step is to research which database will best serve your needs. Many database software packages are available for Linux; some are free, and others cost hundreds of thousands of dollars. Expensive commercial databases, such as Oracle, are beyond the scope of this book. Instead, this chapter focuses on two freely available databases: MySQL and PostgreSQL.

Both of these databases are quite capable, and either one could probably serve your needs. However, each database has a unique set of features and capabilities that might serve your needs better or make developing database applications easier for you.

We should note that Oracle recently bought Sun Microsystems, who owned MySQL. In the short term this may not have any impact, but the database world is watching to see what will happen with MySQL and there is are at least two groups who have forked the code to ensure that the database stays free and open source while still in active development. These groups have released and are working on Drizzle (http://drizzle.org) and MariaDB (http://kb.askmonty.org/v/MariaDB). Although no one really knows yet what will happen, we suggest keeping an eye on these projects and potential replacements for MySQL should the worst fears be realized and Oracle decides that the free MySQL is too much of a competitor to their paid database offerings and kills the project.

Speed

Until recently, the speed choice was simple: If the speed of performing queries was paramount to your application, you used MySQL. MySQL has a reputation for being an extremely fast database. Until recently, PostgreSQL was quite slow by comparison.

Newer versions of PostgreSQL have improved in terms of speed (when it comes to disk access, sorting, and so on). In certain situations, such as periods of heavy simultaneous access, PostgreSQL can be significantly faster than MySQL, as you will see in the next section. However, MySQL is still extremely fast when compared to many other databases.

Data Locking

To prevent data corruption, a database needs to put a lock on data while it is being accessed. As long as the lock is on, no other process can access the data until the first process has released the lock. This means that any other processes trying to access the data have to wait until the current process completes. The next process in line then locks the data until it is finished, and the remaining processes have to wait their turn, and so on.

Of course, operations on a database generally complete quickly, so in environments with a small number of users simultaneously accessing the database, the locks are usually of such short duration that they do not cause any significant delays. However, in environments in which many people are accessing the database simultaneously, locking can create performance problems as people wait their turn to access the database.

Older versions of MySQL lock data at the table level, which can be considered a bottleneck for updates during periods of heavy access. This means that when someone writes a row of data in the table, the entire table is locked so no one else can enter data. If your table has 500,000 rows (or records) in it, all 500,000 rows are locked any time one row is accessed. Once again, in environments with a relatively small number of simultaneous users, this doesn't cause serious performance problems because most operations complete so quickly that the lock time is extremely short. However, in environments in which many people are accessing the data simultaneously, MySQLs table-level locking can be a significant performance bottleneck.

PostgreSQL, on the other hand, locks data at the row level. In PostgreSQL, only the row currently being accessed is locked. The rest of the table can be accessed by other users. This row-level locking significantly reduces the performance impact of locking in environments that have a large number of simultaneous users. Therefore, as a general rule, PostgreSQL is better suited for high-load environments than MySQL.

The MySQL release bundled with Ubuntu gives you the choice of using tables with table-level or row-level locking. In MySQL terminology, MyISAM tables use table-level locking and InnoDB tables use row-level locking.

NOTE

MySQL's data locking methods are discussed in more depth at www.mysql.com/doc/en/Internal_locking.html.

You can find more information on PostgreSQL's locking at www.postgresql.org/idocs/index.php?locking-tables.html.

ACID Compliance in Transaction Processing to Protect Data Integrity

Another way MySQL and PostgreSQL differ is in the amount of protection they provide for keeping data from becoming corrupted. The acronym ACID is commonly used to describe several aspects of data protection:

- **Atomicity**—This means that several database operations are treated as an indivisible (atomic) unit, often called a *transaction*. In a transaction, either all unit operations are carried out or none of them are. In other words, if any operation in the atomic unit fails, the entire atomic unit is canceled.
- **Consistency**—Ensures that no transaction can cause the database to be left in an inconsistent state. Inconsistent states can be caused by database client crashes, network failures, and similar situations. Consistency ensures that, in such a situation, any transaction or partially completed transaction that would cause the database to be left in an inconsistent state is *rolled back*, or undone.
- **Isolation**—Ensures that multiple transactions operating on the same data are completely isolated from each other. This prevents data corruption if two users try to write to the same record at the same time. The way isolation is handled can generally be configured by the database programmer. One way that isolation can be handled is through locking, as discussed previously.
- **Durability**—Ensures that, after a transaction has been committed to the database, it cannot be lost in the event of a system crash, network failure, or other problem. This is usually accomplished through transaction logs. Durability means, for example, that if the server crashes, the database can examine the logs when it comes back up and it can commit any transactions that were not yet complete into the database.

PostgreSQL is ACID-compliant, but again MySQL gives you the choice of using ACID-compliant tables or not. MyISAM tables are not ACID-compliant, whereas InnoDB tables are. Note that ACID compliancy is no easy task: All the extra precautions incur a performance overhead.

SQL Subqueries

Subqueries allow you to combine several operations into one atomic unit, and they enable those operations to access each other's data. By using SQL subqueries, you can perform some extremely complex operations on a database. In addition, using SQL subqueries eliminates the potential problem of data changing between two operations as a result of another user performing some operation on the same set of data. Both PostgreSQL and MySQL have support for subqueries in this release of Ubuntu, but this was not true in earlier releases.

Procedural Languages and Triggers

A *procedural language* is an external programming language that can be used to write functions and procedures. This allows you to do things that aren't supported by simple SQL. A *trigger* allows you to define an event that will invoke the external function or procedure you have written. For example, a trigger can be used to cause an exception if an INSERT statement containing an unexpected or out-of-range value for a column is given.

For example, in the CD tracking database, you could use a trigger to cause an exception if a user entered data that did not make sense. PostgreSQL has a procedural language called PL/pgSQL. Although MySQL has support for a limited number of built-in procedures and triggers, it does not have any procedural language. It does have a feature called stored procedures that is similar, but it doesn't do quite the same thing.

Configuring MySQL

A free and stable version of MySQL is included with Ubuntu. MySQL is also available from the website, www.mysql.com. The software is available in source code, binary, and APT format for Linux. You can use the Synaptic client to add the software to your system. See Chapter 7 for the details on adding (or removing) software.

After you have MySQL installed, you need to initialize the *grant tables* or permissions to access any or all databases and tables and column data within a database. You can do this by issuing `mysql_install_db` as root. This command initializes the grant tables and creates a MySQL root user.

CAUTION

The MySQL data directory needs to be owned by the user that owns the MySQL process, most likely mysql (you may need to changethe directory's owner using the chown command). In addition, only this user should have any permissions on this directory. (In other words, the permissions should be set to 700 by using chmod.) Setting up the data directory any other way creates a security hole.

Running `mysql_install_db` should generate output similar to the following:

```
matthew@seymour:~$ sudo mysql_install_db
Preparing db table
Preparing host table
Preparing user table
Preparing func table
Preparing tables_priv table
Preparing columns_priv table
Installing all prepared tables
020916 17:39:05 /usr/libexec/mysqld: Shutdown Complete
...
```

The command prepares MySQL for use on the system and reports helpful information. The next step is to set the password for the MySQL root user, which is discussed in the following section.

CAUTION

By default, the MySQL root user is created with no password. This is one of the first things you must change because the MySQL root user has access to all aspects of the database. The following section explains how to change the password of the user.

Setting a Password for the MySQL Root User

To set a password for the root MySQL user, you need to connect to the MySQL server as the root MySQL user; you can use the command `mysql -u root` to do so. This command connects you to the server with the MySQL client. When you have the MySQL command prompt, issue a command like the following to set a password for the root user:

```
mysql> SET PASSWORD FOR root = PASSWORD("secretword");
```

`secretword` should be replaced by whatever you want to be the password for the root user. You can use this same command with other usernames to set or change passwords for other database users.

After you enter a password, you can exit the MySQL client by typing `exit` at the command prompt.

Creating a Database in MySQL

In MySQL you create a database by using the `CREATE DATABASE` statement. To create a database, you connect to the server by typing **`mysql -u root -p`** and pressing Enter. After you do so, you are connected to the database as the MySQL root user and prompted for a password. After you enter the password, you are placed at the MySQL command prompt. Then you use the **`CREATE DATABASE`** command. For example, the following commands create a database called `animals`:

```
matthew@seymour:~$ mysql -u root -p
Enter password:
Welcome to the MySQL monitor. Commands end with ; or \g.
Your MySQL connection id is 1 to server version: 3.23.58

Type 'help;' or '\h' for help. Type '\c' to clear the buffer.

mysql> CREATE DATABASE animals;
Query OK, 1 row affected (0.00 sec)
mysql>
```

Another way to create a database is to use the mysqladmin command, as the root user, with the create keyword and the name of a new database. For example, to create a new database named reptiles, you use a command line like this:

```
matthew@seymour:~# mysqladmin -u root -p create reptiles
```

Granting and Revoking Privileges in MySQL

You probably want to grant yourself some privileges, and eventually you will probably want to grant privileges to other users. Privileges, also known as *rights*, are granted and revoked on four levels:

- **Global-level**—These rights allow access to any database on a server.
- **Database-level**—These rights allow access to all tables in a database.
- **Table-level**—These rights allow access to all columns within a table in a database.
- **Column-level**—These rights allow access to a single column within a database's table.

NOTE

Listing all the available privileges is beyond the scope of this chapter. See the MySQL documentation for more information.

To add a user account, you connect to the database by typing `mysql -u root -p` and pressing Enter. You are then connected as the root user and prompted for a password. (You did set a password for the root user, as instructed in the last section, right?) After you enter the root password, you are placed at the MySQL command prompt.

To grant privileges to a user, you use the `GRANT` statement, which has the following syntax:

```
grant what_to_grant ON where_to_grant TO user_name IDENTIFIED BY 'password';
```

The first option, *`what_to_grant`*, is the privileges you are granting to the user. These privileges are specified with keywords. For example, the `ALL` keyword is used to grant global-, database-, table-, and column-level rights for a specified user.

The second option, *`where_to_grant`*, specifies the resources on which the privileges should be granted. The third option, `user_name`, is the username to which you want to grant the privileges. Finally, the fourth option, `password`, is a password that should be assigned to this user. If this is an existing user who already has a password and you are modifying permissions, you can omit the `IDENTIFIED BY` portion of the statement.

For example, to grant all privileges on a database named `sampledata` to a user named `foobar`, you could use the following command:

```
GRANT ALL ON animals.* TO foobar IDENTIFIED BY 'secretword';
```

The user `foobar` can now connect to the database `sampledata` by using the password `secretword`, and `foobar` has all privileges on the database, including the ability to create and destroy tables. For example, the user `foobar` can now log in to the server (by using the current hostname—`shuttle2`, in this example), and access the database like this:

```
matthew@seymour:~$  mysql -h shuttle2 -u foobar -p animals
Enter password:
Welcome to the MySQL monitor. Commands end with ; or \g.
Your MySQL connection id is 43 to server version: 3.23.58

Type 'help;' or '\h' for help. Type '\c' to clear the buffer.

mysql>
```

NOTE

See the section "The MySQL Command-Line Client" for additional command-line options.

Later, if you need to revoke privileges from `foobar`, you can use the `REVOKE` statement. For example, the following statement revokes all privileges from the user `foobar`:

```
REVOKE ALL ON animals FROM foobar;
```

Advanced database administration, privileges, and security are very complex topics that are beyond the scope of this book. See the section "Reference" at the end of this chapter for links to online documentation. You can also check out Luke Welling's and Laura Thompson's book, *PHP and MySQL Development* from Sams Publishing.

Configuring PostgreSQL

If you do not want to use the version of PostgreSQL bundled with Ubuntu, the latest PostgreSQL binary files and source are available at www.postgresql.org. The PostgreSQL packages are distributed as several files. At a minimum, you want the `postgresql` package. You should see the `README` file in the FTP directory ftp://ftp.postgresql.org/pub/ to determine whether you need any other packages.

If you are installing from the Ubuntu package files, a necessary `postgres` user account (that is, an account with the name of the user running the server on your system) is created for you automatically:

```
matthew@seymour:~$  fgrep postgres /etc/passwd
postgres:x:26:26:PostgreSQL Server:/var/lib/postgresql:/bin/bash
```

Otherwise, you need to create a user called `postgres` during the installation. This user shouldn't have login privileges because only root should be able to use `su` to become this user and no one will ever log in directly as the user. (See Chapter 10, "Managing Users," for more information on how to add users to an Ubuntu system.) After you have added the user, you can install each of the PostgreSQL packages you downloaded using the standard `dpkg -i` command for a default installation.

Initializing the Data Directory in PostgreSQL

Installation initializes the database and sets the permissions on the data directory to their correct values.

CAUTION

The `initdb` program sets the permissions on the data directory to `700`. You should not change these permissions to anything else to avoid creating a security hole.

You can start the `postmaster` program with the following command (make sure you are still the user `postgres`):

```
matthew@seymour:~$ postmaster -D /usr/local/pgsql/data &
```

If you have decided to use a directory other than `/usr/local/pgsql/data` as the data directory, you should replace the directory in the `postmaster` command line with whatever directory you are using.

TIP

By default, Ubuntu makes the PostgreSQL data directory `/var/lib/pgsql/data`. This isn't a very good place to store the data, however, because most people do not have the necessary space in the `/var` partition for any kind of serious data storage. Note that if you do change the data directory to something else (such as `/usr/local/pgsql/data`, as in the examples in this section), you need to edit the PostgreSQL startup file (named `postgres`) located in `/etc/init.d` to reflect the change.

Creating a Database in PostgreSQL

Creating a database in PostgreSQL is straightforward, but it must be performed by a user who has permissions to create databases in PostgreSQL—for example, initially the user named `postgres`. You can then simply issue the following command from the shell prompt (not the PSQL client prompt, but a normal shell prompt):

```
matthew@seymour:~# su - postgres
-bash-2.05b$ createdb database
```

where `database` is the name of the database you want to create.

The createdb program is actually a wrapper that makes it easier to create databases without having to log in and use psql. However, you can also create databases from within psql with the CREATE DATABASE statement. Here's an example:

```
CREATE DATABASE database;
```

You need to create at least one database before you can start the pgsql client program. You should create this database while you're logged in as the user postgres. To log in as this user, you need to use su to become root and then use su to become the user postgres. To connect to the new database, you start the psql client program with the name of the new database as a command-line argument, like this:

```
matthew@seymour:~$ psql sampledata
```

If you don't specify the name of a database when you invoke psql, the command attempts to connect to a database that has the same name as the user as which you invoke psql (that is, the default database).

Creating Database Users in PostgreSQL

To create a database user, you use su to become the user postgres from the Linux root account. You can then use the PostgreSQL createuser command to quickly create a user who is allowed to access databases or create new database users, like this:

```
matthew@seymour:~$ createuser heather
Shall the new user be allowed to create databases? (y/n) y
Shall the new user be allowed to create more new users? (y/n) y
CREATE USER
```

In this example, the new user named phudson is created and allowed to create new databases and database users (you should carefully consider who is allowed to create new databases or additional users).

You can also use the PostgreSQL command-line client to create a new user by typing psql along with name of the database and then use the CREATE USER command to create a new user. Here is an example:

```
CREATE USER foobar ;
```

CAUTION

PostgreSQL allows you to omit the WITH PASSWORD portion of the statement. However, doing so causes the user to be created with no password. This is a security hole, so you should always use the WITH PASSWORD option when creating users.

NOTE

When you are finished working in the psql command-line client, you can type \q to get out of it and return to the shell prompt.

Deleting Database Users in PostgreSQL

To delete a database user, you use the `dropuser` command, along with the user's name, and the user's access is removed from the default database, like this:

```
matthew@seymour:~$  dropuser msmith
DROP USER
```

You can also log in to your database by using `psql` and then use the DROP USER commands. Here's an example:

```
matthew@seymour:~$ psql demodb
Welcome to psql, the PostgreSQL interactive terminal.

Type: \copyright for distribution terms
 \h for help with SQL commands
 \? for help on internal slash commands
 \g or terminate with semicolon to execute query
 \q to quit

demodb=# DROP USER msmith ;
DROP USER
demodb=# \q
```

Granting and Revoking Privileges in PostgreSQL

As in MySQL, granting and revoking privileges in PostgreSQL is done with the `GRANT` and `REVOKE` statements. The syntax is the same as in MySQL except that PostgreSQL doesn't use the `IDENTIFIED BY` portion of the statement because with PostgreSQL, passwords are assigned when you create the user with the `CREATE USER` statement, as discussed previously. Here is the syntax of the `GRANT` statement:

```
GRANT what_to_grant ON where_to_grant TO user_name;
```

The following command, for example, grants all privileges to the user `foobar` on the database `sampledata`:

```
GRANT ALL ON sampledata TO foobar;
```

To revoke privileges, you use the `REVOKE` statement. Here is an example:

```
REVOKE ALL ON sampledata FROM foobar;
```

This command removes all privileges from the user foobar on the database `sampledata`.

Advanced administration and user configuration are complex topics. This section cannot begin to cover all the aspects of PostgreSQL administration or of privileges and users. For more information on administering PostgreSQL, see the PostgreSQL documentation or consult a book on PostgreSQL, such as *PostgreSQL* (Sams Publishing).

Database Clients

Both MySQL and PostgreSQL use a client/server system for accessing databases. In the simplest terms, the database server handles the requests that come into the database and the database client handles getting the requests to the server as well as getting the output from the server to the user.

Users never interact directly with the database server even if it happens to be located on the same machine they are using. All requests to the database server are handled by a database client, which might or might not be running on the same machine as the database server.

Both MySQL and PostgreSQL have command-line clients. A command-line client is a very primitive way of interfacing with a database and generally isn't used by end users. As a DBA, however, you use the command-line client to test new queries interactively without having to write front-end programs for that purpose. In later sections of this chapter, you will learn a bit about the MySQL graphical client and the web-based database administration interfaces available for both MySQL and PostgreSQL.

The following sections examine two common methods of accessing a remote database, a method of local access to a database server, and the concept of web access to a database.

NOTE

You should consider access and permission issues when setting up a database. Should users be able to create and destroy databases? Or should they only be able to use existing databases? Will users be able to add records to the database and modify existing records? Or should users be limited to read-only access to the database? And what about the rest of the world? Will the general public need to have any kind of access to your database through the Internet? As DBA, you must determine the answers to these questions.

SSH Access to a Database

Two types of remote database access scenarios are briefly discussed in this section. In the first scenario, the user directly logs in to the database server through SSH (to take advantage of the security benefits of encrypted sessions) and then starts a program on the server to access the database. In this case, shown in Figure 21.4, the database client is running on the database server itself.

In the other scenario, shown in Figure 21.5, the user logs in to a remote host through SSH and starts a program on it to access the database, but the database is actually running on a different system. Three systems are now involved—the user's workstation, the remote host running the database client, and the remote host running the database server.

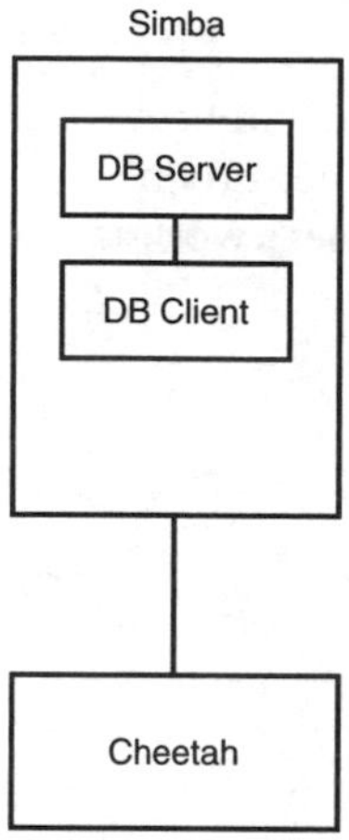

FIGURE 21.4 The user logs in to the database server located on host **simba** from the workstation (**host cheetah**). The database client is running on **simba**.

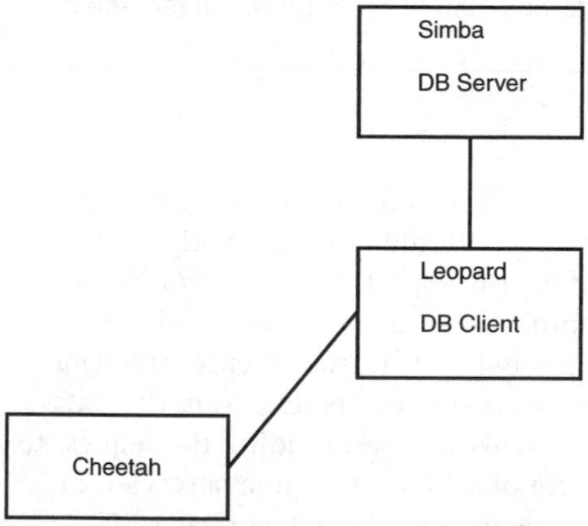

FIGURE 21.5 The user logs in to the remote host **leopard** from the workstation (**host cheetah**) and starts a database client on **leopard**. The client on **leopard** then connects to the database server running on host **simba**. The database client is running on **leopard**.

The important thing to note in Figure 21.5 is the middleman system `leopard`. Although the client is no longer running on the database server itself, it isn't running on the user's local workstation, either.

Local GUI Client Access to a Database

A user can log in to the database server by using a graphical client (which could be running on Windows, Macintosh, or a UNIX workstation). The graphical client then connects to the database server. In this case, the client is running on the user's workstation. Figure 21.6 shows an example.

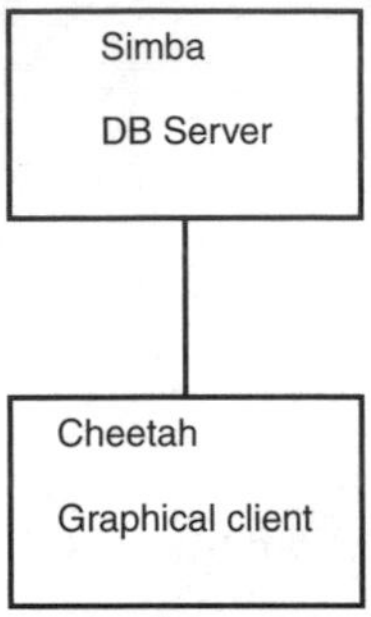

FIGURE 21.6 The user starts a GUI database program on the user's workstation (hostname **cheetah**). This program, which is the database client, then connects to the database server running on the host **simba**.

Web Access to a Database

In this section, we look at two basic examples of web access to the database server. In the first example, a user accesses the database through a form located on the World Wide Web. At first glance, it might appear that the client is running on the user's workstation. Of course, in reality it is not; the client is actually running on the web server. The web browser on the user's workstation simply provides a way for each user to enter the data that the user wants to send to the database and a way for the results sent from the database to be displayed to the user. The software that actually handles sending the request to the database is running on the web server in the form of a CGI script; a Java servlet; or embedded scripting such as the PHP or Sun Microsystems, Inc.'s JavaServer Pages (JSP).

Often, the terms *client* and *front end* are used interchangeably when speaking of database structures. However, Figure 21.7 shows an example of a form of access in which the client and the front end aren't the same thing at all. In this example, the front end is the form displayed in the user's web browser. In such cases, the client is referred to as *middleware*.

In another possible web access scenario, it could be said that the client is a two-piece application in which part of it is running on the user's workstation and the other part is running on the web server. For example, the database programmer can use JavaScript in the web form to ensure that the user has entered a valid query. In this case, the user's query is partially processed on the user's own workstation and partially on the web server. Error checking is done on the user's own workstation, which helps reduce the load on the server and also helps reduce network traffic because the query is checked for errors before being sent across the network to the server.

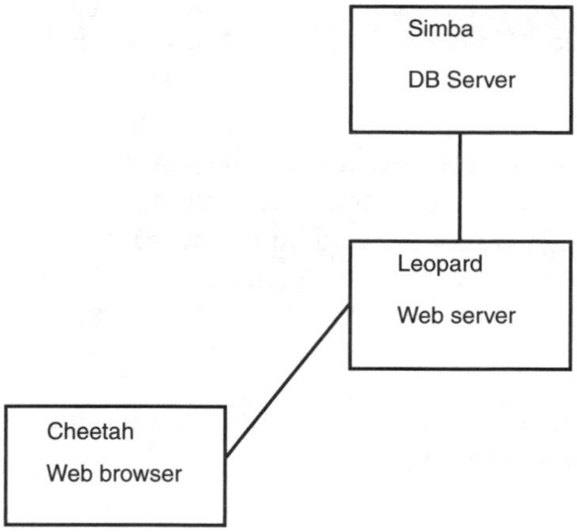

FIGURE 21.7 The user accesses the database through the World Wide Web. The front end is the user's web browser, the client is running on **leopard**, and the server is running on **simba**.

The MySQL Command-Line Client

The MySQL command-line client is `mysql`, and it has the following syntax:

```
mysql [options] [database]
```

Some of the available options for `mysql` are discussed in Table 21.1. *`database` is optional, and if given, it should be the name of the database to which you want to connect.*

TABLE 21.1 Command-Line Options to Use When Invoking **mysql**

Option	Action
`-h hostname`	Connects to the remote host `hostname` (if the database server isn't located on the local system).
`-u username`	Connects to the database as the user `username`.
`-p`	Prompts for a password. This option is required if the user you are connecting as needs a password to access the database. Note that this is a lowercase `p`.
`-P n`	Specifies `n` as the number of the port that the client should connect to. Note that this is an uppercase `P`.
`-?`	Displays a help message.

More options are available than are listed in Table 21.1, but these are the most common options. See the man page for `mysql` for more information on the available options.

CAUTION

Although `mysql` allows you to specify the password on the command line after the `-p` option, and thus allows you to avoid having to type the password at the prompt, you should never invoke the client this way. Doing so causes your password to display in the process list, and the process list can be accessed by any user on the system. This is a major security hole, so you should never give your password on the `mysql` command line.

You can access the MySQL server without specifying a database to use. After you log in, you use the help command to get a list of available commands, like this:

```
mysql> help


MySQL commands:
Note that all text commands must be first on line and end with ';'
help (\h) Display this help.
? (\?) Synonym for 'help'.
clear (\c) Clear command.
connect (\r) Reconnect to the server. Optional arguments are db and host.
edit (\e) Edit command with $EDITOR.
ego (\G) Send command to mysql server, display result vertically.
exit (\q) Exit mysql. Same as quit.
go (\g) Send command to mysql server.
nopager (\n) Disable pager, print to stdout.
notee (\t) Don't write into outfile.
pager (\P) Set PAGER [to_pager]. Print the query results via PAGER.
print (\p) Print current command.
quit (\q) Quit mysql.
rehash (\#) Rebuild completion hash.
source (\.) Execute a SQL script file. Takes a file name as an argument.
status (\s) Get status information from the server.
tee (\T) Set outfile [to_outfile]. Append everything into given outfile.
use (\u) Use another database. Takes database name as argument.
```

You can then access a database by using the use command and the name of a database that has been created (such as `animals`) and that you are authorized to connect to, like this:

```
mysql> use animals
Database changed
mysql>
```

The PostgreSQL Command-Line Client

You invoke the PostgreSQL command-line client with the command `psql`. Like `mysql`, `psql` can be invoked with the name of the database to which you would like to connect. Also like `mysql`, `psql` can take several options. These options are listed in Table 21.2.

TABLE 21.2 Command-Line Options to Use When Invoking **psql**

Option	Action
`-h hostname`	Connects to the remote host `hostname` (if the database server isn't located on the local system).
`-p n`	Specifies n as the number of the port that the client should connect to. Note that this is a lowercase p.
`-U username`	Connects to the database as the user `username`.
`-W`	Prompts for a password after connecting to the database. In PostgreSQL 7 and later, password prompting is automatic if the server requests a password after a connection has been established.
`-?`	Displays a help message.

Several more options are available in addition to those listed in Table 21.2. See the `psql`'s man page for details on all the available options.

Graphical Clients

If you'd rather interact with a database by using a graphical database client than with the command-line clients discussed in the previous section, you're in luck: A few options are available.

MySQL has an official graphical client, called MySQLGUI. MySQLGUI is available in both source and binary formats from the MySQL website at www.mysql.com.

Web-based administration interfaces are also available for MySQL and PostgreSQL. phpMyAdmin and phpPgAdmin are two such products. Both of these products are based on the PHP-embedded scripting language and therefore require you to have PHP installed. Of course, you also need to have a web server installed.

RELATED UBUNTU AND DATABASE COMMANDS

The following commands are useful for creating and manipulating databases in Ubuntu:

- `createdb`—Creates a new PostgreSQL database
- `createuser`—Creates a new PostgreSQL user account

- `dropdb`—Deletes a PostgreSQL database
- `dropuser`—Deletes a PostgreSQL user account
- `mysql`—Interactively queries the mysqld server
- `mysqladmin`—Administers the mysqld server
- `mysqldump`—Dumps or backs up MySQL data or tables
- `psql`—Accesses PostgreSQL via an interactive terminal

Reference

- www.mysql.com—This is the official website of the MySQL database server. Here you can find the latest versions as well as up-to-date information and online documentation for MySQL. You can also purchase support contracts here. You might want to look into this if you will be using MySQL in a corporate setting. (Many corporations balk at the idea of using software for which the company has no support contract in place.)
- http://radar.oreilly.com/2009/07/oscon-the-saga-of-mysql.html—An interesting article describing the fears of the MySQL community and the creation of forks.
- http://drizzle.org/Home.html—The home page for Drizzle, a fork of MySQL.
- http://kb.askmonty.org/v/MariaDB—The home page for MariaDB, another fork of MySQL made by one of the founders of MySQL.
- www.postgresql.org—This is the official website of the PostgreSQL database server.

CHAPTER 22

LDAP

IN THIS CHAPTER

- Configuring the Server
- Configuring Clients
- Administration
- Reference

The *Lightweight Directory Access Protocol* (LDAP, pronounced ell-dap) is one of those technologies that, while hidden, forms part of the core infrastructure in enterprise computing. Its job is simple: It stores information about users. However, its power comes from the fact that it can be linked into dozens of other services. LDAP can power login authentication, public key distribution, email routing and address verification; more recently, it has formed the core of the push toward single-sign-on technology.

TIP

Most people find the concept of LDAP easier to grasp when they think of it as a highly specialized form of database server. Behind the scenes, Ubuntu uses a database for storing all its LDAP information; however, LDAP does not offer anything as straightforward as SQL for data manipulation!

OpenLDAP uses Sleepycat *Software's Berkeley* DB (BDB), and sticking with that default is highly recommended. However, alternatives exist if you have specific needs.

This chapter looks at a relatively basic installation of an LDAP server, including how to host a companywide directory service that contains the names and email addresses of employees. LDAP is a client/server system, meaning that an LDAP server hosts the data, and an LDAP client queries it. Ubuntu comes with OpenLDAP as its LDAP server, along with several LDAP-enabled email clients, including Evolution and Mozilla Thunderbird. We cover all three of these applications in this chapter.

Because LDAP data is usually available over the Internet—or at least your local network—it is imperative that you make every effort to secure your server. This chapter gives specific instruction on password configuration for OpenLDAP, and we recommend you follow our instructions closely.

Configuring the Server

If you have been using LDAP for years, you will be aware of its immense power and flexibility. On the other hand, if you are just trying LDAP for the first time, it will seem like the most broken component you could imagine. LDAP has specific configuration requirements, is vastly lacking in graphical tools, and has a large number of acronyms to remember. On the bright side, all the hard work you put in will be worth it because, when it works, LDAP will improve your networking experience immensely. You should read the entire chapter and understand it before you start. Then, we recommend you read the README file in `/etc/ldap/schema` before you do anything.

The first step in configuring your LDAP server is to install the client and server applications. Install the `slapd` and `ldap-utils` packages from the Ubuntu repositories. This will also install three other packages: `odbcinst`, `odbcinstdebian2`, and `unixodbc`.

By default, Ubuntu configures `slapd` with the minimum options necessary to run the daemon. We are going to configure everything from that bare-bones installation up to where it will be useful.

Now we need to know the fully qualified domain name (FQDN) of your server. In a moment we will begin to write/modify some configuration files, and this will be a vital part of that process. Let's use matthewhelmke.com. Whenever you see this, change it to your FQDN.

From the FQDN we acquire our domain component, which is the name of your domain as stored in DNS. This is abbreviated using dc. LDAP considers each part of a domain name (separated by a dot) to be domain components. In our example, there are two dc items: matthewhelmke and com.

OpenLDAP now uses a separate directory containing the cn=config Directory Information Tree (DIT) to configure the `slapd` daemon dynamically. This allows for modifying schema definitions, indexes, and so on without stopping and restarting the service, as was required in earlier versions. Two files are needed for this configuration: a back end that has only a minimal configuration, and a front end that uses a traditional format that is compatible with and accessed by external programs using established standards.

Creating Your Schema

We will start by loading some premade schema files. This makes configuration faster and easier by preloading some settings. If you are building an enterprise server, you should read the official OpenLDAP documentation and start from scratch so that you know precisely what everything on your server is doing and why. For our example, load these three files into the directory using these commands:

```
$ sudo ldapadd -Y EXTERNAL -H ldapi:/// -f /etc/ldap/schema/cosine.ldif
$ sudo ldapadd -Y EXTERNAL -H ldapi:/// -f /etc/ldap/schema/nis.ldif
$ sudo ldapadd -Y EXTERNAL -H ldapi:/// -f /etc/ldap/schema/inetorgperson.ldif
```


Next, we create a file called `backend.matthewhelmke.com.ldif` with these contents:

```
# Load dynamic backend modules
dn: cn=module,cn=config
objectClass: olcModuleList
cn: module
olcModulepath: /usr/lib/ldap
olcModuleload: back_hdb

# Database settings
dn: olcDatabase=hdb,cn=config
objectClass: olcDatabaseConfig
objectClass: olcHdbConfig
olcDatabase: {1}hdb
olcSuffix: dc=matthewhelmke,dc=com
olcDbDirectory: /var/lib/ldap
olcRootDN: cn=admin,dc=matthewhelmke,dc=com
olcRootPW: changeMEtoSOMETHINGbetter
olcDbConfig: set_cachesize 0 2097152 0
olcDbConfig: set_lk_max_objects 1500
olcDbConfig: set_lk_max_locks 1500
olcDbConfig: set_lk_max_lockers 1500
olcDbIndex: objectClass eq
olcLastMod: TRUE
olcDbCheckpoint: 512 30
olcAccess: to attrs=userPassword by dn="cn=admin,dc=matthewhelmke,dc=com" write by
anonymous auth by self write by * none
olcAccess: to attrs=shadowLastChange by self write by * read
olcAccess: to dn.base="" by * read
olcAccess: to * by dn="cn=admin,dc=matthewhelmke,dc=com" write by * read
```

Make sure you change all instances of matthewhelmke and com to fit your FQDN and change the entry for `olcRootPW` to a more secure password of your choosing. Then, add the new file to the directory (I am assuming you are entering this command from the directory where the file was created).

```
$ sudo ldapadd -Y EXTERNAL -H ldapi:/// -f backend.example.com.ldif
```

Populating Your Directory

The back end is ready. Now we need to populate the front-end directory to make this useful. Create another file called `frontend.matthewhelmke.com.ldif` with the following contents:

```
# Create top-level object in domain
dn: dc=matthewhelmke,dc=com
objectClass: top
objectClass: dcObject
objectclass: organization
o: Example Organization
dc: Example
description: LDAP Example

# Admin user.
dn: cn=admin,dc=matthewhelmke,dc=com
objectClass: simpleSecurityObject
objectClass: organizationalRole
cn: admin
description: LDAP administrator
userPassword: changeMEtoSOMETHINGbetter

dn: ou=people,dc=example,dc=com
objectClass: organizationalUnit
ou: people

dn: ou=groups,dc=matthewhelmke,dc=com
objectClass: organizationalUnit
ou: groups

dn: uid=john,ou=people,dc=matthewhelmke,dc=com
objectClass: inetOrgPerson
objectClass: posixAccount
objectClass: shadowAccount
uid: matthew
sn: Helmke
givenName: Matthew
cn: Matthew Helmke
displayName: Matthew Helmke
uidNumber: 1000
gidNumber: 10000
userPassword: changeMEtoSOMETHINGbetter
gecos: Matthew Helmke
loginShell: /bin/bash
homeDirectory: /home/matthew
shadowExpire: -1
```

```
shadowFlag: 0
shadowWarning: 7
shadowMin: 8
shadowMax: 999999
shadowLastChange: 10877
mail: matthew@matthewhelmke.com
postalCode: 85711
l: Tucson
o: Example
mobile: +1 (520) xxx-xxxx
homePhone: +1 (520) xxx-xxxx
title: System Administrator
postalAddress: I'm not putting it in the book.
initials: MH

dn: cn=example,ou=groups,dc=example,dc=com
objectClass: posixGroup
cn: example
gidNumber: 10000
```

Remember to change the details to fit your information. Then, we add this to the LDAP directory:

```
$ sudo ldapadd -x -D cn=admin,dc=example,dc=com -W -f frontend.example.com.ldif
```

To check that our content has been added to the LDAP directory correctly, we can use: `ldapsearch`.

```
$ ldapsearch -xLLL -b "dc=example,dc=com" uid=john sn givenName cn


dn: uid=matthew,ou=people,dc=matthewhelmke,dc=com
cn: Matthew Helmke
sn: Helmke
givenName: Matthew
```

In this example, dn stands for distinguished name, uid refers to user identification, ou tells us the organizational unit, dc represents domain component, cn is common name, sn is the family or surname, and many cultures know givenName as your first name.

When you use LDAP, you can organize your data in many ways. You can use a number of currently existing schemas, such as in the previous example using the .ldif files we loaded at the start, or you can write your own. The `/etc/ldap/schemas` directory has many fine examples in the files with a `.schema` suffix and a few that have been converted to `.ldif` format. To be used, the file must be in the LDAP Data Interchange Format (LDIF, or when used as a file suffix, `.ldif`). You can convert one of the example schemas or create your own schema.

Configuring Clients

Although Ubuntu comes with a selection of email clients, there is not enough room here to cover them all. So, we discuss the two most frequently used clients: Evolution, the default, and Thunderbird. Both are powerful messaging solutions and so both work well with LDAP. Of the two, Thunderbird seems to be the easier to configure. We have had various problems with Evolution in the past in situations where Thunderbird has worked the first time.

Evolution

To configure Evolution for LDAP, click the arrow next to the New button and select Address Book. A new screen appears; its first option prompts you for the type of address book to create. Select On LDAP Servers.

For Name, just enter `Address book`, and for Server, enter the IP address of your LDAP server (or `127.0.0.1` if you are working on the server), as shown in Figure 22.1. Leave the port as `389`, which is the default for `slapd`. Switch to the Details tab, and set Search Base to be the entire DN for your address book—for example, `ou=People,dc=matthewhelmke,dc=com`. Set Search Scope to be Sub so that Evolution will perform a comprehensive search. To finish, click Add Address Book.

FIGURE 22.1 Configuring Evolution to use LDAP for addresses is easy for anonymous connections.

Thunderbird

Thunderbird is a little easier to configure than Evolution and tends to work better, particularly with entries that have multiple CNs. To enable, go to the Edit menu, click Preferences, and then select Composition from the tabs along the top.

From the Addressing subtab, check the Directory Server box and click the Edit Directories button to its right. From the dialog box that appears, click Add to add a new directory. You can give it any name you want because this is merely for display purposes. As shown in Figure 22.2, set the Hostname field to be the IP address of your LDAP server (or `127.0.0.1` if you are working on the server). Set the Base DN to be the DN for your address book (for instance, `ou=People,dc=matthewhelmke,dc=com`), and leave the port number as `389`. Click OK three times to get back to the main interface.

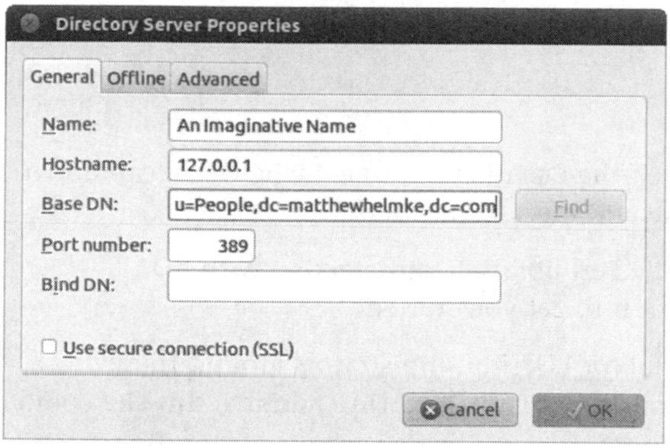

FIGURE 22.2 Thunderbird's options are buried deeper than Evolution's, but it does allow you to download the LDAP directory for offline use.

Administration

After you have your LDAP server and clients set up, they require little maintenance until something changes externally. Specifically, if someone in your directory changes jobs, changes her phone number, gets married (changing her last name [surname]), quits, or so forth, you need to be able to update your directory to reflect the change.

We installed some useful utilities with the `ldap-utils` package earlier. Here are what they do. Each one requires administration privileges, so use sudo.

- `ldapsearch`—Opens a connection to an LDAP server and searches its directory for requested information
- `ldapmodify`—Opens a connection to an LDAP server and allows you to add or modify entries

- `ldapadd`—Opens a connection to an LDAP server and allows you to add an entry
- `ldapdelete`—Opens a connection to an LDAP server and allows you to delete one or more entries

None of these are simple to use, but all come with moderate amounts of documentation in their man pages.

A much smarter option is to use phpLDAPadmin, which is an LDAP administration tool that allows you to add and modify entries entirely through your web browser. The program is available in the Ubuntu software repositories as phpldapadmin.

Starting, stopping, or restarting the slapd daemon is done in the usual way for system daemons (that do not yet have Upstart methods written for them).

```
sudo /etc/init.d/slapd start/stop/restart
```

Reference

- www.openldap.org—The home page of the OpenLDAP project where you can download the latest version of the software and meet other users.
- http://ldap.perl.org/—The home of the Perl library for interacting with LDAP provides comprehensive documentation to get you started.
- www.ldapguru.com/—A gigantic portal for LDAP administrators around the world. From forums dedicated to LDAP to jobs specifically for LDAP admins, this site could very well be all you need.
- https://help.ubuntu.com/10.10/serverguide/C/openldap-server.htmlOfficial Ubuntu Server documentation for OpenLDAP.
- http://phpldapadmin.sourceforge.net/—The official documentation for phpLDAPadmin.
- The definitive book on LDAP is *LDAP System Administration* (O'Reilly), ISBN: 1-56592-491-6. It is an absolute must for the bookshelf of any Linux LDAP administrator. For more general reading, try *LDAP Directories Explained* (Addison-Wesley), ISBN: 0-201-78792-X. It has a much stronger focus on the Microsoft Active Directory LDAP implementation, however.

CHAPTER 23

Linux Terminal Server Project (LTSP)

IN THIS CHAPTER

- Installation
- Interesting Information
- Reference

The *Linux Terminal Server Project* (LTSP) is an add-on package for Linux that allows you to run multiple thin clients, low powered terminals, from one main server. A thin client is a small, energy-efficient, and generally lower powered system designed to be used in conjunction with a more powerful server. The thin client will have limited processing power and speed and limited storage, making it very inexpensive. All it is used for is receiving input from a device such as a keyboard or mouse, communicating with a server, and displaying output to a screen.

Processing of information and the actual running of programs are offloaded to the server, meaning the server does all the hard work and is the only system in the network that has strong requirements for processor power and speed, memory, storage, and so on. Thin clients are also generally smaller in size and quieter, which also make them more convenient to use when space and noise are potential issues. Those of us who have been around longer or who have worked in enterprise environments will see an immediate relationship to big metal servers and dumb client terminals, and it is reasonable to think of an LTSP setup this way. In our case, the server isn't as big or as powerful and the thin clients aren't as dumb and weak, but the idea is the same.

Thin clients are great in places such as classrooms and computer labs where strict control and strong security are desirable, where money for a room of full-powered systems may not be available, and where installing and maintaining core software on one server is preferable to doing so on many systems. For this reason, Edubuntu, a community led official sub-project of Ubuntu, is designed for easy LTSP installation and configuration. We will focus on using LTSP with standard Ubuntu, but if you want to use LTSP in an education-specific context, or if you just want an additional perspective and more information about LTSP, Edubuntu is worth a closer look. Other common places you are likely to find thin clients in use are libraries for catalog access and searches and in some airports that make courtesy terminals for checking email available for travelers.

Links to several thin client hardware sources are included in Reference, although they are included to inform and should not be taken as endorsements—we don't own and have not used equipment from every company listed and can't make any honest recommendations about them. In addition to those mentioned, you are sure to find others. In fact, computers that often make excellent thin clients are not advertised as such. You can look for compact format systems that use an ARM, VIA, or maybe an Intel Atom processor, for example, and are likely to find they make wonderful thin clients. You can even recycle older hardware that would otherwise be bound for the dustbin and make it useful again as a thin client.

Now that you have a sense of why you might use LTSP and how the network is created, it is a good time to fill you in on some of the details of what LTSP is, what it is not, and how it is designed to work. Armed with this knowledge, you will be able to find documentation to help you decide what you can afford to buy, how you want to configure it, and even whether this is a configuration that is applicable and useful to your situation.

LTSP is add-on software for Linux that creates a server that can be used to boot client computers over a network. It allows them to access and run applications on the server while the client remains responsible for input and display and the server handles processing data and storage. This allows many inexpensive hardware clients to be used to do things that would normally be beyond the capability of the hardware and streamlines administration by placing all the configuration and software on one server. The biggest limitations will result from server and networking hardware (for example, switch or hub, 1GB versus 100 MB ports, high-end server and storage or less expensive just-adequate equipment).

Requirements

Our minimum recommended specifications for thin clients are a processor running at 400MHz with 128MB RAM and the ability to boot via PXE (a common network boot protocol). Nearly any system sold today and advertised as a thin client will exceed these requirements by a wide margin. We list them here in case you want to try to reuse old hardware that is otherwise obsolete. Server and other hardware recommendations are listed in the Installation section.

Let's start by looking at several wiring schemes to show appropriate methods of using LTSP. The first one, shown in Figure 23.1, is the default install without an Internet connection and is the simplest way to use LTSP.

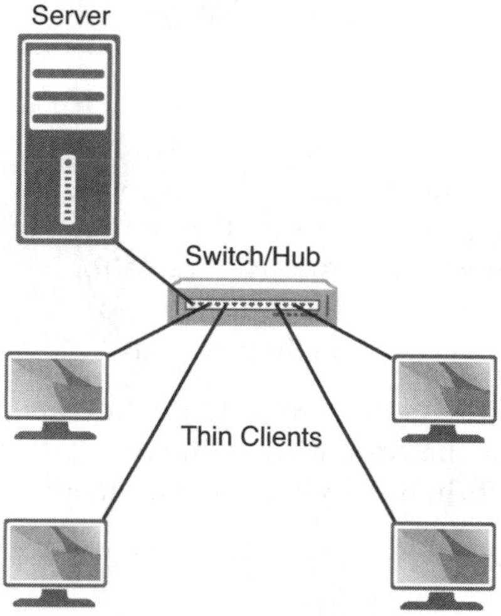

FIGURE 23.1 A default LTSP install without an Internet connection.

From the diagram alone you can see the main pieces of hardware needed: a server, a switch/hub, and a number of thin clients. The switch/hub is the first piece of hardware we discuss.

For simplicity we only show four thin clients in each example, but this is not an actual limit. The number of thin clients is limited by your switch/hub and even an inexpensive hub will support four connections, although it is common for quality enterprise-grade switches to have 48 or more ports. A switch is generally faster and more expensive than a hub and is often preferable for reasons beyond the scope of this chapter, but they both serve the same basic purpose and either can work in an LTSP setting. They are used to control traffic on a network and make sure that communication happens between computers as it is intended.

Ideally, you want a piece of hardware here that will support a GB connection between the server and a switch, with at least 100MB connections between the thin clients and the switch, and enough unused communication ports to make future expansion easy without requiring the addition of another switch or hub and layer of complexity. If money is an issue and ideal performance isn't vital, an inexpensive hub that only had 100MB ports all around and just enough ports to connect everything will certainly work. If you are connecting more than 10 clients to the server, a GB connection to the server is strongly recommended. Life is full of trade-offs and money supplies are not limitless, so use your best judgment and buy the best you can afford.

For the server, recommended specifications depend greatly on the intended use. If everyone will be using the same program on each client, you do not need as much memory and processor speed as you would if everyone is doing different things at the same time. You can easily run LTSP server on a repurposed old machine you have sitting around with 512MB RAM, a 1GHz Celeron processor, and a decent, working hard drive, and it will work, but we don't really recommend that if you are going to have more than a couple of clients doing anything beyond simple and identical tasks.

Our minimum recommendation is the same as the current recommendation for a minimum Ubuntu desktop installation: a 1GHz x 86 processor, 1GB RAM, a 15GB hard drive. At least a 100MB ethernet card is vital. Ideally, you would bump each category up to the highest level you can afford and expect better performance as a result. Our minimum-if-you-want-a-great-experience recommendation is a current-issue fast-as-you-can-afford multicore 64 bit processor, 4GB RAM, at least two fast hard drives in a RAID array for performance and data backup, and at least one and perhaps two GB ethernet cards.

Most of the time you use LTSP you will want the network to be connected to the Internet. There are two main ways to do this. Figure 23.2 shows the network with an Internet connection via an Internet router connected to the switch/hub. This is a common method and will work well.

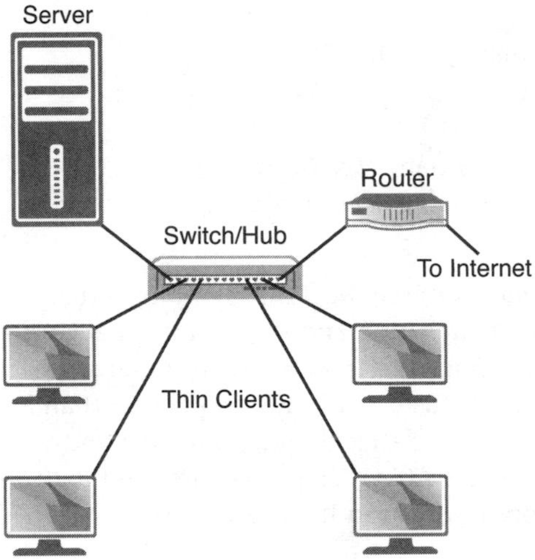

FIGURE 23.2 A typical LTSP install with an Internet connection via an Internet router.

Another common method is to connect the server directly to the Internet router as in Figure 23.3. This has the benefit of allowing you to easily configure and use the server as a gateway to control thin client access to the Internet. To do this, the server must have two network cards, and we again recommend that the one used to connect to the switch is a 1GB card; all the thin client traffic has to travel between the switch and server over that one connection, so this will cause fewer bottlenecks than if you have multiple clients connecting to a switch at 100MB trying to share a single 100MB connection to a server. The card from the server to the Internet router should be adequate for the Internet connection available, but there is no reason to put anything faster in there. If you have only a 100MB connection with your Internet service provider, using a 1GB card will not give any particular benefit.

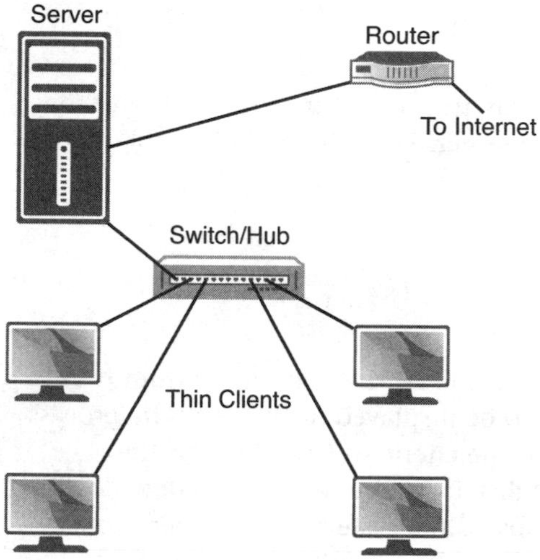

FIGURE 23.3 Using a server with two ethernet cards as a portal to the Internet.

Installation

After you decide how you want to set up your network and connect all the hardware, you can get to the task of installing the software. In Ubuntu, the LTSP software is available for installation in two ways. If you are repurposing a server that already has a current release of Ubuntu installed on it, you install the `ltsp-server-standalone` and `openssh-server` packages from the Ubuntu repositories and run the following to set up the environment:

```
matthew@seymour:~$ sudo ltsp-build-client
```

If your server is a 64-bit system and your thin clients use a different processor architecture, you want to run that command with the `--arch` option, as in

```
matthew@seymour:~$ sudo ltsp-build-client --arch i386
```

Most people will be installing from scratch and not reusing a system with Ubuntu already installed. This is still quite easy. You will need to download the alternate install CD from the Ubuntu website at http://releases.ubuntu.com/. From here, find the release version of Ubuntu you want to use for the server. Some will want the current release (at this writing, 10.10) and some will want to use an LTS release like 10.04 LTS. Click the release version you want to use and then find the link for the alternate install CD for your server's processor architecture, either 32-bit or the 64-bit. Download it and burn the image to a CD as discussed in Chapter 1, "Installing Ubuntu."

Make sure all your thin clients are connected and set to boot from network using PXE, but turned off. Then boot the server using the alternate CD, press F4 for the modes menu, and choose Install an LTSP Server. A regular Ubuntu installation will begin. Near the end of the installation a message will appear that lets you know the thin client system is being built on the server. You will be notified that it is being compressed into an image, and when the process is complete you will reboot your server, removing the CD at the appropriate moment in the process.

After the server has rebooted and is running, you may turn on your thin clients and they will boot from the network using the image on the server. Thin clients will be able to run any programs installed on the server.

Using LTSP

When you boot a thin client in an LTSP network, it retrieves the boot image from the LTSP server and uses it to create the environment to be displayed to the user. The process includes using DHCP to request from and assign to the client an IP address on the network, downloading the kernel and initial RAM disk from the server, then downloading the LTSP configuration and mounting the server-hosted file system, using `chroot` to use this file system as the client's own root file system, and then finishing the boot using the instructions in that file system. This is a highly configurable process. By default the client boots to a login screen using the LTSP Display Manager (LDM) in place of GDM that is used by Ubuntu, KDM that is used by Kubuntu, or others. User accounts are used to limit or control access, and the LDM initializes the details for communication between the server and client, including launching the desktop, mounting storage devices and home directories, and creating menu items. The entire desktop is run on the server and displayed on the client.

By default, LTSP uses inherent abilities in Linux but has configured them to work together smoothly. Details may be modified to suit your needs. For example, communication between an application server and a client is done by tunneling an X11 session over `ssh`, making the sharing of a graphical desktop easy and using a standard method while also being a secure method of communicating user credentials.

One really useful feature in LTSP is that you are not limited to using only one server in a network. If your network of thin clients grows to a point where your current server is being taxed, there is an easy way to configure and add a second or multiple servers to the network to share the load. In this case, the server that a thin client uses to boot is not necessarily the same server that a user will log in to. When you add servers, one server is chosen to be the primary server and controls thin client boots, data storage, and runs additional services. Additional, secondary servers can be much simpler because all they do is host desktop sessions and will be configured to use the central services from the primary server for everything else. In a multiple server network, authentication of users is something that you will need to think through and configure as it becomes a little more complex. There are many ways to do this, including the obvious choice, LDAP.

Creating and maintaining an LTSP network is very useful in specific situations and can be a cost-effective way of using administrator time while providing useful functionality to end users. Although the foundation sounds simple in this introductory chapter, it can be a complex task worthy of an entire book. Our intent with this chapter is to give enough information for you to determine whether LTSP is a technology that will suit your needs and is deserving of a closer look. To that end, we offer several useful links in the Reference section and suggest them as your next step.

Reference

- https://help.ubuntu.com/community/UbuntuLTSP—The Ubuntu community documentation page is easily the best resource for LTSP because it includes an organized and up-to-date set of links to information on any aspect you should need.
- http://edubuntu.com/—The leaders of the Edubuntu community project are very knowledgeable about LTSP and helpful. This site is a great place to start when you are looking for people with experience to help you with questions.

A sampling of companies advertising thin clients:

- www.artecgroup.com/thincan
- www.chippc.com/thin-clients/thin-clients.asp
- www.devonit.com/hardware
- www.disklessworkstations.com/
- http://h10010.www1.hp.com/wwpc/us/en/sm/WF02d/12454-12454-321959.html
- www.lucidatech.com/
- www.wyse.com/products/hardware/thinclients/index.asp
- www.ltsp.org/—The official upstream LTSP website.
- https://help.ubuntu.com/community/UbuntuLTSP/Tour—This gives an overview of the differences between a traditional LTSP installation and the Ubuntu community modifications to the process for ease of installation, software updates, and security.
- https://help.ubuntu.com/community/UbuntuLTSP/ThinClientHowtoNAT/—If you use the network design in Figure 23.3, this will tell you how to configure your server so your thin clients have access to the Internet.
- http://doc.ubuntu.com/edubuntu/edubuntu/handbook/C/—The Edubuntu Handbook provides one of the most clear and complete guides to setting up and using LTSP.

CHAPTER 24

Ubuntu in the Cloud

IN THIS CHAPTER

Cloud computing allows you to build large, flexible systems for on-demand processing of data. When your requirements are low, you use few resources. As the need arises, your processes scale to use multiple systems with optimized performance according to the requirements of the moment. This is an efficient way to utilize hardware and minimize waste.

To accomplish this feat of computer engineering, a special network is set up using on-demand virtual systems that consume resources only as needed and release those resources for use by others when they are not in use. Virtualization is the technology that enables this concept. This may be accomplished using third-party virtualization platforms like VMware, VirtualBox, Parallels, and others. Ubuntu has another option to offer, the Ubuntu Enterprise Cloud, which is the main focus of this chapter.

NOTE

Much of what we discuss here is possible using other forms of virtualization, such as those mentioned previously. What makes Ubuntu Enterprise Cloud unique is that the virtualization is done using KVM, the Kernel-based Virtual Machine that is a part of the Linux kernel, and the capabilities of modern processors containing virtualization extensions in a way that allows easy installation, deployment, integration, and configuration. Canonical certifies Ubuntu on a wide range of equipment from multiple manufacturers and guarantees that Ubuntu Enterprise Cloud will work on them, just as it works with other virtualization providers.

Why a Cloud?

Businesses and enterprises have built computer networks for years. There are many reasons, but usually networks are built because specific computation or data processing tasks are made easier and faster using more than one computer. The size of the network generally depends on the tasks that need to be done. Building a network usually entails taking a detailed survey of needs, analyzing those requirements, and gathering together the necessary hardware and software to fulfill those needs now, perhaps with a little room for growth if money permits.

Cloud computing is designed to make that easier by providing resources such as computing power and storage as services on the Internet in a way that is easy to access remotely, available on demand, simple to provision and scale, and highly dynamic. In the ideal case, this saves both time and money. Hardware, storage, networks, and software are abstracted as services instead of being manually built and configured and are then accessed locally on demand when the additional resources are required. Sometimes these abstractions are referred to as Infrastructure as a Service (IAAS), Platform as a Service (PAAS), and Software as a Service (SAAS).

Some of the greatest benefits are the ease with which new resources may be added to a cloud, the fault tolerance inherent in the built-in redundancy of a large pool of servers, and the payment schedules that charge for resources only when they are used. There is also a great benefit in abstracting the complexity out of the process; clients perform the tasks they want to perform, and the cloud computing platform takes care of the details of adding resources as needed without the end user being aware of the process. Virtual machines are created and used when needed and destroyed immediately after they are no longer needed, freeing up system resources for other purposes.

UEC and Eucalyptus

Ubuntu Enterprise Cloud (UEC) is a stack of applications from Canonical that are included in the Ubuntu Server Edition. These applications make it very easy to install and configure an Ubuntu-based cloud. The software is free and open source, but Canonical offers paid technical support.

UEC is based primarily on Eucalyptus, which is GPL software written to provide cloud computing and cloud storage platforms that are both free (as in freedom and as in beer) and completely compatible with Amazon's EC2 cloud computing and S3 cloud storage platforms. The Eucalyptus services are available through APIs that are compatible with EC2/S3, so client tools written for the Amazon Web Services (AWS) can also be used with Eucalyptus.

An Ubuntu Enterprise Cloud consists of several components. We start with a node, which is a server that is capable of running KVM as its hypervisor. A hypervisor is software that allows multiple virtual machines to run on one piece of hardware by presenting each virtual machine with a virtual platform and monitors each virtual machine for performance, resource use, and needs. This allows multiple operating systems to share hardware resources. Other hypervisors are available, such as Xen, but Ubuntu has chosen KVM as the default.

The next components are the Node Controller (NC) and the Cluster Controller (CC). The NC runs on each node and controls all virtual machines running on that node. The NC runs as a layer between the host operating system and the CC above it, serving as a go-between that queries the operating system to discover physical resources available and the state and number of virtual machines running on the node and reports this information to the CC. The CC then manages the networking for the instances running on that and other nodes and makes sure that the Cloud Controller (CLC) gets that information.

The Cloud Controller is the main front end to the whole cloud. It provides the API for client services and deals with all requests and responses, communicating via web services between the client tool and the UEC components. The CLC also provides a web interface for managing parts of the infrastructure. This is where resource availability is monitored and managed.

Two other controllers are in the interface, the Storage Controller (SC) and the Walrus Storage Controller (WS3). The SC provides a way to create persistent storage devices similar to Amazon's Elastic Block Storage (EBS) devices, which are block storage devices that are created separately from cloud computing instances and are intended to be highly reliable, highly available, and accessible. The WS3 is a simple storage service that uses REST and SOAP APIs that are compatible with Amazon's S3 APIs and that serve to store virtual machine images, snapshots, and store and serve files.

This highly complex system is illustrated in Figure 24.1.

Deploy/Install

There are two ways to deploy UEC: on a private cloud or on a public cloud. Both have benefits and drawbacks. This section presents the things you need to consider when choosing. We also look at a way to mix the two.

A public UEC is built on Amazon's EC2. This means your local hardware requirements are minimal, your startup costs are low, deployment is quick, and growth is easy. The drawback to working this way is that you do not physically control the hardware on which

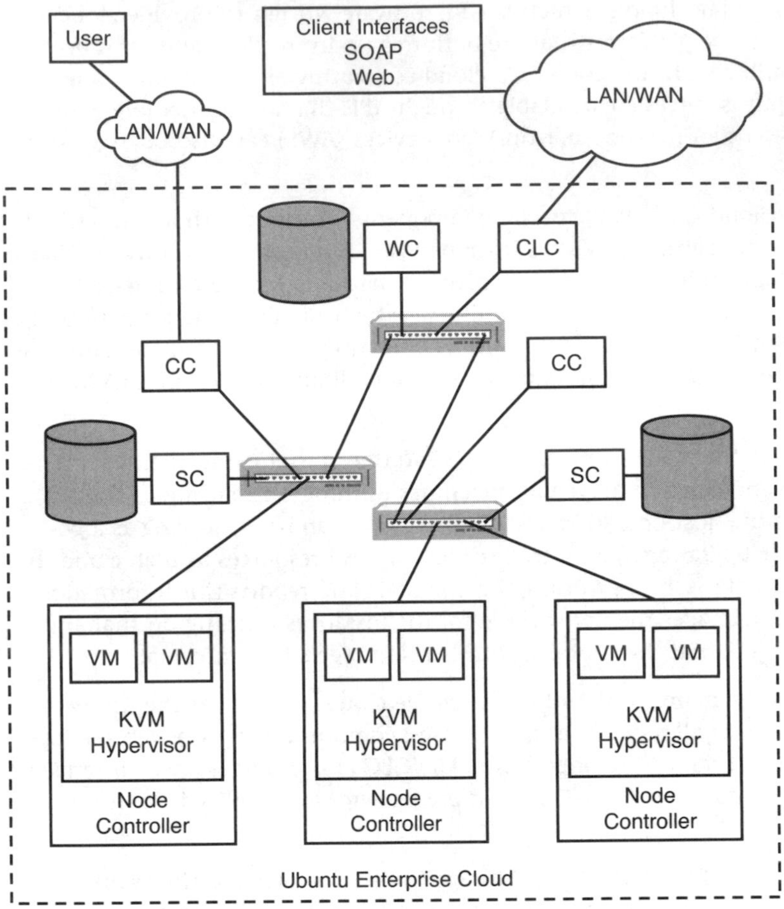

FIGURE 24.1 A sample UEC cloud.

your cloud is running. For many this is a benefit, but this may not be suitable for high security needs. Although you alone control the software and processes on your public cloud, there may be some worry about who has access to the machines. While Amazon would not last long in business if their data centers and machines were not secure, there are some applications and data that are so sensitive you cannot afford to allow any outside risk. There are also legal constraints, such as from the Sarbanes-Oxley Act, that sometimes force IT policy decisions in an organization and make the public option impossible.

A private UEC is created on hardware you own and control. This requires a large upfront commitment, but you have the security of running everything behind a company firewall and with complete knowledge of who is able to physically access your machines and who is listening on the network.

One thing to consider is the possibility of starting your UEC as a private cloud and then creating interfaces from there to public services. Perhaps you prefer to keep all your data stored on the private cloud, but you want to use some services and applications on a public cloud. This is an avenue worth exploring if your company has a mixture of "must be secured and held in-house" and "we still want to keep it away from prying eyes, but if something happens it won't be catastrophic" needs. The big issue with this method is moving data between public and private servers; if you have large amounts of data, this can be prohibitive. As always, do your due diligence.

Public

Deploying a public cloud on Amazon's servers is quick and easy. First, go to http://aws.amazon.com/ and sign up for an account. Then, while logged in, go to Your Account, Security Credentials, and define the security settings to manage and access your service.

Next, you need a tool to allow you to start and stop instances. There are several, but we will focus on two. One is Euca2ools, which are a set of command-line tools from Eucalyptus for interacting with the Amazon EC2 and S3 services via web services. These are installed by default with Ubuntu Server; you can learn more about using them in the Euca2ools User Guide from the link provided in the Reference section. We cover the basic commands for Euca2ools later in this chapter. The other tool is a paid service from Canonical called Landscape. It provides a web-based graphical user interface for interacting with the Amazon cloud services and for managing your UEC. It works with both public deployments on Amazon and private installations on your own equipment. A link to Canonicals website for Landscape is also in the Referencesection.

After your tool is in place, you use it to choose and start your machine instances. You will also use this tool to manage the instances later. Many Ubuntu virtual machine images have already been published to Amazon EC2 and are immediately available for deployment. You can find a list at http://uec-images.ubuntu.com/releases/ under the specific Ubuntu release you are interested in using.

The final step is to access your instances to set up the applications you want to provide on your cloud. You will manage your cloud using the tools mentioned earlier.

Private

Installing UEC on your own machines is more complicated, even though the needs are the same. Much of the complexity is dealt with by Amazon when deploying on its servers. Before you start, you will need to check that you have the hardware required. At a minimum, you will need two servers. One will serve as a front end, and you need one or more nodes.

For the front end, or any system that will run one or more of these, the CLC, the CC, the WS3 and/or the SC, the basic requirements shown in Table 24.1 must be met.

TABLE 24.1 Basic Requirements for CLC, CC, WS3 and SC

Hardware	Minimum	Suggested	Notes
CPU	1GHz	2 x 2GHz	For an all-in-one front end, it helps to have at least a dual-core processor.
Memory	2GB	4GB	The Java web front end benefits from lots of available memory.
Disk	5400rpm IDE	7200rpm SATA	Slower disks will work, but will yield much longer instance startup times.
Disk Space	40GB	200GB	40GB is enough space for only a single image, cache, and so on. Eucalyptus does not like to run out of disk space.
Networking	100Mbps	1000Mbps	Machine images are hundreds of MB and need to be copied over the network to nodes.

For nodes, which will run the node controller and instances, you need to meet the requirements shown in Table 24.2.

TABLE 24.2 Requirements for the Node Controller and Instances

Hardware	Minimum	Suggested	Notes
CPU	VT extensions	VT, 64-bit, Multicore	64-bit can run both i386 and amd64 instances; by default, Eucalyptus will run only 1 VM per CPU core on a node.
Memory	1GB	4GB	Additional memory means more and larger guests.
Disk	5400rpm IDE	7200rpm SATA or SCSI	Eucalyptus nodes are disk intensive; I/O wait will likely be the performance bottleneck.
Disk Space	40GB	100GB	Images will be cached locally; Eucalyptus does not like to run out of disk space.
Networking	100Mbps	1000Mbps	Machine images are hundreds of MB and need to be copied over the network to nodes.

When you have confirmed that your equipment meets or exceeds the requirements, download the Ubuntu Server installation disk from http://releases.ubuntu.com/ and click the release version you want to use (for example, 10.04 LTS or 10.10). Make sure you download the server installation CD. Burn it to a disk.

When you boot, select Install Ubuntu Enterprise Cloud. The installer will check and detect whether you have a Eucalyptus cloud controller or other components. Because none are present, you will need to install a cloud controller (CLC) at a minimum. If this is going to be the only front-end system and will be expected to run all the services, make sure you also tell the installer to include the WS3, CC, and SC components.

You will be asked to name your cluster and supply a range of IP addresses on the LAN that UEC will be able to use and allocate to instances. Typically, this is something like 192.168.1.125—192.168.1.240. Allow the installation to complete.

To install node controller(s), make sure each system you intend to use as a node is connected to the network on which the CLC is running. Boot each one at a time to the same server installation CD and again select Install Ubuntu Enterprise Cloud. It should detect the cluster and preselect Node for you. Confirm it and finish the installation as usual. When the node reboots, it will be ready to be registered.

Node registration should be automatic and will include servers exchanging public SSH keys, configuring services properly, services publishing their existence to the rest of the cloud, running the appropriate version of uec-component-listener for components installed, and verifying registration. Instructions for performing these steps manually are available at https://help.ubuntu.com/community/UEC/CDInstall should you discover a failure.

After installing and booting the CLC, users will need credentials. These can be retrieved using a web browser or from the command line. From a web browser, open https://<cloud-controller-ip-address>:8443/. You must use a secure connection, but you will receive a security certificate warning. You need to add an exception to view the page. If you do not, you will not be able to view the Eucalyptus configuration page.

Use the username "admin" and password "admin" the first time you log in. Follow the onscreen instructions to change the admin password as required and enter a valid email address for the admin. Click the Credentials tab, and from there choose Download Credentials. Save the certificates to ~/.euca and unzip.

You may also retrieve your credentials from the command line. Create ~/.euca and enter that directory; then enter:

```
matthew@seymour:~.euca$ sudo euca_conf —get-credentials mycreds.zip
```

Unzip them and create this link:

```
matthew@seymour:~.euca$ ln -s ~/.euca/eucarc ~/.eucarc
```

Next, you need to set up the EC2 API and AMI tools on your server. Check that `euca2ools` package is installed. If it is, you can get the local cluster availability details this way:

```
matthew@seymour:~.euca/eucarc$ euca-describe-availability-zones verbose
AVAILABILITYZONE    myowncloud                 192.168.1.1
AVAILABILITYZONE    ¦- vm types                free / max   cpu    ram  disk
AVAILABILITYZONE    ¦- m1.small                0004 / 0004   1     192     2
AVAILABILITYZONE    ¦- c1.medium               0004 / 0004   1     256     5
AVAILABILITYZONE    ¦- m1.large                0002 / 0002   2     512    10
AVAILABILITYZONE    ¦- m1.xlarge               0002 / 0002   2    1024    20
AVAILABILITYZONE    ¦- c1.xlarge               0001 / 0001   4    2048    20
```

If everything looks correct, you can start installing images. The easiest way to do this is from the store using the web interface. Access the interface as you did earlier using https://<cloud-controller-ip-address>:8443/ and this time click the Store tab. You will see a list of available images to download and install. Information is also given here about how to run images.

To run an image from the command line, you first need to create a key pair that you can use to log in to that instance as root. Here is an easy way to do that:

```
if [ ! -e ~/.euca/secretkey.priv ]; then
    mkdir -p -m 700 ~/.euca
    touch ~/.euca/secretkey.priv
    chmod 0600 ~/.euca/secretkey.priv
    euca-add-keypair secretkey > ~/.euca/secretkey.priv
fi
```

You can call your key anything you want, and if you forget what keys exist you can run `euca-describe-keypairs` to get a list of created keys stored on the system. You then have to allow access to port 22 in each of your instances using:

```
matthew@seymour:~.euca/eucarc$ euca-authorize default -P tcp -p 22 -s 0.0.0.0/0
```

Then you can create instances of your registered image using:

```
matthew@seymour:~.euca/eucarc$ euca-run-instances $EMI -k mykey -t m1.small
```

You may have more than one instance of the same image. The first time you run an instance, the system will take a while to start up because it will set up a cache of the image. VM images are quite large. You can watch to see if it is up using:

```
matthew@seymour:~.euca/eucarc$ watch -n5 euca-describe-instances
```

When the status changes from pending to running, you want to make a note of the IP address assigned to the instance and connect to it using:

```
matthew@seymour:~.euca/eucarc$ IPADDR=$(euca-describe-instances | grep $EMI | grep
running | tail -n1 | awk '{print $4}')
matthew@seymour:~.euca/eucarc$ ssh -i ~/.euca/mykey.priv ubuntu@$IPADDR
```

When you are done, you can exit your SSH connection and terminate your instance using:

```
matthew@seymour:~.euca/eucarc$ INSTANCEID=$(euca-describe-instances | grep $EMI |
grep running | tail -n1 | awk '{print $2}')
matthew@seymour:~.euca/eucarc$ euca-terminate-instances $INSTANCEID
```

A Euca2ools Primer

Most uses for cloud computing involve custom tools and software by people who know how to read an API and make their program interact without bothering end users with the details. It is no different with UEC. For that reason, we will list some of the commands from euca2ools without a lot of commentary.

Euca2ools contains many commands for managing your resources. Most have numerous configuration options available. After the euca2ools package is installed, the man pages for each command provide valuable information about how to use them. Following is a simple list to help you remember what commands do so that you can look up the details of how to use them:

- `euca-bundle-image`—Bundles an image for use with Eucalyptus, UEC, or Amazon EC2
- `euca-bundle-vol`—Bundles the local file system of a running instance as a bundled image
- `euca-delete-bundle`—Deletes a previously uploaded bundle
- `euca-download-bundle`—Downloads a bundled image from a bucket
- `euca-unbundle`—Unbundles a previously bundled image
- `euca-upload-bundle`—Uploads a previously bundled image to the cloud
- `euca-describe-images`—Shows information about machine images
- `euca-describe-image-attribute`—Shows image attributes
- `euca-register`—Registers a manifest for use with the cloud
- `euca-deregister`—Deregisters an image from the cloud
- `euca-describe-instances`—Shows information about instances
- `euca-reboot-instances`—Reboots specified instances
- `euca-run-instances`—Starts instances
- `euca-terminate-instances`—Stops specified instances
- `euca-confirm-product-instance`—Confirms if instance is running with product code supplied
- `euca-attach-volume`—Attaches a volume to an instance
- `euca-create-volume`—Creates a volume in the specified availability zone
- `euca-delete-volume`—Deletes a volume
- `euca-describe-volumes`—Shows information about existing volumes
- `euca-detach-volume`—Detaches a volume from an instance
- `euca-create-snapshot`—Creates a snapshot from an existing volume
- `euca-delete-snapshot`—Deletes a snapshot
- `euca-describe-snapshots`—Shows information about snapshots
- `euca-allocate-address`—Allocates a public IP address
- `euca-associate-address`—Associates an instance with a public IP address
- `euca-describe-addresses`—Shows information about IP addresses
- `euca-disassociate-addresses`—Disassociates a public IP address from an instance

- `euca-release-address`—Releases a public IP address
- `euca-add-group`—Creates a new security group
- `euca-delete-group`—Deletes a security group
- `euca-describe-groups`—Shows information about groups
- `euca-add-keypair`—Creates a new key pair for use with instances
- `euca-delete-keypair`—Deletes a key pair
- `euca-describe-keypairs`—Shows information about key pairs
- `euca-describe-availability-zones`—Shows information about availability zones
- `euca-describe-regions`—Shows information about regions
- `euca-get-console-output`—Prints console output from a running instance
- `euca-modify-image-attribute`—Modifies attributes of an image
- `euca-reset-image-attribute`—Resets attributes for an image
- `euca-revoke`—Revokes a rule for a security group
- `euca-version`—Shows the Euca2ools version
- `euca-authorize`—Adds a new rule to a security group
- `uec-publish-tarball`—Registers a UEC tarball
- `uec-registration`—Enables or disables automatic component registration
- `uec-run-instances`—Same as euca-run-instances
- `uec-publish-image`—Publishes image to bucket
- `uec-query-builds`—Finds information about a build
- `uec-resize-image`—Resizes UEC image

Reference

- www.ubuntu.com/cloud—The official Ubuntu introduction to cloud computing.
- https://help.ubuntu.com/community/UEC—Ubuntu community documentation for Ubuntu Enterprise Cloud.
- http://eucalyptus.com/resources/overview—Official information resources from Eucalyptus, the system on which UEC is built.
- http://aws.amazon.com/—The Amazon Web Services main page.

- www.linux-kvm.org/page/Main_Page—The main page for KVM, the Kernel-based Virtual Machine.
- http://open.eucalyptus.com/wiki/Euca2oolsGuide_v1.1—The Euca2ools User Guide.
- www.canonical.com/enterprise-services/ubuntu-advantage/landscape/cloud-management—Canonical's Landscape is a commercial management tool for UEC and Amazon EC2 instances.

CHAPTER 25

Opportunistic Development

IN THIS CHAPTER

- Introduction to Opportunistic Development
- Launchpad
- Quickly
- Ground Control
- Desktop Couch
- The Desktop Is the IDE
- Reference

There are some among us who love to write program code. Others are able, but don't particularly enjoy doing so. Most of this section of the book (Part V: Programming Linux) is dedicated to the first group, those who love to code and want to know how to get started using their favorite tool(s) in Ubuntu. However, it also applies to those of us who just want to scratch a specific itch by coding up a quick program to do something useful and make it available to other Ubuntu users, but who aren't interested in learning how to become a package maintainer, upload to the official software repositories, and so on. We call this process opportunistic development, where an end user codes up a quick solution to a problem. This is in direct contrast to system atic development, with professional planning, requirements gathering, design, processes and procedures.

We have a couple of links in the Reference section if serious, sustained development and helping with official packaging is your ultimate goal, but to get started, let's look at an initiative by the Ubuntu community to help scratch that itch—get something written and then make it available to others quickly and easily. This project is quite new and under active development, so what we have here is a short survey to whet your appetite and help you know where to look to get connected and get started.

You have an idea for a program that will save time by automating a repetitive task. You plan for it to have a pretty GUI interface and you think there are probably others out there who would like to use the tool after it is written. The problem is that you work full time, have a family, and already have a ton of side projects that don't get enough attention. You are either not able or not willing to sit down and study how Ubuntu packages programs to get them into the official software repositories. (If you are, see the links in Reference.)

It used to be that you had one simple choice at this juncture: write the program and put it on a website for others to find—and hope that maybe someone would find it useful, make a .deb package, and upload it into either the Debian or Ubuntu repositories. That is no longer the only option if your goal is simply to write your tool and make the software available to Ubuntu users. Now, you still need to be technically proficient at writing whatever code you want to write and understand complex systems, but Ubuntu is lowering the complexity for getting that code written and making it available to the wider community. This allows developers who want only to scratch that one itch to do so without reading tons of documentation about tools they expect to use rarely or only once.

Launchpad

To get started, you need to sign up for an account on Launchpad (Figure 25.1). Launchpad is an infrastructure created to simplify communication, collaboration, and processes within software development. It was developed and is supported by Canonical, the company that supports the Ubuntu community, but it is used by many software projects, including several that are not a part of the Ubuntu community.

FIGURE 25.1 Launchpad is the place to start for development in Ubuntu.

Launchpad is where Ubuntu development takes place. It integrates Bazaar, a version control system that makes keeping track of changes to software code much simpler and permits those changes to be reverted when necessary while tracking who is performing the actions. Launchpad also incorporates Soyuz, which is a distribution and archive management software that handles the automatic package builds within Launchpad.

For developers using Launchpad, this means that the process became a bit simpler. They can concentrate on writing and editing their code and let Launchpad deal with keeping track of the changes and creating their packages. This is useful for active developers who write and maintain big projects that need source code version control and so on. It also hosts bug reporting and tracking, mailing lists, software interface translation, and much more. Most of this is beyond the scope of this chapter but of great interested to the serious developer.

What is of interest to us is that registered Launchpad users can create a personal package archive (PPA). This is a much simpler way to make programs available. Anyone with a PPA can upload source code to be built in to packages. Those packages will then be made available in an apt repository that may be added to any Ubuntu user's list of source repositories and downloaded or removed using any of the standard package management tools in Ubuntu, such as apt, Ubuntu Software Center, and Synaptic. Instructions are included on the web page for each Launchpad PPA, describing how to add that repository, making this an easy method to share software that may be added and removed by even the most nontechnical end user. In Figure 25.2 we show the PPA for the stable version of Google Chromium.

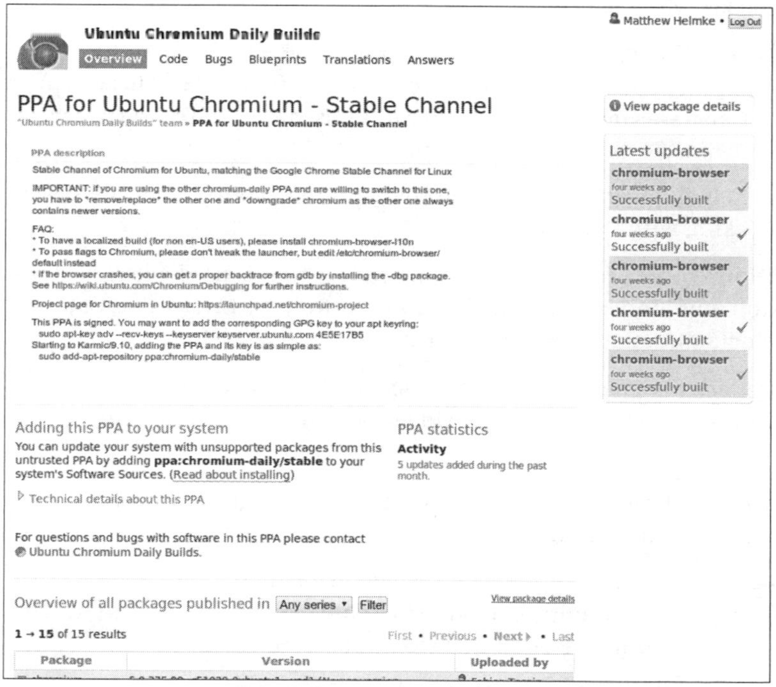

FIGURE 25.2 A Launchpad PPA for the stable version of Google Chromium.

Quickly

Several very knowledgeable and talented Ubuntu developers got together and started talking. These are people who know how to program and who enjoy it. At the same time, they want programming on Linux to be easy and fun and decided that it wasn't terribly fun for some because it can be so hard to learn. There are so many choices, so many tools, so much documentation to read and study just to get started. They had a "what if" moment: What if we could write a program that makes some very opinionated choices about tools and templates and make that available to new programmers and people who just want to write a quick application and who are not interested in studying every available option before choosing? Not everyone cares about the benefits of Gtk versus Qt, or even knows what those are. Why force uninterested people to make those choices? Quickly is the result of these discussions and is the solution created by some of those developers.

Quickly is a tool to help you write and package software programs (and other things) quickly. You can select from a set of application templates and use some simple quickly commands to create, edit code and GUI, and publish your software for others to use. Quickly's templates are easy to write. So if you are a fan of language foo, you can create a foo-project template. Or if you want to help people making plug-ins for your killer app, you can make a killer-app plug-in template. You can even create a template for managing corporate documents, creating your awesome LaTeX helpers. Better yet, if you don't know what some of that means and you just want to make a useful Python tool with a pretty GUI, you can do that quickly with Quickly.

The most popular template is the ubuntu-application template, which is not surprising because the Ubuntu community wrote Quickly and uses it most often so far. This template uses a specific set of tools that are among the most common used for Linux, and specifically Ubuntu, desktop software. They include the following:

- **Python**—An extremely popular, easy-to-learn programming language that we cover in Chapter 28, "Working with Python."
- **GTK**—A cross-platform toolkit for creating GUI interfaces that is used extensively in the GNOME desktop environment, making it a good fit for easy integration of new programs into the default desktop used by Ubuntu.
- **Glade**—A user interface designer for GTK from the GNOME community. It is powerful and quite easy to use to aggregate all the widgets and windows desired for a project.
- **GStreamer**—A media framework used in GNOME for easy integration of audio and video content in desktop applications.
- **Desktop Couch**—A database format built on Apache's CouchDB that allows easy integration of powerful database storage, replication, and synchronization in desktop programs. It is used by Ubuntu One and others for cloud storage.
- **gedit**—The default text editor in the GNOME desktop environment.

Using these very common tools by default eliminates many of the more confusing choices developers need to make when creating a new application. Because each of these choices are very common in Ubuntu, in GNOME, and generally throughout the Linux world, an application created using them is almost guaranteed to blend in beautifully with any end user's desktop.

Quickly is in the Ubuntu repositories as `quickly`. Quickly is run from the command line. After installation, the best way to get going is to run the tutorial and read some basic information:

```
matthew@seymour:~$ quickly tutorial ubuntu-application
```

Some useful commands for quickly include:

```
matthew@seymour:~$ quickly create ubuntu-application matthewsapplication
```

This creates the initial template for an Ubuntu program called `matthewsapplication` and a subfolder from which you will work on your project, and you'll get feedback with a nice pop-up window (Figure 25.3).

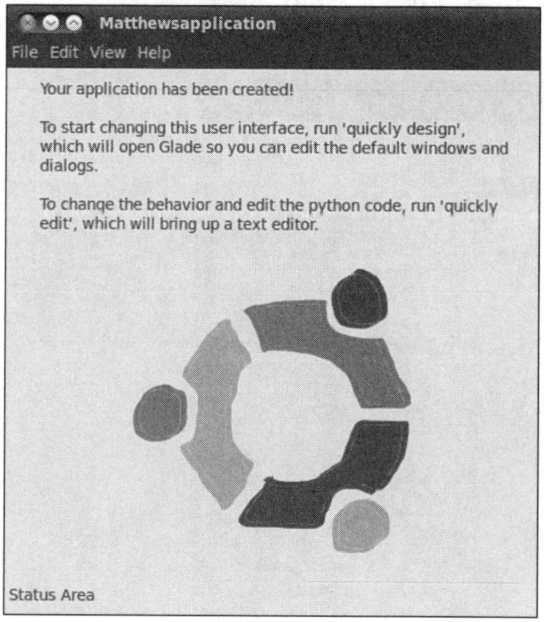

FIGURE 25.3 Quickly lets you know your application has been successfully created.

To verify that the application has been created, you can change to the new application's directory and list its contents.

```
matthew@seymour:~$ cd matthewsapplication
```

```
matthew@seymour:~$ ls -la
total 44
drwxr-xr-x   6 matt matt 4096 2010-07-31 15:42 .
drwxr-xr-x 125 matt matt 4096 2010-07-31 15:42 ..
-rw-r—r—     1 matt matt   45 2010-07-31 15:42 AUTHORS
drwxr-xr-x   2 matt matt 4096 2010-07-31 15:42 bin
drwxr-xr-x   6 matt matt 4096 2010-07-31 15:42 .bzr
drwxr-xr-x   4 matt matt 4096 2010-07-31 15:42 data
drwxr-xr-x   2 matt matt 4096 2010-07-31 15:42 matthewsapplication
-rw-r—r—     1 matt matt  191 2010-07-31 15:42 matthewsapplication.desktop.in
-rw-r—r—     1 matt matt   76 2010-07-31 15:42 .quickly
-rw-r—r—     1 matt matt 2956 2010-07-31 15:42 setup.py
-rw-r—r—     1 matt matt 2837 2010-07-31 15:42 setup.pyc
```

Start editing the default GUI for your new app using Glade with

```
matthew@seymour:~$ quickly design
```

This will bring up a beautiful interface to help you create all the actions, containers, widgets, and so on that you need in your application (Figure 25.4).

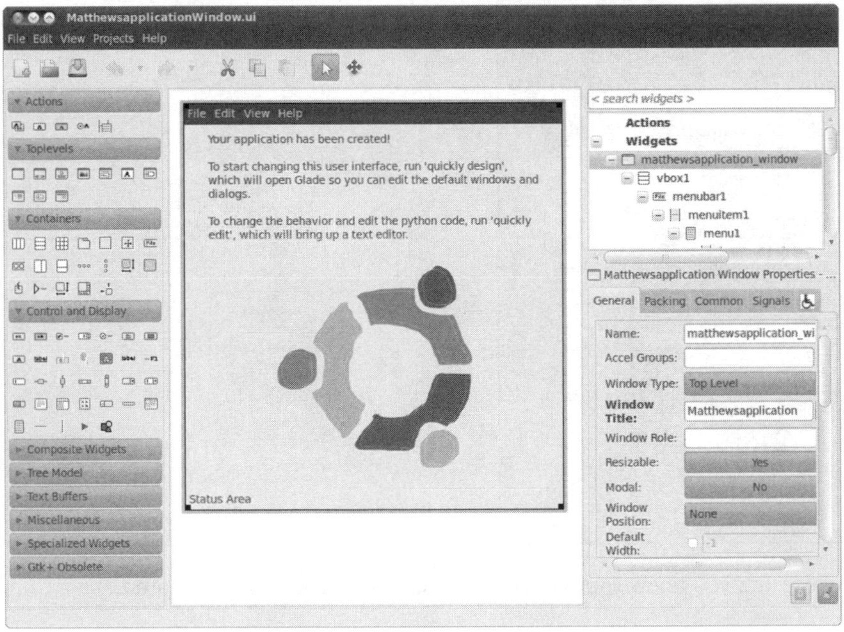

FIGURE 25.4 Quickly uses Glade to help you create your user interface.

Change the application behavior and edit your Python code in gedit (Figure 25.5) with

```
matthew@seymour:~$ quickly edit
```

Test your new application by running it with

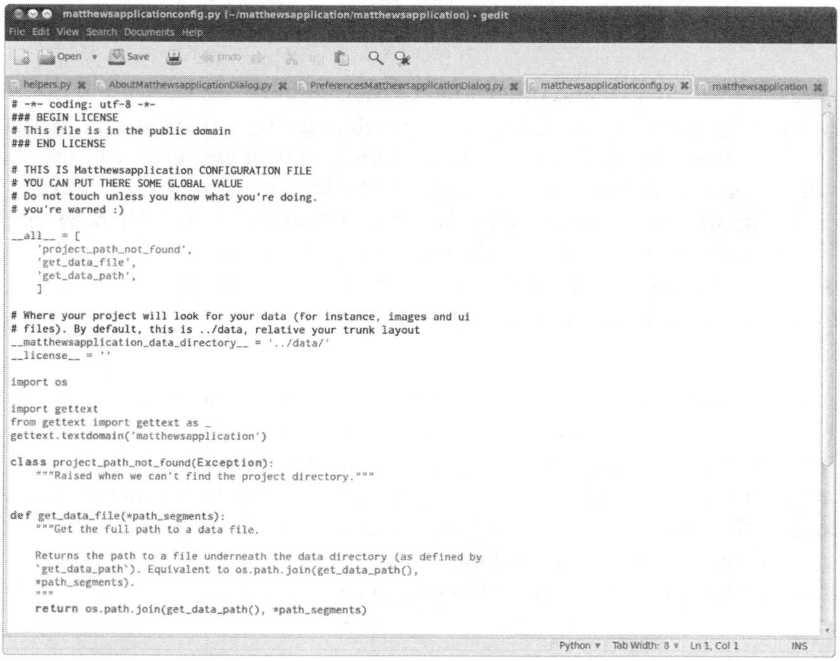

FIGURE 25.5 Code files open in adjacent tabs for quick and easy editing in gedit.


```
matthew@seymour:~$ quickly run
```

You can create a package build of your application, which is recommended for testing, using:

```
matthew@seymour:~$ quickly package
```

One of the most exciting features of Quickly is that it integrates with Launchpad to speed up the process of dealing with PPAs. You will need a Launchpad account. There are two equivalent commands for doing this:

```
matthew@seymour:~$ quickly release
```

and

```
matthew@seymour:~$ quickly share
```

If you have a bit more development experience, you can create templates for Quickly, like the ubuntu-application template, that make specific decisions about programming language and much, much more. Quickly is young and in active development, but is already very usable. Check out the links in the Reference section for more information.

Ground Control

Collaboration on software can be difficult. The bar for entry into that world is set quite high because of the complexity of the tools. Have you ever had a problem with a program and been able to figure out what was wrong—maybe you've even been able to write a quick software patch for it—but not been able to figure out how to submit that patch to the original developer? It happens. Think of the case where someone discovers a misspelled word in a bit of Python code and wants to help save a bit of the developer's time by fixing it.

Ground Control seeks to simplify this and other sorts of collaboration on software projects. It takes the technology and workflows that most developers use and know and makes them available to the Ubuntu desktop where common non-developer end users can use them. It is essentially a version control system built in to the Ubuntu desktop that interacts directly with Launchpad and Bazaar using the standard Ubuntu GNOME file browser. This is also useful when you write the software yourself using Quickly or another method and make it available on Launchpad using a PPA. Then someone comes to you offering a bug fix, someone who may be even less technically proficient with the behind-the-scenes tools.

Install Ground Control (groundcontrol) from the Ubuntu software repositories, from the Ground Control website (https://launchpad.net/groundcontrol), or from the daily build PPA linked from that web page. A program will appear in your menu at System, Preferences, Ground Control Configuration, shown in Figure 25.6, which you need to run to give Ground Control the capability to interact with your Launchpad account. This is also the tool you use to log out when you are done using Ground Control. If you don't have a Launchpad account, Ground Control will help you sign up for one.

FIGURE 25.6 Click Login to Launchpad to get started with Ground Control.

When you sign in, Ground Control will get your Launchpad credentials, including your uploaded ssh key, from Launchpad. An `ssh` key is a special code needed for secure connections; it identifies you personally so that the systems and others using it can be confident of who uploaded the code. You can use an existing `ssh` key that you have uploaded to your Launchpad account. If you do not have an `ssh` key, Ground Control will help you create one. Ground Control will then update your local Bazaar configuration automatically.

Then, when you use the GNOME file browser (aka Nautilus) to view a directory that is related to a Bazaar branch you have previously used, it will give you tools to interact with it. After you have run the Ground Control Configuration tool the first time, you will discover a new folder in your home folder called Projects. From now on, if you want to log in to Ground Control, you can also do so in that folder by clicking the Identify Yourself button, as shown in Figure 25.7.

FIGURE 25.7 Identify yourself to Ground Control within the file manager.

After you are logged in, you will see the confirmation box (Figure 25.8) and notice a change in the file manager. You now have buttons labeled Fix Bug and Fetch Project (Figure 25.9).

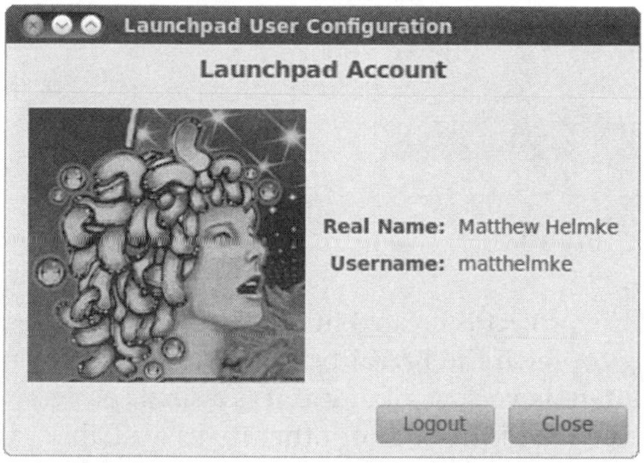

FIGURE 25.8 The confirmation window uses your Launchpad details.

FIGURE 25.9 New abilities appear in Projects.

If you click Fetch Project, you are taken to a search window. Enter the name of a project you want to find, and click Find to begin your search. Figure 25.10 shows the results of a search for "chromium," while looking for the Google open-source browser. Notice that any project with the name you are seeking is returned.

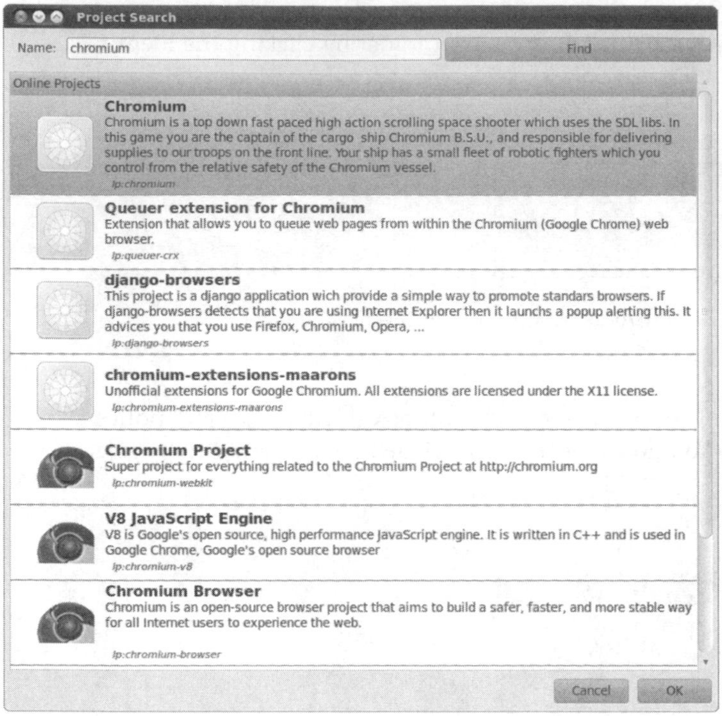

FIGURE 25.10 Searching for Chromium.

When you click to select, a subdirectory for the project is created in your Projects directory. Clicking it enables you to either fix bugs or fetch the Bazaar branch containing the source code for the part of the project that interests you, or all of it if it is a small project (see Figures 25.11 and 25.12). A branch is a version of the code or other items available, such as graphics or documentation.

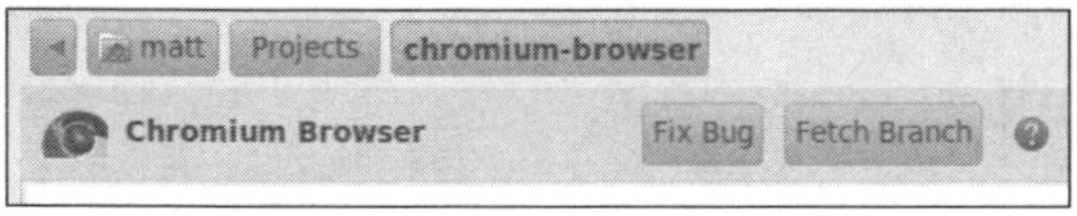

FIGURE 25.11 New options in a new directory.

Suppose you want the main development focus branch, which is the first one listed. However, if you were working with someone on a specific part of the code or something else like icons, you could find and download that branch. Select the branch, give it a local branch name in the bottom right, and click OK. Choose a unique name so that when you upload it later with your modifications, it won't conflict with anything that currently exists. You will need to enter your ssh key password, which you created when you created your `ssh` key, to confirm your identity so that activity on this code can be traced. This

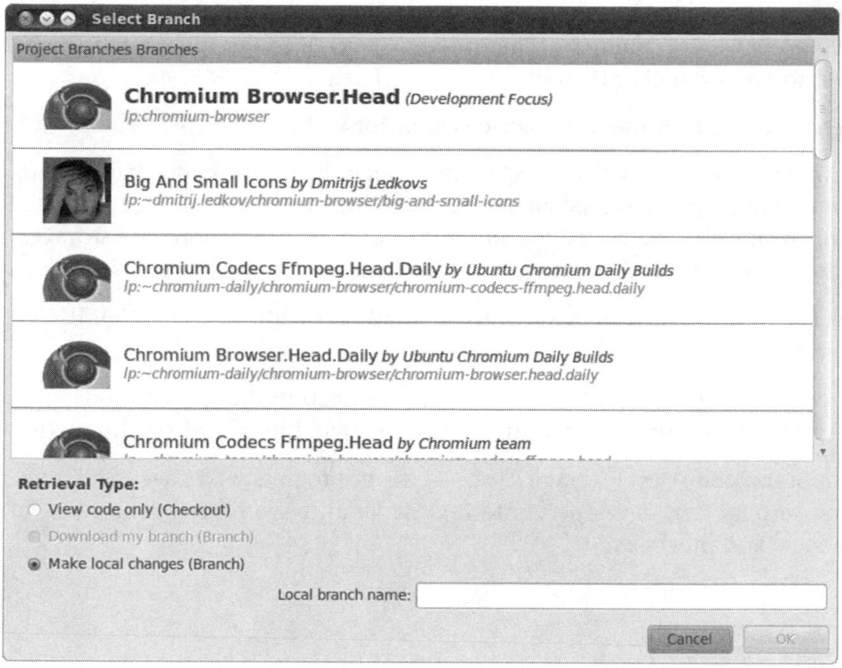

FIGURE 25.12 Selecting which branch from which to download code.

helps prevent, or at least track, sinister activity by people wanting to cause trouble, and it helps track or remove uploaded mistakes. It will find any and all revisions and download the code to your computer. You will now find files on your computer.

That should be enough to get you started. Committing your changes works similarly to submitting bug fixes. Ground Control is rather new and in active development that seems to go in spurts, with flurries of activity separated by months of inactivity, which is normal for a small team running a project on the side. For the latest on features and use instructions, check out the Ground Control website, listed in the Reference section.

Reference

- https://launchpad.net/—Launchpad is an open source website that hosts code, tracks bugs, and helps developers and users collaborate and share.
- http://bazaar.canonical.com/en/—Bazaar is the version control system used by Ubuntu and many other free and open source software projects.
- https://launchpad.net/ubuntu/+ppas—Personal Package Archives allow source code to be uploaded and built in to .deb packages and made available to others as an apt repository.
- https://launchpad.net/quickly and https://wiki.ubuntu.com/Quickly—Quickly makes integrating a graphic toolkit, your code, and the packaging process fast and easy.

- www.pygtk.org/, based on http://www.gtk.org/—PyGTK is the toolkit most used by Ubuntu developers when creating GUI interfaces with GTK in Python, which is what Quickly is set to do in the ubuntu-application template.
- http://glade.gnome.org/—A user interface designer for GTK.
- www.freedesktop.org/wiki/Specifications/desktopcouch, http://couchdb.apache.org/ and https://launchpad.net/desktopcouch—Desktop Couch is a data storage format used by Ubuntu One and many desktop programs for easy integration data storage, replication from one computer to another, and synchronization into programs.
- http://projects.gnome.org/gedit/—gedit is the default text editor in the GNOME desktop environment.
- https://launchpad.net/groundcontrol and http://ground-control.org/—Ground Control integrates the power and usefulness of Launchpad into your Ubuntu desktop.
- https://wiki.ubuntu.com/DeveloperStackTour—This in-progress wiki page is planned to be the first stop for new developers entering the Ubuntu world. Here you will learn about tools and processes.

CHAPTER 26

Helping with Ubuntu Testing and QA

IN THIS CHAPTER

- Community Participation
- Ubuntu Testing
- QA Testing
- Bug Squad
- Test Drive
- Reference

There are many ways to help the Ubuntu community create, refine, and promote the operating system. Some are highly technical, like writing code or packaging programs to be included in the software repositories. Some are less technical, such as helping promote Ubuntu locally or through blogging interesting news items from the community. Somewhere in the middle, leaning toward the technical side, is a task that is wide open for greater community involvement.

This will be a rather brief and intentionally vague chapter. Testing by volunteers is something that requires more than a casual interest if it is going to be helpful to the developers and not an annoyance. For that reason, this chapter covers the basics of how to get involved and some of the opportunities, but not the precise details. If you are interested, and after reading this chapter we hope you are, the next step is to visit the websites listed at the end of the chapter.

Community Teams

There are two community teams that would love to see volunteers who can follow directions, be careful and methodical, and who notice details. Both teams work to refine the distribution during the development cycle to help make Ubuntu the best it can be.

The Ubuntu Testing Team works to collaborate the testing of release ISOs. An ISO is a one-file package that contains everything that goes on either a CD or a DVD, in our case the ISO contains everything needed to make Ubuntu install media. People in this team download install ISO files and use precise methods to try to find any bugs in the installation process. The goal is to ensure that the ISOs released by Ubuntu will boot on as many computer hardware configurations as possible and will work properly. They also perform other tests, as explained next.

The Ubuntu QA Team looks directly at the overall quality of the distribution, trying out default programs and configurations and trying to break things. The goal is to find bugs during the development cycle and make clear reports about them, trying to get them fixed before end users ever know of their existence. The goal here is product improvement and quality control or assurance.

These are big tasks. Even with several Canonical employees working on these full time, it is nearly impossible to test every hardware configuration or use case. It is also impossible to guess what creative ways users will attempt to perform tasks that developers have designed to perform differently. Testing as many of these options as possible is key when the goal is to create a positive experience for as many people as possible. This is why volunteers are both welcome and actively recruited.

These are also exacting tasks. Testing and bug reporting (or fixing) requires careful attention so that problems are reported clearly with steps that can be repeated by developers. This enables them to find where problems lie and more easily fix them. Not everyone is well suited for this sort of thing, but those who are able to be clear and precise and who can follow the directions given in testing plans and procedures are worth their weight in gold. You may not receive public glory for testing, but you will receive honor from those working with you in testing if you are able to do the job well.

You will notice some crossover in the team descriptions that follow. That is because the teams work together closely. Although each has a main focus, each may perform similar tasks from time to time. Even the individual team's web pages link to the others and offer similar information to help coordinate and direct any interested volunteers to the tasks they feel most equipped to help with.

Ubuntu Testing Team

Members of the Ubuntu Testing Team are probably best known for their work during a release week, when they help validate all of the CD and DVD images. They also operate during the release cycle testing beta releases and release candidates. In addition, they test update packages for stable releases before the packages are pushed out to users. They do this by enabling a new software repository called -proposed and trying out the software there before it ends up in the -updates repository. In addition, they help developers by coordinating communications and actively seeking and connecting additional volunteers when specific testing needs are encountered.

To get started, you need a Launchpad account. Then, join the Ubuntu Testing Team via the team's page in Launchpad at https://launchpad.net/~ubuntu-testing. It is also a good idea to subscribe to the team's email list at https://lists.ubuntu.com/mailman/listinfo/ubuntu-qa. When testers are needed, the Launchpad team list and the mailing list are the initial points of contact for those that are asked to help.

There are many ways to get involved in testing; each has varying requirements on time and technical skill. Some tasks are quick and easy, and others may be more involved. Some of the tests are general in nature, and others involve specific features, applications, and hardware. Some tests are automated and require specific test software to be downloaded and installed. Others are given as a list of instructions. Opportunities exist for many skill levels and most time schedules.

QA Testing Team

The QA Testing Team has a stronger focus on developing and using tools to automate the process. This enables people using the tools to run a large battery of tests against a code base very quickly while ensuring they are probing precisely what is needed. Much of their work is useful for hardware certification, logic testing, and bug discovery. They have developed an Ubuntu developer focused suite of tools called `ubuntu-qa-tools`, a library called Mago for the Linux Desktop Testing Project (LDTP) to simplify testing of Ubuntu within the wider realm of Linux desktops, and a framework called Checkbox that tests and sends test data directly to Launchpad.

Bug Squad

One of the first places people become involved in Ubuntu testing is with Bug Squad. These volunteers are the initial point of contact for most bugs filed with Ubuntu. They read bug reports to see if the bug seems legitimate (for example, that it isn't something like "Ubuntu doesn't work," but is rather specific and measurable), that it is filed against the appropriate software package, and that adequate information is included with each report for the developers to be able to figure out the problem. If the bug report meets this criteria, the Bug Squad determines which developer or team should be notified. Sometimes during the triage process they may ask reporters for more information. They attempt to determine the severity of the bug and may assign a priority setting to the report.

Test Drive

One specific tool used by both volunteers and developers that deserves a mention is Test Drive. Dustin Kirkland is an Ubuntu developer on Canonical's Ubuntu Server team. He was looking for an easy way to download and run the latest daily development snapshot of Ubuntu using a virtual machine like KVM or VirtualBox. Like any good developer who doesn't want to repeat tasks unnecessarily, he wrote a tool to automate the process. While creating Test Drive, he made it configurable to use different virtual machines with different settings according to the user's taste. It can even download and run any ISO that may be accessed via a URL, which means it could be used to download and run images from other distributions during their development cycles.

Test Drive is written in a way that enables even a nontechnical Ubuntu user to consistently test Ubuntu development releases. Test Drive is available in the Ubuntu repositories as `testdrive`. It runs from the command line, although a GUI front end is in active development and may be available by the time this book goes to print.

When you run the program, you are offered a menu:

```
matthew@seymour:~$ testdrive

Welcome to Testdrive!

  1. Ubuntu Desktop (maverick-amd64)
  2. Ubuntu Desktop (maverick-i386)
     +-cache—> [2010-07-20 00:08:09] maverick-desktop-i386.iso
  3. Ubuntu Alternate (maverick-amd64)
  4. Ubuntu Alternate (maverick-i386)
  5. Ubuntu Netbook (maverick-i386)
  6. Ubuntu Server (maverick-amd64)
  7. Ubuntu Server (maverick-i386)
  8. Other (prompt for ISO URL)

Select an image to testdrive [1]:
```

Type a number to download and run a specific ISO. As you can see, the preceding example is from the development cycle for Maverick Meercat, which eventually became Ubuntu 10.10.

The Test Drive configuration is stored in a simple text file and is easy to understand and edit (although many using Test Drive will never need to edit it). Test Drive will look several places for the testdriverc file, including the default location `/etc/testdriverc` as well as in the user's home directory at `/home/matthew/.testdriverc` and `/home/matthew/.config/testdrive/testdriverc`.

Here is an example:

```
# This is the global configuration file for the testdrive(1) utility.
[testdrive-common]

# CACHE is the directory to cache the ISOs and disk images
# Default: $HOME/.cache/testdrive
#CACHE = /path/to/your/cache

# CACHE_IMG and CACHE_ISO will default to $CACHE/img and $CACHE/iso, respectively.
# You can set them explicitly if you want (specially interesting if you are
# trying to run the image off /dev/shm.  Make sure you have enough space there!!!
#CACHE_IMG = /dev/shm

# CLEAN_IMG will remove the just-generated image at the end of run. By default the
image
# is kept, unless nothing was changed (i.e., the disk image was created, but no
installation
# was actually tried).
```

```
# If running the image off /dev/shm, then *by default* the image will be removed
(memory is a
# restricted resource, and we should not over-allocate it)
#CLEAN_IMG = False

# VIRT is the type of hypervisor to use
# VIRT can be either 'kvm', 'virtualbox', or 'parallels'
VIRT = kvm
#VIRT = virtualbox
#VIRT = parallels

# MEM is the amount of memory in MB to give to the VM guest
# Default: 384
MEM = 384
#MEM = 512
#MEM = 1024

# SMP is the number of processors to give to the VM guest if
# running in KVM.
# Default is the number of CPUs in the host
#SMP = 1

# DISK_SIZE is the size of the disk image
# Note that this will be a sparse, qcow2 file, so it should not actually
# take that much space on the filesystem.
# Default: 6G
DISK_SIZE = 6G
#DISK_SIZE = 10G

# KVM_ARGS is a string of arbitrary KVM_ARGS to use when launching the VM
# See kvm(1) for a comprehensive list of arguments
KVM_ARGS = -usb -usbdevice tablet -net nic,model=virtio -net user -soundhw es1370 -
vga vmware

# Uncomment the following line if you want to hardcode the Ubuntu release
# and arch; otherwise, TestDrive will try to determine it dynamically.
#r = maverick
#m = i386
u = rsync://cdimage.ubuntu.com/cdimage

# Section for TestDrive (Command-line) specific variables.
[testdrive]

# DISK_FILE is the full path to the disk image
# Default: $CACHE/$ISO.img
#DISK_FILE = /path/to/foo.img
```

```
# The following line determines the default Ubuntu Flavor used by TestDrive.
# Possible flavors are: ubuntu/kubuntu/xubuntu/edubuntu/mythbuntu/ubuntustudio
f = ubuntu

# Section for TestDrive GTK specific variables.
[testdrive-gtk]

# The following line determines the default Ubuntu Flavors used by TestDrive GTK.
# Possible flavors are: ubuntu/kubuntu/xubuntu/edubuntu/mythbuntu/ubuntustudio
f = ubuntu, kubuntu, xubuntu
```

Reference

- www.ubuntu.com/testing—An invitation from the Ubuntu website to get involved in testing
- qa.ubuntu.com/—The starting point for understanding and volunteering for QA Testing
- https://wiki.ubuntu.com/BugSquad—The Ubuntu Bug Squad
- https://launchpad.net/testdrive—The official location for downloading TestDrive and assisting with its development

CHAPTER 27
Using Perl

IN THIS CHAPTER

Perl (the *Practical Extraction and Report Language*, or the *Pathologically Eclectic Rubbish Lister*, depending on who you speak to) is a powerful scripting tool that enables you to manage files, create reports, edit text, and perform many other tasks. Perl is included with and installed in Ubuntu by default and could be considered an integral part of the distribution because Ubuntu depends on Perl for many types of software services, logging activities, and software tools.

Perl is not the easiest of programming languages to learn because it is designed for flexibility. This chapter shows how to create and use Perl scripts on your system. You will see what a Perl program looks like, how the language is structured, and where you can find modules of prewritten code to help you write your own Perl scripts. This chapter also includes several examples of Perl used to perform a few common functions on a computer system.

Using Perl with Linux

Although originally designed as a data-extraction and report-generation language, Perl appeals to many Linux system administrators because it can be used to create utilities that fill a gap between the capabilities of shell scripts and compiled C programs. Another advantage of Perl over other UNIX tools is that it can process and extract data from binary files, whereas `sed` and `awk` cannot.

NOTE

In Perl, "there is more than one way to do it." This is the unofficial motto of Perl, and it comes up so often that it is usually abbreviated as TIMTOWTDI.

You can use Perl at your shell's command line to execute one-line Perl programs, but most often the programs (usually ending in `.pl`) are run as a command. These programs generally work on any computer platform because Perl has been ported to nearly every operating system.

Perl programs are used to support a number of Ubuntu services, such as system logging. For example, if you install the `logwatch` package, the `logwatch.pl` program is run every morning at 6:25 a.m. by the crond (scheduling) daemon on your system. Other Ubuntu services supported by Perl include the following:

- Amanda for local and network backups
- Fax spooling with the `faxrunqd` program
- Printing supported by Perl document filtering programs
- Hardware sensor monitoring setup using the `sensors-detect` Perl program

Perl Versions

As of this writing, the current production version of Perl from the Perl website is 5.12.1 (which is Perl Version 5 point 12, patch level 1). The version that was available at code freeze for the Ubuntu 10.10 release and that is available from the Ubuntu repositories is 5.10.1. Perl is installed from default.

You can download the code from www.perl.com and build the newest version from source if you want to, although a stable and quality release of Perl is already installed by default in Ubuntu and most (all?) Linux and Unix-like distributions, including Mac OSX. Updated versions may appear in the Ubuntu repositories, but generally only security fixes that can be installed by updating your system. See Chapter 32, "Managing Software," to see how to quickly get a list of available updates for Ubuntu.

You can determine what version of Perl you installed by typing **`perl -v` at a shell prompt. If you are installing the latest Ubuntu distribution, you should have the latest version of Perl that was available when the software for your Ubuntu release was gathered and finalized.**

A Simple Perl Program

This section introduces a very simple sample Perl program to get you started using Perl. Although trivial for experienced Perl hackers, a short example is necessary for new users who want to learn more about Perl.

To introduce you to the absolute basics of Perl programming, Listing 27.1 illustrates a simple Perl program that prints a short message.

LISTING 27.1 A Simple Perl Program

```
#!/usr/bin/perl
print "Look at all the camels!\n";
```

Type that in and save it to a file called `trivial.pl`. Then make the file executable using the `chmod` command (see the following sidebar) and run it at the command prompt.

COMMAND-LINE ERROR

If you get the message `bash: trivial.pl: command not found` or `bash: ./trivial.pl: Permission denied`, you have either typed the command line incorrectly or forgotten to make `trivial.pl` executable (with the `chmod` command):

```
matthew@seymour:~$ chmod +x trivial.pl
```

You can force the command to execute in the current directory as follows:

```
matthew@seymour:~$ ./trivial.pl
```

Or you can use Perl to run the program like this:

```
matthew@seymour:~$ perl trivial.pl
```

The sample program in the listing is a two-line Perl program. Typing in the program and running it (using Perl or making the program executable) shows how to create your first Perl program, a process duplicated by Linux users around the world every day!

NOTE

`#!` is often pronounced `she-bang`, which is short for `sharp` (the musicians name for the `#` character), and `bang`, which is another name for the exclamation point. This notation is also used in shell scripts. See Chapter 11, "Automating Tasks," for more information about writing shell scripts.

The `#!` line is technically not part of the Perl code at all. The `#` character indicates that the rest of the screen line is a comment. The comment is a message to the shell, telling it where it should go to find the executable to run this program. The interpreter ignores the comment line.

Exceptions to this practice include when the `#` character is in a quoted string and when it is being used as the delimiter in a regular expression. Comments are useful to document your scripts, like this:

```
#!/usr/bin/perl
# a simple example to print a greeting
print "hello there\n";
```

A block of code, such as what might appear inside a loop or a branch of a conditional statement, is indicated with curly braces ({}). For example, here is an infinite loop:

```
#!/usr/bin/perl
# a block of code to print a greeting forever
while (1) {
        print "hello there\n";
};
```

Perl statements are terminated with a semicolon. A Perl statement can extend over several screen lines because Perl is not concerned about whitespace.

The second line of the simple program prints the text enclosed in quotation marks. `\n` is the escape sequence for a newline character.

TIP

Using the `perldoc` and `man` commands is an easy way to get more information about the version of Perl installed on your system. To learn how to use the `perldoc` command, enter the following:

```
matthew@seymour:~$ perldoc perldoc
```

To get introductory information on Perl, you can use either of these commands:

```
matthew@seymour:~$ perldoc perl
matthew@seymour:~$ man perl
```

For an overview or table of contents of Perl's documentation, use the `perldoc` command like this:

```
matthew@seymour:~$ perldoc perltoc
```

The documentation is extensive and well organized. Perl includes a number of standard Linux manual pages as brief guides to its capabilities, but perhaps the best way to learn more about Perl is to read its `perlfunc` document, which lists all the available Perl functions and their usage. You can view this document by using the `perldoc` script and typing `perldoc perlfunc` at the command line. You can also find this document online at http://perldoc.perl.org/.

Perl Variables and Data Structures

Perl is a *weakly typed* language, meaning that it does not require that you declare a data type, such as a type of value (data) to be stored in a particular variable. C, for example, makes you declare that a particular variable is an integer, a character, a structure, or whatever the case may be. Perl variables are whatever type they need to be, and can change type when you need them to.

Perl Variable Types

Perl has three variable types: *scalars, arrays,* and *hashes*. A different character is used to signify each variable type, so you can have the same name used with each type at the same time.

Scalar variables are indicated with the $ *character*, as in `$penguin`. Scalars can be numbers or strings, and they can change type from one to the other as needed. If you treat a number like a string, it becomes a string. If you treat a string like a number, it is translated into a number if it makes sense to do so; otherwise, it usually evaluates to 0. For example, the string "`76trombones`" evaluates as the number `76` if used in a numeric calculation, but the string "`polar bear`" evaluates to `0`.

Perl arrays are indicated with the `@` character, as in `@fish`. An `array` is a list of values referenced by index number, starting with the first element numbered `0`, just as in C and `awk`. Each element in the array is a scalar value. Because scalar values are indicated with the `$` character, a single element in an array is also indicated with a `$` character.

For example, `$fish[2]` refers to the third element in the `@fish` array. This tends to throw some people off, but is similar to arrays in C in which the first array element is `0`.

Hashes are indicated with the % character, as in `%employee`. A *hash* is a list of name and value pairs. Individual elements in the hash are referenced by name rather than by index (unlike an array). Again, because the values are scalars, the $ character is used for individual elements.

For example, `$employee{name}` gives you one value from the hash. Two rather useful functions for dealing with hashes are *keys* and *values*. The `keys` function returns an array containing all the keys of the hash, and `values` returns an array of the values of the hash. Using this approach, the Perl program in Listing 27.2 displays all the values in your environment, much like typing the bash shell's `env` command.

LISTING 27.2 Displaying the Contents of the **env** Hash

```
#!/usr/bin/perl
foreach $key (keys %ENV)  {
  print "$key = $ENV{$key}\n";
}
```

27

Special Variables

Perl has a variety of special variables, which usually look like punctuation— `$_`, `$!`, and `$]`—and are all extremely useful for shorthand code. $_ is the default variable, $! is the error message returned by the operating system, and `$]` is the Perl version number.

$_ is perhaps the most useful of these. You will see that variable used often in this chapter. $_ is the Perl default variable, which is used when no argument is specified. For example, the following two statements are equivalent:

```
chomp;
chomp($_);
```

The following loops are equivalent:

```
for $cow (@cattle) {
        print "$cow says moo.\n";
}
for (@cattle)         {
        print "$_ says moo.\n";
}
```

For a complete listing of the special variables, you should see the `perlvar` document that comes with your Perl distribution (such as in the `perlvar` manual page).

Operators

Perl supports a number of operators to perform various operations. There are *comparison* operators (used to compare values, as the name implies), *compound* operators (used to combine operations or multiple comparisons), *arithmetic* operators (to perform math), and special string constants.

Comparison Operators

The comparison operators used by Perl are similar to those used by C, `awk`, and the `csh` shells, and are used to specify and compare values (including strings). Most frequently, a comparison operator is used within an `if` statement or loop. Perl has comparison operators for numbers and strings. Table 27.1 shows the numeric comparison operators and their behavior.

TABLE 27.1 Numeric Comparison Operators in Perl

Operator	Meaning
`==`	Is equal to
`<`	Less than
`>`	Greater than
`<=`	Less than or equal to
`>=`	Greater than or equal to
`<=>`	Returns –1 if less than, 0 if equal, and 1 if greater than
`!=`	Not equal to
`..`	Range of >= first operand to <= second operand

Table 27.2 shows the string comparison operators and their behaviors.

TABLE 27.2 String Comparison Operators in Perl

Operator	Meaning
`eq`	Is equal to
`lt`	Less than
`gt`	Greater than
`le`	Less than or equal to
`ge`	Greater than or equal to
`ne`	Not equal to
`cmp`	Returns -1 if less than, 0 if equal, and 1 if greater than
`=~`	Matched by regular expression
`!~`	Not matched by regular expression

Compound Operators

Perl uses compound operators, similar to those used by C or awk, which can be used to combine other operations (such as comparisons or arithmetic) into more complex forms of logic. Table 27.3 shows the compound pattern operators and their behavior.

TABLE 27.3 Compound Pattern Operators in Perl

Operator	Meaning
`&&`	Logical AND
`||`	Logical OR
`!`	Logical NOT
`()`	Parentheses; used to group compound statements

Arithmetic Operators

Perl supports a variety of math operations. Table 27.4 summarizes these operators.

TABLE 27.4 Perl Arithmetic Operators

Operator	Purpose
x**y	Raises x to the y power (same as x^y)
x%y	Calculates the remainder of x/y
x+y	Adds x to y
x-y	Subtracts y from x
x*y	Multiplies x times y
x/y	Divides x by y
-y	Negates y (switches the sign of y); also known as the unary minus
++y	Increments y by 1 and uses value (prefix increment)
y++	Uses value of y and then increments by 1 (postfix increment)
—y	Decrements y by 1 and uses value (prefix decrement)
y—	Uses value of y and then decrements by 1 (postfix decrement)
x=y	Assigns value of y to x. Perl also supports operator-assignment operators (+=, -=, *=, /=, %=, **=, and others)

You can also use comparison operators (such as == or <) and compound pattern operators (&&, ¦¦, and !) in arithmetic statements. They evaluate to the value 0 for false and 1 for true.

Other Operators

Perl supports a number of operators that don't fit any of the prior categories. Table 27.5 summarizes these operators.

TABLE 27.5 Other Perl Operators

Operator	Purpose
~x	Bitwise not (changes 0 bits to 1 and 1 bits to 0)
x & y	Bitwise and
x ¦ y	Bitwise or
x ^ y	Bitwise exclusive or (XOR)
x << y	Bitwise shift left (shifts x by y bits)
x >> y	Bitwise shift right (shifts x by y bits)
x . y	Concatenate y onto x
a x b	Repeats string a for b number of times

TABLE 27.5 Continued

Operator	Purpose
`x, y`	Comma operator—evaluates x and then y
`x ? y : z`	Conditional expression—if x is true, y is evaluated; otherwise, z is evaluated

Except for the comma operator and conditional expression, these operators can also be used with the assignment operator, similar to the way addition (+) can be combined with assignment (=), giving +=.

Special String Constants

Perl supports string constants that have special meaning or cannot be entered from the keyboard.

Table 27.6 shows most of the constants supported by Perl.

TABLE 27.6 Perl Special String Constants

Expression	Meaning
`\\`	The means of including a backslash
`\a`	The alert or bell character
`\b`	Backspace
`\cC`	Control character (like holding the Ctrl key down and pressing the C character)
`\e`	Escape
`\f`	Formfeed
`\n`	Newline
`\r`	Carriage return
`\t`	Tab
`\xNN`	Indicates that NN is a hexadecimal number
`\0NNN`	Indicates that NNN is an octal (base 8) number

Conditional Statements: `if/else` and `unless`

Perl offers two conditional statements, `if` and `unless`, which function opposite one another. `if` enables you to execute a block of code only if certain conditions are met so that you can control the flow of logic through your program. Conversely, `unless` performs the statements when certain conditions are not met.

The following sections explain and demonstrate how to use these conditional statements when writing scripts for Linux.

if

The syntax of the Perl `if/else` structure is as follows:

```
if (condition) {
  statement or block of code
} elsif (condition) {
  statement or block of code
} else {
  statement or block of code
}
```

condition is a statement that returns a true or false value.

Truth is defined in Perl in a way that might be unfamiliar to you, so be careful. Everything in Perl is true except 0 (the digit zero), `"0"` (the string containing the number `0`), `""` (the empty string), and an undefined value. Note that even the string `"00"` is a true value because it is not one of the four false cases.

The statement or block of code is executed if the test condition returns a true value.

For example, Listing 27.3 uses the `if/else` structure and shows conditional statements using the `eq` string comparison operator.

LISTING 27.3 **`if/elsif/else`**

```
if  ($favorite eq "chocolate") {
      print "I like chocolate too.\n";
} elsif ($favorite eq "spinach") {
      print "Oh, I don't like spinach.\n";
} else {
     print "Your favorite food is $favorite.\n";
}
```

unless

`unless` works just like `if`, only backward. `unless` performs a statement or block if a condition is false:

```
unless ($name eq "Rich")         {
  print "Go away, you're not allowed in here!\n";
}
```

NOTE

You can restate the preceding example in more natural language, like this:

```
print "Go away!\n" unless $name eq "Rich";
```

Looping

A *loop* is a way to repeat a program action multiple times. A very simple example is a countdown timer that performs a task (waiting for one second) 300 times before telling you that your egg is done boiling.

Looping constructs (also known as *control structures*) can be used to iterate a block of code as long as certain conditions apply, or while the code steps through (evaluates) a list of values, perhaps using that list as arguments.

Perl has four looping constructs: `for`, `foreach`, `while`, and `until`.

`for`

The `for` construct performs a *statement* (block of code) for a set of conditions defined as follows:

```
for (start condition; end condition; increment function) {
  statement(s)
}
```

The start condition is set at the beginning of the loop. Each time the loop is executed, the increment function is performed until the end condition is achieved. This looks much like the traditional `for/next` loop. The following code is an example of a `for` loop:

```
for ($i=1; $i<=10; $i++) {
      print "$i\n"
}
```

`foreach`

The `foreach` construct performs a statement block for each element in a list or array:

```
@names = ("alpha","bravo","charlie");
foreach $name (@names) {
  print "$name sounding off!\n";
}
```

The loop variable ($name in the example) is not merely set to the value of the array elements; it is aliased to that element. That means if you modify the loop variable, you're actually modifying the array. If no loop array is specified, the Perl default variable $_ may be used:

```
@names = ("alpha","bravo","charlie");
foreach (@names) {
  print "$_ sounding off!\n";

}
```

This syntax can be very convenient, but it can also lead to unreadable code. Give a thought to the poor person who'll be maintaining your code. (It will probably be you.)

NOTE

foreach is frequently abbreviated as for.

while

while performs a block of statements as long as a particular condition is true:

```
while ($x<10) {
     print "$x\n";
     $x++;
}
```

Remember that the condition can be anything that returns a true or false value. For example, it could be a function call:

```
while ( InvalidPassword($user, $password) )        {
        print "You've entered an invalid password. Please try again.\n";
        $password = GetPassword;
}
```

until

until is the exact opposite of the while statement. It performs a block of statements as long as a particular condition is false—or, rather, until it becomes true:

```
until (ValidPassword($user, $password))  {
  print "YSdpgm_m
Sdpgm_m
You have entered an invalid password. Please try again.\n";
Sdpgm_m
  $password = GetPassword;
}
```

`last` and `next`

You can force Perl to end a loop early by using a `last` statement. `last` is similar to the C `break` command—the loop is exited. If you decide you need to skip the remaining contents of a loop without ending the loop itself, you can use `next`, which is similar to the C continue command. Unfortunately, these statements don't work with `do ... while`.

On the other hand, you can use `redo` to jump to a loop (marked by a label) or inside the loop where called:

```
$a = 100;
while (1) {
  print "start\n";
  TEST: {
    if (($a = $a / 2) > 2) {
      print "$a\n";
      if (—$a < 2) {
        exit;
      }
      redo TEST;
    }
  }
}
```

In this simple example, the variable $a is repeatedly manipulated and tested in an endless loop. The word *start* will be printed only once.

`do ... while` and `do ... until`

The `while` and `until` loops evaluate the conditional first. The behavior is changed by applying a `do` block before the conditional. With the `do` block, the condition is evaluated last, which results in the contents of the block always executing at least once (even if the condition is false). This is similar to the C language `do ... while (conditional)` statement.

Regular Expressions

Perl's greatest strength is in text and file manipulation, which is accomplished by using the regular expression (regex) library. Regexes, which are quite different from the wildcard-handling and filename-expansion capabilities of the shell (see Chapter 15), allow complicated pattern matching and replacement to be done efficiently and easily.

For example, the following line of code replaces every occurrence of the string `bob` or the string `mary` with `fred` in a line of text:

```
$string =~ s/bob¦mary/fred/gi;
```

Without going into too many of the details, Table 27.7 explains what the preceding line says.

TABLE 27.7 Explanation of `$string =~ s/bob¦mary/fred/gi;`

Element	Explanation
`$string =~`	Performs this pattern match on the text found in the variable called `$string`.
`s`	Substitute.
`/`	Begins the text to be matched.
`bob¦mary`	Matches the text `bob` or `mary`. You should remember that it is looking for the text `mary`, not the word `mary`; that is, it will also match the text mary in the word `maryland`.
`fred`	Replaces anything that was matched with the text `fred`.
`/`	Ends replace text.
`g`	Does this substitution globally; that is, replaces the match text wherever in the string you match it (and any number of times).
`i`	The search text is not case sensitive. It matches `bob`, `Bob`, or `bOB`.
`;`	Indicates the end of the line of code.

If you are interested in the details, you can get more information using the regex (7) section of the manual.

Although replacing one string with another might seem a rather trivial task, the code required to do the same thing in another language (for example, C) is rather daunting unless supported by additional subroutines from external libraries.

Access to the Shell

Perl can perform for you any process you might ordinarily perform by typing commands to the shell through the \\ syntax. For example, the code in Listing 27.4 prints a directory listing.

LISTING 27.4 Using Backticks to Access the Shell

```
$curr_dir = 'pwd';
@listing = 'ls -al';
print "Listing for $curr_dir\n";
foreach $file (@listing) {
     print "$file";
}
```

NOTE

The \\ notation uses the backtick found above the Tab key (on most keyboards), not the single quotation mark.

You can also use the `Shell` module to access the shell. `Shell` is one of the standard modules that comes with Perl; it allows creation and use of a shell-like command line. Look at the following code for an example:

```
use Shell qw(cp);
cp ("/home/httpd/logs/access.log", "/tmp/httpd.log");
```

This code almost looks like it is importing the command-line functions directly into Perl. Although that is not really happening, you can pretend that the code is similar to a command line and use this approach in your Perl programs.

A third method of accessing the shell is via the `system` function call:

```
$rc = 0xffff & system('cp /home/httpd/logs/access.log /tmp/httpd.log');
if ($rc == 0) {
  print "system cp succeeded \n";
} else {
  print "system cp failed $rc\n";
}
```

The call can also be used with the `or die` clause:

```
system('cp /home/httpd/logs/access.log /tmp/httpd.log') == 0
  or die "system cp failed: $?"
```

However, you can't capture the output of a command executed through the `system` function.

Modules and CPAN

A great strength of the Perl community (and the Linux community) is the fact that it is an open-source community. This community support is expressed for Perl via the *Comprehensive Perl Archive Network (CPAN)*, which is a network of mirrors of a repository of Perl code.

Most of CPAN is made up of *modules*, which are reusable chunks of code that do useful things, similar to software libraries containing functions for C programmers. These modules help speed development when building Perl programs and free Perl hackers from repeatedly reinventing the wheel when building a bicycle.

Perl comes with a set of standard modules installed. Those modules should contain much of the functionality that you will initially need with Perl. If you need to use a module not installed with Ubuntu, use the CPAN module (which is one of the standard modules) to download and install other modules onto your system. At www.perl.com/CPAN, you will find the CPAN Multiplex Dispatcher, which will attempt to direct you to the CPAN site closest to you.

Typing the following command will put you into an interactive shell that gives you access to CPAN. You can type `help` at the prompt to get more information on how to use the CPAN program:

```
$ perl -MCPAN -e shell
```

After installing a module from CPAN (or writing one of your own), you can load that module into memory where you can use it with the `use` function:

```
use Time::CTime;
```

`use` looks in the directories listed in the variable `@INC` for the module. In this example, `use` looks for a directory called `Time`, which contains a file called `CTime.pm`, which in turn is assumed to contain a package called `Time::CTime`. The distribution of each module should contain documentation on using that module.

For a list of all the standard Perl modules (those that come with Perl when you install it), see `perlmodlib` in the Perl documentation. You can read this document by typing **`perldoc perlmodlib` at the command prompt.**

Code Examples

The following sections contain a few examples of things you might want to do with Perl.

Sending Mail

You can get Perl to send email in several ways. One method that you see frequently is opening a pipe to the `sendmail` command and sending data to it (shown in Listing 27.5). Another method is using the `Mail::Sendmail` module (available through CPAN), which uses socket connections directly to send mail (as shown in Listing 27.6). The latter method is faster because it does not have to launch an external process. Note that `sendmail` must be running on your system for the Perl program in Listing 27.5 to work.

LISTING 27.5 Sending Mail Using **Sendmail**

```
#!/usr/bin/perl
open (MAIL, "¦ /usr/sbin/sendmail -t"); # Use -t to protect from users
print MAIL <<EndMail;
```

```
To: you\
From: me\
Subject: A Sample Email\nSending email from Perl is easy!\n
.
EndMail
close MAIL;
```

NOTE

The @ sign in the email addresses must be escaped so that Perl does not try to evaluate an array of that name. That is, dpitts@mk.net will cause a problem, so you need to use dpitts\<indexterm startref="iddle2799" class="endofrange" significance="normal"/>:}]

The syntax used to print the mail message is called a *here document*. The syntax is as follows:

```
print <<EndText;
.....
EndText
```

The EndText value must be identical at the beginning and at the end of the block, including any whitespace.

LISTING 27.6 Sending Mail Using the `Mail::Sendmail` Module

```
#!/usr/bin/perl
use Mail::Sendmail;

%mail = ( To => 'you@there.com',
  From => 'me@here.com',
  Subject => 'A Sample Email",
  Message => "This is a very short message"
  );

sendmail(%mail) or die $Mail::Sendmail::error;

print "OK. Log says:\n", $Mail::Sendmail::log;

use Mail::Sendmail;
```

Perl ignores the comma after the last element in the hash. It is convenient to leave it there; if you want to add items to the hash, you don't need to add the comma. This is purely a style decision.

USING PERL TO INSTALL A CPAN MODULE

You can use Perl to interactively download and install a Perl module from the CPAN archives by using the -M and -e commands. Start the process by using a Perl like this:

```
# perl -MCPAN -e shell
```

After you press Enter, you will see some introductory information and be asked to choose an initial automatic or manual configuration, which is required before any download or install takes place. Type **no** and press Enter to have Perl automatically configure for the download and install process; or, if desired, simply press Enter to manually configure for downloading and installation. If you use manual configuration, you must answer a series of questions regarding paths, caching, terminal settings, program locations, and so on. Settings are saved in a directory named .cpan in current directory.

When finished, you will see the CPAN prompt:

```
cpan>
```

To have Perl examine your system and then download and install a large number of modules, use the install keyword, specify Bundle at the prompt, and then press Enter, like this:

```
cpan> install Bundle::CPAN
```

To download a desired module (using the example in Listing 27.6), use the get keyword like this:

```
cpan> get Mail::Sendmail
```

The source for the module will be downloaded into the .cpan directory. You can then build and install the module using the install keyword, like this:

```
cpan> install Mail::Sendmail
```

The entire process of retrieving, building, and installing a module can also be accomplished at the command line by using Perl's -e option, like this:

```
# perl -MCPAN   -e "install Mail::Sendmail"
```

Note also that the @ sign did not need to be escaped within single quotation marks (''). Perl does not *interpolate* (evaluate variables) within single quotation marks, but does within double quotation marks and here strings (similar to << shell operations).

Purging Logs

Many programs maintain some variety of logs. Often, much of the information in the logs is redundant or just useless. The program shown in Listing 27.7 removes all lines from a file that contain a particular word or phrase, so lines that you know are not important can be purged. For example, you might want to remove all the lines in the Apache error log that originate with your test client machine because you know those error messages were produced during testing.

LISTING 27.7 Purging Log Files

```
#!/usr/bin/perl
# Be careful using this program!
# This will remove all lines that contain a given word
# Usage:  remove <word> <file>
$word=@ARGV[0];
$file=@ARGV[1];
if ($file)  {
  # Open file for reading
  open (FILE, "$file") or die "Could not open file: $!";      @lines=<FILE>;
  close FILE;
  # Open file for writing
  open (FILE, ">$file") or die "Could not open file for writing: $!";
  for (@lines)  {
    print FILE unless /$word/;
  } # End for
  close FILE;
} else {
  print "Usage:  remove <word> <file>\n";
}  #  End if...else
```

The code uses a few idiomatic Perl expressions to keep it brief. It reads the file into an array using the `<FILE>` notation; it then writes the lines back out to the file unless they match the pattern given on the command line.

The die function kills program operation and displays an error message if the open statements fail. `$!` in the error message, as mentioned in the section on special variables, is the error message returned by the operating system. It will likely be something like '`file not found`' or '`permission denied`'.

Posting to Usenet

If some portion of your job requires periodic postings to Usenet—a FAQ listing, for example—the following Perl program can automate the process for you. In the sample code, the posted text is read in from a text file, but your input can come from anywhere.

The program shown in Listing 27.8 uses the `Net::NNTP` module, which is a standard part of the Perl distribution. You can find more documentation on the `Net::NNTP` module by typing **'`perldoc Net::NNTP`' at the command line.**

LISTING 27.8 Posting an Article to Usenet

```
#!/usr/bin/perl
# load the post data into @post
open (POST, "post.file");
@post = <POST>;
```

```
close POST;
# import the NNTP module
use Net::NNTP;
$NNTPhost = 'news';
# attempt to connect to the remote host;
# print an error message on failure
$nntp = Net::NNTP->new($NNTPhost)
  or die "Cannot contact $NNTPhost: $!";
# $nntp->debug(1);
$nntp->post()
  or die "Could not post article: $!";
# send the header of the post
$nntp->datasend("Newsgroups: news.announce\n");
$nntp->datasend("Subject: FAQ - Frequently Asked Questions\n");
$nntp->datasend("From: ADMIN <root\
$nntp->datasend("\n\n");
# for each line in the @post array, send it
for (@post)     {
  $nntp->datasend($_);
} #  End for
$nntp->quit;
```

One-Liners

One medium in which Perl excels is the one-liner. Folks go to great lengths to reduce tasks to one line of Perl code. Perl has the rather undeserved reputation of being unreadable. The fact is that you can write unreadable code in any language. Perl allows for more than one way to do something, and this leads rather naturally to people trying to find the most arcane way to do things.

Named for Randal Schwartz, a *Schwartzian Transform* is a way of sorting an array by something that is not obvious. The sort function sorts arrays alphabetically; that is pretty obvious. What if you want to sort an array of strings alphabetically by the third word? Perhaps you want something more useful, such as sorting a list of files by file size? A Schwartzian Transform creates a new list that contains the information that you want to sort by, referencing the first list. You then sort the new list and use it to figure out the order that the first list should be in. Here's a simple example that sorts a list of strings by length:

```
@sorted_by_length =
  map { $_ => [0] }             # Extract original list
  sort { $a=>[1] <=> $b=>[1] } # Sort by the transformed value
  map { [$_, length($_)] }     # Map to a list of element lengths
  @list;
```

Because each operator acts on the thing immediately to the right of it, it helps to read this from right to left (or bottom to top, the way it is written here).

The first thing that acts on the list is the map operator. It transforms the list into a hash in which the keys are the list elements and the values are the lengths of each element. This is where you put in your code that does the transformation by which you want to sort.

The next operator is the sort function, which sorts the list by the values.

Finally, the hash is transformed back into an array by extracting its keys. The array is now in the desired order.

Command-Line Processing

Perl is great at parsing the output of various programs. This is a task for which many people use tools such as awk and sed. Perl gives you a larger vocabulary for performing these tasks. The following example is very simple, but illustrates how you might use Perl to chop up some output and do something with it. In the example, Perl is used to list only those files that are larger than 10KB:

```
$ ls -la | perl -nae 'print "$F[8] is $F[4]\n" if $F[4] > 10000;'
```

The -n switch indicates that I want the Perl code run for each line of the output. The -a switch automatically splits the output into the @F array. The -e switch indicates that the Perl code is going to follow on the command line.

RELATED UBUNTU AND LINUX COMMANDS

You will use these commands and tools when using Perl with Linux:

- a2p—A filter used to translate awk scripts into Perl
- find2perl—A utility used to create Perl code from command lines using the find command
- perldoc—A Perl utility used to read Perl documentation
- s2p—A filter used to translate sed scripts into Perl
- vi—The vi (actually vim) text editor

Reference

The first place to look is in the Perl documentation and Linux man pages.

Perl, all of its documentation, and millions of lines of Perl programs are all available free on the Internet. A number of Usenet newsgroups are also devoted to Perl, as are shelves of books and a quarterly journal.

Books

Although your local bookstore might have dozens of titles on Perl, the following are some of the more highly recommended of these. You might also look at the *Camel Critiques* (Tom Christiansen; http://language.perl.com/critiques/index.html) for reviews of other available Perl books.

- *Advanced Perl Programming*, by Sriram Srinivasan, O'Reilly & Associates
- *Sams Teach Yourself Perl in 21 Days, Second Edition*, by Laura Lemay, Sams Publishing
- *Sams Teach Yourself Perl in 24 Hours, Second Edition*, by Clinton Pierce, Sams Publishing
- *Learning Perl, third edition*, by Randal L. Schwartz, Tom Phoenix, O'Reilly & Associates
- *Programming Perl, third edition*, by Larry Wall, Tom Christiansen, and Jon Orwant, O'Reilly & Associates
- *Effective Perl Programming: Writing Better Programs with Perl*, by Joseph Hall, Addison-Wesley Publishing Company
- *CGI Programming with Perl, second edition*, by Gunther Birznieks, Scott Guelich, Shishir Gundavaram, O'Reilly & Associates
- *Mastering Regular Expressions*, by Jeffrey Friedl, O'Reilly & Associates

Usenet

Check out the following on Usenet:

- comp.lang.perl.misc—Discusses various aspects of the Perl programming language. Make sure that your questions are Perl specific, not generic CGI programming questions. The regulars tend to flame folks who don't know the difference.
- comp.infosystems.www.authoring.cgi—Discusses authoring of CGI programs, so much of the discussion is Perl specific. Make sure that your questions are related to CGI programming, not just Perl. The regulars are very particular about staying on topic.

Websites

Check these sites on the World Wide Web:

- http://www.perl.com—Tom Christiansen maintains the Perl language home page. This is the place to find all sorts of information about Perl, from its history and culture to helpful tips. This is also the place to download the Perl interpreter for your system.
- http://cpan.perl.org—CPAN (Comprehensive Perl Archive Network) is the place for you to find modules and programs in Perl. If you write something in Perl that you think is particularly useful, you can make it available to the Perl community here.
- http://perldoc.perl.org/index-faq.html—Frequently Asked Questions index of common Perl queries; this site offers a handy way to quickly search for answers about Perl.
- http://learn.perl.org—One of the best places to start learning Perl online. If you master Perl, go to http://jobs.perl.org.
- www.pm.org—The Perl Mongers are local Perl users groups. There might be one in your area. The Perl advocacy site is http://www.perl.org.

- www-106.ibm.com/developerworks/linux/library/l-p101—A short tutorial about one-line Perl scripts and code.

Other

Other valuable resources not falling into any of the preceding categories are Perl-related Internet Relay Chat channels. You can usually find several channels available on an IRC server. However, the questions, discussions, and focus of similarly named channels will vary from server to server.

For example, a `#perlhelp` channel is usually for general questions about installing, using, and learning about Perl. A `#perl` channel is generally for more advanced questions, but on some servers beginner questions might be welcomed. You might also find some helpful answers on `#cgi` and `#html` channels. Browse to http://perl-begin.berlios.de/irc for a list of servers.

CHAPTER 28

Working with Python

IN THIS CHAPTER

- Python on Linux
- The Basics of Python
- Functions
- Object Orientation
- The Standard Library and the Python Package Index
- Reference

As PHP has come to dominate the world of web scripting, Python is increasingly dominating the domain of command-line scripting. Python's precise and clean syntax makes it one of the easiest languages to learn, and it allows programmers to code more quickly and spend less time maintaining their code. Although PHP is fundamentally similar to Java and Perl, Python is closer to C and Modula-3, and so it might look unfamiliar at first.

Most of the other languages have a group of developers at their cores, but Python has Guido van Rossum—creator, father, and *Benevolent Dictator for Life (BDFL)*. Although Guido spends less time working on Python now, he still essentially has the right to veto changes to the language, which has enabled it to remain consistent over the many years of its development. The end result is that, in Guido's own words, "Even if you are in fact clueless about language design, you can tell that Python is a very simple language."

This chapter constitutes a "quick-start" tutorial to Python designed to give you all the information you need to put together basic scripts and to point you toward resources that can take you further.

Two supported version of Python are out in the wild right now. Python Version 2.x (the current production release is 2.7) is the backward-compatible status quo, the version that anyone who has already used Python for more than a year or two has learned and the version most likely to have been used in already written code you discover and read. Python 3.x is the newest branch (the current production release is 3.1.2) with lots of shiny newness.

Python 3.x is not backward compatible, and most programs written in or for 2.x will need some work to run on 3.x. This should be a factor in any decision you make about using Python: Do you want to run your program on many machines, perhaps including some that have only the older version installed? Does the newer version have all the functionality you want and need, including software libraries, because not all of them have been rewritten for 3.x (like Twisted and Django)? If porting is a nontrivial task, you may want to stick with 2.x for now.

Both versions will be supported for some time, but if you expect you will be using what you write for a very long time, you probably want to try to do so in 3.x, but with a readiness to fall back to 2.x if you discover significant blocking limitations currently in 3.x. The language itself is ready for use, though, and is receiving high marks from people who have used both versions. The official Python website will help you make an informed decision; it contains clear discussion of the advantages and disadvantages of each version at http://wiki.python.org/moin/Python2orPython3.

This chapter is centered on the 2.x version of Python because it is what most people are still using in late 2010 when this was written, but we will try to note places where significant differences exist in 3.x that should be considered. If you are learning Python for the first time, you may want to start with a look at the 3.x series because it is the future and is very likely to already have everything you need. Ubuntu 10.10 comes with Python 2.6.6 installed by default with 2.7 available in the repositories, which is another reason for us to focus this chapter on the 2.x series (although the current 3.x is also available in the repositories and available for easy installation).

NOTE

This chapter is a very elementary introduction to Python. For that reason, nearly everything we cover is identical in both 2.x and 3.x. We mention the differences earlier and in a couple of notes that follow so that readers wanting to learn more will not be surprised later. Unless noted otherwise, you should find what we say in this chapter applies well to either version.

Python on Linux

Most versions of Linux and UNIX, including Mac OS X, come with Python preinstalled. This is partially for convenience because it is such a popular scripting language—and it saves having to install it later if the user wants to run a script—and partially because many vital or useful programs included in Linux distributions are written in Python. For example, the Ubuntu Software Center is a Python program.

The Python binary is installed into `/usr/bin/python` (or `/usr/bin/python3`); if you run that, you enter the Python interactive interpreter where you can type commands and have them executed immediately. Although PHP also has an interactive mode (use `php -a` to activate it), it is neither as powerful nor as flexible as Python's.

As with Perl, PHP, and other scripting languages, you can also execute Python scripts by adding a shebang line (#!) to the start of your scripts that point to `/usr/bin/python` and then setting the file to be executable.

The third way to run Python scripts is through `mod_python`, which is an Apache module that embeds the Python interpreter into the http server, allowing you to use Python to write web applications. You can install from the Ubuntu repositories.

For the purposes of this introduction, we use the interactive Python interpreter because it provides immediate feedback on commands as you type them.

We will be using the interactive interpreter for this chapter, so it is essential that you become comfortable using it. To get started, open a terminal and run the command `python`. You should see something like this, perhaps with different version numbers and dates:

```
matthew@seymour:~$ python
Python 2.6.6rc2 (r266rc2:84114, Aug 18 2010, 09:46:34)
[GCC 4.4.5 20100816 (prerelease)] on linux2
Type "help", "copyright", "credits" or "license" for more information.
>>>
```

The `>>>` is where you type your input, and you can set and get a variable like this:

```
>>> python = 'great'
>>> python
'great'
>>>
```

On line one, the variable `python` is set to the text great, and on line two that value is read back from the variable simply by typing the name of the variable you want to read. Line three shows Python printing the variable; on line four you are back at the prompt to type more commands. Python remembers all the variables you use while in the interactive interpreter, which means you can set a variable to be the value of another variable.

When you are done, press Ctrl+D to exit. At this point, all your variables and commands are forgotten by the interpreter, which is why complex Python programs are always saved in scripts!

The Basics of Python

Python is a language wholly unlike most others, and yet it is so logical that most people can pick it up quickly. You have already seen how easily you can assign strings, but in Python nearly everything is that easy—as long as you remember the syntax.

Numbers

The way Python handles numbers is more precise than some other languages. It has all the normal operators—such as `+` for addition, `-` for subtraction, `/` for division, and `*` for multiplication—but it adds `%` for modulus (division remainder), `**` for raise to the power, and // for floor division. It is also specific about which type of number is being used, as this example shows:

```
>>> a = 5
>>> b = 10
>>> a * b
50
>>> a / b
0
>>> b = 10.0
>>> a / b
0.5
>>> a // b
0.0
```

The first division returns `0` because both `a` and `b` are integers (whole numbers), so Python calculates the division as an integer, giving `0`. By converting `b` to `10.0`, Python considers it to be a floating-point number, and so the division is now calculated as a floating-point value, giving `0.5`. Even with b being a floating point, using //—floor division—rounds it down.

Using **, you can easily see how Python works with integers:

```
>>> 2 ** 30
1073741824
>>> 2 ** 31
2147483648L
```

The first statement raises 2 to the power of 30 (that is, 2... times 2 times 2 times 2...), and the second raises 2 to the power of 31. Notice how the second number has a capital *L* on the end of it—this is Python telling you that it is a long integer. The difference between long integers and normal integers is slight but important: Normal integers can be calculated using simple instructions on the CPU, whereas long integers—because they can be as big as you need them to be—need to be calculated in software and therefore are slower.

When specifying big numbers, you need not put the *L* at the end—Python figures it out for you. Furthermore, if a number starts off as a normal number and then exceeds its boundaries, Python automatically converts it to a long integer. The same is not true the other way around: If you have a long integer and then divide it by another number so that it could be stored as a normal integer, it remains a long integer:

```
>>> num = 999999999999999999999999999999999L
>>> num = num / 1000000000000000000000000000000
>>> num
999L
```

You can convert between number types using typecasting, like this:

```
>>> num = 10
>>> int(num)
10
>>> float(num)
10.0
>>> long(num)
10L
>>> floatnum = 10.0
>>> int(floatnum)
10
>>> float(floatnum)
10.0
>>> long(floatnum)
10L
```

You need not worry whether you are using integers or long integers; Python handles it all for you, so you can concentrate on getting the code right. In the 3.x series, the Python integer type automatically provides extra precision for large numbers, whereas in 2.x you would use a separate long integer type for numbers larger than the normal integer type is designed to handle.

More on Strings

Python stores strings as an immutable sequence of characters—a jargon-filled way of saying that "it is a collection of characters that, once set, cannot be changed without creating a new string." Sequences are important in Python. There are three primary types, of which strings are one, and they share some properties. Mutability makes a lot of sense when you learn about lists in the next section.

As you saw in the previous example, you can assign a value to strings in Python with just an equal sign, like this:

```
>>> mystring = 'hello';
>>> myotherstring = "goodbye";
>>> mystring
'hello'
>>> myotherstring;
'goodbye'
>>> test = "Are you really Bill O'Reilly?"
>>> test
"Are you really Bill O'Reilly?"
```

The first example encapsulates the string in single quotation marks, and the second and third in double quotation marks. However, printing the first and second strings shows them both in single quotation marks because Python does not distinguish between the two. The third example is the exception—it uses double quotation marks because the string itself contains a single quotation mark. Here, Python prints the string with double quotation marks because it knows it contains the single quotation mark.

Because the characters in a string are stored in sequence, you can index into them by specifying the character you are interested in. Like most other languages, these indexes are zero based, which means you need to ask for character `0` to get the first letter in a string. For example:

```
>>> string = "This is a test string"
>>> string
'This is a test string'
>>> string[0]
'T'
>>> string [0], string[3], string [20]
('T', 's', 'g')
```

The last line shows how, with commas, you can ask for several indexes at the same time. You could print the entire first word using this:

```
>>> string[0], string[1], string[2], string[3]
('T', 'h', 'i', 's')
```

However, for that purpose you can use a different concept: slicing. A *slice* of a sequence draws a selection of indexes. For example, you can pull out the first word like this:

```
>>> string[0:4]
'This'
```

The syntax there means "take everything from position 0 (including 0) and end at position 4 (excluding it)." So, [0:4] copies the items at indexes 0, 1, 2, and 3. You can omit either side of the indexes, and it will copy either from the start or to the end:

```
>>> string [:4]
'This'
>>> string [5:]
'is a test string'
>>> string [11:]
'est string'
```

You can also omit both numbers, and it will give you the entire sequence:

```
>>> string [:]
'This is a test string'
```

Later you will learn precisely why you would want to do that, but for now there are a number of other string intrinsics that will make your life easier. For example, you can use the + and * operators to concatenate (join) and repeat strings, like this:

```
>>> mystring = "Python"
>>> mystring * 4
'PythonPythonPythonPython'
>>> mystring = mystring + " rocks! "
>>> mystring * 2
'Python rocks! Python rocks! '
```

In addition to working with operators, Python strings come with a selection of built-in methods. You can change the case of the letters with `capitalize()` (uppercases the first letter and lowercases the rest), `lower()` (lowercases them all), `title()` (uppercases the first letter in each word), and `upper()` (uppercases them all). You can also check whether strings match certain cases with `islower()`, `istitle()`, and `isupper()`; that also extends to `isalnum()` (returns `true` if the string is letters and numbers only) and `isdigit()` (returns `true` if the string is all numbers).

This example demonstrates some of these in action:

```
>>> string
'This is a test string'
>>> string.upper()
'THIS IS A TEST STRING'
>>> string.lower()
'this is a test string'
>>> string.isalnum()
False
>>> string = string.title()
>>> string
'This Is A Test String'
```

Why did `isalnum()` return `false—our` string contains only alphanumeric characters, doesn't it? Well, no. There are spaces in there, which is what is causing the problem. More important, we were calling `upper()` and `lower()` and they were not changing the contents of the string—they just returned the new value. So, to change our string from `This is a test string` to `This Is A Test String`, we have to assign it back to the string variable.

Another really useful and kind of cool thing you can do with strings is triple quoting. This lets you easily create strings that include both double and single quoted strings, as well as strings that span more than one line, without having to escape a bunch of special characters. Here's an example:

```
>>>foo = """
```

28

```
..."foo"
...'bar'
...baz
...blippy
..."""
>>>foo
'\n"foo"\n\'bar\'\nbaz\nblippy\n'
>>>
```

Although this is intended as an introductory guide, the capability to use negative indexes with strings and slices is a pretty neat feature that deserves a mention. Here's an example:

```
>>>bar="news.google.com"
>>>bar[-1]
'm'
>>>bar[-4:]
'.com'
>>>bar[-10:-4]
'google'
>>>
```

One difference between 2.x and 3.x is the introduction of new string types and method calls. That doesn't affect what we share here, but is something to pay attention to as you work with Python.

Lists

Python's built-in list data type is a sequence, like strings. However, they are mutable, which means they can be changed. Lists are like arrays in that they hold a selection of elements in a given order. You can cycle through them, index into them, and slice them:

```
>>> mylist = ["python", "perl", "php"]
>>> mylist
['python', 'perl', 'php']
>>> mylist + ["java"]
['python', 'perl', 'php', 'java']
>>> mylist * 2
['python', 'perl', 'php', 'python', 'perl', 'php']
>>> mylist[1]
'perl'
>>> mylist[1] = "c++"
>>> mylist[1]
'c++'
>>> mylist[1:3]
['c++', 'php']
```

The brackets notation is important: You cannot use parentheses, ((and)) or braces ({ and }) for lists. Using + for lists is different from using + for numbers. Python detects you are working with a list and appends one list to another. This is known as *operator overloading*, and it is one of the reasons Python is so flexible.

Lists can be *nested*, which means you can put a list inside a list. However, this is where mutability starts to matter, and so this might sound complicated. If you recall, the definition of an immutable string sequence is that it is a collection of characters that, once set, cannot be changed without creating a new string. Lists are mutable, as opposed to immutable, which means you can change your list without creating a new list.

This becomes important because Python, by default, copies only a reference to a variable rather than the full variable. For example:

```
>>> list1 = [1, 2, 3]
>>> list2 = [4, list1, 6]
>>> list1
[1, 2, 3]
>>> list2
[4, [1, 2, 3], 6]
```

Here we have a nested list. `list2` contains 4, then `list1`, then 6. When you print the value of `list2`, you can see it also contains `list1`. Now, proceeding on from that:

```
>>> list1[1] = "Flake"
>>> list2
[4, [1, 'Flake', 3], 6]
```

In line one, we set the second element in `list1` (remember, sequences are zero based!) to be `Flake` rather than 2; then we print the contents of `list2`. As you can see, when `list1` changed, `list2` was updated, too. The reason for this is that `list2` stores a reference to `list1` as opposed to a copy of `list1`; they share the same value.

We can show that this works both ways by indexing twice into `list2`, like this:

```
>>> list2[1][1] = "Caramello"
>>> list1
[1, 'Caramello', 3]
```

The first line says, "Get the second element in `list2` (list1) and the second element of that list, and set it to be `'Caramello'`." Then `list1`'s value is printed, and you can see it has changed. This is the essence of mutability: We are changing our list without creating a new list. On the other hand, editing a string creates a new string, leaving the old one unaltered. For example:

```
>>> mystring = "hello"
```

```
>>> list3 = [1, mystring, 3]
>>> list3
[1, 'hello', 3]
>>> mystring = "world"
>>> list3
[1, 'hello', 3]
```

Of course, this raises the question of how you copy without references when references are the default. The answer, for lists, is that you use the [:] slice, which we looked at earlier. This slices from the first element to the last, inclusive, essentially copying it without references. Here is how that looks:

```
>>> list4 = ["a", "b", "c"]
>>> list5 = list4[:]
>>> list4 = list4 + ["d"]
>>> list5
['a', 'b', 'c']
>>> list4
['a', 'b', 'c', 'd']
```

Lists have their own collections of built-in methods, such as sort(), append(), and pop(). The latter two add and remove single elements from the end of the list, with pop() also returning the removed element. For example:

```
>>> list5 = ["nick", "paul", "julian", "graham"]
>>> list5.sort()
>>> list5
['graham', 'julian', 'nick', 'paul']
>>> list5.pop()
'paul'
>>> list5
['graham', 'julian', 'nick']

>>> list5.append("Rebecca")
```

In addition, one interesting method of strings returns a list: split(). This takes a character to split by and then gives you a list in which each element is a chunk from the string. For example:

```
>>> string = "This is a test string";
>>> string.split(" ")
['This', 'is', 'a', 'test', 'string']
```

Lists are used extensively in Python, although this is slowly changing as the language matures. The way lists are compared and sorted has changed in 3.x, so be sure to check the latest documentation when you attempt to perform these tasks.

Dictionaries

Unlike lists, dictionaries are collections with no fixed order. Instead, they have a *key* (the name of the element) and a *value* (the content of the element), and Python places them wherever it needs to for maximum performance. When defining dictionaries, you need to use braces ({ }) and colons (:). You start with an opening brace and then give each element a key and a value, separated by a colon, like this:

```
>>> mydict = { "perl" : "a language", "php" : "another language" }
>>> mydict
{'php': 'another language', 'perl': 'a language'}
```

This example has two elements, with keys `perl` and `php`. However, when the dictionary is printed, we find that `php` comes before `perl`—Python hasn't respected the order in which we entered them. We can index into a dictionary using the normal code:

```
>>> mydict["perl"]
'a language'
```

However, because a dictionary has no fixed sequence, we cannot take a slice, or index by position.

Like lists, dictionaries are mutable and can also be nested; however, unlike lists, you cannot merge two dictionaries by using +. This is because dictionary elements are located using the key. Therefore, having two elements with the same key would cause a clash. Instead, you should use the `update()` method, which merges two arrays by overwriting clashing keys.

You can also use the `keys()` method to return a list of all the keys in a dictionary.

There are subtle differences in how dictionaries are used in 3.x, such as the need to make list calls to produce all values at once so they may be printed. Again, be sure to check the latest documentation as you move ahead, because there are several of these changes in functionality with some tools now behaving differently or even disappearing and other new dictionary tools being added. Some of those features have been backported; for example, Python 2.7 has support for ordered dictionaries, backported from Python 3.1 (see http://docs.python.org/dev/whatsnew/2.7.html#pep-0372).

Conditionals and Looping

So far, we have just been looking at data types, which should show you how powerful Python's data types are. However, you cannot write complex programs without conditional statements and loops.

Python has most of the standard conditional checks, such as > (greater than), <= (less than or equal to), and == (equal), but it also adds some new ones, such as `in`. For example, we can use `in` to check whether a string or a list contains a given character/element:

```
>>> mystring = "J Random Hacker"
```

```
>>> "r" in mystring
True
>>> "Hacker" in mystring
True
>>> "hacker" in mystring
False
```

The last example demonstrates how it is case sensitive. We can use the operator for lists, too:

```
>>> mylist = ["soldier", "sailor", "tinker", "spy"]
>>> "tailor" in mylist
False
```

Other comparisons on these complex data types are done item by item:

```
>>> list1 = ["alpha", "beta", "gamma"]
>>> list2 = ["alpha", "beta", "delta"]
>>> list1 > list2
True
```

`list1`'s first element (`alpha`) is compared against `list2`'s first element (`alpha`) and, because they are equal, the next element is checked. That is equal also, so the third element is checked, which is different. The *g* in `gamma` comes after the *d* in `delta` in the alphabet, so `gamma` is considered greater than `delta` and `list1` is considered greater than `list2`.

Loops come in two types, and both are equally flexible. For example, the `for` loop can iterate through letters in a string or elements in a list:

```
>>> string = "Hello, Python!"
>>> for s in string: print s,
...
H e l l o ,   P y t h o n !
```

The `for` loop takes each letter in a string and assigns it to s. This then is printed to the screen using the `print` command, but note the comma at the end; this tells Python not to insert a line break after each letter. The "..." is there because Python allows you to enter more code in the loop; you need to press Enter again here to have the loop execute.

The same construct can be used for lists:

```
>>> mylist = ["andi", "rasmus", "zeev"]
>>> for p in mylist: print p
...
andi
rasmus
zeev
```

Without the comma after the `print` statement, each item is printed on its own line.

The other loop type is the `while` loop, and it looks similar:

```
>> while 1: print "This will loop forever!"
...
This will loop forever!
This will loop forever!
This will loop forever!
This will loop forever!
This will loop forever!
(etc)
Traceback (most recent call last):
  File "<stdin>", line 1, in ?
KeyboardInterrupt
>>>
```

That is an infinite loop (it will carry on printing that text forever), so you need to press Ctrl+C to interrupt it and regain control.

If you want to use multiline loops, you need to get ready to use your Tab key: Python handles loop blocks by recording the level of indent used. Some people find this odious; others admire it for forcing clean coding on users. Most of us, though, just get on with programming!

For example:

```
>>> i = 0
>>> while i < 3:
...     j = 0
...     while j < 3:
...             print "Pos: " + str(i) + "," + str(j) + ")"
...             j += 1
...     i += 1
...
Pos: (0,0)
Pos: (0,1)
Pos: (0,2)
Pos: (1,0)
Pos: (1,1)
Pos: (1,2)
Pos: (2,0)
Pos: (2,1)
Pos: (2,2)
```

You can control loops using the `break` and `continue` keywords. `break` exits the loop and continues processing immediately afterward, and `continue` jumps to the next loop iteration.

Again we find many subtle changes in 3.x. Most conditionals and looping work the same, but since we mention it in this section we should note that print is no longer a statement in 3.x and is now a function call. That provides a nice segue to our discussion of functions.

Functions

Other languages—such as PHP—read and process an entire file before executing it, which means you can call a function before it is defined because the compiler reads the definition of the function before it tries to call it. Python is different: If the function definition has not been reached by the time you try to call it, you get an error. The reason behind this behavior is that Python actually creates an object for your function, and that in turns means two things. First, you can define the same function several times in a script and have the script pick the right one at runtime. Second, you can assign the function to another name just by using =.

Function definition starts with `def`, then the function name, then parentheses and a list of parameters, and then a colon. The contents of a function need to be indented at least one level beyond the definition. So, using function assignment and dynamic declaration, you can write a script that prints the right greeting in a roundabout manner:

```
>>> def hello_english(Name):
...     print "Hello, " + Name + "!"
...
>>> def hello_hungarian(Name):
...     print "Szia, " + Name + "!"
...
>>> hello = hello_hungarian
>>> hello("Paul")
Szia, Paul!
>>> hello = hello_english
>>> hello("Paul")
```

Notice that function definitions include no type information. Functions are typeless, like we said. The upside of this is that you can write one function to do several things:

```
>>> def concat(First, Second):
...     return First + Second
...
>>> concat(["python"], ["perl"])
['python', 'perl']
>>> concat("Hello, ", "world!")
'Hello, world!'
```

That demonstrates how the `return` statement sends a value back to the caller, but also how a function can do one thing with lists and another thing with strings. The magic here is being accomplished by the objects. We write a function that tells two objects to add themselves together, and the objects intrinsically know how to do that. If they don't—if, perhaps, the user passes in a string and an integer—Python catches the error for us. However, it is this hands off, "let the objects sort themselves out" attitude that makes functions so flexible. Our concat() function could conceivably concatenate strings, lists, or *zonks*—a data type someone created herself that allows adding. The point is that we do not limit what our function can do—tacky as it might sound, the only limit is your imagination!

Object Orientation

After having read this far, you should not be surprised to hear that Python's object orientation is flexible and likely to surprise you if you have been using C-like languages for several years.

The best way to learn Python `object-oriented programming (OOP)` is to just do it. So, here is a basic script that defines a class, creates an object of that class, and calls a function:

```
class Dog(object):
    def bark(self):
        print "Woof!"

fluffy = Dog()
fluffy.bark()
```

Defining a class starts, predictably, with the `class` keyword followed by the name of the class you are defining and a colon. The contents of that class need to be indented one level so that Python knows where it stops. Note that the `object` inside parentheses is there for object inheritance, which is discussed later. For now, the least you need to know is that if your new class is not based on an existing class, you should put `object` inside parentheses as shown in the previous code.

Functions inside classes work in much the same way as normal functions do (although they are usually called *methods*); the main difference is that they should all take at least one parameter, usually called `self`. This parameter is filled with the name of the object the function was called on, and you need to use it explicitly.

Creating an instance of a class is done by assignment. You do not need any `new` keyword, as in some other languages—providing the parentheses makes the creation known. Calling a function of that object is done using a period, the name of the class to call, with any parameters being passed inside parentheses.

Class and Object Variables

Each object has its own set of functions and variables, and you can manipulate those variables independently of objects of the same type. In addition, some class variables are set to a default value for all classes and can be manipulated globally.

This script demonstrates two objects of the dog class being created, each with its own name:

```
class Dog(object):
     name = "Lassie"
     def bark(self):
        print self.name + " says 'Woof!'"
     def set_name(self, name):
        self.name = name
fluffy = Dog()
fluffy.bark()
poppy = Dog()
poppy.set_name("Poppy")
poppy.bark()
```

That outputs the following:

```
Lassie says 'Woof!'
Poppy says 'Woof!'
```

There, each dog starts with the name `Lassie`, but it gets customized. Keep in mind that Python assigns by reference by default, meaning each object has a reference to the class's `name` variable, and as we assign that with the `set_name()` method, that reference is lost. This means that any references we do not change can be manipulated globally. Thus, if we change a class's variable, it also changes in all instances of that class that have not set their own value for that variable. For example:

```
class Dog(object):
    name = "Lassie"
    color = "brown"
fluffy = Dog()
poppy = Dog()
print fluffy.color
Dog.color = "black"
print poppy.color
fluffy.color = "yellow"
print fluffy.color
print poppy.color
```

So, the default color of dogs is brown—both the `fluffy` and `poppy` `Dog` objects start off as brown. Then, using `Dog.color`, we set the default color to be black, and because neither of the two objects has set its own color value, they are updated to be black. The third-to-last line uses `poppy.color` to set a custom color value for the `poppy` object—`poppy` becomes yellow, whereas `fluffy` and the `dog` class in general remain black.

Constructors and Destructors

To help you automate the creation and deletion of objects, you can easily override two default methods: `__init__` and `__del__`. These are the methods called by Python when a class is being instantiated and freed, known as the *constructor* and *destructor*, respectively.

Having a custom constructor is great for when you need to accept a set of parameters for each object being created. For example, you might want each dog to have its own name on creation, and you could implement that with this code:

```
class Dog(object):
    def __init__(self, name):
        self.name = name
fluffy = Dog("Fluffy")
print fluffy.name
```

If you do not provide a name parameter when creating the `dog` object, Python reports an error and stops. You can, of course, ask for as many constructor parameters as you want, although it is usually better to ask only for the ones you need and have other functions to fill in the rest.

On the other side of things is the destructor method, which allows you to have more control over what happens when an object is destroyed. Using the two, we can show the life cycle of an object by printing messages when it is created and deleted:

```
class dog(object):
    def __init__(self, name):
        self.name = name
        print self.name + " is alive!"
    def __del__(self):
        print self.name + " is no more!"
fluffy = Dog("Fluffy")
```

The destructor is there to give you the chance to free up resources allocated to the object, or perhaps log something to a file. Note that although it is possible to override the __del__ method, it is a very dangerous idea because it is not guaranteed that __del__ methods are called for objects that still exist when the interpreter exits. The official Python documentation explains this well at http://docs.python.org/reference/datamodel.html#object.__del__.

Class Inheritance

Python allows you to reuse your code by inheriting one class from one or more others. For example, lions, tigers, and bears are all mammals and so share a number of similar properties. In that scenario, you would not want to have to copy and paste functions between them; it would be smarter (and easier!) to have a mammal class that defines all the shared functionality and then inherit each animal from that.

Consider the following code:

```
class Car(object):
    color = "black"
    speed = 0
    def accelerate_to(self, speed):
        self.speed = speed
    def set_color(self, color):
        self.color = color
mycar = Car()
print mycar.color
```

That creates a `Car` class with a default color and also provides a `set_color()` function so people can change their own colors. Now, what do you drive to work? Is it a car? Sure it is, but chances are it is a Ford, or a Dodge, or a Jeep, or some other make—you don't get cars without a make. On the other hand, you do not want to have to define a class `Ford`, give it the methods `accelerate_to()`, `set_color()`, and however many other methods a basic car has and then do the same thing for `Ferrari`, `Nissan`, and so on.

The solution is to use inheritance: Define a `car` class that contains all the shared functions and variables of all the makes and then inherit from that. In Python, you do this by putting the name of the class from which to inherit inside parentheses in the class declaration, like this:

```
class Car(object):
    color = "black"
    speed = 0
    def accelerate_to(self, speed):
        self.speed = speed
    def set_color(self, color):
        self.color = color
class Ford(Car): pass
class Nissan(Car): pass
mycar = Ford()
print mycar.color
```

The `pass` directive is an empty statement—it means our class contains nothing new. However, because the Ford and Nissan classes inherit from the `car` class, they get `color`, `speed`, `accelerate_to()`, and `set_color()` provided by their parent class. Note that we do not need `object` after the class names for `Ford` and `Nissan` because they are inherited from an existing class: `car`.

By default, Python gives you all the methods the parent class has, but you can override that by providing new implementations for the classes that need them. For example:

```
class Modelt(car):
    def set_color(self, color):
        print "Sorry, Model Ts only come in black!"
```

```
myford Ford()
Ford.set_color("green")
mycar = Modelt()
mycar.set_color("green")
```

The first car is created as a Ford, so `set_color()` will work fine because it uses the method from the `car` class. However, the second car is created as a Model T, which has its own `set_color()` method, so the call will fail.

This provides an interesting scenario: What do you do if you have overridden a method and yet want to call the parent's method also? If, for example, changing the color of a Model T was allowed but just cost extra, we would want to print a message saying, "You owe $50 more," but then change the color. To do this, we need to use the class object from which our current class is inherited—`Car` in this case. Here's an example:

```
class Modelt(Car):
    def set_color(self, color):
        print "You owe $50 more"
        Car.set_color(self, color)

mycar = Modelt()
mycar.set_color("green")
print mycar.color
```

That prints the message and then changes the color of the car.

The Standard Library and the Python Package Index

A default Python install includes many modules (blocks of code) that enable you to interact with the operating system, open and manipulate files, parse command-line options, perform data hashing and encryption, and much more. This is one of the reasons most commonly cited when people are asked why they like Python so much—it comes stocked to the gills with functionality you can take advantage of immediately. In fact, the number of modules included in the Standard Library is so high that entire books have been written about them.

28

For unofficial scripts and add-ons for Python, the recommended starting place is called the Python Package Index (PyPI) at http://pypi.python.org/pypi. There you can find well over 10,000 public scripts and code examples for everything from mathematics to games.

Reference

- www.python.org—The Python website is packed with information and updated regularly. This should be your first stop, if only to read the latest Python news.www.jython.org—Python also has an excellent Java-based interpreter to allow it to run on other platforms. If you prefer Microsoft .NET, try http://www.ironpython.com.

- www.pythonline.com—Guido van Rossum borrowed the name for his language from *Monty Python's Flying Circus*, and as a result many Python code examples use oblique *Monty Python* references (spam and eggs are quite common, for example). A visit to the official *Monty Python* site to hone your Python knowledge is highly recommended!
- www.zope.org—The home page of the Zope Content Management System (CMS), it's one of the most popular CMSes around and, more important, written entirely in Python.
- If you want a book, we recommend starting with *Learning Python, by Mark Lutz* (O'Reilly), and for advanced work move to *Programming Python*, also by Mark Lutz (O'Reilly).

CHAPTER 29

Writing PHP Scripts

IN THIS CHAPTER

- Introduction to PHP
- Basic Functions
- Handling HTML Forms
- Databases
- Reference

This chapter introduces you to the world of PHP programming, from the point of view of using it as a web scripting language and as a command-line tool. PHP originally stood for *personal home page* because it was a collection of Perl scripts designed to ease the creation of guest books, message boards, and other interactive scripts commonly found on home pages. However, since those early days, it has received two major updates (PHP 3 and PHP 4), plus a substantial revision in PHP 5, which is the version bundled with Ubuntu.

Part of the success of PHP has been its powerful integration with databases—its earliest uses nearly always took advantage of a database back end. In PHP 5, two big new data storage mechanisms were introduced: SQLite, which is a powerful and local database system, and SimpleXML, which is an *application programming interface (API)* designed to make XML parsing and querying easy. As you will see over time, the PHP developers did a great job: Both SQLite and SimpleXML are easy to learn and use.

NOTE

Many packages for PHP are available from the Ubuntu repositories. The basic package is just called `php5`, but you might also want to add extensions such as `php5-ldap`, `php5-mysql`, or `php5-pgsql`.

Introduction to PHP

In terms of the way it looks, PHP is a cross between Java and Perl, having taken the best aspects of both and merged them successfully into one language. The Java parts include a powerful object-orientation system, the capability to throw program exceptions, and the general style of writing that both languages borrowed from C. Borrowed from Perl is the "it should just work" mentality where ease of use is favored over strictness. As a result, you will find a lot of "there is more than one way to do it" in PHP. This also means that it is possible to accomplish tasks in ways that are less than ideal or without consideration for good security. Many criticize PHP for this, but for simple tasks or if written carefully, it can be a pretty good language and is easy to understand and use, especially for quick website creation.

Entering and Exiting PHP Mode

Unlike PHPs predecessors, you embed your PHP code inside your HTML as opposed to the other way around. Before PHP, many websites had standard HTML pages for most of their content, linking to Perl CGI pages to do back-end processing when needed. With PHP, all your pages are capable of processing and containing HTML. This is a huge factor in PHPs popularity.

Each .php file is processed by PHP that looks for code to execute. PHP considers all the text it finds to be HTML until it finds one of four things:

- <?php
- <?
- <%
- <script language="php">

The first option is the preferred method of entering PHP mode because it is guaranteed to work.

When in PHP mode, you can exit it by using ?> (for <?php and <?); %> for <%) or </script> (for <script language="php">). This code example demonstrates entering and exiting PHP mode:

```
In HTML mode
<?php
  echo "In PHP mode";
?>
In HTML mode
In <?php echo "PHP"; ?> mode
```

Variables

All variables in PHP start with a dollar sign (`$`). Unlike many other languages, PHP does not have different types of variable for integers, floating-point numbers, arrays, or Booleans. They all start with a `$`, and all are interchangeable. As a result, PHP is a weakly typed language, which means you do not declare a variable as containing a specific type of data; you just use it however you want to.

Save the code in Listing 29.1 into the script `ubuntu1.php`.

LISTING 29.1 Testing Types in PHP

```
<?php
  $i = 10;
  $j = "10";
  $k = "Hello, world";
  echo $i + $j;
  echo $i + $k;
?>
```

To run that script, bring up a console and browse to where you saved it. Then type this command:

```
$ php ubuntu1.php
```

If PHP is installed correctly, you should see the output `2010`, which is really two things. The 20 is the result of 10 + 10 (`$i` plus `$j`), and the 10 is the result of adding 10 to the text string `Hello, world`. Neither of those operations are really straightforward. Whereas `$i` is set to the number 10, `$j` is actually set to be the text value `"10"`, which is not the same thing. Adding 10 to 10 gives 20, as you would imagine, but adding 10 to `"10"` (the string) forces PHP to convert `$j` to an integer on-the-fly before adding it.

Running `$i + $k` adds another string to a number, but this time the string is `Hello, world` and not just a number inside a string. PHP still tries to convert it, though, and converting any non-numeric string into a number converts it to 0. So, the second `echo` statement ends up saying `$i + 0`.

As you should have guessed by now, calling `echo` outputs values to the screen. Right now, that prints directly to your console, but internally PHP has a complex output mechanism that enables you to print to a console, send text through Apache to a web browser, send data over a network, and more.

Now that you have seen how PHP handles variables of different types, it is important that you understand the selection of types available to you, as shown in Table 29.1.

TABLE 29.1 PHP Variable Types

Type	*Stores*
`integer`	Whole numbers; for example, 1, 9, or 324809873
`float`	Fractional numbers; for example, 1.1, 9.09, or 3.141592654
`string`	Characters; for example, "a", "sfdgh", or "Ubuntu Unleashed"
`boolean`	True or false
`array`	Several variables of any type
`resource`	Any external data

The first four can be thought of as simple variables, and the last three as complex variables. Arrays are simply collections of variables. You might have an array of numbers (the ages of all the children in a class); an array of strings (the names of all Wimbledon tennis champions); or even an array of arrays, known as a *multidimensional array*. Arrays are covered in more depth in the next section because they are unique in the way in which they are defined.

Objects are used to define and manipulate a set of variables that belong to a unique entity. Each object has its own personal set of variables, as well as functions that operate on those variables. Objects are commonly used to model real-world things. You might define an object that represents a TV, with variables such as `$CurrentChannel` (probably an integer), `$SupportsHiDef` (a Boolean), and so on.

Of all the complex variables, the easiest to grasp are resources. PHP has many extensions available to it that allow you to connect to databases, manipulate graphics, or even make calls to Java programs. Because they are all external systems, they need to have types of data unique to them that PHP cannot represent using any of the six other data types. So, PHP stores their custom data types in resources—data types that are meaningless to PHP but can be used by the external libraries that created them.

Arrays

Arrays are one of our favorite parts of PHP because the syntax is smart and easy to read and yet manages to be as powerful as you could want. There are four pieces of jargon you need to know to understand arrays:

- An array is made up of many *elements*.
- Each element has a *key* that defines its place in the array. An array can have only one element with a given key.
- Each element also has a *value*, which is the data associated with the key.
- Each array has a *cursor*, which points to the current key.

The first three are used regularly; the last one less often. The array cursor is covered later in this chapter in the section "Basic Functions," but we will look at the other three now. With PHP, your keys can be virtually anything: integers, strings, objects, or other arrays. You can even mix and match the keys so that one key is an array; another is a string, and so on. The one exception to all this is floating-point numbers: You cannot use floating-point numbers as keys in your arrays.

There are two ways of adding values to an array: with the `[]` operator, which is unique to arrays; and with the `array()` pseudo-function. You should use `[]` when you want to add items to an existing array and use `array()` to create a new array.

To sum all this up in code, Listing 29.2 shows a script that creates an array without specifying keys, adds various items to it both without keys and with keys of varying types, does a bit of printing, and then clears the array.

LISTING 29.2 Manipulating Arrays

```
<?php
  $myarr = array(1, 2, 3, 4);

  $myarr[4] = "Hello";
  $myarr[] = "World!";
  $myarr["elephant"] = "Wombat";
  $myarr["foo"] = array(5, 6, 7, 8);

  echo $myarr[2];
  echo $myarr["elephant"];
  echo $myarr["foo"][1];

  $myarr = array();
?>
```

The initial array is created with four elements, to which we assign the values 1, 2, 3, and 4. Because no keys are specified, PHP automatically assigns keys for us starting at 0 and counting upward—giving keys 0, 1, 2, and 3. Then we add a new element with the `[]` operator, specifying 4 as the key and `"Hello"` as the value. Next, `[]` is used again to add an element with the value `"World!"` and no key and then again to add an element with the key "elephant" and the value `"wombat"`. The line after that demonstrates using a string key with an array value—an array inside an array (a multidimensional array).

The next three lines demonstrate reading back from an array, first using a numeric key, then using a string key, and then using a string key and a numeric key. Remember, the `"foo"` element is an array in itself, so that third reading line retrieves the array and then prints the second element (arrays start at 0, remember). The last line blanks the array by simply using `array()` with no parameters, which creates an array with elements and assigns it to `$myarr`.

The following is an alternative way of using `array()` that allows you to specify keys along with their values:

```
$myarr = array("key1" => "value1", "key2" => "value2",
7 => "foo", 15 => "bar");
```

Which method you choose really depends on whether you want specific keys or want PHP to pick them for you.

Constants

Constants are frequently used in functions that require specific values to be passed in. For example, a popular function is `extract()`, which takes all the values in an array and places them into variables in their own right. You can choose to change the name of the variables as they are extracted using the second parameter—send it a 0 and it overwrites variables with the same names as those being extracted, send it a 1 and it skips variables with the same names, send it 5 and it prefixes variables only if they exist already, and so on. Of course, no one wants to have to remember a lot of numbers for each function, so you can instead use `EXTR_OVERWRITE` for 0, `EXTR_SKIP` for 1, `EXTR_PREFIX_IF_EXISTS` for 5, and so on, which is much easier.

You can create constants of your own by using the `define()` function. Unlike variables, constants do not start with a dollar sign. Code to define a constant looks like this:

```
<?php
  define("NUM_SQUIRRELS", 10);
  define("PLAYER_NAME", "Jim");
  define("NUM_SQUIRRELS_2", NUM_SQUIRRELS);
  echo NUM_SQUIRRELS_2;
?>
```

That script demonstrates how you can set constants to numbers, strings, or even the value of other constants, although that doesn't really get used much!

References

Using the equal sign (=) copies the value from one variable to another so they both have their own copy of the value. Another option here is to use references, which is where a variable does not have a value of its own; instead, it points to another variable. This enables you to share values and have variables mutually update themselves.

To copy by reference, use the & symbol, as follows:

```
<?php
  $a = 10;
  $b = &$a;
  echo $a . "\n";
  echo $b . "\n";
```

```
  $a = 20;
  echo $a . "\n";
  echo $b . "\n";

  $b = 30;
  echo $a . "\n";
  echo $b . "\n";
?>
```

If you run that script, you will see that updating `$a` also updates `$b`, but also that updating `$b` updates `$a`, too.

Comments

Adding short comments to your code, is recommended and usually a requirement in larger software houses. In PHP you have three options for commenting style: `//`, `/* */`, and `#`. The first option (two slashes) instructs PHP to ignore everything until the end of the line. The second (a slash and an asterisk) instructs PHP to ignore everything until it reaches `*/`. The last (a hash symbol) works like `//` and is included because it is common among shell scripting languages.

This code example demonstrates the difference between `//` and `/* */`:

```
<?php
  echo "This is printed!";
  // echo "This is not printed";
  echo "This is printed!";
  /* echo "This is not printed";
  echo "This is not printed either"; */
?>
```

It is generally preferred to use `//` because it is a known quantity. On the other hand, it is easy to introduce coding errors with `/* */` by losing track of where a comment starts and ends.

NOTE

Contrary to popular belief, having comments in your PHP script has almost no effect on the speed at which the script executes. What little speed difference exists is wholly removed if you use a code cache.

Escape Sequences

Some characters cannot be typed, and yet you will almost certainly want to use some of them from time to time. For example, you might want to use an ASCII character for new line, but you can't type it. Instead, you need to use an escape sequence: `\n`. Similarly, you can print a carriage return character with `\r`. It's important to know both of these because, on the Windows platform, you need to use `\r\n` to get a new line. If you do not plan to run your scripts anywhere else, you need not worry about this!

Going back to the first script we wrote, recall that it printed 2010 because we added 10 + 10 and then 10 + 0. We can rewrite that using escape sequences, like this:

```
<?php
  $i = 10;
  $j = "10";
  $k = "Hello, world";
  echo $i + $j;
  echo "\n";
  echo $i + $k;
  echo "\n";
?>
```

This time PHP prints a new line after each of the numbers, making it obvious that the output is 20 and 10 rather than 2010. Note that the escape sequences must be used in double quotation marks because they will not work in single quotation marks.

Three common escape sequences are `\\`, which means "ignore the backslash"; `\"`, which means "ignore the double quote"; and `\'`, which means "ignore the single quote." This is important when strings include quotation marks inside them. If we had a string such as `"are you really Bill O'Reilly?"`, which has a single quotation mark in, this code would not work:

```
<?php
  echo 'Are you really Bill O'Reilly?';
?>
```

PHP would see the opening quotation mark, read all the way up to the *O* in O'Reilly, and then see the quotation mark following the *O* as being the end of the string. The `Reilly?` part would appear to be a fragment of text and would cause an error. You have two options here: You can either surround the string in double quotation marks or escape the single quotation mark with `\'`.

If you choose the escaping route, it will look like this:

```
echo 'Are you really Bill O\'Reilly?';
```

Although they are a clean solution for small text strings, be careful with overusing escape sequences. HTML is particularly full of quotation marks, and escaping them can get messy:

```
$mystring = "<img src=\"foo.png\" alt=\"My picture\"
width=\"100\" height=\"200\" />";
```

In that situation, you are better off using single quotation marks to surround the text simply because it is a great deal easier on the eye!

Variable Substitution

PHP allows you to define strings using three methods: single quotation marks, double quotation marks, or heredoc notation. Heredoc isn't discussed here because it's fairly rare compared to the other two methods, but single quotation marks and double quotation marks work identically, with one minor exception—variable substitution.

Consider the following code:

```
<?php
  $age = 25
  echo "You are ";
  echo $age;
?>
```

That is a particularly clumsy way to print a variable as part of a string. Fortunately, if you put a variable inside a string, PHP performs *variable substitution*, replacing the variable with its value. That means we can rewrite the code like this:

```
<?php
  $age = 25
  echo "You are $age";
?>
```

The output is the same. The difference between single quotation marks and double quotation marks is that single-quoted strings do not have their variables substituted. Here's an example:

```
<?php
  $age = 25
  echo "You are $age";
  echo 'You are $age';
?>
```

The first `echo` prints `"You are 25"`, but the second one prints `"You are $age"`.

Operators

Now that we have data values to work with, we need some operators to use, too. We have already used + to add variables together, but many others in PHP handle arithmetic, comparison, assignment, and other operators. *Operator* is just a fancy word for something that performs an operation, such as addition or subtraction. However, *operand* might be new to you. Consider this operation:

```
$a = $b + c;
```

In this operation, = and + are operators, and `$a`, `$b`, and `$c` are operands. Along with +, you will also already know – (subtract), * (multiply), and / (divide), but Table 29.2 provides some more.

TABLE 29.2 PHP Operators

<table>
<tr><th>Operator</th><th>What It Does</th></tr>
<tr><td>=</td><td>Assigns the right operand to the left operand.</td></tr>
<tr><td>==</td><td>Returns true if the left operand is equal to the right operand.</td></tr>
<tr><td>!=</td><td>Returns true if the left operand is not equal to the right operand.</td></tr>
<tr><td>===</td><td>Returns true if the left operand is identical to the right operand. This is not the same as ==.</td></tr>
<tr><td>!==</td><td>Returns true if the left operand is not identical to the right operand. This is not the same as !=.</td></tr>
<tr><td><</td><td>Returns true if the left operand is smaller than the right operand.</td></tr>
<tr><td>></td><td>Returns true if the left operand is greater than the right operand.</td></tr>
<tr><td><=</td><td>Returns true if the left operand is equal to or smaller than the right operand.</td></tr>
<tr><td>&&</td><td>Returns true if both the left operand and the right operand are true.</td></tr>
<tr><td>||</td><td>Returns true if either the left operand or the right operand is true.</td></tr>
<tr><td>++</td><td>Increments the operand by one.</td></tr>
<tr><td>—</td><td>Decrements the operand by one.</td></tr>
<tr><td>+=</td><td>Increments the left operand by the right operand.</td></tr>
<tr><td>-=</td><td>Decrements the left operand by the right operand.</td></tr>
<tr><td>.</td><td>Concatenates the left operand and the right operand (joins them together).</td></tr>
<tr><td>%</td><td>Divides the left operand by the right operand and returns the remainder.</td></tr>
<tr><td>|</td><td>Performs a bitwise OR operation. It returns a number with bits that are set in either the left operand or the right operand.</td></tr>
<tr><td>&</td><td>Performs a bitwise AND operation. It returns a number with bits that are set both in the left operand and the right operand.</td></tr>
</table>

At least 10 other operators are not listed; to be fair, however, you're unlikely to use them. Even some of the ones in this list are used infrequently—bitwise AND, for example. Having said that, the bitwise OR operator is used regularly because it allows you to combine values.

Here is a code example demonstrating some of the operators:

```
<?php
  $i = 100;
  $i++; // $i is now 101
```

```
  $i—; // $i is now 100 again
  $i += 10; // $i is 110
  $i = $i / 2; // $i is 55
  $j = $i; // both $j and $i are 55
  $i = $j % 11; // $i is 0
?>
```

The last line uses modulus, which takes some people a little bit of effort to understand. The result of `$i` % 11 is 0 because `$i` is set to 55 and modulus works by dividing the left operand (55) by the right operand (11) and returning the remainder. 55 divides by 11 exactly 5 times, and so has the remainder 0.

The concatenation operator, a period, sounds scarier than it is: It just joins strings together. For example:

```
<?php
echo "Hello, " . "world!";
echo "Hello, world!" . "\n";
?>
```

There are two "special" operators in PHP that are not covered here and yet are used frequently. Before we look at them, though, it's important that you see how the comparison operators (such as <, <=, and `!=`) are used inside conditional statements.

Conditional Statements

In a *conditional statement* you instruct PHP to take different actions depending on the outcome of a test. For example, you might want PHP to check whether a variable is greater than 10 and, if so, print a message. This is all done with the `if` statement, which looks like this:

```
if (your condition) {
  // action to take if condition is true
} else {
  // optional action to take otherwise
}
```

The `your condition` part can be filled with any number of conditions you want PHP to evaluate, and this is where the comparison operators come into their own. For example:

```
if ($i > 10) {
  echo "11 or higher";
} else {
```

29

```
  echo "10 or lower";
}
```

PHP looks at the condition and compares `$i` to 10. If it is greater than 10, it replaces the whole operation with `1`; otherwise, it replaces it with `0`. So, if `$i` is 20, the result looks like this:

```
if (1) {
  echo "11 or higher";
} else {
  echo "10 or lower";
}
```

In conditional statements, any number other than 0 is considered to be equivalent to the Boolean value `true`, so `if (1)` always evaluates to `true`. There is a similar case for strings—if your string has any characters in, it evaluates to `true`, with empty strings evaluating to `false`. This is important because you can then use that `1` in another condition through `&&` or || operators. For example, if you want to check whether `$i` is greater than 10 but less than 40, you could write this:

```
if ($i > 10 && $i < 40) {
  echo "11 or higher";
} else {
  echo "10 or lower";
}
```

If we presume that `$i` is set to `50`, the first condition (`$i, 10`) is replaced with `1` and the second condition (`$i < 40`) is replaced with `0`. Those two numbers are then used by the `&&` operator, which requires both the left and right operands to be *true*. Whereas `1` is equivalent to `true`, `0` is not, so the `&&` operand is replaced with `0` and the condition fails.

=, ==, ===, and similar operators are easily confused and often the source of programming errors. The first, a single equal sign, assigns the value of the right operand to the left operand. However, all too often you see code like this:

```
if ($i = 10) {
  echo "The variable is equal to 10!";
} else {
  echo "The variable is not equal to 10";
}
```

That is incorrect. Rather than checking whether `$i` is equal to 10, it assigns `10` to `$i` and returns true. What is needed is ==, which compares two values for equality. In PHP, this is extended so that there is also === (three equal signs), which checks whether two values are identical—more than just equal.

The difference is slight but important: If you have a variable with the string value `"10"` and compare it against the number value of 10, they are equal. Thus, PHP converts the type and checks the numbers. However, they are not identical. To be considered identical, the two variables must be equal (that is, have the same value) and be of the same data type (that is, both are strings, both are integers, and so on).

NOTE

It is common practice to put function calls in conditional statements rather than direct comparisons. For example:

```
if (do_something()) {
```

If the `do_something()` function returns `true` (or something equivalent to `true`, such as a nonzero number), the conditional statement evaluates to `true`.

Special Operators

The ternary operator and the execution operator work differently from those we have seen so far. The ternary operator is rarely used in PHP, thankfully, because it is really just a condensed conditional statement. Presumably it arose through someone needing to make a code occupy as little space as possible because it certainly does not make PHP code any easier to read!

The ternary operator works like this:

```
$age_description = ($age < 18) ? "child" : "adult";
```

Without explanation, that code is essentially meaningless; however, it expands into the following five lines of code:

```
if ($age < 18) {
  $age_description = "child";
} else {
  $age_description = "adult";
}
```

The ternary operator is so named because it has three operands: a condition to check (`$age < 18` in the previous code), a result if the condition is true ("`child`"), and a result if the condition is false ("`adult`"). Although we hope you never have to use the ternary operator, it is at least important to know how it works in case you stumble across it.

The other special operator is the execution operator, which is the backtick symbol, `. The position of the backtick key varies depending on your keyboard, but it is likely to be just to the left of the 1 key (above Tab). The execution operator executes the program inside the back ticks, returning any text the program outputs. For example:

```
<?php
  $i = 'ls -l';
  echo $i;
?>
```

That executes the `ls` program, passing in `-l` (a lowercase *L*) to get the long format, and stores all its output in `$i`. You can make the command as long or as complex as you like, including piping to other programs. You can also use PHP variables inside the command.

Switching

Having multiple `if` statements in one place is ugly, slow, and prone to errors. Consider the code in Listing 29.3.

LISTING 29.3 How Multiple Conditional Statements Lead to Ugly Code

```
<?php
  $cat_age = 3;

  if ($cat_age == 1) {
    echo "Cat age is 1";
  } else {
    if ($cat_age == 2) {
      echo "Cat age is 2";
    } else {
      if ($cat_age == 3) {
        echo "Cat age is 3";
      } else {
        if ($cat_age == 4) {
          echo "Cat age is 4";
        } else {
          echo "Cat age is unknown";
        }
      }
    }
  }
?>
```

Even though it certainly works, it is a poor solution to the problem. Much better is a `switch/case` block, which transforms the previous code into what's shown in Listing 29.4.

LISTING 29.4 Using a switch/case Block

```
<?php
  $cat_age = 3;

  switch ($cat_age) {
    case 1:
      echo "Cat age is 1";
      break;
```

```
    case 2:
      echo "Cat age is 2";
      break;
    case 3:
      echo "Cat age is 3";
      break;
    case 4:
      echo "Cat age is 4";
      break;
    default:
      echo "Cat age is unknown";
  }
?>
```

Although it is only slightly shorter, it is a great deal more readable and much easier to maintain. A `switch/case` group is made up of a `switch()` statement in which you provide the variable you want to check, followed by numerous `case` statements. Notice the `break` statement at the end of each `case`. Without that, PHP would execute each `case` statement beneath the one it matches. Calling `break` causes PHP to exit the `switch/case`. Notice also that there is a `default case` at the end that catches everything that has no matching case.

It is important that you do not use `case default`: but merely `default:`. Also, it is the last `case` label, so it has no need for a `break` statement because PHP exits the `switch/case` block there anyway.

Loops

PHP has four ways you can execute a block of code multiple times: `while`, `for`, `foreach`, and `do...while`. Of the four, only `do...while` sees little use; the others are popular and you will certainly encounter them in other people's scripts.

The most basic loop is the `while` loop, which executes a block of code for as long as a given condition is true. So, we can write an infinite loop—a block of code that continues forever—with this PHP:

```
<?php
  $i = 10;
  while ($i >= 10) {
    $i += 1;
    echo $i;
  }
?>
```

The loop block checks whether `$i` is greater or equal to 10 and, if that condition is true, adds 1 to `$i` and prints it. Then it goes back to the loop condition again. Because `$i` starts at 10 and we only ever add numbers to it, that loop continues forever. With two small changes, we can make the loop count down from 10 to 0:

```
<?php
  $i = 10;
  while ($i >= 0) {
    $i -= 1;
    echo $i;
  }
?>
```

So, this time we check whether `$i` is greater than or equal to 0 and subtract 1 from it with each loop iteration. `while` loops are typically used when you are unsure of how many times the code needs to loop because `while` keeps looping until an external factor stops it.

With a `for` loop, you specify precise limits on its operation by giving it a declaration, a condition, and an action. That is, you specify one or more variables that should be set when the loop first runs (the *declaration*), you set the circumstances that will cause the loop to terminate (the *condition*), and you tell PHP what it should change with each loop iteration (the *action*). That last part is what really sets a `for` loop apart from a `while` loop: You usually tell PHP to change the condition variable with each iteration.

We can rewrite the script that counts down from 10 to 0 using a `for` loop:

```
<?php
  for($i = 10; $i >= 0; $i -= 1) {
    echo $i;
  }
?>
```

This time we do not need to specify the initial value for `$i` outside the loop, and neither do we need to change `$i` inside the loop—it is all part of the `for` statement. The actual amount of code is really the same, but for this purpose the `for` loop is arguably tidier and therefore easier to read. With the `while` loop, the `$i` variable was declared outside the loop and so was not explicitly attached to the loop.

The third loop type is `foreach`, which is specifically for arrays and objects, although it is rarely used for anything other than arrays. A `foreach` loop iterates through each element in an array (or each variable in an object), optionally providing both the key name and the value.

In its simplest form, a `foreach` loop looks like this:

```
<?php
  foreach($myarr as $value) {
    echo $value;
  }
?>
```

This loops through the `$myarr` array we created earlier, placing each value in the `$value` variable. We can modify that so we get the keys as well as the values from the array, like this:

```
<?php
  foreach($myarr as $key => $value) {
    echo "$key is set to $value\n";
  }
?>
```

As you can guess, this time the array keys go in `$key` and the array values go in `$value`. One important characteristic of the `foreach` loop is that it goes from the start of the array to the end and then stops—and by *start* we mean the first item to be added rather than the lowest index number. This script shows this behavior:

```
<?php
  $array = array(6 => "Hello", 4 => "World",
                 2 => "Wom", 0 => "Bat");
  foreach($array as $key => $value) {
    echo "$key is set to $value\n";
  }
?>
```

If you try this script, you will see that `foreach` prints the array in the original order of 6, 4, 2, 0 rather than the numeric order of 0, 2, 4, 6.

The `do...while` loop works like the `while` loop, with the exception that the condition appears at the end of the code block. This small syntactical difference means a lot, though, because a `do...while` loop is always executed at least once. Consider this script:

```
<?php
  $i = 10;
  do {
    $i -= 1;
    echo $i;
  } while ($i < 10);
?>
```

Without running the script, what do you think it will do? One possibility is that it will do nothing; `$i` is set to 10, and the condition states that the code must loop only while `$i` is less than 10. However, a `do...while` loop always executes once, so what happens is that `$i` is set to 10 and PHP enters the loop, decrements `$i`, prints it, and then checks the condition for the first time. At this point, `$i` is indeed less than 10, so the code loops, `$i` is decremented again, the condition is rechecked, `$i` is decremented again, and so on. This is in fact an infinite loop, and so should be avoided!

If you ever want to exit a loop before it has finished, you can use the same `break` statement, which we used earlier to exit a `switch/case` block. This becomes more interesting if you find yourself with *nested* loops—loops inside of loops. This is a common situation to be in. For example, you might want to loop through all the rows in a chessboard and, for each row, loop through each column. Calling `break` exits only one loop or `switch/case`, but you can use `break 2` to exit two loops or `switch/cases`, or `break 3` to exit three, and so on.

Including Other Files

Unless you are restricting yourself to the simplest programming ventures, you will want to share code among your scripts at some point. The most basic need for this is to have a standard header and footer for your website, with only the body content changing. However, you might also find yourself with a small set of custom functions you use frequently, and it would be an incredibly bad move to simply copy and paste the functions into each of the scripts that use them.

The most common way to include other files is with the `include` keyword. Save this script as `include1.php`:

```
<?php
  for($i = 10; $i >= 0; $i -= 1) {
    include "echo_i.php";
  }
?>
```

```
Then save this script as echo_i.php:
<?php
  echo $i;
?>
```

If you run `include1.php`, PHP loops from 10 to 0 and includes `echo_i.php` each time. For its part, `echo_i.php` just prints the value of `$i`, which is a crazy way of performing an otherwise simple operation, but it does demonstrate how included files share data. Note that the `include` keyword in `include1.php` is inside a PHP block, but we reopen PHP inside `echo_i.php`. This is important because PHP exits PHP mode for each new file, so you always have a consistent entry point.

Basic Functions

PHP has a vast number of built-in functions that enable you to manipulate strings, connect to databases, and more. There is not room here to cover even 10 percent of the functions; for more detailed coverage of functions, check the "Reference" section at the end of this chapter.

Strings

Several important functions are used for working with strings, and there are many more less frequently used ones for which there is not enough space here. We are going to look at the most important here, ordered by difficulty—easiest first!

The easiest function is `strlen()`, which takes a string as its parameter and returns the number of characters in there, like this:

```
<?php
  $ourstring = "  The Quick Brown Box Jumped Over The Lazy Dog  ";
  echo strlen($ourstring);
?>
```

We will be using that same string in subsequent examples to save space. If you execute that script, it outputs 48 because 48 characters are in the string. Note the 2 spaces on either side of the text, which pad the 44-character phrase up to 48 characters.

We can fix that padding with the `trim()` function, which takes a string to trim and returns it with all the whitespace removed from either side. This is a commonly used function because all too often you encounter strings that have an extra new line at the end or a space at the beginning. This cleans it up perfectly.

Using `trim()`, we can turn our 48-character string into a 44-character string (the same thing, without the extra spaces), like this:

```
echo trim($ourstring);
```

Keep in mind that `trim()` returns the trimmed string, so that outputs "`The Quick Brown Box Jumped Over The Lazy Dog`". We can modify that so `trim()` passes its return value to `strlen()` so that the code trims it and then outputs its trimmed length:

```
echo strlen(trim($ourstring));
```

PHP always executes the innermost functions first, so the previous code takes `$ourstring`, passes it through `trim()`, uses the return value of `trim()` as the parameter for `strlen()`, and prints it.

Of course, everyone knows that boxes do not jump over dogs—the usual phrase is "the quick brown fox." Fortunately, there is a function to fix that problem: `str_replace()`. Note that it has an underscore in it; PHP is inconsistent on this matter, so you really need to memorize the function name.

The `str_replace()` function takes three parameters: the text to search for, the text to replace it with, and the string you want to work with. When working with search functions, people often talk about *needles* and *haystacks*—in this situation, the first parameter is the needle (the thing to find), and the third parameter is the haystack (what you are searching through).

29

So, we can fix our error and correct *box* to *fox* with this code:

```
echo str_replace("Box", "Fox", $ourstring);
```

There are two little addendums to make here. First, note that we have specified "`Box`" as opposed to "`box`" because that is how it appears in the text. The `str_replace()` function is a *case-sensitive* function, which means it does not consider "`Box`" to be the same as "box". If you want to do a non-case-sensitive search and replace, you can use the `stri_replace()` function, which works in the same way.

The second addendum is that, because we are actually changing only one character (*B* to *F*), we need not use a function at all. PHP enables you to read (and change) individual characters of a string by specifying the character position inside braces ({ and }). As with arrays, strings are zero based, which means in the `$ourstring` variable `$ourstring{0}` is *T*, `$ourstring{1}` is *h*, `$ourstring{2}` is *e*, and so on. We could use this instead of `str_replace()`, like this:

```
<?php
  $ourstring = "  The Quick Brown Box Jumped Over The Lazy Dog  ";
  $ourstring{18} = "F";
  echo $ourstring;
?>
```

You can extract part of a string using the `substr()` function, which takes a string as its first parameter, a start position as its second parameter, and an optional length as its third parameter. Optional parameters are common in PHP. If you do not provide them, PHP assumes a default value. In this case, if you specify only the first two parameters, PHP copies from the start position to the end of the string. If you specify the third parameter, PHP copies that many characters from the start.

We can write a simple script to print "`Lazy Dog`" by setting the start position to 38, which, remembering that PHP starts counting string positions from 0, copies from the 39th character to the end of the string:

```
echo substr($ourstring, 38);
```

If we just want to print the word "`Lazy`," we need to use the optional third parameter to specify the length as 4, like this:

```
echo substr($ourstring, 38, 4);
```

The `substr()` function can also be used with negative second and third parameters. If you specify just parameter one and two and provide a negative number for parameter two, `substr()` counts backward from the end of the string. So, rather than specifying 38 for the second parameter, we can use –10, so it takes the last 10 characters from the string. Using a negative second parameter and positive third parameter counts backward from the end string and then uses a forward length. We can print "`Lazy`" by counting 10 characters back from the end and then taking the next four characters forward:

```
echo substr($ourstring, -10, 4);
```

Finally, we can use a negative third parameter, too, which also counts back from the end of the string. For example, using "`-4`" as the third parameter means to take everything except the last four characters. Confused yet? This code example should make it clear:

```
echo substr($ourstring, -19, -11);
```

That counts 19 characters backward from the end of the string (which places it at the *O* in Over) and then copies everything from there until 11 characters before the end of the string. That prints "`Over The`". The same thing could be written using –19 and 8, or even 29 and 8—there is more than one way to do it!

Moving on, the strpos() function returns the position of a particular substring inside a string; however, it is most commonly used to answer the question, "Does this string contain a specific substring?" You need to pass it two parameters: a haystack and a needle (yes, that's a different order from `str_replace()`!).

In its most basic use, `strpos()` can find the first instance of "`Box`" in our phrase, like this:

```
echo strpos($ourstring, "Box");
```

This outputs 18 because that is where the *B* in Box starts. If `strpos()` cannot find the substring in the parent string, it returns `false` rather than the position. Much more helpful, though, is the ability to check whether a string contains a substring; a first attempt to check whether our string contains the word *The* might look like this:

```
<?php
  $ourstring = "The Quick Brown Box Jumped Over The Lazy Dog";
  if (strpos($ourstring, "The")) {
    echo "Found 'The'!\n";
  } else {
    echo "'The' not found!\n";
  }
?>
```

Note that we have temporarily taken out the leading and trailing whitespace from `$ourstring` and we are using the return value of `strpos()` for our conditional statement. This reads, "If the string is found, then print a message; if not, print another message." Or does it?

Run the script, and you will see it print the "`not found`" message. The reason for this is that `strpos()` returns `false` if the substring is not found and otherwise returns the position where it starts. If you recall, any nonzero number equates to `true` in PHP, which means that `0` equates to `false`. With that in mind, what is the string index of the first *The* in our phrase? Because PHP's strings are zero based and we no longer have the spaces on either side of the string, the *The* is at position 0, which our conditional statement evaluates to `false—hence`, the problem.

The solution here is to check for identicality. We know that `0` and `false` are equal, but they are not identical because `0` is an integer, whereas `false` is a Boolean. So, we need to rewrite the conditional statement to see whether the return value from `strpos()` is identical to `false`. If it is, the substring was not found:

```
<?php
  $ourstring = "The Quick Brown Box Jumped Over The Lazy Dog";
  if (strpos($ourstring, "The") !== false) {
```

```
    echo "Found 'The'!\n";
  } else {
    echo "'The' not found!\n";
  }
?>
```

Arrays

Working with arrays is no easy task, but PHP makes it easier by providing a selection of functions that can sort, shuffle, intersect, and filter them. As with other functions, there is only space here to choose a selection; this is by no means a definitive reference to PHP's array functions.

The easiest function to use is `array_unique()`, which takes an array as its only parameter and returns the same array with all duplicate values removed. Also in the realm of "so easy you do not need a code example" is the `shuffle()` function, which takes an array as its parameter and randomizes the order of its elements. Note that `shuffle()` does not return the randomized array; it uses your parameter as a reference and scrambles it directly. The last too-easy-to-demonstrate function is `in_array()`, which takes a value as its first parameter and an array as its second and returns `true` if the value is in the array.

With those out of the way, we can focus on the more interesting functions, two of which are `array_keys()` and `array_values()`. They both take an array as their only parameter and return a new array made up of the keys in the array or the values of the array, respectively. The `array_values()` function is an easy way to create a new array of the same data, just without the keys. This is often used if you have numbered your array keys, deleted several elements, and want to reorder it.

The `array_keys()` function creates a new array where the values are the keys from the old array, like this:

```
<?php
  $myarr = array("foo" => "red", "bar" => "blue", "baz" => "green");
  $mykeys = array_keys($myarr);
  foreach($mykeys as $key => $value) {
    echo "$key = $value\n";
  }
?>
```

That prints "`0 = foo`", "`1 = bar`", and "`2 = baz`".

Several functions are used specifically for array sorting, but only two get much use: `asort()` and `ksort()`, the first of which sorts the array by its values and the second of which sorts the array by its keys. Given the array `$myarr` from the previous example, sorting by the values would produce an array with elements in the order bar/blue, baz/green, and foo/red. Sorting by key would give the elements in the order bar/blue, baz/green, and foo/red. As with the `shuffle()` function, both `asort()` and `ksort()` do their work *in place*, meaning they return no value, directly altering the parameter you pass in. For interest's sake, you can also use `arsort()` and `krsort()` for reverse value sorting and reverse key sorting, respectively.

This code example reverse sorts the array by value and then prints it as before:

```
<?php
  $myarr = array("foo" => "red", "bar" => "blue", "baz" => "green");
  arsort($myarr);
  foreach($myarr as $key => $value) {
    echo "$key = $value\n";
  }
?>
```

Previously when discussing constants, we mentioned the `extract()` function that converts an array into individual variables; now it is time to start using it for real. You need to provide three variables: the array you want to extract, how you want the variables prefixed, and the prefix you want used. Technically, the last two parameters are optional, but practically you should always use them to properly namespace your variables and keep them organized.

The second parameter must be one of the following:

- `EXTR_OVERWRITE`—If the variable exists already, overwrites it.
- `EXTR_SKIP`—If the variable exists already, skips it and moves on to the next variable.
- `EXTR_PREFIX_SAME`—If the variable exists already, uses the prefix specified in the third parameter.
- `EXTR_PREFIX_ALL`—Prefixes all variables with the prefix in the third parameter, regardless of whether it exists already.
- `EXTR_PREFIX_INVALID`—Uses a prefix only if the variable name would be invalid (for example, starting with a number).
- `EXTR_IF_EXISTS`—Extracts only variables that already exist. We have never seen this used.

You can also, optionally, use the bitwise `OR` operator, |, to add in `EXTR_REFS` to have `extract()` use references for the extracted variables. In general use, `EXTR_PREFIX_ALL` is preferred because it guarantees name spacing. `EXTR_REFS` is required only if you need to be able to change the variables and have those changes reflected in the array.

This next script uses `extract()` to convert `$myarr` into individual variables, `$arr_foo`, `$arr_bar`, and `$arr_baz`:

```
<?php
  $myarr = array("foo" => "red", "bar" => "blue", "baz" => "green");
  extract($myarr, EXTR_PREFIX_ALL, 'arr');
?>
```

Note that the array keys are "foo", "bar", and "baz" and that the prefix is "arr", but that the final variables will be $arr_foo, $arr_bar, and $arr_baz. PHP inserts an underscore between the prefix and array key.

Files

As you will have learned from elsewhere in the book, the UNIX philosophy is that everything is a file. In PHP, this is also the case: A selection of basic file functions is suitable for opening and manipulating files, but those same functions can also be used for opening and manipulating network sockets. We cover both here.

Two basic read and write functions for files make performing these basic operations easy. They are file_get_contents(), which takes a filename as its only parameter and returns the file's contents as a string, and file_put_contents(), which takes a filename as its first parameter and the data to write as its second parameter.

Using these two, we can write a script that reads all the text from one file, filea.txt, and writes it to another, fileb.txt:

```
<?php
  $text = file_get_contents("filea.txt");
  file_put_contents("fileb.txt", $text);
?>
```

Because PHP enables us to treat network sockets like files, we can also use file_get_contents() to read text from a website, like this:

```
<?php
  $text = file_get_contents("http://www.slashdot.org");
  file_put_contents("fileb.txt", $text);
?>
```

The problem with using file_get_contents() is that it loads the whole file into memory at once; that's not practical if you have large files or even smaller files being accessed by many users. An alternative is to load the file piece by piece, which can be accomplished through the following five functions: fopen(), fclose(), fread(), fwrite(), and feof(). The *f* in those function names stands for *file*, so they open, close, read from, and write to files and sockets. The last function, feof(), returns true if the end of the file has been reached.

The fopen() function takes a bit of learning to use properly, but on the surface it looks straightforward. Its first parameter is the filename you want to open, which is easy enough. However, the second parameter is where you specify how you want to work with the file, and you should specify one of the following:

- r—Read-only; it overwrites the file.
- r+—Reading and writing; it overwrites the file.
- w—Write-only; it erases the existing contents and overwrites the file.
- w+—Reading and writing; it erases the existing content and overwrites the file.

- a—Write-only; it appends to the file.
- a+—Reading and writing; it appends to the file.
- x—Write-only, but only if the file does not exist.
- a+—Reading and writing, but only if the file does not exist.

Optionally, you can also add b (for example, a+b or rb) to switch to binary mode. This is recommended if you want your scripts and the files they write to work smoothly on other platforms.

When you call fopen(), you should store the return value. It is a resource known as a *file handle,* which the other file functions all need to do their jobs. The fread() function, for example, takes the file handle as its first parameter and the number of bytes to read as its second, returning the content in its return value. The fclose() function takes the file handle as its only parameter and frees up the file.

So, we can write a simple loop to open a file, read it piece by piece, print the pieces, and then close the handle:

```
<?php
  $file = fopen("filea.txt", "rb");
  while (!feof($file)) {
    $content = fread($file, 1024);
    echo $content;
  }
  fclose($file);
?>
```

That only leaves the fwrite() function, which takes the file handle as its first parameter and the string to write as its second. You can also provide an integer as the third parameter, specifying the number of bytes you want to write of the string, but if you exclude this, fwrite() writes the entire string.

If you recall, you can use a as the second parameter to fopen() to append data to a file. So, we can combine that with fwrite() to have a script that adds a line of text to a file each time it is executed:

```
<?php
  $file = fopen("filea.txt", "ab");
  fwrite($file, "Testing\n");
  fclose($file);
?>
```

To make that script a little more exciting, we can stir in a new function, filesize(), that takes a filename (not a file handle, but an actual filename string) as its only parameter and returns the file's size in bytes. Using that new function brings the script to this:

```
<?php
  $file = fopen("filea.txt", "ab");
  fwrite($file, "The filesize was" . filesize("filea.txt") . "\n");
  fclose($file);
?>
```

Although PHP automatically cleans up file handles for you, it is still best to use `fclose()` yourself so you are always in control.

Miscellaneous

Several functions do not fall under the other categories and so are covered here. The first one is `isset()`, which takes one or more variables as its parameters and returns `true` if they have been set. It is important to note that a variable with a value set to something that would be evaluated to `false`—such as `0` or an empty string—still returns `true` from `isset()` because it does not check the value of the variable. It merely checks that it is set; hence, the name.

The `unset()` function also takes one or more variables as its parameters, simply deleting the variable and freeing up the memory. With these two, we can write a script that checks for the existence of a variable and, if it exists, deletes it (see Listing 29.5).

LISTING 29.5 Setting and Unsetting Variables

```
<?php
  $name = "Ildiko";
  if (isset($name)) {
    echo "Name was set to $name\n";
    unset($name);
  } else {
    echo "Name was not set";
  }

  if (isset($name)) {
    echo "Name was set to $name\n";
    unset($name);
  } else {
    echo "Name was not set";
  }
?>
```

That script runs the same `isset()` check twice, but it `unset()`s the variable after the first check. As such, it prints "`Name was set to Ildiko`" and then "`Name was not set`".

Perhaps the most frequently used function in PHP is `exit`, although purists will tell you that it is in fact a language construct rather than a function. `exit` terminates the processing of the script as soon as it is executed, meaning subsequent lines of code are not executed. That is really all there is to it; it barely deserves an example, but here is one just to make sure:

```
<?php
  exit;
  echo "Exit is a language construct!\n";
?>
```

That script prints nothing because the `exit` comes before the `echo`.

One function we can guarantee you will use a lot is `var_dump()`, which dumps out information about a variable, including its value, to the screen. This is invaluable for arrays because it prints every value and, if one or more of the elements is an array, it prints all the elements from those, and so on. To use this function, just pass it a variable as its only parameter:

```
<?php
  $drones = array("Graham", "Julian", "Nick", "Paul");
  var_dump($drones);
?>
```

The output from that script looks like this:

```
array(4) {
  [0]=>
  string(6) "Graham"
  [1]=>
  string(6) "Julian"
  [2]=>
  string(4) "Nick"
  [3]=>
  string(4) "Paul"
}
```

The `var_dump()` function sees a lot of use as a basic debugging technique because it is the easiest way to print variable data to the screen to verify it.

Finally, we briefly discuss regular expressions; with the emphasis on *briefly* because regular expression syntax is covered elsewhere in this book and the only unique thing relevant to PHP are the functions you will use to run the expressions. You have the choice of either Perl-Compatible Regular Expressions (PCRE) or POSIX Extended regular expressions, but there really is little to choose between them in terms of functionality offered. For this chapter, we use the PCRE expressions because, to the best of our knowledge, they see more use by other PHP programmers.

The main PCRE functions are `preg_match()`, `preg_match_all()`, `preg_replace()`, and `preg_split()`. We will start with `preg_match()` because it provides the most basic functionality by returning `true` if one string matches a regular expression. The first parameter to preg_match() is the regular expression you want to search for, and the second is the string to match. So, if we wanted to check whether a string had the word *Best*, *Test*, *rest*, *zest*, or any other word containing *est* preceded by any letter of either case, we could use this PHP code:

```
$result = preg_match("/[A-Za-z]est/", "This is a test");
```

Because the test string matches the expression, $result is set to 1 (true). If you change the string to a nonmatching result, you get 0 as the return value.

The next function is preg_match_all(), which gives you an array of all the matches it found. However, to be most useful, it takes the array to fill with matches as a by-reference parameter and saves its return value for the number of matches that were found.

We suggest you use preg_match_all() and var_dump() to get a feel for how the function works. This example is a good place to start:

```
<?php
  $string = "This is the best test in the west";
  $result = preg_match_all("/[A-Za-z]est/", $string, $matches);
  var_dump($matches);
?>
```

That outputs the following:

```
array(1) {
  [0]=>
  array(3) {
    [0]=>
    string(4) "best"
    [1]=>
    string(4) "test"
    [2]=>
    string(4) "west"
  }
}
```

If you notice, the $matches array is actually multidimensional in that it contains one element, which itself is an array containing all the matches to our regular expression. The reason for this is because our expression has no *subexpressions*, meaning no independent matches using parentheses. If we had subexpressions, each would have its own element in the $matches array containing its own array of matches.

Moving on, preg_replace() is used to change all substrings that match a regular expression into something else. The basic manner of using this is quite easy: You search for something with a regular expression and provide a replacement for it. However, a more useful variant is *backreferencing*, using the match as part of the replacement. For our example, we will imagine you have written a tutorial on PHP but want to process the text so each reference to a function is followed by a link to the PHP manual.

PHP manual page URLs take the form www.php.net/<somefunc>—for example, www.php.net/preg_replace. The string we need to match is a function name, which is a string of alphabetic characters, potentially also mixed with numbers and underscores and terminated with two parentheses, (). As a replacement, we will use the match we found, surrounded in HTML emphasis tags (<em></em>), and then with a link to the relevant PHP manual page. Here is how that looks in code:

```
<?php
  $regex = "/([A-Za-z0-9_]*)\(\)/";
  $replace = "<em>$1</em> (<a href=\"http://www.php.net/$1\">manual</A>)";
  $haystack = "File_get_contents()is easier than using fopen().";
  $result = preg_replace($regex, $replace, $haystack);
  echo $result;
?>
```

The $1 is our backreference; it will be substituted with the results from the first subexpression. The way we have written the regular expression is very exact. The [A-Za-z0-9_]* part, which matches the function name, is marked as a subexpression. After that is \(\), which means the exact symbols (and), not the regular expression meanings of them, which means that $1 in the replacement will contain fopen rather than fopen(), which is how it should be. Of course, anything that is not backreferenced in the replacement is removed, so we have to put the () after the first $1 (not in the hyperlink) to repair the function name.

After all that work, the output is perfect:

```
<em>File_get_contents()</em> (<a href="http://www.php.net/
file_get_contents">manual</A>) is easier than using <em>fopen()
</em> (<a href="http://www.php.net/fopen">manual</A>).
```

Handling HTML Forms

Given that PHPs primary role is handling web pages, you might wonder why this section has been left so late in the chapter. It is because handling HTML forms is so central to PHP that it is essentially automatic.

Consider this form:

```
<form method="POST" action="thispage.php">
User ID: <input type="text" name="UserID" /><br />
Password: <input type="password" name="Password" /><br />
<input type="submit" />
</form>
```

When a visitor clicks Submit, thispage.php is called again and this time PHP has the variables available to it inside the $_REQUEST array. Given that script, if the user enters 12345 and frosties as her user ID and password, PHP provides you with

`$_REQUEST['UserID']` set to `12345` and `$_REQUEST['Password']` set to `frosties`. Note that it is important that you use HTTP post unless you specifically want `GET`. `POST` enables you to send a great deal more data and stops people from tampering with your URL to try to find holes in your script.

Is that it? Well, almost. That tells you how to retrieve user data, but you should be sure to sanitize it so users do not try to sneak HTML or JavaScript into your database as something you think is innocuous. PHP gives you the `strip_tags()` function for this purpose. It takes a string and returns the same string with all HTML tags removed.

Databases

The ease with which PHP can be used to create dynamic, database-driven websites is for the key reason to use it for many people. The stock build of PHP comes with support for MySQL, PostgreSQL, SQLite, Oracle, Microsoft SQL Server, ODBC, plus several other popular databases, so you are sure to find something to work with your data.

If you want to, you can learn all the individual functions for connecting to and manipulating each database PHP supports, but a much smarter, or at least easier, idea is to use `PEAR::DB`. `PEAR::DB` is an abstraction layer over the databases that PHP supports, which means you write your code once, and—with the smallest of changes—it will work on every database server.

PEAR is the script repository for PHP and contains numerous tools and prewritten solutions for common problems. `PEAR::DB` is perhaps the most popular part of the PEAR project, but it is worth checking out the PEAR site to see whether anything else catches your eye.

To get basic use out of `PEAR::DB`, you need to learn how to connect to a database, run a SQL query, and work with the results. This is not a SQL tutorial, so we have assumed you are already familiar with the language. For the sake of this tutorial, we have also assumed you are working with a database called `dentists` and a table called `patients` that contains the following fields:

- **ID**—The primary key, auto-incrementing integer for storing a number unique to each patient
- **Name**—A varchar(255) field for storing a patient name
- **Age**—Integer
- **Sex**—1 for male, 2 for female
- **Occupation**—A varchar(255) field for storing a patient occupation

Also for the sake of this tutorial, we will use a database server on IP address 10.0.0.1, running MySQL, with username ubuntu and password `alm65z`. You will need to replace these details with your own—use `localhost for` connecting to the local server.

The first step to using PEAR::DB is to include the standard PEAR::DB file, DB.php. Your PHP will be configured to look inside the PEAR directory for include() files, so you do not need to provide any directory information.

PEAR::DB is object oriented, and you specify your connection details at the same time as you create the initial DB object. This is done using a URL-like system that specifies the database server type, username, password, server, and database name all in one. After you have specified the database server here, everything else is abstracted, meaning you only need to change the connection line to port your code to another database server.

This first script connects to our server and prints a status message (see Listing 29.6).

LISTING 29.6 Connecting to a Database Through PEAR::DB

```
<?php
  include("DB.php");
  $dsn = "mysql://ubuntu:alm65z@10.0.0.1/dentists";
  $conn = DB::connect($dsn);
  if (DB::isError($conn)) {
    echo $conn->getMessage() . "\n";
  } else {
    echo "Connected successfully!\n";
  }
?>
```

You should be able to see how the connection string breaks down. It is server name first, then a username and password separated by a colon, then an @ symbol followed by the IP address to which to connect, and then a slash and the database name. Notice how the call to connect is DB::connect(), which calls PEAR::DB directly and returns a database connection object for storage in $conn. The variable name $dsn was used for the connection details because it is a common acronym standing for data source name.

If DB::connect() successfully connects to a server, it returns a database object we can use to run SQL queries. If not, we get an error returned that we can query using functions such as getMessage(). In the previous script, we print the error message if we fail to connect, but we also just print a message if we succeed. Next, we will change that so we run an SQL query if we have a connection.

Running SQL queries is done through the query() function of our database connection, passing in the SQL we want to execute. This then returns a query result that can be used to get the data. This query result can be thought of as a multidimensional array because it has many rows of data, each with many columns of attributes. This is extracted using the fetchInto() function, which loops through the query result converting one row of data into an array that it sends back as its return value. You need to pass in two parameters to fetchInto() specifying where the data should be stored and how you want it stored.

Unless you have unusual needs, specifying `DB_FETCHMODE_ASSOC` for the second parameter is a smart move.

Listing 29.7 shows the new script.

LISTING 29.7 Running a Query Through PEAR::DB

```
<?php
  include("DB.php");
  $dsn = "mysql://ubuntu:alm65z@10.0.0.1/dentists";
  $conn = DB::connect($dsn);
  if (DB::isError($conn)) {
    echo $conn->getMessage() . "\n";
  } else {
    echo "Connected successfully!\n";
    $result = $conn->query("SELECT ID, Name FROM patients;");
    while ($result->fetchInto($row, DB_FETCHMODE_ASSOC)) {
      extract($row, EXTR_PREFIX_ALL, 'pat');
      echo "$pat_ID is $pat_Name\n";
    }
  }
?>
```

The first half is identical to the previous script, with all the new action happening if we get a successful connection.

Going along with the saying "never leave to PHP what you can clean up yourself," the current script has problems. We do not clean up the query result, and we do not close the database connection. If this code were being used in a longer script that ran for several minutes, this would be a huge waste of resources. Fortunately, we can free up the memory associated with these two by calling `$result->free()` and `$conn->disconnect()`. If we add those two function calls to the end of the script, it will be complete.

Reference

- www.php.net—The best place to look for information is the PHP online manual. It is comprehensive, well written, and updated regularly.www.phpbuilder.net—A large PHP scripts and tutorials site where you can learn new techniques and also chat with other PHP developers.
- www.zend.com—The home page of a company founded by two of the key developers of PHP. Zend develops and sells proprietary software, including a powerful IDE and a code cache, to aid PHP developers.
- http://pear.php.net/—The home of the PEAR project contains a large collection of software you can download and try, and it has thorough documentation for it all.

- www.phparch.com/—There are quite a few good PHP magazines around, but *PHP Architect* probably leads the way. It posts some of its articles online for free, and its forums are good, too.

Quality books on PHP abound, and you are certainly spoiled for choice. For beginning developers, the best available is *PHP and MySQL Web Development* (Sams Publishing), ISBN 0-672-32672-8. For a concise, to-the-point, book covering all aspects of PHP, check out *PHP in a Nutshell* (O'Reilly). Finally, for advanced developers, you can consult *Advanced PHP Programming* (Sams Publishing), ISBN 0-672-32561-6.

CHAPTER 30

C/C++ Programming Tools for Ubuntu

IN THIS CHAPTER

- Programming in C with Linux
- Using the C Programming Project Management Tools Provided with Ubuntu
- Using the GNU C Compiler
- Graphical Development Tools
- Reference

If you're looking to learn C or C++ programming, this part of the book isn't the right place to start—unlike Perl, Python, PHP, or even C#, it takes more than a little dabbling to produce something productive with C, so this chapter is primarily focused on the tools Ubuntu offers you as a C or C++ programmer.

Whether you're looking to compile your own code or someone else's, the GNU Compiler Collection (`gcc`) is there to help—it understands C, C++, Fortran, Pascal, and dozens of other popular languages, which means you can try your hand at whatever interests you. Ubuntu also ships with hundreds of libraries you can link to, from the GUI toolkits behind GNOME and KDE to XML parsing and game coding. Some use C, others C++, and still others offer support for both, meaning you can choose what you're most comfortable with.

Programming in C with Linux

C is the programming language most frequently associated with UNIX-like operating systems such as Linux or BSD. Since the 1970s, the bulk of the UNIX operating system and its applications have been written in C. Because the C language doesn't directly rely on any specific hardware architecture, UNIX was one of the first portable operating systems. In other words, the majority of the code that makes up UNIX doesn't know and doesn't care which computer it is actually running on. Machine-specific features are isolated in a few modules within the UNIX kernel, which makes it easy for you to modify them when you are porting to different hardware architectures.

C is a *compiled* language, which means that your C source code is first analyzed by the *preprocessor* and then translated into assembly language first and then into machine instructions that are appropriate to the target CPU. An assembler then creates a binary, or *object*, a file from the machine instructions. Finally, the object file is linked to any required external software support by the *linker*. A C program is stored in a text file that ends with a `.c` extension and always contains at least one routine, or function, such as `main()`, unless the file is an *include* file (with a `.h` extension, also known as a *header* file) containing shared variable definitions or other data or declarations. *Functions* are the commands that perform each step of the task that the C program was written to accomplish.

NOTE

The Linux kernel is mostly written in C, which is why Linux works with so many different CPUs. To learn more about building the Linux kernel from source, see Chapter 36, "Kernel and Module Management."

C++ is an object-oriented extension to C. Because C++ is a superset of C, C++ compilers compile C programs correctly, and it is possible to write non–object-oriented code in C++. The reverse is not true: C compilers cannot compile C++ code.

C++ extends the capabilities of C by providing the necessary features for object-oriented design and code. C++ also provides some features, such as the capability to associate functions with data structures that do not require the use of class-based object-oriented techniques. For these reasons, the C++ language enables existing UNIX programs to migrate toward the adoption of object orientation over time.

Support for C++ programming is provided by `gcc`, which you run with the name `g++` when you are compiling C++ code.

Using the C Programming Project Management Tools Provided with Ubuntu

Ubuntu is replete with tools that make your life as a C/C++ programmer easier. There are tools to create programs (editors), compile programs (`gcc`), create libraries (`ar`), control the source (Git, Mercurial, Subversion), automate builds (`make`), debug programs (`gdb` and `ddd`), and determine where inefficiencies lie (`gprof`).

The following sections introduce some of the programming and project management tools included with Ubuntu. If you have some previous UNIX experience, you will be familiar with most of these programs because they are traditional complements to a programmer's suite of software.

Building Programs with `make`

You use the `make` command to automatically build and install a C program, and for that use it is an easy tool. If you want to create your own automated builds, however, you need to learn the special syntax that `make` uses; the following sections walk you through a basic `make` setup.

Using Makefiles

The `make` command automatically builds and updates applications by using a makefile. A *makefile* is a text file that contains instructions about which options to pass on to the compiler preprocessor, the compiler, the assembler, and the linker. The makefile also specifies, among other things, which source code files have to be compiled (and the compiler command line) for a particular code module and which code modules are needed to build the program—a mechanism called *dependency checking*.

The beauty of the `make` command is its flexibility. You can use `make` with a simple makefile, or you can write complex makefiles that contain numerous macros, rules, or commands that work in a single directory or traverse your file system recursively to build programs, update your system, and even function as document management systems. The `make` command works with nearly any program, including text processing systems such as TeX.

You could use `make` to compile, build, and install a software package, using a simple command like this:

```
matthew@seymour:~$ sudo make install
```

You can use the default makefile (usually called `Makefile`, with a capital *M*), or you can use `make`'s `-f` option to specify any makefile, such as `MyMakeFile`, like this:

```
matthew@seymour:~$ sudo make -f MyMakeFile
```

Other options might be available, depending on the contents of your makefile. You may have a source file named `hi.c` and just run `make hi`, where make figures out what to do automatically to build the final executable. See make's built in rules with `make -p`.

Using Macros and Makefile Targets

Using `make` with macros can make a program portable. Macros allow users of other operating systems to easily configure a program build by specifying local values, such as the names and locations, or *pathnames*, of any required software tools. In the following example, macros define the name of the compiler (`CC`), the installer program (`INS`), where the program should be installed (`INSDIR`), where the linker should look for required libraries (`LIBDIR`), the names of required libraries (`LIBS`), a source code file (`SRC`), the intermediate object code file (`OBJS`), and the name of the final program (`PROG`):

```
# a sample makefile for a skeleton program
CC= gcc
INS= install
```

```
INSDIR = /usr/local/bin
LIBDIR= -L/usr/X11R6/lib
LIBS= -lXm -lSM -lICE -lXt -lX11
SRC= skel.c
OBJS= skel.o
PROG= skel

skel:  ${OBJS}
	${CC} -o ${PROG} ${SRC} ${LIBDIR} ${LIBS}

install: ${PROG}
	${INS} -g root -o root ${PROG} ${INSDIR}
```

NOTE

The indented lines in the previous example are indented with tabs, not spaces. This is important to remember! It is difficult for a person to see the difference, but `make` can tell. If `make` reports confusing errors when you first start building programs under Linux, check your project's makefile for the use of tabs and other proper formatting.

Using the makefile from the preceding example, you can build a program like this:

```
matthew@seymour:~$ sudo make
```

To build a specified component of a makefile, you can use a target definition on the command line. To build just the program, you use make with the `skel` target, like this:

```
matthew@seymour:~$ sudo make skel
```

If you make any changes to any element of a target object, such as a source code file, make rebuilds the target automatically. This feature is part of the convenience of using make to manage a development project. To build and install a program in one step, you can specify the target of `install` like this:

```
matthew@seymour:~$ sudo make install
```

Larger software projects might have a number of traditional targets in the makefile, such as the following:

- `test`—To run specific tests on the final software
- `man`—To process an include or a `troff` document with the `man` macros
- `clean`—To delete any remaining object files
- `archive`—To clean up, archive, and compress the entire source code tree
- `bugreport`—To automatically collect and then mail a copy of the build or error logs

Large applications can require hundreds of source code files. Compiling and linking these applications can be a complex and error-prone task. The `make` utility helps you organize the process of building the executable form of a complex application from many source files.

Using the `autoconf` Utility to Configure Code

The `make` command is only one of several programming automation utilities included with Ubuntu. There are others, such as `pmake` (which causes a parallel make), `imake` (which is a dependency-driven makefile generator that is used for building X11 clients), `automake`, and one of the newer tools, `autoconf`, which builds shell scripts that can be used to configure program source code packages.

Building many software packages for Linux that are distributed in source form requires the use of GNU's `autoconf` utility. This program builds an executable shell script named `configure` that, when executed, automatically examines and tailors a client's build from source according to software resources, or *dependencies* (such as programming tools, libraries, and associated utilities) that are installed on the target host (your Linux system).

Many Linux commands and graphical clients for X downloaded in source code form include `configure scripts`. To configure the source package, build the software, and then install the new program, the `root` user might use the script like this (after uncompressing the source and navigating into the resulting build directory):

```
matthew@seymour:~$ ./configure ; make ; sudo make install
```

The `autoconf` program uses a file named `configure.in` that contains a basic *ruleset*, or set of macros. The `configure.in` file is created with the `autoscan` command. Building a properly executing `configure` script also requires a template for the makefile, named `Makefile.in`. Although creating the dependency-checking `configure` script can be done manually, you can easily overcome any complex dependencies by using a graphical project development tool such as KDEs KDevelop or GNOME's Glade. (See the "Graphical Development Tools" section, later in this chapter, for more information.)

Managing Software Projects with Subversion

Although `make` can be used to manage a software project, larger software projects require document management, source code controls, security, and revision tracking as the source code goes through a series of changes during its development. Subversion provides source code version control utilities for this kind of large software project management.

The Subversion system is used to track changes to multiple versions of files, and it can be used to backtrack or branch off versions of documents inside the scope of a project. It can also be used to prevent or resolve conflicting entries or changes made to source code files by multiple developers. Source code control with Subversion requires the use of at least the following five command options on the `svn` command line:

- `checkout`—Checks out revisions
- `update`—Updates your sources with changes made by other developers

30

- `add`—Adds new files to the repository
- `delete`—Eliminates files from the repository
- `commit`—Publishes changes to other repository developers

Note that some of these commands require you to use additional fields, such as the names of files. With the `commit` *command*, you should always try to pass the `-m` parameter (lets you provide a message describing the change) followed by some information about your changes. For example:

```
matthew@seymour:~$ svn commit -m "This fixes bug 204982."
```

One of the most impressive features of Subversion is its capability to work offline—any local Subversion checkout automatically has a `.svn` directory hidden in there, which contains copies of all checked-out files. Thanks to this, you can check your current files against the ones you checked out without having to contact the server—it all runs locally.

Debugging Tools

Debugging is both a science and an art. Sometimes, the simplest tool—the code listing—is the best debugging tool. At other times, however, you need to use other debugging tools. Three of these tools are `splint`, `gprof`, and `gdb`.

Using `splint` to Check Source Code

The `splint` command is similar to the traditional UNIX `lint` command: It statically examines source code for possible problems, and it also has many additional features. Even if your C code meets the standards for C and compiles cleanly, it might still contain errors. `splint` performs many types of checks and can provide extensive error information. For example, this simple program might compile cleanly and even run:

```
matthew@seymour:~$ gcc -o tux tux.c
matthew@seymour:~$ ./tux
```

But the `splint` command might point out some serious problems with the source:

```
matthew@seymour:~$ splint tux.c
Splint 3.1.2 —- 29 Apr 2009

tux.c: (in function main)
tux.c:2:19: Return value (type int) ignored: putchar(t[++j] -...
  Result returned by function call is not used. If this is intended, can cast
  result to (void) to eliminate message. (Use -retvalint to inhibit warning)
Finished checking —- 1 code warning
```

You can use the splint commands `-strict` option, like this, to get a more verbose report:

```
matthew@seymour:~$ splint -strict tux.c
```

GCC also supports diagnostics through the use of extensive warnings (through the `-Wall` and `-pedantic` options):

```
matthew@seymour:~$ gcc -Wall tux.c
tux.c:1: warning: return type defaults to 'int'
tux.c: In function 'main':
tux.c:2: warning: implicit declaration of function 'putchar'
```

Using `gprof` to Track Function Time

You use the `gprof` (profile) command to study how a program is spending its time. If a program is compiled and linked with `-p` as a flag, a `mon.out` file is created when it executes, with data on how often each function is called and how much time is spent in each function. `gprof` parses and displays this data. An analysis of the output generated by `gprof` helps you determine where performance bottlenecks occur. Using an optimizing compiler can speed up a program, but taking the time to use `gprof`'s analysis and revising bottleneck functions significantly improves program performance.

Doing Symbolic Debugging with `gdb`

The `gdb` tool is a symbolic debugger. When a program is compiled with the `-g` flag, the symbol tables are retained and a symbolic debugger can be used to track program bugs. The basic technique is to invoke `gdb` after a *core dump* (a file containing a snapshot of the memory used by a program that has crashed) and get a stack trace. The stack trace indicates the source line where the core dump occurred and the functions that were called to reach that line. Often, this is enough to identify a problem. It isn't the limit of `gdb`, though.

`gdb` also provides an environment for debugging programs interactively. Invoking `gdb` with a program enables you to set breakpoints, examine the values of variables, and monitor variables. If you suspect a problem near a line of code, you can set a breakpoint at that line and run `gdb`. When the line is reached, execution is interrupted. You can check variable values, examine the stack trace, and observe the program's environment. You can single-step through the program to check values. You can resume execution at any point. By using breakpoints, you can discover many bugs in code.

A graphical X Window interface to `gdb` is called the Data Display Debugger, or `ddd`.

Using the GNU C Compiler

If you elected to install the development tools package when you installed Ubuntu (or perhaps later on, using `synaptic`), you should have the GNU C compiler (`gcc`). Many different options are available for the GNU C compiler, and many of them are similar to those of the C and C++ compilers that are available on other UNIX systems. Look at the `man` page or information file for `gcc` for a full list of options and descriptions.

When you build a C program using `gcc`, the compilation process takes place in several steps:

1. First, the C preprocessor parses the file. To do so, it sequentially reads the lines, includes header files, and performs macro replacement.
2. The compiler parses the modified code to determine whether the correct syntax is used. In the process, it builds a symbol table and creates an intermediate object format. Most symbols have specific memory addresses assigned, although symbols defined in other modules, such as external variables, do not.
3. The last compilation stage, linking, ties together different files and libraries and then links the files by resolving the symbols that had not previously been resolved.

NOTE

Most C programs compile with a C++ compiler if you follow strict ANSI rules. For example, you can compile the standard `hello.c` program (everyone's first program) with the GNU C++ compiler. Typically, you name the file something like `hello.cc`, `hello.C`, `hello.c++`, or `hello.cxx`. The GNU C++ compiler accepts any of these names.

Graphical Development Tools

Ubuntu includes a number of graphical prototyping and development environments for use during X sessions. If you want to build client software for KDE or GNOME, you might find the KDevelop, Qt Designer, and Glade programs extremely helpful. You can use each of these programs to build graphical frameworks for interactive windowing clients, and you can use each of them to automatically generate the necessary skeleton of code needed to support a custom interface for your program.

Using the KDevelop Client

You can launch the KDevelop client (shown in Figure 30.1) from the application's menu, or from the command line of a terminal window, like this:

```
matthew@seymour:~$ kdevelop &
```

After you press Enter, the KDevelop Setup Wizard runs, and you are taken through several short wizard dialogs that set up and ensure a stable build environment. You must then run `kdevelop` again (either from the command line or by clicking its menu item under the desktop panel's Programming menu). You will then see the main KDevelop window and can start your project by selecting KDevelop's Project menu and clicking the New menu item.

You can begin building your project by stepping through the wizard dialogs. When you click the Create button, KDevelop automatically generates all the files that are normally found in a KDE client source directory (including the `configure` script, which checks dependencies and builds the client's makefile). To test your client, you can either first click the Build menu's Make menu item (or press F8) or just click the Execute menu item (or press F9), and the client is built automatically. You can use KDevelop to create KDE clients, plug-ins for the `Konqueror` *browser*, KDE `kicker` panel applets, KDE desktop themes, Qt library–based clients, and even programs for GNOME.

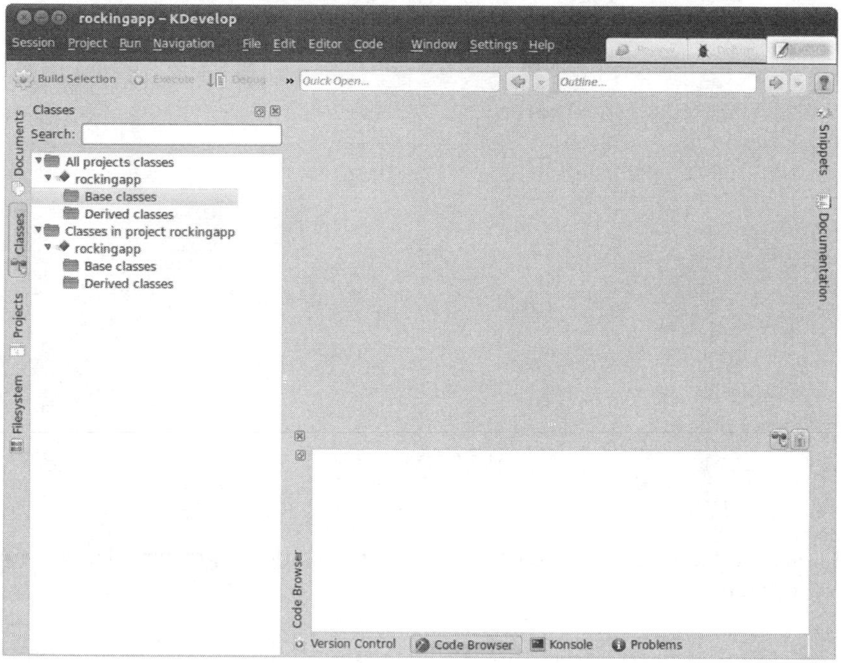

FIGURE 30.1 KDE's KDevelop is a rapid prototyping and client-building tool for use with Linux.

The Glade Client for Developing in GNOME

If you prefer to use GNOME and its development tools, the Glade GTK+ GUI builder can help you save time and effort when building a basic skeleton for a program. You launch Glade from the desktop panel's Programming menu.

When you launch Glade, a directory named `Projects` is created in your home directory, and you see a main window, along with two floating Palette and Properties windows (see Figure 30.2, which shows a basic GNOME client with a calendar widget added to its main window). You can use Glade's File menu to save the blank project and then start building your client by clicking and adding user interface elements from the Palette window. For example, you can first click the Palette window's Gnome button and then click to create your new client's main window. A window with a menu and a toolbar appears—the basic framework for a new GNOME client!

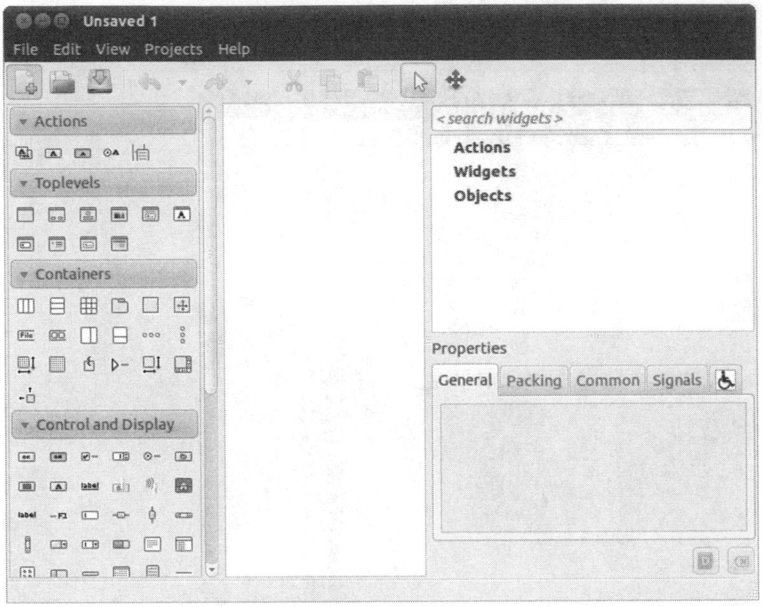

FIGURE 30.2 You can use the GNOME Glade client to build and preview a graphical interface for a custom GNOME program.

Reference

- http://gcc.gnu.org/java/compile.html—More information about GCC's Java support.
- www.gnu.org/software/autoconf/autoconf.html—More information about the GNU Project's `autoconf` utility and how to build portable software projects.
- http://qt.nokia.com—The main Qt website.
- http://glade.gnome.org—Home page for the Glade GNOME developer's tool.
- www.kdevelop.org—Site that hosts the KDevelop Project's latest versions of the KDE graphical development environment, KDevelop.
- *The C Programming Language*, by Brian W. Kernighan and Dennis M. Ritchie, Prentice Hall.
- *The Annotated C++ Reference Manual*, by Margaret A. Ellis and Bjarne Stroustrup, ANSI Base Document.
- *Programming in ANSI C*, by Stephen G. Kochan, Sams Publishing.

- *Sams Teach Yourself C in 21 Days*, by Peter Aitken and Bradley Jones, Sams Publishing.
- *Sams Teach Yourself C++ for Linux in 21 Days*, by Jesse Liberty and David B. Horvath, Sams Publishing.
- *C How to Program and C++ How to Program*, both by Harvey M. Deitel and Paul J. Deitel, Deitel Associates.

CHAPTER 31
Mono

IN THIS CHAPTER

Although Microsoft intended it for Windows, Microsoft's .NET platform has grown to encompass many other operating systems. No, this isn't a rare sign of Microsoft letting customers choose which OS is best for them—instead, the spread of .NET is because of the Mono project, which is a free re-implementation of .NET available under the a GPL license.

Because of the potential for patent complications, it took most distros a long time to incorporate Mono, but it's here now and works just fine. What's more, Mono supports both C# and Visual Basic .NET, as well as the complete .NET 1.0 and 1.1 Frameworks (and much of the 2.0 Framework, too), making it quick to learn and productive to use.

Why Use Mono?

Linux already has numerous programming languages available to it, so why bother with Mono and .NET? Here are my top five reasons:

- .NET is "compile once, run anywhere"; that means you can compile your code on Linux and run it on Windows, or the reverse.
- Mono supports C#, which is a C-like language with many improvements to help make it object-oriented and easier to use.
- .NET includes automatic garbage collection to remove the possibility of memory leaks.

- .NET uses comes with built-in security checks to ensure that buffer overflows and many types of exploits are a thing of the past.
- Mono uses a high-performance just-in-time compiler to optimize your code for the platform on which it's running. This lets you compile it on a 32-bit machine, then run it on a 64-bit machine and have the code dynamically re-compiled for maximum 64-bit performance.

At this point, Mono is probably starting to sound like Java, and indeed it shares several properties with it. However, Mono has the following improvements:

- The C# language corrects many of the irritations in Java, while keeping its garbage collection.
- .NET is designed to let you compile multiple languages down to the same bytecode, including C#, Visual Basic .NET, and many others.
- Mono even has a special project (known as "IKVM") that compiles Java source code down to .NET code that can be run on Mono.
- Mono is completely open source!

Whether you're looking to create command-line programs, graphical user interface apps, or even web pages, Mono has all the power and functionality you need.

Mono is made up of several components including a C# compiler, the Mono Runtime, the Base Class Library and the Mono Class Library.

The C# compiler includes all of the features to compile C# 1.0, 2.0, and 3.0 (ECMA) code. Mono 2.6, which is installed by default in Ubuntu 10.10, includes a preview implementation of C# 4.0, which is expected to be complete in Mono 2.8. The compiler is able to compile itself, is fast, and includes a test suite. The C# compiler gives you your pick of several services that applications may consume:

- `mcs`—References the 1.0-profile libraries and supports C# 1.0 and C# 3.0, minus generics and any features that depend on generics and is called mono-cms in the Ubuntu software repositories.
- `gmcs`—References the 2.0-profile libraries and supports the full C# 3.0 language and is called mono-gcms in the Ubuntu software repositories and is installed by default in Ubuntu 10.10.
- `smcs`—References the 2.1-profile libraries, supports the full C# 3.0 language, and is used for creating Moonlight (the Mono version of Silverlight) applications. It is not available in the Ubuntu software repositories.
- `dmcs`—Targets the C# 4.0 language and is not available in the Ubuntu software repositories.

The first three in that list are all the same compiler, but with different default settings. The last one listed is new and will become the default in Mono 2.8.

The Mono Runtime uses the ECMA Common Language Infrastructure (CIL). This is a runtime similar to the Java Virtual Machine. It provides a Just In Time (JIT) compiler, an

Ahead Of Time (AOT) compiler, a library loader, a garbage collector, a threading system, and interoperability functionality. The execution engine, `mono`, can be used as a stand-alone process. By itself it runs as a JIT or AOT code generator. With `—full-aot`, it can run in fully static mode with no JIT involvement. You can reuse your existing C and C++ code and extend it with Mono either with scripting or by embedding Mono into applications.

The Mono Base Class Library provides a set of foundational classes that are compatible with Microsoft's .Net Framework. It is extended by the Mono Class Library that provides additional functions that are especially useful when building Linux applications, such as classes for Gtk+, LDAP, and POSIX.

Mono runs on many platforms, not just Linux. It is designed as a free-software implementation of Microsoft's C# and can also run on Windows, Mac OSX, BSD, Solaris, Nintendo Wii, Sony PlayStation 3, and the Apple iPhone. It will work on many different types of processors, including the common x86 and x86-64 that Ubuntu targets, and also others like PowerPC, SPARC, ARM, Alpha, and more. The Common Language Runtime (CLR) that comes with Mono allows you to choose other programming languages, write your code using them, and then run the programs in Mono (see mono-project.com/Languages).

MonoDevelop

- Mono should already be installed on your system, however it is installed only for end users rather than for developers—you need to install a couple more packages to make it usable for programming. Install `mono-complete` and `monodevelop` from the Ubuntu repositories.
- These give you the basics to do Mono development.

If you want to do other exciting things with Mono, lots of Mono-enabled libraries are available. Use Synaptic at System, Administration, Synaptic Package Manager to search the Ubuntu software respositories for "sharp" to bring up the list of .NET-enabled libraries that you can use with Mono—the suffix is used because C# is the most popular .NET language, indeed the flagship language in the .NET fleet, written especially for .NET. In this list you'll see things such as gnome-sharp2 and gtk-sharp2—we recommend you at least install the gtk-sharp2 libraries because these are used to create graphical user interfaces for Mono.

Open MonoDevelop from the menu at Applications, Programming, MonoDevelop.

TIP

You don't have to use MonoDevelop to write your code, but it helps—syntax highlighting, code completion, and drag-and-drop GUI designers are just a few of its features.

When MonoDevelop has loaded, open File, New, Solution. From the left of the window that appears, choose C#, then Console Project. Give it a name and choose a location to save it, as in Figure 31.1. When you're ready, click Forward.

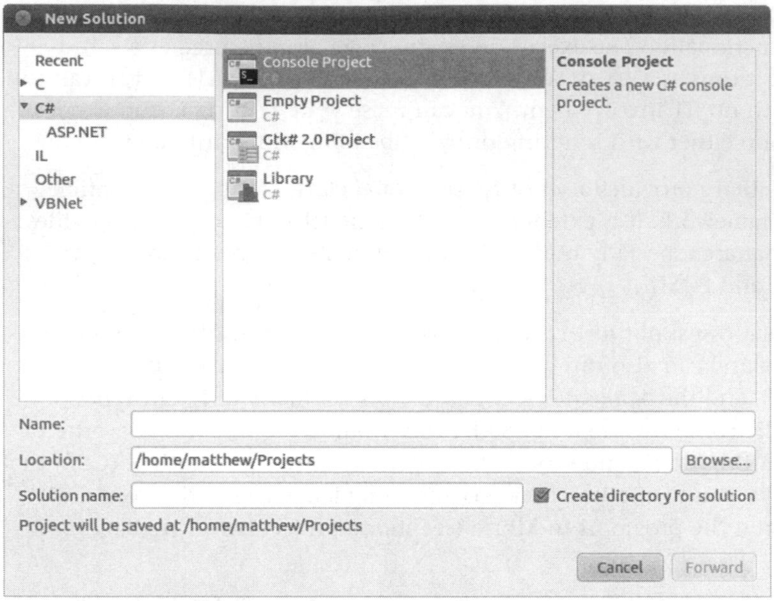

FIGURE 31.1 MonoDevelop ships with a number of templates to get you started, including one for a quick Console Project.

This is a simple command-line project. For our example, select Unix Integration as the only feature to include in Figure 31.2 and click OK. Notice that this generates a launch script by default and allows you to choose to create a .desktop file if desired. You can also create packaging as an archive of binaries or a tarball and enable support for GTK#. We don't need either of these for our example.

The default Console Project template creates a program that prints a simple message to the command line: the oh-so-traditional "Hello World!" Click Build, Build HelloWorld (or F7) to build the project (Figure 31.3). Click Run, Run (or Ctrl+F5) to run the program. A terminal window will appear to show you the output of your program as shown in Figure 31.4.

You can also run and debug at the same time using Run, Debug (or F5). If there are errors in the program code, you will be notified, as seen in Figure 31.5. I created a simple error by removing a letter from the end of a word. If there are no errors, the program will run as it did when we used Run, Run previously.

The Structure of a C# Program

As you can guess from its name, C# draws very heavily on C and C++ for its syntax, but it borrows several ideas from other languages that its creator, Hejlsberg, had experience with like Java, Turbo Pascal, Delphi, Python, Icon, Smalltalk, and Modula-2 and 3. C# is object-oriented. In C# you define a class, which is then instantiated by calling its constructor.

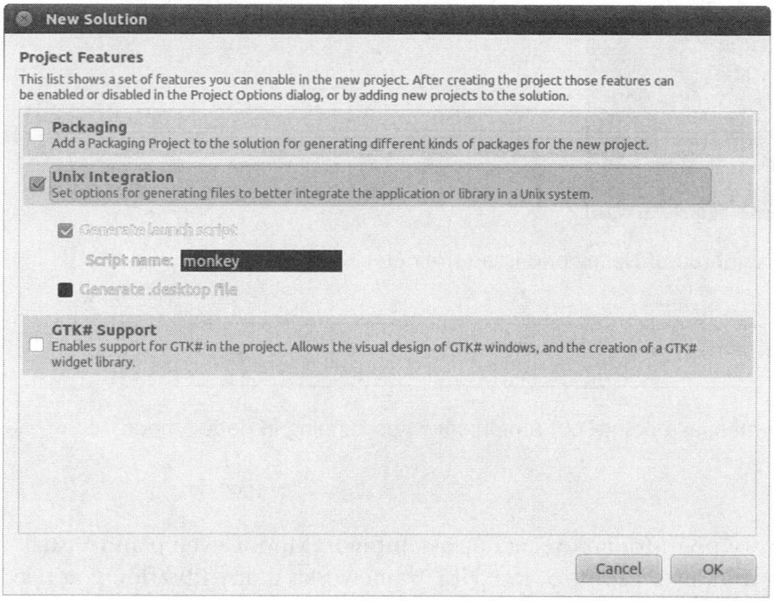

FIGURE 31.2 Choose the Project Features you want to enable in your project.

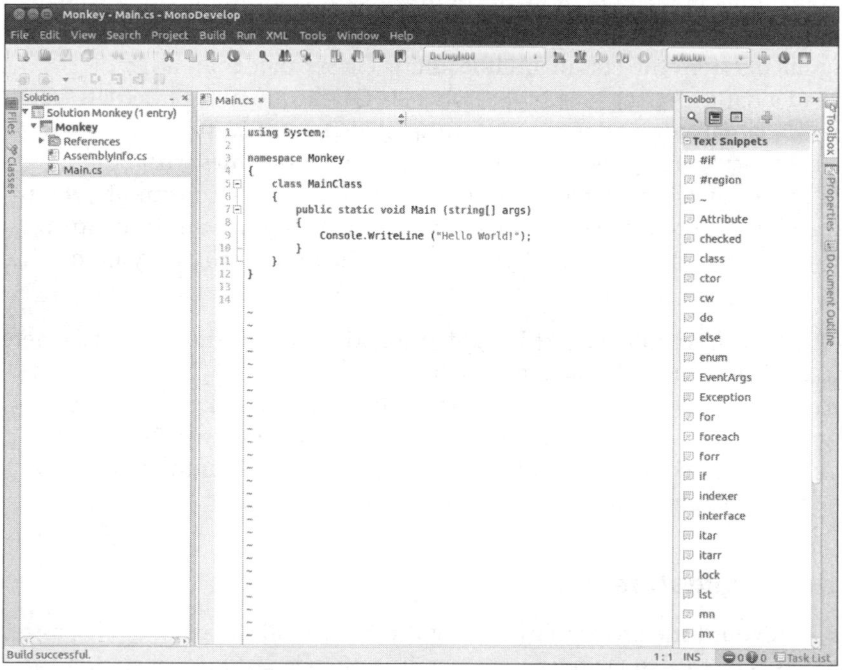

FIGURE 31.3 MonoDevelop with HelloWorld loaded, showing a successful build notice at the bottom.

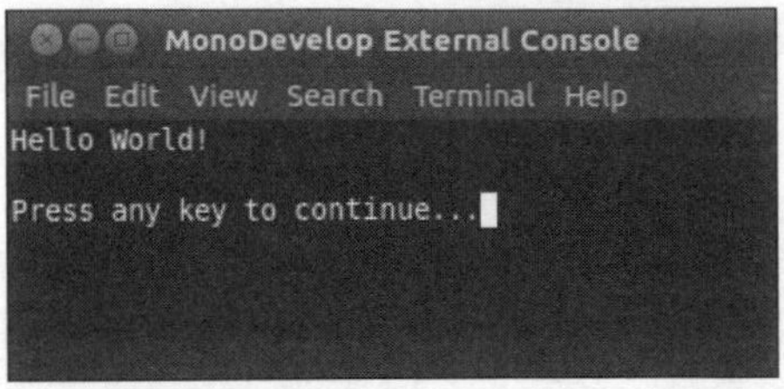

FIGURE 31.4 A successful run of HelloWorld in a terminal.

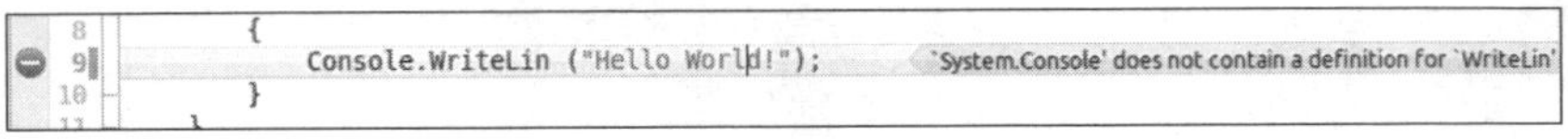

FIGURE 31.5 An error message points out a problem when running in debug mode.

Main() is the default entry point for an executable assembly in MonoDevelop and Visual Studio .NET. To be able to draw on some of the .NET framework's many libraries, you need to add `using` statements at the top of your files—by default only `using System;` is included, enabling you to access the console to write your Hello World! message.

If you have experience with C or C++, you will notice that there are no header files in C#: your class definition and its implementation are all in the same file. You might also have noticed that the `Main()` method accepts the parameter `"string[] args"`, which means we will be passing arguments from the command line and is C#-speak for "an array of strings." C never had a native "string" data type, whereas C++ acquired it rather late in the game, and so both languages tend to use the antiquated `char*` data type to point to a string of characters. In C#, `"string"` is a data type all its own, and comes with built-in functionality such as the capability to replace substrings, the capability to trim off white-space, and the capability to convert itself to upper- or lowercase if you want it to. Strings are also Unicode friendly out of the box in .NET, so that's one fewer thing for you to worry about.

The final thing you might have noticed—at least, if you had looked in the directory where MonoDevelop placed your compiled program (usually `/path/to/your/project/bin/Debug`)—is that Mono uses the Windows-like `.exe` file extension for its programs. because Mono aims to be 100percent compatible with Microsoft .NET, which means you can take your Hello World program and run it unmodified on a Windows machine and have the same message printed out.

Printing Out the Parameters

We're going to expand your little program by having it print out all the parameters passed to it, one per line. In C# this is—amazingly—just one line of code. Add this just after the existing `Console.WriteLine()` line in your program:

```
foreach (string arg in args) Console.WriteLine(arg);
```

The foreach keyword is a special kind of loop designed to iterate over any collection, in this case an array. The for loop exists in C#, and lets you loop a certain number of times; the while loop exists too, and lets you loop continuously until a conditional is no longer true or a break statement is encountered—the conditional controls the loop and a break statement will allow an exit if desired or included. But the foreach loop is designed to loop over a collection from the start to the end. You get each value as a variable of any type you want—the preceding code says string arg in args, which means "for each array element in args, give it to me as the variable arg of type string." Because args is already an array of strings, no datatype conversion will take place here—but it could if you wanted to convert classes or do anything of the like. One reason you might use a for loop over a foreach loop is if you need to determine an index into a collection, as in finding a minimum or maximum value. There is no index available for the current iteration in a foreach loop, much like it is not available in a while loop.

After you have each individual argument, call WriteLine() to print it out. This works whether there's one argument or one hundred arguments—or even if there are no arguments at all (in which case the loop doesn't execute at all).

Creating Your Own Variables

You can have anonymous variable types and "var" variable declarations in C#. You can also specify variable types with great precision. Most of the time you can use int and leave C# to work out the details. Let's modify our program to accept two parameters, add them together as numbers, and then print the result. This gives you a chance to see variable definitions, conversion, and mathematics, all in one. Edit the Main() method to look like this:

```
using System;


namespace AddNumbers
{
        class MainClass
       {
                public static void Main (string[] args)
                 {
                         int num1 = int.Parse(args[0]);
                         int num2 = int.Parse(args[1]);
                         Console.WriteLine("Sum of two parameters is: " + (num1 +
num2)");
                 }
        }
}
```

Run this new code using Run, Run With, Custom Parameter. As you can see, each variable is declared with a type (int) and a name (num1 and num2), so that C# knows how to handle them. The args array contains strings, so we convert the strings to integers with the int.Parse() method. Finally, the actual addition of the two strings is done at the end of the method, while they are being printed out. Note how C# is clever enough to have `integer + integer` be added together (in the case of num + num2), whereas `string + integer` attaches the integer to the end of the string (in the case of `"Sum of two parameters is:" + the result of num1 + num2`). This isn't by accident: C# tries to convert data types cleverly, and warns you only if it can't convert a data type without losing some data. For example, if you try to treat a 64-bit integer as a 32-bit integer, it warns you because you might be throwing a lot of data away. You can use `int.TryParse()` to attempt parsing conditionally, and it would also return a boolean response indicating success or failure. In addition, you can also use checked conversions to perform operations and have the compiler verify that they do not cause overflow (essentially meaning the variable could not represent the value).

Adding Some Error Checking

Right now your program crashes in a nasty way if users don't provide at least two parameters. The reason for this is that we use `arg[0]` and `arg[1]` (the first and second parameters passed to your program) without even checking whether *any* parameters were passed in. This is easily solved: `args` is an array, and arrays can reveal their size. If the size doesn't match what you expect, you can bail out.

Add this code at the start of the `Main()` method:

```
if (args.Length != 2) {
   Console.WriteLine("You must provide exactly two parameters!");
   return;
}
```

The new piece of code in there is `return`, which is a C# keyword that forces it to exit the current method. As `Main()` is the only method being called, this has the effect of terminating the program because the user didn't supply two parameters. You could also specify that the Main() method have a return type of int so that an exit code would be returned instead of returning without any feedback. This would be especially helpful if the executable was to be used in a command line tool chain by another tool that needs feedback after your tool runs.

Using the `Length` property of `args`, it is now possible for you to write your own `Main()` method that does different things, depending on how many parameters are provided. To do this properly, you need to use the `else` statement and nest multiple `if` statements like this:

```
if (args.Length == 2) {
   /// whatever...
} else if (args.Length == 3) {
   /// something else
} else if (args.Length == 4) {
   /// even more
} else {
   /// only executed if none of the others are
}
```

Building on Mono's Libraries

Ubuntu ships with several Mono-built programs such as Tomboy and gBrainy. It also comes with a fair collection of .NET-enabled libraries, some of which you probably already installed earlier. The nice thing about Mono, like many other object-oriented languages, is that it lets you build on these libraries really easily: You just import them with a `using` statement, then get started.

To demonstrate how easy it is to build more complicated Mono applications, we're going to produce one using Gtk#, the GUI toolkit that is the standard for GNOME development.

Creating a GUI with Gtk#

Gtk# was included with Gnome by default for the first time in Gnome 2.16, but it had been used for a couple of years before that and so was already mature. MonoDevelop comes with its own GUI designer called GTK# Designer, which lets you drag and drop GUI elements onto your windows to design them.

To get started, in MonoDevelop go to File, New, Solution, choose C#, then Gtk# 2.0 project. Call it GtkTest, and deselect the box asking MonoDevelop to make a separate directory for the solution. Click Forward. In the New Solution Project Features window, all you need is already selected, so click OK.

You'll find that Main.cs contains a little more code this time because it needs to create and run the Gtk# application. However, the actual code to create your GUI is in the User Interface section in the left pane. If you open that group, you'll see Stock Icons and MainWindow. Double-click MainWindow to bring up MonoDevelop's GUI designer.

Click Toolbox on the left of the screen to drag and drop the different window widgets onto your form to see what properties they have.

For now, drag a button widget onto your form. It automatically takes up all the space on your window. If you don't want this to happen, try placing one of the containers down first, then putting your button in there. For example, if you want a menu bar at the top, then a calendar, then a status bar, you ought to drop the VBox pane onto the window first, then drop each of those widgets into the separate parts of the VPane, the main GUI creation workspace.

Your button will display the text "GtkButton" and use the variable name "button1" by default. Click to select it, then Properties on the right and look for Label in the Button Properties group. Change the label to "Hello." Just at the top of the properties pane is a tab saying Properties (where you are right now), and another saying Signals. Signals are the events that happen to your widgets, such as the mouse moving over them, someone typing, or, of interest to us, when your button has been clicked. Look inside the Button Signals group for Clicked and double-click it. MonoDevelop automatically switches you to the code view, with a pre-created method to handle button clicks.

Type this code into the method:

```
button1.Label = "World!";
```

If you want to change the button's variable name, you do so from the same Properties tab using the first entry, Name. Change the Name value and your variable's name is changed. Press F5 to compile and run, and try clicking the button!

Reference

- www.mono-project.com/—The homepage of the Mono project is packed with information to help you get started. You can also download new Mono versions from here, if there's something you desperately need.
- www.monodevelop.com/—The MonoDevelop project has its own site, which is the best place to look for updates.
- www.icsharpcode.net/OpenSource/SD/—MonoDevelop started life as a port of SharpDevelop. If you happen to dual-boot on Windows, this might prove very useful to you.
- http://msdn.microsoft.com/vcsharp/—We don't print many Microsoft URLs in this book, but this one is important: It's the homepage of their C# project, which can be considered the spiritual home of C# itself.
- Jesse Liberty's *Programming C#* (O'Reilly, ISBN 0-596-00699-3) is compact, it's comprehensive, and it's competitively priced.
- If you're very short on time and want the maximum detail (admittedly, with rather limited readability), you should try *The C# Programming Language*, which was co-authored by the creator of C#, Anders Hejlsberg (Addison-Wesley, ISBN: 0-321-33443-4).
- For a more general book on the .NET framework and all the features it provides, you might find *.NET Framework Essentials* (O'Reilly, ISBN: 0-596-00505-9) useful.

CHAPTER 32

Managing Software

IN THIS CHAPTER

In this chapter, we look at the options you have to manage your software in Ubuntu. If you are used to a Windows environment where you are reliant on visiting different vendor websites to download updates, you are in for a pleasant surprise! Updating a full Ubuntu installation, including all the application software, is as simple as running the Update Manager program. You will discover just how easy it is to install and even remove various software packages.

Ubuntu provides a variety of tools for system resource management. The following sections introduce the graphical software management tools that you will use for most of your software management. This chapter also covers monitoring and managing memory and disk storage on your system.

Ubuntu Software Center

The Ubuntu Software Center is a graphical utility for package management in Ubuntu. You will find it in the Applications menu as Ubuntu Software Center; it is named software-center. The Ubuntu Software Center allows you to easily select and install a large array of applications by using the intuitive built-in search and easy one-click installation. When you open the program, you will see the Package Browsing screen, as shown in Figure 32.1.

Along the left side of the screen, you will see three menu options: Get Software, Installed Software, and History. At the top is a search bar that you can use to search for packages. When you click the Get Software link, you will be presented with options to explore software Provided by Ubuntu or software For Purchase. Clicking the Installed Software link will present you with a list of all the installed applications on your Ubuntu desktop.

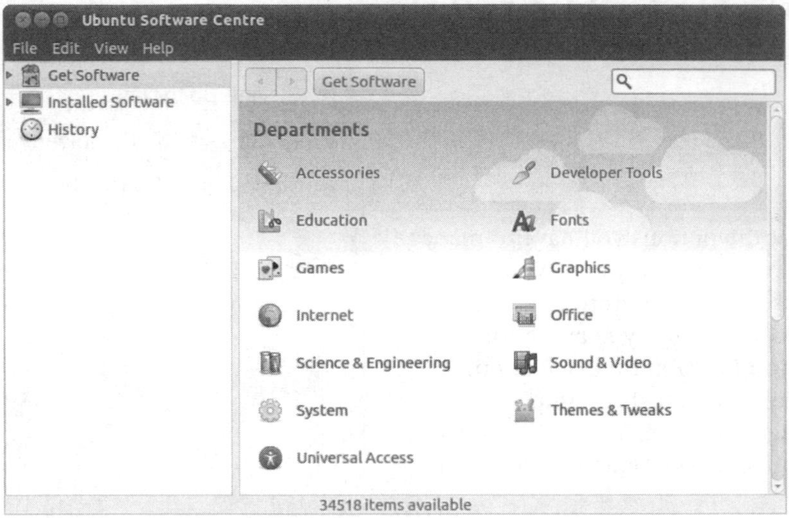

FIGURE 32.1 The initial Ubuntu Software Center screen allows you to browse through packages sorted by groups.

Installing new software via Ubuntu Software Center is as simple as finding it in the package list, double–clicking, and clicking the Install button. When you do so, you may be asked for your password; then the application will be downloaded and installed. You can remove an application by finding it in Ubuntu Software Center and clicking the Remove button.

Use the Search box at the top to search for a specific application in the list. Note that this searches within the current category; so if you are in the Games category and search for "office," you will get no results. The best place to search is within the Get Free Software category, to make sure you search all areas.

Using Synaptic for Software Management

The Add/Remove Applications dialog works just fine for adding applications, but if you need to install something very specific—such as a library—or if you want to reconfigure your installation system, you need to use Synaptic (see Figure 32.2). You can run Synaptic by selecting it from the System, Administration, Synaptic Package Manager menu option.

At first glance, Synaptic looks a little like the Add/Remove Applications window. Along the left are software categories (although this time there are more of them), along the top right are the package selections for that category, and on the bottom right is the Package Information window that shows information about the currently selected package. To install or remove software, click the check box to the left of its name, and you'll see a menu that offers the following options:

- **Unmark**—If you have marked this package for installation, upgrade, or one of the other options, this removes that mark.

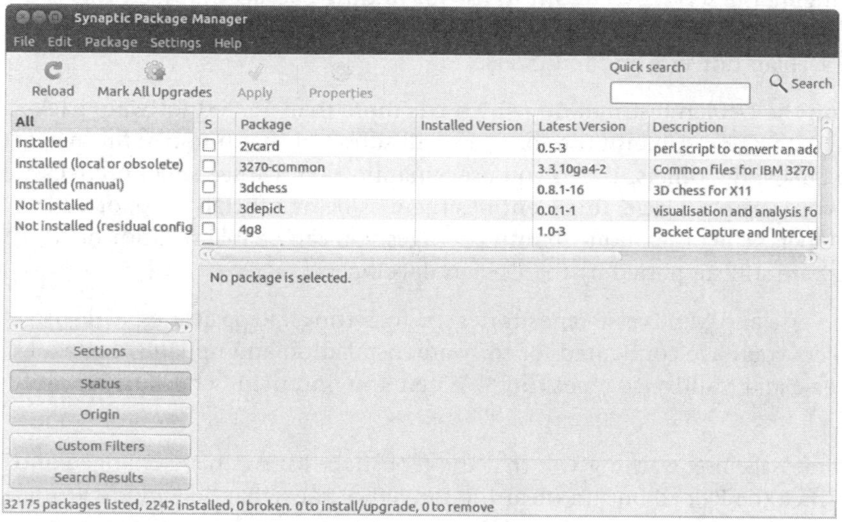

FIGURE 32.2 For more advanced software management, Synaptic is the preferred tool.

- **Mark for Installation**—Add this package to the list that will be installed.
- **Mark for Re-installation**—If you have some software already installed, but for some reason it's not working, this reinstalls it from scratch.
- **Mark for Upgrade**—If the software has updates available, this will download and install them.
- **Mark for Removal**—This deletes the selected package from your system, but leaves its configuration files intact so that if you ever reinstall it you do not have to reconfigure it.
- **Mark for Complete Removal**—This deletes the selected package from your system, but also removes any configuration files, purging everything from the system.

After you have made your changes, click the Apply button to have Synaptic download, install, upgrade, and uninstall as necessary. If you close the program without clicking Apply, your changes will be lost.

Beneath the categories on the left side of the screen, you will see four buttons: Sections, Status, Search, and Custom, with Sections selected. These customize the left list: Sections is the Categories view, Status lets you view packages that are installed or upgradable, Search stores results of your searches, and Custom has some esoteric groupings that are useful only to advanced users.

You can press Ctrl+F at any time to search for a particular package. By default it is set to search by package name, but it is quite common to change the Look In box to Description and Name. As mentioned already, your search terms are saved under the Search view (the button on the bottom left), and you can click from that list to re-search on that term.

As well as providing the method of installing and removing software, Synaptic provides the means to configure the servers you want to use for finding packages. In fact, this is where you can make one of the most important changes to your Ubuntu system: You can open it up to the Debian universe and multiverse.

Ubuntu is based on the Debian distribution, which has more than 15,000 software packages available for installation. Ubuntu uses only a small subset of that number, but makes it easy for you to enable the others. When you use Synaptic, you will see small orange Ubuntu logos next to every package; this identifies them as being officially supported by the Ubuntu developers. The other, non-Ubuntu packages you can enable will not have this logo, but they are still supported by the Debian developers.

To enable the Universe and Multiverse repositories, go to Settings, Repositories. This list shows all the servers you have configured for software installation and updates, and will include the Universe and Multiverse repositories. When you find them, check them, and then click Close.

Synaptic shows a message box warning you that the repository listings have changed and that you need to click the Reload button (near the top left of the Synaptic window) to have it refresh the package lists. Go ahead and do that, and you should see a lot more software appear for your selection. However, notice that only a small number have the official Ubuntu "seal" attached, which means you need to be a bit more careful when installing software!

NOTE

Much of the software discussed in this book is available only through the Universe repository. As such, we highly recommend enabling it to get full use out of this book and your Ubuntu installation.

Staying Up-to-Date

Although you can manage your software updates through Synaptic, Ubuntu provides a dedicated tool in the form of Update Manager (launched through System, Administration, Update Manager, and shown in Figure 32.3). This tool is designed to be simple to use: when you run it, Update Manager automatically downloads the list of updates available and checks them all in the list it shows. If the update list was downloaded automatically not too long ago, you can force Ubuntu to refresh the list of available updates by clicking the Check button. Otherwise, all you need to do is click Install Updates and your system will be brought up-to-date. If you want a little more information about the updates, click Show Details at the bottom to see what has changed in the update.

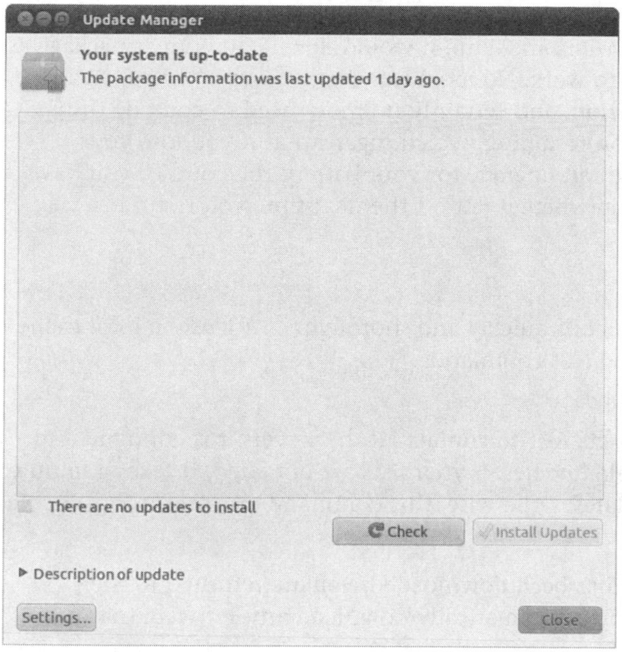

FIGURE 32.3 If you need to update your software to apply bug fixes and security upgrades, use Update Manager.

Ubuntu automatically checks for updates periodically and notifies you when critical updates are available. However, there's no harm running Update Manager yourself every so often, just to make sure; it's better to be safe than sorry.

Working on the Command Line

With so much software available for installation, it is no surprise that Debian-based distros have many ways to manage software installation. At their root, however, they all use Debian's world-renowned Advanced Package Tool (APT). A person posting on Slashdot.com once said, "Welcome to Slashdot. If you can't think of anything original, just say how much APT rocks and you'll fit right in." You see, even though many other distros have tried to equal the power of APT, nothing else even comes close.

Why is APT so cool? Well, it was the first system to properly handle dependencies in software. Other distros, such as Red Hat, used RPM files that had dependencies. For example, an RPM for Gimp would have a dependency on Gtk, the graphical toolkit on which Gimp is based. As a result, if you tried to install your Gimp RPM without having the Gtk RPM, your install would fail. So you grab the Gtk RPM and try again. Aha: Gtk has a dependency on three other things that you need to download. And those three other things have dependencies on 20 other things. And so on, and so on, usually until you can't find a working RPM for one of the dependencies, and you give up.

APT, on the other hand, was designed to automatically find and download dependencies for your packages. So if you wanted to install Gimp, it would download Gimp's package as well as any other software it needed to work. No more hunting around by hand, no more worrying about finding the right version, and certainly no more need to compile things by hand. APT also handles installation resuming, which means that if you lose your Internet connection part-way through an upgrade (or your battery runs out, or you have to quit, or whatever), APT will pick up where it left off the next time you rerun it.

Day-to-Day Usage

To enable you to search for packages both quickly and thoroughly, APT uses a local cache of the available packages. Try running this command:

```
matthew@seymour:~$ sudo apt-get update
```

The apt-get update command instructs APT to contact all the servers it is configured to use and download the latest list of file updates. If your lists are outdated, it takes a minute or two for APT to download the updates. Otherwise, this command executes it in a couple of seconds.

After the latest package information has been downloaded, you are returned to the command line. You can now ask APT to automatically download any software that has been updated, using this command:

```
matthew@seymour:~$ sudo apt-get upgrade
```

If you have a lot of software installed on your machine, there is a greater chance of things being updated. APT scans your software and compares it to the latest package information from the servers and produces a report something like this:

```
mmatthew@seymour:~$  sudo apt-get upgrade
Reading package lists... Done
Building dependency tree
Reading state information... Done
The following packages will be upgraded:
  cabextract google-chrome-beta icedtea6-plugin language-pack-en
  language-pack-en-base language-pack-gnome-en language-pack-gnome-en-base
  libfreetype6 libfreetype6-dev libsmbclient libwbclient0 openjdk-6-jre
  openjdk-6-jre-headless openjdk-6-jre-lib samba-common samba-common-bin
  smbclient upstart winbind xserver-common xserver-xorg-core
21 upgraded, 0 newly installed, 0 to remove and 0 not upgraded.
Need to get 84.8MB of archives.
After this operation, 623kB of additional disk space will be used.
Do you want to continue [Y/n]?
```

Each part of that report tells us something important. Starting at the top, the line "the following packages will be upgraded" gives us the exact list of packages for which updates are available. If you're installing new software or removing software, you'll see lists titled "The following packages will be installed" and "The following packages will be removed." A summary at the end shows a total of 21 packages that APT will upgrade, with 0 new packages, 0 to remove, and 0 not upgraded. Because this is an upgrade rather than an installation of new software, all those new packages will take up only 623KB of additional space. Although we have an 84.8MB download, the packages are overwriting existing files.

It's important to understand that a basic `apt-get` upgrade will never remove software or add new software. As a result, it is safe to use to keep your system fully patched, because it should never break things. However, occasionally you will see the "0 not upgraded" status change, which means some things cannot be upgraded. This happens when some software must be installed or removed to satisfy the dependencies of the updated package, which, as previously mentioned, `apt-get` upgrade will never do.

In this situation, you need to use `apt-get dist-upgrade`, so named because it's designed to allow users to upgrade from one version of Debian/Ubuntu to a newer version—an upgrade that inevitably involves changing just about everything on the system, removing obsolete software, and installing the latest features. This is one of the most-loved features of Debian because it allows you to move from version to version without having to download and install new CDs. Keeping regular upgrades and dist-upgrades separate is very useful for making sure that security updates and simple bug fixes don't change software configurations that you may be counting on, especially on a machine that needs to be consistently available and working, such as a server.

Whereas `apt-get upgrade` and `apt-get dist-upgrade` are there for upgrading packages, `apt-get install` is responsible for adding new software. For example, if you want to install the MySQL database server, you would run this:

```
matthew@seymour:~$  sudo apt-get install mysql-server
```

Internally, APT would query "mysql-server" against its list of software and find that it matches the mysql-server-5.0 package. It would then find which dependencies it needs that you don't already have installed and give you a report like this one:

```
matthew@seymour:~$  sudo apt-get install mysql-server
Reading package lists... Done
Building dependency tree... Done
The following extra packages will be installed:
  libdbd-mysql-perl libdbi-perl libnet-daemon-perl libplrpc-perl
  mysql-client-5.0 mysql-server-5.0
Suggested packages:
  dbishell libcompress-zlib-perl
Recommended packages:
  mailx
The following NEW packages will be installed
  libdbd-mysql-perl libdbi-perl libnet-daemon-perl libplrpc-perl
  mysql-client-5.0 mysql-server mysql-server-5.0
0 upgraded, 7 newly installed, 0 to remove and 11 not upgraded.
Need to get 28.5MB of archives.
After unpacking 65.8MB of additional disk space will be used.
Do you want to continue [Y/n]?
```

This time, you can see that APT has picked up and selected all the dependencies required to install MySQL Server 5.0, but it has also listed one recommended package and two suggested packages that it has not selected for installation. The "recommended" package is just that: The person who made the MySQL package (or its dependencies) thinks it would be a smart idea for you to also have the mailx package. If you want to add it, press N to terminate `apt-get` and rerun it like this:

```
matthew@seymour:~$ apt-get install mysql-server mailx
```

The "suggested" packages are merely a lower form of recommendation. They don't add any crucial features to the software you selected for install, but it's possible that you might need them for certain smaller things.

NOTE

APT maintains a package cache where it stores `.deb` files it has downloaded and installed. This usually lives in `/var/cache/apt/archives` and can sometimes take up many hundreds of megabytes on your computer. You can have APT clean out the package cache by running `apt-get clean`, which deletes all the cached `.deb files.` Alternatively, you can run `apt-get autoclean`, which deletes cached `.deb` files that are beyond a certain age, thereby keeping newer packages.

If you try running `apt-get` install with packages you already have installed, APT considers your command to be `apt-get update` and looks to see whether new versions are available for download.

The last day-to-day package operation is removing things you no longer want. This is done through the `apt-get remove` command, as follows:

```
matthew@seymour:~$ apt-get remove firefox
```

Removing packages can be dangerous, because APT also removes any software that relies on the packages you selected. For example, if you were to run `apt-get remove libgtk2.0-0` (the main graphical toolkit for Ubuntu), you would probably find that APT insists on removing more than a hundred other things. The moral of the story is this: When you remove software, read the APT report carefully before pressing Y to continue with the uninstall.

A straight `apt-get remove` leaves behind the configuration files of your program so that if you ever reinstall it you do not also need to reconfigure it. If you want the configuration files removed as well as the program files, run this command instead:

```
matthew@seymour:~$ apt-get remove —purge firefox
```

That performs a full uninstall.

NOTE

You can see a more extensive list of `apt-get` parameters by running `apt-get` without any parameters. The cryptic line at the bottom, "This APT has Super Cow Powers," is made even more cryptic if you run the command `apt-get moo`.

Finding Software

With so many packages available, it can be hard to find the exact thing you need using command-line APT. The general search tool is called `apt-cache` and is used like this:

```
matthew@seymour:~$ apt-cache search kde
```

Depending on which repositories you have enabled, that tool will return about a thousand packages. Many of those results will not even have KDE in the package name, but will be matched because the description contains the word *KDE*.

You can filter through this information in several ways. First, you can instruct `apt-cache` to search only in the package names, not in their descriptions. This is done with the `-n` parameter, like this:

```
matthew@seymour:~$ apt-cache -n search kde
```

Now the search has gone down from more than 1,000 packages to a few hundred.

Another way to limit search results is to use some basic regular expressions, such as `^`, meaning "start," and `$`, meaning "end." For example, you might want to search for programs that are part of the main KDE suite and not libraries (usually named something like libkde), additional bits (such as xmms-kde), and things that are actually nothing to do with KDE yet still match our search (like tkdesk). This can be done by searching for packages that have a name starting with kde, as follows:

```
matthew@seymour:~$ apt-cache -n search ^kde.
```

Perhaps the easiest way to find packages is to combine `apt-cache` with `grep`, to search within search results. For example, if you want to find all games-related packages for KDE, you could run this search:

```
matthew@seymour:~$ apt-cache search games ¦ grep kde
```

When you've found the package you want to install, run it through `apt-get install` as per usual. If you first want a little more information about that package, you can use `apt-cache showpkg`, like this:

```
matthew@seymour:~$ apt-cache showpkg mysql-server-5.0
```

This shows information on "reverse depends" (which packages require, recommend, or suggest mysql-server-5.0), "dependencies" (which packages are required, recommended, or suggested to install mysql-server-5.0) and "provides" (which functions this package gives you). The "provides" list is quite powerful because it allows different packages to provide a given resource. For example, a MySQL database-based program requires MySQL to be installed, but isn't fussy whether you install MySQL 4.1 or MySQL 5.0. In this situation, the Debian packages for MySQL 4.1 and MySQL 5.0 will both have "mysql-server-4.1" in the provides list, meaning that they offer the functionality provided by MySQL 4.1. As a result, you can install either version to satisfy the MySQL-based application.

Compiling Software from Source

Compiling applications from source is not that difficult. Most source code is available as compressed source *tarballs*—that is, `tar` files that have been compressed using `gzip` or `bzip`. The compressed files typically uncompress into a directory containing several files. It is always a good idea to compile source code as a regular user to limit any damage that broken or malicious code might inflict, so create a directory named `source` in your home directory.

From wherever you downloaded the source tarball, uncompress it into the `~/source` directory using the `-C` option to `tar`:

```
matthew@seymour:~$ tar zxvf packagename.tgz -C ~/source

matthew@seymour:~$ tar zxvf packagename.tar.gz -C ~/source

matthew@seymour:~$ tar jxvf packagename.bz -C ~/source

matthew@seymour:~$ tar jxvf packagename.tar.bz2 -C ~/source
```

If you are not certain what file compression method was used, use the `file` command to figure it out:

```
matthew@seymour:~$ file packagename
```

Now, change directories to `~/source/packagename` and look for a file named `README`, `INSTALL`, or a similar name. Print out the file if necessary because it contains specific instructions on how to compile and install the software. Typically, the procedure to compile source code is as follows:

```
matthew@seymour:~/source/packagename$ ./configure
```

This runs a script to check whether all dependencies are met and the build environment is correct. If you are missing dependencies, the configure script normally tells you exactly which ones it needs. If you have the Universe and Multiverse repositories enabled in Synaptic, chances are you will find the missing software (usually libraries) in there.

When your configure script succeeds, run the following to compile the software:

```
matthew@seymour:~/source/packagename$ make
```

And finally, run the following:

```
matthew@seymour:~/source/packagename$ sudo make install.
```

If the compile fails, check the error messages for the reason and run the following before you start again:

```
matthew@seymour:~/source/packagename$ make clean
```

You can also run the following to remove the software if you do not like it:

```
matthew@seymour:~/source/packagename$ sudo make uninstall
```

Reference

- www.debian.org/doc/manuals/project-history/ch-detailed.en.html—History of the Debian Linux package system www.nongnu.org/synaptic/—Home of the Synaptic package managerwww.ubuntu.com/usn—The official list of Ubuntu security notices

CHAPTER 33

Securing Your Machines

IN THIS CHAPTER

- Understanding Computer Attacks
- Assessing Your Vulnerability
- Protecting Your Machine
- Viruses
- Configuring Your Firewall
- AppArmor
- Forming a Disaster Recovery Plan
- Reference

No computer with a connection to the Internet is 100 percent safe. If this information does not concern you, it should! Although there is no way to guarantee the ability to stop patient, creative, and serious crackers who are intent on getting into your computer or network, there are ways to make it harder for them and to warn you when they do.

In this chapter, we discuss all aspects of securing your Linux machines. You might have wondered why we did not spread this information around the book wherever it was appropriate, but the reason is simple: If you ever have a security problem with Linux, you know you can turn to this page and start reading without having to search or try to remember where you saw a tip. Everything you need is here in this one chapter, and we strongly advise you read it from start to finish.

BUILT-IN PROTECTION IN THE KERNEL

A number of networking and low-level protective services are built in to the Linux kernel. These services can be enabled, disabled, or displayed using the `sysctl` command, or by echoing a value (usually a `1` or a `0` to turn a service on or off) to a kernel process file under the `/proc` directory.

Understanding Computer Attacks

There are many ways in which computer attacks can be divided for classification. Perhaps the easiest dichotomy is to separate attacks as *internal,* which are computer attacks done by someone with access to a computer on the local network, and *external*, which are attacks by someone with access to a computer through the Internet. This might sound like a trivial separation to make, but it is actually important: Unless you routinely hire talented computer crackers or allow visitors to plug computers into your network, the worst internal attack you are likely encounter is from a disgruntled employee.

HACKER VERSUS CRACKER

In earlier days, there was a distinction made between the words *hacker* and *cracker*. A hacker was someone who used technology to innovate in new or unusual ways, whereas a cracker was someone who used technology to attack another's computers and cause harm. In the original definition, hackers did good or cool things and crackers did bad things.

This distinction was lost on the general public, so the term *hacker* has now regretfully come to mean the same thing as *cracker for most people*. However, we recognize the distinction and use the term cracker to mean a malicious person using a computer to cause problems for others. In your real-world conversations, you should realize most people will not make a distinction, and you should be prepared to define your terms if you call yourself a hacker.

Although you should never ignore the internal threat, you should arguably be more concerned with the outside world. The big bad Internet is a security vortex. Machines connected directly to the outside world can be attacked by people across the world, and invariably are, even only a few minutes after having been connected.

This situation is not a result of malicious users lying in wait for your IP address to do something interesting. Instead, canny virus writers have created worms that exploit a vulnerability, take control of a machine, and then spread it to other machines around them. As a result, most attacks today are the result of these autocracking tools; there are only a handful of true clever crackers around, and, to be frank, if one of them ever actually targets you seriously, it will take a mammoth effort to repel the cracker, regardless of which operating system you run.

Autocracking scripts also come in another flavor: prewritten code that exploits a vulnerability and gives its users special privileges on the hacked machine. These scripts are rarely used by their creators; instead, they are posted online and downloaded by wannabe hackers, who then use them to attack vulnerable machines.

So, the external category is itself made up of worms, serious day job crackers, and wannabe crackers (usually called *script kiddies*). Combined they will assault your Internet-facing servers, and it is your job to make sure your boxes stay up, happily ignoring the firefight around them.

On the internal front, things are somewhat more difficult. Users who sit inside your firewall are already past your primary source of defense and, worse, they might even have physical access to your machines. Anyone with malicious intent and physical access to a machine is nearly impossible to stop unless they are simply inept. The situation is only slightly better if they don't have physical access but do have access to your internal network.

Regardless of the source of the attack, you can follow a five-step checklist to secure your box:

1. Assess your vulnerability. Decide which machines can be attacked, which services they are running, and who has access to them.
2. Configure the server for maximum security. Install only what you need, run only what you must, and configure a local firewall.
3. Secure physical access to the server.
4. Create worst-case-scenario policies.
5. Keep up-to-date with security news.

Each of these is covered in the following sections, and each is as important as the others.

Assessing Your Vulnerability

It is a common mistake for people to assume that switching on a firewall makes them safe. This is not the case and, in fact, has never been the case. Each system has distinct security needs, and taking the time to customize its security layout will give you maximum security and the best performance.

The following list summarizes the most common mistakes:

- **Installing every package**—Do you plan to use the machine as a DNS server? If not, why have BIND installed? Go through and ensure that you have only the software you need.
- **Enabling unused services**—Do you want to administer the machine remotely? Do you want people to upload files? If not, turn off SSH and FTP because they just add needless attack vectors. This goes for many other services.
- **Disabling the local firewall on the grounds that you already have a firewall at the perimeter**—In security, depth is crucial: The more layers someone has to hack through, the higher the likelihood the cracker will give up or get caught.
- **Letting your machine give out more information than it needs to**—Many machines are configured to give out software names and version numbers by default, which is just giving crackers a helping hand.
- **Placing your server in an unlocked room**—If so, you might as well just turn it off now and save the worry. The exception to this is if all the employees at your company are happy and trustworthy. But why take the risk?
- **Plugging your machine into a wireless network**—Unless you need wireless, avoid it, particularly if your machine is a server. Never plug a server into a wireless network because it is just too fraught with security problems.

After you have ruled out these, you are onto the real problem: Which attack vectors are open on your server? In Internet terms, this comes down to which services are Internet-facing and which ports they are running on.

Two tools are often used to determine your vulnerabilities: Nmap and Nessus. Nessus scans your machine, queries the services running, checks their version numbers against its list of vulnerabilities, and reports problems.

Although Nessus sounds clever, it does not work well in many modern distributions (Ubuntu included) because of the way patches are made available to software. For example, if you're running Apache 2.0.52 and a bug is found that's fixed in 2.0.53, Ubuntu backports that patch to 2.0.52. This is done because the new release probably also includes new features that might break your code, so the Ubuntu team takes only what is necessary and copies it into your version. As a result, Nessus will see the version 2.0.52 and think it is vulnerable to a bug that has in fact been backported.

The better solution is to use Nmap, which scans your machine and reports on any open TCP/IP ports it finds. Any service you have installed that responds to Nmap's query is pointed out, which enables you to ensure that you have locked everything down as much as possible.

Nmap is available to install from the Ubuntu software repositories. Although you can use Nmap from a command line, it is easier to use with the front end—at least until you become proficient. To run the front end, open a terminal and run `nmapfe`. If you want to enable all Nmap's options, you need to have administrator privileges and run `sudo nmapfe`.

When you run Nmap (click the Scan button), it tests every port on your machine and checks whether it responds. If it does respond, Nmap queries it for version information and then prints its results onscreen.

The output lists the port numbers, service name (what usually occupies that port), and version number for every open port on your system. Hopefully, the information Nmap shows you will not be a surprise. If there is something open that you do not recognize, it could be that a cracker placed a backdoor on your system to allow easy access, so you should check into it further.

You should use the output from Nmap to help you find and eliminate unwanted services. The fewer services that are open to the outside world, the more secure you are. Only use Nmap on systems that you own. It is impolite to scan other people's servers and you may also be accused of doing so in preparation for illegal activity.

Protecting Your Machine

After you have disabled all the unneeded services on your system, what remains is a core set of connections and programs that you want to keep. However, you are not finished yet: You need to clamp down your wireless network, lock your server physically, and put scanning procedures in place (such as Tripwire and promiscuous mode network monitors).

Securing a Wireless Network

Because wireless networking has some unique security issues, those issues deserve a separate discussion here.

Wireless networking, although convenient, can be very insecure by its very nature because transmitted data (even encrypted data) can be received by remote devices. Those devices could be in the same room; in the house, apartment, or building next door; or even several blocks away. Extra care must be used to protect the actual frequency used by your network. Great progress has been made in the past couple of years, but the possibility of a security breech is increased when the attacker is in the area and knows the frequency on which to listen. It should also be noted that the encryption method used by more wireless NICs is weaker than other forms of encryption (such as SSH) and should not be considered as part of your security plan.

TIP

Always use OpenSSH-related tools, such as `ssh` or `sftp`, to conduct business on your wireless LAN. Passwords are not transmitted as plain text, and your sessions are encrypted. See Chapter 15, "Remote Access with SSH and Telnet," to see how to connect to remote systems using `ssh`.

The better the physical security is around your network, the more secure it will be (this applies to wired networks as well). Keep wireless transmitters (routers, switches, and so on) as close to the center of your building as possible. Note or monitor the range of transmitted signals to determine whether your network is open to mobile network sniffing—now a geek sport known as *war driving*. Wireshark is an example of a program that is useful for analyzing wireless traffic (as well as all network activity) and can be installed from the Ubuntu repositories with more information at www.wireshark.org/. An occasional walk around your building not only gives you a break from work, but can also give you a chance to notice any people or equipment that should not be in the area.

Keep in mind that it takes only a single rogue wireless access point hooked up to a legitimate network hub to open access to your entire system. These access points can be smaller than a pack of cigarettes, so the only way to spot them is to scan for them with another wireless device.

Passwords and Physical Security

The next step toward better security is to use secure passwords on your network and ensure that users use them as well. For somewhat more physical security, you can force the use of a password with the GRUB bootloader, remove bootable devices such as floppy and CD-ROM drives, or configure a network-booting server for Ubuntu.

Also, keep in mind that some studies show that as many as 90 percent of network breakins are by current or former employees. If a person no longer requires access to your network, lock out access or, even better, remove the account immediately. A good security policy also dictates that any data associated with the account first be backed up and retained for a set period of time to ensure against loss of important data. If you are able, remove the terminated employee from the system before the employee leaves the building.

Finally, be aware of physical security. If a potential attacker can get physical access to your system, getting full access becomes trivial. Keep all servers in a locked room, and ensure that only authorized personnel are given access to clients.

Configuring and Using Tripwire

Tripwire is a security tool that checks the integrity of normal system binaries and reports any changes to syslog or by email. Tripwire is a good tool for ensuring that your binaries have not been replaced by Trojan horse programs. *Trojan horses* are malicious programs inadvertently installed because of identical filenames to distributed (expected) programs, and they can wreak havoc on a breached system.

There are two versions of Tripwire, an open source version and a commercial product. The free version of Tripwire is available in the Ubuntu repositories. You can find out about the differences at www.tripwire.org.

To initialize Tripwire, use its `—init` option like this:

```
matthew@seymour~:$ sudo tripwire —init
Please enter your local passphrase:
Parsing policy file: /etc/tripwire/tw.pol
Generating the database...
*** Processing Unix File System ***
....
Wrote database file: /var/lib/tripwire/shuttle2.twd
The database was successfully generated.
```

Note that not all the output is shown here. After Tripwire has created its database (which is a snapshot of your file system), it uses this baseline along with the encrypted configuration and policy settings under the `/etc/tripwire` directory to monitor the status of your system. You should then start Tripwire in its integrity checking mode, using a desired option. (See the tripwire manual page for details.) For example, you can have Tripwire check your system and then generate a report at the command line, like this:

```
matthew@seymour~:$ sudo tripwire -m c
```

No output is shown here, but a report is displayed in this example. The output could be redirected to a file, but a report is saved as `/var/lib/tripwire/report/hostname-YYYYMMDD-HHMMSS.twr` (in other words, using your host's name, the year, the month, the day, the hour, the minute, and the seconds). This report can be read using the `twprint` utility, like this:

```
matthew@seymour~:$ sudo twprint —print-report -r \
/var/lib/tripwire/report/shuttle2-20020919-181049.twr ¦ less
```

Other options, such as emailing the report, are supported by Tripwire, which should be run as a scheduled task by your system's scheduling table, `/etc/crontab`, on off-hours. (It can be resource intensive on less powerful computers.) The Tripwire software package also includes a `twadmin` utility you can use to fine-tune or change settings or policies or to perform other administrative duties.

Plan to spend some time reading documentation if you want to use Tripwire. It is powerful, but not simple. We recommend starting with the man pages and www.tripwire.com.

Devices

Do not ever advertise that you have set a NIC to promiscuous mode. Promiscuous mode (which can be set on an interface by using `ifconfig`'s `promisc` option) is good for monitoring traffic across the network and can often allow you to monitor the actions of someone who might have broken into your network. The `tcpdump` command also sets a designated interface to promiscuous mode while the program runs; unfortunately, the `ifconfig` command does not report this fact while `tcpdump` is running!

Remember to use the right tool for the right job. Although a network bridge can be used to connect your network to the Internet, it would not be a good option. Bridges have almost become obsolete because they forward any packet that comes their way, which is not good when a bridge is connected to the Internet. A router enables you to filter which packets are relayed.

Viruses

In the right hands, Linux is every bit as vulnerable to viruses as Windows is. That might come as a surprise to you, particularly if you made the switch to Linux on the basis of its security record. However, the difference between Windows and Linux is that it is much easier to secure against viruses on Linux. Indeed, as long as you are smart and diligent, you need never worry about them. Here is why:

- Linux never puts the current directory in your executable path, so typing `ls` runs `/bin/ls` rather than any program named ls in the current directory.
- A non-root user can infect only the files that user has write access to, which is usually only the files in the user's home directory. This is one of the most important reasons for never using sudo when you don't need to!
- Linux forces you to manually mark files as executable, so you can't accidentally run a file called `myfile.txt.exe`, thinking it was just a text file.
- By having more than one common web browser and email client, Linux has strength through diversity: Virus writers cannot target one platform and hit 90 percent of the users.

Despite saying all that, Linux is susceptible to being a carrier for viruses. If you run a mail server, your Linux box can send virus-infected mails on to Windows boxes. The Linux-based server would be fine, but the Windows client would be taken down by the virus.

In this situation, you should consider a virus scanner for your machine. You have several to choose from, both free and commercial. The most popular free suite is Clam AV (www.clamav.net), but Central Command, BitDefender, F-Secure, Kaspersky, McAfee, and others all compete to provide commercial solutions—look around for the best deal before you commit.

Configuring Uncomplicated Firewall (UFW)

Always use a hardware-based or software-based firewall on computers connected to the Internet. Ubuntu has a firewall application installed by default named UFW or Uncomplicated Firewall. This tool allows you to implement selective or restrictive policies regarding access to your computer or LAN.

UFW is run from the terminal, and you must have administrative privileges to use it. Commands are given like this:

```
matthew@seymour~:$ sudo ufw status
```

The most useful commands are listed in Table 33.1. For others, see `man ufw`. Many are described in greater detail after the table.

TABLE 33.1 Useful commands for UFW

Usage: UFW COMMAND	
Commands:	
enable	enables the firewall
disable	disables the firewall
reload	reloads the firewall to ensure changes are applied
default allow¦deny¦reject sets	default policy
logging on¦off	toggles logging (can also be used to set the level of logging, see manual)
allow ARGS	adds allow rule
deny ARGS	adds deny rule
reject ARGS	adds reject rule
limit ARGS	adds limit rule
delete RULE	deletes RULE
status shows	firewall status
status numbered	shows firewall status as numbered list of RULES
status verbose	shows verbose firewall status
show REPORT	shows firewall report
—version	displays version information

By default the UFW or firewall is disabled. To enable the firewall you will run the following command:

```
matthew@seymour~:$ sudo ufw enable
```

To disable replace enabled with disabled.

Next, we will want to enable firewall logging. Much like the enable command we will run the following command:

```
matthew@seymour~:$ sudo ufw logging on
```

To enable specific ports on the firewall you can run UFW command along with the port number to open. For example if you want to allow port 80 (http) incoming connections to your Ubuntu server you would enter the following:

```
matthew@seymour~:$ sudo ufw allow 80
```

To remove the firewall rule allowing port 80 connections run the following command:

```
matthew@seymour~:$ sudo ufw delete allow 80
```


Many services are already defined in `ufw`. This means you don't have to remember the standard ports those services use and you can allow, deny or delete using the service name, like this:

```
matthew@seymour~:$ sudo ufw allow ssh
```

You can also allow incoming connections from particular IP addresses, for example if you want to let 192.168.0.1 to connect to your server you would enter the following:

```
matthew@seymour~:$ sudo ufw allow from 192.168.0.1
```

To remove the firewall rule allowing the previous IP address to connect you would run the following command:

```
matthew@seymour~:$ sudo ufw delete allow from 192.168.0.1
```

There is also a graphical interface that can be installed from the Ubuntu repositories to manage UFW called GUFW. If you install it, you can open GUFW at System, Administration, Firewall configuration. The same details apply, but the interface is easier and does not require to remember as much, as you can see in Figure 33.1 where I have a rule to allow traffic in on port 22 (for the `ssh` service) and incoming traffic on port 5900 if it uses the `tcp` protocol (for the VNC service).

If you click Add you can add rules for preconfigured services easily, as shown in Figure 33.2, or you can configure your own rules from the Simple and Advanced tabs.

AppArmor

AppArmor is a Manditory Access Control (MAC) system. It is less complicated than the better known SELinux (www.nsa.gov/research/selinux/), a MAC created by the United States' National Security Agency (NSA). AppArmor is designed to limit what specific programs can do by restricting them to the use of predetermined resources and only those resources. This is done via profiles, which are loaded into the kernel at boot. It can be run in complain mode, where information is logged about insecure practices but no action is taken, or in enforce mode where policies and limits are active.

This is a brief introduction to AppArmor. For a fuller introduction, checks the links listed in the Reference section, as well as take a look at this Ubuntu Forums thread: http://ubuntuforums.org/showthread.php?t=1008906.

FIGURE 33.1 The GUFW graphical interface.

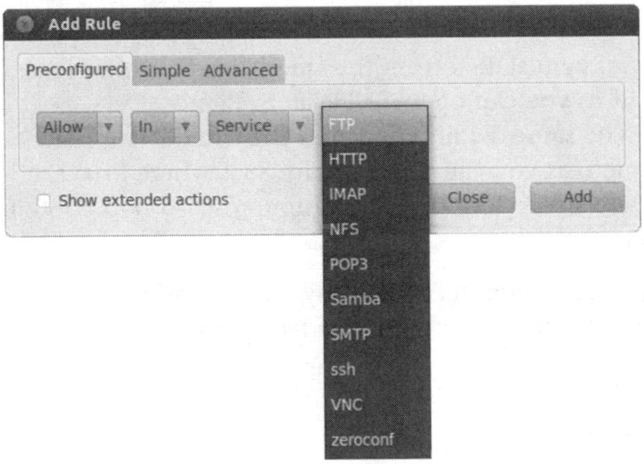

FIGURE 33.2 GUFW preconfigured service options.

By default, AppArmor does very little. You can install some extra profiles from the Ubuntu repositories by installing the `apparmor-profiles` package. These will run in complain mode and log issues in /var/log/messages.

To unleash the power of AppArmor, you need to edit or create text files in /etc/apparmor.d. Profiles are named for the application they restrict, including the full path to the application in the filesystem. For example, the file sbin.syslogd, shown here, restricts the system logging daemon:

```
# $Id$
# ------------------------------------------------------------------
#
#    Copyright (C) 2002-2005 Novell/SUSE
#
#    This program is free software; you can redistribute it and/or
#    modify it under the terms of version 2 of the GNU General Public
#    License published by the Free Software Foundation.
#
# ------------------------------------------------------------------


#include <tunables/global>


/sbin/syslogd flags=(complain) {
  #include <abstractions/base>
  #include <abstractions/nameservice>
  #include <abstractions/consoles>


  capability sys_tty_config,
  capability dac_override,
  capability dac_read_search,
  capability setuid,
  capability setgid,


  /dev/log                       wl,
  /var/lib/*/dev/log             wl,


  /dev/tty*                      w,
  /dev/xconsole                  rw,
  /etc/syslog.conf               r,
  /sbin/syslogd                  rmix,
  /var/log/**                    rw,
  /var/run/syslogd.pid           krwl,
  /var/run/utmp                  rw,
  /var/spool/compaq/nic/messages_fifo rw,
}
```

33

Even without knowing the syntax, we can see from this file that profiles are simple text files that support the use of comments, that absolute paths and globbing (pattern matching for filenames) are supported, that specific capabilities are allowed or disallowed, and what locations and programs in the filesystem may be accessed or used.

Each access rule specifies specific permissions from this list:

```
r    - read
w    - write
ux   - unconstrained execute
Ux   - unconstrained execute — scrub the environment
px   - discrete profile execute
Px   - discrete profile execute — scrub the environment
ix   - inherit execute
m    - allow PROT_EXEC with mmap(2) calls
l    - link
```

These permissions are listed at the end of lines.

Genprof is a program that helps you generate or update a profile. You supply the name of the executable (or the path, if it is not already in the path) and may optionally supply the path to the profiles as well.

```
matthew@seymour~:$ sudo genprof google-chrome
```

You will be asked to start the program and use it for a bit. After it is complete, you will be given an opportunity to choose whether access to each function should be allowed or denied. The program will then write a text file in /etc/apparmor.d using the name of the program and its path, in this case opt.google.chrome.google-chrome, which I installed directly from Google (www.google.com/chrome?platform=linux), so no premade Apparmor profile exists on my system. You may then edit the text file as desired, which you will need to do if you want to change from complain to enforce mode.

After you have a set of profiles that cover what you need, these are the commands you will use most often:

Start :

```
matthew@seymour~:$ sudo service apparmor start
```

Stop :

```
matthew@seymour~:$ sudo service apparmor stop
```

Reload:

```
matthew@seymour~:$ sudo service apparmor reload (or restart)
```

Show status:

```
matthew@seymour~:$ sudo service apparmor status
```

We have only scratched the surface of AppArmor, but hopefully enough to have whetted your appetite to do some further reading. AppArmor is still rather new and is changing. Online documentation is the best way to keep up. A few good places to start are included in the Referencesection.

Forming a Disaster Recovery Plan

No one likes planning for the worst, which is why two thirds of people do not have wills. It is a scary thing to have your systems hacked: One or more criminals has broken through your carefully laid blocks and caused untold damage to the machine. Your boss, if you have one, will want a full report of what happened and why, and your users will want their email when they sit down at their desks in the morning. What to do?

If you ever do get hacked, nothing will take the stress away entirely. However, if you take the time to prepare a proper response in advance, you should at least avoid premature aging. Here are some tips to get you started:

- **Do not just pull the network cable out**—This acts as an alert that the cracker has been detected, which rules out any opportunities for security experts to monitor for that cracker returning and actually catch him.
- **Only inform the people who need to know**—Your boss and other IT people are at the top of the list; other employees are not. Keep in mind that it could be one of the employees behind the attack, and this tips them off.
- **If the machine is not required and you do not want to trace the attack, you can safely remove it from the network**—However, do not switch it off because some backdoors are enabled only when the system is rebooted.
- **Take a copy of all the log files on the system and store them somewhere else**—These might have been tampered with, but they might contain nuggets of information.
- **Check the**

`/etc/passwd` file and look for users you do not recognize—Change all the passwords on the system, and remove bad users.

- **Check the output of**

`ps aux` for unusual programs running—Also check to see whether any cron jobs are set to run.

- **Look in /var/www and see whether any web pages are there that should not be.**
- **Check the contents of the `.bash_history`** files in the home directories of your users—Are there any recent commands for your primary user?
- **If you have worked with external security companies previously, call them in for a fresh audit**—Hand over all the logs you have, and explain the situation. They will be able to extract all the information from the logs that is possible.
- **Start collating backup tapes from previous weeks and months**—Your system might have been hacked long before you noticed, so you might need to roll back the system more than once to find out when the attack actually succeeded.

- **Download and install Rootkit Hunter from www.rootkit.nl/projects/rootkit_hunter.html**—This searches for (and removes) the types of files that bad guys leave behind for their return.

Keep your disaster recovery plan somewhere safe; saving it as a file on the machine in question is a very bad move!

Reference

- https://help.ubuntu.com/community/InstallingSecurityTools—Ubuntu community documentation of and suggestions for various security tools.
- www.insecure.org/nmap/—This site contains information on Nmap.
- www.securityfocus.com/—The Security Focus website.
- www.tripwire.org—Information and download links for the open-source version of Tripwire.
- www.ubuntu.com/usn—The official Ubuntu security notices list; well worth keeping an eye on!
- https://help.ubuntu.com/community/UFW—Ubuntu community documentation for UFW.
- https://wiki.ubuntu.com/UncomplicatedFirewall—Ubuntu documentation for UFW.
- https://help.ubuntu.com/community/AppArmor—Ubuntu community documentation for AppArmor.
- www.novell.com/linux/security/apparmor/—Novell's excellent introduction to and documentation for AppArmor.

CHAPTER 34

Performance Tuning

IN THIS CHAPTER

Squeezing extra performance out of your hardware might sound like a pointless task given how cheap commodity upgrades are today. To a certain degree that is true—for most of us, it is cheaper to buy a new computer than to spend hours fighting to get a 5 percent speed boost. But what if the speed boost were 20 percent? How about if it were 50 percent?

The amount of benefit you can get by optimizing your system varies depending on what kinds of tasks you are running, but there is something for everyone. Over the next few pages we will be looking at quick ways to optimize the Apache web server, both the KDE and Gnome desktop systems, both MySQL and PostgreSQL database servers, and more.

Before we start, you need to understand that *optimization* is not an absolute term: If we optimize a system, we have improved its performance, but it is still possible it could further be increased. We are not interested in getting 99.999 percent performance out of a system, because optimization suffers from the law of diminishing returns—the basic changes make the biggest differences, but after that it takes increasing amounts of work to obtain decreasing speed improvements.

Hard Disk

Many Linux users love to tinker under the hood to increase the performance of their computers, and Linux gives you some great tools to do that. Whereas Moms tell us, "Don't fix what's not broken," Dads often say, "Fix it until it breaks." In this section, you learn about many of the commands used to tune, or "tweak," your file system.

Before you undertake any "under the hood" work with Linux, however, keep a few points in mind. First, perform a benchmark on your system before you begin. Linux does not offer a well-developed benchmarking application, and availability of what exists changes rapidly. You can search online for the most up-to-date information for benchmarking applications for Linux. If you are a system administrator, you might choose to create your own benchmarking tests. Second, tweak only one thing at a time so you can tell what works, what does not work, and what breaks. Some of these tweaks might not work or might lock up your machine.

Always have a working boot disc handy and remember that you are personally assuming all risks for attempting any of these tweaks. If you don't understand what you are doing or are not confident in your ability to revert any changes discussed here, do not attempt any of the suggestions in this chapter. The default settings in Ubuntu work very well for most people and really don't need adjusting; but some people like old 1960s muscle cars and enjoy tweaking and breaking and fixing them. This chapter is for that sort of person. If you don't think you can fix it, don't risk breaking it.

Using the BIOS and Kernel to Tune the Disk Drives

One method of tuning involves adjusting the settings in your BIOS. Because the BIOS is not Linux and every BIOS seems different, always read your motherboard manual for better possible settings and make certain that all the drives are detected correctly by the BIOS. Change only one setting at a time.

Linux provides a limited means to interact with BIOS settings during the boot process (mostly overriding them). In this section, you learn about those commands.

Other options are in the following list, and are more fully outlined in the BOOTPROMPT HOWTO and the kernel documentation. These commands can be used to force the IDE controllers and drives to be optimally configured. However, YMMV (Your Mileage May Vary) because these do not work for everyone.

- `idex=dma`—This will force DMA support to be turned on for the primary IDE bus, where x=0, or the secondary bus, where x=1.
- `idex=autotune`—This command will attempt to tune the interface for optimal performance.
- `hdx=ide-scsi`—This command will enable SCSI emulation of an IDE drive. This is required for some CD-RW drives to work properly in write mode, and it might provide some performance improvements for regular CD-R drives as well.
- `idebus=xx`—This can be any number from 20 to 66; autodetection is attempted, but this can set it manually if `dmesg` says that it isn't autodetected correctly or if you have it set in the BIOS to a different value (overclocked). Most PCI controllers will be happy with 33.

- `pci=biosirq`—Some motherboards might cause Linux to generate an error message saying that you should use this. Look in `dmesg` for it; if you do not see it, you don't need to use it.

These options can be entered into `/etc/lilo.conf` or `/boot/grub/grub.conf` or GRUB2's `/boot/grub/grub.cfg` in the same way as other options are appended.

The hdparm Command

The `hdparm` utility can be used by root to set and tune the settings for IDE hard drives. You would do this to tune the drives for optimal performance.

Once a kernel patch and associated support programs, the `hdparm` program is now included with Ubuntu. You should only experiment with the file systems mounted read-only because some settings can damage some file systems when used improperly. The `hdparm` command also works with CD-ROM drives and some SCSI drives.

The general format of the command is this:

```
matthew@seymour:~? hdparm command device
```

This command runs a hard disk test:

```
matthew@seymour:~? hdparm -tT /dev/hda
```

You will need to replace `/dev/hda` with the location of your hard disk. `hdparm` will then run two tests—cached reads and buffered disk reads. A good IDE hard disk should be getting 400–500MB/sec for the first test, and 20–30MB/sec for the second. Note your scores, then try this command:

```
matthew@seymour:~? hdparm -m16 -d1 -u1 -c1 /dev/hda
```

That enables various performance-enhancing settings. Now try executing the original command again—if you see an increase, you should run this command:

```
matthew@seymour:~? hdparm -m16 -d1 -u1 -c1 -k1 /dev/hda
```

The extra parameter tells `hdparm` to write the settings to disk so they will be used each time you boot up—ensuring optimal disk performance in the future.

The man entry for `hdparm` is extensive and contains useful detailed information, but because the kernel configuration selected by Ubuntu already attempts to optimize the drives, it might be that little can be gained through tweaking. Because not all hardware combinations can be anticipated by Ubuntu or by Linux, and performance gains are always useful, you're encouraged to try.

TIP

You can use the hdparm command to produce a disk transfer speed result with

```
matthew@seymour:~? hdparm -tT device
```

Be aware, however, that although the resulting numbers appear quantitative, they are subject to several technical qualifications beyond the scope of what is discussed and explained in this chapter. Simply put, do not accept values generated by `hdparm` as absolute numbers, but only as a relative measure of performance.

File System Tuning

Never content to leave things alone, Linux provides several tools to adjust and customize the file system settings. The belief is that hardware manufacturers and distribution creators tend to select conservative settings that will work well all the time, leaving some of the potential of your system leashed—that's why you have chosen *Ubuntu Unleashed* to help you.

The Linux file system designers have done an excellent job of selecting default values used for file system creation, and the 2.6 version of the Linux kernel now contains new code for the IDE subsystem that significantly improves I/O (input/output) transfer speeds over older versions, obviating much of the need for special tweaking of the file system and drive parameters if you use IDE disks. Although these values work well for most users, some server applications of Linux benefit from file system tuning. As always, observe and benchmark your changes.

SYNCHRONIZING THE FILE SYSTEM WITH SYNC

Because Linux uses buffers when writing to devices, the write will not occur until the buffer is full, until the kernel tells it to, or if you tell it to by using the `sync` command. Traditionally, the command is given twice, as in the following:

```
matthew@seymour:~? sync ; sync
```

To do it twice is overkill. Still, it can be helpful before the unmounting of certain types of media with slow write speeds (such as some USB hard drives or PCMCIA storage media), but only because it delays the user from attempting to remove the media too soon, not because two syncs are better than one.

The `tune2fs` Command

With `tune2fs`, you can adjust the tunable file system parameters on an `ext2` or `ext3` file system. A few performance-related items of note are as follows:

- To disable file system checking, the `-c 0` option sets the maximal mount count to zero.
- The interval between forced checks can be adjusted with the `-i` option.
- The `-m` option will set the reserved blocks percentage with a lower value, freeing more space at the expense of fsck having less space to write any recovered files.
- Decrease the number of superblocks to save space with the `-O sparse_super option`. (Modern file systems use this by default.) Always run `e2fsck` after you change this value.
- More space can be freed with the `-r` option that sets the number of reserved (for root) blocks.

Note that most of these uses of `tune2fs` free up space on the drive at the expense of the capability of `fsck` to recover data. Unless you really need the space and can deal with the consequences, just accept the defaults; large drives are now relatively inexpensive.

The `e2fsck` Command

This utility checks an `ext2/ext3` file system. Some useful arguments taken from `man e2fsck` are as follows:

- `-c`—Checks for bad blocks and then marks them as bad.
- `-f`—Forces checking on a clean file system.
- `-v`—Verbose mode.

The `badblocks` Command

Although not a performance tuning program per se, the utility `badblocks` checks an (preferably) unmounted partition for bad blocks. It is not recommended that you run this command by itself, but rather allow it to be called by `fsck`. It should be used directly only if you specify the block size accurately—don't guess or assume anything.

The options available for `badblocks` are detailed in the `man` page. They allow for very low-level manipulation of the file system that is useful for data recovery by file system experts or for file system hacking, but are beyond the scope of this chapter and the average user.

Disabling File Access Time

Whenever Linux reads a file, it changes the last access time—known as the `atime`. This is also true for your web server: If you are getting hit by 50 requests a second, your hard disk will be updating the atime 50 times a second. Do you really need to know the last time a file was accessed? If not, you can disable the atime setting for a directory by typing this:

```
matthew@seymour:~? chattr -R +A /path/to/directory
```

The `chattr` command changes file system attributes, of which "don't update atime" is one. To set that attribute, use +A and specify –R so that it is recursively set. `/path/to/directory` gets changed, and so do all the files and subdirectories it contains.

Kernel

As the Linux kernel developed over time, developers sought a way to fine-tune some of the kernel parameters. Before `sysctl`, those parameters had to be changed in the kernel configuration, and then the kernel had to be recompiled.

The `sysctl` command can change some parameters of a running kernel. It does this through the `/proc` file system, which is a "virtual window" into the running kernel. Although it might appear that a group of directories and files exist under `/proc`, that is only a representation of parts of the kernel. When we're the root user (or using the sudo command), we can read values from and write values to those "files," referred to as *variables*. We can display a list of the variables as shown in the following. (An annotated list is presented because roughly 250 items, or more, exist in the full list.)

```
matthew@seymour:~? sysctl -A
net.ipv4.tcp_max_syn_backlog = 1024
```

```
net.ipv4.tcp_rfc1337 = 0
net.ipv4.tcp_stdurg = 0
net.ipv4.tcp_abort_on_overflow = 0
net.ipv4.tcp_tw_recycle = 0
net.ipv4.tcp_syncookies = 0
net.ipv4.tcp_fin_timeout = 60
net.ipv4.tcp_retries2 = 15
net.ipv4.tcp_retries1 = 3
net.ipv4.tcp_keepalive_intvl = 75
net.ipv4.tcp_keepalive_probes = 9
net.ipv4.tcp_keepalive_time = 7200
net.ipv4.ipfrag_time = 30
```

The items shown are networking parameters, and tweaking these values is beyond the scope of this book. If we wanted to change a value, however, the `-w` parameter is used:

```
matthew@seymour:~? sysctl -w net.ipv4.tcp_retries 2=20
```

This increases the value of that particular kernel parameter.

If you find that a particular setting is useful, you can enter it into the `/etc/sysctl.conf` file. The format is as follows, using the earlier example:

```
net.ipv4.tcp_retries 2=20
```

Of more interest to kernel hackers than regular users, `sysctl` is a potentially powerful tool that continues to be developed and documented.

TIP

The kernel does a good job of balancing performance for graphical systems, so there's not a great deal you can do to tweak your desktop to run faster.

Both GNOME and KDE are "heavyweight" desktop systems: They are all-inclusive, all-singing, and all-dancing environments that do far more than browse your file system. The drawback is that their size makes them run slow on older systems. On the flip side, Ubuntu has others available in the repositories like the Xfce desktop, which is a great deal slimmer and faster than the other two. If you find GNOME and KDE are struggling just to open a file browser, Xfce is for you.

Apache

Despite being the most popular web server on the Internet, Apache is by no means the fastest. Part of the "problem" is that Apache has been written to follow every applicable standard to the letter, so much of its development work has been geared toward standards-compliancy rather than just serving web pages quickly. However, with a little tweaking we can convert an inexpensive middle-of-the-road server into something capable of surviving the Slashdot Effect.

NOTE

Slashdot.org is a popular geek news website that spawned the Slashdot Effect—the result of thousands of geeks descending on an unsuspecting website simultaneously.

The first target for your tuning should be the `apache2.conf` file in `/etc/apache2`, as well as the other files in `/etc/apache2`. The more modules you have loaded, the more load Apache is placing on your server—take a look through the LoadModule list and comment out (start the line with a #) the ones you do not want. Some of these modules can be uninstalled entirely through the Add or Remove Packages dialog.

As a rough guide, you will almost certainly need `mod_mime` and `mod_dir`, and probably also `mod_log_config`. The default Apache configuration in Ubuntu is quite generic, so unless you are willing to sacrifice some functionality you may also need `mod_negotiation` (a speed killer if there ever was one), and `mod_access` (a notorious problem). Both of those modules can and should work with little or no performance decrease, but all too often they get abused and just slow things down.

Whatever you do, when you are disabling modules you should ensure that you leave either `mod_deflate` or `mod_gzip` enabled, depending on your Apache version. Your bottleneck is almost certainly going to be your bandwidth rather than your processing power, and having one of these two compressing your content will usually turn 10KB of HTML into 3KB for supported browsers (most of them).

Next, ensure keepalives are turned off. Yes, you read that right: turn keepalives off. This adds some latency to people viewing your site, because they cannot download multiple files through the same connection. However, it reduces the number of simultaneous open connections and so allows more people to connect.

If you are serving content that does not change, you can take the extreme step of enabling MMAP support. This allows Apache to serve pages directly from RAM without bothering to check whether they have changed, which works wonders for your performance. However, the downside is that when you do change your pages you need to restart Apache. Look for the `EnableMMAP` directive—it is probably commented out and set to off, so you will need to remove the comment and set it to on.

Finally, you should do all you can to ensure that your content is static: avoid PHP if you can, avoid databases if you can, and so on. If you know you are going to get hit by a rush of visitors, use plain HTML so that Apache is limited only by your bandwidth for how fast it can serve pages.

TIP

Some people, when questioned about optimizing Apache, will recommend you tweak the HARD_SERVER_LIMIT in the Apache source code and recompile. While we agree that compiling your own Apache source code is a great way to get a measurable speed boost if you know what you are doing, you should need to change this directive only if you are hosting a huge site.

The default value, 256, is enough to handle the Slashdot effect, and if you can handle that then you can handle most things.

MySQL

Tuning your MySQL server for increased performance is exceptionally easy to do, largely because you can see huge speed increases simply by getting your queries right. However, you can tune various things in the server itself to help it cope with higher loads as long as your system has enough RAM.

The key is understanding its buffers—there are buffers and caches for all sorts of things, and finding out how full they are is crucial to maximizing performance. MySQL performs best when it is making full use of its buffers, which in turn places a heavy demand on system RAM. Unless you have 4GB RAM or more in your machine, you do not have enough capacity to set very high values for all your buffers—you need to pick and choose.

Measuring Key Buffer Usage

When you add indexes to your data, it enables MySQL to find data faster. However, ideally you want to have these indexes stored in RAM for maximum speed, and the variable `key_buffer_size` defines how much RAM MySQL can allocate for index key caching. If MySQL cannot store its indexes in RAM, you will experience serious performance problems. Fortunately, most databases have relatively small key buffer requirements, but you should measure your usage to see what work needs to be done.

To do this, log in to MySQL and type `SHOW STATUS LIKE '%key_read%';` That returns all the status fields that describe the hit rate of your key buffer—you should get two rows back: `Key_reads` and `Key_read_requests`, which are the number of keys being read from disk and the number of keys being read from the key buffer. From these two numbers you can calculate the percentage of requests being filled from RAM and from disk, using this simple equation:

```
100 - ((Key_reads / Key_read_requests) &infin; 100)
```

That is, you divide `Key_reads` by `Key_read_requests`, multiply the result by 100 and then subtract the result from 100. For example, if you have `Key_reads` of 1000 and `Key_read_requests` of 100000, you divide 1000 by 100000 to get 0.01; then you multiply that by 100 to get 1.0, and subtract that from 100 to get 99. That number is the percentage of key reads being served from RAM, which means 99 percent of your keys are served from RAM.

Most people should be looking to get more than 95 percent served from RAM, although the primary exception is if you update or delete rows very often—MySQL can't cache what keeps changing. If your site is largely read-only, this should be around 98 percent. Lower figures mean you might need to bump up the size of your key buffer.

If you are seeing problems, the next step is to check how much of your current key buffer is being used. Use the `SHOW VARIABLES` command and look up the value of the `key_buffer_size` variable. It is probably something like 8388600, which is eight million bytes, or 8MB. Now, use the `SHOW STATUS` command and look up the value of `Key_blocks_used`.

You can determine how much of your key buffer is being used by multiplying `Key_blocks_used` by 1024, dividing by `key_buffer_size`, and multiplying by 100. For example, if `Key_blocks_used` is 8000, multiply that by 1024 to get 8192000; then divide that by your `key_buffer_size` (8388600) to get 0.97656, and finally multiply that by 100 to get 97.656. Thus, almost 98 percent of your key buffer is being used.

34

Now, the important part: You have ascertained that you are reading lots of keys from disk, and you also know that the reason for reading from disk is almost certainly because you do not have enough RAM allocated to the key buffer. A general rule is to allocate as much RAM to the key buffer as you can, up to a maximum of 25 percent of system RAM—128MB on a 512MB system is about the ideal for systems that read heavily from keys. Beyond that, you will actually see drastic performance decreases because the system has to use virtual memory for the key buffer.

Open `/etc/my.cnf` in your text editor, and look for the line that contains `key_buffer_size`. If you do not have one, you need to create a new one—it should be under the line `[mysqld]`. When you set the new value, do not just pick some arbitrarily high number. Try doubling what is there right now (or try 16MB if there's no line already); then see how it goes. To set 16MB as the key buffer size, you would need a line like this:

```
[mysqld]
set-variable = key_buffer_size=16M
datadir=/var/lib/mysql
```

Restart your MySQL server with service mysqld restart, and then go back into MySQL and run `SHOW VARIABLES` again to see the `key_buffer_size`. It should be 16773120 if you have set it to 16M. Now, because MySQL just got reset, all its values for key hits and the like will also have been reset. You need to let it run for a while so you can assess how much has changed. If you have a test system you can run, this is the time to run it.

After your database has been accessed with normal usage for a short while (if you get frequent accesses, this might be only a few minutes), recalculate how much of the key buffer is being used. If you get another high score, double the size again, restart, and retest. You should keep repeating this until your key buffer usage is below 50 percent or you find you don't have enough RAM to increase the buffer further—remember that you should never allocate more than 25 percent of system RAM to the key buffer.

Using the Query Cache

Newer versions of MySQL allow you to cache the results of queries so that, if new queries come in that use the same SQL, the result can be served from RAM. In some ways the query cache is quite intelligent: If, for example, part of the result changes due to another query, the cached results are thrown away and recalculated next time. However, in other ways it is very simple. For example, it uses cached results only if the new query is exactly the same as a cached query, even down to the capitalization of the SQL.

The query cache works well in most scenarios. If your site has an equal mix of reading and writing, the query cache will do its best but will not be optimal. If your site is mostly reading with few writes, more queries will be cached (and for longer), thus improving overall performance.

First, you need to find out whether you have the query cache enabled. To do this, use `SHOW VARIABLES` and look up the value of `have_query_cache`. All being well, you should get `YES` back, meaning that the query cache is enabled. Next, look for the value of `query_cache_size` and `query_cache_limit`. The first is how much RAM in bytes is allocated to the query cache, and the second is the maximum result size that should be cached. A good starting set of values for these two is 8388608 (8MB) and 1048576 (1MB).

Next, type `SHOW STATUS LIKE 'Qcache%';` to see all the status information about the query cache. You should get output like this:

```
mysql> SHOW STATUS LIKE 'qcache%';
+--------------------------+---------+
| Variable_name            | Value   |
+--------------------------+---------+
| Qcache_free_blocks       | 1       |
| Qcache_free_memory       | 169544  |
| Qcache_hits              | 698     |
| Qcache_inserts           | 38      |
| Qcache_lowmem_prunes     | 20      |
| Qcache_not_cached        | 0       |
| Qcache_queries_in_cache  | 18      |
| Qcache_total_blocks      | 57      |
+--------------------------+---------+
8 rows in set (0.00 sec)
```

From that, we can see that only 18 queries are in the cache (`Qcache_queries_in_cache`); we have 169544 bytes of memory free in the cache (`Qcache_free_memory`), 698 queries have been read from the cache (`Qcache_hits`), 38 queries have been inserted into the cache (`Qcache_inserts`), but 20 of them were removed due to lack of memory (`Qcache_lowmem_prunes`), giving the 18 from before. `Qcache_not_cached` is 0, which means 0 queries were not cached—MySQL is caching them all.

From that, we can calculate how many total queries came in—it is the sum of `Qcache_hits`, `Qcache_inserts`, and `Qcache_not_cached`, which is 736. We can also calculate how well the query cache is being used by dividing `Qcache_hits` by that number and multiplying by 100. In this case, 94.84 percent of all queries are being served from the query cache, which is a great number.

In our example, we can see that many queries have been trimmed because there is not enough memory in the query cache. This can be changed by editing your `/etc/my.cnf` file and adding a line like this one, somewhere in the `[mysqld]` section:

```
set-variable = query_cache_size=32M
```

An 8MB query cache should be enough for most people, but larger sites might need 16MB or even 32MB if you are storing a particularly large amount of data. Very few sites will need to go beyond a 32MB query cache, but keep an eye on the `Qcache_lowmem_prunes` value to ensure you have enough RAM allocated.

Using the query cache does not incur much of a performance hit. When MySQL calculates the result of a query normally, it throws it away when the connection closes. With the query cache, it skips the throwing away, and so there is no extra work being done. If your site does have many updates and deletes, be sure to check whether you get any speed boost at all from the query cache.

Miscellaneous Tweaks

If you have tuned your key buffer and optimized your query cache and yet still find your site struggling, you can make a handful of smaller changes that will add some more speed.

When reading from tables, MySQL has to open the file that stores the table data. How many files it keeps open at a time is defined by the `table_cache` setting, which is set to 64 by default. You can increase this setting if you have more than 64 tables, but you should be aware that Ubuntu imposes limits on MySQL about how many files it can have open at a time. Going beyond 256 is not recommended unless you have a particularly DB-heavy site and know exactly what you are doing.

The other thing you can tweak is the size of the read buffer, which is controlled by `read_buffer_size` and `read_buffer_rnd_size`. Both of these are allocated per connection, which means you should be very careful to have large numbers. Whatever you choose, `read_buffer_rnd_size` should be three to four times the size of `read_buffer_size`, so if `read_buffer_size` is 1MB (suitable for very large databases), `read_buffer_rnd_size` should be 4MB.

Query Optimization

The biggest speed-ups can be seen by reprogramming your SQL statements so they are more efficient. If you follow these tips, your server will thank you:

- Select as little data as possible. Rather than `SELECT *`, select only the fields you need.
- If you need only a few rows, use `LIMIT` to select the number you need.
- Declare fields as `NOT NULL` when creating tables to save space and increase speed.
- Provide default values for fields, and use them where you can.

- Be very careful with table joins because they are the easiest way to write inefficient queries.
- If you must use joins, be sure you join on fields that are indexed. They should also preferably be integer fields, because these are faster than strings for comparisons.
- Find and fix slow queries. Add `log-long-format` and `log-slow-queries = /var/log/slow-queries.log` to your `/etc/my.cnf` file, under `[mysqld]`, and MySQL will tell you the queries that took a long time to complete.
- Use `OPTIMIZE TABLE tablename` to defragment tables and refresh the indexes.

Reference

- www.coker.com.au/bonnie++/—The home page of bonnie, a disk benchmarking tool. It also contains a link to RAID benchmarking utilities and Postal, a benchmarking utility for SMTP servers.
- www.phoronix-test-suite.com/—The Phoronix Test Suite was created by a website that does automated performance testing and comparisons and is a quality benchmarking software to consider.
- http://httpd.apache.org/docs-2.0/misc/perf-tuning.html—The official Apache guide to tuning your web server.
- http://dev.mysql.com/doc/refman/5.6/en/optimization.html—Learn how to optimize your MySQL server direct from the source, the MySQL manual.
- One particular MySQL optimization book will really help you get more from your system if you run a large site—*High Performance MySQL*, by Jeremy Zawodny and Derek Balling (O'Reilly), ISBN: 0-596-00306-4.

CHAPTER 35

Command Line Masterclass

IN THIS CHAPTER

- Why Use the Shell?
- Basic Commands
- Combining Commands
- Multiple Terminals
- Reference

Some Linux users like to focus on the graphical environments that are available—they rush to tell new users that the command line isn't vital when using Linux. Although there are some amazing GUI desktops and this statement is mostly true, avoiding the command line limits your options and makes some tasks more difficult. The command-line interface is where the greatest power and flexibility are found, and those who actively avoid learning how to use it are also actively limiting their abilities and options. You learned the basics earlier in Chapter 4, "Command Line Quickstart." In this chapter we will dig in deeper.

In his book *The Art of Unix Programming,* Eric Raymond wrote a short story that perfectly illustrates the power of the command line versus the GUI. It's reprinted here with permission, for your reading pleasure:

> One evening, Master Foo and Nubi attended a gathering of programmers who had met to learn from each other. One of the programmers asked Nubi to what school he and his master belonged. Upon being told they were followers of the Great Way of Unix, the programmer grew scornful.
>
> "The command-line tools of Unix are crude and backward," he scoffed.
>
> "Modern, properly designed operating systems do everything through a graphical user interface."
>
> Master Foo said nothing, but pointed at the moon. A nearby dog began to bark at the master's hand.
>
> "I don't understand you!" said the programmer.
>
> Master Foo remained silent, and pointed at an image of the Buddha. Then he pointed at a window.

> "What are you trying to tell me?" asked the programmer.
>
> Master Foo pointed at the programmer's head. Then he pointed at a rock.
>
> "Why can't you make yourself clear?" demanded the programmer.
>
> Master Foo frowned thoughtfully, tapped the programmer twice on the nose, and dropped him in a nearby trash can.
>
> As the programmer was attempting to extricate himself from the garbage, the dog wandered over and piddled on him.
>
> At that moment, the programmer achieved enlightenment.

Whimsical as the story is, it does illustrate that there are some things that the GUI just does not do well. Enter the command line: It is a powerful and flexible operating environment and—if you practice—can actually be quite fun, too!

In this chapter, you will learn how to master the command line so that you are able to perform common tasks through it, and also link commands together to create new command groups. We will also be looking at the two most popular Linux text editors: Vim and Emacs. The command line is also known as the shell, the console, the command prompt, and the command-line interpreter (CLI). For the purposes of this chapter, these are interchangeable, although fine-grained differences exist between them!

Why Use the Shell?

Moving from the GUI to the command line is a conscious choice for most people, although it is increasingly rare that it is an either choice. While using a graphical desktop on top of the X server, you can press Ctrl+Alt+F1 (or any of F2 to F6) at any time to switch to a terminal, but most people tend to run an X terminal application that allows them to have the point-and-click applications and the command-line applications side by side, such as the default one found in the menu at Applications, Accessories, Terminal.

Reasons for running the shell include the following:

- You want to chain two or more commands together.
- You want to use a command or parameter available only on the shell.
- You are working on a text-only system.
- You have used it for a long time and feel comfortable there.

Chaining two or more commands together, or piping, is what gives the shell its real power. Hundreds of commands are available and, by combining them in different ways, you get tons of new options. Some of the shell commands are available through the GUI, but these commands usually have only a small subset of their parameters available, which limits what you are able to do with them.

Working from a text-only system is also useful both for working locally with a broken GUI and also for connecting to a remote, text-only system. If your Linux server is experiencing problems, the last thing you want to do is load it down with a GUI connection—working in text mode is faster and more efficient.

The last use is probably the most common: many people use the shell simply because it is familiar to them. Some people even use the shell to start GUI applications just because it saves them taking their hands off the keyboard for a moment! This is not a bad thing; it provides fluency and ease with the system and is a perfectly valid way of working. Working from the command line is faster. The mouse is slow and taking your fingers away from the keyboard makes your work even slower. Anyone looking to achieve the zen-like power-user state hinted at by Eric Raymond will understand this after making the effort to learn.

Basic Commands

It is impossible to know how many commands the average shell citizen uses, but if we had to guess, we would place it at about 25:

- `cat`—Prints the contents of a file
- `cd`—Changes directories
- `chmod`—Changes file access permissions
- `cp`—Copies files
- `du`—Prints disk usage
- `emacs`—Text editor
- `find`—Finds files by searching
- `gcc`—The C/C++/Fortran compiler
- `grep`—Searches for a string in input
- `less`—Filter for paging through output
- `ln`—Creates links between files
- `locate`—Finds files from an index
- `ls`—Lists files in the current directory
- `make`—Compiles and installs programs
- `man`—The manual page reader
- `mkdir`—Makes directories
- `mv`—Moves files
- `ps`—Lists processes
- `rm`—Deletes files and directories
- `ssh`—Connects to other machines
- `tail`—Prints the last lines of a file
- `top`—Prints resource usage

- vim—A text editor
- which—Prints the location of a command
- xargs—Executes commands from its input

Many other commands also are available to you that get used fairly often—diff, gzip, history, ping, su, tar, uptime, who, and so on—but if you are able to understand the 25 listed here, you will have sufficient skill to concoct your own command combinations.

Note that we say understand the commands—not know all their possible parameters and usages. This is because several of the commands, though commonly used, are used only in any complex manner by people with specific needs. gcc and make are good examples of this: Unless you plan to become a programmer, you need not worry about these beyond just typing make and make install now and then. If you want to learn more about these two, see Chapter 30, "C/C++ Programming Tools for Ubuntu."

Similarly, both Emacs and Vim are text editors that have a text-based interface all of their own, and SSH has already been covered in detail in Chapter 15, "Remote Access with SSH and Telnet."

What remains is 20 commands, each of which has many parameters to customize what it actually does. Again, we can eliminate much of this because many of the parameters are esoteric and rarely used, and, the few times in your Linux life that you need them, you can just read the manual page.

We will be going over these commands one by one, explaining the most common ways to use them. There is one exception: The xargs command requires you to understand how to join commands together.

Printing the Contents of a File with cat

Many of Ubuntu's shell commands manipulate text strings, so if you want to be able to feed them the contents of files, you need to be able to output those files as text. Enter the cat command, which prints the contents of any files you pass to it.

Its most basic use is like this:

```
matthew@seymour:~$ cat myfile.txt
```

That prints the contents of myfile.txt. For this usage there are two extra parameters that are often used: -n numbers the lines in the output, and -s ("squeeze") prints a maximum of one blank line at a time. That is, if your file has 1 line of text, 10 blank lines, 1 line of text, 10 blank lines, and so on, -s shows the first line of text, a single blank line, the next line of text, a single blank line, and so forth. When you combine -s and -n, cat numbers only the lines that are printed—the 10 blank lines shown as one will count as 1 line for numbering.

This command prints information about your CPU, stripping out multiple blank lines and numbering the output:

```
matthew@seymour:~$ cat -sn /proc/cpuinfo
```

You can also use cat to print the contents of several files at once, like this:

```
matthew@seymour:~$ cat -s myfile.txt myotherfile.txt
```

In that command, cat merges myfile.txt and myotherfile.txt on the output, stripping out multiple blank lines. The important thing is that cat does not distinguish between the files in the output—there are no filenames printed, and no extra breaks between the 2. This allows you to treat the 2 as 1 or, by adding more files to the command line, to treat 20 files as 1.

Changing Directories with cd

Changing directories is surely something that has no options, right? Not so. cd is actually more flexible than most people realize. Unlike most of the other commands here, cd is not a command in itself—it is built in to bash (or whichever shell interpreter you are using), but it is still used like a command.

The most basic usage of cd is this:

```
matthew@seymour:~$ cd somedir
```

That looks in the current directory for the somedir subdirectory, then moves you into it. You can also specify an exact location for a directory, like this:

```
matthew@seymour:~$ cd /home/matthew/stuff/somedir
```

The first part of cd's magic lies in the characters (- and ~, a dash and a tilde). The first means "switch to my previous directory," and the second means "switch to my home directory." This conversation with cd shows this in action:

```
matthew@seymour:~$  cd /usr/local
matthew@seymour/usr/local$  cd bin
matthew@seymour/usr/local/bin$  cd -
/usr/local
matthew@seymour/usr/local$  cd ~
matthew@seymour:~$
```

In the first line, we change to /usr/local and get no output from the command. In the second line, we change to bin, which is a subdirectory of /usr/local. Next, cd - is used to change back to the previous directory. This time Bash prints the name of the previous directory so we know where we are. Finally, cd ~ is used to change back to our home directory, although if you want to save an extra few keystrokes, just typing cd by itself is equivalent to cd ~.

The second part of cd's magic is its capability to look for directories in predefined locations. When you specify an absolute path to a directory (that is, one starting with a /), cd always switches to that exact location. However, if you specify a relative subdirectory—for example, cd subdir—you can tell cd where you would like that to be relative to. This is accomplished with the CDPATH environment variable. If this variable is not set, cd always uses the current directory as the base; however, you can set it to any number of other directories.

This next example shows a test of this. It starts in /home/matthew/empty, an empty directory, and the lines are numbered for later reference:

```
1 matthew@seymour:~/empty$ pwd
2 /home/matthew/empty
3 matthew@seymour:~/empty$ ls
4 matthew@seymour:~/empty$ mkdir local
5 matthew@seymour:~/empty$ ls
6 local
7 matthew@seymour:~/empty$ cd local
8 matthew@seymour:~/empty/local$ cd ..
9 matthew@seymour:~/empty$ export CDPATH=/usr
10 matthew@seymour:~/empty$ cd local
11 /usr/local
12 matthew@seymour:/usr/local$ cd -
13 /home/matthew/empty
14 matthew@seymour:~/empty$ export CDPATH=.:/usr
15 matthew@seymour:~/empty$ cd local
16 /home/matthew/empty/local
17 matthew@seymour:~/empty/local$
```

Lines 1–3 show that we are in /home/matthew/empty and that it is indeed empty—ls had no output. Lines 4–6 show the local subdirectory being made, so that /home/matthew/empty/local exists. Lines 7 and 8 show you can cd into /home/matthew/empty/local and back out again.

In line 9, CDPATH is set to /usr. This was chosen because Ubuntu has the directory /usr/local, which means our current directory (/home/matthew/empty) and our CDPATH directory (/usr) both have a local subdirectory. In line 10, while in the /home/matthew/empty directory, we use cd local. This time, Bash switches us to /usr/local and even prints the new directory to ensure we know what it has done.

Lines 12 and 13 move us back to the previous directory, /home/matthew/empty. In line 14, CDPATH is set to be .:/usr. The : is the directory separator, so this means Bash should look first in the current directory, ., and then in the /usr directory. In line 15 cd local is issued again, this time moving to /home/matthew/empty/local. Note that Bash has still printed the new directory—it does that whenever it looks up a directory in CDPATH.

Changing File Access Permissions with chmod

Your use of chmod can be greatly extended through one simple parameter: -c. This instructs chmod to print a list of all the changes it made as part of its operation, which means we can capture the output and use it for other purposes. For example:

```
matthew@seymour:~$ chmod -c 600 *
mode of '1.txt' changed to 0600 (rw-------)
mode of '2.txt' changed to 0600 (rw-------)
mode of '3.txt' changed to 0600 (rw-------)
matthew@seymour:~$ chmod -c 600 *
matthew@seymour:~$
```

There the chmod command is issued with -c, and you can see it has output the result of the operation: Three files were changed to rw------- (read and write by user only). However, when the command is issued again, no output is returned. This is because -c prints only the changes that it made. Files that already match the permissions you are setting are left unchanged and therefore are not printed.

There are two other parameters of interest: `--reference` and `-R`. The first allows you to specify a file to use as a template for permissions rather than specifying permissions yourself. For example, if you want all files in the current directory to have the same permissions as the file `/home/matthew/myfile.txt`, you would use this:

```
chmod --reference /home/matthew/myfile.txt *
```

You can use `-R` to enable recursive operation, which means you can use it to `chmod` a directory and it will change the permissions of that directory as well as all files and subdirectories under that directory. You could use `chmod -R 600 /home` to change every file and directory under `/home` to become read/write to their owner.

Copying Files with cp

Like `mv`, which is covered later, `cp` is a command that is easily used and mastered. However, two marvelous parameters rarely see much use (which is a shame!) despite their power. These are `--parents` and `–u`. the first copies the full path of the file into the new directory; the second copies only if the source file is newer than the destination.

Using `--parents` requires a little explanation, so here is an example. You have a file, `/home/matthew/desktop/documents/work/notes.txt`, and want to copy it to your `/home/matthew/backup folder`. You could do a normal `cp`, but that would give you `/home/matthew/backup/notes.txt`, so how would you know where that came from later? If you use `--parents`, the file is copied to `/home/matthew/backup/desktop/documents/work/notes.txt`.

The `-u` parameter is perfect for synchronizing two directories because it allows you to run a command like `cp -Ru myfiles myotherfiles` and have `cp` recopy only files that have changed. The `-R` parameter means recursive and allows you to copy directory contents.

Printing Disk Usage with du

The `du` command prints the size of each file and directory that is inside the current directory. Its most basic usage is as easy as it gets:

```
matthew@seymour:~$ du
```

That outputs a long list of directories and how much space their files take up. You can modify that with the `-a` parameter, which instructs `du` to print the size of individual files as well as directories. Another useful parameter is `-h`, which makes `du` use human-readable sizes like 18M (18MB) rather than 17532 (the same number in bytes, unrounded). The final useful basic option is `-c`, which prints the total size of files.

So, using `du` we can get a printout of the size of each file in our home directory, in human-readable format, and with a summary at the end, like this:

```
matthew@seymour:~$ du -ahc /home/matthew
```

Two advanced parameters deal with filenames you want excluded from your count. The first is `--exclude`, which allows you to specify a pattern that should be used to exclude files. This pattern is a standard shell file matching pattern as opposed to a regular expression, which means you can use ? to match a single character or * to match 0 or many characters. You can specify multiple `—exclude` parameters to exclude several patterns. For example:

```
matthew@seymour:~$ du --exclude="*.xml" --exclude="*.xsl"
```

However, typing numerous `--exclude` parameters repeatedly is a waste of time, so you can use `-X` to specify a file that has the list of patterns you want excluded. The file should look like this:

```
*.xml
*.xsl
```

That is, each pattern you want excluded should be on a line by itself. If that file were called `xml_exclude.txt`, we could use it in place of the previous example, like this:

```
matthew@seymour:~$ du -X xml_exclude.txt
```

You can make your exclusion file as long as you need, or you can just specify multiple `-X` parameters.

TIP

Running du in a directory where several files are hard-linked to the same inode counts the size of the file only once. If you want to count each hard link separately for some reason, use the `-l` parameter (lowercase L).

Finding Files by Searching with `find`

The `find` command is one of the darkest and least understood areas of Linux, but it is also one of the most powerful. Admittedly, the `find` command does not help itself by using X-style parameters. The UNIX standard is `-c`, `-s`, and so on, whereas the GNU standard is `—dosomething`, `—mooby`, and so forth. X-style parameters merge the two by having words preceded by only one dash.

However, the biggest problem with `find` is that it has more options than most people can remember—it truly is capable of doing most things you could want. The most basic usage is this:

```
matthew@seymour:~$ find -name "*.txt"
```

That searches the current directory and all subdirectories for files that end in .txt. The previous search finds files ending in `.txt` but not `.TXT`, `.Txt`, or other case variations. To search without case sensitivity, use `-iname` instead of `-name`. You can optionally specify where the search should start before the `-name` parameter, like this:

```
matthew@seymour:~$ find /home -name "*.txt"
```

Another useful test is `-size`, which lets you specify how big the files should be to match. You can specify your size in kilobytes and optionally use + or - to specify greater than or less than. For example:

```
matthew@seymour:~$ find /home -name "*.txt" -size 100k
matthew@seymour:~$ find /home -name "*.txt" -size +100k
matthew@seymour:~$ find /home -name "*.txt" -size -100k
```

The first brings up files of exactly 100KB, the second only files larger than 100KB, and the last only files under 100KB.

Moving on, the `-user` option enables you to specify the user who owns the files you are looking for. So, to search for all files in `/home` that end with `.txt`, that are under 100KB, and that are owned by user `matthew`, you would use this:

```
matthew@seymour:~$ find /home -name "*.txt" -size -100k -user matthew
```

You can flip any of the conditions by specifying `-not` before them. For example, you can add a `-not` before `-user matthew` to find matching files owned by everyone but `matthew`:

35

```
matthew@seymour:~$ find /home -name "*.txt" -size -100k -not -user matthew
```

You can add as many `-not` parameters as you need, even using `-not -not` to cancel each other out! (Yes, that is pointless.) Keep in mind, though, that `-not -size -100k` is essentially equivalent to `-size +100k`, with the exception that the former will match files of exactly 100KB whereas the latter will not.

You can use `-perm` to specify which permissions a file should have for it to be matched. This is tricky, so read carefully. The permissions are specified in the same way as with the `chmod` command: u for user, g for group, o for others, r for read, w for write, and x for execute. However, before you give the permissions, you need to specify either a plus, a minus, or a blank space. If you specify neither a plus nor a minus, the files must exactly match the mode you give. If you specify -, the files must match all the modes you specify. If you specify +, the files must match any the modes you specify. Confused yet?

The confusion can be cleared up with some examples. This next command finds all files that have permission `o=r` (readable for other users). Notice that if you remove the `-name` parameter, it is equivalent to * because all filenames are matched.

```
matthew@seymour:~$ find /home -perm -o=r
```

Any files that have `o=r` set are returned from that query. Those files also might have `u=rw` and other permissions, but as long as they have `o=r`, they will match. This next query matches all files that have o=rw set:

```
matthew@seymour:~$ find /home -perm -o=rw
```

However, that query does not match files that are `o=r` or `o=w`. To be matched, a file must be readable and writeable by other users. If you want to match readable or writeable (or both), you need to use +, like this:

```
matthew@seymour:~$ find /home -perm +o=rw
```

Similarly, this next query matches only files that are readable by user, group, and others:

```
matthew@seymour:~$ find /home -perm -ugo=r
```

Whereas this query matches files as long as they are readable by the user, or by the group, or by others, or by any combination of the three:

```
matthew@seymour:~$ find /home -perm +ugo=r
```

If you use neither + or -, you are specifying the exact permissions to search for. For example, the next query searches for files that are readable by user, group, and others but not writeable or executable by anyone:

```
matthew@seymour:~$ find /home -perm ugo=r
```

You can be as specific as you need to be with the permissions. For example, this query finds all files that are readable for the user, group, and others and writeable by the user:

```
matthew@seymour:~$ find /home -perm ugo=r,u=w
```

To find files that are not readable by others, use the `-not` condition, like this:

```
matthew@seymour:~$ find /home -not -perm +o=r
```

Now, on to the most advanced aspect of the find command: the `-exec` parameter. This enables you to execute an external program each time a match is made, passing in the name of the matched file wherever you want it. This has very specific syntax: Your command and its parameters should follow immediately after `-exec`, terminated by `\;`. You can insert the filename match at any point using `{}` (an opening and a closing brace side by side).

So, you can match all text files on the entire system (that is, searching recursively from / rather than from `/home` as in our previous examples) over 10KB, owned by `matthew`, that are not readable by other users, and then use `chmod` to enable reading, like this:

```
matthew@seymour:~$ find / -name "*.txt" -size +10k -user matthew -not -perm
+o=r -exec chmod o+r {} \;
```

When you type your own `-exec` parameters, be sure to include a space before `\;`. Otherwise, you might see an error such as `missing argument to '-exec'`.

Do you see now why some people think the `find` command is scary? Many people learn just enough about `find` to be able to use it in a very basic way, but hopefully you will see how much it can do if you give it chance.

Searches for a String in Input with grep

The `grep` command, like `find`, is an incredibly powerful search tool in the right hands. Unlike `find`, though, grep processes any text, whether in files, or just in standard input.

The basic usage of grep is this:

```
matthew@seymour:~$ grep "some text" *
```

That searches all files in the current directory (but not subdirectories) for the string `some text` and prints matching lines along with the name of the file. To enable recursive searching in subdirectories, use the `-r` parameter, like this:

```
matthew@seymour:~$ grep -r "some text" *
```

Each time a string is matched within a file, the filename and the match are printed. If a file contains multiple matches, each of the matches is printed. You can alter this behavior with the `-l` parameter (lowercase L), which forces `grep` to print the name of each file that contains at least one match, without printing the matching text. If a file contains more than one match, it is still printed only once. Alternatively, the `-c` parameter prints each filename that was searched and includes the number of matches at the end, even if there were no matches.

You have a lot of control when specifying the pattern to search for. You can, as we did previously, specify a simple string like `some text`, or you can invert that search by specifying the `-v` parameter. For example, this returns all the lines of the file `myfile.txt` that do not contain the word `hello`:

```
matthew@seymour:~$ grep -v "hello" myfile.txt
```

You can also use regular expressions for your search term. For example, you can search `myfile.txt` for all references to cat, sat, or mat with this command:

```
matthew@seymour:~$ grep "[cms]at" myfile.txt
```

Adding the `-i` parameter to that removes case sensitivity, matching `Cat`, `CAT`, `MaT`, and so on:

```
matthew@seymour:~$ grep -i [cms]at myfile.txt
```

The output can also be controlled to some extent with the `-n` and `—color` parameters. The first tells `grep` to print the line number for each match, which is where it appears in the source file. The `—color` parameter tells `grep` to color the search terms in the output, which helps them stand out when among all the other text on the line. You choose which color you want using the `GREP_COLOR` environment variable: `export GREP_COLOR=36` gives you cyan, and export `GREP_COLOR=32` gives you lime green.

This next example uses these two parameters to number and color all matches to the previous command:

```
matthew@seymour:~$ grep -in —color [cms]at myfile.txt
```

Later you will see how important `grep` is for piping with other commands.

Paging Through Output with `less`

The `less` command enables you to view large amounts of text in a more convenient way than the `cat` command. For example, your `/etc/passwd` file is probably more than a screen long, so if you run `cat /etc/passwd`, you are not able to see what the lines at the top were. Using `less /etc/passwd` enables you to use the cursor keys to scroll up and down the output freely. Type q to quit and return to the shell.

On the surface, `less` sounds like a very easy command; however, it has the infamy of being one of the few Linux commands that have a parameter for every letter of the alphabet. That is, `-a` does something, `-b` does something else, `-c`, `-d`, `-e ... -x`, `-y`, `-z`—they all do things, with some letters even differentiating between upper- and lowercase. Furthermore, these parameters are only used when invoking `less`. After you are viewing your text, even more commands are available. Make no mistake—`less` is a complex beast to master.

Input to `less` can be divided into two categories: what you type before running `less` and what you type while running it. The former category is easy, so we shall start there.

We have already discussed how many parameters `less` is capable of taking, but they can be distilled down to three that are very useful: `-M`, `-N`, and `+`. Adding `-M` (this is different

35

from `-m!`) enables verbose prompting in `less`. Rather than just printing a colon and a flashing cursor, `less` prints the filename, the line numbers being shown, the total number of lines, and the percentage of how far you are through the file. Adding `-N` (again, this is different from `-n`) enables line numbering.

The last option, +, allows you to pass a command to `less` for it to execute as it starts. To use this, you first need to know the commands available to you in `less`, which means we need to move to the second category of `less` input: what you type while `less` is running.

The basic navigation keys are the up, down, left, and right cursors; Home and End (for navigating to the start and end of a file); and Page Up and Page Down. Beyond that, the most common command is /, which initiates a text search. You type what you want to search for and press Enter to have `less` find the `first` match and highlight all subsequent matches. Type / again and press Enter to have `less` jump to the next match. The inverse of that is `?`, which searches backward for text. Type `?`, enter a search string, and press Enter to go to the first previous match of that string, or just use `?` and press Enter to go to the next match preceding the current position. You can use `/` and `?` interchangeably by searching for something with `/` and then using `?` to go backward in the same search.

Searching with `/` and `?` is commonly used with the `+` command-line parameter from earlier, which passes `less` a command for execution after the file has loaded. For example, you can tell `less` to load a file and place the cursor at the first match for the search `hello`, like this:

```
matthew@seymour:~$ less +/hello myfile.txt
```

Or, to place the cursor at the last match for the search `hello`:

```
matthew@seymour:~$ less +?hello myfile.txt
```

Beyond the cursor keys, the controls primarily involve typing a number and then pressing a key. For example, to go to line 50 you type 50g, or to go to the 75 percent point of the file you type 75p. You can also place invisible mark points through the file by pressing `m` and then typing a single letter. Later, while in the same `less` session, you can press ' (a single quote) and then type the letter, and it will move you back to the same position. You can set up to 52 marks, named a–z and A–Z.

One clever feature of `less` is that you can, at any time, press v to have your file opened inside your text editor. This defaults to Vim, but you can change that by setting the `EDITOR` environment variable to something else.

If you have made it this far, you can already use `less` better than most users. You can, at this point, justifiably skip to the next section and consider yourself proficient with `less`. However, if you want to be a `less guru`, there are two more things to learn: how to view multiple files simultaneously and how to run shell commands.

Like most other file-based commands in Linux, `less` can take several files as its parameters. For example:

```
matthew@seymour:~$ less -MN 1.txt 2.txt 3.txt
```

That loads all three files into `less`, starting at `1.txt`. When viewing several files, `less` usually tells you which file you are in, as well as numbering them: `1.txt (file 1 of 3)` should be at the bottom of the screen. However, certain things will make that go away, so you should use `-M` anyway.

You can navigate between files by typing a colon and then pressing `n` to go to the next file or press p to go to the previous file; these are referred to from now on as `:n` and `:p`. You can open another file for viewing by typing `:e` and providing a filename. This can be any file you have permission to read, including files outside the local directory. Use Tab to complete filenames. Files you open in this way are inserted one place after your current position, so if you are viewing file 1 of 4 and open a new file, the new file is numbered 2 of 5 and is opened for viewing straight away. To close a file and remove it from the list, use `:d`.

Viewing multiple files simultaneously has implications for searching. By default, `less` searches within only one file, but it is easy to search within all files. When you type `/` or `?` to search, follow it with a `*`—you should see `EOF-ignore` followed by a search prompt. You can now type a search and it will search in the current file; if nothing is found, it looks in subsequent files until it finds a match. Repeating searches is done by pressing Esc and then either `n` or `N`. The lowercase option repeats the search forward across files, and the uppercase repeats it backward.

The last thing you need to know is that you can get to a shell from `less` and execute commands. The simplest way to do this is just to type `!` and press Enter. This launches a shell and leaves you free to type all the commands you want, as per normal. Type `exit` to return to `less`. You can also type specific commands by entering them after the exclamation mark, using the special character `%` for the current filename. For example, `du -h %` prints the size of the current file. Finally, you can use `!!` to repeat the previous command.

35

Creating Links Between Files with `ln`

Linux allows you to create links between files that look and work like normal files for the most part. Moreover, it allows you to make two types of links, known as hard links and symbolic links (symlinks). The difference between the two is crucial, although it might not be obvious at first.

Each filename on your system points to what is known as an inode, which is the absolute location of a file. Linux allows you to point more than one filename to a given inode, and the result is a hard link—two filenames pointing to the same file. Each of these files shares the same contents and attributes. So, if you edit one, the other changes because they are both the same file.

On the other hand, a symlink—sometimes called a soft link—is a redirect to the real file. When a program tries to read from a symlink, it automatically is redirected to what the symlink is pointing at. The fact that symlinks are really just dumb pointers has two advantages: You can link to something that does not exist (and create it later if you want), and you can link to directories.

Both types of links have their uses. Creating a hard link is a great way to back up a file on the same disk. For example, if you delete the file in one location, it still exists untouched in the other location. Symlinks are popular because they allow a file to appear to be in a different location; you could store your website in `/var/www/live` and an under-construction holding page in `/var/www/construction`. Then you could have Apache point to a symlink `/var/www/html` that is redirected to either the live or construction directory, depending on what you need.

TIP

The `shred` command overwrites a file's contents with random data, allowing for safe deletion. Because this directly affects a file's contents, rather than just a filename, this means that all filenames hard linked to an inode are affected.

Both types of link are created using the `ln` command. By default, it creates hard links, but you can create symlinks by passing it the `-s` parameter. The syntax is `ln [-s] <something> <somewhere>`, for example:

```
matthew@seymour:~$ ln -s myfile.txt mylink
```

That creates the symlink mylink that points to `myfile.txt`. You don't see it here, but the file I created is 341 bytes. This is important later. Remove the `-s` to create a hard link. You can verify that your link has been created by running `ls -l`. Your symlink should look something like this:

```
lrwxrwxrwx  1 matthew matthew    5 Feb 19 12:39 mylink -> myfile.txt
```

Note how the file properties start with l (lowercase L) for link and how `ls -l` also prints where the link is going. Symlinks are always very small in size; the previous link is 5 bytes. If you created a hard link, it should look like this:

```
-rw-rw-r   2 matthew matthew   341 Feb 19 12:39 mylink
```

This time the file has normal attributes, but the second number is 2 rather than 1. That number is how many hard links point to this file, which is why it is 2 now. The file size is also the same as that of the previous filename because it is the file, as opposed to just being a pointer.

Symlinks are used extensively in Linux. Programs that have been superseded, such as `sh`, now point to their replacements (in this case `bash`), and library versioning is accomplished through symlinks. For example, applications that link against `zlib` load `/usr/lib/libz.so`. Internally, however, that is just a symlink that points to the actual `zlib` library: `/usr/lib/libz.so.1.2.1.2`. This enables multiple versions of libraries to be installed without application developers needing to worry about these specific details.

Finding Files from an Index with `locate`

When you use the `find` command, it searches recursively through each directory each time you request a file. This is slow, as you can imagine. Fortunately, Ubuntu ships with a `cron` job that creates an index of all the files on your system every night. Searching this index is extremely fast, which means that if the file you are looking for has been around since the last index, this is the preferable way of searching.

To look for a file in your index, use the command `locate` followed by the names of the files you want to find, like this:

```
matthew@seymour:~$ locate myfile.txt
```

On a relatively modern computer (1.5GHz or higher), `locate` should be able to return all the matching files in under a second. The trade-off for this speed is lack of flexibility. You can search for matching filenames, but, unlike `find`, you cannot search for sizes, owners, access permissions, or other attributes. The one thing you can change is case sensitivity; use the `-i` parameter to do a search that is not case sensitive.

Although Ubuntu rebuilds the filename index nightly, you can force a rebuild whenever you want by running the command `updatedb` with sudo. This usually takes a few minutes, but when it's done the new database is immediately available.

Listing Files in the Current Directory with `ls`

The `ls` command, like `ln`, is one of those you expect to be very straightforward. It lists files, but how many options can it possibly have? In true Linux style, the answer is many, although again you need only know a few to wield great power!

The basic usage is simply `ls`, which lists the files and directories in the current location. You can filter that using normal wildcards, so all these are valid:

```
matthew@seymour:~$ ls *
matthew@seymour:~$ ls *.txt
matthew@seymour:~$ ls my*ls *.txt *.xml
```

Any directories that match these filters are recursed into one level. That is, if you run `ls my*` and you have the files `myfile1.txt` and `myfile2.txt` and a directory `mystuff`, the matching files are printed first. Then `ls` prints the contents of the `mystuff` directory.

The most popular parameters for customizing the output of `ls` are

- `-a`—Includes hidden files.
- `-h`—Uses human-readable sizes.
- `-l`—A lowercase L, it enables long listing.
- `-r`—Reverse order.
- `-R`—Recursively lists directories.
- `-s`—Shows sizes.
- `—sort`—Sorts the listing.

All files that start with a period are hidden in Linux, so that includes the `.gnome` directory in your home directory, as well as `.bash_history` and the `.` and `..` implicit directories that signify the current directory and the parent. By default, `ls` does not show these files, but if you run `ls` -a, they are shown. You can also use `ls -A` to show all the hidden files except `.` and `..`.

The `-h` parameter needs to be combined with the -s parameter, like this:

```
matthew@seymour:~$ ls -sh *.txt
```

That outputs the size of each matching file in a human-readable format, such as 108KB or 4.5MB.

Using the `-l` parameter enables much more information about your files. Instead of just providing the names of the files, you get output like this:

```
drwxrwxr-x 24 matthew matthew  4096 Dec 24 21:33 arch
-rw-r--r--  1 matthew matthew 18691 Dec 24 21:34 COPYING
-rw-r--r--  1 matthew matthew 88167 Dec 24 21:35 CREDITS
drwxrwxr-x  2 matthew matthew  4096 Dec 24 21:35 crypto
```

That shows four matches and prints a lot of information about each of them. The first row shows the `arch` directory; you can tell it is a directory because its file attributes starts with a d. The `rwxrwxr-x` following that shows the access permissions, and this has special meanings because it is a directory. Read access for a directory allows users to see the directory contents, write access allows you to create files and subdirectories, and execute access allows you to `cd` into the directory. If a user has execute access but not read access, the user will be able to cd into the directory but not list files.

Moving on, the next number on the line is 24, which also has a special meaning for directories: It is the number of subdirectories, including . and .... After that is `matthew matthew`, which is the name of the user owner and the group owner for the directory. Next is the size and modification time, and finally the directory name itself.

The next line shows the file `COPYING`, and most of the numbers have the same meaning, with the exception of the 1 immediately after the access permissions. For directories, this is the number of subdirectories, but for files this is the number of hard links to this file. A `1` in this column means this is the only filename pointing to this inode, so if you delete it, it is gone.

Ubuntu comes configured with a shortcut command for `ls -l: ll`.

The `--sort` parameter allows you to reorder the output from the default alphabetical sorting. You can sort by various things, although the most popular are extension (alphabetically), size (largest first), and time (newest first). To flip the sorting (making size sort by smallest first), use the `-r` parameter also. So, this command lists all `.ogg` files, sorted smallest to largest:

```
matthew@seymour:~$ ls --sort size -r *.ogg
```

Finally, the -R parameter recurses through subdirectories. For example, typing `ls /etc` lists all the files and subdirectories in /etc, but `ls -R /etc` lists all the files in and subdirectories in /etc, all the files and subdirectories in /etc/acpi, all the files and subdirectories in /etc/acpi/actions, and so on until every subdirectory has been listed.

Reading Manual Pages with man

Time for a much-needed mental break: The man command is easy to use. Most people use only the topic argument, like this: `man gcc`. However, two other commands work closely with man that are very useful—whatis and apropos.

The whatis command returns a one-line description of another command, which is the same text you get at the top of that command's man page. For example:

```
matthew@seymour:~$  whatis ls
ls     (1) - list directory contents
```

The output there explains what ls does but also provides the man page section number for the command so you can query it further.

On the other hand, the apropos command takes a search string as its parameter and returns all man pages that match the search. For example, `apropos mixer` returns this list:

```
alsamixer (1) - soundcard mixer for ALSA soundcard driver
mixer (1) - command-line mixer for ALSA soundcard driver
aumix (1) - adjust audio mixer
```

So, use apropos to help you find commands and use whatis to tell you what a command does.

One neat trick is that many of the tips and tricks we learned for less also work when viewing man pages. For example, using / and ? to search. This is one of the beautiful things about UNIX systems, gaining knowledge in one area often benefits you in other areas.

Making Directories with mkdir

Making directories is as easy as it sounds, although there is one parameter you should be aware of: -p. If you are in /home/matthew and you want to create the directory /home/matthew/audio/sound, you will get an error like this:

```
mkdir: cannot create directory 'audio/sound': No such file or directory
```

At first glance this seems wrong; mkdir cannot create the directory because it does not exist. What it actually means is that it cannot create the directory sound because the directory audio does not exist. This is where the -p parameter comes in: If you try to make a directory within another directory that does not exist, like the previous, -p creates the parent directories, too. So:

```
matthew@seymour:~$ mkdir -p audio/sound
```

35

That first creates the audio directory and then creates the sound directory inside it.

Moving Files with `mv`

This command is one of the easiest around. There are two helpful parameters to `mv: -f`, which overwrites files without asking, and `-u`, which moves the source file only if it is newer than the destination file. That is it!

Listing Processes with `ps`

This is the third and last "command that should be simple, but isn't" that is discussed here. The `ps` command lists processes and gives you an extraordinary amount of control over its operation.

The first thing to know is that `ps` is typically used with what are known as BSD-style parameters. Back in the section "Finding Files by Searching with `find`," we discussed UNIX-style, GNU-style, and X-style parameters (`-c`, `--dosomething`, and `-dosomething`, respectively), but BSD-style parameters are different because they use single letters without a dash.

So, the default use of `ps` lists all processes that you are running that are attached to the terminal. However, you can ask it to list all your processes attached to any terminal (or indeed no terminal) by adding the `x` parameter: `ps x`. You can ask it to list all processes for all users with the `a` parameter or combine that with `x` to list all processes for all users, attached to a terminal or otherwise: `ps ax`.

However, both of these are timid compared with the almighty `u` option, which enables user-oriented output. In practice, that makes a huge difference because you get important fields like the username of the owner, how much CPU time and RAM are being used, when the process was started, and more. This outputs a lot of information, so you might want to try adding the `f` parameter, which creates a process forest by using ASCII art to connect parent commands with their children. You can combine all the options so far with this command: `ps faux` (yes, with a little imagination you spell words with the parameters!).

You can control the order in which the data is returned by using the `--sort` parameter. This takes either a `+` or a `-` (although the `+` is default) followed by the field you want to sort by: `command`, `%cpu`, `pid`, and `user` are all popular options. If you use the minus sign, the results are reversed. This next command lists all processes, ordered by CPU usage descending:

```
matthew@seymour:~$ ps aux --sort=-%cpu
```

There are many other parameters for `ps`, including a huge amount of options for compatibility with other UNIXes. If you have the time to read the man page, you should give it a try.

Deleting Files and Directories with `rm`

The `rm` command has only one parameter of interest: `—preserve-root`. By now, you should know that issuing `rm -rf /` with sudo will destroy your Linux installation because -r means recursive and `-f` means force (do not prompt for confirmation before deleting). It is possible for a clumsy person to issue this command by accident—not by typing the command on purpose, but by putting a space in the wrong place. For example:

```
matthew@seymour:~$ rm -rf /home/matthew
```

That command deletes the home directory of the user `matthew`. This is not an uncommon command; after you have removed a user and backed up the user's data, you will probably want to issue something similar. However, if you add an accidental space between the `/` and the h in "home", you get this:

```
matthew@seymour:~$ rm -rf / home/matthew
```

This time the command means "delete everything recursively from `/` and then delete `home/matthew`"—quite a different result! You can stop this from happening by using the `--preserve-root` parameter, which stops you from catastrophe with this message:

```
rm: it is dangerous to operate recursively on '/'
rm: use --no-preserve-root to override this failsafe.
```

However, no one wants to keep typing `--preserve-root` each time they run `rm`, so you could add this line to the `.bashrc` file in your home directory:

```
alias rm='rm --preserve-root'
```

That alias automatically adds `--preserve-root` to all calls to `rm` in future Bash sessions. Ubuntu (and Debian, and perhaps other distributions now) have done this by default, not by adding an alias in `bashrc`, but by making `-preserve-root` the default for the command.

Printing the Last Lines of a File with `tail`

If you want to watch a log file as it is written to, or want to monitor a user's actions as they are occurring, you need to be able to track log files as they change. In these situations you need the `tail` command, which prints the last few lines of a file and updates as new lines are added. This command tells tail to print the last few lines of `/var/log/httpd/access_log`, the Apache hit log:

```
matthew@seymour:~$ tail /var/log/httpd/access_log
```

To get tail to remain running and update as the file changes, add the `-f` parameter (follow):

```
matthew@seymour:~$ tail -f /var/log/httpd/access_log
```

You can tie the lifespan of a tail follow to the existence of a process by specifying the `--pid` parameter. When you do this, `tail` continues to follow the file you asked for until it sees that the process identified by PID is no longer running, at which point it stops tailing.

If you specify multiple files on the command line, `tail` follows both, printing file headers whenever the input source changes. Press Ctrl+C to terminate `tail` when in follow mode.

Printing Resource Usage with top

The top command is unusual in this list because the few parameters it takes are rarely, if ever, used. Instead, it has a number of commands you can use while it is running to customize the information it shows you. To get the most from these instructions, open two terminal windows. In the first, run the program yes and leave it running; in the second run top.

The default sort order in top shows the most CPU-intensive tasks first. The first command there should be the yes process you just launched from the other terminal, but there should be many others also. First, we want to filter out all the other users and focus on the user running yes. To do this, press u and enter the username you used when you ran yes. When you press Enter, top filters out processes not being run by that user.

The next step is to kill the process ID of the yes command, so you need to understand what each of the important fields means:

- PID—The process ID
- User—The owner of the process
- PR—Priority
- NI—Niceness
- Virt—Virtual image size in kilobytes
- Res—Resident size in kilobytes
- Shr—Shared memory size in kilobytes
- S—Status
- %CPU—CPU usage
- %Mem—Memory usage
- Time+—CPU time
- Command—The command being run

Several of them are unimportant unless you have a specific problem. The ones we are interested in are PID, User, Niceness, %CPU, %MEM, Time+, and Command. The Niceness of a process is how much time the CPU allocates to it compared to everything else on the system: 19 is the lowest, and –19 is the highest.

With the columns explained, you should be able to find the process ID of the errant yes command launched earlier; it is usually the first number below PID. Now type k, enter that process ID, and press Enter. You are prompted for a signal number (the manner in which you want the process killed), with 15 provided as the default. Signal 15 (also known as SIGTERM, for "terminate") is a polite way of asking a process to shut down, and all processes that are not wildly out of control should respond to it. Give top a few seconds to update itself, and hopefully the yes command should be gone. If not, you need to be more forceful: type `k` again, enter the PID, and press Enter. When prompted for a signal to send, enter `9` and press Enter to send `SIGKILL`, or "terminate whether you like it or not."

You can choose the fields to display by pressing `f`. A new screen appears that lists all possible fields, along with the letter you need to press to toggle their visibility. Selected fields are marked with an asterisk and have their letter, for example:

```
* A: PID        = Process Id
```

If you press the a key, the screen changes to this:

```
a: PID        = Process Id
```

When you have made your selections, press Enter to return to the normal top view with your normal column selection.

You can also press `F` to select the field you want to use for sorting. This works in the same way as the field selection screen, except that you can select only one field at a time. Again, press Enter to get back to `top` after you have made your selection, and it will be updated with the new sorting.

If you press `B`, text bolding is enabled. By default, this bolds some of the header bar as well as any programs that are currently running (as opposed to sleeping), but if you press `x` you can also enable bolding of the sorted column. You can use `y` to toggle bolding of running processes.

The last command to try is `r`, which allows you to renice—or adjust the nice value—of a process. You need to enter the PID of the process, press Enter, and enter a new nice value. Keep in mind that 19 is the lowest and –20 is the highest; anything less than 0 is considered "high" and should be used sparingly.

Printing the Location of a Command with `which`

The purpose of `which` is to tell you the exact command that would be executed if you typed it. For example, `which mkdir` returns `/bin/mkdir`, telling you that running the command `mkdir` runs `/bin/mkdir`.

Combining Commands

So far, we have been using commands only individually, and for the large part that is what you will be doing in practice. However, some of the real power of these commands lies in the capability to join them together to get exactly what you want. There are some extra little commands that we have not looked at that are often used as glue because they do one very simple thing that enables a more complex process to work.

All the commands we have looked at have printed their information to the screen, but this is often flexible. There are two ways to control where output should go: piping and output redirection. A pipe is a connector between one command's output and another's input. Instead of sending its output to your terminal, using a pipe sends that output directly to another command as input. Output redirection works in a similar way to pipes but is usually used for files. We will look at pipes first and then output redirection.

Two of the commands we have looked at so far are ps and grep: the process lister and the string matcher. We can combine the two to find out which users are playing Nethack right now:

```
matthew@seymour:~$ ps aux | grep nethack
```

That creates a list of all the processes running right now and sends that list to the grep command, which filters out all lines that do not contain the word nethack. Ubuntu allows you to pipe as many commands as you can sanely string together. For example, we could add in the wc command, which counts the numbers of lines, words, and characters in its input, to count precisely how many times Nethack is being run:

```
matthew@seymour:~$ ps aux | grep nethack | wc -l
```

The -l parameter (lowercase L) to wc prints only the line count.

Using pipes in this way is often preferable to using the -exec parameter to find, simply because many people consider find to be a black art and so anything that uses it less frequently is better! This is where the xargs command comes in: It converts output from one command into arguments for another.

For a good example, consider this mammoth find command from earlier:

```
matthew@seymour:~$ find / -name "*.txt" -size +10k -user matthew -not -perm
+o=r -exec chmod o+r {} \;
```

That searches every directory from / onward for files matching *.txt that are greater than 10KB, are owned by user matthew, and do not have read permission for others. Then it executes chmod on each of the files. It is a complex command, and people who are not familiar with the workings of find might have problems understanding it. So, what we can do is break it up into two—a call to find and a call to xargs. The most conversion would look like this:

```
matthew@seymour:~$ find / -name "*.txt" -size +10k -user matthew -not -perm
+o=r | xargs chmod o+r
```

That has eliminated the confusing {} \; from the end of the command, but it does the same thing, and faster, too. The speed difference between the two is because using -exec with find causes it to execute chmod once for each file. However, chmod accepts many files at a time and, because we are using the same parameter each time, we should take advantage of that. The second command, using xargs, is called once with all the output from find, and so saves many command calls. The xargs command automatically places the input at the end of the line, so the previous command might look something like this:

```
matthew@seymour:~$ xargs chmod o+r file1.txt file2.txt file3.txt
```

Not every command accepts multiple files, though, and if you specify the `-l` parameter, `xargs` executes its command once for each line in its input. If you want to check what it is doing, use the `-p` parameter to have `xargs` prompt you before executing each command.

For even more control, the `-i` parameter allows you to specify exactly where the matching lines should be placed in your command. This is important if you need the lines to appear before the end of the command or need it to appear more than once. Either way, using the `-i` parameter also enables the `-l` parameter so each line is sent to the command individually. This next command finds all files in `/home/matthew` that are larger than 10,000KB in size (10MB) and copies them to `/home/matthew/archive`:

```
matthew@seymour:~$ find /home/matthew -size +10000k ¦ xargs -i cp {}
./home/matthew/archive
```

Using find with `xargs` is a unique case. All too often, people use pipes when parameters would do the job just as well. For example, these two commands are identical:

```
matthew@seymour:~$ ps aux --sort=-%cpu ¦ grep -v 'whoami'
matthew@seymour:~$ ps -N ux --sort=-%cpu
```

The former prints all users and processes and then pipes that to `grep`, which in turn filters out all lines that contain the output from the program `whoami` (our username). So, line one prints all processes being run by other users, sorted by CPU use. Line two does not specify the `a` parameter to `ps`, which makes it list only our parameters. It then uses the `-N` parameter to flip that, which means it is everyone but us, without the need for `grep`.

The reason people use the former is often just simplicity: Many people know only a handful of parameters to each command, so they can string together two commands simply rather than write one command properly. Unless the command is to be run regularly, this is not a problem. Indeed, the first line would be better because it does not drive people to the manual to find out what `ps -N` does!

Multiple Terminals

Many Linux veterans have enjoyed and use the `screen` command. Screen was designed to allow you to use one terminal to control several terminal sessions easily. While `screen` has been a welcome and useful tool, a better one has appeared called Byobu which is an enhanced version of Screen. The name Byobu is a Japanese term for decorative, multipanel vertically folding screens that are often used as room dividers.

Picture this scene: You connect to a server via SSH and are working at the remote shell. You need to open another shell window so you can have the two running side by side; perhaps you want the output from top in one window while typing in another. What do you do? Most people would open another SSH connection, but that is both wasteful and unnecessary. Like Screen, Byobu is a terminal multiplexer, which is a fancy term for a program that lets you run multiple terminals inside one terminal.

The best way to learn Byobu is to try it yourself, so open a console, type `byobu`, and then press Enter. Your display will blank momentarily and then be replaced with a new console with new information in a panel at the bottom. Now, let's do something with that terminal. Run `top` and leave it running for the time being. Press F2. Your prompt will clear again, leaving you able to type. Run the `uptime` command.

Pop quiz: What happened to the old terminal running `top`? It is still running, of course. You can type F3 to return to it. Type F4 to go back to your `uptime` terminal. While you are viewing other terminals, the commands in the other terminals carry on running as normal so you can multitask. Here are some of the basic commands in Byobu:

- F2—Create a new window
- F3—Go to the previous window
- F4—Go to the next window
- F9—Open Byobu menu for help and configuration

To close a terminal within Byobu, simply log out of it normally using `exit` or `ctrl-d`. When you exit the last terminal session that is open in Byobu, the program closes as well and drops you to the regular terminal session you used to start Byobu.

However, there are two alternatives to quitting a Byobu session: locking and disconnecting. The first, activated with F12, locks access to your screen data until you enter your system password.

The second is the most powerful feature of Screen that also works beautifully in Byobu: you can exit it and do other things for a while and then reconnect later—and both Screen and Byobu will pick up where you left off. For example, you could be typing at your desk, detach from a session and go home, reconnect, and carry on as if nothing had changed. What's more, all the programs you ran from Screen or Byobu carry on running even while Screen or Byobu is disconnected. It even automatically disconnects for you if someone closes your terminal window while it is in a locked state (with Ctrl+a+x).

To disconnect, press F6. You are returned to the prompt from which you launched Screen or Byobu and can carry on working, close the terminal you had opened, or even log out completely. When you want to reconnect, run the command screen -r or byobu -r. You can, in the meantime, just run `screen` or `byobu` and start a new session without resuming the previous one, but that is not wise if you value your sanity! You can disconnect and reconnect the same session as many times you want, which potentially means you need never lose your session again.

Although this has been a mere taste of what Byobu/Screen can do, hopefully you can see how useful it can be. Check the man pages for each to learn more.

Reference

- http://www.gnu.org/—The website of the GNU project, it contains manuals and downloads for lots of command-line software.
- http://oreilly.com/linux/command-directory/—A wide selection of Linux commands and explanations of what they do take from O'Reilly's excellent book *Linux in a Nutshell*, which is a dictionary of Linux commands.
- http://www.tuxfiles.org/linuxhelp/cli.html—Several short command-line tutorials.
- http://www.linuxcommand.org/—Describes itself as "your one-stop command line shop!" It contains a wealth of useful information about the console.
- Understanding the way UNIX works at the nuts and bolts level can be both challenging and rewarding, and there are several good books that will help guide you on your way. Perhaps the best is *The Art of Unix Programming* by Eric Raymond (Addison-Wesley, ISBN: 0-13-142901-9), which focuses on the philosophy behind UNIX and manages to mix in much about the command line.
- O'Reilly's *Unix CD Bookshelf* (ISBN: 0-596-00392-7) contains seven highly respected books in one, although it retails for more than $120 as a result! However, it is incomparable in its depth and breadth of coverage.

CHAPTER 36

Kernel and Module Management

IN THIS CHAPTER

A kernel is a complex piece of software that manages the processes and process interactions that take place within an operating system. As a user, you rarely, if ever, interact directly with it. Instead, you work with the applications that the kernel manages.

The Linux kernel is Linux. It is the result of years of cooperative (and sometimes contentious) work by numerous people around the world. There is only one common kernel source tree, but each major Linux distribution massages and patches its version slightly to add features, performance, or options. Each Linux distribution, including Ubuntu, comes with its own precompiled kernel as well as the kernel source code, providing you with absolute authority over the Linux operating system. In this chapter, we will examine the kernel and learn what it does for us and for the operating system.

In this chapter, you also learn how to obtain the kernel sources, as well as how and when to patch the kernel. The chapter leads you through an expert's tour of the kernel architecture and teaches you essential steps in kernel configuration, how to build and install modules, and how to compile drivers in Ubuntu. This chapter also teaches you important aspects of working with GRUB2, the default Ubuntu boot loader. Finally, the chapter's troubleshooting information will help you understand what to do when something goes wrong with your Linux kernel installation or compilation process. As disconcerting as these problems can seem, this chapter shows you some easy fixes for many kernel problems.

Almost all users find that a precompiled Ubuntu kernel suits their needs (and there are several to choose from). At some point, you might need to recompile the kernel to support a specific piece of hardware or add a new feature to the operating system, although the Ubuntu kernel team works very hard to backport or enable any feature possible (as a module) so it is highly unlikely you will ever have a need to do this. They are also approachable and will gladly discuss specific needs and features. Sometimes features are not enabled simply because no one has ever asked for or needed them. Occasionally there are things not enabled because of a conflict with another feature. The Ubuntu Kernel Team can help you discover what is going on in those cases (but don't abuse their kindness and availability, they already work quite hard and for long hours).

Really, the main reason today for people compiling their own kernel is because they want to learn to be a kernel developer. If you have heard horror stories about the difficulties of recompiling the Linux kernel, you can relax; this chapter gives you all the information you need to understand how to painlessly work through the process if you are interested in learning a new skill. This is a complex and detail-oriented task, but it is within the grasp of most technical users, even if it is completely unnecessary.

WARNING

Building and using a custom kernel will make it very difficult to get support for your system. Although it is a learning experience to compile your own kernel, you will not be allowed to file bugs in Ubuntu on the custom-built kernel (if you do, they will be rejected without further explanation) and if you have a commercial support contract with Ubuntu/Canonical, this will void the contract.

The Linux Kernel

The Linux kernel is the management part of the operating system that many people call "Linux." Although many think of the entire distribution as Linux, the only piece that can correctly be called Linux is the kernel. Ubuntu, like many Linux distributions, includes a kernel packaged with add-on software that interacts with the kernel so that the user can interface with the system in a meaningful manner.

The system utilities and user programs enable computers to become valuable tools to a user.

THE FIRST LINUX KERNEL

In 1991, Linus Torvalds released version .99 of the Linux kernel as the result of his desire for a powerful, UNIX-like operating system for his Intel 80386 personal computer. Linus wrote the initial code necessary to create what is now known as the Linux kernel and combined it with Richard Stallman's GNU tools. Indeed, because many of the Linux basic system tools come from the GNU Project, many people refer to the operating system as GNU/Linux. Since then, Linux has benefited from thousands of contributors adding their talents and time to the Linux project. Linus still maintains the kernel, deciding on what will and will not make it into the kernel as official releases, known to many as the "vanilla" or "Linus" Linux kernel.

The Linux Source Tree

The source code for the Linux kernel is kept in a group of directories called the kernel source tree. The structure of the kernel source tree is important because the process of compiling (building) the kernel is automated; it is controlled by scripts interpreted by the `make` application. These scripts, known as makefiles, expect to find the pieces of the kernel code in specific places or they will not work. You will learn how to use make to compile a kernel later in this chapter.

It is not necessary for the Linux kernel source code to be installed on your system for the system to run or for you to accomplish typical tasks such as email, web browsing, or word processing. It is necessary that the kernel sources be installed, however, if you want to compile a new kernel. In the next section, we will show you how to install the kernel source files and how to set up the special symbolic link required. That link is `/usr/src/linux-2.6`, and it is how we will refer to the directory of the kernel source tree as we examine the contents of the kernel source tree.

The `/usr/src/linux-2.6` directory contains the `.config` and the `Makefile` files among others. The `.config` file is the configuration of your Linux kernel as it was compiled. There is no `.config` file by default; you must select one from the `/configs` subdirectory. There, you will find configuration files for each flavor of the kernel Ubuntu provides; simply copy the one appropriate for your system to the default directory and rename it `.config`.

We have already discussed the contents of the `/configs` subdirectory, so let us examine the other directories found under `/usr/src/linux-2.6`. The most useful for us is the Documentation directory. In it and its subdirectories, you will find almost all the documentation concerning every part of the kernel. The file `00-INDEX` (each `Documentation` subdirectory also contains a `00-INDEX` file as well) contains a list of the files in the main directory and a brief explanation of what they are. Many files are written solely for kernel programmers and application writers, but a few are useful to the intermediate or advanced Linux user when attempting to learn about kernel and device driver issues. Some of the more interesting and useful documents are:

- `devices.txt`—A list of all possible Linux devices that are represented in the /dev directory, giving major and minor numbers and a short description. If you have ever gotten an error message that mentions `char-major-xxx`, this file is where that list is kept.
- `ide.txt`—If your system uses IDE hard drives, this file discusses how the kernel interacts with them and lists the various kernel commands that can be used to solve IDE-related hardware problems, manually set data transfer modes, and otherwise manually manage your IDE drives. Most of this management is automatic, but if you want to understand how the kernel interacts with IDE devices, this file explains it.
- `initrd.txt`—This file provides much more in-depth knowledge of initial ramdisks, giving details on the loopback file system used to create and mount them and explaining how the kernel interacts with them.
- `kernel-parameters.txt`—This file is a list of most of the arguments that you can pass at boot time to configure kernel or hardware settings, but it does not appear too

useful at first glance because it is just a list. However, knowing that a parameter exists and might relate to something you are looking for can assist you in tracking down more information because now you have terms to enter into an Internet search engine such as www.google.com/linux.

- `sysrq.txt`—If you have ever wondered what that key on you keyboard marked "SysRq" was used for, this file has the answer. Briefly, it is a key combination hard-wired into the kernel that can help you recover from a system lockup. Ubuntu disables this function by default for security reasons. You can re-enable it by entering the command `# echo "1" > /proc/sys/kernel/sysrq` and disable it by echoing a value of `0` instead of `1`.

In the other directories found in Documentation, you will find similar text files that deal with the kernel modules for CD-ROM drivers, file system drivers, gameport and joystick drivers, video drivers (not graphics card drivers—those belong to X11R6 and not to the kernel), network drivers, and all the other drivers and systems found in the Linux operating system. Again, these documents are usually written for programmers, but they can provide useful information to the intermediate and advanced Linux user as well.

The directory named `scripts` contains many of the scripts that `make` uses. It really does not contain anything of interest to anyone who is not a programmer or a kernel developer (also known as a kernel hacker).

After a kernel is built, all the compiled files will wind up in the arch directory and its subdirectories. Although you can manually move them to their final location, we will show you later in this chapter how the `make` scripts will do it for you. In the early days of Linux, this post-compilation file relocation was all done by hand; you should be grateful for `make`.

NOTE

The `make` utility is a very complex program. Complete documentation on the structure of `make` files, as well as the arguments that it can accept, can be found at www.gnu.org/software/make/manual/make.html.

The remainders of the directories in /usr/src/linux-2.6 contain the source code for the kernel and the kernel drivers. When you install the kernel sources, these files are placed there automatically. When you patch kernel sources, these files are altered automatically. When you compile the kernel, these files are accessed automatically. Although you never need to touch the source code files, they can be useful. The kernel source files are nothing more than text files with special formatting, which means that we can look at them and read the programmers' comments. Sometimes, a programmer will write an application, but cannot (or often will not) write the documentation. The comments the programmer puts in the source code are often the only documentation that exists for the code.

Small testing programs are even "hidden" in the comments of some of the code, along with comments and references to other information. Because the source code is written in a language that can be read as easily—almost—as English, a nonprogrammer might be able to get an idea of what the application or driver is actually doing (see Chapter 30, "C/C++ Programming Tools for Ubuntu"). This information might be of use to an intermediate to advanced Linux user when the user is confronted by kernel- and driver-related problems.

NOTE

The interaction and control of hardware is handled by a small piece of the kernel called a `device` driver. The driver tells the computer how to interact with a modem, a SCSI card, a keyboard, a mouse, and so on in response to a user prompt. Without the device driver, the kernel does not know how to interact with the associated device.

Types of Kernels

In the early days of Linux, kernels were a single block of code containing all the instructions for the processor, the motherboard, and the other hardware. If you changed hardware, you were required to recompile the kernel code to include what you needed and discard what you did not. Including extra, unneeded code carried a penalty because the kernel became larger and occupied more memory. On older systems that had only 4MB–8MB of memory, wasting precious memory for unnecessary code was considered unacceptable. Kernel compiling was something of a "black art" as early Linux users attempted to wring the most performance from their computers. These kernels compiled as a single block of code are called *monolithic kernels*.

As the kernel code grew larger and the number of devices that could be added to a computer increased, the requirement to recompile became onerous. A new method of building the kernel was developed to make the task of compiling easier. The part of the kernel's source code that composed the code for the device drivers could be optionally compiled as a module that could be loaded and unloaded into the kernel as required. This is known as the *modular* approach to building the kernel. Now, all the kernel code could be compiled at once—with most of the code compiled into these modules. Only the required modules would be loaded; the kernel could be kept smaller, and adding hardware was much simpler.

The typical Ubuntu kernel has some drivers compiled as part of the kernel itself (called *in-line* drivers) and others compiled as modules. Only device drivers compiled in-line are available to the kernel during the boot process; modular drivers are available only after the system has been booted.

NOTE

As a common example, drivers for SCSI disk drives must be available to the kernel if you intend to boot from SCSI disks. If the kernel is not compiled with those drivers in-line, the system will not boot because it will not be able to access the disks.

A way around this problem for modular kernels is to use an initial Ram disk (`initrd`) discussed later in "Creating an Initial RAM Disk Image." The `initrd` loads a small kernel and the appropriate device driver, which then can access the device to load the actual kernel you want to run.

Some code can be only one or the other (for technical reasons unimportant to the average user), but most code can be compiled either as modular or in-line. Depending on the application, some system administrators prefer one way over the other, but with fast modern processors and abundant system memory, the performance differences are of little concern to all but the most ardent Linux hackers.

When compiling a kernel, the step in which you make the selection of modular or in-line is part of the `make config` step that we will detail later in this chapter. Unless you have a specific reason to do otherwise, we suggest that you select the modular option when given a choice. The process of managing modules is addressed in the next section because you will be managing them more frequently than you will be compiling a kernel.

Managing Modules

When using a modular kernel, special tools are required to manage the modules. Modules must be loaded and unloaded, and it would be nice if that were done as automatically as possible. We also need to be able to pass necessary parameters to modules when we load them—things such as memory addresses and interrupts. (That information varies from module to module, so you will need to look at the documentation for your modules to determine what, if any, information needs to be passed to it.) In this section, we will cover the tools provided to manage modules and then look at a few examples of using them.

Linux provides the following module management tools for our use. All these commands (and `modprobe.conf`) have `man` pages:

- `lsmod`—This command lists the loaded modules. It is useful to pipe this through the less command because the listing is usually more than one page long.
- `insmod`—This command loads the specified module into the running kernel. If a module name is given without a full path, the default location for the running kernel, `/lib/modules/*/`, will be searched. Several options are offered for this command—the most useful is `-f`, which forces the module to be loaded.
- `rmmod`—This command unloads (removes) the specified module from the running kernel. More than one module at a time can be specified.
- `modprobe`—A more sophisticated version of `insmod` and `rmmod`, it uses the dependency file created by `depmod` and automatically handles loading, or with the -r option, removing modules. There is no force option, however. A useful option to modprobe is –t, which causes `modprobe` to cycle through a set of drivers until it finds one that matches your system. If you were unsure of what module would work for your network card, you would use this command:

  ```
  matthew@seymour:~$ sudo modprobe -t net
  ```

- The term `net` is used because that is the name of the directory (`/lib/modules/*/kernel/net`) where all the network drivers are kept. It will try each one in turn until it loads one successfully.
- `modinfo`—This will query a module's object file and provide a list of the module name, author, license, and any other information that is there. It often is not very useful.

- `depmod`—This program creates a dependency file for kernel modules. Some modules need to have other modules loaded first; that is, they "depend" on the other modules. (A lot of the kernel code is like this because it eliminates redundancy in the code base.) During the boot process, one of the startup files contains the command `depmod -a` and it is run every time you boot to re-create the file /lib/modules/*/modules.dep. If you make changes to the file `/etc/modprobe.conf`, run `depmod -a` manually. The `depmod` command, its list of dependencies, and the `/etc/modprobe.conf` file enable kernel modules to be automatically loaded as needed.
- `/etc/modprobe.conf`—This is not a command, but a file that controls how `modprobe` and `depmod` behave; it contains kernel module variables. Although the command syntax can be quite complex, most actual needs are very simple. The most common use is to alias a module and then passes it some parameters. For example, in the following code, we alias a device name (from `devices.txt`) to a more descriptive word and then pass some information to an associated module. The `i2c-dev` device is used to read the CPU temperature and fan speed on our system. These lines for `/etc/modprobe.conf` were suggested for our use by the program's documentation. We added them with a text editor.

```
alias char-major-89 i2c-dev
options eeprom ignore=2,0x50,2,0x51,2,0x52
```

A partial listing of `lsmod` is shown here, piped through the `less` command, allowing us to view it a page at a time:

```
matthew@seymour:~$ sudo lsmod | less
Module                  Size  Used by
parport_pc             19392  1
Module                  Size  Used by
parport_pc             19392  1
lp                      8236  0
parport                29640  2 parport_pc,lp
autofs4                10624  0
sunrpc                101064  1
```

The list is actually much longer, but here we see that the input module is being used by the joydev (joystick device) module, but the joystick module is not being used. This computer has a joystick port that was auto detected, but no joystick is connected. A scanner module is also loaded, but because the USB scanner is unplugged, the module is not being used. You would use the `lsmod` command to determine whether a module was loaded and what other modules were using it. If you examine the full list, you would see modules for all the devices attached to your computer.

To remove a module, joydev in this example, use:

```
matthew@seymour:~$ sudo rmmod joydev
```

or

```
matthew@seymour:~$ sudo modprobe -r joydev
```

A look at the output of lsmod would now show that it is no longer loaded. If we removed input as well, we could then use `modprobe` to load both input and joydev (one depends on the other, remember) with a simple

```
matthew@seymour:~$ sudo modprobe joydev
```

If Ubuntu balks at loading a module (because it had been compiled using a different kernel version from what we are currently running; for example, the NVIDIA graphics card module), we could force it to load like this:

```
matthew@seymour:~$ sudo insmod -f nvidia
```

We would ignore the complaints (error messages) in this case if the kernel generated any.

When to Recompile

Ubuntu systems use a modified version of the plain vanilla Linux kernel (a modified version is referred to as a *patched* kernel) with additional drivers and other special features compiled into it.

Ubuntu has quite an intensive testing period for all distribution kernels and regularly distributes updated versions. The supplied Ubuntu kernel is compiled with as many modules as possible to provide as much flexibility as possible. A running kernel can be further tuned with the sysctl program, which enables direct access to a running kernel and permits some kernel parameters to be changed. As a result of this extensive testing, configurability, and modularity, the precompiled Ubuntu kernel does everything most users need it to do. Most users only need to recompile the kernel to:

- Accommodate an esoteric piece of new hardware.
- Conduct a system update when Ubuntu has not yet provided precompiled kernels.
- Experiment with the system capabilities.

Ubuntu supplies precompiled versions of the kernel for 32 and 64 bit processors. For each architecture, they compile a generic kernel that will work well for most uses, a server kernel that is optimized for server use, a preempt kernel designed for use in low latency servers, and an `rt` kernel for times when instant response is more important than balanced use (such as in professional audio/visual recording and editing). There is also a special kernel available for use in virtual machines called virtual. These are all available from the Ubuntu software repositories.

Also available are a series of packages called linux-backports-modules-, each with a specific set of kernel modules backported from newer mainline kernels into current version Ubuntu kernels. If you need an updated driver for a piece of hardware, you should look at the backported modules first.

Kernel Versions

The Linux kernel is in a constant state of development. As new features are added, bugs are fixed, and new technology is incorporated into the code base, it becomes necessary to provide stable releases of the kernel for use in a production environment. It is also important to have separate releases that contain the newest code for developers to test. To keep track of the kernels, version numbers are assigned to them. Programmers enjoy using sequential version numbers that have abstract meaning. Is version 8 twice as advanced as version 4 of the same application? Is version 1 of one application less developed than version 3 of another? The version numbers cannot be used for this kind of qualitative or quantitative comparison. It is entirely possible that higher version numbers can have fewer features and more bugs than older versions. The numbers exist solely to differentiate and organize sequential revisions of software.

For the latest development version of the kernel at the time of writing, for example, the kernel version number from the Linux developers is `2.6.35.3`. Ubuntu 10.10 ships with a recent version of 2.6.35 with Ubuntu specific patches applied. It will receive consistent updates throughout the release's lifecycle.

The kernel version can be broken down into four sections:

- `major version`—This is the major version number, now at `2`.
- `minor version`—This is the minor version number, now at `6`.
- `sublevel number`—This number indicates the current iteration of the kernel; here it is number `15`.
- `extraversion level`—This is the number representing a collection of patches and additions made to the kernel by the Ubuntu engineers to make the kernel work for them (and you). Each collection is numbered, and the number is indicated here in the kernel name. From our preceding example, it is `23`.

Typing `uname -r` at the command prompt displays your current kernel version:

```
matthew@seymour:~$ uname -r
2.6.35-14-generic
```

Obtaining the Kernel Sources

The Linux kernel has always been freely available to anyone who wants it. If you just want to recompile the existing kernel, install the linux-source package from the Ubuntu repositories. To get the very latest "vanilla" version, open an FTP connection to ftp.kernel.org using your favorite FTP client and log in as anonymous. Because you are interested in the 2.6 kernel, change directories to `/pub/linux/kernel/v2.6`. The latest stable kernel as of this writing is `2.6.35`.

NOTE

ftp.kernel.org receives more than its share of requests for download. It is considered a courtesy to use a mirror site to reduce the traffic that ftp.kernel.org bears. www.kernel.org/mirrors/ has a list of all mirrors around the world. Find one close to your geographic location and substitute that address for ftp.kernel.org.

A number of different entries are on the FTP archive site for each kernel version, but because you are interested only in the full kernel, it is necessary to get the full package of source code: for example, linux-2.6.35.bz2.

The `.bz2` extension is applied by the `bzip2` utility, which has better compression than `gzip`.

After it is downloaded, move the package to a directory other than `/usr/src` and unpack it. The `bzip2` unpack command is `tar -xjvf linux-2.6.35.tar.bz2`. After it is unpacked, the package will create a new directory, `linux-2.6.35`. Copy it to /usr/src or move it there. Then, create a symbolic link of `linux-2.6` to `linux-2.6. 35` (otherwise, some scripts will not work). Here is how to create the symbolic link:

```
matthew@seymour:~$ sudo rm /usr/src/linux-2.6
matthew@seymour:~$ sudo ln -s /usr/src/linux-2.6.35 /usr/src/linux-2.6
```

By creating a symbolic link to `/usr/src/linux-2.6`, it is possible to allow multiple kernel versions to be compiled and tailored for different functions: You will just change the symbolic link to the kernel directory you want to work on.

CAUTION

The correct symbolic link is critical to the operation of `make`. Always have the symbolic link point to the version of the kernel sources you are working with.

Patching the Kernel

It is possible to patch a kernel to the newest Linux kernel version as opposed to downloading the entire source code. This choice can be beneficial for those who are not using a high-speed broadband connection. Whether you are patching existing sources or downloading the full source, the end results will be identical.

Patching the kernel is not a mindless task. It requires the user to retrieve all patches from the current version to the version the user wants to upgrade to. For example, if you are currently running `2.6.30` (and have those sources) and want to upgrade to `2.6.35`, you must retrieve the `2.6.31` and `2.6.32` patch sets, and so on. After they are downloaded, these patches must be applied in succession to upgrade to `2.6.35`. This is more tedious than downloading the entire source, but useful for those who keep up with kernel hacking and want to perform incremental upgrades to keep their Linux kernel as up-to-date as possible.

To patch up to several versions in a single operation, you can use the patch-kernel script located in the kernel source directory for the kernel version you currently use. This script applies all necessary version patches to bring your kernel up to the latest version.

The format for using the patch-kernel script looks like this:

```
patch-kernel source_dir patch_dir stopversion
```

The source directory defaults to `/usr/src/linux` if none is given, and the `patch_dir` defaults to the current working directory if one is not supplied.

For example, assume that you have a 2.6.33 kernel code tree that needs to be patched to the 2.6.35 version. The 2.6.34 and 2.6.35 patch files have been downloaded from ftp.kernel.org and are placed in the /patch directory in the source tree. You issue the following command in the `/usr/src/linux-2.6` directory:

```
matthew@seymour:~$ sudo scripts/patch-kernel /usr/src/linux-2.6.33
/usr/src/linux-2.6.33/patch
```

Each successive patch file is applied, eventually creating a `2.6.35` code tree. If any errors occur during this operation, files named `xxx#` or `xxx.rej` are created, where xxx is the version of patch that failed. You will have to resolve these failed patches manually by examining the errors and looking at the source code and the patch. An inexperienced person will not have any success with this because you need to understand C programming and kernel programming to know what is broken and how to fix it. Because this was a stock `2.6.33` code tree, the patches were all successfully applied without errors. If you are attempting to apply a nonstandard third-party patch, the patch might likely fail.

When you have successfully patched the kernel, you are ready to begin compiling this code tree as if we started with a fresh, stock `2.6.35` kernel tree.

USING THE PATCH COMMAND

If you have a special, nonstandard patch to apply—such as a third-party patch for a commercial product, for example—you can use the patch command rather than the special patch-kernel script that is normally used for kernel source updates. Here are some quick steps and an alternative method of creating patched code and leaving the original code alone.

1. Create a directory in your home directory and name it something meaningful, like `mylinux`.
2. Copy the pristine Linux source code there with

   `cp -ravd /usr/src/linux-2.6/* ~/mylinux`
3. Copy the patch file to that same directory with

   `cp patch_filename ~/mylinux`
4. Change to the ~/mylinux directory with

   `cd ~/mylinux`
5. Apply the patch with

   `-patch -p1 < patch_filename  > mypatch.log 2>&1`

   (This last bit of code saves the message output to a file so that you can look at it later.)
6. If the patch applies successfully, you are done and have not endangered any of the pristine source code. In case the newly patched code does not work, you will not have to reinstall the original, pristine source code.
7. Copy your new code to `/usr/src` and make that special symbolic link described elsewhere in the chapter.

Compiling the Kernel

If you want to update the kernel from new source code you have downloaded, or you have applied a patch to add new functionality or hardware support, you will need to compile and install a new kernel to actually use that new functionality. Compiling the kernel involves translating the kernel's contents from human-readable code to binary form. Installing the kernel involves putting all the compiled files where they belong in `/boot` and `/lib` and making changes to the bootloader.

The process of compiling the kernel is almost completely automated by the make utility like the process of installing. By providing the necessary arguments and following the steps covered next, you can recompile and install a custom kernel for your use.

Here are the steps to compile and configure the kernel:

1. Do not delete your current kernel, so that you will have a backup that you can use to boot if there is a problem with the one you compile.
2. Apply all patches, if any, so that you have the features you desire. See the previous section for details.
3. Back up the .config file, if it exists, so that you can recover from the inevitable mistake. Use the following cp command:

   ```
   matthew@seymour:~$ sudo cp .config .config.bak
   ```

NOTE

If you are recompiling the Ubuntu default kernel, the `/usr/src/linux-2.6/configs` directory contains several versions of configuration files for different purposes.

Ubuntu provides a full set of `.config` files in the subdirectory configs, all named for the type of system they were compiled for. If you want to use one of these default configurations as the basis for a custom kernel, simply copy the appropriate file to `/usr/src/linux-2.6` and rename it `.config`.

4. Run the `make mrproper` directive to prepare the kernel source tree, cleaning out any old files or binaries.
5. Restore the `.config` file that the command `make mrproper` deleted, and edit the Makefile to change the `EXTRAVERSION` number.

NOTE

If you want to keep any current version of the kernel that was compiled with the same code tree, manually edit the Makefile with your favorite text editor and add some unique string to the `EXTRAVERSION` variable.

You can use any description you prefer.

6. Modify the kernel configuration file using `make config`, `make menuconfig`, or `make xconfig`—we recommend the latter.
7. Run make dep to create the code dependencies used later in the compilation process.

TIP

If you have a multiprocessor machine, you can use both processors to speed the make process by inserting `-jx` after the `make` command, where as a rule of thumb, `x` is one more than the number of processors you have. You might try a larger number and even try this on a single processor machine (we have used `-j8` successfully on an SMP machine); it will only load up your CPU. For example,

```
matthew@seymour:~$ sudo make -j3 bzImage
```

All the make processes except make dep will work well with this method of parallel compiling.

8. Run `make clean` to prepare the sources for the actual compilation of the kernel.
9. Run `make bzImage` to create a binary image of the kernel.

NOTE

Several choices of directives exist, although the most common ones are the following:

- `zImage`—This directive compiles the kernel, creating an uncompressed file called `zImage`.
- `bzImage`—This directive creates a compressed kernel image necessary for some systems that require the kernel image to be under a certain size for the BIOS to be able to parse them; otherwise, the new kernel will not boot. It is the most commonly used choice. However, the Ubuntu kernel compiled with `bzImage` is still too large to fit on a floppy, so a smaller version with some modules and features removed is used for the boot floppies. Ubuntu recommends that you boot from the rescue CD-ROM.
- `bzDisk`—This directive does the same thing as `bzImage`, but it copies the new kernel image to a floppy disk for testing purposes. This is helpful for testing new kernels without writing kernel files to your hard drive. Make sure that you have a floppy disk in the drive because you will not be prompted for one.

10. Run `make modules` to compile any modules your new kernel needs.
11. Run `make modules_install` to install the modules in `/lib/modules` and create dependency files.
12. Run `make install` to automatically copy the kernel to /boot, create any other files it needs, and modify the bootloader to boot the new kernel by default.
13. Using your favorite text editor, verify the changes made to `/etc/lilo.conf` or `/boot/grub/grub.conf`; fix if necessary and rerun /sbin/lilo if needed.

36

14. Reboot and test the new kernel.
15. Repeat the process if necessary, choosing a Configuration Interface.

Over time, the process for configuring the Linux kernel has changed. Originally, you configured the kernel by responding to a series of prompts for each configuration parameter (this is the `make config` utility described shortly). Although you can still configure Linux this way, most users find this type of configuration confusing and inconvenient; moving back through the prompts to correct errors, for instance, is impossible.

The `make config` utility is a command-line tool. The utility presents a question regarding kernel configuration options. The user responds with a `Y`, `N`, `M`, or `?`. (It is not case sensitive.) Choosing `M` configures the option to be compiled as a module. A response of `?` displays context help for that specific options, if available. (If you choose `?` and no help is available, you can turn to the vast Internet resources to find information.) We recommend that you avoid the `make config` utility, shown in Figure 36.1.

```
Kernel .config support (IKCONFIG) [N/y/?]
Initramfs source file(s) (INITRAMFS_SOURCE) []
Optimize for size (Look out for broken compilers!) (CC_OPTIMIZE_FOR_SIZE) [N/y/?
]
*
* Configure standard kernel features (for small systems)
*
Configure standard kernel features (for small systems) (EMBEDDED) [N/y/?]
  Load all symbols for debugging/kksymoops (KALLSYMS) [Y/?] (NEW) y
    Include all symbols in kallsyms (KALLSYMS_ALL) [N/y/?]
    Do an extra kallsyms pass (KALLSYMS_EXTRA_PASS) [N/y/?]
*
* Loadable module support
*
Enable loadable module support (MODULES) [Y/n/?] y
  Module unloading (MODULE_UNLOAD) [Y/n/?] y
    Forced module unloading (MODULE_FORCE_UNLOAD) [N/y/?] n
  Module versioning support (EXPERIMENTAL) (MODVERSIONS) [Y/n/?]
  Source checksum for all modules (MODULE_SRCVERSION_ALL) [Y/n/?]
  Automatic kernel module loading (KMOD) [Y/n/?] y
*
* Block layer
*
Support for Large Block Devices (LBD) [Y/n/?] █
```

FIGURE 36.1 The make config utility in all its Spartan glory.

If you prefer to use a command-line interface, you can use `make menuconfig` to configure the Linux kernel. `menuconfig` provides a graphical wrapper around a text interface. Although it is not as raw as `make config`, `menuconfig` is not a fancy graphical interface either; you cannot use a mouse, but must navigate through it using keyboard commands. The same information presented in make config is presented by `make menuconfig`, but as you can see in Figure 36.2, it looks a little nicer. Now, at least, you can move back and forth in the selection process in case you change your mind or have made a mistake.

In `make menuconfig`, you use the arrow keys to move the selector up and down and the spacebar to toggle a selection. The Tab key moves the focus at the bottom of the screen to either Select, Exit, or Help.

If a graphical desktop is not available, `menuconfig` is the best you can do. However, both `menuconfig` and `xconfig` (see the following explanation of each) offer an improvement over editing the `.config` file directly. If you want to configure the kernel through a true graphical interface—with mouse support and clickable buttons—`make xconfig` is the best configuration utility option. To use this utility, you must have the X Window System running. The application `xconfig` is really nothing but a Tcl/Tk graphics `widget set` providing borders, menus, dialog boxes, and the like. Its interface is used to wrap around data files that are parsed at execution time. Figure 36.3 shows the main menu of `xconfig`.

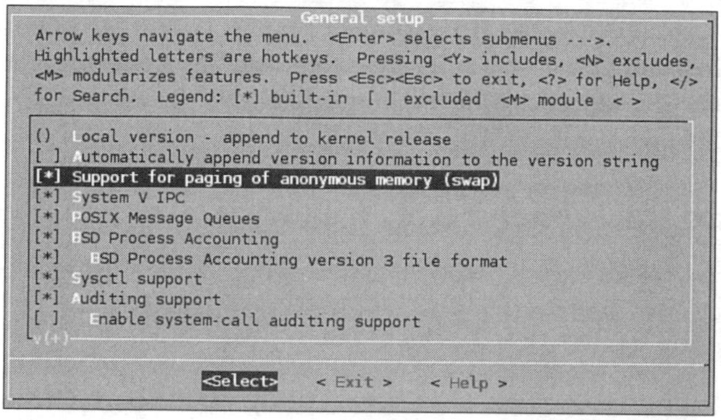

FIGURE 36.2 The make menuconfig utility, a small improvement over make config.

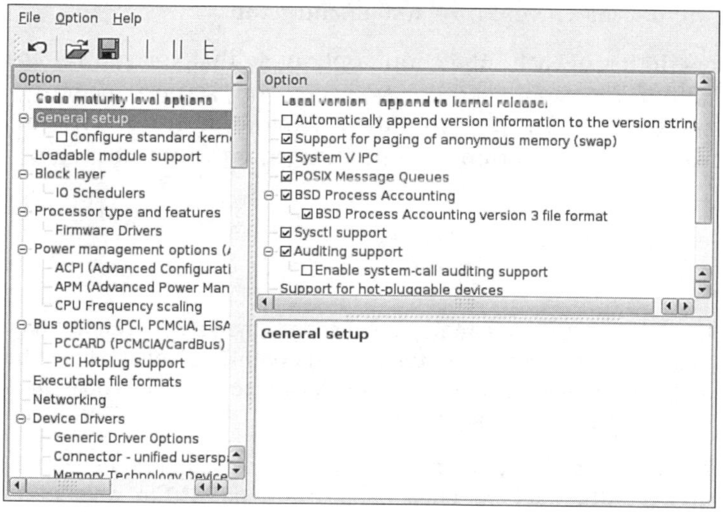

FIGURE 36.3 The much nicer make xconfig GUI interface. We recommend that you use this interface if you are able.

After loading this utility, you use it by clicking each of the buttons that list the configuration options. Each button you click opens another window that has the detail configuration options for that subsection. Three buttons are at the bottom of each window: Main Menu, Next, and Prev(ious). Clicking the Main Menu button closes the current window and displays the main window. Clicking Next takes you to the next configuration section.

When configuring a kernel from scratch, click the button labeled Code Maturity Level Options, and then continue to click the Next button in each subsection window to proceed through all the kernel configuration choices. When you have selected all options, the main menu is again displayed. The buttons on the lower right of the main menu are for saving and loading configurations. Their functions are self-explanatory. If you just want to have a look, go exploring! Nothing will be changed if you elect not to save it.

If you are upgrading kernels from a previous release, it is not necessary to go though the entire configuration from scratch. Instead, you can use the directive `make oldconfig`; it uses the same text interface that `make config` uses, and it is noninteractive. It will just prompt for changes for any new code.

Using `xconfig` to Configure the Kernel

For simplicity's sake, during this brisk walk-through, we will assume that you are using `make xconfig`. Prior to this point, we also assume that you will have completed the first five steps in our kernel compilation checklist shown previously.

As you learned in the preceding section, you configure the kernel using `make xconfig` by making choices in several configuration subsection windows. Each subsection window contains specific kernel options. With hundreds of choices, the kernel is daunting to configure. We cannot really offer you detailed descriptions of which options to choose because your configuration will not match your own system and setup.

Table 36.1 provides a brief description of each subsection's options so that you can get an idea of what you might encounter. We recommend that you copy your kernel's `.config` file to `/usr/src/linux-2.6` and run `make xconfig` from there. Explore all the options. As long as you do not save the file, absolutely nothing will be changed on your system.

TABLE 36.1 Some Kernel Subsections for Configuration

Name	Description
Code maturity level options	Enables development code to be compiled into the kernel even if it has been marked as obsolete or as testing code only. This option should be used only by kernel developers or testers because of the possible unusable state of the code during development.
General setup	This section contains several different options covering how the kernel talks to the BIOS, whether it should support PCI or PCMCIA, whether it should use APM or ACPI, and what kind of Linux binary formats will be supported. Contains several options for supporting kernel structures necessary to run binaries compiled for other systems directly without recompiling the program.
Loadable module support	Determines whether the kernel enables drivers and other nonessential code to be compiled as loadable modules that can be loaded and unloaded at runtime. This option keeps the basic kernel small so that it can run and respond more quickly; in that regard, choosing this option is generally a good idea.

TABLE 36.1 Continued

Name	Description
Processor type and features	Several options dealing with the architecture that will be running the kernel.
Power management options	Options dealing with ACPI and APM power management features.
Bus options	Configuration options for the PCMCIA bus found in laptops and PCI hotplug devices.
Memory Technology Devices	Options for supporting flash memory devices, such as (MTD) EEPROMS. Generally, these devices are used in embedded systems.
Parallel port support	Several options for configuring how the kernel will support parallel port communications.
Plug-and-play configu-ration	Options for supporting Plug and Play PCI, ISA, and plug-and-play BIOS support. Generally, it is a good idea to support plug-and-play for PCI and ISA devices.
Block devices	Section dealing with devices that communicate with the kernel in blocks of characters instead of streams. This includes IDE and ATAPI devices connected via parallel ports, as well as enabling network devices to communicate as block devices.
ATA/IDE/MFM/RLL support	Large collection of options to configure the kernel to communicate using different types of data communication protocols to talk to mass storage devices, such as hard drives. Note that this section does not cover SCSI.
SCSI device support	Options for configuring the kernel to support Small Computer Systems Interface. This subsection covers drivers for specific cards, chipsets, and tunable parameters for the SCSI protocol.
Old CD-ROM drivers	Configuration options to support obscure, older CD-ROM devices that do not conform to the SCSI or IDE standards. These are typically older CD-ROM drivers that are usually a proprietary type of SCSI (not SCSI, not IDE).
Multidevice support	Options for enabling the kernel to support RAID devices in (RAID and LVM) software emulation and the different levels of RAID. Also contains options for support of a logical volume manager.
Fusion MPT device support	Configures support for LSI's Logic Fusion Message Passing Technology. This technology is for high performance SCSI and local area network interfaces.
IEEE1394 (firewire) support	Experimental support for Firewire devices.

TABLE 36.1 Continued

Name	Description
I20 device support	Options for supporting the Intelligent Input/Output architecture. This architecture enables the hardware driver to be split from the operating system driver, thus enabling a multitude of hardware devices to be compatible with an operating system in one implementation.
Networking support	Several options for the configuration of networking in the kernel. The options are for the types of supported protocols and configurable options of those protocols.
Amateur radio support	Options for configuring support of devices that support the AX25 protocol.
IrDA (infrared) support	Options for configuring support of the infrared Data Association suite of protocols and devices that use these protocols.
Bluetooth support	Support for the Bluetooth wireless protocol. Includes options to support the Bluetooth protocols and hardware devices.
ISDN subsystem	Options to support Integrated Services Digital Networks protocols and devices. ISDN is a method of connection to a large area network digitally over conditioned telephone lines, largely found to connect users to ISPs.
Telephony support	Support for devices that enable the use of regular telephone lines to support VoIP applications. This section does not handle the configuration of modems.
Input device support	Options for configuring Universal Serial Bus (USB) Human Interface Devices (HID). These include keyboards, mice, and joysticks.
Character devices	Configuration options for devices that communicate to the server in sequential characters. This is a large subsection containing the drivers for several motherboard chipsets.
Multimedia devices	Drivers for hardware implementations of video and sound devices such as video capture boards, TV cards, and AM/FM radio adapter cards.
Graphics support	Configures VGA text console, video mode selection, and support for frame buffer cards.
Sound	Large subsection to configure supported sound card drivers and chipset support for the kernel.
USB support	Universal Serial Bus configuration options. Includes configuration for USB devices, as well as vendor-specific versions of USB.
File system	Configuration options for supported file system types.
Additional device driver support	A section for third-party patches.
Profiling support	Profiling kernel behavior to aid in debugging and development.

TABLE 36.1 Continued

Name	Description
Kernel hacking	This section determines whether the kernel will contain advanced debugging options. Most users will not want to include this option in their production kernels because it increases the kernel size and slows performance by adding extra routines.
Security options	Determines whether NSA Security Enhanced Linux (SELinux) is enabled.
Cryptographic options	Support for cryptography hardware (Ubuntu patches not found in the "vanilla" kernel sources).
Library routines	Contains zlib compression support.

After you select all the options you want, you can save the configuration file and continue with Step 7 in the kernel compiling checklist shown earlier.

Creating an Initial RAM Disk Image

If you require special device drivers to be loaded in order to mount the root file system (for SCSI drives, network cards, or exotic file systems, for example), you must create an initial RAM disk image named `/boot/initrd.img`. For most users, it is not necessary to create this file, but if you are not certain, it really does not hurt. To create an `initrd.img` file, use the shell script `/sbin/mkinitrd`.

The format for the command is the following, where `file_name` is the name of the image file you want created:

```
/sbin/mkinitrd file_name kernel_version
```

`mkinitrd` looks at `/etc/fstab`, `/etc/modprobe.conf`, and `/etc/ raidtab` to obtain the information it needs to determine which modules should be loaded during boot. For our system, we use

```
matthew@seymour:~$ sudo mkinitrd initrd-2.6.7-1.img 2.6.7-1
```

When Something Goes Wrong

Several things might go wrong during a kernel compile and installation, and several clues will point to the true problem. You will see error messages printed to the screen, and some error messages will be printed to the file `/var/log/messages`, which can be examined with a text editor. If you have followed our directions for patching the kernel, you will need to examine a special error log as well. Do not worry about errors because many problems are easily fixed with some research on your part. Some errors may be unfixable, however, depending on your skill level and the availability of technical information.

Errors During Compile

Although it is rare that the kernel will not compile, there is always a chance that something has slipped though the regression testing. Let's take a look at an example of a problem that might crop up during the compile.

It is possible that the kernel compile will crash and not complete successfully, especially if you attempt to use experimental patches, add untested features, or build newer and perhaps unstable modules on an older system.

At this juncture, you have two options:

- Fix the errors and recompile.
- Remove the offending module or option and wait for the errors to be fixed by the kernel team.

Most users will be unable to fix some errors because of the complexity of the kernel code, although you should not rule out this option. It is possible that someone else discovered the same error during testing of the kernel and developed a patch for the problem: check the Linux kernel mailing list archive. If the problem is not mentioned there, a search on Google might turn up something.

The second option, removing the code, is the easiest and is what most people do in cases in which the offending code is not required. In the case of the NTFS module failing, it is almost expected because NTFS support is still considered experimental and subject to errors. This is primarily because the code for the file system is reverse-engineered instead of implemented via documented standards. Read-only support has gotten better in recent kernels; write support is still experimental.

Finally, should you want to take on the task of trying to fix the problem yourself, this is a great opportunity to get involved with the Linux kernel and make a contribution that could help many others.

If you are knowledgeable about coding and kernel matters, you might want to look in the `MAINTAINERS` file in the `/usr/src/linux-2.6/` directory of the kernel source and find the maintainer of the code. The recommended course of action is to contact the maintainer to see if the maintainer is aware of the problems you are having. If nothing has been documented for the specific error, submitting the error to the kernel mailing list is an option. The guidelines for doing this are in the `README` file in the base directory of the kernel source under the section, "If Something Goes Wrong."

Runtime Errors, Boot Loader Problems, and Kernel Oops

Runtime errors occur as the kernel is loading. Error messages are displayed on the screen or written to the `/var/log/messages` file. Bootloader problems display messages to the screen; no log file is produced. `Kernel oops` are errors in a running kernel, and error messages are written to the `/var/log/messages` file.

Excellent documentation on the Internet exists for troubleshooting just about every type of error that GRUB2 or the kernel could give during boot. The best way to find this documentation is to go to your favorite search engine and type in the keywords of the error you received. You will need to adjust the keywords you use as you focus your search.

If you have GRUB problems, the GRUB manual is online at www.gnu.org/software/grub/manual/ and further information is available at https://help.ubuntu.com/community/Grub2.

TIP

For best results, go to www.google.com/linux to find all things Linux on the Internet. Google has specifically created a Linux area of its database, which should allow faster access to information on Linux than any other search engine.

Reference

- www.kernel.org/—Linux Kernel Archives. The source of all development discussion for the Linux kernel.
- www.kerneltraffic.org/kernel-traffic/index.html—Linux Kernel Traffic. Summarized version and commentary of the Linux Kernel mailing list produced weekly.
- www.gnu.org/—Free Software Foundation. Source of manuals and software for programs used throughout the kernel compilation process. Tools such as `make` and `gcc` have their official documentation here.
- https://wiki.ubuntu.com/Kernel—The starting point for anything you want to know about both Ubuntu and its use of the Linux kernel.
- https://wiki.ubuntu.com/Kernel/FAQ—The Ubuntu Kernel Team answers the most commonly asked questions about Ubuntu's use of Linux kernels.
- www.tldp.org/—The Linux Documentation Project. The Mecca of all Linux documentation. Excellent source of HOWTO documentation, as well as FAQs and online books, all about Linux.
- www.minix.org/—The unofficial minix website. It contains a selection of links to information about minix and a link to the actual homepage. Although minix is still copyrighted, the owner has granted unlimited rights to everyone. See for yourself the OS used to develop Linux.

APPENDIX A

Ubuntu Under the Hood

IN THIS APPENDIX

As with any new thing, it's worthwhile finding out a bit about its history. Ubuntu is no different, and in this appendix you'll learn a little more about where Linux (and Ubuntu) came from.

What Is Linux?

Linux is the core, or kernel, of a free operating system first developed and released to the world by Linus Benedict Torvalds in 1991. Torvalds, then a graduate student at the University of Helsinki, Finland, is now a Fellow at the Linux Foundation (www.linuxfoundation.org/). He is an engineer and previously worked for the CPU design and fabrication company Transmeta, Inc. before leaving in 2003 to work for Open Source Development Labs (ODSL), a consortium created by many high-tech companies to support Linux development and which has enabled him to focus on the Linux kernel full time. Fortunately for all Linux users, Torvalds chose to distribute Linux under a free software license named the GNU General Public License (GPL).

NOTE

The free online resource Wikipedia has a great biography of Linus Torvalds that examines his life and notable achievements. You can find it at http://en.wikipedia.org/wiki/Linux_Torvalds.

The GNU GPL is the brainchild of Richard M. Stallman, the founder of the Free Software Foundation. Stallman, the famous author of the Emacs editing environment and GCC compiler system, crafted the GPL to ensure that software that used the GPL for licensing would always be free and available in source-code form. The GPL is the guiding document for Linux and its ownership, distribution, and copyright. Torvalds holds the rights to the Linux trademark, but thanks to a combination of his generosity, the Internet, thousands of programmers around the world, GNU software, and the GNU GPL, Linux will remain forever free and unencumbered by licensing or royalty issues.

DISTRIBUTION VERSION AND KERNEL NUMBERING SCHEMA

There is a numbering system for Linux kernels, kernel development, and Ubuntu's kernel versions. Note that these numbers bear no relation to the version number of your Ubuntu Linux distribution. Ubuntu distribution version numbers are assigned by the Ubuntu developers, whereas most of the Linux kernel version numbers are assigned by Linus Torvalds and his legion of kernel developers.

To see the date your Linux kernel was compiled, use the `uname` command with its `-v` command-line option. To see the version of your Linux kernel, use the `-r` option. The numbers, such as 2.6.32-24-generic, represent the major version (2), minor version (6), and patch level (32). The final number (24-generic) is the developer patch level and is assigned by the Ubuntu developers.

Even minor numbers are considered "stable" and generally fit for use in production environments. You will find only stable versions of the Linux kernel included with this book. You can choose to download and install a beta (test) version of the kernel, but this is not recommended for a system destined for everyday use. When used, beta kernels are installed by developers to test support of new hardware or operating system features.

Linux, pronounced "lih-nucks," is free software. Combining the Linux kernel with GNU software tools—drivers, utilities, user interfaces, and other software such as the X.Org Foundation's X Window System—creates a Linux distribution. There are many different Linux distributions from different vendors, but many derive from or closely mimic the Debian Linux distribution, on which Ubuntu is founded.

NOTE

To see just how many distributions are based on Debian Linux, go to www.linux.org/, click Distributions, and search for "Debian-based." At the time of writing, 38 distributions owe their existence to Debian.

Why Use Linux?

Millions of clever computer users have been putting Linux to work for more nearly 20 years. Over the past year, many individuals, small office/home office (SOHO) users, businesses and corporations, colleges, nonprofits, and government agencies (local, state, and federal) in a number of countries have incorporated Linux with great success. And, today, Linux is being incorporated into many information service/information technology (IS/IT) environments as part of improvements in efficiency, security, and cost savings. Using Linux is a good idea for a number of reasons, including the following:

- Linux provides an excellent return on investment (ROI)—There is little or no cost on a per-seat basis. Unlike commercial operating systems, Linux has no royalty or licensing fees, and a single Linux distribution on CD-ROM or network shared folder can form the basis of an enterprise wide software distribution, replete with applications and productivity software. Custom corporate CD-ROMs can be easily crafted or network shares can be created to provide specific installs on enterprise-wide hardware. This feature alone can save hundreds of thousands, if not millions, of dollars in IS/IT costs—all without the threat of a software audit from the commercial software monopoly or the need for licensing accounting and controls of base operating system installations.
- Linux can be put to work on the desktop—Linux, in conjunction with its supporting graphical networking protocol and interface (the X Window System), has worked well as a consumer UNIX-like desktop operating system since the mid-1990s. The fact that UNIX is ready for the consumer desktop is now confirmed with the introduction, adoption, and rapid maturation of Apple Computer BSD UNIX—based on Mac OS X—supported, according to Apple, by more than 3,000 Mac OS X-specific programs that are known as native applications. This book's disc contains more than 800 software packages, including Internet connection utilities, games, a full office suite, many fonts, and hundreds of graphics applications.
- Linux can be put to work as a server platform—Linux is fast, secure, stable, scalable, and robust. The latest versions of the Linux kernel easily support multiple-processor computers, large amounts of system memory (up to 64GB RAM), individual file sizes in excess of hundreds of gigabytes, a choice of modern journaling file systems, hundreds of process monitoring and control utilities, and the (theoretical) capability to simultaneously support more than four billion users. IBM, Oracle, and other major database vendors all have versions of their enterprise software available for Linux.
- Linux has a low entry and deployment cost barrier—Maintenance costs can also be reduced because Linux works well on a variety of PCs, including legacy hardware, such as some Intel-based 486 and early Pentium CPUs. Although the best program performance will be realized with newer hardware, because clients can be recompiled and optimized for Pentium-class CPUs, base installs can even be performed on lower-end computers or embedded devices with only 8MB of RAM. This feature provides for a much wider user base; extends the life of older working hardware; and can help save money for home, small business, and corporate users.
- Linux appeals to a wide audience in the hardware and software industry—Versions of Linux exist for nearly every CPU. Embedded-systems developers now turn to Linux when crafting custom solutions using ARM, MIPS, and other low-power processors. Linux is the first full operating system available for Intel's Itanium CPU,

as well as the AMD64 group of CPUs; ports have also been available for HP/Compaq's Alpha and Sun Microsystems SPARC CPUs for some time. PowerPC users regularly use the PPC port of Linux on IBM and Apple hardware.

- Linux provides a royalty-free development platform for cross-platform development—Because of the open-source development model and availability of free, high-quality development tools, Linux provides a low-cost entry point to budding developers and tech industry start-ups.
- Big-player support in the computer hardware industry from such titans as IBM now lends credibility to Linux as a viable platform—IBM has enabled Linux on the company's entire line of computers, from low-end laptops through "Big Iron" mainframes. New corporate customers are lining up and using Linux as part of enterprise-level computing solutions. It has been used on some of the world's fastest computers, including IBM's Blue Gene/L. HP also certifies Linux across a large portion of its hardware offering.

Look forward to even more support as usage spreads worldwide throughout all levels of business in search of lower costs, better performance, and stable and secure implementations.

What Is Ubuntu?

Ubuntu is an operating system based on the Linux kernel; created, improved, refined, and distributed by the Ubuntu Community at www.ubuntu.com/. Ubuntu, sponsored by Canonical Software, is an open-source project supported by a worldwide community of software developers.

Ubuntu is one of the newer Linux distributions currently available today, having released its first version in October 2004. It quickly gained a reputation for ease of installation and use, combined with the slightly wacky code names given to each release. However, Ubuntu itself is based on Debian, which is a much older distribution steeped in respect from the wider Linux community. Ubuntu describes Debian as being the rock on which it is founded, and this is a good way to describe the relationship between the two. It is also worth noting that Debian garnered a reputation for infrequent releases. The move from Debian 3.0 to 3.1 took almost three years, during which time many other Linux distros had moved far ahead of Debian.

Sponsored by Canonical Software and with the formidable resources of Mark Shuttleworth, Ubuntu got off to a great start with version 4.10, the Warty Warthog. From the start, Ubuntu specified clear goals: to provide a distribution that was easy to install and use, that did not overly confuse the user, and that came on a single CD (something increasingly rare these days when a distro can occupy four or five CDs). Releasing every six months, Ubuntu made rapid progress into the Linux community and is now one of the most popular Linux distros across the world.

UBUNTU VERSIONS

As mentioned earlier, Ubuntu has chosen some peculiar code names for their releases since the first launch in October 2004. Doing away with the typical version numbering found elsewhere, Ubuntu decided to take the month and year of release and reverse them. Hence, the first release in October 2004 became 4.10, followed quickly by 5.04 (April 2005), 5.10, 6.06LTS, and so on up to the current 10.10.

The version covered in this book was released in October 2010, and thus bears the version number 10.10. What's even more special about some releases is that they also carries the LTS (Long Term Support) label, meaning that Canonical will support LTS versions for three years on the desktop and a total of five years for the server version after its release. The most recent LTS version was 10.04.

The code names during development are even better: 4.10 was christened the Warty Warthog in recognition that it was a first release, warts and all. The second release, 5.04, was dubbed the Hoary Hedgehog. Things got slightly better with 5.10, code-named the Breezy Badger. 6.06 was announced as the Dapper Drake and was the first Ubuntu distribution to carry the LTS badge. Beyond Dapper, there was the Edgy Eft (6.10) followed by the Feisty Fawn (7.04), and more, up to what was known during development as the maverick meercat (10.10), which is what this book covers.

Ubuntu for Business

Linux has matured over the years, and features considered essential for use in enterprise-level environments, such as CPU architecture support, file systems, and memory handling, have been added and improved. The addition of virtual memory (the capability to swap portions of RAM to disk) was one of the first necessary ingredients, along with a copyright-free implementation of the TCP/IP stack (mainly due to BSD UNIX being tied up in legal entanglements at the time). Other features quickly followed, such as support for a variety of network protocols.

Ubuntu includes a Linux kernel that can use multiple processors, which allows you to use Ubuntu in more advanced computing environments with greater demands on CPU power. This kernel will support at least 16 CPUs; in reality, however, small business servers typically use only dual-CPU workstations or servers. However, Ubuntu can run Linux on more powerful hardware.

Ubuntu will automatically support your multiple-CPU Intel-based motherboard, and you will be able to take advantage of the benefits of symmetric multiprocessors (SMPs) for software development and other operations. The Linux kernels included with Ubuntu can use system RAM sizes up to 64GB, allow individual file sizes in excess of 2GB, and host the demands of—theoretically—billions of users.

Businesses that depend on high-availability, large-scale systems can also be served by Ubuntu, along with the specialist commercial support on offer from hundreds of support partners across the world.

However, Ubuntu can be used in many of these environments by customers with widely disparate computing needs. Some of the applications for Ubuntu include desktop support; small file, print, or mail servers; intranet web servers; and security firewalls deployed at strategic points inside and outside company LANs.

Commercial customers will also benefit from Debian's alliances with several top-tier system builders, including Hewlett-Packard.

Debian itself is also available for multiple architectures, and until recently was developed in tandem on 11 different architectures, from x86 to the older Motorola 680x0 chips (as found in the Commodore Amiga), along with several other architectures.

Small business owners can earn great rewards by stepping off the software licensing and upgrade treadmill and adopting a Linux-based solution. Using Ubuntu not only avoids the need for licensing accounting and the threat of software audits, but also provides viable alternatives to many types of commercial productivity software.

Using Ubuntu in a small business setting makes a lot of sense for other reasons, too, such as not having to invest in cutting-edge hardware to set up a productive shop. Ubuntu easily supports older, or *legacy*, hardware, and savings are compounded over time by avoiding unnecessary hardware upgrades. Additional savings will be realized because software and upgrades are free. New versions of applications can be downloaded and installed at little or no cost, and office suite software is free.

Ubuntu is easy to install on a network and plays well with others, meaning it works well in a mixed-computing situation with other operating systems such as Windows, Mac OS X, and, of course, UNIX. A simple Ubuntu server can be put to work as an initial partial solution or made to mimic file, mail, or print servers of other operating systems. Clerical staff should quickly adapt to using familiar Internet and productivity tools, while your business gets the additional benefits of stability, security, and a virus-free computing platform.

By carefully allocating monies spent on server hardware, a productive and efficient multiuser system can be built for much less than the cost of comparable commercial software. Combine these benefits with support for laptops, PDAs, and remote access, and you will find that Ubuntu supports the creation and use of an inexpensive yet efficient work environment.

Ubuntu in Your Home

Ubuntu installs a special set of preselected software packages onto your hard drive; these are suitable for small office/home office (SOHO) users. This option provides a wealth of productivity tools for document management, printing, communication, and personal productivity.

The standard installation requires nearly 2GB of hard drive space but should easily fit onto smaller hard drives in older Pentium-class PCs. The install also contains administrative tools, additional authoring and publishing clients, a variety of editors, a GNOME-based X11 desktop, support for sound, graphics editing programs, and graphical and text-based Internet tools.

64-Bit Ubuntu

Advances in computing saw the introduction of 64-bit x86-compatible CPUs from AMD in the spring of 2003. Intel's EM64T extensions for x86, which largely mirror the advances made by AMD, have further increased the availability of commodity x86-64 hardware.

Ubuntu fully supports AMD64 processors, and you are encouraged to use the 64-bit version of Ubuntu to get the maximum from these advanced processors.

As far as the Intel Itanium architecture goes, unfortunately Ubuntu does not currently support ia64. However, you may want to investigate Debian, which is available for the ia64 platform and several others.

Getting the Most from Ubuntu and Linux Documentation

Nearly all commercial Linux distributions include shrink-wrapped manuals and documentation covering installation and configuration. You will not find official documentation included on the DVD provided with this book. However, you can read or get copies of assorted manuals or topic discussions online at www.ubuntu.com/. There you will find the links to various Ubuntu documentation projects.

Documentation for Ubuntu (and many Linux software packages) is distributed and available in a variety of formats. Some guides are available in Portable Document Format (PDF) and can be read using Adobe's Acrobat Reader for Linux or the `evince` client. Guides are also available as bundled HTML files for reading with a web browser such as links, KDE's Konqueror, GNOME's Epiphany, or Firefox. Along with these guides, Ubuntu provides various tips, frequently asked questions (FAQs), and HOWTO documents.

You will find traditional Linux software package documentation, such as manual pages, under the `/usr/share/man` directory, with documentation for each installed software package under `/usr/share/doc`.

Linux manual pages are compressed text files containing succinct information about how to use a program. Each manual page generally provides a short summary of a command's use, a synopsis of command-line options, an explanation of the command's purpose, potential caveats or bugs, the name of the author, and a list of related configuration files and programs.

For example, you can learn how to read manual pages by using the `man` command to display its own manual page, as follows:

```
matthew@seymour:~$ man man
```

After you press Enter, a page of text appears on the screen or in your window on the desktop. You can then scroll through the information using your keyboard's cursor keys, read, and then press the Q key to quit reading.

Many of the software packages also include separate documents known as HOWTOs that contain information regarding specific subjects or software.

If the HOWTO documents are simple text files in compressed form (with filenames ending in `.gz`), you can easily read the document by using the `zless` command, which is a text pager that enables you to scroll back and forth through documents. (Use the `less` command to read plain-text files.) You can start the command by using `less`, followed by the complete directory specification and name of the file, or *pathname*, like this:

```
matthew@seymour:~$ less /usr/share/doc/httpd-2.0.50/README
```

To read a compressed version of this file, use the zless command in the same way:

```
matthew@seymour:~$ zless /usr/share/doc/attr-2.4.1/CHANGES.gz
```

After you press Enter, you can scroll through the document using your cursor keys. Press the Q key to quit.

If the HOWTO document is in HTML format, you can simply read the information using a web browser, such as Firefox. Or if you are reading from a console, you can use the links or lynx text-only web browsers, like this:

```
matthew@seymour:~$ links /usr/share/doc/stunnel-4.0.5/stunnel.html
```

The links browser offers drop-down menus, accessed by clicking at the top of the screen. You can also press the Q key to quit.

If the documentation is in PostScript format (with filenames ending in `.ps`), you can use the `gv` client to read or view the document like this:

```
matthew@seymour:~$ gv /usr/share/doc/iproute-2.4.7/ip-crefs.ps
```

Finally, if you want to read a document in Portable Document Format (with a filename ending in .pdf), use the evince client, as follows:

```
matthew@seymour:~$ evince /usr/share/doc/xfig/xfig-howto.pdf
```

NOTE

This book was developed and written using the standard Ubuntu CD. You can use the disc included with this book for your install or download your own copy, available as ISO9660 images (with filenames ending in `.iso`), and burn it onto a 700MB CD-R or a DVD. You can also order prepressed CDs directly from Ubuntu at http://shipit.ubuntu.com.

Along with the full distribution, you will get access to the complete source code to the Linux kernel and source for all software in the distribution—more than 55 million lines of C and nearly 5 million lines of C++ code. Browse to www.ubuntu.com/download/ to get started.

Ubuntu Developers and Documentation

If you are interested in helping with Ubuntu, you can assist in the effort by testing beta releases (known as preview releases, and usually named after the animal chosen for the release name), writing documentation, and contributing software for the core or contributed software repositories. You should have some experience in installing Linux distributions, a desire to help with translation of documentation into different languages, or be able to use various software project management systems, such as CVS.

Mailing lists are also available as an outlet or forum for discussions about Ubuntu. The lists are categorized. For example, general users of Ubuntu discuss issues on the ubuntu-users mailing list. Beta testers and developers via the ubuntu-devel, and documentation contributors via the ubuntu-doc mailing list. You can subscribe to mailing lists by selecting the ones you are interested in at http://lists.ubuntu.com/mailman/listinfo/. Be warned; some of the mailing lists have in excess of 200 to 300 emails per day!

Reference

- www-1.ibm.com/linux/—Information from IBM regarding its efforts and offerings of Linux hardware, software, and services.
- www.ubuntu.com/—Home page for Ubuntu, sponsored by Canonical Software, and your starting point for learning more about Ubuntu.
- http://help.ubuntu.com/—Web page with links to current Ubuntu documentation and release notes.
- www.tldp.org/—The definitive starting point for the latest updates to generic Linux FAQs, guides, and HOWTO documents.
- www.justlinux.com/—One site to which new Linux users can browse to learn more about Linux.
- www.ubuntuforums.org/—A popular site that allows users to communicate and support each other with questions and problems.

APPENDIX B
Ubuntu and Linux Internet Resources

IN THIS APPENDIX

- Websites and Search Engines
- Usenet Newsgroups
- Mailing Lists
- Internet Relay Chat

Ubuntu enjoys a wealth of Internet support in the form of websites with technical information, specific program documentation, targeted whitepapers, bug fixes, user experiences, third-party commercial technical support, and even free versions of specialized, fine-tuned clone distributions.

This appendix lists many of the supporting websites, FTP repositories, Usenet newsgroups, and electronic mailing lists that you can use to get more information and help with your copy of Ubuntu.

IF YOU NEED HELP 24/7

Whether you are an individual, small business, corporate, or enterprise-level Ubuntu user, don't forget that you can always turn to the source, Canonical, or third-party companies who supply Ubuntu support for commercial technical support on a 24/7 onsite basis, by phone, by electronic mail, or even on a per-incident basis. Canonical Software offers a spectrum of support options for its software products. You can read more about support options from the Ubuntu website: www.ubuntu.com/support.

The appendix is divided into the following sections:

- Websites with Linux information arranged by category
- Usenet newsgroups pertaining to Linux
- Mailing lists providing Linux user and developer discussions
- Internet Relay Chat groups for Linux information

This appendix also lists websites that might be of general interest when using Ubuntu or specific components such as Xorg. Every effort has been made to ensure the accuracy of the URLs, but keep in mind that the Internet is always in flux!

KEEP UP-TO-DATE

Keeping informed about bug fixes, security updates, and other errata is critical to the success and health of an Ubuntu system. To keep abreast of the most important developments when using Ubuntu, be sure to register with the Ubuntu Announcements mailing list. From there, you will learn which updates have been issued and what has been fixed as a result. Go to https://lists.ubuntu.com/mailman/listinfo/ubuntu-security-announce to register for this mailing list. You should also keep an eye out for Update Manager notifications in order to keep up with bug fixes, new software packages, and security updates.

Websites and Search Engines

Literally thousands of websites exist with information about Linux and Ubuntu. The key to getting the answers you need right away involves using the best search engines and techniques. Knowing how to search can mean the difference between frustration and success when troubleshooting problems. This section provides some Internet search tips and lists Ubuntu- and Linux-related sites sorted by various topics. The lists are not comprehensive, but have been checked and were available at the time of this writing.

Web Search Tips

Troubleshooting problems with Linux by searching the Web can be an efficient and productive way to get answers to vexing problems. One of the most basic rules for conducting productive searches is to use specific search terms to find specific answers. For example, if you simply search for "Ubuntu Linux," you will end up with too many links and too much information. If you search for "Ubuntu sound," however, you are more likely to find the information you need. If you've received an error message, use it; otherwise, use the Linux kernel diagnostic message as your search criterion.

Other effective techniques include the following:

- Using symbols in the search string, such as the plus sign (+) to force matches of web pages containing both strings (if such features are supported by the search engine used by web search site)
- Searching within returned results
- Sorting results (usually by date to get the latest information)
- Searching for related information
- Stemming searches; for example, specifying returns for not only "link" but also "linking" and "linked"

Invest some time and experiment with your favorite search engine's features—the result will be more productive searches. In addition to sharpening your search skills, also take the time to choose the best search engine for your needs.

Google Is Your Friend

Some of the fastest and most comprehensive search engines on the Web are powered by Linux, so it makes sense to use the best available resources. Out of the myriad number of websites with search engines, http://google.com stands out from the crowd, with millions of users per month. The site uses advanced hardware and software to bring speed and efficiency to your searches. If you are looking for specific Linux answers, take advantage of Google's Linux page at http://google.com/linux.

Why is Google (named after a math number) so powerful? You can get a quick overview from the Google folks at www.google.com/corporate/tech. Part of its success is because of great algorithms, good programming, and simple interface design; but most users really seem to appreciate Google's uncanny capability to provide links to what you are looking for in the first page of a search return. Google's early success was also assured because the site ran its search engine on clusters of thousands of PCs running a version of Red Hat Linux! It is also rumored that an Ubuntu-based distribution is in use on desktops at Google, with the informal moniker of Goobuntu.

Google has the largest database size of any search engine on the Web, with many billions of web pages searched and indexed. The database size is important because empty search results are useless to online users, and the capability to return hits on esoteric subjects can make the difference between success and failure or satisfaction and frustration.

To get a better idea of what Google can offer you, browse to www.google.com/options/. You will find links to many services and tools covering specialized searches, databases, information links, translators, and other helpful browsing tools.

Ubuntu Package Listings

You can quickly and easily view a list of the installed packages on your Ubuntu system, along with a short description of each package, by using the Ubuntu Software Center or Synaptic. Each also shows you descriptions of each package so you can decide whether you want it installed. For more information see Chapter 32, "Managing Software."

Certification

Linux certification courses are part of the rapidly growing information technology training industry. Hundreds of different vendors now offer courses about and testing of Linux skill sets. However, because Linux is open-source software, there are no formal rules or mandates concerning what knowledge or level of expertise is required for certification. If you are interested in certification and want to pursue a career or obtain employment with a company using Linux, you really should seek training. You can find a good list of companies that can provide training at www.ubuntu.com/support/training/, along with other resources.

Commercial Support

Commercial support for Ubuntu is an essential ingredient to the success of Linux in the corporate and business community. Although hundreds, if not thousands, of consultants well versed in Linux and UNIX are available on call for a fee, here is a short list of the best-known Linux support providers:

- www.ubuntu.com/support/services—Go straight to the source for a range of support options. You can get help on Ubuntu direct from Canonical software, or from a local support provider.
- www.hp.com/linux—HP offer a comprehensive package of Linux services and hardware that cover almost everything that you would want to do, including consultancy, business solutions, and hardware specification and implementation.
- www.ibm.com/linux/—Linux services offered by IBM include e-business solutions, open-source consulting, database migration, clustering, servers, and support.

In addition to service-oriented support companies, nearly every commercial distributor of Linux has some form of easily purchased commercial support. There are various ways in which to take advantage of support services (such as remote management, onsite consulting, device driver development, and so on), but needs will vary according to customer circumstances and installations.

THE BENEFITS OF JOINING A LINUX USER GROUP

Join a local Linux Users Group (LUG)! Joining and participating in a local LUG has many benefits. You will be able to get help, trade information, and learn many new and wonderful things about Linux. Most LUGs do not have membership dues, and many often sponsor regular lectures and discussions from leading Linux, GNU, and open-source experts. For one great place to start, browse to www.tux.org/luglist.html. For Ubuntu specific groups, check out Ubuntu Local Community, or LoCo Teams at http://loco.ubuntu.com/.

Documentation

Nearly all Linux distributions include thousands of pages of documentation in the form of manual pages, HOWTO documents (in various formats, such as text and HTML), mini-HOWTO documents, or software package documentation (usually found under the `/usr/share/doc/` directory). However, the definitive site for reading the latest versions of these documents is the Linux Documentation Project, found at www.tldp.org.

Linux Guides

If you are looking for more extensive and detailed information concerning a Linux subject, try reading one of the many Linux guides. These guides, available for a number of subjects, dwell on technical topics in more detail and at a more leisurely pace than a HOWTO. You can find copies of:

- "Advanced Bash-Scripting Guide," by Mendel Cooper; a guide to shell scripting using bash
- "LDP Author Guide," by Mark F. Komarinski; how to write LDP documentation
- "Linux Administration Made Easy," by Steve Frampton
- "Linux Consultants Guide," by Joshua Drake; a worldwide listing of commercial Linux consultants
- "Linux from Scratch," by Gerard Beekmans; creating a Linux distribution from software
- "Linux Kernel Module Programming Guide," by Peter J Salzman, Michael Burian, and Ori Pomerantz; a good guide to building 2.4 and 2.6 series modules
- "Securing and Optimizing Linux," by Gerhard Mourani
- Linux certification
- "The Linux Network Administrator's Guide, Second Edition," by Olaf Kirch and Terry Dawson; a comprehensive Net admin guide

B

Ubuntu

The best place to start for Ubuntu-specific information are Ubuntu-focused websites. Where better to start than the main website for the distribution and the official web forums? While these are not the only official Uubntu resources, they are the most likely to be immediately useful. Others are easily found under the Support tab on the Ubuntu.com website.

- www.ubuntu.com—Home page for Ubuntu, Canonical's community-based free Linux distribution. Ubuntu is the main release of this Linux distribution and includes thousands of software packages that form the core of an up-to-date, cutting-edge Linux-based desktop. You can also find links to the other *buntus, such as Kubuntu, Xubuntu, and edubuntu.
- www.ubuntuforums.org—A good place to go if you need specific Ubuntu support.

Mini-CD Linux Distributions

Mini-CD Linux distributions are used for many purposes. Some distributions are used to boot to a read-only firewall configuration; some are used to provide as complete a rescue environment as possible; whereas others are used to either install or help jumpstart an install of a full distribution. Mini-CDs are available in a variety of sizes, such as 3CD-Rs (or CD-RW) with sizes ranging from 185MB to 210MB. You can also download an `.iso` image and create a Linux bootable business card, typically fitting on a 40MB or 50MB credit-card–size CD-R. (Consider using a mini–CD-RW, especially if you want to upgrade your distribution often.) Here are some links to these distributions:

- www.lnx-bbc.com—Home page for the Linux BBC, a 40MB image hosting a rather complete live Linux session with X, a web browser, and a host of networking tools.
- http://crux.nu/—Home page of the CRUX i686–optimized Linux distribution.
- www.smoothwall.org—The 69MB SmoothWall distribution is used to install a web-administered firewall, router, or gateway with SSH, HTTP, and other services.

Various Intel-Based Linux Distributions

Choosing a Linux *distribution (distro)* for an Intel-based PC is generally a matter of personal preference or need. Many Linux users prefer Red Hat's distro because of its excellent support, commercial support options, and widespread use around the world. However, many different Linux distributions are available for download. One of the best places to start looking for a new distro or new version of your favorite distro is www.distrowatch.com:

- www.debian.org—The Debian Linux distribution, consisting only of software distributed under the GNU GPL license. Ubuntu, itself, is based upon Debian.
- www.slackware.com—Home page for download of the newest version of one of the oldest Linux distributions, Slackware.
- www.opensuse.org—Home page for SUSE Linux.
- http://fedoraproject.org/—A popular distribution closely related to Red Hat.
- www.redhat.com/—One of the most used distributions in the corporate and server world.

PowerPC-Based Linux Distributions

PowerPC processors were created by an alliance between Apple, IBM, and Motorola. They have been used extensively in video game consoles, embedded applications, and were the processors used in Apple's Macintosh computers from 1994 to 2006.

- http://penguinppc.org/—Home page for the PowerPC GNU/Linux distribution
- www.yellowdoglinux.com—Home page for Terra Soft Solutions's Yellow Dog Linux for the PowerPC, which is based on Fedora

Linux on Laptops and PDAs

One of the definitive sites for getting information about running Linux on your laptop is Kenneth Harker's Linux Laptop site. Although not as actively updated as in the past, this site (www.linux-laptop.net) still contains the world's largest collection of Linux and laptop information, with links to user experiences and details concerning specific laptop models.

Another site to check is Werner Heuser's Tuxmobil-Mobile UNIX website at www.tuxmobil.org. You will find links to information such as IrDA, Linux PDAs, and cell phones. Linux Zaurus PDA users can browse to www.openzaurus.org to download a complete open-source replacement operating system for the Zaurus 5000 and 5500 models.

The X Window System

Although much technical information is available on the Internet regarding the X Window System, finding answers to specific questions when troubleshooting can prove problematic. If you are having a problem using X, first try to determine whether the problem is software or hardware related. When searching or asking for help (such as on Usenet's `comp.os.linux.x` newsgroup, which you can access through Google's Groups link; see the next section for other helpful Linux newsgroups), try to be as specific as possible. Some critical factors or information needed to adequately assess a problem include the Linux distribution in use; the kernel version used; the version of X used; the brand, name, and model of your video card; the names, brands, and models of your monitor and other related hardware.

Definitive technical information regarding X is available from www.X.org.

Usenet Newsgroups

Linux-related Usenet newsgroups are another good source of information if you're having trouble using Linux. If your ISP does not offer a comprehensive selection of Linux newsgroups, you can browse to http://groups.google.com/.

The primary Linux and Linux-related newsgroups are as follows:

- `alt.os.linux.dial-up`—Using PPP for dial-up
- `alt.os.linux.mandriva`—All about Mandriva Linux
- `alt.os.linux.slackware`—Using Slackware Linux
- `alt.os.linux.ubuntu`—Using Ubuntu Linux
- `comp.os.linux.advocacy`—Heated discussions about Linux and other related issues
- `comp.os.linux.alpha`—Using Linux on the Alpha CPU
- `comp.os.linux.announce`—General Linux announcements
- `comp.os.linux.answers`—Releases of new Linux FAQs and other information
- `comp.os.linux.development.apps`—Using Linux development tools
- comp.os.linux.development.system—Building the Linux kernel
- `comp.os.linux.embedded`—Linux embedded device development
- `comp.os.linux.hardware`—Configuring Linux for various hardware devices
- `comp.os.linux.m68k`—Linux on Motorola's 68K-family CPUs

- comp.os.linux.misc—Miscellaneous Linux topics
- comp.os.linux.networking—Networking and Linux
- comp.os.linux.portable—Using Linux on laptops
- comp.os.linux.powerpc—Using PPC Linux
- comp.os.linux.security—Linux security issues
- comp.os.linux.setup—Linux installation topics
- comp.os.linux.x—Linux and the X Window System
- comp.windows.x.apps—Using X-based clients
- comp.windows.x.i386unix—X for UNIX PCs
- comp.windows.x.intrinsics—X Toolkit library topics
- comp.windows.x.kde—Using KDE and X discussions
- comp.windows.x.motif—All about Motif programming
- comp.windows.x—Discussions about X
- linux.admin.*—Two newsgroups for Linux administrators
- linux.debian.*—30 newsgroups about Debian
- linux.dev.*—25 or more Linux development newsgroups
- linux.help—Get help with Linux
- linux.kernel—The Linux kernel

Mailing Lists

Mailing lists are interactive or digest-form electronic discussions about nearly any topic. To use a mailing list, you must generally send an email request to be subscribed to the list, and then verify the subscription with a return message from the master list mailer. After subscribing to an interactive form of list, each message sent to the list will appear in your email inbox. However, many lists provide a digest form of subscription in which a single- or half-day's traffic is condensed in a single message. The digest form is generally preferred unless you have set up electronic mail filtering.

The main Ubuntu mailing lists are detailed here, but there are quite a few Linux-related lists. You can search for nearly all online mailing lists by using a typical mailing list search web page, such as the one at www.lsoft.com/lists/list_q.html.

GNOME AND KDE MAILING LISTS

GNOME users and developers should know that more than two dozen mailing lists are available through http://mail.gnome.org/. KDE users will also benefit by perusing the KDE-related mailing lists at www.kde.org/mailinglists.html.

Ubuntu Project Mailing Lists

The Ubuntu Project is always expanding, as many new users continue to find Ubuntu for the first time. You will find many other knowledgeable users with answers to your questions by participating in one of Ubuntu's mailing lists. The lists are focused on using, testing, and developing and participating in Ubuntu's development:

- http://lists.ubuntu.com/mailman/listinfo/ubuntu-security-announce—Security announcements from the Ubuntu developers
- http://lists.ubuntu.com/mailman/listinfo/ubuntu-announce—Announcements concerning Ubuntu
- http://lists.ubuntu.com/mailman/listinfo/ubuntu-users—Discussions among users of Ubuntu releases
- http://lists.ubuntu.com/mailman/listinfo/ubuntu-devel—Queries and reports from developers and testers of Ubuntu test releases

Internet Relay Chat

Internet Relay Chat (IRC) is a popular form and forum of communication for many Linux developers and users because it allows an interactive, real-time exchange of information and ideas. To use IRC, you must have an IRC client and the address of a network and server hosting the desired chat channel for your discussions.

You can use the `irc.freenode.net` IRC server, or one listed at www.freenode.net/ to chat with other Ubuntu users. Some current channels are as follows:

- `#Ubuntu`—General chat about Ubuntu
- `#edubuntu`—General chat about EdUbuntu
- `#xubuntu`—General chat about Xubuntu
- `#kubuntu`—General chat about Kubuntu

For more channels to look at, head over to https://help.ubuntu.com/community/InternetRelayChat for an exhaustive list of "official" channels.

However, Google can help you find other channels to explore. Enter the distro name and IRC into the search options to retrieve information on any IRC channels relevant to your requirements. To get help with getting started with IRC, browse to www.irchelp.org/. Some of the channels of interest might be

- `#linux`—General discussions about Linux.
- `#linuxhelp`—A help chat discussion for new users.
- Most IRC networks provide one or more Linux channels, although some providers require signup and registration before you can access any chat channel.

Index

Symbols

A

B

C

D

E

F

G

H

I

J

K

M

N

O

P

S

T

V

W

X-Z

HEALTH PSYCHOLOGY

HEALTH PSYCHOLOGY

THEORY, RESEARCH AND PRACTICE

DAVID F MARKS, MICHAEL MURRAY,
BRIAN EVANS & EMEE VIDA ESTACIO

4TH EDITION

SAGE

Los Angeles | London | New Delhi
Singapore | Washington DC | Boston

SAGE

Los Angeles | London | New Delhi
Singapore | Washington DC | Boston

SAGE Publications Ltd
1 Oliver's Yard
55 City Road
London EC1Y 1SP

SAGE Publications Inc.
2455 Teller Road
Thousand Oaks, California 91320

SAGE Publications India Pvt Ltd
B 1/I 1 Mohan Cooperative Industrial Area
Mathura Road
New Delhi 110 044

SAGE Publications Asia-Pacific Pte Ltd
3 Church Street
#10-04 Samsung Hub
Singapore 049483

Editor: Luke Block
Editorial assistant: Katie Norton
Production editor: Imogen Roome
Marketing manager: Alison Borg
Cover design: Wendy Scott
Typeset by: C&M Digitals (P) Ltd, Chennai, India
Printed and bound in Great Britain by Ashford Colour Press Ltd

MIX
Paper from responsible sources
FSC www.fsc.org FSC® C011748

First edition 1999; reprinted 2002, 2003. Second edition 2005; reprinted 2008, 2009, 2010. Third edition 2010; reprinted 2011, 2013, 2014

This edition printed 2015

Library of Congress Control Number: 2014950223

British Library Cataloguing in Publication data

A catalogue record for this book is available from the British Library

ISBN 978-1-4462-9506-9
ISBN 978-1-4462-9507-6 (pbk)

Contents

Author Biographies

DAVID F. MARKS served as Head of the School of Psychology at Middlesex Polytechnic, and as Head of the Department of Psychology at City University, London, UK. Previously David held positions at the University of Sheffield, UK, at the University of Otago, New Zealand and at University College London. His other books include *The Psychology of the Psychic* (1980, with R. Kammann), *Theories of Image Formation* (1986), *Imagery: Current Developments* (1990, with J.T.E. Richardson and P. Hampson), *The Quit For Life Programme: An Easier Way to Stop Smoking and Not Start Again* (1993), *Improving the Health of the Nation* (1996, with C. Francome), *Dealing With Dementia: Recent European Research* (2000, with C.M. Sykes), *The Psychology of the Psychic* (revised edition) (2000), *The Health Psychology Reader* (2002), *Research Methods for Clinical and Health Psychology* (2004, with L. Yardley) and *Overcoming Your Smoking Habit* (2005). David is the Editor of the *Journal of Health Psychology* and *Health Psychology Open.*

MICHAEL MURRAY is Professor of Psychology at the University of Keele, UK. Previously he was Professor of Social and Health Psychology in the Division of Community Health, Memorial University of Newfoundland, Canada, and has held positions at St Thomas' Hospital Medical School, London, UK and at the University of Ulster, Northern Ireland. His previous books include *Smoking Among Young Adults* (1988, with L. Jarrett, A.V. Swan and R. Rumen) and *Qualitative Health Psychology: Theories and Methods* (1999, with K. Chamberlain). Michael is Associate Editor of *Psychology and Health* and an editorial board member of the *Journal of Health Psychology*, *Health Psychology Review*, *Health Psychology and Medicine* and *Arts and Health.* His current research interests include the use of participatory and arts-based methods to promote social engagement among older people.

BRIAN EVANS is a Visiting Lecturer at Middlesex University, UK, having previously served there as programme leader of the MSc degree in Health Psychology. Brian has also held positions at City University London and the University of Sussex, UK, and at Concordia University, Montreal, Canada. He is interested in the analysis of psychological research and theory in its socio-political context; his previous publications include *IQ and Mental Testing: An Unnatural Science and Its Social History* (1981, with B. Waites). Brian is an editorial board member of the *Journal of Health Psychology.*

EMEE VIDA ESTACIO is a Lecturer in Psychology at Keele University. She completed her Bachelor's degree in Psychology (magna cum laude) at the University of the Philippines, and her MSc and PhD in Health Psychology at City University London. Emee specializes in health promotion and community development and has facilitated action research projects in some of the most deprived areas in the UK and in the Philippines. As a scholar activist, she became actively involved in supporting activities for Oxfam, the Association for International Cancer Research, CRIBS Philippines and Save the Children UK. Emee is a steering group member of Health Literacy UK and sits on the editorial board of the *Journal of Health Psychology*, *Health Psychology Open*, *Community, Work and Family* and the *Philippine Journal of Psychology*.

Copyright Acknowledgements

The authors and publishers wish to thank the following for permission to use copyright material:

CHAPTER 1

The World Health Organization for 'Plot showing total health expenditures as % of gross domestic product (GPD) versus GPD per capita (191 countries)' (Musgrove, Zeramdini and Carrin, 2002, Basic patterns in national health expenditure. *Bulletin of the World Health Organization*, 80: 134–42).

The King's Fund for Figure 1.4, 'A framework for the determinants of health' (Dahlgren, G. and Whitehead, M., 1991, *Policies and Strategies to Promote Equity in Health*, p. 23).

The Institute of Health Metrics and Evaluation for Figure 1.3, 'Percent change in total DALYs, 1990–2010' (http://www.healthdata.org/infographic/percent-change-total-dalys-1990-2010).

CHAPTER 2

BMJ Publishing Group for Figure 2.1 World population and annual increments , 8000 BC to 2050 AD from Raleight, V.S. (1999). World population and health in transition. BMJ 319:981-984.

Medknow Publications for Figure 2.3 originally published in Anjana, Ali, Pradeepa, Deepa, Datta, Unnikrishnan, Rema and Mohan (2011) "The need for obtaining accurate nationwide estimates of diabetes prevalence in India – Rationale for a national study on diabetes". Open access licence.

The Lancet for Figure 2.4 showing a plot of data from the EuroMonitor industry data 2011 edition originally published by Moodie et al. (2013).

APS for Figure 2.6 'Female life expectancy in the record-holding country' (Oeppen and Vaupel, 2002, Broken limits to life expectancy. Science, 206 (5570): 1029–31).

The US Census Bureau for 'World population 1950–2050' (International Database, April 2004, www.census.gov/ipc/www/img/worldpop.gif) and Figure 2.7 'A population pyramid for the Chinese population for the years 2000 and 2050' (International Database, www.census.gov/cgi-bin/ipc/idbpyrs.pl?cty=USandout=sandymax=250).

AVERT for Figure 2.8.

CHAPTER 4

Figure 4.1, 'Similarities and differences of health and illness conceptions in Eastern European, South American and Italian care workers' (Pace, C.S., Velotti, P. and Zavattini, G.C., 2012).

Art Gallery of South Australia, www.artgallery.sa.gov.au.

CHAPTER 5

Blackwell Publishers for 'Participatory Action Research' (Chataway, C., 1997, An examination of the constraints on mutual inquiry in a Participatory Action Research project. *Journal of Social Issues*, 53 (4): 747–65).

CHAPTER 6

Blackwell Publishers for 'Contraceptive method used in the last year by age group' and 'Contraceptive method used in the last year by marital status' (Johnson, A.M., Wadsworth, J., Wellings, K. and Field, J., 1994, *Sexual Attitudes and Lifestyles*, pp. 300–1).

CHAPTER 7

BMJ Publishing Group for 'Environmental influences on food intake and physical activity' (Egger, G. and Swinburn, B., 1997, *BMJ*, 315: 478).

CHAPTER 9

Blackwell Publishers for 'Six domains of the determinants of tobacco use' (Conrad, K.M., Flay, B.R. and Hill, D., 1992, Why children start smoking: predictors of onset. *British Journal of Addiction*, 87: 1711–24).

CHAPTER 10

Sage Publications for Box 10.5, 'Reactions to participating in an exercise programme for disabled people' (Graham, R., Kremer, J. and Wheeler, G., 2008, Physical activity and psychological well-being among people with chronic illness and disability. *Journal of Health Psychology*, 13: 447–58).

CHAPTER 11

Figure 11.2, 'Examples of loss-framed and gain-framed messages for smoking cessation' (source: www.yalescientific.org).

Figure 11.3, 'Health literacy levels in eight European nations' (HLS-EU Consortium, 2012, *Comparative Report of Health Literacy in Eight EU Member States: The European Health Literacy Survey*, http://ec.europa.eu/eahc/documents/news/Comparative_report_on_health_literacy_in_eight_EU_member_states.pdf).

CHAPTER 12

Pressdram Ltd for 'Coping with a life event stressor' (*Private Eye*, 4 October 1996, p. 22).

Palgrave Macmillan for Figure 12.1, 'Flowchart for an interactional model of stress' (Cox, 1978, *Stress*, p. 19).

CHAPTER 14

Figure 14.1, Protesters outside of St Paul's Cathedral in London (source: http://en.wikipedia.org/wiki/Occupy_London).

Figure 14.2, 'Key elements of the development and evaluation process' (Craig, P., Dieppe, P., Macintyre, S., Michie, S., Nazareth, I. and Petticrew, M., 2008, Developing and evaluating complex interventions: the new Medical Research Council guidance. *BMJ*, 337, doi: http://dx.doi.org/10.1136/bmj.a1655).

CHAPTER 15

Figure 14.1, Sage Publications for Box 15.3, 'HIV as a controllable infection' (Ranjbar, V., McKinlay, A. and McVittie, C., 2014, The micro and the macro: how discourse of control maintains HIV-related stigma. *Journal of Health Psychology*).

CHAPTER 17

Sage Publications for Figure 17.1, 'Dynamic extended model of treatment and illness representations' (Bishop, F.L., Yardley, L. and Lewith, G.T., 2008, Treatment appraisals and beliefs predict adherence to complementary therapies. *Journal of Health Psychology*, 13: 701–18).

Every effort has been made to trace the copyright holders but if any have been inadvertently overlooked the publishers will be pleased to make the necessary arrangement at the first opportunity.

Preface

This textbook provides an in-depth introduction to the field of health psychology. It is designed for undergraduate and postgraduate courses in health psychology, medicine, nursing and health promotion, and for all other readers wishing to update their knowledge about psychology and health. The authors strive to present a balanced view of the field, its theories, research and applications. We aim to present the mainstream ideas, theories and studies within health psychology and also to examine the underlying theoretical assumptions and critically analyse methods, evidence and conclusions.

All mainstream domains and topics relevant to health psychology are included. A key feature of this textbook is the priority given to social meanings and contextual, environmental determinants of health, illness and health care alongside the genetic and biological determinants. The authors argue that meanings and context are as important to health as genes and germs. This book locates health psychology within its global, social and political context. It attempts to provide a snapshot of the 'bigger picture' using a wide-angle lens, as well as giving detailed analyses of the 'nitty-gritty' of theory, research and practice.

This textbook introduces readers to the field of health psychology, the major theoretical approaches, contemporary research on core topics, and how this theory and evidence is being applied in practice. In this fourth edition, we have improved the structure, updated the text, enhanced the pedagogical features, and expanded the Companion Website.

Health psychology is relatively new, having developed as a sub-discipline of psychology in the 1970s and 1980s. The primary focus has been to develop theories and models about social and cognitive processes concerned with health beliefs and behaviours. This approach has yielded thousands of research publications testing theories and models about the causes of health behaviour change. The growth of interest in this subject has been truly amazing. Similar to psychology more generally, the primary focus of health psychology has been the behaviour, beliefs and experiences of individuals.

The book introduces alternative approaches to health psychology which are not yet part of the mainstream. We advance the case that psychological issues are embedded in human social structures in which economics and social justice play crucial roles. The minutiae of 'social cognition' may be of limited relevance in a world where people are struggling to survive, with large debts, to find water, food, shelter, education and health care for their families. This is a world where poverty, social injustice and inequalities are a reality for billions of human beings, and psychological processes are, for many, conditioned by these basic limitations of capability, freedom and power (Marks, 1996, 2002a, 2004; Murray and Campbell, 2003; Murray, 2014a, b).

To contribute to international health, theory and practice in health psychology need to engage with the real economy, develop approaches for industrial-scale behaviour change, and engage with communities and the struggle of the dispossessed. A reinvigorated agenda for health psychology work will aim to produce '*actionable* understandings of the complex individual–society dialectic underlying social inequalities' (Murray and Campbell, 2003: 236). Preliminary thoughts on 'actionable understandings', and of the 'individual–society dialectic' are presented in this book. By having access to mainstream and alternative perspectives in a single volume, lecturers and students can reach an assessment of the field and how it might progress in the future.

We explain the significance of the social context, and review theory and methods (Part 1), analyse the complexity and diversity of health behaviour (Part 2), discuss health promotion and disease prevention (Part 3), and explicate the significance of clinical health psychology work (Part 4).

Table P1 A multi-level framework or 'Onion Model' for health psychology

Level	Description	Where covered
Core	Age, sex and hereditary factors	Various parts of the book
Level 1	Individual lifestyle	Part 2
Level 2	Social and community influences	Whole book
Level 3	Living and working conditions; health care system	Parts 3 and 4
Level 4	General socio-economic, cultural and environmental conditions	Part 1

Source: adapted from Dahlgren and Whitehead (1991: 23)

The book uses a multi-level framework that takes into account the social context of health-related experience and behaviour. This multi-level framework, the 'Onion Model', assumes different levels of influence and mechanisms for bringing about change (see Table P1 and Chapter 1 for details).

Health psychology is a rich field requiring an appreciation of the cultural, socio-political and economic roots of human behaviour and experience. The authors apply an international, cultural and interdisciplinary perspective. We suggest that social, economic and political changes have not kept pace with industrial, scientific and medical achievements. As the gaps between the 'haves' and the 'have-nots' widen, and the world population grows larger, the impacts of learned helplessness, poverty and social isolation are increasingly salient features of society.

Those concerned with health promotion and disease prevention require in-depth understanding of the lived experience of health, illness and health care. By integrating research using quantitative, qualitative and action-oriented approaches, we take a step in that direction.

MAKING THE BEST USE OF THIS BOOK

This fourth edition has been completely revised and updated, with more than one quarter of the 1,000-plus references from the five years 2010–2015. Lecturers may recommend the chapters in any order according to the requirements of any particular course, and personal interests and preferences. Chapters are written as free-standing documents. No prior reading of other chapters is assumed.

Each chapter begins with an **Outline** and ends with a detailed **Summary** of key ideas and suggestions for **Future Research**. The text will be interspersed with **boxed definitions**. Each chapter contains tables, figures and boxes, and recent examples of key studies to guide student understanding using highlighted **key study** boxes. Highlighted **case studies** present works by key people living in different parts of the world showing how context, culture and the environment affect health and behaviour.

Key terms are identified by **bold** and defined in the **Glossary** at the end of the book.

A useful companion reader to this textbook is *The Health Psychology Reader* (Marks, 2002b), which reprints and discusses 25 key articles accompanied by introductions to the main themes. You can also refer to the 85 key articles in *New Directions in Health Psychology* (Murray and Chamberlain, 2015).

Acknowledgements

DFM: To Michael, Brian and Emee, my co-authors, for friendship and collaboration over many years; more specifically, MM for his unstinting support and lively humour, in spite of a heavy administrative burden, BE for pleasant walks, talks and pub lunches over heath and by river; EVE for cake, songs and smiles. To Ziyad Marar for his enthusiastic skills of persuasion that drew me into the SAGE fold two decades ago. To many colleagues at SAGE, especially: Michael Carmichael, the original commissioning editor, for his enthusiastic skills of persuasion (must be a SAGE thing), Luke Block and Keri Dickens, who took over the editor role for this edition, Imogen Roome and David Hemsley, copyeditors of the manuscript, Alison Borg for marketing, Wendy Scott for the cover design and many other colleagues who produced the first three editions. To Catherine Sykes for friendship, inspiration, and a co-author of the second edition. To Carla Willig for friendship, a co-author of the first two editions. To Cailine Woodall for contributing to and co-authoring the second edition. To Jane Ogden for reviewing an early draft of Chapter 7. To generations of students and academic colleagues at universities, from Otago in the Deep South and Tromsø in the Arctic North, from Hokkaido, Hamamatsu, and Kyushu in the Far East and Oregon, Washington and Stanford in the Far West, and, closer to home at Sheffield, UCL, Cambridge and Middlesex Universities. To my father, Victor, for providing the quiet refuge I still call 'home', away from the hustle and bustle of London. Thank you all – this book couldn't have happened without you!

MM: Thanks, as always, to Anne for her continuing love, kindness and inspiration.

BE: To Tessa, Alex, Dan and David for valuable advice, and to many health psychology students at Middlesex and City Universities for their feedback enabling me to focus more clearly on key areas of current interest.

EVE: To my parents for life, to my Andy for love, and to my mentor, DFM for guidance – thanks!

PART 1

HEALTH PSYCHOLOGY IN CONTEXT

This book provides an in-depth, critical overview of the field of health psychology. In Part 1 we are concerned with the social, cultural and psychological context of the health and illness experience. Chapter 1 introduces and discusses the concept of health and reviews the development of health psychology as a field of inquiry. Health and health psychology are defined and approaches and problems to measurement and to the scaling of subjective well-being are presented. The role of frameworks, theories and models is discussed and the 'Health Onion' framework is described.

Chapter 2 discusses the contextual factors of the macro-social environment: the demographic, economic and societal factors which operate globally to structure the health experience of populations, communities and individuals. The chapter uses a wide-angle lens to explore the bigger picture of the global context for human health and suffering. The focus is on human health variations across societies and the chapter considers population growth, poverty and increasing longevity as determinants of health status. Research on gender, ethnicity and disability suggest that *inequality* is a persistent characteristic of our health care systems.

Chapter 3 examines the influence of social inequalities and social injustice in health outcomes. The universal existence of health gradients in developing and industrialized societies shows how much of health experience is determined by social, cultural and economic circumstances and how little by health care systems. Measures to tackle social injustice are required at a political/policy level and health psychologists can play a role as agents of change. There is substantial evidence linking poor social conditions with ill health. The explanations for this include material, behavioural and psychosocial factors. The explanation of health inequalities creates many important challenges for theory and research in health psychology.

Chapter 4 examines the ways in which health and illness have been construed across time and place. Western biomedical procedures often tend to be viewed as 'scientific' and 'evidence based' while the medical systems of other cultures and 'complementary' therapies are seen as 'unscientific' or 'magical'. These assumptions need to be evaluated in the light of studies conducted with participants from different cultures and ethnic groups who make their own accounts of health and illness and act upon them in positive and functional ways. Anthropological and sociological studies of health and medicine have generated a range of theories and concepts that enhance the understanding of health and illness.

Chapter 5 presents an A–Z of the most useful methods for carrying out research in health psychology. Three categories of methods are quantitative, qualitative and action research methods. These types of methods all have potential in assessing, understanding and improving health, illness and health care outcomes. Research designs that are quantitative in nature place emphasis on reliable and valid measurement in controlled experiments, trials and surveys. Multiple sources of evidence are synthesized in systematic reviews and meta-analyses. Qualitative methods use interviews, focus groups, narratives or texts to explore health and illness concepts and experience. Action research enables change processes to feed back into plans for improvement and emancipation.

1 HEALTH PSYCHOLOGY: AN INTRODUCTION

The desire for the prolongation of life we may take to be one of the most universal of all human motives.

(Kenneth Arrow, 1963: 75)

OUTLINE

In this chapter we introduce health psychology as a field of inquiry. The concept of health is introduced from a historical perspective. Health psychology is defined and theories of need-satisfaction and subjective well-being are reviewed. We present a theory of well-being with a life-span perspective that includes the constructs of attachment, life satisfaction, affect and consumption. The scope and rationale of health psychology are discussed. Problems with measurement are discussed and a framework we call the 'Health Onion' is described.

WHAT DO WE MEAN BY 'HEALTH'?

It seems natural to discuss what is meant by '**health**' in a book about health psychology. Otherwise, how do we understand the subject? To unravel the origin of the word, a quick dip into etymology is called for. The word 'health' is derived from Old High German and Anglo-Saxon words meaning whole, hale and holy. The etymology of 'heal' has been traced to a Proto-Indo-European root 'kailo-' (meaning whole, uninjured or of good omen). In Old English this became 'hælan' (to make whole, sound and well) and the Old English 'hal' (health), the root of the adjectives 'whole', 'hale' and 'holy', and the greeting 'Hail'. The word became 'heil' in German (unhurt, unharmed), 'Heil' (good luck or fortune), 'heilig' (holy) and 'heilen' (to heal). In Old Norse there was 'heill' (health, prosperity, good luck). From the same roots, 'Hello' in English, 'Hallo' in German, or 'Hi' are everyday greetings.

Ancient links exist between the concepts of 'health', 'wholeness', 'holiness', 'hygiene', 'cleanliness', 'goodness', 'godliness', 'sanitary', 'sanity' and 'saintliness', as in: 'Wash you, make you clean; put away the evil of your doings from before mine eyes; cease to do evil' (Isaiah, 1:16, King James Bible) and: 'O you who believe! when you rise up to prayer, wash your faces and your hands' (Quran). The concept of health as wholeness existed in ancient China and classical Greece where health was seen as a state of 'harmony', 'balance', 'order' or 'equilibrium' with nature. Related ideas are found in many healing systems today. On the other hand, there are traditional associations between concepts of 'disease', 'disorder', 'disintegration', 'illness', 'crankiness' (or 'krankheit' in German), 'uncleanness', 'insanity', 'chaos' and 'evil'.

Galen (CE 129–200), the early Roman physician, followed the Hippocratic tradition with *hygieia* (health) or *euexia* (soundness) as a balance between the four bodily humours of black bile, yellow bile, phlegm and blood. Galen believed that the body's 'constitution', 'temperament' or 'state' could be put out of equilibrium by excessive heat, cold, dryness or wetness. Such imbalances might be caused by fatigue, insomnia, distress, anxiety, or by food residues resulting from eating the wrong quantity or quality of food. For example, an excess of black bile would cause melancholia. The theory was related to the four elements: earth, fire, water and air (Table 1.1).

In the winter, when it is chilly and wet, people worry about catching a cold, caused by a build up of phlegm. In summer, when a person is hot and sweaty, they may worry about not drinking enough water because they could otherwise become 'hot and bothered' (bad tempered). It is remarkable that some common beliefs today are descendants of early Greek and Roman theories of medicine from 2,000-plus years ago.

Universal interest in health is fuelled by a continuous torrent of content in the media about health and medicine, especially concerning the 'dread' diseases. In 1946 the **World Health Organization (WHO)** defined health as: 'the state of complete physical, social and spiritual well-being, not simply the absence of illness'. It is doubtful whether 'complete physical, social and spiritual well-being' can ever be reached by anyone. Apart from this idealism, the WHO

Table 1.1 Galen's theory of humours

Humour	Season	Element	Organ	Qualities	Personality type	Characteristics
Blood	spring	air	liver	warm and moist	sanguine	amorous, courageous, hopeful
Yellow bile	summer	fire	gall bladder	warm and dry	choleric	easily angered, bad tempered
Black bile	autumn	earth	spleen	cold and dry	melancholic	despondent, sleepless, irritable
Phlegm	winter	water	brain/ lungs	cold and moist	phlegmatic	calm, unemotional

definition overlooks the *psychological*, *cultural* and *economic* aspects of health. Psychological processes, the main subject of this book, are a key factor in health and are embedded in a social context. For this reason, the term 'psychosocial' is often used to describe human behaviour and experience as an influence on well-being. Social inequalities and poverty are also strongly associated with health outcomes and warrant explicit inclusion in any definition of health. With these thoughts in mind, we define health in the light of five key elements (Box 1.1).

BOX 1.1
DEFINITION OF HEALTH

Health is a state of well-being with satisfaction of physical, cultural, psychosocial, economic and spiritual needs, not simply the absence of illness.

NEED SATISFACTION, HAPPINESS AND SUBJECTIVE WELL-BEING

To be useful, the above definition of health needs to be unpacked. Philosophers, psychologists, songsters and others have had much to say about what makes a person feel well. A key concept is that of **need satisfaction**, immortalized by Mick Jagger and Keith Richards in the 1965 Rolling Stones release '(I Can't Get No) Satisfaction'. In Maslow's (1943) **hierarchy of needs** (Figure 1.1), a person is healthy if all of their needs are satisfied, starting with the most basic needs for air, food, water, sex, sleep, homeostasis and excretion. Then as need satisfaction moves toward the top of the pyramid, the epitome of need satisfaction, a person becomes more and more 'satisfied', and thus physically and mentally healthy to the point of self-actualization.

Maslow's hierarchy framework has been highly influential. It puts at the top of the pyramid the concept of 'self-actualization', a state in which the person feels they have achieved a 'peak experience' of meaningful and purposeful existence. Maslow's needs hierarchy emphasizes the great importance of safety, love and belonging, and self-esteem. For every good principle in psychology, there are always exceptions; human needs do not always fall into any fixed hierarchy. For example, an extreme sports enthusiast who is into mountain climbing may put 'esteem' and 'self-actualization' ahead of 'safety'. We read about it in the news the next morning. Few would disagree about the value of the five levels of need within the pyramid. However, there are key elements of human fulfilment that are not explicitly mentioned in Maslow's hierarchy, for example, **agency** and **autonomy** – the freedom to choose – and the often-neglected **spirituality** – the feeling that not all that is significant is of the physical world.

Scholars have attempted to improve on Maslow's hierarchy. Doyal and Gough (1991: 4) argued that: '"health" and "autonomy" are the most basic of human needs that are the same for everyone . . . all humans have a right to optimum need-satisfaction . . . For this to occur . . . certain societal preconditions – political, economic and ecological – must be fulfilled.' The satisfaction

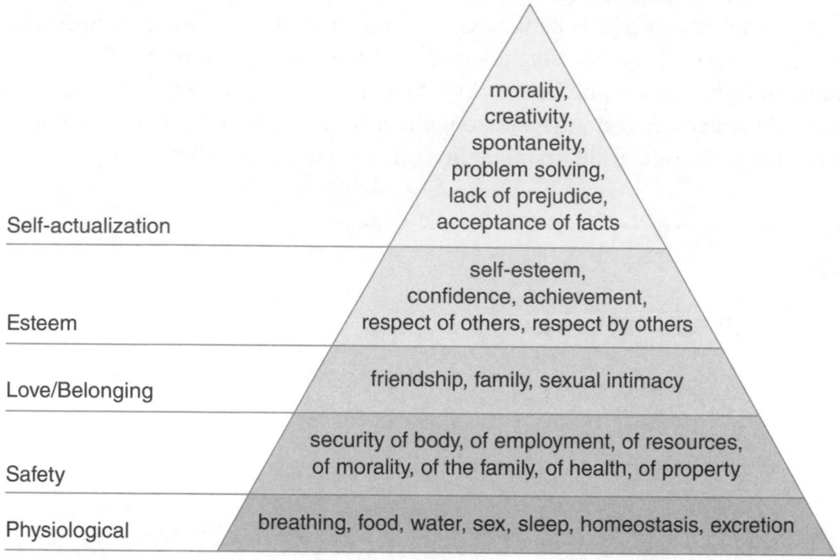

Figure 1.1 Maslow's hierarchy of human needs

of three basic needs – physical health, autonomy of agency, and critical autonomy – are necessary to achieve the avoidance of serious harm as a universal goal in all cultures. If or when a person has reached this universal goal, he/she will then be able to experience 'minimally disabled social participation' (p. 170) and be free to participate in his/her chosen forms of life. The form of the latter will depend upon culture, interests and education. A related psychological theory called 'Self-Determination Theory' suggested three basic human needs: competence, relatedness and autonomy (Ryan and Deci, 2000), but Maslow's hierarchy suggests a more nuanced set of needs than just these three.

Throughout history, philosophers have discussed the nature of a *good and happy life* or what, in health care, is termed '**quality of life**' **(QoL)**. For Aristotle, happiness was viewed as 'the meaning and the purpose of life, the whole aim and end of human existence'. For utilitarians such as Jeremy Bentham, happiness was pleasure without pain. To individuals suffering from cancer or other conditions with pain, unpleasant symptoms and treatment options, and uncertain prognosis, QoL has special relevance.

QoL has been defined by WHO as (take a deep breath):

> An individual's perception of their position in life, in the context of the culture and value systems in which they live, and in relation to their goals, expectations, standards, and concerns. It is a broad ranging concept, affected in a complex way by the person's physical health, psychological state, level of independence, social relationships, and their relationship to salient features of their environment.
>
> (WHOQoL Group, 1995: 1404)

A sixth domain on spirituality, religiousness and personal beliefs, was later added to these five domains by the WHOQoL Group (1995). The Collins dictionary defines QoL more simply as: 'The general well-being of a person or society, defined in terms of health and happiness, rather than wealth.' The QoL concept overlaps with that of **subjective well-being (SWB)**, which has been defined by a leader in the field, Ed Diener, known as 'Dr Happiness', as: 'An umbrella term for different valuations that people make regarding their lives, the events happening to them, their bodies and minds, and the circumstances in which they live' (Diener, 2006: 400). The evidence linking SWB with health and longevity is strong and plentiful.

With a global population of more than seven billion unique individuals in diverse cultures, religions and social circumstances, can QoL ever be assessed using a single yardstick? A few courageous individuals and organizations have given it a try and, since the 1970s, many scales and measures have been constructed. A few examples are listed in Table 1.2.

Table 1.2 Examples of QoL, subjective well-being and happiness scales

Authors	Year	Title	Domains	Samples
Andrews and Withey	1976	Social indicators of well-being	Job satisfaction	Adults
Flanagan	1978	The QoL scale (QoLS)	Material and physical well-being Relationships Social, community and civic activities Personal development and fulfilment Recreation	Healthy adults and patients with chronic illnesses
Kammann Kammann and Flett	1979 1983	Affectometer 1 Affectometer 2	Happiness/subjective well-being	Adults
Diener et al.	1985	Satisfaction with Life Scale (SWLS)	Satisfaction with life	Adults
European Organization for Research and Treatment of Cancer (EORTC)	1986	QLQ-C30	Physical Role Cognitive Emotional Social Global QoL	Patient samples

(Continued)

Table 1.2 (Continued)

Authors	Year	Title	Domains	Samples
Ware and Sherbourne	1992	Short-Form Health Survey (SF-36)	Vitality Physical functioning Bodily pain General health perceptions Physical role functioning Emotional role functioning Social role functioning Mental health	Healthy adults and patients with chronic illnesses
WHOQoL group	1995	WHOQoL	Physical Psychological Level of independence Social relationships Environment Spirituality	Healthy adults and patient groups

By far, the most utilized scale is the SF-36, which accounts for around 50% of all clinical studies (Marks, 2013). These 'happiness scales' are diverse and consist of items about what makes a 'good life'. For example, Diener et al.'s (1985) brief *Satisfaction With Life Scale* (SWLS) uses a seven-point Likert scale with five items:

In most ways my life is close to my ideal.

The conditions of my life are excellent.

I am satisfied with my life.

So far I have gotten the important things I want in life.

If I could live my life over, I would change almost nothing.

Using the 1–7 scale below, testees indicate their agreement with each item by placing the appropriate number on the line preceding that item. They are asked to 'be open and honest' in their responding.

7 Strongly agree

6 Agree

5 Slightly agree

4 Neither agree nor disagree

3 Slightly disagree

2 Disagree

1 Strongly disagree

Luhmann et al. (2012) distinguished between 'cognitive' and 'affective' well-being. They carried out a meta-analysis to examine whether life events have different effects on cognitive and affective well-being and how the rate of adaptation varies across different life events. They integrated longitudinal data from 188 publications that had reported studies on 313 samples with 65,911 people to describe the reaction and adaptation to four family events (marriage, divorce, bereavement, child birth) and four work events (unemployment, re-employment, retirement, relocation/migration). The findings showed that, for most events, the effects on cognitive well-being are stronger and more consistent across samples.

Diener and Chan (2011) review evidence that *having high SWB adds four to ten years to life*. The evidence for an association between SWB and all-cause mortality is mounting. As always, there could be a mysterious third variable influencing both SWB and mortality (e.g. fetal nutrition, social support, lifestyle) and, if the relationship between SWB and mortality did prove to be causal, the possible mediating processes would be a matter for speculation. One of the principal goals of health psychology, then, is to understand the links between subjective well-being and health. A general theory of well-being, physical health and life satisfaction is summarized in Box 1.2.

BOX 1.2
THEORY OF WELL-BEING

The Theory of Well-Being (TWB) shows causal links between some significant determinants of physical and mental well-being. In addition to emotion, and the role of income, restraint and consumption, the TWB places emphasis on the developmentally important construct of attachment (Bowlby, 1969, 1973, 1980). The manner in which a baby attaches to its mother, father and/or other caregiver creates a template for life based on the infant's need to maintain proximity to an anchor person who provides a 'secure base' for exploring the environment. The availability and responsivity of the anchor person to attachment are internalized as mental models of the world that are generalized to relationships throughout life until the individual's death (Ainsworth, Blehar, Waters & Wall, 1978). The different ways of attaching to anchor figures is termed 'attachment style'.

(Continued)

(Continued)

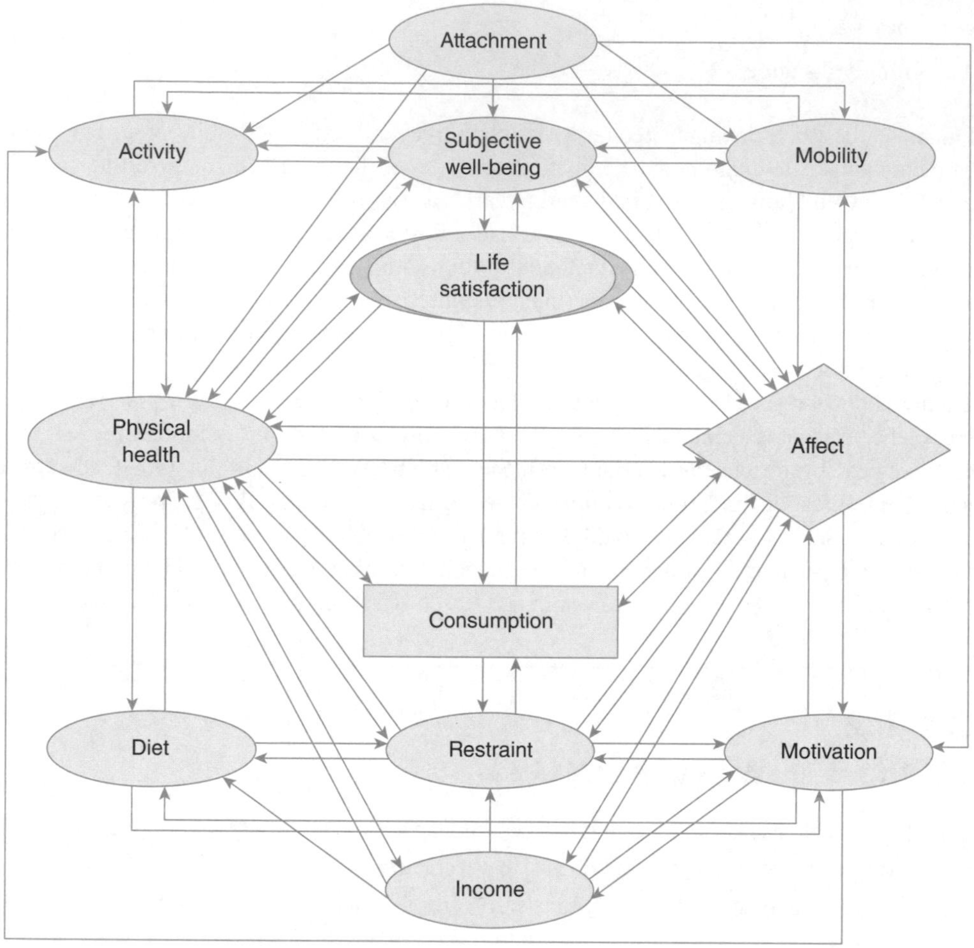

Figure 1.2 General Theory of Well-Being

Evidence from several domains suggests that there is a causal link between life satisfaction, positive affect, moderate levels of consumption and well-being, as indicated in the theory. Attachment style has been shown to influence life satisfaction and a gamut of health-related behaviours including alcohol abuse, drug abuse, smoking, insomnia, accidental injury, trauma, grief, chronic illness, and responses to natural disasters. The literature shows that a significant mediator of the association between life satisfaction and positive health outcomes is a moderate level of consumption. As that well-worn cliché states: 'Anything in moderation'.

The hedonic conception of SWB of Diener and Chan (2011) can be contrasted with the **eudaimonic** approach that focuses on meaning and self-realization and defines well-being in terms of the degree to which a person is fully functioning (Ryan & Deci, 2001). Waterman (1993) has argued that eudaimonic well-being occurs when people are living in accordance with their 'daimon' or authentic self. Eudaimonia is thought to occur when people's life activities mesh with deeply held values and are fully engaged in authentic personal expression.

An important aspect of life satisfaction is the search for eudaimonic meaning. Empirical studies suggest that there exists a strong and stable relationship between meaning in life and subjective well-being (Zika & Chamberlain, 1992). People who believe that they have meaningful lives tend to be more optimistic and self-actualized (Compton et al., 1996), and experience more self-esteem (Steger et al., 2006) and positive affect (e.g. King et al., 2006), as well as less depression and anxiety (Steger et al., 2006) and less suicidal ideation (Harlow et al., 1986). The 'Salutogenic Theory' of Antonovsky (1979) also emphasized the relationship between meaning and purpose in life assessed by the Sense of Coherence scale and positive health outcomes (Eriksson & Lindström, 2006).

Source: Marks (2015).

THE NATURE OF HEALTH PSYCHOLOGY

The importance of psychosocial processes in health and illness is becoming increasingly recognized as the evidence on the role of behaviour and emotion in morbidity and mortality is steadily accumulating. Much research has been conducted to investigate the possible role of stress and psychological characteristics on the onset, course and management of physical illness. Health psychology is growing rapidly and health psychologists are in increasing demand in health care and medical settings. Psychologists have become essential members of multidisciplinary teams in rehabilitation, cardiology, paediatrics, oncology, anaesthesiology, family practice, dentistry, and other medical fields.

Although the primary focus for health psychology has been clinical settings, increasing interest is also being directed towards interventions for disease prevention, especially with reference to sexual health, nutrition, smoking, alcohol, inactivity and stress. A popular view in Western societies is that of '**individualism**' in which individuals are viewed as 'agents' who are personally responsible for their own health. From this viewpoint, a person who smokes 40 a day and develops lung cancer is held responsible for causing their own costly, disabling and terminal illness. Traditional health education has consisted of campaigns providing a mixture of exhortation, information and advice to persuade people to change their unhealthy habits. By telling people to 'Just say no' policy makers have expected people to make the 'right' choices and change unhealthy choices into healthy ones. There has been some notable success in tobacco control that provides a benchmark for what may be achieved through health education and policy (see Chapter 9).

Against the view that keeping ourselves healthy means making responsible choices, there is little convincing evidence, beyond the example of smoking, that people who change their lifestyle actually *do* live longer or have a greater quality of life than people who 'live and let live' and make no real attempt to live healthily. Consider an example: a prospective study suggests that vegetarians live longer than meat eaters. But vegetarians may differ from the meat-eaters in many ways other than their choice of diet, e.g. religious beliefs, use of alcohol, social support. Also a statistical association between two variables such as a vegetarian diet and longevity can never prove causality or allow a prediction about any particular individual case. A vegetarian could still die of stomach cancer and becoming vegetarian does not necessarily lengthen the life of any specific individual. Epidemiology is a statistical science that can only provide a statistical statement to which there will always be inconvenient exceptions, such as 90-year-old smokers.

The assumption that a person must 'live well to be well' is prevalent in contemporary society. The moral aspect of this assumption leads to victim blaming. If people get ill it is often seen as 'their own fault' because they smoke, drink, eat a poor diet, fail to exercise or use screening services, do not cope with stress in a healthy way by joining a gym and so on. Health policy is run through with the blaming and shaming of individuals for their own poor health. The 'smoking evil' has been replaced by the 'obesity evil'. A person who smokes, eats fatty foods, drinks alcohol and watches TV many hours every day is represented as a 'couch potato'. Fitzpatrick (2001) compares disease with sin, and health with virtue. Medicine is portrayed as a quest against gluttony, laziness and lust. Diets are seen as moral choices, in which a 'balanced' and healthy diet is a moral imperative.

Health campaigns are often based on the idea that by informing people they can make responsible choices. People are presumed to be free agents with self-determination. Yet human behaviour is influenced by so many factors in the social and economic environment and especially by role models among family and friends or in the mass media. The herd instinct is as strong in humans as it is in bees, birds or sheep. Christakis and Fowler (2007) reported evidence that behaviour changes such as quitting smoking or putting on weight are associated with similar changes in networks of friends. Imitation is an important influence in human behaviour and a successful change approach, social cognitive theory, is based on this principle (Bandura, 1995).

The built environment, the sum total of objects placed in the natural world by human beings, is another influence. Included within this are the images and messages from advertisers in mass media, and the digital environment. A 'toxic environment' has been engineered to draw people towards unhealthy products, habits and behaviours (Brownell, 1994). The **obesogenic** environment contains affordable but nasty, fatty, salty and sugary foods that readily cause weight gain and obesity on an industrial scale. Items for sale include foods such as 'hot dogs' containing 'mechanically recovered meat' and 0% real meat, and 'chicken nuggets' with 0% chicken. The proliferation of such low-priced items in supermarkets and 24/7 stores offer low-income consumers an unhealthy selection of options.

Another kind of social 'poisoning' of the environment begins early in life. Garbarino (1997) discussed the 'socially toxic environment', in which 'Children's social world has become poisonous, due to escalating violence, the potentially lethal consequences of sex, diminishing adult supervision, and growing child poverty' (Garbarino, 1997: 12). The potential for toxicity is extended to all of the major determinants of health and well-being.

In this book, arguments are presented on different sides of the 'freedom and choice' debate. It is accepted that our present understanding of health behaviour is far from definitive. However, we also adopt a critical position towards the discipline. Health psychology is still relatively young as a discipline and there are many issues to be addressed. For the most part health psychology has been formulated within an ideology of **individualism** embedded in mass culture. Yet the evidence in this book suggests that change approaches that target internalized processes in the form of hypothetical 'social cognitions' are ineffectual and too small-scale (Marks, 1996, 2002a, 2002b). Mass dissemination of such approaches through the health care system is unavailable and unaffordable. Although an idealized wholistic approach represented by the *biopsychosocial* model of health care is more evident, the medical model still remains the dominant foundation of health care, and is likely to remain so in the future.

Health psychologists can work at different levels of the health care system: carrying out research; systematically reviewing research; designing, implementing and evaluating health interventions; training and teaching; doing consultancy; providing and improving health services; carrying out health promotion; designing policy to improve services; and advocating social justice for people and communities to act on their own terms. In this book, we give examples of all of these activities, and suggest opportunities to make further progress.

A **communitarian** perspective to health work, instead of an individualistic approach, offers the prospect of more effective interventions. In working towards social justice and reducing inequalities, people's rights to health and freedom from illness are, quite literally, *a life and death matter*; it is the responsibility of all planners, policy makers and leaders of people wherever they may be to fight for a fairer, more equitable system of health care (Marks, 2004; Murray, 2014).

Our definition of health psychology is given in Box 1.3. In discussing this definition, we can say that the objective of health psychology is the promotion and maintenance of well-being in individuals, communities and populations.

BOX 1.3
DEFINITION OF HEALTH PSYCHOLOGY

Health psychology is an interdisciplinary field concerned with the application of psychological knowledge and techniques to health, illness and health care.

There has been an unfortunate *medicalization* of everyday experience. Human behaviour, thoughts and feelings are given *medicalized* terminology, e.g. a love of shopping is termed as an 'addiction', a person worrying about their debts is said to suffer from 'chronic anxiety', a person who is profoundly sad after the loss of a loved one is 'clinically depressed' and so on. Over millennia, the health care system has been dominated by medical doctors practising in different specializations. With the exception of nursing, the traditional 'hand-maiden to medicine', other health care professionals (HCPs), including health psychologists, are referred to as 'paramedical'.

Although there are diverse points of view, health psychologists generally hold a holistic perspective on individual well-being, that all aspects of human nature are interconnected. While the primary focus of health psychology is *physical* rather than *mental* health, the latter being the province of clinical psychology, it is acknowledged that mental and physical health are actually 'two sides of one coin'. When a person has a physical illness for a period of time then it is not surprising if they also experience worry (= anxiety) and/or sadness (= depression). If serious enough, 'negative affect' (sadness and/or worry) may become classified as 'mental illness' (severe depression and/or anxiety), and be detrimental to subjective well-being and also to aspects of physical health. Each side of the 'well-being coin' is bound to the other. The distinction between 'health psychology' and 'clinical psychology' is an unfortunate historical accident that is difficult to explain to non-psychologists (or even to psychologists themselves). There is also significant overlap between health and clinical psychology with 'positive psychology' as an integrative new field (Seligman and Csikszentmihalyi, 2000; Seligman et al., 2005) although not without critiques of exaggerated claims (Coyne and Tennen, 2010).

RATIONALE AND ROLE FOR HEALTH PSYCHOLOGY

There is a strong rationale and role for the discipline of **health psychology**. First, the behavioural basis for illness and mortality requires effective methods of behaviour change. Second, a holistic system of health care requires expert knowledge of the psychosocial needs of people.

In relation to point 1, *all* of the leading causes of illness and death are *behavioural*. This means that many deaths are preventable if effective methods of changing behaviour and/or the environment can be found. The mortality rates for different conditions in younger and older people are shown in Table 1.3.

Table 1.3 Leading causes of mortality among adults worldwide, 2002

Rank	Cause	Deaths (000)
Mortality: adults aged 15–59		
1	HIV/AIDS	2,279
2	Ischaemic heart disease	1,332
3	Tuberculosis	1,036
4	Road traffic injuries	814
5	Cerebrovascular disease	783

Rank	Cause	Deaths (000)
6	Self-inflicted injuries	672
7	Violence	473
8	Cirrhosis of the liver	382
9	Lower respiratory infections	352
10	Chronic obstructive pulmonary disease	343
Mortality: adults aged 60 and over		
1	Ischaemic heart disease	5,825
2	Cerebrovascular disease	4,689
3	Chronic obstructive pulmonary disease	2,399
4	Lower respiratory infections	1,396
5	Trachea, bronchus, lung cancers	928
6	Diabetes mellitus	754
7	Hypertensive heart disease	735
8	Stomach cancer	605
9	Tuberculosis	495
10	Colon and rectum cancers	477

Source: www.who.int/whr/2003/en/Facts_and_Figures-en.pdf

BOX 1.4
KEY STUDY: THE GLOBAL BURDEN OF DISEASE STUDY

An important epidemiological perspective comes from measures of '**disability**' or 'disablement'. The Global Burden of Disease (GBD) study projected mortality and disablement over 25 years. The trends from the GBD study suggest that disablement is determined mainly by ageing, the spread of HIV, the increase in tobacco-related mortality and disablement, psychiatric and neurological conditions, and the decline in mortality from communicable, maternal, perinatal and nutritional disorders (Murray and Lopez, 1997).

(Continued)

(Continued)

The GBD study was repeated in 2010 and figures were prepared by age, sex and region for changes that had occurred between 1990 and 2010. Global figures for life expectancy show increases for all age groups (Figure 1.3).

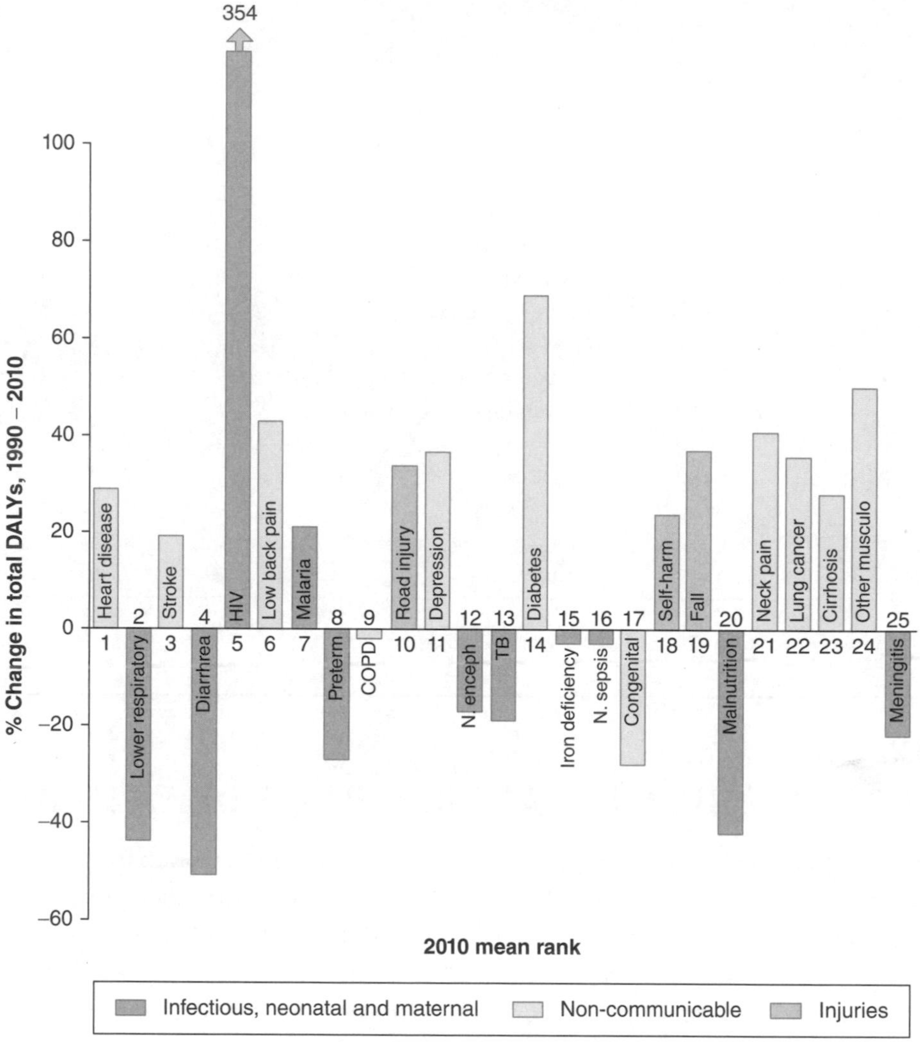

Figure 1.3 Percent change in total DALYs, 1990–2010.

Source: Institute for Health Metrics and Evaluation (2014), www.healthdata.org/infographic/percent-change-total-dalys-1990-2010

The GBD uses the **disability-adjusted life year (DALY)** as a quantitative indicator of burden of disease that reflects the total amount of healthy life lost that is attributed to all causes, whether from premature mortality or from some degree of disablement during a period of time. The DALY is the sum of years of life lost from premature mortality plus years of life with disablement, adjusted for severity of disablement from all causes, both physical and mental (Murray and Lopez, 1997).

Source: Murray and Lopez (1997)

The data in Table 1.4 indicate that nearly 30% of the total global burden of disease is attributable to five risk factors. The largest risk factor (underweight) is associated with poverty (see Chapters 2 and 3). The remaining four risk factors are discussed in Part 2 of this book (see Chapters 6–10).

There were changes in the total DALYs attributable to different causes between 1990 and 2010 as shown in Figure 1.3. Good progress is evident in DALYs for the lower respiratory tract and diarrhoea but a huge increase of 354% occurred in DALYs for HIV patients. Moderate but significant increases in DALYs occurred for heart disease, stroke, low back pain, depression and diabetes.

The statistics on death and disablement indicate the significant involvement of behaviour and therefore provide a strong rationale for the discipline of health psychology in all three of its key elements: theory, research and practice. If the major risk factors are to be addressed, there is a pressing need for effective programmes of environmental and behaviour change. This requires a sea change in policy. The dominant ideology that makes individuals responsible for their own health may not be the most helpful approach. The environment is a hugely important factor. In our opinion, a psychological approach in the absence of environmental change is like whistling in the wind.

Table 1.4 The five leading risk factors for global disease burden computed in DALYs

Risk factor	Number of DALYs (millions)	Percentage of DALYs
Childhood and maternal underweight	138	9.5
Unprotected sex	92	6.3
High blood pressure	64	4.4
Tobacco	59	4.1
Alcohol	58	4.0
Totals	411	28.3

Source: Ezzati et al. (2002)

Health psychologists are at the 'sharp end' of the quest to produce health behaviour change on an industrial scale. The fact that people are highly constrained by their environment and socio-economic circumstances militate against such change. In a sense, without adaptations of the environment, this effort is disabled. There are strong constraints on the ability of health care systems to influence health outcomes at a population level because of the significant social and economic determinants that structure the health of individuals and communities. The environment must change, and by that route, there can be behaviour change on a societal scale. Attempting to change behaviour without first attending to the environment is akin to 'the tail wagging the dog'.

A second rationale for health psychology is growing recognition that a purely medical approach to health care is failing to meet the psychosocial needs of many patients. This has led to a search for an alternative perspective which values holistic care of patients and attempts to improve services through higher quality psychosocial care. In spite of their very high costs, health care systems are often perceived to be inefficient, ineffective and unfit for purpose. This is especially the case in the USA where the largest per capita expenditure is producing some unimpressive outcomes.

The dominance of the **medical model** has been criticized since the 1970s (Illich, 1976). While medical experts want to give modern medicine the credit for the decline of disease in the twentieth century, critics have suggested that health improvements are due mainly to better hygiene, education and reduced poverty (McKeown, 1979).

High costs and increasing levels of dissatisfaction, together with a growing awareness of psychosocial influences, led to concepts such as the **biopsychosocial model** (Engel, 1977), which we discuss in Chapter 3. Since that suggestion, health psychology has developed distinctive approaches. Before discussing these, we need to take a quick look at measurement.

MEASUREMENT

In the natural sciences, attributes of the physical world such as space, time, temperature, velocity and acceleration are all measured quantitatively. Psychologists, concerned with behaviour and experience, are unable to measure many of the most interesting psychological attributes in the same objective manner and have struggled to justify the discipline as a science.

Psychology's early years as an infant science were spent developing psychophysics and ability testing. In spite of some apparent successes in these two areas, the measurement problem in psychology had not been satisfactorily resolved. In the 1950s the influential *Handbook of Experimental Psychology* was published by a professor at Harvard, S.S. Stevens (1951). Stevens proposed a solution, or so he hoped, to the measurement problem by invoking the principle of **operationism**. Since that time, psychologists have assumed that measurement is simply what Stevens said it was: the assignment of numbers to attributes according to rules. Unfortunately, Stevens' solution is illusory.

It is apparent that numbers can be readily allocated to attributes using a non-random rule (the operational definition of measurement) that would generate 'measurements' that are not quantitatively meaningful. For example, numerals can be allocated to colours: red = 1, blue = 2, green = 3, etc. The rule used to allocate the numbers is clearly not random, and the allocation therefore counts as measurement, according to Stevens. However, it would be patent nonsense to assert that 'green is 3 × red' or that 'blue is 2 × red', or that 'green minus blue equals red'. Intervals and ratios cannot be inferred from a simple ordering of scores along a scale. Yet this is how psychological measurement is usually carried out.

In spite of its obvious flaws, Stevens' approach circumvented the requirement for quantitative measurement that only quantitative attributes can be measured (Michell, 1999). This is because psychological constructs such as the quality of a person's life are nothing at all like physical variables that are quantitative in nature. However, psychometricians treated psychological constructs *as if they are quantitative in nature and as amenable to measurement as physical characteristics.* For more than 60 years psychology has been living in a make-believe world where making rules for applying numbers to attributes has been treated as if it were proper measurement. This fundamental issue cuts off at its very roots the claim that psychology is a quantitative science on a par with the natural sciences.

However, this would be a very short textbook, if we were to give up at this point! We must soldier on as if we have solid ground to walk upon rather than boggy sand …

Measurement can be defined as the estimation of the magnitude of a quantitative attribute relative to a unit (Michell, 2003). Before quantification can happen, it is first necessary to obtain evidence that the relevant attribute is quantitative in structure. This has rarely, if ever, been carried out in psychology. Unfortunately, it is arguably the case that the definition of measurement within psychology since Stevens' (1951) operationism is incorrect and psychologists' claims about being able to measure psychological attributes can be questioned (Michell, 1999, 2002). Contrary to common beliefs within the discipline, psychological attributes may not actually be quantitative at all, and hence not amenable to coherent numerical measurement and statistical analyses that make unwarranted assumptions about the numbers collected as data.

The situation is akin to the 'Emperor has no clothes' story. Psychometricians are forced to make the inference that the ordering of scores is a reflection of an underlying quantity and therefore that psychological attributes are measurable on interval scales. Otherwise there would be no basis for quantitative measurement in psychology. Michell (2012) argued that: 'the most plausible hypothesis is that the kinds of attributes psychometricians aspire to measure are merely ordinal attributes with impure differences of degree, a feature logically incompatible with quantitative structure. If so, psychometrics is built upon a myth' (p. 255). This view is supported by Sijtsma (2012) who argued that the real measurement problem in psychology is the absence of well-developed theories about psychological attributes and a lack of any evidence to support the assumption that psychological attributes are continuous and quantitative in nature. This fundamental measurement problem exists within health psychology as it does within psychology as a whole.

BOX 1.5
MEASURING A PSYCHOLOGICAL ATTRIBUTE – WHAT THE MAJORITY OF TEXTBOOKS DON'T TELL YOU AND ABOUT WHICH YOU ARE NOT SUPPOSED TO ASK

A typical study requires participants to complete a set of ratings on questionnaire scales that are designed to measure a psychological attribute. The essential issue is whether the total score obtained from the numbers (ratings) provided by an individual are in any way measures of an attribute along a quantitative scale like the readings from a tape measure, which reflect the quantity of distance. Distance has an absolute zero and different objects can be placed at equal distances from each other or in fixed ratios. Now let's consider the example of Dr Ed Diener's *Satisfaction With Life Scale* (SWLS) (Table 1.2). The total scores on the SWLS are obtained by summing the seven-point ratings of each of five items. Thus a maximum score is 35 and the minimum score is 5. The scoring scheme is given here:

31–35	Extremely satisfied
26–30	Satisfied
21–25	Slightly satisfied
20	Neutral
15–19	Slightly dissatisfied
10–14	Dissatisfied
5–9	Extremely dissatisfied

Is there any basis for assuming the total scores on the SWLS are measures of a quantitative attribute 'Life Satisfaction' such that there is an absolute zero (as there would be in any ratio scale) and a person with a score of 20 has exactly double the life satisfaction of a person who has a score of 10 and/or that two people with scores of 30 and 25 have a life satisfaction that is the same 'distance' apart (5 points) as in the case of two people with scores of 20 and 15? If the 5-point differences were shown to be the same then the SWLS would be an interval scale. However, *neither of the hypotheses is plausible*. We can only infer a person's life satisfaction from their answers to items on the SWLS. *This is because we have no independent definition of life satisfaction, and no evidence that life satisfaction is a quantitative attribute, apart from the SWLS scores themselves*. This measurement problem cuts through the entire discipline of psychology. We infer or, in truth, are forced to act on the unproven assumption that a person's score on the SWLS is a measure of her/his life satisfaction on a continuously quantitative interval scale.

The total scores on the SWLS really only allow respondents to be placed along an ordinal scale, yet it is common practice to treat the scores as if they are interval scale data that can be added together, subtracted, averaged and compared between groups using standard deviations and variance scores in statistical analyses.

[Nobody promised you a rose garden! . . . We said at the outset, we would adopt a critical stance and the measurement problem we have described here, which, for obvious reasons, is not normally talked about, is a good start. The situation is not completely hopeless, however, so please do read on ...]

Fortunately, for an intrinsically practical domain like health psychology, it is possible to 'get by' without having a solution to the measurement problem discussed above. This is because one of the main goals of health psychologists is to design interventions that are effective solutions to problems that require behaviour change. Normally we can find ways to objectively compare different interventions to see what works and what doesn't work. The associations between interventions and outcomes can be observed and measured in quantitative terms. Additionally, a patient seeking treatment for an unpleasant condition can express their thoughts, feelings and motives using plain words by answering questions or items on a questionnaire. In the vast majority of cases, psychological measures are either assumed, for the sake of convenience, to lie along an interval scale or the data are purely categorical.

Health psychologists are concerned with patient–practitioner interactions, public health promotion, or working in communities where actions are carried out, all with observable inputs and outputs. Outcomes in these various scenarios are all objectively observable and measurable, even if the measurements themselves are not shown to have an underlying quantitative attribute. In addition, it is the experiences of the actors that are important, and these are amenable to qualitative methods where the presumption of quantitative attributes and the associated measurement problem do not apply.

A CULTURAL PERSPECTIVE

There are wide variations in health beliefs between cultures and significant individual and group differences within each culture. Folk beliefs, knowledge and practices among individuals from different communities and social groups rub shoulders with each other and with those of health care professionals in a Tower of Babel. These diverse beliefs meld with practices and lifestyles in accord with people's worldviews and values.

Theories in health psychology provide accounts of how psychosocial processes affect individual health experience. In reviewing such theories (e.g. see Chapter 6) it must be acknowledged that they are principally products of the USA and British Commonwealth, together with inputs from Continental Europe and Scandinavia. Many of health psychology's theories are adaptations of US/European cognitive and social psychology from the last 50 years. The resurgence of research in laboratory environments used structured psychometric instruments, questionnaires and performance tests designed to reveal the mechanisms underlying human behaviour. These methods lacked **ecological validity**, or, in other words, the findings could not be generalized to the world outside of the laboratory. Critics have suggested that the laboratory experiment and the questionnaire are both subject to significant biases.

Cross-cultural psychology emphasizes cultural diversity and casts a skeptical eye over the **ethnocentrism** of contemporary psychology. It considers national or large group samples as the unit of analysis rather than individuals. Research has focused primarily on mental health (e.g. Dasen et al., 1988) and relatively little attention has been paid to physical health. A truly cultural approach to health psychology is at an early stage of development. We discuss the role of culture in health in more depth in Chapter 4.

BOX 1.6
INTERNATIONAL EXAMPLE: HEALTH PSYCHOLOGY IN AFRICAN SETTINGS – A CULTURAL-PSYCHOLOGICAL ANALYSIS

This study reveals how the individualistic nature of mainstream health psychology is not applicable to settings in Africa. The mainstream Western approach assumes a worldview in which the causes of illness are attributed to atomistic, physiological processes within the individual. This construction of reality is associated with a view of a person as an individual with his/her own internalized assumptions that he/she is a separate individual. In African cultures, however, each person is seen as interconnected to other people, including living relatives and dead ancestors, and also to places and spiritual forces. Markus et al. (1997) refer to cultural assumptions about self-hood as '**selfways**'. Selfways include what it means to be a good or bad person, and what causes us to become healthy or ill.

Adams and Salter give as an example of African selfways the idea of 'enemyship' – the belief that hatred of another can lead to bad things happening to oneself. The belief in the power of malevolent others is manifest through such practices as divination, infant seclusion, sorcery and witchcraft. They quote the following example: 'I don't know my enemies, but I know that I have them. One day something will happen to me, and then I will know that this person has been after me all along' (Adams and Salter, 2007: 541).

There are implications of selfways for health care provision. In the West we assume that social support and caregiving are generally a source of comfort and coping. Indeed, social support is a major focus for health psychology research and services. We need to consider how intimate family members could also be viewed as *a source of danger, stress, worry and sadness*. In highlighting 'enemyship', the selfways of African cultures shows social embeddedness as an 'inevitable fact of social existence' (Adams and Salter, 2007: 542).

Source: Adams and Salter (2007)

A FRAMEWORK FOR HEALTH PSYCHOLOGY

Theoretical thinking in health psychology consists of three broad types that vary according to their level of generality: **frameworks**, **theories** and **models**. Frameworks have some of the characteristics of paradigms (Kuhn, 1970) as they refer to a complete system of thinking about a field of inquiry. Paradigms explicitly state assumptions, laws and methods. Frameworks are much looser than paradigms but they are a way of organizing information about a field. Figure 1.4 shows a framework about the main influences on the health of individual human beings. It has been adapted from the work of Dahlgren and Whitehead (1991) and we call this the 'Health Onion'.

The 'Health Onion' has a multi-layered structure with the individual at its core, surrounded by four layers of influence:

Core: age, sex and hereditary factors (covered throughout this book).

Level 1: individual lifestyle (Part 2 of this book).

Level 2: social and community influences (Part 1 of this book).

Level 3: living and working conditions and health care services (covered by Parts 3 and 4 of this book).

Level 4: general socio-economic, cultural and environmental conditions (Part 1 of this book).

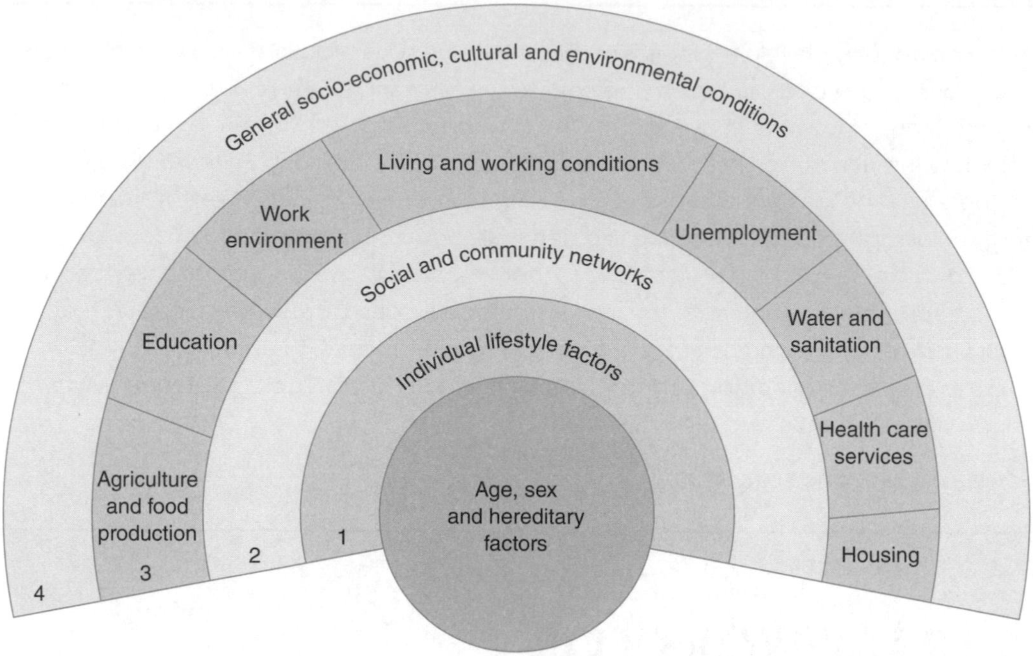

Figure 1.4 The 'Health Onion': a framework for health psychology

Source: Dahlgren and Whitehead (1991). Reproduced by permission

The Health Onion has seven characteristics:

It is holistic – all aspects of human nature are interconnected.

It is concerned with all health determinants, not simply with events during the treatment of illness.

The individual is at the core with health determinants acting through the community, living and working conditions, and the socio-economic, cultural and physical environment.

It places each layer in the context of its neighbours, including possible structural constraints upon change.

It has an interdisciplinary flavour that goes beyond a medical or quasi-medical approach.

It makes no claim for any one level being more important than others.

It acknowledges the complex nature of health determinants.

Different theories and models are needed for each setting and context. However, there is also a need for a general paradigm for individual health within which specific theories and models can be nested. Such a paradigm should attempt to represent in an explicit, detailed and meaningful way the constraints upon and links between individual well-being, the surrounding community and the health care system (Marks, 1996). No such general paradigm exists. We are waiting for a Hippocrates, Darwin or Einstein. Or perhaps the sheer diversity of issues and perspectives makes the field non-amenable to a single paradigm?

BOX 1.7
FILTERING OF EVIDENCE IN EVIDENCE-BASED PRACTICE

Some believe we have a paradigm for all of health care in the form of evidence-based medicine or **evidence-based practice (EBP)**. In EBP, randomized controlled trials are used to produce conclusions about the effectiveness of different methods and treatments. In theory the approach sounds wonderful. In practice it is far from perfect. Evidence on effectiveness in EBP is assumed to have an objective, inviolable status that reflects 'reality'. It is given an iconic status. In some undefined ways this evidence about 'reality' not only aids decision-making, but also determines it. In truth, evidence is never absolutely certain. It consists of negotiable, value-laden and contextually dependent items of information. Evidence (= knowledge) for a technique or treatment in health care is not an accident, but the outcome of a series of 'gates' or 'filters' that must be passed before the technique is deemed to be useful (Marks, 2005).

Consider the sequence of processes from conception to application through which evidence must pass if it is to be considered admissible in EBP. The filtering is so selective that, typically, systematic reviewers will be able to find only a dozen or fewer primary studies that fulfil the inclusion criteria from a field of several thousand. Oakley (2001) described a systematic review of peer health promotion for young people that found 5,124 citations of which exactly 12 (0.234%) were judged to have carried out 'sound' outcome evaluations. She compared this search process to 'finding needles in haystacks' (Oakley, 2001: 22–4). Another analogy is making a pot of filter coffee – the stronger the filtering, the less fresh and flavourful the coffee. EBP is somewhat similar: there are no guarantees the end-product will be fit for purpose. The filtering process involved in EBP consists of seven levels listed below:

(Continued)

(Continued)

1 current knowledge, theory and paradigms taught in universities and schools;
2 funding priorities of government, industry and charities;
3 hypotheses considered important by the funders;
4 methodology approved by funders;
5 journal publication;
6 systematic reviews;
7 translated into EBP.

To be judged 'sound', evidence must pass through all seven of the filters that are disposed towards the preservation of existing practices, knowledge and myths. In confirming the 'sound' status of the chosen techniques that have passed through the filters, the 'unsoundness' of the unfiltered techniques is established by default. Undeniably, this filtering of evidence is systematic and evidence will be considered 'sound' or 'unsound' according to established criteria.

However, EBP is contentious on a number of grounds. First, it is wasteful that so much evidence is 'thrown away'. Many unfiltered techniques are quite possibly as effective as techniques that have been filtered. Second, the filtering process gives a high weighting to techniques that conform to beliefs and values of the knowledge establishment. For example, pharmacotherapy will be established ahead of psychological therapies (pharmaceutical industry sponsorship at filters 1–4), quantitative techniques will be preferred to qualitative techniques (filters 5–6), and patient treatment care will be about outputs and outcomes, rather than feeling they have been cared for as human beings (filters 7). Third, innovation may have difficulty breaking through.

In this book we review the results of many studies using the approach of EBP. Studies that have *not* been based on EBP are also reviewed. Many such studies have been situated in settings where EBP would be unethical, impractical or impossible. We also include qualitative studies because the information yielded illuminates the psychosocial experience of health and illness.

Source: Marks (2005, 2009)

FUTURE RESEARCH

1. Progress in health psychology requires a solution to the measurement problem: there is no evidence that psychological attributes are continuous quantitative variables, as assumed in the majority of health psychology research.

2. Trans-cultural studies of health, illness and health care are needed to facilitate communication and understanding of systems of healing among different cultural, ethnic and religious groups.
3. Apart from smoking cessation, evidence needs to be gathered to confirm the assumption that lifestyle changes cause positive changes to life expectancy and quality of life.
4. The limits of evidence-based practice require innovative evaluation methods of interventions.

SUMMARY

1 Health is a state of well-being with physical, cultural, psychosocial, economic and spiritual attributes, not simply the absence of illness.

2 The fundamental *sociality* of individual behaviour demands a social orientation to health psychology, which must be studied in the context of society and culture.

3 To be healthy in body and mind a person's needs to interconnect and to act autonomously as an agent must be satisfied and as well as their biological needs.

4 Alternative approaches to change are required that go beyond the edicts of individualism.

5 Behaviour is not the only necessary target for change; the toxic environment needs to be given equal priority in interventions.

6 Health psychology has grown rapidly with the increasing: (a) evidence that much illness and mortality are caused by behaviour; (b) awareness of the psychosocial aspects of health and illness.

7 The 'Health Onion' is a useful framework for the investigation of health and illness. The core of the onion is an individual's current health status with particular age, sex and hereditary factors.

8 Within the Health Onion, four layers of analysis that immediately surround the core are individual lifestyle (level 1), social and community influences (level 2), living and working conditions (level 3), and general socio-economic, cultural and environmental conditions (level 4).

9 Concepts about health and disease are embedded in culturally diverse ways, which show significant differences in health experience and behaviour between cultures and places.

10 Organization of knowledge in health psychology occurs at three levels: (a) frameworks; (b) theories; (c) models. It is helpful to notice the difference between these three constructs and to treat them differently.

2 MACRO-SOCIAL INFLUENCES

As in earlier times, advances in the 21st century will be won by human struggle against divisive values – and against the opposition of entrenched economic and political interests.

(Human Development Report, 2000: 6)

OUTLINE

We employ a wide-angle lens to explore the macro-social context for human health. We discuss the fact that what individuals can do to change their lives is not simply a matter of personal choice – choices are constrained culturally, economically and educationally. In spite of medical and technological advances, population growth, globalized promotion of unhealthy commodities, increasing poverty, and shrinking availability of natural resources, especially safe drinking water, are bringing a worsening of health globally. Universal gradients both within and between nations are persistent over time and space. The 'doom and gloom' described in this chapter is not an inevitability, however. The prospects could be improved if elected governments took appropriate action to intervene independently from corporate interests.

FACTS OF LIFE AND DEATH

Where a baby is born and the mother's access to water, food and education determine whether the baby lives or dies. A baby in Sierra Leone has a 72% chance of making it to age 5. A Japanese baby has a 96% chance of reaching 5. Robust health inequalities have always existed both within and between societies; in this chapter, we examine why.

Each individual human is a creation of genetics and environmental experience. The environment can be broken down into macro and micro levels. The macro-social environment affects health and well-being in a huge variety of ways. The term **macro-social** refers to large-scale social, economic, political and cultural forces that influence the life course of masses of people simultaneously. Macro-social influences include actions and policies of governmental organizations, non-governmental organizations (NGOs), cultures, historical legacies, organized religions, multinational corporations and banks, and unpredictable, large-scale environmental events, all of which have the potential to influence huge sectors of the entire human race.

First, devastating 'acts of God' can have severe consequences for individuals and communities. The short- and long-term health impacts of these events are moderated by international readiness to respond. Health psychologists have a role within interdisciplinary teams to ameliorate the impact of natural disaster and extreme weather events, including earthquakes (Ding and Xia, 2013; Gan et al., 2013); tsunamis (Cassim et al., 2014), volcanic activity (Lowe and de Lange, 2000), droughts and famines (Wisner, 2004), floods (Alderman et al., 2012), hurricanes (Brodie et al., 2006; Scheib and Lykes, 2013) and typhoons (Cranmer and Biddinger, 2014). Extreme weather events are becoming more common as a consequence of global warming.

Second, a variety of pandemics that spread across continents include typhoid, cholera, avian flu (Shinya et al., 2006), influenza (Karademas et al., 2013; Mo and Lau, 2014) and HIV (Pellowski et al., 2013). How societies respond is crucial to the impact of such pandemics.

Third, the scourges of war, genocide, sectarian violence and terrorism take a significant toll with multiple deaths, injuries and trauma (De Jong and Kleber, 2007; Medeiros, 2007; Ciccone et al., 2008; Maguen et al., 2010; Zerach et al., 2013).

Fourth, the legacies of colonial genocide take centuries to heal. Indigenous 'First Nations' communities have consistently disproportionate rates of psychiatric distress that are associated with historical experiences of European colonization (Gone, 2013). Aboriginal children experience a greater burden of ill health compared with other children, and these health inequities have persisted for hundreds of years (Greenwood and de Leeuw, 2012). Effective partnerships between Aboriginal and 'mainstream' health services can be 'tenuous and unproductive' owing to tensions from historical race relations (Taylor and Thompson, 2011) (see Figure 2.1).

Fifth, human recklessness with fossil fuels is causing global warming, climate change, rising sea temperatures, acid rain, coral bleaching, global dimming, ozone depletion, biodiversity loss and rising water levels, all transforming life on this planet as we know it (Pearce, 2009).

Sixth, use of fossil fuels is peaking and, as oil and gas reserves run out, and become more costly, the world economy could go into decline with significantly decreased agriculture and food production (Murphy and Hall, 2011; Pfeiffer, 2013).

Seventh, increasing poverty makes life a struggle for survival for a billion people. In spite of progress, almost 870 million people were chronically undernourished in 2010–2012, the majority living in developing countries, where 850 million people, or 15% of the population, were estimated to be undernourished (Food and Agriculture Organization, 2012).

Eighth, clean drinking water is a major cause of suffering, disease and early deaths: 3.4 million people die each year from a water-related disease with 780 million people lacking access to clean drinking water; 2.5 billion people have no access to a toilet (water.org, 2014; http://bit.ly/1aa4eri).

The message of this chapter is summarized thus: what individuals can do to change their lives is not simply a matter of personal choice – such changes are constrained politically, economically and culturally. In the globalized economy, everything is inter-connected. Macro-social economic, political and cultural factors create the context for everything else, including health, illness and health care.

Figure 2.1 The legacy of genocide takes centuries to heal. Trucanini, the last survivor of British genocide of Tasmanian Aboriginal People, died on 8 May 1876. Trucanini's body was exhumed in 1878, exhibited by the Royal Society of Surgeons of England until 1976, then cremated; finally, samples of her hair and skin were laid to rest in her homeland in 2002

Source: 'God Save Our Queen', © David F Marks, 2006

POLICY, IDEOLOGY AND DISCOURSE

The dominant discourse within neo-liberal health policy has been that of the autonomous individual in which each individual is an agent, responsible for his/her own health. The ideology of *individualism* dictates that each person is motivated by self-interest to elevate his/her well-being with the least effort and resources possible. Deep within the ideological substratum of modern culture lurks the credo of individualism – 'each man for himself' – making his/her choices, taking the consequences, as in: 'You made your bed, now lie in it.' Theories in health psychology are imbued with this cultural presumption. The existential truth of 'do or die' is embellished in polite language as 'making informed choices'.

The cult of the individual has spawned the notion of the **responsible consumer** (RC). The RC is an active processor of information and knowledge concerning health and illness. He/she makes rational decisions and responsible choices to optimize well-being. The epitome of the RC is the hypothecated 'anything in moderation' person who eats five-a-day, never smokes, drinks alcohol in moderation, exercises vigorously for at least 30 minutes three times a week, always uses a condom when having sex, and sleeps 8 hours a day. The stereotype of the more common 'irresponsible consumer' (IC) is the so-called 'couch potato' who enjoys beer and cola, smokes, eats junk food, watching TV for many hours each day, and rarely takes exercise. Accordingly, responsibility for illness relating to personal lifestyle is seen as the fault of the individual, not an inevitable facet of a social, corporate, economic environment designed to maximize shareholder profits.

Using a mixture of well-intentioned pleading, information and advice, the traditional approach to health education aimed to persuade people to change their habits and lifestyles. Information campaigns designed to sway consumers into healthier living were the order of the day. Health education has been defined as: 'any combination of planned learning experiences based on sound theories that provide individuals, groups, and communities the opportunity to acquire information and the skills needed to make quality health decisions' (Joint Committee on Terminology, 2001). Combining with policy and taxation, by fighting against a tide of commercial interests, health education justifiably could claim some limited success over the last 50 years, e.g. the fall in lung cancer rates. Tobacco control has become a low, but noteworthy, benchmark for what may be achieved through consistent public policy, educational campaigns and behaviour change. However, the health gains made by this route were extremely hard won. A major public health call today is for a vigorous campaign to halt the obesity epidemic. If similar methods are deployed to those used for tobacco (i.e. voluntary controls, advertising restrictions, product labelling, health education), then the evidence suggests that it could take at least 50–70 years before obesity rates can be expected to go into any noticeable decline.

In recent decades, appealing to the right-minded 'anything in moderation' consumer has been prevalent throughout health care. The prescription to live well has always had a distinctively moral tone. Health promotion policy has been portrayed as a quasi-religious quest, a war against the deadly old sins of gluttony, laziness and lust. Discourse analysis of public health policy statements makes this fact all too clear (Sykes et al., 2004).

The demise of the construct of the RC may be imminent within health policy. Common observation and decades of research show that people are really pushed and pulled in different directions while exercising their 'freedom of choice'. Emotions and feelings are as important in making choices as cognition. The beneficial satisfaction of needs and wants must be balanced against perceived risks and costs. Health policy is beginning to acknowledge both the complexity of health and the power of the market. Witness the huge scale of the advertising industry: $279.6 billion or 2.0% of GDP in the USA alone (Coen Structured Advertising Expenditure Dataset, 2011). An inevitable compromise exists between what any individual wants and needs and the available means to satisfy those wants and needs ('satisficers'; Simon, 1956). The conditions for need satisfaction are seldom optimum and, for many, they are chronically sub-optimum.

Human activity is a reflection of the physical, psychosocial and economic environment. The built environment, the sum total of objects placed in the natural world, dramatically influences health. The 'toxic environment' propels people towards unhealthy behaviours, directly causing mortality and illness (Brownell and Fairburn, 1995).

Recent government policy documents in the UK indicate that the previously strong reliance on consumers as responsible decision makers has been waning but remains a primary strategy. The environment and corporations are being given a larger role. In *Healthy Lives, Healthy People: Our Strategy for Public Health in England* (2010: 29), the Government stated:

> 2.29 Few of us consciously choose 'good' or 'bad' health. We all make personal choices about how we live and behave: what to eat, what to drink and how active to be. We all make trade-offs between feeling good now and the potential impact of this on our longer-term health. In many cases, moderation is often the key.
>
> 2.30 All capable adults are responsible for these very personal choices. At the same time, we do not have total control over our lives or the circumstances in which we live. A wide range of factors constrain and influence what we do, both positively and negatively.
>
> 2.31 The Government's approach to improving health and wellbeing – relevant to both national and potential local actions – is therefore based on the following actions, which reflect the Coalition's core values of freedom, fairness and responsibility. These are:

- strengthening self-esteem, confidence and personal responsibility;
- positively promoting 'healthier' behaviours and lifestyles; and
- adapting the environment to make healthy choices easier.

In the above policy document, *personal responsibility* remains at the top of the agenda. The statement that 'we do not have total control over our lives or the circumstances in which we live' is a small step forward but, unfortunately, taking two steps back negates this. Only holistic public policies can lower the toxicity of the environment and to declare otherwise is a cop-out. Yet large corporations are engaged as the new allies of health promotion in the twenty-first century. The UK government enlisted the food industry, including McDonald's and Kentucky Fried Chicken, among other corporations, to help to write policy on obesity, alcohol and diet-related disease (*Mail Online*, 2011). Processed food and drinks manufacturers including PepsiCo, Kellogg's, Unilever, Mars and Diageo were contributors to five 'responsibility deal' networks set up by Health Secretary Andrew Lansley. In a similar sponsorship arrangement to previous Olympic Games, McDonald's and Coca Cola sponsored the 2012 London Olympics. This is putting foxes in charge of the hen house!

In the USA there has been a similar shift in thinking: the 'anything in moderation' philosophy of responsible consumption is no longer the principal foundation for public health interventions. *The Surgeon General's Vision for a Healthy and Fit Nation* states:

> Interventions to prevent obesity should focus not only on personal behaviors and biological traits, but also on characteristics of the social and physical environments that offer or limit

opportunities for positive health outcomes. Critical opportunities for interventions can occur in multiple settings: home, child care, school, work place, health care, and community.

(US Surgeon General, 2010: 5)

In twenty-first-century health care, the opportunities for health psychological interventions to assist within the major settings has never been greater. But one must ask whether the discipline is fit to meet these challenges. Alternative methods must be tried and tested if we are to make in-roads into the massive scale of issues on the public health agenda.

Economic analyses use gross domestic product (GDP) as a measure of *output* and, to a degree, an indicator of welfare also (Oulton, 2012). GDP measures the value of goods and services produced for final consumption, private and public, present and future. Across countries, GDP per capita is highly correlated with important social indicators. GDP is positively correlated with life expectancy and negatively correlated with infant mortality and inequality. One of the most traumatic events in anybody's life is the loss of a child, and infant mortality rates might be thought of as a proxy indicator of happiness. Figure 2.2 plots infant mortality against per capita GDP for a large sample of countries. The graph shows that richer countries tend to have greater life expectancy, lower infant mortality and lower inequality. As always, it is important to state that correlation is not necessarily causation, although there is strong evidence that higher GDP per capita leads to improved health (Fogel, 2004).

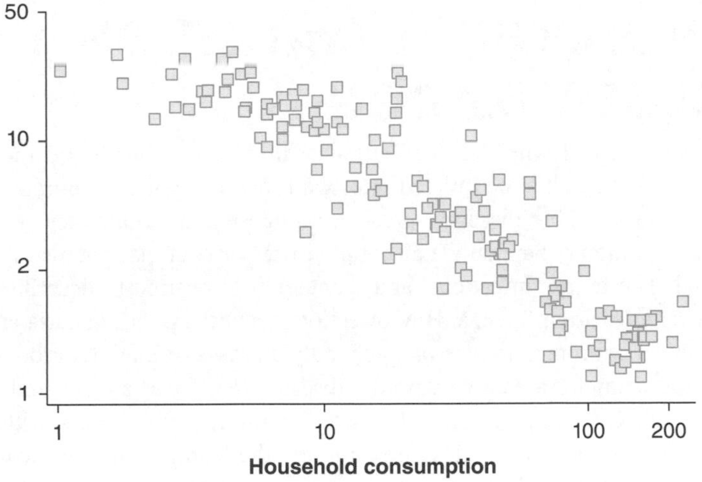

Figure 2.2 Infant mortality versus household consumption per head across 146 countries

Source: Oulton (2012)

Economic downturns trigger social ills that spread globally. Witness the impact of the 2008 'Credit Crunch' in the USA, which triggered a global financial crisis with banks all over the world going into meltdown, leading to many job losses and low interest rates everywhere from the USA to China. The US, UK and other European governments injected trillions into financial institutions and increased their regulation of the financial markets to prevent short selling by banks and hedge fund managers. When the Icelandic banking system collapsed in 2008, managers of a Wessex children's hospice in England worried about the future of the hospice, a specialist cancer hospital in Manchester redesigned its research programme, and millions worried about their pensions.

A key component of subjective well-being and quality of life is employment. A strong relationship exists between these factors. Unemployment brings stigma, lowered self-esteem and mental health problems, especially depression and feeling of low self-worth (Warr et al., 1988). In some cultures, for example, in Japan, a particularly strong correlation exists between the suicide rate and unemployment rate among men (Chen et al., 2012). Under a blanket of statistics lies a multitude of individual calamities.

Demographic changes, population growth and the scourges of increased access to unhealthy commodities, combined with unemployment, poverty and inequality, place their fingerprints all over human existence. In charting the macro-social environment for health we consider the transitions that have accompanied globalization of unhealthy commodities, population growth and widespread poverty; we briefly discuss inequalities both within and between societies, and the inequities that exist between genders and ethnic groups. In the following chapters, we take up social justice issues in more detail (Chapter 3) and explore the significance of culture (Chapter 4).

EPIDEMIOLOGICAL TRANSITION AND GLOBALIZATION

Epidemiology is concerned with the distribution of disease and death and their determinants and consequences. Diseases can be divided into two broad categories: communicable and non-communicable. Communicable diseases spread from one person to another or from an animal to a person. This spread may happen via airborne viruses or bacteria, but also through blood or other bodily fluid. The terms 'infectious' and 'contagious' are used to describe communicable disease. Major examples are influenza, HIV infection, hepatitis, polio, malaria and tuberculosis. Non-communicable, or chronic, diseases are generally diseases of long duration and have a slow progression. Major examples are cardiovascular diseases (e.g. heart attacks and stroke), cancer, chronic respiratory diseases (e.g. chronic obstructed pulmonary disease and asthma) and diabetes. Non-communicable diseases (NCDs) are currently the leading cause of death in the world, representing 63% of all annual deaths (World Health Organization, 2014). NCDs kill at least 36 million people each year, some 80% of which occur in low- and middle-income countries.

Omran (1971) described what he termed the '**epidemiological transition**'. This refers to a reduction in prevalence of communicable diseases and an increase in the prevalence of NCDs that occurs as a country becomes economically stronger. NCDs are lifestyle-related chronic diseases that accompany increased usage of unhealthy commodities such as alcohol, tobacco and processed foods. During this transition, countries that have low or middle incomes face a heavy burden from both communicable and non-communicable diseases. In industrial countries such as the USA, Germany, the UK and Japan, the prevalence of communicable diseases is much lower compared to chronic NCDs. In India, and other low- and middle-income countries, while communicable diseases are still present, the rise of NCDs has been rapid (Anjana et al., 2011). Low- and middle-income countries like India, therefore, are currently facing an epidemiological transition with a 'double burden' of disease.

The major driver of the transition towards widespread prevalence of NCDs is corporate globalization. From the point of view of human health, **globalization** flies a banner of progress and freedom yet brings illness and an early death to millions of people. Transnational corporations are indeed the major drivers of NCD 'pandemics' as they scale up their promotion of, and huge profits from, tobacco, alcoholic and other beverages, ultra-processed food and other unhealthy commodities throughout low- and middle-income countries.

Stuckler et al. (2012) observed that the sales of unhealthy commodities across 80 low- and middle-income countries are strongly interrelated. They argue (see Figure 2.3) that:

> in countries where there are high rates of tobacco and alcohol consumption, there is also a high intake of snacks, soft drinks, processed foods, and other unhealthy food commodities. The correlations of these products with unhealthy foods suggest they share underlying risks associated with the market and regulatory environment.

Referring to these data, Moodie et al. (2013) argued in *The Lancet* that:

> Alcohol and ultra-processed food and drink industries are using similar strategies to the tobacco industry to undermine effective public health policies and programmes.
>
> Unhealthy commodity industries should have no role in the formation of national or international policy for non-communicable disease policy.
>
> Despite the common reliance on industry self-regulation and public–private partnerships to improve public health, there is no evidence to support their effectiveness or safety.
>
> In view of the present and predicted scale of NCD epidemics, *the only evidence-based mechanisms that can prevent harm caused by unhealthy commodity industries are public regulation and market intervention.*

POPULATION GROWTH

The US Census Bureau (2014) publishes a daily best estimate of the world's population on its website (www.census.gov/cgi-bin/ipc/popclockw). According to the Bureau, the total world population, projected to 3 December 2014 at 08:00 GMT (EST+5), was 7,208,893,140. That

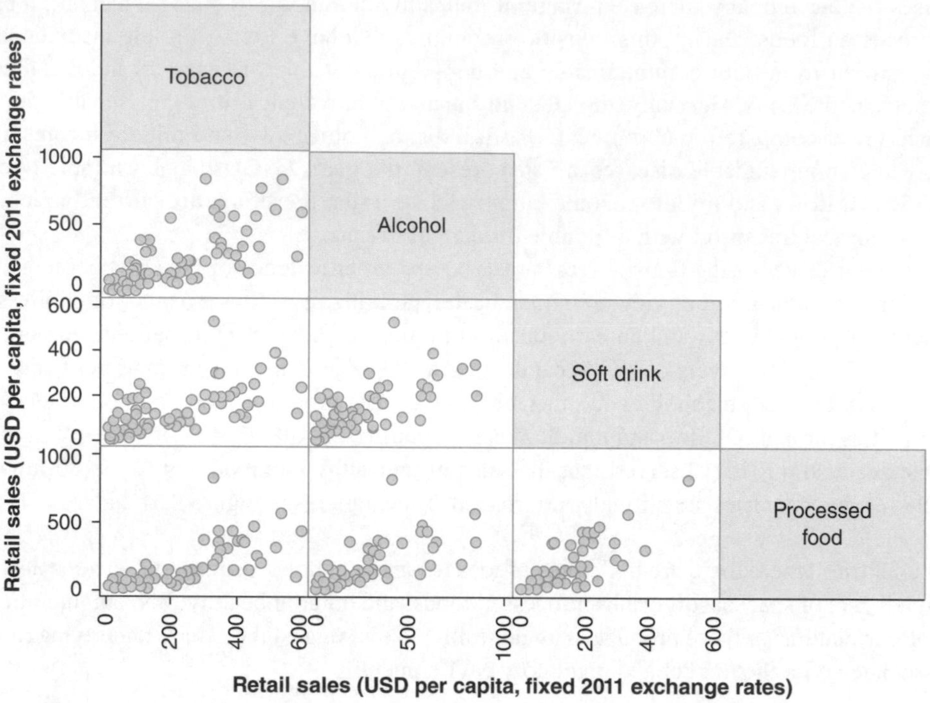

Figure 2.3 Associations of sales of tobacco, alcohol, soft drink and processed food markets, 80 countries, 2010

Source: Stuckler et al. (2012)

figure was increasing at *a rate of 2.4 extra people every second. Slightly scary!* By 2025 there will be 8 billion people on Earth. Approximately 6% of all the people ever born are alive today. As stewards of Planet Earth, human beings hold the keys to planetary survival.

Dividing the globe into regions, the most populous region is China. With 1.355 billion people in 2014, China contains 19% of all people on Earth. Chinese President, Mao Zedong (1893–1976) was keen to allow the Chinese population to grow to enable a large national defence against future enemies. Later, the population reached almost 25% of the world total while arable land suitable for food production was only 7% of the world total.

The second most populous country is India, with 1.236 billion in 2014. It is expected that India's population will surpass China's in the next few decades, with around 1.5 billion by 2040. Fertility is falling in most of the developing world but there is a huge variation between countries (Raleigh, 1999). In 2005, India's fertility rate was running at 2.8. A large generation bulge of future parents already exists so that the population will continue to rise in spite of a reduction in fertility.

One obvious intervention for population growth, birth control, is practised in many countries. However, religious edicts influence sexual and reproductive practices leading to population growth. This issue is difficult to ignore. Consider the position of the Roman Catholic Church as one example. On 25 July 1968, Pope Paul VI's encyclical *Humanae Vitae* ('Of Human Life', subtitled 'On the Regulation of Birth') reinforced the traditional values of the Church by forbidding abortion and artificial contraception. In 2008, Pope Benedict XVI stated: 'What was true yesterday is true also today' (Benedict XVI, International Congress, 12 May 2008). The human failure to practise abstinence as the *only* acceptable method for birth control in South America and Africa is adding to population growth, poverty, and the spread of HIV infection and AIDS.

Fertility is highest in sub-Saharan Africa, not only the poorest region in the world, but where the prevalence of AIDS is at a maximum. This is also the region with the highest growth in numbers of Roman Catholics. The evidence shows a strong association between the spread of Catholicism and HIV infections.

According to the *Statistical Yearbook of the Church* (Vatican Publishing House, 2008), world numbers of Roman Catholics remained stable at around 17.3% from 2000 to 2006 but, in Africa, numbers increased from 130 million in 2000 to 158.3 million in 2006, an increase of 22%.

Economic analyses suggest that birth control is cheaper than other methods of reducing carbon emissions. A report from the London School of Economics (LSE) estimated a $7 cost of abating a tonne of CO_2 (tCO_2) using family planning compared with $24 for wind power, $51 for solar power and $57–83 for coal plants with carbon capture and storage (Wire, 2009). Tickell (2008) estimated that each avoided unwanted birth in the USA reduces emissions by 1,500 tCO_2 (based on the per capita annual emissions of 20 tCO_2 and a life expectancy of 75 years). Assuming a health care cost of $150, this equates to an abatement cost of $0.10/$tCO_2$m, a very good deal. Failing to prevent unwanted births needlessly increases the population and causes poverty and malnutrition, and the physical climate becomes more unstable.

INCREASING LIFE EXPECTANCY

Life expectancy has been increasing almost everywhere due to dramatic decreases in infant and adult mortality from infectious diseases. In Britain life expectancy is currently around 75 years for men and 80 years for women. In 2010 in England a working man could expect, on average, about 10 years of pensioned retirement while a working woman can anticipate around 20 years. Recent research suggests that life expectancy will continue to increase in the twenty-first century and that, by 2060, it could reach 100 years (Oeppen and Vaupel, 2002). Life expectancy is said to be increasing by 3 months every year in developed countries. If life expectancy increases to 85, 90 or even 100, social, health and pensions systems will be difficult to maintain in their current form.

The age profile of any population is displayed as a '**population pyramid**' in which numbers in each age group are plotted on a vertical axis. In the United Kingdom the number of people older than 85 is increasing dramatically. Inflows and outflows suggest that, by 2050, the UK will be the largest country in Europe. In 2050, like many other places, the country will be both crowded and warm.

China has the fastest changing demographic profile in the world with the largest population of senior citizens. Currently China has more than 130 million senior citizens who are above 60, more than 10% of the total population. By the middle of this century senior citizens in China will exceed 400 million, one quarter of the total population. There will be a significant shift in the demographic profile of the Chinese population between 2010 and a projection for 2050. The population pyramids show the ageing process is changing China's pyramid with much larger segments in the higher age brackets.

In 1979 China adopted a one-child policy aimed towards keeping the population at around 1.2 billion in 2000. Family sizes in China are typically smaller in cities than in rural areas where the two-child family is the preferred norm. China's total fertility rate currently is running at around 1.7, with women giving birth to an average of 1.7 offspring. China's one-child policy succeeded in reducing family sizes but led to a rising proportion of males, traditionally favoured in Asian cultures, through sex-selection abortion. The reported female/male ratio went from 1.06 in 1979 to 1.17 in 2001 with ratios up to 1.3 in rural Anhui, Guangdong and Qinghai provinces (Hesketh and Xing, 2006). It is predicted that by 2020, China's population will reach 1.4 billion.

POVERTY

Of 7.2 billion people alive in 2014, approximately 5 billion (70%) live in so-called 'developing' countries, i.e. low- and middle-income countries, the word 'developing' being a polite euphemism for 'poor'. **Poverty**, by whatever name, exists on a massive scale. One-and-one-half billion people live on less than 1.25 dollars per day – i.e. more than one person in every five. For them, clean drinking water, flushing toilets, health services, and modern medicines are completely out of reach. Initiatives that have attempted to improve the health of people in extreme poverty mostly have failed.

The UN Development Programme defined poverty as 'a level of income below that people cannot afford a minimum, nutritionally adequate diet and essential non-food requirements' (United Nations Development Programme, 1995). Half of the world's population lacks regular access to medical care and most essential drugs. International organizations such as the UN state with some justification that poverty is the greatest cause of ill health and early mortality. The health effects of poverty are tangible and the biological and economic mechanisms are everywhere the same. The major impacts of poverty on health are caused by the absence of:

safe water;

environmental sanitation;

adequate diet;

secure housing;

basic education;

income generating opportunities;

access to medication and health care.

These are familiar themes. The most common health outcomes of poverty are infectious diseases, malnutrition and reproductive hazards (Anand and Sen, 2000). Poverty implies lack of access to necessary medicines. HIV infection and AIDS provide a good example. A major killer disease is **AIDS (acquired immune deficiency syndrome)**. In 2004, 6 million people living with HIV infection and AIDS in developing countries urgently needed access to antiretroviral therapy (HAART). The World Health Organization (WHO) began the '3 by 5 Initiative' in 2004 when less than 10% of sufferers had access to HAART. The WHO set a target of providing HAART to 3 million people living with HIV infection or AIDS by the end of 2005. The data show that this figure was half met. However, the number of people accessing antiretroviral therapy in low- and middle-income countries has risen, and reached an estimated 6.6 million at the end of 2010. The major barrier to increasing access to HAART is cost. The pharmaceutical industry holds the patents and loses profits if patent rights are relinquished to enable generic production of HAART medication. Further discussion of HAART can be found in Chapters 6 and 19.

Economic growth refers to the rate of increase in the total production of goods and services within an economy. Such growth increases the capacity of an economy to produce new goods and services allowing more needs and wants to be satisfied. A growing economy increases employment, and stimulates business enterprise and innovation. Sustained growth is fundamental to the raising of living standards and to providing greater QoL. A key concept is **gross national income (GNI)**, which is the monetary value of all goods and services produced in a country over a year. GNI is therefore a useful indicator for measuring growth.

Poverty reduction has been a priority for many international organizations. At the United Nations in 2000, 189 countries adopted the 'Millennium Development Goals', including halving poverty rates by 2015, reducing child mortality, decelerating the growth of AIDS and educating all children. Greatest progress is being made in China, India and Brazil. It is expected that the world poverty rate of 28% as it was in 1990 will be reduced by half by 2015, a tremendous achievement. However, poverty in sub-Saharan Africa is still getting worse. In September 2008, world leaders pledged to reinvigorate 'global partnership of equals' to end poverty, hunger and underdevelopment in Africa. United Nations Secretary-General Ban Ki-moon asserted that 'the current trends . . . indicate that no African country will achieve all the Goals by 2015' (United Nations, 2008). Depressing reading!

BOX 2.1
INTERNATIONAL EXAMPLE: REDUCING POVERTY IN BRAZIL

The Brazilian economy came under the media spotlight in June 2014 when it hosted the FIFA World Cup. In spite of its anti-hunger programme, protests and strikes in Brazil's cities were a prominent feature of the 2014 World Cup. Life in the favelas was shown in TV

(Continued)

(Continued)

documentaries as exotic, entrepreneurial and exciting, in spite of the child prostitution, drug trafficking and extremely impoverished communities. Graffiti art was used to draw attention to the contradiction between the lavish expenditure on 12 new stadia and the chronic levels of extreme poverty among a large proportion of the Brazilian population.

The Millennium Development Goal previously had set the target to halve poverty and hunger from 2000 to 2015. In the early 2000s Brazil was working towards, and expected to reach, these targets using the *Bolsa Família* (family stipend) and *Fome Zero* (zero hunger) programmes (Galindo, 2004). Doctors at a local health clinic in Brazil observed that their patients who regularly came in with health problems related to poverty were visiting less often. This can be reasonably attributed to the national, anti-hunger *Fome Zero* (zero hunger) programme that aimed to give every Brazilian at least three meals a day. With one quarter of Brazil's 170 million people below the poverty line, this goal was a challenge. To date, the government has provided emergency help to 13 million families.

The scheme involved giving 'something for something' by making cash transfers conditional upon regular school attendance, health checks, and participation in vaccination and nutrition programmes. Almost three-quarters of benefits reached the poorest 20% of the population and absolute poverty halved from 21% in 2001 to 11% in 2008 (Hall, 2012). Opinions vary about the success of the programme. Commentators suggested that the Workers' Party gained many extra votes as one consequence of *Bolsa Família* and also that there was shift in policy towards short-term solutions to poverty rather than long-term investments in health and education (Hall, 2008, 2012).

The production of good population health requires much more than simply providing doctors, nurses and hospital services. Basic economic, educational and environmental foundations need to be put into place. This means that some fairly dramatic economic changes are needed if we are to see health improvements during the twenty-first century. Among these changes, the cancellation of unpaid debts of the poorest countries and trade justice have potential to bring health improvements to match those of the last 50 years.

A case can be made that health improvements are a necessary precondition of economic growth. This was suggested by the WHO Commission on Macroeconomics and Health. The Commission Report stated: 'in countries where people have poor health and the level of education is low it is more difficult to achieve sustainable economic growth' (World Health Organization, 2002). If current trends continue, health in sub-Saharan Africa will worsen over the next decades. If the

Millennium Development Goals are going to have any chance of success in Africa, health must be given a higher priority in development policies. Sub-Saharan Africa contains 34 of the 41 most indebted countries, and the proportion of people living in absolute poverty (on under one dollar per day) is growing. The health of sub-Saharan Africans is among the worst in the world. Consider the following indicators:

Two-thirds of Africans live in absolute poverty.

More than half lack safe water.

Seventy per cent are without proper sanitation.

Forty million children are not in primary school.

Infant mortality is 55% higher than in other low-income countries.

Average life expectancy at 51.

The incidence of malaria and tuberculosis is increasing.

These figures indicate the very large gaps that exist between the 'haves' and 'have-nots' on the international stage. International debt is a significant factor in poverty. Rich nations will need to honour pledges they have given to cancel debts and establish fair trade to produce reductions in poverty and hunger in Africa.

INEQUALITIES WITHIN A COUNTRY

The existence of health gradients within health care is a universal constant. Many of the determinants of ill health were identified by Edwin Chadwick in his studies of public health in Victorian England: poverty, housing, water, sewerage, the environment, safety and food. In addition, we recognize today that illiteracy, tobacco, AIDS/HIV, immunization, medication and health services are also important (Ferriman, 2007).

Recent studies of the social determinants of health have pinpointed various kinds of inequity. The first of these is based on **socio-economic status (SES):** people who are higher up the 'pecking order' of wealth, education and status have better health and live longer than those at the lower end of the scale. To illustrate this, Figure 2.4 shows a map of the Jubilee Line, which travels along an east–west axis across London. If you travel eastwards along this tube line from Westminster to Canning Town, the life expectancy of the local population is reduced by one year for every stop.

Health gradients are found in all societies. Wealthier groups always have the best health; poorer groups have the worst health. These differentials occur in both illness and death rates, and health gradients are equally dramatic in both rich and poor countries. The majority of studies have been carried out in rich countries.

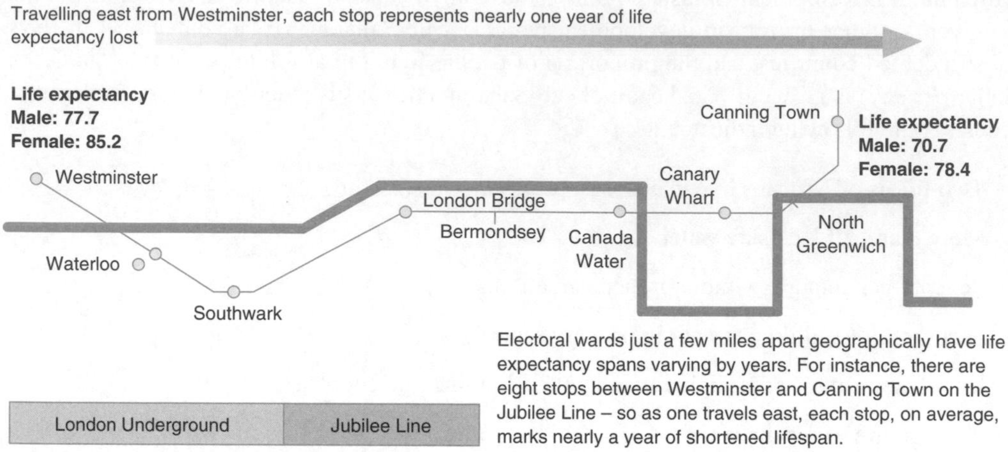

Figure 2.4 Differences in life expectancy within a small area of London

Source: Department of Health (2008)

BOX 2.2
KEY STUDY: THE WHITEHALL STUDIES

The Whitehall studies investigated social class, psychosocial factors and lifestyle as determinants of disease. The first Whitehall study of 18,000 men in the Civil Service was set up in the 1960s. The Whitehall I study showed a clear gradient in which men employed in the lowest grades were much more likely to die prematurely than men in the highest grades.

The Whitehall II study started in 1985 with the aim of determining the causes of the social gradient and also included women, including potential psychological mediators. A total of 10,308 employees participated, two-thirds men and one-third women. The cohort were followed up over time with medical examinations and surveys. Most participants are now retired or approaching retirement.

There have been many phases of data collection, alternating postal self-completion questionnaires with medical screenings and questionnaires. In addition to cardiovascular measures, blood pressure, blood cholesterol, height, weight and ECGs were taken, along with tests of walking, lung function and mental functioning, questions about diet, and diabetes screening.

The Whitehall studies found that an imbalance between demands and control lead to illness. Control is less when a worker is lower in the hierarchy and so a worker in a lower position is unable to respond effectively if demands are increased, supporting Karasek and Theorell's (1990) demand-control model. Other mechanisms can buffer the effect of work stress on mental and physical health: **social support** (Stansfeld et al., 2000), **effort–reward balance** (Kuper and Marmot, 2003), **job security** (Ferrie et al., 2002) and **organizational stability** (Ferrie et al., 1998). Figure 2.5 shows the gradient of death rates vs. employment grades over a 25-year period in men from the Whitehall studies. The death rate is shown relative to the whole Civil Service population (reproduced from Ferrie, 2004).

Virtanen et al. (2014) examined whether midlife adversity predicts post-retirement depressive symptoms in 3,939 Whitehall II participants (mean age 67.6 years at follow-up). Strong associations occurred between midlife adversities and post-retirement depressive symptoms including low occupational position, poor standard of living, high job strain and few close relationships. Associations between socio-economic, psychosocial, work-related or non-work-related exposures and depressive symptoms were of similar strength. The data suggest that socio-economic and psychosocial risk factors for symptoms of depression post-retirement can be detected midlife.

Source: Ferrie (2004)

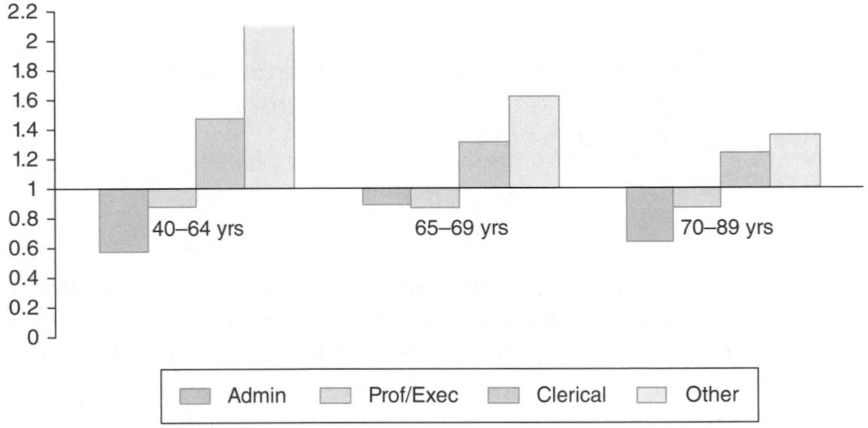

Figure 2.5 Death rates (%) vs. employment grades over a 25-year period in the Whitehall studies

Source: Ferrie (2004). Reproduced with permission

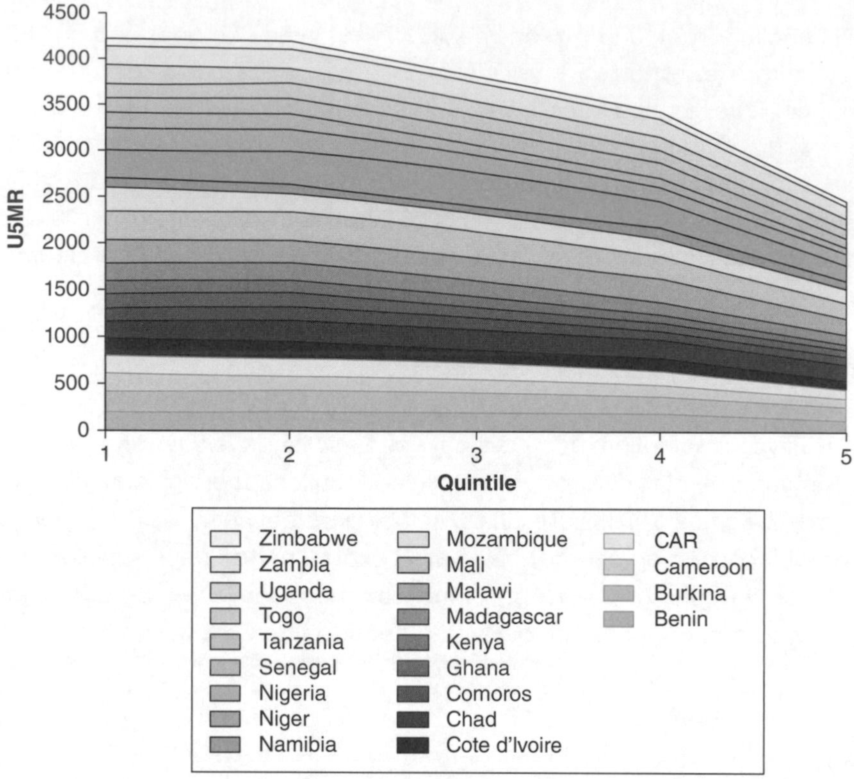

Figure 2.6 Under-5 mortality gradients for sub-Saharan Africa plotted against asset quintile. The area under each line represents the individual country rates. Quintile 1 has least assets, quintile 5 the most

Source: Marks (2004)

There are relatively few studies of health gradients in poor countries. The data are cross-sectional rather than longitudinal, but show a similar pattern to those observed with Whitehall civil servants. One of the authors analysed data from the Demographic and Health Surveys (DHS) programme of the World Bank (2002) (Marks, 2004). These are large-scale household sample surveys carried out periodically in 44 countries across Asia, Africa, the Middle East, Latin America and the former Soviet Union. Socio-economic status was evaluated using answers about assets given by the head of each household. The asset score reflected the household's ownership of consumer items ranging from a fan to a television and car, dwelling characteristics such as flooring material, type of drinking water source and toilet facilities used, and other characteristics related to wealth. Each household was assigned a score for each asset and scores were summed for each household, and individuals were ranked according to the total score of the household in which they reside. The sample was divided into population wealth quintiles – five groups with the same number of individuals in each.

The gradient of under-5 mortality rates (U5MRs) for 22 countries in sub-Saharan Africa are shown collectively in Figure 2.6. The U5MR indicator is the number of deaths to children under 5 years of age per 1,000 live births. This figure shows gradients in all countries. A wide gap in health outcomes exists between the rich and the poor even within these very poor countries. Similar gradients exist for countries in Latin America and the Caribbean and throughout the 44 countries included in the DHS. Infant mortality is halved between quintiles 1 and 5, representing the poorest of the poor and the wealthiest of the poor.

An interesting set of relationships was observed between the U5MRs, literacy and resources (Marks, 2004). The U5MRs in 44 countries were positively correlated with female illiteracy rates (0.69, $p < 0.0001$) and the proportion of households using bush, field or traditional pit latrines (0.60, $p < 0.0001$), and negatively correlated with the proportion of households having piped domestic water (–0.65, $p < 0.0001$), national health service expenditure (–0.33, $p < 0.01$), the number of doctors per 100,000 people (–0.51, $p < 0.0001$), the number of nurses per 100,000 people (–0.35, $p < 0.01$) and immunization rates (–0.27, $p < 0.05$).

The most important predictors of infant survival are educational and environmental. The most effective long-term structural interventions to combat inequality are to improve the educational opportunities for women and to improve the supply of drinking water. High literacy among mothers and access to water supplies and toilets are highly associated with low infant mortality. High numbers of doctors and nurses, immunization rates and health service expenditure are associated with lower mortality rates, but these health service variables are less influential statistically speaking than literacy, domestic water and sanitation. These latter provide the foundations of good health, while health services are the bricks and mortar.

GENDER

Significant differences exist in health outcomes between men and women. Attitudes have changed a little over the last 100 years. A medical textbook from the nineteenth century stated: 'child-bearing is essentially necessary to the physical health and long life, the mental happiness, the development of the affections and whole character of women. Woman exists for the sake of the womb' (Holbrook, 1871: 13–14; cited in Gallant et al., 1997).

In industrialized societies men die earlier than women, but women generally have poorer health (Macintyre and Hunt, 1997). Men in the USA suffer more severe chronic conditions, have higher death rates for all 15 leading causes of death, and die nearly 7 years younger than women (Courtenay, 2000). Similar figures exist in the UK. In 1996 UK boys had a life expectancy of 74.4 years compared with 79.7 years for girls. This excess mortality of 5.3 years in males in 1996 increased over the course of the twentieth century from only 3.9 years in 1900–1910.

Evidence suggests that from the Paleolithic period to the industrial revolution men lived longer than women, 40 years as compared to 35. Also, in less developed countries (e.g. India, Bangladesh, Nepal and Afghanistan) men still live longer than women (World Health Organization, 1989). To complicate the picture further, the health gradient is steeper for men than for women, while illness rates, treatment rates, absenteeism and prescription drug use are generally higher for women (Macintyre and Hunt, 1997). Women suffer more non-fatal chronic illnesses and more acute illnesses. They also make more visits to their family physicians and spend more time in hospital. Women suffer more from hypertension, kidney disease and autoimmune diseases such as rheumatoid arthritis and lupus (Litt, 1993). They also suffer twice the rate of depression. Men, on the other hand, have a shorter life expectancy, and suffer more injuries, suicides, homicides and heart disease.

Psychosocial and lifestyle differences play a role in gender-linked health differences. In industrialized societies women suffer more from poverty, stress from relationships, childbirth, rape, domestic violence, sexual discrimination, lower status work, concern about weight and the strain of dividing attention between competing roles of parent and worker. Financial barriers may prevent women from engaging in healthier lifestyles and desirable behaviour change (O'Leary and Helgeson, 1997).

Social support derived from friendships, intimate relationships and marriage, although significant, appears to be of less positive value to women than to men. Although physical and mental well-being generally benefit from social support, women often provide more emotional support to their families than they receive. Thus, the loss of a spouse has a longer and more devastating effect on the health of men than on that of women (Stroebe and Stroebe, 1983). The burden of caring for an elderly, infirm or dementing family member also tends to be greater for females in the family than for males, especially daughters (Grafstrom, 1994). Gallant et al. (1997) reviewed psychological, social and behavioural influences on health and health care in women.

Gender is a social construction and social constructions of masculinity and femininity have relevance in particular to young men's and young women's health-seeking behaviour. The concept of 'hegemonic masculinity' as a locally dominant ideology of masculinity has been a focus of research (Connell, 2005). Hegemonic masculinity includes the demonstration of 'machismo' through the possession of physical and emotional strength, predatory heterosexuality, being a breadwinner and being unafraid of risk. Recent studies have focused on the health of men, why they suffer more from alcoholism and drug dependency, and why they are so reluctant to seek health from professionals. Gender-specific beliefs and behaviours are likely contributors to these differences (Courtenay, 2000). Men are more likely than women to adopt risky beliefs and behaviours, and less likely to engage in health-protective behaviours that are linked with longevity. Practices that undermine men's health are used to signify masculinity and to negotiate power and status. Social and institutional structures often reinforce the social construction of men as the 'stronger sex'.

One of the cornerstones of masculinity is violence, especially violence against women. This violence cuts across culture and, with only a few exceptions, is a near-universal constant. Kaufman

(1987) argues that violence by men against women is one corner of a triad of men's violence. The other two corners are violence against other men and violence against self. Kaufman asserted that the social context of this triad of violence is the institutionalization of violence in most aspects of social, economic and political life:

> The first corner – violence against women – cannot be confronted successfully without simultaneously challenging the other two corners of the triad. And all this requires a dismantling of the social feeding ground of violence: patriarchal, heterosexist, authoritarian, class societies. These three corners and the societies in which they blossom feed on each other. And together, we surmise, they will fall.
>
> (Kaufman, 1987: 485)

Highly publicized cases, such as the 2002 rape of Mukhtar Mai in Pakistan, the 2012 Delhi gang rape, and rape used as a weapon of war in the Democratic Republic of Congo in 2014 (and throughout history everywhere) have led to an international campaign against rape. Violence against girls and women is the most extreme example of a spectrum of ills with hegemonic masculinity. Risk taking with alcohol (Lemle and Mishkind, 1989), tobacco (Pachankis et al., 2011), drugs (Liu and Iwamoto, 2007) and sexual predation (Prohaska and Gailey, 2010), and presentations about homophobia (Kimmel, 2004), are examples.

Alternative constructions that subvert normative ideas of masculinity include non-drinking. A study of non-drinkers' discourse examined the manner in which not drinking alcohol is construed in relation to the masculine identity. Three prominent discourses about non-drinking were revealed: (i) as something strange requiring explanation; (ii) as simultaneously, unsociable, yet reflective of greater sociability, (iii) as something with greater negative social consequences for men than for women (Conroy and de Visser, 2013).

Constructions of masculinity extend to young men's help-seeking and health service use online. In one study, 28 young men took part in two online focus groups investigating understandings of health, help-seeking and health service use. Discourse analysis was used to explore the young men's framing of health-related practices. Young men are interested in their health and construct their health practices as justified while simultaneously maintaining masculine identities surrounding independence, autonomy and control over their bodies (Tyler and Williams, 2014).

ETHNICITY

The health of minority ethnic groups is generally poorer than that of the majority of the population. This pattern has been consistently observed in the USA between African-Americans ('blacks') and Caucasian-Americans ('whites') for at least 150 years (Krieger, 1987). There has been an increase in income inequality in the USA that has been associated with a levelling-off or even a decline in the economic status of African-Americans. The gap in life expectancy between blacks and whites widened between 1980 and 1991 from 6.9 years to 8.3 years for males and from 5.6 years to 5.8 years for females (National Center for Health Statistics, 1994). Under the age of 70, cardiovascular disease, cancer and problems resulting in infant mortality account for 50% of the excess deaths for black males and 63% of the excess deaths for black females (Williams and Collins, 1995). Similar findings exist in other countries. Analyses of three censuses from 1971 to 1991 have shown that people born in South Asia are more likely to die from ischaemic heart disease than the majority of the UK population (Balarajan and Soni Raleigh, 1993).

There are many possible explanations for these persistent health differences between people of different races who live in the same country and are served by the same educational, social, welfare and health care systems (Williams and Collins, 1995; Williams et al., 1997). First, the practice of **racism** means that minority ethnic groups are the subject of discrimination at a number of different levels. Such discrimination could lead directly or indirectly to health problems additional to any effects related to SES, poverty, unemployment and education. Discrimination in the health care system exacerbates the impacts of social discrimination through reduced access to the system and poorer levels of communication resulting from language differences.

Second, ethnocentrism in health services and health promotion unofficially favours the needs of majority over minority groups. The health needs of members of minority ethnic groups are less likely to be appropriately addressed in health promotion that in turn leads to lower adherence and response rates in comparison to the majority population. These problems are compounded by cultural, lifestyle and language differences. For example, if interpreters are unavailable, the treatment process is likely to be improperly understood or even impaired and patient anxiety levels will be raised. The lack of permanent addresses for minority ethnic group families created by their high mobility makes communication difficult so that screening invitations and appointment letters are unlikely to be received.

Third, health status differences related to race and **culture** are to a large extent mediated by differences in SES. Studies of race and health generally control for SES, and race-related differences frequently disappear after adjustment for SES. Race is strongly correlated with SES and is even sometimes used as an indicator of SES (Williams and Collins, 1995; Modood et al., 1997).

Fourth, differences in health-protective behaviour may occur because of different cultural or social norms and expectations. Fifth, differences in readiness to recognize symptoms may occur also as a result of different cultural norms and expectations. Sixth, differences could occur in access to services. There is evidence that differential access to optimal treatment may cause poorer survival outcomes in African-Americans who have cancer, in comparison to other ethnic groups (Meyerowitz et al., 1998; see Box 2.2). Seventh, members of minority ethnic groups are more likely to inhabit and work in unhealthy environments because of their lower SES. Eighth, there are genetic differences between groups that lead to differing incidence of disease, and some diseases are inherited. There are several well-recognized examples, including sickle cell disorder affecting people of African-Caribbean descent; thalassaemia, another blood disorder that affects people of the Mediterranean, Middle Eastern and Asian descent; and Tay–Sachs disease which affects Jewish people.

Other possible mechanisms underlying **ethnicity** differences in health are differences in personality, early life conditions, power and control, and stress (Williams and Collins, 1995; Taylor et al., 1997). Research is needed with large community samples so that the influence of the above variables and the possible interactions between them can be determined. Further research is needed to explore the barriers to access to health care that exist for people from different groups. We will return to this topic in other chapters.

CONCLUSIONS

Macro-social conditions determine how the single set of resources in this world are shared. Perfect equality will never happen but currently the shares are extremely far from equal. Macro-social conditions require radically different policies if the health of five billion-plus people living in poverty is ever to be improved. The next 50 years is a thin slice of time in which the world population is expected to expand by 25% to around nine billion. The lion's share of this expansion will be in the poorest countries. Eleven million homeless children today live in India alone. Poverty and AIDS/HIV are not abating in sub-Saharan Africa, and life expectancy will continue to be in decline there for some time to come. Policy changes are necessary if AIDS prevention and poverty reduction are going to be more successful than has been achieved to date.

Globalized expansion of transnational industries that promote widespread use of unhealthy commodities has accelerated an epidemiological transition towards high prevalence of non-communicable diseases. The only mechanisms that can be used to prevent harm caused by unhealthy commodity industries are public regulation and market intervention (Moodie et al., 2011). The prospects can be improved if we want to intervene. It all depends on what actions are taken by our elected governments. The electorate puts them there and receives what it demands. If the population wants a world filled with Walmarts, fast food and Big Brand cigarettes, that is what it will get. Unless prevented from doing so, then, inexorably, the globalization steamroller will follow its own course.

Sadly, the research that fills the majority of psychology textbooks is almost all irrelevant to the social and economic issues of today. For the Brave New Worlds of 2050 and 2100, we wonder if priorities will have changed. Will global warming, population, poverty, ideologies of oppression, survival and suffering be on the agenda? Will concepts such as 'stress', 'coping', 'resilience', 'hardiness' and 'change' be given wider interpretation and meaning? Will theories and research concerned with compassion, empathy, emancipation, altruism, sharing, cooperation, sustainability, and cultural, spiritual and religious understanding be more the fore? Will new concepts, theories and methods have been created to deal with the social and psychological problems of the day? The answer to all of these questions must be 'Yes!' – but ultimately it depends on you, and your successors.

FUTURE RESEARCH

1. The causes of poverty and interventions to ameliorate poverty should be *the* priority for economic and social research.
2. Studies in psychology and sociology must be designed to understand humanitarian values, altruism, oppression, fear, aggression and cross-cultural issues.
3. Possible mechanisms underlying ethnicity differences in health, such as differences in early life conditions, power and control, and stress must be explored.
4. Research is needed with large community samples so that the influence of the above variables and their possible interactions can be determined.

SUMMARY

1 The world population is increasing dramatically. From one billion in 1800, it will reach nine billion in 2050.

2 As the global population climbs to nine billion by 2050, the amount of drinkable water available per person will fall by 33%. The increased shortage will affect mainly the poor where the water shortage is already most chronic.

3 Transnational corporations make huge profits from the increased consumption of tobacco, alcohol, ultra-processed food, drink and other unhealthy commodities throughout the low- and middle-income countries. Globalized promotion of unhealthy commodities has driven a huge increase in non-communicable diseases.

4 The greatest influence on health for the majority of people is poverty. Half of the world's population lacks regular access to treatment of common diseases and most essential drugs. Globally, the burden of death and disease is much heavier for the poor than for the wealthy.

5 In developed countries life expectancy is increasing by three months every year. If this trend continues, life expectancy will approach 100 years by 2060. This will place social, health and pensions systems in a perilous position.

6 Economic growth does not reduce disparities in wealth across a society.

7 Health gradients are a universal feature of the health of populations in both rich and poor countries.

8 The UN Millennium Development Goals on poverty and health require rich countries to allocate more resources to poor countries, cancel debts of the poorest countries, and establish fair trade.

9 Gender differences in health, illness and mortality are significant and show striking interactions with culture, history and socio-economic status.

10 The health of minority ethnic groups is generally poorer than that of the majority of the population. Possible explanations include racial discrimination, ethnocentrism, SES differences, behavioural and personality differences, cultural differences and other factors.

11 The 'doom and gloom' described in this chapter is not an inevitability. The prospects can be improved if we, or rather our elected representatives, want to intervene. The future health of populations all depends on what actions are taken by governments and corporations.

3 SOCIAL JUSTICE

Life is unfair.

(John F. Kennedy)

OUTLINE

There is substantial evidence linking poor social conditions with ill health. The explanations for this include material, behavioural and psychosocial factors. In this chapter we consider health inequalities in the context of social justice, the competing explanations and the role of health psychologists in creating a healthier society. The explanation of health inequalities creates many important challenges for theory and research in health psychology.

SOCIAL INEQUALITIES AND HEALTH

As shown in Chapter 2, substantial evidence from dozens of countries has linked social inequalities with health. Consistently these studies show that people of lower **socio-economic status (SES)** have more illness and lower longevity than those in higher socio-economic groups. There is a gradient such that those one step down the ladder are unhealthier than those above. This persistent gradient is often referred to as a '**health gradient**'. When mortality is the measure, a more apposite term would be 'mortality' or '**death gradient**'. 'Death gradients' have been observed in all human societies in both rich/developed countries and poor/developing countries (Marks, 2004). Such gradients are normally continuous throughout the range of economic variation. If the gradient were stepped or flat at one end of the range and steep at the other, it could be inferred that the causative mechanism(s) had a threshold value before any of the 'ill-effects' could appear. However, there is no evidence of such thresholds; the gradient is a continuous one.

One of the earliest reports on the health gradient was by the French physician Louis-René Villermé (1782–1863) who, in the 1820s, examined the health of residents in different neighbourhoods of Paris. From a careful review of the data, Villermé concluded that there was a relationship between the wealth of the neighbourhood and the health of its residents. Those living in the poorer neighbourhoods had a higher death rate, and military conscripts from those neighbourhoods were smaller and had more illnesses and disabilities (Krieger and Davey Smith, 2004). Shortly afterwards, Frederich Engels published his classic work on *The Condition of the Working Class in England in 1844* (Engels, 1845). This book provided a detailed description of the appalling conditions and the limited health care of working-class residents of Manchester (Figure 3.1). He wrote:

> All of these adverse factors combine to undermine the health of the workers. Very few strong, well-built, healthy people are to be found among them. Their weakened bodies are in no condition to withstand illness and whenever infection is abroad they fall victims to it. This is proved by the available statistics of death rates.
>
> (Engels, 1845/1958: 118–19)

When Engels compared death rates within the city he found that they were much higher in the poorer districts. Further, he realized the importance of early development and noted: 'common observation shows how the sufferings of childhood are indelibly stamped on the adults' (p. 115). Although these early researchers realized the importance of the impact of adverse social conditions, interest in the social aspects of health was marginalized with the rise of germ theory and the growth of **Social Darwinism** (Krieger and Davey Smith, 2004). The former theory focused on controlling specific pathogens rather than social reform whereas the second argued that innate

Figure 3.1 Engraving of Manchester in the 1870s

inferiority, not social injustice, was the cause of ill health. However, the growth of social movements in the 1960s rekindled interest in social justice.

The foundation of the National Health Service (NHS) in the UK in 1947 was an attempt to remove inequalities that existed in health care provision. Health services were provided for all free at the point of delivery. Titmuss (1968) observed after 15 years' experience of the NHS that the higher income groups:

> know how to make better use of the service; they tend to receive more specialist attention; occupy more of the beds in better equipped and staffed hospitals; receive more elective surgery, have better maternal care, and are more likely to get psychiatric help and psychotherapy than low-income groups – particularly the unskilled.

These continued disparities led Tudor Hart (1971) to describe the 'inverse care law': the availability of good medical care tends to vary inversely with the need for the population served.

In 1977 the UK government established a working group to further investigate social inequalities in health. The subsequent **Black Report** (Townsend and Davidson, 1982), named after Sir Douglas Black, the working group's chair, summarized the evidence on the relationship between occupation and health. It showed that those classified as unskilled manual workers (Social class V) consistently had poorer health status compared with those classified as professionals (Social class I). Further, the report graphically portrayed an inverse relationship between mortality and occupational rank for both sexes and at all ages. A class 'gradient' was also observed for most causes of death, particularly respiratory, infective and parasitic diseases. Inequalities in terms of utilization of health care, especially among preventive services, were also apparent. It concluded:

> Present social inequalities in health in a country with substantial resources like Britain are unacceptable and deserve to be so declared by every section of public opinion . . . we have no doubt that greater equality of health must remain one of our foremost national objectives and that in the last two decades of the twentieth century a new attack upon the forces of inequality has regrettably become necessary.
>
> (Townsend and Davidson, 1982: 79)

In a follow-up study, similar trends persisted in the 1980s as social inequalities in health continued to widen (Townsend et al., 1992). As discussed in Chapter 2, the Whitehall studies provided supporting evidence on the relationship between SES and health. As Marmot (2002) explained:

> The first finding was that the social gradient in health was as steep as it had been twenty years previously, hadn't got any less, and that fitted with national data. Then what we saw was there were clear social gradients in smoking and lack of physical activity, and so on, as we found in Whitehall I, but in addition now, we showed very clear social differences in people's experience of the workplace – how much control they had at work, how fairly

> they were treated at work, how interesting their work was. We found clear social gradients in people's participation in social networks. We found social gradients in psychological attributes like hostility.
>
> (Marmot, 2002: 3)

Marmot argued that tackling health inequalities is not about eliminating the hierarchy – rather, it is more about understanding the pathways of inequalities and how these can be addressed. Marmot continued:

> All societies may have hierarchies, but we know that the social gradient in disease is not fixed. It's bigger in some places than others, and it can change over time. That could be because the magnitude of the hierarchies change, but there are always hierarchies. But, more importantly, it suggests what is it about where you are in the hierarchy that's related to disease, and can we do something about that? So you ask, is it money? Is it prestige, self-esteem? And, in fact, what I think is, it has much more to do with how much control you have over life circumstances, and the degree to which you're able to participate fully in society; what Amartya Sen calls capabilities.
>
> (Marmot, 2002: 3)

In understanding and dealing with health inequalities, it is important to recognize all determinants of health – from micro to macro levels – and to consider how many of these are within the control of individuals in society. The idea of capabilities is related with the actual freedom and rights enjoyed by people (Sen, 1999). In this respect, freedom does not only entail one's freedom to choose; rather it also involves freedom from the barriers that restrain people from reaching their fullest human potential. Only when individuals have the 'capability' to exert control over the factors that influence their health can they truly exercise their 'right to health'. The vast levels of social inequalities pose serious questions regarding the capacity of individuals to exercise their human rights. The emergence of new centres of power extends the issue to the international scale where the capacity of nation states to protect and promote their citizens' right to health is also being threatened.

The Acheson Report (1998) outlined recommendations to address health and social inequalities in the UK. In 2008, the WHO Global Commission on the Social Determinants of Health published a report to address health equity by taking action into the social determinants health. In the same year, the Scottish Government (2008) published the *Equally Well Report*, which provided substantial evidence on the relationship between health and socio-economic deprivation in Scotland. The UK Government commissioned Sir Michael Marmot to review current trends and to propose the most effective evidence-based strategies to reduce health inequalities in England. In 2010, Marmot's report entitled *Fair Society, Health Lives* recognized the reduction of health inequalities as a matter of fairness and social justice (Marmot, 2013). The report underlined that solely focusing action on the most disadvantaged will be inadequate. Fair distribution of health, well-being and sustainability are more important measures of success than economic growth. As expressed in the final report of the Commission on Social Determinants of Health, inequities in power, money and resources were to blame for much of the inequities in health within and between countries. To address inequities in health effectively, cross-government commitment to action is needed across all of the social determinants of health (Marmot et al., 2013).

EXPLANATIONS FOR SOCIAL INEQUALITIES IN HEALTH

Health inequalities can be considered from an **ecological approach** or **systems theory approach**. Bronfenbrenner's (1979) ecological approach conceptualized developmental influences in terms of four nested systems:

microsystems: families, schools, neighbourhoods;

mesosystems: peer groups;

exosystems: parental support systems, parental workplaces;

macrosystems: political philosophy, social policy.

These systems form a nested set, like a set of Russian dolls, microsystems within mesosystems, mesosystems within exosystems and exosystems within macrosystems.

Ecological theory assumes that human development can only be understood in reference to the structural ecosystems. The 'Health Onion', a general systems framework for understanding the determinants of health and illness, was presented in Chapter 1 (Figure 1.4). Of key importance is the *perceived environment*, not the so-called 'objective' environment. In Box 3.1 we list some of the characteristics of low SES using Bronfenbrenner's (1979) systems approach. The box shows the many different disadvantages across all four systems of the social, physical and economic environment. In addition, we can add the high levels of perceived injustice that many people with low SES may feel.

BOX 3.1
BEHAVIOURS AND EXPERIENCES ASSOCIATED WITH LOW SES

Microsystems: families, schools, neighbourhoods

- Low birth weight
- Family instability
- Poor diet/nutrition

- Parental smoking and drinking
- Overcrowding
- Poor schools and educational outcomes
- Poor neighbourhoods

Mesosystems: peer groups

- Bullying, gangs and violence
- Smoking
- Drinking
- Drugs
- Unprotected sex

Exosystems: parental support systems, parental workplaces

- Low personal control
- Less social support
- Unemployment or unstable employment
- High stress levels
- Low self-esteem
- Poorer physical and mental health

Macrosystems: political philosophy, social policy

- Poverty
- Poor housing
- Environmental pollution
- Unemployment or unstable employment
- Occupational hazards
- Poorer access to health services
- Inadequate social services

SCIENTIFIC EXPLANATIONS

Any explanation of the SES–health gradient needs to consider psychosocial systems that structure inequalities across a broad range of life opportunities and outcomes, health, social and educational. As illustrated in Box 3.1, in comparison to someone at the high end of the SES scale, the profile of a low SES person is one of multiple disadvantage. The disadvantages of low SES accumulate across all four ecosystems. It is this kind of *accumulation* and *clustering* of adverse physical, material, social and psychological effects that could explain the health gradient. While each factor alone can be expected to produce a relatively modest impact on mortality, the combination and interaction of many kinds of ecosystem disadvantage are likely to be sufficiently large to generate the observed gradient. The socio-economic conditions that contribute to the health gradient can also be experienced by individuals across the life course (Pavalko and Caputo, 2013).

While the Black Report (Townsend and Davidson, 1982) clearly documented the link between social position and health, it also detailed four possible explanations for health inequalities:

An artefact: the relationships between social position are an artefact of the method of measurement.

Natural and social selection: the social gradient in health is due to those who are already unhealthy falling downwards while those who are healthy rising upwards.

Materialist and structuralist explanations: emphasize the role of economic and socio-structural factors.

Cultural and/or behavioural differences: 'often focus on the individual as the unit of analysis emphasizing unthinking, reckless or irresponsible behaviour or incautious lifestyle as the moving determinant' (p. 23).

While accepting that each explanation may contribute something, the report emphasized the importance of the materialist explanations and developed a range of policy options that could address the inequalities. Contemporary research into explanations for social inequalities in health has been reviewed by Macinko et al. (2003). Their classification extends the four-fold explanation developed in the Black Report.

Psychosocial explanations are considered at the individual (micro) and social (macro) levels. At the micro level it is argued that 'cognitive processes of comparison', in particular perceived relative deprivation, contribute to heightened levels of stress and subsequent ill health. Additionally, the Whitehall studies suggested that it was lack of perceived control over working conditions that increases stress at the lower end of the social scale. At the macro level psychosocial explanations focus on impairment of social bonds and limited civic participation, so-called social capital (see below), that flows from income inequality.

The **neo-material explanations** have drawn increased support in critiques of the psychosocial approaches (see Macleod and Davey Smith, 2003; Marks, 2004; Stephens, 2014). They focus on the importance of income and living conditions. At the micro level, it is argued that in more unequal societies those worse off have fewer economic resources, leading to increased vulnerability to various health threats. At the macro level, high income inequality contributes to less investment in the social and physical environment. Those who favor the neo-material explanations argue that the psychosocial explanations ignore the broad political context within which social and health inequalities are nested.

There are also the artefact and selection explanations of the social inequalities in health. Although these initially attracted attention, there is less support for these arguments today.

Contemporary research has focused on the relationship between the extent of social inequality in a particular society and the extent of ill health. Wilkinson (1996) argued that health was poorer in more unequal societies. In their book, *The Spirit Level*, Wilkinson and Pickett (2009) provided a comprehensive analysis of the empirical association that exists between health/social problems and inequality among rich countries. For example, higher infant mortality rates were shown in countries where income inequality is high. The same index of health/social problems was found to be only very weakly related to national income but strongly related to inequality. Wilkinson and Pickett (2009) hypothesized that the structural inequality in society causes people to become more anxious, stressed, ashamed, untrusting, and unhappy. In the same year that *The Spirit Level* was published, the Equality Trust was founded by the authors and Bill Kerry. This charity aims to develop and promote policies to reduce social inequalities. The group is currently working on a documentary to widely disseminate key messages from the book (for a trailer, see www.equalitytrust.org.uk).

Torre and Myrskylä (2014) examined the relationship between income inequality and health using data from 21 developed countries over a 30-year period. Findings suggested that income inequality was positively related with the mortality of males and females at ages 1–14 and 15–49. The positive correlation between income inequality and mortality of females was also found at ages 65–89, although this relationship was weaker than for the younger age groups. These findings suggest that narrowing the income inequality gap may be an effective way to promote health, especially among children and young-to-middle-aged groups. However, we need to remember, once again, that correlation does not mean causation. As previously argued, the relationship between income inequality and health is not as straightforward as was initially conjectured (Lynch et al., 2004). However, as Lynch and Davey Smith (2002) also warned, we should be careful not to throw the 'social inequality baby' out with the 'income inequality bathwater'. There is much more to social inequality than inequality of income.

LAY EXPLANATIONS

What do lay people have to say about social inequalities in health? This literature connects with the broader literature on popular health beliefs (Chapter 4). In an early qualitative study with working-class women in England, Calnan (1987) found that women were reluctant to accept that they were less healthy than middle-class people. As one working-class woman said: 'I think as long as they eat the right foods and do have a proper balanced diet, I mean, even the poorest of people can be just as healthy as the others' (p. 76). Those who did accept that wealthy people had better health attributed it to differential access to health care. Conversely, professional women were more likely to accept the existence of a health gradient and attributed the poorer health of working-class people to low job satisfaction, low wages, poor diet and the hazards of the working environment.

The reluctance of working-class people to attribute the cause of social variation in ill health to structural factors was explored by Blaxter (1997). Her secondary analysis of a large survey of British health and lifestyle found limited evidence of popular discussion about health inequalities. This was especially the case among people from poorer backgrounds.

Lofters et al. (2014) explored how residents from Ontario attributed income-related health inequalities. They conducted a telephone survey (n = 2,006) and found that the majority of respondents were most willing to attribute income-related health inequalities to differences in employment, social status, income and food security, and least willing to attribute inequalities to differences in early childhood development, social exclusion, the social gradient and personal health practices and coping skills. Findings also suggested that participants were more willing to accept messages that framed inequalities around privilege of the rich or the plight of the poor and were less likely to agree with messages that implied blaming the poor.

SOCIAL JUSTICE

Critics of research into social inequalities in health often charge that social inequalities are both an inevitable part of life and also are necessary for social progress. An alternative perspective is to consider not simply inequalities per se but inequities in health. According to Dahlgren and Whitehead (1991), health inequalities can be considered as inequities when they are avoidable, unnecessary and unfair. The issue of fairness leads us to consider the issue of **social justice**.

A useful starting point is the theory of 'justice as fairness' developed by the moral philosopher John Rawls (1999). He identified certain underlying principles of a just society, as follows:

Assure people equal basic liberties including guaranteeing the right of political participation.

Provide a robust form of equal opportunity.

Limit inequalities to those that benefit the least advantaged.

Daniels et al. (2000) argued that adhering to these principles would address the basic social inequalities in health. They detailed a series of implications for social organization that flow from the acceptance of these principles. First, assuring people equal basic liberties implies that everyone has an equal right to fully participate in politics. In turn, this will contribute to improvements in health since, according to social capital theory, political participation is an important determinant of health.

Second, providing measures actively to promote equal opportunities implies the introduction of measures to reduce socio-economic inequalities and other social obstacles to equal opportunities. Such measures would include comprehensive childcare and childhood interventions to combat any disadvantages of family background (Daniels et al., 2000). They would also include comprehensive health care for all including support services for those with disabilities.

Finally, a just society would allow only those inequalities in income and wealth that would benefit the least advantaged. This requires direct challenge to the contemporary neo-liberal philosophy that promotes the maximization of profit and increasing the extent of social inequality. A Framework Convention on Global Health (FCGH) grounded in the human right to health could help to reconstruct global governance for health and offer a new vision post-Millennium Development Goals (Gostin and Friedman, 2013).

To an increasing extent, psychological organizations have been recognizing the links between poor social conditions and physical and mental health. Somewhat belatedly, they are catching up with Villermé's and Engels' findings from the 1840s. But why is awareness of social justice issues among the psychology profession so slow in the making? The American Psychological Association was founded in 1892, but it took more than 100 years for the Association to pass a resolution on 'Poverty and Socio-economic Status' in the year 2000. The resolution called for a programme of research on the causes and impact of poverty, negative attitudes towards people living in poverty, strategies to reduce poverty, and the evaluation of anti-poverty programmes. The resolution has been followed by a few new initiatives, including interventions facilitated by critical and community health psychologists (see Chapter 14). A special issue on poverty reduction was published in the *Journal of Health Psychology* in October 2010.

Much more could be achieved if psychologists were more willing to engage with social justice issues 'in their own backyards'. Shamefully, in our opinion, societies like the British Psychological Society have maintained a stance of neutrality on the grounds that the society is a charity and that it is prohibited from engaging in political issues. Yet social justice isn't simply a political issue, it's a life and death issue, affecting the mental and physical well-being of billions of people. It is a problem that is too important to leave to politicians. It affects everybody; everybody can do something towards creating a more just society.

THE UNIVERSAL RIGHT TO HEALTH

Justice is about rights and freedoms. People talk about rights and freedoms of different kinds, e.g. the freedom of expression, the right to vote, having equal rights, and so on. 'Human rights' refer to the fundamental moral and legal social norms necessary for people to live a minimally good life. Every individual is entitled to human rights simply because that person is human. International declarations and legal conventions have been issued by governments and international organizations to ensure that such rights are respected and protected. The Universal Declaration of Human Rights (UDHR) is an example of an international standard that outlines our most basic human rights (United Nations General Assembly, 1948). It affirms that all human beings are 'born free and equal in dignity and rights' (Article 1). These rights are universal and indiscriminate of 'race, color, sex, language, religion, political or other opinion, national or social origin, property, birth or other status' (Article 2).

Can we talk about rights to health, in a similar way? In 1946, the World Health Organization first expressed the right to health as a fundamental human right. Although not legally binding, the UDHR two years later provided the foundation for succeeding laws and policies adopted by governing bodies and states around the world. It is formed of 30 articles consisting of the most comprehensive statements concerning human rights that include security, liberty, political, equality, economic and social rights. In particular, Article 25 affirmed the human right to a standard of living for adequate health and well-being through the provision of food, clothing, housing and medical and social services. The promotion and protection of these rights are prerequisites to a dignified, free and secure way of living.

The right to health is intricately linked with other civil liberties and freedoms. To illustrate this link, it is worth considering the effects of human rights violations on the health and well-being of its victims. Just think of the consequences of ethnic cleansing, slavery, war, genocide and other forms of social aggression and cruelty. The histories of countries such as the USA and the UK and other European powers show many well-known examples of these kinds of abuses. These crimes against humanity reflect how violations of human rights can lead to debilitating consequences for the physical, psychological and social well-being of others. As shown in Box 3.2, the development of effective interventions in the context of violence and conflict need to take into account historical and psychosocial factors that influence health and well-being.

BOX 3.2 INTERNATIONAL CASE STUDY: USING A PSYCHOSOCIAL AND PARTICIPATORY APPROACH TO HEALTH IN THE CONTEXT OF VIOLENCE AND CONFLICT

Background

While several studies have been conducted to explore the relationship between health and physical activity, most of these have been conducted in Western contexts. In communities where violence and conflict are prevalent, it is important to also consider the impact of historical and sociocultural factors and the prevailing incidence of racism, violence, sexual abuse and discrimination experienced by community members.

The programme

The project described by Ley and Rato Barrio (2013) was called *Acción Psicosocial a través del Movimiento, juego y deporte* (Psychosocial Action through Movement, Play and Sport). This project was based in a rural area of Guatemala with two groups of women who had suffered from violence. It used a psychosocial and participatory approach to develop the use of sports and games as educational and therapeutic tools. The methods of movement, games and sports used in the project included *physical* (e.g. progressively increased physical activity of middle-low intensity, stretching and relaxation exercises) and *psychosocial and educative activities* (e.g. cooperative games; modified sports; role-play; verbalization of experiences and perceptions). A mixed method approach was used combining questionnaires, participatory observation and interviews to examine the effectiveness of the programme in promoting health.

Findings

Quantitative findings reflected improvements in sense of coherence and self-esteem among participants. Results suggest that the programme provided opportunities for women who suffered from violence to socialize and offer mutual support. Modified sport, games and participatory group activities that were conducted in an active and enjoyable way also facilitated group interaction. By enabling participants to share their experiences of violence and domestic conflicts in a safe and protective space, they were able to express their feelings and to explore potential solutions with others. This process contributed to mutual learning and enabled participants to reconstruct their perceptions of the world and to reflect on how their circumstances can be improved.

Conclusion

Using a psychosocial and culturally grounded use of games and sports as participatory tools may be useful in promoting health in the context of violence and conflict.

Source: Ley and Rato Barrio (2013)

People with poor health may also suffer from an increased vulnerability to human rights violations due to their fragile state. The stigma associated with their condition may increase their vulnerability from discrimination and maltreatment as discussed below.

STIGMA

Stigma refers to unfavourable reactions towards people when they are perceived to possess attributes that are denigrated. Stigmatization is universal, found in all cultures throughout history. The majority of people will experience it at some time, as both the young and the elderly are stigmatized groups. In addition, people can be multiply stigmatized, as in the case of HIV infection and AIDS, which is associated with certain highly stigmatized groups (e.g. homosexuals, sex workers, intravenous drug users) and adds a further source of stigma as well as intensifying existing stigma(s) (see Chapter 19). Stigma involves a pattern of discrediting, discounting, degradation and discrimination, directed at stigmatized people and extending to their significant others, close associates and social groups. Link and Phelan (2014) used the term 'stigma power' to refer to instances whereby exploitation, control and exclusion of others enable people to obtain what they want. They argued that stigmatization is most effective in achieving its prejudiced aims when it is hidden or 'misrecognized'.

Stigmatization devalues the whole person, ascribing them a negative identity that persists (Miles, 1981), even when the basis of the stigma disappears (e.g. when someone recovers from mental illness they remain characterized forever as a person who had mental health problems). It is a form of social oppression and operates to disqualify and marginalize stigmatized individuals from full social acceptance and participation. Health care professionals are as likely to stigmatize as any other group, influencing their behaviour and decision-making in the provision of health care. The consequences of stigma include physical and psychological abuse, denial of economic and employment opportunities, non-seeking or restricted access to services and social ostracism.

It is not surprising then that individuals frequently expend considerable effort to combat stigmatization and manage their identities, including passing (acting as if they do not have the stigmatized attribute), covering (de-emphasizing difference), resistance (e.g. speaking out against discrimination) and withdrawal. They may also internalize the stigmatization, feeling considerable guilt and shame and devaluing themselves. Kadianaki (2014) argued that coping with stigma could be seen as a meaning-making effort to enable those who are being stigmatized to transform the way they see themselves and to orient themselves in society.

The pervasive Western idealization of physical perfection, independence and beauty may play an important role in the constant devaluation of disabled people and people who are ill. Particular characteristics of illness or disablement increase stigmatization including perceptions that the condition is the person's own fault (e.g. obesity), incurable and/or degenerative (e.g. Alzheimer's disease), intrusive, compromises mobility, contagious (e.g. HIV infection and AIDS) and highly visible. Goffman (1963) distinguished between 'discredited' and 'discreditable' categories of stigma. 'Discredited' refers to conditions that are self-evident, in which the stigma is visible. 'Discreditable' conditions relate to conditions where the stigma is not visible but may be discovered, at which point they would become stigmatized. Stigma is also increased when it is perceived to be threatening or disruptive (Neuberg et al., 2000), which may account for the high level of stigma associated with mental illness, intellectual disabilities, and HIV infection and AIDS.

The lower value placed on the lives of disabled people can be seen in the way disabled people are segregated from the general population including education, housing, employment and transportation. It is also apparent in the way crimes against disabled people are minimized (e.g. discourses of abuse rather than theft/fraud/rape, acquittals and light sentences in cases of 'acceptable' euthanasia). For both disabled people and those with severe or terminal illness, stigma may be central to debates around suicide/euthanasia and abortion (see below). Stigma is a powerful determinant of social control and exclusion. By devaluing certain individuals and groups, society can excuse itself for making decisions about the rationing of resources (e.g. HIV antiretroviral drugs), services (e.g. health insurance exclusions), research funding/efforts and care (e.g. denying operations to individuals who are obese) to these groups. In terms of the social model of disablement, stigmatization may be the main issue concerning disablement.

Multidisciplinary research is needed to further explore how stigma is related to health, disablement and social justice. Why is recognition of the similarities between stigmatized and non-stigmatized individuals over-ridden and obscured by perceived differences that are devalued? How do different stigmas, particularly health-related stigmas, interact? How is stigma manifested by health care professionals and what interventions might mitigate the negative effects of stigma?

LIVES WORTH LIVING VERSUS THE RIGHT-TO-DIE

The pervasive devaluation of people with disabilities, and the negative assumptions about their lower quality of life, are central to the current debates about abortion of impaired fetuses and legalization of assisted suicide/euthanasia or the right-to-die. Disablement rights organizations champion the argument that abortion decisions should not be made on the basis of fetal impairment indicators whereas they challenge the 'right-to-die' rhetoric on the basis of disablement.

The disablement movement argues against abortion on the grounds of potential impairment due to the eugenic implications of such a practice (Sharpe and Earle, 2002). The reason for their concern is encapsulated in Singer's quote: 'the killing of a defective infant is not morally equivalent to the killing of a person; very often it is not morally wrong at all' (Singer, 1993: 184). The new genetic testing and selection technologies allow the identification of suspected fetal impairment during pregnancy and subsequent fetal termination. Shakespeare (1998: 669) argues that such technologies operate as a weak form of eugenics 'via non-coercive individual choices' based on the assumed unacceptable quality of life of disabled people. The rationales for screening and termination include assumptions that people with disabilities are more costly to society, that the lives of children with disabilities are harmful to their families, and that some impairments involve a level of suffering and misery that makes life not worth living.

The way professionals describe test results and the influence of the advice they give is also a concern. There is substantial evidence that the advice given, while often subtle, most frequently encourages termination in response to potential impairment results, and most testing takes place within a plan-to-abort context. There is a tension between this argument and the feminist position that women have a categorical right to make decisions about their own bodies including the decision to terminate an unwanted pregnancy. However, the disablement movement position is not against abortion itself, rather it revolves around the bases upon which the decision is made. Aborting a specific fetus on the basis of a devalued attribute is different from aborting any fetus on the basis of not wanting to have a child at that time (Fine and Asch, 1982). It is unlikely that a woman would be encouraged to terminate a pregnancy because a test indicated the child is likely to have ginger hair; however, the same is not true when a test suggests a possibility of impairment. It is this difference that makes it an issue of discrimination. The disablement movement also asserts the rights of disabled women to have children. This fundamental human right is denied to many women, particularly those with cognitive and emotional impairments, as the additional support and resources that they need to allow them to raise a child are often not available. In some countries, forced sterilization still occurs, including Australia, Spain and Japan.

The right-to-die debate revolves around the argument that people with severe or terminal illness and people with disabilities have the right to end their lives when they feel they have become unbearable, and that assisting them to do so should not be illegal. In May 2013, the Assisted Dying Bill was tabled at the UK House of Lords and recently received its second reading in July 2014. Modelled on a law in the US state of Oregon, the bill proposed to enable adults who are expected to live six months or less to request and be provided with assistance to end their own life. It requires two doctors to confirm that the person (1) is terminally ill; (2) is capable of making this decision; and (3) has formed a settled intention to die. This decision must have been reached as an informed choice, made voluntarily and without force. Both doctors must also confirm that the person has been fully informed of available care options. As soon as the doctors have the signed the declaration, the life-ending drug will be prescribed and dispensed after

14 days. This period can be shortened to six days if the prognosis is less than a month. The person who made the request to end his/her life will administer the drug. We discuss this issue in more detail in Chapter 19.

The argument against the right-to-die lobby, although implicitly anti-suicide, is not necessarily about whether suicide is right or wrong per se. It should be viewed as being about the differential treatment of the issue for people with disabilities and severe illnesses as opposed to 'healthy' people. Morally sanctioning assisting people with incurable terminal or non-terminal conditions to end their lives or withholding life-sustaining treatment/support, while morally opposing the right of suicidal 'healthy' individuals to end their lives (and offering them suicide prevention interventions), equates to a severe form of discrimination based on stigmatization of these individuals.

REDUCING INEQUALITIES

If inequalities can be reduced at all, the evidence suggests that this will only happen by adopting a thoroughly multi-layered approach. Dahlgren and Whitehead (1991) identified four different levels for tackling health inequalities:

Strengthening individuals.

Strengthening communities.

Improving access to essential facilities and services.

Encouraging macroeconomic and cultural change.

These four levels correspond to the four layers of influence in Whitehead's 'Onion Model' of the determinants of health outlined in Chapter 1 (see Figure 1.4). Extra microsystem and mesosystem levels as in Bronfenbrenner's model could perhaps be added to Whitehead's list. Psychologists do not usually talk quite so simplistically about 'strengthening' individuals; we analyse the personal characteristics and skills associated with positive health (e.g. self-efficacy, hardiness, sense of coherence, social skills). Developing interventions aimed at individual health beliefs and behaviours is a core feature of psychological theory, research and practice.

Interventions aimed at tackling inequalities at an individual level have shown mixed results. There are four possible reasons. First, people living and working in disadvantaged circumstances have fewer resources (time, space, money) with which to manage the process of change. Second, health-threatening behaviours such as smoking tend to increase in difficult or stressful circumstances as they provide a means of coping. Third, there may have been a lack of sensitivity to the difficult circumstances in which people work and live that constrain the competence to change. Fourth, there has been a tendency to blame the victim. For example, cancer sufferers may be blamed for the disease if they are smokers on the grounds that they are responsible for the habit that caused it.

Overall, efforts directed at the individual level have been inconclusive and small scale. Because many health determinants are beyond the control of the individual, psychological interventions aimed at individuals are likely to have limited impact on public health problems when considered on a wider scale. This suggests that there is a need for psychologists to work beyond the individual level, with families, communities, work sites and community groups. We are not alone in thinking that structural changes at a societal level are ultimately required if the prevalent inequities are ever going to be reduced. Anything else is simply tinkering, a case of 'fiddling while Rome burns'.

SOCIAL CAPITAL

There is increasing interest in **social capital** as an aid to explaining social variations in health. The concept was especially promoted by Robert Putnam who used it to characterize civic life in Italy (Putnam et al., 1993). He argued that certain communities had higher degrees of civic engagement, levels of interpersonal trust and norms of reciprocity. Together, these characteristics contributed to a region's degree of social capital. Putnam (2000) subsequently explored the extent of social capital in the USA and argued that over the past generation there has been a steady decline in participation in social organizations and thus a steady decline in social capital. An important distinction that Putnam (2000) makes is that between 'bridging' and 'bonding' social capital. 'Bridging' social capital refers to links with diverse groups and provides an opportunity for community members to access power and resources outside their community; whereas 'bonding' social capital refers to inward-looking social ties that bond the community together. Campbell (2004) stresses that both forms of social capital are essential in building healthy communities.

There has been a series of studies investigating variations in social capital and its connection with health. For example, in a national cohort of Open University adults in Thailand ($n = 82{,}482$), self-assessed health was shown to be significantly associated with social trust and social support (Ylengprugsawan et al., 2011). Gilbert et al. (2013) conducted a meta-analysis of social capital, self-reported health and mortality. A total of 39 studies were included in the analysis. Findings suggested that high social capital can increase the odds of good health by 27%. Furthermore, social capital variables such as reciprocity and trust increased the odds of good health by 39% and 32% respectively.

Recent studies have explored the pathways linking social capital with health. In a study with church-going Latinas in California, Martinez et al. (2013) explored the relationship between leisure/physical activity and social cohesion. Leisure/physical activity and neighbourhood cohesion were assessed at baseline, three months and six months after the implementation of a *promotora*-delivered pilot intervention. *Promotoras* are community health leaders who help with the dissemination of health information to community members. They are locally based and have very similar characteristics as the target population. They were given training on how to lead walking groups, general information on the health benefits of physical activity, and information on the barriers to and facilitators of physical activity especially among the Latino community. Evaluation of this intervention showed that social cohesion was an important predictor of physical activity (i.e. social cohesion at three months can predict levels of physical activity at six months). The authors suggested that it is possible that the *promotoras* enhanced social cohesion by providing participants with a sense of belonging and friendship while facilitating these activities. Considering the effectiveness of this approach in promoting leisure-time physical activity, it was argued that intervention coordinators can learn to maximize the benefits of working with community-based facilitators to promote health and well-being.

Participatory and community-based approaches that involve community participation can help to address issues related with poverty and health by empowering individuals and communities more widely (Ng, 2010). For example, Lawson et al. (2014) explored the benefits of participating in a community arts project among people living with mental health problems. The community members selected artwork and curated a public exhibition. Interviews suggested that participants had improved self-worth, and lost some of the stigma associated with mental health issues. The project also offered a sense of belonging and helped participants to develop new knowledge and skills.

Scheib and Lykes (2013) facilitated a participatory action and photo elicitation research in post-Katrina New Orleans from 2007 to 2010. Eleven African-American and Latina women took part in the project. Findings suggested that in developing ties and new ways to respond to consequences of an 'unnatural disaster', the participants developed intra- and inter-group empathy and the capacity to critically examine the social and structural determinants of health inequities.

Other studies have explored the relationship between economic deprivation and social capital. For example, Cramm et al. (2010) examined the effects of income, health, social capital and other socio-economic factors on the subjective well-being (SWB) of poor communities in the Eastern Cape of South Africa. Findings showed that income was positively associated with SWB and that social capital can predict SWB in all income groups. Similarly, Ahnquist et al. (2012) examined the interactions between economic hardships and social capital on health outcomes. Data were derived from the 2009 Swedish National Survey of Public Health. Findings showed that economic capital and low social capital were significantly associated with poor health outcomes. There were also significant interactions between economic hardships and all types of social capital.

Social capital, or its lack, has been linked with health inequalities. Uphoff et al. (2013) systematically reviewed evidence on the associations and interactions between social capital and socio-economic inequalities in health. Of the 60 studies that met the inclusion criteria, 56 showed significant correlations between social capital and socio-economic inequalities in health. Twelve studies showed how social capital can act as a buffer against the negative effects of low SES on health, while five concluded that social capital has a stronger positive effect for people with a lower SES.

Exploring the wider impact of social capital on health, Campbell et al. (2013) examined the role of social capital in managing HIV infection and AIDS in rural Zimbabwe. They reviewed six qualitative studies and found that community membership is often, although not always, associated with decreased HIV incidence and reduced stigma. It is also associated with better access to services, especially among women. Findings suggest too that participation in community groups, whether these are formal or informal, provides opportunities for critical dialogue that enable community members to reflect upon social norms and personal experiences and to discuss potential action to address community issues. However, despite critical engagement, plans for community improvement are usually constrained by social and economic factors. Although raising critical awareness and capacity-building are important in reducing health inequalities, it is crucial that unbalanced power relations and unfair structures are also considered since participatory and community-based action research projects are prone to problems of resistance from dominant social groups (Estacio, 2013; Stephens, 2014; see Chapter 14).

There has been a wide range of criticisms of social capital as an explanatory concept (e.g. Lynch et al., 2000). These include confusion over what exactly the term implies, debates over ways of measuring it, and ignorance of the broader political context. Bjørnskov and Sønderskov (2013) argued that social capital is not a good concept since contemporary research either conceptualizes it as several distinct phenomena or constructs it using other terms. Baum (2000) also emphasizes caution in the use of the concept in that 'there are dangers that the promotion of social capital may be seen as a substitute for economic investment in poor communities particularly by those governments who wish to reduce government spending' (p. 410).

COMMUNITY MOBILIZATION AND POWER

Considering that current global economic processes restrain the capacity of grassroots organization to respond to structural challenges in health, it is important for future interventions to develop new methods to leverage power for such organizations (Speer et al., 2014). It is important to recognize the need to transform power relationships, not just at individual and community levels, but also at macro levels (Ansell, 2014). As shown in the case presented in Box 3.3, developing strategic alliances can help grassroots organizations to strengthen their political power to affect policy change. Developing partnerships for health and community development 'must be understood not as a tool for intervention, but as part of the interventions and definition of success' (Aveling and Jovchelovitch, 2014: 34). The process of building partnerships involves critical reflection and is influenced by institutional and sociocultural contexts.

BOX 3.3
INTERNATIONAL CASE STUDY: CREATING SOCIAL ALLIANCES TO INFLUENCE POSITIVE POLICY CHANGE

Speer et al. (2014) presented the case of ISAIAH, a faith-based community organizing group based in the Minneapolis–St. Paul metropolitan area. It was formed in 2000 when three faith-based groups merged after recognizing that small groups do not

(Continued)

(Continued)

have sufficient political power to influence change. It is now composed of 90 different organizations and uses a social action approach to affect positive policy change to address social inequity. The group had been instrumental in preventing the elimination of three stops for a light rail line being built in Minneapolis–St Paul. The communities that would potentially benefit from these transit stops were predominantly ethnic minority groups. The group influenced planning decisions and funding legislations by collaborating with neighbourhood groups and highlighting the link between transportation and health. As the authors noted:

> Pursuing a deeper appreciation of the connection between health and transportation led ISAIAH leaders to policy professionals who emphasized the role of transportation for community vitality – through access to grocery stores, employment, schools, and affordable neighborhoods. Simultaneous to this discernment, ISAIAH responded to the Governor's vetoes by revisiting state legislators and pushing back against the Governor's neoliberal articulation of scarcity and limited resources. (Speer et al., 2014: 165)

To maintain the momentum of the group's efforts, ISAIAH and its allies are currently working on a health impact assessment to explore land use policies to prevent the negative consequences of the rail line on marginalized neighbourhoods.

Source: Speer et al. (2014)

Campbell et al. (2010) showed that it is possible for people from disadvantaged communities to mobilize themselves to demand for better social and economic conditions to improve health. They presented three successful pro-poor social movements in Brazil, India and South Africa wherein social groups demanded access to land, health services and life-saving medical treatment. A similar case is presented in Box 3.4, wherein *pobladores* successfully mobilized themselves to demand for better living and working conditions in Chile (Hadjez-Berrios, 2014). In these case studies, although enabling disadvantaged groups to make their concerns heard were important aspects of the movement, the willingness of those in power to take these demands seriously proved crucial to the success of these campaigns. As Stephens (2010) argued, health promotion research and practice need to recognize how those in more advantaged social positions maintain and perpetuate unequal power relations in society. She noted:

> Using social theories will enable us to develop research questions with a focus on making visible the practices of those with privilege that work to simultaneously preserve and increase power and access to resources while denying access to other groups. (p. 997)

BOX 3.4
INTERNATIONAL CASE STUDY: COMMUNITY PARTICIPATION IN HEALTH DURING THE UNIDAD POPULAR GOVERNMENT – SANTIAGO DE CHILE (1970–1973)

Context

The organization and mobilization of popular classes had a significant impact on the improvement of living and working conditions in overcrowded cities in Chile. In addition to the creation of the National Health System in 1952 and its later institutional development until 1973, active participation of disadvantaged and marginalized communities, a.k.a. *pobladores*, had mobilized social action to address local health problems in poor urban settlements. Community participation in health in Chile saw its peak with the arrival of the *Unidad Popular Government* in 1970. This ended abruptly in September 1973 due to a military coup that lasted for 17 years.

Method

This qualitative study aimed to explore the experiences of community participation in health during the Unidad Popular Government in Santiago de Chile from 1970 to 1973. Participants included three former health government officials, three primary health care workers and six *pobladores* who were directly involved with the movement.

Findings

Participants constructed community participation in health from 1970 to 1973 as multiple and dynamic in response to the health and political challenges faced by communities. Three different moments in community participation in health were highlighted in the analysis. The first moment aimed to expand health care coverage, prevent diseases, educate pregnant women and prevent alcoholism through the development of 'Health Brigades' inside settlements. 'Health Brigades' were relatively autonomous organizations (mostly composed of young women) who were trained by health workers. The second moment was characterized by improvements in autonomy and widening of the scope of participation through grassroots participation in health decisions. In this context, health issues were no longer conceptualized in biomedical terms. Finally, the third moment in community participation in health

(Continued)

(Continued)

was characterized by a growing understanding of the wider determinants of health and the development of comprehensive definitions of health related to the democratization of health services.

Conclusion

Community participation in health in Chile during the Unidad Popular Government contributes to a critical understanding of community participation, conceived as a dialectic and transformative action. In this context, the *pobladores* constituted themselves as social subjects who actively transformed Chilean health institutions by challenging the dominant and oppressive hierarchies in society.

Source: Hadjez-Berrios (2014)

It is the development of such 'receptive social environments' that pro-poor advocates need to pay more attention to in future interventions (Campbell et al., 2010). Working with Papua New Guinean young people, Vaughan (2014) argued that while facilitating critical thinking is useful, this process does not inevitably lead to action, thus highlighting the 'need to shift the focus of participatory research from supporting "safe social spaces" to supporting "transformative action in context"' (p. 184). Campbell (2014) argued that lessons from the 'new left' and the burgeoning global protest movements can provide useful insights into community mobilization in the current globalized environment.

FUTURE RESEARCH

1. There is a need to clarify the character of the psychosocial explanations for the social inequalities in health.
2. Research on social inequalities needs to be combined with further research on ethnic and gender inequalities in health. Qualitative studies of the health experiences of people from different socio-economic backgrounds are of particular importance to our understanding of the psychological mechanisms underlying health variations. Further qualitative studies are also needed to explore the relationship between social positioning and health experience.
3. Forms of research on social inequalities in health need to explicitly consider how they can contribute to reducing them.
4. An essential aspect of future research is to consider the social and psychological obstacles to movements to alleviate social inequalities in health.

SUMMARY

1 Health and illness are determined by social conditions.
2 There is a clear relationship between income and health leading to the development of a social gradient.
3 Psychosocial explanations of these social variations include perceived inequality, stress, lack of control and less social connection.
4 Material explanations of the social gradient in health include reduced income and reduced access to services.
5 Political factors connect both psychosocial and material explanations in a broader causal chain.
6 Lay explanations of social inequalities in health include people's immediate social and physical environment.
7 Social environment includes the character of people's social relationships and their connection with the community.
8 Social justice is concerned with providing equal opportunities for all citizens. Socio-economic status (SES) and wealth are strongly related to health, illness and mortality. These gradients may be a consequence of differences in social cohesion, stress and personal control.
9 A health psychology committed to social justice needs to orient itself to address the needs of the most disadvantaged in society.

4 CULTURE AND HEALTH

There is no such thing as human nature independent of culture.

(Clifford Geertz, 1973)

OUTLINE

The way people think about health, become ill and react to illness is rooted in broader health belief systems that are immersed in culture. In this chapter we provide examples of different health belief systems that have existed historically and popular belief systems of today. We consider several indigenous health systems and those of complementary and alternative medicine. Finally, we discuss some issues related to rapid cultural change in contemporary society including racism and how culturally competent health care systems help to bridge cultural, social and linguistic barriers.

WHAT IS CULTURE?

We are cultural beings and an understanding of health beliefs and practices requires an understanding of the historical and sociocultural context that gives human lives meaning. An inclusive definition of **culture** has been provided by Corin (1995):

> a system of meanings and symbols. This system shapes every area of life, defines a world view that gives meaning to personal and collective experience, and frames the way people locate themselves within the world, perceive the world, and believe in it. Every aspect of reality is seen as embedded within webs of meaning that define a certain world view and that cannot be studied or understood apart from this collective frame. (p. 273)

Culture has been viewed principally in two different ways: (A) as a fixed system of beliefs, meanings and symbols that belong to a group of people who speak a common language and may also adhere to a common religion and system of medicine; (B) as a developmental and dynamic system of signs that exists in continuously changing narratives or stories. People's reactions to illness are driven by a constant struggle for meaning in light of beliefs that are evolving across space and time. These two approaches yield very different kinds of psychological investigation.

Within psychology the study of culture that uses approach A is that of **cross-cultural psychology**. Samples of populations said to be from different cultures are compared in terms of attitudes, beliefs, values, and behaviours that are viewed as stable and essential characteristics of particular cultures. This approach is illustrated by research on individualism vs. collectivism by Triandis (1995) and Hofstede and Bond (1988). The study of culture that uses approach B is that of **cultural psychology** illustrated by the work of Valsiner (2013), who views cultural psychology as:

> a science of human conduct mediated through signs from beginning to end, and from one time moment to the next in irreversible time . . . All phenomena of manifest kind – usually subsumed under the blanket term behavior – are subordinate to that cultural process of irresistible meaning-making (and re-making). Behavior is not objective, but subjective – through the meanings linked with it . . . Human psychology is the science of human conduct and not of behavior, or of cognition. (p. 25)

The concept of **belief** is a core concept in health psychology but rarely is it defined. Beliefs are viewed as:

> durable and implicit; as associated with practices, choices and activities; and as bearing personal significance and import . . . Belief tends to reproduce cultural norms, the precepts, expectations and values of particular times and places . . . Simultaneously, within such broad cultural patternings, the belief of any given individual is produced through the mediation of that person's particular history of social relations – with parents, carers, teachers, significant others – with which these acquired norms get inflected.
>
> (Cromby, 2012: 944–6)

Belief is viewed in social cognition models such as the theory of planned behaviour (TPB; Ajzen, 1985) as a fundamental theoretical construct, with each of the TPB's three core constructs, attitude, subjective norm and perceived behaviour control, all being underpinned by belief, an enduring, cognitive entity employed in rational thought and detached from feelings. It is often constructed and expressed as a part of discourse and narrative when asked for an account of one's views about a topic in conversation. Beliefs are therefore constructed 'on the hoof' as much as they are a fixed piece of dogma that underlies decisions and actions.

Yet, as we argue elsewhere in this book, beliefs are almost always associated with affect. This is the view of Cromby (2012) who states:

> Belief arises when social practice works up structures of feeling in contingent association with discourse and narrative . . . Believing is not merely information-processing activity, and belief is not an individual cognitive entity. Belief is the somewhat contingent, socially co-constituted outcome of repeated articulations between activities, discourses, narratives and socialized structures of feeling. (p. 954)

Beliefs are at the core of what we mean when we talk of culture.

HEALTH BELIEF SYSTEMS

As societies evolve, **health belief systems** develop as bodies of knowledge are constructed and exchanged among those who undergo specialized training. This gives rise to the separation of *expert* or *technical* beliefs systems from *traditional*, *folk* or *indigenous* systems. These two types of systems are not discrete but interact and are in a process of constant evolution. Although the majority of people in any society organize meaning-making through the use of loosely organized indigenous belief systems, the character of these is connected in some form with expert belief systems.

Kleinman (1980) described three overlapping sectors of any health care system:

> The *popular sector* refers to the lay cultural arena where illness is first defined and health care activities initiated.
>
> The *professional sector* refers to the organized healing professions, their representations and actions.
>
> The *folk sector* refers to the non-professional, non-bureaucratic, specialist sector that shades into the other two sectors.

Although this three-fold division is widely cited, other researchers (e.g. Blumhagen, 1980) have preferred a simpler two-fold division into professional and popular realms. The former are said to consist of systematicity, coherence and interdependence (Blumhagen, 1980: 200). Conversely, a lay health belief system can appear disconnected, inconsistent and at times plainly contradictory. This broad classification avoids an accusation that certain specialized health belief systems are classified as 'folk' when they have limited status in society although they may offer an extensive classification of health complaints and treatments. These two broad kinds of belief systems interact such that the lay person can draw upon more specialized knowledge but also the specialist will make use of more popular knowledge. Further, both ways of thinking about health draw upon a more general world-view located within particular local socio-political contexts. Blumhagen

(1980) argues that these two kinds of health belief systems should be considered distinct from an individual belief system that a person employs to understand their personal experience of illness. Dominant expert health belief systems have the tendency to become doctrinal in nature with principles and guidelines that inform practitioners and specialists in systems of treatment for different illnesses.

WESTERN HEALTH BELIEF SYSTEMS

Classical Views of Health

The classical view of health and illness in the West is derived from the Graeco-Arabic medical system known as **Galenic medicine**. This provided an expert system developed from the Greeks, in particular the work of Hippocrates and his colleagues. As we discussed in Chapter 1, the central concept in Galen's formulation is the *balance* of four bodily fluids or humours: yellow and black bile, phlegm and blood. Balance is equated with health and imbalance implied ill health. The bodily fluids have been linked with: the *four seasons* (e.g. an excess of phlegm was common in the winter leading to colds, while an excess of bile led to summer diarrhoea); the *four primary conditions* (i.e. hot, cold, wet and dry); and the *four elements* (i.e. air, fire, earth and water). Medieval scholars added *four temperaments* (i.e. choleric, sanguine, melancholic, and phlegmatic).

Besides focusing on understanding natural processes, the Galenic tradition placed responsibility on individuals to look after themselves. Ill health was viewed as one consequence of natural processes, not a result of divine intervention. In many ways Galen's ideas not only prefigured but also continue to influence much of contemporary health beliefs.

Christian Ideas

Galenic ideas dominated medicine in Europe for almost two millennia. However, during the Middle Ages in Europe, Galen's work became confined more to the learned few and other ideas based upon religion became more commonplace. Illness was often seen as punishment for humankind's sinfulness. The Church's *seven deadly sins* came to be associated with pathological conditions of the body. For example, pride was symbolized by tumours and inflammations while sloth led to dead flesh and palsy (Thomas, 1979).

Christianity drew upon different traditions. The *ascetic tradition* scorned concern for the body and instead promoted acts such as fasting and physical suffering, which supposedly led to spirituality. With the *Protestant Reformation* this belief was replaced with the idea that the body had been given to humans by God. It was the individual's religious duty to look after and care for the body. Illness was seen as a sign of weakness and neglect. To honour God required living a healthy life and abstaining from excess, especially in terms of sex and diet. Wear (1985) noted that religious writers frequently made reference to the body. For example, Robert Horne described the body as the 'Temple of God' and that it was necessary to keep it pure and clean. These ideas were widely promulgated in the new Protestant Reformation. The way to heaven was through attention to health behaviour and was strongly linked to a social morality. The poor were expected to take responsibility for their condition while at the same time the rich were wrong to indulge themselves while there was so much poverty and suffering.

Despite the authority of the Church, these religious interpretations began to decline with the growth of medical science. While in terms of the expert belief system there has been increasing acceptance of a naturalistic view of disease, the moral basis of health continues to underlie much of contemporary health belief.

Biomedicine

Two streams of thought in knowing the world dominated during the Enlightenment. The first was the acceptance of the distinction between superstition and reason. The second was the emergence of **positivism**, which emphasized that science based upon direct observation, measurement and experimentation gave direct access to the real world. This approach concentrated attention on material reality and a conception of the body as distinct from the mind. A central figure was Descartes (1596–1650), who conceived of the human being as composed of mind and body. The former was not open to scientific investigation whereas the latter could be conceived as a machine.

The eighteenth century saw the rise of **individualism** in Western society. In previous eras the group or collective organized ways of thinking and acting, which in turn was interconnected with the physical and spiritual world. Professional understanding of health and illness became more closely entwined with knowledge of the individual physical body. Foucault (1976) described how between the mid-eighteenth and mid-nineteenth centuries the 'medical gaze' came to focus on the interior of the human body. The symptoms of illness now became signs of underlying pathophysiology. Foucault noted that the change in perspective of the physician was illustrated in the change in the patient query from 'How do you feel?' to 'Where does it hurt?' For this new physician the stethoscope became the symbol of having insight into the bodily interior. Treatment centred on changing the character of this physiology by either medical or surgical means.

This approach to the study of health and illness has become known as **biomedicine**, or cosmopolitan or allopathic medicine (Leslie, 1976). It came to dominance for several reasons, including the fact that it was in accord with a broader view of humans, its alliance with physical science and the steady improvement in the health of the population that was attributed to medical intervention. The focus on the body is in accord with the Western emphasis on the individual. Further, the separation of mind and body 'offers a subtle articulation of the person's alienation from the body in Western society, but this alienation is found, as well, in every sphere of economic and political life' (Benoist and Cathebras, 1993: 858). Biomedicine separates the person from the body.

Friedson (1970) described how the coming to dominance of the biological approach was not without resistance. It required strong political action to organize the profession of medicine and to take legal action against other health practitioners. Throughout there was the dismissal of alternative perspectives and the assertion that biomedicine was the central force that had led to the substantial improvements in society's health. Biomedicine was based upon a positivist epistemology that supposedly gave it access to an outside reality. Only this approach was the true approach. All other approaches could be disparaged.

The Biopsychosocial Model of Health

The dominance of this biomedical system has come in for substantial challenge both from the scientific establishment and the public. Initially, this was reflected in a call for more attention to the psychological and social aspects of health. This led to the development of the **biopsychosocial model** of health and illness (Engel, 1977). According to Engel (1980) the various aspects of health and illness can be organized in a hierarchy from the biosphere and society down through the individual's level of experience and behaviour to the cellular and subatomic level. All of these levels interact and need to be considered if we are to understand health and illness. With varying degrees of enthusiasm this model has in some respects replaced the basic biomedical model (see Chapter 1).

In addition, the increasing evidence of the link between social and behavioural factors and health has led to the promulgation of a health promotion ethic by the medical establishment with an emphasis on personal responsibility for health. Crawford (1980: 365) argued that 'in an increasingly "healthist" culture, healthy behaviour has become a moral duty and illness an individual moral failing'. Admittedly, the adoption of a more biopsychosocial approach to health care, especially by general practitioners, is sometimes met with hostility by patients who have accepted and may even feel more comfortable with 'the doctor knows best' model of biomedicine. This might explain why some people feel concerned if, apparently, their physician/GP is becoming too involved in their 'personal'/psychosocial problems.

Criticisms of the biomedical model led the World Health Organization to propose an extensive definition of health as a state of complete physical, mental and social well-being, not the mere absence of disease or infirmity. This definition widened the scope of health care to consider the well-being not only of the individual but also of the community. In Chapter 1 an even wider definition was offered, encompassing the economic, political and spiritual domains. Currently, much of health care in Western society is attempting to shift from a concern with bodily processes to concern with the wider concept of quality of life.

Popular Views of Health

Evidence from a series of studies of popular beliefs about health and illness in Western society illustrates the interaction of what can be described as the classic, the religious, the biomedical and the lifestyle approaches to health and illness. Probably the most influential study of Western lay health beliefs was carried out by Herzlich (1973). She conducted interviews with a sample of French adults and concluded that health was conceived as an attribute of the individual – a state of harmony or balance. Illness was attributed to outside forces in our society or way of life. Lay people also referred to illness in terms of both organic and psychosocial factors. On their own organic changes did not constitute illness. Rather, for the layperson, 'physical facts, symptoms and dysfunctions have, of course, an existence of their own, but they only combine to form an illness in so far as they transform a patient's life.' The ability to participate in everyday life constitutes health, whereas inactivity is considered the true criterion of illness. Herzlich's study was seminal because it provoked further research into popular health beliefs.

Blaxter (1990) analysed the definitions of health provided by over 9,000 British adults in a health and lifestyles survey. She classified the responses into nine categories:

1. Health as not-ill (the absence of physical symptoms).
2. Health despite disease.
3. Health as reserve (the presence of personal resources).
4. Health as behaviour (the extent of healthy behaviour).
5. Health as physical fitness.
6. Health as vitality.
7. Health as psychosocial well-being.
8. Health as social relationships.
9. Health as function.

In analysing the responses across social classes, Blaxter (1990) noted considerable agreement in the emphasis on behavioural factors as a cause of illness. She commented on the limited reference to structural or environmental factors, especially among those from working-class backgrounds. Williams and Calnan (1996) suggest that the growth of the self-help consumer movement in health care is another symbol of popular opposition to the passive patient model of biomedicine. They noted that this opposition 'can be located within the broader socio-cultural and political framework of self-determination and a reclaiming of control over the body, self and wider environment' (p. 1617).

However, health beliefs go beyond descriptive dimensions to consider underlying aetiology. In a discussion of **social representation theory**, Moscovici (1984) suggested that people rarely confine their definition of concepts to the descriptive level. Rather, lay descriptions often include reference to explanations. Lay perceptions of health and illness can be rooted in the social experience of people, in particular sub-cultures. A study of East and West German workers found similar findings to that of Herzlich but with an added emphasis on health as lifestyle (Flick, 1998). Similarly, in a study of Canadian baby-boomers, Murray et al. (2003) found a very activity-orientated conception of health. They defined health in terms of lifestyle, functionality, social engagement and attitude as well as reserve. It was suggested that this conception reflected a greater self-responsibility for health that is promoted in Canadian culture. However, there was also evidence of a certain resistance to this stance among those from working-class backgrounds.

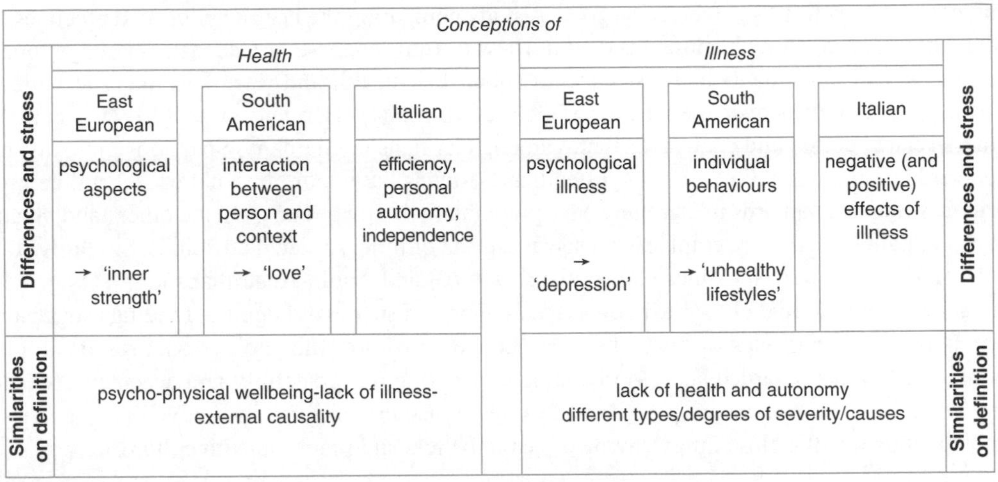

Figure 4.1 Similarities and differences of health and illness conceptions in Eastern European, South American and Italian care workers

Source: Pace et al. (2012)

Health beliefs are influenced by social and cultural contexts. Figure 4.1 shows a diagram of three different conceptions of health and illness held by health care workers from East European, South American and Italian backgrounds. The findings from intra-ethnic focus groups suggested that Eastern Europeans focused on 'inner strengths' vs. 'depression', South Americans on 'love' vs. 'unhealthy lifestyles' and Italians on 'personal autonomy' vs. 'negative effects of illness' for their conceptions of health and illness respectively.

In another example, Goins et al. (2010) explored the perceptions and definitions of health among older adults in six rural communities in West Virginia. Qualitative analyses highlighted four general themes into the meaning of health: (1) health as a value; (2) dimensions of life; (3) holistic nature of health; and (4) health care use and adherence. These findings reflect the multidimensional nature of health. It is important for health care professionals to be able to recognize how these lay constructions could influence patients' subjective experiences of health and health care.

In Western society a metaphor that is frequently applied to health is that of *self-control*. This metaphor is in turn infused with moral connotations such that to become ill is not to 'take care of oneself' (Crawford, 1980). Admittedly, health is a contested arena since release from certain controls, or even the rejection of them, can be considered a sign of good health. Conversely, the person who abides by certain controls can be perceived as unhealthy. In her study of lay people's views of health and illness, Crossley (2003) found, for some, that to transgress the moral imperative to health was perceived as good. A study comparing the health beliefs and practices of adults living in Japan with adults resident in Hawaii from Japanese or Caucasian heritage found that the Japanese residents had less concern about their health and were less likely to believe that they had control over their health (Gotay et al., 2004). Bermejo et al. (2012) compared illness-related causal and control attributes among Germans in Germany, Spaniards in Spain and Spaniards in Germany. Findings suggested that Germans have more internal causal and control beliefs, whereas Spaniards in Germany have more fatalistic attributions. On the other hand, Spaniards in Spain placed more emphasis on social aspects of illness-related attributes. Similarly, Tan et al. (2010) interviewed Chinese-Australians (n = 10) and Anglo-Australians (n = 11) aged 55 to 78 years to explore their life experiences and views on successful ageing. Findings suggested that, although both groups associated successful ageing with health and personal responsibility, Anglo-Australians regarded successful ageing as growing old gracefully and acceptance of old age, while Chinese-Australians placed more value on financial security and active lifestyle. These findings illustrate the close interweaving of health beliefs and practices with culture.

NON-WESTERN VIEWS OF HEALTH

Chinese Views of Health

Traditional Chinese Medicine (TCM) is greatly influenced by the religion and philosophy of **Taoism**. According to this view the universe is a vast and indivisible entity and each being has a definite function within it. The balance of the two basic powers of yin and yang governs the whole universe including human beings. *Yang* is considered to represent the male, positive energy that produces light and fullness, whereas the *yin* is considered the female, negative force that leads to darkness and emptiness. A disharmony in yin and yang leads to illness. A variety of methods including *acupuncture* and *herbal medicines* can be used to restore this harmony. There are at least 13,000 medicinal substances with 50 fundamental herbs including the roots, twigs and leaves of cannabis, ginseng, ginger, licorice, peony and rhubarb.

Confucianism is influential in the traditional Chinese views on health. Within this culture, human suffering is traditionally explained as the result of destiny or *ming*. Cheng (1997) quotes the Confucian teacher Master Meng: ‘A man worries about neither untimely death nor long life but cultivates his personal character and waits for its natural development; this is to stand in accord with Fate. All things are determined by Fate, and one should accept what is conferred’ (p. 740). An important part of your destiny depends upon your horoscope or *pa-tzu*. During an individual’s life, his or her pa-tzu is paired with the timing of nature. Over time these pairings change and create the individual’s luck or *yun*.

Buddhist beliefs are also reflected in Chinese medical belief systems. Good deeds and charitable donations for example are promoted. Heavenly retribution is expected for those who commit wrongs. This retribution may not be immediate but it will be inevitable. An important concept in this respect is *pao* which has two types: (1) reciprocity and (2) retribution (Cheng, 1997). In mutual relationships reciprocity is expected. When this does not occur some form of retribution will take place.

These influences are not only codified within Chinese medicine but also influence everyday lay beliefs about health and illness both in China and in Chinese communities around the world. For example, Chen et al. (2009) discussed how these three philosophical foundations influence Chinese patients' perspectives on cancer pain and its management.

These lay belief systems remain strong within immigrant communities. In a qualitative study on social representations, Jovchelovitch and Gervais (1999) showed that despite differences related to age and degrees of acculturation, Chinese people in England share common representational systems relating to health and illness that are still based on the notions of 'balance' and 'harmony' of the yin and yang.

Similarly, in a quantitative study examining cultural health beliefs held by older Chinese in Canada, Lai and Surood (2009) reported that their health beliefs are loaded onto factors related with traditional health practices, beliefs about traditional Chinese medicine, and beliefs about preventive diet. More recently, Rochelle and Marks (2010) explored the extent of medical pluralism among Chinese people in London. The thematic analysis suggests that Chinese medicine and Western medicine were perceived as two systems of health provision and that these two systems could be used concurrently. Generally, the National Health Service was perceived to be difficult to use and concerns were expressed around communication and trust with health care providers due to language barriers.

Like orthodox medicine, TCM raises ecological and ethical concerns. TCM is a private industry worth billions of dollars and the efficacy of the treatments is largely unknown. Many rare and endangered species currently face extinction owing to the harvesting of animal parts such as tiger bone, rhinoceros horn, turtle shell and seahorses and there is suffering of cruel conditions by animals used as a source of medicines, e.g. the harvesting of bile from thousands of captive Asiatic black bears being held in small cages. However, the bile is the main source of ursodeoxycholic acid used to treat kidney problems and stomach and digestive disorders (Lindor et al., 1994). Cruelty to animals to generate medicines within TCM is paralleled by the use of animals in the testing of new medicines in orthodox medicine.

Ayurvedic Medicine

The Ayurvedic system of medicine is based upon the Sanskrit words *ayus* (life) and *veda* (science). This system remains extremely extensive in India. It is estimated that 70% of the population of India and hundreds of millions of people throughout the world use Ayurvedic medicine which is based on Hindu philosophy (Schober, 1997). Both the cosmos and each human being consists of a female component, *Prakrti*, which forms the body, and a male component, *Purusa*, which forms the soul. While the Purusa is constant, the Prakrti is subject to change. The body is defined in terms of the flow of substances through channels. Each substance has its own channel. Sickness occurs when a channel is blocked and the flow is diverted into another channel. When all channels are blocked the flow of substances is not possible and death occurs. At this stage the soul is liberated from its bodily prison. The task of Ayurvedic medicine is to identify the blockages and to get the various essences moving again. The different forms of imbalance can be corrected through both preventive and therapeutic interventions based on diet, yoga, breathwork, bodywork, meditation and/or herbs (Schober, 1997). The use of herbs plays a major role in treatment and prevention of illnesses (see Table 4.1).

As in TCM, the Ayurvedic system informs beliefs about health and illness through the Indian sub-continent and among Indian communities everywhere. However, Ayurvedic medicine has not gained the domination of Western biomedicine, even within India. There is a variety of other competing health belief systems in a pluralistic health culture. In an interview study of a community in northern India, Morinis and Brilliant (1981) found evidence not only of Ayurvedic beliefs, but also 'unami' (another indigenous health system), allopathic, homeopathic, massage, herbalist, folk, astrologic and religious systems. They note that while these systems may formally seem to conflict, participants could draw on some or all of them to help explain different health problems. Further, the strength of these beliefs is related to the immediate social situation and the roles and expectations of the community. For example, for women in some parts of Pakistan, the health belief system is a mixture of biomedicine and 'unami' medicine that is a version of Galenic medicine.

African Health Beliefs

A wide range of traditional medical systems continues to flourish in Africa. These include a mixture of herbal and physical remedies intertwined with various religious belief systems. As Porter (1997) notes, belief systems that attribute sickness to 'ill-will, to malevolent spirits, sorcery, witchcraft and diabolical or divine intervention still pervade the tribal communities of Africa, the Amazon basin and the Pacific' (p. 9). In a more developed assessment Chalmers (1996) summarized the African view as reflecting 'a belief in an integrated, independent, totality of all things animate and inanimate, past and present' (p. 3). As with other traditional health systems a central concept is balance: 'Disturbances in the equilibrium be they emotional, spiritual or interpersonal may manifest in discordance at any level of functioning' (p. 3).

Two dimensions are paramount in understanding African health beliefs: *spiritual influences* and a *communal orientation*. It is common to attribute illness to the work of ancestors or to supernatural forces. Inadequate respect for ancestors can supposedly lead to illness. In addition, magical influences can be both negative and positive, contemporary and historical. Thus, illness can be attributed to the work of some malign living person. The role of the spiritual healer is to identify the source of the malign influence. African culture has a communal orientation. Thus, the malign influence of certain supernatural forces can be felt not just by an individual but also by other members of his or her family or community. Thus intervention may be aimed not only at the sense of balance of the individual but also at the family and community.

Mulatu (1995) investigated the illness causal beliefs of a large sample of adults from Ethiopia. Four dimensions were identified: (1) psychological stressors; (2) supernatural retribution; (3) biomedical defects; and (4) social disadvantage. Psychological stressors and supernatural retribution were considered more important causes of psychological than of physical illnesses. A relationship between these causal beliefs and treatment choices, attitude to patients, and demographic characteristics has also been found. For example, belief in supernatural retribution is associated with use of religious prayer, holy water, consulting traditional healers, and both traditional and modern medicine. There is also a relationship between education and causal beliefs such that the less educated placed more emphasis on supernatural causes.

In Uganda, Martin et al. (2014) examined the measurement and conceptualization of 'adjustment' among people living with HIV. Participants ($n = 263$) completed a translated Mental Adjustment to HIV Scale, depression items from the Hopkins checklist and demographic questions. The factor analysis revealed four factors: (1) active coping, (2) cognitive–social adjustment, (3) hopelessness and (4) denial or avoidance. This reflects how mental adjustment to HIV can be conceptualized as both process and outcome in this context.

Culture also influences perceptions of personal body image and its perceived impact on health. Whaley et al. (2011) tested whether African-American adolescents accept larger body size more than their European-American counterparts. Data from the 2009 Youth Risk Behavior Survey showed that obese African-American adolescents reported significantly better physical health than obese European-American participants. However, obese African-Americans reported significantly poorer health when compared with healthy-weight participants. The authors suggested that health care professionals could consider within-race instead of between-race differences when discussing health risks associated with obesity among African-American adolescents.

COMPLEMENTARY AND ALTERNATIVE MEDICINE

The biomedical perspective has come to a position of dominance throughout the world, reflecting 'globalization' more generally. Alternative health care systems tend to be disparaged and marginalized by advocates of biomedicine. Based on a positivist, reductionist perspective, practitioners of biomedicine believe that the material existence of medical science is independent of any patient's psychological search for meaning, understanding and control. As such, alternative perspectives are seen as basically flawed. In spite of this resistance from orthodoxy, alternative professional systems of health care continue to exist in large parts of the world, especially in Asia. As migrants have moved to other countries they have taken their health beliefs with them. In the major Western metropolitan centres there is extensive availability of health care systems other than biomedicine. This has fed back into Western ways of thinking about health and illness, especially among those who are disenchanted with biomedicine. Increasingly, **complementary and alternative medicine** (CAM) is gaining popularity and respectability in Western health care. CAM encompasses all health systems and practices other than those of the established health system of a society.

CAM is viewed as one further example of patient empowerment, as evidenced by a statement made by EU Commissioner Tonio Borg (2013) to the European Parliament:

> Patient empowerment is on the increase. It progressively serves to put patients in the driver's seat – taking charge and control of their own health. Patients often know what treatment works for them, and which healthcare is efficient for their condition. This can include the use of complementary medicine.

In the USA, the National Center for Complementary and Alternative Medicine (NCCAM, 2013) categorizes CAM into two subgroups: (1) natural products; and (2) mind and body practices. *Natural products* often include the use of herbs, vitamins, minerals and probiotics. These products are marketed widely and are commonly sold as dietary supplements. *Mind and body practices* cover a diverse range of procedures that are often administered by a trained practitioner. Examples include acupuncture, massage therapy, meditation techniques, movement therapies (e.g. Feldenkrais method, Alexander technique, Pilates), relaxation techniques, spinal manipulation, tai chi, qi gong, reiki and hypnotherapy.

Harris et al. (2012) reviewed the 12-month prevalence of CAM use by the general public in 51 published reports from 49 surveys in 15 countries. Estimates of CAM use ranged from 9.8% to 76%; and from 1.8% to 48.7% for visits to CAM practitioners. In surveys using consistent measurement methods, CAM rates have been stable, particularly in Australia (49%, 52%, 52%; 1993, 2000, 2004) and USA (36%, 38%; 2002, 2007). The three highest rates of CAM use in this systematic review were reported in Japan (76%), South Korea (75%) and Malaysia (56%). More recently, Posadzki et al. (2013a) conducted a systematic review to examine the prevalence of CAM use among patients in the UK. The review included 89 surveys, with a total of 97,222 participants between January 2000 and October 2011. Findings showed that the average one-year prevalence of CAM use was 41.1%, while the average lifetime prevalence was 51.8%. Herbal medicine was the most popular CAM, followed by homeopathy, aromatherapy, massage and reflexology.

Herbal Medicine

Herbal medicine involves the use of plants and plant extracts to treat illnesses or to promote well-being. This practice has been used for thousands of years, with the first recorded use in China in 2800 BC (Brown, 2007). It is believed that this practice was derived from the Ayurvedic tradition and then later adopted by the Chinese, Greeks and Romans. With the growth of the pharmaceutical industry, herbal medicine can now be produced and marketed on a massive scale. In the UK, about 1 in 3 adults take herbal medicine (Posadzki et al., 2013b), while in the USA, it is about 20% (Bent, 2008). Some of the most commonly used herbal products, and their purpose, efficacy and risks, are summarized in Table 4.1.

More recent systematic reviews show inconsistent evidence on the efficacy of herbal medicine in treating various conditions. While some reviews did not have substantial evidence to support the use of herbal supplements during pregnancy (Dante et al., 2013) or to treat depression (Butler and Pilkington, 2013), some showed support for treatment of tic disorders (Yun et al., 2014), gout (Li et al., 2013) and irritable bowel disease (Ng et al., 2013). More recently, a systematic review by Li et al. (2014) showed how the use of herbal medicine can help to improve the quality of life among chronic heart failure patients. However, reviews that showed substantial findings also raised concerns regarding small sample sizes, high clinical heterogeneity, and poor methodological quality in some trials. We return here to a refrain from other chapters concerned with the evidence base for treatments: more large-scale randomized controlled trials (RCTs) are required to provide robust evidence on the efficacy of herbal medicine. At present, there is limited support for a few specific treatments but the evidence is inconclusive for many of the most popular herbal remedies.

Table 4.1 Commonly used herbal medicines

Herb	Purpose†	Evidence for efficacy‡	Risks	References
Echinacea	Upper respiratory tract infection	Inconclusive	Side effects similar to placebo	Lindeet et al. (2006)
Ginseng	Physical and cognitive performance	Inconclusive	Limited data; hyperactivity and restlessness in case reports	Vogler et al. (1999)
Ginkgo biloba	Dementia Claudication	Likely effective Likely effective	Side effects similar to placebo; case reports of bleeding	Oken et al. (1998); Pittler and Ernst (2000); Bentet et al. (2005); Birks and Grimley Evans (2009)
Garlic	Hyper-cholesterolaemia	Likely effective	Mild gastro-intestinal side effects and garlic odour; case reports of bleeding	Rose et al. (1990); Burnham (1995); Stevinson et al. (2000)
St. John's wort	Depression	Likely effective for mild–moderate depression	Drug interactions	Hammerness et al. (2003); Linde et al. (2008)
Peppermint	Upset stomach/ irritable bowel syndrome	Inconclusive	Limited data, but side effects appear to be mild	Pittler and Ernst (1998)
Ginger	Nausea	Inconclusive	No known side effects	Ernst and Pittler (2000); Rotblatt and Ziment (2002)
Soy	Menopausal symptoms	Not effective	Concerns regarding long-term oestrogenic effects	Lethaby et al. (2007); Taku et al. (2007)
	Hyper-cholesterolaemia	Effective		
Chamomile	Insomnia/ gastrointestinal problems	No high-quality data	Rare allergic reactions	Ulbricht and Basch (2005)
Kava kava	Anxiety	Likely effective	Case reports of severe hepatotoxicity	CDCP (2002); Pittler and Ernst (2003)

Source: adapted from Bent (2008: 856)

Data sources: † Rotblatt and Ziment (2002), Fugh-Berman (2003) and Ulbricht and Basch (2005); ‡ systematic review by Bent and Ko (2004)

Homeopathy

Homeopathy is a form of CAM which involves the use of highly diluted substances to trigger the body's natural healing system. It is based on the Latin principle *similia similibus curentur*, which means 'let like be cured by like'. This means that a substance which can cause symptoms when taken in large doses can also be used to treat the same symptoms when taken in smaller doses. Its origins can be traced back to the work of German physician, Samuel Hahnemann (1755–1843). During his time, medical treatments often relied on harsh procedures such as blood-letting, purging and the use of poisons. Hahnemann refused to use these techniques and experimented on himself and other healthy volunteers. He recorded the physiological effects of toxic materials such as mercury, arsenic and belladonna and then latter collated reports of 'cured symptoms' based on homeopathic prescriptions of these substances. In recent years, more than 2,500 homeopathic medicines have been recorded (Whitmarsh, 2007).

In the UK, there are currently four homeopathic hospitals, in London, Bristol, Liverpool and Glasgow. It is much more widely used on the European continent especially in France and Germany. Homeopathy has been used for a variety of health conditions, including asthma, ear infections, hay fever, allergies, dermatitis, arthritis and high blood pressure, and for mental health conditions such as depression, stress and anxiety. However, recent systematic reviews on the effectiveness of homeopathy showed inconclusive results and trials are of poor quality (Ernst, 2012; Saha et al., 2013; Peckham et al., 2013). Posadzki et al. (2012) have also commented on the potential harm of homeopathy to patients in direct and indirect ways.

Aromatherapy

Aromatherapy involves the use of essential oils from plant extracts for therapeutic purposes. This practice dates back to ancient Egyptian, Chinese and Indian traditions. French chemist and scholar, René-Maurice Gattefossé (1881–1950), is considered the father of modern aromatherapy. He discovered the healing properties of lavender when he accidentally burned his hand while working in his laboratory. He continued to experiment on essential oils including thyme, lemon and clove and used these with First World War soldiers as antiseptics. In recent years, aromatherapy is being used for stress and pain relief, headaches, digestive and menstrual problems. The essential oils can be massaged into the skin, added to warm bath water, blended into lotions or creams, or inhaled through a diffuser, vaporizer or candles. Consumers can buy oils at pharmacies or health shops or attend an aromatherapy session with a trained therapist. However, as with other CAMs, systematic reviews on the efficacy of aromatherapy have produced inconclusive results (Hur et al., 2012; Lee et al., 2012).

Reflexology

Reflexology involves the application of pressure and massage to specific reflex areas in the body. These reflex areas are usually on the feet, but can also be applied on the hands and ears.

It is based on the belief that certain areas of the hands and feet correspond to other parts of the body. It is believed that accumulated waste can be felt in these areas and thus massaging these can help to dissolve blockages in the body to encourage the free flow of vital energy and to restore the balance between the yin and yang. Reflexology is currently being applied to relieve symptoms of various chronic health conditions such as asthma, back pain, irritable bowel disorder, headaches and stress (Skinner, 2007). A recent systematic review has shown that reflexology can be effective in treating insomnia (Yeung et al., 2012). However, authors also advised that this conclusion may need to be treated with caution due to methodological limitations of the studies.

Perspectives on CAM

Debates around the efficacy of CAM have polarized researchers. The most simple, basic explanation for the popular appeal of CAM is the **placebo effect**. The generous time, warm glow of personal attention and friendly conversation received by each individual patient with many CAM practitioners compares favourably to the brief and business-like encounters of mainstream medicine. This aspect seems particularly true in the case of cancer. For example, one Australian study found that: 'CAM use appeared to be associated with high patient acceptance and satisfaction which was not related to either cancer diagnosis or prognosis' (Wilkinson and Stevens, 2014: 139). Another positive factor in favour of CAM is that patients: 'find these health care alternatives to be more congruent with their own values, beliefs, and philosophical orientations toward health and life' (Astin, 1998: 1548). Arguably, the specific treatment effects per se are of marginal relevance. In light of the inconclusive evidence base, Segar (2012) outlined two main discussions around this topic. First, there were concerns regarding evidence-based medicine and whether CAM can be assessed appropriately using the currently available methods which are based on positivist, biomedical approaches that may be incongruent with the underlying principles of CAM. Second, there were questions concerning whether CAM should be advocated considering that its effect may be no different from a placebo. While some commentators are concerned that CAM is pseudo-scientific, MacArtney and Wahlberg (2014) argued that 'this form of problematization can be described as a flight from social science' (p. 114) and could negatively represent CAM users as 'duped, ignorant, irrational or immoral' (p. 114). While there is insufficient evidence from RCTs to support the efficacy of CAM, findings from qualitative research suggest that the use of CAM can promote feelings of control, empowerment and agency (Sointu, 2013).

Contrary to the polarized views among researchers, Segar (2012) found through a qualitative study that therapists and patients tend to be 'pragmatic pluralists' who have opinions as to when CAM may be appropriate to use or not. In relation to patients' perspectives towards CAM integration in primary care, findings from a mixed methods study by Jong et al. (2012) suggest that a majority of patients preferred a GP who is informed about CAM and if necessary, works alongside CAM practitioners. Furthermore, a systematic review by Nissen et al. (2012) suggested that in many European countries, many hold positive attitudes towards CAM and would like to widen access and provision, including clear regulatory frameworks to ensure quality and safety. Reliable information and more involvement from biomedical health care professionals were called for to help patients to make informed choices about CAM.

In the UK, the Department of Health provides clinical guidelines for health care professionals on CAM. A recent systematic review by Lorenc et al. (2014) showed that a total of 60 guidelines have been produced in relation to CAM therapies. About 44% were inconclusive, mostly due to insufficient empirical evidence, while there was almost an equal proportion of guidelines either recommending or advising against CAM (19%). Recently, the WHO launched a Strategy on Traditional Medicine (2014–2023) to support the development of policies and action plans to strengthen the role of CAM to improve health, well-being and people-centred health care, and to promote quality and safety of CAM through regulation and better training and skills development of practitioners. The strategy aims to build a knowledge base around CAM, regulate products, therapies and practitioners, and integrate CAM into national health care systems.

Changing Cultures and Health

In a world of rapid change and interpenetration of cultural groups and belief systems and an increasingly globalized society, health psychologists need to recognize the complexity and diversity of dynamic and interlocking systems rather than assume that our health belief systems are fixed (MacLachlan, 2000).

BOX 4.1
THE FALSE STEREOTYPE OF THE 'DRUNKEN ABORIGINAL'

Traditionally Aboriginal people consumed weak alcohol made from various plants. Their problems with alcohol began with the colonial invasions of the eighteenth century. Contrary to all popular stereotypes, surveys find that roughly similar proportions of Aboriginal people drink alcohol as the European colonial population. The media distort the facts and reinforce stereotyping.

Evidence shows that the lifetime risk of alcohol consumption for Australian Aboriginal and Torres Strait Islanders is similar to that of the non-indigenous population for both males and females. Similar proportions of Aboriginal and Torres Strait Islander people and non-indigenous people of the same age and sex exceed lifetime risk guidelines, apart from women aged 55-plus where Aboriginal and Torres Strait Islanders are significantly *less* likely than non-indigenous women to exceed lifetime risk guidelines (7% compared with 10%) (Australian Bureau of Statistics, 2014).

So where did the false stereotyping come from? One answer lies in early colonial art. The lithograph was created by Augustus Earle (1793–1838) and printed by C. Hullmandel, London, in 1830. A group of bedraggled indigenous Australians are sitting in a Sydney street. They wear ragged remnants of European clothing or simply material wraps. Empty 'grog' bottles are scattered on the ground. Behind them there is a two-storey hotel with a kangaroo sign and another sign on the side of the building says 'George Street'. Fashionably dressed British settlers promenade down the street or stand near the hotel. Beyond is a glimpse of Sydney Harbour, with masts and rigging of sailing ships. The picture references the 'grog culture' of the early colonial years – 'grog' being a mid-eighteenth-century term meaning cheap alcohol; two men gather round a bucket of 'bull', a cheap source of alcohol made by soaking and fermenting old sugar bags.

Indigenous Health

There are almost 400 million indigenous people from thousands of different cultures in all continents of the planet (Gracey and King, 2009). While indigenous communities cannot be encapsulated within a single definition, the United Nations (2009) used Martinez Cobo's (1987) conceptualization of indigenous groups as:

> peoples and nations which, having a historical continuity with pre-invasion and pre-colonial societies that developed on their territories, consider themselves distinct from other sectors of the societies now prevailing on those territories, or parts of them. They form at present non-dominant sectors of society and are determined to preserve, develop and transmit to future generations their ancestral territories, and their ethnic identity, as the basis of their continued existence as peoples, in accordance with their own cultural patterns, social institutions and legal system.
>
> (United Nations, 2009: 4)

Generally, indigenous people experience poorer health outcomes than their non-indigenous counterparts (Stephens et al., 2005). They have lower life expectancies and mortality rates for specific diseases such as heart disease, tuberculosis, cancer, respiratory disease, stroke and diabetes (Horton, 2006; Woods et al., 2012; Tollefson et al., 2013). Even after adjustment for stage at diagnosis, treatment, and comorbidity, non-indigenous cancer patients survive longer than indigenous ones

(Valery et al., 2006). Indigenous populations are six times more likely to die from injuries (Desapriya et al., 2006), and have worse access to health services and education (Horton, 2006; Stephens et al., 2006). The alleged health profile of indigenous groups has been distorted by racism and racial stereotypes. This is illustrated by the alleged alcoholism rates of Australian Aboriginals (Box 4.1). Similar stereotyping occurs regarding the alcohol use of Native Americans. Direct comparisons to published alcohol consumption data from other US populations indicated that American Indians in two reservation samples may be *less likely to use alcohol* than are others in the United States. However, among American Indian drinkers, more alcohol was consumed per drinking occasion (Beals et al., 2003).

Poorer health outcomes are evident among indigenous communities in Australia, New Zealand and the Pacific (Anderson et al., 2006), Latin America and the Caribbean (Montenegro and Stephens, 2006), and Africa (Ohenjo et al., 2006).

Governmental efforts aim to address inequalities that disadvantage indigenous communities but, in some instances, these efforts are tokenistic or symbolic in nature. Living with a legacy of conquest and culture, they may even continue to subjugate indigenous people to unjust and unfair economic and educational systems (Fredericks et al., 2014). Stephens and colleagues (2005) pointed out that interventions targeting indigenous communities often fail because of a lack of understanding of indigenous notions of health. Indigenous health belief systems are typically characterized by 'a combination of practices and knowledge about the human body, and coexistence with other human beings, with nature, and with spiritual beings' (Cunningham, 2009: 157). It is important to recognize indigenous ways of knowing and to value indigenous stories and narratives within their socio-cultural context (Kendall et al., 2013).

In designing interventions, it is essential to actively involve community members in action plans to address issues. **Participatory action research** can be used to facilitate the process of surfacing knowledge that is relevant, respectful and useful (Tobias et al., 2013; Starkes and Baydala, 2014; see also Chapters 5 and 14). The process of involving indigenous participants helps to establish rapport and trust, as well as facilitate equal power sharing between researchers and community members (Christopher et al., 2011). Genuine participation helps to develop personal and community skills that can strengthen community capacity. Enabling community members to engage meaningfully in the research process also gives them a sense of ownership of the project and can help to raise critical awareness (Kelly et al., 2012). This can enhance social participation and encourage community engagement through dialogue and action to transform shared social realities (Campbell and Scott, 2011).

Adams et al. (2012) used the PhotoVoice method to facilitate action with an urban Aboriginal community to explore the meaning of food and food insecurity. There were ten participants, most of whom were women in their twenties and thirties, with one older woman and one young man. The participants received photography training with an Aboriginal photographer and were given one week to take photographs of the food they eat, food sources, cooking methods, people they eat with, and other things they think are important about food. Then the group met to discuss the photographs and common themes. Findings suggested that food selection in this community was influenced by family harmony and collectivism. Although participants expressed pride for their hunter-gatherer heritage, it seemed that cheap high-carbohydrate and fatty foods were also commonly chosen to satisfy hunger. Based on the community-based knowledge generated from this research, action recommendations were then developed that included developing a cooking television series, a specialized cook book, healthy food plates and social cooking opportunities. The process involved working in partnership with the Wathaurong Aboriginal Cooperative, which helped to ensure that the action plans were relevant to the community's needs.

In another Australian study, Thompson et al. (2013) facilitated an arts-based participatory action research to explore the experiences and meaning of physical activity in two remote Northern Territory communities in Australia. Semi-structured interviews were conducted with community members ($n = 23$) and supplemented by five commissioned paintings by community-based artists and ethnographic observations. Physical activities were often linked with work, diet, social relationships and being active 'on country'. They also were associated with educating younger generations about indigenous traditions, as exemplified in the quote below on bush walking:

> That's why we have to take them [kids, bush walking] so the old people can show them the country and the names of the place. They need to talk about and learn about the name of the places and who belongs to that place. That's why myself and [my husband] always join in for the bush walks so when we go there they always tell us, 'well this is your great, great, great, grandmother country, or grandfather'. Like when we stayed there, [at the] first camp, we told [them] 'this place here you call your grandfather country'.
>
> (Bininj woman, aged 26–35, quoted in Thompson et al., 2013: 7)

Culturally appropriate physical activities such as bush walking, dancing and art making contribute to health promotion of the community. It is important that indigenous beliefs, knowledge and traditions are considered in the process. Furthermore, social and political issues, including those that are related with racism and discrimination, need to be taken into account since these may compound experiences and access to health care and promotion (Denison et al., 2014). Ranzijn (2010) raised concerns that the concept of 'active ageing' could inadvertently devalue the life experiences of Australian Aboriginal elders. He argued that expecting older adults to continue to be physically active could marginalize such groups. Thus culturally appropriate ageing policies and alternative conceptions of ageing (e.g. 'ageing well' or 'authentic ageing') were recommended to promote diversity and social inclusion.

Working in the Philippines, Estacio and Marks (2012) facilitated a participatory action research project with the indigenous Ayta community to generate community knowledge about notions and experiences of health to inform action plans. The research methods were culturally sensitive and people-oriented (Pe-Pua, 2006) and guided by the principles of *Sikolohiyang Pilipino* (Enriquez, 1993). These included community visits, *kwentuhan* (story-telling sessions), workshops and stakeholder meetings. Findings suggested that the Ayta community have a holistic concept of health that incorporates factors such as livelihood stability, good social relations, cleanliness, and spiritual wellness. Health is deeply embedded within their socio-economic and political environment wherein everyday discourses revolved around the need to generate sufficient income to sustain their families' daily needs. In the process, health promotion and education activities were developed through an alternative learning system that integrated indigenous culture-based livelihood and literacy initiatives into the action recommendations.

Racism and Health

Racism contributes to poor mental and physical health among migrants, ethnic minority groups and indigenous peoples. Research evidence suggests that everyday experiences of discrimination are related to stress that could potentially lead to chronic illnesses (Gee et al., 2007; Williams et al., 1997). Systematic reviews examining the impact of racial discrimination on health have shown how perceived discrimination is linked with physical ill health, including cardiovascular disease, hypertension, respiratory conditions, obesity and diabetes (Cuffee et al., 2012; Nadimpalli and Hutchinson, 2012; Dolezsar et al., 2014). Strong associations were also shown between racial discrimination and common mental health problems (Schulz et al., 2006). Interpersonal racism and perceived racism can increase the risk of developing psychiatric disorders even after controlling for demographic factors (Karlson et al., 2005). More recently, Anderson (2013) used data from the 2004 Behavioral Risk Factor Surveillance System (BRFSS) to examine the relationship between stress symptoms from perceived racism and overall health ($n = 32{,}585$). The analyses suggest that stress from perceived racism can have substantial negative consequences that contribute to poor mental and physical health days in adults. Among young people, Grollman (2012) used data from the African-American Youth Culture Survey ($n = 1{,}052$) to examine the prevalence, distribution, and mental and physical health consequences of multiple forms of perceived discrimination. Findings suggest that young people from disadvantaged backgrounds are more susceptible from experiencing multiple forms of discrimination than their more privileged counterparts. As with the findings from the adult population, a systematic review showed that the relationship between perceived racial discrimination and mental health can be observed among children and young people from minority ethnic groups (Priest et al., 2013).

Another response to the chronic stress of racism is smoking. Low socio-economic status, racial discrimination, and low acculturation (i.e. being immersed in African-American culture and communities) are known to be the major sociocultural correlates of smoking among African-American adults (Landrine and Corral, 2015). From a study with a random sample of 2,118 adult African-Americans in California, Landrine and Corral studied the influence of all three variables together. They reported that low education and low acculturation predicted smoking but, surprisingly, racial discrimination did not. For women, low acculturation was the sole predictor of smoking, whereas for men, socio-economic status variables were the sole predictors. Therefore, as low acculturation may be associated with smoking among African-American women only, Landrine and Corral suggested that culturally specific smoking cessation programmes designed for low-acculturated African-Americans might be effective for African-American women alone.

DeLilly and Flaskerud (2012) suggested that the poor health outcomes related to perceived racial discrimination are associated with negative feelings of low self-worth and subordination. This can sometimes be manifested as depression or can be expressed through anger, hostility and aggression. Cultural values further complicate the impact of perceived racial discrimination on health outcomes by placing the emphasis on individual determination and hard work (i.e. the belief that individuals can succeed if they have the will power or persevere enough).

Imposing culturally insensitive health promotion activities may exacerbate the social exclusion that is already being experienced by minority ethnic groups. Ochieng (2013) conducted a qualitative study exploring the beliefs and perceptions of healthy lifestyle practices among African-Caribbean men and women. In-depth interviews were conducted with 18 participants from the north of England. Findings suggest that participants felt that messages around healthy lifestyle practices were not applicable to their everyday lived experiences since these often ignored issues related with their experiences of social exclusion, racism and ethnic identity. Health promotion programmes that use individualistic approaches are inappropriate for, and isolate, those from ethnic minority communities who practise more collectivist traditions to express their beliefs, values and identity. Thus campaigns that try to promote healthy lifestyles need to consider socio-economic and cultural contexts, including issues related with disadvantage, racism and marginalization to enable African-American and other minority ethnic groups to incorporate these messages and practices into their everyday lives (see Chapter 14).

Landrine (1997) criticized studies of North American health beliefs that have largely ignored the distinctive culture of African-Americans. African slaves maintained their pre-slavery health beliefs, practices and indigenous healers. When they gained emancipation African-Americans found they were denied access to medical care. As a consequence they relied on their indigenous healers and over time developed a unique African-American folk medicine. She suggested that, in contemporary North America, many people from African backgrounds are returning to this medical system as they feel rejected or excluded by what they perceive as the racism of white American health care.

Representations of minority ethnic groups play a role in this process. For example, in a study exploring the impact of social constructions of ethnic identities on community participation, Campbell and McLean (2002, 2003) found that stereotypical representations of ethnic minority groups acted as a barrier for community members to engage with local community networks. The media contributes to this process in the way it portrays particular communities in society (Nairn et al., 2006). An open-peer commentary in the *Journal of Health Psychology* raised a debate concerning racist humour in the media and what health psychologists can contribute to challenge such oppressive social practices (see Box 4.2).

BOX 4.2
OPEN-PEER COMMENTARY ON RACIST HUMOUR, THE MEDIA AND HEALTH

This debate was sparked by the controversial airing of the BBC comedy show 'Harry and Paul' which portrayed a Filipino domestic worker as a sex object. Outraged members of the Filipino community in London demanded an apology from the BBC and the producers of the show for inciting racial discrimination. It has been argued that the sketch in question insensitively touched on social issues that are widely experienced by vulnerable migrant communities (e.g. human rights abuses, third world poverty and labour migration) (Estacio, 2009). Although it was generally acknowledged that racist humour in the media is unacceptable, Hodgetts and Stolte (2009) highlighted the complexity of media content which can contain both racist and anti-racist social representations and warned health psychologists not to overstate the negative influence of the media on racism in society. Nonetheless, it was agreed in these discussions that health psychologists need to take a more active stance in challenging oppressive social representation and its consequences by prioritizing 'concrete', real-world social issies (Cornish, 2009) and by carrying out research at micro (McVittie and Goodall, 2009), community (Stephens, 2009), and macro levels (MacLachlan, 2009).

Source: *Journal of Health Psychology* (2009)

Culturally Competent Health care Systems

In the ever changing demographic and cultural trends of 'globalized' society, health care systems need to be able to adapt flexibly to such changes and develop **cultural competence**.

Culturally competent health care involves developing (1) *culturally sensitive staff* who are able to reflect about their own beliefs and practices and acknowledge diversity in the community, and (2) *culturally appropriate materials, activities and systems* that address linguistic, cultural and social barriers. Cultural competence in health care asserts the importance of health service users and providers being able to communicate clearly with each other. As Anderson et al. (2003) argued, 'when clients do not understand what their health care providers are telling them, and providers either do not speak the client's language or are insecure to cultural differences, then the quality of health care can be compromised' (p. 68). This resonates with key ideas of effective communication and the role of **health literacy** in health care and promotion (see Chapter 11). Training health care professionals to develop skills that enable them to deal with communication issues associated with cultural, linguistic and health literacy differences may be a good way to reduce inequities in health (Lie et al., 2012). Culturally competent health care systems can do this by helping health care professionals to develop cultural sensitivity, knowledge and skills and by instilling processes that will enable them to engage meaningfully with culturally diverse patients (Anderson et al., 2003). Systematic reviews suggest that interventions that aim to improve cultural competence among health care professionals can help to increase their knowledge of cultural issues in health care (Renzaho et al., 2013) and improve patient and clinical health outcomes (Truong et al., 2014).

In addition to culturally competent health care, diversity and inclusivity can be promoted in other social contexts. For example, Andreouli et al. (2014) explored the role of schools in promoting inclusive communities. The authors argued that intercultural exchange can be promoted by examining how communities resist stigma and discrimination on a local level. Whilst starting on a micro level, such approaches can be endorsed to build the foundations of health-promoting communities.

FUTURE RESEARCH

1. Through access to historical documents, research psychologists can assist understanding of the evolution of health beliefs.
2. Understanding popular health beliefs requires an appreciation of their social and cultural context.
3. The increasing development of alternative health care in Western society requires ongoing research.
4. Comprehensive and accurate measurement of perceived discrimination and its mechanisms that contribute to poor health.

SUMMARY

1. Human thought and practices are culturally immersed.
2. The Western view of health has moved through various stages from the classic to the religious and then the scientific.
3. The scientific view of health, or biomedicine, is the dominant view in contemporary society but other health belief systems remain popular.
4. Traditional Chinese Medicine remains popular in China and among Chinese migrants in other societies.
5. Ayurvedic medicine remains popular in parts of southern Asia.
6. In Africa a wide variety of health belief systems emphasize spiritual aspects and a communal orientation.
7. In contemporary society there is increasing interest in various complementary and alternative (CAM) therapies such as herbal medicine, homeopathy, aromatherapy and reflexology.
8. While debates are on-going about the efficacy of CAM, guidelines and policies are being developed to ensure quality and safety.
9. Interventions aiming to promote indigenous health need to reflect the holistic notion of health among these communities and the voice of the community itself.
10. Racism continues to contribute to poor health among migrants, ethnic minority groups and indigenous peoples.
11. Culturally competent health care must aim to adapt to changing demographic and cultural trends

5 A–Z OF RESEARCH METHODS AND ISSUES IN HEALTH PSYCHOLOGY

OUTLINE

In this chapter we present an A–Z of methods and issues within health psychology research. Not all letters have an associated method, but those that do generally fall into one of three categories: quantitative, qualitative or action research. Quantitative researchers place emphasis on reliable and valid measurement in controlled experiments, trials and surveys. Qualitative researchers use interviews, focus groups, narratives or texts to explore health and illness concepts and experience. Action researchers facilitate change processes, improvement, empowerment and emancipation.

INTRODUCTION

As the field grows, health psychologists generate a diverse array of research questions. These questions require a wide range of research methods to answer them. Human curiosity to understand how things work remains the overarching motive for any new piece of research. Theories, models and hypotheses play a crucial role in guiding that curiosity along worthwhile avenues. We would not know where to start without these guiding theories, models and hypotheses. Using sound methodology is of equal importance in testing theories and models, putting theory into practice, and evaluating the consequences of doing so. In applying health psychology in making interventions or taking actions to produce change, we need to know what works, what doesn't work, and why.

Many of psychology's traditional methods and research designs are quantitative, placing emphasis on reliable and valid measurement in controlled investigations with experiments, trials and surveys. Multiple sources of such evidence are integrated or synthesized using systematic reviews and meta-analysis. Case studies are more suited to unique, one-off situations that merit investigation. Qualitative methods use interviews, focus groups, narratives or texts to explore health and illness concepts and experience. Action research enables change processes to feed back into plans for improvement, empowerment and emancipation. Interest in qualitative methods and action research has been increasing. These different kinds of method complement each other, and all are necessary if we want to a complete picture of psychology and health. Which method is appropriate in any given situation depends entirely upon the question being asked and the context.

Research in health psychology has been growing exponentially. Figure 5.1 plots the growth in studies over the period 1990–2009. The ISI Web of Knowledge database was searched using each of the following main terms: self-efficacy, cultural differences, poverty, spirituality, cognitive behavioural therapy, motivational interviewing and mindfulness, in combination with all of the

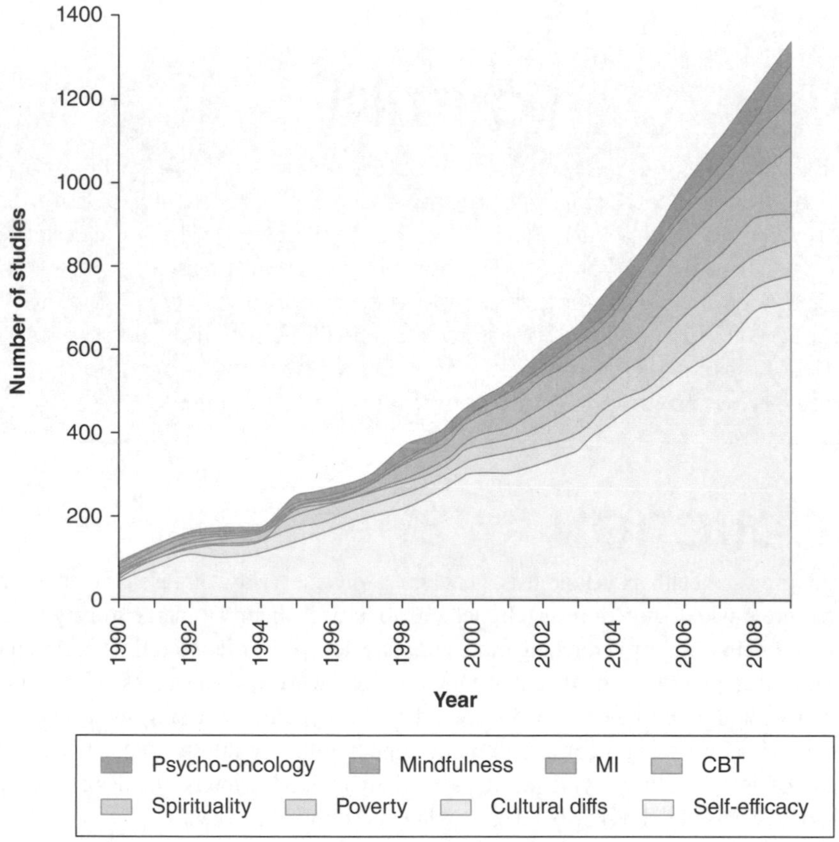

Figure 5.1 Trends in numbers of health psychology studies, 1990–2009

Source: Marks (2013)

health issues of drinking, smoking, pain, weight control, diet, exercise or condoms. Another search counted the items in the field of psycho-oncology. In total, approximately 8,000 published studies in these topic areas appeared in print in 2009 as compared to about 800 in 1990, a ten-fold increase in just 20 years! That level of growth continues, and there is no sign of any levelling off. Each study in the survey used a specific participant or patient population (P), an intervention or issue of interest (I), a comparison of interest (C) and an outcome of interest (O) or 'PICO'. Every study also used a specific research method to collect the data.

The sections below present an A–Z of the most commonly used research methods and issues that arise in health psychology. The majority of studies use the methods or designs or approaches described below.

ACTION RESEARCH

Action research is about the process of change and what stimulates it. The investigator acts as a facilitator, collaborator or change-agent who works with the stakeholders in a community or organization to help a situation to develop or make a change of direction. Action research is particularly suited to organizational and consultancy work when a system or service requires improvements. In a community it aims to be emancipatory, helping to empower members to take more control over the way things work in their local community.

Action research can be traced back to the Gestalt psychology of Kurt Lewin (1936): 'Every psychological event depends upon the state of the person and at the same time the state of the environment . . . One can hope to understand the forces that govern behaviour only if one includes in the representation the whole psychological situation' (p. 12). Lewin later wrote about what he called 'Feedback problems of social diagnosis and action' (1947) and presented a diagram of his method (see Figure 5.2).

A series of action steps with feedback loops allow each action step to be 'reconnoitred' before further action steps. The military tone of Lewin's terminology may have come from his First World War experience when he served in the German army and wrote afterwards about the soldier's experience of trench warfare. Disciples of Lewin (e.g. Argyris, 1975) interpret Lewin in terms of increasing collaboration of community members, stakeholders and researchers in the design and interpretation of the study. Feedback of early results to participants often leads to redesign in light of consultation about the findings.

Participant action research (PAR) is a prominent method in community health psychology (Campbell and Cornish, 2014). In PAR, researchers share power and control with participants and need to tolerate the uncertainty that rolls out of power-sharing. PAR is a suitable research approach in direct social actions that are organized to create change in entrenched scenarios where power imbalances are disadvantaging many of the actors. For example, Yeich (1996) described how housing campaigns with groups for homeless people involved assisting in the organization of demonstrations and working with the media to raise broad awareness of people's housing needs. Action research takes time, resources, creativity and courage. It requires collaboration with different agencies. It is an approach that does not follow a straight line but proceeds in a halting,

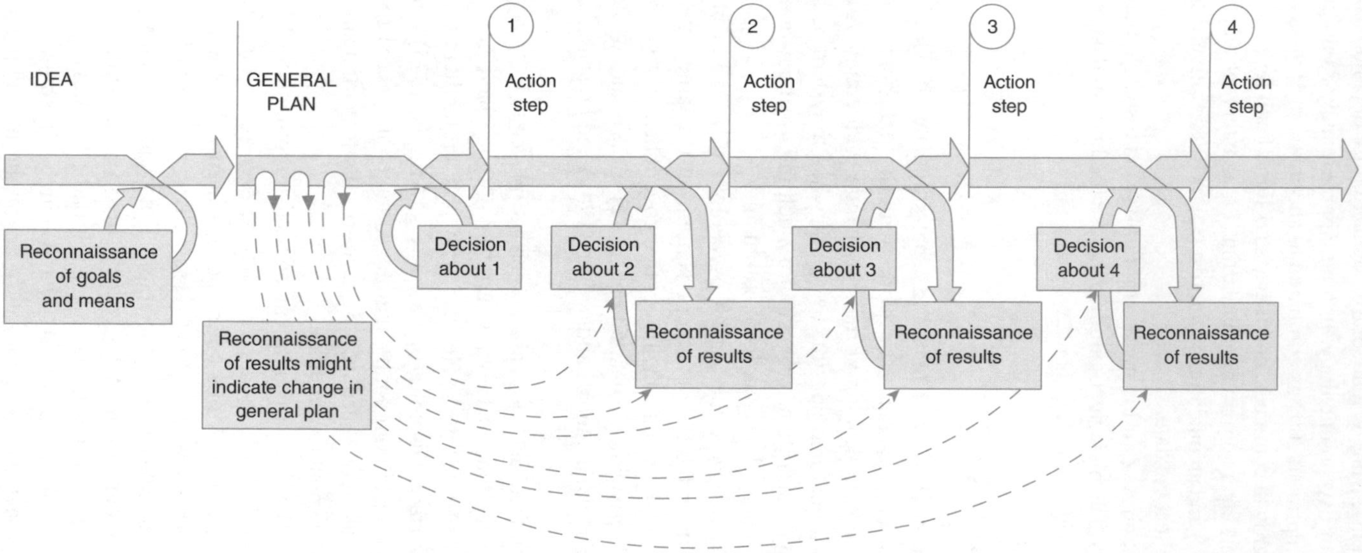

Figure 5.2 Planning, fact-finding and execution as described by Kurt Lewin (1947)

zig zag format. Often there are personal challenges and disappointments for the researcher who must devote substantial emotional and intellectual energy to the project (Brydon-Miller, 2004). Cornish et al. (2014) proposed the Occupy movement as a paradigm example of community action that they labelled 'trusting the process' (see Chapter 14).

PAR researchers also use arts and performance as vehicles for envisioning and promoting change. Two examples are the photo-novella (Wang et al., 1996; Lykes, 2001) and PhotoVoice (Haaken and O'Neill, 2014; Vaughan, 2014). These techniques create a space where people meaningfully participate and exert control in the research process. Research participants can reflect on how they make their way within the community through photography. By taking and displaying photographs people can became more reflectively aware and are able to mobilize around personal and local issues. Tucker and Smith (2014) developed a Lewinian approach to the investigation of life situations and a specific example of self-care in a service user's home. The service-user's own photographs indicated the possibility of open and closed regions, boundaries, and multiple psychological life spaces. A study of accidents in a fishing community used the PAR approach (Murray and Tilley, 2004) as did Gray and his colleagues (Gray et al., 2001; Gray and Sinding, 2002) by transforming interviews with cancer patients into plays that were subsequently performed to support groups.

BETWEEN GROUPS DESIGNS

A **between groups design** allocates matched groups of people to different treatments. If the measures are taken at one time this is called a cross-sectional design, in contrast to a longitudinal design where the groups are tested at two or more time-points. When we are comparing only treatment groups, a failure to find a difference between them on the outcome measure(s) might be for one of three reasons: they are equally effective; they are equally ineffective; they are equally harmful. For this reason, one of the groups should be a control group that will enable us to discover whether the treatment(s) show a different effect from no treatment.

Ethical issues arise over the use of control groups. Not treating someone in need of treatment is unacceptable. However, if there is genuine uncertainty about what works best, it is better to compare the treatments with a control condition than to continue for ever applying a treatment that may be less effective than another. Once it has been determined which therapy is the most effective, this can be offered to the control group and to all future patients (Clark-Carter and Marks, 2004).

The choice of the control condition is important. The group should receive the same amount of attention as those in the treatment condition(s). This type of control is known as a placebo control (see below) as treatment itself could have a non-specific effect to 'please' the client and enhance his/her well-being.

If all of the various groups' responses are measured only after an intervention, then we haven't really measured change. All groups, including the control group, could have changed but from different starting positions, and failing to find a difference between the groups after the treatment could miss this. We can help to deal with this problem by using a mixed design when we measure all groups before and after the treatment. However, we would be introducing some of the difficulties mentioned above for a cross-over or within-subjects design (Clark-Carter, 1997).

CASE STUDIES

The term 'case study' is used to describe a detailed descriptive account of an individual, group or collective. The purpose of such case studies is to provide a 'thick description' (Geertz, 1973) of a phenomenon that would not be obtained by the usual quantitative or qualitative approaches. It requires the researcher to be expansive in the type of data collected with a deliberate aim to link the person with the context, e.g. the sick person in the family. The researcher usually attempts to provide a chronological account of the evolution of the phenomenon from the perspective of the central character.

A challenge for the researcher is in establishing the boundaries of the case. These need to be flexible to ensure that all information relevant to the case under investigation is collected. The major strength of the case study is the integration of actor and context and the developmental perspective. Thus the phenomenon under investigation is not dissected but rather maintains its integrity or wholeness and it is possible to map its changes over time.

There are several different types of case study. The empirical case study is grounded in the data. The theoretical case is an exemplar for a process that has already been clarified. The researcher can conduct interviews, or repeat interviews and observe the case in different settings. The process of analysis can be considered the process of shaping the case. Thus the researcher selects certain pieces of information and discards others so as to present a more integrated case. One example is De Visser and Smith's (2006) investigation of the links between masculine identity and social behaviour with a 19-year-old man living in London. The case study indicated the perceived importance of health-related behaviours such as drinking, drug use, physical activity, sport and sexual behaviour in the construction of a masculine identity.

CONFIDENCE INTERVAL

A confidence interval (CI) is the interval around the mean of a sample that one can state with a known probability contains the mean of the population. A population parameter is always estimated using a sample. The reliability of the estimate varies according to sample size. A confidence interval specifies a range of values where a parameter is estimated to lie. The narrower the interval, then the more reliable the estimate. Typically the 95% or 99% CI is stated in the results of a study that has obtained a representative sample of values, e.g. the mean heart rate for a sample might be 75.0 with a 95% CI of 72.6 to 77.4. Confidence intervals are normally reported in tables or graphs along with point estimates of the parameters, to indicate the reliability of the estimates.

CROSS-OVER OR WITHIN-PARTICIPANTS DESIGNS

The cross-over or within-participants design is used when the same people provide measures of a dependent variable at more than one time and differences between the measures at the different times are recorded. An example would be a measure taken before an intervention (pre-treatment) and again after the intervention (post-treatment). Such a design minimizes the effect of individual differences as each person acts as his or her own control.

There are a number of problems with this design. Any change in the measure of the dependent variable may be due to other factors having changed. For example, an intervention designed to improve quality of life among patients in a long-stay ward of a hospital may be accompanied by other changes, for example, a new set of menus introduced by the catering department. In addition, the difference may be due to some aspect of the measuring instrument. If the same measure is being taken on both occasions, the fact that it has been taken twice may be the reason that the result has changed. We have already discussed the most basic problem in psychological measurement in Chapter 1, the fact that usually we have no proof that the attribute we are measuring is quantitative in the first place.

Failure to find a difference between the two occasions doesn't tell you very much; in a worsening situation the intervention still might have been effective in preventing things from worsening more than they have already. The counterfactual scenario in which nothing changed is an unknown entity. Additionally, if a cross-over design is used to compare two or more treatments, the particular results could be an artefact of the order in which the treatments were given. To counter order effects one can use a baseline or 'washout period' before and after treatment periods. Also one can randomly assign people to different orders or, if one is interested in seeing whether order does have an effect, then a more systematic allocation of participants to different orders can be employed: for example, if there are only two conditions participants could be alternately placed in the two possible orders, or if there are more than two conditions a Latin square design can be employed (Clark-Carter and Marks, 2004).

CROSS-SECTIONAL DESIGNS

Cross-sectional studies obtain responses from respondents on one occasion only. With appropriate randomized sampling methods, the sample can be assumed to be a representative cross-section of the population under study and it is possible to make comparisons between sub-groups (e.g. males vs. females, older vs. younger people, etc.). However, cause and effect can never be inferred between one variable and another and it is impossible to say whether the observed associations are caused by a third background variable not measured in the study.

Cross-sectional designs are popular because they are relatively inexpensive in time and resources. However, there are serious problems of interpretation, not only about causality, but about generalizability whenever there is doubt about the randomness and representativeness of the samples. Many studies are done with students as participants and we can never be sure that the use of a non-random, non-representative sample of students is methodologically rigorous. The ecological validity of the findings is strongly contentious in the sense that they are unlikely to be replicated in a random sample from the general population. We recommend that any study with a non-random student sample be repeated with a representative sample from which generalizations to a known population can be made.

Cross-sectional designs are also unsuited to studies of behaviour change and provide weak evidence in the testing of theories.

DIARIES AND BLOGS

Diaries and **diary techniques** frequently have been used as a method for collecting information about temporal changes in health status. These diaries can be prepared by the researcher or participant or both, and can be quantitative or qualitative or both. They can be compared to the time charts that have been used by health professionals for generations to track changes in the health status of individuals. Blogs also provide a rich source of data on different illnesses and conditions and lay ideas on 'healthy living'.

A summary of the current uses of the diary in health research is reproduced in Table 5.1.

Diaries and blogs have benefits for the participant irrespective of the researcher (Murray, 2009). Research by Pennebaker (1995) and others has demonstrated that expressive writing can be psychologically beneficial. A series of studies has provided evidence that journal writing can lead to reduction in illness symptoms and in the use of health services (e.g. Smyth et al., 1999). There are a number of explanations for this including release of emotional energy, cognitive processing and assistance with narrative restructuring.

Table 5.1 The applicability of a diary or blog in health psychology research

Type of diary or blog	Description of use	Participant(s)	Reference
Validation of questionnaires	Examining the same behavioural change or psychological characteristics as recorded in diary	Chronic headache sufferers	Stewart et al. (1999)
Reflective understanding	Personal and scholarly reflections on experience of struggling with meaning-making	Cancer sufferer	Willig (2009)
Communication device	Provides a voice for the patient and an insight into how the patient interprets illness and treatment	Patients with longstanding illness	Stensland and Malterud (1999)
Evolving methodology	Provides an opportunity to gain qualitative data that can inform hypothesis generation and testing	ICU patients and families	Berghom et al. (1999)
Developing or testing theories	Constructs from a theoretical model and behaviour are measured	Patients	Ferguson and Chandler (2005)

Type of diary or blog	Description of use	Participant(s)	Reference
Tracking/time series	Psychological, behavioural and physiological data can be collected to map changes over time	Non-clinical and clinical samples	Eissa et al. (2001)
Efficacy of treatment	Outcome measure	Behavioural therapy for irritable bowel syndrome	Heyman-Monnikes et al. (2000)
Bloggers' experiences with disease or condition	Virtual social support and sharing of information	Patients	Miller and Pole (2010)
Personal experiences of health professionals	Virtual social support and sharing of information	Health care professionals	Miller and Pole (2010)
Healthy living blogs	Advice on improving physical and mental health, eating, exercise, and self-image	Various	Boepple and Thompson (2014)

The Internet provides a resource for blogs, diaries and forums in which individuals share their experiences, seek information, and provide virtual social support. Anonymity may be used by bloggers to foster self-disclosure in describing embarrassing conditions. Chiu and Hsieh (2013) explored how cancer patients' writing and reading on the Internet play a role in their illness experience using focus group interviews with 34 cancer patients. They found that personal blogs enabled cancer patients to reconstruct their life stories, and express closure of life and how they expected to be remembered after death. Reading fellow patients' stories significantly influenced their perceptions and expectations of their illness prognosis, which was sometimes a greater influence than their doctors.

DIRECT OBSERVATION

The simplest kind of study involves directly observing behaviour in a relevant setting, for example, patients waiting for treatment in a doctor's surgery or clinic. **Direct observation** may be accompanied by recordings in written, oral, auditory or visual form. Several investigators may observe the same events and reliability checks conducted. Direct observation includes casual observation, formal observation and participant observation. However, ethical issues are raised by planned formal observational study of people who have not given informed consent to such observations.

DISCOURSE ANALYSIS

Discourse analysis is a set of procedures for analysing language as used in speech or texts. It focuses on the language and how it is used to construct versions of 'social reality' and what is gained by constructing events using the particular terms being used. It has links with ethnomethodology, conversation analysis and the study of meaning (semiology). There are two forms of discourse analysis. The first, discursive psychology, evolved from the work of Potter and Wetherell (1987) and is concerned with the discursive strategies people use to further particular actions in social situations, including accounting for their own behaviour or thoughts. This approach has been used to explore the character of patient talk and the character of doctor–patient interactions. There is a particular preference for naturally occurring conversations, e.g. mealtime talk (Wiggins et al., 2001). Locke and Horton-Salway (2010) analysed how class leaders talked to antenatal class members about pregnancy, childbirth and infant care in 'golden age' or 'bad old days' stories variably to contrast the practices of the past with current practices. The second type of discourse analysis, Foucauldian discourse analysis (FDA), was developed by Ian Parker (1997) and others who criticized the previous approach as evading issues of power and politics. FDA aims to identify the broader discursive resources that people in a particular culture draw upon in their everyday lives. This approach has been used to explore such issues as smoking (Gillies and Willig, 1997) and masculine identity (Tyler and Williams, 2014).

DOUBLE-BLIND CONTROL

A **double-blind control** is used in randomized controlled trials to prevent bias: both the investigator and the participant (subject) are prevented from knowing whether they are in the treatment or control condition. A single-blind is when only the participant is unaware of the condition they have been allocated to.

EFFECT SIZE

An **effect size** is the strength of the association between study variables and outcome as measured by an observed difference or correlation. Cohen's d and Person's r are the most popular indices of effect size in psychological studies. The effect size is a measure of the importance of an effect rather than its statistical significance. Effect sizes are used in meta-analysis as a means of measuring the magnitude of the results obtained over different studies. Effect size is related to the power of a study to detect a difference that really exists. A weak study cannot detect a real difference because it has samples that are too small relative to the magnitude of the difference that exists, a common problem in psychology. It is estimated that 60–70% of published studies in psychology journals lack sufficient power to obtain statistical significance.

ETHICAL APPROVAL

This is a necessary requirement before any research can be started. Ethics boards and research review panels in all research institutions and universities have been established for this purpose. Any research project must present before a panel of experts on ethical issues, and have the panel's explicit approval of: the full details of the aims, design, the participants, and how they will be chosen; the information provided to the participants; the method of consent used; methods of data analysis; nature and timing of debriefing of participants; and methods of dissemination. Funding and publication are normally contingent on ethical approval being obtained.

ETHNOGRAPHIC METHODS

Ethnographic methods seek to build a systematic understanding of a culture from the viewpoint of the insider. Ethnographic methods are multiple attempts to describe the shared beliefs, practices, artefacts, knowledge and behaviours of an intact cultural group. They attempt to represent the totality of a phenomenon in its complete, naturalistic setting. Detailed observation is an important part of ethnographic fieldwork. Ethnography can provide greater ecological validity. The processes of transformation can be observed and documented, including how the culture becomes embodied in participants, alongside the recording of their narratives. It is more labour-intensive, but combining ethnography with narrative interviews can produces richer information than qualitative interviews alone (Paulson, 2011).

The observation can be either overt or covert. In the overt case the researcher does not attempt to disguise his/her identity but rather is unobtrusive such that the phenomenon under investigation is not disturbed. In this case the researcher can take detailed notes, in either a prearranged or discursive format. In certain cases the researcher may decide that his/her presence may disturb the field. In this case two forms of covert observation may be used. In one form the focus of observation is not aware at all of the presence of the researcher. An alternative approach is when the person observed may be aware of the researcher's presence but is unaware that he/she is a researcher. In both of these forms the researcher needs to consider whether such covert surveillance is ethically justified. A form of participant observation that is not covert is when the researcher accompanies the person but tries not to interfere with the performance of everyday tasks. Priest (2007) combined grounded theory and ethnography to explore members' experience of a mental health day service walking group, including psychological benefits of the physical activity, the outdoor environment and the social setting. Stolte and Hodgetts (2013) used ethnographic methods to study the tactics employed by a homeless man in Central Auckland, New Zealand, to maintain his health and to gain respite while living on the streets, an unhealthy place.

FOCUS GROUPS

Focus groups comprise one or more group discussions in which participants 'focus' collectively upon a topic or issue usually presented to them as a group of questions, although sometimes as a film, a collection of advertisements, cards to sort, a game to play, or a vignette to discuss. The distinctive feature of the focus group method is its generation of interactive data (Wilkinson, 1998). Focus groups were initially used in marketing research. As its title implied they had a focus that was to clarify the participants' views on a particular product. Thus from the outset the researcher had set the parameters of the discussion and as it proceeded he/she deliberately guided the discussion such that its focus remained limited. More recent use of the focus group has been much more expansive. In many cases the term discussion group is preferred to give an indication of this greater latitude. The role of the researcher in the focus group is to act as the moderator for the discussion. The researcher can follow similar guidelines as those with an interview by using a guide, except that the discussion should be allowed to flow freely and not be constrained too much by the investigator's agenda. The researcher needs to ensure that all the group participants have opportunity to express their viewpoints. The method is often combined with interviews and questionnaires.

At the beginning of the discussion the researcher should follow the usual guidelines. It is important that the group is briefed on the basic principles of confidentiality and respect for different opinions. It is useful for them to know each others' first names and to have name badges. This facilitates greater interaction. It is also useful to have some refreshments available.

Although it is usual for the moderator to introduce some themes for discussion, this can be supplemented with a short video extract or pictures relevant to the topic being investigated. As the discussion proceeds, the researcher can often take a background role, but ensuring that the discussion does not deviate too far from the focus of the research and that all the participants have an opportunity to express their views. An assistant can help completing consent forms, providing name-tags, organizing refreshments, keeping notes on who is talking (this is useful for transcription), and monitoring the recording equipment. The focus group recording should be transcribed as soon as possible afterwards since it is often difficult to distinguish speakers.

A few examples: Jones et al. (2014) carried out a focus group and telephone interviews with patients in rural areas to examine diabetes management in a rural areas; Liimakka (2014) drew upon focus group discussions to explore how young Finnish university students viewed the cultural ideals of health and appearance; Griffiths et al. (2014) used pre- and post-intervention focus groups to test a website, Realshare, for young oncology patients in the south-west of England; and Bogart (2014) examined the social experiences of ten adolescents aged 12–17 years with Moebius Syndrome, a rare condition involving congenital facial paralysis.

GROUNDED THEORY ANALYSIS

Grounded theory analysis is a term used to describe a set of guidelines for conducting qualitative data analysis. It was originally developed by Glaser and Strauss (1967) and has subsequently gone through various revisions. In its original form qualitative researchers were asked to dispense with theoretical assumptions when they began their research. Rather they were encouraged to adopt a stance of disciplined naivety. As the research progresses, certain theoretical concepts are discovered and then tested in an iterative fashion. In the case of the qualitative interview, the researcher is encouraged to begin the analysis at a very early stage, even as the interview is progressing. Through a process of abduction the researcher begins to develop certain theoretical hypotheses. These hypotheses are then integrated into a tentative theoretical model that is tested as more data is collected.

This process follows a series of steps beginning with generating data. At this stage the researcher may have some general ideas about the topic but this should not restrict the talk of the participant. From the very initial stages the researcher is sifting through the ideas presented and seeking more information about what are considered to be emerging themes. From a more positivist perspective it is argued that the themes emerge from the data and that the researcher has simply to look for them. This approach is often associated with Glaser (1992). From a more social constructionist perspective, certain theoretical concepts of the researcher will guide both the data collection and analysis. This approach is more associated with the symbolic interactionist tradition (Strauss, 1987; Charmaz, 2003).

Having collected some data the researcher conducts a detailed coding of it followed by the generation of bigger categories. Throughout the coding the researcher follows the process of constant comparative analysis. This involves making comparison of codes within and between interview transcripts. This is followed by the stage of memo-writing that requires the researcher to begin to expand upon the meaning of the broader conceptual categories. This in turn can lead to further data generation through theoretical sampling. This is the process whereby the researcher deliberately selects certain participants or certain research themes to explore further because of the data already analysed. At this stage the researcher is both testing and strengthening the emergent theory. At a certain stage in this iterative process the researcher feels that he/she has reached the stage of data saturation – no new concepts are emerging and it is considered fruitless to continue with data collection.

A few examples: DiMillo et al. (2014) used grounded theory methodology to examine the stigmatization experiences of six BRCA1/2 gene mutation carriers following genetic testing; Searle et al. (2014) studied participants' experiences of facilitated physical activity for the management of depression in primary care; Silva et al. (2013) used the method to study the balancing of motherhood with drug addiction in addicted mothers.

HISTORICAL ANALYSIS

Health and illness are socially and historically located phenomena. As such psychologists have much to gain by detailed historical research (**historical analysis**) on the development of health beliefs and practices. They can work closely with medical or health historians to explore the evolution of scientific and popular beliefs about health and illness or they can work independently (see Chapter 3). An example is the work of Herzlich and Pierret (1987). Their work involved the detailed analysis of a variety of textual sources such as scientific medical writings but also popular autobiographical and fictional accounts of the experience of illness. They noted the particular value of literary works because of their important contribution to shaping public discourse. Such textual analysis needs to be guided by an understanding of the political and philosophical ideas of the period.

Health psychologists need also to be reflexive about the history of their own discipline. It arose at a particular historical period sometimes described as late modernity. Initially it was seen as providing a complement to the excessive physical focus of biomedicine. Now some see it as part of the broader lifestyle movement.

There are different approaches to the writing of history. There are those who can be broadly characterized as descriptive and who often provide a listing of the growth of the discipline in laudatory terms (e.g. Stone et al., 1987). Conversely there are those who adopt a more critical approach and attempt to dissect the underlying reasons for the development of the discipline. Within health psychology, this latter approach is still in its early stages (e.g. Stam, 2014).

INTERPRETATIVE PHENOMENOLOGICAL ANALYSIS

Phenomenological research is concerned with exploring the lived experience of health, illness and disability. Its aim is to understand these phenomena from the perspective of the particular participant. This in turn has to be interpreted by the researcher. A technique that addresses this challenge is **interpretative phenomenological analysis** (IPA) (Smith, 2004). IPA focuses on the cognitive processing of the participant. Smith (2004) argues that it accords with the original direction of cognitive psychology that was concerned with exploring meaning-making rather than information-processing. IPA provides a guide to conducting the researcher's making sense or meaning of reported experiences. It begins by accessing the participant's perceptions through the conduct of an interview or series of interviews with a homogeneous sample of individuals. The interview is semi-structured and focuses on the particular issue of concern.

Data analysis in IPA goes through a number of stages. Initially the researcher reads and re-reads the text and develops a higher order thematic analysis. Having identified the key themes or categories the researcher then proceeds to look for connections between them by identifying clusters. At this stage the researcher is drawing upon their broader understanding to make sense of what has been said. Once the researcher has finished the analysis of one case they can proceed to conduct an analysis of the next case in a similar manner. Alternatively, the researcher can begin to apply the analytic scheme developed in the previous case. The challenge is to identify repeating patterns but also to be alert to new patterns. Further details of this form of analysis are available in Smith et al. (1999) and Smith and Osborn (2003).

A few examples: Conroy and De Visser (2014) studied the importance of authenticity for student non-drinkers; Mackay and Parry (2013) studied two perspectives on autistic behaviours; Burton et al. (2014) used an interpretative phenomenological analysis of sense-making within a dyadic relationship of living together with age-related macular degeneration; Ware et al. (2014) used IPA to study the experience of hepatitis C treatment for people with a history of mental health problems; Levi et al. (2014) investigated phenomenological hope among perceptions of traumatized war veterans.

INTERVENTIONS

Interventions are deliberate attempts to facilitate improvements to health. The idea for the intervention can come from a theory or model, from discussions with those who are knowledgeable about the condition or situation that needs to be changed, or from 'out of the blue'.

A key aspect of designing and/or implementing any intervention is evaluation – attempting to prove whether or not the intervention is effective or efficacious. Furthermore, reports of intervention studies are typically brief, opaque descriptions of what can often be complex interventions.

Reports of behaviour change studies typically provide brief summaries of what in reality may be a highly complex and unique intervention. One problem is that there is no meaningful method of classifying interventions for behaviour change into any single theory or method of description. There is no accepted taxonomy for methods and techniques employed in interventions designed to change behaviour. This means that the researcher does not know how to label what they have done in a way that communicates this in any precise manner.

There is no meaningful method of relating the practice of behaviour change to any single theory or taxonomy. This means that the researcher does not know how to label what they have done in a way that communicates this in any precise manner to others (Marks, 2009). A key criterion for the reporting of an intervention must be transparency. Can another person or group repeat the study in his/her/their own setting with his/her/their own participants? The need to be concise in publishing studies means that the level of detail required for successful replication may often be missing. It is, therefore, almost impossible for new investigators to repeat a published intervention with any exactitude in their own settings.

INTERVIEWS (SEMI-STRUCTURED)

Semi-structured interviews are designed to explore the participant's view of things with the minimal amount of assumptions from the interviewer. A semi-structured interview is more open ended than a structured interview and allows the interviewee to address issues that he/she feels relevant to the topics raised by the investigator (see Qualitative research methods below). Open-ended questions are useful in this kind of interview. They have several advantages over closed-ended questions. The answers will not be biased by the researcher's preconceptions as much as closed-ended questions can be. The respondents are able to express their opinions, thoughts and feelings freely using their own words in ways that are less constrained by the particular wordings of the question. The respondents may have responses that the structured interview designer has overlooked. They may have in-depth comments that they wish to make about the study and the topics that it is covering that would not be picked up using the standard questions in a structured interview.

In preparing for the interview the researcher should develop an interview guide. This can include a combination of primary and supplementary questions. Alternatively, the researcher may prefer to have a list of themes to be explored. However, it is important that the researcher does not formally follow these in the same order but rather introduces them at the appropriate time in the interview. Prior to the interview, the researcher should review these themes and order them from the least invasive to the more personal.

INTERVIEWS (STRUCTURED)

A structured interview schedule is a prepared, standard set of questions that are asked in person, or perhaps by telephone, of a person or group concerning a particular research issue.

LITERATURE SEARCH

An essential skill in any research project is to carry out a **literature search**. Usually this will be best achieved using keywords. The key data in all scholarly publications consist of the title, the abstract, which is a summary of 100 to 250 words, and the keywords that are listed with the data about the article. By inserting keywords into any search engine it is possible to obtain a comprehensive list of scholarly research reports, dissertations, and conference papers, books and monographs. One popular search engine is Google Scholar. Another major database for researchers is the 'ISI Web of Knowledge'. This contains a large selection of peer-reviewed publications from journals with a proven track record of high-quality publications. Examples of the results from searches of the health psychology literature are shown in Figures 5.1 and 5.3.

LONGITUDINAL DESIGNS

Longitudinal designs involve measuring responses of a single sample on more than one occasion. The measurements may be prospective or retrospective. Prospective longitudinal designs allow greater control over the sample, the variables measured and the times when the measurements take place. Such designs are superior to cross-sectional designs because one is more able to investigate hypotheses of causation when the associations between variables are measured over time. Longitudinal designs are among the most powerful designs available for the evaluation of treatments and of theories about human experience and behaviour, but they are also the most costly in labour, time and money.

META-ANALYSIS

Meta-analysis is the use of statistical techniques to combine the results of primary studies addressing the same question into a single pooled measure of effect size, with a confidence interval. The analysis is often based on the calculation of a weighted mean effect size in which each primary study is weighted according to the number of participants. A meta-analysis follows a series of steps as follows: (1) develop a research question; (2) identify all relevant studies; (3) select studies on the basis of the issue being addressed and methodological criteria; (4) decide which dependent variables or summary measures are allowed; (5) calculate a summary effect; and (6) reach a conclusion in answer to the original research question.

NARRATIVE APPROACHES

This approach is concerned with the desire to seek insight and meaning about health and illness through the acquisition of data in the form of stories concerning personal experiences. The **narrative approach** assumes that human beings are natural storytellers and that the principal task of the psychologist is to explore the different stories being told (Murray, 2015). The most popular source of material for the narrative researcher is the interview. The focus of the narrative interview is the elicitation of narrative accounts from the interviewee. This can take various forms. The life-story interview is the most extended form of the narrative interview. As its name implies, the life-story interview seeks to obtain an extended account of the person's life. The primary aim is to make the participant at ease and encourage him/her to tell their story at length.

A particular version of the narrative interview is the episodic interview in which the researcher encourages the participant to speak on a variety of particular experiences. This approach assumes that experiences are often stored in memory in narrative-episodes and that the challenge is to reveal these without integrating them into a larger narrative. Throughout the interview the role of the interviewer is to encourage sustained narrative accounting. This can be achieved through a variety of supportive remarks. The researcher can deliberately encourage the participant to expand upon remarks about particular issues.

Narrative analysis (NA) can take various forms. It begins with a repeated reading of the text to identify the story or stories within it. The primary focus is on maintaining the narrative integrity of the account. The researcher may develop a summary of the narrative account that will help identify the structure of the narrative, its tone and the central characters. It may be useful to engage in a certain amount of thematic analysis to identify some underlying themes. But this does not equate with narrative analysis. NA involves trying to see the interconnections between events rather than separating them. Having analysed one case the researcher can then proceed to the next, identifying similarities and differences in the structure and content of the narratives.

OBSERVATIONAL STUDIES

This term is used to describe research carried out to evaluate the effect of an intervention or treatment that does not have the advantages of a control group. A single group of patients are observed at various points before, during and after the treatment in an attempt to ascertain the changes that occur as a result of the treatment. There are strict limitations on the conclusions that can be reached as a consequence of the lack of control group (e.g. see Randomized controlled trials later in the chapter). However, there are occasions when a randomized controlled trial is impossible to carry out because of ethical or operational difficulties.

PARTICIPATORY ACTION RESEARCH

Participatory action research (PAR) is a version of action research (see above) that deliberately seeks to provoke some form of social or community change.

POWER ANALYSIS

Power refers to the ability of a study to find a statistically significant effect when a genuine effect exists. The principal method of increasing power is to choose the size of a sample using **power analysis**. Cohen (1972) found that psychology studies had about a 50% chance of finding a genuine effect owing to their lack of statistical power. The situation has changed in the last 40 years but it remains problematic. This lack of power is caused by study samples being too small to permit definite conclusions. Given the easy availability of free software online, there can be little excuse for not doing a power analysis before embarking on a research project. Also, funding agencies, ethics boards and research review panels normally require a power analysis as a condition of funding.

QUALITATIVE RESEARCH METHODS

Qualitative research methods aim to understand the meanings, purposes and intentions of behaviour, not its amount or quantity. A huge variety of methods are available and these are described in this A–Z under the following headings: diaries and blogs; discourse analysis; focus groups; grounded theory; historical analysis; interpretative phenomenological analysis; interviews, especially semi-structured; and narrative approaches. Figure 5.3 shows the rapid growth of qualitative research in health psychology over the last few decades. This is a trend that is expected to continue.

QUESTIONNAIRES

Questionnaires in health psychology consist of a standard set of questions with accompanying instructions concerning attitudes, beliefs, perceptions or values concerned with health, illness or health care. Ideally, a questionnaire will have been demonstrated to be a reliable and a valid measure of the construct(s) it purports to measure.

Questionnaires vary in objectives, content, especially in their generic versus specific content, question format, the number of items, and sensitivity or responsiveness to change. Questionnaires may be employed in cross-sectional and longitudinal studies. When looking for changes over time, the responsiveness of a questionnaire to clinical and subjective changes is a crucial feature. A questionnaire's content, sensitivity and extent, together with its reliability and validity, influence a questionnaire's selection. Guides are available to advise users on making a choice that contains the appropriate generic measure or domain of interest (e.g. Bowling, 2001, 2004). These guides are useful as they include details on content, scoring, validity and reliability of dozens of questionnaires for measuring all of the major aspects of psychological well-being and quality of life, including disease-specific and domain-specific questionnaires and more generic measures.

The investigator must ask: What is it that I want to know? The answer will dictate the selection of the most relevant and useful questionnaire. The most important aspect of questionnaire selection is therefore to match the objective of the study with the objective of the questionnaire. For example, are you interested in a disease-specific or broad-ranging research question? When this question is settled, you need to decide whether there is anything else that your research objective will require you to know. Usually the researcher needs to develop a specific block of questions that will seek vital information concerning the respondents' socio-demographic characteristics that can be placed at the beginning or the end of the main questionnaire.

Questionnaire content may vary from the highly generic (e.g. *How has your health been over the last few weeks? Excellent, Good, Fair, Poor, Very Bad*) to the highly specific (e.g. *Have you had any arguments with people at work in the last two weeks?*). Questionnaires vary greatly in the number of items that are used to assess the variable(s) of interest. Single-item measures use a single question, rating or item to measure the concept or variable of interest. For example, the now popular single verbal item to evaluate health status: *During the past 4 weeks 85 how would you rate your health in general? Excellent, Very good, Good, Fair, Poor.* Single items have the obvious advantages of being simple, direct and brief.

Questionnaires remain one of the most useful and widely applicable research methods in health psychology. A few questionnaire scales have played a dominant role in health psychology research over the last few decades. Figure 5.3 shows the number of items in the ISI Web of Knowledge database for three of the most popular scales. Over the 20-year period 1990–2009, usage of scales designed to measure health status has been dominated by three front-runners: the McGill Pain Questionnaire (Melzack, 1975), the Hospital Anxiety and Depression Scale (HADS; Zigmond and Snaith, 1983), and the SF-36 Health Survey (Brazier et al., 1992). The SF-36 is by far the most utilized scale in clinical research, accounting for around 50% of all clinical studies (Figure 5.3).

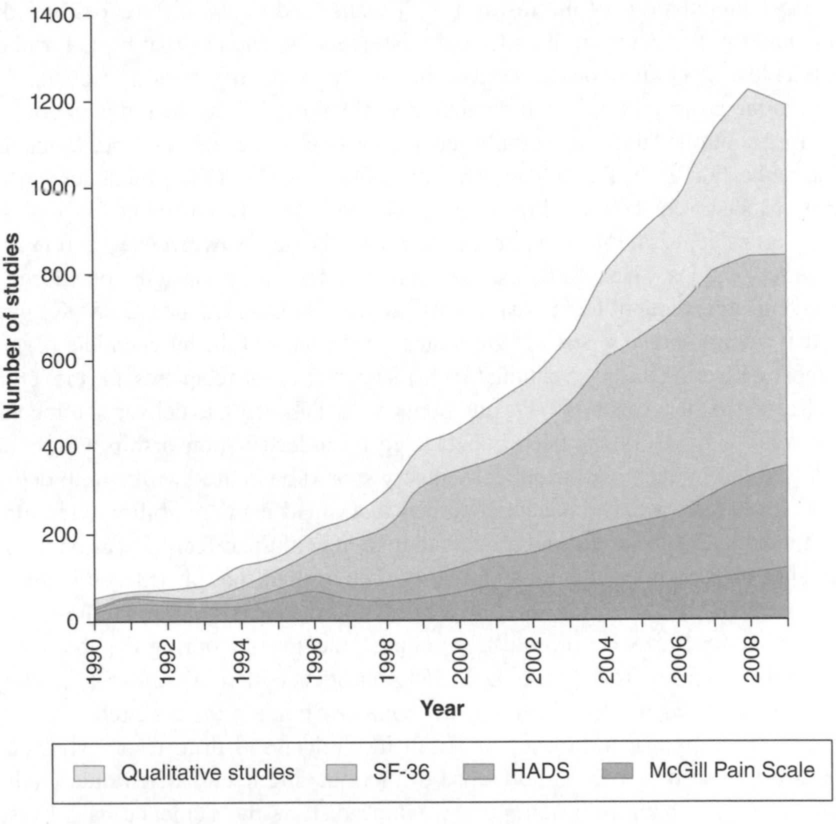

Figure 5.3 Trends in numbers of health psychology studies using different research measures and methods, 1990–2009

Source: Marks (2013)

RANDOMIZED CONTROLLED TRIALS

Randomized controlled trials (RCTs) involve the systematic comparison of interventions using a fully controlled application of one or more 'treatments' with a random allocation of participants to the different treatment groups. The statistical tests that are available have as one of their assumptions that participants have been randomly assigned to conditions. In real world settings of clinical and health research, the so-called 'gold standard' of the RCT cannot always be achieved in practice, and, in fact, may not be desirable for ethical reasons.

We are frequently forced to study existing groups that are being treated differently rather than have the luxury of being able to allocate people to conditions. Thus, we may in effect be comparing the health policies and services of a number of different hospitals and clinics. Such 'quasi-experimental designs' are used to compare treatments in as controlled a manner as possible, when, for practical reasons, it is impossible to manipulate the independent variable, the policies, or allocate the participants.

The advantage of an RCT is that differences in the outcome can be attributed with more confidence to the manipulations of the researchers, because individual differences are likely to be spread in a random way between the different treatments. As soon as that basis for allocation of participants is lost, then questions arise over the ability to identify causes of changes or differences between the groups; in other words, the internal validity of the design is in question.

Randomized controlled trials are complex operations to manage and describe, which has led to a difficulty in replication of RCTs. To help solve this problem, CONSORT guidelines for RCTs were published by Moher, Schultz and Altman (2001) and the TREND statement for non-randomized studies (Des Jarlais et al., 2004) were intended to bridge the gap between intervention descriptions and intended replications. These guidelines have driven efforts to enhance the practice of reporting behaviour change intervention studies. Davidson et al. (2003) expanded the CONSORT guidelines in proposing that authors should report: (1) the content or elements of the intervention; (2) characteristics of the those delivering the intervention; (3) characteristics of the recipients; (4) the setting; (5) the mode of delivery; (6) the intensity; (7) the duration; and (8) adherence to delivery protocols/manuals.

Another issue with RCTs has been bias created by industry sponsorship. Critics claim that research carried out by the pharmaceutical industry should be treated with a high degree of suspicion as the investigators may have a hidden bias that can affect their ability to remain independent. Lexchin et al. (2003) carried out a systematic review of the effect of pharmaceutical industry sponsorship on research outcome and quality. They found that pharmaceutically sponsored studies were less likely to be published in peer-reviewed journals. Also, studies sponsored by pharmaceutical companies were more likely to have outcomes favouring the sponsor than were studies with other sponsors (odds ratio 4.05; 95% confidence interval 2.98–5.51). They found a systematic bias favouring products made by the company funding the research.

There have been significant abuses of RCTs in clinical and drug trials. Many trials have not been registered so that there is no record of them having been carried out. Trials showing non-significant effects have been unreported, which distorts the evidence base by suggesting that a drug is better than it actually is. Placebo control conditions have been manipulated to enhance drug effects. The double-blind requirements for RCTs have been broken. Investigators who have received funding from drug companies have written biased or misleading reports.

Ghost writers have been employed to write glowing reports. These abuses have led to wastage of public funds on ineffective drugs and treatments, missed opportunities for improving treatments, and trials being repeated unnecessarily.

The AllTrials movement is campaigning to remove these abuses and to obtain publication of all clinical trials (see www.alltrials.net/).

REPLICATION

Replication is one of the most important research methods in existence. Yet it is hardly used and mentioned in textbooks about research methods. Replication refers to the attempt by an investigator to repeat a study purely to determine whether the original findings can be repeated. Essentially, the researcher wants to know whether the original findings are reliable or whether they have been produced by some combination of chance or spurious factors. If study findings can be replicated then they can be accepted as reliable and valuable to knowledge and understanding. However, if the findings of a study cannot be replicated, then the findings cannot be accepted as a genuine contribution to knowledge.

Lack of replication has been a bone of contention in many areas of psychology, including health psychology. Traditionally, a low priority has been given to replication of other researchers' results. Perhaps researchers believe that they will not be perceived as sufficiently creative if they replicate somebody else's research. In a similar vein, journal editors do not give replications of research, especially failed replications, the same priority as novel findings. This bias towards new positive results, and away from failed replications, produces a major distortion in the academic literature.

SINGLE CASE EXPERIMENTAL DESIGNS

Single case experimental designs are investigations of a series of experimental manipulations with a single research participant.

SURVEYS

Surveys are systematic methods for determining how a sample of participants respond to a set of standard questions attempting to assess their feelings, attitudes, beliefs or knowledge at one or more times. For example, we may want to know how drug users' perceptions of themselves and their families differ from those of non-users, or better understand the experiences of patients receiving specific kinds of treatment, how health and social services are perceived by informal carers of people with dementia, Parkinson's, multiple sclerosis (MS) or other chronic conditions, or learn more about how people recovering from a disease such as coronary heart disease feel about their rehabilitation. The survey method is the method of choice in many of these types of study.

The survey method, whether using interviews, questionnaires, or some combination of the two, is versatile, and can be applied equally well to research with individuals, groups, organizations, communities or populations to inform our understanding of a host of very different types of research issues and questions. Normally a survey is conducted on a sample of the study population of interest (e.g. people aged 70+; women aged 20–44; teenagers who smoke; carers of people with dementia, etc.). Issues of key importance in conducting a survey are: the objective(s); the mode of administration; the method of sampling; the sample size; and the preparation of the data for analysis.

As in any research, it is essential to have a clear idea about the objective, why we are doing our study (the theory or policy behind the research), what we are looking for (the research question), where we intend to look (the setting or domain), who will be in the sample (the study sample), and how we use the tools we have at our disposal. The investigator must be cautious that the procedures do not generate any self-fulfilling prophecies. Lack of clarity about purposes and objectives is one of the main stumbling blocks for the novice investigator to overcome. This is particularly the case when carrying out a survey, especially in a team of investigators who may have varying agendas with regard to the why, what, who, where and how questions that must be answered before the survey can begin.

Modes of administration include: face-to-face interview, telephone interview, social media, group self-completion, and postal self-completion. Next you need to decide who will be the sample for your survey and also where you will carry it out. Which population is your research question about? The sample should represent the study population as closely as possible. In some cases, the sample can consist of the entire study population, e.g. every pupil in a school; every student at a university; every patient in a hospital. More usually however, the sample is likely to be a random selection of a proportion of the members of a population, e.g. every tenth person in a community, or every fourth patient admitted into a hospital. This method is called simple random sampling (SRS). A variation on SRS is systematic sampling. In this case the first person in the sampling frame is chosen at random and then every *n*th person on the list from there on, where *n* is the sample fraction being used.

In stratified sampling the population is divided into groups or 'strata' and the groups are randomly sampled, but in different proportions so that the overall sample sizes of the groups can be made equal, even though they are not equal in the population (e.g. the 40–59, 60–79 and 80–99 age groups in a community sample, or men and women in a clinical sample). These groups will therefore be equally represented in the data. Other methods include non-probability sampling of six kinds: convenience samples, most similar/dissimilar samples, typical case samples, critical case samples, snowball samples, and quota samples.

All such sampling methods are biased; in fact there is no perfect method of sampling because there will always be a category of people that any sampling method under-represents. In any survey it is necessary to maximize the proportion of selected people who are recruited. If a large proportion of people refuse to participate, the sample will not represent the population, but be biased in unknown ways. As a general principle, surveys that recruit at least 70% of those invited to participate are considered representative. The sample size is a key issue. The variability of scores obtained from the sampling diminishes as the sample size increases, so the larger the sample, the more precise will be the estimates of the population scores, but the more the survey will cost.

SYSTEMATIC REVIEWS

A **systematic review** (SR) is a method of integrating the best evidence about an effect or intervention from all relevant and usable primary sources. What counts as relevant and usable is a matter for debate and judgement. Rules and criteria for selecting studies and for extracting data are agreed in advance by those carrying out the review. Publishing these rules and criteria along with the review enables such reviews to be replicable and transparent. Proponents of the SR therefore see it as a way of integrating research that limits bias. Traditionally the method has been applied to quantitative data. Recently, researchers have begun to investigate ways and means to synthesize qualitative studies also.

Knowing how to carry out and to critically interpret an SR report are essential skills in all fields of health research. They enable researchers and clinicians to integrate research findings and make improvements in health care.

Systematic reviews act like a sieve, selecting some evidence but rejecting other evidence. To retain the metaphor, the reviewers act as a filter; what they see and report depends on how the selection process is operated. Whenever there is ambiguity, the process may well tend to operate in confirmatory mode, seeking positive support for a position, model or theory rather than disconfirmation. It is essential to be critical and cautious in interpreting and analysing SRs of biomedical and related topics. If we want to implement new practice as a direct consequence of such reviews, we had better make certain that the findings are solid and not a mirage. This is why the study of the method itself is so important. Systematic reviews of the same topic can produce significantly different results, indicating that bias is difficult to control. Like all forms of knowledge, the results of an SR are the consequences of a process of negotiation about rules and criteria, and cannot be accepted without criticism and debate. There are many examples of how SRs cause controversy, e.g. Law et al. (1991), Swales (2000), Marks (2002c), Dixon-Woods et al. (2006), Millett (2011), Roseman et al. (2011) and Coyne and Kok (2014).

TAXONOMY FOR INTERVENTION STUDIES

This section describes an idea for a **taxonomy** designed to help solve a variety of issues mentioned elsewhere in this A–Z, namely: the description of interventions, replication and transparency. As noted, lack of replication has been a major issue in psychology. One reason for the failure to replicate is the sheer complexity of different interventions that are available. A vast array of interventions and techniques can be delivered in multitudinous combinations enabling literally millions of different interventions designed to change behaviour (Marks, 2009).

If interventions are incompletely described, it is not possible to (1) determine all the necessary attributes of the intervention; (2) classify the intervention into a category or type; (3) compare and contrast interventions across studies; (4) identify which specific intervention component was responsible for efficacy; (5) replicate the intervention in other settings; or (6) advance the science of illness prevention by enabling theory testing in the practice of health care.

One way to put order into the chaos is to use a taxonomic system similar to those used to classify organisms or substances. Taxonomies for living things have been constructed since the time of Aristotle, with the periodic table in chemistry being the best-known example. Some researchers approached this issue by generating 'shopping lists' of interventions used in different studies. For example, Abraham and Michie (2008) described 26 behaviour change interventions, which they claimed provided a 'taxonomy' of generally applicable behaviour change techniques. Michie et al. (2008: Appendix A) also produced a list of 137 heterogeneous techniques. However, these lists are not useful as taxonomies because they do not demonstrate any systematic structure or organization of classification. A list of techniques is no more useful than a list of chemicals. Only when there is an organization like the periodic table do we gain an understanding of the underlying structure and the relationship between the various elements that lie in the table.

Psychology lacks a system for classifying interventions into a single system consisting of all known techniques and sub-techniques. In an effort to fill this gap, one of the authors has described a taxonomy with six levels, as illustrated in Figure 5.4. This taxonomic system includes six nested levels:

1. Paradigms, e.g. individual, community, public health, critical.
2. Domains, e.g. stress, diabetes, hypertension, smoking, weight, exercise, etc.

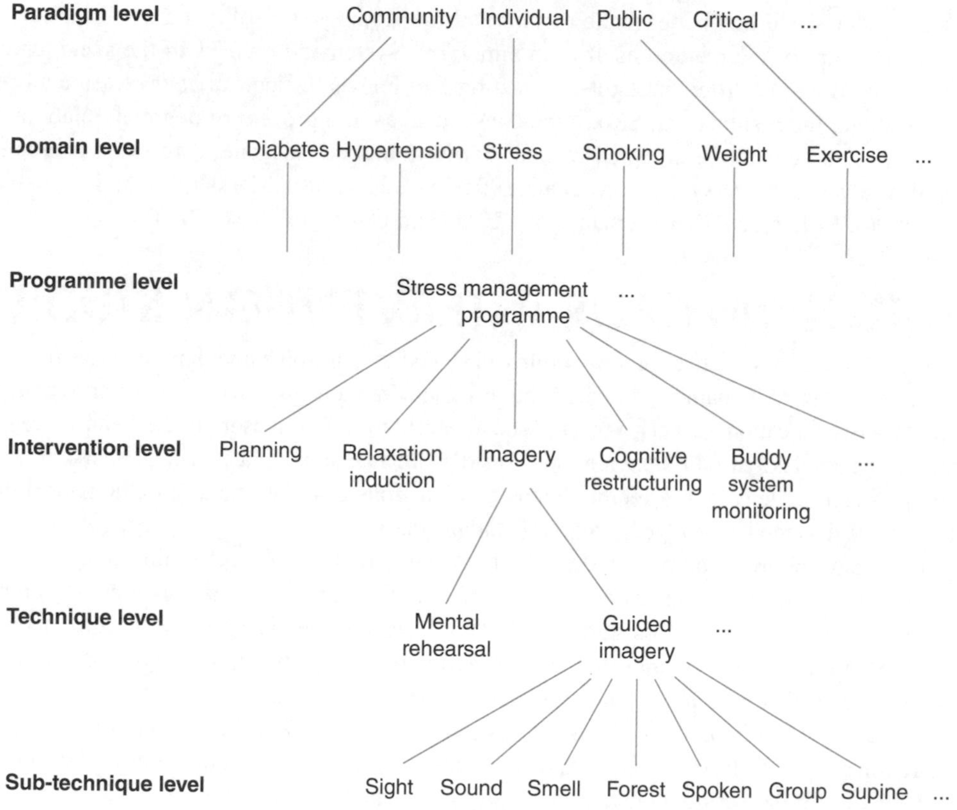

Figure 5.4 Tree diagram showing paradigm, domain, programme, intervention, technique and sub-technique levels of description

Source: Marks (2009)

3. Programmes, e.g. smoking cessation, obesity management, stress management and assertiveness training.
4. Intervention types, e.g. relaxation induction, imagery, planning, cognitive restructuring, imagery, buddy system monitoring.
5. Techniques, e.g. within imagery there are a large number of techniques such as mental rehearsal, guided imagery, flooding in imagination, and systematic sensitization.
6. Sub-techniques, e.g. within guided imagery there exist a variety of sensory modalities (sight, sound, smell, taste, touch, warmth/coldness), scenarios (e.g. beach, forest, garden, air balloon), delivery methods (e.g. spoken instruction, self-administered by reading, listening to audio tapes), settings (e.g. individual, group) and participant positions (e.g. supine, sitting on floor, sitting on chair).

This taxonomic system is capable of including all health psychology paradigms, domains, programmes, intervention types, techniques and sub-techniques as defined with universal reference in the form of a tree diagram. Any research design that is sufficiently specific can be placed within this taxonomic system to enable any imaginable intervention to be constructed, delivered, evaluated, labelled, reported and replicated in an unambiguous fashion. This system, or something similar, is needed to remove some basic problems that hold back progress in psychology as a discipline.

TRANSPARENCY

A key issue in designing and reporting research studies in health psychology is **transparency**. This refers to the ability to accurately and openly describe in full detail the participants or patient population (P), intervention (I), comparison (C) and outcome (O) ('PICO'). Above, we have mentioned the CONSORT and TREND guidelines that were designed to improve transparency of the descriptions of interventions. Intervention studies are typically designed to compare one, two or, at most, three treatments with a control condition consisting of standard care, a waiting list control, a placebo, or no treatment.

The standard designs are simple because precious resources must be stretched across a large number of trials. Rarely, if ever, does an intervention include only one technique, with practically all trials including two or more techniques in combination. If an intervention domain such as smoking has, say, 500 techniques, then there would be 2.5 million possible two-technique combinations, 124 million three-technique combinations and 62 billion four-technique combinations! These eye-watering figures may help to explain why replication so often fails. Which specific combination is used in any individual case, and in what order, depends on the subjective choices of the practitioner.

Only if the 'PICO' description is fully detailed and transparent can an independent investigator have the opportunity to reproduce a replica of the study.

UNCONTROLLED VARIABLE

An **uncontrolled variable** is the bête noire of any research study. This is a background variable that, unknown to the investigator, operates within the research environment to affect the outcome in an uncontrolled manner. As a consequence, the study will contain the risk of producing a false set of findings. For example, a study concerning the J-shaped association between alcohol and mortality might conclude that light drinkers were protected by their moderate levels of alcohol use from diseases caused by alcohol. However, that conclusion would be false if it was also the case that light drinkers were generally from a higher socio-economic group than moderate and heavy drinkers of alcohol (see Chapter 8 for more details) because low socio-economic status is a significant predictor of higher mortality.

FUTURE RESEARCH

1. More studies using qualitative and action research methods will help to broaden the focus on quantitative research in health psychology.
2. More research is needed on the health experiences and behaviour of children, ethnic minority groups, disabled people and older people.
3. The evidence base on effectiveness of behaviour change interventions needs to be strengthened by larger-scale randomized controlled trials.
4. More extensive collaboration with health economists is needed to carry out cost-effectiveness studies of psychosocial interventions.
5. If health psychology is to achieve its full potential, policy-relevant research must be publicized and more widely disseminated through the media.

SUMMARY

1 The principal research methods of health psychology fall into three categories: quantitative, qualitative and action research.

2 Quantitative research designs emphasize reliable and valid measurement in controlled experiments, trials and surveys.

3 Qualitative methods use interviews, focus groups, narratives, diaries or texts to explore health and illness concepts and experience.

4 Action research enables change processes to feed back into plans for improvement, empowerment and emancipation.

5 Evaluation research to assess the effectiveness of interventions generally is on too small a scale and of insufficient quality. There is a need for much larger scale studies that are methodologically rigorous.

6 Multiple sources of evidence may be synthesized in systematic reviews and meta-analyses.

7 Health psychology research of the highest quality should be widely disseminated at all levels of society.

PART 2

HEALTH BEHAVIOUR AND EXPERIENCE

In Part 2 we review both theory and research concerned with the health-related behaviours and experiences most relevant to the major causes of illness and death. We also consider the environmental influences, both physical and social, that affect these health-relevant behaviours. Each chapter offers practical recommendations on how theory and research in health psychology can be applied to improve current systems of health care. In each case the focus is on behaviour and its ecological determinants. Changes in living conditions as human societies adapted from hunter-gathering to post-industrial, post-electronic sedentary living have generated a toxic ecology in affluent societies.

In Chapter 6 we focus on sexual health, prevention of unintended pregnancies, STIs and HIV infections. The principal theories and models of health behaviour with particular relevance to sexual health are described. These individual-level theories are based on constructs, intended to be universally applicable, concerning how behaviours are adopted, maintained and changed. The models have yielded disappointing results yet they continue to dominate the research in the field. Our critique of the approach indicates the need for fresh lines of inquiry.

In Chapter 7 we examine the part played by food, diets and dieting in the changing patterns of illnesses and deaths associated with the obesity pandemic. The sub-optimal food environment has generated high levels of obesity, diabetes, cardiovascular diseases, cancers, osteoporosis and dental disease. We describe four theories of obesity and the evidence for and against each of them. This evidence includes the observed effects of diets with differing proportions of macronutrients in the form of fats, sugars and proteins. We review available interventions for obesity and overweight and the evidence on their effectiveness.

In Chapter 8 we discuss theories and research concerned with alcohol consumption and the causes, prevention and treatment of drinking problems. We begin with a discussion of the ambivalent attitudes to alcohol which have characterized many cultures from the distant past to the present day. An analysis of the physical and psychosocial dangers of drinking leads on to an examination of contrasting theories about the causes of excessive drinking. The chapter concludes with a discussion of the relative merits of different approaches to the prevention and treatment of drinking problems.

In Chapter 9 we document the extent of smoking, its major health impacts, and factors that help to explain its continued popularity. Smoking is a complex practice involving a mixture of biopsychosocial processes. Three main theories, the biological, psychological and social, are outlined. The primary methods to assist smokers to quit are reviewed together with the results of evaluation studies. Methodological issues with placebos and vested interests of industry suggest caution in interpreting studies funded by the pharmaceutical industry.

In Chapter 10 we review evidence on the increasing prevalence of sedentary behaviour and its potential impact on health. We consider the social and psychological factors associated with participation, the varying meanings of different forms of physical activity, and strategies that have been used to promote greater participation.

6 SEXUAL HEALTH: THEORIES, MODELS AND INTERVENTIONS

A fresh approach is needed yielding new theories and interventions that work.

(Fine and Feinman, 2004)

OUTLINE

In this chapter we focus on sexual health, and prevention of unintended pregnancies, STIs and HIV infections. In spite of educational campaigns, knowledge and awareness of risks and dangers of unprotected sexual contact remain at low levels and statistics on STIs and teenage pregnancies show increasing prevalences. The principal theories and models of health behaviour with particular relevance to sexual health are described. These individual-level theories are based on constructs, intended to be universally applicable, concerning how behaviours are adopted, maintained and changed. The models have yielded disappointing results yet they continue to dominate the research in the field. Our critique of the approach indicates the need for fresh lines of inquiry.

Sexual behaviour is any activity that arouses sexual arousal for pleasure or procreation. Sexual intimacy can have life-changing consequences: unintended pregnancy, HIV and sexually transmitted infections (STIs). The latter cause serious medical complications including chronic illness, infertility, disability and death. Issues within sexual health are associated with significant problems of stigma and discrimination. This chapter focuses on models and theories applied to sexual health with the aim of preventing STIs, HIV infection and unintended pregnancy.

INCIDENCE AND PREVALENCE OF STIs, HIV AND AIDS

Sexually transmitted infections (STIs) are passed on through intimate sexual contact. They can be passed on during vaginal, anal and oral sex, as well as through genital contact with an infected partner. Common STIs are chlamydia, genital warts and gonorrhoea. Two of the most serious, but fortunately more rare STIs, are syphilis and HIV. The greatest affected age group for the common STIs is young people aged 16–24 years. Even though they account for just 12% of the population, more than half of all STIs diagnosed in the UK occur in young people. This includes 65% of new chlamydia cases and 55% of new genital warts cases. In the UK, the incidence of STI has been rising steadily since the 1990s. By the end of 2012, an estimated 98,400 people were living with HIV infection in the UK, including about 77,610 people diagnosed with HIV infection and 21,900 who were infected but undiagnosed. United States statistics are similar. The Centers for Disease Control (CDC, 2013) reported that there are more than 110 million total STIs among men and women across the nation and 20 million new ST infections in the USA each year, costing the American health care system nearly $16 billion in direct medical costs alone. The CDC estimated that half of all new STIs in the country occur among young men and women. Young people in general suffer from two potentially fatal ideas: (1) they think that they know it all when, in fact, they are ignorant of risks; and (2) they think that bad things won't happen to them (so-called 'optimistic bias').

The **prevalence** of HIV infection across the globe has been rising steadily with the majority (69%) of cases in sub-Saharan Africa (see Figure 6.1).

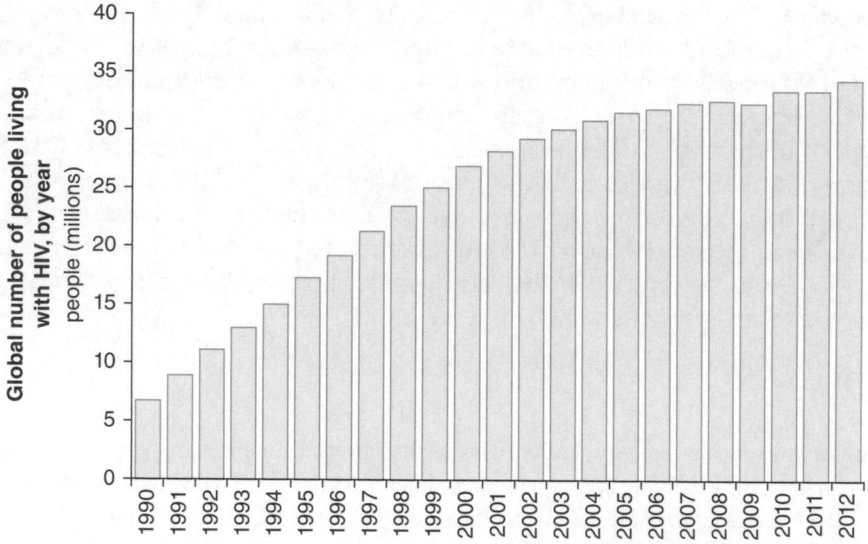

Figure 6.1 The number of people living with HIV infection has risen from around 8 million in 1990 to around 35 million, and is still growing

Source: AVERT Organization (2014), www.avert.org/. Reproduced by permission

These worrying statistics show that unprotected sexual behaviour is creating a considerable health care burden from people with HIV infection, AIDS, STIs and unintended pregnancies. The figures for developing countries are high, and the high cost of medicines is prohibiting the most effective forms of treatment. Much of the limited funds that exist for HIV infection and STI prevention programmes are committed to poster and condom campaigns for which there is little evidence of effectiveness.

KNOWLEDGE, AWARENESS AND CONDOM USE

In spite of decades of health education about STIs and HIV, there is still widespread ignorance about these diseases. The National AIDS Trust (2011) reported that one in five people still did not realize that HIV infection can be passed on through sex without a condom between a man and a woman and, worryingly, knowledge of this fact had fallen by 11% in the last decade. In addition, one in ten people incorrectly believed HIV infection can be transmitted through impossible routes such as kissing (9%) and spitting (10%) and these figures had doubled since 2007 (from 4% and 5% respectively).

A research survey involving 1,566 young people from 99 countries was carried out by the student organization AIESEC International (2009). A press release on 12 August 2009 announced that: 'Half the world's teenagers admit to being dangerously ignorant about risks of HIV infection – and many do not use condoms.' The report stated that one in three youngsters apparently do not believe using protection stops the spread of sexually transmitted diseases. Yet half of the world's new HIV infections are among 15- to 24-year-olds. Fifty-seven per cent of youngsters in south-east Asia admit to knowing little about HIV infection or AIDS as compared to 74.3% of young Africans, with sub-Saharan Africa having the world's highest AIDS rate (AIESEC International, 2009).

Risky sexual behaviour has been studied in relation to social and educational status, and to habits such as drinking alcohol and taking drugs. Health risks are often associated with, for example, smoking, drinking, drugs and alcohol. Sexual risk taking has been associated with poorer academic performance. Poor academic performance at high school predicts risky sexual behaviour after high school (Bailey et al., 2008). Bogart et al. (2006) found that poor grades in high school predicted health risk behaviour in adulthood, including high-risk sexual behaviour. The reasons for the association between academic performance and sexual risk behaviour remains unclear. A possible mediator would be alcohol and drug use.

Hittner and Kryzanowski (2010) investigated academic performance, residential status, class rank, and gender as predictors of risky sexual behaviour under two different substance use contexts, being 'drunk or high' and 'not drunk or high'. Results indicated that gender moderated the association between residential status and risky sex, such that males living on-campus engaged in more frequent casual sex than males living off-campus. The data for females did not differ on- or off-campus, possibly resulting from the under-reporting of sexual behaviour by females. All studies on sexual behaviour using self-reports tend to find disparities between the males' and females' reports in line with gender stereotypes in which it has traditionally been 'macho' to report plenty of encounters and 'feminine' to report few, a well-known 'double standard'.

Randrianasolo et al. (2008) studied barriers to the use of diaphragms and implications for woman-controlled prevention of sexually transmitted infections in Madagascar. The researchers approached women seeking care for vaginal discharge at a public health clinic for a semi-structured interview or focus group discussion. Of 46 participating women, 70% reported occasional use of male condoms, while only 14% reported using hormonal contraception. Three barriers to using modern contraceptives were: gaps in knowledge; misinformation and negative perceptions; and concern about social opposition from male partners.

One group receiving a lot of research attention is college students. Partly this is because academic researchers have access to limitless numbers of students. Students are taught a mantra that university life isn't purely about studying and learning, it's about the good 'social life' too. (For 'social life', in many cases, you had better read 'sex'.) The majority of students have multiple sex partners and yet report inconsistent condom use (Lewis et al., 2009). The American College Health Association (2005) found 52% of college students had vaginal intercourse at least once in the past 30 days with 63% reporting inconsistent condom use. Alcohol and drug use prior to sexual activity is a predictor of unsafe sex (Hittner and Kennington, 2008; Lewis et al., 2009) because it compromises sexual decision-making (Wechsler et al., 1994) and increases unsafe sexual contact (Bon et al., 2001). Negative psychological consequences, guilt and reduced self-esteem tend to follow unplanned sexual activity (Paul et al., 2000). Ma et al. (2009) investigated behavioural and psychosocial predictors of condom use among students in eastern China using a questionnaire survey. Among 1850 sexually active participants, frequent condom use was reported by about only 40% of men and women. Given the strict laws on procreation in China, these data illustrate the low adoption of condom use among students in Eastern as well as Western countries. The evidence suggests that putting on a condom just seems like too big an effort before having a screw!

An important barrier to risk behaviour reduction is low literacy. Kalichman et al. (1999) tested the significance of health literacy relative to other predictors of adherence to treatment for HIV infection and AIDS. Kalichman et al. studied a community sample of HIV-seropositive men and women taking a triple-drug combination of antiretroviral therapies for HIV infection; 60% were from ethnic minorities, and 73% had been diagnosed with AIDS. The findings showed that education and health literacy were significant predictors of treatment adherence after controlling for age, ethnicity, income, symptoms of HIV infection, substance abuse, social support, emotional distress and attitudes toward primary care providers. They found that people who are low in literacy were more likely to miss treatment doses because of confusion, depression, and desire to cleanse their body than were participants with higher health literacy. The authors concluded: 'People of lower literacy may benefit from pictorial displays of their medications, accurate in color and size, with graphic illustration of the instructions including the number of pills to be taken, and at what times. In addition, videotapes tailored to different levels of comprehension may provide a more effective medium than pamphlets and brochures for educating patients about their treatments. Intensive case management and assertive assistance programs may be required for those persons with the greatest difficulty understanding their treatment regimen and the importance of adherence' (Kalichman et al., 1999: 271).

A more insidious barrier to risk behaviour reductionism is pseudoscience and 'denialism', the organized, widespread form of denial such as occurred in South Africa and to a lesser extent in other regions including the USA. The idea that HIV infection is a myth, or that HIV infection treatments are poison, is fuelled by pseudoscience, faulty logic, conspiracy theories, homophobia and racism, the subject of Seth Kalichman's (2009) book, *Denying AIDS*. Individuals may refuse to be tested, ignore their diagnoses, or reject the treatments that could save their lives based on the dangerous, pseudoscientific misinformation put out by denialists such as President Mbeki in South Africa. Against the consensus of scientific opinion, Mbeki argued that HIV infection was not the cause of AIDS and that antiretroviral (ARV) drugs were not useful for patients, and so he declined to accept freely donated nevirapine and grants from the Global Fund. It has been estimated that more than 330,000 lives or approximately 2.2 million person-years were lost because a feasible and timely ARV treatment programme was not implemented in South Africa between 2000 and 2005 (Chigwedere et al., 2008).

As we have seen, low condom usage and other risk behaviours are not caused simply by a lack of awareness or knowledge, or optimistic bias (e.g. Chapin, 2001), but can be caused by misinformation and phony science. Motivational and emotional factors play a very significant role, as does culture. Explaining and reducing sexual risk taking is therefore a significant challenge for all of health care. The need to put theory into cost-effective practice has never been greater. In the rest of this chapter we explore the main theoretical approaches and evaluate their success with data from controlled studies and meta-analyses.

INDIVIDUAL-LEVEL THEORIES AND MODELS

Individual-level approaches use theoretical concepts and models as a basis for studying people's actions and choices. Because interventions using this approach are based on preconceived theoretical ideas, they are described as '**top-down**'. The interventions using this approach are constructed without any involvement of the intended participants. The psychologist decides what makes people behave the way that they do, using internalized concepts, and then tests the theory to see if it fits controlled data. Many theories and models have been applied to the study of contraceptive use and safer sex practices.

In this section, we outline eight theories that have informed interventions targeted at individual sexual risk: the health belief model, protection motivation theory, the theory of reasoned action, the theory of planned behaviour, the information–motivation–behavioural skills model, the common sense model or self-regulation theory, the transtheoretical or stages of change model, and social cognitive theory. (We apologise in advance if this section exceeds your 'boredom threshold', but we have to include them somewhere, so we decided to put them in the sex chapter.)

These theories and models have been fashionable, with dozens of researchers forging successful careers in the pursuit of a well-tested theory (even if the theory itself is fairly 'crap'). Unfortunately, elaborate in-depth and in-detail testing has not gone well for many of the models that are now little more than 'museum pieces' presented here for their historical role in the development of the field. Some are still actively being worked on and may yet yield results in the field of prevention. However, there are serious flaws in the assumptions behind many of these theories and models, which does not augur well for a successful outcome. As we indicate here and in other chapters, there is a vast scope for new approaches that are grounded in the social and economic circumstances of contemporary living.

THE HEALTH BELIEF MODEL

The **health belief model (HBM)**, developed by Rosenstock (1966), is an influential cognitive model that examines the predictors and precursors to health behaviour. The HBM (see Figure 6.2) contains four constructs:

1. Perceived susceptibility (an individual's assessment of their risk of getting the condition).
2. Perceived severity (an individual's assessment of the seriousness of the condition, and its potential consequences).
3. Perceived barriers (an individual's assessment of the influences that facilitate or discourage adoption of the promoted behaviour).
4. Perceived benefits (an individual's assessment of the positive consequences of adopting the behaviour).

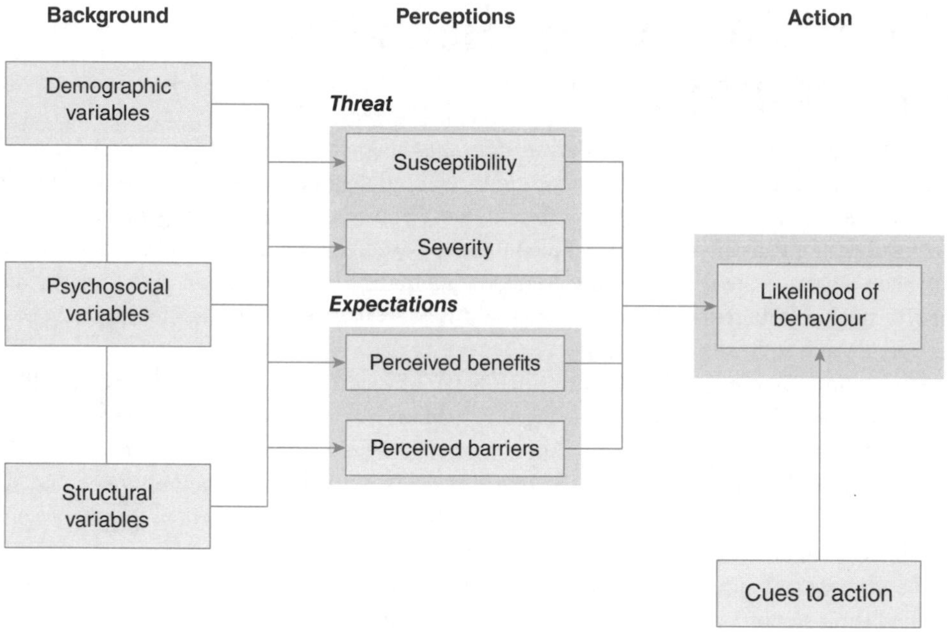

Figure 6.2 The health belief model

The likelihood of a behaviour is influenced also by **cues to action** that are reminders or prompts to take action consistent with an intention. These cues to action can be *internal* (e.g. feeling fatigued can trigger actions to take time out or relax) or *external* (e.g. seeing health promotion leaflets/posters, personal communication from health professionals, family members, peers, etc.)

The HBM takes these factors into account to predict the likelihood of implementing health-related behaviour. The HBM has been developed over the years and additional factors have been included in the model (Becker, 1974; Rosenstock et al., 1994). For example, demographic factors (e.g. age, sex and socio-economic background), psychosocial factors (e.g. personality traits, peer influence, family, etc.) and structural factors (e.g. knowledge of the health condition or previous contact to the disease) have been added into the model.

The HBM has been tested in several studies of sexual health and has been used as a theoretical framework for interventions. A few examples follow, showing modest and sometimes inconsistent results. Lollis et al. (1997) investigated the efficacy of the health belief model for predicting condom usage and risky sexual practices in 122 white heterosexual college students (aged 17 to 33 years). The findings suggested that HBM did not significantly explain condom usage in the 58 men and 64 women surveyed and only partially explained the variance in sexual risk behaviours. The HBM explained 9% of the variance in the likelihood of women being intoxicated or high during sex and 18% of the variance in the number of sexual risk behaviours endorsed by women. These authors concluded that the HBM had limited utility for predicting sexual practices in university students, suggesting the need for more comprehensive models of behaviour change.

Wiggers et al. (2003) investigated social-cognitive determinants of condom use among ethnic minority communities in Amsterdam. Wiggers et al. tested the predictive utility of the health belief model and the theory of planned behaviour (TPB, see below) with a sample of 537 Surinamese, Antillean and sub-Saharan African heterosexual men and women. Participants were interviewed and donated saliva for HIV infection testing. Consistent condom use was reported in only 23% of primary partnerships and in 77% of the casual partnerships. Controlling for socio-demographic and behavioural factors, analyses showed that perceived behavioural control and subjective norms regarding condom use were the main social-cognitive determinants of consistent condom use, confirming the TPB. However, perceived susceptibility and severity of HIV infection, perceived benefits of condom use, and cues to action did not help to explain condom use, disconfirming the HBM in this sample.

Downing-Matibag and Geisinger (2009) studied how ‘hooking up’ with friends, strangers and acquaintances enabled students to experience sexual intimacy without committing to a romantic relationship, preferably not even exchanging names. ‘Hooking up’ often involves risky behaviours because it frequently occurs in situations in which prophylactics are unavailable or judgment is impaired through drinks or drugs. The authors carried out 71 semi-structured interviews with students about their experiences of hooking-up. The authors found the health belief model to be a useful framework for understanding sexual risk taking, and sexual risk-prevention programmes on college campuses. Students’ self-assessments of susceptibility to STIs are often misinformed, enabling situational characteristics, such as spontaneity, to influence their sexual self-efficacy.

BOX 6.1
GET YOURSELF TESTED CAMPAIGN

The Get Yourself Tested (GYT) campaign was launched in the USA in 2009 to reduce stigma and promote STD communication and testing. Media, communication and public relations/outreach resources are informed by the health belief model and the Theory of Planned Behaviour. As young people often do not perceive that they are at risk for STDs and often fear STD testing, e.g. uncomfortable procedures and stigma, the campaign is directed towards accurate information and increased rates of testing. GYT campaign messages were developed to increase STD awareness and perceived risk, reduce fear and stigma, and promote open communication with sex partners and health care providers. GYT uses television, the Web, SMS, print and on-the-ground efforts to reach young people with information and link them to testing. The hub of the campaign is the website www.GYTNOW.org. Through this site, young people can access nearby, free/low-cost and teen-friendly STD testing services (www.findSTDtest.org). National promotions and celebrity endorsements further incentivize testing. The GYT campaign runs year-round, with refreshed messaging each April. GYT toolkits containing promotional materials are provided each year to facilitate state and local efforts.

Friedman et al. (2014) assessed the first two years of campaign engagement and associations with STD testing among young people. The evidence suggests positive, but modest, results. On-the-ground events reached an estimated 20,000 young people in 2009 and 52,000 in 2010. Across 2009 to 2010, GYT's Facebook page gained 4,477 fans, its Twitter feed gained 1,994 followers, and more than 140,000 referrals were made to the STD testing locator. From April 2008 to 2010, there was a 71% increase in STD testing and a 41% increase in chlamydia testing at 118 health centres. Chlamydia case positivity rates during this period were stable at 6.6% (2008) and 7.3% (2010). The authors concluded that data quality was limited in a manner similar to many STD prevention efforts. However, they reported that the evidence suggests GYT reaches young people and is associated with increased STD testing.

Campaigns such as GYT are based on the HBM in assuming that human beings are rational information processors who make systematic use of the information available to them. This assumption is questionable in mature adults and even more so in young people, the target group for campaigns to promote safe sex practices and prevent unintended pregnancies.

PROTECTION MOTIVATION THEORY

Protection motivation theory (PMT) was developed by Rogers (1975) to describe coping with a health threat in light of two appraisal processes, threat appraisal and coping appraisal. It introduces a most basic human emotion into health protection: *fear.* Fear is widely used in campaigns and behavioural change interventions, yet empirical support for its use remains unconvincing.

According to PMT the appraisal of the health threat, basically one's fear of the consequences of one's actions, and the possible coping response result in an intention, or 'protection motivation', to perform either an adaptive response or a maladaptive response. According to PMT, behaviour change is best achieved by appealing to an individual's fears. The PMT proposes four constructs, which are said to influence the intention to protect oneself against a health threat:

1. The perceived *severity* of a threatened event (e.g. HIV infection).
2. The perceived probability of the occurrence, or *vulnerability* (e.g. the perceived vulnerability of the person to HIV).
3. The efficacy of the recommended preventive behaviour (i.e. how effective is the wearing of a condom?).
4. The perceived *self-efficacy* (e.g. the person's confidence in putting a condom in place) (see Figure 6.3).

This theory takes account of both costs and benefits of behaviour in predicting the likelihood of change. PMT assumes that protection motivation is maximized when:

the threat to health is severe;

the individual feels vulnerable;

the adaptive response is believed to be an effective means for averting the threat;

the person is confident in his or her abilities to complete successfully the adaptive response;

the rewards associated with the maladaptive behaviour are small;

the costs associated with the adaptive response are small.

Such factors produce protection motivation and subsequently an adaptive, or coping, response (Figure 6.3).

Li et al. (2004) studied HIV/STD risk behaviours and perceptions among 2,153 sexually active rural-to-urban migrants in China. Migration often places individuals at increased risk for HIV infection and STI. The applicability of the constructs of the PMT to the study population was evaluated. The authors measured migrant mobility, sexual risk, and the seven constructs of the PMT. The data confirmed that the high mobility among the rural-to-urban migrant population was associated with increased sexual risk. The PMT constructs were found to be applicable in identifying perceptions and attitudes associated with sexual risk behaviours in this population. Increased sexual risk was associated with increased perceptions of extrinsic rewards, intrinsic rewards, and response cost. Also consistent with PMT, increased sexual risk was associated with perceptions of decreased severity, vulnerability, response efficacy and self-efficacy. After controlling for

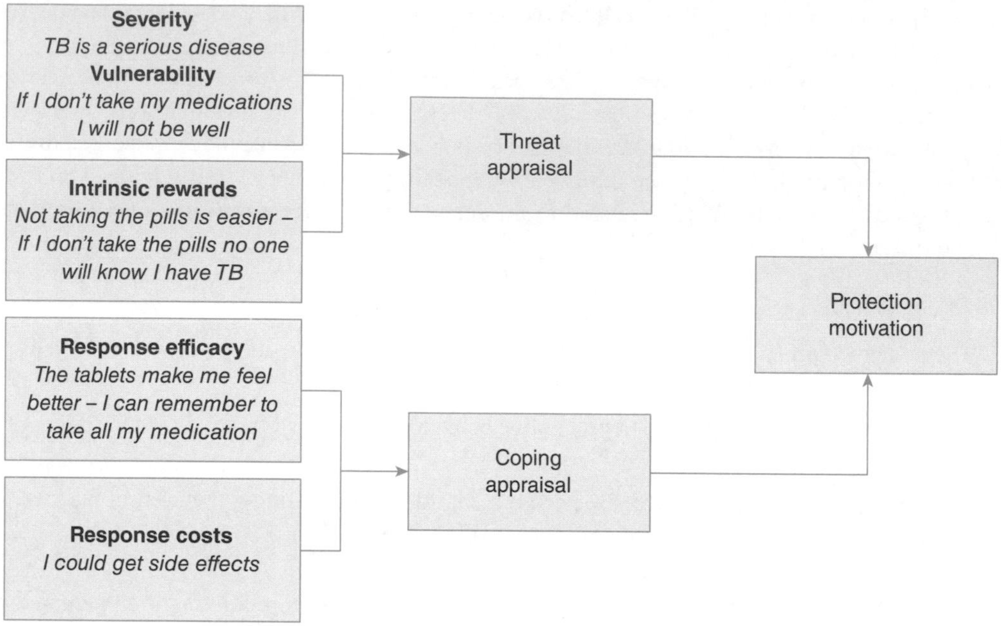

Figure 6.3 The four constructs and the two appraisal processes that result in protection motivation

Source: adapted from Stroebe (2000)

a number of confounding factors, all seven PMT constructs were found to be associated with sexual risk in the manner posited by the theory. The association between mobility and sexual risk emphasizes the importance of having effective HIV/STD prevention efforts among this vulnerable population. The PMT could form a rational basis for interventions targeting migrants.

Floyd et al. (2000) carried out a meta-analysis of research on PMT. The review included 65 relevant studies that represented over 20 health issues. The mean overall effect size ($d+ = 0.52$) was of moderate magnitude. In general, increases in threat severity, threat vulnerability, response efficacy, and self-efficacy facilitated adaptive intentions or behaviours while decreases in maladaptive response rewards and adaptive response costs increased adaptive intentions or behaviours. This held true whether the measures were based on intentions or behaviours, and suggests that PMT components may be useful for both individual and community interventions.

Ruiter et al. (2014) reviewed empirical evidence on the effectiveness of fear appeals in light of six meta-analytic studies on the effectiveness of fear appeals. They concluded that coping information aimed at increasing perceptions of response effectiveness and especially self-efficacy is more important than presenting health information aimed at increasing risk perceptions and fear arousal. Attempts to change behaviour by appealing to fear have received only limited empirical support. Alternative methods are likely to be more fruitful.

THEORY OF REASONED ACTION

The theory of reasoned action (TRA) includes three constructs: behavioural intention, attitude, and subjective norm. The TRA is based on the assumption that a person is likely to do what he or she intends to do. The theory assumes that a person's behavioural intention depends on the person's attitude about the behaviour and subjective norms. The model is illustrated in Figure 6.4.

Recent studies of the TRA include: Patterson et al. (2005) developing an HIV-prevention intervention for sex workers in Tijuana, Mexico; Koniak-Griffin and Stein (2006) using TRA predictors of sexual risk behaviours among adolescent mothers in a human immunodeficiency virus prevention programme; Randolph et al. (2009) developing an STI-prevention for seriously mentally ill women using the theory of reasoned action.

In spite of efforts to apply the TRA to sexual health, it fails to capture the complexity of sexual experience. The TRA is based on the flawed assumption of rationality, that human beings ordinarily can make systematic and logical use of available information. It also assumes that human behaviour is determined by free choice in a manner that is unrestrained by political or economic factors, neglects the role of emotion and feelings in sexual intimacy, and does not incorporate factors such as self-efficacy and self-esteem, which are of crucial importance in negotiating safe sex practices. For these reasons, the theory failed to provide an explanatory account of health behaviour. Yet, in spite of its obvious weaknesses, the TRA approach spawned other, similarly flawed theories, as we shall see below.

THE THEORY OF PLANNED BEHAVIOUR

Behaviour is complex and rarely controlled with the rationality implied by the TRA. Sex, smoking, eating and alcohol use are all good examples of behaviour that people have difficulty controlling in a free and voluntary way. Ajzen (1985) added the variable of **perceived behavioural control** to produce the theory of planned behaviour (TPB) (see Figure 6.5). The TPB is the most cited theory in the history of psychology, cited even more than Freud's theory of psychoanalysis. It has become as 'sacred' as the Holy Cow itself, shot right through with holes.

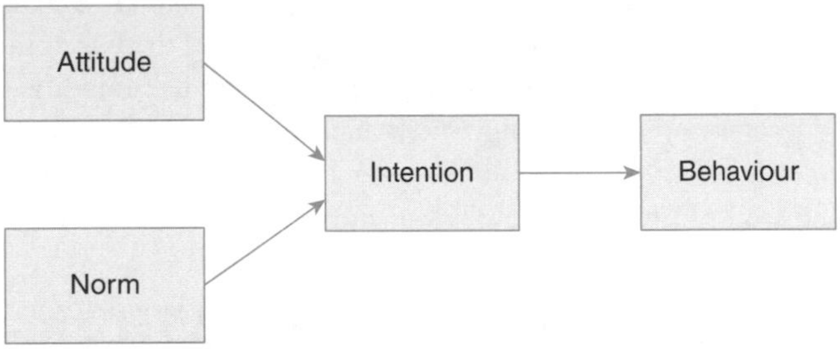

Figure 6.4 The theory of reasoned action

Source: Fishbein and Ajzen (1975)

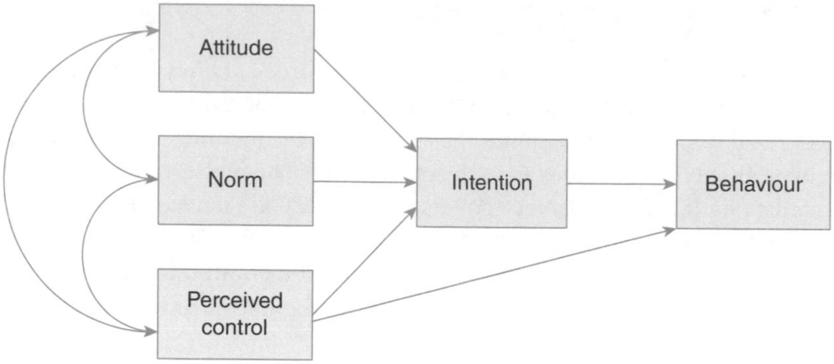

Figure 6.5 The theory of planned behaviour

Source: Ajzen (1991)

Perceived behavioural control refers to one's perception of control over the behaviour, and reflects the obstacles and successes encountered in past experience with this behaviour. The TPB proposes that perceived behavioural control can influence intentions and behaviour directly. For example, in the college student population, attitudes towards safe sex, condom use self-efficacy and beliefs about peer norms have all been shown to predict unsafe sexual activity (Lewis et al., 2009; Hittner and Kryzanowski, 2010). The success of the TPB in predicting safer sexual behaviour was reviewed in a meta-analysis published by Albarracín et al. (2001) (see below).

Important factors of culture and religion that are influential on behaviour are missing from the TPB. Sinha et al. (2007) studied sexual behaviour and relationships amongst black and minority ethnic (BME) teenagers in East London. The authors wanted to learn how these relationships are shaped by culture, gender, peer norms and religion. They collected data from 126 young people, aged 15–18, mainly using focus groups in the London boroughs of Hackney, Newham and Tower Hamlets. The findings suggested that sexual behaviour is mediated by gender, religion and youth in multiple ways not included in the TPB. A recent systematic review of 237 independent prospective tests found that the TPB accounted for only 19% of the variability in health behaviour (McEachan et al., 2011).

The findings from multiple studies concur that the TPB, and its many extensions and versions, have consistently failed to account for more than a meagre 20% of the variability in health behaviour. This means that at least 80% of the variance in sexual health behaviour is unexplained by the TPB. Its stalwart adherents notwithstanding, Sniehotta et al. (2014) suggested that it was 'time to retire' the TPB. Unperturbed by its difficulties, Ajzen (2014) remains steadfastly convinced that the THP is 'alive and well'. Every holy cow has its guru.

THE INFORMATION–MOTIVATION–BEHAVIOURAL SKILLS MODEL

The information–motivation–behavioural skills (IMB) model was proposed by Fisher and Fisher (1992, 2000). The IMB model focuses on informational, motivational and behavioural skills factors that are found to be associated with sex-related problem-prevention and wellness-promotion behaviours. According to the IMB model, the learning of sexuality-related information is a prerequisite to action in these areas. HIV-related information is likely to include facts about HIV infection (e.g. 'Oral sex is safer than vaginal or anal sex') that could facilitate preventive behaviour performance. The IMB model assumes that having the motivation to practise specific sex-related behaviours is necessary for the production of problem-prevention or wellness promotion. Finally, sexuality-related behavioural skills are a third fundamental determinant of acting effectively to avoid sexual problems and achieving sexual well-being. The behavioural skills construct focuses on the person's self-efficacy in performing sexual problem-prevention or well-being-related behaviours including insisting on abstinence from intercourse, discussing and practising contraceptive use, and sexual behaviours that optimize a couple's sexual pleasure. Barak and Fisher (2001) proposed an Internet-driven approach to sex education using the Internet based on the IMB model. An illustration of the IMB model applied to adherence in using HAART medication for HIV infection is shown in Figure 6.6.

There have been several studies of the IMB model in different settings. Carey et al. (2000) carried out a randomized clinical trial of an IMB-based intervention using information, motivational enhancement, and skills training to reduce the risk of HIV infection for low-income urban women in Syracuse, New York. Risk markers in the past year included a non-monogamous partner (82%), more than one partner (62%), sex trading (32%), an STI (24%), a bisexual partner (23%), and a partner who had injected drugs (5%); only 1% reported needle-sharing. Participants

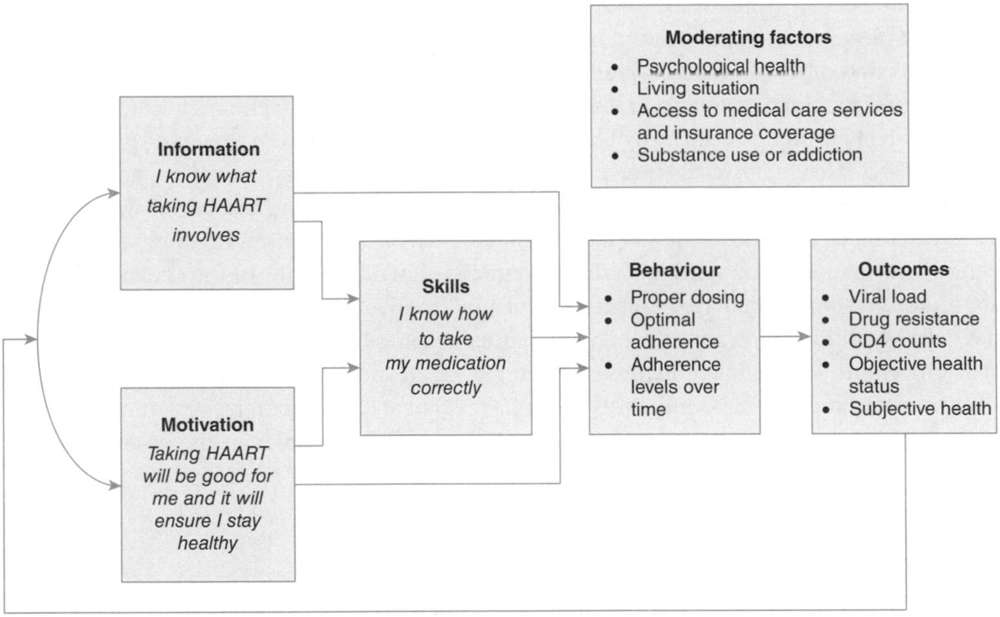

Figure 6.6 The information–motivation–behavioural skills model

Source: adapted from Fisher et al. (2006)

completed a questionnaire on their demographics, HIV-related information, motivation (risk perception, behavioural intentions) and risk-related behaviour. Carey et al. offered two interventions randomly to the participants: (i) the HIV-Risk Reduction (HIV-RR) intervention was designed to reduce HIV-related risk behaviours by first enhancing motivation for behaviour change by using motivational interviewing strategies (Miller and Rollnick, 1991); (ii) a health-promotion control group. Women in the HIV-RR programme were found to have enhanced their knowledge and strengthened their risk reduction intentions relative to controls.

Eggers et al. (2013) tested the IMB model to assess the hypothesized motivational pathways for the prediction of condom use during last sexual intercourse with 1,066 students from Cape Town, South Africa. Knowledge of how to use a condom and how STIs are transmitted directly predicted behaviour as hypothesized by the IMB model. However, an alternative model had a higher proportion of significant pathways.

Scott-Sheldon et al. (2010) found that the IMB model provided a good fit to data collected from 1,474 STD patients. They found that information was unrelated to condom use but motivation and behavioural skills both had a positive effect on condom use. Stronger associations between motivation and condom use occurred among participants reporting no prior STD treatment.

Mongkuo et al. (2012) highlighted that African-Americans continue to be the most severely burdened with HIV infection of all racial groups in the USA (US CDC, 2011). In 2009, despite representing only 14% of the US population, African-Americans accounted for 44% of all new cases of HIV infection. Furthermore, African-Americans accounted for a higher proportion of HIV infections at all stages of the disease – from new infections to deaths. They applied the IMB model to assess the effects of prevention education, prevention personal motivation and prevention knowledge on HIV infection prevention behavioural skills among black college students. The research examined motivation and knowledge to explain HIV infection prevention behaviour among students from the historically black colleges and universities. Survey data of indicators of the three IMB latent constructs – prevention information, prevention motivation, and prevention behavioural skills – were collected. Structural equation modelling (SEM) analysis was performed to estimate the overall model fit and the magnitude of effects of prevention motivation and prevention information or knowledge on the prevention behavioural skills of the students. The analysis found that prevention HIV infection education motivation and HIV infection prevention knowledge had no significant effect on prevention behavioural skills, while HIV infection personal prevention knowledge emerged as having a significantly large effect in explaining HIV infection prevention behavioural skills among the students. The authors suggested that future studies using the IMB model should expand the exogenous variables in the model to include exposure to violent living conditions.

THE COMMON SENSE MODEL

The common sense model (CSM), also known as the self-regulatory model (SRM), or Leventhal's model, was developed by Howard Leventhal and colleagues (Leventhal et al., 1980, 2003). A key construct within the CSM is the idea of illness representations or 'lay' beliefs about illness. These representations integrate with normative guidelines that people hold, to make sense of their symptoms and guide any coping actions. Five components of illness representations in the CSM are: *identity*, *cause*, *time-line*, *consequences* and *curability/controllability*. For further discussion of the CSM, see Chapter 16.

THE TRANSTHEORETICAL MODEL OR STAGES OF CHANGE MODEL

The transtheoretical model (TTM), otherwise known as the stages of change model, was developed by Prochaska and DiClementi (1983). It has been highly influential in the literature on health behaviour change. The TTM hypothesizes six discrete stages of change (see Figure 6.7), which people are alleged to progress through in making a change:

Pre-contemplation – a person is not intending to take action in the foreseeable future, usually measured as the next six months.

Contemplation – a person is intending to change in the next six months.

Preparation – a person is intending to take action in the immediate future, usually measured as the next month.

Action – a person is making specific overt modifications in his/her lifestyle within the past six months.

Maintenance – a person is working to prevent relapse, a stage that is estimated to last from six months to about five years.

Either *termination* – an individual has zero temptation and 100% self-efficacy, or *relapse* – an individual reverts to the original behaviour.

The TTM has been tested in multiple studies with mixed results. For example, Velasquez et al. (2009) carried out a trial designed to reduce sexual risk behaviours and alcohol use among HIV-positive men who have sex with men. They used a stages of change-based intervention and also the technique of motivational interviewing (MI). Valasquez et al. found reductions in the number of drinks per 30-day period, number of heavy drinking days per 30-day period, and the number of days on which both heavy drinking and unprotected sex occurred. Chacko et al. (2009) tested the efficacy of a motivational/behavioural intervention to promote chlamydia and gonorrhea screening in young women, which is critical to reduction of asymptomatic cervicitis and its complications. Three hundred and seventy-six sexually active, young women were randomized to two groups: intervention plus standard care or standard care alone. The intervention used the TTM and MI. However, no significant differences occurred between the two groups.

A meta-analysis by Noar et al. (2009) indicated that interventions using the Stages of Change Model were relatively effective. However, critics have suggested that the model contains arbitrary time periods and that the supportive evidence is meagre and inconsistent (e.g. Sutton, 2000). The TTM has remained a resilient and popular model of change in health psychology.

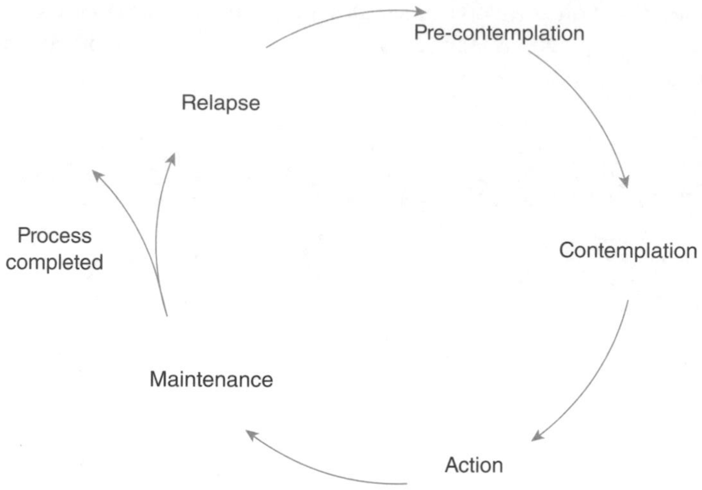

Figure 6.7 The transtheoretical model or stages of change model

Source: Prochaska and DiClementi (1982)

SOCIAL COGNITIVE THEORY

Bandura's (1986) social cognitive theory (SCT) examines the social origins of behaviour in addition to the cognitive thought processes that influence human behaviour and functioning. Bandura's social-cognitive approach proposes that learning can occur in the absence of direct reinforcement through observation of models in the absence of any overt reinforcement. The acquisition of skill and knowledge have an intrinsic reinforcement value independent of biological drives and needs. The basic constructs within SCT are described in this section.

Observational Learning

According to Bandura, people can learn by watching or observing others, by reading about what people do, and by making general observations of the world. This learning may or may not be demonstrated in the form of behaviour. Bandura proposed a four-step conceptual scheme for observational learning:

Step 1: attentional processes including certain model characteristics that may increase the likelihood of the behaviour being attended to and the observer characteristics such as sensory capacities, motivation and arousal levels, perceptual set, and past reinforcement.

Step 2: retention processes including the observer's ability to remember and to make sense of what has been observed.

Step 3: motor reproduction processes including the capabilities that the observer has to perform the behaviours being observed. Specific factors include physical capabilities and availability of responses.

Step 4: motivational processes including external reinforcement, vicarious reinforcement and self-reinforcement. If a behaviour is to be imitated, an observer must be motivated to perform that behaviour.

Self-Efficacy

Bandura (1994) defined the concept of 'perceived self-efficacy' as:

> People's beliefs about their capabilities to produce designated levels of performance that exercise influence over events that affect their lives. Self-efficacy beliefs determine how people feel, think, motivate themselves and behave. Such beliefs produce these diverse effects through four major processes. They include cognitive, motivational, affective and selection processes. (p. 71)

Self-efficacy is a person's belief that they have behavioural competence in a particular situation. Self-efficacy is related to whether or not an individual will undertake particular goal-directed activities, the amount of energy that he or she will put into their effort, and the length of time that the individual will persist in striving to achieve a particular goal. Among the sources of self-efficacy are:

performance accomplishments: past experiences of success and failure;

vicarious experience: witnessing others' successes and failures;

verbal persuasion: being told by others that one can or cannot competently perform a particular behaviour;

emotional arousal: when engaging in a particular behaviour in a specific situation.

The concept has been widely applied in studies of, and interventions for, health protecting behaviours. The concept mirrors the self-help literature of the kind Dale Carnegie founded on the principle that people can achieve great things by believing that they can do so, so-called 'positive thinking'. Carnegie (1913) was an erudite scholar of the art of rhetoric who believed that reading yielded priceless knowledge. There can be little doubt that ideas about positive thinking and self-efficacy are very prevalent in popular culture. Bandura has made some extremely important observations about human learning and thought. Observational learning and self-efficacy are invaluable concepts. However, critics argue that the relationship between the concepts is not clear.

APPLYING SOCIAL COGNITIVE THEORY IN MASS COMMUNICATION

Bandura's (1986) theory of vicarious learning can be applied to the use of role models in the mass media as a method for shaping cultural attitudes and behaviour. Of particular interest are the use of serial melodramas, 'telenovelas' and 'soaps' using the methodology developed by Sabido (1981) in Mexico that aim to reinforce social values through the use of drama. Ryerson's (2010) Population Media Centre has been actively promoting reproductive health in many different countries. Research is carried out prior to the development of TV programmes to measure audience attitudes and norms. Characters for the soaps are developed to reflect the interests of the audience. Through the evolution of characters as they respond to problems that many audience members are also facing, soap operas can show the adoption of new, non-traditional behaviours in a way that generates no negative response and little resistance from the audience. Audience members form bonds with soap characters, and adopt them as role models. Evaluation of these methods has shown excellent results (Ryerson, 2010).

Galavotti et al. (2001) describe a successful approach to prevent HIV infection and AIDS using modelling and reinforcement to combat HIV infection (MARCH). This approach combines individual behaviour change with efforts to change social norms by using entertainment as a vehicle for education (long-running serialized dramas on radio or television portray role models evolving towards the adoption of positive behaviours) and interpersonal reinforcement at the community level (support from friends, family members, and others can help people initiate behaviour changes; support through changes in social norms is necessary for behavioural effects to be sustained over time). Galavotti et al. argue that media and interpersonal intervention activities should be linked to existing community resources and, wherever possible, provide increased access to preventive services, supplies, and other supporting elements.

Kuhlmann et al. (2008) examined the use of radio role models for the prevention of mother-to-child transmission of HIV infection and HIV infection testing among pregnant women in Botswana. A programme for the prevention of mother-to-child-transmission of HIV infection (PMTCT) suffered from low uptake. Using 2003 survey data from 504 pregnant and post-partum women, Kuhlmann et al. assessed associations between exposure to a long-running radio serial drama that encourages use of the PMTCT programme and HIV infection testing during pregnancy. Controlling for demographic, pregnancy and other variables, women who spontaneously named a PMTCT character in the serial drama as their *favourite* character were nearly twice as likely to test for HIV infection during pregnancy as those who did not. The authors concluded that identification with characters in the radio serial drama is associated with testing during pregnancy.

Nambiar et al. (2011) studied a mass media campaign in Tamil Nadu, India. They studied the effect of Nalamdana's radio and theatre programme on knowledge, stigma, and behavioural outcomes among antiretroviral therapy patients. The study compared patients at consecutive stages of receiving antiretroviral treatment, coinciding with exposure to a radio-and-theatre-based educational programme at three levels: unexposed ($n = 120$), just exposed ($n = 77$) and exposed for one month ($n = 60$). Exposure was associated with significantly higher HIV-related knowledge, lower levels of stigma, and over four times the adjusted odds of asking doctors questions about HIV. Higher exposure was associated with lower felt stigma, greater odds of consistent condom use, doctor–patient communication, peer advice-giving and HIV-related advocacy. Coupled with other supporting elements, serial dramas could make a helpful contribution to HIV infection prevention, treatment and care initiatives.

In spite of the huge amount of research on self-efficacy over the last few decades, fundamental issues about the theory remain unresolved. Williams (2010) discussed a contradiction in that self-efficacy – defined as perceived capability to perform a behaviour – is meant to causally influence expected outcomes of behaviour, not vice versa. However, research has shown that expected outcomes causally influence self-efficacy judgments. Critics have argued that this relationship invalidates self-efficacy theory. Bandura (2007) rebutted these arguments by saying that self-efficacy judgments are not invalidated when influenced by expected outcomes. Williams (2010) points out that Bandura has argued that (a) expected outcomes cannot causally influence self-efficacy, but (b) self-efficacy judgments remain valid when causally influenced by expected outcomes. If you find this argument confusing, you are not alone.

META-ANALYSES

Munro et al. (2007) provided a summary of meta-analyses carried out until February 2005 concerned with long-term medication adherence. The effects were modest and highly variable with theoretical constructs accounting for anywhere between 0 and 25% of the variance in behaviour. This means that the theoretical models left anything between 75 and 100% of the variations in medication adherence behaviour unaccounted for, a rather depressing conclusion. Is the outcome of meta-analyses of sexual health behaviour any more encouraging?

Albarracín et al. (2001) meta-analysed data on the ability of the TRA and TPB to predict condom use. In total, 96 data sets with over 22,000 participants were analysed. Consistent with the TRA: (a) condom use correlated with intentions with a mean coefficient, r, of 0.45; (b) intentions were based on attitudes ($r = 0.58$) and subjective norms ($r = 0.39$); (c) attitudes were correlated with behavioural beliefs ($r = 0.56$) and norms were correlated with normative beliefs ($r = 0.46$). Consistent with the TPB: perceived behavioural control was related to condom use intentions ($r = 0.45$) and condom use ($r = 0.25$), but, contrary to the TPB, it did not correlate significantly to condom use. However, the strength of these associations was influenced by the consideration of past behaviour. It must be borne in mind that the correlation coefficient needs to be squared to compute the variance explained by a variable. Thus the strongest relationship observed by Albarracín et al. (2001), the correlation of 0.58 between attitudes and subjective norms, accounted for 0.58×0.58 or 34% of the variance, which is certainly no cause for celebration. In fact, one might be excused a certain degree of surprise at how weak this relationship actually is.

Noar et al. (2009) carried a meta-analysis of the efficacy of computer technology-based HIV infection prevention interventions aimed at increasing condom use among at-risk populations. The overall effect size for condom use was moderate ($d = 0.259$) but indicated a statistically significant impact of the interventions. The findings showed that interventions were more efficacious when directed at single-sex groups (men or women) rather than mixed-sex groups, with individualized tailoring, using the stages of change model. On the basis of these data, HIV infection prevention using computer technology may have similar efficacy to traditional human-delivered interventions, which, if true, leaves one wondering what possible role is left for the therapist.

BOX 6.2
KEY STUDY: WHAT WORKS BEST IN PREVENTION?

In the largest meta-analysis of HIV-prevention strategies ever conducted, Albarracín et al. (2005) tested the main theoretical assumptions in models of behaviour change in contrasting 'passive' and 'active' HIV-prevention interventions (Figure 6.8). The investigators compared the effectiveness of different intervention strategies and attempted to look at the sequence of psychological change that different interventions produce, e.g. behavioural skills training should first increase behavioural skills that promote condom use. Another objective was to investigate the generalizability of different intervention strategies to different populations. They reviewed 194 research reports from 1985 to 2003, the most comprehensive review to date.

Albarracín et al. (2005) studied the impact of interventions to increase condom use on (a) attitudes, (b) norms, (c) control perceptions, (d) intentions, (e) HIV knowledge, (f) behavioural skills, (g) perceived severity of HIV, (h) perceived susceptibility to HIV, and ultimately (i) condom use. They also compared 'passive' and 'active' interventions. Passive interventions involve minimal participation by using messages to (a) induce pro-condom attitudes, (b) induce pro-condom norms, (c) increase relevant knowledge, (d) verbally model skills that promote condom use, and (e) increase perceived threat. Active interventions include client-tailored counselling, HIV testing, or activities to increase behavioural skills, such as role-playing of behaviours related to condom use.

There were two main conclusions from this extensive review. First, the most effective interventions were those that contained attitudinal arguments, educational information, behavioural skills arguments, and behavioural skills training. The least effective were those that attempted to induce fear of HIV. The impact of the interventions and the different strategies behind them was found to vary according to gender, age, ethnicity, risk group, and past condom use.

Source: Albarracín et al. (2005)

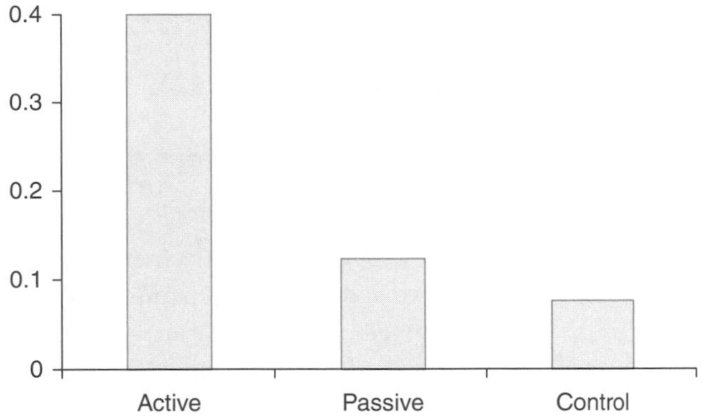

Figure 6.8 Mean behaviour change for active interventions, passive interventions, and control groups. The difference between active and passive interventions was highly significant ($p < 0.001$)

Source: adapted from Albarracín et al. (2005, Figure 1)

CRITIQUE OF INDIVIDUAL-LEVEL APPROACHES

The position regarding social cognition theories of sexual behaviour has not changed since previous editions. The evidence does not justify any confidence in the scientific value of these theories. The overall outcome of meta-analyses of theory testing provides a somewhat mixed but disappointing picture. The overall pattern of evidence suggests that current psychological theories of sexual health do not provide a viable foundation for effective interventions. We analyse the reasons for this in the following paragraphs. Alternative approaches are necessary if there is to be any significant progress in stemming the tide of STIs, HIV and unintended pregnancies.

Individualistic Bias

The individual-level approaches of traditional health psychology fall under the umbrella of individualism (see Chapter 1). The processes of choice and responsibility are internalized inside each individual's head as processes similar to the operating system of a computer. The human 'operating system' is assumed to be universal and rational, following a fixed set of formulae that the models attempt to describe. Along with the individualism comes the baggage of the positivist assumptions of a purely quantitative empirical approach. Yet even within its own terms, the programme of model testing and confirmation is failing to meet the goals it has set for itself.

Lack of Ecological Validity and Questionable Statistical Methods

Thousands of published studies – and an imponderable number unpublished – have used null hypothesis testing with small samples of college students or smaller samples of patients. The power, ecological validity and generalizability of these studies is questionable, yet we do not really know their true merit because of uncertainties about representativeness, sampling, and statistical assumptions. Rarely are alternative and arguably superior approaches to theory testing utilized, for example, by using Bayesian statistics and power analyses carried out to assess the *importance* of the effects rather than their *statistical significance* (Cohen, 1994).

Neglect of Culture, Religion and Gender

Key factors such as religion, culture and gender are not included in the social cognition models. We have seen above that studies of sexual behaviour (e.g. Sinha et al., 2007) show the importance of these factors and yet the models neglect them. The models are aiming at universal application that is unwarranted and implausible.

Tautological and Unfalsifiable

Critics of social cognition models have suggested that they are **tautological** and, therefore, irrefutable (Smedslund, 2000; Ogden, 2003). A tautology is a statement that is necessarily true, e.g. 'Jill will either stop or not stop smoking'. Whatever data we obtain about Jill's smoking, the statement will always be true, a very safe prediction. Smedslund (2000) further deduced that, if tautological theories are disconfirmed or only partially supported by empirical studies, then the studies themselves must be flawed for not 'discovering' what must be the case! Bad models can only be supported by bad research. Others have argued that behavioural beliefs (attitudes) and normative beliefs are basically the same thing. Ogden (2003) analysed empirical articles published between 1997 and 2001 from four health psychology journals that tested or applied one or more social cognition models (theory of reasoned action, theory of planned behaviour, health belief model, and protection motivation theory). Ogden concluded that the models do not enable the generation and testing of hypotheses because their constructs are unspecific. Echoing Smedslund (2000), she suggested that the models focus on analytic truths that must be true by definition.

However, not all theorists agree that SCMs are tautological and/or unfalsifiable. Trafimow (2009) claimed to have demonstrated that the TRA and TPB are falsifiable because these theories makes risky predictions. He furthermore claimed to have falsified one of the assumptions of the TPB, namely, that perceived control is a worse predictor of behavioural intentions than perceived difficulty (Trafimow et al., 2002). Yet perceived behavioural control is usually measured by items evaluating control and items evaluating difficulty. If empirical falsification of the TPB has actually occurred then the theory must, ipso facto, be falsifiable, and one of the main criticisms has been eliminated.

Unsupported Assumptions

The transtheoretical model has received particular criticism. Sutton (2000b) argued that the stage definitions are logically flawed, and that the time periods assigned to each stage are arbitrary. Herzog (2008) suggested that, when applied to smoking cessation, the TTM does not satisfy the criteria required of a valid stage model and that the proposed stages of change 'are not qualitatively distinct categories'.

Procedural Issues

French et al. (2007) investigated what people think about when they answer TPB questionnaires using the 'think aloud' technique. French et al. found problems relating to information retrieval and to participants answering different questions from those intended and they concluded that: 'The standard procedure for developing TPB questionnaires may systematically produce problematic questions' (p. 672).

Neglect of Motivation

Another common complaint about the SCMs is that they do not adequately address the motivational issues about risky behaviours. Surely it is their very riskiness that in part is responsible for their adoption. Willig (2008) questioned the assumption that lies behind behind much of health and sex education 'that psychological health is commensurate with maintaining physical safety, and that risking one's health and physical safety is necessarily a sign of psychopathology' (p. 690). Flowers et al. (1999) studied gay men's concept of 'risk' in the context of public sex environments (parks) using semi-structured, in-depth interviews. Flowers et al. reported that: Risk reduction, danger and safety figured frequently in men's accounts of sex and sexual decision-making. However, the risks men reported related more directly to the threat of attack or arrest rather than the avoidance of sexually transmitted infections. Indeed, danger itself was occasionally something to be sought and enjoyed (Flowers et al., 1999: 483). If risk taking is actually a key part of the excitement in having sex, then theories that assume risk taking is a deterrent are doomed. The failure of theories of sexual behaviour to deal adequately with the multiple contexts and manners in which people have sex and construct sexuality is a major shortcoming. On the basis of current evidence, grand theories claiming universal application are lacking any empirical support.

Other Criticisms

Studies measuring social cognitions about sexual practices rely upon questionnaires which presuppose that cognitions are stable entities residing in people's heads. They do not allow for contextual variables which may influence social cognitions. For example, an individual's attitude towards condom use may well depend upon the sexual partner with whom they anticipate having sexual contact. It may depend upon the time, place, relationship and physiological state (e.g. intoxication) within which sex takes place. As a result, the attempt to predict actual behaviour from decontextualized attitude measures is unlikely to succeed. In addition, it can be argued that sexual intercourse, which is a joint activity, is less likely to be shaped by individual cognitions than solitary health behaviours such as flossing or exercising . . . the vast majority of social cognition studies of sexual behaviour has focused upon young heterosexual people and gay men, who are perceived to be most vulnerable to HIV infection. However, Johnson and Wellings (1994) found that people who are divorced, widowed or separated report higher rates of risky sexual practices than those who are single. Also, most heterosexual women in the USA suffering from STI infections have become infected by a partner with whom they have had a long-term involvement (Reiss, 1991). Thus, there is a need for studies of older and/or cohabiting/married heterosexuals' sexual decision-making.

THE ELEPHANT IN THE ROOM – THE PERSISTENCE OF ERROR

There is an embarrassing, unanswered question about theories and models in psychology that is screaming to be answered. If the evidence in support of SCMs is so meagre and feeble, how come they have survived for such a long time? The scientific method is intended to be a fail-safe procedure for abandoning disconfirmed hypotheses and progressing with hypotheses that appear not to be disconfirmed. The psychologists who dream up these theories and test them claim to be scientists, so what the heck is going on?

One reason that theories and models become semi-permanent features of textbooks and degree programmes is that the simple rules of logical inference that are the very heart of science are persistently broken. If a theory is tested and found wanting, then one of two things happens: either (1) the theory is revised and retested or (2) the theory is abandoned. The history of science suggests that (1) is far more frequent than (2). Investigators become attached to the theories and models that they are working with, not to mention their careers, and they invest significant amounts of time, energy and funds in them, and are loath to give them up, a bit like a worn-out but comfortable armchair. Nothing dishonest seems to be happening in such cases, simply an unwitting bias to confirm one's theoretical predilections. This is the well-known *confirmation bias* studied by, yes, you guessed it, *psychologists* (e.g. Nickerson, 1988).

The process of theory or model testing is illustrated in Figure 6.9. The diagram shows how the research process insulates theories and models against negative results, leading to the persistence of error over many decades. Continuous cycles of revisions and extensions following meagre or negative results protect the model from its ultimate abandonment until every possible amendment and extension has been tested and tried and found to be wanting. Several methods of protection are available to investigators in light of 'bad' results: (1) Amend the model and test it again, a process that can be repeated indefinitely. (2) Test and retest the model ignoring the 'bad' results until some positive results appear that can happen purely by chance (a type 2 error). (3) Carry out some 'statistical wizardry' to concoct a more favourable-looking outcome. (4) Do nothing, i.e. do not publish the findings. And/or (5) look for another theory or model to test and start all over again! Beside all of these issues, there is increasing evidence of lack of replication, selective publication of positive findings, and outright fraud in psychological research, all of which militate against authentic separation of fact from fantasy (Yong, 2012).

Little attention has been paid to the cultural, socio-political and economic conditions that create the context for individual health experience and behaviour (Marks, 1996). Thousands of studies have accumulated to the evidence base that is showing that social cognition theory is a woefully inadequate theory of health behaviour change. Any theory that does not reflect the complex interaction of socio-economic, cultural and political conditions is unable to provide a satisfactory account of any one individual's health experience. Furthermore, as discussed in previous editions, current health psychology theories have not been grounded on a level that is connected to the known cultural, socio-political, and community contexts within which individual health behaviour and experience are embedded (Marks, 2002). Slowly but surely these issues are becoming more widely recognized across the discipline.

Critics of the social cognition approach have suggested that SCMs are tautological and effectively irrefutable (Smedslund, 2000; Ogden, 2003). If this is true, then no matter how many studies are carried out to investigate a social cognitive theory, there will be no genuine progress in understanding, a prospect too gloomy to contemplate. Weinstein (1993: 324) summarized the state of health behaviour research as follows: 'despite a large empirical literature, there is still no consensus that certain models of health behaviour are more accurate than others, that certain variables are more influential than others, or that certain behaviours or situations are understood better than others.' Unfortunately, there has been little improvement since then. The individual-level approach to health interventions focuses on theoretical models, piloting, testing and running randomized controlled trials to demonstrate efficacy. It has been estimated that the time from conception to funding and completing the process of demonstrated effectiveness can take at least 17 years (Clark, 2008). The meta analyses, reviewed above, suggest that the 'proof

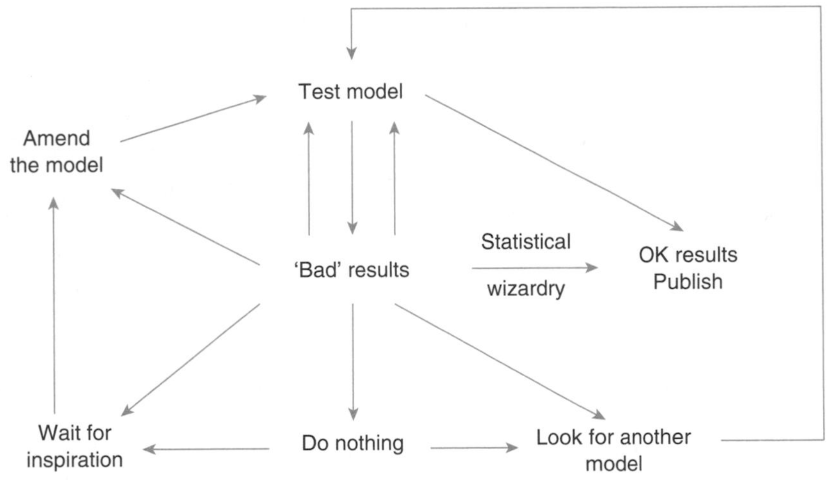

Figure 6.9 Another thing most textbooks don't tell you: the persistence of error – the manner in which a model or theory becomes insulated against negative results

of the pudding' in the form of truly effective individual-level interventions is yet to materialize. Alternative means of creating interventions for at-risk communities are needed.

Fresh Approach Needed

To quote Fine and Feinman (2004), 'a fresh approach is needed yielding new theories and interventions that work'. Where will this new approach come from? One alternative approach is offered by community health psychology. This approach challenges harmful social inequalities and looks at the role played by marginalized groups and supportive allies in tackling these (Campbell and Cornish, 2014). An example is intervention at a community level to modify risk behaviour norms via key opinion leaders to bring about reductions in HIV infection risk behaviour (Kelly et al., 1991). This approach induces the concept of 'empowerment' which can be considered as a relational approach that recognizes the need to transform power relationships at multiple levels (Ansell, 2014). Knowledge is power, as is the skill to persuade power brokers that their interests are best served by engaging the inert resources of communities. We discuss this approach in Chapter 14. We also discuss interventions to enhance the effectiveness of treatments for people suffering with HIV infection and AIDS in Chapter 19.

Another approach with potential is the use of e-health and digital technology. The Internet, text messaging, and social networking are new tools for engaging young people in sexual health promotion and risk reduction. This is an emerging area of research and is rapidly changing. One example is an initiative in San Francisco, California, 'SEXINFO', a sexual health text messaging service for young people (Levine et al., 2008). In the first 25 weeks of service (April–October 2006), more than 4,500 inquiries were received with 2,500 inquiries leading to access to more information and referrals. The top three messages accessed were: (1) 'what 2 do if ur condom broke'; (2) '2 find out about STDs'; and (3) 'if u think ur pregnant'. Social networks can produce a 'viral'-like spread of information among the target population, leading to a wider reach of the intervention and greater effectiveness due to peer-influence. Peer-to-peer text messages, pictures and videos can 'go viral' through word-of-mouth and forwarding of text messages and emails, mimicking the spread of a virus from person to person.

Guse et al. (2012) searched eight public databases across multiple disciplines for all peer-reviewed studies published between January 2000 and May 2011 that evaluated the impact of digital media-based interventions on the sexual health knowledge, attitudes and/or behaviours of adolescents aged 13–24 years. Ten studies met inclusion criteria, with seven in the USA. Two interventions significantly delayed initiation of sex, and one successfully encouraged users of a social networking site to remove sex references from their public profile. Guse et al. reported that seven interventions significantly influenced psychosocial outcomes such as condom self-efficacy and abstinence attitudes, but 'at times the results were in directions unexpected by the study authors'. Six studies increased knowledge of HIV, sexually transmitted infections, or pregnancy. More data from controlled studies with longer (>1 year) follow-up and measurement of behavioural outcomes will provide a more robust evidence base from which to judge the effectiveness of new digital media in changing adolescent sexual behaviour. Future research is needed to evaluate the cost-effectiveness of new approaches in systematic trials, with long (>1 year) follow-up, to improve the effectiveness of interventions in ways that are transferable and transparent.

FUTURE RESEARCH

1. A fresh approach is needed yielding new theories and interventions that work.
2. People are social and emotional beings and these features need to be restored into theories, models and interventions of sexual behaviour.
3. Future research must look at the potential of the Internet, text messaging and social networking as tools for engaging young people in sexual health promotion and risk reduction.

SUMMARY

1 Sexual activity, whether for pleasure or procreation, is associated with risks in the form of STIs, HIV infections and unplanned pregnancies.

2 In spite of efforts by health authorities at global, national and local levels, the incidence and prevalence of STIs and HIV infection is increasing in most regions of the world.

3 Individual-level theories and models are based on universal constructs concerning behavioural adoption, maintenance, and change.

4 Thousands of studies and meta-analyses have tested individual-level, social cognitive theories and models with mixed success. Only modest amounts of variation in intentions and behaviour are accounted for using the social cognitive approach.

5 Critics have suggested that individual-level theories and models of social cognition are fundamentally flawed, unfalsifiable and tautological.

6 Seemingly insulated from the disappointing results, these theories and models continue to be the main focus for research and interventions.

7 The 'Holy Cow' effect preserves the high status of a theoretical approach even when the evidence for its effectiveness is disappointingly lacking.

8 An alternative approach used by community psychologists challenge social inequalities by engaging with marginalized groups and supportive allies.

9 Another approach with potential is the use of e-health and digital technology. The Internet, text messaging and social networking are new tools for engaging young people in sexual health promotion and risk reduction.

10 Future research is needed to evaluate the cost-effectiveness of new approaches in systematic trials, to carry out cross-cultural comparisons, and to improve the effectiveness of interventions in ways that are transferable and transparent.

7 FOOD, DIETS AND OBESITY

Although millions seek treatments for obesity, the benefits of treatment have been overstated. For most people, treatment is not effective; the majority of the obese struggle in vain to lose weight and blame themselves for relapses . . . Many therapists may be contributing to this psychologic damage by giving their patients false hope for success and by failing to recognize that seeking treatment for obesity may be triggered by psychologic problems that are not addressed in obesity treatment.

(Wooley and Garner, 1991, p. 1248)

OUTLINE

In this chapter, we examine the part played by food, diets and dieting in the changing patterns of illnesses and deaths associated with the obesity pandemic. People are oversupplied by foods that are calorie-dense and nutrient-poor. The sub-optimal food environment has generated high levels of obesity, diabetes, cardiovascular diseases, cancers, osteoporosis and dental disease. We address the obesity problem as a biopsychosocial issue with biological, environmental and psychological determinants. The evidence for and against different theories includes the observed effects of diets with differing proportions of macronutrients in the form of fats, sugars and proteins. We review available interventions for obesity and overweight and the disappointing evidence on their effectiveness. It is concluded that legislation to change the food environment is required to combat the obesity pandemic.

Eating and drinking are pleasurable and social activities that provide essential energy to the body. They satisfy hunger and thirst, and are steeped in cultural, moral and symbolic meaning. Food and drink form part of culture itself, a 'food and drink culture' with its own associated beliefs, values and customs. Food consumption consists of a complex set of processes that includes genetic and environmental factors, conditioning, and customs. There are many interesting aspects of food, diets and dieting, enough for many volumes. The central issue of the chapter is a phenomenon that overshadows all of the rest: *the global obesity pandemic*. We review here recent research on food, diets and dieting relevant to the prevention and treatment of obesity.

Authorities decree that a 'balanced diet' with regular physical activity is of crucial importance to a healthy body. Yet, in spite of thousands of studies, hundreds of campaigns, and scores of dedicated institutes and journals, there are currently no validated public health interventions able to achieve sustained long-term weight loss. Today the much-touted idea of the 'balanced diet' seems little more that an interesting academic myth. Some basic questions require answers: *What is causing the obesity pandemic? What can be done about it? What is the role, if any, for health psychology?*

In applying the biopsychosocial approach to obesity, we must keep a balance between the three major elements of the biological, psychological and social. Each of these is a necessary component to any explanation of obesity. It is recognized that a complex interplay of biological, behavioural and societal factors contribute to the causes of obesity. The Foresight Report (2007) referred to a 'complex web of societal and biological factors that have, in recent decades, exposed our inherent human vulnerability to weight gain'. The report presented an obesity map with energy balance at its centre *with over 100 variables* directly or indirectly influencing energy balance. One page of this book would be unable to contain it. This complex mapping was divided into seven cross-cutting themes in four categories which provides a useful framework for the understanding of overweight and obesity (Figure 7.1). In this chapter, we consider all seven themes.

The obesity pandemic is comparable in importance to the smoking pandemic. It took 50 years of consolidated pressure to reduce the prevalence of smoking related diseases. There is enough scientific knowledge now to tackle the obesity pandemic. A crucial issue is that our system of governance is market-led so that food policy and regulation are based on economic imperatives as much as by scientific evidence. There can be little doubt that if the food chain could be rationally developed, the obesity pandemic, and other food issues, could be solved.

DEFINITION AND PREVALENCE

Obesity has been defined as a chronic, relapsing, neurochemical disease (Bray, 2003a). It manifests itself by an increase in size and number of fat cells (**adipose tissue**). The definition of obesity is based on a measure known as the **body mass index (BMI)**, the most widely used method of measuring body size. The BMI is a person's weight in kilograms divided by the square of his/her height in metres (kg/m^2). A BMI greater than or equal to 25 is classified as overweight; a BMI greater than or equal to 30 is classified as obesity.

The prevalence of overweight and obesity (OAO) in adults doubled from 6% in 1980 to 12% in 2008 (Stevens et al., 2012). By 2050, it is predicted that obesity will affect 60% of adult men,

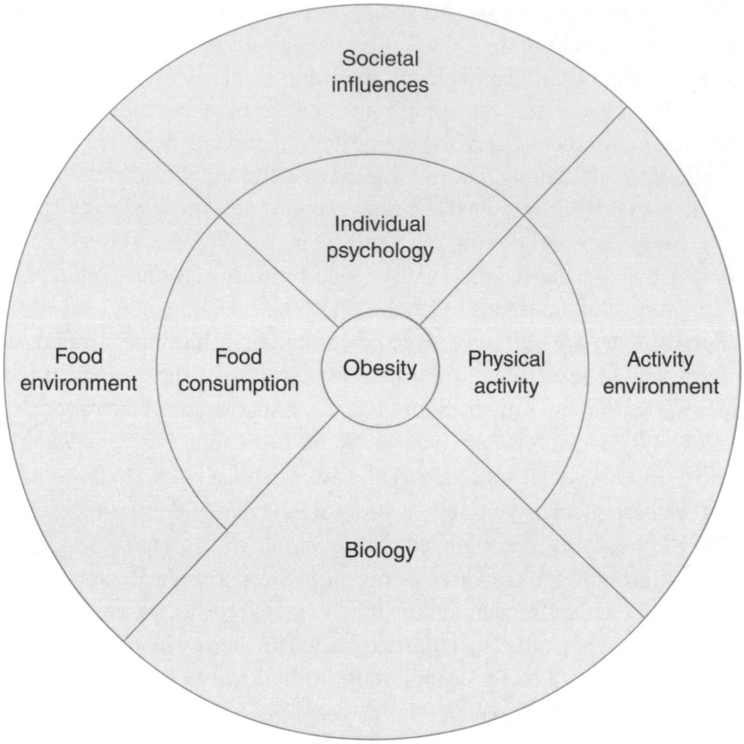

Figure 7.1 Seven influences on overweight and obesity

Source: Foresight Report (2007)

50% of adult women and 25% of children, making Britain *a mainly obese society* (Butland et al., 2007). Similar projections apply to the USA and other European countries. The medical complications of obesity are extensive and lead to higher mortality. Obesity is a marker for insulin resistance, type 2 diabetes and the **metabolic syndrome (MS)**, a collection of cardiovascular risk factors that includes hypertension, dyslipidaemia and insulin resistance (see Figure 7.2).

The Prospective Studies Collaboration (2009) analysed data from almost one million people who were followed from middle age in 57 prospective studies. A J-shaped mortality curve was obtained with optimal survival at a BMI level of 22.5–25 kg/m^2. Above this range, mortality from several causes – especially vascular diseases – increased. Moderate obesity (BMI 30–35) is associated with three years' loss of life while the extremely obese (BMI 40–50) lose ten years of life, equivalent to the years lost by a lifetime of smoking. Obesity is also a risk factor for cancer, cancer recurrence and survival (Boeing, 2013).

There have been many hotly debated controversies about food, diets and dieting. Different dietary interventions for obesity have been extensively explored yet a review of the literature indicates that outcomes have been universally modest. Many interventions, from simple trials of

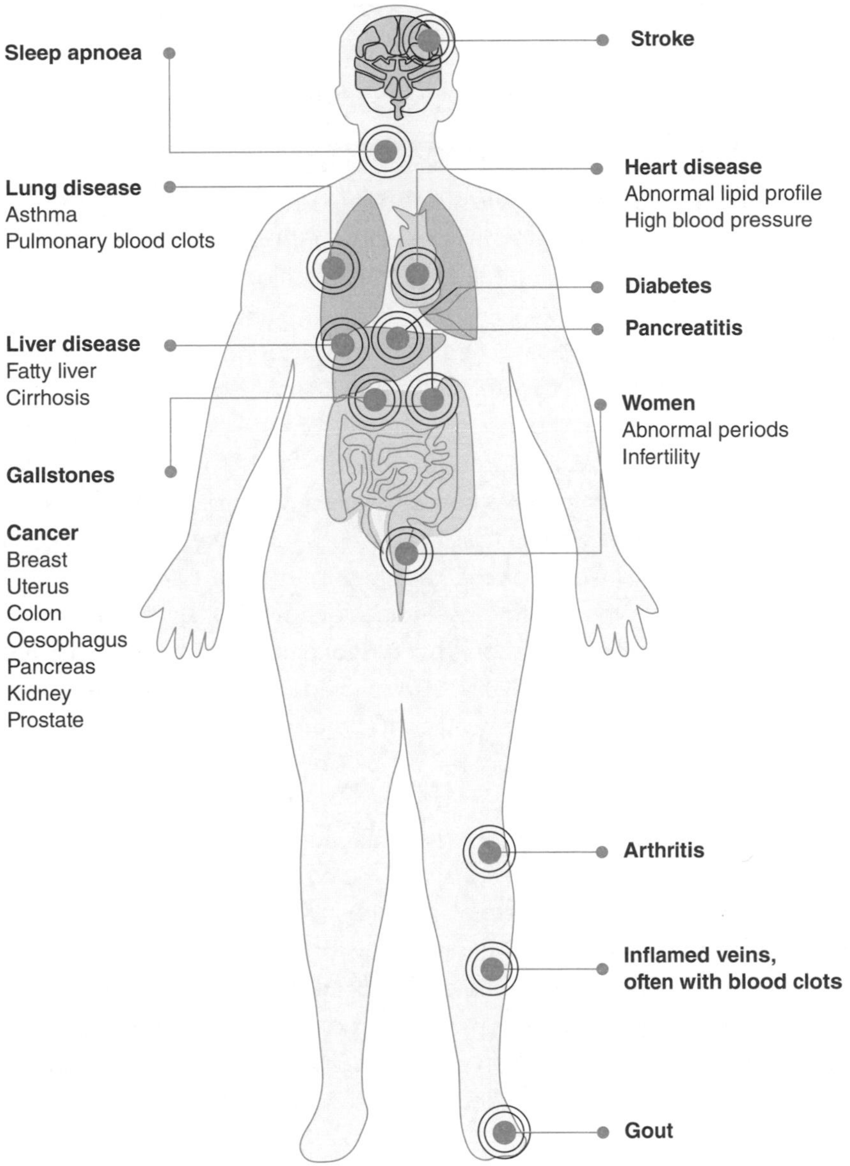

Figure 7.2 The medical complications of obesity

Source: Yale University Rudd Center for Food Policy and Obesity

a single method to complex multi-component treatments, have yielded unexciting results. In this chapter we attempt to address the issue of why this could be. We begin by considering the issue of measuring obesity (Box 7.1) and then review the many different theories of obesity.

BOX 7.1
HOW ARE OVERWEIGHT AND OBESITY MEASURED?

The BMI is a proxy measure of body fat that does not measure directly. Because BMI is easy to measure, shows high test-retest reliability, is inexpensive, and correlates with health risk markers and diseases, it is considered the measurement of choice for large-scale studies. However, as a method of classification for OAO, it suffers from serious problems.

To start with, the body consists of four compartments: bone, muscle, subcutaneous fat (about 80% of body fat) and **visceral fat** (about 20% of body fat). The latter consists of fat in organs such as the liver that causes insulin resistance and MS. The BMI does not distinguish between the four bodily compartments. While some people can have a BMI in the obese range and yet have normal levels of visceral fat (e.g. fit gymnasts), approximately 20% of people with normal BMI have clinical levels of visceral fat. A physician who uses only BMI waves on the latter group to an early grave.

Studies have compared the BMI to other indices of body fat. Shah and Braverman (2012) compared BMI and body fat scores using **dual energy X-ray absorptiometry (DXA)** on 1,393 patients from 1998 to 2009. DXA, originally used to measure bone density and total body composition, can alse be used to determine abdominal fat mass. There was agreement for only 60% of the sample, with 39% misclassified as non-obese using BMI. 48% of women and 25% of men were misclassified as non-obese by BMI, but were obese by percentage body fat scores (Figure 7.3). Other researchers using regression suggested that BMI predicts risk markers in white males as well as skin-fold thickness and DXA (Hariri et al., 2013). Yet the scatterplot in Figure 7.3 shows the huge room for error even when the correlation between BMI and body fat percentage is quite strong.

Medical diagnosis is based on cut-offs, e.g. BMI > 30 or body fat > 30%. These cut-offs give different outcomes and have low concordance. For accurate measurement of adiposity, DXA or MRI, in combination with leptin, should be used. Researchers and physicians who continue to use BMI as the sole basis for classifying OAO are prone to error and putting patients at risk.

Another indicator of OAO is **waist circumference**. The correlation between waist circumference and intra-abdominal adipose tissue (IAAT) is 0.8. Abdominal subcutaneous (ASAT), IAAT, and IAAT/ASAT ratio all increase significantly by age and BMI group (Thomas et al., 2012). Belt size may be used as a proxy for waist circumference: > 40 inches for males and 35 inches for females indicate excess visceral fat. The body adiposity index (BAI) may also be used: waist circumference as a percentage of height. Another measure, **skin-fold thickness**, is obtained using calipers in different bodily areas.

For accurate diagnosis of obesity, DXA and MRI need to be used as they provide direct images of adiposity throughout the body.

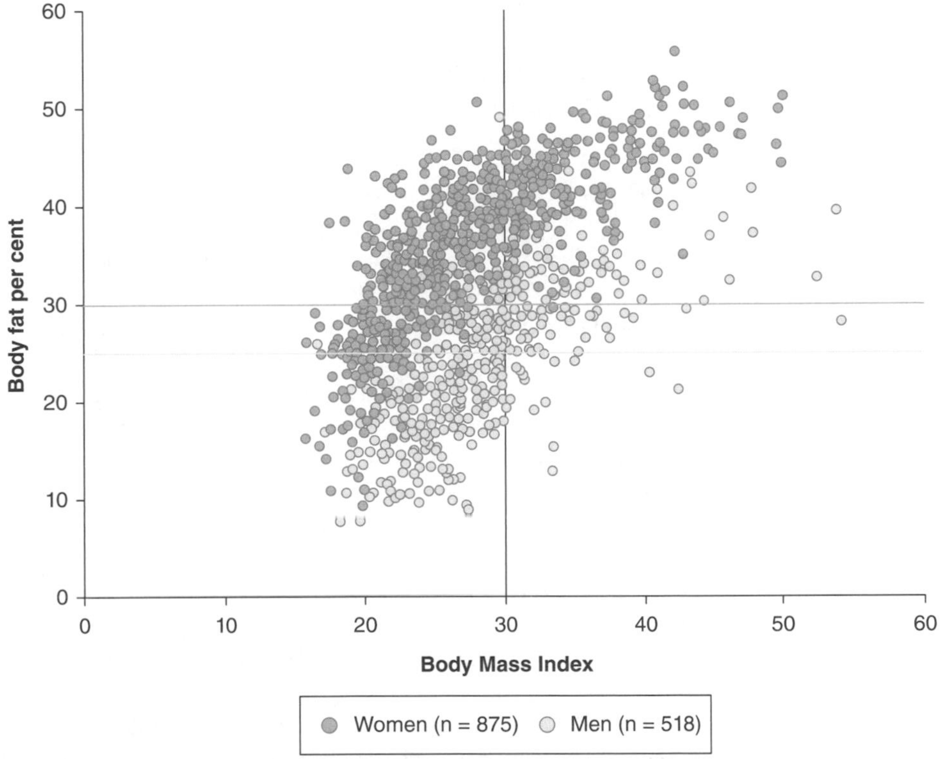

Figure 7.3 BMI vs. per cent body fat in scatter plot. Women who fall above the line are obese according to American Society of Bariatric Physicians criteria (DXA per cent body fat: approx. 30%). Men who fall above the horizontal line are obese according to American Society of Bariatric Physicians criteria (DXA per cent body fat: approx. 25%). The upper left quadrant bordered by the horizontal line (30% body fat) and vertical line (BMI = 30) demonstrates large number of women misclassified as 'non-obese' by BMI yet 'obese' by per cent body fat

Source: Shah and Braverman (2012)

CAUSES OF OBESITY

In considering the complex issue of causation, we need to bear in mind the likelihood that obesity has multiple causes, a familiar principle in psychology.

Looking at the prevalence figures, and at the costs to society, the increasing prevalence of obesity is *the* major public health concern of the age. To consider the example of the US, what has caused obesity rates to rise from around 15% in 1980 to the high level of 55% reached today? To answer this question, we need to consider in turn the main explanations of obesity. We consider biological theories concerning evolutionary and genetic predispositions towards the storage of body fat and the nutritional consequences of different diets, the theory of the obesogenic environment, social and developmental factors, and psychological explanations of the role of conditioning, emotion, depression and body dissatisfaction.

Evolutionary Hypothesis

The genetic make-up of humans is adapted to a nomadic existence of hunting and gathering in which the body stores fat. Early humans have been traced to sites in Africa dating approximately 2.5 million years ago; the tool-making *Homo habilis* ('handy man') lived in the Olduvai Gorge in Tanzania. These Olduvai hominids were hunter-gatherers, killing and processing their food with weapons and tools fashioned from pieces of volcanic obsidian (Lamb and Sington, 1998). Allowing 25 years for each generation, 100,000 generations of humans separate contemporary *Homo sapiens* from *Homo habilis*. In evolutionary terms this is not many generations for major changes to occur. The vast majority of humans alive today live and work in cities where an ecology of food and inactivity is generating ill health and disease on a mass scale.

Natural ecosystems provide a diet of wild plant-based foods that is both varied and plentiful. For example, North American Indians used hundreds of plants in their diets including stinging nettle, common purslane, milkweed, clover, pond-lily, dandelions and fiddleheads (Fieldhouse, 1996). In addition to plants, hunter-gatherers would harvest insects and fish, and hunt for meat. Over 13,000 insects have been classified as edible. This diet was adequate both in quality of nutrients and quantity of energy supplied. A review by Cordain et al. (2000) suggested that whenever it was ecologically possible, hunter-gatherers would have consumed high amounts (45–65% of total energy) of animal food. Most (73%) hunter-gatherer societies worldwide derived > 50% (56–65%) of their subsistence from animal foods, whereas only 13.5% of these societies derived more than half (56–65%) of their subsistence from gathered plant foods. Until human beings settled in villages and towns around 10,000 years ago, humans consumed only wild and unprocessed food collected from their environment. They will have walked or ran 5–10 miles daily searching for their food, drinking only fresh water, and their diet was high in lean protein, poly-unsaturated fats (especially omega-3 fatty acids), mono-unsaturated fats, fibre, vitamins, minerals, antioxidants and other beneficial phytochemicals (O'Keefe and Cordain, 2004). The 'diseases of affluence' of the modern age would have been almost unknown.

For a few million years of evolution, the capacity to store fat easily was advantageous for survival. Ice Age hunter-gatherers needed to store fat to survive the winters and long journeys in search of food. When the ice retracted and temperatures increased, foods became more accessible and activity levels declined. Thus a metabolic feature designed to promote survival became a risk factor for diseases that rarely existed in history but are commonplace today.

Genetic Predisposition

It is a common observation that size, whether large or small, runs in families. This observation has led to many studies of the heritability of excess weight in twins and adoptees. Heritability is the proportion of observed differences in a trait among individuals that is due to genetic differences. Evidence from multiple studies indicates that the tendency to put on weight is inherited and beyond any individual's personal control.

A systematic review explored genetic studies on BMI in pre-adolescence, young adulthood and late adulthood (Nan et al., 2012). Nan et al. searched for studies reporting intra-pair correlations of healthy twin pairs who were raised together, finding data on 8,179 monozygotic (MZ, i.e. identical) and 9,977 dizygotic (DZ, non-identical) twin pairs from twelve studies in addition to data for 629 MZ and 594 DZ pairs from four twin registries. They used heritability scores of BMI that they found ranged from 61 to 80% for male and female participants combined, while unique environmental influences increased from 14 to 40% with increasing age. The authors concluded that: 'Environmental changes over time do not seem to have as big a relative impact on an individual's weight as previously reported, suggesting a mainly genetic influence on variation in BMI over the years' (Nan et al., 2012: 248).

The existence of a genetic predisposition to develop overweight and obesity is a biological fact. However, the human genome has not altered in the last few thousand years and so a genetic predisposition, although necessary, is insufficient to explain the dramatic increase in the prevalence of obesity over the last few decades. To understand this, we must turn to other theories.

The Energy Balance Theory

The 'energy balance theory' (EBT) has dominated obesity research over the last 50 years. According to EBT, obesity is caused by an imbalance between energy intake and energy expenditure. The **energy balance equation (EBE)** states:

energy intake = internal heat produced + external work + energy stored

Energy is consumed in the diet through intake of three macronutrients: protein, carbohydrate and fat. In the presence of excess food, the body will convert and store nutrients as triglycerides in adipose tissue. Translating the EBE in terms of fat, the equation becomes:

rate of change of fat stores in the body = rate of fat intake – rate of fat oxidation

First, consider energy intake. The standard unit of energy, the **calorie**, is defined as the energy needed to increase the temperature of 1 kg of water by 1°C, which is about 4.184 kJ. Fat contributes 9 calories per gram, alcohol 7 calories per gram and carbohydrates 4 calories per gram. The fat content of a food item is the sum of four different fats: saturated fats: trans-saturated (trans), poly-unsaturated and mono-unsaturated fats. For sedentary adults, every 22 kcal per day increase in energy intake will increase body weight by roughly 1 kg after several years. As a person gets fatter, they need to expend more energy to lose it again.

Eating itself expends calories, the 'thermic effect' of food, which is the energy expended in order to consume (bite, chew and swallow) and process (digest, transport, metabolize and store) food. Processing protein, carbohydrate and fat requires 20–35%, 5–15% and 2–3% of energy consumed respectively. A gram of fat not only gives you more calories, but a smaller percentage is burned off by the thermic effect.

The majority of diets are based on counting calories. The diet designers assume that diets of equal caloric content result in identical weight change *independent of macronutrient composition*. 'A calorie is a calorie', so the saying goes. Actually, this assumption is false because it violates the second law of thermodynamics. Feinman and Fine (2004) proposed that a misunderstanding of the second law accounts for the controversy about the role of macronutrients on weight loss: 'Attacking the obesity epidemic will involve giving up many old ideas that have not been productive. "A calorie is a calorie" might be a good place to start' (Feinman and Fine, 2004). All calories are *not* equal. If you eat an equal number of calories of protein, fat and carbohydrates, the metabolic processes are different and calories in the fat are more likely to end up on your waist as fewer calories are burned off by the thermic effect.

Almost all authorities subscribe to the dictum that obesity is caused by eating too many calories (gluttony) and failing to burn off enough calories (sloth). This belief creates both victim-blaming and stigmatization, which have done little to reduce the incidence of overweight and obesity.

Inactivity

Let's turn to the energy expenditure side of the energy balance theory. Energy expended in exercise is measured in joules. One joule in everyday life represents approximately the energy required to lift a small apple (with a mass of approximately 100 g) vertically through one metre. Do this a million times and you have used 1 megajoule (MJ) of energy or 239 calories.

The use of exercise is a recommended part of any weight loss programme. However, this has proven to be an ineffective procedure. The impact of increased activity is slow-acting and hard to sustain. In spite of its almost universal prescription as a means of controlling body weight, simple mathematics suggests that the amount of exercise necessary for significant long-term weight loss maintenance far exceeds the capacity of most individuals. While the case for increasing activity levels to lose weight is technically correct, in practice, aiming for weight loss by this method alone is almost impossible to achieve.

Hall et al. (2011) mathematically simulated energy expenditure adaptations during weight loss. They estimated that a persistent daily energy imbalance gap between intake and expenditure of about 30 kJ per day underlies the observed average weight gain in the US population. In addition, energy intake must have risen to keep pace with increased expenditure associated with increased weight. A heavier person expends more energy to move a certain distance. They calculated that the average increase of energy intake needed to sustain the increased weight (the maintenance energy gap) amounted to about 0.9 MJ per day.

A 100 kg man would need to run about 20 km, almost a half-marathon each week, or reduce energy intake by 1.2 MJ per day, to reach a weight of around 85 kg. However, *this would take approximately 5 years to achieve using exercise alone*. That regimen would require running 5,000 km over 5 years to lose 15 kg. Therefore, it is hardly surprising that obese people find exercise an ineffective method of weight loss, and attrition rates in exercise programmes are so high.

Similar findings have been obtained in other systematic reviews (SRs), e.g. by Loveman et al. (2011) and in an SR carried out by a Swedish expert committee (Swedish Council on Health Technology Assessment, 2013). The latter concluded:

> adding physical activity to a dietary intervention for obese individuals has a marginal – if any – effect on weight loss at group level. The lack of effect can be explained by compensatory mechanisms, such as a lower degree of physical activity throughout the rest of the day or increased hunger and less of a sense of satiety in connection with meals.

In spite of all the advice coming from health authorities to exercise more to lose weight, it is extremely unlikely that the obesity pandemic would ever be reversed by individuals increasing their daily amount of exercise, unless they also make major dietary changes.

Other critics argue that it is not excess calories that cause obesity, but the quantity and quality of carbohydrates consumed (Taubes, 2012). We turn to this theory next.

The Insulin Theory

> The **insulin theory** claims that obesity is caused by a chronic elevation in insulin in a diet that contains too much carbohydrate (Taubes, 2009): This alternative hypothesis of obesity constitutes three distinct propositions. First . . . is the basic proposition that obesity is caused by a regulatory defect in fat metabolism, and so a defect in the distribution of energy rather than an imbalance of energy intake and expenditure. The second is that insulin plays a primary role in this fattening process, and the compensatory behaviours of hunger and lethargy. The third is that carbohydrates, and particularly refined carbohydrates – and perhaps the fructose content as well, and thus perhaps the amount of sugars consumed – are the prime suspects in the chronic elevation of insulin; hence, they are the ultimate cause of common obesity.
>
> (Taubes, 2009: 359)

Carbohydrate is a high **glycaemic index (GI)** food that produces insulin that, in turn, causes the body to store fat. Carbohydrates include starch, which is found in rice, wheat, maize, potatoes and cassava, and all sources of sugar, specifically natural sugars and added sugars and fibre. Sugary beverages including alcohol, sweets, sugary cereals, dried fruits, low-fat crackers, rice cakes, potato crisps, flour, cakes, cookies, jams, preserves, potato products, pickles, sauces, salad dressings and pizzas are all high in carbohydrates.

According to the insulin theory, the carbohydrate content of a person's diet must be rectified to restore health (Taubes, 2012). This is because blood levels of insulin are mainly determined by carbohydrate intake, and insulin regulates fat accumulation. The more digestible the carbohydrates that we eat (i.e. the higher their glycaemic index) and the sweeter they are (the higher their fructose content), the higher our blood insulin level goes, and the more fat we accumulate in our bodies. Box 7.2 summarizes the new WHO guidelines on sugar.

BOX 7.2
NEW WHO GUIDELINES ON SUGAR

The consumption of sugar has grown continuously over the last 200 years and continues to grow. In 2014 the WHO launched a new draft guideline on sugars intake in light of scientific studies on the consumption of sugars and its impact on excess weight gain and tooth decay. Systematic reviews were carried out by Te Morenga et al. (2013), who showed that sugar is a determinant of body weight, and Moynihan and Kelly (2014), who found that 47 of 55 studies reported a positive association between sugars and caries. Yang et al. (2014) examined time trends of added sugar consumption as percentage of daily calories in the USA. Yang et al. observed a significant relationship between added sugar consumption and increased risk for CVD mortality. The highest sugar group had a risk of death from a cardiovascular event almost three times higher than those whose sugar consumption was 10% or lower of daily calories.

The WHO's previous recommendation from 2002 was that sugars should make up less than 10% of total energy intake per day. *The new guideline proposes that a reduction to below 5% of total energy intake per day would be beneficial.* Five per cent of total energy intake is equivalent to around 25 grams (around 6 teaspoons) of sugar per day for an adult with normal BMI.

Sugar includes monosaccharides (such as glucose, fructose) and disaccharides (such as sucrose or table sugar) that are added by the manufacturer, cook or consumer, and naturally present sugars in honey, syrups, fruit juices and fruit concentrates. Much of the sugars consumed today are 'hidden' in processed foods that are not usually viewed as sweets. For example, 1 tablespoon of ketchup contains around 4 grams (around 1 teaspoon) of sugars. A single can of sugar-sweetened soda contains up to 40 grams (around 10 teaspoons). A Yeo Valley Family Farm 0% Fat Vanilla Yogurt contains 20.9 grams (around 5 teaspoons).

Sugar has become a new watchword, along with fat.

The dangers of sugar were highlighted in the 1970s by John Yudkin in *Pure, White and Deadly* (1972). Following this publication, there should have been a reduction of sugar in the diet; however, food consumption and diets do not follow reason or scientific evidence and consumption of sugar-sweetened beverages has risen rapidly ever since.

Food consumption data from the National Health and Nutrition Examination Survey (NHANES) between 1971 and 2004 indicate that the observed increase in energy intake in the USA is accounted for almost completely by increased carbohydrate consumption, with a 67.7 g increase per day in men and a 62.4 g increase per day in women within that time frame (Lim et al., 2010). Meals composed predominately of high GI foods induce hormonal events that stimulate hunger and cause overeating in adolescents. A high GI diet has been linked with risk for central adiposity, cardiovascular disease and type 2 diabetes (Ebbeling et al., 2002). Low-carbohydrate diets show a metabolic advantage. An isocaloric diet, which has a fixed number of calories, can be used to compare diets that vary in the percentage of carbohydrate (CHO) that they contain. If a calorie really was a calorie, then the weight loss obtained in a low-CHO isocaloric diet would be identical to that in a high CHO isocaloric diet. However, in nine out of ten studies, more weight loss occurred in the low-carb diet (Fine and Feinman, 2004). This research led to the conclusion that a good way to take off weight is to switch to a low-carb diet.

Two recent SRs reviewed the effects of a low-carbohydrate diet (LC). Santos et al. (2012) studied the effect of LC on weight loss and cardiovascular risk factors. LC was associated with significant decreases in body weight (7.04 kg), body mass index, abdominal circumference, blood pressure, and a variety of cardiovascular risk factors. In a meta-analysis of RCTs, Bueno et al. (2013) compared a very-low-carbohydrate ketogenic diet (VLCKD) to a low-fat diet (LF) for long-term weight loss. The VLCKD was defined as a diet with no more than 50 g carbohydrates per day and a conventional low-fat diet as a restricted-energy diet with less than 30% of energy from fat. Individuals using a VLCKD showed a greater weight loss (20.91 kg; 1,415 patients) than those assigned to an LF diet in the long term.

While a low-carbohydrate diet provides a helpful method of reducing body fat, the insulin hypothesis has not been confirmed in scientific studies (Guyenet, 2012).

Developmental Hypothesis

There is an increasing body of evidence that suggests that obesity starts in the womb. The baby is highly sensitive to the environment experienced within the womb. A relationship has been observed between the weight of a mother-to-be and her child. For example, Modi et al. (2011) used MRI to monitor fat levels in 105 unborn babies and found that 30% had more abdominal adipose tissue than expected. The amount of fat was proportional to the mother-to-be's BMI. These findings were reinforced by Schellong et al. (2012) who found that infants with a birth weight in excess of 4 kg were twice as likely to suffer from obesity in later life as normal-weight babies. Preventing *in-utero* overnutrition by avoiding maternal over-nutrition, overweight and/or diabetes during pregnancy might be a promising strategy to prevent overweight and obesity globally.

Risk of overweight and obesity continues to develop in the crib and accelerates during the first few years of life. A consistent association occurs between faster infant weight gain (from birth to age one year) and later overweight or obesity. Druet et al. (2012) assessed the ability of infant weight gain to predict subsequent obesity by performing a meta-analysis of individual-level data on 47,661 participants from ten cohort studies. Each +1 unit increase in weight SD scores between 0 and 1 year conferred a two-fold higher risk of childhood obesity and a 23% higher risk of adult obesity (Figure 7.4). Infant weight gain showed a consistent positive association with subsequent obesity.

Childhood and adolescence are critical periods for the adoption of a healthful lifestyle. By age 15 many adolescents show consistent behaviour patterns that will influence their chances of OAO in later years. Clark et al. (2007) studied how parents' child-feeding behaviours influence child weight. Parents reported using a wide range of child-feeding behaviours, including monitoring, pressure to eat and restriction. Interestingly, *restriction of children's eating* has most frequently and consistently associated with child weight gain. The authors found evidence for a causal relationship between parental restriction and childhood overweight indicating that, inadvertently, parents may promote excess weight gain in childhood by using inappropriate child-feeding behaviours.

The evidence suggests that early parental **attachment** plays a critical role in the regulation of emotion and in the formation of drinking habits, substance abuse and food consumption (Marks, 2015; Figure 7.8). Future emotion regulation, associated with attachment patterns, plays a critical

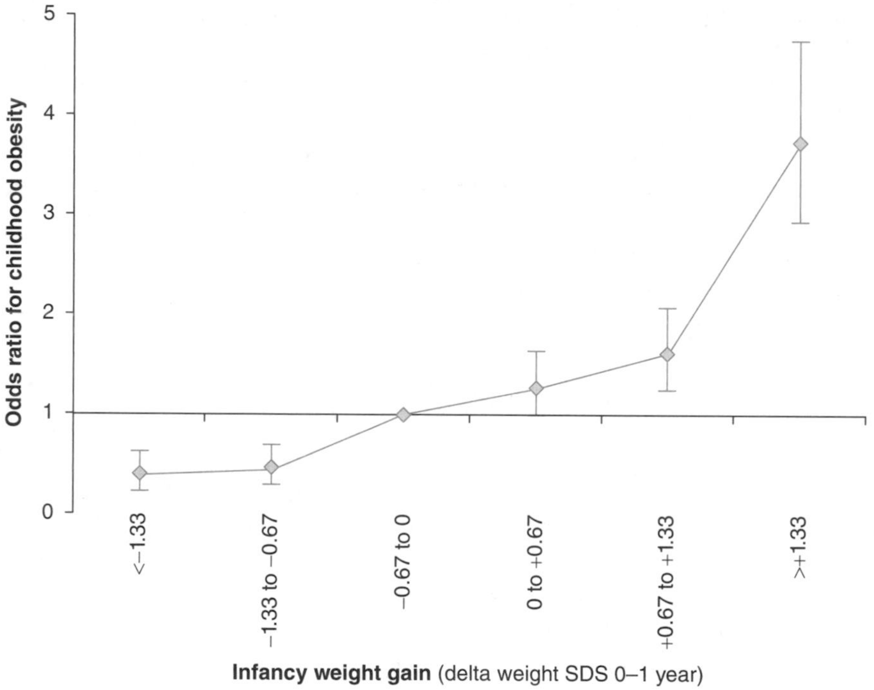

Figure 7.4 Odds ratios for childhood obesity by infant weight gain, 0–1 year, Adjusted for sex, age and birth weight

Source: Druet et al. (2012)

role in the production of ill health. DeSteno, Gross and Kubzansky (2013) summarized the evidence that chronic high childhood distress at age 7 or 8 years is associated with a range of adult physical health outcomes such as obesity, number of physical illnesses and inflammation. Dietary habits from childhood tend to persist in adulthood once formed, and parental influences can be internalized and enacted throughout the lifespan. Goossens, Braet, Van Durme, Decaluwé and Bosmans (2012) examined the role of attachment towards mother and father as a predictor of eating pathology and weight gain among 8–11-year-old boys and girls. Insecure attachment towards the mother was predictive of increases in dietary restraint, eating concerns, weight concerns, and shape concerns, and adjusted BMI in children 1 year later. An insecure attachment toward father was predictive of persistence in children's subjective binge eating episodes. Faber and Dubé (2015) investigated the role of caregiver–child attachment quality and its associations with high caloric food consumption in middle socio-economic status children and adults. Data from 213 children and 216 parents showed that an insecure parental attachment, whether actual or recalled, significantly and positively predicted HCF consumption in both samples. Faber and Dubé (2015) concluded that: 'From an intervention standpoint, parents-to-be could receive a short information sheet teaching them that responding to a child's attention-seeking does not make the child needy, but rather teaches him or her to become trusting and independent. From a counselling and clinical standpoint, children and parents of children with eating issues could benefit greatly from developing secure and trusting relationships.'

Lanigan (2012) studied the association between child-care provider practices, knowledge and beliefs in supporting children's healthful eating using a longitudinal design. Variables included the feeding environment, nutrition education, family communication, efficacy, knowledge and misconceptions about child feeding, and the priority placed on supporting children's healthful eating. Lanigan's results showed that efficacy and feeding knowledge accounted for significant variance in nutrition education changes (R^2 = 0.59) and family communication changes (R^2 = 0.29). A reduction in misconceptions was significantly associated with improved feeding practices.

Knowledge about child-feeding is one aspect of parenting and child-care that could benefit from training. Training could be designed to increase provider knowledge and self-efficacy and remove misconceptions as well as educate providers about feeding, nutrition education, and family communication. Another area of concern is children's sleeping patterns.

An interesting association exists between obesity and sleep loss. Padez et al. (2009) studied the association between sleep duration, overweight and body fat in a sample of Portuguese children. Prevalence of overweight decreased with a longer night sleep times. Laboratory and epidemiological studies point to short sleep duration and poor sleep quality as factors associated with obesity (Beccuti and Pannain, 2011). A meta-analysis of cross-sectional studies has shown that there is an almost two-fold higher prevalence of obesity in children and adults who have a short sleep duration (Miller et al., 2014). These are correlational data and the precise reasons behind the association remain unclear.

Perhaps there is a simple explanation. **Obstructive sleep apnoea (OSA)**, which is associated with sleep fragmentation, is more common with OAO. Increased visceral adiposity tends to reduce the airway size while lying down. OSA is also known to trigger hypertension, insulin resistance, type 2 diabetes, and possibly, MS. OSA causes daytime sleepiness and impaired memory and concentration (Dempsey et al., 2010). Sleep deprivation makes a person less attentive and careful in their food choices, reducing their fruit and vegetable consumption but increasing their consumption of fast food (Kruger et al., 2014). In these circumstances, daytime sleepiness and OAO form a vicious circle: OAO → OSA → daytime sleepiness → poor diet → OAO. This hypothesis warrants further study.

Conditioning and Early Experience

Why do some people develop a 'sweet tooth', a strong preference for candy, sweet foods, cakes and drinks, and others prefer savoury foods? And why do some children and adults have a strong aversion to new foods and flavours? One way to answer these questions is through the process of conditioning. Following Pavlov's (1927) studies of conditioned reflexes, learning and conditioning are the main focus of research on food preferences and aversions. Although experience generally determines food choices, sweet tastes and possibly fatty tastes are innately attractive while bitter tastes are innately avoided. Capaldi (1996) suggested that preferences for foods are modifiable in four ways:

Mere exposure.

Flavour–flavour learning: flavours that are repeatedly associated with an already preferred flavour such as saccharin will themselves become preferred. A sweetener produces liking in almost any other food with which it is mixed.

Flavour–nutrient learning: flavours that are repeatedly associated with a nutrient such as a protein become preferred.

Taste aversion learning: this occurs when a novel taste solution (the conditioned stimulus or CS) is followed by an unpleasant stimulus (the unconditioned stimulus or UCS) that produces transient gastrointestinal illness or vomiting (the unconditioned response or UR) (Garcia et al., 1966). This type of learning is adaptive in animals that need to learn rapidly to differentiate between positive and toxic foods. However, taste and food aversions are also quite common in humans, for example with specific types of alcohol (gin or whisky), as a result of nausea caused by over-imbibing on the first occasion of use.

The flavour of food is conveyed by taste, smell and chemical irritation. The foetus receives its first nutrients in the amniotic fluid, which is a potential carrier of flavour and odour (Mennella and Beauchamp, 1996). By term, the human foetus has swallowed quite large amounts of amniotic fluid (200–760 ml daily) and has been exposed to glucose, fructose, lactic acid, pyruvic acid, citric acid, fatty acids, phospholipids, creatinine, urea, uric acid, amino acids, proteins and salts (Mennella and Beauchamp, 1996). The amniotic fluid and mother's milk are both primed by a maternal diet that is unique and so may have similar aromatic profiles providing a 'thread of chemical continuity between the pre- and postnatal niches' (Schaal and Orgeur, 1992). Studies of foetal swallowing and of preterm infant sucking even suggest that a preference for sweet flavours is evident before birth (Tatzer et al., 1985). This evidence suggests that preferences for flavour and smell are influenced very early in life. In fact the earliest and most emotional life events revolve around eating and drinking and, as Rozin states, the taking and giving of food are, from the very first, 'exquisitely social' (Rozin, 1996: 235). A strongly conditioned preference for and overindulgence in sweet foods and drinks is one of the foundation stones for OAO later in life.

Learning and conditioning are also involved in encountering novel foods and in the treatment of food neophobia, the fear of novel foods, which can be a barrier to a well-balanced diet. Pliner and Hobden (1992) developed a scale to measure food neophobia. Birch et al. (1987) investigated the effectiveness of 'look' or 'taste' exposures to seven novel fruits in 2- to 5-year-old children. Foods were exposed five, 10 or 15 times, and one food remained novel. Following the exposures, children made two judgments of each of the 21 pairs: one based on looking, the other on tasting the foods. Looking without tasting was not sufficient to produce enhanced taste preferences. The results suggest that the perception of safety of a novel food is learned by exposure to confirm that a novel taste is not followed by negative gastrointestinal consequences. This is supported by studies showing a correlation between food neophobic items, family resemblances, and lack of exposure at the table (Hursti and Sjödén, 1997). This leads to a consideration of culture and cuisine.

Culture and Cuisine

Culturally shared eating habits provide a sense of belonging; they are an affirmation of cultural and social identity, kept with pride and not readily altered. Food preferences and eating habits are acquired in the context of family dynamics, moral values, culture and cuisine. Culture is the major determinant of what and when we eat and, to a lesser degree, how much we eat. Food habits and preferences are among the last characteristics of a culture to be lost during immigration into a new culture. Rozin suggests that socio-cultural factors are so important in determining food choices that if you can ask only one question, the question should be: 'What is your culture or ethnic group?' (Rozin, 1996: 235). A second useful question would be: 'What is your religion?'

Culture is the sum total of a group's learned behaviour and preserved traditions, especially those concerned with eating habits: 'Culture is learned. Food habits are acquired early in life and once established are likely to be long-lasting and resistant to change. Hence the importance of developing sound nutritional practices in childhood as a basis for life-long healthy eating' (Fieldhouse, 1996: 3).

Eating and drinking habits are central to the socialization that occurs during infancy in the family, and they are influenced principally by mothers. The immediate family is the dominant influence on the child, establishing cultural and culinary practices and preferences and the rules by which different foods may be eaten in particular combinations or meals.

Recent studies have explored the role of family dynamics and parental influences on the food choices of adolescents. The evidence suggests that food preferences established by mid-adolescence appear to continue well into adult life (Kelder et al., 1994). Of particular interest is the establishment of preferences for snacks, sweet foods, fruit and vegetables. Boureaudhuij (1997) investigated the establishment of family food rules in infancy and its impact on food choices and consumption in adolescence. Adolescents and young adults aged 12 to 22 who reported more permissiveness in their family at age 10 were found to be eating more fat and sweet foods and more snacks. They reported more unhealthy food choices in their families.

In industrialized societies, variations in family structures have occurred as a result of social changes and new working patterns. These changes have brought more variation to traditional patterns of eating communal family meals. However, meal structures are adhered to rather inflexibly and the scope for innovations may be more limited than nutritional health education desire (Douglas and Nicod, 1974). Studies have shown that television watching and frequency of family meals are predictive of overweight onset and persistence in children (e.g. Gable, Chang, and Krull, 2007).

The atmosphere around the table may be as important as the food itself in producing healthful outcomes. Recent studies have explored the role of the family mealtime as a joint family activity that can have knock-on effects in adolescent behaviours above and beyond eating. For example, White and Halliwell (2010) examined family meal frequency, family connectedness, perceived priority, atmosphere and structure of mealtimes as predictors of alcohol and tobacco consumption, using data from 550 adolescents (age 11–16). They found that frequent family meals were associated with a lower alcohol and tobacco use. This association was explained by adolescents' perception of the atmosphere at mealtimes as a positive experience, which suggests that positively experienced family meals can have a generalized protective effect. Thus enjoyable family meals can provide the perfect setting for family bonding which promotes security in children and adolescents.

Windlin and Kuntsche (2012) explored differences in the impact of the frequency and enjoyment of joint family activities (JFA) on adolescent substance use and violence. In this Swiss study, a national sample of 3,467 13- to 16-year-olds revealed that JFA enjoyment rather than JFA frequency is consistently related to low adolescent substance use and violence. By choosing JFA that their children enjoy, parents can provide opportunities for disclosure, strengthen family bonds and reduce the likelihood of adolescent problem behaviours. The findings of Windlin and Kunsche (2012) have implications for prevention in suggesting that a shift in focus towards the quality of JFA rather than the quantity could prove effective.

Encouraging children to be more involved in home meal preparation can also be an effective health promotion strategy. Chu et al. (2013) asked grade 5 children in Canada how often they helped prepare food at home and rated their preference for 12 fruits and vegetables. Self-efficacy was measured by asking children their level of confidence in selecting and eating healthful foods at home and at school. A majority (83–93%) of the children reported helping in home meal preparation at least once monthly. A high frequency of helping to prepare and cook food at home was associated with higher fruit and vegetable preference and with higher self-efficacy for selecting and eating healthy foods.

A significant role in promotion of cohesion is played by cuisine, a style of cooking with particular ingredients, flavours and modes of preparation and rules about orders and combinations (Rozin, 1982). The type of cuisine defines written or oral rules concerning how food sources are gathered or killed, prepared and combined into meals. Fieldhouse stated: 'Our unwillingness to accept just anything as food betrays the notion that food is consumed for nourishment of the body alone. Food also nourishes the heart, mind and soul' (1996: 76). This leads us to consider the rewarding qualities of food and the links between how food reward is coded in the brain and the development of overweight and obesity.

Food Reward theory

This theory is based on the fact food has a reward or reinforcement value that strengthens the desire to eat. The **food reward theory** of obesity argues that the reward value of food influences food intake and body fatness, contributing to the development of obesity (Guyenet, 2012, 2014). Cues such as the sight or smell of food stimulate appetite and promote higher consumption. Studies of conditioning carried out by Pavlov and many others show that animals and people learn to associate non-food cues with eating. Exposure to the conditioned stimuli then elicits salivation and changes in blood glucose, and can initiate food intake even in people that are already sated.

To help explain obesity, the food reward theory is paired with the idea that a breakdown can occur in the brain's ability to switch off eating when the stomach is full. As early as 1840, a German physician, Bernard Mohr, suggested that obesity is associated with abnormalities of the basal hypothalamus. The food reward theory hypothesizes that obese people may have impairments in the dopaminergic pathways of their brains that regulate neuronal systems associated with reward sensitivity, conditioning and control (Volkow et al., 2011). Dopamine is involved in reward functions, and is a major regulator of food intake and body fatness. Dopamine signalling in the striatum regulates the motivation to obtain food (wanting), but not the enjoyment or palatability of food (liking). The theory suggests that neuropeptides responsible for regulating energy balance through the hypothalamus also modulate the activity of dopamine cells and their projections into regions involved in the reward process in food intake. Volkow et al. hypothesize the breakdown of feedback mechanisms and increased resistance to homoeostatic signals in obese people impairs the function of circuits involved in reward sensitivity, conditioning and cognitive control.

Thaler et al. (2012) studied the effect of hypothalamic injury in rodents and humans to look for an association with the development of obesity. MRI was used to image and quantify gliosis, a process leading to scars in the central nervous system, in the brains of 34 young humans undergoing clinical examination. Thaler et al. found evidence of increased gliosis in the mediobasal hypothalamus of obese humans and concluded that, in both humans and rodent models, obesity is associated with neuronal injury in a brain area crucial for body weight control.

This theory has been extended to incorporate the notion of 'food addiction' that may or may not be helpful. However, the food reward theory has implications for obesity prevention and treatment via decreasing the reward value of food and enhancing the reward value of alternative activity.

The Protein Leverage Hypothesis

The '**protein leverage hypothesis**' predicts that humans prioritize protein when regulating food intake (Simpson and Raubenheimer, 2005). They use a geometric framework (GF) theory to describe and predict the food intake. There is an optimal mixture of these nutrients or *intake target*. Figure 7.5(a) shows the two-dimensional nutrient space indicating the daily intake of protein (P) and carbohydrate (C) + fat (F) (the 'intake target') necessary to maintain energy balance on a diet containing 14% of energy as P and 86% as C + F, for a moderately active, 45-year-old male (BMI 23.5). A balanced daily diet is the line that runs from the origin to intersect the intake

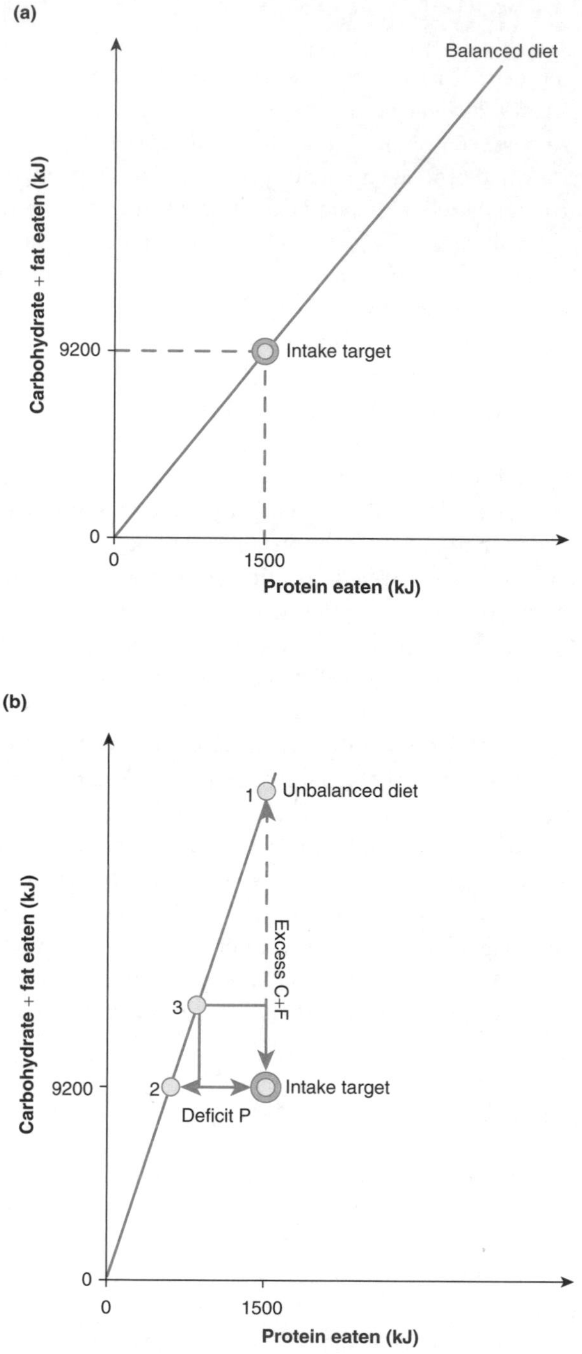
(a)
Balanced diet
9200
Intake target
0
0
1500
Carbohydrate + fat eaten (kJ)
Protein eaten (kJ)
(b)
1
Unbalanced diet
Excess C+F
3
2
9200
Intake target
Deficit P
0
0
1500
Carbohydrate + fat eaten (kJ)
Protein eaten (kJ)

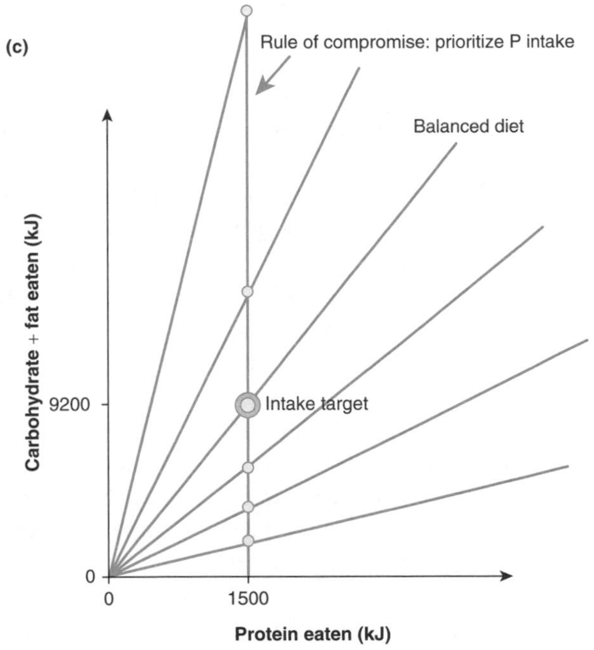

Figure 7.5 (a) A geometric framework indicating a balanced daily diet, the line that runs from the origin to intersect the intake target. (b) An unbalanced diet (one that does not intersect the intake target). If the subject eats until point 1, he/she would have achieved the intake target level of P but ingested an excess of C + F. At point 2, he/she would have gained the intake target amount of C + F, but undereaten P. At point 3 a balance is struck between overeating C and F in excess and undereating P. (c) Five unbalanced diets showing the rule of compromise in which intake of P is prioritized over that of C + F

Source: Simpson and Raubenheimer (2005)

target. Figure 7.5(b) and (c) show the different consequences of an unbalanced diet between P and C + F. The rule of compromise prioritizes protein intake with the consequence that a person will eat as much food as necessary to arrive at the intake target for protein.

A wide variety of data provide empirical support to the GF. Martinez-Cordero et al. (2012) carried out a longitudinal analysis from a large sample of Filipino women showing that calories of dietary protein remained more constant over time than calories of dietary carbohydrates or fat. Martens and Westerterp-Plantenga (2014) found that a protein intake of 0.8–1.2 g/kg/day is sufficient to sustain satiety, energy expenditure, and fat-free mass, independent of a dietary 'low-carb' content. A diet that aimed at a moderately high daily average amount of protein could have potential in curtailing obesity.

Evidence suggests that overconsumption of animal protein is hazardous to human health. A meta-analysis comparing high protein (HP) versus low-protein (LP) diets with a duration between 28 days and 12 months observed favourable effects of HP diets on biomarkers of obesity as well as cardiovascular risk factors such as HDL-cholesterol (HDL-C), triacylglycerols (TG) and blood pressure (Santesso et al., 2012). However, these were short-term effects that might not extend to the longer term.

Rohrmann et al. (2013) examined the association of red meat, processed meat and poultry consumption with the risk of early death in 448,568 men and women without prevalent cancer, stroke or myocardial infarction between 35 and 69 years old. Poultry consumption was unrelated to all-cause mortality. However, a positive association occurred between processed meat consumption and mortality, in particular due to cardiovascular diseases, but also to cancer.

Recent studies by Levine et al. (2014) combined an epidemiological study of 6,381 US men and women aged 50 and above from the National Health and Nutrition Examination Survey (NHANES III) with mouse and cellular studies. People with high protein diets were four times more likely to die an early death from cancer and 74% more likely to die of any cause compared to people who ate a low protein diet. Systematic reviews of long-term protein diets are inconclusive, however, e.g. Lepe, Bacardi Gascon and Jimenez Cruz (2011) and Schwingshackl and Hoffmann (2013).

The protein leverage hypothesis is not supported by US nutrition data. According to the 2005–2006 National Health and Nutrition Examination Survey (NHANES), men were taking in 101.9 g and women 70.1 g (NCHStats, 2014). Unless the body requires amounts of protein well in excess of 70 g for women and 102 g for men, which seems highly unlikely, then over-consumption of carbohydrate and fat is not being driven by protein.

To understand obesity, we need to turn to a theory that focuses on the food environment.

The Obesogenic Environment

With the agricultural revolution came deleterious changes in diet and lifestyle. Diets became less varied and balanced, fat consumption increased, and average levels of activity and energy expenditure decreased. Today's modern food environment, containing large amounts of processed food, has been deliberately engineered to maximize sales. Processed foods have been carefully engineered to maximize food reward. Consumers select foods for their palatability, convenience and cost. Such palatable and cheap convenience foods are typically highly obesogenic, i.e. they contain sufficient amounts of sugar and fat to produce overweight and obesity when consumed regularly over months or years. Producers have influenced the palatability of foods by increasing quantities of sugar and salt in combination with fats and flavourings.

A summary of overall food intake is the number of calories consumed in the daily diet. Data for the USA on calories consumed and obesity prevalence over the period 1960–2010 show a 17% increase in daily calories over the 50-year period that corresponds almost perfectly with the increase in obesity prevalence. Coincidence?

According to this theory, obesity is the end-product of an 'obesogenic' environment created by a food industry that has been given free reign to promote fattening, unhealthful foods (Swinburn et al., 1999). Obesity is in the category of non-communicable diseases (NCDs), which also includes cancer, heart disease, diabetes and dementia. Through the sale of unhealthy commodities – tobacco, alcohol, and ultra-processed food and drink – transnational corporations are major drivers of global epidemics of NCDs.

It would be naïve to expect highly profitable industries and supermarket chains to curb their activities unless forced to do so by legislation. Moodie et al. (2013) discuss the rise in sales of unhealthy commodities that is occurring in low-income and middle-income countries compared to high-income countries where sales tended to level off between 1997 and 2009. There is a high concentration in these industries of processed foods and relatively few companies are dominating the market. For example, 75% of world food sales are of processed foods, whose largest manufacturers control more than a third of the global market.

Common strategies are used by the transnational corporations to deliberately undermine NCD prevention and control. For example, companies hire doctors to ghost-write scientific papers that cast doubt about findings linking unhealthy products to illness. They also infiltrate governmental committees responsible for regulation. Moodie et al. (2013) point out that industry self-regulation and public–private partnerships have yielded a complete lack of effective control and safety. It is plainly evident that unhealthy commodity industries *should not have any role in the formation of national or international NCD policy*. Only public regulation and intervention can be effective in preventing harm caused by obesity and other NCDs that are the direct result of unhealthy commodity industries.

Research on eating behaviour has shown that calorie consumption is higher when meals consist of a variety of foods compared with a single food type, when the food is more palatable, and when it is presented in more energy-dense formulations. More palatable and energy-dense diets result in greater weight gain (Wardle, 2007). Opinions about the optimum **macronutrient** composition of a healthful diet have been strongly divided. However, there has been a convergence of evidence over time. Three macronutrients have been linked to OAO: fats, sugars and proteins. One of the biggest changes associated with the increase in calories consumed has been the widespread availability of snack and fast foods. These contain high amounts of fat, sugar or protein, and salt is often used to enhance flavour. In addition to changes in eating habits, portion sizes of main meals have increased substantially. 'Supersizing' increases consumption: doubling of portion size increases consumption by 35% (Zlatevska, Dubelaar, and Holden, 2014).

Epidemiological studies show an association between dietary fat and body fat (adiposity). Lee Hooper et al. (2012) reviewed studies that compared lower versus usual total fat intake on body fatness. Low-fat diets were associated with lower relative body weight but the difference in weight was fairly slight – *only 1.6 kg*. Moreover, the prevalence of obesity has greatly increased, despite an apparent decrease in proportion of total calories consumed as fat in the diet of US children (Ebbeling et al., 2002).

In prospective studies, Mozaffarian et al. (2011) studied data collected from 120,877 US women and men with follow-up periods from 1986 to 2006. Within each 4-year period, participants gained an average of 1.52 kg – this would be 7.60 kg over 20 years. Four-year weight change was most strongly associated with the intake of: potato chips (0.76 kg), potatoes (0.58 kg), sugar-sweetened beverages (0.45 kg), unprocessed red meats (0.43 kg) and processed meats (0.42 kg). Weight gain was inversely associated with the intake of: vegetables (–0.10 kg), whole grains (–0.17 kg), fruits (–0.22 kg), nuts (–0.26 kg) and yogurt (–0.37). 'Lifestyle' factors associated with weight change included: physical activity (–0.80 kg), alcohol use (0.19 kg per drink per day), smoking (new quitters, 2.35 kg; former smokers, 0.06 kg), sleep (more weight gain with < 6 or > 8 hours of sleep) and television watching (0.14 kg per hour per day).

Mozaffarian et al.'s data lead to an interesting inference. If the 'couch potato diet' of red meat, potatoes, chips and cola (+2.31 kg) is replaced by a 'hairy shirt' diet of vegetables, grains, fruits, nuts and yogurt (–1.12) plus some physical activity (–0.80) there could be an average weight reduction of 4.15 kg every four years. That comes to a massive 20.4 kg over 20 years. With this rate of change, the obesity pandemic could be solved. Unfortunately, the human tendency to 'go with the flow' is a more attractive option than to be a lean and restrained spartan. Until the first heart attack, that is.

Food producers have used fats, sugars and salts to tinker with our taste buds while playing havoc with public health. They have experimented with trans fats (a partially hydrogenated oil, PHO), sugars, corn syrup and salt. In 2013, the US Centers for Disease Control and Prevention estimated that a reduction of trans fat could prevent 7,000 deaths from heart disease and up to 20,000 heart attacks each year in the USA. The high risks associated with PHOs led the FDA to suggest that PHOs are no longer 'generally recognized as safe' (GRAS). With the removal of GRAS status, trans fats will all but disappear from the US food chain.

High-fructose corn syrup (HFCS) accounts for 40% of sweeteners used in the US. The product is in sodas, ketchups and condiments, salad dressings, canned soups, bread, and many other places you possibly don't expect to find it. Consumption of HFCS increased to 27 kg per person per year between 1970 and 2000, a trend mirrored by the figures for obesity. Studies in endocrinology have suggested a causal relationship between sugar intake and weight gain (e.g. Lustig, 2013).

To summarize the obesity story thus far, we have seen that there is a complex array of genetic, nutritional, developmental, and environmental factors that influence the development of overweight and obesity. None seems to 'tell the whole story' on its own. Obesity is a clear case of multiple causation. We need to explain not only *how* obesity can develop in a susceptible individual. We also need to understand *why some individuals develop it and not others*. We turn now to consider social and psychological explanations for obesity.

Societal Influences: The Thin Ideal, Body Dissatisfaction and Stigmatization

Society places a high value on the '**thin ideal**', a body image that is slim and slender with a narrow waist and little body fat. Yet, for many, the thin ideal is in direct opposition to both a natural predisposition to become obese and to an obesogenic food environment. Psychologist Kelly Brownell (1992) discussed the search for the perfect body as an instance where physiology and culture collide:

> Modern society breeds a search for the perfect body. Today's aesthetic ideal is extremely thin, and now, superimposed on this, is the need to be physically fit. People seek the ideal, not only because of expected health benefits, but because of what the ideal symbolizes in our culture (self-control, success, acceptance). Two assumptions are widespread with regard to body weight and shape. One is that the body is infinitely malleable, and that with the right combination of diet and exercise, every person can reach the ideal. The second is that vast rewards await

> the person who attains the ideal. Research has shown that biological variables, particularly genetics, are influential in the regulation of body weight and shape. Hence, there are limits to how much a person can change. This places culture in conflict with physiology. In addition, the rewards of being attractive are less than most would expect. There are serious consequences of seeking the ideal and falling short, some psychological and others physiological (e.g. increased health risk for weight cycling). Clinical and research efforts are necessary to help individuals establish reasonable weight and shape goals, and to educate the public accordingly.
>
> (Brownell, 1992: 1)

The psychological impact of OAO can be measured in terms of the stigma, lowered self-esteem and reduced well-being. The size of the thin ideal is decreasing as the rate of obesity is increasing, making the thin ideal difficult to maintain (Pinhas et al., 1998). Depending on the degree to which the thin body ideal is internalized, the perceived gap between the actual body and the thin ideal can have serious psychological effects (Ahern et al., 2011). Thin ideal internalization is associated with body-image and eating disturbances, especially in conjunction with dieting and negative affect (Thompson and Stice, 2001). The thin ideal is a global phenomenon. The influence of the media, especially the representation of the female body on magazine covers, is huge.

Rodgers et al. (2009) noted that: 'In Western society, body image concerns are so prevalent among young women they have been called normative, with body dissatisfaction appearing in girls as young as 5 years old' (pp. 89–95). The thin ideal is 'transmitted' from mother to child. Yamazaki and Omori (2014) asked early adolescents (175 girls and 198 boys) in Japan to complete a questionnaire to assess their drive for thinness and perceptions of mothers' attitudes and behaviours related to body shape. The questionnaire for mothers (n = 206) measured mothers' thin ideal internalization. The authors found that mothers' thin ideal internalization was associated with girls' drive for thinness through the perception of mothers' attitudes directed to the girls, and with boys' drive for thinness through observation of their mothers' weight-loss behaviour.

Bojorquez et al. (2013) examined the bodily experiences of Mexican women to investigate their acceptance of the thin ideal and body dissatisfaction. They conducted semi-structured individual interviews with 30 adult participants in Mexico City. The interviewees accepted the thin body ideal, but experienced their bodies as 'signifiers of motherhood' that protected them from body dissatisfaction. Thus perception of overweight may predict body dissatisfaction and weight loss intentions better than weight status itself.

Fredrickson et al. (2015) examined the association of weight perception and weight satisfaction with body change intentions and weight-related behaviours in 928 overweight adolescents (aged 11–18; 44% female). Accurate perception of weight and dissatisfaction with weight were associated with trying to lose weight, but were negatively associated with some healthy weight-related behaviours. Awareness of overweight and body dissatisfaction may be detrimental to the adoption of healthy weight control behaviours. The authors concluded that interventions with overweight adolescents should encourage body satisfaction. Overweight and obesity are rarely, if ever, a deliberate or conscious choice. Yet the blaming, shaming and stigmatization of people with OAO is very common; it heightens the stress of OAO individuals that, in turn, leads to increased eating. People with OAO are openly stigmatized and often incur more open forms of prejudice and discrimination than other stigmatized social groups (Brochu and Esses, 2011). Obesity is often the butt of jokes and cartoons.

In reviewing earlier research, Puhl and Brownell (2004, p. 69) stated:

> Research is clear in showing that obese individuals are highly stigmatized, and that bias and discrimination are often a consequence. Given that half the [American] population is overweight, the number of people potentially faced with discrimination and stigmatization is immense. The consequences of being denied jobs, disadvantaged in education, or marginalized by health care professionals because of one's weight can have a profound impact on family life, social status, and quality of life. Obese individuals can suffer terribly from this, both from direct discrimination and from other behaviours (e.g. teasing and social exclusion) that arise from weight-related stigma.

In an updated review in 2009, Puhl and Heuer (2009) found no evidence that negative attitudes towards obese people were becoming less prevalent. The authors concluded that weight bias will remain a social injustice and public health issue, impairing the quality of life for both present and future generations of obese individuals.

Pearl et al. (2014) investigated the effects of weight bias experiences and internalization on exercise among 177 women with OAO in a cross-sectional study. Participants completed questionnaires assessing exercise behaviour, self-efficacy and motivation; experiences of weight stigmatization; weight bias internalization; and weight-stigmatizing attitudes toward others. Pearl et al. found that weight stigma experiences positively correlated with exercise behaviour, but weight bias internalization was negatively associated with all exercise variables.

Seacat et al. (2014) studied daily diaries to assess female weight stigmatization. They recruited 50 overweight/obese women from public weight forums to complete week-long daily diaries. A total of 1,077 weight-stigmatizing events were reported. Results indicated that body mass index, education, age, daily activities and interpersonal interactions can all can influence individual levels of stigmatization.

Stigma-based bullying is associated with significant negative mental and physical health outcomes. In a longitudinal study, Rosenthal et al. (2013) used surveys and physical assessments with mostly Black and Latino, socio-economically disadvantaged, urban students. Rosenthal et al. reported greater weight- and race-based bullying as being indirectly associated with increased blood pressure and BMI. Bullying was associated with decreased self-rated health across two years.

We turn now to consider some of the main psychological processes associated with obesity.

Emotion, Personality, Body Dissatisfaction and Depression

In this section we review studies on emotional/impulsive eating, body dissatisfaction and depression.

One psychological hypothesis to explain obesity has been to attribute overeating to emotionality. People are said to eat to calm themselves, assuage sadness or guilt, or reduce feelings of loneliness.

In spite of its intuitive appeal, the evidence for this theory is positive but inconsistent. The initial research was done in laboratory studies with students. Lowe and Fisher (1993) compared the emotional reactivity and emotional eating of normal-weight and overweight female college students in a natural environment. Their participants self-monitored food intake and pre-eating mood at each episode of eating for 12 consecutive days. The obese students were more emotionally reactive and more likely to engage in emotional eating than normal-weight individuals with snacks but not with meals. Emotional distress was associated with snack eating, and emotional eating was related to their percentage overweight.

Polivy et al. (1978) compared the emotional responsiveness of dieters and non-dieters in a sample of male college students. Dieters were found to be more extreme emotional responders. When an internal source of arousal (i.e. caffeine) was provided, non-dieters became more emotional and dieters became less emotional.

Rodin (1973) studied the effects of distraction on performance of obese and normal-weight participants. Male undergraduates worked on tasks requiring concentration, while competing, irrelevant material was also used to distract them. Rodin found that overweight students were more disrupted than normal-weight students by interesting, emotionally toned material, while they performed better than normals when there were no distracting events. Rodin suggested that obese people may have a heightened responsiveness to external cues. This finding led to a theory that obese people were not only more responsive to external cues but also ate more when feeling anxious, bored or depressed (Schachter and Rodin, 1974). This is the theory that obesity is related to emotional eating.

The above-mentioned studies were conducted with student samples. More recent studies have explored the role of emotional eating and regulation in obese young people from non-student populations and in adults. They have also looked at family and peer relational factors as a source of the emotion and feeling. For example, Vandewalle, Moens and Braet (2014) explored the association between parental rejection and emotional eating in 110 obese young people aged 10 and 16 years attending a Belgian treatment centre for obesity. Participants completed questionnaires assessing maternal and paternal rejection, emotion regulation strategies and emotional eating. Vandewalle and colleagues found that the use of maladaptive emotion regulation strategies mediated the relation between maternal rejection and emotional eating. Paternal rejection itself was not found to be associated with emotion regulation or with emotional eating in the young people.

Personality traits can contribute to unhealthy weight increases and difficulties with weight management. Of particular interest are possible links between weight increases and personality in people with obesity. Sutin et al. (2011) studied the association between personality and obesity across the adult life span. Their data came from a longitudinal study with 1,988 participants that spanned more than 50 years to investigate personality associations with adiposity and fluctuations in BMI. They modelled the BMI trajectory across adulthood and tested whether personality predicted its rate of change.

Participants with higher scores on neuroticism or extraversion or lower scores on conscientiousness had higher BMI, more body fat, and larger waist and hip circumferences. The strongest association was found for impulsivity. Participants who scored in the top 10% of impulsivity weighed, on average, 11 kg more than those in the bottom 10% (Figure 7.6). Longitudinally, high neuroticism and low conscientiousness, and difficulty with impulse control, were associated with weight fluctuations, measured as the variability in weight over time. Low scores on agreeableness and impulsivity predicted a greater increase in BMI across the adult lifespan. Overall, BMI was mostly unrelated to changes in personality traits.

The findings that impulsiveness and emotional eating both are associated with a tendency to develop obesity make good psychological sense, as does the finding that obesity is associated with low agreeableness.

Another psychological factor that has been investigated is dietary restraint, the attempt to hold back from eating. Some studies have found that restraint can create a rebound effect in the form of binge eating. In a cross-sectional study, Marcus et al. (1985) determined the prevalence and severity of binge eating among 432 women seeking behavioural treatment for obesity and to assess the relationship between binge eating and dietary restraint; 46% of women reported serious binge eating, especially younger and heavier women, in whom binge eating severity was related to overall dietary restraint. A prospective study by Johnson and Wardle (2005), however, found no evidence that dietary restraint causes bulimic binge eating. A survey of 1,177 adolescent girls explored whether emotional eating, binge eating, abnormal attitudes to eating and weight, low self-esteem, stress and depression are associated with dietary restraint or body dissatisfaction.

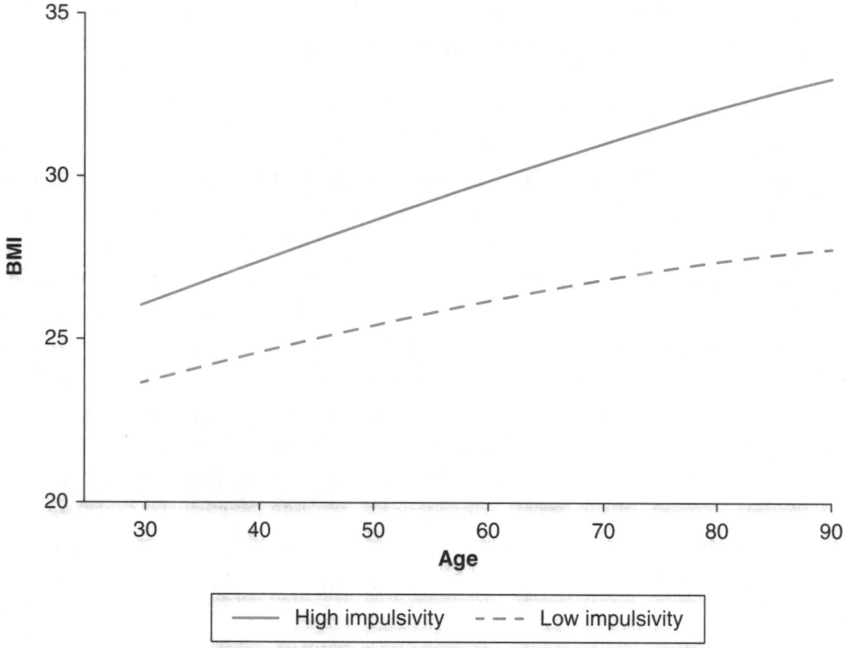

Figure 7.6 Estimated BMI for participants 1 SD above and below the mean on impulsiveness

Source: Sutin et al. (2011)

They found that restraint was associated only with more negative attitudes to eating, whereas body dissatisfaction was significantly associated with all adverse outcomes, casting doubt on the hypothesis that restrained eating is a primary cause of bulimic symptoms and emotional eating. Body dissatisfaction was the key factor. Many studies have shown that body dissatisfaction is associated with depression (e.g. Paxton et al., 2006).

Psychiatric studies indicate a strong and reliable association between depression and obesity. This association occurs both in cross-sectional and prospective studies. In a cross-sectional study, Onyike et al. (2003) studied rates of depression in the past month for both men and women as a function of BMI (Figure 7.7). The data came from 9,997 respondents to the National Health and Nutrition Examination Survey (NHANES), an interview survey of the US population. Depression was assessed using the Diagnostic Interview Schedule, based on the criteria for major depression outlined in the *DSM-III*.

Obesity was associated with increased rates of depression. Being overweight or mildly obese was not associated with substantially increased rates of depression; however, the severely obese (BMI ≥ 40) suffered markedly higher rates. This study provides no evidence about causation. However, it seems likely that causation runs in both directions, which is confirmed in prospective studies.

Luppino et al. (2010) conducted a systematic review and meta-analysis on the longitudinal relationship between depression, overweight and obesity to identify possible influencing factors.

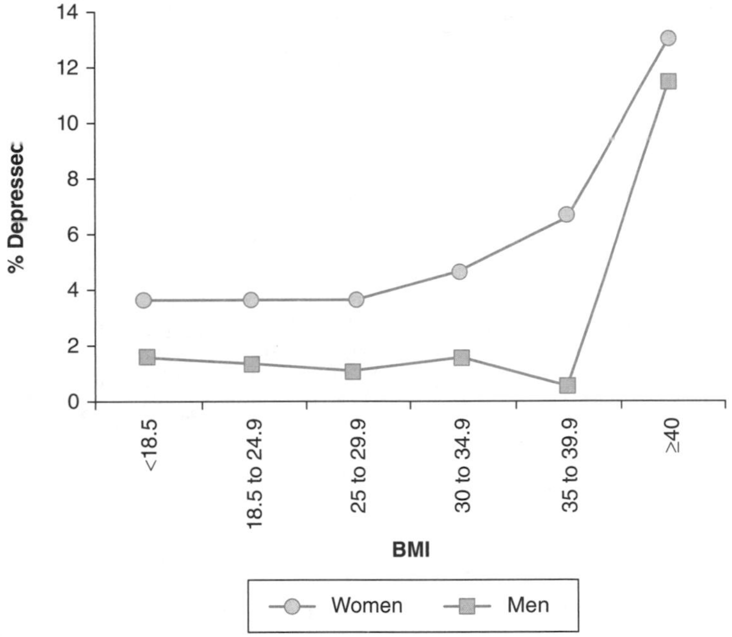

Figure 7.7 The relationship between depression and BMI

Source: Onyike et al. (2003)

They reviewed studies examining the longitudinal relationship between depression and overweight (BMI 25–29.99) or obesity (BMI $\geq$ 30). Obesity at baseline increased the risk of onset of depression at follow-up by 55%. Overweight also increased the risk of onset of depression at follow-up by 27%. This association was statistically significant among adults (aged 20 or above) but not among younger persons under 20. Baseline depression was not found to be predictive of overweight over time. However, depression increased the odds for developing obesity by 58%. Luppino et al. (2010) concluded that: 'This meta-analysis confirms a reciprocal link between depression and obesity. Obesity was found to increase the risk of depression, most pronounced among Americans and for clinically diagnosed depression. In addition, depression was found to be predictive of developing obesity' (p. 220).

The evidence we have reviewed from studies of the psychological influences on obesity suggests the causal chain illustrated in a homeostatic system (Figure 7.8). Empirical evidence of this 'vicious circle' in adolescents and obese women is present in the literature (e.g. Wardle et al., 2001; Chaiton et al., 2009; Goldfield et al., 2010; Sonneville et al., 2012); it certainly exists among smokers; and it may well flow over into the drinking and drug-taking patterns of both men and women. This 'circle of discontent' requires systematic investigation using prospective studies (Marks, 2015).

How do doctors and lay people themselves explain obesity? Ogden and Flanagan (2008) explored general practitioners' (GPs') beliefs about the causes and solutions to obesity and compared them to those held by a lay sample. Interestingly, the GPs tended to favour psychological, behavioural and social explanations, which they felt lay outside their expertise, while lay people

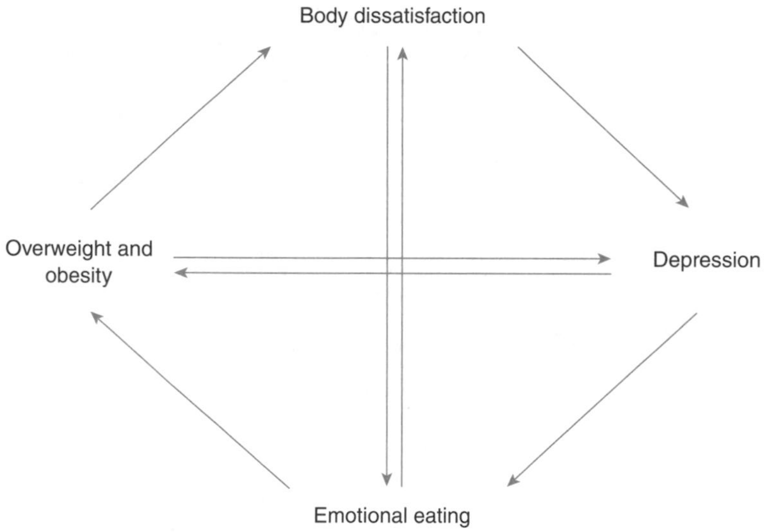

Figure 7.8 A model linking body dissatisfaction, depression, emotional eating, and overweight and obesity

Source: Marks (2015)

preferred more biological explanations and looked to doctors for help. Such differing models can lead to conflictual problems between patients and their GPs. Jane Ogden's research suggested that while 'patients prefer a more professional based approach, GPs would prefer a more patient-led one' (Ogden et al., 2001). These results suggest that if an intervention can be negotiated, success rates would tend to be low as either the patient or the GP would be acting in contradiction to their beliefs about the nature of obesity.

This apparent 'culture clash' was born out in a qualitative study of GPs' views on treating obesity by Epstein and Ogden (2005). They found that GPs believed that obesity was the patient's responsibility rather than a medical problem. This conflict was perceived as potentially detrimental to the doctor–patient relationship. GPs described using a range of strategies to maintain a good relationship including offering anti-obesity drugs, in which they had little faith, as a means of meeting patients' expectations, listening to the patients' problems, despite not having a solution, and offering understanding of the overweight problem. Epstein and Ogden (2005) concluded: 'GPs believe that although patients want them to take responsibility for their weight problems, obesity is not within the GP's professional domain. Until more effective interventions have been developed GPs may remain unconvinced that obesity is a problem requiring their clinical expertise and may continue to resist any government pressure to accept obesity as part of their workload' (p. 750).

One suspects that little has changed since then.

INTERVENTIONS

Dietary Guidelines

One of the main strategies for preventing obesity and overweight at a societal or population level is the publication of dietary guidelines. Guidelines are produced on a regular basis by many national governments. The *Dietary Guidelines for Americans* (DGA) is updated every five years as a blueprint for nutrition policies such as School Lunch. The 2010 *DGA* emphasized three things: balancing calories with physical activity to manage weight; consuming more fruits, vegetables, whole grains, fat-free and low-fat dairy products, and seafood; consuming less sodium (salt), saturated fats, trans fats, cholesterol, added sugars and refined grains. A pictorial aid called 'MyPlate' shows a place setting divided into five food groups (Figure 7.9).

The 2010 DGA committee report emphasized an urgent need to address obesity at every stage of the lifespan (especially in childhood), while preventing nutrient deficiencies and imbalance, and changing the overall 'food environment' to encourage and allow all people to choose healthier food patterns (Dietary Guidelines Advisory Committee, 2010). The 2010 DGA called for moderate- to high-carbohydrate consumption that includes six one-ounce servings of grain foods each day, at least half from whole grain sources. In spite of the accumulating evidence about the benefits of low-carb diets, the 2010 DGA promoted a high-carbohydrate diet. Critics responded: 'MyPlate mixes science with the influence of powerful agricultural interests, which is not the recipe for healthy eating.' Moreover, its protein section offered no indication that some high-protein foods – fish, poultry, beans, nuts – are healthier than red meats and processed meats; it recommended dairy at every meal; and it said nothing about sugary drinks (Datz, 2011).

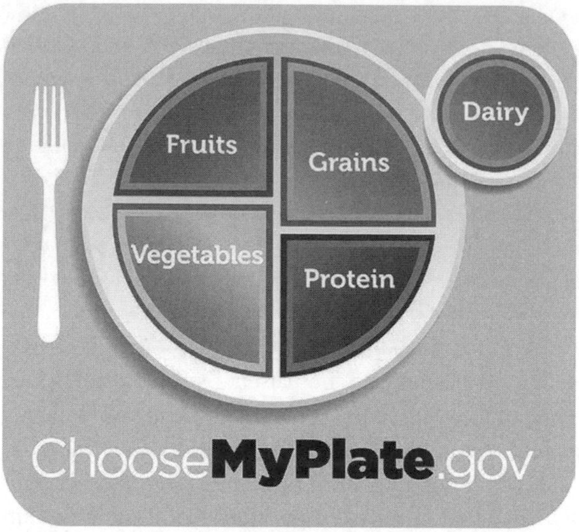

Figure 7.9 MyPlate showing the American population how to keep a 'balanced diet'

Attempts by health authorities to promote healthy eating through guidelines has sometimes led to public confusion about portion sizes, dietary fat, percentage energy and certain nutrients. Nutritional messages in public health and commercial sources are perceived as conflicting and food guides are used minimally by consumers (Boylan et al., 2013). To be usefully applied as a guide to eating behaviour, guidelines need to clearly and consistently inform people what, when and where to eat, not only how much they should consume. This point was addressed by De Ridder et al. (2013) who argue that people's ability to regulate their eating is compromised by a lack of clear, shared standards that guide eating behaviour. They hypothesize that the availability of clear, credible, shared eating appropriateness standards will decrease the uncertainty resulting from the current lack of such standards, and provide effective guidance of eating behaviour.

The idea that clear, socially shared norms promote healthful eating is supported by laboratory studies of social norms that operated to moderate people's tendency to maximize eating (Leone et al., 2007). A normative model might assume that people will follow one of two possible norms for 'appropriate' eating behaviour: the norm to eat minimally and the norm to avoid eating excessively. Without clear norms people tended to overeat; clear norms in the same situation exerted a restraining effect. Leone et al. observed that individuals are more likely to eat in accordance with their own desires (i.e. to be 'greedy') when social norms are not apparent.

The presence of other people may facilitate or inhibit intake, depending on how much the other people eat. In the presence of palatable food, external cues about how much we have eaten can influence our food intake as much as internal cues of satiety. Social norms can account for either increased or decreased intake in the presence of others, depending on how much the others eat and the extent to which one is eager to impress the others (Herman et al., 2003).

Wansink et al. (2005) used self-refilling soup bowls to examine whether visual cues related to portion size influence intake volume without altering estimated intake or satiation. The experiment used two visibility levels: (1) an accurate visual cue of a food portion (normal bowl) vs. (2) a biased visual cue (self-refilling bowl). The soup eating apparatus was situated in a restaurant-style table in which two of four bowls imperceptibly refilled as their contents were consumed. The participants who unknowingly ate from self-refilling bowls consumed 73% more soup than those eating from normal soup bowls. However, they did not believe they had consumed more, nor perceive themselves as more sated than those with normal bowls. Apparently, the amount of food on a plate or bowl increases intake because it influences consumption norms and expectations and it lessens one's reliance on self-monitoring.

The tendency to overeat is difficult to restrain even with training and education. Cavanagh et al. (2013) found that the portion size effect, the tendency to eat more when there's more to eat on the plate, is quite hard to change. Neither education nor mindfulness was effective in reducing the effect of portion size.

Norms acting as guidelines, and vice versa, could be an underutilized resource in the prevention of overeating and OAO. If a guideline is to become socially normative, however, it must be accepted as a credible source that is deservedly worth following. Turati et al. (2012) studied adherence to the European Food Safety Authority (EFSA) dietary guidelines and cancer risk in Italy. They used a 'EFSA index' by adding 1 point for adherence to each EFSA guideline. They found that overall adherence to the EFSA dietary guidelines was not associated with colorectal, colon and rectal cancer risk. We discuss the issue of adherence in Chapter 17.

Vegetarianism and Veganism

One underutilized intervention for overweight and obesity is switching to a vegetarian or vegan diet. **Vegetarian** diets include eggs and/or dairy but no other foods derived from animal sources. **Vegan** diets exclude all animal-based foods. Such diets can be motivated by ethical beliefs against animal cruelty, by concerns for the environment, or by an interest in improved health including the desire to lose weight. Total consumption of meat and dairy by meat eaters is striking. Each year a US meat eater consumes: 130 shellfish, 40 fish, 26 chickens, one turkey, nearly half a pig and a little more than a tenth of a cow. That's nearly 200 animals a year or 16,000 animals over a lifetime (Mohr, 2012). To provide all of this livestock, the agri- and aquacultural systems degrade land and water, biodiversity and climate both directly through pasture and indirectly through its use of feed and forage, and the methane expelled by cattle (Foley et al., 2011). Ruminants (cattle, water buffalo, sheep and goats) use 86% of the world's agricultural land and consume 71% of its total biomass, yet produce only 8% of its food (Smith et al., 2013). The Union of Concerned Scientists (2012) argued that a diet shift from beef toward chicken would greatly reduce the pressure on land and the resulting pressure for deforestation. It would also have health benefits, particularly in developed countries where beef consumption is already at levels leading to heart disease, cancer and other illnesses.

Early human food cultures were plant-based (Leitzmann, 2014). Major religions such as Hinduism and Buddhism always recommended a vegetarian way of life since their conception.

Recent scientific evidence has indicated that a vegetarian diet reduces the risk of most contemporary diseases and that vegetarianism is being increasingly accepted owing to health concerns and ethical, environmental, and social issues including the need for a sustainable nutrition for the future well-being of humankind. Leitzmann states: 'An increasing number of people do not want animals to suffer nor do they want climate change; they want to avoid preventable diseases and to secure a livable future for generations to come' (2014).

Key et al. (1998) compared the mortality rates of vegetarians and non-vegetarians among 76,000 men and women who had participated in five prospective studies. This meta-analysis collated the entire body of evidence collected in prospective studies in Western countries from 1960 to 1981. The original studies were conducted in California (2), Britain (2) and Germany (1) and provided data concerning 16- to 89-year-olds for whom diet and smoking status information was available. Vegetarians were defined as those who did not eat any meat or fish (n = 27,808). Participants were followed for an average of 10.6 years when 8,330 deaths occurred. The results showed that vegetarians as a group contained a lower proportion of smokers and current alcohol drinkers but a higher proportion of high exercisers, and had a consistently lower BMI. The death rate ratio for ischaemic heart disease for vegetarians versus non-vegetarians across the five studies was 0.76 (95% CI 0.62–0.94). The all cause mortality ratio was 0.95 (95% CI 0.82–1.11). When non-vegetarians were subdivided into regular meat eaters and semi-vegetarians who ate fish only or ate meat less than once a week, there was evidence of a significant dose-response. The death rate ratio for ischaemic heart disease, caused by a narrowing of the arteries, for semi-vegetarians and vegetarians compared to regular meat eaters was 0.78 and 0.66 respectively. Vegetarians have a lower risk of dying from ischaemic heart disease than non-vegetarians.

A meta-analysis with over 120,000 participants reported a 29% lower risk of death from cardiovascular disease in vegetarians (those eating meat or fish less than once a week) and an 18% lower incidence of cancer overall in vegetarians (Huang et al., 2012). Vegetarians have a lower risk of hospitalization or death from ischaemic heart disease (Crowe et al., 2013); lower blood pressure and a lower risk of having hypertension (Pettersen et al., 2012; Yokoyama et al., 2013); lower risk of developing MS (Rizzo et al., 2011); and a lower risk of some cancers than do meat eaters. Vegetarians and fish eaters had a lower risk of cancer compared to meat eaters (Key et al., 2009). Vegetarians have a lower risk of diverticular disease compared to meat eaters or fish eaters; vegans have an even lower risk (Crowe et al., 2011). Vegetarians, especially vegans, have a lower risk of developing type 2 diabetes (Tonstad et al., 2009, 2013). However, vegans require dietary supplements of vitamin B12, B6, D and iodine.

A neglected factor has been fibre. Keys Seven Countries study found fibre intake was inversely related to body weight. Large-scale studies by the European Prospective Investigation into Cancer and Nutrition (EPIC) produced data that could be applied to the study of obesity. Fogelholm et al. (2012) examined the role of dietary macronutrient composition, food consumption and dietary patterns in predicting weight or waist circumference change, with and without prior weight reduction. The results show that dietary fibre, especially cereal fibre, fruit/vegetable intake and the Mediterranean dietary pattern were inversely associated with weight or waist change. A mechanism for the protective effect of fibre was elucidated in 2014 (De Vadder et al., 2014). It involves the intestinal flora and the ability of the intestine to produce glucose between meals.

Nath (2011) explored the impact of hegemonic masculinity upon the adoption of meatless diets. The evidence suggested that the belief that meat provides strength and vigour to men and the enforcement of meat-eating as a social norm help to explain why vegetarianism is not viewed as an appealing choice for men. However, evidence suggests that this concern is becoming less evident as vegetarianism is gaining in popularity among both men and women.

Vegetarian and vegan diets are affordable and environmentally friendly. One UK study has shown that changing from a non-vegetarian to a vegetarian or vegan diet could reduce greenhouse gas emissions by 22% and 26% respectively. Any of these changes would be less expensive than the average diet in the UK and would have adequate protein (Berners-Lee et al., 2012). On current evidence, vegetarian and vegan diets provide a sustainable and effective means for achieving healthful levels of nutrition and body weight.

Drug Therapies and Bariatric Surgery

Long-term safety concerns limit the use of drugs to bring about weight loss. Five major drugs have been withdrawn owing to safety concerns. The two remaining drugs are phentermine, a derivative of amphetamine (an appetite suppressant), and orlistat, which reduces the amount of fat absorbed from food eaten. Orlistat has negative side effects that have resulted in poor tolerability, low adherence and varied effectiveness. Orlistat is currently available over the counter in European countries and elsewhere.

An average weight loss of 5% is regarded as the minimum threshold for approval guidelines issued by regulatory authorities, yet the majority of patients will often set much higher targets of 10–15%. Modest efficacy offered by currently drug therapies for obesity but a history of poor tolerability and lack of safety, a paucity of novel therapies, and lack of reimbursement have substantially constrained developers of new drugs for obesity (Wong et al., 2012).

At least 25% of people in the UK are obese, yet only 1.3% (2.1% of females, 0.6% of males) received anti-obesity medication (Patterson et al., 2014). The relationship between medication rates and age differs by gender with prescriptions higher in younger females and older males. While the prevalence of obesity worsens with age, younger females are more likely to be prescribed anti-obesity medication, suggesting an element of patient demand.

Medication gives patients an imperfect solution to OAO while perpetuating feelings of learned helplessness. Hollywood and Ogden (in press) studied ten participants' experiences of gaining weight after taking orlistat using thematic analysis. They found that the participants attributed their failure to lose weight to the medication and emphasized a medical model of obesity. Their weight gain was fatalistically considered an inevitable part of their self-identity, that of a perpetual dieter.

Bariatric surgical procedures forcibly induce a drastic lifestyle change and can elicit up to 20% weight loss, but carry inherent medical risks and high cost. Bariatric surgery is the most effective treatment for the severely obese but it does not work for everyone (Husted and Ogden, 2014). MackSense (2014) reported a huge jump in the number of NHS-funded bariatric procedures in England from 261 in 2000/01 to 8,087 in 2010/11. It estimated that for 2001–2011 less than 1% of people eligible for bariatric surgery received the treatment, i.e. 5,000–10,000 (MackSense, 2014).

In the US, the incidence of bariatric surgery plateaued by 2010 at approximately 113,000 cases per year (Livingston, 2010). Complication rates fell from 10.5% in 1993 to 7.6% of cases in 2006. Bariatric surgery costs the health economy at least $1.5 billion annually.

A recent study suggests that a significant variable in predicting the success of bariatric surgery is a person's investment in the operation – i.e. the extent to which they are committed and also the effort that they undertake, in time, finance, emotion, or physical and behavioural effort. In an RCT, Husted and Ogden (2014) found that success following surgery was related to individuals' sense of investment in the surgery, with failure being linked to hedonic motivation to consume food and greater susceptibility to food in the environment. The intervention raised the salience of personal investment in having weight-loss surgery by reducing automatic hedonic thoughts about food to aid weight loss. By three months, the intervention group had a mean weight loss of 6.77 kg compared to 0.91 kg for the control participants. This simple, cost-effective psychological intervention facilitated weight loss and changed hedonic thoughts about food in bariatric patients.

Significant weight loss after bariatric surgery creates a high demand for body contouring surgery. In a qualitative study, Gilmartin et al. (2014) observed two major quality-of-life perception changes for patients who had undergone contouring surgery after dramatic weight loss: 'identity transformation', which embraced improved physical function and enhanced self-esteem, confidence and quality of life, and a 'changed lifestyle'. The participants talked about 'discarding stigmatised identities' and transitioning toward new identity meanings that are perceived as 'normal' in comparison to their former stigmatized 'fat/ugly' categorization. One female 58-year-old explained: 'A new powerful self emerged. I am happy with my body shape and self-perception. The surgery dramatically altered my physical appearance and my inner world too. The journey has birthed a new personality and identity' (Gilmartin et al., in press).

Behavioural Interventions

A variety of interventions have been tried at the individual level of influence. The quality of the research used to evaluate the interventions is of varied quality but mostly rather poor. Sample sizes are small, power analyses are rarely if ever carried out, and designs are overall poor. Recent systematic reviews on effectiveness will be briefly summarized to illustrate the crisis situation that exists in dealing with obesity using behavioural methods.

Traditional approaches have used a combination of diets and exercise. Behavioural programmes have produced weight losses of 10 kg on average at the end of six months (Wing, 2004). Adherence to such programmes is typically low and attrition high. Those who most need to reduce their weight show the least adherence; e.g. Pedro et al. (2015) found an association between waist circumference percentile and non-adherence. Long-term follow-up of interventions for weight loss show gradual regaining of weight such that four years after initial treatment only a modest amount of weight loss remained evident ($M = 1.8$ kg) (Perri and Foreyt, 2004).

The use of temporary diets and activity programmes produce only temporary effects. People who wish to maintain a lower weight over their entire lifetime need to commit to permanent lifestyle change. Evidence suggests that only a small percentage of people are willing to make such a commitment. There is no magic bullet.

Lifestyle modifications of diet and exercise remain the safest means of prevention and treatment of OAO but they are also the least effective. The EBT model and dietary guidelines may have been useful communication aids, but they have not proved to be a secure basis for interventions. For example, Stice et al. (2006) carried out a meta-analytic review of obesity prevention programmes for children and adolescents. The findings were mediocre: numerous prevention programmes have been evaluated, yet most (79%) did not produce statistically reliable weight gain prevention effects. Indeed, the average intervention effect size was an *r* of 0.04, which would be considered trivial by most researchers and clinicians.

Dozens of SRs have evaluated the effectiveness of clinical behavioural treatment interventions with a multiplicity of different OAO groups. The outcomes have been modest with average amounts of weight loss rarely exceeding 5% of body weight. Follow-up over a few years suggests that maintenance of weight loss in such programmes is almost non-existent.

Some recent findings on self-help weight loss interventions are more encouraging. In a prospective study of self-help, group behavioural treatment, participants reported a mean of 5.1 prior weight-loss attempts and lost 13.8% of initial weight in their current treatment (Latner and Ciao, 2014). Based on the last observation carried forward, participants lost a mean of 13.8% (7.8%) of their pretreatment weight (13.05 kg) at the last meeting they attended (for dropouts) or at 24 months (for those still in treatment at that time). A greater number of past attempts independently predicted greater 6-month, 18-month, and intent-to-treat weight losses. The correlation between number of attempts and 24-month weight loss was 0.51 ($p < 0.01$). However, attrition rate was high with 65% of participants remaining in treatment for less than 24 months. Latner and Ciao suggested that, in contrast to studies on professional treatment, group self help participants might benefit from repeated weight-loss efforts despite previous failures.

Systematic reviews have attempted to evaluate techniques that are effective. Dombrowski et al. (2012) reviewed RCTs of interventions targeting dietary and/or physical activity change for obese adults with follow-up data for at least 12 weeks. Results indicated that interventions using increasing numbers of techniques are not necessarily associated with better outcomes. Bull et al. (2014) carried out SRs on trials with low-income groups effective which investigated interventions for changing healthy eating, physical activity and smoking behaviours. They found only small positive effects on healthy eating, physical activity and smoking which weakened substantially over 6–12 months.

The basis for dietary interventions often appears to be the existing dietary guidelines themselves rather than the result of active collaboration with experts in the appropriate basic sciences. Hafekost et al. (2013) suggested that reliance on dietary guidelines to inform the scientific basis of interventions may be a significant factor in holding back progress as there are very few public health interventions testing alternative models. They point out that a range of alternative interventions, such as carbohydrate restricted, low glycaemic index, and low fructose, have been proposed based on more plausible models than energy balance.

As early as 1991, the competence of therapists to help obese patients to lose weight was being questioned:

> Although millions seek treatments for obesity, the benefits of treatment have been overstated. For most people, treatment is not effective; the majority of the obese struggle in vain to lose weight and blame themselves for relapses . . . Many therapists may be contributing to this psychologic damage by giving their patients false hope for success and by failing to recognize that seeking treatment for obesity may be triggered by psychologic problems that are not addressed in obesity treatment.
>
> (Wooley and Garner, 1991: 1248)

Hafekost et al. (2013) questioned whether 'the public health message' matches scientific knowledge of obesity. They examined the models of energy balance underpinning current research about weight-loss intervention from the field of public health, and determined whether they are consistent with the model provided by basic science. Most public health interventions were based on the energy balance theory, and attempted to reduce caloric consumption and/or increase physical activity in order to create a negative energy balance. Hafekost et al. (2013) concluded that: 'Public health weight-loss interventions seem to be based on an outdated understanding of the science . . . Instead of asking why people persist in eating too much and exercising too little, the key questions of obesity research should address those factors (environmental, behavioural or otherwise) that lead to dysregulation of the homeostatic mechanism' (p. 41).

They also raise an important ethical point: is it really right to continue to offer interventions that have not worked in the past?

> Despite the extensive literature on their long-term ineffectiveness, interventions based on this simplistic understanding of energy balance continue to be advocated under the assumption that previous interventions have not been pursued sufficiently vigorously or that participants have failed to follow the prescriptions of the intervention . . . Continuing to promote a model that is unlikely to be successful in the longer term, and may result in individuals becoming discouraged, is both unproductive and wasteful of resources that could be better spent on investigating more plausible alternatives to improving weight control.
>
> (Hafekost et al., 2013)

The evidence of effectiveness of behavioural interventions is so weak, we can only hope the old dictum 'prevention is better than cure' will one day be acted on by those with the power to do so. This will require legislation to make the choice of healthful foods more affordable and fatty foods and sugary drinks less attractive to consumers (Marks, 2015).

FUTURE RESEARCH

1. Redesign of dietary guidelines that are clear, credible and science-based to provide effective guidance of eating behaviour.
2. Finding the best methods for giving dietary guidance during pregnancy and maternity.
3. Methods of facilitating long-term dietary change towards plant-based diets and reduced consumption of processed foods and red meats.
4. Improvements in the transparency and usability of food labelling.
5. Critical thinking about basic nutritional science, food fads and diets that lack any basis in science.

SUMMARY

1 Eating and drinking are pleasurable, social activities that are necessary for survival. They are steeped in cultural and symbolic meaning.

2 Human beings spent 95.5% of evolutionary history as hunter-gatherers and are genetically endowed to store excess food energy as fat. Contemporary processed food is a poor match for the human metabolic system and creates an 'obesogenic' environment with excessive amounts of fats and sugars.

3 Obesity is a chronic, relapsing, neurochemical disease that manifests itself by an increase in size and number of fat cells. Increasing prevalence of overweight and obesity is a global pandemic. By 2050, it is predicted that obesity will affect the majority of adults and 25% of children, to create a mainly obese society.

4 According to energy balance theory, obesity is caused by an excess of calories: an imbalance between energy intake and energy expenditure. This theory has been a dominant influence in theory, research and practice for half a century. It has led to a 'blame and shame' culture around overweight and obesity, and interventions based upon the theory have failed to control the pandemic. A new approach is needed.

5 Alternative nutritional theories have been suggested: the insulin theory claims that obesity is caused by a chronic elevation in insulin in a diet that contains too much carbohydrate; the food reward theory explains obesity as a breakdown in the hedonic systems of the brain; the protein leverage hypothesis proposes that protein intake is prioritized with the consequence that a person will eat as much food as necessary to arrive at the intake target for protein. None of these theories has yielded a breakthrough.

(Continued)

(Continued)

6 Childhood obesity begins in the womb, continues to develop in the crib, and accelerates during the first few years of life. Attachment patterns, body dissatisfaction and negative affect influence eating and food preferences in early adolescence and continue into adulthood in a circle of discontent.

7 The 'thin ideal' pervades popular culture with narratives and images of thinness. This influence has an entirely negative effect on both young and adult people the world over. At the same time, discrimination against people who are overweight or obese causes stress and socio-economic disadvantage.

8 Research on different diets suggests that a plant-based diet containing low amounts of sugar, little or no red meat and the minimum of fats promotes weight loss and prevents obesity, diabetes, metabolic syndrome, coronary heart disease and cancer. A vegan diet with no meat, fish or dairy is especially anti-obesogenic.

9 Behavioural interventions in obesity prevention and treatment have yielded disappointing outcomes. Raising false hopes among people with OAO by continuing to offer interventions that have such poor outcomes is a questionable practice that should be terminated. Drug therapies also have poor outcomes. The most effective treatment remains bariatric surgery but this is costly and unavailable to many people who would benefit from it. Also, there can be unwanted, long-term effects.

10 Governmental actions that are independent of corporate interests are urgently required at all levels of society to reduce the prevalence of obesity and other chronic diet-based conditions. Of particular relevance are: the design of evidence-based dietary guidelines; accessible, accurate food labelling; improved education and training of parents and child-care providers; and legislation to change the balance of the obesogenic environment towards healthier food choices.

8 ALCOHOL AND DRINKING

Dionysus discovered and bestowed on men the service of drink, the juice that streams from the wine-clusters; men have but to take their fill of wine, and the sufferings of an unhappy race are banished, each day's troubles are forgotten in sleep – indeed this is our only cure for the weariness of life.

(Euripides, *The Bacchae*, trans. P. Vellacott, 1954/414 BC)

OUTLINE

In this chapter we discuss theories and research concerned with alcohol consumption and the causes, prevention and treatment of drinking problems. It begins with a discussion of the ambivalent attitudes to alcohol which have characterized many cultures from the distant past to the present day. An analysis of the physical and psychosocial dangers of drinking is followed by an examination of contrasting theories about the causes of excessive drinking. The chapter concludes with a discussion of the relative merits of different approaches to the prevention and treatment of drinking problems.

THE BLESSING AND CURSE OF ALCOHOL: PAST AND PRESENT ATTITUDES

Ambivalence towards alcohol is characteristic of many past civilizations and is illustrated in Euripides' tragedy, *The Bacchae*, written in 414 BC and quoted at the beginning of this chapter.

The tragedy revolves around the conflict between the stern killjoy attitude of the protagonist Pentheus and the wild abandon of the Bacchic women, a conflict orchestrated by Dionysus, the god of wine. Modern views on alcohol as a social problem can be traced back to the eighteenth century when distilled spirits became available for the first time in Europe. Because of their relative cheapness, they were popular with the English working class. This was the subject of much concern, at least among the educated middle classes. William Hogarth's 1751 prints *Beer Street* and *Gin Lane* (see Figure 8.1) illustrate the prevailing view by contrasting the pleasant and supposedly harmless effects of drinking beer with the dire consequences of drinking spirits. Notice the general sense of industriousness and well-being in Beer Street; many people are working and the only shop that is boarded up is the pawnbrokers. In Gin Lane nobody is working except the busy pawnbroker and there is a grim depiction of emaciation, death and the neglect of children.

Since the early nineteenth century popular beliefs about the dangers of alcohol have been shaped by organizations known as **temperance societies**. Beginning with the formation of the

Figure 8.1 Hogarth's *Beer Street* and *Gin Lane*. Trusler, J., Hogarth, J. and Nichols, J. (1833). *The Works of William Hogarth*. London: Jones & Co

American Temperance Society in 1826 and then spreading to many other countries, their influence has been enormous not only in bringing about the era of American prohibition from 1920 to 1934 but also in helping to establish as the standard medical opinion, especially in the USA, the belief that alcoholics can never return to moderate drinking but can only be cured by remaining abstinent for the rest of their lives. A range of sometimes conflicting views can be found among different temperance societies, some simply preaching moderation and the avoidance of excess, some taking the view that spirits are intrinsically dangerous while weaker alcoholic drinks are harmless; some believing that alcohol is highly addictive for everyone, others that it only presents dangers for a small minority of individuals with a predisposition to become addicted. Of particular historical importance were the Washingtonians in the USA in the 1840s, self-help associations running regular meetings along the lines of religious revivalist groups with an emphasis on the confessions of the repentant sinner and an appeal to a 'Higher Power' for support. This particular tradition remains strong today in Alcoholics Anonymous which has branches in almost every North American and British town of any size and in many other countries.

With the exception of some countries with majority Muslim populations, alcohol is legally obtainable nowadays in most parts of the world. The predominant view seems to be that it is 'all right in moderation, harmful in excess'. We review the evidence for this view in the next section. For the time being we focus on the undisputed harm that occurs as a consequence of regular heavy drinking and of 'binge drinking', both now seen as major problems in many countries. In 2007 the World Health Organization estimated that 3.7% of global mortality and 4.4% of disease was attributable to alcohol, noting also that this does not include social harm such as family and interpersonal problems, work problems, violence and other crimes (World Health Organization, 2007). Room et al. (2005) estimated the global burden of disease attributable to alcohol as 4%, varying from 1.3% in the poorest countries with low consumption to 12.1% in the former socialist countries. Rehm et al. (2009) estimated that 3.8% of global deaths could be attributed to alcohol, adding that 'Disease burden is closely related to average volume of alcohol consumption, and, for every unit of exposure, is strongest in poor people and in those who are marginalized from society.' Reviewing the situation in the European Union, Anderson and Baumberg (2006) pointed out that, among young people (aged 15 to 29), 25% of male mortality and 10% of female mortality is attributable to alcohol.

Alcohol problems and approaches to prevention and treatment vary greatly from country to country. The example of India, described briefly in the case study below, illustrates the extent to which specific cultural and historical circumstances need to be taken into account. In Britain in recent years the major source of concern has been binge drinking, with many city centres on weekend evenings notorious for the presence of large numbers of extremely drunk and disorderly young people (Raistrick, 2005; Plant and Plant, 2006). The British government has been much criticized for contributing to this by liberalizing the drinking laws under the influence of the Portman Group, a drinks industry public relations organization, while ignoring medical and other professional opinion opposed to liberalization.

BOX 8.1
INTERNATIONAL CASE STUDY: ALCOHOL CONSUMPTION IN INDIA

It is misleading to characterize India as a 'dry' or 'abstaining' culture. Prior to British colonial rule, a relaxed attitude to alcohol prevailed. British attempts to profit from the production and sale of alcohol led to opposition. Gandhi and the nationalist movement campaigned against alcohol as a symbol of colonial oppression, and demands for prohibition were associated with the desire for the ritual purity of the Indian nation. In practice, since independence, alcohol policy has varied from state to state and, although there have been periods of national prohibition, currently most states permit the sale of alcohol, and in fact derive 15% to 20% of their income from alcohol tax. Although alcohol is stigmatized in many sectors of society, an ambivalent attitude can be seen from the fact that many states stimulate the production of alcohol by demanding that increasing sales quotas be met by manufacturers as a condition of renewing licences. The drinks industry in turn seeks to influence government by making contributions to political parties.

The majority of Indians abstain from alcohol; in 2005 it was estimated that 21% of men and less than 5% of women drink. However, of those that do drink, half drink at levels known to be hazardous. The drinks industry is increasingly seeking to make drinking more popular among women by lifestyle advertising and the types of drink they produce. Local manufacturers are also being taken over by multinationals who view India as a key target for expansion. Attempts to control levels of consumption by increased taxation tend to have a weak effect because illegal production and smuggling are rife. There is also opposition to the publication of 'safe' drinking advice, because it is felt that this may prove counterproductive by encouraging consumption in the currently abstinent majority.

Source: Benegal (2005)

Babor and Winstanley (2008) reviewed papers on the alcohol experiences of 18 countries commissioned for the journal *Addiction* from 2004 to 2007. One problem already mentioned is the high level of consumption prevalent in the former socialist countries. In Russia, during the Gorbachev era from 1985, public health initiatives led to a 25% reduction in consumption followed by dramatic increases in male life expectancy. These reforms were subsequently abandoned and consumption increased again with concomitant increases in health problems (Zaridze et al. (2014). A problem confronting many countries wishing to address alcohol problems is the powerful influence of international drinks companies. Babor and Winstanley (2008) noted that potentially expanding markets such as India, Nigeria, China and Brazil are being targeted with 'highly sophisticated western marketing techniques.' At the same time, the papers which they review mention specifically that the drinks industry is an obstacle to effective alcohol policy in India, Nigeria, the UK, Thailand, South Africa and Mexico. We examine approaches to prevention and treatment for alcohol problems later in this chapter.

THE DANGERS AND POSSIBLE HEALTH BENEFITS OF DRINKING ALCOHOL

In this section we consider evidence of the health risks associated with the consumption of alcohol as well as the possible health benefits. A brief summary of the major risk factors is given in Box 8.2.

BOX 8.2
RISKS INCURRED BY THE CONSUMPTION OF ALCOHOL

Risks that can be incurred on any single occasion of heavy drinking:

- Driving, industrial and household accidents: falls, fires, drowning.
- Domestic and other forms of violence as perpetrator.
- Domestic and other forms of violence as victim.
- Unwanted pregnancies; HIV or other sexually transmitted diseases following unprotected sexual exposure.

Risks incurred by regular heavy drinking:

- Death from liver cirrhosis and acute pancreatitis.
- Increased risk of cardiovascular disease and certain cancers.
- Problems caused by alcohol dependence.
- Exacerbation of pre-existing difficulties such as depression and family problems.
- Loss of employment; reduced career prospects.

Risks incurred by women who drink during pregnancy:

- Fetal alcohol syndrome.
- Miscarriages and premature babies.
- Cognitive and behavioural problems of the developing child.

An analysis of the research findings on the health hazards of drinking is considerably more complicated than is the case for smoking. Whereas smoking is dangerous even for low levels of consumption, and increasingly so for heavy smokers, the dangers to health of alcohol consumption are not always found for light and moderate drinkers, who may even experience health benefits compared with non-drinkers. We therefore examine the evidence for risk associated with heavy drinking, and go on to consider the possible benefits of light and moderate drinking.

To begin with, it is necessary to be a little more precise about what is meant by 'light', 'moderate' and 'heavy' drinking. We will adopt the British system of informal measurement in which one 'unit' is assumed to equal 8 g of alcohol or one glass of wine of average strength, half a pint (250 cc) of normal strength beer, and a single measure (25 ml) of spirits. It is important to bear in mind that strong wines and beers may contain up to twice this amount of alcohol. We will consider moderate drinking to be at the average level of 3/2 units a day for men/women respectively; less than half of that level will be regarded as light drinking and anything over 7/5 regular daily units will be regarded as heavy drinking.

Liver Cirrhosis and Acute Pancreatitis

Prolonged heavy drinking is known to be the main cause of **liver cirrhosis**, a serious condition that frequently results in death. Using figures provided by the British Department of Health, the Academy of Medical Sciences (2004) noted a four- to five-fold increase in deaths from chronic liver disease in the UK from 1970 to 2000, with over nine-fold increases among young men and women. Using more recent figures, the UK Office for National Statistics estimated that mortality from liver disease had doubled from 1991 to 2007 (Office for National Statistics, 2008). While some of these changes are attributable to increased rates of hepatitis C infection, effects that are themselves exacerbated by alcohol consumption, the main reason for the changes are increases in levels of heavy drinking. Although it receives much less publicity than liver cirrhosis, acute pancreatitis is another frequently fatal disease that is often caused by heavy drinking. Goldacre and Roberts (2004) surveyed hospital admissions for this disease in England from 1963 to 1998, noting that they have more than doubled over the 35-year period, with particularly large increases among the younger age groups. These changes closely parallel the patterns of increased alcohol consumption over this period of time.

Cancer

The evidence linking alcohol consumption to cancer has been reviewed in detail by Bagnardi et al. (2001). They considered the evidence for three levels of consumption, 14, 21 and 28 units a week, and found associations increasing at each level for cancers of the oral cavity and pharynx, larynx, breast, liver, colo-rectum and stomach. In a more recent study of 109,118 men and 254,870 women from eight European countries, Schütze et al. (2011) estimated that 10% of all cancer cases in men and 3% of cases in women are attributable to alcohol consumption. The most strongly associated are those of the upper aerodigestive tract (44% and 25% of male and female cases respectively), liver (33% and 18%) and colorectum (17% and 4%). The association with breast cancer is weaker, but of particular importance because this is one of the most common causes of premature death in women. Schütze et al. estimated that 5% of cases are attributable to alcohol. This corresponds closely to an earlier estimate by Hamajima et al. (2002), who conducted a detailed re-analysis of data from 53 studies with a total sample size of over 150,000. They found that there was a clear relationship with risk increasing steadily from teetotallers through to those drinking more than five units a day. They concluded that alcohol could be the cause of about 4% of deaths from breast cancer. A similar finding of a small increase in risk at low levels of consumption was reported by Chen et al. (2011) in a 28-year follow-up of 105,986 US nurses. However, the increase in risk was quite modest and, as Hamajima et al. (2002) pointed out, it needs to be interpreted in the context of the possible beneficial effects of moderate alcohol consumption, which is discussed later in this chapter.

A significant proportion of regular alcohol-using males are also smokers. Survey data indicate that approximately 7% of 15–54-year-olds in the USA are co-dependent on alcohol and tobacco (Anthony and Echeagaray-Wagner, 2013). Since 1957 it has been established that the joint exposure to high amounts of alcohol and tobacco on risk of oral cancers confers an excess risk of major proportions, with one estimate being an excess risk of 18.4:1 (Rothman and Keller, 1972). The effects of alcohol and tobacco on excess risk of cancer are not simply additive: they actually multiply. A recent meta-analysis showed that there is a positive synergistic (multiplicative) effect of alcohol and tobacco use for cancer of the oesophagus (Prabhu et al., 2014). The observed combined effect of alcohol and tobacco was almost double the effect that would be expected if synergy did not happen.

Drinking During Pregnancy

This has been the subject of much controversy in recent years. US medical authorities invariably recommend that pregnant women should avoid alcohol completely, while in many other countries the usual advice is that low levels of consumption do no harm. Very heavy drinking is the cause of **fetal alcohol syndrome**, in which the child suffers from a particular type of facial abnormality as well as mental impairment and stunted growth. It has also been established that heavy drinking is associated with miscarriages, premature births, low birth weight and a variety of cognitive and behavioural problems in the developing child. While it may seem tempting to infer from this that there must be some increase in risk even for light drinking, there is in fact surprisingly little evidence that this is the case.

In a report for the British Department of Health, Gray and Henderson (2006) reviewed research on the fetal effects of low-to-moderate alcohol consumption and binge drinking, concluding that, for most outcomes, there was no consistent evidence of adverse effects from low alcohol consumption, although there was some evidence of harmful effects on neurodevelopment of binge drinking. More recently, in a useful and challenging review of research findings on many dos and don'ts for pregnant women, Oster (2013) notes that there has been much research but few findings of harmful effects of low-to-moderate levels of alcohol consumption. In a large-scale Australian study Robinson et al. (2010) obtained data on weekly alcohol consumption at 18 and 34 weeks for 2900 women with follow-up testing for child behavioural problems when the children were aged 2, 5, 8, 10 and 14. They found no evidence of an increase in behavioural problems where mothers drank up to 10 units a week as compared with those who were abstinent. In a recent Danish study of 1,628 women and their children, Skogerbø et al. (2012) found that low-to-moderate alcohol consumption in early pregnancy had no statistically significant associations with assessments of cognitive functioning of the children at age 5. Similarly Kelly et al. (2013) carried out a seven-year follow-up of 10,534 children born in the

UK between 2000 and 2002 and found no evidence of unfavourable cognitive or behavioural effects on children whose mothers were light drinkers during pregnancy compared with abstainers. In fact the children of light drinkers performed slightly better on a number of measures.

In contrast to these studies, which may be regarded as good news for women wishing to drink lightly or moderately during pregnancy, two recent studies indicate that light drinking, especially in the first trimester, is associated with some negative birth outcomes. Andersen et al. (2012) investigated outcomes for 92,719 Danish women and reported that light drinkers, as compared with abstainers, showed an increased risk of miscarriage during weeks 13–16, but no increase later in the pregnancy. Nykjaer et al. (2014) investigated outcomes for 1,303 UK women and found that light drinkers in the first trimester were more likely than abstainers to have premature and low-birth-weight babies. Experts in the field have pointed out a number of methodological weaknesses in these studies, which make interpretation of the results difficult (Savitz, 2012; Science Media Centre, 2014). However, given the importance of the issue and the current state of uncertainty about the evidence, women would probably be best advised to adopt the cautious approach of abstinence, at least in the first trimester of their pregnancy.

Health Benefits of Drinking

The possible benefits of light-to-moderate drinking have been the subject of a great deal of research and considerable controversy over more than 50 years. The main focus of attention has been cardiovascular disease (CVD), where most studies have reported a U- or J-shaped function, with light and moderate drinkers having substantially lower risk than both abstainers and heavy drinkers. In a detailed review of publications from 1950 to 2009, Ronksley et al. (2011) found the evidence supporting the protective effect of light-to-moderate drinking to be compelling. Overall the relative risk for alcohol drinkers for CVD mortality was 25% lower than for non-drinkers, with the lowest risk for light drinkers with consumption levels between 7 and 14 units a week. In the case of mortality from strokes, there was relatively little indication of a protective effect for light drinkers and a very pronounced negative effect for heavy drinkers. In a review of papers published from 1980 to 2010, Roerecke and Rehm (2012) found that light drinking was associated with a reduced risk of ischaemic heart disease incidence and mortality but they were cautious in their interpretation of this finding, pointing out that there was considerable variation in the extent of the apparent protective effects reported in different studies.

In addition to an association with reduced risk of CVD there is also some evidence that light drinking is associated with a reduced risk of death from cancer when compared with abstainers. This is surprising in view of the evidence which we have already noted, that cases of some types of cancer are more frequent among light drinkers. However, in a meta-analysis combining data from 18 studies published up to April 2012, Jin et al. (2013) found that light drinkers (up to 11 units a week) had a 9% reduction in all-cancer mortality, while heavy drinkers (over 44 units a week) had a 31% increase when compared with non/occasional drinkers.

After considering the costs and benefits of alcohol consumption in relation to different diseases, the natural question to ask is, how is consumption related to all-cause mortality? In addition to their analysis for CVD, Ronksley et al. (2011) also examined this evidence. Of the 84 studies that provided data for CVD, 31 also provided data for all-cause mortality, indicating that there was a J-shaped relationship, with light drinkers having a 13% reduction in mortality compared with abstainers, and heavy drinkers a 30% increase.

The results of these and other studies are not entirely consistent with each other, especially for the purpose of establishing upper limits for safe drinking, but they are at least consistent with the statement that men and women in good health who drink moderately are not taking any significant risk with their physical health. The additional claim that light-to-moderate drinking is actually beneficial to health is more open to doubt. Although non-drinkers do have higher mortality rates than drinkers, this may be only because the category of non-drinkers includes a substantial number of individuals who have given up drinking because of poor health. This is a useful illustration of the statistician's dictum that 'correlation does not entail causation'. It could be that not drinking is a cause of poorer health but, equally well, it could be that poor health is a cause of not drinking. The latter view was first analysed in detail by Shaper et al. (1988), using data from 7,000 middle-aged men, confirming that those who suffered from health problems cut down or abstained from drinking. The argument was subsequently developed by a number of other critics, notably Fillmore and her associates (Fillmore et al., 2007). An alternative possibility is that a third, 'background' variable could be the cause of both good health and moderate drinking. An example of such a background variable might be having an optimistic style of personality. We discuss the links between personality and health in Chapter 16.

Recent reviews have gone some way towards meeting these criticisms, by dividing abstainers into ex-drinkers and lifelong abstainers, and still finding a protective effect for light drinkers. However, a range of further criticisms of this interpretation have been put forward by Fekjær (2013). He points out that light drinking has been shown by various studies to have an apparent protective effect not only against CVD but also against a wide range of diseases, many of which have no obvious physiological connection with alcohol consumption. Thus while plausible biological mechanisms have been proposed for protective effects against CVD (Brien et al., 2011), it is difficult to imagine that this could also be done for such diverse conditions as asthma, gallstones, osteoporosis, hearing loss and Alzheimer's disease. Since the peak protective effects always seem to occur at very similar levels of light drinking, there are grounds for suspecting that we are not dealing with a panacea so much as a flaw in research design. Fekjær argues that the latter is the case. He points out that most studies have been conducted in countries where light or moderate alcohol consumption is very much the prevailing norm, and statistically associated with high social status, while non-drinkers are on average of lower social status and education with less healthy diets and levels of exercise, and many other characteristics which are correlated with poor health. As discussed in Chapters 2 and 3 social inequalities are strongly associated with health.

Accidents and Psychosocial Problems

The importance of drink-driving as a cause of road traffic accidents, and the deaths of drivers, passengers and pedestrians, is universally acknowledged. The risk begins even at the lowest blood-alcohol levels and increases proportionately thereafter (Anderson and Baumberg, 2006). Legislation lowering the maximum permitted level of blood-alcohol, increasing the amount of police attention paid to drink driving, and the introduction of random breath testing are all measures which have been shown to reduce fatalities (Room et al., 2005).

The legalization of marihuana in many states of the USA has meant a higher incidence of combining recreational use of alcohol with cannabis. Since the 1970s it has been known that skilled performance is worse under the influence of alcohol and cannabis together than with either drug alone, with some evidence of synergistic effects (Casswell and Marks, 1973; Marks and MacAvoy, 1989). Brady and Li (2014) studied trends in alcohol and other drugs detected in drivers who were killed within one hour of a motor vehicle crash in six US states (California, Hawaii, Illinois, New Hampshire, Rhode Island and West Virginia) over the period 1999–2010. Of 23,591 drivers studied, it was reported that 39.7% tested positive for alcohol and 24.8% for other drugs. The prevalence of non-alcohol drugs rose from 16.6% in 1999 to 28.3% in 2010, whereas the prevalence of positive results for alcohol remained stable.

Alcohol consumption has also been shown to be a factor in many other kinds of injuries, including deaths from falls, fires, industrial accidents and drowning. In a 16-year follow-up study of Finnish men, Paljärvi et al. (2005) found that heavy drinking was associated with an increased frequency of fatal injury, the risk being highest among those who reported the highest annual number of heavy drinking occasions. In a study of 11,536 patients with non-fatal injuries attending 28 emergency departments in 16 countries, Borges et al. (2006) found the relative risk to be considerably greater among those who had been drinking within six hours of injury.

Anderson and Baumberg (2006) reviewed an extensive range of studies from many countries demonstrating an association between heavy drinking and a variety of personal and social problems, including violent assaults and homicide, marital violence and marital breakdown, child abuse, impaired work performance, depression and suicide. To what extent is alcohol to blame? This raises all of the usual chicken-and-egg problems of interpreting statistical correlations. For example, does drinking incite people to commit crimes or do criminals drink to reduce their fear before carrying out the crimes which they have already decided to commit? Do people take to drink in an effort to ameliorate their psychological problems, or are these problems caused by heavy drinking? These issues of correlation and causation are difficult to resolve, but are neatly circumvented by the following excellent and fully valid health education slogan: 'If you drink because you have a problem, then you will end up with two problems.'

THE EFFECTS OF ALCOHOL AND CAUSES OF ALCOHOL DEPENDENCE

To understand the motivation for drinking and problems of dependence it is best to begin by considering the psychological effects of alcohol. These effects are much influenced by culture and by people's expectations about potential benefits, including enjoyment, stress reduction and increased sociability (Anderson and Baumberg, 2006). This explains why it is consumed in social gatherings such as parties and weddings, when people wish to interact in a much more relaxed and informal way than they might otherwise, and also why heavy drinking is common among people with psychological problems. Alcohol dependence is widespread among people suffering from anxiety disorders, and the use of alcohol to induce sleep is also known to aggravate sleep disorders, because it leads to increased wakefulness and arousal a few hours later (Anderson and Baumberg, 2006).

Let us now look more closely at the question of why some people develop drinking problems while others do not. Here a number of contrasting theoretical perspectives need to be considered. They are not mutually exclusive in the sense that this can sometimes be said of theories in the natural sciences. The discerning reader will notice various ways in which elements of each can be consistent with elements of the others. They are best thought of as reference points that are useful aids to thinking about the issues. A brief summary of the main theoretical views is given in Table 8.1.

Genetic Theories

Genetic theories propose that some people have an inherited predisposition to develop drinking problems. Those who are convinced of the overwhelming importance of heredity believe that certain people are 'born alcoholics', destined to succumb to alcoholism almost as soon as they take their first drink. Perhaps surprisingly, this 'biological determinist' view is also attractive to manufacturers of alcoholic drinks. They can argue that the born alcoholic is bound to have a drink and become alcoholic sooner or later, however much the availability of drink is restricted. The rest of us can drink as we wish without running the risk of becoming alcoholic.

While it is certainly true that alcohol problems tend to run in families, this is not in itself enough to prove the existence of genetic influences. Drinking habits can be passed on from parents to children as the result of upbringing and imitation just as much as they may be passed on through genes. The most widely cited evidence for genetic influences comes from twin and adoption studies. Twin studies are based on comparisons of the concordance rates for drinking patterns in *monozygotic* (MZ, identical)

Table 8.1 Theories of problem drinking

Type of theory	Causes of problem drinking
Genetic theories	DNA variations possibly associated with the metabolism of alcohol mean that certain individuals are much more likely than most to develop alcohol problems if they drink
Addiction, disease and dependence theories	Individuals who drink heavily may develop a physiological addiction and psychological dependence which can only be effectively treated by lifelong abstinence
Learning theories	Mechanisms of conditioning and social learning can explain the development of excessive consumption and the phenomena of dependence, craving, increased tolerance and withdrawal symptoms

and *dizygotic* (DZ, fraternal) *twins*. The theory behind this is that both types of twin grow up in the same family environment, so that a greater concordance for the 100% genetically similar MZ twins than for the 50% similar DZ twins is evidence of genetic effects. Adoption studies examine whether adopted children grow up to acquire similar drinking habits to their biological parents, or whether they are more influenced by their adopting parents.

Twin and adoption studies have been used to estimate 'heritability', a statistical assessment of the relative importance of hereditary and environmental influences which can take values from 100% for fully inherited characteristics to 0% for those which are purely environmentally determined. In practice heritability estimates for drinking patterns have varied greatly from study to study, partly as the result of methodological problems which are difficult to overcome, and partly because the estimates vary as a function of what is measured. The highest estimates have sometimes been found for 'chronic alcoholism' and sometimes for 'teetotalism'; some have found greater heritability for males than females, and some the exact opposite (see for example Heather and Robertson, 1997). Insofar as generalizations have been made about the heritability of alcohol problems, figures of 50–60% have sometimes been suggested (Anderson and Baumberg, 2006); however, Walters (2002) carried out a meta-analysis of 50 studies and concluded that heritability was quite low, unlikely to be higher than 30–36%.

Given the increasing popularity of DNA-based research, it is not surprising that there have been a number of attempts to demonstrate specific genetic loci for alcohol problems, but these have only met with modest success (Cook and Gurling, 2001; Anderson and Baumberg, 2006). As with other forms of human behaviour, there are likely to be a multitude of complex genetic routes that may make some individuals more likely than others to become problem drinkers (Palmer et al., 2012). For example, there may be inheritable differences in the way that alcohol is metabolized, so that some people find its effects pleasant, others unpleasant, some find it takes more alcohol, others less, to achieve the same effect. There may be differences in genetic predisposition to experience anxiety, so that some are predisposed to drink more than others on discovering that it temporarily suppresses anxiety.

On the basis of existing research evidence, there is certainly no reason to suppose that some people are 'born alcoholics'. Although there is enough evidence to show that there is some degree of genetic predisposition towards different patterns of drinking, it seems unlikely that this is as important an influence as environmental factors. To appreciate what this means, take as an analogy the fact that some people may have an inherited proneness to develop heart disease, but whether or not they will do so still depends on whether they smoke, eat fatty foods, avoid exercise and so on. The risks are just greater for some people than for others. Similarly, there could be many environmental reasons why drinking problems develop in those who have an inherited predisposition and also in those who do not.

Addiction, Disease and Dependence Theories

The history of these theories has been examined in a broad social and historical context by Thom (2001). **Addiction theories** can be traced back to the classic works of Benjamin Rush of Philadelphia and Thomas Trotter of Edinburgh, published respectively in 1785 and 1804. Rush and Trotter replaced the traditional view of habitual drunkards as moral degenerates by one in which they are victims of an addiction. Once the addiction is established, the victims lose all voluntary control over their drinking. They have become incapable of resisting their craving for the 'demon drink'. Rush and Trotter succeeded in popularizing their belief that alcohol is a highly addictive substance 70 years before the case was made for opium.

Later **disease theories** focused increasingly on the at-risk individual who has a predisposition to become alcoholic once he or she starts drinking. Although a predisposition to become alcoholic does not have to be hereditary (we have already mentioned that it may be the result of upbringing), nevertheless the concept of the born alcoholic proved attractive to disease theorists. In common with earlier addiction theories, disease theories emphasized craving and loss of control. The difference was that, for the later disease theorists, alcohol is only highly addictive for a small number of people. The rest of us can drink with impunity. This change of emphasis proved attractive, especially to a North American society that had abandoned prohibition, embraced personal liberty and responsibility and has a powerful drinks industry.

BOX 8.3
SYMPTOMS OF ALCOHOL DEPENDENCE SYNDROME

According to Griffith Edwards, this includes some or all of the following symptoms:

- tolerance (a diminished effect of alcohol, usually accompanied by increased consumption);
- withdrawal symptoms following reduced consumption;
- consumption of larger amounts or for a longer time period than was intended;
- persistent desire or unsuccessful efforts to cut down or control drinking;
- excessive time spent obtaining, consuming or recovering from the effects of alcohol;
- reduction of important activities due to drinking; and
- continued drinking despite knowing that it is causing or exacerbating a physical or psychological problem.

Source: Sayette (2007)

From the mid-1970s, the disease theory was being revised and extended, notably by Griffith Edwards and Milton Gross, to become the **alcohol dependence syndrome**. In this new conceptualization, the sharp distinction which had previously been made between physical addiction and psychological dependence was abolished and the syndrome was viewed instead as a psycho-physiological disorder. The descriptions given by Edwards and Gross are not always very clear and tend to change from one publication to another. Box 8.3 lists the main aspects of Edwards' more recent accounts as summarized by Sayette (2007).

The concept of the alcohol dependence syndrome has been much criticized, originally by Shaw (1979) who pointed out that much woolly thinking lies behind it. Most people, on reading the list of symptoms in Box 8.3, would conclude that anyone who drinks regularly would exhibit one or more of them to some degree. As a list, it seems consistent with the idea that, rather than being a disease, alcohol dependence is an arbitrary point that can be chosen on a continuum from the light social drinker to the homeless street drinker. Yet proponents of the syndrome insist that it is a clinical entity, admittedly with somewhat varying symptoms, which only applies to a relatively small number out of all the people who drink heavily.

One should not, of course, 'throw out the baby with the bath water'. No theory of alcohol use can afford to neglect the phenomena of physical dependence associated with prolonged heavy drinking and most clearly manifested in the spectacular withdrawal symptoms that can occur following sudden abstinence. These include some of the most unpleasant to be found among all types of drug withdrawal, including tremors ('the shakes'), sweating, nausea, vomiting, hallucinations ('pink elephants') and convulsions. Indeed, Lerner and Fallon (1985) noted that, in a significant number of cases, sudden withdrawal can actually prove fatal. The phenomenon of psychological dependence also need to be addressed by any theory of alcohol use. While alcohol dependence syndrome may be poorly defined as a clinical entity, the psychological problems that are often associated with heavy drinking certainly need to be explained.

Learning Theories

Learning theorists consider drinking problems to develop as a result of the same learning mechanisms that are at work in establishing patterns of 'normal drinking'. They argue that the reasons why some people become problem drinkers and others do not lie in their particular personal histories of learning to drink, their present social environment insofar as it provides opportunities and encouragement to drink, and in physiological variables that may make the effects of alcohol more pleasurable or positively reinforcing for some people than others.

Operant conditioning is the type of learning that occurs when animals are trained to respond in a particular way to a stimulus by providing rewards after they make the appropriate response. In the classic experiment, hungry rats were confined in small boxes and trained to press a bar in order to obtain food pellets. This phenomenon, which was of course well known to animal trainers, pet owners and the parents of small children long before it was 'discovered' by psychologists, has some applicability to the understanding of problem drinking. Of particular importance is the **gradient of reinforcement**, the fact that reinforcement which occurs rapidly after the response is much more effective in producing learning than delayed reinforcement. In the case of drinking alcohol, a small amount of positive reinforcement, such as reduced anxiety, that occurs fairly soon after drinking, may cause a strong habit to develop in spite of the counterbalancing effect of a large amount of punishment (hangover, divorce, loss of employment) that occurs much later.

Drinking, eating, smoking, drug and sexual addictions all have the 'irrational' characteristic that the total amount of pleasure gained from the addiction seems much less than the suffering caused by it. According to learning theorists, the reason for this lies in the nature of the gradient of reinforcement. Addictive behaviours are typically those in which pleasurable effects occur rapidly while unpleasant consequences occur after a delay. The simple mechanism of operant conditioning and the gradient of reinforcement functions, as it were, to overpower the mind's capacity for rational calculation. Bigelow (2001) discussed the applicability of operant conditioning principles to the understanding and treatment of alcohol problems. He concludes that they have considerable relevance but notes that there has been little interest in them in the alcohol field in recent years, in contrast to the field of illegal substance use where they continue to play quite a dominant role.

Classical conditioning refers to the process whereby a response that occurs as a natural reflex to a particular stimulus can be conditioned to occur to a new stimulus. In Pavlov's early experiments a bell was rung shortly before food was placed in a dog's mouth, thereby eliciting salivation as a physiological reflex. After a number of pairings of bell and food Pavlov found that the dog salivated when the bell was rung unaccompanied by food.

A number of interesting models have been developed by applying classical conditioning principles to addictions, and Drummond et al. (1995) provided a useful survey of this now highly technical subject. One application to explain the phenomena of drug dependence, tolerance and withdrawal is the **compensatory conditioned response model**. Initially, when a drug is taken, a physiological 'homeostatic' mechanism comes into operation to counteract its effects. In the case of alcohol, which has a depressing effect, the homeostatic mechanism activates the nervous system in order to maintain the normal level of activation. In the regular drinker this gradually produces tolerance so that increasingly large quantities of alcohol are required to produce the same effect. Furthermore, the homeostatic response of nervous activation may become conditioned to stimuli normally associated with drinking, such as situations where drinking has frequently taken place in the past. If conditioned drinkers avoid alcohol in these situations, the conditioned response of nervous activation will not be balanced by the effects of alcohol and the resultant unpleasant state of excessive activation is what is known as a withdrawal state. In this way classical conditioning can account for the close connection observed between the phenomena of tolerance and withdrawal.

The compensatory conditioned response model has considerable intuitive plausibility but there is a lack of convincing evidence for its applicability to problem drinking. Drobes et al. (2001) discussed this model and a range of alternative classical conditioning models with specific reference to alcohol dependence and they conclude that, in all cases, there is a lack of empirical evidence to support the approach.

Social learning theorists argue that classical and operant conditioning provide incomplete explanations of human learning, which also frequently depends on observation and imitation. Bandura (1977) has been particularly influential in emphasizing the importance of learning by imitation and linking it to his concept of **self-efficacy**, a personality trait consisting of having confidence in one's ability to carry out one's plans successfully. People with low self-efficacy are much more likely to imitate undesirable behaviour than those with high self-efficacy. Collins and Bradizza (2001) reviewed applications of social learning theory to drinking, noting that the evidence points to parents having the strongest influence on the initiation of adolescent alcohol use while peers are most influential in determining subsequent frequency of use.

Freud's concept of 'secondary gain' can also be usefully applied to alcohol problems as an extension of the learning theory perspective. Just as hypochondriacs are often seen to be using their condition to avoid work and to get people at their beck and call, so can it be seen that sufferers from many kinds of neurosis often exploit their condition in order to gain attention, avoid things that they do not wish to do and generally manipulate people around them. It is easy to see how patterns of drinking can function in this way, and not only in the regular heavy drinker: 'It's your fault for getting me drunk' or 'I only did it because I was drunk' can provide a convenient way of evading responsibility for the person who commits a sexual indiscretion or beats their partner. Here alcohol has the double function of releasing the inhibitions that might otherwise prevent the impulse from being acted on, while simultaneously being held to blame as if it were the drink that performed the action rather than the drinker. In the case of the alcoholic, it is possible to see here some dangers in adopting the medical or disease model. If alcoholics think of themselves as victims of a disease over which they have no control, not only will they avoid taking responsibility for actions carried out while under the influence of drink, but also they will avoid taking responsibility for drinking, which may make it difficult or impossible to help them.

BOX 8.4
THE CONTROLLED DRINKING CONTROVERSY

Can individuals with severe drinking problems ever resume moderate levels of drinking, or is total abstinence their only realistic goal? Because they regard heavy drinking as essentially a habit rather than a disease, learning theorists have taken the view that a return to moderate drinking can, at least in some cases, be a viable objective. Disease theorists, on the other hand, believe that lifelong abstinence is the only realistic goal for the alcoholic. This issue has been highly controversial over the last 50 years (see, for example, Heather and Robertson, 1997).

In a significant contribution to the debate Miller et al. (2001) analysed data from seven large studies looking at how people fare during the year after treatment for alcoholism. Their findings were:

- one in four clients were abstinent;
- one in ten used alcohol moderately without problems;
- the remaining two-thirds made significant improvements reducing their overall alcohol consumption by 87% on average.

They conclude that 'This substantial level of improvement in "unremitted" clients tends to be overlooked when outcomes are dichotomized as successful or relapsed.'

PREVENTION AND TREATMENT OF ALCOHOL PROBLEMS

Prevention

Approaches to the prevention of alcohol problems have been the subject of intense controversy in recent years. On the one hand, specialists in this field are generally in favour of measures to reduce overall levels of consumption by increasing prices and imposing restrictions on advertising, promotions and general availability; on the other hand, the drinks industry campaigns against all these approaches and in favour of educational initiatives and self-regulation. The main issues are summarized in Box 8.5. Here we briefly review the evidence in support of the 'population-based approach', and also consider the position of the drinks industry and its influence on government policies.

BOX 8.5
POPULATION-BASED PREVENTION: EXPERT OPINION VERSUS THE DRINKS INDUSTRY

- Specialists on the prevention of alcohol problems are almost unanimous in their support for the population-based approach, which incorporates the principle that the most effective policies for reducing alcohol problems are those which reduce overall levels of consumption. These policies include higher levels of taxation on alcoholic drinks, restrictions on advertising and sponsorship, limiting opening hours for bars and imposing tight controls on which shops can sell alcohol and the hours during which they can do so.
- The population-based approach is opposed by the drinks industry because reduced overall consumption means smaller profits. They propose that 'sensible drinking' can be encouraged by self-regulation of the drinks industry and educational initiatives. They argue that the population-based approach penalizes the majority of sensible drinkers in order to discourage the minority of irresponsible drinkers.
- Critics of the drinks industry suggest that the drinks industry claims are disingenuous because it has been clearly shown that educational initiatives are ineffective at curbing heavy drinking, and also because the drinks industry makes most of its profit from the minority of drinkers who consume well above recommended limits.
- In many countries the drinks industry has been much more successful than the alcohol experts at influencing government policies. This may be because governments do not wish to risk unpopularity by adopting population-based policies.

Sources: Babor et al. (2003); Academy of Medical Sciences (2004); Anderson and Baumberg (2006); WHO (2007)

The detailed reviews of the evidence cited at the foot of Box 8.5 were variously commissioned by the World Health Organization, the European Commission and the British Academy of Medical Sciences and published between 2003 and 2007. These reports concur in finding much evidence that overall levels of consumption in populations are closely associated with the extent of alcohol problems. Rossow and Norström (2013) provide a recent and thoughtful analysis of the evidence together with other related epidemiological issues in alcohol studies. Earlier in this chapter we indicated some evidence coming from the dramatic impact of changes which occurred in Russia during the Gorbachev era. We also noted the huge increase in deaths from chronic liver disease in the UK tracking increases in levels of alcohol consumption in the period from 1970 to 2007. More generally, comparisons of different countries and of changes occurring within countries over lengthy periods of time all arrive at the same result. The World Health Organization (WHO) (2007) noted that half of the world's consumption of alcohol is by the 10% heaviest drinkers and that 75% of the variation across different regions in the extent of alcohol dependence can be predicted from overall levels of consumption. Much as this must disappoint the drinks industry, there are no examples of countries which have managed to maintain population levels of consumption while at the same time reducing alcohol problems.

Probably the most effective measure for reducing population levels of consumption is increased taxation. This is a policy which requires careful analysis and attention to the specific conditions of individual countries, particularly poor countries where large increases in taxation may lead to increases in the production of illicit and potentially lethal distilled liquor. But in relatively wealthy countries, increases in taxation generally lead to proportionate decreases in consumption. The WHO (2007) noted that young people's drinking is particularly sensitive to increases in price, which can therefore reduce underage drinking as well as the extent of binge drinking among teenagers. Furthermore, and contrary to widespread belief, price increases have also been shown to have an impact on the amount consumed among older frequent and heavy drinkers.

Anderson and Baumberg (2006) examined the impact of restrictions on the sale of alcohol including increases in the minimum legal age for purchase and measures to restrict number of outlets and days and hours where sale is permitted. These measures have all been shown to reduce the extent of alcohol problems in a number of countries.

Each of the reports referred to in Box 8.5 note that the global drinks industry is deploying sophisticated modern marketing techniques aimed at young people including lifestyle advertising, promotions involving sporting teams and events, rock concerts and festivals, fashion shows and carnivals, as well as the development of new products specifically aimed at young people, such as 'alcopops' and 'pre-mix cocktails'. Agostinelli and Grube (2002) reviewed advertising on alcohol counters, including warnings on alcoholic products, with a number of interesting proposals. Unfortunately research to date has been mainly concerned with participants' assessments of the impact of this type of advertising rather than its effectiveness in reducing misuse. It can also be argued that such efforts are a drop in the ocean in comparison with the amount of money that the drinks industry spends on product promotion. An alternative approach, deeply unpopular with the drinks industry, is the introduction of bans on advertising and sponsorship. Although earlier research had indicated that bans have little or no effect on overall consumption, Saffer and Dave (2002) argued that this research is flawed. They use an economic model to analyse pooled data from 20 countries over 26 years and conclude that advertising and sponsorship bans can reduce overall consumption by 5% to 8%. They note that increases in levels of consumption often stimulate the introduction of bans, but that reductions in consumption often lead to the rescinding of bans, as has happened in recent years in Canada, Denmark, New Zealand and Finland.

One area of legislation to control the dangers of alcohol use, which more and more countries are adopting, is strictly enforced drink-driving laws with severe penalties for offenders. It is now almost universally agreed that this has played an important role in reducing traffic fatalities. It even commands the support of the drinks industry, which, in view of the high level of public support for the laws, would be foolish to oppose it.

The other main preventive measures that have been much analysed are health education initiatives with the aim of preventing alcohol misuse. Unfortunately, the evidence here indicates that they are not very effective. Health education generally appears to improve knowledge about the effects of alcohol and attitudes to it, but has no effect on the amounts actually consumed. Midford and McBride (2001) reviewed alcohol education programmes in schools, noting that, in the USA, efforts have been hampered by excessive emphasis on abstinence, while in Europe and Australasia the emphasis has been on 'sensible drinking'. Although they detect a few promising signs in recent developments, the general finding is that these programmes have either failed to achieve any effects or, at best, have produced very small effects. Foxcroft et al. (2003) reviewed reports of 56 interventions aimed at young people aged 25 or under with substantially similar conclusions.

The ineffectiveness of educational campaigns designed to encourage sensible drinking perhaps explains why the drinks industry is happy to support them and even participate in them. Although this may seem an unnecessarily cynical view, there are some reasons for taking it seriously. Heather and Robertson (1997) pointed out that the drinks industry derives a good part of its profits from very heavy drinkers. In a 1978 survey of Scottish drinking habits, it was estimated that 3% of the population were responsible for 30% of total alcohol consumption. The loss of this source of profits would be crippling to the drinks industry. Hence the continued profitability of the industry requires the existence of a substantial percentage of very heavy drinkers. This provides another salient example of a conflict of interest between good public health and profits in industry.

In considering international perspectives at the beginning of this chapter we noted that the drinks industry is often mentioned as an obstacle to effective alcohol policy. A good example is provided by the UK in recent years. Heather and Robertson (1997) described attempts by the Portman Group, an organization funded by the British drinks industry, to influence academic debate on alcohol policy by financial offers to academics to encourage them to mount critiques of research supporting the population-based approach. The Institute of Alcohol Studies (2003) commented on the influence of the Portman Group on a decision of the British government to extend permitted drinking hours in England and Wales. The Portman Group was also a key influence on the British government's 2004 alcohol harm reduction strategy (Plant, 2004). This document is replete with positive references to the drinks industry and the Portman Group, emphasizing the value of educational programmes and other drinks industry initiatives, while rejecting any increases in taxation or legislation to control advertising and availability. In 2009, the Chief Medical Officer, Sir Liam Donaldson, proposed in his annual report that the government should introduce a minimum price policy for alcohol, stating that 'Implementing this minimum price-per-unit policy would save an estimated £1 billion every year, impact high-risk drinkers more than others and eliminate cheap supermarket drink that young people binge on' (HMSO, 2009). The Prime Minister, Gordon Brown, promptly rejected this proposal, saying it is important to protect the interests of 'the sensible majority of moderate drinkers', a comment that accords perfectly with the views of the British drinks industry. In 2006 the Portman Group set up a sister organization, Drinkaware, apparently with some government support, and whose activities, like those of its parent organization, seem designed to 'divert attention away from population-level strategies that limit the availability, price and promotion of alcohol, and thus threaten corporate profits, towards those focused on individual responsibility' (McCambridge et al., 2014). The authors also note that these organizations are continuing to enjoy success in countering the one government policy which is most feared by the drinks industry, the introduction of minimum unit pricing. Although rejected by Gordon Brown, this policy was again considered favourably, but then rejected by the present government led by David Cameron.

Paralleling the activities of the Portman Group in the UK, Jernigan (2012) analysed the activities of the International Center for Alcohol Policies (ICAP), funded by the international drinks industry and established in the USA in 1995. Jernigan argued that much of the material published by ICAP appears to be a direct attempt to counter the publications being put out concurrently by the World Health Organization (WHO). While superficially mirroring the WHO publications, those of ICAP were heavily dependent on research involving collaborations with the drinks industry and highly selective literature reviews which typically arrive at conclusions either supporting the position of the drinks industry or at least emphasizing high levels of disagreement among researchers. The ICAP publications frequently recommend alcohol policies known to be ineffective. The WHO went to some lengths to distance itself from ICAP and similar organizations as is evident from the following extracts from a 2013 letter from its director to the *British Medical Journal*:

> The development of alcohol policies is the sole prerogative of national authorities. In the view of WHO, the alcohol industry has no role in the formulation of alcohol policies, which must be protected from distortion by commercial or vested interests.
>
> WHO is grateful to the many researchers and civil society organizations that keep careful watch over the behaviour of the alcohol industry. This behaviour includes direct industry drafting of national alcohol policies, or drafting through the International Center for Alcohol Policies and other entities or 'public health consultants', which it funds. As documented in recent reports, some of the most effective policy options to reduce the harmful use of alcohol, as defined by WHO, are conspicuously absent in these policies.
>
> (Chan, 2013)

Treatment

A brief synopsis of alternative approaches to treatment is given in Table 8.2.

One of the most striking features of the treatment of alcohol problems is the contrasting approaches taken in different countries. In the USA and Canada, treatment is usually aimed at total abstinence, while in Britain most agencies regard a return to moderate drinking as a legitimate treatment goal

Table 8.2 Alternative approaches to the treatment of problem drinking

Type of treatment	Approach to treatment
In-patient treatment	'Drying out centres' and private clinics which focus on the alleviation of withdrawal symptoms followed by counselling and therapy to maintain abstinence following discharge
Alcoholics Anonymous	Self-help groups run by ex-alcoholics using the '12-step facilitation programme' to maintain lifelong abstinence. May receive individuals on discharge from in-patient treatments
Counselling and psychotherapy	Encompasses many approaches deriving from different psychotherapeutic models with the shared aim of helping clients to achieve insight into the causes and effects of problem drinking, seen as an essential basis for change
Cognitive behavioural therapies	Often based on learning theories and sometimes aiming to reduce levels of drinking rather than promoting abstinence as the treatment objective. Popular current approaches include motivational interviewing and mindfulness-based relapse prevention
Brief interventions	Advice on reducing consumption given by general practitioners and other health professionals, including 'opportunistic interventions' given to individuals who have attended for other reasons, such as for screening programmes

for some clients, mainly those with lower levels of dependence. North American programmes are often based on specialist treatment centres with a strong medical orientation. In Finland, on the other hand, alcohol problems are regarded as essentially social problems and dealt with primarily by social workers. These differences have been shaped by social forces and, until recently, have rarely involved any serious critical analysis of the evidence for the efficacy of the approaches.

Miller and Wilbourne (2002) provided an extensive review of the amount and quality of the evidence concerning the efficacy of different treatment programmes. They examined studies of 48 different types of treatment, rating each study for its methodological adequacy and then placing the treatments in rank order. The rather surprising result is that brief interventions, often consisting of advice given by general practitioners and at hospital emergency departments, are particularly well supported by the evidence. This finding, which was based on a large number of studies (see the Key Study below for an important example), was confirmed in a further review by Whitlock et al. (2004) who also noted that reductions in amount consumed, and in the proportion of participants who reduced their drinking to moderate or safe levels, were maintained up to four years after the interventions. Bertholet et al. (2005) reviewed **opportunistic interventions**, brief treatments given at primary care facilities to individuals attending for reasons other than alcohol-related problems. After examining 19 trials that included 5,639 individuals, they conclude that these interventions were effective in reducing alcohol consumption measured at 6 and 12 months after the interventions.

BOX 8.6
KEY STUDY: BRIEF TREATMENTS – PROJECT MATCH

In a large five-year study in the USA, known as Project MATCH, 1,726 people with drinking problems were divided into three groups receiving respectively: (a) a treatment based on the '12-step facilitation programme' of Alcoholics Anonymous; (b) coping skills therapy based on social learning theory; (c) motivation enhancement therapy, based on the techniques of motivational interviewing (described below). Motivation enhancement therapy proved just as effective as the other two, although it consisted of only four as against 12 sessions over a 12-week period. This finding applied equally across clients with problems of relatively high and low degrees of severity.

Developed by Miller and his associates over the last 30 years (see Miller and Rollnick, 2013), the motivational interviewing (MI) approach is in direct contrast to the confrontational tactics traditionally adopted by therapists treating addictions, in which every effort is made to overcome the client's supposed resistance to acknowledging that he or she has a problem, to challenge aggressively any dishonesty and to break down his or her defences. Instead the motivational therapist tries to create a warm empathic relationship with the client and uses a gentle and indirect approach in order to elicit, rather than impose, an increase in motivation to change behaviour, improve self-esteem and develop the feeling of self-efficacy for putting changes into practice.

The successful use of MI in Project MATCH is consistent with the findings of meta-analyses indicating its effectiveness (e.g. Lundahl and Burke, 2009).

Source: Project MATCH Research Group (1997)

Because brief interventions are effective as well as being much less expensive than other forms of treatment, they are becoming increasingly popular. The main problem that has been identified by researchers is the difficulty that has been experienced in persuading general practitioners to undertake them. After discussing this issue, Roche and Freeman (2004) proposed as a solution that practice nurses could take over the function of general practitioners. However, it remains to be seen whether this is equally effective. For example, it could be that the high status of general practitioners and doctors in hospital clinics is a key reason for the effectiveness of brief interventions.

Of the other types of treatment reviewed by Miller and Wilbourne, there is a considerable quantity of evidence for the effectiveness of **motivational interviewing** (see Project MATCH Key Study above). None of the remaining 46 types of treatment considered by Miller and Wilbourne receive much support from outcome studies, although **cognitive behavioural therapies (CBT)** appear to be more effective than psychotherapeutic approaches. Furthermore, and in spite of its enduring popularity, there are few good quality studies which provide support for the approach of Alcoholics Anonymous and their abstinence-based '12-step facilitation programme'. However, to be fair to Alcoholics Anonymous, it should be emphasized that their perfectly reasonable insistence on anonymity and the associated difficulty of forming properly randomized control groups make it difficult to evaluate.

Since Miller and Wilbourne published their review in 2002, there has been some interest in applying the methods of **mindfulness-based relapse prevention (MBRP)** to problem drinking as well as other substance use disorders, with encouraging early findings. Mindfulness-based therapies are considered in more detail in Chapter 12 (pp. 314–15). Their application to relapse prevention was first proposed by Witkiewitz et al. (2005), and Bowen et al. (2014) have reported a full trial in which 286 participants, having successfully completed an initial treatment for alcohol and substance use disorders, were randomly assigned to one of three groups: traditional 12-step facilitation, cognitive behavioural relapse prevention (CBRP) and MBRP. At six-month follow-up the CBRP and MBRP groups both had lower relapse rates than the 12-step group, and after 12 months MBRP was outperforming both of the other groups. Following this finding and the general high level of current interest in mindfulness-based approaches, it can be expected that further studies along these lines will be undertaken.

FUTURE RESEARCH

1. Clarification of the health risks and possible benefits of light-to-moderate drinking, including heart disease and risks to the unborn child.
2. Studies to examine the role of learning processes, including classical and operant conditioning and social learning in the development of alcohol dependence and problem drinking.
3. Studies to assess the relative merits of abstinence versus controlled drinking as an objective for people with drinking problems. What types of client are best advised to aim respectively for abstinence and for moderation?
4. Investigations to establish what the physiological and psychological mechanisms are of dependence, tolerance and withdrawal symptoms.
5. Research into barriers to the adoption of policies which are known to be effective in reducing levels of alcohol problems, including taxation, restrictions on availability, and advertising, and reasons for the persistence of policies known to be ineffective, including educational initiatives. Such research should be designed to take account of socio-economic and other cultural differences applicable in different countries and social groups.
6. Evaluation of the relative effectiveness of different approaches to the treatment of problem drinking, including brief and opportunistic interventions, motivational interviewing, mindfulness-based relapse prevention, and self-help organizations.

SUMMARY

1. Most cultures both past and present have an ambivalent view of the use of alcohol, its benefits and undesirable effects. This ambivalence is often associated with the view that alcohol is harmless, possibly beneficial, in moderation, but harmful in excess.
2. There is a sharp conflict between addiction and disease models of alcoholism, particularly prevalent in North America, where lifelong abstinence is considered to be the only cure for the alcoholic, and psychological models, more common in Europe, where drinking in moderation is sometimes considered to be a viable objective.
3. Drinking has been shown to cause liver cirrhosis, pancreatitis, strokes, various cancers and, in the case of drinking during pregnancy, damage to the unborn child. Most of these physical health risks are confined to the heavy drinker.
4. There is some evidence that light alcohol consumption may be protective against heart disease. The greatest physical risk taken by the moderate drinker and by the occasional binge drinker is the risk of accidental injury or death, especially, but not exclusively, traffic accidents.
5. Heavy drinking has been shown to be associated with a substantial proportion of violent assaults and homicide, marital violence, marital breakdown and child abuse. It is not clear to what extent drinking problems cause psychological disorders or are a consequence of pre-existing disorders. However, whichever is the case, drinking has the effect of exacerbating these disorders and making them more difficult to treat
6. It has proved difficult to assess the relative contribution of hereditary and environmental factors to the development of different patterns of drinking; on balance, the evidence suggests that both factors make a substantial contribution but that environmental factors play the larger role.
7. The nature of physical and psychological dependence on alcohol is not well understood; at present, conditioning and learning models represent the most promising approach.
8. The most effective methods for preventing alcohol problems are measures that have the effect of reducing overall levels of consumption, including high taxation, advertising bans and restricted availability. However, in many countries the drinks industry acts as a powerful lobby against these measures and few politicians would risk unpopularity by introducing them.
9. Educational programmes have had little effect in reducing alcohol problems.
10. Brief interventions from general practitioners, including 'opportunistic interventions' given to individuals attending for other reasons, have been shown to be particularly effective in producing substantial reductions in levels of consumption.
11. For individuals seeking treatment for alcohol problems, motivational interviewing and mindfulness-based relapse prevention have both been shown to be effective. These approaches contrast sharply with traditional confrontational approaches.

9 TOBACCO AND SMOKING

This vice brings in one hundred million francs in taxes every year. I will certainly forbid it at once – as soon as you can name a virtue that brings in as much revenue.

(Napoleon III, 1808–1873)

OUTLINE

With the accumulation of evidence on the negative aspects of smoking, Western governments have promoted measures to reduce smoking prevalence. These measures have met with substantial success, in spite of attempts by the tobacco industry to deliberately misinform the public. Smoking prevalence is increasing throughout the developing world and many people continue to smoke in the industrialized world. This chapter documents the extent of smoking, its major health impacts, and factors that help to explain its continued popularity. Smoking is a complex practice involving a mixture of biopsychosocial processes. Three main theories, the biological, psychological and social, are outlined. The primary methods to assist smokers to quit are reviewed, together with the results of evaluation studies. Methodological issues with placebos and vested interests of industry suggest caution in interpreting studies funded by the pharmaceutical industry.

BRIEF HISTORY OF TOBACCO AND SMOKING

Among recreational drugs, tobacco is by far the biggest killer and the nicotine it contains is the most addictive substance known. Yet it has been in use for millennia and, in spite of the certain knowledge that it can kill, it is used by around two billion people, six million of whom die each year. If discovered for the first time today, tobacco would definitely be banned. How did the fatal attraction to tobacco begin?

In the first century BC the Mayans in Central America are alleged to have smoked the tobacco in religious ceremonies. The Aztecs took the smoking custom from the Mayans, who later settled in the Mississippi Valley, and smoking was adopted by neighbouring tribes (Figure 9.1). Amazonian Indians also used tobacco in their religious rituals. This group colonized the Bahamas, later discovered by Columbus in 1492.

The English adventurer Sir Walter Raleigh is alleged to have introduced both potatoes and tobacco to England. Raleigh's public health legacy of tobacco and potato (chips/fries) would be hard to rival. Raleigh popularized tobacco at court, and apparently believed that it was a good cure for coughs and so he often smoked a pipe. Indeed, it is alleged that Raleigh's final request before his beheading by James I at the Tower of London in 1618 was a smoke of tobacco, a legacy to all subsequent prisoners facing execution.

Cigarette smoking was reintroduced to England by British soldiers returning from Wellington's Napoleonic campaigns in the Iberian Peninsula (1808–1814). Following this, veterans returning from the Crimean War (1853–1856) increased cigarette smoking in Britain. In addition

Figure 9.1 Aztec guests being presented with a tobacco tube and a sunflower

Source: The Florentine Codex

to bringing many millions of deaths and injuries to service personnel, war has always been a great addicter to tobacco and, in the case of the Royal Navy, to rum.

The economics and politics of tobacco are complicated with many dilemmas and contradictions. Over the last 450 years tobacco has been a major contributor to the economy. Tobacco tax makes a significant contribution to wealth, exceeding the cost of treating smoking-related diseases in health systems. Tax revenue from tobacco products in the UK reached £12.3 billion in 2012/13. Until 2010, tobacco farmers in 12 EU countries including Bulgaria, Greece, Romania and Italy were receiving £260 million in subsidies. At the same time the EU has a policy of discouraging smoking by restricting tobacco advertising, and mandating health warnings on cigarette packets.

Although many other factors are involved, the greatest disincentive to smoking, especially among children, has been increased taxation to raise the retail price (Figure 9.2).

PREVALENCE AND DISTRIBUTION

Although tobacco was popular during the nineteenth century, it was largely smoked using pipes and confined to men. The development of cigarettes towards the end of the nineteenth century

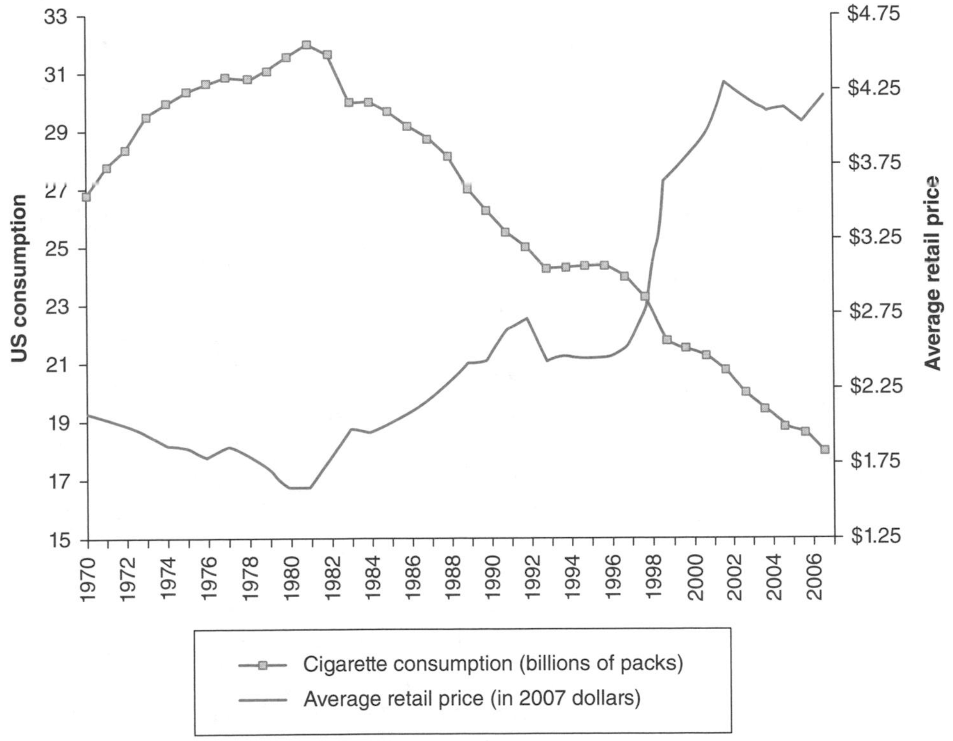

Figure 9.2 Tobacco consumption by price in US, 1970–2007

Source: www.tobaccofreekids.org/research/factsheets/pdf/0146.pdf

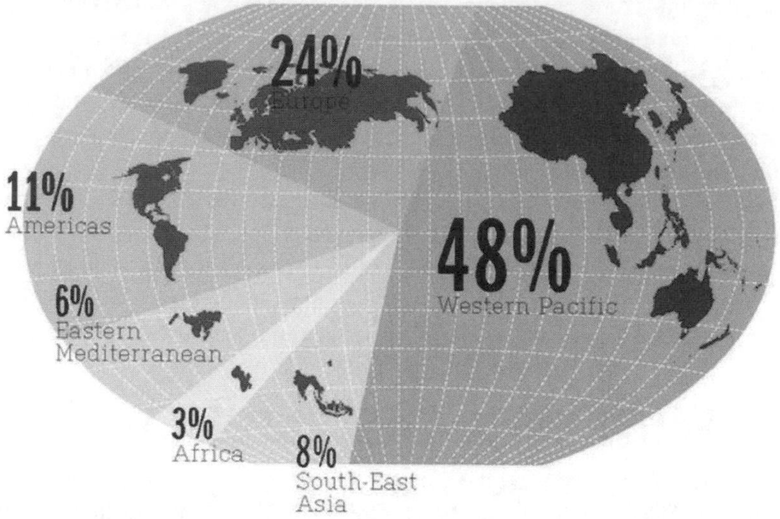

Figure 9.3 World cigarette consumption by region, 2009

Source: *The Tobacco Atlas*, 4th edition

was followed by a rapid increase in tobacco consumption. In the first half of the twentieth century, cigarette smoking became a hugely popular activity, especially among men in the Western world. In the USA cigarette consumption doubled in the 1920s and again in the 1930s and peaked at about 67% in the 1940s and 1950s. However, between 1965 and 2004, cigarette smoking among adults aged 18 and older declined by half from 42% to 21% and rates declined to 20% in 2007. An estimated 43.4 million Americans currently smoke (American Cancer Society, 2009). In recent years smoking prevalence has been highest in China (Figure 9.3).

In Britain it was estimated that the **prevalence** among men reached almost 80% during the 1940s and 1950s (Wald et al., 1988). Since then, the prevalence has declined overall, with sex, social class, regional and other differences. There are about 10 million adult cigarette smokers in Great Britain and about 15 million ex-smokers. Since 1990 there has been a steady increase in the number of smokers using mainly hand-rolled tobacco. In 1990, 18% of male smokers and 2% of female smokers said they smoked mainly hand-rolled cigarettes but by 2011 this had risen to 40% and 26% respectively.

The 2012 Opinions and Lifestyle Survey found that 38% of men and 24% of women smoked hand-rolled cigarettes (Action on Smoking and Health, 2014). Much of the tobacco used by hand-rollers is smuggled across borders duty free.

The World Health Organization (2013) estimated that tobacco kills approximately six million people and causes more than half a trillion dollars of economic damage each year. The WHO report in 2013 estimated that tobacco will kill as many as one billion people this century if the

WHO Framework Convention on Tobacco Control is not implemented rapidly. Prevalence in developing countries is rising dramatically where there is extensive promotion of smoking by the tobacco industry.

Although fewer women than men are smokers, there have been dramatic increases in smoking among women and the gap in smoking rates between men and women is narrowing in most places. In Europe, there was a consistent decline in the prevalence of smoking among men from about 70–90% to about 30–50% between 1950 and 1990. However, among women the same period saw a rise in the prevalence of smoking followed by a slow decline reaching 20–40% in 1990. The initial rise in prevalence was led by women from professional backgrounds, but they have also led the decline such that today smoking is more common among women from poorer backgrounds.

National surveys have established a growing link between smoking and various indicators of social deprivation. In Britain a national survey of health and lifestyles found that smoking is more prevalent among people on low incomes, the unemployed and those who are divorced or separated.

HEALTH EFFECTS OF SMOKING

The health effects of smoking have been studied for over 100 years. There is hardly a single organ in the body that is not deleteriously influenced by tobacco smoking.

Effects on Active Smokers

The classic study by Doll and Hill (1952) linking smoking with cancer was followed by reports by the Royal College of Physicians in Britain (1962) and the Surgeon General in the United States (US Department of Health, Education and Welfare, 1964) demonstrating the harmful effects of smoking. The US Centers for Disease Control and Prevention (2005) give a useful guide to the health impacts of smoking. Cigarette smoking accounts for more than 440,000 deaths each year in the United States and 120,000 deaths in the UK, nearly one of every five deaths. More deaths are caused each year by tobacco than all deaths from human immunodeficiency virus (HIV), illegal drug use, alcohol use, motor vehicle injuries, suicides and murders combined. The risk of dying from lung cancer is at least 22 times higher among men who smoke, and about 12 times higher among women who smoke, compared with those who have never smoked.

Chemicals and radiation that are capable of triggering the development of cancer are called 'carcinogens'. **Carcinogens** initiate a series of genetic alterations ('mutations') that stimulate cells to proliferate uncontrollably. A delay of several decades occurs between exposure to carcinogens in tobacco smoke and the onset of cancer. People exposed to carcinogens from smoking cigarettes generally will not develop cancer for 20 to 30 years. In the USA there have been 29 Surgeon General's reports on smoking and health during the period 1964–2006. Tobacco is the leading preventable cause of illness and death in the United States, resulting in an annual cost of more than $75 billion in direct medical costs. Nationally, smoking results in almost 6 million years of potential life lost each year. More than 6.4 million children living today will die prematurely because of their decision to smoke cigarettes.

The 2004 US Surgeon General's report on smoking and health revealed that smoking causes diseases in nearly every organ of the body (US Department of Health and Human Services, 2004). Published 40 years after the Surgeon General's first report on smoking – which had concluded that smoking was a definite cause of three serious diseases – the 2004 report found that cigarette smoking is conclusively linked to leukaemia, cataracts, pneumonia and cancers of the cervix, kidney, pancreas and stomach. On average, men who smoke cut their lives short by 13.2 years, and female smokers lose 14.5 years. Statistics indicate that more than 12 million Americans have died from smoking since the first (1964) Surgeon General's report, and another 25 million Americans alive today are likely to die of a smoking-related illness. The report concluded that quitting smoking has immediate and long-term benefits, reducing risks for diseases caused by smoking and improving health in general. Quitting smoking at age 65 or older reduces by nearly 50% a person's risk of dying of a smoking-related disease.

BOX 9.1
INTERNATIONAL STUDY: SMOKING DEATHS IN INDIA

In an epidemiological study, Jha et al. (2008) estimated that smoking accounts for 900,000 deaths a year in India. It is predicted that 1.5 million people a year will die from tobacco smoking in India by 2020. The Jha et al. study warned that smoking could soon account for 20% of all male deaths and 5% of all female deaths in India between the ages of 30 and 69. The data showed a 6-year reduction in longevity for male smokers and an 8-year reduction for females.

Smokeless tobacco, including chewing products such as gutkha, zarda, paan masal and khaini, is the most common form of tobacco use, with poorer people and women preferring these to smoking cigarettes or bidis – small, cheap, locally made cigarettes.

Source: Jha et al. (2008)

Effects on Passive Smokers

For obvious reasons, tobacco smoke does most damage to the person who is actively inhaling. However, those consistently breathing **second-hand smoke** (SHS) also have a higher risk of cancer, heart disease, and respiratory disease, as well as sensory irritation. The Surgeon General estimated that exposure to SHS killed more than 3,000 adult non-smokers from lung cancer each year, approximately 46,000 from coronary heart disease, and an estimated 430 newborns from sudden infant death syndrome. In addition, SHS causes other respiratory problems in non-smokers such as coughing, phlegm and reduced lung function. Passive smoking causes the premature death of thousands of non-smokers worldwide.

The Scientific Committee on Tobacco and Health (SCOTH, 1998) commissioned a review of the impact of secondary smoking on lung cancer. This review analysed 37 epidemiological studies of lung cancer in women who were lifelong non-smokers living with smokers. The review found that the women had a statistically significant excess risk of lung cancer of 26%. The analysis also showed that there was a dose response relationship between the risk of lung cancer and the number of cigarettes smoked by a person's partner, as well as the duration over which they had been exposed to their smoke. The report also concluded that parental smoking caused acute and chronic middle ear disease in children. Furthermore, it concluded that **sudden infant death syndrome** (SIDS), the main cause of post-neonatal death in the first year of life, is associated with exposure to environmental tobacco smoke. The association was judged to be one of cause and effect.

Tobacco Industry Campaign of Disinformation

The tobacco industry carried out a disinformation campaign over several decades. The campaign deliberately sought to create doubt in the minds of legislators and the public about the effects of smoking. However, through litigation and the action of whistleblowers and with the release of thousands of tobacco industry documents, the details of the disinformation campaign were revealed. The anti-tobacco organization, Action on Smoking and Health (ASH), carried out a survey of the documents, extracted 1,200 relevant quotes, and grouped these under common themes (Action on Smoking and Health, 2010), summarized in the Key Study below.

BOX 9.2
KEY STUDY: ANALYSIS OF TOBACCO INDUSTRY DOCUMENTS ON SMOKING AND HEALTH

Publicly the tobacco industry denied that smoking causes lung cancer – yet it has understood the carcinogenic nature of its product since the 1950s, e.g.: 'A demand for scientific proof is always a formula for inaction and delay and usually the first reaction of the guilty . . . in fact scientific proof has never been, is not and should not be the basis for political and legal action'

(S.J. Green, 1980, cited by Action on Smoking and Health, 2010).

Nicotine and addiction

The industry routinely denied that tobacco is addictive, yet it has known this since the 1960s. The idea of nicotine **addiction** destroyed the industry's stance that smoking is a matter of personal choice, e.g.: 'the entire matter of addiction is the

(Continued)

(Continued)

most potent weapon a prosecuting attorney can have in a lung cancer/cigarette case. We can't defend continued smoking as "free choice" if the person was "addicted"' (The Tobacco Institute, 1980, cited by Action on Smoking and Health, 2010).

Marketing to children

The companies deny that they target the young. Yet company documents revealed the companies' preoccupation with teenagers and younger children and methods to influence smoking behaviour in these age groups, e.g.: 'If the last ten years have taught us anything, it is that the industry is dominated by the companies who respond most to the needs of younger smokers' (Imperial Tobacco, Canada, cited by Action on Smoking and Health, 2010).

Advertising

The industry maintains that advertising is used only to fight for brand share, not to increase total consumption, while academic research shows otherwise, e.g.: 'I am always amused by the suggestion that advertising, a function that has been shown to increase consumption of virtually every other product, somehow miraculously fails to work for tobacco products' (Emerson Foote, former Chairman of McCann-Erickson, which handled US$20m of tobacco industry accounts, cited by Action on Smoking and Health, 2010).

Cigarette design

The industry promoted 'low-tar' cigarettes knowing that they were lacking any health benefits, or even made cigarettes more dangerous, e.g.: 'Are smokers entitled to expect that cigarettes shown as lower delivery in league tables will in fact deliver less to their lungs than cigarettes shown higher?' (BAT in 1977, cited by Action on Smoking and Health, 2010).

Passive smoking

The industry refused to accept the evidence of the harm caused by SHS, e.g.: 'All allegations that passive smoking is injurious to the health of non-smokers, in respect of the social cost of smoking as well as unreasonable demands for no smoking areas in public places, should be countered strongly' (BAT in 1982, cited by Action on Smoking and Health, 2010).

'Emerging markets'

With reducing smoking levels in the West, the companies moved aggressively into developing countries and Eastern Europe, e.g.: 'They have to find a way to feed the monsters they've built. Just about the only way will be to increase sales to the developing world' (ex-tobacco company employee, R. Morelli, cited by Action on Smoking and Health, 2010).

Source: Action on Smoking and Health (2010)

Another study reached similar conclusions. Tong et al. (2005) discuss the tobacco industry's use of scientific consultants to attack the evidence that SHS causes disease, including lung cancer. SHS has been linked causally with sudden infant death syndrome (SIDS) in major reports such as the 2004 US Surgeon General's report. Tobacco industry documents included 40 million pages of internal memos and reports made available in litigation settlements against the tobacco industry in the United States. From their analyses of these documents, Tong et al. concluded:

> PM executives responded to corporate concerns about the possible adverse effects of SHS on maternal and child health by commissioning consultants to write review articles for publication in the medical literature. PM executives successfully encouraged one author to change his original conclusion that SHS is an independent risk factor for SIDS to state that the role of SHS is 'less well established'.
>
> (Tong et al., 2005: 356)

Balbach et al. (2006) argue that the health belief model (see Chapter 6) helps the tobacco industry through its theoretical stance regarding individual choice, and 'information'. Balbach et al. analysed trial and deposition testimony of 14 high-level tobacco industry executives from six companies plus the Tobacco Institute to determine how they used the concepts of 'information' and 'choice' in relation to theoretical models of health behaviour change. They concluded that tobacco industry executives deployed the concept of 'information' to shift full moral responsibility for the harms caused by tobacco products to consumers. The industry executives characterized the tobacco industry as: 'that of impartial supplier of value-free 'information', without regard to its quality, accuracy and truthfulness . . . Over-reliance on individual and interpersonal rational choice models may have the effect of validating the industry's model of smoking and cessation behaviour, absolving it of responsibility and rendering invisible the 'choices' the industry has made and continues to make in promoting the most deadly consumer product ever made' (Balbach et al., 2006). Discourses about smoking have a powerful influence on attributions of responsibility, whether the consumer or the provider is ultimately to blame. Our 'blame culture' can easily swing in either direction.

Tobacco Promotion and the Social and Economic Context of Smoking

The tobacco industry spends billions worldwide on advertising and promoting tobacco products. Research shows that tobacco advertising encourages children to start smoking and reinforces the social acceptability of the habit among adults. The US Surgeon General (1989) stated that tobacco advertising increases consumption by:

- encouraging children or young adults to experiment with tobacco and thereby slip into regular use;
- encouraging smokers to increase consumption;
- reducing smokers' motivation to quit;
- encouraging former smokers to resume;
- discouraging full and open discussion of the hazards of smoking as a result of media dependence on advertising revenues;
- muting opposition to controls on tobacco as a result of the dependence of organizations receiving sponsorship from tobacco companies;
- creating, through the ubiquity of advertising and sponsorship, an environment in which tobacco use is seen as familiar and acceptable and the warnings about its health are undermined.

Hastings and MacFadyen (2000) analysed internal tobacco company documents and found that the companies worked with advertising agencies to target young people. The companies used advertising to increase overall consumption as well as brand share, in contrast to their public assertions that they only advertise to encourage existing smokers to switch brands.

Most econometric studies have found that increased expenditure on tobacco advertising increases demand for cigarettes, while banning advertising leads to a reduction in tobacco consumption. In 1991, a meta-analysis of 48 econometric studies found that tobacco advertising significantly increased tobacco sales. The UK Department of Health's Chief Economic Adviser found that there was a drop in tobacco consumption of between 4% and 16% in countries that had implemented a tobacco-advertising ban (Smee et al., 1992). Given the huge numbers of people who die from smoking related diseases, it seems illogical that tobacco companies are allowed legally to advertise their harmful products. However, many issues are intertwined and the abolition of tobacco advertising has not been as simple and straightforward as it might first appear.

First, there is the argument that there is a lack of evidence to suggest that tobacco advertising significantly influences smoking behaviour. The 'magical potency' of tobacco advertising could be questioned since most advertisements are directed to target audiences who already use the product. Researchers claimed that econometric studies have found either no overall relationship between advertising and sales or a small, statistically significant positive relationship. However, this view can be contested and the results of such studies are equivocal, as much depends on who supplies data for the studies: the tobacco industry or the public health authorities.

The issue of banning tobacco advertising is further tangled when politics are included. The epitome of this can be seen within the European Union (EU) which, on the one hand, has supported and finances the tobacco industry through the Common Agricultural Policy, and on the other, recognizes the health effects of tobacco in funding its 'Europe Against Cancer' campaign. However, in financial terms, the former greatly exceeds the latter. Despite this, attempts have been made to persuade tobacco growers to change their crops. Yet the fact remains that in 2000 the EU provided €984.5 million in tobacco subsidies and a mere €64 million to the 'Europe Against Cancer' campaign. The 15-fold greater expenditure on tobacco subsidies surely cancelled out any benefit from the anti-cancer campaign. Crazy!

THEORIES OF SMOKING

The resistance shown by smokers to large-scale campaigns to discourage the practice has prompted a massive amount of research to help to explain the continuing popularity of smoking. It is agreed that smoking is an extremely complex practice involving a mixture of processes. The biopsychosocial model indicates three influences on health that are mirrored in theories of smoking: the biological, the psychological, and social theories of smoking (Table 9.1). The theories are complementary and slightly overlapping, hence the term 'biopsychosocial' being an apt one in this context.

BIOLOGICAL THEORY

Nicotine, the main active ingredient in tobacco smoke, is a substance that if taken in large quantities can be toxic and even fatal. However, delivered in small amounts via cigarette smoke it has a range of psychophysiological effects including tranquillization, weight loss, decreased irritability, increased alertness and improved cognitive functioning. However, tolerance to the effect of nicotine develops such that there is less evidence of performance improvements among regular smokers (Jarvis, 2004). Over time the smoker develops a **physical dependence** on nicotine. In 1997 the smallest of the big five US tobacco companies (the Liggett Group) admitted that it had raised the nicotine content in cigarettes to increase their addictiveness. Nicotine is a naturally occurring colourless liquid that turns brown when burned and smells of tobacco when exposed to air. It has complex but predictable effects on the brain and body. Most cigarettes contain 10 milligrams (mg) or more of nicotine. The typical smoker takes in 1 to 2 mg of nicotine per cigarette. Nicotine is absorbed through the skin and lining of the mouth and nose or by inhalation in the lungs. In cigarettes nicotine reaches peak levels in the bloodstream and brain rapidly, within 7–10 seconds of inhalation. Cigar and pipe smokers, on the other hand, typically do not inhale the smoke, so nicotine is absorbed more slowly through the mucosal membranes of their mouths. Nicotine from smokeless tobacco also is absorbed through the mucosal membranes.

Nicotine is addictive because it activates brain circuits that regulate feelings of pleasure, the 'reward pathways' of the brain. A key chemical involved is the neurotransmitter **dopamine** that nicotine

Table 9.1 The three main theoretical approaches to the understanding of smoking

Theory	Main elements of the theory
Biological	1. Tobacco contains nicotine, an addictive substance 2. Nicotine activates brain circuits that regulate feelings of pleasure, the 'reward pathways' of the brain 3. Nicotine increases the amounts of the neurotransmitter dopamine 4. The acute effects of nicotine disappear in a few minutes, causing the smoker to repeat the dose of nicotine 5. Smoking is an addiction that is repeatedly and immediately reinforced with each new intake of nicotine
Psychological	1. Smoking is a learned habit, which becomes an automatic response to stimuli following repeated reinforcement – a conditioned response 2. The pleasant associations of smoking generalize to a range of settings and situations 3. The smoker learns to discriminate between those situations in which smoking is rewarded and those in which it is punished 4. The smoker develops responses to a number of conditioned stimuli (internal and external 'triggers') that elicit smoking 5. Smoking is an escape/avoidance response to certain aversive states. The smoker will light up a cigarette to escape or avoid an uncomfortable situation
Social	1. Initially, smoking is physically unpleasant but this is overruled because of social reinforcement from peers 2. Smoking is a social activity in which the smoker identifies with others who smoke. There is a rebellious feeling associated with the activity 3. The social identity of the smoker is changed once he/she forms the habit 4. Smokers group together socially and share their experiences, which smokers find pleasurable and empowering. The in-group feeling is heightened by social norms and health advice to quit 5. The strong associations between social identity, in-group feelings, and a smoking sub-culture are difficult to change

increases. The acute effects of nicotine disappear in a few minutes, causing the smoker to repeat the dose of nicotine to maintain the drug's pleasurable effects and prevent withdrawal symptoms.

The cigarette is an efficient and highly engineered drug-delivery system. By inhaling, the smoker can get nicotine to the brain rapidly with each and every puff. A typical smoker will take ten puffs on a cigarette over a period of 5 minutes that the cigarette is lit. Thus, a person who smokes 30 cigarettes daily gets 300 'hits' of nicotine every day. That is over 100,000 hits a year or one million every ten years! This is why cigarette smoking is so highly addictive. Smoking behaviour is rewarded and reinforced hundreds of thousands or millions of times over the smoker's lifetime.

An enzyme called monoamineoxidase (MAO) shows a marked decrease during smoking. MAO is responsible for breaking down dopamine. An ingredient other than nicotine causes the change in MAO, since it is known that nicotine does not dramatically alter MAO levels. Smokers may be increasing central dopamine levels by reducing monoamineoxidase inhibitor activity, reinforcing smoking by keeping high satisfaction levels through repeated tobacco use.

There is evidence that tobacco is a highly addictive drug. More than 30% of people who try tobacco for the first time develop a dependency on tobacco, while for other drugs, this percentage is generally lower. However, there are variations in the speed and strength of **addiction** to nicotine among smokers. One obvious way to explain individual differences in smoking is our genetic makeup. Genetic factors could play a role in several aspects of nicotine addiction, from the tendency to begin smoking, to the chances of quitting.

Twin studies produced evidence of a genetic link to smoking. Heath and Madden (1995) found that genetic factors increased the likelihood of becoming a regular smoker ('initiation') and of these smokers becoming long-term smokers ('persistence'). In a large follow-up survey of male twin pairs from the US Vietnam Era Twin Registry, True et al. (1997) found that genetic factors account for 50% of the risk of smoking and environmental factors accounted for a further 30%. In addition, genetic factors accounted for 70% of the risk variance of becoming a regular smoker whereas environmental factors were not important.

With the decline in the overall prevalence a group of 'refractory' smokers has emerged who are more likely to have other problems such as depression, anxiety and bulimia (Pomerlau, 1979). In ancient times these patterns may have been biologically adaptive or neutral. However, in contemporary society, a more active fight or flight response is inappropriate. Smoking would be valuable to this population because it can produce small but reliable adjustments to levels of arousal. Evolutionary approaches to addictions tend to ignore the psychological and social influences that create the conditions for tobacco use (Marks, 1998). It is to these influences that we now turn.

PSYCHOLOGICAL THEORY

Probably the most frequently used model of smoking is that based on learning theory. Basically, it argues that people become smokers because of the positive reinforcement they obtain from smoking. The mechanisms are similar to those described in Chapter 8 in reference to alcohol drinking. Initially, smoking is physically unpleasant (to a greater extent than is the case for alcohol) but this is overruled because of the social reinforcement from peers. The pleasant associations of smoking then generalize to a range of other settings. In addition, the smoker learns to discriminate between those situations in which smoking is rewarded and those in which it is punished. He or she also develops responses to **conditioned stimuli** (both internal and external) that elicit smoking. Smoking can be conceptualized as an escape/avoidance response to certain aversive states (Pomerlau, 1979). The smoker will light up a cigarette to escape or avoid an uncomfortable situation.

In 1966 Tomkins proposed his 'affect management model' of smoking that was subsequently revised and extended by Ikard et al. (1969) who conducted a survey of a national (US) probability sample. In a factor analysis of the responses they identified six smoking motivation factors: reduction of negative affect, habit, addiction, pleasure, stimulation and sensorimotor manipulation. Subsequent surveys produced similar factors. Women more than men report that they smoked for reduction of negative affect and pleasure.

In their study of smoking among young adults, Murray et al. (1988) added two additional reasons: boredom and nothing to do. In a survey they asked young adults to indicate which of these factors were important reasons for smoking in different situations. In all situations relaxation and control of negative affect were considered the most important reasons. At home boredom was also considered important, perhaps reflecting these young people's frustration with family life. At work, addiction was considered important, perhaps reflecting the extent to which it disrupted their work routine, while socially, habit was rated as important.

According to Zuckerman (1979) individuals engage in **sensation seeking** so as to maintain a certain level of physiological arousal. More specifically, Zuckerman emphasized that sensation seeking was designed to maintain an optimal level of catecholaminergic activity. In a French sample, smokers score higher on a measure of sensation seeking, in particular on disinhibition, experience seeking and boredom susceptibility sub-scales. From a physiological perspective these sensation seekers have a low level of tonic arousal and seek exciting, novel or intense stimulation to raise the level of cortical arousal. This argument is similar to that of Eysenck et al. (1960) who found that smokers scored higher on measures of *extraversion*. This personality dimension is also supposed to reflect a lower level of cortical arousal that could be raised by engaging in risky activities such as smoking.

Besides sensation seeking and extraversion, a variety of personality characteristics have been found to be associated with smoking. In a sample of Scottish adults, Whiteman et al. (1997) found that smoking was associated with hostility. However, they accept that 'presence of an association does not help in determining if the relationship is causal'. Indeed, they hypothesize that deprivation of smoking that was required for the study may have increased hostility.

A variety of different types of studies have found that stress is associated with smoking. For example, among smokers, consumption is higher in experimental, stressful laboratory situations. In surveys, people with higher self-reports of stress are more likely to be heavy smokers. In a study of nurses' smoking practices, Murray et al. (1983) found that those who reported the most stress were more likely to smoke. This relationship remained after controlling for the effect of family and friends' smoking practices. Finally, in a macro-social study, US states that have the highest levels of stress as measured by a range of social indicators also have the highest levels of smoking and of smoking related diseases.

Other researchers have looked for evidence of personality differences between people who smoke and non-smokers. Sensation seeking, neuroticism and psychoticism are all correlated with smoking (Marks, 1998). However, the relationships are fairly weak and it can be concluded that anybody has the potential to become addicted to nicotine.

SOCIAL THEORY

Smoking is a social activity. Even when the smoker smokes alone he or she still smokes in a society where cigarettes are widely available and promoted. A number of qualitative studies have considered the social meaning of smoking. Murray et al. (1988) conducted detailed interviews with a sample of young adults from the English Midlands. These suggested that smoking had different meanings in different settings. For example, at work going for a cigarette provided an opportunity to escape from the everyday routine. For these workers, to have a cigarette meant to have a break and conversely not to have a cigarette meant not to have a break. The cigarette was a marker, a means to regulating their work routine.

Outside work, smoking was perceived as a means of reaffirming social relationships. For those young people who went to the pub, the sharing of cigarettes was a means of initiating, maintaining and strengthening social bonds. Those who did not share cigarettes were frowned upon.

Graham's (1976) series of qualitative studies has provided a detailed understanding of the meaning of smoking to working-class women. In one of her studies, she asked a group of low-income mothers to complete a 24-hour diary detailing their everyday activities. Like the young workers in the study by Murray et al. (1988), smoking was used as a means of organizing these women's daily routine. Further, for these women smoking was not just a means of resting after completing certain household tasks but also a means of coping when there was a sort of breakdown in normal household routines. This was especially apparent when the demands of childcare became excessive. Graham describes smoking as 'not simply a way of structuring caring: it is also part of the way smokers re-impose structure when it breaks down' (Graham, 1987: 54).

Graham (1987) argued that for these women smoking is an essential means of coping with everyday difficulties. It is also a link to an adult consumer society. Through smoking the women were reaffirming their adult identity. Similarly, in Bancroft et al.'s (2003) Scottish study, both men and women reported integrating smoking into contrasting periods of their lives. They smoked as a means of coping with stress at work and often because of boredom at home.

Smoking is not only embedded in the immediate material circumstances in which the smoker lives, but also in the wider social and cultural context within which smoking is widely promoted. Admittedly, in most Western societies there are considerable restrictions on the sale and promotion of cigarettes. Despite these, tobacco manufacturers continue to find ways to promote their products, e.g. through the sponsorship of sporting and cultural activities. In the USA it is estimated that the tobacco companies spend approximately $6 billion per annum on advertising and promotion. As illustrated above, the tobacco industry is a powerful lobby group having considerable influence on government and policymaking.

SMOKING CESSATION

In the last ten years smoking prevalence in adults has been driven down in many Western countries to around 15–30%. Yet millions are still harmed by tobacco, and to an increasing extent in developing countries, deepening health inequalities. This has led to attempts to develop a more sophisticated understanding of the process of giving up smoking. There is more clarity today about the best ways to proceed in helping individual smokers.

The majority of smokers spend a considerable portion of their smoking career wishing they could quit. When they do finally quit, the vast majority do so on their own, without professional help, and they quit using 'cold turkey', i.e. by abrupt withdrawal. The American Cancer Society (2003) reports that 91.4% of former smokers quit 'cold turkey' or by slowly decreasing the amount smoked. Doran et al. (2006) surveyed adult patients attending Australian GPs in 2002 and 2003. Over a quarter of patients were former smokers and one in five were current smokers. Doran et al. reported that 92% of former and 80% of current smokers used only one method in their last quit attempt, 'cold turkey' being the most common method used by both former (88%) and current (62%) smokers.

For those who seek help, guidelines such as those of the Surgeon General can be followed (Fiore, 2008). For smokers who are willing to quit, the 'five as' are a useful framework:

> *Ask about tobacco use*: Identify and document tobacco use status for every patient at every visit.
>
> *Advise to quit*: In a clear, strong and personalized manner urge every tobacco user to quit.
>
> *Assess willingness to make a quit attempt*: Is the tobacco user willing to make a quit attempt at this time?
>
> *Assist in quit attempt*: For the patient willing to make a quit attempt, offer medication and provide or refer for counselling or additional treatment to help the patient quit. For patients unwilling to quit at the time, provide interventions designed to increase future quit attempts.
>
> *Arrange follow-up*: For the patient willing to make a quit attempt, arrange for follow-up contacts, beginning within the first week after the quit date. For patients unwilling to make a quit attempt at the time, address tobacco dependence and willingness to quit at next clinic visit.

For smokers unwilling to quit, it is recommend to implement the 'five **R**s': explain the relevance, risks, rewards, run over the roadblocks, and repeat at every available opportunity. In the following sections we review the three main approaches to smoking cessation which are available singly or in combination: pharmacological, psychological and social.

PHARMACOLOGICAL APPROACH TO CESSATION

The first paragraph to read in any paper reporting a drug study is the 'Declaration of Interests'. Some authors are paid lucrative sponsorship deals by the pharmacological industry which should be declared in this section. Frequently, the reader will find that the authors have received *honoraria* (= *money*) from companies such as Pfizer®, Novartis®, GlaxoSmithKline®, AstraZeneca® and Roche®, and that they act as speakers, undertake consultancy and research, receive travel funds and hospitality from manufacturers of medications, or receive an unrestricted research grant (= *more money*) from one or more companies. These financial relationships between corporations and researchers are not conducive to unbiased, impartial science. It has been shown that pharmaceutical industry sponsorship of drug studies is associated with findings that are favourable to the sponsor's product (Lexchin et al., 2003; Bero, 2013).

Pharmacological approaches aim to minimize the unpleasant symptoms of withdrawal, i.e. the irritability, difficulty concentrating, anxiety, restlessness, increased hunger, depressed mood and a craving for tobacco that accompanies cessation. These **withdrawal symptoms** are relieved by administration of nicotine but not of **placebo**. There are three kinds of pharmacological treatment for nicotine withdrawal that aim to raise the chances of cessation.

Nicotine replacement therapy (NRT) reduces symptoms of nicotine withdrawal, thereby, in theory, increasing the likelihood of cessation. Six forms are available: gum, patch, nasal spray, inhaler, tablet and lozenge. Evidence from clinical trials has been interpreted as demonstrating that NRT is effective (e.g. Stolerman and Jarvis, 1995). NRT company websites, and 'independent' sites that are viewed as authoritative, proclaim that the nicotine patch, available over the counter, 'doubles the chances of quitting'. Such sites are unreliable, sadly, even those by government departments. For example, the NHS Smokefree website makes the unsupported claim that: 'If you also use medicines such as patches or gum to manage your cravings, you are up to four times more likely to successfully go smokefree!' (National Health Service, 2010).

Methodological problems exist within many RCTs that compare NRT to placebos. This is because smokers in the placebo condition *can detect that they are not receiving any nicotine* (Mooney et al., 2004; Polito, 2008). Dar et al. (2005) found that control group members were 3.3 times more likely to correctly guess that they had received placebo than to incorrectly guess that they had received nicotine (54.5% vs. 16.4%). If the trials in an RCT are not double blind, the findings give a misleading picture of treatment effectiveness. Cochrane Reviews, which assess the quality of trials from the written reports (e.g. Cahill et al., 2013), have no way of checking whether double blind requirements have been broken. This fact may help to explain why real world results for NRT are worse than those obtained in RCTs. The issue of the safety of NRT and other drug therapies also needs to be considered. **Bupropion** (Zyban) is a weak dopamine and noradrenaline (norepinephrine) reuptake inhibitor. Initially employed as an antidepressant, bupropion was found to have potential as a smoking treatment. Bupropion treatment normally lasts for 7 to 12 weeks, with the patient halting the use of tobacco about ten days into the course. Wu et al.'s (2006) meta-analysis claimed that after one year of treatment, the odds of maintaining quitting were 1.5 times higher in the bupropion group than in a placebo group. A third pharmacotherapy is **varenicline** (Champix), which is a nicotinic acetylcholine receptor partial agonist. Agonists at this receptor may stimulate the release of dopamine to reduce craving and withdrawal while simultaneously acting as a partial antagonist by blocking the binding and consequent reinforcing effects of smoked nicotine. In a direct comparison of buproprion with varenicline, Jorenby et al. (2006) claimed varenicline had superior efficacy: after one year, the rate of continuous abstinence was 10% for placebo, 15% for bupropion and 23% for varenicline.

BOX 9.3
CASE STUDY: THE NATIONAL HEALTH SERVICE (NHS) IN ENGLAND'S SMOKING CESSATION SERVICE

Pharmacologically mediated cessation, primarily NRT, has been promoted through guidelines that have a questionable evidence base. The English NHS smoking cessation service is based on pharmacotherapy in combination with counselling support. The claims for high efficacy and cost-effectiveness of NRT have not been substantiated in real-world effectiveness studies (e.g. Pierce and Gilpin, 2002; Ferguson et al., 2005; Doran et al., 2006). Pierce and Gilpin (2002) stated: 'Since becoming available over the counter, NRT appears no longer effective in increasing long-term successful cessation' (p. 1260). Efficacy studies, using randomized controlled trials, do not transfer well to real-world effectiveness. Bauld et al. (2009) reviewed 20 studies the effectiveness of intensive NHS treatments for smoking cessation published between 1990 and 2007. Quit rates showed a dramatic decrease between four weeks and one year. A quit rate of 53% at four weeks fell to only 15% at one year. Younger smokers, females, pregnant smokers and more deprived smokers had lower quit rates than other groups.

The NHS evaluation data prove that NRT produces *poorer* outcomes than non-pharmacological methods (Health and Social Care Information Centre, Lifestyles Statistics, 2008). In 2007/08, 680,000 people set a quit date and 88% of these had received pharmacotherapy at a cost of £61 million. Of these, 49% successfully quit for four weeks compared to 55% of people who had received no pharmacotherapy. Smokers who used NRT had a lower quit rate than those who did not use NRT. The NRT system needs to be replaced by a more effective system.

Another issue concerning NRT is lack of safety. In 2005 the MHRA relaxed the restrictions on NRT use, allowing the combined use of patches and gum, and permission for its use by pregnant and young smokers, smokers with cardiovascular disease and smokers who want to reduce their smoking. However, a critical review concluded that NRT use by pregnant women and children would pose a significant risk to neurological development in infants and children (Ginzel et al., 2007). That NRT is used so widely in health care systems in spite of the poor outcomes and lack of safety is profitable for the pharmaceutical industry, but a poor return for taxpayers and smokers. This review suggests that a therapeutic strategy for smoking should look beyond a purely medical model. A psychosocial model would yield a radically different approach. Efficacy and cost-effectiveness will be higher when treatment strategies address the causes, not the symptoms.

PSYCHOLOGICAL APPROACH TO CESSATION

Quitting smoking or, if that is impossible, reducing cigarette consumption, are both viable targets for a smoking cessation programme. In order to achieve these aims, it is necessary for an intervention to help smokers to control both their physical and their **psychological dependency** on smoking. The US Surgeon General's (2008) guidelines on 'Treating Tobacco Use and Dependence' recommended the use of individual, group and telephone counselling (Fiore, 2008). The report concluded that two components of counselling are especially effective: practical counselling concerning problem solving and skills training, and social support. The results of the meta-analysis are shown in Table 9.2. While counselling and medication are effective alone, a combination of counselling and medication is the most effective. The report found a strong association between the number of sessions of counselling, when combined with medication, and smoking abstinence. The best abstinence rate was obtained with more than eight sessions of counselling and behaviour therapy plus medication, giving an odds ratio of 1.7 and an abstinence rate of 32.5%.

The guidelines give specific recommendations about particular behavioural and social elements to include in smoking treatments (see Table 9.3). There has been increasing interest in the use of cognitive behavioural therapy (CBT) for the control of smoking and other health-related behaviours. These therapies can be delivered as a brief intervention in one or more sessions to groups of smokers who are at the action stage. One example of a treatment programme which

Table 9.2 Meta analysis of the effectiveness of and estimated abstinence rates for various types of counselling and behavioural therapies (*n* = 64 studies)

Type of counselling and behavioural therapy	Number of arms	Estimated odds ratio (95% CI)	Estimated abstinence rate (95% CI)
No counselling/behavioural therapy	35	1.0	11.2
Relaxation/breathing	31	1.0 (0.7, 1.3)	10.8 (7.9, 13.8)
Contingency contracting	22	1.0 (0.7, 1.4)	11.2 (7.8, 14.6)
Weight/diet	19	1.0 (0.8, 1.3)	11.2 (8.5, 14.0)
Cigarette fading	25	1.1 (0.8, 1.5)	11.8 (8.4, 15.3)
Negative affect	8	1.2 (0.8, 1.9)	13.6 (8.7, 18.5)
Intra-treatment social support	50	1.3 (1.1, 1.6)	14.4 (12.3, 16.5)
Extra-treatment social support	19	1.5 (1.1, 2.1)	16.2 (11.8, 20.6)
Other aversive smoking	19	1.7 (1.04, 2.8)	17.7 (11.2, 24.9)
Rapid smoking	19	2.0 (1.1, 3.5)	19.9 (11.2, 29.0)

Source: US Surgeon General (2008)

integrates a variety of effective behavioural techniques is the **Quit For Life (QFL) programme** (Sulzberger and Marks, 1977). This multi-modal programme includes all of the methods listed in Table 9.3 (Marks, 1993, 2005) and encourages a steady reduction of cigarette consumption over seven to ten days followed by complete abstinence. The QFL programme is delivered in several alternative ways: as a group therapy of ten sessions, as a self-help programme following a single, one-hour group therapy session, or on the Internet. A preliminary observational study suggested that the therapy could be particularly effective when delivered to groups of self-referring smokers (Marks, 1992). Randomized controlled trials showed that the QFL programme is capable of delivering relatively high quit rates among lower SES smokers with only one intensive session (Marks and Sykes, 2000; Sykes and Marks, 2001). These results suggest that this CBT intervention can reduce smoking among lower SES smokers at relatively low cost.

Table 9.3 Elements of problem-solving and skills training recommended in the Surgeon General's (2008) guidelines

Practical counselling (problem-solving/skills training) treatment component	Examples
Recognize danger situations – identify events, internal states, or activities that increase the risk of smoking or relapse	Negative affect and stress
	Being around other tobacco users
	Drinking alcohol
	Experiencing urges
	Smoking cues and availability of cigarettes
Develop coping skills – identify and practise coping or problem-solving skills. Typically, these skills are intended to cope with danger situations	Learning to anticipate and avoid temptation and trigger situations
	Learning cognitive strategies that will reduce negative moods
	Accomplishing lifestyle changes that reduce stress, improve quality of life, and reduce exposure to smoking cues
	Learning cognitive and behavioural activities to cope with smoking urges (e.g. distracting attention; changing routines)
Provide basic information about smoking and successful quitting	The fact that any smoking (even a single puff) increases the likelihood of a full relapse
	Withdrawal symptoms typically peak within one to two weeks after quitting but may persist for months. These symptoms include negative mood, urges to smoke, and difficulty concentrating
	The addictive nature of smoking

The most popular method of smoking cessation remains 'cold turkey' (abrupt cessation). The Australian study by Doran et al. (2006) reported success rates among 2,207 former smokers and 928 current smokers as follows: cold turkey 77.2%; nicotine patch 35.9%; nicotine gum 35.9%; nicotine inhaler 35.3%; and bupropion 22.8%. According to these data, NRT and bupropion *reduced* the odds of quitting when considered across the whole population of quitters. Health care professionals tend to see only those smokers who have the most difficulty quitting by themselves. It is therefore likely that, as the smoking population shrinks over time, those who seek help become harder to treat.

SOCIAL APPROACH TO CESSATION

Smoking is deeply embedded in everyday social activities. Today, smoking has become almost taboo, and smokers are seen as 'outsiders'. Cessation attempts must take these aspects into consideration, including the increasing social gradient in smoking prevalence. Smoking cessation efforts not only need to provide social support but also attempt to enhance people's sense of control and mastery through changing their social conditions. Smoking cessation may thus form part of a more general community intervention to promote empowerment and health advocacy (see Chapters 6 and 14).

Many group treatment programmes use the 'buddy system' in which smokers are paired up to provide mutual support. A variety of organizations also offer group support for quitters. These are organized at a local level by health care providers and charities. The NHS Stop Smoking Services offer free local group sessions which start a week or two before the official quit date. The group then meets weekly for four weeks to give advice and motivation. Some people prefer to talk one-to-one with a professional advisor, but many find the group support helpful. Many support systems are provided by hospitals and clinics.

The Internet provides social networking through specialized forum sites that aim to support quitters using diverse methods. A few non-commercial sites are listed in Box 9.4. WhyQuit's Freedom from Nicotine is informative and acts as a counter to bias on other sites like Quit.

BOX 9.4
INTERNET SITES SUPPORTING QUITTERS

WhyQuit's Freedom from Nicotine: A high-quality site that is critical and reflective. It is designed for 'cold turkey' quitters only without use of any product, pill or procedure. This leading site has an archive of more than 100,000 member posts on 19 subject message boards. http://whyquit.com/

(Continued)

(Continued)

Quit: The pharmaceutical industry must love this site. It perpetuates three myths: (1) that the only successful way to quit is via pharmaceutical methods; (2) 'only 3% of smokers succeed by willpower alone' and (3) that smokers can increase their chances by four times 'with the right support.' www.quit.org.uk/

KillTheCan.org: advocates quitting dipping for smokeless and chewing tobacco users but provides support for all methods including NRTs. www.killthecan.org/

Quit Smokeless.org: for smokeless tobacco quitters only. www.quitsmokeless.org/index.php

ADOLESCENTS, SPECIAL POPULATIONS AND MOBILE PHONE APPS

In this section we review a few meta-analyses on smoking cessation efforts with adolescents, special populations and new technology. First, we summarize a review of studies of adolescent smoking cessation. Garrison et al. (2003) reviewed controlled trials for adolescent smoking cessation up to June 2002. The authors found only limited evidence demonstrating efficacy of smoking-cessation interventions in adolescents, and no evidence on the long-term effectiveness of such interventions.

Ranney et al. (2006) systematically reviewed smoking cessation intervention strategies for adults and adults in special populations. Research findings counselling and pharmacotherapy used either alone or in combination can improve rates of success with quit attempts. There were few studies focused on ways to reach or treat special populations.

Recent reviews have examined the use of electronic media in smoking cessation, specifically mobile phones and the Internet. Whittaker et al. (2009) reviewed trials of mobile phones used as a medium for smoking cessation. Participants were smokers of any age who wanted to quit. In a meta-analysis the text message programme trials showed a significant increase in short-term self-reported quitting (RR 2.18, 95% CI 1.80 to 2.65). This review found text message mobile phone programmes to be effective in the short term (six weeks), and a combined Internet–mobile phone programme to be effective up to 12 months.

Shahab and McEwen (2009) reviewed the efficacy and acceptability of online, interactive interventions for smoking cessation and identified moderators and mediators of treatment effects in the literature from 1990 to 2008. Shahab and McEwan found 11 relevant randomized controlled trials of variable quality. Web-based, tailored, interactive smoking cessation interventions were found to be effective compared with untailored booklet or e-mail interventions. The web-based interventions were considered acceptable and user satisfaction was generally high. The authors concluded that interactive, web-based interventions for smoking cessation can be an effective aid in smoking cessation.

QUITTING WITHOUT HELP

As is the case with problem drinking, gambling, and narcotics use, studies show that at least 90% of smokers who permanently stop smoking do so without any form of assistance (Chapman and MacKenzie, 2010). In 2003, 20 years after the introduction of cessation pharmacotherapies, smokers trying to stop unaided were twice as numerous as those using pharmacotherapies, and only 8.8% of US quit attempters used a behavioural treatment. Yet the most common method used by people who successfully stopped smoking is unassisted cessation (cold turkey or reducing before quitting). Great gains could be made if public health authorities highlighted this fact.

ELECTRONIC CIGARETTES

Electronic or e-cigarettes were first developed in China in 2003. E-cigarettes are battery-operated cylindrical devices designed to replicate smoking without the use of tobacco. Some look like conventional cigarettes, while others appear more like an electronic gismo. They use heat to vaporize a liquid-based solution containing nicotine and flavouring into an aerosol mist, and have been proposed as a way to help smokers quit the habit. They are actively promoted throughout the world as a smokeless and safe way to inhale nicotine without being exposed to tar and the many toxic components of standard cigarettes, and as an aid to smoking cessation.

The industry started on the Internet and at shopping-mall kiosks and has rocketed from thousands of users in 2006 to several million worldwide who have more than 200 brands to choose from. Sales of e-cigarettes in the UK rose by 340% to £193 million between 2012 and 2013 and an estimated 1.3 million people in Britain use them. Sales in the USA are estimated to have reached nearly $2 billion in 2013. Tobacco companies have jumped into the business with many appealing flavours being offered.

They are subject to limited regulation, and are not licensed as a medicine in the UK. In 2014, under regulations by the Food and Drug Administration, the US federal government banned sales of electronic cigarettes to minors and required approval for new products and health warning labels. Researchers are still unsure how effective e-cigarettes are as a quitting aid in comparison to other therapies such as nicotine patches.

Glynn (2014) has summarized current concerns about e-cigarettes. There is a lack of sufficient scientific data about: their safety (Bassett et al., 2014, reported nicotine poisoning in an infant who consumed a quantity of e-cigarette liquid); their effectiveness as smoking cessation aids; their ability to deliver enough nicotine to satisfy withdrawal effects; the potential for e-cigarette use to reverse the decades-long public health effort to 'denormalize' combusted cigarette use; the effects of second-hand vapour from e-cigarettes, as well as the desire of most people to avoid being exposed to this vapour in public places such as restaurants, movie theatres and aeroplanes, whether proven to be a health hazard or not; whether the use of e-cigarettes encourages smokers who might have otherwise quit to continue smoking and only use e-cigarettes when they are in no-smoking environments (i.e. the 'dual use' concern); and whether young people may use e-cigarettes as an introduction to smoking regular combusted cigarettes. Until we have answers to these questions, buyer beware.

CANDY-FLAVOURED TOBACCO AND BLUNTS

Flavoured tobacco products have been marketed worldwide for some time. Since the majority of adult smokers begin their smoking careers as teenagers, flavoured cigarettes are a new 'gateway' for children and young adults to become regular smokers. US legislation bans sales of cigarettes with flavours other than menthol, but that ban does not apply to products not categorized as cigarettes such as cigars, cigarillos and 'blunts', large cigars composed of a tobacco-based paper overwrap holding shredded tobacco. Also excluded are conventional rolled-leaf cigars, 'roll-your-own' tobacco, 'blunt wraps' (i.e. tobacco-based wraps – often flavoured – that are often used to roll cannabis), hookah tobacco, moist snuff for 'dipping,' and electronic cigarettes (Brown et al., 2014).

Some cannabis smokers use the shell of a blunt cigar to 'roll a blunt', which combines tobacco use with cannabis, a practice that also occurs when hash is mixed with tobacco in joints. Some cigars are very similar to cigarettes, and so the ability to flavour cigars translates into the availability of flavoured cigarette-like products. According to Brown et al. (2014), flavoured smoking products are used by 42% of middle-school and high-school students who smoke. Their analysis of the chemicals in flavoured smoking products suggested that the same sensory cues associated with fruit flavours in popular candy and drink products are being exploited in candy-flavoured tobacco.

FUTURE RESEARCH

1. There is still limited understanding of cigarette smoking among young people. In particular, there is a need for increased understanding of the social, ethnic and gender variations in smoking among young people.
2. More research on the influence of tobacco advertising on the uptake of smoking in young people is necessary in those countries where advertising is permitted. This evidence will be significant in eventually gaining a worldwide advertising ban.
3. More research funding on smoking prevention and cessation is necessary from bodies independent of the tobacco industry.
4. Research on e-cigarettes is needed to clarify their impact on the smoking careers of users.

SUMMARY

1 About 25% of adults smoke, with increasing prevalence in the developing world. The prevalence of smoking varies according to sex, social class and ethnicity.

2 Biological, psychological and social factors contribute to the smoking epidemic.

3 Effective tobacco control requires a multi-level approach including economic, political, social and psychological interventions.

4 Most smokers report difficulty in quitting the habit. However, significant progress has been made in our understanding of smoking cessation.

5 Efficacy and cost-effectiveness are higher when treatment strategies address the causes, not the symptoms.

6 Smokers wishing to quit are helped using the 'five **A**s': **A**sk about tobacco use; **A**dvise to quit; **A**ssess willingness to make a quit attempt; **A**ssist in quit attempt; **A**rrange follow-up.

7 Smokers unwilling to quit are helped using the 'five **R**s': explain the **R**elevance; **R**isks; **R**ewards; run over the **R**oadblocks; and **R**epeat at every available opportunity.

8 Doubts exist about the methodology and funding of clinical trials of pharmaceutical products such as NRT in smoking cessation. Studies sponsored by pharmaceutical companies are more likely to have outcomes favouring the sponsor's products.

9 Evaluation studies using real world observation produce outcomes that are significantly less favourable to products such as NRT than randomized trials.

10 A biopsychosocial model focuses on the experience of smoking, its motivation, and its emotional and social associations.

11 The most effective strategy for smoking cessation to date uses elements from each of the biological, psychological and social approaches, a combination of medication, cognitive behavioural therapy, and social support.

12 The vast majority of quitters quit on their own. Health authorities could utilize this fact by giving self-quitting a stronger endorsement.

10 PHYSICAL ACTIVITY AND EXERCISE

By equating certain types of behaviour with virtue and others with vice, the secular moralists . . . threaten to undermine the critical task of educating the public in general . . . to the very real dangers lurking behind everyday behavioural choices.

(Leichter, 1997: 360–1)

OUTLINE

Recent years have seen an increased official concern at the apparent widespread decline in the participation of people in all types of physical activity. In this chapter we review evidence on the increasing prevalence of sedentary behaviour and its potential impact on health. We consider the social and psychological factors associated with participation, the varying meanings of different forms of physical activity, and strategies that have been used to promote greater participation.

EXTENT OF PHYSICAL ACTIVITY

Evidence from a variety of social surveys has confirmed the increasingly sedentary lifestyle of modern society. The most recent summary of physical activity statistics in the UK (British Heart Foundation Research Group, 2013) found that the majority of adults did not reach recommended levels of physical activity. In Scotland only 45% of men reported meeting recommended levels of physical activity, compared to 39% in England, 37% in Wales and 33% in Northern Ireland. Women were less active than men, with 33% reporting meeting recommended levels in Scotland, 29% in England, 24% in Wales and 28% in Northern Ireland. Only 14% of adults in the UK were found to exercise or play sport regularly, higher than the EU average of 9% but lower than Ireland, which has the highest prevalence of 23%.

The latest data from Europe show some recent changes in participation, but nothing to 'write home about' (Figure 10.1). In England in 2008, the most common form of occupational and non-occupational physical activity was walking. In England 56% of women did not spend any time in sports and exercise in 2008. There was also evidence of reduced physical activity in the workplace and in terms of mode of travel to work. In England 24% of men reported moderate to vigorous occupational activity for at least 30 minutes per day compared to 10% of women. In Great Britain the average distance travelled on foot or by bike by each person per year has decreased from 306 miles in 1975/76 to 221 miles in 2010. The most common barriers to doing more physical activity identified by adults in England were work commitments and a lack of leisure time.

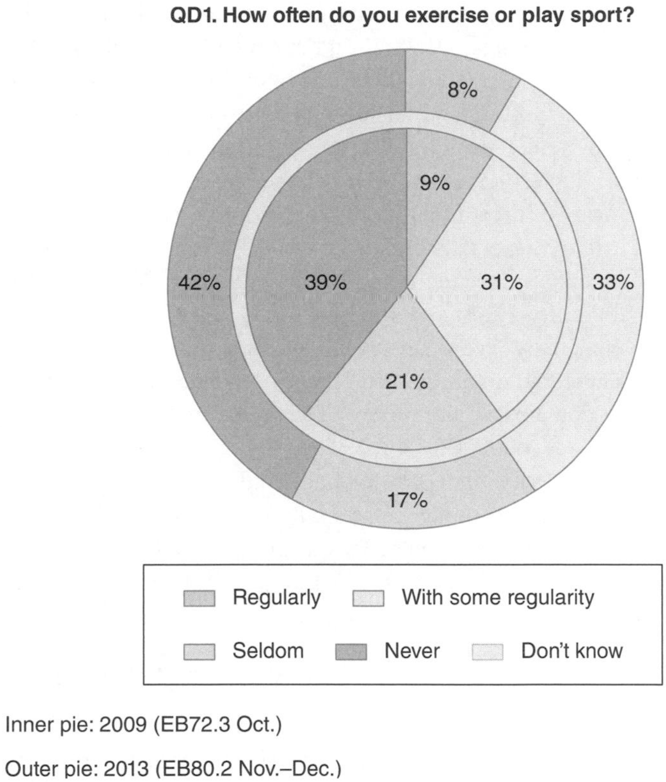

Figure 10.1 Data from the Eurobarometer on Participation in Sport and Physical Activity

Source: European Commission (2014)

According to the UK Time Use Survey 2000, among those who are most active the most common activities are walking, gardening, DIY and 'ball games'. However, there is evidence that even walking is becoming less common. For example, according to the National Travel Survey the total miles walked per annum fell by 26% between 1975 and 2001 and the amount travelled by bicycle fell by a similar amount during the same period. It was estimated that this meant approximately 66 fewer miles walked per annum per person in that period. There is some lesser evidence that people are taking up more leisure-time physical activity such as walks over two miles, swimming, keep fit and yoga.

Data from Europe suggest that the main reasons people give for engaging in sport or physical activity are to improve health, to improve fitness and to relax (European Commission, 2014). To have fun comes fourth in the list of reasons (Figure 10.2).

VARIATION IN PARTICIPATION

Most studies confirm that the extent of participation in physical activity is linked not only to age and sex but also to socio-economic and education background. The Health Survey for England (Prescott-Clarke and Primatesta, 1998) found that men from manual social classes are more active, but this was due to greater occupational activity. In general, adults from manual social classes participated less in sporting and leisure-related exercise activities. Several studies have confirmed the class and gender variations in sports participation with men from middle-class backgrounds having the highest levels of participation (Lim et al., 2011).

One problem with many of the estimates of participation of physical activity is that they often focus on leisure time activity, especially organized sports. Attempts to measure the extent of physical activity is work are at home are more limited. The study by Cochrane et al. (2000) used the International Physical Ability Questionnaire (www.ipaq.ki.se/downloads.htm), which requires participants to complete a daily record for seven days of activity in four domains: work related, active transport, gardening and domestic, and leisure. It is then possible to obtain a measure of energy in each of these domains. In the survey of a sample of residents of an English Midlands city they found that work accounted for 44% of reports of physical activity, compared to 32% for garden and domestic activity, and 12% for both active transport (walking and cycling) and leisure. However, the median level of physical activity at work was zero for both men and women and also zero for leisure activity for women. This would suggest that the majority of people have very sedentary working styles and most women participate little in leisure-time physical activity.

PHYSICAL ACTIVITY AND HEALTH

The reason for governmental interest in this apparent decline in physical activity is the increasing evidence of the negative impact on health. The World Health Organization (2004a) has identified the decreasing level of physical activity as a major cause of death and chronic disease worldwide. Rates of the following diseases have been found to be associated with higher rates of physical inactivity: cardiovascular disease, colon cancer, type 2 diabetes, stroke and breast cancer. The WHO

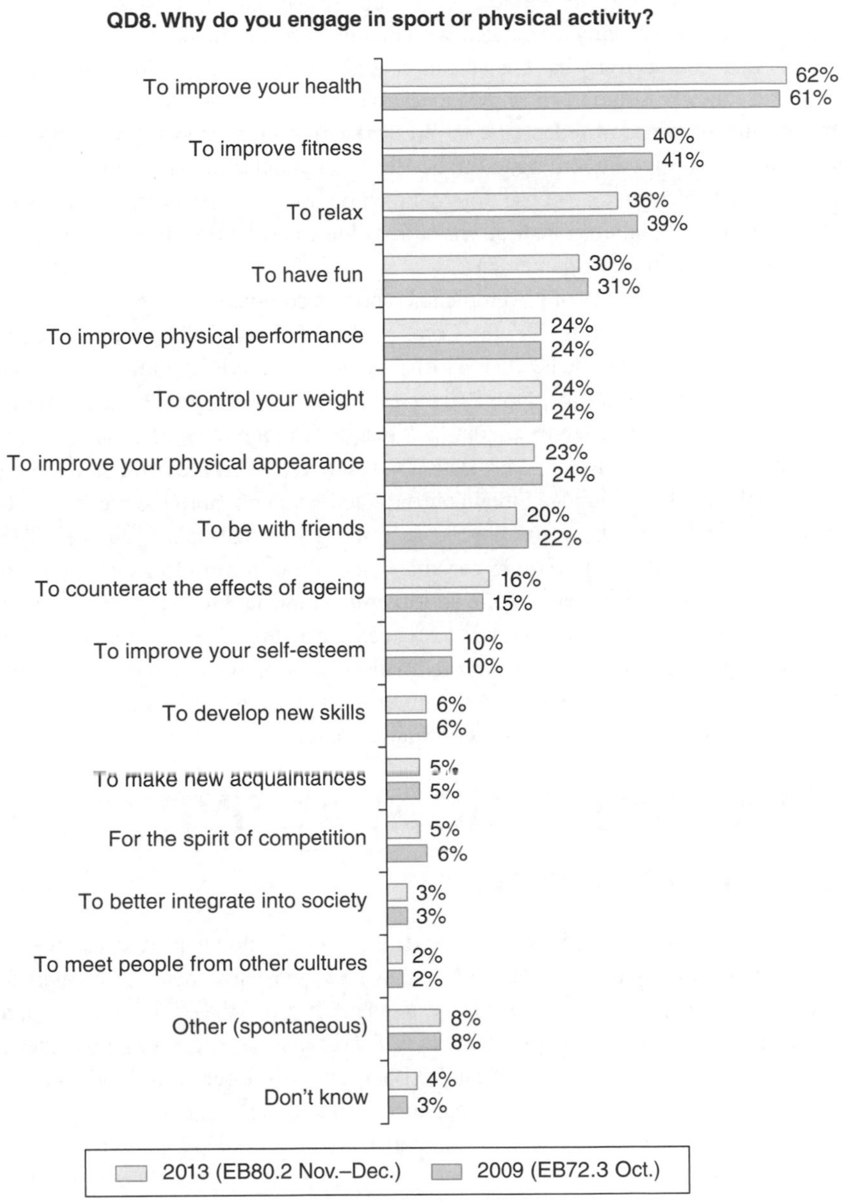

Figure 10.2 Data from the Eurobarometer on Motivation for Sport and Physical Activity

Source: European Commission (2014)

also highlighted the dose–response character of this activity–disease relationship with the greater amounts of physical activity being associated with greater levels of health.

A particular impact of inactivity has been the increase in levels of obesity in the population. Since increased levels of obesity is due to an imbalance between energy intake and energy expenditure it is not surprising that evidence of a decrease in physical activity has been followed by evidence of an increase in rates of obesity. According to Public Health England approximately one in four adults in the country are now classified as obese. International comparisons show that while the USA has the highest rates of obesity other industrialized nations are catching up. (For further discussion of the obesity pandemic, please see Chapter 7.)

This evidence has led to a series of governmental reports recommending increased participation in physical activity. For example, in the UK the Chief Medical Officers issued a joint report (Department of Health, 2011) identifying the health risks of a sedentary lifestyle including chronic conditions such as coronary heart disease, stroke, type 2 diabetes, cancer, obesity, mental health problems and musculo-skeletal conditions. The report emphasized that even relatively small increases in physical activity are associated with at least some protection for all ages. Often these reports adopt a victim-blaming stance to those who participate little in physical activity and ignore the broad social context.

Much psychological research in this field is far removed from 'rocket science'. Typically, it is based on very basic models and simple variables, and often, the findings are self-evident, no more than 'common sense'. Because of the shortcomings and lack of sophistication in models and theories, our ability to provide a satisfactory account of the bigger issues remains limited. In our view it is important to consider in a more nuanced fashion how social, environmental and psychological processes work together in explaining participation in physical activities. Of key importance is the meaning of exercise, not its actual amount.

CONTEXT OF PHYSICAL ACTIVITY

Socio-cultural Context

As noted, an understanding of the variations in the extent of participation in physical activities requires attention to the socio-cultural and political context within which they have meaning and which promote or discourage involvement in such pursuits. We discussed in Chapter 6 the evidence that human beings traditionally required considerable energy expenditure for survival. In ancient times hunter-gatherers needed to expend substantial energy on a regular basis so as to ensure access to food and shelter. This need to expend significant amounts of energy remained well into the twentieth century and continues in much of the developing world. However, the rapid increase in technology in industrialized societies over the past generation has led to a much more sedentary lifestyle. This decline in physical activity is a consequence of the reduced need for energy expenditure in all spheres of human life, including work, transportation and home maintenance (Eaton and Eaton, 2003). Technological developments in entertainment have reduced the role of physical activity in leisure time (King, 1994).

Increasing attention has been paid to the influence of neo-liberalism on everyday lives. One concept that has gained interest is **affluenza**, a combination of the concepts influenza and affluence.

In modern consumer society we are constantly persuaded that the key to success is greater consumption of commodities. Everything is offered for sale, including a certain lifestyle and a certain body shape. According to James (2006), the growth of 'affluenza' is one of the symptoms of the broader move towards increasing social inequality. He defined 'affluenza' as the increasing value placed on money, possessions and appearance. Part of this is the trend towards a more passive consumerist lifestyle and the belief that it is possible to purchase physical health through health supplements and membership of sports clubs. However, increasing social inequality has placed many of these products outside the reach of an increasing number of people who initially bought into this dream. Nowadays there is more evidence that people are increasingly resisting the myths peddled by advertisers (Hamilton and Denniss, 2010). While more empirical research is needed on this concept, it highlights the importance of the broader socio-cultural context.

Physical activities are also conducted within a cultural context that promotes different ideals about physicality. For example, the muscular physique is presented as the ideal male form in Western societies. As Luschen et al. (1996) noted, the emergence of bodybuilding exercises aimed at building muscular strength and fitness 'reflects a bodily culture that is in line with American values of masculine prowess' (p. 201). He continued: 'activities like American football, weightlifting, and boxing set a premium on brute physical force and place much less emphasis on endurance and relaxation' (p. 202). The ability to attain this physical shape is promised to those who participate in various fitness gyms. However, access to these somewhat elite facilities is often restricted to those with money. In addition, aggressive sporting activities are also promoted among the middle class as a training ground for developing an aggressive business attitude, not to mention the making of useful social contacts. This begins at an early age as is illustrated in studies of school sporting activities (Wright et al., 2003).

An important aspect of culture is religion. Different religions have different concepts of the body (see Chapter 4). For example, certain forms of Christianity traditionally held a negative view of excessive concern about the body. It has been suggested that this is a reason for the poorer performance of athletes from more Catholic countries in sporting events (Curtis and White, 1992). Conversely, in more Protestant or secular societies concern with body shape and performance is promoted. Indeed, Turner (1984) has argued that contemporary concern for the body could be described as the 'new Protestant ethic'. As health psychologists we need to engage with research into these broad socio-cultural processes.

Environmental Context

Environmental psychologists emphasize the importance of considering the **behavioural setting** or the physical and social context within which the behaviour occurs (Stokols, 1996). This includes the built environment, the buildings in which we live and work, and the communities in which we reside. The contemporary urban environment is 'passivogenic'. Modern buildings certainly are not designed with increasing physical activity in mind. Architects have created environments that foster inactivity and obesification (see Chapter 6). For example, stairways are often more difficult to access than either escalators or elevators. Airports use 'travelators' that allow people to stand still while being moved from A to B. Suburban bus services take shoppers directly from a nearby bus-stop to superstores. Huge shopping malls have replaced high streets. Communities often have poor play facilities and unaffordable fitness centres, which is especially the case in low-income neighbourhoods. The most common means of transport is cars; cycling and walking are discouraged or dangerous (Sallis et al., 1998). In a city such as London there is a high rate of fatalities among cyclists, who still have to navigate their way on the same roads as heavy goods vehicles (HGVs). In November 2013, six cyclists were killed on London's streets within two weeks, with 14 killed in London in that year, nine involving HGVs (BBC, 2013). In this respect, countries such as Germany and the Netherlands are more progressive.

A study of participation levels among residents of an English Midlands city helped clarify the relative importance of the physical environment. Cochrane et al. (2009) obtained environmental data from various official sources, including data on access to shops, traffic density and crime statistics, and combined this data with information from a community survey of participation in physical activity and attitudes towards physical activity. They identified environmental predictors of physical activity including ease of access to shops and to work suggesting that, the more accessible those places, the more likely people are to walk to them. Other factors of importance identified included moderate levels of road traffic and lower rates of road traffic accidents, suggesting that such environments are more conducive to walking. However, although these environmental factors were important, the researchers found that they were of lesser importance than beliefs and intentions about participation in physical activity as measured in the community survey.

An Australian study by Salmon et al. (2003) produced similar findings. They found that personal barriers such as lack of time, other priorities, work and family commitments predicted extent of involvement in physical activities more than environmental barriers such as weather, cost and safety. It is worth noting that these immediate personal barriers are a reflection of broader social demands. Another Australian study by Giles-Corti and Donovan (2002) also found that individual and social environmental factors were more important than physical environmental factors in predicting exercise participation. They found that the most important predictors of participation in recreational physical activity were perceived behavioural control, behavioural intention, habit and exercising peers. The most important environmental predictor was accessibility to recreational facilities.

In the United States, Wilson et al. (2007) conducted a telephone survey of physical activity among residents of South Carolina. They found that those residents who reported that they lived in a pleasant neighbourhood were trusting of their neighbours and had sidewalks in their neighbourhood were less likely to report being physically inactive. A study in Chicago found that residents of suburbs and those who had high levels of fear about their neighbourhoods were less likely to walk (Ross, 2000).

Humpel et al. (2002) conducted a review of 19 studies that looked at the relationship between physical activity and objectively determined physical environments. They found that physical activity was greater where there was evidence of accessibility, opportunities and aesthetic features of the neighbourhood including safety. While these studies demonstrate the importance of environmental factors, it is important to consider the limited activity-friendly features and the greater exposure to various environmental threats for residents of disadvantaged neighbourhoods.

PSYCHOLOGICAL MODELS

Various SCMs of health behaviour have been used to account for variations in the extent of participation in physical activity among adults. The four that have attracted most research interest are the theory of reasoned action, theory of planned behaviour, the social cognitive model, and the transtheoretical model. We provide further details of these models in Chapter 6. Here we illustrate the application of the models to exercise behaviour.

Theories of Reasoned Action and Planned Behaviour

The theory of reasoned action (TRA) was developed by Ajzen and Fishbein (1980). As described in Chapter 6, this theory proposes that behaviour, such as physical activity and exercise, is predicted by intention to engage in such behaviour, which in turn is predicted by the individual's attitude towards exercise and the perceived social norm. The attitudinal component is a function of the perceived consequences of participating and a personal evaluation of those consequences, while the perceived norm is a function of the perceived expectations to participate and the motivation to comply with those expectations.

The theory of planned behaviour (TPB) developed by Ajzen (1985) introduced *perceived behavioural control* into the basic TRA theory and suggested that, besides the attitudinal and social norm components, whether someone intended to behave in a certain way depended upon the extent to which they believed they had control over a particular behaviour. There have been several meta-analytic studies that have used the TPB to account for involvement in physical activity. In a review of more than 30 studies, Hausenblas et al. (1997) found that there were significant mean correlations between exercise intention and attitude, subjective norm and perceived behavioural control. A subsequent review by Hagger et al. (2002) also found significant but lower correlations. However, a large proportion of the variance in studies of physical activity remains unaccounted for.

Hamilton and White (2010) explored the role of salient behavioural, normative, and control beliefs among mothers and fathers of young children, drawing on the TPB framework. Interview data were analysed using thematic content analysis. Hamilton and White identified a range of advantages (e.g. improves parenting practices), disadvantages (e.g. interferes with commitments), barriers (e.g. time) and facilitators (e.g. social support) to performing physical activity, and also normative pressures.

Extensions of the TPB have investigated the role of a range of other psychological factors such as moral norms, affect, self-efficacy and past behaviour (Conner and Armitage, 1998). An example of the use of an extended TPB is the study by Abraham and Sheeran (2004). This found that **anticipated regret** accounted for an additional proportion of the variance in exercise intentions besides the core TPB variables.

Social Cognitive Theory

Bandura's (1986, 2001) social cognitive theory has been used extensively to account for participation in physical activity. In particular, Bandura's argument that self-efficacy is the common cognitive mechanism that mediates behavioural responses has been applied. It is argued that whether a person persists in a particular behaviour in different circumstances depends upon his/her perception of individual mastery over the behaviour. This sense of self-efficacy develops through personal experiences of success, but also from verbal support from others and the perceived level of physiological arousal. This theory is bidirectional such that not only can self-efficacy contribute to increased behavioural effort, but also success in the behaviour can contribute to increased self-efficacy.

In physical activity and exercise research it has been found that self-efficacy predicts greater involvement (e.g. McAuley and Jacobson, 1991). Variants of self-efficacy have been found to predict involvement. These include *barrier self-efficacy* or the confidence in ones' ability to overcome barriers to regular exercise attendance (Brawley et al., 1998), *scheduling self-efficacy* (DuCharme and Brawley, 1995) and *exercise self-efficacy* (Poag-DuCharme and Brawley, 1993). Some studies have found a negative relationship such that lower levels of self-efficacy statistically predicted more physical activity. Rimal (2001) in a longitudinal study found evidence of this and suggested that those with lower self-efficacy improved their self-efficacy over time which, in turn, led to greater exercise behaviour. Together these findings would confirm the interactive nature of self-efficacy beliefs and physical activity.

A related factor to self-efficacy is **self-determination**. According to Deci and Ryan's (1985) self-determination theory people will engage in many activities simply because of pure enjoyment or *intrinsic motivation*. A study in Wales (Ingledew et al., 1998) found that participants in the early stages of exercising attributed participation more to extrinsic motives (e.g. appearance/weight management) whereas in the later stages they referred to intrinsic motives such as enjoyment. It was concluded that intrinsic motives are important for progression to and maintenance of the exercise.

Bandura distinguished between three forms of agency or efficacy: personal, collective and proxy. *Proxy efficacy* is the belief in the role of others in aiding achievement of desired outcomes. Although at first this might seem to be the converse of self-efficacy, evidence suggests that it can be an important complement. The proxy is seen as someone who will provide assistance and help a person to achieve their goals. A study of participants in a fitness class found that *fitness instructor efficacy* as well as self-efficacy beliefs were predictive of class attendance for initiates (Bray et al., 2001). However, Bandura (1997) cautioned that an over-reliance on the proxy may reduce the cultivation of personal competencies. In a study to test this possible negative effect Shields and Brawley (2007) conducted a questionnaire study of participants in an exercise class. They found an interactive effect such that those participants who preferred proxy assistance expressed lower self-regulatory and task self-efficacy when faced with a class without a proxy. In order to promote sustainability of exercise behaviour, they concluded that proxy-agents (exercise instructors) should balance between providing assistance to participants and encouraging greater self-regulation.

Transtheoretical Model

The transtheoretical model (TTM) was developed by Prochaska and DiClemente (1983) to explain why anti-smoking messages were more successful for some people than others. According to the TTM, people adopting a new behaviour move through a series of stages of change within which they utilize different processes to support the changes. These stages are described in Chapter 6. Movement across the stages is dependent on *decisional balance* and *perceived self-efficacy*. *Decisional balance* is a cognitive assessment of the relative merits of the pros and cons of the exercise behaviour while *self-efficacy* is the belief in one's ability to perform the exercise. This model has been applied to physical activity by many researchers to describe the so-called five stages of exercise behaviour change (Marcus et al., 1992):

Pre-contemplation: sedentary, no intention of becoming active within six months.

Contemplation: still sedentary but does not accept the value/need for physical activity.

Preparation: person is intending to become more active in the very near future.

Action: person is physically active but only in the last six months.

Maintenance: person has been active for more than six months.

In addition to these five stages, an integral part of the TTM is the processes of change that describe movement from one stage to the next. Box 10.1 describes the character of the five experiential and the five behavioural processes of exercise behaviour change. Marcus et al. (1992) found that the five experiential change processes were more important in predicting progress in the early stages of exercise behaviour change while the five behavioural processes were more important in the later stages.

BOX 10.1
PROCESSES OF EXERCISE BEHAVIOUR CHANGE

Cognitive

Consciousness raising: gathering information about benefits of exercise.

Dramatic relief: feelings about inactivity and its consequences.

Environmental re-evaluation: consideration of consequences of inactivity on others.

Self re-evaluation: reconsidering consequences of physical activity for self.

Social liberation: awareness of social norms.

(Continued)

(Continued)

Behavioural

Counter-conditioning: substituting alternatives to sedentary behaviours.
Helping relationships: support of others becoming physically active.
Reinforcement management: rewards for physical activity.
Self-liberation: commitment to physical activity.
Stimulus control: avoiding environmental stimuli associated with physical activity.

Source: derived from Marcus et al. (1992)

A Scottish study found support for the role of these processes in describing exercise behaviour change (Lowther et al., 2007). Over 300 urban residents who had volunteered to participate in an exercise programme were assessed by questionnaire prior to the programme and at various intervals after the programme. They found that self-liberation was the most important change process at every stage movement but other processes were more important at particular stage movements. Stimulus control was more important when progressing from contemplation to preparation while social liberation and helping relationships were more important progressing from action to maintenance. The authors recommended that exercise interventions should be matched to the particular stage of change of the participants and target specific change processes.

Moving across the stages is said to depend on '**decisional balance**', the balance of pros and cons. In a study that compared reasons for and against participation in exercise in groups of non-exercisers and regular exercisers, Cropley et al. (2003) found that the pre-contemplators provided relatively more *con* reasons while the maintainers provided relatively more *pro* reasons. It was concluded that one reason why people do not exercise is that they cannot think of good reasons to do so.

Evidence of the importance of self-efficacy was provided by Marcus et al. (1992), who found that those who were regularly participating in physical activity (action or maintenance stages) scored higher on this measure. They concluded that this suggests that those who are at the early stages (pre-contemplation and contemplation) have little confidence in their ability to exercise.

Although the TTM continues to attract research interest it has also attracted ongoing criticism. Sutton (2000) argued that the TTM is not really a theoretical model at all but merely a description of 'pseudo stages' that are really arbitrary steps on a continuum of motivation. Armitage (2009) is sympathetic to this critique and suggests an alternative two-stage motivational-volitional model. However, he also argued that the focus of the critique on the stages of change has diverted attention away from the more interesting processes of change. West (2005) suggested moving on to develop a more theoretically coherent approach.

SELF-CONCEPT

Recent social cognition modellers have suggested introducing a variety of additional psychological variables. Hagger et al. (2003) suggested introducing *perceived competence* (similar to self-efficacy) and **self-concept**. There is evidence that there is a positive relationship between physical self-concept and participation in physical activity. It is supposed that a person who feels positively about him- or herself in one domain (physical) is more likely to perform well in that domain. Marsh (1990) argued that this relationship is reciprocal such that prior self-concept affects subsequent physical activity and vice versa. Marsh et al. (2006) confirmed this reciprocal relationship and found that physical self-concept had an independent effect in prediction of exercise intention beyond perceived control.

COMMENTS

Health psychologists have tended to focus their attention on SCMs, such as those described above, as the prime determinants of physical activity. These models continue to attract substantial research interest. As noted in Chapter 6, these models have attracted criticism for their methodological and theoretical shortcomings (Sniehotta et al., 2014). On the one hand, there are those who argue that there is a need for greater integration of these models with environmental models. On the other hand, there are those who argue that the cognitive models are insufficient because they rely on a restrictive individualistic and rationalistic view of humans (e.g. Marks, 1996; Mielewczyk and Willig, 2007; Murray, 2014). They locate thinking in the head of the individual rather than as something that unfolds in interaction with others leading to an individualistic focus in health promotion.

Integrating Psychological and Environmental Models

There have been increasing attempts to develop a more integrative ecological view of physical activity that combines environmental and psychosocial factors. For example, in a Canadian study it was found that access to recreational facilities was associated with enhanced physical activity among those with high levels of intention to be active (Rhodes et al., 2007). In a US study, it was found that a combination of psychosocial factors (perceived social support, perceived barriers and self-efficacy) together with environmental supports (walkability, aesthetics, walking facilities) was the best predictor of physical activity among older adults (Carlson et al., 2012).

In an extensive three-country study (Belgium, USA and Australia) Van Dyck et al. (2014) examined the interaction of psychosocial and environmental factors in predicting the extent of walking and leisure time physical activity. They found that perceived social support from friends and perceived barriers were the strongest psychosocial correlates of these activities. They also found that the role of perceived social support from family was more important for women. However, even after controlling for the psychosocial attributes, environmental factors emerged as important. These included perceptions of residential density, proximity of destinations, and aesthetics.

A social interactionist views the individual as part of a group and of a society. His or her behaviour, thoughts and beliefs can be considered as unfolding in interaction with the groups and society as a means of adapting to changing circumstances. Their decision to become involved in physical activity is the result of an ongoing engagement with their immediate social world. Further criticisms of SCMs can be found in Chapter 6. There is increasing critical and qualitative research that considers the various meanings of physical activity and considers these within varying social and cultural contexts.

Meanings of Physical Activity among Adults

Understanding the extent of participation in physical activity requires an understanding of the different meanings of physical activity. This depends upon the character of everyday social experience.

Social Class

People from diverse social backgrounds perceive physical activity differently. Calnan and Williams (1991) conducted detailed interviews with a sample of middle-aged men and women from south-east England. The participants were from different social backgrounds. They found clear social class differences in perceptions of exercise. Those from working-class backgrounds perceived exercise in relation to everyday tasks, activities and duties at home and at work. They adopted a functional definition of health and fitness. For them their ability to 'exercise' their everyday tasks both confirmed and reaffirmed their health. For example, one farm-worker said: 'I get enough exercise when I am working on the farm shovelling corn all day, you get enough exercise. In the garden out there, I take the dog for a walk, yet I get enough exercise' (p. 518). They tended to be satisfied with their physical health which they could enhance during their everyday activities.

Middle-class people tended to perceive exercise as not being part of their everyday activities. They preferred to define it with reference to recreational or leisure activities that they sometimes felt they could not engage in because of lack of time. Fitness for these individuals was defined in terms of athleticism not in ability to perform everyday tasks. This group also made more reference to the health-promoting effects of exercise in terms of 'well-being' and relief from routine daily obligations. In discussing these class differences in perceptions of exercise, Calnan and Williams (1991) referred to the work of Bourdieu (1984) who suggested that whereas working-class people express an instrumental relation to their bodily practices, middle-class people engage in health practices that are 'entirely opposed to (such) total, practically oriented movements' (p. 214).

In a large-scale survey of young people's physical activity in Norway, Oygard and Anderssen (1998) also considered the importance of the meaning of exercise and the physical body. In discussing the relationship between social class and exercise they also refer to the work of Bourdieu (1984) who suggested that this relationship derives from social class differences in attitude towards the body. In our society the legitimized body emphasizes both inner and outer characteristics. While the former is concerned with the healthy body, the latter refers to the fit and slim body. The middle and upper classes are more able to produce this legitimized body since it requires investment in time and money. Working-class people with less time free from necessity have a more instrumental view of their body and view concern with exercise and fitness as pretentious. Conversely, middle-class people with more leisure time and resources to expend promote a cult of health and a concern with physical appearance.

Gender

Men and women perceive physical activity differently depending upon their social and cultural background. In their survey Oygard and Anderssen found that level of education was positively associated with extent of participation in physical activity among females but not among males. In reviewing this finding, they refer to the suggestion that concern with the body is more common among those belonging to the cultural elite who are more anxious about their appearance and their 'body for others' (Bourdieu, 1984: 213). Oygard and Anderssen (1998) concluded: 'For females in higher social positions, it may be of importance to show others who they are by developing healthy and "delicate" bodies, i.e. they are more concerned with the inner and outer body than females in lower social positions' (p. 65). However, they also added more prosaically that the lesser involvement of less-educated females in physical activity may be due to them having limited access to leisure facilities. They found little relationship between education and physical activity among males and suggest that this may reflect the greater promotion of male sporting activities and the greater integration of physical activity into male culture.

Age

It is well established that participation in physical activity declines steadily with age. This may reflect a variety of factors including limited socialization into physical activity among that generation to perceived social exclusion. A study in New Zealand found that older people who participated in sporting activities reported that they were often confronted by a discouraging stance from younger people (Grant, 2001). This negative social value regarding seniors and sports would seem to be internalized such that many elderly people report limited participation for fear that they might incur an injury (O'Brien Coussins, 2000). Hardy and Grogan (2009) investigated older adults' influences and motivations to engage in physical activity in forty-eight 52–87-year-old participants. Preventing disability through exercise was a key factor in determining physical activity participation. Other influences included enjoyment of exercise, having support from others as motivators to exercise and a perception of limited appreciation for older people's needs.

Ethnicity

People from ethnic minorities participate less in various physical activities. This is due both to the social and environmental constraints and differences in the perceived nature of physical activity. Henderson and Ainsworth (2003) conducted interviews with African-American and American-Indian women about their perception of physical activity. These women emphasized not only the physiological but also the spiritual benefits of physical activity. As one woman said: 'I love being outside. Mostly I love taking walks. I love the quietness with that' (p. 319). Despite this positive view of physical activity these women identified various obstacles to participation.

This included perceived lack of time, although they also wondered about the legitimacy of this perceived obstacle. As one woman said: 'I talk about lack of time, et cetera, but you know, time is the sort of thing you can make available when you want' (p. 315). Other perceived constraints included job demands, tiredness, illness, family needs and safety issues. These constraints are not peculiar to women form ethnic minorities. Other studies (e.g. Verhuef et al., 1992) have identified similar constraints as being common among other groups of women.

Culture

In an intensive qualitative study of adults from the Netherlands, the USA and Korea, Lim et al. (2011) explored the importance of both individual and structural factors in sports participation and how this differed between countries. In the US sample, the participants reported involvement in team sports while at school but this declined as they moved into adulthood. Those who continued with sports tended to be involved in more individualistic activities such as running, working-out or golf. They recalled fondly the social aspects of youth sports (e.g. 'Probably the thing I loved most about childhood sports was [that] "the neighbourhood" played whatever sport was in season'). However, they felt that this was less obvious among modern young people ('This is long gone in today's culture for most children and certainly for most adults'; p. 212). Among US adults the predominant form of sport experience was passive – they watched sports on television and perhaps at a stadium. This was an opportunity for social interaction since it was easier to find people who had shared fanship rather than shared sports involvement. In the Netherlands sample there was evidence of greater continuity of sports participation from youth to adulthood. There was less evidence of the passive participation evident in the US sample. Conversely the Korean sample was more like the US sample. Together this cross-country comparison reveals the cultural variation in sports participation with passive sporting participation, being more extensive in the USA and Korea.

In terms of individual motivations for sports participation there was also evidence of cultural variations. The Korean adults referred to social, business, health and entertainment factors. While the American adults also referred to the importance of social and health reasons they also referred to competition. In addition, they detailed more reasons for non-participation such as career and family commitments and lack of time. This need for justifying non-participation could perhaps be interpreted as evidence of personal conflict with a great cultural expectation of participation. They also referred more to their children as a barrier to their own participation – as Lim et al. (2011) put it 'Either my child plays or I play' (p. 219). Thus while they may be letting down national expectations they ensured that their children were living up to them. Finally, the greater extent of passive participation in the USA and Korea could be interpreted as evidence of the importance attached to the social as opposed to the health value of sport in those societies.

Body image

There is growing interest in the concept of 'body image' or, more precisely, 'body imaging', and its relation with physical activity. The term 'body image' is defined by Grogan (2006) as 'a person's perceptions, feelings and thoughts about his or her body'. There has been extensive research exploring the relationship between exercise participation and body image. In an extensive review of over 100 studies, Hausenblas and Fallon (2006) concluded that exercise participation was associated with a more positively perceived body image. In addition, this relationship was apparent not only in correlational studies but also in intervention studies such that those who participated in physical exercise programmes reported an enhanced body image following the programme. This led Hausenblas and Fallon (2006) to conclude that exercise programmes may be an effective intervention for people with poor body image. However, they also caution that there may be a negative effect with some sub-groups. For example, Slater and Tiggermann (2006) found that women who exercise a lot have higher levels of body dissatisfaction and a great drive for thinness. This follows the general critique of modern representations of women equating beauty with slimness. Not surprisingly, it has been found that women and girls who weigh more are more dissatisfied with their body (Healey, 2006) although this relationship depends upon various social and cultural factors.

There is less research on male body image. Most studies have investigated the dimensions of adiposity and muscularity. As expected, males have reported a greater desire than females to become more muscular (Grogan and Richards, 2002). The covers of men's health magazines show a globalized obsession with muscularity.

Adolescents who engage in sporting activities typically report a more positive body image (Ferron et al., 1999). However, it would seem that there is less investment in body image for males (Hargreaves and Tiggemann, 2005) than for females, although this is influenced by social and cultural factors.

In addition to male muscularity, the media pay a great deal of attention to penis size, equating a man's penis size with his power and masculinity. Internet pornography plays an increasing role. In a Dutch study, Peter and Valkenburg (2014) found that males who watched more Internet pornography were dissatisfied with their body and stomach size but this was unrelated to males' satisfaction with their penis size. However, watching Internet pornography was unrelated to females' body satisfaction. Lever, Frederick and Peplau (2006) assessed views about penis size in an Internet survey of 52,031 heterosexual men and women. They reported that 85% of women were satisfied with their partner's penis size, while only 55% of men were satisfied with their penis size, with 45% wanting a larger penis, and 0.2% wanting a smaller one. Men reporting larger-than-average penises rated their appearance more favourably, suggesting a more positive body image. Flowers et al. (2013) explored contemporary understandings and representations of the penis. Traditionally, medical discourse focused upon the functionality of the penis, and more recently on the use of Viagra. However, Flowers et al. suggest the 'emergence of a new penile discourse, a penile aesthetic that focuses upon penile appearance as much as function. This shift has been facilitated by the Internet, the deregulation of pornography and changes in sexual mores' (Flowers et al., 2013: 121).

However, penis size is not everything. Tiggemann et al. (2008) investigated several different aspects of the male body image: head hair, body hair, height and penis size, in addition to body weight and muscularity. Online questionnaires were completed by 200 heterosexual men. Men were dissatisfied with all six aspects of their bodies, but particularly concerned about their body weight, penis size and height. Men's weight, muscularity, height and penis size, but not head or body hair, were related to overall self-esteem about appearance. This study suggests that men's body image is more nuanced than is often assumed in media accounts.

Campbell and Hausenblas (2009) conducted a meta-analysis of the effects of exercise interventions on body image and also participant, intervention, and design features associated with larger effects. They identified 57 interventions with pre-and post-data for the exercise and control groups and found a small random effect indicating that exercise interventions had improved body image compared to control conditions.

In our view, body imaging is not a fixed and static, intra-psychic phenomenon; like beliefs more generally, it develops in interaction and conversation with others and is embedded within a specific socio-cultural context (for more discussion of beliefs, see Chapter 4). As Gleeson and Frith (2006) emphasize: 'it is more useful to consider body imaging as a process, an activity, rather than a product' (p. 88). This re-orientation away from a static definition of body image emphasizes the need for more sophisticated qualitative work to explore the connection between the evolution of body imaging and physical activity.

EXERCISE AMONG CHILDREN

In the UK it has been estimated that among 2–15 year olds, four out of ten boys and six out of ten girls are not participating sufficiently in physical activity (Prescott-Clarke and Primatesta, 1999). As with adults the extent of participation varies substantially. In Norway, Oygard and Andersen (1998) found that teenage girls with higher levels of education were more physically active whereas among boys there was less evidence of a relationship with level of education.

Physical activity levels established in childhood are maintained to some degree across the lifespan. Friedman et al. (2008) extracted data from the American Terman Life-Cycle Study that began in 1922 and collected data on participants at regular intervals in subsequent decades. People with high active levels in childhood tended to report greater participation in physical activity in adulthood. This was especially the case for males. The longevity of activity levels added to governmental concern at the evidence of a decline in recent decades of involvement of children in physical activity and exercise.

Several studies have confirmed the importance of family and friends. Coleman et al. (2008) found that parents and siblings served as important role models for children's physical activity. Wheeler (2012) found that this socialization of activity occurs through direct and indirect strategies and practices. Direct strategies include telling the child about the benefits of physical activity while indirect strategies include parents' modelling physical activity. Downward et al. (2014) found a gender linkage in these relationships, in particular for boys. In a longitudinal study, Bunke et al. (2013) identified the importance of social support from outside the family, including involvement in sports clubs and schools' informal connections.

Several psychosocial factors have been associated with participation including physical competence, social acceptance and enjoyment. One can't help thinking that *joy* or *fun* must be *the* key element in participation in physical activities and exercise for people of all ages. Frederick and Ryan (1993) identified 'fun, skill development, challenge and fitness' as important factors. The opportunity to enhance competence and skill level were identified by Weis and Williams (2004) as other factors in maintaining involvement in sports. Conversely factors that deterred involvement included expense, travel, limited choice of activity, experience, adult support, familiarity with the environment, and knowledge of activities (Girginov and Hills, 2008). Factors predicting drop-out included negative experiences such as *lack of fun*, coach conflicts and lack of playing time (Fraser-Thomas et al., 2008).

A decline in participation in physical activities occurs as children enter adolescence. This is particularly pronounced among girls. Not to put too fine a point upon it, looking 'cool' isn't easy in a sweaty T-shirt, Lycra shorts and trainers with your hair in a mess and your make-up all smudged! It just isn't cool for adolescent girls to do sport (Slater and Tiggemann, 2010). The Scottish Health Survey 2012 (Chambers, 2013) found that while eight out of ten 5–7-year-old children met the physical activity guideline, by 13–15 years this had dropped to 55%. The drop was most pronounced between 11–12 (68%) and 13–15 years (55%), especially among girls who showed a 21% drop in participation between these age groups from 66% to 45%. Reasons for a growing disinterest in physical activity among girls included perceptions of their femininity, fears about looking stupid and fears about safety (Dwyer et al., 2006).

Research has also explored the socio-economic background of children's physical activity. In Denmark, Nielsen et al. (2012) found that children from higher SES families were more involved in sporting activities, although there was little difference in general physical activity. The lower SES boys may have been doing their paper rounds or kicking a ball around in the back alleys. They identified differences in material, social, educational and sporting capital as being important correlates of sporting participation.

MEANING OF PHYSICAL ACTIVITY FOR YOUNG PEOPLE

An increasing number of qualitative studies have begun to clarify the changing experiences of physical activity among young people. Kunesh et al. (1992) investigated school play activities of 11- to 12-year-old girls in central USA. In interviews the girls reported that they found physically active games at home and at school enjoyable. However, in the school playground the girls preferred to stand in a group and talk while the boys participated in various games. When the girls did participate in games often they got criticized by the boys for their supposed inferior performance. To avoid this negative treatment, the girls excluded themselves. The girls reported that when playing at school they felt nervous and embarrassed. These findings suggest that while at an early age, boys and girls both enjoy physical activities, by the time they reach puberty the girls feel that they are being excluded or they exclude themselves for other reasons.

As they enter adolescence the gender difference in participation in physical activities becomes more pronounced. From a series of interviews with young people living in south-east London, Coakley and White (1992) identified five factors that help explain young people's decisions about participation in sporting activities (Box 10.2).

BOX 10.2 YOUNG PEOPLE'S DECISIONS ABOUT SPORT PARTICIPATION

Consideration of the future, especially the transition to adulthood.
Desire to play and extend personal competence and autonomy.
Constraints related to money, parents and opposite-sex friends.
Support and encouragement from parents, relatives and peers.
Past experiences in school sports and physical education.
Perceived identity was a central concern in the extent and character of sports preferred. Young people actively sought out or rejected involvement in certain physical activities dependent upon a variety of factors including previous experiences and ongoing changing circumstances. As Coakley and White (1992) state: 'young people become involved in sport through a series of shifting, back-and-forth decisions made within the structural, ideological, and cultural context of their social worlds' (p. 21).

Source: Coakley and White (1992). Reproduced by permission

Qualitative studies have investigated gender and social class factors associated with different forms of participation of children in various forms of physical activity. In a study of the images in teenage girls' magazines, Cockburn (2001) found two polarized female images: one actively involved in romantic activities vs. the aberrant female involved in physical activity. Teenage girls who she interviewed resented these stereotypical images and felt that it did not accord with the everyday conflicts they experienced. However, they also voiced concern at the increasing social restraints on their involvement in sporting activities. For example, one girl said: 'when I was at primary school I just used to go out there and I'd do anything . . . I wouldn't care what other people thought, I'd just go out and enjoy it . . . now it's more, "Oh my god can I do this?" And you know, like everybody's looking at you . . . I hate it.'

Together, these studies confirm the importance of the various meanings associated with physical activity among children and young people. For teenagers, being cool and looking cool is the main issue.

Promoting Physical Activity

With the growing evidence on the health benefits of physical activity and exercise, governments and health authorities have become keen to promote greater participation. For example, in the UK, the Department of Health requires all health authorities to contribute to local programmes designed to promote greater physical activity (Department of Health, 2001). These have included population-, community-, school- and clinic-based interventions.

POPULATION-BASED STRATEGIES

Population-based strategies are designed to promote more widespread participation in physical activity in society. The strategies range from ones with an environmental focus, such as the introduction of cycle lanes in cities and reducing traffic speed, to mass media campaigns; the impact of these interventions varies. An evaluation of an intervention designed to promote physical activity (Sallis et al., 2007) found that it had a greater impact among women in the area that reported no unattended dogs and low crime in their neighbourhood, and among men who reported often seeing people being active in their neighbourhood.

However, these environmental supports for physical activity are not equally distributed in society. In a review of the literature, Taylor et al. (2006) identified the strong inverse relationship between what they termed physical activity-friendly environments and low-income and ethnic minority groups. To promote an activity friendly environment requires an 'environmental' or 'social justice' approach that aims to redress social inequalities in exposure to environmental hazards. We covered this issue in detail in Chapter 3.

In public buildings physical strategies have been employed to promote greater physical activity. It isn't rocket science: simply displaying posters near stairwells promotes greater usage (e.g. Anderson et al., 1998). A variant of this is the positioning of health promotion messages on the actual stair rises. A study of a shopping centre in England found that such an initiative more than doubled stair usage (Kerr et al., 2001). While these cheap and simple measures are important, the many occupational hazards in the workplace, which are again unfairly distributed, cannot be ignored. An example of a participatory approach to challenging occupational and environmental hazards is given in Box 10.3.

BOX 10.3
INTERNATIONAL CASE STUDY:

Promoting environmental justice through 'Theatre of the Oppressed'

Environmental justice is concerned with building a campaign to challenge the environmental hazards in any community. An example of an environmental justice campaign is that developed by John Sullivan and his colleagues in several low-income communities in Texas.

(Continued)

(Continued)

The campaigns were participatory and informed by Augusto Boal's Theatre of the Oppressed. This approach uses drama as a means of expressing the community's dissatisfaction with current environmental arrangements and demanding improved living and working conditions. During the drama, or Forum, the participants are encouraged to reflect upon the environmental hazards and what can be done about them. The Forum is not expected to be a passive affair but rather the spectator is transformed into a 'spect-actor' who is prepared to take action after to Forum to campaign for environmental justice.

'There is no place for passivity at a Forum; Theatre of the Oppressed primes spectators to apply their powers to deconstruct what they see and 'prepare for action' (Sullivan et al., 2008: 171).

The third population-based strategy is mass media campaigns. A survey of European countries found that residents of those countries who perceived that public policy was promoting physical activity were more likely to report participating in such activity (Von Lengerke et al., 2004). However, moves to promote exercise through healthy public policy must be distinguished from the further promotion of the ideology of individualistic self-control (Marks, 1996). Although middle-class adults may be attracted to this message, many people from working class and more deprived backgrounds may treat it with cynicism (Crossley, 2003). Often, there seems to be a disconnection between healthy public policies and the material circumstances of people's everyday lives (Murray and Campbell, 2003) and it invites the same 'victim-blaming' criticism as traditional health education (Crawford, 1985). An inactive and obese person might well feel that they are to blame, and feel more than their fair share of stigma and shame.

COMMUNITY-BASED STRATEGIES

Interventions that have attempted to increase participation in communities have often been based upon SCMs, especially the TTM. Marcus et al. (1992) designed an exercise intervention for volunteers recruited from a community. The character of the intervention was matched to the initial stage of change of the volunteers. On follow-up there was evidence of a significant increase in involvement in exercise commensurate with the initial stage. In a subsequent randomized controlled trial, Marcus et al. (1994) found further supportive evidence. At three-month follow-up the participants in the stage-matched group showed stage progression (i.e. greater interest or involvement in exercise) while those in the standard group showed stage stability or regression.

Clarke and Eves (1997) found partial support for the TTM in describing the willingness of sedentary adults to participate in an exercise programme prescribed by their family doctor. They classified the participants into the pre-contemplation, contemplation and preparation stages reflecting the fact that at this stage they had not begun the programme. As predicted, the cons of participation in the exercise programme decreased across the stages, although there was little change in the pros. The barriers to participation identified were lack of support, lack of facilities, dislike of exercise and lack of time. The importance of dislike of exercise declined across the stages while the importance of lack of facilities increased. The finding that lack of time was used as frequently by those in the pre-contemplation as those in the preparation stage was interpreted as evidence that it is more a justification for lack of participation rather than a convincing reason.

Other studies have expanded the basic TTM to consider the importance of *outcome expectancies* (Williams et al., 2005). For example, Fridlund et al. (2008) investigated the role of anticipated positive and negative emotions. This study was a three-month follow-up of a sample of healthy, community dwelling adults who agreed to participate in an exercise programme. Fridlund and colleagues found that anticipated emotions interacted with stage of behaviour change in predicting activity adoption and maintenance. At baseline, they found that anticipated positive emotions of success were lowest in those classed in the pre-contemplation stage while anticipated negative emotions of failure were highest in those classed in the maintenance stage. Further, anticipated positive emotions of success predicted physical activity adoption and maintenance.

Hutchison et al. (2013) presented an alternative to the dominant SCMs of physical activity promotion derived from in-depth interviews with a sample of previously sedentary adults who had successfully completed a physical activity course. This alternative model consists of cues, leading to certain cognitions and action determinants and then to behavioural responses (physical activity). Underlying this model were intervening core values that were the key to behaviour change. The most important values that were associated with uptake of physical activity were social orientation (importance of close interpersonal relations), competence orientation (importance of personal success or competence), control orientation (importance of independence of action) and health orientation (importance of health). It is argued that the derivation of this model from detailed interviews provided ecological validity. However, absent from their model is the broader socio-cultural and political context within which the values draw meaning.

Finally, a large number of studies have considered the role of body image in evaluating the impact of exercise interventions. A review of 41 such studies by Hausenblas and Fallon (2006) concluded that exercisers had a more positive body image and that participants had a more positive body image post-intervention.

SCHOOL-BASED ACTIVITIES

Since children and young people spend much of their daily lives at schools or colleges they have become the focus in promoting physical activity. The two main opportunities for children to participate in physical activity at school are during less-supervised breaks and during physical education classes.

Some research has focused on the less-organized physical activity that occurs during break times. It has been found that the larger the schoolyard, the more physical activity. Also, if there are playground markings indicative of sporting/play activities, children are more likely to engage in physical activity (Escalante et al., 2012).

There is a long history of physical education (PE) in schools. This tradition, especially in British schools, has been based upon a nineteenth century model of teaching children to perform a range of very masculinistic and militaristic physical exercises where discipline and stoicism are key features (Paechter, 2003). Perhaps girls and less 'macho' or 'sporty' boys are rather more reluctant to give their all to many of these exercises. In their study of teenage girls, Cockburn and Clarke (2002) noted that: 'Many of these traditional and stereotypical rituals in PE contradict the notion of acceptable/desirable "appearance" within the teenage feminine culture and cause conflict for girls' (p. 654). Indeed, this conflict with the dominant image of femininity can lead to a clash between what Cockburn and Clarke describe as two polarized identities:A girl can identify herself as a masculinized 'doer' of PE (a 'tomboy'), or a feminized ('girlie') 'non-doer' of sport and physical activity. It is highly unlikely that girls can achieve both physically active and (heterosexually) desirable, so they are obliged to choose between these images (p. 661). Further, in her study Paechter (2003) found that some girls demonstrate their femininity through deliberate resistance to PE.

Boys who are poor at school sporting activities also often attract ridicule from their more athletic peers. This is especially the case in those schools that emphasize the more physical sports. These games in which the boys are expected to demonstrate their strength have many similarities with military exploits (Paechter, 2003)

In a study of PE in Australian schools, Wright et al. (2003) showed how its character was clearly related to social class. Boys, especially those from affluent backgrounds, participated in organized team sports from an early age. For these boys, participation in sports was a very important part of the school ethos and identity. This led Wright et al. (2003) to describe the social practices around sport as 'powerful disciplinary technologies (Foucault, 1980) whereby particular kinds of citizens, forms of masculinity and ways of interacting with physical activity are shaped' (p. 25). In this setting the young people are being trained to strongly identify with their school team and to act in a particularly aggressive way towards others. Sport thus becomes part of the training for a form of officer class and, indeed, competitions between teams representing schools, colleges or even nations take on some of the characteristics of battle or warfare.

In an Australian study of participation in sports and physical activity by rural teenage girls, Casey et al. (2009) found that the girls reported that they were more keen to participate if the activities were fun, involved being with their friends, and were supported by family and friends through role modelling and feedback.

An alternative to this technology of disciplining young people through physical activity is one that offers emancipatory potential. This approach is one informed by Freire's pedagogy and that aims to enhance the children's experience of themselves as physical beings in the world (Lloyd, 2008). It is an approach infused with happiness and laughter in the present as well as a questioning and curiosity about the future. This approach is designed to experiment with forms of physical activity and explore new ways through which the students can enhance their bodies. An example of this was the study by Holt et al. (2013) that considered the importance of after-school programmes. Their study used a participatory action design deliberately working with the children to identify the activities they liked. They found that the children especially enjoyed those activities that provided challenges and 'adventures' and engaged with their imaginations.

Finally, in a comprehensive review of school-based physical activity programmes, Erwin et al. (2012) drew attention to the many difficulties involved in conducting comparative evaluations. They highlight the many difficulties of integrating physical activities into the school day especially with the increasing attention to improving academic performance.

CLINIC-BASED PHYSICAL ACTIVITY PROGRAMMES

Exercise interventions are often targeted at certain sub-groups of the population including people who are overweight, elderly or who suffer from particular health problems. The evaluations of these programmes have often been quantitative in design and have identified a limited number of social cognition variables that predict adherence to the programmes. In a review of the impact of exercise programmes for coronary heart disease, Woodgate and Brawley (2008) identified the importance of personal efficacy. They distinguished between task self-efficacy and self-regulatory-efficacy.

A common problem with exercise programmes is that while many people sign up for such programmes it has been estimated that 50% or more drop out after a short period of participation (Dishman, 1986). Box 10.4 provides a summary of four behavioural strategies identified by Robinson and Rogers (1994) as being associated with increased adherence. However, this is a very schematic outline and there is a need for further research into the dynamic nature of the exercise behaviour change process.

BOX 10.4
BEHAVIOURAL STRATEGIES TO IMPROVE ADHERENCE TO EXERCISE PROGRAMMES

Stimulus control: providing cues that remind people of the programme.

Consequent control: providing rewards and punishments for participation.

Cognitive behavioural modification: increasing people's belief that they have control over the design and conduct of the programme.

Behavioural treatment packages: combining behavioural and cognitive strategies.

Source: Robinson and Rogers (1994). Reproduced by permission

Most of the interventions targeted at enhancing physical activity have used quantitative assessments. This restricts the opportunity to clarify what the participants actually feel about the various interventions. Several recent evaluations that have used qualitative methods have emphasized the importance of perceived enjoyment. A study by Daley et al. (2008) included a qualitative study within the larger randomized controlled trial of an exercise intervention for obese adolescents. This revealed that the participants expressed a variety of feelings including feeling more energetic and pleased about potential weight loss. The research emphasized the importance of positive feelings and enjoyment in the programme as being central to its success. The researchers concluded that 'it is unlikely that young people who are obese will commit to a regular active lifestyle unless they have opportunities to experience positive feelings from engagement' (p. 816).

Another qualitative study (Graham et al., 2008) explored the experiences of people with chronic illness and disability who participated in a physical exercise programme. Analysis of the interviews identified three polarized themes, which are summarized in Box 10.5. In reviewing these themes it is apparent that the intervention is effective not just through improving physical ability but also on more social and psychological processes, in particular, the value of the activity intervention in enhancing mood, social connections and identity.

BOX 10.5
REACTIONS TO PARTICIPATING IN AN EXERCISE PROGRAMME FOR DISABLED PEOPLE

Passive distress vs. active mood management: whereas disability can contribute to a passive inactive lifestyle, participation can enhance mood and reduce patterns of rumination. For example: 'My energy wasn't great. I would get into the house and just sit down and say, "I can't be bothered", I was doing nothing at all. I was just going home, watching TV all day. I don't do that now because I think of the exercises . . . I imagine myself within the group and I do a few [exercises] at home. I'm sort of motivated now.'

Identity erosion vs. identity renewal: whereas disability and chronic illness can lead to feelings of identity loss, participation in physical activity contributed to a new identity of physical competence. For example, 'From being an outgoing, physical sort of person you whether bedridden. That was mind-blowing. Terrible. Shattered. Suddenly this residual bit of fitness I had all my life was going out the window.' The exercise programme stopped that slide into inactivity.

Detachment vs. connection: while disability can lead to detachment from familiar valued aspects of everyday life such as friends and familiar bodily functioning the intervention provided new connections. For example, 'Since getting so unwell I have lost contact with a lot of people I would have met when I was out and about. Now I don't have those kinds of contacts because I'm inside most of the time. I meet people here [day centre]. It's a bit like being exiled or being cast out – you think I'd leprosy sometimes! [laughs] Maybe I'll get a bell to warn people off.'

Source: Graham et al. (2008). Reproduced by permission

Further, these strategies are largely focused at the individual level. They ignore the social context and the social meaning of exercise and physical activity. Social approaches attempt to widen the traditional individual change approach to include 'changes in social networks and structures, organizational norms, regulatory policies, and the physical environment as a means of enhancing long-term maintenance of the target behavior' (King, 1994: 1406).

ALTERNATIVE FORMS OF PHYSICAL ACTIVITY

There is increasing challenge to the dominance of the functional approaches to promoting physical activity with its attendant emphasis on physical health. Alternative strategies consider such issues as the more social, emotional and aesthetic aspects of physical activity. Three such alternative forms are dance, walking groups and lifestyle sports.

Dance

There has been a recent growth of interest in the health benefits of dance. It is considered a very non-intrusive means of promoting participation in physical activity. However, participation in dance is more than just a means of enhancing physical health. Fensham and Gardner (2005) argue that within dance 'the body is not simply an object upon or through which discipline or utility must be imposed, but [. . .] through which values, meanings and pleasures are enacted and created' (p. 15). Dancing can be considered a means of developing cultural capital (Bourdieu, 1986). This form of capital allows one to withdraw from the economic necessities of life and distance oneself from 'practical urgencies'.

Dance is attractive to men and women from different social backgrounds. For example, Baker (2002) notes that especially for younger people dance is an important way of playing being sexual in which 'they try a more sexual presence on for size' (p. 18). Among older people it is a very enjoyable means of developing social interaction (Paulson, 2005).

Walking Groups

Walking, especially in natural, semi-rural or rural settings, can be both physically and mentally exhilarating. Priest (2007) investigated what she termed the 'healing balm effect' of using a walking group to feel better. Priest combined methods from grounded theory and ethnography to explore members' experience of a mental-health day-service walking group. An overall model, the healing balm effect, integrated seven categories to describe the 'healing' properties of the experience: Closer to what is more natural; Feeling safe; Being part; Striving; Getting away; Being me; and Finding meaning. Several of the features reported by Priest would not be present, or only partially present, walking in towns or cities. The most beneficial urban walking places are likely to be commons or parks.

Cauwenberg et al. (2012) used walk-along interviews to identify environmental factors that influence walking for transportation among older adults. Access to facilities, walking facilities, traffic safety, familiarity, safety from crime, social contact, aesthetics and weather were frequently mentioned as influencing walking among participants.

Kassavou et al. (2013) studied environmental factors that influence walking in groups using a walk-along interview procedure with ten leaders of walking groups. The leaders took groups to parks, city centres, or did laps. Kassavou et al. identified the characteristics of place that influenced the type of walking that people do in groups and the processes used by walkers to find meaning in the places they walk. They found that the walking places were 'nodes' where people formed social networks, not restricted to the specific place (e.g. the park during walks) but expanded beyond that to other places for socializing. Walking alone would seemingly serve a different function, that of reflection, problem solving and creative thinking.

Lifestyle Sports

Over the past 10–20 years a counter-establishment form of sporting activity has grown in popularity. A report by Tomlinson et al. (2005) collectively termed these activities as 'lifestyle sports'. They are also frequently termed *extreme sports* and include such activities as bungee jumping, white-water rafting, rock-climbing and surfing. These activities are especially popular among young people.

There is a growing body of research on who participates in these activities and the perceived character of the experience. Willig (2008a) analysed detailed interviews with a small sample of eight extreme sports practitioners. The interviews were phenomenological in orientation and sought to grasp the meaning of the sports to the practitioners. Willig identified what she described as four constitutive themes and five other themes in these interviews. These are summarized in Box 10.6.

BOX 10.6
MEANINGS OF EXTREME SPORTS

Constitutive themes

Context: the environment or social context within which the sport has a particular enhanced meaning, e.g. solitude and the experience of mountain climbing.
Challenge: the opportunity to push oneself to the limits both physically and mentally, e.g. overcoming the fear of jumping from a great height.
Suffering: the possibility of pain, injury or death.
Other people: other people being aware that they were practising these sports, e.g. being different from others.

Additional themes

Mastery and skill: the need for specialized knowledge and skill.
Contrasts: the presence of two apparently contradictory qualities, e.g. the beauty/calmness of the landscape and the challenge of the sport.
Being in the present: the focus on the immediate to the exclusion of other thoughts.
Compulsion: the strongly felt need to engage in these activities.
Pleasure: the enlightened feelings of pleasure and excitement.

Source: Willig (2008a)

Unlike populist characterizations of these activities as reckless or sensation seeking it was apparent from these interviews that the participants carefully considered them. Willig suggested that participation in these activities enabled the participants to attain a particular state of being comparable to what Csikszentmihalyi (1997) has termed 'flow'. This is the experience of a sort of unity of the self, world and activity in which the more mundane, everyday worries and concerns become less important. As such, it could be argued that participation in these sports is a reaction to broader cultural demands on young people in our consumer society, which provides limited opportunity for such experiences. However, the individualistic nature of such activities can pose potential threats. For example, Willig cautions that while participation in these activities may be therapeutic, they may also lead to dependency.

AFTER ALL THAT

The past generation has seen the promotion within Western societies of a neo-liberal philosophy promoting greater individual responsibility and minimal government intervention together with market fundamentalism (Ayo, 2012). This is particularly apparent within the physical activity arena. Harrington and Fullagar (2013) detailed how the promotion of the active living agenda by many Western governments positions the individual as responsible and ignores the other social and material constraints on participation. They note that 'the decline of the welfare state and the rise of liberal notions of responsibility have occurred alongside an increased reliance on market forces and voluntary organizations with stretched resources to provide opportunities for active leisure and sport' (Coalter, 2007). In their study of Australian sport and recreation workers they found that, while the workers were very committed to promoting enhanced participation, they were unsure of their impact in the light of limited resources. Instead people from disadvantaged backgrounds found it difficult to engage with these activities. In particular, this led to victim-blaming of those such as overweight women, migrants, low income families, older people, and those with disabilities who found it difficult to participate in organized physical activities.

Ayo (2012) noted the pervasiveness of the active living agenda within Western societies. This ranges from marketing of membership of sports clubs to sportswear. This promotion of an active health agenda contributes to what Galvin (2002) has termed a 'consumerist frenzy'. People join sports clubs and wear sports clothes but do not participate in sporting activities. Membership of elite sports clubs and purchase of expensive sportswear form part of a process of gaining enhanced social status and reinforcing social inequalities.

BOX 10.7
HAVING A PET DOG

Unsurprisingly, having a dog to walk contributes greater physical activity to owners. A Canadian study found that dog owners walked almost twice as much as non-dog owners (300 min/week compared with 168 min/week; Brown and Rhodes, 2006). The benefits of dog ownership can also extend beyond physical health. There is evidence that it is associated with improved psychological health (Serpell, 1991). Taking the dog for a walk also leads to greater opportunity for social interaction. There is evidence that dog owners report more social contact and having longer conversations when out walking than non-dog owners (Beck and Meyers, 1996). It has also been suggested that dog ownership strengthens commitment to weight loss programmes. While most of the evidence is for adults there is also evidence that children in families with dogs report more time walking (Owen et al., 2010) and that they are less likely to be overweight (Timperio et al., 2008). Salmon and Timerio (2011) suggest that other social and psychological benefits of dog ownership for children include enhanced feelings of well-being and fewer feelings of loneliness. Boisvert and Harrell (2014) further suggest a range of spiritual benefits of dog ownership for children including increased feelings of joy, creativity, hopefulness and sense of connectedness with self and others, and a sense of wholeness with the universe. They also report social and psychological benefits of dog ownership for children who are overweight.

Figure 10.3

FUTURE RESEARCH

1. Public participation in physical activity is continuing to decline, including children and young people. We need to know more about why.
2. There is still a need to explore the specific impact of exercise interventions on the health of different population groups to demonstrate that increased activity actually improves health.
3. Research is needed to develop our understanding of the different meanings for different sub-groups of the population.
4. Participatory action research offers an opportunity to increase our understanding of different perceptions of various types of physical activity programmes.

SUMMARY

1 Interest in exercise has waxed and waned over the years. The past generation has witnessed increasing interest in the health benefits of exercise.

2 A large proportion of the populations of Western societies is sedentary.

3 Results of several comprehensive surveys indicate that moderate degrees of physical activity have both physical and psychological benefits.

4 There is some evidence to suggest that excessive exercise can have negative health effects. It may even prove fatal.

5 The degree of participation declines during adolescence, especially among girls.

6 In adulthood, participation is lesser among females, those from poorer social positions and those from ethnic minorities.

7 Various psychological factors have been found to be associated with participation in both childhood and adulthood.

8 The meaning of exercise is linked to the varying social contexts. For young people, if it isn't perceived as 'cool' or as 'fun', they won't do it.

9 Exercise participation programmes can be either population based or aimed at high-risk groups. The main problem with both forms of programme is adherence that is generally low.

10 Alternative methods of activity such as dance, group walking and lifestyle sports are capable of evoking joy, excitement and pleasure, which means that the activity is more likely to be repeated.

PART 3

HEALTH PROMOTION AND DISEASE PREVENTION

In this part of the book we review some of the main lines of inquiry into health promotion and disease prevention. We critically analyse theory, research and practice, and recommend improvements in health care that flow out of this psychological perspective.

In Chapter 11 we discuss health information, communication and the role of health literacy. We begin with an introduction to communication theory and discuss the e-health revolution, research about health care professional–patient communication and health message framing. We consider how health literacy can influence people's ability to access, understand and use health information. Finally, we examine strategies to make health communication more effective by enhancing the skills of health care providers and service users, simplifying the health care system and promoting health-sustaining environments.

In Chapter 12 we explore theoretical approaches to the study of stress and coping, and research on stress as a cause of physical illness. We begin with an account of stimulus, response and interactional perspectives, together with a critical analysis of them. We look at alternative approaches to stress management and assessments of their effectiveness. After discussing methodological problems confronting research on stress and illness, we examine the evidence linking stress to cardiovascular disease, cancer and infectious diseases.

In Chapter 13 we consider two main forms of disease prevention available within health care systems: screening and immunization. Screening programmes are designed to identify individuals who, because of certain personal characteristics, are considered at risk of developing a certain disease. Immunization programmes are designed to vaccinate people who are at risk because of their exposure to environmental pathogens. Various social and psychological processes are involved in explaining the pros and cons of these different processes of risk management.

In Chapter 14 we focus on the psychological dimensions of health promotion. We describe two contrasting approaches: the behaviour change approach and the community development approach. Examples of interventions using each approach are critically examined and criteria for evaluating the effectiveness of health promotion interventions are presented. We conclude with a discussion of 'healthist' discourse in health promotion and its implications.

11 INFORMATION, COMMUNICATION AND HEALTH LITERACY

The problem with communication is the illusion that it has been accomplished.

(George Bernard Shaw)

OUTLINE

Here we discuss health information, communication and the role of health literacy. We begin with an introduction to communication theory and discuss the e-health revolution, research about health care professional–patient communication and health message framing. We consider how health literacy can influence people's ability to access, understand and use health information. Finally, we examine strategies to make health communication more effective by enhancing the skills of health care providers and service users, simplifying the health care system and promoting health-sustaining environments.

WHAT IS HEALTH COMMUNICATION?

Health communication refers to all interpersonal, organizational or mass communication that concerns health. It can occur in various *contexts* (e.g. doctor–patient communication, public health campaigns); be applied in a variety of *settings* (e.g. clinics, schools, workplaces, online communities); use a variety of *channels* (e.g. face-to-face communication, posters, social media); deliver a variety of *messages* (e.g. healthy eating, smoking cessation, safe sex); and serve a variety of *purposes* (e.g. risk assessment, communication of diagnosis, service awareness, advocacy).

To understand the nature of health communication, first we need to understand what is meant by the term 'communication'.

Communication refers to the exchange of information between one person, or 'entity', and one or more others. There is a magic to excellent communication that can be instantly recognized but precisely how this 'magic' is achieved is slightly mysterious. To describe how messages are transmitted in the communication process, Shannon and Weaver (1949) proposed one of the best-known (and longest lasting) models of communication. As we have seen, most models have a shelf life of about 15 or 20 years, but this model has been mentioned in dispatches for 65 years and is about to draw its pension. The model has five basic components:

- *Source* – where the message is coming from.
- *Transmitter* – something that 'encodes' the message into signals.
- *Channel* – where encoded signals are transmitted.
- *Receiver* – something that 'decodes' the signal back into the message.
- *Destination* – where the message goes.

As an example, writing and reading this book form part of a communication process. As authors (source), we have a message to communicate to you, our reader (destination). We transmit this message through printed text (transmitter) using this book (channel). You read the book with your eyes and then decode the message with your brain (receiver). Hopefully the message will reach you as we originally intended! However, *noise* can also interfere in the communication process. Noise can be translated literally as *physical noise* (e.g. a crackly phone line or loud music in the background), *cognitive noise* (e.g. being distracted by other concerns such as remembering to telephone a friend, feed the cat, or water the pot plants), *affective noise* (e.g. you may be feeling anxious about a forthcoming meeting with your instructor), or *socio-cultural noise* (e.g. we write 'cool' as in 'temperature' and you read 'sick' as in 'awesome'). Considering these factors, it is important that all forms of noise are minimized.

Originally developed in a technical report for a telephone company, Shannon and Weaver's model evolved over time and is the simplest and most influential model of communication. As a receiver of health information, it is important to consider the *message* and its *source*. This is a useful descriptive model that serves a didactic function but precious little more. What is the message being communicated? How reliable and accurate is the source? For health information providers, it is important to consider the *purpose* of communication and the target *destination* – who are they trying to reach and why? How will they effectively reach their audience considering personal backgrounds, capabilities, and socio-cultural contexts in which they operate? What would be the best mode of communication to transmit information? How can distortions (noise) be minimized and clarity in understanding maximized? What are the factors that compete for the recipients' attention and what strategies can be used to ensure that the communication aims are achieved? These are some questions health communication researchers look into.

In this chapter, we discuss health care professional–patient communication, health-message framing and e-health. We also consider how health literacy influences effective health communication and the strategies that can be used to promote it.

HEALTH CARE PROFESSIONAL–PATIENT COMMUNICATION

Effective communication between health care professionals (HCPs) and patients is integral to health promotion, disease prevention and treatment, and is an essential skill that can greatly improve the quality and efficiency of care (Mauksch et al., 2008). A systematic review by Rodin et al. (2009) suggested that the way HCPs relate to and communicate with service users can have a profound impact on their psychosocial adjustment, decision making, treatment compliance and satisfaction. As shown in Figure 11.1, there are direct and indirect pathways that link effective communication with health outcomes (Street et al., 2009). The direct path highlights benefits related to improved survival and remission rates, enhanced emotional well-being, pain control, functional ability, vitality and reduced suffering. Good communication may also facilitate better HCP–patient relationships that can improve intermediate outcomes such as access to care, treatment adherence, self-management, support and trust in the health care system.

In a 'classic' study, Byrne and Long (1976) identified different doctors' styles of communicating with patients. They analysed audiotape interactions from 71 GPs and about 2,500 patients. They identified four diagnostic styles and seven prescriptive styles used by the doctors. These styles constituted a continuum from 'patient-centred' to 'doctor-centred' styles. A **patient-centred communication style** makes use of the patient's knowledge and experience through techniques such as silence, listening and reflection; whereas a **doctor-centred communication style** makes use of the doctor's knowledge and skill with minimal input from the patient. Using leadership theory Huynh and Sweeny (2013) updated these communication styles and outlined three patterned approaches to patient care among clinicians: (1) *laissez-faire* (negligent and unsympathetic

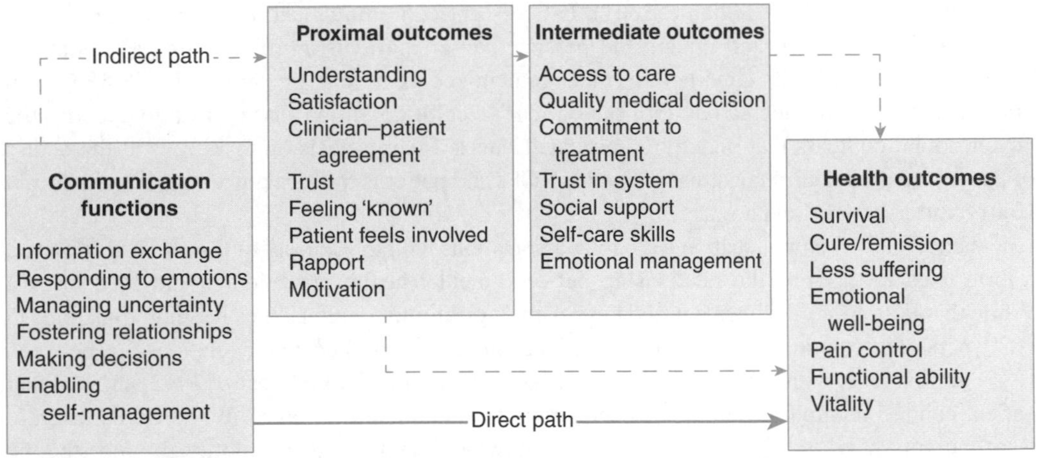

Figure 11.1 Communication and health outcomes (Adapted from Street et al., 2009)

towards patients); (2) *transactional* (sets health goals and provides patients with instructions, feedback, and reinforcement to pursue these behaviour goals); and (3) *transformational* (provides health goals, inspires and motivates patients to be personally engaged in those goals).

Communication styles between HCPs and patients have evolved immensely over the past 50 years, moving from a doctor-centred style towards a more patient-centred approach (Taylor, 2009). The evolution of HCP–patient communication has been the product of shifting social norms and expectations of the role of HCPs and patients. There has been a transformation in the way doctors are perceived by many patients, and by doctors themselves.

Since the 1970s there has been a movement towards a consumerist model of health care that places patients to the fore. While doctors and HCPs were once viewed as figures of authority, patient empowerment has become a trend that encourages service users to question authority, demand more from practitioners and be more proactive in their own health. The major criticism of doctors' traditional communication style was that it was characterized by working to rigid agendas and little listening to patients' accounts and discussion of treatment options. Thus a more patient-centred approach has been called for and, to varying degrees across different settings, this has been received. Of course, like anything else, there are huge cultural variations and wide individual differences between physicians and also in what any individual patient actually needs and wants. For example, a patient who has high internal locus of control and high health value is more likely to seek health information that he or she can use to improve their health chances (Wallston et al., 1976).

PATIENT-CENTRED COMMUNICATION

Patient-centred communication refers to communication among HCPs, service users and their families intended to promote patient-centred care. The ethos of patient-centred care lies within 'compassionate, empathetic and responsive care that reflects the needs, values and preferences of patients' (Institute of Medicine, 2001). Patient-centred communication is a communications style that aims to elicit and understand perspectives of patients and their families about the patient's particular health condition, its management and treatment (Epstein et al., 2005). Its aim is to reach a shared understanding of the patient's health condition that takes into account the psychosocial contexts that underpin their experiences. Shared-decision making is at the centre of patient-centred communication; it enables HCPs and patients to share power and responsibility (Barry and Edgman-Levitan, 2012).

Patient-centred communication has strong associations with the concept of **therapeutic alliance**, a term used to describe the relationship between mental health practitioners and their clients. While this term has often been confined to psychological interventions, the changing dynamics in HCP–patient interactions has led to the emergence of the idea of therapeutic relationships between HCPs and patients with physical illnesses. A systematic review by Pinto et al. (2012) showed that patient-centred communication can indeed strengthen therapeutic alliance. When HCPs listen to what patients have to say, ask questions and show sensitivity to their emotional concerns, the therapeutic alliance is reinforced. Evidence from a systematic review also suggests that having a good therapeutic alliance between HCPs and patients can positively influence treatment outcomes through improvements in symptoms and general health status (Hall et al., 2010). While there were mixed findings concerning the impact of patient-centred communication on clinical outcomes, it was shown that this style of communication can facilitate patient satisfaction and self-management (Rathert et al., 2013). It has also been shown that tailoring communication for patients can improve medicine adherence (Linn et al., 2014). Furthermore, taking time for reciprocal discussion and alleviating patient anxiety has also been shown to promote greater referral for cardiovascular rehabilitation (Pourhabib et al., 2014).

Patient-centred communication promotes knowledge, trust, loyalty and positive regard between HCPs and patients. The depth of the therapeutic relationship can also be strengthened through longitudinal care (i.e. seeing the same doctor over time). Ridd et al. (2009) suggest that having positive consultations with the same doctor over time can build depth to the HCP–patient relationship. However, longitudinal care alone is not enough to develop deeper HCP–patient relationships; it must also engender positive experiences with the care received. Unsurprisingly, when given the choice, patients are unlikely to choose the same doctor if the experience is negative.

Although the rhetoric around patient-centred communication is used to signify patient participation and autonomy, it also implies greater personal responsibility for health (Coulter, 1999). Therefore caution is necessary when promoting discourses of patient-centred care to avoid disproportionate burdens of care and responsibility being placed on patients and families. A balance must be reached between patient empowerment and responsibility, while leaving HCPs accountable.

E-HEALTH AND TELEMEDICINE

With the arrival of the World Wide Web, individuals were able to gain instant access to almost *any* information from any source at their fingertips. This amazing technical achievement created the '**e-health** revolution'. 'E-health' is a general term referring to the application of digital information and communication technology (ICT) to health care. The health care world is experiencing a paradigm shift like no other as a consequence of a virtual 'explosion' in digital technology. West and Miller (2009) described the situation in the USA as follows:

> Websites such as WebMD.com, MedlinePlus.gov, MerckSource.com, HealthFinder.gov, and MayoClinic.com answer health-related questions and provide links to discussion groups about particular illnesses. In states such as Massachusetts, California, New York, and Michigan, consumers can visit state health department sites and compare performance data on the quality of care. The US government has a website that evaluates 2,500 hospitals on mortality rates, room cleanliness, and call button response and on how their patients judge the quality of the care that they provide. Some physicians encourage patients to use e-mail or web messaging instead of telephone calls or in-office visits for simple issues such as appointments, prescription renewals, referrals, or brief consultations. And digital diagnostic systems, decision-support software for health care providers, telemedicine (medical care provided by televideo or telephone), and computer-aided self-help tools also are available.
>
> (West and Miller, 2009: 1)

Initially, in the 1990s, Internet access was slow and 'clunky' because it required dial-up access. By the 2000s, many users had faster, broadband access that allowed continuous browsing, downloading, telephoning, videoconferencing, teaching and learning, public or private networking, commercial marketing, buying and selling, and gaming. The capabilities in health care referred to by West and Miller are expanding daily and, to an increasing extent, have global reach. By 30 June 2012, there were approximately 2.5 billion users from a population of 7 billion (35%). Penetration varies by region and there is still a long way to go in Africa and Asia, although one billion Asians were already using the Internet by mid-2012. Access and penetration are projected to increase (Internet World Stats, 2014). The Internet is bringing a shift in the patient role from *passive recipient* to *active consumer* of information. In fact, many patients are far more than *consumers*; they are among the most innovative *creators* of information and *critics* of health care provision through their personal websites, social media, blogging, forums, noticeboards and chat rooms. There has never existed such a powerful and sophisticated technology to boost and foster patient empowerment and engagement in health care. The aphorism 'knowledge is power' has never been more apt.

One review begins with the words:

> The right person in the right place and at the right time is not always possible; telemedicine offers the potential to give audio and visual access to the appropriate clinician for patients. Advances in information and communication technology (ICT) in the area of video-to-video communication have led to growth in telemedicine applications in recent years. For these advances to be properly integrated into healthcare delivery, a regulatory framework, supported by definitive high-quality research, should be developed.
>
> (Amadi-Obi et al., 2014)

Who can disagree with these sentiments? As the potential for the expansion of telemedicine is huge, there will be an increasing role for health psychology researchers to climb aboard. This has implications for health psychology training. Courses in e-health should become a mandatory component.

The doctor is no longer the fount of all wisdom that he/she once was. By 2013 in the USA, more than a third of adults were already using the Internet to self-diagnose (Kuehn, 2013). Based on the US Health Information National Trends Survey (HINTS) ($n = 2{,}338$), those using the Internet for health information tend to be younger, more educated, higher income and prefer numbers rather than words to describe risk (Koch-Weser et al., 2010). These trends will shift over time as the entire population becomes computer literate and Internet savvy. McMullan (2006) found that the majority of health-related Internet searches by patients are usually carried out before a clinical encounter. The usual purpose of these searches is to gather information before deciding whether to implement self-care and/or get professional help. The Internet is also helpful in formulating better informed questions to ask the doctor, saving precious clinical time. Additionally, Internet searches may be carried out after the clinical encounter for reassurance or to appease dissatisfaction with the information provided by the HCP.

Similar results were found in an EU survey ($n = 7{,}022$) in which those who frequently used the Internet for health information were usually more inquisitive and self-reliant about their health (Santana et al., 2011). As access to the Internet expands through the population, many more people everywhere will be able to become curious and self-reliant.

As Internet access expands to an even broader spectrum of society, and a greater proportion of people globally become computer-literate, there is almost limitless potential for e-health and telemedicine. Like the bank clerks and bus conductors of Merrie Olde England, some doctors and nurses may soon be in fear for their jobs! Fortunately for them, in spite of health information being widely available online, HCPs generally are still seen as the main sources of reliable information by patients/service users. For example, Kivits (2006) explored the impact of online information-seeking of patients on interactions with HCPs. She found that patients still acknowledged the primary role of HCPs in delivering health and medical information and that Internet searches complemented rather than opposed medical expertise. Similarly, Suziedelyte (2012) found that people who use e-health tend to consult HCPs more often, especially among those who have good health care coverage. Using data from the HINTS, Chung (2013) also found that men were more likely than women to have a conversation about information found on the Internet with HCPs. Ironically, those who had trouble understanding or trusting online health information were found to be no more likely to ask questions or seek guidance from HCPs.

Online platforms are widely used to share health data. There is a wide variety of available platforms including social media, Facebook, Twitter, wikis, forums, blogs, virtual communities and conferencing technology. These social networks are open for people who would like to talk, share information or find other individuals who have similar experiences to themselves. Some websites have chat rooms, discussion boards, email listings, information sheets and links to other useful websites for further information regarding the health condition, relevant treatments and services. In a qualitative study of an Internet forum for patients with systemic lupus erythematosus, Mazzoni and Cicognani (2014) found that participants post messages online to start new relationships, seek information, receive emotional support and contribute to discussions. This highlights how online support groups provide multiple benefits to suit the needs of its users.

Research has shown the benefit of empowerment obtained from online health support groups. For example, Van Uden-Kraan et al. (2008) interviewed 32 participants from breast cancer, arthritis and fibromyalgia online support groups. Members felt empowered by participating in these groups and felt that they helped to facilitate information exchange, encounter emotional support, find recognition, share experiences, help others and be amused together. Participants also felt that they were better informed, were more confident in their relationship with their physician, their treatment and their social environment. They felt more able to accept their condition, more optimistic and in control, and reported better self-esteem and social well-being. Furthermore, the use of online support groups fostered collective action among members. Although disempowering processes were also mentioned in this study (e.g. being unsure about the quality of the information, being confronted with negative sides of the disease, or being confronted with complainers) these were far less mentioned in comparison to its positive consequences. Chiu and Hsieh (2013) found that writing online blogs enabled cancer patients to reconstruct their life story, express closure of life and hope they will be remembered after their death. Reading other patients' stories influenced their own experiences of living with cancer. Sometimes, other patients influenced their perceptions of their prognosis more than their doctors.

Online health communities also facilitate self-management. Willis (2013) explored how patients with arthritis (n = 8,231) use online support groups to better manage their condition. By facilitating exchange of information and experience, online groups can act as peer-led self-management programmes that can help to improve the health literacy and experience of members concerning arthritis.

Apart from online support groups that support coping, there are also websites that encourage 'unhealthy' behaviours. For example, Mulveen and Hepworth (2006) explored participation in pro-anorexia websites and the relationship with disordered eating using interpretative phenomenological analysis. They found that some participants in 'pro-anorexia' websites routinely reported their attempts of losing weight and passed on tips and techniques to other members. Members of the pro-anorexia community appear to distinguish between *anorexia as a mental illness* versus *anorexia as a lifestyle choice* (also referred to as 'ana'). Describing anorexia as a personal choice is often backed up with challenges to medical authority, comparing it with earlier psychiatric discourses that defined homosexuality as a mental illness. Members feel that the web enables the freedom to speak openly within a safe and supportive space. Similarly, online spaces exist for non-suicidal self-injury groups. Lewis and Michal (2014) found that these e-community users are often motivated by the need to obtain and offer support to others.

The range of activities that can be carried out online offers numerous benefits. Moorhead et al. (2013) showed how online social media can be used to increase interactions, facilitate, share and obtain health information with other users. It widens access to health information and has the potential to influence health policy in the long run. However, the review also suggested that, despite its benefits, online users are still cautious about the lack of reliability, confidentiality and privacy of online health communication platforms.

The e-health revolution has many profound implications for health care systems. HCPs need to acknowledge that patients generally want to be fully informed about their concerns, illnesses, treatments and prognosis, and this information, whether reliable or not, will be available, searched and accessed by patients online. **Patient informatics** is becoming an increasingly useful addition to the training of HCPs by, first, increasing their own awareness, knowledge and skills through access to the Internet and, second, in learning how best to engage with the growing use of online health information by, and sophistication of, many service users.

GENDER AND SOCIAL DIFFERENCES IN HCP–PATIENT COMMUNICATION

Several studies have been carried out to explore gender and social differences in HCP–patient communication. Bertakis (2009) examined the influence of both physician and patient gender. New adult patients (n = 509) were prospectively and randomly assigned to family practice or internal medicine clinics at a university medical centre and followed-up after one year. The consultations were videotaped and analysed to examine doctor–patient communication styles. Bertakis found significant gender differences with female doctors providing more preventive services and psychosocial counselling while male doctors spent more time on technical practice behaviours (e.g. medical history taking and physical examination). Patient demographics, self-reported health status, patient satisfaction and use of health care services were also measured. Even after adjusting for patient characteristics and doctors' communication style, the patients of female doctors were more satisfied.

Researchers have also looked into gender dyads to understand whether the gender of both doctors and patients can influence these interactions. Sandhu et al. (2009) showed that same-sex dyads were characterized by friendlier and calmer tones than opposite-sex dyads. *Male doctor/male patient* (M/M) dyads were characterized by relative ease and equality between doctors and patients, with talk focused on the patients' social agenda more than other dyads. *Female doctor/female patient* (F/F) dyads were the most patient-centred and had longer consultations containing the most psychosocial aspects and bio-medical talk (medical and therapeutic issues); whereas *male doctor/female patient* (M/F) dyads were the least patient-centred. In M/F dyads, doctors spent more time discussing screening services and conducting physical examinations than in other dyads. Doctors in M/F dyads also made more presumptions about patients' histories. *Female doctors/male patient* (F/M) dyads were characterized by less ease between doctors and patients. In F/M dyads, doctors had the least friendly voice tone and patients were the most bored, compared with other dyads. Although these findings suggest tension around gender role conflict, there is also evidence that both doctors and patients try to collaborate despite the tension. This is reflected through frequent smiling among female doctors and least use of technical language; while male patients try to make partnering statements.

Researchers have also explored social factors in HCPs' use of patient-centred communication. Street et al. (2007) examined whether GPs' perceptions of patients influenced their use of patient-centred communication and the influence of socio-demographic characteristics. Audio-recordings of consultations between GPs (n = 29) and patients (n = 207) from ten outpatient settings in the USA were examined. GPs used patient-centred communication more among patients whom they perceived as more satisfied, more likely to adhere and those with better communication skills. GPs also used patient-centred communication among patients who expressed positive affect, were more involved, and who were perceived to be less contentious. Racial background also played a role. GPs in this study were more contentious with Black patients than patients from other racial backgrounds.

It is perhaps the on-going discussions around social inequities in health, discussed in Chapter 3, that has re-sparked interest in social differences in HCP–patient relationships. Verlinde et al. (2012) examined literature published between 1965 and 2011 on the social gradient in doctor–patient communication. Socio-economic status (SES) was operationalized by patients' income, education and occupation. Patients with lower SES received less socio-emotional talk and a more doctor-centred style from GPs. These interactions were characterized by less involvement in shared-decision making and more biomedical talk. Doctors also asked more questions, engaged in more physical examination, and gave less information and patient control over communication. On the other hand, patients from higher SES groups were given more information, more explanations and more emotional support. Doctors were more patient-centred with higher SES patients.

While several factors contribute to health gradients (Chapters 2 and 3), health inequities are evident even at a micro level in one-to-one interactions between patients and HCPs. Patients from higher SES groups have more confidence, are more opinionated, and ask for more explanations from HCPs than lower SES patients (Street, 1991; 1992; Street et al., 2005). While it may be convenient to simply examine patient characteristics and personal communication styles, it is important to recognize that these interactions are embedded in institutional and cultural contexts. Thus an ecological approach to HCP–patient communication is helpful in unravelling the factors that influence these interactions (Street et al., 2007).

Protheroe et al. (2013) explored perceptions of health care in different SES groups. Interviews with 35 patients from GP practices in socio-economically diverse areas of north-west England explored reasons why SES groups participate differently in health care. Patients from lower SES groups generally felt less able to ask questions when at the doctor's. Lower SES patients felt that asking questions could be construed as challenging the doctor. More proactive questioning and shared-decision making was evident among higher SES patients. To participate actively in health care, people must feel free to question or challenge doctors and other HCPs. In addition, and this is equally important, HCPS need to communicate effectively and answer the questions that are asked accurately and clearly.

MESSAGE FRAMING

The way messages are framed influences people's intentions and willingness to change their behaviour (Rothman and Salovey, 1997). Tversky and Kahneman's (1981) **prospect theory** proposed that people consider their 'prospects' (i.e. potential gains and losses) when making decisions and, therefore, people's preferences are sensitive to the framing of information. People tend to avoid risks when considering potential gains, but will be willing to take risks when considering potential losses. Gain- or loss-framed messages can be tailored to specific behaviours to maximize message effectiveness. **Gain-framed messages** give information about a health behaviour that emphasizes the benefits of taking action; whereas **loss-framed messages** give information that emphasizes the costs of failing to take action (see Figure 11.2).

Research into message framing has grown dramatically over recent years. Studies have been carried out to examine the effectiveness of health-message framing on improving breast screening uptake (Consedine et al., 2007), condom use (Garcia-Retamero and Cokely, 2011), maternal influenza immunization (Frew et al., 2014), physical activity (Berry and Carson, 2010) and reducing salt intake (Riet et al., 2010). While findings from a meta-analytic review by Gallagher and Updegraff (2012) showed no significant differences in screening behaviours between loss- and gain-framed messages, gain-framed messages were more likely than loss-framed messages to encourage prevention behaviours such as smoking cessation and physical activity. Subsequently, Updegraff and Rothman (2013) identified two major approaches in message framing research:

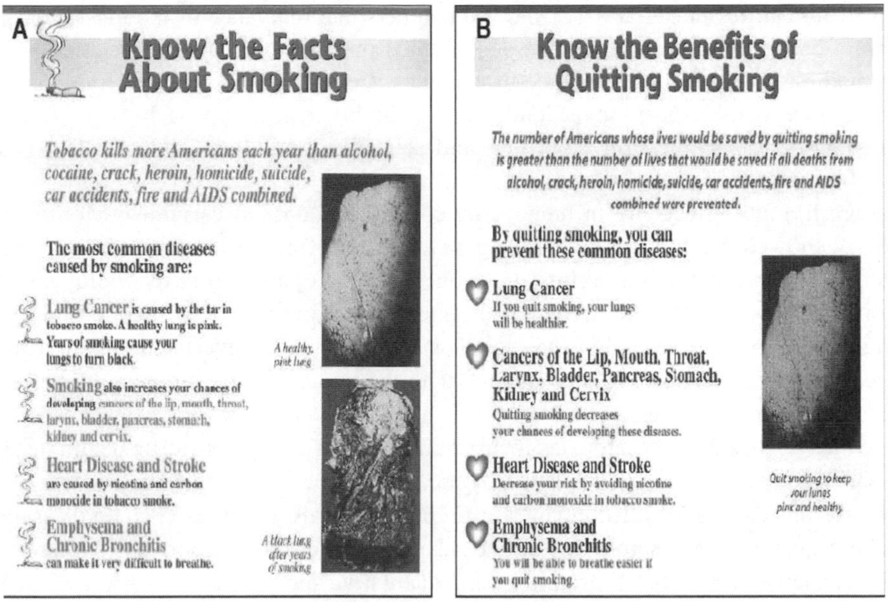

Figure 11.2 Examples of loss-framed (A) and gain-framed (B) messages for smoking cessation

Source: Benjamin Toll, www.yalescientific.org/2011/04/smoking-cessation-a-gain-framed-counseling-approach

(1) exploring the perceived risks and uncertainties of the health behaviour; and (2) exploring the motivational orientation of the recipient.

Both the perceived effectiveness of behaviour and perceived susceptibility to and severity of health risks can moderate the effects of message framing. For example, Hwang et al. (2012) examined how perceived effectiveness of sun safety behaviours and perceived susceptibility to skin cancer can moderate message-framing effects. Loss-framed messages were more effective when perceived effectiveness was low, whereas gain-framed messages were more effective when perceived effectiveness was high. Intention to use sunscreen and to wear long trousers to prevent skin cancer were also moderated by perceived susceptibility to skin cancer (i.e. loss-framed messages were more effective when perceived susceptibility was high). This was consistent with Bassett-Gunter et al.'s (2013) study which found loss-framed messages to be more effective in promoting physical activity beliefs and intentions than gain-framed messages. In a study of women's perceptions of the human papillomavirus (HPV) vaccine, Gainforth and Latimer (2012) found that appropriately framing messages can alleviate the negative consequences of risk information on coping appraisal.

The motivational orientation of the recipient also has been found to moderate message-framing effects on dietary calcium intake (Gerend and Shepherd, 2013), sun protection behaviour (Hevey and Dolan, 2013) and fruit and vegetable consumption (Churchill and Pavey, 2013).

Findings from van't Riet et al. (2012) showed that personal relevance of the message can moderate the effect of message framing, i.e. loss-framed messages are only more persuasive than gain-framed message for low-relevance participants. Covey's (2014) review found significant moderating effects of dispositional factors such as ambivalence, approach-avoidance motivation, regulatory focus, need for cognition and self-efficacy beliefs on the effectiveness of message framing.

Message framing effects are influenced by cortical and optical variables. McCormick and Seta (2012) showed that loss-framed messages were more effective than gain-framed messages when these were presented in the right hemisphere. Using eye-tracking technology, O'Malley and Latimer-Cheung (2013) showed that the number of fixations, dwell time and recall for gain-framed messages were higher than loss- or neutral-framed advertisements. Furthermore, message recall was also positively associated with the number of fixations and dwell time for gain- and neutral-framed messages.

While message framing research has focused on efforts to promote specific health behaviours, practitioners frequently face the challenge of encouraging people to perform a series of behaviours and sustain such actions (Rothman et al., 2006). The majority of research on message framing has been quantitative in nature. It would be useful for future research to also explore people's subjective experience of message framing using qualitative approaches.

Strategies that aim to inform and educate patients also need to consider whether their target audiences are able to access and understand the information being provided. Having access to information is necessary but not sufficient; people need to be able to read, understand or use the information provided, i.e. to be health literate. McInnes and Haglund (2011) examined the readability of information about various health conditions online. On average, health information on the Internet has a readability suitable for US Grade 12, which is too high for people with literacy issues. Not a single website was found to be written at or below the recommended Grade 6 level. About 45% of the websites were considered 'difficult' to read, while 13% were 'very difficult'. Websites on stroke, depression, bronchitis and pneumonia were significantly more readable than websites on cardiovascular disease, major depressive disorder and lower respiratory tract infection. Websites on dementia, Alzheimer's disease and alcoholism were also significantly harder to read than others.

Information dissemination alone is insufficient. The information must be understood by its intended recipients; the recipients must have the necessary skills to use the information; and the environmental and structural conditions must support the behaviours advocated. This is where the concept of health literacy comes in.

HEALTH LITERACY

What is Health Literacy?

There is no universal definition of **health literacy**. Early definitions focused on the application of *literacy skills* (e.g. reading and numeracy) to *understand* and *use* information to enable individuals to *function* in the health care setting (Kirsch et al., 1993). Later definitions expanded the concept to include *social skills* and application of these skills to include the ability to *access* information to *promote* and *maintain* health (Nutbeam, 1998). More recent definitions incorporate ideas from health promotion and patient empowerment to include evaluation and communication skills to enable people to make informed decisions, increase control and take responsibility for health in various contexts (Kickbusch et al., 2005; Murray, 2007; Rootman and Gordon-El-Bihbety, 2008; Sorensen et al., 2012). For the purposes of this chapter, health literacy is defined as: the capacity to access, understand, appraise, and apply health information and services, and to make appropriate health decisions to promote and maintain health.

Health literacy may be categorized into three levels (Nutbeam, 2000):

- *Functional health literacy* refers to the basic reading, writing and numeracy skills that enable individuals to function effectively in health care. Activities associated with this level of health literacy often involve communication of health information to improve patient knowledge, e.g. leaflets, websites and other available media.
- *Interactive health literacy* refers to the development of personal skills to improve personal capacity to act independently based on knowledge. It focuses on improving motivation and self-confidence to act upon the advice received, i.e. self-efficacy. Examples include tailored health communication, community self-help and social support groups.
- *Critical health literacy* refers to the ability to critically evaluate and use information to actively participate in health care. Activities include cognitive and social skills development and capacity-building to influence the wider, social health determinants.

Health literacy skills are not limited to functional reading and numeracy skills. People need a skill-set that enables them to handle the complex nature of promoting and maintaining health. Table 11.1 lists skills and tasks required for health promotion and management.

Table 11.1 Skills and tasks relevant to health promotion and management

Skills	Examples of tasks relevant to health promotion and management
Reading and comprehension	Understanding written health information materials
	Making sense of doctor's prescription, food labels, health risk precautions
	Understanding policies on patients' rights
Listening and comprehension	Understanding spoken medical advice
	Making sense of significant others' health concerns
	Listening to specific health issues relevant to the community
Speaking	Reporting health status to health professional
	Asking for clarifications regarding health condition or treatment
	Communicating health information with others
	Providing patient perspectives on how to improve health care

(Continued)

Table 11.1 (Continued)

Skills	Examples of tasks relevant to health promotion and management
Writing	Keeping personal records of medication intake
	Communicating with health professional by email
	Writing a petition to improve equal access to health care for all
Numeracy	Timing and applying appropriate dosage for prescribed medications
	Budgeting personal finances to accommodate 'healthy living'
	Interpreting relevance of statistical information concerning a public health issue
Analytical	Making sense of medical test results
	Evaluating credibility and accuracy of health information
	Assessing implications of public issues on health
Decision-making	Providing informed consent for treatment procedures
	Working as partners in the design, implementation and evaluation of health programmes
	Voting on organizational or government policies affecting health
Navigation	Locating health facilities
	Navigating oneself through the health care system
	Scheduling doctor's appointments
Negotiation	Negotiating treatment options
	Negotiating ways to improve personal and public health
Awareness	Being aware of physical symptoms and personal health status
	Recognizing social barriers and opportunities to promote health
	Recognizing shared social beliefs to around the social determinants of health
Advocacy	Obtaining information and resources needed to promote health
	Mobilization of action to address public health issues

Why is Health Literacy Important?

The National Assessment of Adult Literacy in 2003 showed that 77 million people in the USA had basic or below-basic health literacy – more than one-third of the population. Europeans have similar levels of health illiteracy. The European Health Literacy Survey (HLS-EU) showed that 12% of the population had inadequate health literacy and 35% problematic health literacy (Figure 11.3). These are worrying findings, considering that inadequate levels of health literacy can have damaging repercussions.

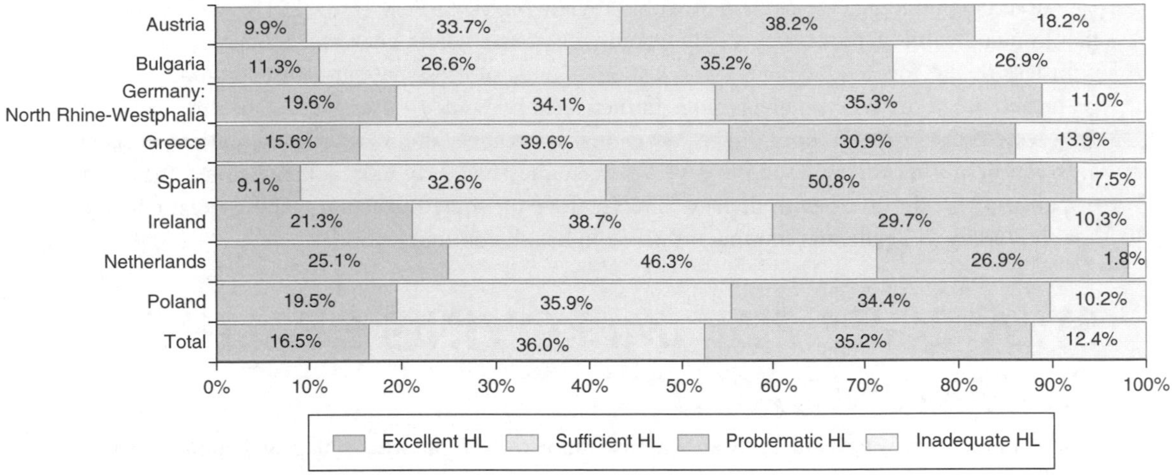

Figure 11.3 Health literacy levels in eight European nations

Source: HLS-EU Consortium (2012) (reproduced with permission)

The associations between health literacy, access to health care and health outcomes are well-established. Berkman et al. (2011) showed how poor health literacy was consistently associated with higher hospitalization rates, greater use of emergency care and poorer access to immunization and screening services. People with inadequate health literacy were less able to take medications appropriately and interpret labels. Among elderly persons, limited health literacy was associated with poorer overall health and higher mortality. Even after adjusting for SES and health status, people with limited health literacy make fewer visits to their doctors, prefer emergency care, and have more preventable hospital admissions than those with adequate literacy skills (Schumacher et al., 2013).

Ochieng (2013) examined the experiences of Black African migrant families in accessing health promotion services using self-administered questionnaires in Arabic, English, French and Swahili. Limited literacy and proficiency in English were perceived as the main barriers to accessing services among migrant families. Because of communication difficulties with HCPs, participants felt reluctant to seek health promotion information and support in the first place. Health literacy differences, therefore, help to explain both the health gradient and also ethnicity differences.

Health literacy also can influence people's willingness to participate in shared-decision making. Aboumatar et al. (2013) recruited 41 primary care physicians and 275 of their patients in an RCT that aimed to improve patient adherence to hypertension treatments. The physicians were allocated to either minimal intervention or communication skills training, while patients received a minimal, control intervention or a pre-visit coaching session. Patients with low health literacy skills were less likely to experience shared-decision making than those with adequate health literacy. Patients with limited health literacy were also less likely to ask questions and were less able to respond to patient-centred communication.

These latter findings are consistent with a review by McCaffery et al. (2013), which showed that limited health literacy was not only linked with poorer health knowledge, but also associated with less desire for involvement, less question-asking, and less patient-centred communication with their doctors. When patients with limited health literacy do engage in health decisions, they were more likely to report higher decisional uncertainty and regret. While patient decision aids can help, this review found that very few studies had explicitly acknowledged the needs of patients with limited health literacy. Interventions on shared-decision making must consider health literacy as a potential limiting influence in health communication.

STRATEGIES FOR IMPROVING HEALTH COMMUNICATION

In spite of the increasing availability and sophistication of ICT, the weak link in any communication system remains the human being. There are diverse ways to improve health communication, which is hardly ever perfect, but effective communication is not 'rocket science' either. Unless human HCPs are replaced by robots in some future universe (which seems, to us, highly unlikely), people always will play a crucial role in the delivery of health care. In a recent study in two clinics in Dallas, Texas, Gutierrez et al. (2014) observed that, regardless of health literacy, patients relied on their HCPs to obtain health information.

HCPs everywhere need to take into account the *messenger*, the *receiver*, the *message* and the *context*. Interventions that aim to promote effective health communication must consider the best ways to: (1) improve HCP communication skills; (2) promote individual and community capabilities; and (3) simplify and clarify all health care information.

IMPROVING HCP COMMUNICATION SKILLS

HCPs and patients often have very different perceptions of how well an episode of HCP–patient communication actually went (Kenny et al., 2010). Often physicians have not been sufficiently aware of the difficulties that some patients have with their lack of health literacy (Baker et al., 1996). Similar to doctors, Dickens et al. (2013) found that nurses tend to overestimate patients' health literacy skills. HCPs also have a tendency to overestimate the clarity of their own oral communication skills. Probably this is true of the majority of human beings. For example, in a study comparing self-reported and actual use of clear verbal communication among medical residents, Howard et al. (2013) found that although the majority of the medical residents reported using plain language when communicating with patients (88%), on average, while completing a standardized low literacy patient encounter, they used *two jargon terms per minute.* Similarly, while 48% reported using the *teach-back technique* (i.e. confirming that the delivered information was understood by asking patients to repeat or demonstrate what they had been told), only 22% used it in the standardized encounter. They failed to translate their training into everyday practice.

To enable patients to make informed choices, HCPs need to take steps to communicate in a manner that patients can understand. Protheroe and Rowlands (2013) argue that HCPs need to adapt their communication techniques to take into account the patients' different levels of health literacy. To promote effective interactions with patients, HCPs need to improve their communication skills and be aware of the varying levels of health literacy that exists across patients. Weiss (2007) suggested the following communication strategies:

- *Slow down.* Spend some time talking with patients using plain language. In a study by Sadeghi et al. (2013), it was found that time constraints and use of medical jargon are the main barriers that impede HCP–patient communication. It is important for HCPs to speak slowly and use language that is easy to understand.
- *Show or draw pictures.* Visual aids can help to enhance understanding and recall. Simple line drawings and cartoons will suffice. As an example, Choi (2012) developed simple line drawings and used these to enhance clarity and understanding of complex breast health care instructions among patients with limited literacy skills. Similarly, Mohan et al. (2013) have shown how illustrated medication instructions can be used to improve medication management among Latino patients with diabetes in the USA.
- *Limit the amount of information provided and repeat it.* This is particularly important for patients with limited literacy skills since health literacy can significantlyinfluence people's ability to remember verbal instructions and to recall information (McCarthy et al., 2012; Miller et al., 2013). Information is easier to understand and to remember when given in small doses. Repeating and highlighting key tasks can help enhance recall.
- *Create a shame-free environment.* Some patients may feel embarrassed to share their literacy difficulties because of stigma (see Box 11.1). It is important for HCPs to promote a culture of helpfulness in their everyday practice by encouraging patients to ask questions. The *Ask Me 3*™ programme can be a useful guide for patients and HCPs. This is a patient education programme advocated by the US National Patient Safety Foundation, designed to promote communication between patients and HCPs. In this programme, patients are encouraged to ask HCPs three questions:

    1. What is my problem?
    2. What do I need to do?
    3. Why is it important for me to do this?

Ask Me 3 has demonstrated encouraging outcomes. For example, Miller et al. (2008) carried out a pretest-posttest study to evaluate the *Ask Me 3* programme in a community pharmacy context. One-hundred and six community-dwelling, well but elderly participants were recruited from senior centres in Polk County between March 2006 and February 2007. Information on demographic characteristics, regularity of health care and medication use, health literacy level and multidimensional health locus of control were collected. Participants were randomly allocated to one of the three groups: (1) pretest-posttest; (2) pretest only; and (3) posttest only during each of the 12 *Ask Me 3* educational sessions. The evaluation showed that the *Ask Me 3* programme increased the proportion of participants planning to or actively bringing a list of current medications when visiting the pharmacist. It was concluded that this programme was a practical tool that could reinforce the principles of clear health communication. Similarly, Michalopoulou et al. (2010) showed that the *Ask Me 3* programme can improve patient satisfaction and perceptions of physician cultural competency among African-American patients. Participants also found all the questions to be helpful and reported knowing more about their medical condition after visiting their GP.

BOX 11.1
KEY STUDY: STIGMA OF LOW LITERACY AND SPOKEN INTERACTIONS BETWEEN PATIENTS AND HCPs

Aim

This qualitative study explored how limited literacy could influence access to health care, self-management and health outcomes.

Method

Participants were recruited from a community-based adult learning centre in Dundee, Scotland. Participants (n = 29) were working-age adults who had English as a first language and had sought support for literacy difficulties. Using interviews, researchers explored personal experiences of literacy, health care (including self-care) and self-reported health outcomes. The interviews were supplemented with focus group discussions to further explore ideas about how health services could be improved to support people with literacy difficulties. The interviews and focus groups were transcribed and analysed using framework analysis.

Findings

Participants explained that limited literacy skills impaired their interactions with HCPs. These difficulties were expressed in terms of understanding written information, complex explanations and instructions that subsequently ripple onto their broader health care experiences and ability to self-care. For some, interactions with HCPs were so bad that they described these scenarios as all 'gobbledygook' to them. Some participants also felt that HCPs did not make any effort to help them to understand what was being said. This is reflected in the quote below:

> ... and he [hospital consultant] was 'blah blah blah' and he knew fine I didn't have the foggiest idea what he was talking about. (Harry, male, 40s, quoted in Easton et al., 2013: 6).

Findings also suggest that some of the communication difficulties experienced by patients were further exacerbated by the stigma associated with limited literacy. The participants' narratives revealed how they have tried to conceal their limited literacy from their HCPs and in other social contexts. Some participants felt the need to hide their literacy difficulties because of the negative experiences they had in the past. In the fear of revealing their limited literacy skills, some participants would detract from engaging in the process, as reflected in the quote below:

> I couldn't spell it. I just went, 'You know what, I'm going to have to go. I'm not feeling very good. I'll come back, I will come back' and I grabbed it [the form] and ran out. (Barbara, female, 50s, quoted in Easton et al., 2013: 7)

Conclusion

Limited literacy can seriously impair interactions between HCPs and their patients. However, it is not only the difficulties associated with reading and understanding information that can interfere with the process. The stigma associated with limited literacy often exacerbates problems when patients try to hide the difficulties they experience to avoid embarrassment. Complex processes and HCP-communication styles that are littered with medical jargon often can drive some patients to avoid these interactions to prevent exposing their literacy difficulties in public. It is important for HCPs to recognize the needs of people with limited literacy skills by communicating effectively (without jargon) and by creating a shame-free and non-judgmental environment.

Source: Easton et al. (2013)

There is sufficient evidence to support the effectiveness of communication skills training courses to improve communication styles and attitudes among HCPs (Barth and Lannen, 2011). In particular, programmes that last for at least a day, are learner-centred, focus on practising skills and include activities such as role-play, feedback and small group discussions are shown to be most effective for training communication skills among GPs (Berkhof et al., 2011).

Promoting Individual and Community Capabilities

Health promotion requires the development of skills necessary to enable individuals and communities to take control over the determinants of health. In an attempt to improve health equity, Chervin et al. (2012) worked in partnership with adult education centres to incorporate health literacy into the curriculum. The project was based on the premise that social disparities in health can be reduced by enhancing the capacity of adult learners from marginalized communities to navigate the health care system and to manage their health conditions. Six adult education centres that served ethnic minority, immigrant and low-income learners in a small north-eastern state in the USA received a grant to deliver health literacy sessions as part of their curriculum. Quantitative and qualitative methods were used to assess its processes and outcomes. Health literacy instruction was found to have a positive impact on the learners' knowledge and understanding of health issues, the health care system, medical terminology and patient rights and responsibilities. Furthermore, the centres reported that learners were able to apply the health literacy skills they had developed in practice, such as healthier eating, scheduling doctor's appointments, communicating effectively with HCPs and following medical instructions. Levels of self-efficacy had also increased. Towards the end of the project, nearly three-quarters of the centres included health literacy sessions in the curriculum, with almost half of the teachers continuing to attend professional development activities for health literacy. Over the course of the project, each centre also developed partnerships with health care providers that provided the infrastructure for further knowledge and opportunities for teachers and learners.

Health literacy interventions, however, do not need to be isolated within the education setting. Considering that difficulties associated with limited health literacy are often exacerbated by social, cultural and historical contexts, it is important that interventions consider alternative environments to ensure that these are appropriate and relevant to the target audience. A creative example of such an intervention is the Barbershop Hypertension Screening programme in Phoenix, Arizona. This project was designed to improve health literacy and knowledge among Black barbershop owners and their male clients about the screening, treatment, and control of high blood pressure (Davis, 2011). Barbers were trained by HCPs to monitor and record customers' blood pressure scores. They were also trained to identify customers with untreated hypertension and to be able to advise those who might need to seek further medical attention. Barbers were given information about blood pressure disparities within African-American communities and the impact of tobacco use on cardiovascular health so that they could inform their customers about these issues as well. The customers were offered on-going monitoring every time they came to the barber's, along with written information to supplement open discussions around hypertension, blood pressure and the screening process. In this innovative project, the barbershop was redefined as a social space where health messages could be communicated 'man to man' in a supportive and engaging manner. This project illustrates nicely how vital health information can be delivered in the community and in a culturally grounded manner that is accessible and appropriate to the target audience.

A word of caution, however – promoting health literacy does not necessarily lead to patient empowerment. As Schulz and Nakamoto (2013) argue, although health literacy and empowerment may be related, they are distinct concepts, and one may not necessarily lead to the other. Presuming this to be the case can lead to deleterious consequences. As shown in Figure 11.4, high levels of health literacy without improving patient empowerment can lead patients to become overly dependent on HCPs. On the other hand, improving patient empowerment without corresponding improvements in health literacy potentially can lead to dangerous self-management among patients. When aiming to help patients become effective self-managers of health, interventions need to encompass methods for improving *both health literacy and empowerment.* Only these two in combination can ensure patients have the knowledge, skills and confidence to use appropriate resources effectively to promote and maintain their health.

One way to improve health literacy, build capacity and promote empowerment is by actively engaging participants themselves in the intervention process. **Participatory action research (PAR)** (Chapters 5 and 14) is one approach that can help to develop skills and raise critical consciousness at the same time. For example, Stewart et al. (2008) facilitated participatory action research with a group of Canadian indigenous young people and their teachers to enhance skills and expand health literacy through the use of videos. Developed over a span of six years, the project aimed to facilitate indigenous student investigation on topics around healthy living and injury prevention. In producing the videos, the participants developed critical consciousness about community, confidence, control and culture (the six 'C's). Video making gave participants the opportunity to express their ideas, hopes, metaphors, and rituals about health that were in line with their indigenous heritage and culture. In the process, this PAR helped to improve health literacy, not only by raising awareness on health and wellness, but also by enhancing personal and community capabilities and highlighting the importance of community knowledge and connecting to the community as a healthy way of life.

SIMPLIFYING AND CLARIFYING HEALTH INFORMATION AND THE WIDER HEALTH CARE SYSTEM

Using text-based materials containing lengthy, complex information can be difficult for people with limited literacy skills. It is important that information materials are clear and easy to understand. However, simplifying health information is not just about improving its readability by using shorter words. Designing effective health information needs to consider the materials' cultural appropriateness, relevance and context to narrow the gap between the health message, the messenger and its intended recipients (Zarcadoolas, 2011). It is also important to consider what information patients actually need, based on their goals and circumstances in line with a patient-centred approach (Ormandy, 2011). For example, Hingle et al. (2013)

		Empowerment	
		Low	High
Health literacy	Low	'High-needs patient'	'Dangerous self-manager'
	High	'Needlessly dependent patient'	'Effective self-manager'

Figure 11.4 Health literacy, empowerment and patient behaviour

Source: Schulz and Nakamoto (2013)

piloted text messages for young people to influence their knowledge, attitudes and behaviour towards nutrition and physical activity. Based within youth programmes in Arizona, nine focus groups, four classroom discussions, and an eight-week pilot study were conducted over a 12-month period to engage young people in discussing the message content, format, origin and message delivery of the text messages. These young people preferred text messages that were in an active voice referencing teens. They also preferred two text messages a day from nutrition professionals that provided advice on specific and achievable behaviours. By engaging young people in the process, more than 300 text messages that were relevant, acceptable and suitable to this target group were developed and tested.

Kennedy et al. (2014) evaluated a series of self-management guidebooks using cartoons for people with inflammatory bowel disease, irritable bowel syndrome, diabetes, chronic obstructive pulmonary disease and chronic kidney disease. The content was informed by qualitative research to obtain lay views and experiences. In general, the cartoons depicted common patient situations and dilemmas, decision-making choices and uncertainties associated with these conditions. After the guidebooks had been piloted, in-depth interviews and 'think-aloud' methods were used to evaluate them. The cartoons invoked amusement, recognition and reflection and helped provide clarity and understanding that, otherwise, may have been impossible.

Creative methods can also be used to improve health communication. Beacom and Newman (2010) suggested that strategies that included technology (e.g. programs aiming to increase computer and Internet access, skills, and comprehension), focus on interpersonal communication (e.g. community health worker model), and use mass media channels (e.g. 'edutainment') are useful in disadvantaged communities. Nambiar et al. (2011) examined how radio-and-theatre-based educational programmes can improve knowledge, attitudes and behaviour among antiretroviral therapy patients in India. Exposure to these programmes was associated with higher HIV-related knowledge, lower levels of stigma, consistent condom use, better doctor–patient communication, peer-advice giving and HIV-related advocacy.

Storybooks also can be used to communicate complex health information. Scott et al. (2012) explored how storybooks can support parents of children who are going through treatment of croup. Parents received a set of three storybooks, each depicting different severity levels of croup (mild, moderate and severe). Findings from the evaluation suggest that reading the storybooks helped parents to gain a better understanding of progressions and treatment of croup. This helped to alleviate their anxiety by reducing the uncertainty concerning their child's condition. The parents also felt reassured and empowered, and gained a sense of normalization of their experiences.

Contemporary health care systems often rely on overly complex processes that can be tedious to operate even to those with high levels of health literacy (DeWalt, 2007). There is often a mismatch between the demands of health care and the skills of patients, thus highlighting the need to simplify these systems to enable both patients and practitioners to operate effectively within this environment (Rudd, 2013). For example, Herndon et al. (2011) examined the health literacy level of patients in an emergency department (ED) and the readability of ED information materials. They found that 40% of patients had health literacy skills at Grade 8 or below while, on average, ED materials had readability levels suitable for or above Grade 9. This meant that a substantial proportion of ED materials were too complex for its target audience.

It is important that information pamphlets are a clear and appropriate match to the needs and skills of end-users. In England, for example, the Information Standard is used to ensure that the quality of health and social care information is clear, accurate, impartial, evidence-based and up-to-date. The Information Standard is an independent certification programme commissioned by NHS England and run by Capita on their behalf. Any organization producing evidence-based health and social care information for the public across England can apply for a mark. Organizations that pass this rigorous assessment are awarded the Information Standard Quality Mark.

In the USA, Paasche-Orlow et al. (2006) suggested that adopting a patient-centred system could address the service-systems complexity issue and the mismatch with patient capabilities. They argued that health promotion and health care services could improve their effectiveness by tailoring health care messages and interventions to the needs of patients and by actively involving patients in goal-setting and decision-making. Procedures also need to be simplified and explained clearly to enable both patients and HCPs to navigate through the system. Minimizing bureaucratic procedures and using plain and simple language to explain how the system operates would be beneficial to all, regardless of literacy level. Furthermore, the authors argued that developing structures that incentivize programmes that meet quality standards for vulnerable populations would help to address health inequalities by rewarding investment in technologies and interventions that support patient education, engagement and self-management, especially among those most in need.

In addition to reducing complexity in the health care system, there is also a need to consider the wider social and environmental conditions that influence health. Considering that health literacy is about having the capability and skills to implement informed choices to promote health, it is important that the environment is supportive of the decisions made by individuals to enhance healthy living. One way forward is the *WHO Healthy Cities Movement* which aims to promote healthy environments. This programme is a long-term international initiative that aims to create health-supportive environments through comprehensive local strategies for health protection and sustainable development. It capitalizes on community participation, inter-sectoral partnerships and participant equity to ensure that health is placed high on the agenda of key decision makers. The success of a Healthy City is therefore dependent upon the political, economic and social will to improve the local environment to promote health. Thousands of cities from all WHO regions are now part of this network, and sub-networks are currently being formed to promote Health Literate Cities. This initiative of the WHO acknowledges the concept, endorsed throughout this book, that the improvement of human health requires multi-sectoral interventions at international, governmental, community, family, and individual levels.

Individual HCPs – health psychologists included – may be small cogs in a huge wheel, but, without effective cogs, the huge wheel quickly grinds to a halt. Improving communication skills is, by far, the best and most cost-efficient way to 'oil the cogs', keeping this marvelous 'wheel' of the health care system moving in a positive direction – providing patients with the best possible care.

FUTURE RESEARCH

1. How to use health-message framing to promote the initiation and maintenance of health behaviours, including qualitative explorations of people's subjective experiences of behaviour change.
2. How health literacy can be incorporated into the design of patient decision aids to foster better shared-decision making.
3. More participatory action research projects to develop interventions to narrow social inequities in health information.
4. Robust evaluation of processes and outcomes to examine its effectiveness and impact on health service users' and providers' experiences.
5. Exploring how the WHO Healthy Cities Movement is succeeding in promoting health-sustaining environments.

SUMMARY

1 Health communication refers to all interpersonal, organizational or mass communication that concerns health. It can occur in various contexts, settings and channels, and deliver a variety of messages for a variety of reasons.

2 Shannon and Weaver's telephone model of communication considers six key components to communication: (1) source, (2) transmitter, (3) channel, (4) receiver, (5) destination and (6) noise. This is a basic descriptive model that serves a didactic function and little more.

3 Good communication between HCPs and patients is essential to health promotion, disease prevention and treatment and serves as the foundation for effective HCP–patient partnership.
4 Message framing can be used to influence people's motivation to undertake specific health behaviours.
5 E-health refers to the application of ICT to health or health care. The role of the patient is shifting from a 'passive consumer' to an 'active consumer of information' who is able to access an almost unlimited amount of health information and support, free at the point of delivery, online.
6 Health literacy refers to the capacity to access, understand, appraise and apply health information and services to make appropriate health decisions to promote and maintain health. It has three general levels: (a) functional, (b) interactive and (c) critical.
7 There are a number of skills concerning health literacy that are relevant to health promotion. These skills include reading, writing, numeracy, analysis, decision-making, navigation, negotiation, awareness and advocacy.
8 Low literacy has been associated with poor health outcomes, including knowledge, intermediate disease markers, measures of morbidity, general health status and use of health resources. Patients with low literacy may also be reluctant seek assistance due to the stigma and shame attached with it.
9 HCPs need to be aware of health literacy levels when communicating information to ensure effective interactions with patients.
10 Building HCPs' and patients' skills, simplifying the health care system and promoting health-sustaining environments are useful ways to improve health communication.

12 STRESS AND COPING

Though the faculties of the mind are improved by exercise,
yet they must not be put to a stress beyond their strength.

(John Locke, *Of the Conducting of the Understanding*, 1706)

OUTLINE

In this chapter we discuss theoretical approaches to the study of stress and coping, and research on stress as a cause of physical illness. It begins with an account of stimulus, response and interactional perspectives, together with a critical analysis of them. Consideration is given to alternative approaches to stress management and assessments of their effectiveness. A discussion of the methodological problems confronting research on stress and illness is followed by an examination of the evidence linking stress to cardiovascular disease, cancer and infectious diseases.

WHAT IS STRESS?

It is often asserted that **stress** has become a major feature of modern living, as a result of changes in the type of work that we do, the increased pace of life, and many features of the contemporary urban environment. Life today may be less obviously stressful than the life of our hunter-gatherer ancestors, but it seems that modern humans have created an environment that is far from optimal for mental and physical health. Stress is thought to be a principal cause of psychological distress and physical illness and millions of working days every year are believed to be lost as a consequence of this. The ability to cope successfully with stress is frequently held to be the key to human happiness.

But what exactly do we mean by the term 'stress', and how convincing is the evidence in support of these popular beliefs? If you ask people what they mean by stress you will find that their answers fall into one of three categories, each of which finds its echo in the academic literature. These three categories are summarized in Table 12.1.

The first answer is that stress occurs 'when you are under a lot of pressure', or 'when things are getting on top of you'. This is essentially the position taken by researchers who adopt stimulus-based perspectives. It is assumed that individuals have a certain tolerance for stress but will become ill when the stress is too great (Bartlett, 1998). Stimulus theorists have tried to devise measures of the relative stressful impact of different life events, ranging in severity from bereavement, divorce and job loss to problems in personal relationships, work pressures and environmental disturbances. These measures have in turn been used to investigate the role of stress as a cause of physical illness. Stimulus-based perspectives are associated with the work of occupational and environmental psychologists, seeking to reduce levels of stress by changing the structuring of jobs, and reducing stressful aspects of the physical environment.

The second answer concentrates on the physical and psychological feeling of 'being stressed' or 'completely stressed out', with symptoms such as anxiety, poor concentration, insomnia, bodily tension and fatigue. This position is taken by theorists who adopt response-based perspectives. They concentrate on the psychophysiology of stress and investigate possible mechanisms linking stress to physical illnesses such as coronary disease and viral infections, by way of the cardiovascular and immune systems respectively. Response-based perspectives have also provided the impetus for the introduction of stress management programmes that focus on controlling the psychophysiology of stress using techniques such as relaxation and breathing exercises, yoga, aerobics and other forms of physical exercise.

Table 12.1 Alternative perspectives on stress

Theoretical perspective	Popular conception	Major theories and techniques	Approaches to stress management
Stimulus-based	'When things are getting on top of you'	Life event stress scales; studies of workplace and environmental stress	Making jobs and physical environments less stressful
Response-based	'When you feel stressed-out'	Measuring physiological effects of stress; post-traumatic stress disorder	Biofeedback; relaxation and breathing exercises; yoga
Interactional	'When you think that you cannot cope'	Interactional theories; coping scales	Stress inoculation training; mindfulness-based stress reduction

The third answer is that stress is 'when you think you can't cope' or 'when you have too much strain put on you and you do not have the ability to deal with it'. This is the position developed in interactional perspectives by theorists who argue that stress occurs when there is an imbalance between the perceived demands placed on the individual and the ability to meet those demands, often described as *coping resources*. These theories are attractive because they overcome a problem inherent in stimulus and response perspectives; individuals differ as to what events or demands they find stressful and in the way that they respond to them. Interactional perspectives have led to the study of coping and to the development of techniques such as **stress inoculation training** (Meichenbaum, 1985, 1996, 2014) aimed at helping individuals to overcome stress by increasing the effectiveness of their coping strategies.

The above three perspectives are not mutually exclusive and it is possible to contemplate the emergence of a very broad 'general theory of stress' which incorporates elements of all of them. However, the classification is useful because it enables us to focus on the rather different styles of research which have emanated from each and to discuss the major criticisms that have been directed at them.

STIMULUS-BASED PERSPECTIVES AND LIFE EVENT SCALES

Holmes and Rahe (1967) conducted some influential research into the types of life events that people rate as being most stressful. They began by choosing 43 probably stressful life events, and then asked 400 US adults to rate the relative amount of readjustment that they judged would be required by each of the 43 events. The ten highest rated of these are listed in Box 12.1. They then used their results to construct a social readjustment rating scale (SRRS) that assigns point values to different kinds of stress and which is still being used in research on the relationship between stress and physical illness.

Some researchers felt dissatisfied with the SRRS because many of the events listed in it occur relatively rarely in anyone's life. There was a need for a scale that reflected to a greater degree the day-to-day variation experienced by people in the levels of the stress to which they are exposed. This led Kanner et al. (1981), using similar techniques to those of Holmes and Rahe, to devise two further scales, a **hassles scale** consisting of everyday events that cause annoyance or frustration, and an **uplifts scale** consisting of events that make them feel good. Of the two, the hassles scale has been the more widely used for research which parallels that using the SRRS. Box 12.1 lists, as an example, the findings of Chamberlain and Zika (1990), using an adaptation of the Kanner et al. scale, of the ten most frequently endorsed hassles by a sample of 161 students in New Zealand.

BOX 12.1
STRESSFUL LIFE EVENTS AND DAILY HASSLES SCALES

Listed below in order of severity are the ten life events rated as highly stressful by a sample of the US adult population studied by Holmes and Rahe (1967), and the ten daily hassles endorsed most frequently by a New Zealand student population studied by Chamberlain and Zika (1990) using a scale derived from Kanner et al. (1981).

Life events		*Daily hassles*	
1	Death of spouse	1	Not enough time
2	Divorce	2	Too many things to do
3	Marital separation	3	Troubling thoughts about future
4	Jail term	4	Too many interruptions
5	Death of close family member	5	Misplacing or losing things
6	Personal injury or illness	6	Health of a family member
7	Marriage	7	Social obligations
8	Fired at work	8	Concerns about standards
9	Marital reconciliation	9	Concerns about getting ahead
10	Retirement	10	Too many responsibilities

The SRRS, the hassles scale and research using them have been the subject of extensive criticism since their original publication (e.g. Schroeder and Costa, 1984). These criticisms focus on the choice of items for inclusion in the scale, items that often seem highly arbitrary, vague, ambiguous, insensitive to individual differences and sometimes likely to assess the individual's level of neuroticism rather than experienced life event stress.

The arbitrariness of items included in the scales is probably inevitable. It is trivially easy to think of stressful life events and hassles that have not found their way into the existing scales, but a complete listing of all such events would be endless. The vagueness and ambiguity of some items is another serious problem. Items such as *change in recreation* or *change in responsibilities at work*, taken from the SRRS, and most items on the hassles scale, can be criticized in this way. Items such as bereavement may also create problems because bereavement may have very different stressful impacts on different people as a function of length and quality of relationship, whether or not the death was unexpected, and so on.

Much of the research linking physical illness to stressful life events has consisted of retrospective studies in which participants are asked about events occurring prior to the onset of physical illness. These studies have been criticized because people who have recently been ill may very well-be predisposed to recollect and report recent stressful events to a greater extent than control group individuals who have remained well. Any such tendency will obviously lead to an overestimation of the association between stress and illness. The inclusion of vague and ambiguous items in the scales is clearly likely to maximize the differential reporting of stressful events.

The question as to whether the scales may be partially measuring neuroticism arises because they include a lot of items such as *too many things to do* or *troubling thoughts about the future* which could equally find a place in scales designed to measure anxiety or depression. This leads to a problem in interpreting the results even of prospective studies that investigate the association between scores on life events and hassles scales and subsequently occurring physical illness over a period of time. In principle this can establish whether stress really does predict the development of illness. Most prospective studies have relied on self-reports of illness; but it is highly probable that neurotic individuals will not only give high scores on life events and hassles scales but also be more likely to interpret minor symptoms as indicative of physical illness in comparison with individuals low on neuroticism. Here an empirical association between stress and illness may occur as a result of a reporting bias rather than a genuine causal link. A better approach is to rely on biologically verified assessments of illness.

An improvement on the traditional life events stress scales is the structured interview techniques developed by Brown and Harris. Their **life events and difficulties schedule (LEDS)** is used to assess, classify and rate the severity of each stressful event, making allowance for individual circumstances. Originally developed to study the social origins of depression in women, the LEDS has since been used to study links between life event stress and physical illness (Harris, 2007).

RESPONSE-BASED PERSPECTIVES AND THE PHYSIOLOGY OF STRESS

Since any catalogue of potentially stressful events is endless, and individuals differ greatly as to what they find stressful, an alternative is to seek to identify characteristic responses that occur for a range of stressful circumstances. This could theoretically include physiological, psychological and behavioural consequences of stress, although in practice researchers have tended to concentrate on physiological effects, especially those that may be associated with the development of physical illness. We will briefly consider the work of two historically significant contributors to this field, and then survey contemporary developments.

A pioneer in studying the physiology of stress was Hans Selye whose work extended from the early 1930s until shortly before his death in 1982 (Selye, 1976). He argued for the existence of a generalized response, known as the **general adaptation syndrome (GAS)**, which is triggered by exposure to stress. The GAS occurs primarily in the pituitary-adrenocortical system and consists of three stages, an *alarm reaction* in which the body's defences are mobilized, a *resistance stage* in which the body adapts to the cause of stress, and an *exhaustion stage* in which the body's capacity to resist finally breaks down. Selye drew particular attention to the abnormal physiology which develops during the resistance stage that, if protracted, could lead to what he called the *diseases of adaptation*. These include ulcers, cardiovascular disease and asthma. Although Selye's views have been very influential in the history of stress research, they are no longer widely accepted following extensive criticism, particularly that of Mason (1971, 1975).

The tradition of psychosomatic medicine, which is described in more detail in Chapter 16, spans a similar historical period as the work of Selye. A key figure was Franz Alexander (1950), who drew a distinction between the temporary and biologically adaptive changes in the physiology of the animal facing an emergency necessitating flight or fight, and the protracted and maladaptive physiological changes taking place in the anxious or stressed human being. Of particular significance are the physiological changes that are activated by the sympathetic branch of the autonomic nervous system. The proponents of psychosomatic medicine emphasized the effects of stress and anxiety on the cardiovascular, gastro-enteritic and respiratory systems. Some of their theories have an attractive plausibility, but their broad theoretical sweep and the range of physiological mechanisms proposed were never matched by an appropriate level of careful empirical research (Holroyd and Coyne, 1987).

A useful brief summary of contemporary research findings on physiological pathways that may link stress to disease has been provided by Cohen et al. (2007). This research is based on physiological measures taken from stressed laboratory animals, and from human participants who have experienced a range of types of stress, both long term, such as caring for a relative with dementia, and brief but traumatic, such as experiencing a sexual assault. Cohen et al. note that the effects of stress have been demonstrated on two major endocrine systems which act in conjunction with the hypothalamus and autonomic nervous system. These are the *hypothalamic-pituitary-adrenocortical axis* (*HPA*) and the *sympathetic-adrenal-medullary* (*SAM*) *system*. Of specific relevance for links between stress and diseases to be considered in this chapter, both HPA and SAM influence the functioning of the immune and cardiovascular systems. Cohen et al. also point out that stress has demonstrable effects on *vagal tone*, a key component of parasympathetic activity and strongly linked to cardiovascular processes.

While contemporary research on the psychophysiology of stress is of a much higher quality than that of the early pioneers, there is at least agreement that the proposed mechanisms could lead to higher rates of cardiovascular disease (CVD) for individuals who experience stress, particularly long-term stress. Of course it is necessary not only to find evidence of plausible physiological mechanisms but also to show that there actually is a demonstrable link between stress and CVD. The evidence for this will be discussed later in the chapter. In recent years there has also been a great deal of research into the effects of stress on the immune system, which indicates that stress may be responsible for a range of other diseases. This research is now known by the name of a new sub-discipline, referred to as **psychoneuroimmunology (PNI)**.

Psychoneuroimmunology (PNI)

The AIDS epidemic was one reason for an increased interest in psychological influences on the immune system, but there are also other considerations. The immune system is implicated not only in the body's defences against all infectious diseases but also in cancer and in autoimmune diseases such as rheumatoid arthritis. If psychological factors can be shown to have a significant role as causes of upregulation and downregulation of the immune system, then it is possible that psychological interventions could play an important role in the treatment of a very wide range of diseases.

Reviews of modern research findings in PNI have been provided by Evans et al. (2000), Segerstrom and Miller (2004), Bachen et al. (2007) and Kemeny (2011). At a theoretical level, Maier and Watkins (1998) attempt to synthesize current knowledge from an evolutionary perspective to account for psychological and behavioural effects of physical illness as well as the effects of stress on the immune system. These authors all emphasize that the immune system is a very complicated one involving a range of different types of cell with distinct functions. A brief synopsis of these is given in Box 12.2.

BOX 12.2
CELLS OF THE HUMAN IMMUNE SYSTEM

The main cells of the immune system are *leucocytes*, usually known as white blood cells. The three most important types of leucocytes are *granulocytic cells*, *monocytes/macrophages* and *lymphocytes*. These in turn divide into the following categories.

- *Granulocytic leucocytes*: the main types are *neutrophils*, which are *phagocytes* (eating cells) that engulf and destroy bacteria; *eosinophils*, which similarly engulf antigen-antibody complexes; and *basophils*, which have effects that promote the migration of other immune cells to the region.
- *Monocytes/macrophages*: these cells have a number of functions including 'recognition' of certain carbohydrates on the surfaces of micro-organisms.
- *Lymphocytes*: these cells have the function of attacking specific targets. They can be subdivided into *B cells*, *NK cells* and *T cells*. B cells produce antibodies that proliferate rapidly, thereby controlling infection. NK (natural killer) cells destroy virus-infected and tumour cells. T cells further subdivide into *T helper cells*, which enhance immune responses by stimulating the replication of immune system cells and antibodies, *cytotoxic T cells*, which destroy virus-, parasite- and tumour-infected cells, and *T suppressor cells*, which inhibit immune responses.

It can be seen that the human immune system is not simple. Much as one might like to do so, it is not possible to talk in a general sense of heightened or reduced immunity, because the immune system is volatile with changes constantly taking place in one or more of its parts. At any particular time one measure may indicate heightened immunity while another may indicate reduced immunity. An important example is the distinction between *cell-mediated immunity* and *humoral immunity*. In recent years there has been considerable interest in the relationship between psychological stress and increases in levels of the hormone cortisol, which has the effect of inhibiting cell-mediated immunity while enhancing humoral immunity (Evans et al., 2000; Dickerson and Kemeny, 2004). This provides some support for the much earlier conjecture of the psychosomatic schools (see Chapter 16) that asthma and other allergic conditions can have psychological origins. High levels of cortisol are associated with these conditions (Evans et al., 2000). Further support for this conjecture comes from the research of Sandberg et al. (2000), which demonstrated that acute and chronic stress is associated with subsequent asthma attacks in children who suffer from the condition.

A major difficulty when interpreting PNI research is that the preponderance of different kinds of immune cells varies considerably among healthy individuals and in the same healthy individual from day to day. O'Leary (1990) was one of the first to point out that the demonstration of statistically significant effects of stress on one or more parameters of the immune system does not necessarily entail that these changes have clinical significance as regards disease outcomes. Changes that have been shown to occur are invariably within the normal range of variation to be found in healthy individuals. There has been little progress on this important issue as is evident from the fact that 17 years later Bachen et al. (2007) make exactly the same point.

Research on stress and immunity can be broadly divided into studies of the short-term effects of *acute stress* and of the longer-term effects of *chronic stress*. Types of acute stress that have been studied include sleep deprivation, space flight, taking examinations, exposure to the objects of phobias (such as snakes), violent exercise, loud noises, electric shocks and attempting to solve difficult or impossible problems. Types of chronic or long-term stress that have been studied include bereavement, unemployment, marital conflict, separation and divorce, and caring for relatives suffering from Alzheimer's disease. No study has investigated the effects of any one kind of stress on all aspects of immune function and it is therefore necessary to piece together findings from different studies in order to obtain a general picture.

It has been a fairly consistent finding that chronic stress is associated with some degree of downregulation of immune systems with changes found particularly in the number of NK cells, the total number of T cells and the proportion of T helper cells to T suppressor cells. Findings for the effects of acute stress have been more variable, with some indications of upregulation, some of downregulation, and some null findings (Evans et al., 2000; Segerstrom and Miller, 2004). Segerstrom and Miller also note that subjective reports of stress are not usually associated with immune changes.

While most of the research in this field has been concerned with establishing the effects of stress on the immune system, there have also been a number of studies investigating the effects of psychological interventions, including stress management, on immune measures. If successful these interventions could obviously have considerable potential benefit in reducing susceptibility to disease and improving recovery rates. Miller and Cohen (2001) reviewed 85 studies with rather disappointing conclusions. Positive findings were mainly for interventions using hypnosis and conditioning while stress management and relaxation techniques rarely produced substantial effects. However, they warn against jumping to the conclusion that the immune system cannot be much influenced by psychological interventions, pointing out a range of research problems that need to be solved before firm conclusions can be drawn.

There is general agreement that a number of methodological difficulties need to be overcome before we can safely conclude that stress has direct effects on the immune system with disease consequences. First, it is important to distinguish between direct effects of stress and other physiological pathways that may be activated by stressful experiences such as sleep deprivation and space flight. Second, it is necessary to rule out indirect effects that may be obtained when stress provokes health hazardous behaviour, such as smoking and alcohol consumption, which may in turn have effects on the immune system. Third, where significant effects of stress on immune function have been adequately demonstrated, it is also necessary to show that these effects have clinical significance as regards disease outcomes. We shall return to this last point later in this chapter when we examine research on the relationship between stress and biologically verified disease.

Post-Traumatic Stress Disorder (PTSD)

Can a characteristic response to stress be found in individuals who have been subjected to extreme levels of stress, such as soldiers in battles, victims of rape and other violent crimes and survivors of disasters such as earthquakes, floods and nuclear accidents? The term 'PTSD' was introduced by researchers studying psychological symptoms reported by soldiers returning to the USA from the Vietnam War and it was subsequently extended to studies of other types of traumatic stress. It was first accepted as a diagnostic label by the American Psychiatric Association in 1980. The symptoms that are most often used to characterize PTSD are insomnia, nightmares, flashbacks, problems of memory and concentration, acting or feeling as if the event is recurring and a greatly increased sensitivity to new stressful events (Posluszny et al., 2007). A variety of physiological changes have also been found in persons suffering from PTSD.

As in the other areas of enquiry that focus on reactions to stress, our understanding of PTSD is complicated by the existence of large individual differences. Only a minority of individuals exposed to traumatic stress go on to develop the symptoms of PTSD. Prevalence rates vary widely according to the nature of the stress, most commonly from 10% to 30%. There are also large individual differences in the types of symptoms encountered and their severity. Some recent attempts have been made to review the voluminous literature on PTSD to establish whether differences in emotional reactions occurring at the time of and immediately after traumatic stress can predict the subsequent development of PTSD, although so far with little agreement (Harvey and Bryant, 2002; Ozer et al., 2003). Neither is it clear whether reactions to different kinds of traumatic stress are basically the same or whether they depend on the particular type of stress involved.

The psychophysiological differences found between those who suffer from PTSD and those who do not are real enough, but it has not been established whether they have occurred purely as a result of exposure to traumatic stress, or whether they are at least partly determined by pre-existing characteristics of the individuals who develop PTSD. It is quite often found that these individuals have a history of psychological problems, including childhood trauma, abnormal adolescent development, depression and anxiety disorders (Posluszny et al., 2007). This in turn raises the question, in any particular case, as to whether the traumatic stress is the primary cause of subsequent psychological reactions or the final trigger at the end of a series of causal influences.

To what extent is PTSD associated with the development of physical illness in addition to psychological problems? A number of studies have sought to answer this question but with mixed results. The main focus has been on cardiovascular disease (CVD). Qureshi et al. (2009) analysed a selection of studies published between 1981 and 2008 and found a conflicting mixture of positive and negative findings. Dedert et al. (2010) conducted a detailed review of research published between 2002 and 2009, concluding there was evidence of an association but that it could not be relied on because the research had a range of methodological shortcomings. Other studies of PTSD and physical illness have usually found positive associations where the measures of illness are patients' subjective reports, but little or no associations where objective physicians' reports have provided the data. Rytwinski et al. (2014) utilized both subjective and objective measures for a sample of 200 PTSD sufferers. They found that PTSD severity is associated with subjectively assessed but not with objectively assessed health, a finding which suggests that the effects of traumatic stress are primarily psychological. At the same it should be noted that long-term psychological problems, especially anxiety and depression, have themselves been found to be associated with CVD (see Chapter 16).

While there has been at least one attempt to develop a theoretical model of PTSD (Brewin et al., 1996), others question its usefulness as a clinical diagnosis. A trenchant critique is given by the Canadian anthropologist Allan Young (1995), who combines an historical analysis of the concept with an ethnographic study conducted in a psychiatric unit specializing in the treatment of PTSD. He argues that PTSD is not, as its proponents would have us believe, a psychiatric condition that has been vividly described throughout human history, but a cultural phenomenon of the modern era. He traces it to the work of Freud and others in the late nineteenth century, work that has contributed to the **medicalization** of certain types of human unhappiness. While not disputing the extent of the suffering that is caused by traumatic experiences, he does challenge the usefulness of the diagnosis of PTSD as a step towards helping people to deal with their suffering.

Summerfield (2001) took some of these criticisms further. He pointed out that the diagnosis of PTSD has an important legal advantage for people seeking financial compensation for distress suffered while performing functions that might be thought to be part of their job, such as ambulance personnel attending road accidents and police officers on duty at disasters. He comments:

> There is a veritable trauma industry comprising experts, lawyers, claimants and other interested parties. It is a kind of social movement trading on the authority of medical pronouncements. An encounter between a sympathetic psychiatrist and a claimant is primed to produce a report of post-traumatic stress disorder if that is what the lawyer says the rules require and what has, in effect, been commissioned. In the United Kingdom awards for psychological damage based on the diagnosis can be several times higher than, say, the £30,000 to £40,000 limit that the Criminal Injuries Compensation Authority applies for the traumatic loss of a leg.
>
> (Summerfield, 2001: 95)

Mezey and Robbins (2001) challenged Summerfield's view. While agreeing that the diagnosis of PTSD has been used indiscriminately in civil litigation, they argued that PTSD involves a level of distress that transcends ordinary human misery and unhappiness and that the diagnosis has the positive function of taking away blame from the sufferer who experiences guilt, shame and failure, so that the symptoms can be experienced as a normal response to an abnormal event rather than a pathological condition. They also argued that the psychophysiological characteristics of PTSD can be clearly distinguished from those associated with other psychiatric diagnoses.

INTERACTIONAL PERSPECTIVES AND COPING SCALES

It is clear that a key problem for both stimulus and response based perspectives on stress is individual differences. Different people find different things stressful, and react to the same potentially stressful events and circumstances in different ways. A number of theorists have sought to overcome this problem by conceptualizing stress as a relationship between the individual and the environment and developing *interactional models*. The most influential of these was first put forward by Lazarus and developed by Lazarus and Folkman (1984). In this model psychological stress is defined as ‘a particular relationship between the person and the environment that is appraised by the person as taxing or exceeding his or her resources and endangering his or her well-being’ (p. 10). A distinction is made between *primary appraisal* whereby an event may be perceived as benign and non-threatening, potentially harmful, threatening to one’s self-esteem, or challenging, and *secondary appraisal* in which an assessment is made of one’s ability to cope with the threat or challenge. Stress occurs whenever the perceived threat exceeds the perceived ability to cope.

These ideas have been developed at considerable length in a number of books and articles, but they do raise the question as to whether they amount to much more than just another way of saying that stress is when you think you cannot cope. Although this may seem a modest enough assertion, it can in fact be criticized for its implication that stress results only from a purely subjective mismatch between demands and coping resources. One can ask, what about the person who thinks that they can cope when objectively the demands of the situation exceed their actual ability to cope? Are such optimists not stressed? This problem was partially solved by Trumbull and Appley (1986) who extended the model of Lazarus and Folkman by proposing that stress can occur whenever either the real or the perceived demands exceed either the real or the perceived capacity to cope. It might be felt that Trumbull and Appley’s definition is so broad and all-encompassing that it amounts to no more than a statement of the obvious. A critical question might be, what is the relative importance of mismatches between real demands and coping resources and those between perceived demands and coping resources in determining whether an individual suffers the effects of stress?

A thoughtful and influential analysis of problems for interactional approaches has been given by Monroe and Simons (1991). While their analysis is primarily concerned with depressive disorders, it also has broader implications for stress theories. In particular they devote their attention to the problems of separating the influence on stressed reactions of pre-existing individual characteristics, including personality, and of current stressors in all their variety. We have already touched on these issues in considering methods of measuring life events stress and on analysing the causes of post-traumatic stress disorder. The problems are further confounded if we bear in mind that pre-existing characteristics may very well determine not only whether people experience specific events as stressful, but also whether they actively seek stress, as is the case for some competitive personalities, or whether they seek to avoid it. We will consider these issues further later in this chapter, when examining the relationship between stress and physical illness, and also in Chapter 16, which is concerned with illness and personality.

In some ways it is probably better to think of interactional models of stress as *frameworks* for thinking about the subject rather than as specific and testable theories or models. Another way of representing an interactional framework is the flowchart of Cox (1978) shown in Figure 12.1. One of the useful features of this flowchart is that it incorporates feedback between responses, demands and appraisal. For example, behavioural responses, depending on whether they are appropriate or inappropriate, may result in a reduction or an increase in actual demand; psychological defence mechanisms may become activated, leading to changes in the cognitive appraisal of mismatches between perceived demand and perceived capability, and so on.

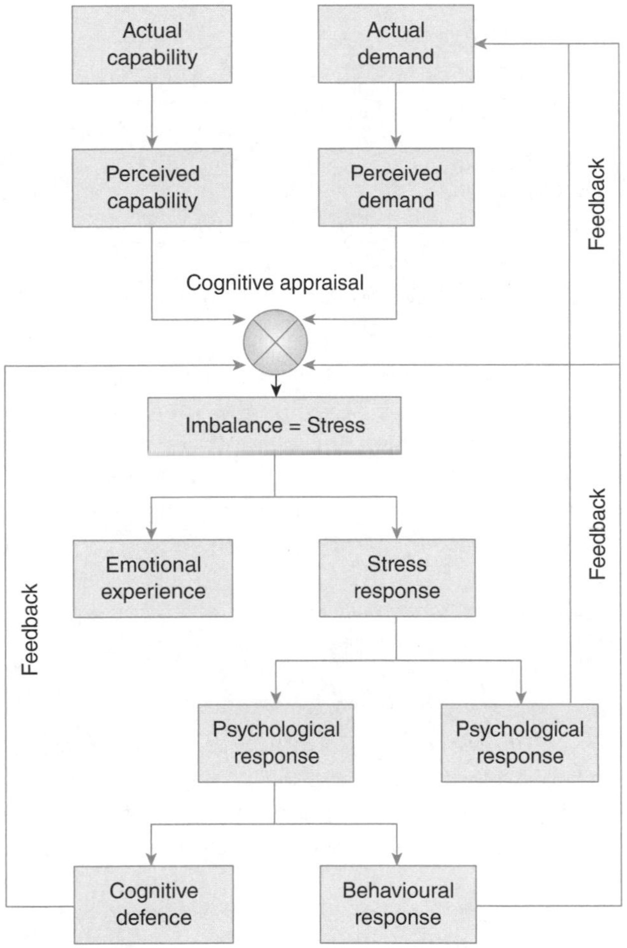

Figure 12.1 Flowchart for an interactional model of stress

Source: Cox (1978: 19). Reproduced with permission

One consequence of the emergence of interactional models of stress has been the development of checklists designed to assess the individual's predominant coping strategies. An example is the COPE questionnaire devised by Carver et al. (1989) that consists of 15 sub-scales each made up of a number of items for which the individual indicates agreement or disagreement on a four-point scale. The 15 sub-scales with an example of a checklist statement from each are shown in Box 12.3.

BOX 12.3
ASSESSING COPING STRATEGIES: THE COPE SCALE

In the COPE scale, you are asked how you respond when confronting difficult or stressful events in your life. To each item you use the following rating system:

- I usually don't do this at all.
- I usually do this a little bit.
- I usually do this a medium amount.
- I usually do this a lot.

The 15 COPE sub-scales with an example of a checklist from each (the complete version contained four items per sub-scale) are:

- *Active coping*: I take additional action to get rid of the problem.
- *Planning*: I try to come up with a strategy about what to do.
- *Suppression of competing activities*: I put aside other activities in order to concentrate on this.
- *Restraint coping*: I force myself to wait until the right time to do something.
- *Seeking social support for emotional reasons*: I ask people who have had similar experience what they did.
- *Seeking social support for instrumental reasons*: I talk to someone about how I feel.
- *Positive reinterpretation and growth*: I look for something good in what is happening.
- *Acceptance*: I learn to live with it.
- *Turning to religion*: I seek God's help.
- *Focus on and venting of emotions*: I get upset and let my emotions out.
- *Denial*: I refuse to believe that it has happened.
- *Behavioural disengagement*: I give up the attempt to get what I want.
- *Mental disengagement*: I turn to work or other substitute activities to take my mind off things.
- *Alcohol-drug disengagement*: I drink alcohol, or take drugs, in order to think about it less.
- *Humour*: I make fun of the situation.

Source: Carver et al. (1989)

Problems and issues for coping research were discussed by Folkman and Moskovitz (2004). Coping scales have been criticized for adopting a 'blunderbuss' approach to the complex mechanisms involved in coping with different types of stress, and failing to take account of the fact that individuals may vary greatly in the way they cope with different stressful situations (Somerfield, 1997; Aldwin and Park, 2004). They may also be criticized for relying too much on introspective judgements unsupported by other types of evidence. If it is a feature of the psychology of stress that people tend to behave irrationally when exposed to high levels of stress, then the reports of individuals about their personal ways of coping may be particularly inaccurate. For example, *denial*, the refusal to acknowledge the existence of a real danger, may be observed when an individual ignores or denies the significance of symptoms of life-threatening disease, but it is unlikely to be a fully conscious process. How is such an individual likely to respond to the denial items on the COPE questionnaire when asked, for example, how often when confronted with stressful life events, he or she 'refuses to believe that it has happened'? Surely the whole point about denial is that it only works as a defence if the person does not realize that she/he is doing it.

STRESS MANAGEMENT

The most obvious approach to stress management is to deal with the causes of stress. For example, an important part of the work of the occupational psychologist is to analyse the nature of stress in the workplace in order to advise on how restructuring could be carried out to reduce the amount of stress experienced by employees. In principle this would be of benefit not only to employees, but also to employers on the assumption that employees will be more productive when less stressed. It is not possible to make generalizations about this approach to stress management because everything will depend on the specific nature of the job and the workplace environment. The approach of the environmental planner is also highly task specific, when considering features of the design of housing, thoroughfares and public spaces to reduce levels of stress that may be related to noise, pollution, overcrowding, and exposure to crime and other physical dangers. At the other end of the stress spectrum, where stress is unavoidable, stress management may be based on efforts to modify the psychophysiology of stress, including the use of physical exercise, breathing and relaxation techniques. In practice these methods have normally been incorporated into the main interactional approaches to stress management, a topic to which we now turn.

The more widely applicable methods of stress management often make use of the techniques of **cognitive behavioural therapy (CBT)**. They are all fairly similar in their approach, but one which has been developed rather more thoroughly than most is **stress inoculation training (SIT)** (Meichenbaum, 1985, 1996). Using an interactional perspective, the aim of SIT is to help people to cope after exposure to stressful events and to improve already existing coping skills so that they become more readily available for dealing with continuing and future stressors. In the first or *conceptualization* phase, the therapist/trainer aims to educate the client to treat threats as soluble problems and to clarify those stressors and responses which are potentially changeable and those which are not. The second phase then concentrates on *skills acquisition* and *rehearsal*, in which effective skills are practised, first in training sessions and subsequently in real situations. Skills may include methods for relaxation and anxiety reduction, cognitive restructuring and interpersonal skills using social support networks. In the third and final phase of *application* and *follow-through*, clients are taught to apply their expanded coping skills to increasingly high levels of stress, using imagery, rehearsal, modelling and role playing. They are also taught how to identify high-risk situations to prevent relapse to previous and inadequate methods of coping, and to deal with relapse if and when it does occur. At this stage they may be encouraged to help others with similar problems. SIT has been used for individuals and in groups of various sizes, and for a range of time scales, from single 20-minute sessions when preparing patients for stressful surgery to regular weekly and bi-weekly one-hour sessions, up to 40 sessions in some cases.

A rather different method of stress management, which has become increasingly widely used in recent years, is based on the concept of *mindfulness*. An influential pioneer of this approach is Jon Kabat-Zinn, a molecular biologist and Buddhist, who introduced his programme known as **mindfulness-based stress reduction (MBSR)** in 1979. Since then he has written a series of popular accounts (see, for example, Kabat-Zinn, 1990). Mindfulness is a central feature of Buddhist meditation, especially in Theravada Buddhism, but Kabat-Zinn and practitioners of similar programmes, now collectively referred to as *mindfulness-based therapies*, emphasize that they can be practised with equally good effect without any commitment to Buddhist beliefs. Keng et al. (2011) describe the practice as follows:

> The elements of mindfulness, namely awareness and nonjudgmental acceptance of one's moment-to-moment experience, are regarded as potentially effective antidotes against common forms of psychological distress – rumination, anxiety, worry, fear, anger, and so on – many of which involve the maladaptive tendencies to avoid, suppress, or over-engage with one's distressing thoughts and emotions.
>
> (Keng et al., 2011: 1042)

Mindfulness-based therapists, like Buddhist teachers, may recommend the initial practice of hatha yoga and concentration on breathing as a preliminary step in developing attention, but the practice of observing the mind is regarded as the central therapeutic procedure. It is instructive to contrast this with traditional forms of cognitive behavioural therapy, stress management and self-help manuals, in which the emphasis is on the cultivation of positive thinking and desirable habits, and the elimination of negative ones. For the mindfulness-based therapist the practice of self-observation will inevitably lead to beneficial outcomes as the practitioner becomes increasingly aware of the maladaptive nature of his or her problematic states of mind. They may simply be dropped with no further effort required. For Buddhist monks the cultivation of mindfulness is often regarded as a preliminary to deeper spiritual practices, perhaps leading to the ultimate goal of enlightenment/salvation, while for the mindfulness-based therapist, as indeed for many Buddhists, mindfulness may be regarded as sufficient in itself. The non-directional character of mindfulness training is in some ways comparable with the psycho-analytic procedure of free association, although without the additional requirement for analysis and interpretation. Perhaps the results of observing the mind are self-evident.

There have been a number of recent reviews of studies into the efficacy of mindfulness-based therapies, including MBSR. Keng et al. (2011) examined 18 randomized controlled studies of MBSR and 14 of mindfulness-based cognitive therapy (MBCR) and found evidence of increased subjective well-being and reduced levels of anxiety, depression, anger and perceived stress. Khoury et al. (2013) examined 209 studies, of which 109 were randomized controlled studies. They concluded that mindfulness therapies are moderately or largely effective for treating anxiety, depression and stress, but no more effective than traditional cognitive behavioural therapies (CBT). Goyal et al. (2014) examined 47 studies, concluding that mindfulness is moderately effective for anxiety, depression and pain control, but less effective for stress and mental-health-related quality of life. They found no evidence that meditation is more effective than drugs, exercise and other behavioural therapies.

The picture that emerges from comparative studies of stress management methods is much the same as that which has been commented on for many years as a typical finding of research into the effectiveness of psychotherapies for a wide range of problems. Rosenzweig (1936) was among the first to note that they all seem to be equivalent in achieving better results than no therapy, but are largely indistinguishable from each other. He referred to this as leading to the Dodo argument, derived from the Caucus race in *Alice's Adventures in Wonderland*. In this race, the participating animals, which are initially distributed around the course in no particular order, begin running in whatever direction they please and stop whenever each chooses. When the Dodo calls out that the race has finished, and the animals want to know who has won, the Dodo declares 'Everyone has won and all must have prizes'. Since 1936, meta-analyses of therapy outcomes have regularly made reference to the Dodo argument and have usually found that the evidence continues to support it (Luborsky et al., 1975, 2002; Stiles et al., 1986).

ARE STRESS THEORIES NECESSARY?

The stress theories which we have been considering in this chapter were, for the most part, fully developed by the mid-1980s. Since that time there has been a decline in interest in the development of general theories in favour of a piecemeal approach to research, mostly concerning possible links between specific types of stress and susceptibility to physical illness. Many critics have argued that the development of general theories of stress is not a viable scientific objective. For example, while it seems worthwhile to study the effects respectively of bereavement, living in noisy environments and of poor role definition at the workplace, it is not necessarily the case that such studies would yield results that have enough in common to be incorporated into a broad general theory. Critics have pointed out that stress is an umbrella term that has been applied to so many quite different phenomena as to become virtually meaningless from a scientific point of view (for example, Pollock, 1988; Brown, 1996). In an effort to encompass such diverse phenomena theories have become so vague and ambiguous that they lack any practical value. But if the stress concept is such a nebulous one, why has it come to play such a significant role in popular discourse and media presentations? Pollock, Brown and others have attempted to answer this question by analysing stress as a social construct. Here are two examples of the way in which this approach can be revealing.

First, stress is often used as a device for legitimating behaviour that might otherwise be seen as the result of anxiety, neurosis or personal inadequacy. For example, to phone up your workplace to say that you will not be coming in today, or to excuse yourself for not sitting an examination, on the grounds that you are too worried, not sleeping well, too tired, or simply feel inadequate would not be considered acceptable. To give as the reason that you are suffering from stress, preferably supported by a letter from a doctor or counsellor, could be considered perfectly reasonable. In spite of the differences between stimulus, response and interactional models of stress, what they all have in common is that they draw attention to current events in one's life or one's immediate environment as provoking a reaction, rather than focusing exclusively on the individual. But it may very well be that an inability to cope with the demands of everyday life is more appropriately seen as indicative of a long-standing psychological problem such as anxiety or depression.

Second, stress often has the function of explaining the otherwise inexplicable, whether this be psychological or physical symptoms or actual illness. Suppose that someone has a consultation with the doctor after suffering a heart attack. The doctor is expected to provide an explanation as to why the heart attack occurred. Does the patient smoke, avoid exercise, drink a lot of alcohol, eat too much fatty foods, have high blood pressure or a family history of heart disease? If the answer to all these questions is 'no', the next question is likely to be, 'Have you been experiencing a lot of stress lately?', a question to which most people are likely to reply, 'yes', especially if they are urgently seeking an explanation for an otherwise inexplicable complaint. But is the explanation a valid one or merely a convenient pseudo-explanation? Clearly the role of stress in the aetiology of physical illness needs to be investigated just as carefully as any other proposed causal agent.

For a more detailed review of arguments against stress theories and analysis of the concept as a social construct, the reader is referred to the useful summaries which have been provided by Bartlett (1998) and Jones and Bright (2001). For the rest of this chapter we will focus on the evidence for associations between stress and physical illness.

DOES STRESS MAKE US MORE SUSCEPTIBLE TO PHYSICAL ILLNESS?

This topic has generated a great deal of research and it is easy to see why. If stress can be shown to be an important influence on our susceptibility to disease, then the possibility exists that interventions designed to reduce stress, or to help individuals to cope better with unavoidable stress, may lower the incidence of disease and assist the recovery of those who are already ill. The popular belief that stress is a major cause of physical illness is not convincingly supported by existing research findings, but neither is the opposite belief that stress plays only an insignificant role. The problem is that it is extremely difficult to carry out well-controlled research in this area and most of what has been done is open to a range of possible interpretations. We have already noted two shortcomings that apply to the majority of studies. First, retrospective studies may have a substantial response bias because people are more likely to recall experiencing stress in periods preceding illness than at other times. Second, all studies that rely on self-reports of illness may have a response bias because people who consider themselves to be suffering from stress are more likely than non-stressed individuals to interpret minor ailments as symptoms of illness.

The better designed studies that investigate the association between exposure to stress and subsequent and biologically verified illness may still present problems of interpretation. For example, it has been shown that people who are experiencing stress are more likely than others to indulge in health hazardous behaviour such as heavy smoking, a high-fat diet and lack of exercise (Ng and Jeffery, 2003). Thus it could be that stress acts only indirectly as a cause of illness insofar as it influences health behaviour, rather than through direct physiological pathways.

The methodological problems which we have discussed so far are all likely to lead to inflated estimates of the strength of the association between stress and illness. Further issues have been raised that point in the opposite direction, to the possibility that current research may produce underestimates. These issues derive partly from work on the relationship between personality and illness considered in Chapter 16. One argument is that some individuals possess personal characteristics that make them resistant to the effects of stress. Among the personal characteristics that have been suggested as having this function are **conscientiousness**, **self-efficacy**, **hardiness** and **sense of coherence**. If stress only causes illness in people with vulnerable personalities, then it may be misleading to calculate the size of the effect of stress on illness by using general population samples that include many who are relatively insensitive to these effects. A further issue is the potential mediating effect of *social support* on the relationship between stress and illness. There is extensive evidence that people with strong networks of social support live longer and enjoy better health than relatively isolated individuals (Cohen, 2004). In seeking to explain this relationship, Cohen argues that social support has a *buffering effect* against the effects of stress, so that stress is only likely to cause illness among individuals with relatively low levels of support.

If the above considerations are valid, then stress is only likely to have a strong effect on susceptibility to illness among individuals who score low on conscientiousness, self-efficacy, hardiness and sense of coherence, and who have a low level of perceived social support. Therefore, studies of stress–illness links that are based on representative population samples may greatly underestimate the potential effects of stress because they include many individuals for whom the effect is likely to be small. Would-be researchers, who consider these issues alongside our previous observations on factors that may lead to overestimates, could be excused if they were to throw up their hands in despair. As a research topic it is not an easy one and certainly no study published to date has succeeded in overcoming all or even most of the potential problems. Nevertheless, recent and relatively well-designed studies have thrown up a number of interesting findings, particularly in the areas of **coronary heart disease (CHD)**, cancer and infectious diseases, and to these we now turn. For further discussion of chronic conditions, see Chapter 19.

Coronary Heart Disease (CHD)

Studies of the relationship between stress and subsequent CHD have produced a mixture of positive and negative findings. In a 12-year follow-up study of 6,935 healthy men, Rosengren et al. (1991) found that those who had initially reported substantial stress were more likely to experience coronary artery disease subsequently, after controlling for the effects of smoking, alcohol consumption and lack of physical exercise. In contrast, in a six-year follow-up of 12,866 men who were at high risk,

Hollis et al. (1990) found no relationship between stress and subsequent mortality. Macleod et al. (2002) described a 21-year follow-up study of 2,623 Scottish men in which self-reported stress was strongly associated with subsequent angina but not with objective measures of CHD, including mortality. However, the diagnosis of angina is usually based on self-reported chest pain and Macleod et al. conclude that the stress–angina relationship probably results from a tendency of participants reporting higher stress to also report more symptoms.

There has also been extensive research into the possible relationship between occupational stress and CHD (Byrne and Espnes, 2008). Studies of workers in European countries, with follow-up periods ranging from five to ten years, all found an association between assessments of job strain and subsequent risk of CHD (e.g. Kivimäki et al., 2002; Kuper and Marmot, 2003), but Reed et al. (1989) found no association in an 18-year follow-up of 8,006 Hawaiian men of Japanese ancestry and Eaker et al. (2004) found no association in a 10-year follow-up of 1,711 men and 1,328 women in the USA.

In view of the conflicting nature of these findings it is obviously not possible to draw any definite conclusions as to whether stress increases susceptibility to CHD. However, two recent meta-analyses concur in finding a modest prospective relationship between perceived stress and objective measures of CHD, including mortality. Richardson et al. (2012) analysed studies with a combined total of 118,696 participants and found that individuals with high perceived stress were 27% more likely than those with low perceived stress to be diagnosed with or die as a result of CHD at least six months later. Kivimäki et al. (2012) pooled results from 13 European studies comparing risk of heart attack for people in high stress vs. low stress jobs. Out of a total of 197,473 participants there were 2,358 heart attacks in an average follow-up period of 7.5 years, with those reporting high job strain at a 23% increased level of risk compared with those reporting no job strain, an increased risk which is quite similar to that estimated by Richardson et al. Kivimäki et al. conclude that prevention of workplace stress might decrease disease incidence but to a much smaller extent than tackling standard risk factors, such as smoking.

Cancer

Studies that have considered that the subsequent occurrence of all forms of cancer following periods of stress have generally failed to find evidence of an association. The few positive findings have come from small and poorly designed studies, whereas large prospective studies have produced negative findings. There is, for example, no indication of a higher cancer rate among the bereaved (Jones et al., 1984; Fox, 1988), and Keehn (1980) found no increased rate of cancer among former prisoners of war, men who had suffered extreme forms of mental and physical hardship. Joffress et al. (1985) found no relationship between stressful life events and subsequent cancer in a study of Japanese men living in Hawaii. Recently Heikkilä et al. (2013) conducted a meta-analysis of 12 European cohort studies including 116,056 participants who were initially free from cancer when assessed for self-reported job strain. The follow-up period was for a median time of 12 years, during which 5,765 cases of cancer were recorded from hospital admission and death registers. Heikkilä et al. found no clear evidence for an association between job strain and risk of cancer.

With regard to the prognosis for individuals already suffering from cancer, the most impressive study involved over 14,000 women in Norway and found no increased risk of recurrence or death for those who had lost a spouse or had been divorced (Kvikstad et al., 1995) or who had lost a child (Kvikstad and Vatten, 1996). Reviewing the evidence from 26 studies on coping styles and survival and recurrence in people with cancer, Petticrew et al. (2002) conclude that there are few indications of significant associations.

Over the last 20 years particular attention has been given to the possible relationship between stress and breast cancer. This is understandable because breast cancer is the most common cause of premature death in women, and epidemiological studies have so far failed to establish its causes. McGee (1999) notes that speculation about stress as a cause of breast cancer may be found in medical opinion at least as far back as 1893. He gives examples of relatively recent poorly designed studies which sometimes produce dramatic positive findings, while large prospective studies have not found an association. Duijts et al. (2003) confirmed this conclusion in a detailed meta-analysis, with the single exception that there was a significant, albeit modest, association with death of a spouse. In a further quite surprising finding, Nielsen et al. (2005) found evidence that stress may actually reduce the likelihood of women developing breast cancer (see Box 12.4).

BOX 12.4
INTERNATIONAL CASE STUDY: DATA ON STRESS AND BREAST CANCER – SURPRISING RESULTS FROM A MAJOR DANISH STUDY

Nielsen et al. (2005) followed up 6,689 initially healthy women over 18 years after obtaining self-reported stress measures in 1981–1983, when the women were participants in the Copenhagen City Heart Study. During follow-up 251 women were diagnosed with breast cancer. Surprisingly, the women with high stress levels were significantly less likely to be subsequently diagnosed with breast cancer than those with low stress levels. For each increase in stress level on a six-point scale an 8% lower risk of primary breast cancer was found. However, the authors caution that lower breast cancer risk may be counterbalanced by possible effects of stress in increasing risks of other diseases

In addition to research into the relationship between stress and the subsequent diagnosis of breast cancer, there has also been a good deal of interest in studies of the relationship between stressful life events and survival and recurrence for women who have already been diagnosed and treated. Some dramatic findings of a poorer prognosis for patients who experience stressful events after diagnosis were given considerable publicity although other researchers were reporting negative findings (see Petticrew et al., 1999). All of these studies had serious methodological flaws that have been largely overcome in a major prospective study by Graham et al. (2002). They carried out a five-year follow-up of 170 women who had received surgery for breast cancer and found no evidence of a positive relationship between stressful events and increased risk of relapse; in fact they found a significant decrease in recurrence for women who had experienced one or more severely stressful events since diagnosis, a finding of the possible beneficial effects of stress which parallels that of Nielsen et al. (2005) described in Box 12.4.

It is unfortunate that occasional positive findings concerning stress and cancer are given a great deal of publicity while the many negative findings are ignored. Studies with negative findings may also not be submitted or accepted for publication. The assumption that stress is a cause of cancer plays a major role in justifying complementary therapies of dubious efficacy. But, as McGee (1999) pointed out:

> Recriminations over real or imagined life stress may be counterproductive for individuals with cancer and their families. They should be reassured that the available scientific evidence does not support any direct role for stressful life events leading to a diagnosis of cancer.
>
> (McGee, 1999: 1016)

Infectious Diseases

If stress causes changes in the immune system, then this could obviously lead to altered susceptibility to infectious diseases. We have already seen that there is extensive evidence that stress does have statistically significant effects on a variety of measures of immune functioning, but that these effects are generally well within the range of normal variation for healthy people. This leaves the question open as to whether they are sufficiently large to lead to altered susceptibility to disease. The obvious way to find out is to examine the evidence for a direct relationship between stress and the incidence of infectious disease. Over the last 28 years Sheldon Cohen and his associates have been conducting a thorough and detailed analysis of this issue.

Cohen and Williamson (1991) dismissed evidence drawn from retrospective studies and all studies that rely on self-reported illness for reasons which we have already explained. Much of the research in this area is concerned with minor viral infections, such as the common cold, and these are likely to be particularly susceptible to reporting bias. For example, a mild sore throat and headache may be self-diagnosed as a viral infection by the more hypochondriacal individual while others will attribute the same symptoms to staying up too late at a party or pollution from traffic fumes. It is easy to see how correlations may occur between such self-reported illness and perceived levels of stress, even if there is no true causal relationship between stress and susceptibility to viral infections.

A further problem pointed out by Cohen and Williamson is that stress may be associated with greater exposure to viruses, perhaps because stressed individuals seek the company of others to a greater extent than non-stressed individuals. An illustration of this methodological problem is given in Box 12.5. An ingenious way of avoiding the difficulty comes from **viral challenge studies** in which volunteers are deliberately exposed to viruses, usually cold viruses, and then followed up to determine whether those reporting high levels of stress prior to exposure are more likely than others to catch the virus, biologically verified by the researchers.

BOX 12.5
STRESS AND EXPOSURE TO VIRAL INFECTIONS: A RESEARCH PROBLEM

A popular source of volunteers for researchers studying stress and illness has been medical students taking examinations, no doubt because they are the most readily available and co-operative participants to be found at institutions where medical research is conducted. However, as a method for studying the effect of stress on susceptibility to viral infections, the method is deeply flawed. Can you see why?

While it is true that taking examinations is very stressful for medical students, it is also the case that sitting in an examination hall with a large number of other students for several hours is likely to provide a high level of exposure to whatever minor viruses happen to be around at the time. Note also that, prior to taking examinations, for several days or more, students are likely to spend a lot of time alone in their own rooms preparing for the examinations, and relatively little time socializing with other students. They are unlikely to be exposed to viruses. After the examinations the reverse is the case. Students spend very little time on their own and a great deal of time socializing, once again at the mercy of whatever viruses are around. Researchers are likely to find that the students develop the symptoms of viral infections consistent with exposure at or shortly after the high stress period of taking examinations but only rarely consistent with exposure in the period prior to the examinations. They might draw the unwarranted conclusion that students have a heightened level of immunity in the stressful period prior to the examinations and a much reduced level afterwards.

Since 1986 Cohen and his associates have been conducting viral challenge studies on stress and the common cold, and Cohen and Miller (2001) summarized their findings. The first major study was conducted in the UK, where 394 participants were exposed to one of five different cold viruses. It was found that stress levels predicted increased likelihood of catching a cold, that this was equally true for all five viruses, and that the higher the level of reported stress, the greater the susceptibility. They also found that this relationship remained the same after controlling for the effects of smoking, drinking, diet, exercise and sleep quality. In a second major study, this time conducted in the USA, 276 participants were exposed to one or other of two types of cold virus, after completing the LEDS semi-structured interview, described earlier in this chapter. The main purpose of the study was to ascertain what types of stress were associated with increased susceptibility to the cold viruses. It was found that, the longer the duration of stress, the greater the probability of catching a cold, and that interpersonal problems with family and friends and work problems were the main culprits. Short-term acute stress did not appear to increase susceptibility.

A question discussed frequently in recent years is whether stress is a factor in the onset or development of HIV/AIDS. Not everyone exposed to the HIV virus becomes infected and the rate at which the disease progresses varies from person to person. Since much of this variability is currently unexplained it is not surprising that there has been considerable interest in the possibility that stress is a factor. Unfortunately the topic is an extremely difficult one to investigate. It is rarely possible to know when an individual was initially exposed to the HIV virus with any degree of precision, and subsequent diagnosis and disease progression is associated with much stress, lifestyle changes and the occurrence of other infections, so that it is not easy to disentangle the variables.

Following a detailed review of studies conducted from 1990 to 2007, Leserman (2008) found consistent evidence that the occurrence of stressful life events is associated with a range of indicators of disease progression, including mortality. However, it is unclear whether this is the result of direct effects of stress on the immune system or changes in stress-related behaviour; Gore-Felton and Koopman (2008) noted that the demands of coping with the side-effects of medication and related illnesses may influence behaviour such as adherence to medication, substance use, sexual risk taking and lack of exercise, all of which may cause more rapid disease progression.

FUTURE RESEARCH

1. Studies focusing on the psychological and physiological effects of different types of stress (e.g. bereavement, excessive work load, physical assault). Such research need not proceed on the assumption that very general psychophysiological models of stress are being tested.
2. Prospective stress-disease studies that combine measures of a wide variety of physiological characteristics (e.g. of the immune system) with biologically verified assessments of disease status.
3. Research into the effects of stress on the gastro-enteric and respiratory systems in addition to its effects on the cardiovascular and immune systems.
4. Assessment of the effectiveness of stress management programmes for those already suffering from stress-related diseases. This research should examine the psychological benefits of the programmes as well as their effect on disease prognosis.
5. Clarification of the relationship between stress, physiological reactions, health behaviours, social support and stress-immunizing personality characteristics using large-scale population-based studies.

SUMMARY

1. Stress is sometimes conceptualized as environmental stimuli or life events that impinge on the individual, sometimes as a particular type of response or reaction to stressful events, and sometimes as a mismatch between demands placed on the individual and the perceived ability to cope with these demands.
2. Various methods have been proposed for assessing life events stress. The main problem is that individuals differ greatly as to what they find stressful. For this reason structured interviews are to be preferred to standardized questionnaires.
3. Investigations into physiological reactions to stress have identified many different types of reaction. Physiological reactions vary considerably from individual to individual and according to the nature of the stressor.
4. Significant effects of stress on the immune system have been demonstrated although it is not yet clear whether these effects are large enough to alter susceptibility to disease.
5. A variety of physiological and psychological effects associated with exposure to traumatic stress have been shown to exist, although it is arguable whether they can be used to establish post-traumatic stress disorder as a clinical syndrome.
6. Interactional models of stress are intrinsically attractive because they take account of individual differences in reactions to stress and methods of coping. They have the disadvantage that they depend very much on the reliability of subjective assessments and, for this reason, may not be scientifically testable.
7. Empirical studies of the relationship between stress and disease have frequently been unsatisfactory because they are retrospective and rely on self-reported stress and illness. They also frequently fail to distinguish between physiological effects of stress and influences on health behaviour.
8. Theoretical models of the relationship between stress and disease are difficult to test because they involve complex interactions between stress, social support and personality variables.
9. There is conflicting evidence as to whether stress does or does not contribute to risk of coronary heart disease. Recent meta-analyses concur in finding a moderate increase in risk, although much less than major risks such as smoking.
10. There is no convincing evidence for a significant role of stress in the aetiology and prognosis for cancer.
11. Viral challenge studies have established that stress does increase susceptibility to some infectious diseases, especially colds and flu. It has not yet been established whether this association is the direct result of effects on the immune system or indirectly caused by changes in health behaviour.
12. There is evidence that occurrence of stressful life events is associated with HIV disease progression but it is unclear whether this is the direct result of stress on the immune system or changes in stress-related behaviour.

13 SCREENING AND IMMUNIZATION

We are living in a world that is beyond controllability.

(Ulrich Beck)

OUTLINE

We consider two forms of disease prevention available within health care systems: screening and immunization. These programmes are premised on the basis of controlling risk. Screening programmes are designed to identify individuals who, because of certain personal characteristics, are considered at risk of developing a certain disease. Immunization programmes are designed to vaccinate people who are at risk because of their exposure to environmental pathogens. Various social and psychological processes are involved in explaining these processes of risk management.

RISK AND RISK CONTROL

According to various sociologists we live in a 'risk society' (Beck, 1986), by which is meant that people feel that they are under threat from an increasing range of hazards. The role of the state in this later modern era is promoted as being to identify and bring under control these many hazards. Joffe (1999) argued that while risk in general is defined in the language of science, behind it is a 'more moralistic endeavour, one that routes dangers back to those responsible for them' (p. 4). This follows the well-trodden blame and shame path of personal responsibility.

The control of risk is a central theme in contemporary health care. Once again, the dominant language of science conceals a more moralistic message about personal responsibility. Preventive health care has been predicated upon epidemiological research that has estimated the statistical importance of various so-called 'risk factors'. According to these statistical models, individuals or groups who are exposed to certain pathogens, either internally or externally, or who behave in a certain manner are at higher risk of developing a particular health problem. The task of preventive health programmes then becomes one of identifying individual risks for particular health problems and bringing these risks under control. A central challenge is the extent to which people are willing to participate in these programmes.

Health psychologists have contributed to attempts to explore this issue by investigating cognitive and other psychological processes that can help clarify risk control actions. Research on preventive health services such as screening and immunization has been dominated by the cognitive approach, which focuses on the information-processing model of the single individual, in contrast to a more sociocultural approach, which considers the interaction between the individual and the sociocultural context. Both of these approaches are considered below.

SCREENING

One of the main forms of health risk management is the early detection of disease through screening. This is the procedure whereby those sections of the population that are considered statistically more at risk of developing a particular disease are examined to see whether they have any early indications of that disease. The rationale behind this strategy is that the earlier the disease is identified and treated, the less likely it is to develop into its full-blown form. Within public health circles there has been sustained debate as regards the value of this strategy. A variety of criteria have been identified for deciding to implement screening (Wilson and Jungner, 1968). These include the character of the evidence with regard to its effectiveness, benefits, harms and costs.

In Western countries there have been several attempts to introduce mass screening for a limited number of conditions that satisfy all or most of these criteria. However, despite the supposed benefits of these programmes there has been a variety of problems in their implementation. It was generally assumed by their proponents that the major problem would be the introduction of the programmes. However, the challenge has been not a technical one of implementing the programme but rather a human one concerned with the reluctance of at least a proportion of the targeted population to make use of these programmes and the unexpected negative side effects of participation. In addition, there continues to be debate about the effectiveness of particular forms of screening.

Screening for Cancer

Over the past decade there has been a concerted effort in most industrialized societies to introduce screening programmes for breast cancer. The reason for this was that it is a common health problem and there was evidence that those detected and treated at an early stage had better survival prospects. It is currently one of the most prevalent forms of female cancer in Western society.

It is estimated that one in nine women will develop breast cancer at some point in their lives. In the UK about 49,000 new cases were diagnosed in 2011 and about 11,500 died from the disease (Cancer Research UK, 2013).

Partly in response to the epidemiological and medical evidence about the widespread prevalence of the disease and the association between stage of identification and success of treatment, there has been a demand not only from health authorities but also from women's organizations for the introduction of breast cancer screening programmes. Initially, the method favoured was breast self-examination (BSE) but due to debate about the accuracy of this procedure most health authorities now favour mammography coupled (sometimes) with clinical breast examination by a health professional. In most industrialized countries mammography programmes have been targeted at all women aged 50 to 69 years who are invited on a 2–3 year basis to undergo the procedure.

Although mammography is widely promoted by health authorities, evaluations of its effectiveness have not been conclusive. The Cochrane Collaboration review estimated that the breast cancer mortality reduction due to mammography was 15% rather than the 29% previously reported (Gøtzsche and Nielsen, 2009). They concluded that while on a societal level mammography may be beneficial, 'the chances that a woman will benefit from attending screening is very small, and considerably smaller than the risk that she will experience harm.' The authors refer to a range of harmful consequences of mammography that often have been ignored in evaluations including heightened levels of distress among the women, harmful effects of radiation, and overdiagnosis (i.e. cases that would never become clinically detectable or pose a threat to health without screening) leading to surgery and other forms of treatment. A recent commentary noted that 'it seems likely that little of the decline in breast cancer mortality since 1990 is due to mammography screening, and nearly all to improved therapy of breast cancer' (Miller, 2008: 485).

A review of 11 randomized trials concluded that the relative risk of breast cancer mortality for women invited to screening compared with controls was 0.80 (95% CI 0.73–0.89), which is a relative risk reduction of 20% (Independent Panel, 2012). The Panel concluded that 20% was still a reasonable estimate of the relative risk reduction. Despite widespread support for mammography there is concern that some of the evidence on the effectiveness of alternative approaches to detection may be underestimated. Kearney and Murray (2009) highlighted the limitations of previous evaluative research, suggesting that BSE was of limited benefit in reducing mortality on the grounds that the evidence was drawn from trials of BSE education, not of BSE practice. It has been discouraged because BSE would also lead to heightened anxiety among women and unnecessary visits to the family doctor. However, there is little evidence for the latter. Rather, there is evidence that the majority of breast cancer tumours are discovered by the women themselves.

Cervical cancer is a much less prevalent condition. In 2011, over 3,000 new cases of cervical cancer were diagnosed in the UK, making it the twelfth most common cancer in women and accounting for around 2% of all female cancers (Cancer Research UK, 2013). The incidence rate for cervical cancer is highest for those aged 30–40, reaching around 17 per 100,000 women. In 2011, there were 972 deaths from cervical cancer in the UK. It has been established that the human papillomavirus (HPV) is the main risk factor and a necessary cause of cervical cancer. This virus is spread particularly through sexual activity. There is evidence that the precancerous stage of the disease can be detected at an early stage using a simple cervical smear test (pap test).

Most Western countries have introduced campaigns to encourage women to attend for regular smear tests, usually at least once every three to five years. Another prevention strategy has been the introduction of HPV vaccination. In many countries an HPV immunization programme has been introduced into schools for teenage girls (see later).

Evidence from several countries suggests that a large proportion of women do not use cancer screening programmes. Approximately 2.75 million women aged 50–70 were invited for breast cancer screening in 2009–2010 in the UK. Of these, approximately 2.02 million were screened and 16,500 cancers and tumours were detected (Cancer Research UK, 2013). The cervical smear test has been around for a longer period but it also has encountered a reluctance of a substantial proportion of targeted women to participate. More recently there have been attempts to introduce screening for other forms of cancer. There has been particular interest in developing screening for colorectal cancer, which is the second major cause of cancer in Western society and affects both men and women. However, the uptake of the test has not been high.

HEALTH BELIEFS AND CANCER SCREENING

The dominant approach used by health psychologists to explain participation in screening programmes has been underpinned by SCMs, especially the health belief model (HBM) and the theory of reasoned action (TRA). (For further details, please see Chapter 6.) These models argue that it is possible to identify a certain typical belief pattern that will predict the use of health services such as screening.

In the case of breast cancer screening, most of the studies have considered participation in mammography programmes and fewer have considered BSE. The most frequently cited predictors of participation in both are perceived susceptibility and perceived barriers. A meta-analysis of a large number of US studies (McCaul et al., 1996) found a strong relationship between family history (actual risk) and mammography utilization but also a moderate relationship between perceived vulnerability (perceived risk) and use of mammography. In a UK study, Sutton et al. (1994) also found a relationship between perceived risk and attendance. Stein et al. (1992) found that perceived susceptibility to breast cancer was the best predictor of future intention to participate in mammography. However, they add that 'it is questionable . . . whether heightened feelings of susceptibility alone will sufficiently motivate women to obtain mammograms in the absence of a physician's recommendation' (p. 458).

Various barriers to attendance for mammography, both physical and psychological, have been reported. Rimer et al. (1989) found in their survey of women in the USA that those who did not attend for mammography had a stronger belief that screening was not necessary in the absence of symptoms, a preference not to think about it and a worry about the effect of radiation. Murray and McMillan (1993) found that perceived barriers were the most important predictor of attendance for a smear test. The barriers they considered included dislike of the health service, fear of the examination, and fear of the result. Moore et al. (1998) found that the main barriers to both breast and testicular self-examination were embarrassment, perceived unpleasantness and difficulty, reliability concerns and concerns about the findings.

McCaul et al. (1996) found that women who worry about breast cancer are more likely to engage in self-protective actions such as BSE and attendance for mammography. Sutton et al. (1994) found a non-linear relationship with the highest attendance among women who were 'a bit worried', while those at the two extremes of worry were less likely to attend. They concluded that health promotion campaigns must balance advice to women on perceived risk with the negative impact of excessive worry. Other barriers reported include belief that a mammogram is appropriate only when there are symptoms, concern about radiation exposure, cost and access-related factors (Slenker and Grant, 1989).

With respect to benefits, several studies have indicated that the most frequently given reason for non-participation in cancer screening is that the women do not feel it necessary – they were healthy so they did not feel it was necessary to use it. It was thought that it was only necessary to have mammograms when one was sick. Potvin et al. (1995) found that perceiving one's health as good was inversely associated with recent mammography. Harlan et al. (1991) found that the most frequently given reason for not having a cervical smear was not believing it necessary.

Although the HBM has been widely used in studies designed to predict attendance for breast cancer screening the results have not always been consistent. Bernstein Hyman et al. (1994) found that women who never scheduled a mammogram were more likely to perceive both fewer benefits of and barriers to mammography. They did not find any relationship between perceived susceptibility and mammography usage. They suggested that possibly other variables such as knowledge were a more important overriding factor. Many women are either unaware of the availability of the services or do not understand the character of the investigation. For example, Gregory and McKie (1991) found that many women did not understand that the early stages of *cervical carcinoma* are not accompanied by any symptoms. Similarly, Harlan et al. (1991) found that the main reason for non-participation in cervical screening was that women did not think it necessary because they did not have any symptoms. Rimer (1990) argues that since mammography occurs when there are no symptoms of breast cancer it takes 'almost an act of faith' to participate.

A criticism of many of these studies of breast cancer screening is that they used a cross-sectional design. One study that used a longitudinal design (Norman and Brain, 2005) found that previous experience of BSE was the best predictor of the practice. Of the HBM factors considered the best predictors were perceived emotional barriers (e.g. 'Finding breast cancer is emotionally distressing') and perceived self-efficacy barriers (e.g. 'I am confident that I can examine my own breasts regularly'). This would suggest that the barriers dimension should be considered in more detail. In addition, this study found that those women who scored low on perceived self-efficacy barriers and high on breast cancer worries and perceived severity of cancer were more likely to conduct BSE excessively. It was suggested that these women may carry out more frequent but less thorough BSE.

In a survey of a large sample of Scottish residents invited to participate in colorectal cancer screening Wardle et al. (2004) found that interest in participating in screening was predicted by perceived higher risk, worry and benefits, and lower perceived barriers, fears and fatalism. They also found that those from lower SES backgrounds perceived the benefits of screening less and the barriers to it more. Although their study was not formally based on the HBM, it does agree with other studies of cancer screening.

The TRA and TPB have met with some success in predicting cancer screening behaviour. Cooke and French (2008) conducted a large meta-analysis of 33 studies that used this approach. They found that attitudes had a large-sized relationship with intention to participate in screening, while subjective norms and perceived behavioural control had medium-sized relationships. Intention had a medium-sized relationship with participation. They also considered the role of moderator variables and identified (a) type of screening, (b) location of recruitment, (c) screening cost, and (d) invitation to screen as important.

Several researchers have used the transtheoretical model (TTM) of change (Prochaska and DiClemente, 1983) to explore the extent of participation in screening programmes. Rakowski et al. (1992) found that women who were classified as pre-contemplators (i.e. those who never had a mammogram and did not plan to have one) scored higher on a measure of negative beliefs including the beliefs that mammograms lead to unnecessary surgery and that they are only advisable if you have some breast symptoms. Skinner et al. (1997) found that action/maintainers were less likely to agree with the psychological and physical barriers to screening.

SOCIAL VARIATIONS IN PARTICIPATION

The growth of research on health gradients (see Chapter 3) has confirmed that not only do people from poorer backgrounds experience worse health but also they make less use of preventive health services such as screening. The US Centers for Disease Control and Prevention (2012) reported on a National Health Interview Survey on colorectal screening in 2000, 2003, 2005, 2008 and 2010 with the civilian non-institutionalized population aged 50–75. The data showed that the overall percentage of adults ages 50–75 who reported receiving colorectal cancer screening significantly increased from 34% in 2000 to 59% in 2010 and that rates increased among all racial and income groups. However, in all years except 2008, Asians were less likely to receive colorectal cancer screening than Whites. Since 2005, Blacks have also been less likely than Whites to receive screening. In 2005 and 2008, AI/ANs were less likely than whites to receive screening. In all years, poor, low-income and middle-income adults were less likely to receive colorectal cancer screening than high-income adults .

This evidence is supported by data from other countries. Moser et al. (2009) found that women who did not own a car were less likely to have had a mammography and women from ethnic minorities were less likely to have participated in cervical cancer screening. The introduction of a home testing kit for colorectal cancer followed a similar pattern. Early indications are that in trials of different forms of screening for colorectal cancer the uptake has been lower among people from lower SES backgrounds (Wardle et al., 2004). One study found that while 49% of test kits sent to homes were returned from more affluent neighbourhoods only 32% of kits were returned from the more disadvantaged neighbourhoods (von Wagner et al., 2009).

A framework for integrating the psychological evidence on the relationship between SES and use of screening has been developed by von Wagner et al. (2011). Box 13.1 shows that this framework classified the evidence into two broad categories: corollaries of SES and attitudinal mediators. In the former category they group a mixture of social stressors that they argue reduce the perceived importance of preventive health behaviours. It also includes educational opportunities that contribute to health literacy and the ability to access and process information about preventive and other health services.

The third social corollary is illness experience. It is suggested that this corollary is associated with lower use of cancer prevention services via three pathways. The first is cancer fatalism. A study by Wardle et al. (2004) found that people from lower SES were more likely to agree with the statement 'It's not worth having the test because "what will be will be"'. The second illness experience pathway was characterized by a lack of confidence in dealing with the medical system. It is known that people of lower SES have less confidence and express greater dissatisfaction with the medical system. Low rates of participation in screening are more common among those who express dissatisfaction with health care (Ackerson and Preston, 2009). The third proposed pathway was low perceived personal value of cancer screening. Since people from lower SES have lower life expectancies and have what Barrett (2003) described as 'older identities' they are more sceptical of the benefits of preventive health care such as screening.

In reviewing the evidence for the psychosocial mediators von Wager et al. (2011) expressed surprise that despite the large amount of research on social cognitive processes a limited amount of research had connected these processes with details of the SES status of the study participants. Despite these limitations they suggested three broad blocks of attitudinal mediators. These were the perceived threat of unpleasant or invasive medical procedures, self-efficacy for participating in cancer screening, and response efficacy for screening to detect cancer early, prolong life or minimize treatment.

These attitudinal mediators are then hypothesized to contribute to the low uptake of cancer screening among low SES adults through inadequate information processing (e.g. lack of information seeking) and limited goal setting (e.g. prioritization of alternative activities).

Although the von Wagner framework integrated a large amount of empirical work there is still a tendency to adopt a *deficit model* to explain non-participation in screening. Those who do not use the service tend to be characterized as lacking in knowledge and concern about their health. An alternative perspective is to view this non-attendance within its socio-cultural context and as a form of *resistance* to what is perceived as an unnecessary interference in their lives or even of something that could increase the likelihood of cancer.

MEANING OF CANCER AND CANCER SCREENING

Despite the advances in the treatment of cancer, or indeed partly due to the character of these advances, cancer remains the most feared disease. Murray and McMillan (1993) conducted a survey of a random sample of adults resident in Northern Ireland. They found that cancer was the most feared disease especially among women. The reason for this fear was because cancer was perceived as incurable and as leading to a painful death. Slenker and Spreitzer (1988) conducted a survey of a random sample of adults in Ohio. They found that not only was cancer the most feared disease but approximately half the respondents felt there was little you could do about the disease.

BOX 13.1
SOCIAL COROLLARIES AND PSYCHOSOCIAL MEDIATORS OF CANCER SCREENING

Corollaries of socio-economic status

- Stressors and resources for change
- Educational opportunities
- Illness experiences

Attitudinal mediators

- Perceived threat of unpleasant or invasive medical procedures and cancer diagnosis
- Self-efficacy for participating in cancer screening
- Response efficacy for screening to detect cancer early, prolong life, or minimize treatment

Non-participation in cancer screening

- Information processing
- Goal setting and behavioural translation

Source: adapted from von Wagner et al. (2011)

Several qualitative studies have explored women's fear of cancer and their reluctance to use the screening services. Blaxter (1983) conducted interviews with women from Glasgow about their views on health and illness. She found that the women were reluctant to talk about cancer. Blaxter suggested that this lack of reference to cancer was a coping strategy used by the women to protect themselves from cancer: 'to talk about it was to invoke it, to speak briefly or in a lowered voice was to leave it sleeping'. Participation in screening would threaten this form of psychological defence.

Murray and McMillan (1988) conducted interviews with a sample of working-class women from Northern Ireland. Again they found evidence of a fear of cancer and a reluctance to interfere. One woman explained why she had not had a smear test taken:

> I think you have the fear, you see, of it. But they say they can get it in time . . . but sure how do they know they've got it in time? They don't know until they start opening you up and if they open you up, it would spread. So I would say, leave well enough alone.
>
> (Murray and McMillan, 1988: 42).

A similar finding was reported by Gregg and Curry (1994). They conducted detailed interviews with a sample of African-American low-income women on their beliefs about cancer. Not surprisingly, they had a very negative image of the disease. They not only believed that cancer was deadly but also felt that if the cancer could be detected by mammography then it was already beyond cure. An example of this attitude is the case of a 62-year-old woman who had received a negative result from her pap test. Her reaction was a refusal to obtain a follow-up test:

> My last pap didn't come back good and they want me to go over to Grady, but I didn't go because I'm afraid they're going to tell me that I've got cancer. I've just had so much experience with cancer, and I know that if they operate on me it's going to get worse. So I'm just going to prolong it as much as I can . . . We all going to die anyway . . . It's too late now.
>
> (Gregg and Curry, 1994: 524)

Balshem (1991) linked these negative beliefs about cancer with the life experiences of the women. She conducted an ethnographic study of a working-class community in Philadelphia that seemed very resistant to a health promotion campaign aimed at encouraging healthier lifestyles including attendance for breast cancer screening. When she interviewed these women, Balshem found that the health promotion message was counter to their experience. They believed that fate determined who got cancer and who survived. To look for cancer was to tempt fate; it was 'looking for trouble'. To quote Balshem: 'Challenging fate is a risky business. Cancer inspires not challenge but taboo.' Thus the women preferred not to think about cancer.

Other qualitative work suggests that some women would prefer to conduct self-examination rather than attend a medical centre for investigation. For example, Tessaro et al. (1994) interviewed a sample of older African-American women and found that they did not think it necessary to use the health service since after self-examination they had found no lumps. Other women felt that they accepted lumps and bumps as part of life and were more concerned about other people's health rather than their own. One woman had this to say:

> I think the black woman don't realize herself she has a tendency to leave herself alone and worry about other people. So she doesn't have a chance to examine her body and see what is really wrong with it because she is so used to bumps and knocks and hurts until she ignores it.
>
> (Tessaro et al., 1994: 291)

Another important issue to consider is the sexual connotations of both breast and cervical cancer. Breasts are at the centre of a woman's sexual identity. Women fear breast cancer partly because of the threat to this identity (Murray and McMillan, 1988). Also, the evidence that a sexually transmitted virus may contribute to cervical cancer has been widely discussed. This has contributed to some women's reluctance to have a smear test. McKie (1993, 1995) considered the views of a sample of English working-class women. She found that in the minds of some of the women the test was associated with sexual promiscuity, a label that they did not want to have. By avoiding the test they sought to avoid the label.

Kearney (2006) conducted focus groups with women about their perceptions of cancer and cancer screening. This study used action research with the two groups of women meeting regularly to discuss the issues over several weeks. Over the course of this study the women became more critical of the medical establishment. One woman described the promotion of mammography as the preferred method for breast cancer screening as an example of 'boys with toys' and as reflecting the masculine preference for technology within health care in general. Another woman described as 'chilling' her growing awareness of the role of medical technology.

The women in these studies were generally from lower socio-economic backgrounds or from ethnic minorities who tend to have a higher rate of cancer but a lower uptake of mammography. Rather than acquiescing with scientific medical advice these women protected themselves from the threat of cancer either by refusing to discuss it, by associating it with other people, or by characterizing cancer screening as a potential cause of the disease itself. This accords with Joffe's (1999) argument that 'people are motivated to represent the risks that they face in a way that protects them, and the groups with which they identify, from threat. They make meaning of the threat in line with self-protective motivations rather than with rational dictums' (p. 10).

Another screening programme within the UK NHS is screening for bowel cancer using a faecal occult blood test that people carry out in their own homes using cardboard spatulas and sending samples through the post. Uptake is relatively low, ranging from 35% in the most deprived to 61% in the least deprived areas. Palmer et al. (2014) used focus groups to explore reasons for this low non-uptake. Participants described sampling faeces and storing faecal samples as crossing a cultural taboo, and causing shame. Having to complete the test kit within the home rather than a formal health setting was felt to be unsettling and reduced the perceived importance of the test. One participant said:

> Why don't they send you t'doctors or hospital to have it done there? . . . if the doctor sent for me and said I want to do so and so for you I'd go, or the hospital but doing that meself, I didn't like it at all.

Not knowing the screening results was reported to be preferable to the implications of a positive screening result. Feeling well was associated with low perceived relevance of screening, and talking about bowel cancer screening with family and peers emerged as the key to subsequent participation in screening after receiving the test kit through the post. Palmer et al. (2014) concluded that: 'Initiatives to normalise discussion about bowel cancer screening, to link the (screening) to general practice, and to simplify the test itself may lead to increased uptake across all social groups' (p. 1705).

EXPERIENCE OF CANCER SCREENING

Most of the research on cancer screening has concentrated on describing those factors associated with initial attendance for mammography. However, according to current guidelines women are expected to attend not once but on a regular basis. Fewer studies have examined this process of re-attendance although the evidence does suggest that rate of attendance for follow-up is lower than for initial examination (Sutton et al., 1994). One important factor in re-attendance is the woman's reaction to the initial test. Evidence suggests that this is not always positive.

Women often find mammography screening painful. Keefe et al. (1994) reviewed studies on the experience of pain during mammography and found that the percentage of women reporting pain varied widely across studies with a range of 1–62%. Admittedly, four of the eight studies reviewed by Keefe et al. (1994) found that at least one-third of the women reported some degree of pain during mammography. Lightfoot et al. (1994) reported that 40% out of a sample of 315 women undergoing screening mammography agreed that it hurt. Admittedly, it would seem that many accept the pain and discomfort since it is short term and has long-term benefits. However, some are less accepting and indeed feel that the pain may actually increase their risk of cancer. For example, one woman commented in Eardley and Elkind's (1990) study: 'The straight answer is – if I don't have cancer now, I'll have it after this [the pressure of the machine].' Such a viewpoint may act as a disincentive for repeat mammography. Despite this evidence, recent findings confirm that women still report pain during mammography and more intense pain is associated with reduced re-attendance. Whelehan et al. (2013) found in a review of 20 studies that 25–46% of women who had not re-attended cited pain as a reason.

There is also evidence that cervical screening can be uncomfortable for some women. Schwartz et al. (1989) found in her survey of women in the East End of London that 54% rated having a smear test as painful or uncomfortable and 46% found it embarrassing. Similarly, in a qualitative study (Waller et al., 2012) it was found that the women often talked about the test in terms of embarrassment, violation or pain. Again, such experiences would not be expected to encourage re-attendance.

In her study in the East Midlands of England, Armstrong (2007) contrasted the official discourse on cervical screening with that of the women. Whereas the former presented the smear test as a simple, painless and non-intrusive procedure the women characterized it as invasive and very uncomfortable. Armstrong, using Foucauldian discourse analysis, referred to three resources on which the women drew to challenge the official discourse. The first of these was their emotional experiences through which the women could explain how their particular feelings. For example, one woman said:

> It's just something that I just hate, I think it's, you know I don't know what it is and I know to the nurse it's nothing but I think it's just, perhaps because I'm such a private person. (p. 77)

In this case the woman is emphasizing her particular 'private' nature that led to her feeling particularly uncomfortable about the test. A second resource was the actual physical experiences in that the women drew attention to their particular physical experiences. For example, one woman said:

> every time uncomfortable and painful, they're just horrible . . . apparently, erm, I've got a funny shape so when the instrument is put in it goes in to open your cervix up it doesn't always go properly because of the shape. (p. 79)

The third resource was the changing body that was an extension to the physical experiences. In talking about the smear test these women were not trying to find a way to avoid attending for the test but rather challenging the official medical discourse of smear test as routine.

Psychological Consequences of Cancer Screening

In the initial haste to establish screening programmes, the psychological cost in terms of increased anxiety was overlooked. There are obvious adverse psychological consequences for women from being recalled following screening even if they are subsequently cleared. In the UK about 5% of women who undergo breast cancer screening are called back for further tests. This is termed a 'false positive' diagnosis. Although recalled women may be given the 'all-clear' following the further tests, they often still harbour uncertainty and anxiety.

The false positive result is followed by further anxiety-provoking investigation that will include clinical examination and possibly surgery. In a ten-year follow-up, Elmore et al. (1998) found that as many as one-third of women who obtained positive results were required to undergo additional investigations, including biopsies, even though it turned out that they did not have breast cancer.

Several studies have suggested that this anxiety remains even after the women have been cleared. Lerman and Rimer (1993) found that distress and anxiety continued after further examination had excluded cancer. Admittedly, not all women continue to experience anxiety. Although most cancer agencies will attempt to reduce anxiety by speeding up the process between evidence of a positive finding on the mammogram and subsequent surgical clearance, this is not always possible. An analysis of the tests conducted on a sample of women eventually declared false positive in Sweden found that they sometimes took up to two years (Lidbrin et al., 1996).

In a large Danish study, women who underwent screening for breast cancer were surveyed at baseline, 1, 6, 18 and 36 months (Brodersen and Siersma, 2013). The women were classified into three groups – those with a diagnosis of breast cancer, the false positives and the normal women. Those with the diagnosis of breast cancer had the most psychological disruption, followed by those with the false positive diagnosis. Even at 36 months after they had been given the all-clear, the women who had been false-positively diagnosed still reported substantial psychological disruption. An earlier UK study found similar findings. Women who had initially been falsely diagnosed but then were cleared of having breast cancer were found still to be suffering psychological symptoms three years later (Brett and Austoker, 2001). Further, those women who had undergone the most further tests experienced greater anxiety.

Moving beyond false positives are those women who are actually diagnosed and treated for cancer and found not to have it. The term 'overdiagnosis' is used to describe the diagnosis of cancer at screening that would not have been clinically apparent in the woman's lifetime. There is debate about the extent of such overdiagnosis with most estimates around 19–35%. An independent UK panel (2011) reviewed the evidence and concluded that for every 10,000 UK women aged 50 years invited for screening over the next 20 years, a total of 43 deaths would be prevented while 129 cases would be overdiagnosed, i.e. one breast cancer death prevented for every three overdiagnosed cases. A focus group study of women concluded that the benefits still outweighed the risks. The Panel concluded that information should be made available in a transparent and objective way to women invited to screening so that they can make informed decisions.

A qualitative study conducted in Australia further extended this discussion from a woman's perspective (Hersch et al., 2013). A sample of 50 women participated in focus group discussions. This showed that the majority of women were unaware that some women were being misdiagnosed with breast cancer. They were reluctant to accept the concept of overdiagnosis. As one woman said:

> How do we know that things are being overdetected? How do we know that there are some cancers that move more quickly or become more malignant than others? . . . Overdiagnosis assumes that these women, who have been overdiagnosed, have a cancer that is not necessarily aggressive . . . Who determines what's an aggressive and non-aggressive cancer?

Some of the women, especially younger women, indicated that this knowledge of the prospect of misdiagnosis deterred them from participating in screening. As one said:

> Turns me off further . . . I'm just adding the things that we've learnt together . . . and all the doctors not knowing if it is malignant or not, you add them all together and you think, 'Why bother?'

However, most women said that even with an estimated 30% overdiagnosis they were still willing to participate.

Health Service Organization for Cancer Screening

Several studies have found that the most important factor in explaining variation in participation is the extent to which the woman's doctor recommends participation (National Cancer Institute, 1990). Further, Lurie et al. (1993) found that women are more likely to undergo screening with pap smears or mammograms if they see female rather than male physicians. There is evidence to suggest that some physicians are reluctant to advise mammography for a variety of reasons, including scepticism about its effectiveness in general or for certain groups of women and fear of the effect of radiation. Smith and Herbert (1993) found that family physicians did not recommend mammography because they did not think the patients would participate, because the test was not available, because they were concerned about the radiation risk and because of the cost. Physicians are especially less likely to refer older women for screening (Costanza, 1992). Further, Frazier et al. (1996) found that Black women were more likely to report that their physician had not recommended participation.

A further reason for the hesitancy among some physicians in the USA as to recommending screening is fear of litigation. It has been suggested in the USA that many physicians may be reluctant to talk about screening with their patients because of the public controversy about screening guidelines (Leitch, 1995). This could lead to anxiety among some physicians, bearing in mind that delayed diagnosis of breast cancer is one of the most common causes of malpractice complaint. In the USA women who have developed cervical or uterine cancer after smear tests have won legal cases because of inappropriate treatment. In commenting on these cases, Austin and McLendon (1997) state that 'this trend is having a chilling effect on those professionals in the field of cytotechnology and cytopathology and potentially threatens the availability of this procedure for many of our patients' (p. 754).

More countries and regions are now establishing dedicated cancer screening programmes with postal invitations to women to attend on a regular basis. Despite these moves a proportion of women are still reluctant to participate in screening. Similarly, some women do not participate even when they are personally encouraged to attend by their physician (May et al., 1999). Sharp et al. (1996) found that a personal invitation by a woman's family doctor was as effective as a home visit from a nurse conveying the same message. However, despite the best intentions of family doctors, many women fail to receive such personal invites because of inaccurate registers (McEwan et al., 1989).

MEN AND CANCER SCREENING

Most of the research on psychological aspects of cancer screening has been on women and their use of breast and cervical cancer screening programmes. Since there are no similar programmes for men it is not surprising that there is less research. However, there is increasing discussion about the potential value of screening for both colorectal and prostate cancers among men. The limited psychological research has often been from a social cognition framework. These studies have referred to the importance of such factors as attitude, perceived behavioural control and perceived social norms as important predictors of intention to participate in such screening (e.g. Sieverding et al., 2010).

Several studies have confirmed the lower rates of uptake of screening programmes among men from low SES and ethnic minority backgrounds (e.g. von Wagner et al., 2011). In a study of US Hispanic males, Goodman et al. (2006) identified a series of perceived barriers to participation in screening for colorectal cancer. These included low levels of knowledge and awareness, lack of understanding of the screening test, and language and communication challenges.

The importance of the cultural context was identified in a qualitative study of New Mexico Hispanic men and women (Getrich et al., 2012) that considered the meaning of machismo – or the 'tough guy' attitude. They found that it was particularly important among the Mexicans interviewed. One woman said: 'Yes, machismo's a problem. I think that [men] are all the same. They feel that they are not sick – they say, "Nothing hurts me!"' Conversely, this was less evident among the Hispanos interviewed. For example, one man said: 'Macho is gone, those days are gone. It's a lot different than it was before . . . people get together and talk.' A qualitative study of Latino men's views of prostate cancer screening (Rivera-Ramos and Buki, 2011) also identified the importance of machismo as a deterrent to participation. The men interviewed in this study frequently referred to the digital rectal examination that is part of the prostate cancer screening as being a threat to their masculinity. As one participant said: 'It's almost the worst thing that can happen to a man.'

GENETIC SCREENING

The rapid advances in genetic research now hold out the prospect of genetic screening for different diseases. This can take various forms (see Lerman, 1997). Carrier testing investigates people who are likely to be carriers of the genes for such diseases as cystic fibrosis or Tay–Sachs disease. This form of testing is usually conducted in the context of reproductive decision-making. Presymptomatic testing allows the identification of a disease before the symptoms actually develop. This form of testing is used to determine the person's risk of developing such late-onset diseases as Huntington's disease. Susceptibility testing is designed to test for a person's susceptibility to develop a disease, although whether or not that disease develops depends upon a variety of environmental and nutritional factors partly outside the person's control.

Although the general principles underlying genetic screening are similar to those of other forms of screening there are certain unique features. Lerman (1997) described several distinguishing features that need to be taken into consideration when investigating the psychological aspects (Box 13.2). These factors need to be accounted for in exploring the development of these services.

BOX 13.2
FEATURES OF GENETIC SCREENING

Type of information

Genetic information is probabilistic and uncertain. In some cases you can say with certainty that a person will develop a disease but *when* is less clear (e.g. Huntington's disease). In other cases it is unclear whether the person will develop the disease at all (e.g. cancer).

Medical value

Control over disease onset is limited for certain diseases (e.g. cancer) and non-existent for others (e.g. Huntington's disease).

Timescale

The timescale is variable in that the results of genetic testing concern events that may occur far in the future.

Impact of results

The results affect not only the individual but also the family since genetic susceptibility is transmitted within families.

Source: Lerman (1997: 4)

An extension of cancer screening programmes has been genetic testing for cancer. This is still not a very common procedure but has attracted substantial interest among certain population subgroups. In a study in New Zealand, Cameron and Reeve (2006) found that worry about cancer was associated with interest in obtaining such a test although perceived risk was not. It was suggested that this may be due to perceived risk leading to more cautious appraisals of the benefits of genetic testing.

The importance of the patients' assessment of the benefit of the test was shown in a qualitative study of patients, patient group representatives and health professionals involved in clinical genetic services (McAllister et al., 2008). This study found that a common integrating theme in the patients' accounts was perceived *empowerment*. By this was meant that participating in the genetic testing enhanced the patients' feelings of control over their disease. As one patient group representative said:

> Information is power, [you're] powerless if you don't have information and that's one of the problems that we've come across. Families feel isolated, they have anxiety because they have no information therefore they have no power . . . I mean power to make the right decisions.

PSYCHOLOGICAL CONSEQUENCES OF GENETIC SCREENING

Unlike cancer screening, genetic testing is often initiated by individuals when they suspect that because of family history they may be carriers. Thus they would be expected to be in a heightened state of anxiety. Several studies have found a reduction in such anxiety following testing (e.g. Tibben et al., 1993). However, some studies have reported evidence of subsequent psychological distress. Lawson et al. (1996) found that of 95 individuals receiving the results of a test for Huntington's disease, two made plans for suicide and seven had clinical depression. Interestingly, there was no difference between those tested positive and those tested negative. Tibben et al. (1993) found that carriers tended to minimize the impact of the test results on their futures.

In a large systematic literature review, Broadstock et al. (2000) found no evidence of increased distress (general and situational distress, anxiety and depression) in carriers or non-carriers within 12 months after testing. Rather, both carriers and non-carriers showed decreased distress after testing; this was greater and more rapid among non-carriers. However, they point out that the studies were on self-selected populations who had agreed to participate in psychological assessment and that there was a need for further research.

There is some evidence that the positive effect of screening may only be short term. At six-month follow-up Tibben et al. (1993) found that one-quarter of the carriers exhibited signs of psychopathology. They continued to follow the group for three years (Tibben et al., 1997) and found that for the first six months there was a rise in avoidant thoughts and a decrease in intrusive feelings. This was followed by a reversal of this pattern. It was suggested that this was evidence of a coping strategy whereby the carriers 'dose themselves' with tolerable levels of intrusive thoughts as they begin to process and accept the test results.

Genetic screening can also have a dramatic impact on the family of the carrier. Hans and Koeppen (1989) found that partners often reacted with disbelief and denial. However, this turned to resentment and hostility as they became aware of the threat of transmission to their children. The partners can play an important role in helping the carrier cope with the diagnosis (Tibben et al., 1993).

The evidence of psychological impact of genetic screening has been followed by calls for greater provision of psychological support services (Marteau, 1990). It is suggested that such services be made available both prior to testing such that the testees are fully aware of the issues and also afterwards so that they and their families can begin to come to terms with the findings.

The prospect of widespread genetic screening has provoked sustained debate about the ethical issues. Harper (1992) voiced concern that the needs of individuals and families are being made subservient to broader eugenic goals. Stone and Stewart (1996) claimed that the voice of the public is rarely heard in this debate. They argue that the advocates of genetic screening often falsely claim that their programmes are based on the public's right to know. Yet there is little evidence that the public wants to know. Stone and Stewart also raised a variety of other questions about genetic screening such as the ability of lay people to interpret genetic information, the competence of health personnel in explaining aspects of genetic screening and the use made of genetic information.

In a review of the social impact and ethical implications of genetic testing, Davison et al. (1994) identified three areas of popular perception that have implications for predictive testing for Huntington's disease:

1. Both positive and negative results can lead to personal and family anguish. While the former is expected there is also evidence that those who are cleared suffer from survivor guilt and a feeling they do not belong to their family.

2. Some families who inherit the gene have developed ways of deciding who in the family will be sufferers. This lay procedure is undermined by medical investigation.

3. Knowing about possible futures may decrease the quality of a person's life. They note that this finding 'is not easily accommodated within the essentially rationalist or utilitarian philosophy underlying the idea of screening' (p. 354).

One particular aspect of remaining ignorant is that it allows the maintenance of hope. Many lay people are happy to tolerate uncertainty because of the hope that they will survive.

The premise of much genetic testing is that people understand the basic principles of inheritance. However, this may not always be the case. In an interview study of members of families at risk of familial adenomatous polyposis (FAP), which geneticists consider almost 100% genetic, Michie et al. (1996) found that many referred to what they considered to be the vital role of the environment. Many of the family members also minimized the threat posed by the disease. While advising these people that they are at risk may be formally correct, it has immense implications for the future quality of their lives.

Riley et al. (2012) present recommendations on the essential elements of genetic cancer risk assessment, counselling, and testing on behalf of the National Society of Genetic Counsellors in the USA. They argue that psychosocial assessment should be part of both the pre-test and post-test genetic counselling process, beginning by identifying the patient's primary reason for seeking the consultation and enquiring about the patient's current understanding of cancer genetics risk assessment and testing process. The skills required by genetic counsellors are complex and far-reaching. The counsellor should address any misconceptions in a sensitive manner and help the patient with his/her cancer worry, intrusive thoughts, depression, anger, fear, guilt, family experiences with cancer, perception of risk for self and others, competence for giving informed consent, social stressors and supports and networks, family communications, and readiness for testing.

IMMUNIZATION

Immunization is the procedure whereby those individuals who are most susceptible to contracting certain communicable diseases are administered a vaccine. This procedure is aimed at both immediate protection of individuals and also immunity across the whole community where the uptake rate is high. Over the years various vaccines have been developed for specific diseases.

In the mid- to late nineteenth century several countries began to introduce vaccines to prevent specific diseases. In the UK laws were passed making smallpox vaccination of children compulsory. However, this was not always met with approval and in some countries led to the development of anti-vaccination societies (Blume, 2006). This was perhaps not surprising in view of the organization of public health practice at that time but gradually this opposition declined and a range of vaccines have been introduced over the past century. According to current public health agencies immunization is now one of the most successful examples of the primary prevention of disease. However, as McKeown (1979) emphasized, the specific impact of vaccination programmes should not be confused with the health benefits of improvements in living and working conditions.

Despite the apparent success of mass immunization programmes (Figure 13.1), a large proportion of individuals are not immunized against certain diseases. Indeed, this has given rise to what

Figure 13.1 Immunization is an effective method for saving lives. Measles killed 2.6 million people before 1980 when the vaccine was introduced. That figure has dropped to around 100,000

Source: poster produced by the World Health Organization (2014)

has been described as a new anti-vaccination movement (Blume, 2006). An understanding of this participation of people in mass vaccination programmes requires an exploration of individuals' perceptions and the broader social context.

Psychological Models of Immunization

There is a large body of research using different SCMs to predict uptake of vaccination. A common feature of these models is risk perception. In a meta-analysis of 48 such studies, Brewer et al. (2007) distinguished between three dimensions of risk that were termed perceived likelihood, perceived susceptibility and perceived severity. These dimensions are detailed in Table 13.1. A fourth dimension – perceived risk if you do not take the health-protection action – was also noted. However, since this dimension was seldom reported in research, it was not included in the meta-analysis.

The results of the meta-analysis showed that:

- Those perceiving a higher likelihood of getting an illness were more likely to be vaccinated.
- Those who perceived themselves to be more susceptible to a particular illness were more likely to be vaccinated.
- Those who perceived the severity of the particular illness to be higher were more likely to be vaccinated.

Table 13.1 Dimensions of risk

Dimension	Description	Example
Perceived likelihood	Probability that one will be harmed by the hazard	'If I don't get immunized, there is a high chance I'll get the flu'
Perceived susceptibility	Constitutional vulnerability to a hazard	'I get sick more easily than others my age'
Perceived severity	Extent of harm that the hazard would cause	'The flu can kill you'

Source: Brewer et al. (2007)

It could be argued that these relationships were simply post-hoc rationalizations for receiving the vaccinations, i.e. after being vaccinated the individuals justified their actions by emphasizing their perceived risk. However, the effect sizes for the prospective studies were larger than for the cross-sectional studies, suggesting that this was not the case.

It was also noted that the effect sizes were larger for influenza vaccination than for other forms of vaccination. This may have been due to a variety of factors including:

- The non-flu studies included a wide range of vaccines, each with particular perceived characteristics.
- Flu vaccination is more familiar and contributes to a clearer perceived risk.
- The non-flu vaccines (e.g. hepatitis) require multiple vaccinations that may attenuate the risk perception.

A final result of this meta-analysis was that the effect sizes were smaller for medical personnel. Brewer et al. suggest that this may be due to the fact that perceived risk to the medical personnel themselves may be a lesser motivator than reducing the risk to their patients. In addition, it may be the case that medical personnel are required by their employers to be vaccinated. Some evidence on the importance of health professional identity was provided by a study conducted by Falomir-Pichastor et al. (2008) conducted in Switzerland. This study conducted a survey of nurses' intention to receive the flu vaccination. They found that the more the nurses identified with their profession the more likely were they to perceive vaccination as a professional duty and the more likely were they to have been vaccinated.

Findings on the role of risk perception in explaining vaccination can be contradictory. For example, in an online experiment, Betsch and Sachse (2013) found that strong 'no risk' messages were followed by a higher perceived vaccination risk than weak 'no risk' messages. Further, there is evidence that the role of risk depends upon who the risk is for – self or someone else. For example, in a survey of parents, Tang et al. (2014) found that they were more willing to vaccinate their child than themselves. It was suggested that parents were likely to take a risk of non-vaccination for themselves but they were anxious about doing similar for their child. Some evidence of this was found in a Q-methodology study of parental understandings of child vaccination (Harvey et al., 2014). In this study parents completed a Q-sort task after their two-month-old infant had been immunized. Four factors were identified in the Q-sort as being important: A: 'Because the doctor told me to'; B: 'I know what's best for my baby'; C: 'Will they really be OK?'; and D: 'Why wouldn't you protect them?'. While there were differences between parents in which factors they stressed, all agreed that vaccination provided unrivalled protection against disease. However, those parents with factor C also had feelings of uncertainty about vaccine safety and its side effects.

Recently there have been attempts to expand SCMs of health behaviour to include emotional components. In the case of immunization, this has included emotions such as worry and regret. In a study of university employees, Chapman and Coups (2006) found that anticipated regret and worry were stronger predictors of vaccination than perceived risk. This would confirm that humans are less concerned about statistical estimates of risk and more with how they feel about the likelihood of something happening.

SOCIO-CULTURAL CONTEXT OF IMMUNIZATION

As with our earlier discussion of screening, there is a need to locate the cognitive view of the risk associated with immunization within a broader understanding of the meaning of immunization and infectious diseases and the particular socio-cultural context.

The widespread introduction of immunization programmes over the past two centuries is a major example of the power of medical science. However, this power has not been accepted unquestionably. Blume (2006) has reviewed the growth of anti-vaccination movements over the past two centuries. When compulsory vaccination was introduced in the mid-nineteenth century it was opposed by a wide range of groups of people including the middle class, who were concerned with threats to individual liberty, but especially by the organized working class, who opposed the growing power of the state in the disciplining of the body. In the 1970s the public concern about the safety of the pertussis vaccine led to a substantial fall in its uptake. More recently, moves to introduce a range of new vaccines have been met with varying degrees of support.

The swine flu vaccine was introduced into many countries in 2009. Although in some countries it was enthusiastically received, in others this was not the case. For example, in North America there were active campaigns for mass vaccination against swine flu, whereas in the UK, after some initial debate, support for it declined as evidence for the severity of the epidemic declined. This is probably a reflection of the greater medicalization of American society.

Dew (1999) in his review of changing media representations of measles argues that the dominant approach of the media has been an acceptance of the medical viewpoint. However, in this age of risk (Beck, 1986) the media can become a forum for challenging the accepted medical approach. A review of British newspapers during the 1990s found a substantial increase in reportage of vaccine-related topics (Cookson, 2002). Of particular note was the finding that an increasing proportion of these articles dealt specifically with concerns about the safety of vaccines. In addition, there are an increasing number of websites devoted to critical views of vaccination. This would suggest that the debates about the value of immunization that were current in the nineteenth century are again growing. It is within this context of confusion that individuals attempt to develop an approach that is personally and socially responsible.

HEALTH CARE PROVIDERS AND IMMUNIZATION

Besides the media, health professionals also have a very important role to play in creating a climate of support or opposition to immunization. Several projects have illustrated the variable view of medical practitioners. While public health officials may enthusiastically promote immunization other health professionals may be less supportive. For example, there is evidence that family doctors have played a role in spreading fear about particular vaccines. A report in Britain (Peckham et al., 1989) concluded that the main obstacle to parents having their child immunized was misconceptions concerning contra-indications by the family doctor.

New and Senior (1991) in their interview study of mothers in north-west England found that 53 out of 71 mothers who had not had their children fully immunized claimed that either their child was contra-indicated to the pertussis vaccine or their doctor had advised them against it. Further, many of the mothers said they had received conflicting advice from different health professionals that led to confusion and loss of confidence in such advice. Indeed, some mothers said it was the actual attempt by the health professionals to convince them of the minimal risk that deterred them. As one mother said: 'Until they find a safe vaccine, one in 300,000 is still too large; I wouldn't play Russian roulette with my child.'

In addition to the family doctor, ancillary health staff can contribute to parents' anxiety about immunization. For example, Reddy (1989) conducted a survey of parents in a town in south-east England. He found that a frequent reason given for non-vaccination was that their child was ill at the appointed time. However, Reddy found that when he telephoned the parents most of those children who were supposedly ill only had a minor cold. When questioned the parents said they were concerned about the dangers of vaccinating a sick child and that this concern had been shared by the health centre receptionist, leading the parent to defer the appointment.

IMMUNIZATION AMONG CHILDREN

Much of the debate and research on immunization has focused on children and their parents. The reason for this is that from a very early age it is expected that children receive immunization against a range of diseases such as whooping cough, polio and measles. Despite substantial health care expenditure immunization uptake among children is not comprehensive. For example, more than two-thirds of Primary Care Trusts (PCTs) in England (221 of 294) reported less than 85% coverage for MMR during 2003–2004. Indeed, the coverage fell below 70% in 19 PCTs (Henderson et al., 2008). As with adults, rates of immunization have been found to be lower among children from more disadvantaged communities and from certain minority ethnic communities.

New and Senior (1991) conducted detailed interviews with over 250 mothers from north-west England. They found that mothers with lower educational qualifications, mothers living alone, mothers with large families and mothers with a sick child were the best predictors of non-immunization. A study in the north of England (Reading et al., 1994) found that even after the establishment of an immunization programme, the relationship between immunization uptake and social deprivation remained. In this study the immunization of four birth cohorts between 1981 and 1990 was examined. Although there was an overall increase in uptake, the rates remained lowest among the children from the most disadvantaged areas.

Several studies have identified a variety of reasons expressed by parents for not having their children immunized. These have been summarized by Meszaros et al. (1996) under five categories that, similar to the meta-analysis of Brewer et al. (2008), focused on perceptions of risk and risk management (Table 13.2).

In their study, Meszaros et al. (1996) attempted to assess the relative importance of each of these explanations in a questionnaire survey of readers of *Mothering*, a popular magazine read by mothers in the USA. They found that the most important predictors of parents having their child immunized were the perceived dangers of the vaccine, doubts about medical claims that vaccines are effective, omission bias, belief that physicians overestimate the dangerousness of the disease, perceived ability to protect their child, and perceived assessment of the likelihood of their child contracting the disease.

Table 13.2 Parental reasons for non-immunization

Risk/benefit ratio	Perception that the risks of contracting the disease outweigh the benefits of being immunized
Individual risk	Belief that the societal statistics that public health planners use do not apply to their child. Further, the parents believe that they can protect the child from exposure
Ambiguity aversion	Aversity to options with ambiguous outcomes such that parents will prefer a straightforward Yes/No assessment of the likelihood of their child contracting a disease. When there is disagreement about potential risk they will err on the side of caution. Further, some parents may already be sceptical of medical information
Omission bias	Preference for acts of omission over acts of commission
'Free riding'	Assumption that since most of their children's peers have been vaccinated they are protected

Source: Meszaros et al. (1996: 698)

Following a series of reports in the 1990s of a possible link between childhood vaccination and autism, vaccination rates dropped. Subsequent reports have been strongly challenged and vaccination rates have subsequently recovered (Recamme, 2012). However, anti-vaccination organizations continue to report this link, promoting fear and anxiety among parents. According to a Swedish study by Dannetun et al. (2005) parents report obtaining information on vaccination from the media (82%) and the Internet (36%). A study of websites on vaccination found that nearly half contained vaccine critical information (Davies et al., 2002). Further these websites often use emotional appeals and personal stories coupled with photographs and pictures. In an experimental study Betsch et al. (2010) found that accessing a vaccine critical website increased the perception of risk due to vaccination.

This fear of the adverse effect of immunization may be particularly high in certain communities. In a study in England (Loewenthal and Bradley, 1996) it was found that the uptake of childhood immunization was particularly low among orthodox Jews. It was suggested by mothers interviewed that the main reason for their low uptake was their fear of a negative reaction, logistical difficulties and unsympathetic treatment by health staff. According to the health professionals, the mothers' fears were exaggerated because they lived in a close-knit community that perpetuated tales of bad reactions. A more recent study of a similar community by Henderson et al. (2008) emphasized the importance of the closed nature of the community within which rumours about the harm done by immunization were combined with a general concern about the negative influence of the outside world on the Jewish community. Table 13.3 summarizes the main findings of the study.

Besides these factors, an additional factor is the perceived relative risk. In a qualitative investigation of the views of a sample of inner-city parents in Baltimore, Keane et al. (1993) found that although some parents accepted that they or their children might be vulnerable to infectious diseases, other threats such as drugs, street violence and 'the wrong crowd' were considered more severe. Further, vaccines were viewed as only partly successful. The continued occurrence of chickenpox was frequently cited as evidence of vaccine failure.

A frequent explanation given by mothers in several studies is the natural/unnatural distinction. New and Senior (1991) found that whereas vaccination was perceived by some mothers

Table 13.3 Childhood immunization in an orthodox Jewish community

Social network	Advice circulated through local networks
Media	Stories from mass media coupled with negative feelings about outside world
Safety	Separation of community from outside influence led to feelings of safety
Danger	Immunization was perceived a 'putting the disease in the child'

Source: Henderson et al. (2008)

as unnatural, by implication whooping cough was natural and therefore acceptable. Admittedly, some other women had weighed up the benefits and risks of immunization and decided in favour of immunization. It would be expected that these were the women who were more accepting of the medical viewpoint.

This natural/unnatural distinction was also alluded to in a large German study by Weitkunat et al. (1998). They found that the most significant predictors of measles immunization were parental natural health orientation, advice of paediatrician, birth order position, dangerousness of measles, marital status, reliability of vaccination and smoking. They suggested that natural health orientation and advice of paediatricians may be interactive since individuals with a natural health orientation may select like-minded physicians. In a more detailed analysis of what they described as the subjective relevance of measles they found that those who assessed the likelihood of contracting measles as high and the latency as low were more likely to have their children immunized. A more recent German study of Facebook groups (Betsch and Sachse, 2013) reported finding that those with a preference for conventional medicine also tended to have a positive attitude to vaccination.

Parental concern about the possible risks of vaccination is expressed too in homeopathic beliefs. In a survey of parents of children in south-west England (Simpson et al., 1995) it was found that the commonest reasons given for non-immunization of their children were homeopathy and religious beliefs. With regard to homeopathy, one parent said:

> I believe that the body's defences are best strengthened by optimum nutrition and good hygiene and by allowing the body to experience normal illnesses without suppression during the normal course of events. To enhance this process I consult our family homeopath for acute and chronic assistance as necessary. I am actually thoroughly opposed to current practices in vaccination programmes; the onslaught of several vaccinations at once on a tiny body for the sake of convenience and getting them done, I find very disturbing. I am sure high prices are paid for this in terms of autoimmune diseases and weakened immune systems.
>
> (Simpson et al., 1995: 227)

Taken together these findings would suggest that while parents may be hesitant about having their child immunized because of their anxiety about the potential risk, this image is compounded by media speculation and by the contradictory advice they sometimes receive from health professionals.

A final point needs to be made about a more recent form of childhood immunization. The recent introduction of HPV immunization for 11–12-year-old girls has attracted substantial media and increasing research interest. A survey of parents of adolescent girls resident in North Carolina (Reiter et al., 2009) found that the dimensions of the HBM were predictors of vaccine uptake by their daughters. Parents who reported their daughter had been vaccinated were more likely to perceive the HPV vaccine as effective, perceived fewer barriers and harms and were also likely to be confident their insurance covered the cost. Although there has been media discussion about the sexual connotations of HPV immunization they did not find that anticipated regret about greater sexual activity by their daughter was an independent predictor of HPV uptake although another study did find some evidence of such a relationship (Ziarnowski et al., 2009).

There remains considerable uncertainty about this new vaccine. A survey of mothers of teenage girls conducted in Texas (Baldwin et al., 2012) found that those parents who perceived their daughters as being vulnerable were more likely to talk with others and their physician about the vaccine. However, people from ethnic minorities were less likely to discuss this vaccine with others. This is a new form of immunization and the role of socio-cultural factors is of obvious importance.

Despite considerable efforts to promote this vaccine several studies have confirmed that parents remain apprehensive. In a review of studies, Jacobson et al. (2013) identified the three main perceptions discouraging mothers were the perception that the vaccine was not needed by their daughter, that it was potentially harmful, and that their child was too young because they were not sexually active. Related to the latter perception was the anxiety that having the vaccine might promote earlier sexual activity. There is no evidence for this concern. A survey of college-age women in the USA (Ziemer and Hoffman, 2012) found that although perceived benefits was the major predictor of vaccination intentions, many of the unvaccinated women expressed the view that it was not necessary for them since they did not perceive themselves as being at risk.

The role of industry in promoting the uptake of HPV, despite limited evidence on its effectiveness, also draws attention to the importance of the socio-cultural context. A large amount of money has been used by industry to promote this vaccine and further medicalize the lives of people (Porta, 2009). While psychology can identify the immediate factors that promote its uptake it needs also to consider these contextual factors.

ANTI-VACCINE CONSPIRACY THEORIES

One factor in people's resistance to vaccination stems from the belief that vaccinations are actually dangerous. This idea is promoted quite heavily on anti-vaccination websites and blogs on the Internet. There are many prominent alleged conspiracies to be found there, such as the NASA moon landings of 1969 being televised from a film studio, President J.F. Kennedy murdering Marilyn Monroe, the CIA, in turn, murdering President Kennedy, the Duke of Edinburgh murdering Princess Diana, 9:11 being cleverly arranged by President Bush so companies he had an interest in could grab some oil wells in Iraq, and global warming being a total myth. Vaccination programmes have been the subject of some equally popular conspiracy theories, one of the main ones being that Big Pharma has created evidence supporting vaccinations purely to promote expensive but ineffective vaccines.

The potential impact of anti-vaccination conspiracy theories on vaccination intentions was investigated empirically by Jolley and Douglas (2014). The results suggest that conspiracy theories can be influential. In one study, British parents completed a questionnaire measuring beliefs in anti-vaccine conspiracy theories and the likelihood that they would have a fictitious child vaccinated. A significant negative relationship was found between anti-vaccine conspiracy beliefs and vaccination intentions mediated by the perceived dangers of vaccines, and feelings of powerlessness, disillusionment and mistrust in authorities. In a second study, participants read information that either supported or refuted anti-vaccine conspiracy theories, or a control condition. Participants who were exposed to material supporting anti-vaccine conspiracy theories showed less intention to vaccinate than those in the anti-conspiracy condition or controls. The effect was mediated by the same variables as in Study 1. Jolley and Douglas' findings pointed to the potentially detrimental impact of anti-vaccine conspiracy theories, and highlight their potential role in shaping health-related behaviours. Disinformation can be an effective influence on behavioural intentions, so it would seem.

CONCLUSION ABOUT DISEASE PREVENTION

The development of screening and immunization programmes designed to prevent the onset of specific diseases is premised upon a scientific model of risk with less attention given to the social and psychological features. While psychological research has tended to focus on the role of individual perceptions of risk, these need to be studied within the broader socio-cultural context.

FUTURE RESEARCH

1. There is a need for further research on breast self-examination.
2. Modern health care is pervaded by notions of risk control. There is a need to critique the relative contribution of prevention programmes.
3. There are substantial social and ethnic variations in participation in screening and immunization programmes. Research needs to explain the varying meanings of these programmes to particular population sub-groups.
4. The media plays an important role in shaping lay people's understanding of vaccination. There is a need for research to consider the influence of different forms of media, including conspiracy theories.
5. Genetic research has rapidly produced a host of social, psychological and ethical issues. There is a need for an expanded programme of research to investigate both professional and public perceptions of genetic screening and the impact on different populations.

SUMMARY

1 Many countries have implemented screening programmes for different forms of cancer. Participation in these programmes varies substantially.

2 Psychological factors associated with use of these programmes connect with the socio-cultural context.

3. The health professional – especially the family doctor – is central to explaining participation in these programmes.
4. The so-called 'genetic' revolution has many implications for screening.
5. Both the general public and people who are at risk of certain diseases have a variety of concerns about genetic screening.
6. A wide range of immunization programmes have been developed for adults and children.
7. A central feature in the uptake of immunization is perceived risk but this needs to be considered within its socio-cultural context.
8. The health professional plays a central role in deciding whether parents have their children immunized.
9. Parents have a range of fears and anxieties about childhood immunization.
10. Irrational fears and beliefs exert a powerful influence on intentions and decisions.

14 HEALTH PROMOTION

Imagination lights the fuse of possibility.

(Emily Dickinson)

OVERVIEW

This chapter focuses upon the psychological dimensions of health promotion. Two contrasting approaches to health promotion are described: the behaviour change approach and the community development approach. Health promotion interventions informed by each approach are described and critically examined. Criteria for the evaluation of the effectiveness of health promotion interventions are also presented. We conclude with discussions concerning healthist discourses in health promotion and its wider implications on subject positioning and experience.

WHAT IS HEALTH PROMOTION?

Health promotion is any event, process or activity that facilitates the protection or improvement of the health status of individuals, groups, communities or populations. The objective is to prolong life and to improve quality of life, that is, to prevent or reduce the effects of impaired physical and/or mental health in those individuals who are directly (e.g. patients) or indirectly (e.g. carers) affected. Health promotion practice is often shaped by how health is conceptualized. While early models focused primarily on disease prevention (as influenced by the biomedical model), more recent models are influenced by the biopsychosocial model which takes into account the psychological and social determinants of health.

In 1986, the Ottawa Charter for Health Promotion defined health promotion as 'the process of enabling people to increase control over, and to improve, their health' (World Health Organization, 1986: 1). The charter recognized that this process requires the strengthening of skills and capabilities of individuals, communities and social groups. This involves building healthy public policy, creating supportive environments, strengthening community actions, developing personal skills and reorienting health services. The Ottawa Charter also acknowledged that health is a *resource for everyday life*, not the object for living. It affirmed that the prerequisites for this state of well-being should include peace, shelter, education, food, income, a stable ecosystem, sustainable resources, social justice and equity. To achieve its goals, health promotion needs to: (1) advocate for health and create favourable social conditions; (2) enable individuals to achieve their fullest health potential by reducing inequalities and ensuring equal opportunities; and (3) mediate between all sectors of society and coordinate with people from all walks of life. A weighty agenda indeed!

In this chapter, we present two commonly used approaches to health promotion: the **behaviour change approach** and the **community development approach**. While these approaches pursue different goals, utilize different means to achieve the goals and propose different criteria for **evaluation**, both aim to promote good health and to prevent or reduce the effects of ill health. Health promotion interventions informed by each approach are described and critically examined.

BEHAVIOUR CHANGE APPROACH

The goal of the behaviour change approach is to bring about changes in individual behaviour through changes in their cognitions. Based on the assumption that humans are rational decision makers, this approach relies heavily upon the provision of information about risks and benefits of certain behaviours. As such, this approach to health promotion is synonymous with health education as it aims to increase individuals' knowledge about the causes of health and illness. Health information can be disseminated through leaflets, mass and social media campaigns, visual displays or one-to-one advice. Information is often presented as factual and attributed to an expert source. Health messages can be framed positively by highlighting the benefits of the behaviour; or negatively by emphasizing health risks (see Chapter 11). This approach had been a fundamental aspect of health promotion work in England and was highlighted as a priority in the White Paper, *Saving Lives: Our Healthier Nation* (Department of Health, 1999). Through the provision of health information, this approach gives the illusion of patient empowerment by enabling individuals to make informed choices and to allow them to take more responsibility for their own health.

Social Cognition Models and Behaviour Change

As we saw in Chapter 6, theories about the relationship between knowledge, attitudes and behaviour are known as **social cognition models (SCMs)**. These have been researched in a wide range of preventive health behaviours such as vaccination uptake, breast self-examination and contraceptive use. SCMs aim to predict the performance of behaviours and, by implication, to provide guidance as to how to facilitate their uptake by manipulating relevant variables (such as beliefs, attitudes and perceptions). It is suggested that there is a close relationship between people's beliefs, attitudes and their intentions to act in particular ways. Consequently, by bringing about changes in knowledge and beliefs, it is hoped to bring about behaviour change. Now that sounds as easy as falling off a log, but is it really?

To give an example, Cassidy et al. (2014) used the health belief model (HBM; Becker, 1974) to design an information-based intervention to promote HPV vaccine uptake. A brochure was given to parents of preteen girls, and electronic alerts promoted telephone reminders for dose completion. Using a quasi-experimental design to evaluate outcomes, results showed that parents who received the intervention were 9.4 times more likely to have HPV vaccine uptake and 22.5 times more likely to complete the dose. If these kind of outcomes could be obtained everywhere, that would be really exciting! Similarly, Jalilian et al. (2014) applied the HBM as a theoretical framework to understand and predict patients' attitudes towards diabetes and how this understanding can be used to design an educational programme to promote diabetes self-management among patients in Iran. The programme was run as six weekly teaching sessions (45–60 minutes each) which included discussions on type 2 diabetes complications (to improve patients' perceived susceptibility), foot care (to improve patients' perceived severity), physical activity and diet education (to improve patients' self-efficacy). Using a randomized controlled trial design to evaluate project outcomes, results showed that patients who received the intervention had higher scores on perceived susceptibility, severity, benefit and self-management than those in the control group.

The theory of reasoned action (TRA; Fishbein and Ajzen, 1975) and its revised version, the theory of planned behaviour (TPB; Ajzen, 1985, 2002) have also been used extensively to predict health relevant behaviours and to use these as a framework to develop behaviour change interventions. For example, Giles et al. (2014) used the TPB to develop an intervention to improve young people's motivations to breastfeed. PowerPoint slides developed by the Health Promotion Agency (Northern Ireland) were initially used in the programme. This was further developed using information from focus groups and questionnaires with young people exploring their cognitions around breastfeeding. The findings were integrated into the final intervention. This was delivered as part of the Year 10 Home Economics curriculum in the school. To evaluate outcomes, questionnaires which included key components of the TPB were administered to control and intervention schools. Findings showed that female pupils from the intervention group had increased intentions to breastfeed, improved their knowledge, and had more positive attitudes and perceptions of subjective norms towards breastfeeding than those in the control group. The only trouble is we never know if those good intentions will cash out in actual behaviour, as quite frequently they do not. This is known as the 'intention–behaviour' gap.

Theoretical developments in the use of SCMs to predict health-relevant behaviours have also seen extensions of existing models by incorporating additional variables (see Chapter 6). For example, Rogers' (1975) protection motivation theory expanded upon the HBM to include the role of fear in promoting behaviour intentions. This model had been influential in the use of fear tactics in persuading people to modify behaviours. One example is the use of graphic warnings in anti-smoking campaigns.

Ruiter et al. (2014) reviewed 60 years of fear appeal research and concluded that fear tactics may not be the most appropriate strategy to promote healthy behaviour. Presenting coping information that increases perceptions of response effectiveness may be more effective than presenting fear-arousing stimuli. Ethical issues also must be taken into consideration when using fear-arousing stimuli in health communication. Brown and Whiting (2014) argued that the use of fear tactics poses the potential risk of harming audiences who do not consent to being exposed to these campaigns and are unable to withdraw from them. Gagnon et al. (2010) also argued that the use of fear can be understood as society's way of managing citizens' behaviours. Drawing upon Foucault's concept of 'governmentality', the authors critically analysed a sexual health campaign, 'Condoms: They aren't a luxury', and examined how young adults are encouraged to 'consume' fear and to practise self-discipline to avoid suffering the adverse consequences of unsafe sex. The authors were concerned that 'young adults are more likely to capture the undertow of the prevention campaign and internalize the invisible messages – hereby referring to the discourses of punishment and moral disgrace surrounding STIs and those who contract them' (p. 253).

This resonates with Lupton's (1995) critique of the discourse of risk prevalent in contemporary health promotion. She proposed that 'risk, in contemporary societies, has come to replace the old-fashioned (and in modern secular societies now largely discredited) notion of sin' (p. 89). This is achieved through the practice of health risk appraisals and screening programmes. Lupton likened these practices to religious confessions where sins are confessed, judgment is passed and penance is expected. Lupton pointed out that risk discourse attributes ill health to personal characteristics such as lack of will power, laziness or moral weakness. In this way those 'at risk' become 'risk takers' who are responsible for their own ill health as well as its effects upon others and society as a whole. Lupton argued that risk discourse can have detrimental consequences for those positioned within it: being labelled at risk can become a self-fulfilling prophecy since people may feel reluctant to seek medical advice for fear of being reprimanded. Also, it can give rise to fatalism, as well as anxiety, uncertainty and fear, as, for example, for women 'at risk' of breast cancer who can experience their 'at risk' status as a half-way house between health and illness (Gifford, 1986, cited in Lupton, 1995).

Despite the risks and criticisms associated with the use of fear tactics in health promotion, several campaigns still adopt this approach to influence behaviour change. To explore the reasons for the wide application of fear appeals in health risk communication, Peters et al. (2014) conducted semi-structured interviews with 33 stakeholders in behaviour change interventions in the Netherlands. The analysis suggested that the main reasons for using fear arousal were to attract attention and to encourage audiences to reflect about risks. Social dynamics and power structures in intervention development play a role. While those who were more closely involved in developing and implementing interventions were convinced that fear arousal should be avoided, often they were unable to convince funders who preferred the use of fear appeals in health risk communication. Furthermore, non-researchers were unable to understand the research evidence about the use of fear tactics and the cognitive processes involved in behaviour change. The psychologist must learn the best ways to communicate evidence to programme investors in a convincing fashion, otherwise there can be conflicts.

SOCIAL MARKETING AND BEHAVIOUR CHANGE

Social marketing (SM) is the application of consumer-oriented marketing techniques in the design, implementation and evaluation of programmes aimed towards influencing behaviour change. Social marketing draws upon concepts from behavioural theory, persuasion psychology and marketing science, and incorporates the 'four Ps' of marketing: place, price, product and promotion (Evans, 2006). The key concepts are as follows (Department of Health, 2008):

- *Consumer orientation*: the consumer is at the core of this approach; it uses consumer research to gain insight into their knowledge, attitudes and beliefs, and the social context in which they live and work.
- *Existing behaviour and behavioural goals*: behaviour change strategies are based on existing behaviours and the factors that influence it. Behavioural change goals are developed which are divided into actionable and measurable steps and phased over time.
- '*Intervention mix*' *or* '*marketing mix*': this approach uses a range of interventions or methods to achieve its goals.
- *Audience segmentation*: the audience is segmented so that the intervention can be tailored to the specific needs of each segment.
- *Exchange*: this approach takes into consideration what people must give up or pay to receive the benefits of behaviour change by maximizing perceived benefits and minimizing perceived costs.
- *Competition*: this approach takes into consideration all other factors that compete for people's attention and willingness to adopt the behaviour being promoted.

A recent systematic review by Truong (2014) reflected on the growth of the social marketing approach over the past decade. This review included 867 articles published from 1998 to 2012, typically based in the USA or UK. Qualitative methods were frequently used, although quantitative and mixed method approaches were also becoming more common. Public health was the most common topic of interest. Discussions on 'downstream' social marketing (e.g. media campaigns) were prevalent, with limited attention given to 'upstream' (e.g. structural workplace interventions, provision of resources and fiscal interventions) and critical dimensions.

Box 14.1 gives an example of a smoking cessation intervention in Nottingham, UK, designed to reduce smoking in adults living in its most deprived areas. Insights into the smoking behaviour of the target groups were developed through 'geo-demographic' profiling, literature review, and qualitative research through semi-structured and street interviews. A marketing agency developed the intervention mix, using billboards, adverts on buses and trams, posters, and beer mats.

BOX 14.1
'LISTENING TO REASON': A SOCIAL MARKETING STOP-SMOKING CAMPAIGN IN NOTTINGHAM

Context

Nottingham City NHS Primary Care Trust (PCT) established a multidisciplinary team to coordinate a campaign to persuade adults to quit smoking, targeting the over-40 population living in the most deprived areas of the city.

Consumer research

Data from the geo-demographic classification system (Mosaic) was supplemented with local information to profile the target group. A marketing research company helped gain insights into the incentives and barriers to quitting, what could be offered in exchange, and the competing personal behaviours and external factors that would be likely to limit the interventions. Qualitative research explored consumer profiles. Three smoker groups were identified: those who would give up now, those who would give up some time, and those who would never give up.

Developing the campaign

Using the information from the consumer research, the team considered the benefits of giving up smoking compared to its costs. Respondents reported that they were aware that the cost of stopping smoking may be putting on weight. Thus including testimonies of people losing weight was an important element of the campaign. Other benefits included financial savings, having the health and energy to spend time with children and grandchildren (both short and longer term), and being fitter and able to do more leisure activities. Internal and external 'competitions' were also considered.

Based on group profiling, it was considered that the target groups were more likely than the general population to feel negatively about impending legislation on smoke-free

(Continued)

(Continued)

public places. Thus the team delayed the launch of the campaign to distance it from this new legislation. Another issue was the use of the NHS brand. While the team was aware that the target groups resisted health professionals telling them to quit, the NHS brand was viewed as helpful in offering free support to quitters. The campaign was therefore explicitly linked to the NHS stop-smoking service.

A 'media mix' developed by a marketing agency used the by-line 'listen to reason', the idea of knowing the arguments for quitting and considering the testimony of local people about why they had given up smoking and the benefits received (i.e. 'My reason is . . .'). The following strategies were based on accessibility to the target audience and cost:

- A3 posters using the testimonies of nine local volunteers.
- Adverts for trams, buses and billboards carrying the same visual images of the volunteers on the posters and shortened testimonies.
- Beer mats for pubs.
- A campaign website (www.listentoreason.com) providing free access to supportive materials and information about smoking.

Implementing the campaign

The campaign was launched in mid-August 2007. Local people whose images appeared in the campaign were asked to participate in the launch. The campaign was also covered in the local media. Distribution of posters by front-line NHS staff aided their engagement and improved distribution to appropriate venues. Beer mats were distributed by the marketing agency to 75 pubs in target areas. The website was accessed by over 350 people during the eight weeks of the campaign.

Source: De Gruchy and Coppel (2008)

CRITIQUE OF BEHAVIOUR CHANGE APPROACHES TO HEALTH PROMOTION

The behaviour change approach has attracted many criticisms. First, it is unable to target the major causes of ill health. Individual behaviour change, even when successfully implemented, cannot address socio-economic factors such as poverty, unemployment or environmental pollution. Its objective is change within the individual rather than change in the individual's environment.

Neglecting wider determinants of health poses the risk of generating further inequalities in health. For example, a review of systematic reviews by Lorenc et al. (2013) suggests that some 'downstream' interventions can increase social inequalities in health, while 'upstream' interventions aim to reduce these.

Second, the choice of which behaviour to target lies with 'experts' whose task it is to communicate and justify this choice to the public. As a result, recommendations and advice provided 'from above' can be seen as incompatible with community norms. Receiving health advice in a top-down fashion can be disempowering, as Ayo (2012) argued:

> Health promotion messages such as 'be active', 'eat healthy' and 'lose weight', are boisterously propagated throughout Western neoliberal societies as the panacea to modern day health concerns of chronic diseases. Under this logic, it is individuals who are placed at the centre of health promotion strategies, as opposed to overarching social systems that also determine health outcomes. They are seen as being both the cause and the solution to potential health problems and thus are made to be accountable for their own health. However, when exercising one's autonomy and freedom, it is expected that the responsible citizen will allow his or her lifestyle to be guided under the auspices of knowledgeable experts and normative prescriptions of what it means to be healthy. This requires attending to one's own health in ways which have been socially approved and politically sanctioned. (p. 104)

Third, the behaviour change paradigm does not address the many variables other than cognitions that influence human actions. Despite the increasing range and complexity of SCMs, there are a number of shared characteristics on which to base a critique of the genre. For example, SCMs conceptualize the individual as a rational decision maker and are only concerned with conscious, cognitively mediated health behaviours (e.g. the decision to buy a smoke alarm). However, it has been pointed out that many health habits occur routinely (Bennett et al., 1995) (e.g. brushing one's teeth in the morning) and do not involve conscious decision making.

Furthermore, with one notable exception which makes a questionable use of fear (protection motivation theory), SCMs generally do not take the role of impulse and/or emotion into account. Even where models do include the variable of 'volitional control' (e.g. TPB; Ajzen, 1985), this is conceptualized as a conscious belief (in one's own efficacy) that the individual includes in his/her rational appraisal. However, emotional needs and 'urges' as well as power relations can have a strong and direct influence on behaviours. Consider, as one example, the deeply felt cravings of the quitting smoker or heroin user.

SCMs also assume that the same variables are universally relevant to diverse groups of people. Yet there is evidence to the contrary from studies that have identified different psychological antecedents of HIV preventive behaviour for men and women, people of different ages, as well as people with different amounts of sexual experience (e.g. Abraham and Sheeran, 1994). The behaviour change paradigm tends to assume homogeneity among the receivers of its health messages. However, information is not received or processed uniformly by those to whom it is directed: mood, motivation, past experience, interest, perceived relevance, lay beliefs, group membership and many other factors mediate the way in which a message is 'heard' and interpreted. Translating and communicating information in a meaningful way is a complex undertaking affected by a multiplicity of factors including health literacy, the media and the ubiquity of health information (see Chapter 11).

Considering all of these criticisms, it is not surprising that outcomes from interventions based on SCMs are unimpressive, so much so that they show no significant improvements beyond those obtained with interventions lacking any theoretical basis whatsoever. As the authors of one study concluded, 'interventions based on Social Cognitive Theory or the Transtheoretical Model were similarly effective and no more effective than interventions not reporting a theory base' (Prestwich et al., 2014). This is the disappointing legacy of 40 years of research with SCMs. Alternative approaches need to be considered as the SCMs are quietly retired.

COMMUNITY DEVELOPMENT APPROACH

Health psychologists have explored different ways of understanding health and illness and engaged with different strategies for intervention with health and well-being. Throughout this book we emphasize the value of broadening the scope of health psychology by considering the social and cultural context within which health and illness are located and developing more socially collective strategies for promoting health. Recently there has been increasing interest in community development approaches within health psychology.

Community development approaches aim to improve and promote health by addressing socio-economic and environmental determinants of health within the community. These recognize the close relationship between individual health and its social and material contexts, which consequently become the target for change. Individuals act collectively in order to change their environment rather than themselves. Thus, it constitutes the interface between the environmental and the behavioural approaches to health promotion in that it is concerned with the ways in which collectivities can actively intervene to change their physical and social environment. The psychologist serves as an agent of change.

Over the past decade there has emerged increasing interest in developing a **community health psychology**. This has been defined as 'the theory and method of working with communities to combat disease and to promote health' (Campbell and Murray, 2004: 187). As in community psychology itself, there are different orientations. The more *accomodationist approach* focuses on processes within the community while the more *critical approaches* aim to connect intra-community processes with the broader socio-political context. A primary aim of critical community psychologists is:

> to promote analysis and action that challenges the restrictions imposed by exploitative economic and political relationships and dominant systems of knowledge production, often aligning themselves with broad democratic movements to challenge the social inequalities which flourish under global capitalism.
>
> (Campbell and Murray, 2004: 190)

McLeroy et al. (2003) distinguish between four different forms of community-based health promotion. These are community as setting, community as target, community as agent and community as resource. *Community as setting* is largely defined in geographical terms. This is a very common definition and assumes outside experts who are targeting a clearly defined community. The *community as target* is somewhat similar but is particularly concerned with creating a healthy environment through largely systemic changes. The *community as resource* is concerned with outside experts identifying and promoting the community strengths. Finally, the *community as agent* emphasizes working with the community to identify needs and resources and to support them in the processes of change. This approach is the most similar to that of community health psychology. It is its activist orientation which distinguishes community health psychology from other forms of community-based health interventions.

THEORETICAL INFLUENCES IN COMMUNITY HEALTH PSYCHOLOGY

Community health psychology has deliberately attempted to connect with other developments in critical social and health psychology and with developments in community psychology. Paulo Freire's (1910–1990) critical pedagogy is one of the key theoretical influences of this approach. Freire was a Brazilian educator who argued that the campaign to increase literacy was a political struggle and contrasted the traditional approach to literacy education with a more critical approach. In the former approach the all-knowledgeable educator pours her/his wisdom into the empty vessels, who are the students. 'Education thus becomes an act of depositing, in which the students are the depositories and the teacher is the depositor' (Freire, 1970: 53). He described this as the 'banking' model of education. In the more critical approach the educator engages with the student in an active dialogical manner to encourage them to consider the broader social and structural restraints on their lives and how they can begin to challenge these through collective action.

Freire used the term *conscientization* to describe this process of developing **critical consciousness**. He stressed that his work was 'rooted in concrete situations' and emphasized the collaborative nature of his work. He described the radical as someone who:

> does not become the prisoner of a 'circle of certainty' within which reality is also imprisoned ... This person does not consider himself or herself the proprietor of history or of all people, or the liberator of the oppressed; but he or she does commit himself or herself, within history, to fight at their side.
>
> (Freire, 1970: 21)

These ideas were also developed further in the **liberation psychology** of Ignacio Martin-Baro (Box 14.2). While acknowledging Freire's ideas as a powerful starting point for advocacy and community development, Campbell (2014) also encouraged contemporary community health psychologists to develop approaches suitable for new century problems.

BOX 14.2
LIBERATION PSYCHOLOGY

This approach draws its inspiration from the liberation theology developed by the worker-priest movement in different countries in Latin America during the 1950s and 1960s. This movement argued that it was the duty of Catholics to fight against social injustice and to adopt a *preferential option for the poor*. These ideas were given wider currency within psychology by Ignacio Martin-Baro (1942–1989), who was murdered by the Salvadoran army for his campaigning work in defence of the poor.

He developed a form of liberation psychology that set as its primary task the interests of the poor and oppressed. He criticized mainstream psychology for its scientistic mimicry and its lack of an adequate epistemology (including positivism, individualism and ahistoricism). This focus on individualism 'ends up reinforcing the existing structures, because it ignores the reality of social structures and reduces all structural problems to personal problems'.

Instead he argued that psychologists need to 'redesign our tools from the standpoint of the lives of our own people: from their sufferings, their aspirations, and their struggles' (Martin-Baro, 1994: 25). He proposed three elements in this new liberation psychology:

1 *A new horizon*: psychology must stop focusing on itself and being concerned about its scientific and social status but rather focus on the needs of the masses.
2 *A new epistemology*: psychology needs to consider what psychosocial processes look like from the perspective of the dominated.
3 *A new praxis*: psychology needs to consider itself as 'an activity of transforming reality that will let us know not only about what is but also about what is not, by which we may try to orient ourselves toward what ought to be' (Martin-Baro, 1994: 29).

Eliot Mishler states in the preface to the collection of his writings that they '*challenge us to align ourselves, as he did in El Salvador, with those struggling for equality and justice in our own country*' (Martin-Baro, 1994: xii).

For example, Cornish et al. (2014) proposed new ways of thinking about community mobilization by using the Occupy movement as an example (see Box 14.3). The authors argued that modernist conceptualizations of community mobilization tend to 'follow a linear logic, establishing a set of goals, objectives, indicators of success, and a clearly defined and hierarchical division of labour, with leaders on the top and front line workers at the bottom' (p. 62). However, as reflected in many community-based health interventions, processes tend to be messier and less straightforward than planned. Thus the authors encouraged community health psychologists to explore alternatives to instrumental rationality. They suggested to 'trust the process' and to create mechanisms that enable people to decide on outcomes themselves.

BOX 14.3
USING THE OCCUPY MOVEMENT TO RE-CONCEPTUALIZE COMMUNITY MOBILIZATION

The Occupy movement is a global protest against corporate greed and the unjust distribution of economic and political power in society. It was inspired by the Indignados' occupation of Madrid's Sol Square in mid-May 2011. The movement gained vast media attention when Occupy Wall Street began on 17 September 2011. United by the slogan 'We are the 99%', thousands of protesters camped in hundreds of cities around the world. On 15 October 2011, thousands gathered in London with the aim to occupy the London Stock Exchange (Figure 14.1). As the police blocked their access, the group settled and erected 250 tents in front of St Paul's Cathedral instead. The protesters were evicted four months later. However, during the course of their 'occupation', the group managed to establish a 'community', with common facilities, networks and processes in place to organize themselves.

This is a concrete example of a process-focused community mobilization wherein goals were developed as part of a process rather than being imposed from above. This movement also re-conceptualizes the notion of community wherein shared practices define what it means to be part of a community rather than by similarities of identity, interest or geographical location.

Source: Cornish et al. (2014)

Figure 14.1 Protesters outside of St Paul's Cathedral in London

Source: http://en.wikipedia.org/wiki/Occupy_London

More recently, important developments in South Africa and other countries have served to revitalize community psychology in terms of its socio-political project. This includes projects concerned with the health challenges faced by indigenous people and also the issues of colonialism and post-colonialism (Duncan et al., 2007). These developments have introduced important ideas such as those of Frantz Fanon who developed a sophisticated understanding of the psychology of political oppression, in particular the processes by which oppressed people internalize ideas of inferiority and worthlessness.

Another concept relevant to this approach is that of **social capital**, referring to the community's ability to support empowerment through participation of local organizations and networks. Putnam (2000) discussed two kinds of social capital: *bonding social capital* which refers to within-group social capital; and *bridging social capital* which is concerned with linking with outside bodies with the power and resources to enable mutually interesting benefits to accrue. He argued that in modern society there has been a steady decline in social capital which he characterized as the character of civic participation, trust in others and reciprocity within a community. Other work by Bourdieu has characterized social capital in terms of resources that can be drawn upon. However, after initial enthusiasm about this concept, confusion over its definition and its lack of connection with broader political processes have led researchers to consider other more specific concepts.

PROMOTING HEALTHY BEHAVIOUR IN COMMUNITIES

While the traditional focus of health psychology has been on promoting individual behaviour change, there have been various attempts to explore more community-based strategies. Previously we have discussed how there have been various strategies designed to encourage behaviour change. However, these strategies have adopted the traditional individualist focus. Community health psychology attempts to work with groups or communities to identify how they see the issue and to explore opportunities for change.

A sustained example of this approach is the work of Catherine Campbell in South Africa where she has been involved in several projects designed to reduce HIV infection. A central feature of her work has been the use of peer educators. These are people from the community who take a leading role in educating the residents about the risk of HIV infection. The ideal role adopted by the peer educators is to engage in participatory learning through, for example, games, drama and role-playing. Following the model of Friere the educator engages in a process of dialogue with the co-learners rather than imposing certain ideas. The participants are then active participants in the learning.

Despite considerable resources being expended in the development of such community interventions, Campbell (2006) did not encounter sustained success. She identified a variety of reasons for this limited success both in the programme delivery and in the broader community context. The traditional didactic model of teaching in the schools meant that both the peer educators and the other students were unfamiliar with the participatory approach that underlay the programme. In addition, the strongly negative attitude of the community residents to HIV/AIDS discouraged the students from participating in the programme.

In her subsequent work Campbell has been involved in programmes designed to promote AIDS-competent communities (Campbell et al., 2007). These are communities where a large proportion of the residents have HIV/AIDS. In these communities the aim is to reduce the stigma associated with the disease and to encourage support for sexual behaviour change and care of those with the disease. They have identified six factors that promote these sorts of community:

- Building knowledge and basic skills.
- Creating social spaces for dialogue and critical thinking.
- Promoting a sense of local ownership of the problem and incentives for action.
- Emphasizing community strengths and resources.
- Mobilizing existing formal and informal networks.
- Building partnerships between marginalized communities and more powerful outside actors and agencies.

Although these factors were specifically developed in the context of building AIDS-competent communities they have broader relevance in other contexts.

PROMOTING SOCIAL WELL-BEING

The growth of interest in the connection between social interaction and health status has contributed to a more expansive definition of health including the extent and character of people's everyday social relationships. Approaches in community health psychology have been used to promote social well-being by enhancing the social interactions of individuals in the community. For example, in a study conducted in Australia, Bradley et al. (2004) facilitated a participatory action research project with rural youth. Theoretically they situated this project within Beck's concept of a risk society. According to this theory one of the consequences of modernization is the breakdown of established certainties which has a particular impact on young people who have no clear identity maps. This confusion can contribute to such problems as homelessness, suicide, unemployment, drug-use, crime and single parenthood. In this context the authors argue it is extremely important that young people have the opportunity to participate in community planning.

Their project involved three stages. In the first they organized a public conversation involving city councillors and various providers of services for young people. This led to little change in the provision of council support for young people. In the second stage young people themselves were invited to participate in a collaborative theatre group. This group used the theatrical techniques developed by Boal's Theatre of the Oppressed. In the third stage the young people had the opportunity of performing to a large audience. Later one member of the group had an opportunity of describing the project and the impact it had had on her and other participants. This led the council to reverse their earlier decision and fund a youth officer.

This project showed the deliberate attempt of the psychologists to not only work with their community of interest (young people) but also to involve them in a process of challenging the established authority (town council). Thus the project had an impact not only on the immediate participants but also on the wider audience. It was through the process of collective meaning making and action that the young people grew in confidence and were prepared to take further action to transform their situation. A further point stressed by Bradley et al. was the power of public display of the young people's experiences. The greater impact of this public display compared with previous scientific evidence provided some confirmation for Beck's argument on the declining power of expert knowledge.

Similarly, Murray and Crummett (2010) facilitated a community arts-based project with a group of older residents in a disadvantaged industrial city in England. They found that while the participants were reluctant to access resources outside their immediate neighbourhood, they were prepared to participate in locally organized social activities. The project involved participants in weekly meetings which engaged them in a variety of artistic activities including painting, writing and pottery. At the close of the project the participants organized an exhibition to which they invited other local residents and representatives of various local agencies. Reviewing the project the participants were extremely enthusiastic. A particular strength of this intervention was its collective nature. The enjoyment of art was a shared activity and as such strengthened social bonds between the participants.

Hodgetts et al. (2014) worked in partnership with service providers and families living in poverty in Auckland. The project, Family 100, aimed to promote the social well-being of people in need by exploring the everyday lived experience of communities and how residents make sense of their experiences. The project involved exploration of topics central to poverty, including education, employment, housing, health, agency supports, income and debt and social justice. Influenced by Simmel's (1903/1964) *principle of emergence* of social phenomena, Family 100 assumed that wider systemic elements in society can be understood by exploring micro-level processes in community settings. By engaging community members in dialogue and by documenting these interactions, critical reflections were encouraged which were then used to form the basis for action. Thus, this approach repositions academic researchers into academic scholars (Murray, 2012) whereby researchers work in collaboration with community members and other stakeholders to achieve change.

COMBATTING STRUCTURAL DETERMINANTS OF HEALTH INEQUALITIES

A more critical community health psychology attempts at all times to connect local action with broader social change. The extent to which community health psychologists make connections with the broader social context depends upon opportunity as well as orientation. Indeed, while community action projects can enthuse the participants they are often apprehensive about taking larger social action. The magnitude of the task is apparent in the various community projects that have sought to challenge social inequalities in health.

In previous chapters we have outlined the substantial social inequalities in wealth and health that exist both within and between societies. As we have argued the traditional individualistic lifestyle approach to addressing these inequalities has met with limited success. There is an obvious need to address the material and wider social factors within which these unhealthy lifestyles are located. For example, using the conceptual apparatus of therapeutic citizenship, Kagee et al. (2014) underlined the importance of historical, political and other structural barriers to antiretroviral therapy (ART) adherence. By outlining the struggle for access to ART in South Africa, they demonstrated how medication costs, local political factors and global flow of funds contribute to the challenges associated with the organization and delivery of ART, especially in resource-constrained countries.

An example of a health promotion intervention that deals with the wider structural determinants of health inequalities is Lubek et al.'s (2003, 2014) multi-sectoral participatory action research (PAR) project which aimed to confront the HIV infection and AIDS pandemic in Cambodia (see Box 14.4). The PAR approach emphasizes empowerment of local women and others increasingly at risk, as well as the development of a culturally and gender-sensitive health intervention/research programme, which eventually can be made self-sustaining. This approach succeeds best by facilitating collaboration between grass-root organizations and local and international corporate industries. All of these stakeholders need to take responsibility for prevalence reductions in HIV infections.

BOX 14.4
INTERNATIONAL CASE STUDY: CONFRONTING HIV INFECTION AND ALCOHOL IN CAMBODIA

Context

In rural Cambodia, where non-literacy rates are as high as 75%, female workers face health and safety risks selling international beer brands in restaurants. These so-called 'beer girls' or 'beer promotion women' are underpaid by about 50%, and are sometimes forced to trade sex for money. Twenty per cent are HIV-seropositive, quickly die, and are replaced by younger girls from the countryside. 'Beer girls' must wear the uniforms of the international beer brands that they sell in restaurants and beer gardens.

In 2002, 'beer girls' were set a sales quota of twenty-four 33cl. cans/small bottles per night – each selling at US$1.50 on average totalling US$36's worth of beer daily or US$13,000 annually. In 2004–2005, Heineken and Tiger Beer promotion women were

(Continued)

(Continued)

put on fixed salaries of around US$55 per month. This amount is about half the income they need to support their families. One-third of the women support children as single mothers, and 90% support rural families. About half become indirect sex workers, exchanging money for sex to supplement their income.

'Beer girls' consume unsafe quantities of alcohol when working, drinking over 1.2 litres of beer (about 5 standard drinks) nightly 27 days a month (Schuster et al., 2006). Condom use following beer drinking is lowered, increasing risks for HIV infections, AIDS and STIs. Averaged over the seven years, 20% of the female beer promotion women in Cambodia are seropositive for HIV/AIDS (Lubeck, 2005). It is estimated that there are approximately 200,000 people living with HIV infections and AIDS (PLWHAs) in Cambodia, with 10,000 in Siem Reap.

A clone of the life-prolonging anti-retroviral therapy (ARVT) costs approximately US$360 per year. The annual wage of US$600–US$800 means that ARVT is not an option for HIV-positive 'beer girls'. Death can follow three months to two years after diagnosis. Médicins Sans Frontières and other NGOs provide free clone ARVT for a small number of Cambodians with HIV infections and AIDS.

The spread of HIV infections and AIDS is accelerated by sexual tourism, poverty, and lack of condom use. HIV sero-positivity rates have averaged 32.7% (1995–May, 2005) for brothel-based (direct) sex workers. Siem Reap is the largest tourist site in Cambodia and hosted 354,000 people in 2001, and over 1,000,000 in 2004. Many of the male tourists are 'sexual tourists'. In 2001, 23 brothels were registered in the 100% condom use programme, employing 250 direct sex workers. An additional 350 indirect sex workers were 'beer promotion women', or worked as massage workers and karaoke singers (Lubek, 2005). Infection patterns reflect a 'bridging' pattern involving sexual tourists, indirect and direct sex workers, local men, their wives and newborns. Married women, men and young persons are increasingly at risk, with less than 10% of the estimated 10,000 persons living with HIV infection or AIDS in Siem Reap in 2006 being given anti-retrovirals.

The intervention

In 2006–2008, the Siem Reap Citizens for Health, Educational, and Social Issues (SiRCHESI) organization partnered with three Siem Reap hotels in a hotel apprenticeship programme. This removed women from risky beer-selling jobs, sending them every morning to SiRCHESI's school to learn English, Khmer reading, health education, social and life skills. New advocacy, political and policy-formation skills and activism include trade union activities for beer sellers, meetings with government legislators, supplying data to ethical shareholders groups, and debating international beer executives in the press and scientific journals. Multiple actions were organized to tackle the issue on a number of different levels:

- workshops training women at risk for HIV infection and AIDS to be peer educators about health and alcohol overuse;
- workshops to prevent the sexual exploitation and trafficking of children;
- company sponsorship of HIV infection prevention health education;
- fair salaries to enable the women to adequately support their dependents;
- monitoring voluntary HIV testing (serology);
- free anti-retroviral therapy (ARVT) for 'promotion girls' who are HIV positive;
- breathalyzer testing in bars;
- changes in community health behaviours and attitudes;
- fund raising through the sale of fair-trade souvenirs.

Evaluation of project outcomes showed changes in health-related knowledge, behaviour, self-image and empowerment (Lee et al., 2010). As reflected in this case study, Lubek et al. (2014) demonstrated how community health psychology can help to address critical community health issues by adjusting its research and practices to approaches that are guided by grassroots and locally defined interventions.

Source: Lubek et al. (2014)

CRITIQUE OF COMMUNITY DEVELOPMENT APPROACHES TO HEALTH PROMOTION

It is clear that approaching health promotion using community health psychology as a framework is deeply political. It involves the collective organization of those who are traditionally excluded from decision-making processes and a direct and active challenge to power relations associated with health and illness. As a result, health promotion initiatives using this approach have the potential to come into conflict with interests that lie with the status quo such as industry, employers, government departments and local councils that aim to make financial savings.

Consequently, community action as a form of health promotion is vulnerable to lack of public funding and is subject to resistance from dominant social groups (Stephens, 2014).

There is also a danger of '*professionalization creep*' whereby those involved in the initiative become removed from the grassroots concerns of those they set out to represent (Homans and Aggleton, 1988). Self-appointed community leaders or representatives can emerge who claim to speak for all members of the community but in reality represent the dominant elites. Alternatively, because of the huge personal effort and sacrifice needed to make this type of project work, professionals tend to become emotionally involved, which may lead to *burn-out*. Community change also occurs as a consequence of a complex interplay of actors, circumstances and actions. The aims and objectives may well be noble and virtuous, but the consequences are not predictable or certain. The outcome could possibly be to the benefit of some and to the detriment of others in unpredictable ways (Estacio and Marks, 2010).

The notion of 'community', upon which this approach depends, is problematic. For example, people who live in the same geographical space (or those who share a sexual preference, language, ethnic background, age group or social class) do not constitute homogeneous groups. The use of the term 'community' obscures the diversity of lifestyles that exist within groups, posing the risk of failure to address the diverse needs of under-served members of a community.

While community-based methods are useful in surfacing local insights about health-related issues, these projects have been scrutinized for limited measurable outcomes when evaluating impact. For example, a systematic review by Milton et al. (2011) examined the impact of community engagement on health and social outcomes. Data were extracted from 14 papers on 13 projects. The analysis found no significant evidence of positive impact on population health or quality of services. However, improvements in social outcomes were reported. For example, the evidence suggested that community-managed social housing performed better than local authority housing on a number of key indicators. Community engagement initiatives also showed potential to improve information communication and engagement with hard-to-reach groups in the local area. Several studies also reported improved well-being at community level, including gains in social capital, social cohesion, partnership working, capacity building and empowerment. Since community-based interventions are complex, the authors of the review argued for methodological developments in evaluating these interventions to provide more robust evidence on impact.

The ability of an intervention to improve the health of individuals suffering from an illness needs to be evaluated if we are to place any confidence in the community psychology approach in health care. Ideally, a similar, robust level of proof is required for all types of intervention. However, there is an uneven playing field because the same high level of proof available for individual-level interventions is not feasible for the vast majority of community-level interventions. Individual-level interventions of the top-down variety can be studied in randomized controlled trials and the data can be synthesized in meta-analysis. This is because the parameters can be systematically varied in the design of any trial and the conditions controlled accordingly. Bottom-up community interventions are by definition unique to each particular community and circumstance and the intervention(s) designed in light of the circumstances arising as the various stakeholders influence what actually happens.

A community intervention often feels very messy, fluid, and difficult to control, and certainly not amenable to a randomized controlled trial. In fact, it is almost impossible to run trials using matched controlled conditions in bottom-up interventions of the kind reviewed here. When any intervention is truly bottom-up, there is hardly ever going to be the opportunity to provide a controlled evaluation. However, evaluation using other types of design is not precluded, and should ideally be carried out (e.g. processes and outcomes can be monitored and compared at different time points). Drawing upon Freire's later work, the *Pedagogy of Hope*, Nolas (2014) encouraged community health psychologists to engage with the messiness of practice and argued for a 'journey' approach to collective action.

HEALTH PROMOTION EVALUATION

As discussed earlier, evaluation of the effectiveness of health promotion initiatives can be an extremely difficult undertaking. First of all, we need to differentiate between **outcome evaluation**, i.e. an assessment of changes brought about by the intervention, and **process evaluation**, i.e. an understanding of how and why the intervention worked. In addition, outcome evaluation can focus on a range of different criteria, such as behavioural (e.g. how many people have stopped smoking) or cognitive (e.g. the extent to which people's knowledge about the health risks of smoking has increased) or health status (mental or physical). Furthermore, there may be unintended consequences of an intervention, such as increases in anxiety that may be generated by provision of information about particular risks.

French and Adams (1986) specified evaluation criteria that are appropriate for different types of health promotion interventions. For example, a mass media campaign based on the principles of the behaviour change model would be best evaluated by measuring changes in compliance, morbidity and mortality rates, as well as knowledge increases, attitude and behaviour change, whereas an intervention using a community development approach would be assessed through self-reports and community discussions around well-being, social capital and empowerment. However, it is important to bear in mind both that a health promotion evaluation should only assess the extent to which a campaign has achieved its objectives and that these can be limited. For example, a campaign whose purpose it is to warn people about potential risks should not be evaluated by measuring behaviour change. In other words, campaign objectives and evaluation criteria need to be carefully matched.

In recent years, increasing emphasis has been placed upon evaluation and the need for evidence-based health promotion. Within a climate of financial pressures and budget cuts, public service expenditure needs to be cost effective. Governments and funding bodies are more likely to invest in health promotion projects that can be shown to work. In addition, there are ethical reasons for systematic evaluations: ineffective or counter-productive interventions should not be repeated, while effective interventions should be made available as widely as possible.

Everitt and Hardiker (1997) stated that health promotion evaluations should look at multiple perspectives. Nutbeam (1999) gave examples of the different perspectives and emphases on what represents 'success' for a health promotion programme. For policy makers and budget managers, success is often defined in terms of the relationship between investment and the achievement of health outcomes in the short term. Shannon (2004) reported the inherent difficulties in demonstrating a cause and effect link between public health interventions and clinical outcomes highlighted by Ian Kennedy, the chairman of the NHS Healthcare Commission. He stated 'You will have to persuade the least readily persuadable people in the land – the Treasury – that this money (for public health programmes) is well spent' (p. 1). For health promotion practitioners, Nutbeam (1999) suggested success may be defined in terms of the practicality of implementation of a programme and the possibilities of engaging people and organizations in action for health. For the population who are to benefit from health promotion action, relevance to perceived needs and opportunities for community participation may define success. For academic researchers, success is likely to be defined in terms of the methodological rigour, maintenance of programme integrity and achievement of predetermined outcomes.

Evaluation of health promotion interventions can be complex, as some interventions may require multiple components, involving several partners, contexts, target groups or behaviours. Datta and Petticrew (2013) examined the challenges described by researchers when evaluating such interventions. Using extracts from published journal articles ($n = 207$) from January 2002 to December 2011, the analysis suggests that the content and standardization of interventions, development of outcomes measures and methods used for evaluation were common issues in evaluation. Challenges associated with organizational factors such as the impact of the people involved (i.e. staff and patients) and the organizational context were also described.

In the UK, the Medical Research Council (MRC) (2000, 2008) developed a framework for funders, developers and evaluators of complex interventions (see Figure 14.2). It recognized the complexity of developing and evaluating interventions and acknowledged that this process will require several phases which may not necessarily follow a linear sequence. While experimental designs are preferred, particularly randomized controlled trials, the MRC framework also acknowledged that using experimental designs may not always be feasible. Thus alternatives have been proposed such as quasi-experimental and observational designs (Craig et al., 2013).

As well as adopting a pluralistic approach to developing and evaluating interventions, evaluators need to be pragmatic by using data that can be realistically obtained yet remain meaningful and useful to the many key players in implementing the learning from evaluations. Often, this is not an easy task. Failure to translate research evidence into practice and policy is not uncommon in clinical and health services (Grimshaw et al., 2012). Research evidence may not be accessible to practitioners and policy makers. It is also possible that practice is informed by other sources of knowledge apart from research (e.g. personal experience and interaction with others).

To bridge the evidence–practice gap, Klinner et al. (2014) recommended that conceptions of health promotion evidence need to be expanded. Furthermore, 'relationship-based' methods need to be harnessed to enable practitioners to document community interactions and to use these as research evidence. This requires developing organizational capacity to enhance practitioners' skills. Reforms in the research-to-practice pipeline are also needed to make research evidence more relevant and actionable in real-life contexts (Green, 2014).

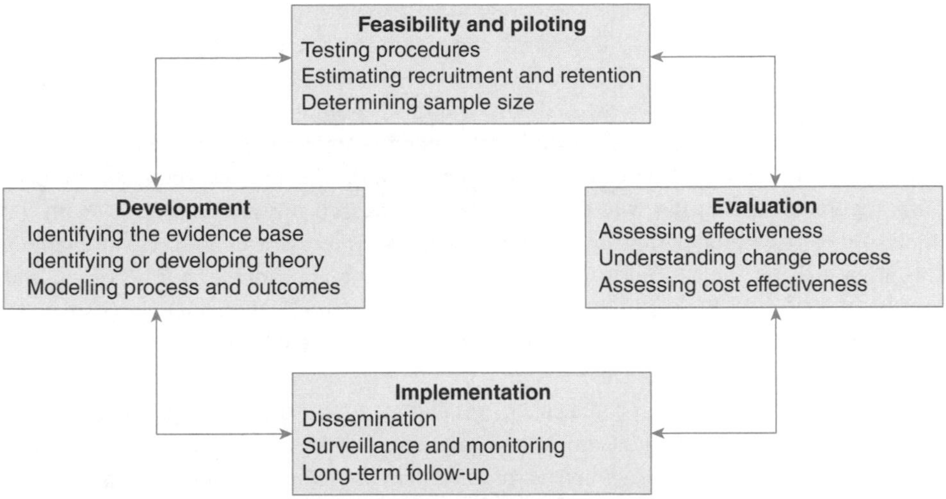

Figure 14.2 Key elements of the development and evaluation process

Source: Craig et al. (2013: 589)

Challenging Healthism in Health Promotion

Health promotion is concerned with strategies for promoting health. It is assumed that (a) good health is a universally shared objective; (b) there is agreement on what being healthy means, and (c) there is a scientific consensus about which behaviours facilitate good health. From this perspective, the real (and only) challenge for health experts and educators is to find effective ways of helping people to maximize their health.

However, there have been criticisms of this contemporary 'ideology of health promotion'. In 1980, Crawford coined the term '**healthism**', which refers to the ideology that situates health and disease within the context of the individual. He raised concerns regarding how healthist ideas could lead to the 'medicalization of everyday life' and reinforce neo-liberal ideals by placing the emphasis on personal responsibility for health (see Chapter 2 for further critique of the ideology of the 'responsible consumer').

Evans (1988) argued that such an ideology can also begin to drive health promotion interventions that instead ought to be informed by scientific evidence (both biomedical and psychosocial). Evans drew attention to programmes directed at lifestyle changes that are not unequivocally justified by biomedical research evidence, such as the recommendation to reduce cholesterol levels in the blood to prevent heart disease. Evans worried that 'by increasingly promoting presumably non-risky behaviours, we may be contributing to a type of mass hypochondriasis resulting in an increasingly diminished freedom in human lifestyle and quality of life' (p. 207). This, he suggested, can result in an unhealthy obsession with exercise, an inability to enjoy a meal, as well as a reduction in spontaneity of lifestyle.

Recent critics of the healthist ideology draw upon critical theory to highlight how healthism is propagated in society and how this is used as a method of social control. For example, using critical discourse analysis and Bourdieu's theoretical framework, Lee and Macdonald (2010) explored how healthist discourses are maintained through young people's experiences in school physical education (PE). They interviewed rural young women and examined these alongside discourses from their school PE head of department (HOD). The analysis suggests that healthist discourses were evident in the way the participants discussed physical activity, health, fitness and their bodies. Health and fitness were constructed as important elements that enable them to control body shape and to conform to the 'ideal' feminine appearance. Furthermore, findings suggest that the school's PE curriculum is also being influenced by the HOD's own engagement with healthist discourses and that these too impact upon young people's understandings of health, wellness and their bodies.

The adoption of healthist ideas can also support and maintain social segregation. For example, Gurrieri et al. (2013) examined the impact of healthism-based social marketing campaigns on how women's bodies are portrayed, and its implications on subject positioning and experience. Drawing upon embodiment theory, the authors argued that some health promotion campaigns (e.g. breastfeeding, weight management and physical activity) may inadvertently construct women's bodies as sites of control. Using critical visual analysis, the authors showed that such campaigns could represent certain body types as less acceptable. Women who do not fit within the ideal body type or those who engage in activities that counter dominant health messages could become subject to stigmatization and exclusion. Thus the authors urged the emerging field of critical social marketing to develop a broader social justice agenda to address the societal impacts of health promotion campaigns.

Similarly Barker-Ruchti et al. (2013) interviewed second-generation girls of immigrant background in Switzerland and examined how participants drew upon healthist ideologies to construct sport as a way to achieve good health and the ideal, feminine body. While alternative discursive resources exist, the authors found that the participants did not use these. It was argued that the use of healthist discourses provided participants with a way to construct their position as being integrated with Western knowledge and cultures, thus maintaining predominantly White healthist ideas and contributing to the promotion of the 'othering' of foreign migrants.

While healthist ideas can be used as a form of social control, Ayo (2012) argued that in the context of modern neo-liberalism, healthism is shaping individuals into health conscious citizens who willingly abide by society's prescribed norms. Healthy lifestyles are now 'being sold' by health promotion campaigners and other private companies wherein the responsible consumer is expected to buy into this lifestyle in the free market. Thus social control is no longer constructed as something that is delivered forcefully. Rather, autonomous individuals wilfully obey the state and regulate their own behaviour as 'good and responsible citizens'.

Healthist ideas in health promotion have not gone unchallenged, however. Recent publications have explored the function and position of contemporary health promotion in an attempt to formulate alternatives to individualistic risk-based approaches (e.g. Stephens, 2008). Debates concerning the use of healthist ideas to promote neo-liberal agendas have also sparked discussions and research into the politics of health promotion. For example, Lovell et al. (2014) examined how political changes have impacted on health promotion in New Zealand. They conducted interviews and focus groups with health promotion practitioners between January 2008 and March 2009. While neo-liberal reforms have been adopted to increase efficiency in the health care sector, participants from this study have responded critically to government restrictions. In the face of limited resources and budget constraints, health promotion practitioners often have become community advocates when neo-liberal agendas come into conflict with community priorities. In this respect, it is important for health promotion developers and practitioners to reflect upon their position and how their work impacts upon the lived experiences of individuals and on society as a whole. Health promotion that is guided by evidence, ethics and values may be a good way forward (Carter, 2011).

FUTURE RESEARCH

1. Further development of critical social marketing is needed to encourage more discussion and consideration of wider social determinants of health in social marketing-based health promotion interventions.
2. Methodological developments in community-based research are needed to generate more robust evidence into the impact of community health promotion interventions.
3. Exploration of reforms is needed to encourage effective translation of research evidence into practice.

SUMMARY

1 Health promotion is any event, process or activity that facilitates the protection or improvement of the health status of individuals, groups, communities or populations.

2 Two commonly used approaches in health promotion are the behaviour change approach and the community development approach. Each pursues different goals, utilizes different means to achieve its goals and proposes different criteria for intervention evaluation.

3 The behaviour change approach aims to bring about changes in individual behaviour through changes in the individual's cognitions. Social cognition models are utilized in order to make the link between knowledge, attitudes and behaviour. However, attempts by SCMs to predict behaviour on the basis of cognitions has led to disappointing results.

(Continued)

(Continued)

4 Criticisms of the behaviour change approach include its inability to target socio-economic causes of ill health, its top-down approach to education, its exclusive focus upon cognitions, its assumption of homogeneity among receivers of health messages and its individualism.

5 The community development approach recognizes the close relationship between individual health and socio-economic factors. It aims to remove the socio-economic and environmental causes of ill health through the collective organization of members of the community.

6 Health promotion interventions that use the community development approach can encounter a number of difficulties. They can come into conflict with powerful bodies and they are vulnerable to lack of public funding and official opposition. Other problems include creeping professionalization and difficulties associated with defining and identifying communities.

7 Evaluation of the processes and outcomes of health promotion interventions can be a complex task as interventions may involve multiple components, involving several partners, contexts, target groups or behaviours.

8 Healthist discourses have sparked discussions concerning their role in social governance and control. It is important for health promotion developers and practitioners to reflect upon their values and the impact of their work on the lived experiences of individuals and on society as a whole.

PART 4

ILLNESS EXPERIENCE AND HEALTH CARE

Part 4 is concerned with what people think and believe about illness, whether their illness experience might be related to their personality, what efforts are made within the health care system to prevent people from becoming ill, the experience of pain, and what happens when a person becomes seriously ill.

In Chapter 15 we contrast research that has used a cognitive approach to the study of illness representations with those that have adopted phenomenological, discursive and social approaches.

In Chapter 16 we examine the influence of individual differences in personality and other psychological characteristics on susceptibility to illness. We begin with a brief history of the contrasting approaches of orthodox and holistic medicine. We examine historically significant Freudian ideas on hysteria and contemporary approaches to medically unexplained symptoms such as chronic fatigue syndrome. We look at the evidence on research on personality and illness with particular reference to coronary heart disease and cancer.

In Chapter 17 we explore the extent to which patients adhere or comply with recommended treatment regimens. The assumptions underlying the term *compliance* imply an authoritarian stance that has been challenged by recent changes within health care systems. We consider the extent and character of treatment non-adherence and the issue of medical error. We look at patient-centred health care that focuses on shared decision making and patient *empowerment.*

In Chapter 18 we discuss the complex nature of pain, initially discussing the direct line of transmission, pattern and multidimensional gate control theories. We examine the psychological and social processes that mediate and moderate pain behaviour and experience. We summarize the pros and cons of different pain assessment methods and review the fear-avoidance model. Finally, we explore psychological techniques for pain management and evidence on their effectiveness.

In Chapter 19 we consider three life-threatening and disabling diseases: cancer, coronary heart disease, and HIV infection or AIDS from five points of view: 'What is xx?'; 'Interventions for xx'; 'Living with xx'; 'Adaptation to xx'; and 'Caring for someone with xx'. The contribution of psychosocial interventions for patients suggests that psychosocial interventions have not yet demonstrated their full potential. We discuss the importance of end-of-life care and research on the quality of death and dying, and suggest ways to improve the psychological understanding of treatment and care and ways of improving the quality of death and dying.

15 LAY REPRESENTATIONS OF ILLNESS

As long as a particular disease is treated as an evil, invincible predator, not just a disease, most people with cancer will indeed be demoralized by learning what disease they have. The solution is hardly to stop telling cancer patients the truth, but to rectify the conception of the disease, to de-mythicize it.

(Susan Sontag, [1978] 2002: 11)

OUTLINE

The traditional biomedical approach to illness defines it in terms of physical symptoms and underlying physical pathology. However, to the lay person, illness is a much more complicated process. In this chapter we contrast research that has used a cognitive approach to the study of illness representations with those that have adopted phenomenological, discursive and social approaches. Whereas the former adopts a positivist perspective, the others adopt constructivist perspectives.

One of the core tenets of health psychologists is that health and illness are more than biomedical phenomena. A particular research trajectory has been to explore what 'ordinary' people think of health and illness as a means of grasping their social and psychological dimensions. Psychologists have used a variety of theoretical perspectives to investigate popular representations of illness.

COGNITIVE APPROACHES

Illness Perceptions

The most developed cognitive model of illness was initially proposed by Howard Leventhal and his colleagues (Leventhal et al., 1989). This was derived from their work on the impact of fear communication. They found that, irrespective of the level of fear, the message conveyed was effective if it produced a plan of action. This led them to infer that the key factor was the way the threat was represented or understood. They developed a *dual processing model* to accommodate the representation of fear and of the threat (Figure 15.1), an influential model that has undergone some elaboration by Leventhal (1999).

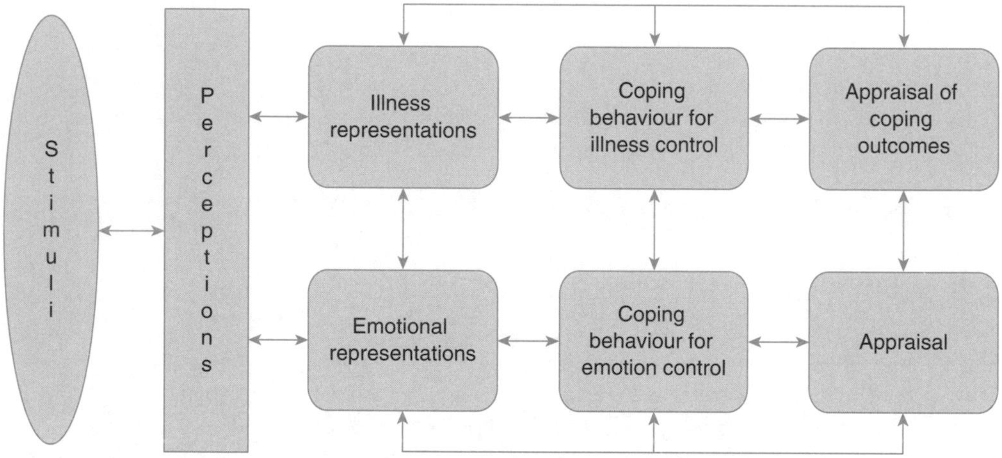

Figure 15.1 Leventhal's self-regulation model of illness cognitions and behaviour (after Leventhal, 1979)

Basically the model suggests that when faced with a threat the person forms a cognitive and emotional representation of that threat. They will cope with that threat depending upon the character of the threat representation. The consequences of these coping strategies will then be appraised and the representations and coping strategies revised accordingly. This model led the Leventhal group to explore how lay people represented specific threats such as illness. They conducted open-ended interviews with a sample of patients suffering from various diseases. From this information they proposed a *self-regulation model* of illness that suggested that lay people's thoughts on illness could be organized along four dimensions. Lau and Hartman (1983) suggested that since these dimensions were derived from a sample of patients with an acute, time-limited illness experience it was necessary to introduce a fifth dimension to cover those illnesses that were resistant to treatment (Box 15.1). These five dimensions are often termed the common sense model (CSM) of illness.

BOX 15.1
DIMENSIONS OF COMMON SENSE ILLNESS PERCEPTIONS

Identity: The signs, symptoms and the illness label.

Consequence: The perceived physical, social and economic consequences of the disease and the felt emotional consequences.

Causes: The perceived causes of the disease.

Timeline: The perceived time frame for the development and duration of the illness threat.

Cure/control: The extent to which the illness is responsive to treatment.

Source: Leventhal et al. (1980); Lau and Hartman (1983)

This model has provoked considerable research over the past 30 years. Indeed, it was suggested as offering a new framework for psychosomatic research (Weinman and Petrie, 1997). A major impetus to research into this CSM was the development of the Illness Perception Questionnaire (IPQ) by Weinman et al. (1996) to measure the original five illness dimensions. This measure has been used extensively on a wide range of populations with varying degrees of success. It was originally used in a longitudinal study to investigate the relationship between illness representations and work behaviour after myocardial infarction (Petrie et al., 1996). This study found that attendance at a cardiac rehabilitation course was significantly predicted by a stronger belief during admission that the illness could be cured. Return to work was predicted by perception that the illness would last a short time and have less serious consequences. In conclusion, it was argued that these popular illness beliefs 'seem to be largely formed by information before becoming ill [and] are quite consistent over time'. A recent meta-analysis of 45 studies using this measure found some evidence that confirmed the five-fold structure of the CSM and also the relationship between the other components of the self-regulation model (Hagger and Orbell, 2003).

A revision of this questionnaire (Revised Illness Perception Questionnaire, IPQ-R) introduced a measure of *illness coherence* and of emotional representations of illness (Moss-Morris et al., 2002). The former considers how the illness 'makes sense' as a whole to the patient. The emotional representations had been ignored in the previous model although they were explicit in the original formulation of the self-regulation model of illness. In addition, the IPQ-R divided the cure/control dimension into *personal control* and *treatment control*. This enabled researchers to distinguish between perceived control of the illness from perceived control of the treatment.

There continues to be research to explore the structure of this cognitive model of illness representations. Recent researchers have attempted to expand the basic model. For example, in a study of patients undergoing surgery for coronary heart disease (Hirani et al., 2006) using the original IPQ confirmed what are considered the three core dimensions of the model which they labelled illness impact (consequences), duration (timeline) and control (cure/control). They also identified a fourth dimension labelled 'self-image' that they argued has been ignored in much research. They suggest that in the same way as the IPQ-R added an additional illness coherence component to the basic cognitive model, future research should consider the overall impact of the disease on self-image.

A weakness in many early studies that have used this framework was that they were correlational. Thus although the CSM components were found to be interrelated they did not provide firm evidence to support the self-regulation model. More recent studies have attempted to overcome this deficiency. An example is the work by Searle et al. (2007) in which they investigated the connection between illness representations (measured by the IPQ-R), illness cognitions and coping behaviours in a prospective study of patients with type 2 diabetes. They found that the illness representations were direct predictors of both coping cognitions and coping behaviours. In study of patients receiving treatment for head and neck cancer, Llewellyn et al. (2007) found that beliefs about the chronicity of the disease (timeline beliefs on the IP-Q) predicted depression after surgery. Using a Danish translated version of the IPQ-R in a study of primary care patients, Frostholm et al. (2007) also found evidence that illness perceptions predicted changes in health status two years later.

French et al. (2006) conducted a systematic review and meta-analysis of studies of predictors of attendance at cardiac rehabilitation. They found that four illness perceptions (positive identity, cure/control, consequences and coherence) all predicted attendance.

Some researchers have attempted to explore in more detail the mediating processes between illness perceptions and subsequent health status. For example, in a cross-sectional study, Knibb and Horton (2008) considered the relationship between coping strategies and illness beliefs in a sample of people who suffered from allergy. They found that those with strong personal-control coping strategies reported less emotional distress. Further this coping strategy partly mediated the link between the illness beliefs and

It is increasingly accepted among CSM researchers that illness representations are not simply the property of individual patients but reflect interpersonal and cultural experiences. For example, it has been found that the illness representations of patients and family are often similar (Weinman et al., 2000), reflecting their shared experiences. Further, when they differ there is evidence to suggest that this has implications for the patients. An example of the consequences of conflicting perceptions is illustrated in the study of women's and men's perceptions of infertility by Benyamini et al. (2009). They found different patterns in the relationship of illness perceptions between partners that were associated with different levels of distress. The highest distress was found among women who reported low levels of controllability whereas their partner reported high controllability. An awareness of these different perceptions could be used to provide psychological counselling for couples.

There have recently been attempts to use the CSM approach in investigations of lay representations of illness in developing countries. For example, Kart et al. (2007) conducted an interview survey of 3,000 residents of Kathmandu, Nepal who had been diagnosed as having diabetes. They included two standardized assessment instruments: the revised version of the Illness Perception

Questionnaire (IPQ-R) and the Summary of Diabetes Self-Care Activities (SDSCA) questionnaire. Both measures were translated into Nepali. Factor analysis of the responses to the IPQ-R revealed a similar structure to that in the original formulation of the measure (Morris et al., 2002). Only the 'Illness coherence' dimension was not identified. When the participants' ratings of the 18 causal categories in the IPQ-R were examined it revealed three causal clusters again similar to that found in other countries. Despite finding such similarities the authors were cautious in their conclusion. Their sample was educated and urban, in many ways unrepresentative of Nepal and more similar to people in developed countries. Also, they commented on the limitations of the quantitative assessment and concluded that there was a need for more qualitative research that could identify the particular cultural dimensions of Nepali illness representations.

A nine item measure of illness perceptions (known as the Brief IPQ) has been developed by Broadbent et al. (2006). Recent articles using this measure have found relationships between illness perceptions and adjustment to illness (Price et al., 2012). Scores on the scale dimensions were also found to change following cardiac diagnosis (Devcich et al., 2008) suggesting that diagnostic tests can effect how patients perceive their illness. Wilson et al. (2011) found that burn perceptions measured using the Brief IPQ predicted recovery from the burn as assessed from clinic notes several weeks later.

Although the development of standardized measures of lay representations of illness have contributed to a large body of research in this area it has also restricted its development. Some researchers using this framework have begun to explore other measures. For example, in a substantial study considering the differences between lay and professional representations of breathlessness, Insel et al. (2005) administered a 'Perceived Experience of Breathlessness' scale to participants. This scale was not structured around the five dimensions of the CSM but rather inductively from concepts people with breathlessness used to describe the experience. A network analysis was conducted to explore the relationship between these concepts. This revealed a different network for the four groups of participants such that while for those with COPD the two central concepts were 'awareness of breathing' and 'worry about the next breath' the pulmonologists had a single central concept, 'breathlessness'. There were similarities in some of the nodes of the network with the dimensions of the CSM. This study illustrated new ways of investigating lay representations of illness but also connections between the various dimensions. Of particular note was the conclusion that there was need to integrate qualitative research with quantitative findings to develop a more sophisticated understanding of lay representations of illness.

Causes of Disease

Perceived cause is considered one of the central components in Leventhal's original model of lay illness representations. Psychological interest in how lay people explain the onset of disease derives from attribution theory (Heider, 1958). According to the basic tenets of attribution theory, people attempt to provide a causal explanation for events in their world particularly if those events are unexpected and have personal relevance. Thus it is not surprising that people will generally seek a causal explanation for an illness, particularly one that is serious.

Swartzman and Lees (1996) considered the character of the causal explanations of various physical symptoms. Initial classification of the suggested causes revealed 14 categories. Multidimensional scaling analysis of the scores suggested three dimensions, which they labelled non-physical–physical, stable–unstable, and controllable–uncontrollable. The latter two labels are comparable to two of the original attributional dimensions while the first label is specific to explanations of illness. Physical causes included 'physical activity' and 'physical constitution' while non-physical causes included personality, mood and stress.

Murray and McMillan (1993) asked a sample of over 700 adults to rate the relative importance of 24 potential causes of cancer. Factor analysis of their ratings revealed five factors:

- stress (which contained items referring to stress, worry, loneliness and unemployment);
- environment (including such items as air pollution, work conditions, asbestos, nuclear radiation, a knock or hurt, X-rays and promiscuity);
- health-related (such factors as childbirth, antibiotics, breast-feeding, virus or infection);
- behaviour (fatty foods, smoking, drinking).

Although some of these factors could be redefined along the classic attributional dimensions, others (e.g. health-related) were more specific and would suggest that people combine general and specific causal explanations.

In the development of their Revised Illness Perception Questionnaire (IPQ-R), Moss-Morris et al. (2002) identified four causal dimensions: psychological attributions, risk factors, immunity, and accident or chance. They stressed that these four factors should not be considered universal or prescriptive but depending upon the illness, the culture and the population.

Other recent studies have used the causal dimension scale of the IPQ to explore illness attributions. For example, Rief et al. (2004) administered an expanded version of the scale to patients with unexplained symptoms attending health care. Factor analysis of the scores identified four causal dimensions that they labelled vulnerability, psychological, organic and stress. They found that patients with somatoform disorders scored higher on the vulnerability and organic causes. They concluded that these patients have more organically oriented illness models that would lead them to seek more health care. However, in a subsequent study the team (Hilbert et al., 2010) found that while there was a relationship between illness attributions and symptom severity when studied cross-sectionally, illness attributions did not predict symptom severity six months later.

Comment

The common sense model of illness has attracted considerable research effort. The enthusiasm for this approach is partly explained by the development of standardized assessment instruments. There is considerable theoretical and methodological debate about this approach. The first concerns the broad limitations of the cognitivist approach with its positivist epistemological assumptions and the information-processing model of thinking. The second concerns the neglect of social and cultural factors as well as the limitations of using standardized instruments to assess a dynamic process. Some recent research shows an interest in exploring connections with more qualitative approaches.

PHENOMENOLOGICAL APPROACHES

A major criticism of the cognitive approach is that it adopts an information-processing approach and loses sight of the person who is actively trying to make sense of their world. One attempt to recover the person is the phenomenological approach. Here we will briefly consider, in particular, two forms of this approach – interpretative phenomenological analysis (IPA) and the narrative approach. These approaches share epistemological constructivist assumptions and a preference for qualitative methods of investigation. It is argued that since phenomenology is concerned with exploring the participant's perspective on the world rather than confirming that of the observer/researcher, the researcher should adopt an open-ended qualitative approach to research. The concern is with trying to understand the subjective experience of the patient in their own words.

Interpretative Phenomenological Analysis

The IPA approach has attracted considerable attention over the past decade. It was originally developed by Smith (1996) and since then has been applied extensively in health psychology. This approach argues that a human characteristic is a tendency towards self-reflection, an ongoing process in which humans try to make sense of their worlds. There is no presumed structure to this subjective experience and the challenge faced by the researcher is trying to describe the world from the perspective of the other. The primary source of information on the subjective world of the other is their verbal reports of their experiences.

Smith has provided detailed advice on how to obtain and analyse these verbal reports. In particular, he notes the importance of the researchers being explicit about their own interpretative framework. He has described this approach as being a double hermeneutic in that the researcher is trying to make sense of the patient's sense making. It is for this reason that the approach is described as interpretative because 'a person's thoughts are not transparently available from, for example, interview transcripts, [so, the researcher] engages in the analytic process in order, hopefully, to be able to say something about the thinking' (Smith, 1996: 219).

A series of studies have illustrated the value of this approach for exploring the experience of illness. Kay et al. (2009) explored the experiences of young women living with type 1 diabetes. Using IPA as their analytic frame they identified four main superordinate themes:

- *The relationship with the body*: this theme was concerned with how the women viewed their bodies, especially the importance of weight and how diabetes impacted on their health.
- *Personal challenges*: this theme was concerned with the impact of diabetes on their everyday lives.

- *Impact of relationship*: this theme focused especially on the impact of diabetes on relationships.
- *Changing and adapting*: this theme was concerned with how the young women managed the disease.

The young people are particularly concerned with the impact of the disease on their lives and on their relationships and how they manage both of these. Diabetes is perceived by the young people not as a fixed unchanging thing but an ongoing process with which they engage on a daily basis. The character of the experience of these young people depends upon who they are and the various supports available. It also depends upon broader societal expectations. The young women were particularly concerned with the impact of the illness on their body image and interpersonal relationships.

Diabetes is a long-term condition and the accounts of the young people in this study emphasized the importance of how they integrated the disease into their lives and their ongoing management of it. Other diseases are more life threatening and the experiences of those suffering from them are quite different. For example, Moore et al. (2008) conducted an IPA study of a sample of women suffering from venous thromboembolic disease (VTE), a life-threatening condition. The women in their sample had received a diagnosis of inherited thrombophilia. The researchers indentified three main themes in the interviews they conducted with these women:

- *Causal models*: the women participants identified multi-causal models of VTE including surgery, stress and HRT.
- *Primary control efforts*: there were a variety of self-protective behaviours (e.g. walking, compression tights) that reduced the risk of recurrence.
- *Secondary control efforts*: these were concerned with the broader acceptance of having the disease.

Once again, the IPA revealed the ongoing phenomenological process involved in having a disease, in this case a life-threatening one. The illness representations were not fixed but dynamic. The women identified a complex model of causes of the disease and linked this to their everyday lives. They talked about the reassurance provided by having established a biological cause of the disease but the additional causes they identified meant that they could potentially exert some control over the disease. They also mentioned their anxiety of passing it onto their children but managed that anxiety by identifying other possible, more controllable causes of the disease. The primary control strategies they mentioned were not single strategies but ongoing processes of maintaining some control over the disease and reducing the likelihood of recurrence. The third theme labelled secondary control was more an ongoing attitude that was in turn related to the broader social and religious beliefs of the women involved. A central theme in this study was the emphasis on the ongoing tension involved in having a life-threatening disease and still trying to lead a normal life.

Most IPA studies have used semi-structured interviews as their primary source of information about the lived experience of particular health problems. More recent studies have begun to explore additional sources of subjective information. An example is the study by Murray (2005) on the social meanings of prosthesis use. In this study three sources of information were used:

semi-structured face-to-face interviews, e-mail interviews, and an analysis of the posts made on an Internet discussion group. The researcher then integrated the three sources of information. In doing so he was aware of the different character of the three datasets. Murray (2005) noted that:

> the use of e-mail interview extracts allows the representation of temporal experiences, while the use of Listserv posts provides in a more direct way the social contexts in which the social meanings of prosthesis use arise while also supplementing the more 'public' account of the one-on-one interview with the 'private' accounts of persons with a common membership (see Cornwell, 1984). (p. 430)

From this detailed analysis of these different sources of information he identified four themes concerned with the social meaning of prosthesis use:

- prosthesis use and social rituals;
- being a leper – reactions of others;
- social meanings of concealment and disclosure;
- feelings and experiences regarding romantic and sexual relationships.

Once again, it is apparent that the experience of prosthesis use was not a fixed event but an ongoing process that the IPA study revealed was part of the person's involvement in the social world. Thus having the prosthesis changed not only the way the person acts in the world but also the way others act towards them. The IPA study provided a vivid description of this process that in turn the researcher interpreted. Murray drew especially on the work of Irving Goffman (1963) who described the process of stigmatization and how the person with a stigma develops a range of strategies to manage everyday social interaction. The study by Murray illustrates the value of using multiple sources of data to reveal the lived experience of people with a particular health problem.

IPA continues to attract an increasing amount of research. As an evolving approach it has also attracted discussion about its theoretical and methodological assumptions. For example, Willig (2001) noted that the concern with trying to describe cognitive or thinking processes may not be compatible with some forms of phenomenology that are concerned with non-propositional, pre-cognitive forms of knowledge. IPA is often compared with grounded theory (Glaser and Strauss, 1967) although that approach has a greater focus on method than on theory. Willig adds that grounded theory is more suitable for understanding social processes whereas the focus of IPA is on personal experiences. Admittedly, the distinction between these foci is not very clear, as is apparent in the previously described studies.

An extensive review of the literature by Brocki and Wearden (2006) identified 55 articles using this approach with a further seven identified subsequently. They noted a series of methodological concerns including lack of clarity as regards the role of the researcher in data collection and analysis, the inconsistency in sample sizes in reported studies, and the role of theory in interpretation. The original developers are aware of these and other criticisms and are keen to extend discussion about refining and further developing this approach (Smith et al., 2009).

In a recent review and commentary, Smith (2011a) identified certain best practices for researchers planning to adopt this approach. These are summarized in Table 15.1. Although these practices are not specific to studies of illness they still provide a useful guide for conducting and evaluating IPA research on illness perceptions.

Table 15.1 Best practices in IPA articles

Clear focus	Focus on a particular aspect
Strong data	Good interviews
Rigorous	Careful selection of extracts
Theme elaboration	Clear justification of themes
Interpretation	Interpretation not description of themes
Convergence and divergence	Similarity and uniqueness
Well written	Well-wrought sustained narrative

In his subsequent commentary, Smith (2011b) made clear the need to connect the individual experience with the social context. As he emphasizes: 'Clearly individuals do not live in hermetically sealed bubbles. Their experience takes place in a context and is influenced by the social, historical, linguistic milieu' (p. 56). This connecting the personal experience of illness to the social context is apparent in a study of the experience of living with severe back pain by Smith and Osborn (2007) who conducted detailed interviews with six middle-aged men and women. In their analysis they placed pain as an assault on the self at the centre of their interpretation but it is apparent from their analysis that this self is in relationship with others. Box 15.2 provides a summary of the findings. It shows that pain is conceptualized by the sufferer as a challenge to the sense of self but this challenge is more pronounced in the presence of others.

BOX 15.2
PAIN AS AN ASSAULT ON THE SELF

The negative impact of pain on the self

This theme describes the effect of pain on a patient's sense of self and identity:

> It's not who I am it's just who I am if you know what I mean, it's not really me, I get like that and I know like, you're being mean now but I can't help it. It's the pain, it's me, but it is me, me doing it but not me do you understand what I'm saying?

Continuum and trajectory?

This theme describes the possibility of a developmental process beginning with fight to retain positive self, then beginning to doubt this and finally resigning to less desirable self:

> It's like living with this guy who follows you around all the time […] You're cursed with him and he gets in the way, he embarrasses me, he's unsociable and sometimes downright rude.

The public arena makes it worse

This theme describes the negative effect of pain in the presence of others:

> I'd love that [being alone on a desert island] […] but to be away from people and not have to be something else you're not, that would be bliss.

Directing it at others

This theme describes how the negativity about the pain becomes directed at others:

> If something sad happens to someone, I'm not sad, sometimes I'm pleased.

The sting in the tail

This theme is concerned with the fear of social judgement being strong:

> I need to be careful about people and a bit worried what's going to happen to me. Are we all going to get rounded up and taken to a camp somewhere?

Source: Smith and Osborn (2007)

Illness Narratives

Another phenomenological approach is that of narrative psychology. According to narrative psychologists (e.g. Sarbin, 1986) *narrative* construction is an intrinsic part of making sense of the world. The process of creating a narrative enables the person to give meaning to their constantly changing world. Before the narrative there is merely a disjointed sequence of events. In creating the narrative the person selects some pieces of information and ignores others and pieces a story together. Admittedly this process is not conducted in isolation but as part of a wider process of social engagement.

According to narrative psychology people generate stories about illness experiences (Murray, 1999). The construction of these narrative accounts enables the person to grasp its meaning and to begin to exert some control over it. The character of these stories varies depending upon a variety of factors such as previous experience and public repertoires. In terms of orientation, some stories may offer the prospect of advancement, while others are more pessimistic. In terms of emotional valence, some stories may convey excitement whereas others are more placid or depressing.

Research into illness narratives was initially taken up by medical sociologists and anthropologists. Frank (1993) suggested that the central point in any crisis narrative is an epiphany when the actors begin to reassess their position in the world. This can occur at any time during the course of an illness but subsequently the sick person sees the illness in a new light. It is at this stage that the illness story turns from a regressive narrative into a progressive narrative. Admittedly not all sick persons encounter such an epiphanous moment. As Frank (1993) stated: 'Insofar as changing your life is a historically defined project, so the general possibility of epiphanies is also socially constructed. To experience an epiphany requires a cultural milieu in which such experiences are at least possibilities, if not routine expectations' (p. 42).

Frank (1995) developed a three-part typology of illness narratives:

1. *Restitution narrative*: the participant minimizes the experience of illness, rather considering it a temporary interruption that will be overcome.
2. *Chaos narrative*: the ill person loses a sense of order in their life and is unable to develop a way of dealing with the illness experience.
3. *Quest narrative*: the illness is a challenge to be met.

Subsequently, Ezzy (2000) proposed an extension to this typology to take into consideration the temporal dimension:

1. Restitutive linear narratives in which the future is controlled through current actions.
2. Chaotic linear narratives in which there is no prospect of exerting control.
3. Polyphonic narratives in which the emphasis is on the present rather than the future, which is portrayed as uncertain.

These typologies have attracted substantial interest, although like all typologies they should not be considered definitive but rather loose characterizations.

Another sociologist, Michael Bury, characterized the onset of illness as a period of *biographical disruption*. This term was developed by Bury (1982) to describe the experience of people diagnosed with rheumatoid arthritis (RA). The onset of this disease disrupted plans and hopes for the future. For these people their life-story no longer fit with their everyday experiences and it needed to be recast. This process of reworking the parameters of the self has been termed *narrative reconstruction* by Williams (1984). Again working with people suffering from RA, Williams identified a pattern in the casual reasoning adopted by these individuals. They were attempting to integrate RA into their life plans. According to Williams this process of narrative reconstruction helped the sufferers 'reconstitute and repair ruptures between body, self, and world by linking and interpreting different aspects of biography in order to realign present and past and self and society' (p. 197).

These concepts of biographical disruption and narrative reconstruction have increasingly been used by a wide range of health practitioners and researchers including health psychologists. An example is the work of Mathieson and Stam (1995). They conducted detailed interviews with a sample of women who had had breast cancer. Their analysis of these interviews identified three major concerns and activities themes in the participants' accounts:

- *Disrupted feelings of fit*: those bodily changes and other events in the woman's life that threatens their identity.
- *Renegotiating identity*: the realization that there is a stigma associated with cancer and they will have to renegotiate their identity.
- *Biographical work*: this is particularly concerned with how the events around the cancer make up a more or less coherent theme among the other events in their lives.

In developing Bury's concept of biographical disruption, Mathieson and Stam described the biographical work engaged by the women in their study as the process of integrating the illness events into their larger narrative identities. A challenge faced by the cancer patients was that they felt rejected by their peers because of the social and moral stigma attached to cancer. They felt deprived of opportunities for conversations within which they could conduct this biographical work.

In a follow-up study Yaskowich and Stam (2003) described the role of cancer support groups as providing such an opportunity for biographical work. They conducted interviews with women who participated in support groups. Analysis of these interviews identified five preliminary categories that were labelled 'talking safely', 'demystifying the unknown', 'deciding', 'hoping' and 'finding a separate space'. These categories were then transformed into two broader categories: 'a unique and separate social space' and 'biographical work'. It was within the support groups that the women felt they had the opportunity to engage in biographical work that was not available elsewhere. As one woman said:

> Now you've done it [the treatment], everybody's sick and tired of talking about it. You're fixed. It's over with . . . I don't want to be burdening [my husband] with it. (p. 732)

A study by Murray (2007) of the narrative accounts of injured workers identified four narrative structures:

- disability as devastation;
- disability as challenge;
- disability as phenomenon;
- disability as opportunity.

The four structures are somewhat similar to those identified by Gergen and Gergen (1986) who described the main orientations in narratives as being regressive, stable or progressive. The devastation narrative was very much regressive; the challenge and phenomenon narratives were more stable while the opportunity narrative was progressive (see Murray, 2002). These narrative orientations were not fixed but connected to how long the worker had the disability. At the outset, the workers emphasized the devastation narrative but then as they began to grasp the character of the disability and how it could be managed they began to view it partly as an opportunity.

One feature of narrative psychology is the focus on the individual account of illness experience or on that of a small number of individuals. An example is the study by Gray et al. (2005) on the narrative accounts of cancer provided by two Black men. Four in-depth interviews were conducted with each of the participants. Between interviews the research team reflected on their content and identified particular issues to be pursued in subsequent interviews. In analysing the accounts Gray et al. were partially guided by Frank's three-part narrative typology. However, they were aware that such typologies can 'simplify and potentially distort'. Although there were elements of the restitution narrative in their accounts it was more an ongoing process and as such more similar to Ezzy's restitutive linear narrative. In the content of their narratives the two men intertwined personal and societal factors that made their accounts unique rather than abstract.

Although the dominant approach within narrative psychology has been the semi-structured interviews there is a growing body of research that has explored written narratives of various sorts. An example is the work by McGowan et al. (2007) in which they examined the accounts written by women with chronic pelvic pain, a disabling condition with unclear underlying pathophysiology and resistant to various forms of medical intervention. Following a newspaper article the researchers approached over 100 women who were interested in describing their experiences. Subsequently they received hand-written letters from 26 women and a further six e-mail letters. Analysis of these letters revealed that they all followed the same chronological structure from initial awareness, through seeking medical advice and then receiving various treatments. Further analysis revealed one major theme that was labelled 'pathways to disengagement' that encompassed the various factors that disrupted or impeded the flow of the diagnostic cycle. This pathway was a passive process that occurred when the women felt they just could not face continued engagement with a health system that denied their pain. Unlike some of the other illness narratives, this narrative account did not have any end. Rather the women continued to experience pain and were frustrated at the lack of recognition of that pain. There is a need for health care to develop strategies to help these women re-engage with the health system or offer alternative forms of management of the pain.

Another source of illness narratives is the published accounts of people who have experienced various health problems. These are written not only by established writers but also by those with limited experience of writing. They are written both by patients and a variety of health practitioners. The increased popularity of this genre of writing has given rise to a descriptive term – pathography. A number of health psychologists have become interested both in the content of these published accounts but also in the whole process of writing about illness.

Murray (2009) analysed the written accounts of a sample of women who had breast cancer. These accounts were organized into a similar storyline with a beginning, a middle and an end.

The beginning was the period before cancer that was often characterized as a time of innocence. The middle of the story was the diagnosis and the subsequent medical treatment. The end was the period of reassessment of identity and reintegration into society. In closing their story the women frequently emphasized the positive features of having cancer – it had given them an opportunity to reassess their lives. It was also apparent that the women were aware of the therapeutic benefits in telling their stories. They explicitly referred to this process of sense making.

This self-consciousness of the writers about the potential value of telling one's story has contributed to the growth of creative writing and drama classes in hospitals and health centres (Murray, 2009). This growth in what is termed 'therapeutic writing' is partly informed by the work of Pennebaker and Beall (1986) who reported evidence from experimental trials of the health benefits of short periods of writing. More recent reviews of the benefits of this so-called 'expressive writing' suggest that the effect is not large (Frattaroli, 2006). However, research in this field is limited through its focus on short periods of controlled writing. There is a need to explore the value of the more extensive creative writing (Nicholls, 2009).

A recent methodological development has been the growth of autoethnography, which is a disciplined reflection on the researcher's own experiences. In some ways this is a return to some of the earliest forms of psychological research. As an example, let us consider a researcher's writing about their own illness. Carla Willig (2009) reported her analysis of her own written accounts of the experience of having skin cancer. In this study she was explicitly guided by Heidigger's (1962) philosophical phenomenology. In particular, she was concerned with the concept of being 'thrown' into the world. According to Heidigger, as humans we are thrown into life circumstances that are changing and of which we have to make sense and act. Admittedly, in everyday life we do not experience this feeling of 'thrownness' but every so often crises occur when we are forced to reflect upon our position. Willig took this as the starting point for a reflection on her skin cancer diary.

She described how the process of writing helped her to make sense of this threat to her life. On initial diagnosis she noted how 'meaning-making – something that had always seemed more or less effortless, even playful at times – felt like hard physical labour involving my whole body in the struggle against the black hole of meaninglessness' (p. 183). In the following days she developed what she described as a 'serviceable narrative'. This was one based upon confronting her mortality head-on rather than trying to evade it. This narrative gave her 'a sense of peace born from accepting where [she] had been "thrown"' but it was not easy to maintain. However, it was a narrative that she pursued since 'integrating the possibility of death into life as it was lived in the here and now seemed to remove some of the horror surrounding the idea of terminal illness' (p. 185).

Fortunately, the treatment for Willig's skin cancer was successful. Now that it was over she reflected not simply on the content of her narrative making but also on the idea that perhaps from an existential perspective, meaning-making may not always be helpful. As she noted, 'attempts to find meaning (especially backward-looking meanings such as the search for a cause) can interfere with accepting that life is, and always will be, uncertain, unpredictable and (to a large extent) uncontrollable'(p.189).

Comment

Overall, it is apparent that these different phenomenological approaches provide an insight into the processes by which the individual attempts to make sense of illness. These approaches have grown in popularity and sophistication. Unlike the cognitivist approach they are much more open-ended and aim to connect personal representations of illness with changing everyday experiences. They also draw upon different philosophical traditions.

SOCIAL APPROACHES

Illness Discourse

The discursive turn in psychology has highlighted a problem with cognitive and phenomenological approaches to the study of illness representations in that they are concerned with trying to infer something about inner mental worlds from a study of verbal reports. An alternative approach is to focus on the character of the *discourse* itself and the context within which it occurs rather than on the structure of inferred inner mental phenomena. Within this approach the communicative nature of language is the focus of attention rather than inferred underlying beliefs (Potter and Wetherell, 1987).

Two main orientations have been identified in contemporary discourse analysis – discursive psychology and Foucauldian discourse analysis (Willig, 2004; McKinlay and McVittie, 2008). The former places emphasis on unpacking the various discursive strategies such as 'footing' and 'disclaiming' and their functions within a particular discursive context. The focus of this approach is on what the discourse is doing. The latter, more critical form focuses on the particular discursive resources available within a culture and the implications for those who live there. These resources enable us to construct and live in the world in particular ways. It has been argued that these two orientations should not be seen as distinct approaches but rather complementary (Potter and Wetherell, 1987, 1995). Individuals are both producers and the products of discourse. More critical psychologists are wary at the assumed autonomy of the individual actor and the ignorance of issues of politics and power by discursive psychologists (Parker, 1997). Here we consider both approaches in a little more detail.

Discursive Psychology

Discursive psychologists have been concerned with how people talk about illness in different contexts. Detailed analysis of this discourse has provided insight into how illness is constructed through everyday language. An early example of this approach is the study by Middleton (1996) in which he explored the talk in a parent group for children with chronic renal failure. He argued that this talk is more than 'a display of inner workings of minds' but is 'part of the process of making [their] health care experiences socially intelligible' (p. 244). Rather than breaking the talk down into elemental beliefs, he attempted to understand it as part of the process of making sense of illness within a social context. He stressed that an important component of such talk is that it contains many contradictory elements and expressions of uncertainty. These elements are not deficiencies but rather are seen as being 'used to establish common understandings concerning what it is to care for chronically ill children' (p. 257). Further, the talk is more than self-presentation that can be ironed out by careful assessment but is rather part of the broader collective process of meaning making.

An example of the use of discursive psychology is the study by Radtke and Van Mens-Verhulst (2001) of mothers with asthma. Interviews with a number of these women revealed the dominance of the traditional medical discourse to describe asthma. Further, they identified certain causes of the disease in their everyday lives but distinct from their role as mothers. In discussing an exemplar case the authors noted that by avoiding any suggestion of a link between her asthma symptoms and mothering allowed the woman to do two things: 'first she positioned herself as a competent mother despite living with asthma' and 'second, it justified her claim that her previous employment situation and problems with her extended family were unjust and harmful and thereby had contributed to her illness.' In interpreting these findings Radtke and Van Mens-Verhulst emphasize that the women are both producers and products of discourse: 'As producers of discourse, the women do not draw upon the cultural resources available to them in some straightforward way, but rather use them strategically to accomplish certain actions' (p. 381).

Discursive psychologists are particularly interested in how discourse is oriented to social action. According to discourse analysts, discourse constructs different versions of reality that lead to particular actions. An example of this is the study by Ranjbar et al. (2014) of the discourses HIV/AIDS care workers. In this study a sample of care workers were interviewed about their work. Prior to the analysis the researchers carefully transcribed the interviews following a version of the transcription method developed by Jefferson (2004) that enabled them to consider not only the words used but also the various para-linguistics such as pauses and coughs. The extract from one of the interviews provided in Box 15.3 illustrates how the care worker perceives the infection as controllable and avoidable.

BOX 15.3
HIV AS A CONTROLLABLE INFECTION

Interviewer: And how do you feel about (...) working with (0.2) individuals who are HIV positive or who have AIDS or TB.

Care worker: Mm (0.6) uhm I don't have a problem with that at all (1.1) uhm but as I said my background I've dealt with (.) a lot of people with different disabilities mental physical (0.6) uhm (1.1) >and I've always been< raised

(Continued)

(Continued)

to treat people equally (0.8) so (0.2) that doesn't affect me at all like I'd (1.5) ((coughs)) I don't have concerns about myself catching it because I know (0.7) I'm extremely careful and I take precautions (0.8) uhm >all the safety precautions that you're supposed to take<

Transcription symbols (from Jefferson, 2004):

°...°	speech that is quieter
>...<	speech that is faster
(.)	brief pause
(1.1)	Time of pause

Source: Ranjbar et al. (2014)

This strategic use of discourse in everyday social interaction was developed further by Radley and Billig (1996) in their detailed commentary on the discursive context within which talk about health and illness is generated. In particular they contrasted the different positionings of healthy and sick people: 'The healthy have much to say about their illness experience, while the sick are often at pains to show their "normality"' (p. 225). Since the interviewer is usually a healthy person, the sick person feels strongly 'the need to *legitimate* [their] position'. This emphasizes that the 'accounts are situated in a rhetorical context of potential justification and criticism' (p. 226). Although this commentary was aimed at qualitative interview research, a similar comment can be made about quantitative questionnaire studies of health and illness beliefs.

Other studies have explored the dominant discourses that we draw upon to construct our sense of particular health issues. Drawing upon the concept of *interpretative repertoire* (Potter and Wetherell, 1987: 139), Benveniste et al. (1999) explored lay theories of anorexia nervosa. Interviews with five men and five women in Australia revealed three dominant themes that were labelled as a socio-cultural discourse, a discourse of the individual and a discourse of femininity. Drawing upon the socio-cultural discourse enabled participants to attribute a source of blame for anorexia nervosa to factors external to the individual. Conversely, the individual discourse located the cause of anorexia within the individual. However, it is argued that both of these discourses are premised upon a humanist conception of the individual as an autonomous rational being. This separation of socio-cultural factors from individual psychology maintains the idea that anorexia nervosa is a manifestation of psychopathology.

Foucauldian Discourse Analysis

The internalization of dominant discourses of health and illness can be considered part of disciplinary power by which social norms are accepted (Foucault, 1979). Deviation from such norms can cause severe distress to the individual concerned. An example is the case of hirsutism: a medical term used to describe an excess of hair on the female body. In Western society, women spend a substantial amount of money to remove such hair. A study of women who had self-perceived hirsutism found that the women had strongly internalized the dominant discourse around female bodily hair and adopted a range of personal strategies to reduce the associated distress (Keegan et al., 2004): 'Through self-surveillance and correction to such norms, and the regulation of bodies through body practices such as depilitatory regimes, women are rendered less socially oriented and more focused on self-modification' (p. 338). A particular point of interest was the way removal of hair was perceived as 'looking-after', an example of how body regulation is seen as self-care rather than a process of gender control.

A similar study of women with bulimia (Burns and Gavey, 2004) revealed the importance of the dominant discourse of healthy weight. This interacted with the dominant discourse on female body shape. The authors argue that both 'bulimic' and 'healthy' female bodies are underwritten by 'normalizing discourses that derogate female fat and amplitude and that promote engaging in regulatory practices designed to promote a slender body'. They continue that by focusing on healthy weight rather than a broader concept of health, current health promotion campaigns are 'paradoxically implicated in the shaping and production of subjectivities, practices and bodies for some women in ways that are antithetical to an overt health message' (p. 562).

A particular feature of FDA is exploring how dominant ideas become embodied in the person. Thus FDA researchers are not simply investigating discourses as things in themselves but how they become material reality through a process of negotiation by the person. An example of this is the work by Willig and Paulson (2008) on older women's talk about their ageing bodies. They initially identified through a literature review four dominant discourses about the ageing body. These were:

- A biological discourse that emphasizes the vulnerability of the ageing body through physical degeneration.
- A social constructionist/historical and personal agency discourse that considers the tension between discourses of contextual determinism and personal agency.
- A female beauty discourse that considers older women's talk about losing control of their appearance.
- A feminist discourse that considers women's ageing bodies threatened by the male gaze in patriarchal society and by the beauty industry.

Considering these four 'expert' discourses Willig and Paulson conducted qualitative interviews with ten older women about their perceptions of their bodies. These interviews were subsequently analysed following the six stages developed by Willig (2001):

1. Highlighting the transcript for references to the body.
2. Coding each section for wider cultural discourses.
3. Specifying the action-orientation of each section of the text.

4. Identifying the various subject positions.
5. Considering the practical implications of each section of text.
6. Identifying the 'ways of being' made possible by each section of text.

This analysis contributed to a detailed understanding of how the women engaged with dominant discourses about the ageing body. An important feature was the tension within the older women's use of the dualist constructions of the ageing body. On the one hand, the women could talk about their body as something separate that was in decline physically. On the other hand, this separation of body and mind could be considered functional in that the women could exert their active mind to control these ageing bodies. Willig and Paulson concluded that this demonstrates how the cultural discourses of personal agency are as important as those of biological and contextual determinism in shaping the ageing body.

Social Representations of Health and Illness

Unlike some of the previous approaches to our understanding of illness representations, social representation (SR) theory places the social at the centre of the process of sense making. The other approaches tend to focus more on individual experiences of illness or the immediate discourses around illness. Social representations are concerned with the socio-cultural understanding of the phenomenon that is revealed not only in language but in everyday social practices. Social representation theory is concerned with both the content of these representations and how they operate to shape our engagement with the world. According to Moscovici (1973): 'They do not represent simply "opinions about", "images of" or "attitudes towards", but "theories" or "branches of knowledge" in their own right, for the discovery and organization of reality' (p. xiv).

An increasing number of researchers have explored the character of SRs of illness. The early classic study was conducted by Claudine Herzlich (1973). From her interviews with a sample of French adults, Herzlich concluded that a central concept in the popular definitions of health and illness is activity. For most lay people to be active means to be healthy, while to be inactive means to be ill. Herzlich distinguished between three lay reactions to illness:

- *Illness as destructive*: the experience of those actively involved in society.
- *Illness as liberator*: the experience of those with excessive social obligations.
- *Illness as an occupation*: the experience of those who accept illness and feel they must contribute to its alleviation.

Lay people are aware of these different reactions and not only adopt one or another of these strategies depending upon time and circumstance, but also characterize other individuals as belonging to a particular category. The study of injured workers described earlier (Murray, 1997) reveals the inter-penetration of personal narratives with these social representations.

The original formulation of SR theory emphasized the important role of science in shaping everyday common sense (Moscovici, 1984). More recent formulations have indicated a much more dynamic interaction between science and common sense (Joffe, 2002). In Western society, biomedicine is extremely important in shaping our understandings of health and illness. As Herzlich and Pierret (1987) stress: 'in our society the discourse of medicine about illness is so loud that it tends to drone out all others' (p. xi). The media plays a very important role in acting as a conduit of scientific medical ideas to the general public. As such, SR researchers are interested in both what lay people have to say about illness but also in how the media report these ideas. The media help to transform scientific thinking into more everyday terms. In doing so they transform illness from something that is impersonal into something that is personal and is infused with particular cultural norms and values. Of course, since scientists are lay people too their language can also reflect these values.

An important characteristic of SRs is that they are not passive characteristics of the individual but part of the dialectical process of engagement between the individual and the social world. Moscovici (1984) refers to two particular processes, *anchoring* and *objectification*, which underlie the process of developing SRs. The first is the process whereby unfamiliar concepts are given meaning by connecting them with more familiar concepts, whereas the second is the process whereby a more abstract concept acquires meaning through association with more everyday phenomena.

Several researchers have used these concepts to explore popular views of particular illnesses. Joffe (1996) conducted detailed interviews about AIDS with a sample of young adults from London and from South Africa. She also conducted a content analysis of media campaigns. She notes that historically mass incurable illnesses have been anchored to the 'other'. In the case of AIDS this process is shown in the anchoring of that disease in the supposed aberrant behaviour of others. This process serves a protective function by distancing the person from the risk of contracting the disease. However, a certain amount of 'leakage' has occurred as it became apparent that AIDS could be spread via the blood supply and among heterosexuals. The process of objectification transforms an abstract concept into an image. Joffe (1996) noted that the media images of tombstones and coffins concretized the fear associated with AIDS.

Forming SRs helps to define a group and also to promote in-group solidarity and to defend group members from out-group threats. Consider the case of the Ebola virus that can be deadly if contracted. Interviews conducted in Britain about this virus found that most lay people portrayed it as an African disease and that they are very unlikely to contract it. As one woman said:

> It just seemed like one of those mythical diseases, sort of thing, science fiction like thing, that happens in places like Africa and underdeveloped countries and doesn't come here.
>
> (Joffe and Haarhoff, 2002: 965)

By clearly characterizing the disease in fantastical terms the lay public is symbolically protecting itself from this outside threat.

In a comparable study of representations of AIDS in Zambia (Joffe and Bettega, 2003) it was found that young residents distanced themselves from the risk of the disease by representing it as originating in Western society and in deviant sexual and scientific practices. These findings highlighted the challenge of encouraging young people to take personal action to protect themselves against AIDS. Health campaigns designed to curtail the spread of AIDS would need to challenge these SRs.

The internal dynamic within SRs was explored in a study by Moloney and Walker (2002). Their study explored how people in Australia talk about organ donation and transplantation. Their analysis of focus group discussions suggested that SRs of were organized around what they characterized as two dialectically opposed images – the gift of life and the mechanistic removal and replacement of body parts. However, the participants were extremely comfortable with this apparent opposition. According to Moloney and Walker this illustrated the role of conflict and debate within the production of SRs: 'Through the process of debate, members were able to articulate and discuss the conflicting nature of the donation dilemma and, in so doing, either reach a position that was slightly different from that held at the beginning of the discussion, or consolidated how they felt' (p. 317).

SR theory is not just concerned with language but also with non-linguistic representations of phenomena such as illness. Joffe (2003) links this broader concern with the use of images and symbols to understand health and illness, for example the ribbons used to convey support for particular diseases or the various metaphors that are associated with illness. The classic analyses by Sontag of the metaphors used to describe cancer (Sontag, 1978) and AIDS (Sontag, 1988) illustrate how difficult it is to talk and think about illness without reference to certain metaphors.

Other researchers have accessed a range of other sources to explore the changing nature of SRs of illness. For example, Porto (2007) considered social representations of tuberculosis through an analysis of different literary documents. In the mid-nineteenth century tuberculosis was popularly seen as a disease that provided the sufferer with an aura of exceptionality and even a certain refinement. This aura was something that was perceived as a positive quality by some of the literary establishment. Porto quotes from Casimiro de Abreu, a Brazilian poet of that period:

> I desire a serious, severe, long-term disease indeed for I am tired of this good health monotony. However, I would like to have the phthisis with all its unexpected incidents; I would like to wither lyrically, always singling the last chants of life, and afterwards, to expire around perfumes under Italy's bluish sky, or around this sublime nature that surrounds Queimado.

This use of such a wide range of resources provides an opportunity for health psychologists to connect with scholars from other disciplines.

According to Joffe (1996) the potential for modifying SRs of disease is limited since they serve the function of preserving the status quo in a culture. They not only make the social world remain familiar and manageable but also maintain the dominance of certain ideas. Admittedly, certain organized groups within society can subvert these dominant ideas. The gay movement in Britain contributed to a reassessment of the dominant image of AIDS as belonging to a supposedly deviant minority group that in terms of religious beliefs were themselves to blame for contracting the disease (Markova and Wilkie, 1987). Instead, it was recharacterized as a disease that could affect heterosexual as well as gay individuals.

Other researchers have explored the potential of challenging the character of restrictive SRs of illness through various forms of social action. For example, Krause (2003) conducted a participant action research project with a group of individuals who had inflammatory bowel disease. Interviews were conducted with them before and after the participatory intervention. At the outset, the participants had a very negative SR of the disease. The disease pervaded all aspects of their lives: family, work and social relations. Figure 15.2 provides a summary of the SR of the disease before and after the participatory intervention. It shows how SR theory is concerned with developing an understanding of the lay theories of illness and how these can change over time.

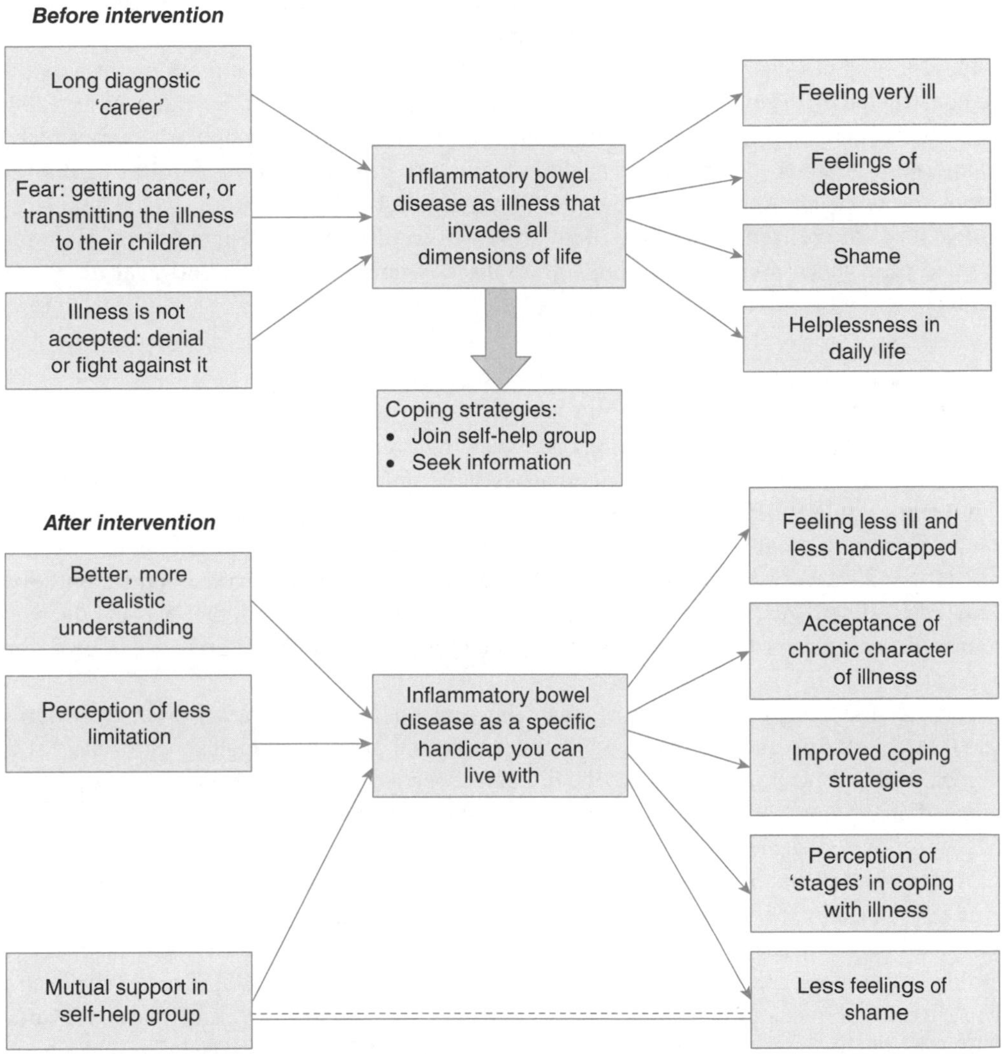

Figure 15.2 Social representations of inflammatory bowel disease

Source: Krause (2003)

MEDIA REPRESENTATIONS

An important part of studies of SRs has been concerned with how particular phenomena are represented in the media. The initial study of Moscovici considered how psychoanalysis was represented in the Catholic and the communist press in France in the 1950s. Today, the media is much more extensive. It can range from newspapers and television through to the Internet and zines. Public surveys have confirmed the extent of popular interaction with different forms of media. There is an obvious need to explore not only the character of illness representations in the various media but also how lay people engage with these representations and who sets the agenda in illness media production (Hodgetts and Chamberlain, 2006).

Further, it is not just illness representations in themselves that are important but how they are constructed with reference to other social phenomena. For example, Nairn et al. (2006) have commented on how ethnic minorities and indigenous groups are popularly represented in a denigratory manner in the popular media. This in turn has implications for the health of the groups so portrayed. Recently, Estacio (2009) has highlighted the need for critical health psychologists to move from describing these processes to directly challenging them. Her study reported on a successful activist campaign to directly challenge media portrayal of Filipino workers.

CONCLUSIONS

The study of lay illness representations is a growing area within health psychology. Different theoretical and methodological approaches have guided research in this area. One way of integrating these different approaches to the study of illness beliefs is by considering the levels of psychological analysis proposed by Doise (1986). Doise suggested that a reason for the confusion between different social psychologists was that they operated at different levels of analysis. He suggested that we should distinguish between research that was conducted at the *intrapsychic* level of analysis from that which is conducted at the *interpersonal*, *group* and *societal* levels.

This classification provides a way of organizing research on representations of illness (Murray, 1993). At the intrapsychic level are both the cognitive and phenomenological approaches; at the interpersonal and positional levels are the discursive accounts while at the societal level are the Foucauldian discourse analytic and social representational approaches. The challenge is to explore the connection across these levels.

An example of the integration of the different levels was the study by Crossley (1999) who noted the connection between personal and cultural stories. Similarly Murray (2003) explored the connection between narrative and social representation theory. Detailed analysis of the three-fold typology of social representations of illness developed by Herzlich (1978) revealed their narrative structure. Conversely, narratives can also be explored at different levels of analysis (Murray, 2000). The challenge is to see the social and political in the personal accounts of illness and to explore the implications of this for strategies to improve health (Murray, 2011).

FUTURE RESEARCH

1. Illness representations evolve over time. There is a need for a greater understanding of their evolution.
2. Illness representations are connected with people's social world. Health psychologists need to be involved in mapping these connections within specific cultures.
3. Theoretically, health psychologists need to explore the conceptual connections between illness and health discourse.
4. The interconnectedness of illness discourse and bodily processes is still poorly understood. There is a need for a concerted programme of theoretical work in this area.
5. Lay representations of illness, or of groups of people, can have negative impact on the health of particular groups. Health psychology has a role in challenging these representations.

SUMMARY

1 Psychologists have used a variety of theoretical perspectives to investigate lay representations of illness. The major approaches have been the cognitive, phenomenological, discursive and socio-cultural perspectives.

2 Cognitive approaches have attempted to identify a limited number of dimensions of illness representations including identity, causes, time line, consequences and control/cure. The cognitive approach has generated a substantial body of empirical research using various standardized measures.

3 The phenomenological approach is concerned with describing the subjective experiences of the individual patient. It is less concerned with identifying a limited number of illness dimensions but more with developing a sophisticated interpretative model. This approach prefers to use qualitative interviews to collect data.

4 Narrative psychology is a particular phenomenological approach that is concerned with the narrative character of people's accounts of illness.

5 Discourse analysis focuses on the character of the language used to talk about illness and the context within which it occurs rather than on the structure of inferred beliefs.

6 Social representation theory is concerned with the lay theories that underlie popular understandings of illness.

16 ILLNESS AND PERSONALITY

Ills of the body may be cured by physical remedies or by the power of the spirit acting through the soul.

(Paracelsus)

OUTLINE

In this chapter we examine the influence of individual differences in personality and other psychological characteristics on susceptibility to illness. It begins with a brief history of the contrasting approaches of practitioners of orthodox and holistic medicine. It goes on to consider Freud's work on hysteria and contemporary approaches to medically unexplained symptoms such as chronic fatigue syndrome. After an account of some of the ways in which Freud's theories became applied to organic illness by the psychosomatic schools of psychoanalysis, there is an analysis of the problems involved in investigating and explaining links between personality and physical illness. The chapter concludes with an assessment of contemporary research on personality and illness with particular reference to coronary heart disease and cancer.

ORTHODOX MEDICINE AND HOLISTIC APPROACHES

Orthodox Western medicine has always been based on the belief that physical illness has physical causes and requires physical treatment. While there is increasing acceptance of the importance to be attached to health behaviours among the causes of illness, the assumption remains that the actual mechanisms are physical, including such things as viruses, bacteria, carcinogens and physiological abnormalities. Partly as a result of DNA research and the influence of the pharmaceutical industry, this *physicalist* approach is increasingly being applied to psychological disorders, and conditions ranging from schizophrenia to mild cases of depression are commonly attributed to biochemical imbalances, often thought to be genetic. On the other hand, there are popular beliefs, supported to some extent by health psychologists, that people with certain kinds of personality

Figure 16.1 Albrecht Dürer, *Melancholia*. Durer's 1514 etching is a superb representation of the condition we now refer to as depression. In addition to its devastating psychological effects, depression has been found to be associated with subsequent physical illness, including coronary heart disease

may be particularly susceptible to heart disease or cancer and that psychological disturbances may be a cause of much physical illness. The research on stress and illness discussed in Chapter 12 is one aspect of this. Holistic treatments and complementary therapies for physical diseases often have a psychological component including stress management programmes, relaxation, breathing exercises and meditation. It is claimed by the proponents of such treatments that they are capable of correcting 'psychic' or 'energy' imbalances that have triggered the symptoms in the first place.

While holistic approaches can be traced back at least as far as Plato (Bass, 2007), it is quite clearly shown in Roy Porter's history of medicine from its earliest origins to the present day (Porter, 1997) that most professional practitioners of medicine from many different cultures throughout the world have taken a physicalist approach. In the history of Western medicine, the most influential doctrine has been the Hippocratic one, which dates back to the fifth century BC and which presupposes that there is a physical basis for all disorders, whether physical or psychological. As we saw in Chapter 1, according to Galen (born AD 129), a key figure in the Hippocratic tradition, psychological and physical disorders were both attributable to an imbalance of the four bodily humours, blood, phlegm, black bile and yellow bile. Little scope was left for psychological causation and this theory only really lost its hold on Western thinking in the 1850s. When Galen noted that *melancholy* women were more likely to get breast cancer than *sanguine* women he was not putting forward a psychological hypothesis. Although the psychological characteristics of melancholy correspond to some extent to the modern concept of depression, Galen took the view that breast cancer and melancholy were jointly attributable to humoral imbalance, in this case to an excess of black bile (see Sontag, 2002).

As an indication of the grip these ideas had on medical thinking in western Europe, the black bile theory of depression was still being articulated in 1836 by Johannes Freidreich, professor of psychiatry in Würzburg, together with the view that mania was caused by an excess of yellow bile, psychosis by an excess of blood, and dementia by an excess of phlegm (see Shorter, 1992). One feature of the doctrine of the four humours that even in recent times finds its echo in psychological theory is Galen's description of the four *classical temperaments* already described in Table 1.1 (see Box 16.1).

The humoral theory was eventually abandoned following the rapid development of physiology in the nineteenth century, and notably the founding of the modern science of cellular pathology by Rudolf Virchow in the 1850s. This was the key that opened the door to our contemporary understanding of physical diseases. Since there were no obvious indications that cellular pathology could account for psychological disorder, the door was also open for the development of purely psychological explanations, notably by Sigmund Freud. The historical dominance of the humoral theory and the modem ascendancy of organic medicine has not entirely inhibited speculation of the opposite kind, that psychological factors may play a part in causing physical diseases and influencing recovery. An early example is provided by Dogen (1200–1253), the founder of the Soto school of Japanese Buddhism. Admonishing his pupils not to regard illness as a hindrance to performing their spiritual practices, he remarked:

BOX 16.1 THE FOUR HUMOURS AND MODERN PERSONALITY THEORY

In the second century AD Galen described four temperaments that characterize individuals possessing an excess of each of the four humours. The *sanguine* has an excess of blood, the *choleric* of yellow bile, the *phlegmatic* of phlegm and the *melancholic* of black bile (see Table 1.1). As descriptions of personality types they were still in use during the second half of the twentieth century. In his influential theory of personality the late Hans Eysenck proposed two basic dimensions of personality, extravert–introvert and stable–unstable, and developed a personality test to measure them. Both dimensions were assumed to be measurable along a continuum, with extreme examples towards each end and the average person in the middle. Although he considered the reduction of personality to four qualitatively different types to be an oversimplification, Eysenck (1965/1970) pointed out that the classical temperaments do correspond quite closely with four extremes that can be identified using his personality test: the stable extravert (sanguine), unstable extravert (choleric), stable introvert (phlegmatic) and unstable introvert (melancholic), an interesting convergence of classical and contemporary personality theories.

> I suspect that the occurrence of illness stems from the mind . . . Some years ago when I went to China, I suffered from diarrhoea while aboard ship. A violent storm arose, causing great confusion; before I knew it, my sickness was gone. This makes me think that if we concentrate on study and forget about other things, illness will not arise.
>
> (*Dogen's Shobogenzo Zuimonki*, translated by R. Masunaga, 1972: 91.)

Sontag (2002) provided many European and North American examples. In England in the late sixteenth and seventeenth centuries it was widely believed that the happy man would not get plague. In 1871 the physician who treated Alexander Dumas for cancer wrote that, among the principal causes of cancer, were 'deep and sedentary study and pursuits, and feverish and anxious agitation of public life, the cares of ambition, frequent paroxysms of rage, violent grief' (Sontag, 2002: 52). At about the same time in England, one doctor advised patients that they could avoid cancer by being careful to bear the ills of life with equanimity; above all things, not to 'give way' to any grief. At this time also, tuberculosis (TB) was often thought to come from too much passion afflicting the reckless and sensual, or else to be a disease brought on by unrequited love.

In fact TB was often called *consumption*, and hence the appearance in the English language of metaphors such as *consuming passion*.

BOX 16.2
HYSTERIA: THE CASE OF 'ANNA O'

Psychological theories of hysteria first came to prominence as a result of the collaboration between Sigmund Freud and the Viennese physiologist Josef Breuer. From 1880 to 1882 Breuer treated a patient who became known as 'Anna O' and who proved to be of great importance in the history of psychoanalysis. Anna suffered from a spectacular range of hysterical and other symptoms, including paralysis and loss of sensation mainly on the right side of her body, disturbances of eye movements and vision, occasional deafness, multiple personality and loss of the ability to speak her native German. As a result of this last symptom, Breuer was obliged to talk to her in English over which she retained a perfect command. When she was asked to recall previous occurrences of each of her symptoms while under hypnosis, Anna invariably arrived at previously forgotten memories of distressing incidents that had occurred while she had nursed her dying father. As a result of this the symptom temporarily disappeared. For example, the paralysis of Anna's right arm disappeared after she recalled having had the hallucination of a large black snake while sitting at her father's bedside. Anna O's true identity was much later revealed to be Bertha Pappenheim and she went on to become a well-known feminist who campaigned on problems of single mothers, children in orphanages, prostitution and the white slave trade. Just how successful was her treatment for hysteria is still a matter of controversy and she herself remained ambivalent about the value of psychoanalysis, once remarking that it depends very much on the ability of the psychoanalyst whether it is a good instrument or a double-edged sword. For further details, see Sulloway (1980).

FREUD, HYSTERIA AND MEDICALLY UNEXPLAINED SYMPTOMS

Having had a top quality orthodox medical education in the 1880s, Freud was not inclined to propose psychological explanations for organic disorders. His psychoanalytic theories, which were eventually to encompass the whole of human psychology, originated in the study of **hysteria**, symptoms that appeared to indicate serious neurological or other physical disorder, but for which no underlying physical cause could be found (see Box 16.2). The medical theorists of ancient Greece first used the word 'hysteria' to refer to anomalous physical complaints that they believed occurred only in women. They regarded it as a gynaecological disorder caused by the womb moving away from its normal position. By the end of the nineteenth century, as a result of the pioneering work of Charcot, Breuer and Freud, it had become widely accepted that hysterical disorders are not restricted to women and that the causes are psychological rather than physiological. By using the newly discovered techniques of hypnosis, these pioneers were able to show that hysteria may be caused psychologically, but outside the awareness of the sufferer. Hysterical symptoms could be induced in any hypnotizable person by the use of hypnotic suggestion, and the symptoms of hypnotizable patients could often be relieved, unfortunately only temporarily, in this way. While this does not actually rule out the possibility that there is an organic basis to hysteria, it certainly made it a lot easier for Freud to put forward his bold psychological hypotheses. (For detailed accounts of this early work on hysteria and subsequent developments in the twentieth century, see Sulloway, 1980, and Shorter, 1992.)

Psychosomatic Disorders

The term *hysteria* is not very often used nowadays, having been largely replaced by two different diagnostic categories in the DSM-III, **psychosomatic (or somatoform) disorder**, subsequently termed *somatic symptom disorder* (DSM-5), and **borderline** *personality disorder* (Meares, 2012), but it remains implicit in the new terminology that sufferers are somehow *somatising* problems that are intrinsically psychological in nature. Freud found it difficult to convince his patients that they were not suffering from an organic disease and it is equally true today that sufferers from a variety of conditions are hostile to suggestions that these conditions may be psychological rather than organic in origin.

Among the conditions that provoke controversy are **myalgic encephalomyelitis (ME)** or **chronic fatigue syndrome** (CFS; see Box 16.3), irritable bowel syndrome, repetitive strain injury, fibromyalgia, Gulf War syndrome, total allergy syndrome, migraine, and a variety of types of pain in the back, chest, abdomen, limbs and face. Arguments for believing that these are all contemporary forms of hysteria have been forcefully put by Shorter (1992) and Showalter (1997). On the other hand, there are many who share the views of the sufferers themselves that a failure to find an organic basis for a condition is not a convincing reason for asserting that one does not exist. Sufferers of the above mentioned conditions are offended by the idea that the cause of their suffering is 'all in the mind'.

Certainly, the technical literature is confusing. For example, with regard to ME and CFS, many experts use the two terms 'ME' and 'CFS' interchangeably. Others have suggested that ME and CFS may not be identical conditions, as alleged. Jason et al. (2014) found that patients who met the Myalgic Encephalomyelitis International Consensus Criteria were more impaired and had more severe symptoms than those who met the internationally accepted criteria for CFS. The jury is still out on this issue.

One of the most striking but least understood aspects of the history of psychosomatic medicine is the large differences in the types of symptoms that have been found in different historical periods. The spectacular examples reported by Charcot, Freud and others in the nineteenth century, apparently indicating an underlying neurological condition, are nowadays encountered by neurologists only rarely in a working lifetime. While Charcot certainly exaggerated the dramatic character of these symptoms, and encouraged his patients to do so, there is little doubt that they were common enough, and that their disappearance is a real change. The shifting character of the symptoms, and the intense controversies about their organic basis, are elegantly and plausibly explained by Shorter (1992). He accepts the view that the symptoms are produced by the action of the unconscious mind, and argues that an essential feature of the condition is a need to convince doctors of the organic reality of the patients' illness. He states:

> One factor that conveys a history is the doctor's attitude. Patients want to please doctors, in the sense that they do not want the doctor to laugh at them and dismiss their plight as imaginary. Thus they strive to produce symptoms the doctor will recognise. As doctors' own ideas about what constitutes 'real' disease change from time to time due to theory and practice, the symptoms the patients present will change as well. These medical changes give the story of psychosomatic illness its dynamic: the medical 'shaping' of symptoms.
>
> (Shorter, 1992: 1)

In a medical environment in which brain scans are readily available, hysterical patients are unlikely to convince neurologists that they are suffering from a brain tumour; but in a world in which new viruses continue to appear, sometimes not easy to isolate in the laboratory, then plausible symptoms of infectious disease, for example, are much more likely to be taken seriously.

BOX 16.3
MYALGIC ENCEPHALOMYELITIS AND CHRONIC FATIGUE SYNDROME

In July 1955, 200 people were admitted to the Royal Free Hospital, London, with symptoms similar to those nowadays referred to either as ME or CFS. Subsequently 70 doctors and nurses at the hospital were also taken ill and the hospital had to close for two months. No cause was ever discovered and psychiatrists concluded that it was a case of mass hysteria. CFS first appeared in the USA in 1984 when 160 cases of a new mystery illness were diagnosed in Incline Village, a prosperous small town near Lake Tahoe, Nevada.

The symptoms reported were quite diffuse but suggestive of a viral infection together with prolonged and debilitating fatigue. As in the case of the Royal Free syndrome, extensive laboratory tests failed to identify any pathological agent. Since then a huge number of further cases of ME/CFS have been reported together with a failure to identify any organic cause, leading many doctors and medical researchers to conclude that the condition is psychosomatic. Although the terms ME and CFS are modern ones, the actual symptoms are more or less identical to those referred to as neurasthenia in the period around the beginning of the twentieth century. This widespread phenomenon was also investigated by researchers who failed to find a viral cause.

Although there is still no clear evidence of an organic disease basis for CFS/ME, there are medical hypotheses (e.g. Anderson et al., 2012) and most patients' organizations remain committed to the belief that there is a purely physical basis, in opposition to current medical opinion. In a survey of the websites of UK patients' organizations and medical websites and textbooks, Hossenbaccus and White (2013) reported that 89% of the patient organizations viewed the condition as purely physical, as compared with only 24% of the medical websites and textbooks. They point out that the propaganda of patients' organizations may have the effect of discouraging sufferers from embarking on behavioural and cognitive behavioural treatments, which have been shown to be moderately effective. For example, in a study involving 641 patients, White et al. (2011) found that cognitive behavioural therapy (CBT) and graded exercise therapy (GET) were reasonably effective treatments.

Medically Unexplained Symptoms

Bass (2007) noted that, perhaps in deference to patients' sensitivities with regard to suggestions of psychological causation, the currently fashionable terms replacing *psychosomatic disorders* are the relatively neutral *functional somatic symptoms* and *medically unexplained symptoms*. He pointed out that they account for nearly half of all primary care consultations, but that only 10–15% are subsequently shown to have an organic basis. Furthermore, Nimnuan et al. (2001) found that the symptoms of apparently distinct syndromes such as chronic fatigue syndrome and irritable bowel syndrome were sufficiently intercorrelated in a sample of 550 individual sufferers that the authors doubt whether they can be regarded as clinically distinct. This evidence of overlap was also found in a review by Aaron and Buchwald (2001).

Brown (2004) reviewed earlier explanations of medically unexplained symptoms and attempted to integrate them into a modern neuropsychological theory. The main earlier explanations, each of which he considers to be partially true, are based on the concepts of (a) *disassociation* – a loss of awareness, following traumatic experiences, of cognitive processes which are nevertheless still active; (b) *conversion* – the unconscious suppression (or *repression*) of traumatic memories that retain a neural energy which becomes *converted* into somatic symptoms that were either present at the time of the original trauma or represent it symbolically; and (c) *somatization* – the tendency to experience or express psychological distress as the symptoms of physical illness. He then presented a new integrative model that utilizes elements of each of these while locating his theory in modern conceptions of *attention*, *consciousness*, *control*, *personality*, *illness beliefs* and the *misattribution of symptoms*. He considered his model to be consistent with the use of cognitive behavioural therapy for treatment, but argued that it is also consistent with the use of psychodynamic psychotherapy, physiotherapy, occupational therapy and antidepressants – all treatments currently in use for medically unexplained symptoms.

PSYCHOSOMATIC MEDICINE AND ORGANIC ILLNESS

The rapid development of organic medicine from the 1850s led to a declining enthusiasm among medical practitioners for speculation about possible psychological causes of organic diseases. Freud was no exception. He insisted that psychoanalytic training should be restricted to those already qualified in medicine, on the grounds that only the medically trained psychoanalyst would have the skills necessary to decide whether or not a patient's symptoms needed to be investigated as indicating possible organic disorder. It was not until the period from the 1920s to the 1950s that Freud's theories were applied to physical illness by theorists who developed the *psychosomatic approach* in psychoanalysis.

A useful survey of this approach was given by Brown (1964). One of its most colourful representatives was George Groddeck, who believed that all illness is unconsciously motivated and has a meaning for the sufferer. Just as a hysterical pregnancy might be motivated by an unconscious wish to have a baby, so might a case of laryngitis be motivated by a desire not to speak. To take an extreme example, a heart attack might be viewed as an unconscious attempt to commit suicide. Another equally colourful representative was Wilhelm Reich, who believed, among many other extraordinary things, that repressed sexual feelings could cause a blocking of mysterious forms of organic energy leading to the development of cancer. Reich's cancer theories were pseudoscientific and absurd, but his idea that cancer may be caused by some block in the individual's normal flow of emotional energy has proved influential. The belief that psychological factors play an important part in the initial causation and subsequent disease course of cancer was widely held by many psychosomatic thinkers. By the mid-1950s when the influence of the psychosomatic approach was at its height, Leshan and Worthington (1956), reviewing research in this area for the *British Journal of Medical Psychology*, drew the following conclusions:

> As one examines these papers, one is struck by the fact that there are consistent factors reported in studies that gathered material in different ways. There appear to be four

> separate threads that run through the literature. These are (1) the patient's loss of an important relationship prior to the development of the tumour; (2) the cancer patient's inability successfully to express hostile feelings and emotions; (3) the cancer patient's unresolved tension concerning a parental figure; (4) sexual disturbance. (p. 54)

Views such as these are still widely held, although seldom by cancer specialists. They are often used to justify complementary therapies that aim to teach sufferers how to beat cancer by the power of the mind. This is all very well if they work, if psychological dispositions really do play a significant part in the causation and development of cancer. If not, as Sontag and others have pointed out, the propagation of these beliefs may be profoundly undesirable:

> In Karl Menninger's more recent formulation: 'Illness is in part what the world has done to a victim, but in larger part it is what the victim has done with his world, and with himself . . .'. Such preposterous and dangerous views manage to put the onus of the disease on the patient and not only weaken the patient's ability to understand the range of plausible medical treatment but also, implicitly, direct the patient away from such treatment.
>
> (Sontag, 2002: 47–8)

Of all the theorists in the psychosomatic tradition, the one who has contributed most to modern health psychology is Franz Alexander, the Chicago psychoanalyst who, in *Psychosomatic Medicine* (1950), combined psychoanalytic theory with hypotheses about physiological mechanisms, principally those involving the *autonomic nervous system* (ANS). He emphasized the distinction between the *sympathetic* division of the ANS that, roughly speaking, controls emotional arousal and the fight-or-flight emergency reactions of the organism, and the *parasympathetic* division that, again roughly speaking, controls relaxation and the slowing down of functions activated by the sympathetic division. According to Alexander, sustained activity in either branch of the ANS without the counterbalancing effect of the other can have disease consequences. Excessive sympathetic activity contributes to cardiovascular disease, diabetes and rheumatoid arthritis, while excessive parasympathetic activity contributes to gastrointestinal disorders including dyspepsia, ulcers and colitis. Excessive sympathetic activity may occur as a consequence of prolonged stress (see Chapter 12), but Alexander also thought that some personalities may be predisposed to the excessive activation of one of the two branches of the ANS at the expense of the other.

Alexander's theories led both to the development in contemporary health psychology of the distinction between the **Type A** and **Type B personalities** and their differential susceptibility to cardiovascular disease, and to recent related work on hostility and cardiovascular disease. We consider this work shortly but, before doing so, it is necessary to examine the logic underlying empirical research linking personality to physical disease and some of the pitfalls in its interpretation.

EXPLAINING LINKS BETWEEN PERSONALITY AND PHYSICAL ILLNESS

It is generally agreed today that the psychosomatic approach in psychoanalysis and the proponents of **psychosomatic medicine** failed to produce convincing evidence of causal connections between psychological characteristics and physical illness, or to demonstrate that their therapeutic interventions were effective (Holroyd and Coyne, 1987). They were criticized for much the same reasons that psychoanalysis has been criticized more generally (MacMillan, 1997). Their theories were highly speculative and relied on elaborate interpretations of clinical data rather than controlled statistical studies. They also suffered from the defect of being retrospective, seeking to 'explain' patients' illnesses as 'caused' by psychological characteristics already known to the clinician, rather than prospective, making predictions about future illness on the basis of present psychological assessments.

The period since the 1960s has seen the growth of a large empirical literature on the statistical relationship between personality, as assessed by a wide variety of standardized tests, and physical illness. These studies often derive their hypotheses from the earlier speculations of the psychosomatic approach but seek to rectify its defects by carefully analysing statistical evidence. There is, however, one major defect that cannot be overcome because it is intrinsic to this type of research. The evidence is obtained from correlational investigations rather than true experiments and, as a consequence, findings are open to a wide range of interpretations. Obviously no investigator can assign personalities at random to experimental participants and then study their subsequent proneness to illness. All that the investigator can do is to administer personality tests to the participants and obtain measures of their illness status. Statisticians constantly remind us that it is not possible

Table 16.1 Problems of interpretation in research on personality and illness

Type of problem	Statement of the problem
Direction of causality	Cross-sectional studies are correlational and so there can be no certainty as to the direction of causality, as to what may be a cause and what may be an effect. There may be no causal relationship between the two variables
Background variables	Two variables (A and B) that are associated together may both be related to a third, background variable (C) that has not been measured and may not even be known to be relevant
Self-reporting of illness	Health psychology research often relies upon self-reported illness that has not been verified by objective medical tests
Dimensions of personality	The number of different personality variables to evaluate remains controversial
Physiological mechanisms versus health behaviour	It is difficult to determine whether associations between personality and illness are mediated by physiological differences or health behaviour or something else altogether

to infer causation from correlation and, in the case of personality–illness correlations, it is possible to illustrate this by considering a range of important problems of interpretation. The issues are perennial problems in the health psychology literature and are essentially logical in nature. We have summarized these in Table 16.1.

These problems will now be considered in more detail.

Direction of Causality

Psychological characteristics may be a cause of physical illness but they can also be a consequence of it. This is a particular problem for cross-sectional studies that simultaneously assess personality traits and illness. For example, if patients with a history of coronary illness have higher scores on anxiety and depression than healthy controls, should we conclude that anxiety and depression are risk factors for coronary illness or that a history of coronary problems can cause people to become more anxious and depressed? Obviously the existence of any causal relationship cannot be inferred from this type of study. The flaw may seem trivially obvious but it is surprising how many cross-sectional studies are to be found in the research literature on associations between personality and illness.

The problem cannot always be resolved by conducting prospective studies to investigate the extent to which the current personalities of healthy participants are predictive of future illness. The reason for this is that many major illnesses take a long time to develop and it is frequently the case that patients have experienced unusual and disturbing symptoms for some time before a diagnosis is given. It is therefore possible that psychological characteristics that appear to be a cause of subsequent illness are in fact a consequence of symptoms of developing illness occurring prior to diagnosis. Prospective studies are clearly far superior to cross-sectional studies but they do not necessarily eliminate the problem of how to determine the direction of causality.

Background Variables

A correlation may be found between two variables A and B when there is neither a direct effect of A on B, nor of B on A, but because a third *background* variable C has an effect on both. Galen's explanation for the association he believed to exist between melancholy and breast cancer is a good illustration. Here an excess of black bile is the background variable that he hypothesized to be a cause of both melancholy and breast cancer. As a further illustration, suppose that some people have a history of childhood illness that leaves them constitutionally weak and prone to further illness. Suppose also that this history of childhood illness has had a deleterious effect on their personality development, perhaps by limiting their opportunities for social development. The inclusion of a number of such individuals in a sample along with constitutionally stronger individuals who have had a healthy childhood could produce a non-causal correlation in the sample between adult personality and adult proneness to illness, because both are influenced by childhood illness. Further examples of background variables, notably genetic predispositions, are discussed by Holroyd and Coyne (1987) and Suls and Rittenhouse (1990).

Self-Reporting of Illness

Stone and Costa (1990) and Cohen and Williamson (1991) pointed out that much health psychology research relies on self-reported illness rather than biologically verified disease. This does not only apply to minor ailments such as colds and flu. The diagnosis of angina pectoris, for example, is frequently based solely on patients' reports of chest pain. Stone and Costa argue that this reliance on self-reported illness is particularly unsatisfactory when considering research into links between personality and illness. They point out that there is extensive evidence that psychological distress is associated with somatic complaints but not with organic disease. Since many personality test scores may be interpreted, at least to some extent, as measures of distress, it follows that correlations between test scores and self-reported illness may provide a false indication of a link between personality and disease when all that they really show is that neurotic individuals are the ones most likely to complain of being ill. Friedman and Kern (2014) consider these issues in some detail, and recommend that personality–illness research should focus primarily on mortality and longevity as outcome measures. However, it should not be assumed that any discrepancy between self-reported illness and biologically verified illness is necessarily an indication of neuroticism. Adler and Matthews (1994) noted that there is evidence that perceived health predicts mortality independently of biological risk factors, leading them to conclude that self-reported health provides useful information over and above direct biological indications. The association between perceived health and mortality has now been confirmed by many studies, and Jylhä (2009) provides a detailed analysis of possible reasons for it.

Dimensions of Personality

Personality testing is not an exact science and there is little agreement as to what the basic dimensions of personality really are, or even whether the question is worth asking. Three influential theories have been those of Eysenck, who argued initially that there were only two dimensions, extraversion and neuroticism (see Box 16.1), and subsequently added a third, psychoticism; Cattell, who believed he had identified 16; and McCrae and Costa (2003) who settled for five. These so-called 'Big Five' personality traits, which have generated a considerable amount of recent research, consist of extraversion/introversion, agreeableness/antagonism, conscientiousness, neuroticism/emotional stability, and openness to experience.

A problem that arises in research using personality tests is that similar items can often be found included in tests that are supposed to be measuring different traits so that, not surprisingly, scores for the same group of individuals given both tests may be highly intercorrelated. Consider some of the measures that are frequently used in research into the links between personality and illness. The individual who scores high on anxiety is also likely to score high on depression, neuroticism and **pessimistic explanatory style**, and correspondingly low on **self-esteem**, **self-efficacy**, **hardiness** and **sense of coherence**. The common element that may run through all of these measures is probably best labelled, following Stone and Costa (1990), as *distress* *proneness*. Suls and Bunde (2005) discuss this issue in a detailed review of research linking anger/hostility, anxiety and depression with cardiovascular disease. They note that strong correlations exist between all three traits that make it difficult to establish which of the associations with cardiovascular disease is of primary importance, or whether a more general trait of negative affectivity is the key variable.

Physiological Mechanisms versus Health Behaviour

Psychological characteristics may be linked to illness, either by way of physiological variables with which they are associated, or more indirectly, by way of their relationship to health behaviour. The proponents of psychosomatic medicine, especially Franz Alexander, believed in the existence of physiological mechanisms linking personality to illness, often involving differences in the functioning of the sympathetic and parasympathetic divisions of the autonomic nervous system. Health psychologists who conduct research into the relationship between personality and illness are also primarily interested in physiological pathways. However, it is generally acknowledged that more prosaic explanations for correlations between personality and illness may be derived from the fact that personality differences are often associated with differences in health behaviour (Suls and Rittenhouse, 1990; Miller et al., 1996; Stone and McCrae, 2007). Characteristics such as anxiety, depression, neuroticism and hostility have been variously shown to be associated with levels of smoking and alcohol consumption, diet and exercise, sleep disturbance, likelihood of seeking medical advice in the early stages of a disease and the likelihood of adhering to recommendations subsequently. Any of these variables, or some combination of them, could be invoked to account for an empirical correlation between personality and illness.

The Importance of Intervention Studies

The following brief survey of statistical studies of the associations between personality and physical illness indicates that there are a number of promising findings. However, for the reasons that have just been presented, all of these findings are subject to a range of interpretations so that true causal links have not yet been definitively established. Friedman and Kern (2014) concluded that, in order to make a convincing case for causality, it is necessary not only to demonstrate the existence of an association, but also to show that interventions designed to reduce a 'toxic' aspect of personality, or enhance a beneficial one, have the effect of reducing disease risk and increasing longevity. Interventions may obviously be of value in reducing distress in individuals suffering from serious illness, but the question that also needs to be addressed is, can they produce an improved prognosis for the disease in question? Sadly this has not yet been convincingly shown in any study. We now review the evidence in order to indicate the areas that look most promising for future research using interventions.

THE TYPE A PERSONALITY, HOSTILITY AND CORONARY HEART DISEASE

Type A and B Personalities

Speculation about an association between the Type A and Type B personalities and coronary heart disease (CHD) has a history that dates back more than 50 years (Riska, 2000). The distinction between the two personalities was introduced in the mid-1950s by the cardiologists Meyer Friedman and Ray Rosenman, although, as already noted, their ideas can be traced back further to the work of Alexander in psychosomatic medicine. The Type A personality, thought to be at greater risk of CHD, is described as highly competitive and achievement oriented, not prepared to suffer fools gladly, always in a hurry and unable to bear delays and queues, hostile and aggressive, inclined to read, eat and drive very fast, and constantly thinking what to do next, even when supposedly listening to someone else. In contrast to this the Type B personality is relaxed, laid back, lethargic, even-tempered, amiable and philosophical about life, relatively slow in speech and action, and generally has enough time for everyone and everything. The Type A personality has much in common with Galen's choleric temperament, the Type B with the phlegmatic (see Table 1.1. and Box 16.1). It is well known that men are at greater risk of CHD than women, and Riska (2000) made an interesting argument for the view that the concept of the Type A personality was an attempt to 'medicalize' and 'pathologize' traditional concepts of masculinity.

The key pioneering study of Type A personality and CHD was the Western Collaborative Group Study (WCGS) in which over 3,000 Californian men, aged from 39 to 59 at entry, were followed up initially over a period of eight-and-a-half years, and later extending over 22 years. When results were reported at the eight-and-a-half-year follow-up, it appeared that Type As were twice as likely compared with Type Bs to suffer from subsequent CHD. Of the sample 7% developed some signs of CHD and two-thirds of these were Type As. This increased risk was apparent even when other risk factors assessed at entry, such as blood pressure and cigarette smoking, were statistically controlled for. Similar results were subsequently published from another large-scale study conducted in Framingham, Massachusetts, this time with both men and women in the sample and, by the early 1980s, it was confidently asserted that Type A characteristics were as much a risk factor for heart disease as high blood pressure, high cholesterol levels and smoking.

However, later research failed to support these early findings. When Ragland and Brand (1988) conducted a 22-year follow-up of the WCGS, using CHD mortality as the crucially important measure, they failed to find any consistent evidence of an association. Much further research continued to be published up to the late 1980s, yielding few positive findings. Reviewing this evidence, Myrtek (2001) suggests that the modest number of positive findings that did exist were the result of over-reliance on angina as the measure of CHD. As we have already pointed out, this is an unreliable measure because it is frequently based solely on self-reported chest pain. Considering studies that adopted hard criteria, including mortality, Myrtek concludes that we can be confident that the Type A personality is not a risk factor for CHD.

Hostility

It can take a long time for a popular belief to fade away when there is a lack of evidence to support it. The extensive coverage still given to the Type A–CHD hypothesis by textbook writers is a good illustration of this. Researchers may be a little quicker to react as is indicated by the decline in publications in this field from the early 1990s. In fact it was largely replaced by an alternative hypothesis that was itself generated by the analysis of Type A–CHD research. This hypothesis is that hostility is the key dimension of personality that is associated with CHD.

The Type A personality, as described briefly in the last section, contains a number of components that are not necessarily closely correlated. Measures of Type A and B personalities often included sub-components that could be separately analysed for their association with subsequent CHD. When this was done it emerged that there was only one component that did seem to have some predictive power, and this component was anger or hostility. Research into links between anger/hostility and CHD became as popular in the 1990s as Type A research had been in previous years, but unfortunately with a very similar conclusion. By the end of the decade a number of reviews, including that of Myrtek (2001), found the studies to be of very mixed quality, with inconsistent results. There was some evidence of a statistically significant but very weak relationship for prospective studies of initially healthy individuals, but not for studies that have followed up patients already diagnosed with CHD.

In a curious mirroring of the breakdown of the Type A personality into sub-components, which led to the hostility–CHD research, the hostility researchers themselves reacted to disappointing findings by breaking hostility down into separate components. These included cynicism, mistrust, verbal and physical aggressiveness, and overt and experienced aggressiveness. It was proposed that more attention should be given to these sub-components in order to discover which are the most hazardous for health. However, when reviewing this area of research, Suls and Bunde (2005) noted that there is considerable overlap between measures of these sub-components of anger/hostility, with similar items being included in ostensibly different measures. Suls and Bunde also confirm Myrtek's earlier conclusion that evidence of an association between hostility, however measured, and subsequent CHD suggests a weak relationship, possibly no more than a side effect of the correlation of hostility measures with anxiety and depression, characteristics that will be considered later in this chapter because they appear to have a more substantial association with CHD.

SUPPORT OF THE TOBACCO INDUSTRY FOR PERSONALITY–ILLNESS RESEARCH

In view of the disappointing results achieved by research into the Type A personality, hostility and CHD, it may well be asked why it obtained so much publicity over more than 40 years. The reason may be connected with the high level of support this research has received from the US tobacco industry. Petticrew et al. (2012) have established this by analysing material lodged at the Legacy Tobacco Documents Library, a vast collection of documents that the companies were obliged to make public following litigation in 1998. These documents show that, for over 40 years from the 1950s, the industry heavily funded research into links between personality and both CHD and cancer, hoping to demonstrate that these personality variables were associated with cigarette smoking, thereby undermining claims about causal links between smoking and disease. Thus, for example, if it could be shown that Type A personalities were both more likely to smoke than Type Bs, and more likely to develop CHD, then it could be argued that smoking might be just an innocent background variable. Further to this, the Philip Morris company funded Meyer Friedman, the originator of Type A research, for the Meyer Friedman Institute, conducting research aiming to show that Type A personalities could be changed by interventions, thereby presumably reducing proneness to CHD even if they continued to smoke. Petticrew et al. also show that, while most Type A–CHD studies were not funded by the tobacco industry, most of the ones that found positive results were tobacco-funded. As has been pointed out in many areas of science, positive findings invariably get a great deal more publicity than negative findings and rebuttals.

Another researcher who found an association with the tobacco industry to be a useful source of funding was the late H.J. Eysenck. Pringle (1996) reported that he received nearly £800,000 to support his research on personality and cancer, with results that were a spectacular exception to the general run of negative findings in this field, findings that are discussed later in this chapter. Eysenck (1988) claimed that personality variables are much more strongly related to death from cancer than even cigarette smoking. In two subsequent papers, with R. Grossarth-Maticek, the two researchers appeared to have identified personality types that increase the risk of cancer by about 120 times and heart disease by about 25 times (Grossarth-Maticek and Eysenck, 1991; Eysenck and Grossarth-Maticek, 1991). They also claimed to have tested a new method of psychological treatment that can reduce the death rate for disease prone personalities over the next 13 years from 80% to 32%.

These extraordinary claims were not received favourably by others working in this field. In a comprehensive and highly respected review of the subject, Fox (1988) dismissed earlier reports by Eysenck and Grossarth-Maticek as 'simply unbelievable' and the 1991 papers, which were the first moderately detailed accounts of their research, were subjected to devastating critiques by Pelosi and Appleby (1992, 1993) and by Amelang and Schmidt-Rathjens (1996). The 'cancer prone personality' was not clearly described and seems to have been an odd amalgam of emotional distance and excessive dependence. After pointing out a large number of errors, omissions, obscurities and implausible aspects of the data, in a manner reminiscent of Leon Kamin's now-legendary analysis of Cyril Burt's twin IQ data (Kamin, 1977), Pelosi and Appleby comment:

> It is unfortunate that Eysenck and Grossarth-Maticek omit the most basic information that might explain why their findings are so different from all the others in this field. The methods are either not given or are described so generally that they remain obscure on even the most important points . . . Also essential details are missing from the results, and the analyses used are often inappropriate.
>
> (Pelosi and Appleby, 1992: 1297).

ANXIETY, DEPRESSION AND CORONARY HEART DISEASE

There have been a number of reviews that have concluded, on the basis of prospective studies, that there are substantial associations between both anxiety and depression and subsequent CHD (Hemingway and Marmot, 1999; Krantz and McCeney, 2002; Wulsin and Singal, 2003; Lett et al., 2004; Suls and Bunde, 2005). These associations have been found in studies of patients with clinically diagnosed distress and in general population studies. Anxiety seems to predict sudden cardiac death rather more than other types of CHD, and phobic, panic-like anxiety is a particularly strong predictor: Haines et al. (1987) found that sufferers were three times more at risk of sudden cardiac death over the next seven years compared with non-sufferers. Very similar results were subsequently found by Kawachi et al. (1994) in a two-year follow-up of 33,999 initially healthy US male health professionals. Box 16.4 gives a further example from a Taiwanese study together with mention of an important caution when interpreting research in this area.

BOX 16.4
INTERNATIONAL CASE STUDY: PANIC DISORDER AND HEART ATTACKS – DATA FROM TAIWAN

Chon et al. (2009) carried out a one-year follow-up investigation of 9,641 Taiwanese patients who had been diagnosed with panic disorder compared with 28,923 matched control participants. Approximately 1 in 21 of the panic disorder patients suffered from *acute myocardial infarctions* (heart attacks) in the follow-up period compared with 1 in 37 of the comparison cohort. The samples were matched for a number of relevant variables, but the possibility cannot be excluded that the panic disorders could have been provoked by cardiac symptoms preceding the heart attack, such as irregularities in heartbeats, rather than having a causal role.

Depression is predictive of a wider range of CHD than anxiety. In a UK study with 19,649 participants who were initially free of clinical manifestations of heart disease, Surtees et al. (2008) found, with an average follow-up period of 8.5 years, that those assessed as suffering from a major depressive disorder were 2.7 times more likely to die from ischaemic heart disease over the follow-up period than those who did not, independently of age, sex, smoking, systolic blood pressure, cholesterol, physical activity, body mass index, diabetes, social class, heavy alcohol use and antidepressant medication use. In a very large prospective study of 96,376 post-menopausal women, Wassertheil-Smoller et al. (2004) report that depressive symptoms were substantially associated with death from cardiovascular disease after adjusting for age, race, education, income, diabetes, hypertension, smoking, cholesterol level, body mass index and physical activity.

These findings for anxiety and depression are impressive, but they should be considered alongside our earlier discussion of problems in interpreting personality–illness correlations. Hemingway and Marmot (1999) point out that these problems are particularly acute in this area. Anxiety and depression are certainly consequences of CHD as well as possible causes of it. Furthermore, symptoms of incipient CHD, such as breathlessness and chest pains, may occur for years prior to diagnosis, and lead in turn to experienced anxiety and depression. In this way, prospective studies could give the impression that anxiety and depression are causes of CHD, when in fact the direction of causality is the other way round.

As Miller et al. (2009) pointed out, one practically useful way of resolving some of the methodological problems in interpreting findings in this area would be a robust demonstration that interventions designed to reduce anxiety and depression in patients suffering from CHD could produce an improved prognosis. Unfortunately the two most substantial trials that have been conducted so far, each targeting depression and with more than 2,000 participants, showed no effect of interventions. Berkman et al. (2003) evaluated a programme that included cognitive behavioural therapy supplemented with antidepressants for the more severely depressed patients; van Melle et al. (2007) evaluated an intervention consisting simply of treatment with antidepressants. Neither study found any evidence of an improvement in event-free survival for the intervention groups compared with controls. One type of intervention that deserves further study in this field is mindfulness-based therapy, an increasingly popular treatment that is described and discussed in Chapter 12 (pp. 314–15). Whether or not it is effective in improving the prognosis for CHD, the current evidence is that it is reasonably effective for alleviating the symptoms of anxiety and depression, and this in itself is obviously a worthwhile gain from an intervention programme.

Some studies have indicated that the relationship between emotional distress and illness is not restricted to heart disease. Mykletun et al. (2007) examined data from a population-based health study of 61,349 participants. With a mean follow-up of 4.4 years, they found that depression was equally associated with all disease-related causes of death, not just CHD. They did not find any evidence of an association with anxiety. On the other hand, Grossardt et al. (2009), in a follow-up of 7,080 participants originally tested between 1962 and 1965, found that pessimistic, anxious and depressive personality traits were each predictive of all-cause mortality. Further research is obviously needed to clarify reasons for the differences between the findings of the two studies. However, they both suggested that the association between psychological distress and disease-related death extends beyond CHD.

DEPRESSION AND CANCER

The widely held belief that depression is an important factor in the onset and subsequent development of cancer has received little support from research. Adler and Matthews (1994) reviewed three large-scale prospective studies of the relationship between depression and both the incidence of and mortality from cancer. In these studies, initially healthy samples of up to 9,000 were followed up over periods ranging from 10 to 20 years and no associations were found between depression and either cancer onset or mortality. Since then two large-scale studies have produced conflicting results. Penninx et al. (1998) carried out a prospective study of 1,708 men and 3,117 women aged 71 and over. They found a significantly increased incidence of cancer for those who were diagnosed as suffering from chronic depression, indicated by repeated assessments of symptoms over six years. On the other hand, Whooley and Browner (1998) undertook a prospective study over six years of 7,519 women aged 67 or over and analysed the relationship between depression and subsequent mortality from (a) cancer, (b) cardiovascular disease and (c) all other diseases. They found no relationship between depression and cancer but a strong relationship with both cardiovascular disease and all other diseases.

Negative findings have also been reported from follow-up studies of patients who have been treated for cancer. For example, Barraclough et al. (1992) followed up 204 patients who had received surgery for breast cancer over 42 months after surgery. They used a very detailed interview schedule, which included the assessment of prolonged major depression before surgery and during the follow-up period. They found no relationship at all between depression and relapse. Relapse was also unrelated to stress, including bereavement, long-term social difficulties and lack of a confiding relationship.

Coyne et al. (2007) noted the persistence of the belief that psychotherapy promotes survival in people with cancer in the face of contradictory findings. They provide a systematic critical review of the relevant literature and conclude:

> No randomized clinical trial designed with survival as a primary endpoint and in which psychotherapy was not confounded with medical care has yielded a positive effect. Among the implications of the review is that an adequately powered study examining effects of psychotherapy on survival after a diagnosis of cancer would require resources that are not justified by the strength of the available evidence. (p. 367)

POSITIVE PSYCHOLOGY AND HEALTH

In contrast to the focus on the health consequences of negative characteristics, such as anxiety and depression, a considerable amount of recent research has been concerned with the potential health benefits of positive characteristics such as optimism, life satisfaction and self-esteem. A good example is the work of Surtees et al. (2003) on sense of coherence and health. Originally proposed as a measurable characteristic by Antonovsky (1979), sense of coherence is described as the ability to perceive one's world as meaningful and manageable. Surtees et al. carried out a prospective study over six years of the relationship between sense of coherence and mortality from all causes for a very large UK sample of 20,579 participants aged 41–80 years. They found that a strong sense of coherence was associated with a 30% reduction in mortality from all causes and also more specifically for cardiovascular disease. The explanation for this probably lies in the fact that sense of coherence is inversely correlated with anxiety and depression. In a study conducted in Finland of 4,642 men and women aged from 25 to 74, Konttinen et al. (2008) found inverse correlations of 0.62 between sense of coherence and depression for both men and women; the inverse correlations between sense of coherence and anxiety were 0.57 for men and 0.54 for women. It follows that the findings of Surtees et al. could be basically the corollary of the positive correlations already discussed between anxiety and depression and both cardiovascular disease and all-cause mortality.

Boehm and Kubzansky (2012) provide a broad critical review of research on the association between psychological well-being and cardiovascular health. They note the existence of many findings that confirm this association, while pointing out the potential significance of the correlations between psychological well-being and the health behaviours that are already known to be associated with cardiovascular health. It has not been demonstrated that changes to an individual's psychological well-being, whether the result of interventions or for other reasons, have a direct effect on cardiovascular health, independently of known risk factors such as smoking, diet and exercise.

In a combative paper in *The Lancet*, Sloan (2011) notes that beliefs in the health benefits of positive thinking have been widespread in the USA since the middle of the nineteenth century and are especially prevalent today. They have been promoted both by religious organizations and, in a secular form, by the ever-popular self-help manuals. They may seem harmless enough even if there is a lack of convincing evidence in their favour, but, as Sloan points out, they are associated with the view that individuals are largely responsible for their own health, which is convenient for governments wishing to minimize spending on public health services. They may also be doubly pernicious if they are false. As Coyne and Tennen (2010) argue, in the case of cancer, there is no evidence that dispositions such as a 'fighting spirit' are associated with a better prognosis, or that interventions based on the belief that cancer can be beaten by the power of the mind have any effect at all on mortality. If this were more widely appreciated, sufferers might be spared from wasting their money on expensive private treatments based on these claims and also, perhaps more seriously, be spared from blaming themselves for having become ill in the first place, and for failing to get better.

CONSCIENTIOUSNESS AND LONGEVITY

Conscientiousness is one of the five factors of personality proposed by McCrae and Costa in their influential theory that was originally developed in 1985. A considerable amount of research has shown that this characteristic is associated with longevity. In a meta-analysis that pooled the results of 20 independent samples, Kern and Friedman (2008) found a modest but significant correlation of 0.11 between conscientiousness and longevity. In a subsequent review, Friedman and Kern (2014) draw attention to much further research which confirms the existence of this relationship, which also extends from childhood through adult life. They suggest a number of pathways mediating the association. An important one is health behaviour. For example, Bogg and Roberts (2004) pooled the results from 194 studies that incorporated measures of conscientiousness-related traits and assessments of any of the leading behavioural contributors to mortality (tobacco use, diet and activity patterns, excessive alcohol use, violence, risky sexual behaviour, risky driving, suicide and drug use). They found that conscientiousness-related traits were negatively related to all risky health-related behaviours and positively related to all beneficial health-related behaviours.

Other factors may also be at work in mediating the relationship between conscientiousness and health. While it seems clear that health behaviour is a major one, social environmental correlates of conscientiousness, including social status, may also be important. In a 17-year follow-up of a UK sample of 6,800 participants, aged from 34 to 55 at recruitment, Hagger-Johnson et al. (2012) found that health behaviours and socio-econonmic status both played a significant part, but that the relationship was not fully accounted for by these factors. Other possibilities are considered by Friedman and Kern (2014) and by Bogg and Roberts (2013). For example, conscientiousness may ameliorate the effects of stress on health (see Chapter 12, p. 317). A question that naturally arises at this point is, can interventions be developed to increase conscientiousness, thereby potentially leading to improved health? Here there are grounds for scepticism. Given that health behaviours play an important role in mediating the association, it might seem more productive to focus on health promotion campaigns and interventions aimed directly at specific behaviours, such as smoking, drinking, diet and exercise, rather than the development of programmes with a very broad focus aimed at conscientiousness as a general characteristic.

FUTURE RESEARCH

1. Studies to assess the role of psychological factors in medically unexplained symptoms, such as chronic fatigue syndrome, including empirical testing of modern neuropsychological theories.
2. Research to clarify the structure of personality with particular reference to health, in order to reduce or eliminate the problem of overlapping measures.
3. Investigations to distinguish between personality variables that are associated with biologically verified illness, as distinct from those that are associated only with self-reported illness.
4. Studies to establish which dimensions of personality are directly associated with health-relevant physiological variables, and to distinguish them from those that are primarily associated with health behaviours.
5. Outcome studies to assess the effectiveness of interventions designed to modify psychological characteristics that are suspected of being health hazardous. It would be particularly valuable to assess whether interventions can improve the prognosis for those already diagnosed as suffering from organic disease. In the case of anxiety and depression, interventions would obviously be worthwhile if they relieve these conditions, whether or not they influence health outcomes.
6. Where personality variables are linked primarily to health behaviours, it would be useful to establish whether interventions designed to modify health behaviour (e.g. smoking cessation programmes) could be more effective if they took account of personality assessments of participants.

SUMMARY

1 From the ancient Greeks to modern times, orthodox medical practitioners have usually believed that there is a physical basis to all illness, including psychological disorders. In contrast to this, there has also been a holistic tradition that has placed an emphasis on the role of psychological factors.

2 The modern history of psychological explanations for physical symptoms begins with Freud's analysis of hysteria, physical symptoms of illness for which no organic basis could be discovered. These conditions are often referred to nowadays as 'medically unexplained symptoms', and recent theories about them have drawn on neuropsychological research and theories.

3 The psychosomatic approach was developed by psychoanalysts who extended Freud's theories of hysteria to provide psychological explanations for the causation of organic disorders such as heart disease and cancer.

4 Proponents of the psychosomatic approach generally failed to produce convincing evidence to support their hypotheses. However, the theories of Franz Alexander on the physiological mechanisms that could underlie the relationship between the psychology of the individual and organic disease have led to modern conceptions of the associations between personality and health.

5 Health psychologists have found it very difficult to determine whether personality is associated with susceptibility to physical disease directly through physiological mechanisms, indirectly by way of health behaviour, or whether the data are best explained by statistical artefacts and flaws in the design of the studies from which they are obtained.

6 Early indications that the Type A personality is a risk factor for CHD were not confirmed by later studies. Attention then shifted to hostility but this variable now seems only to be a weak predictor.

7 Anxiety, especially phobic panic-like anxiety, and depression are both associated with an increased risk of CHD, although a number of different interpretations of these associations are possible.

8 There is very little clear-cut evidence to support the view that personality variables are associated with risk of cancer or of relapse following treatment. Interventions based on treatment for depression have not been shown to improve the survival chances of cancer sufferers.

9 There is substantial evidence that 'positive' psychological characteristics, including sense of coherence, are associated with reduced risk of CHD and all-cause mortality. This may be primarily the inverse of the parallel findings for anxiety and depression, which have strong negative correlations with positive characteristics.

10 Conscientiousness has been shown in many studies to be predictive of longevity. A major reason seems to be that this characteristic is negatively related to many risky health-related behaviours and positively related to beneficial health-related behaviours.

17 MEDICINE TAKING: ADHERENCE AND RESISTANCE

Drugs don't work in patients who don't take them.

(Former US Surgeon General C. Everett Koop)

OUTLINE

Adherence and compliance are terms used to describe the extent to which patients adhere or comply with recommended treatment regimens. It is one of the most widely researched forms of health-related behaviour. The assumptions underlying the term 'compliance' implies an authoritarian stance on the part of the physician or other health professional that is challenged by recent changes within health care systems. This chapter considers the extent and character of treatment non-adherence and the issue of medical error. It also considers the patient-centred formulation of health care that focuses on shared decision making and patient empowerment.

WHAT IS ADHERENCE?

Character of Adherence

The prescription of medicines is the most common form of medical treatment. Indeed, the terms for the profession and the form of treatment are interchangeable. However, a challenge faced by medicine is that most patients do not fully comply with the prescribed medication. This non-compliance can take various forms including not having prescriptions filled, not taking the correct dosage, not taking the medicine at the correct times, and stopping the medication before the course of treatment is completed. This incomplete medicine taking has attracted a massive research effort and given rise to a range of competing claims.

The terms used to describe the process have changed over the years. Initially the most popular descriptive term was **compliance**, which referred to the extent to which the patient passively accepted the physician's instructions on medicine taking. With the growing challenge to the power of medicine the term **adherence** has become more popular, because it is considered a more neutral expression. More recently, the term **concordance** has been introduced because it implies a more cooperative relationship between physician and patient. In this chapter we will start with the popular term adherence and then consider some more critical options.

In addition, there has been discussion about the use of the term patient with its implications of passivity and acceptance. Frankenberg (1982) in his classic work on time in the health care setting extends this discussion. He notes that in the traditional health care setting the patient is expected to be 'patient' and to 'wait' in the waiting room for the medical doctor. The longer the patient has to wait for an appointment is an indication of how important the medical doctor is. Indeed, the medical doctor can manipulate this arrangement. In their extensive review of research on adherence Horne et al. (2005) noted that especially in the mental health context there is a preference for the term service user. However, there have been moves to reassert the role of the patient with patient rights groups and the introduction of the 'expert patient' into health decision making. Within the research literature on medical adherence the preference is to use the term patient although as we will see there is also discussion about patient empowerment – even a move towards the impatient.

Adherence to correctly prescribed medications is essential for good outcomes of patient care and properly controlled evaluation of different modes of drug treatment. Satisfactory adherence includes timely initiation of dosing plus punctual and persistent execution of the dosing regimen throughout the specified duration of treatment. Electronic methods for compiling drug dosing histories are now the recognized standard for quantifying adherence. Prior to electronic data collection, methods of assessing adherence consisted of counting returned, untaken doses, questionnaires, histories, diaries, assays of drug concentration in blood samples, and audits of prescription refills. Such methods 'gave only fragmentary glimpses of an ambulatory patient's dosing history, typically indicating that doses must have been omitted but at indeterminable times' (Blaschke et al., 2012: 276). Thus, the frequency of inadequate adherence is probably underestimated by these pre-electronic methods and would generally be unnoticed as a cause of failed treatment or underestimated effectiveness.

Although there is extensive literature on adherence outside the medical setting this literature is not discussed in this chapter. Further details can be found in the discussion of smoking cessation and exercise involvement.

Figure 17.1 *Taking Physick*, by James Gillray, 1800

EXTENT OF ADHERENCE

The extent of adherence varies across the different forms of recommended medication-related behaviours. In general, most people do not adhere to specific medical or health care directives – at least not fully. While non-adherence would seem to be the norm, its extent varies. It has been estimated that 50–75% of patients do not adhere to medical advice (Wertheimer and Santella, 2003). Some further estimates include:

- 14–21% of patients do not fill their prescriptions;
- 60% of all patients cannot identify their own medication;
- 30–50% of all patients ignore or compromise medication instructions;
- 12–20% of patients take other people's medication.

Recent evidence based on electronic recording of dosing has been reviewed by Blaschke et al. (2012). Their review suggests that only 55% of patients correctly adhered to their prescribed medication over a one year period.

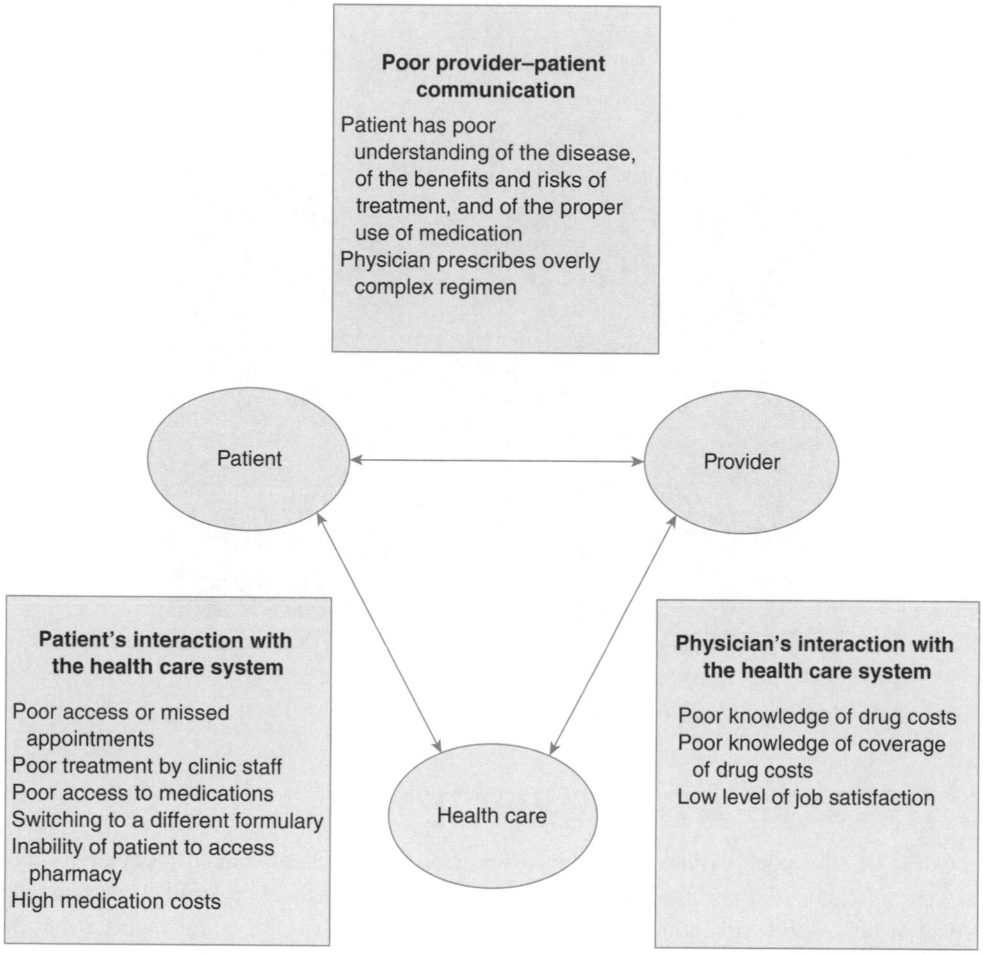

Figure 17.2 Health care barriers to adherence (derived from Osterberg and Blaschke, 2005)

From a medical treatment perspective this high rate of non-adherence reflects a major failure in the system. There have been attempts to document the negative impact of non-adherence. For example, Wertheimer and Santella (2003) estimated that each year in the USA:

- approximately 125,000 people with treatable ailments die of inappropriate medication usage;
- approximately one-quarter of nursing home admissions are due to inappropriate medication usage;
- hospital costs due to medication non-adherence were then $8.5 billion.

Other researchers have calculated even higher costs. For example, Osterberg and Blaschke (2005) reported that 30–69% of medication-related hospital admissions in the USA were due to poor adherence and this amounted to additional health care costs of up to $100 billon.

Certain forms of non-adherence are potentially more dangerous than others. One common health problem that has a high rate of non-adherence is asthma. Despite the large number of drug education programmes the proportion of people with asthma who do not comply with the recommended treatment remains high (Bender et al., 1997). In the USA it has been estimated that the direct and indirect costs of asthma in 1990 were over $6 billion (Weiss et al., 1992). It has been suggested that a large proportion of this cost could be eliminated if adherence with medication was improved (Bender et al., 1997).

This low rate of adherence has attracted a massive research effort to identify what factors are associated with the process and how it can be enhanced. In an extensive review of the research literature, Vermeire et al. (2001) concluded there has been limited consistent success in identifying factors that predict adherence, due to a lack of concern with the patient's perspective and a preference for quantitative methods. We will start by summarizing some of the evidence from the more quantitative research before considering alternative approaches.

A French study assessed demographic and psychological characteristics of patients with irritable bowel disease (IBD), many of whom were members of the French association for IBD sufferers (Nahon et al., 2011). Patients belonging to the French IBD patients' association (AFA) were found to be more adherent to treatment than those who did not. The AFA helped patients to increase their knowledge about IBD and provided psychological support. Adherence to treatment was associated with psychological distress as measured by high anxiety scores on the HADS but not with high depression scores and not with socio-economic deprivation.

FACTORS ASSOCIATED WITH NON-ADHERENCE

Patient Characteristics

There has been some success in identifying the social and personal characteristics of the non-adherent patient. In general, the less social support and the more socially isolated the patients are, the less likely they are to follow medical directives. For example, in a study of treatment adherence in an outpatient clinic for people with tuberculosis, it was found that homelessness was the only factor that predicted non-completion of therapy (Brainard et al., 1997). Further, individuals who came from unstable families were also found to be less compliant with medical treatment (Bender et al., 1997). A study of adherence among diabetes patients found that adherence to medication was associated with higher levels of social support (Gray-Sevilla et al., 1995).

There has been much effort to identify the so-called 'non-compliant' personality. However, like much personality research in general, this effort has met with limited success. In reviewing the evidence, Hulka (1979) found no consistent relationship between age, sex, marital status, education, number of people in the household, social class and adherence. Admittedly, this is not to deny that specific groups of patients may be resistant to accepting certain types of treatment. For example, certain cognitive deficits or emotional upsets may reduce adherence. There is also evidence that people with a range of psychological problems are less likely to adhere to treatment (e.g. Christiannse et al., 1989; Stilley et al., 2004). Table 17.1 summarizes some of the patient characteristics associated with adherence.

Table 17.1 Patient characteristics associated with adherence

Social characteristics	Personal characteristics	Health beliefs
Characteristics of individual's social situation	Demographics	Inappropriate or conflicting health beliefs
Lack of social supports	Sensory disabilities	Competing socio-cultural and ethnic folk concepts of disease and treatment
Family instability or disharmony	Type and severity of psychiatric disorder	Implicit model of illness
Patient's expectations and attitudes towards treatment	Forgetfulness	
Residential instability	Lack of understanding	
Environment that supports non-adherent behaviour		
Competing or conflicting demands		
Lack of resources		

Source: Meichenbaum and Turk (1987: 43)

It has been argued that the more the prescribed medication accords with the patients' belief systems, the more likely they are to comply with the treatment. In an attempt to coordinate this research beyond the extensive listings of variables, some investigators have turned to the popular social cognition models. Probably the most frequently used such model has been the health belief model (HBM). Indeed, this model was originally formulated to explain compliance with medical recommendations (Becker and Mainman, 1975). According to the HBM, the extent to which a person complies or adheres with certain medication advice depends upon perceived disease severity, susceptibility to the disease, benefits of the treatment recommended and barriers to following the treatment (see also Chapter 13).

Varying degrees of support have been found for this model. For example, Masek (1982) found that the more the patients perceive their condition to be serious, the more likely they will be to comply with the recommended treatment. However, Glasgow et al. (1997) found that perceived seriousness of diabetes was not predictive of adherence. In a study of drug therapy defaulting, Fincham and Wertheimer (1985) found that belief in the benefits of medical care and low barriers to care predicted high adherence. Glasgow et al. (1997) found that the perceived effectiveness of the treatment was a better predictor of adherence in diabetes than the perceived barriers.

In a meta-analysis of 47 independent studies, Gonzalez et al. (2008) found a significant association between depression and treatment non-adherence in patients with diabetes. Studies that used stronger methodologies were found to have larger effects. Gonzalez et al. concluded that treatment non-adherence may be an important pathway between depression and worse diabetes clinical outcomes.

In a review of non-adherence in dialysis patients, Clark et al. (2014) suggested that it is difficult to compare the results from different studies because of the complex nature of non-adherence and the variety of methods and criteria that are employed. They suggested that large-scale, prospective studies are needed to investigate the association between psychological factors and non-adherence.

Social learning theory has also been used with varying degrees of success to explain non-adherence. Tillotson and Smith (1996) found that although internal **locus of control** predicted adherence to a weight control programme for patients with diabetes, its importance was small and depended on the degree of social support. In a study of patients with rheumatoid arthritis Beck et al. (1988) found that patients' predictions concerning their adherence (**self-efficacy** expectations) with treatment predicted actual adherence. There has been a growing literature on adherence to HIV antiretroviral treatments. Some of these have found support for some of the social-cognitive dimensions. For example, a study in New York found that self-efficacy for adherence to HIV treatment significantly predicted adherence (Halkitis et al., 2005). However, this relationship may have been complicated by the role of recreational drugs that are common among individuals who are HIV positive and which, in turn, are associated with poorer adherence and also with avoidant coping. This led the authors to conclude that there is a need to consider the complex relationship between intrapsychic and socio-cultural realities in order to explain HIV treatment adherence.

The social cognition models of adherence describe the beliefs that are associated with or predict adherence. These models can be criticized on both empirical and theoretical grounds. On empirical grounds the major problem is that the beliefs have been found to predict only a small proportion of the variance of adherence behaviour. Theoretically, the major problem is that these models reify the phenomenon. As such it characterizes the behaviour as fixed and abstracted from the changing social relations and the broader social context within which adherence occurs. Treatment is not usually a one-off event but extends over a period of time. In the case of chronic illness this period can be a lifetime. To understand adherence fully therefore requires an understanding of the social context and how the patient integrates the treatment into his/her everyday life. Literacy is also an important facilitating factor in adherence

Wolf et al. (2007) explored the relationship between patient literacy level and self-reported HIV medication adherence among 204 patients receiving care at infectious disease clinics in Shreveport, Louisiana, and Chicago, Illinois. Approximately one-third of patients (30.4%) were found to be less than 100% adherent to their regimen, and 31.4% had marginal to low literacy skills. The low-literate patients were 3.3 times more likely to be non-adherent to their antiretroviral regimem. Self-efficacy was a significant mediator of this relationship.

Disease Characteristics

Certain disease characteristics have been found to be associated with adherence. Perhaps the most frequently mentioned disease characteristics are the severity of the disease and visibility of the symptoms. The relationship with disease severity would appear not to be linear. A number of studies have found that patients with asymptomatic chronic diseases frequently do not comply with treatment (e.g. Miller, 1997). When the symptoms are obvious and unwanted, the person is more likely to comply with treatment that offers a promise of removing them. However, when the prognosis is poor there is evidence that the rate of adherence is reduced. For example, Dolgin et al. (1986) found adherence lower in those cancer patients whose survival prospects were poor.

Treatment Factors

There are a large number of treatment factors associated with adherence. These are summarized in Table 17.2 under four broad temporal headings. Before the patient is actually prescribed a treatment, she/he has to obtain an appointment with the physician. The character of this process prepares or sets the scene for the physician's recommendations. Lengthy or inconvenient waiting times can lead to considerable frustration and an unwillingness to comply.

The more complicated the treatment prescribed, the less likely the patient is to comply fully. Admittedly, there have been attempts to simplify treatment regimens by providing patients with detailed information. However, the evidence suggests that adherence is still poor. One reason is information overload (Meichenbaum and Turk, 1987). In an attempt to cope with a very complicated treatment regimen the patient simply gets confused or ignores much of the information. Although physicians may explain the treatment, patients frequently forget or do not understand the instructions provided. Ley (1979) found that patients forget at least one-third of the information given by their physician. A variety of factors influences understanding. Basically, the more extensive and complex the instructions given, the less likely the patient is to recall it subsequently.

Besides complexity, an important treatment characteristic is the actual length of the treatment regimen. Adherence declines with an increase in the number of medications or doses and with the length of recommended treatment (Hulka et al., 1976). Sackett and Snow (1979) estimated that adherence with long-term therapy declines to approximately 50%, irrespective of illness or setting. Masur (1981) suggests that it is not the length of treatment that is the reason for this decline

Table 17.2 Treatment factors associated with non-adherence

Preparation for treatment	Immediate character of treatment	Administration of treatment	Consequences of treatment
Characteristics of treatment setting	Characteristics of treatment recommendations	Inadequate supervision by professionals	Medication side effects
Long waiting time	Complexity of treatment regimen	Absence of continuity of care	Social side effects
Long time elapsed between referral and appointment	Duration of treatment regimen	Failure of parents to supervise drug administration	
Timing of referral	Degree of behavioural change		
Absence of individual appointment times	Inconvenience		
Lack of cohesiveness of treatment delivery systems	Expense		
Inconvenience associated with operation of clinics	Characteristics of medicine		
Poor reputation of treatment facility	Inadequate labels		
	Awkward container design		

Source: Meichenbaum and Turk (1987: 43)

in adherence but rather the absence of symptoms. Long-term therapy is often recommended for chronic medical conditions that have few symptoms or for which there is no definite improvement in symptoms as a result of medication. In these cases the patient has no feedback on the benefits of medication. This lack of feedback undermines any motivation to comply with the medication. Leventhal (1986) found that when patients with hypertension were able to identify symptoms of their disease that were controlled by medication they were more likely to comply with it.

The actual character of the treatment is also important. For example, some people with asthma do not like taking inhaled medication while others do not follow the correct inhalation procedure, thus reducing overall adherence (McFadden, 1995). Understanding how the patient feels about a particular procedure or treatment is a necessary step in improving adherence.

It would perhaps be expected that those drugs with few *physical side effects* would be associated with higher adherence. It would seem that the social side effects, in terms of stigma, are just as important (see section on empowerment). A related factor is the extent to which the treatment disrupts the patient's everyday life.

There has been considerable research on the extent of adherence to medical treatment among people with HIV. The treatment requires taking medication twice a day and missing no more than two doses a month. If this regime is not followed then there is the prospect of the development of drug resistance and more rapid disease progression. Parson et al. (2007) conducted a study of adherence among HIV patients who were undergoing antiretroviral treatment. Using questionnaires they examined the role of alcohol, affective factors (e.g. anxiety), cognitive factors (e.g. attitudes, self-efficacy) and social factors (e.g. social norms) in predicting the extent of adherence. They found that self-efficacy, which they defined as the belief in the ability to follow the treatment despite the medication, was the best predictor.

Interpersonal Factors

The character of the physician–patient relationship has been at the centre of research into adherence. Physician styles in physician–patient communication have been classified as either 'patient-centred' or 'authoritarian' (see Chapter 12). The *patient-centred* or affiliative style is designed to promote a positive relationship and includes behaviours such as interest, friendliness and empathy. The *authoritarian* or control-oriented style is designed to maintain the physician's control in the interaction. Not surprisingly, patients prefer those physicians who adopt the more affiliative style (Buller and Buller, 1987). Various related styles of physician interaction have been associated with adherence. In behavioural terms the physician keeps good eye contact, smiles a lot and leans in towards the patient – all behaviours that are interpreted as demonstrating interest and consideration. Hall et al. (1988) found in their meta-analysis of 41 studies that patient satisfaction was associated with perceived interpersonal competence, social conversation and better communication as well as more information and technical competence.

Several studies have found an association between physician job satisfaction and aspects of adherence. McGlynn (1988) found that patients were more satisfied with those physicians who had high job satisfaction. A related factor is the physician's sense of security. Since many conditions are resistant to standard medical interventions many physicians can experience a sense of inadequacy. This, in turn, could lead to reduced job satisfaction and more conflict with patients. Indeed, when general practitioners receive complaints from their patients, they initially feel out of control, and may experience feelings of shock, panic and indignation (Jain and Ogden, 1999).

Physicians and patients have a different view of health and illness. For example, St Clair et al. (1996) compared the definitions of health provided by a sample of family physicians and those provided by a sample of patients with asthma. Whereas the former defined health in terms of absence of disease, the latter referred to 'being able', 'taking action' and 'physical well-being'. The more understanding the physician is of the patient's belief system, the more compliant the patient is. For example, Ruiz and Ruiz (1983) found that Hispanic patients tend to comply more when their physician is more understanding of their cultural norms and practices.

An important although less explored factor is the physician's view of the patient. This factor overlaps with the physician's understanding of the patient's health beliefs and suggests that when the physician has a positive view of the patient then she/he will adopt a much more affiliative style of communication. This helps to explain the well-established social class effect that upper and middle-class patients receive more information and attention from physicians. For example, Taira et al.

(1997) conducted a large survey of state employees in Massachusetts. According to the responses physicians were more likely to discuss healthy lifestyle issues such as diet and exercise with high-income patients but they discussed smoking more with low-income patients. Physicians frequently report more frustration with and less interest in lower and working-class patients (Hall et al., 1988).

An interesting additional factor is the effect of a physician's 'tactile contact' with the patient. In a recent study in France (Guéguen and Vion, 2009) a group of physicians were instructed to lightly touch their patients when giving advice on medication. It was found that compared with a control group of patients the 'touched' patients were significantly more likely to consume more of the prescribed tablets. This effect was apparent seven days after the consultation. It was suggested that this effect may be due to those physicians who lightly touched their patients being perceived as more competent. However, in view of the potential misinterpretation of touch there is a need to advise caution in applying these findings particularly in societies where there are clear professional restrictions on tactile behaviour towards patients.

SOCIAL AND ORGANIZATIONAL SETTING

The medical consultation takes place in a social setting. Meichenbaum and Turk (1987) identified ten setting characteristics potentially associated with non-adherence. Adherence is greater when the referral to a specialist is seen as part of the assessment rather than as a last resort, when care involves follow-up and is personalized, when appointments are individualized and waiting times are reduced, when treatment is available on site, when treatment is carefully supervised through home visits, special nursing care, etc., when there are good links between inpatient and outpatient services, and when staff have a very positive attitude towards the treatment. In particular with long-term therapy, there is evidence that regular follow up by the physician increases adherence (Bond and Monson, 1984).

It is not just the immediate medical context but also the local social context, in terms of family and friends, which is important. If family members remind and assist the patient concerning their medication it would only be expected that the patient would be more compliant. Indeed, it has been suggested that the patient's partner's views of the medication prescribed is the most important factor in explaining adherence. In a meta-analysis of 122 studies on the impact of social support, DiMatteo (2004) found that practical support had a high correlation with adherence. He also found that adherence was higher in cohesive families and lower in families in conflict. This concern with social context requires consideration of the broader socio-political context that conditions the character of health care and of adherence.

In a review of the empirical research on factors contributing to reduced levels of adherence to medication Osterberg and Blaschke (2005) developed a model of some of the key health care factors that are a barrier to adherence. This model identified three key processes:

1. poor patient–provider communication (e.g. patient has poor understanding of the disease; patient has poor understanding of the benefits and risks of treatment);
2. poor quality of patient interaction with the health care system (e.g. poor access to clinic appointments, poor treatment by staff, poor access to medication);

3. poor physican interaction with the health care system (e.g. poor knowledge of drug costs, low level of job satisfaction).

There is an ongoing interaction between the patient, the provider and the health care system.

ALTERNATIVES TO ADHERENCE

While the extensive quantitative literature on non-adherence has provided some insight into the character of the phenomenon, it has not contributed to its reduction (Vermiere et al., 2001). One of the main reasons for this lack of progress is that the majority of adherence research has been based upon a static model of the phenomenon that ignores the broader social context of health care and the dynamic nature of health and illness behaviour. An alternative, more social and psychological approach requires an understanding of the role of medicine in our society and of the actual lived experience of illness and of managing illness.

MODERN MEDICINE

In Western society medicine has been based upon power and authority. Since it is founded on the assumption that it has the monopoly on truth, it follows that patient non-adherence is a result of ignorance and/or deviance. Thus it is not surprising that Trostle (1998) describes the literature on compliance as 'a literature about power and control' (p. 1299). He argues that the increasing research interest in medical compliance is a reflection of 'a concern for market control combined with a concern for therapeutic power' (p. 1301). However, this very concern with maintaining power may carry with it an equal and opposite reaction evidenced by a reluctance of patients to comply.

According to **reactance theory** (Brehm, 1966), individuals believe they have the right to control their own behaviour. When this right is threatened they react and attempt to regain control over that behaviour and to prevent the loss of other freedoms. Basically, people do not like being pushed around and will attempt to subvert attempts to do so. In a revision of the original theory, Brehm and Brehm (1981) defined the concept of freedom as equivalent to that of control. People like to feel in control of their lives. Any attempt to reduce the sense of control over specific areas of our lives is a threat to the sense of freedom and is generally resisted.

The theory of psychological reactance has been used as an explanatory framework for non-compliance. The more extensive and complex the treatment prescribed, the greater the threat to perceived freedom (Fogarty, 1997). Admittedly, this threat would be accepted if there was an indication that it was worthwhile. However, the very complexity of some regimens may sensitize the patient to additional threats to their freedom such that patients may become resistant to additional demands. Non-compliance can thus be interpreted as a means of resisting medical dominance.

Admittedly, not all patients are critical of the traditional authoritarian stance of the physician or feel the need to resist or not comply. Some people are more accepting of authority than others. In recent years there has been more public opposition to the idea of the all-powerful doctor, and demands for greater control over health care. Despite this apparent change in public attitudes, several researchers have found that many people are reluctant to adopt a more resisting, consumerist attitude. Haug and Lavin (1983) found that while younger and more educated patients are more consumerist in their attitude regarding their role in the doctor–patient encounter, older patients are more accepting and accommodating.

Lupton (1997) investigated the impact of the supposed cultural shift on the attitudes of patients in Australia. She argued that contemporary popular advice is that the patient should adopt an active consumerist attitude to health care. In her interviews with a sample of patients, Lupton found a more mixed picture. Many of the patients, especially the older ones, still preferred the passive patient role. Admittedly, they accepted that the traditional authoritarian image of the doctor had been challenged over the past generation as a result of publicity about medical negligence and sexual harassment. This resulted in ambivalence about the doctor and a tension between adopting the consumerist or passive patient role. Thus while some patients would demand a more active role in their treatment and would be frustrated if they were denied it, many patients still preferred to adopt the traditional passive patient role.

The more consumerist stance of certain patients is not always welcomed by physicians. Although several studies have shown that patients generally express a desire for information about their condition, many physicians are reluctant to disclose much information. In his study, West (1984) found that physicians often ignored patients' requests for information. Indeed it was found that patients' requests for more information were often met by challenges to their intelligence.

ROLE OF THE PHYSICIAN

Trostle (1998) suggested that 'the last decade's preoccupation with adherence is a consequence of the declining authority of the [medical] profession' (p. 1303). In traditional non-Western societies the physician maintains the dominant role and the patient is more inclined to adopt a compliant stance. For example, Matsumoto et al. (1995) found that first-generation Japanese-Americans were much more likely to report a willingness to comply than their second-generation peers. Conversely, in Western society the demand for greater control over one's life conflicts with the traditional passive role and leads to greater resistance to medical advice.

Another feature of medical dominance is the power of the physician to define sickness. It is often assumed that the doctor typically makes the correct diagnosis and prescribes appropriate treatment. This is the ideal medical model. Thus non-adherence is the patient's fault. However, the evidence suggests that there are many sources of error on the part of the physician. For example, patients frequently attend with a variety of psychosocial problems, but physicians often ignores these. Bertakis et al. (1991) estimated that as many as 85% of patients who come to see their family doctor have some degree of psychological distress. As Mishler (1984) has emphasized, scientific medical discourse does not contain language to handle these issues so the physician prefers to focus concern on biomedical matters that may be of limited concern to the patient.

In a large study conducted over 11 sites in the USA, Bertakis et al. (1991) analysed the verbal content of 550 physician–patient interviews. They found that physician questions about biomedical topics were negatively related to patient satisfaction while physician questions about psychosocial topics were positively associated with patient satisfaction. In addition, those patients whose physician dominated the interview reported less satisfaction. Bertakis et al. concluded that 'patients are most satisfied by interviews that encourage them to talk about psychosocial issues in an atmosphere that is characterized by the absence of physician domination'.

However, Waitzkin (1989) argues that the exclusion of discussion of the social context of health complaints is a 'fundamental feature of medical language . . . a basic part of what medicine is in our society' (p. 232). Not only does medical language ignore these social issues but also medical treatment does not address these social issues. He suggests a redirection for medicine: 'By suggesting collective action as a meaningful option, medical professionals might begin to overcome the impact that its exclusion exerts.' To do this it needs to recognize the 'limits of medicine's role and the importance of building links to other forms of praxis that seek to change the social context of medical encounters' (p. 237).

The movement towards patient-centred models of medical treatment indicates that the medical profession is well aware of the growing criticism. So too are pharmacists who play a central role in dispensing medication. A report by the Royal Pharmaceutical Society of Great Britain (1997) called for a new approach to patient care. In a commentary on the report, Marinker (1997) noted that 'compliance may have been appropriate within a welfare state rooted in the values and thinking of society in the 1930s, when services were driven by benign paternalism and the practice of patients trusting their doctors' (p. 7082). The alternative that the report proposed was *concordance*, which is a model of the doctor–patient relationship based upon mutual respect (Vermeire et al., 2001). Marinker (1997) concluded: 'The price of compliance was dependency – it belongs to an older world. The price of concordance will be greater responsibility' (for both the doctor and the patient). While this vision of shared responsibility seems commendable, as we shall discuss subsequently, it also holds the potential of medical neglect.

Overall, there is much evidence to suggest that non-adherence is an integral component of the contemporary medical-dominated health care system. To reduce non-adherence thus requires a reassessment of this system. It also requires an understanding of what it means to the patient to be ill.

LIVED EXPERIENCE OF CHRONIC ILLNESS

The extent to which people, especially those with chronic illness, comply with recommended treatment is enmeshed in their experience of living with illness. Adherence is not a fixed event but a changing process. An increasing number of qualitative studies of illness help us to understand the processes by which people make sense of the prescribed treatment regimens. Some of these processes are considered here.

Self-Regulation

Individuals with chronic illness actively monitor and adjust their medication on an ongoing basis. It is not that they are recklessly ignoring professional advice but rather they are carefully regulating it according to a variety of factors. This is illustrated in the study conducted by Conrad (1985). Over a three-year period he conducted interviews with 80 individuals who had epilepsy about their life experiences with the disease. He noted that the individuals developed a personal 'medication practice' that best fitted with their self-image and their lifestyle. The patients realized the benefits of medication for seizure control and frequently stated that the medication helped them be more 'normal'. However, simultaneously the medication was seen as a daily reminder that they had epilepsy. They felt that reducing the medication was evidence that they were 'getting better'. Side effects were a frequently given justification for not complying with the recommended treatment. However, although side effects were mentioned they rarely referred to bodily side effects. Rather, they referred to social side effects. If the people with epilepsy felt that the medication was impairing their ability to handle routine social activities, they modified the medication to reduce this impact.

BOX 17.1
REASONS FOR SELF-REGULATION OF MEDICATION

- *Testing*: the way patients test the impact of varying dosages.
- *Controlling dependence*: the way patients assert to themselves and others that they are not dependent on the prescribed medication.
- *Destigmatization*: an attempt to reject the illness label and to be 'normal'.
- *Practical practice*: the way patients modified their dosage so as to reduce the risk of seizures, e.g. increasing the dosage in high stress situations.

Source: Conrad (1985: 34–5)

Box 17.1 summarizes four reasons that Conrad suggested underlie individuals' preference to self-regulate the treatment rather than comply fully with the recommended regimen. These illustrate how non-adherence is a rational process whereby the individual carefully adjusts the medication to maximize its impact.

People carefully monitor the impact of prescribed medication and adjust the dosage accordingly. They do not simply follow the standardized instructions provided by the physician but rather adjust them to suit their own personal needs. This is illustrated in a study by Hunter et al. (1997) who looked at middle-aged women's usage of hormone replacement therapy (HRT). They interviewed 45 women and identified three broad themes within which the women talked about HRT:

1. *Hot flushes and night sweats*: the women would not take the medication when there were no symptoms, e.g. one woman said: 'I have no extraordinary symptoms, therefore I have no need of HRT' (p. 1544).

2. *Doctors' opinions and behaviour*: the women listened carefully to their doctor's advice and decided whether or not to take HRT, e.g. one woman said: 'I came to the doctor and had a discussion. I felt that I weighed up the advantages and disadvantages' (p. 1544).
3. *Taking hormones or medication for a 'natural' process*: the women were reluctant to take medication for something that they felt was natural. They sometimes referred to a similar concern with taking the contraceptive pill, e.g. 'I might consider it if I was suffering from symptoms which I felt I could not put up with. I'm a bit wary. I never really wanted to go on the pill because I'm always a bit wary of interfering with nature' (p. 1545).

This study illustrates that the patient's attitude to the recommended treatment is interwoven with their attitude to the illness and their attitude to their physician.

The **self-regulatory model** of illness developed by Leventhal and Cameron (1987) provides a framework to explore patients' medication beliefs. This model considers health-related decisions as dynamic rather than static. According to the model whether a person adopts a certain coping procedure (e.g. adherence with medication) depends upon perception of illness threat and the perceived efficacy of the coping strategy. According to the model, concrete symptom experience is important both in formulating representations of the disease and in monitoring medication efficacy. Thus, a perceived lack of evidence of the disease or of the efficacy of the medication would encourage non-adherence. For Leventhal, the patient can best be considered as an active problem-solver.

An extension of this approach was developed by Horne and Weinman (1999). They developed a measure of medication beliefs that distinguished between the perceived benefits and harms of the medication. They found that patients' beliefs about the efficacy and necessity of medication were tempered by concerns about the potential for harm. A study of patients with chronic illness found that there was a strong relationship between perceived necessity of the medication and reported adherence to the treatment (Horne and Weinman, 1999). In a recent extension of this work with individuals who had asthma it was found that there was a relationship between illness perceptions (see Chapter 11), medication beliefs and adherence (Horne and Weinman, 2002). Those individuals with strong medication necessity beliefs also perceived asthma as having a lengthy timeline and that its consequences were serious. A statistical model found that treatment concerns and necessity and illness consequences were significant predictors of reported medication adherence.

A study using the Beliefs about Medicines Questionnaire (BMQ; Horne et al., 1999) found further supporting evidence of the importance of the patients' medication beliefs. The study considered medication adherence among individuals suffering from chronic arthritis (Treharne et al., 2004). It found that those who perceived their medications as being more necessary and those who perceived medications as not being overused were more adherent to the prescribed medication.

Similar findings were found in a study of non-pharmacological treatment for dizziness (Yardley et al., 2001). In this study patients were interviewed about the treatment. It was found that those patients who did not adhere to the recommended treatment attributed their symptoms to causes inconsistent with the rationale for the therapy. However, some other patients who did adhere also attributed inconsistent causes but emphasized trust in their physician or a willingness to try anything that might help. These patients reported an improvement in symptoms during the treatment period although they were hesitant about attributing the cause of this to the treatment. Yardley et al. concluded that while this study provided some evidence for Leventhal's illness regulation model there were also inconsistencies. It was suggested that these might be explained by considering the role of the therapist. They concluded that their findings 'highlight the reciprocal interactions between subjective experiences of bodily symptoms, abstract images of illness and treatment and social interactions between patient and therapist' – in other words between the 'material' (i.e. concrete, embodied) and the discursive (i.e. symbolic, socio-culturally mediated) aspects of health care (Yardley, 1997). Together these findings would extend the illness regulation model to include the discursive and social context within which the illness and the treatment are situated.

Finally, a recent study of adherence to complementary therapies developed a dynamic extended model of treatment and illness representations (Bishop et al., 2008). This model conceives of the patient as being involved in an ongoing review of the treatment to assess its effectiveness and the value of continued treatment. Using this model to test adherence to complementary therapies it was found that positive perceptions of one's therapist as well as a belief that the illness was not caused by mental factors predicted adherence to appointments. In addition, beliefs about the value of holistic health and difficulty attending appointments predicted adherence to remedies prescribed.

FEAR OF MEDICATION

From the physician's perspective, non-adherence can seem a foolhardy process. However, to the layperson non-adherence can be perceived as a means of reducing a variety of fears. This is illustrated in the findings of a study conducted by Donovan and Blake (1992). They investigated the extent to which a sample of people with various forms of arthritis complied with the recommended treatment. The study involved interviews and observations of 44 patients over a period of several years. They found that about half the patients did not follow the prescribed treatment. Detailed questioning of these patients revealed that they were carefully considering the implications of this non-adherence. It was not just a matter of obeying instructions or not – they were experimenting with dosages and timing. They were reluctant to follow the prescribed treatment for these reasons:

- fear of side effects;
- fear of dependency;
- fear of reduced effectiveness;
- did not fit with lifestyle;
- drugs as a sign of weakness;
- drugs do not fit with health beliefs.

Similarly, Britten (1994) in her study of lay people's perceptions of medicines found that many people have a range of fears and anxieties about medication. This was especially the case among those people who reported that they often did not comply with prescribed medication. In her discussion, Britten comments on the physicians' urge to prescribe and suggests they should consider other options than medication.

In the development of the Beliefs about Medicines Questionnaire, Horne (1997) distinguished between 'general overuse' (beliefs that medicines in general are over-used by doctors) and 'general harm' (beliefs that medicines in general are harmful addictive poisons). These two beliefs were found to be closely related. Subsequent work found that in a sample of British students, males, those with less experience of medication and those from an Asian background had a stronger belief in the general harm of medicines (Horne et al., 2004). This would indicate that medication beliefs are closely intertwined with gender and cultural identity and with experience of medication.

IDENTITY CONTROL

Medication adherence is also tied to the extent to which the patient accepts that she/he has an illness and wishes to control it. This is illustrated in the study by Adams et al. (1997). They conducted detailed interviews with a sample of asthma sufferers registered with a general practice in South Wales. Analysis of these interviews revealed that the extent to which the individuals complied with the recommended treatment (daily use of a curative and a prophylactic inhaler) was intimately bound up with how they defined themselves and their attitude to the illness. Three groups of patients, each with a particular pattern of medication, were identified:

1. *Deniers/distancers*: these were the individuals who argued that despite the medical diagnosis they did not have asthma but rather just 'bad chests'. They would fall into Goffman's (1963) 'discreditable' category and took steps to ensure that others were not aware of their diagnosis. They generally had a negative view of people with asthma (e.g. 'weakling' or 'wimp') and wished to avoid such a label. Although they took reliever medication when necessary, they were reluctant to take prophylactic medication regularly. While the former helped their 'bad chest', the latter was a symbol that they were 'asthmatic'.
2. *Accepters*: these individuals reluctantly accepted that they had asthma. They also held a variety of negative associations of people with asthma. They emphasized that they were not stereotypical asthmatic people but rather more like certain individuals who were able to achieve despite having asthma, e.g. certain athletes. They defined asthma as a 'condition' that needed to be controlled. As such they not only took the reliever medication but also the prophylactic medication. However, these individuals emphasized that although they took their medication regularly they were not dependent on their doctor. Rather, they were proud that they controlled their asthma themselves, using the drugs, with limited contact with their physician.

3. *Pragmatists*: these individuals did not fall neatly into the previous two categories although they were closer to the accepters. All of them accepted that they had asthma but their notions of asthma and medication usage were somewhat idiosyncratic. Unlike the secrecy of the deniers and the public stance of the accepters this group adopted a more pragmatic attitude and practised what Adams et al. described as a strategic policy of disclosure. This was related to their self-medication practices to which they adopted a pragmatic stance.

MEANING OF ILLNESS

Within the phenomenological and narrative literature there has been substantial discussion on the role of perceived meaning. For example, within narrative psychology it has been argued that the creation of a narrative account helps bring order and meaning to events that are confusing (Murray, 2007; see Chapter 13). There is a substantial research literature on the perceived meaning of illness. In a study of published accounts of breast cancer it was shown that many women search for meaning in their disease (Murray, 2009). It has been argued that greater narrative coherence is associated with feelings of well-being (Baerger and McAdams, 1999). It is possible that it is also linked to treatment adherence.

Recent research on writing has suggested that the process of writing can provide an opportunity for people to clarify the meaning of events in their lives. In a study by Westland et al. (2007) women with HIV were asked to participate in a regular writing task over one month. Analysis of what they had written found that those women who, during the writing task, had found some personal meaning in having HIV were more likely to have greater adherence to the medication prescribed at the end of the project. In this case, discovery of meaning was defined as 'a major shift in values, priorities, or perspectives'. There is ongoing discussion about what is going on in such writing activities (Nicholls, 2007). The growth of creative writing classes in health care settings provides an opportunity for further research.

Resistance to Medicine Taking

A common feature in qualitative research into medicine taking is the active role of the patient in assessing the value of the prescribed medication and deciding to what extent they should accept or resist it. In an extensive review of the qualitative research, Pound et al. (2005) concluded that 'the urge to evaluate suggests widespread caution about taking medicines as well as distrust in the information given about medicines' (p. 149).

They developed a model of medicine taking that highlighted the active role of the patient in decision making. Figure 17.3 shows that people will resist medication for a variety of reasons, especially concern about adverse drug reactions. They conclude that if the term resistance sounds strong 'It should be remembered that the huge literature on "non-compliance" only exists because so many people have continued to resist taking medicines in the face of sustained advice, interventions and admonishments' (Pound et al., 2005: 152).

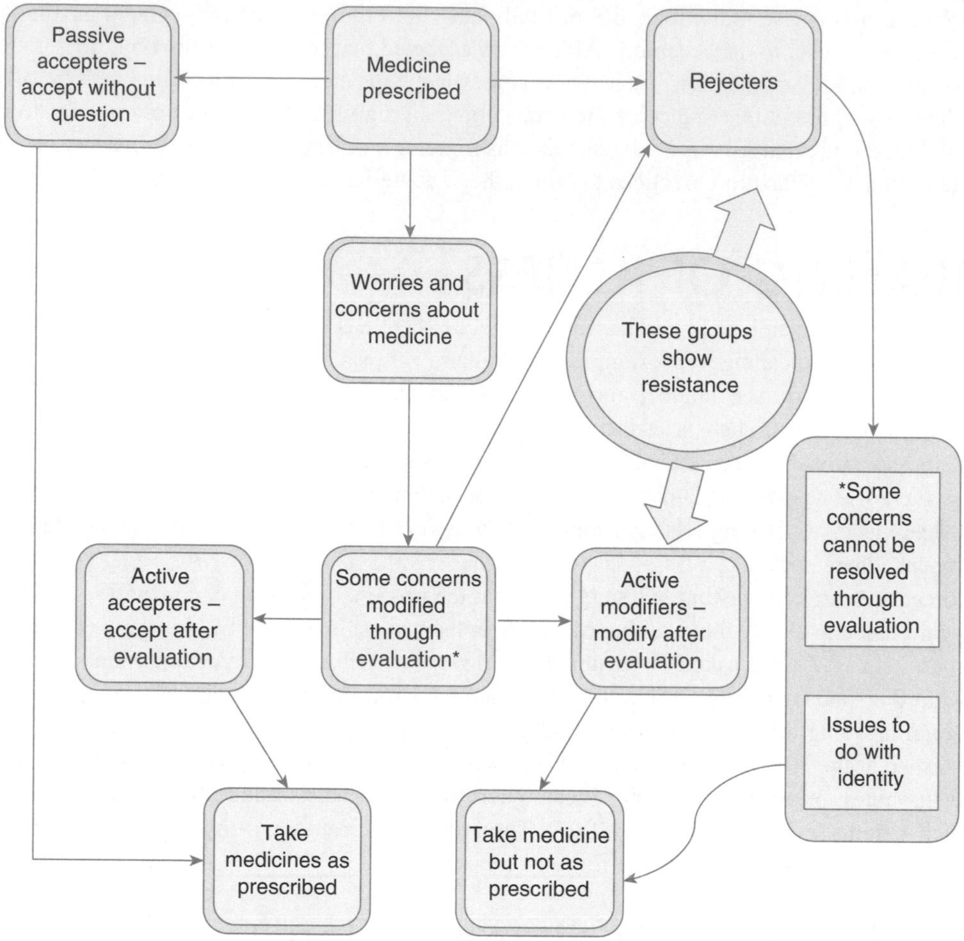

Figure 17.3 Model of medicine taking

Source: Pound et al. (2005: 139)

SOCIAL SETTING

These studies illustrate that the extent of adherence with the recommended treatment is intertwined not only with the character of the disease but also with the patient's self-definition and the perceived meaning of the illness. Adherence or non-adherence is a means not only of managing symptoms but also of managing self-identity. The patient does not simply follow the advice of the physician but rather acts depending upon how she/he interprets it. However, these processes take place in a particular social setting. This setting can range from the immediate family setting to the broader societal setting.

Consider the case of juvenile diabetes. It is established that parents assume the responsibility for ensuring their child follows the treatment regimen but as the child enters adolescence they transfer responsibility across. However, it is known that adherence to diabetes treatment begins to decline in adolescence (Miller and Drotar, 2007). The reasons for this decline include lack of parental involvement (Nansel et al., 2009) and lack of self-management skills (Modi et al., 2012).

An opportunity to ensure the transfer of self-management skills would seem to enhance adherence among adolescents with diabetes. Evidence to support this was found in a study by Miller and Jawad (2014) who found that those parents who reported that their youth expressed opinions and information during discussion about the illness management were more likely to report that their youth adhered to the treatment. Thus a family setting which encouraged and also facilitated self-management would be one in which the young people developed a sense of themselves as being responsible for the management of their illness.

Adherence can also be located in the broader socio-political setting. An example of this is given in Box 17.2.

BOX 17.2
INTERNATIONAL CASE STUDY: THERAPEUTIC CITIZENS – THEORIZING BEYOND THE INDIVIDUAL

The importance of broader political and historical context in explaining treatment adherence for HIV/AIDS is detailed in this collection of studies from Africa. Nguyen (2004) has developed the concept of the therapeutic citizen to describe the extent to which people actively participate as social and political beings in the use of medications. This concept has been taken up by Kagee et al. (2014) to explore the changing adherence to antiretroviral treatment for HIV/AIDS in South Africa over the past ten years. They begin by drawing attention to a range of more immediate structural barriers to adherence including poor transport, food insecurity, over-burdened health care facilities, limited access to mental health services, and difficulty accessing adequate counselling (Kagee et al., 2008; Kagee and Delport, 2010).

Kagee et al. (2014) refer to the period around 2008 when the political leadership in South Africa accused 'White' science as colluding with the ideas of apartheid. The government refused to make antiretrovirals (ARVs) available in the public health system since it was argued that AIDS was not caused by HIV but by poverty. This contributed to AIDS denialism (see Chapter 19). This in turn meant that the ART users were located in

(Continued)

(Continued)

opposition to the state. As Kagee et al. (2014) state: 'Part of that political identity was the daily action of being adherent to ART. Medication taking during this historical period was not only a health-promoting behaviour at the time but also an overtly political act' (p. 106).

However, due to overwhelming pressure from AIDS activists and others this AIDS denialism was rejected and now ART is widely available such that it has become more of a personal rather than a political act. Instead, adherence is presented as a pro-social act that is aimed at promoting the common good.

The current political context of lack of political direction and limited sign in improvement in the lives of people has created a new therapeutic context within which ART is located. Kagee et al. (2014) conclude that 'without a sense of a viable future, it may be more difficult to adhere to the demands of an ARV regimen, which in the short term may offer no benefits at all and is associated with inconvenience, stigma and side effects' (pp. 107–8).

Together these studies highlight the importance of moving from a personal to a political perspective to understand the changing use of certain medications.

Source: Kagee et al. (2014); Nguyen (2004)

PHARMACEUTICAL INDUSTRY

The elephant in the room in all discussion of medication adherence is the pharmaceutical industry (Big Pharma). This industry is one of the largest and most powerful industries in the world. It is dedicated to maximizing its profits through the promotion and sales of all forms of medication. Moynihan et al. (2002) describe their business as 'selling sickness'. They go further to argue:

> Some forms of medicalizing ordinary life may now be better described as disease mongering: widening the boundaries of treatable illness in order to expand markets for those who sell and deliver treatments . . . The social construction of illness is now being replaced by the corporate construction of disease. (p. 886)

The drug industry expend massive resources not just in developing new drugs, many of which are little different from other drugs, but in marketing these drugs to both the lay public and professionals. They do this through both direct and indirect marketing campaigns. In the process of medicalizing human health and personal problems they promote drugs as being the only method of promoting health. Those approaches which characterize many such problems as being benign or self-limiting are rejected as being insufficient and instead both patients and health professionals are convinced that medication is necessary.

Gøtzsche (2013) has detailed the multiple legal and illegal methods that Big Pharma uses to promote sales. He compares their methods to that of the Mafia or the Mob. Further, he argues that the industry has corrupted science by its promotion of the limited benefits of many drugs. He details how the drug companies exert massive influence in the direction of research to the extent that they can be said to have 'bought doctors, academics, professional and patient organisations, university departments, journalists, regulators, and politicians' (Smith, 2013). There have been many editorials in medical journals condemning the nefarious influence of drug companies but governments have only taken limited steps to control them. As Davis and Abraham (2013) state 'Such timid regulatory behaviour may be symptomatic of the extent to which regulators have been encouraged by governments to be responsive to the commercial interests of industry and to view large drug firms as clients whose fees increasingly fund these agencies' (p. 755).

With such widespread promotion of drugs worldwide it is not surprising that medication use is so widespread. According to the most recent Health Survey for England – 2013 (Health and Social Care Information Centre, 2014) 43% of men and 50% of women reported that they had taken at least one prescribed medicine in the last week. Even more alarmingly, 22% of men and 24% of women reported that they had taken at least three prescribed medicines in the last week. Among older people these figures were even higher with more than 70% of those aged 75 and over having taken at least three prescribed medicines. While many drugs have a beneficial impact on health, others have little impact or, of increasing concern, a negative impact.

MEDICAL ERROR

The desire of patients to evaluate the impact of the medication prescribed on their health is supported by the evidence on the extent of medical error. The term **iatrogenesis** was developed by Ivan Illich (1976) to describe health problems that are caused by medicine. While this term applies to the overall negative effects of the medical system, a particular issue is the extent of preventable **medical error**. Over the past 15 years there has been increasing awareness of the extent of medical error. In 2000 the US Institute of Medicine (IOM) published a report summarizing the growing evidence on the risk to the health of patients due to medical error (Institute of Medicine, 2000). This report highlighted two studies – one in Colorado and Utah and the other one in New York (Brennan et al., 1991) – that found that adverse events occurred in 2.9% and 3.7% of hospitalizations, respectively. Extrapolating to the whole of the USA the report estimated that 44,000 to 98,000 Americans die each year as a result of medical error. That is more than die each year from motor-vehicle accidents, breast cancer or AIDS.

Since the publication of the IOM report, other countries have produced similar reports. For example, in 2001 the UK Chief Medical Officer produced a report entitled *An Organisation with a Memory* (Department of Health, 2000) and a subsequent action report detailing specific recommendations (Department of Health, 2001). This was followed by a report by the UK Chief

Pharmaceutical Officer (Smith, 2004). These reports also referred to the high rate of adverse medical events. They highlighted one British study (Vincent et al., 2001) that found that 10% of patients admitted to two London teaching hospitals had experienced an adverse event, of which half were preventable. It was estimated that such adverse events generated up to £2 billion in additional costs to the NHS (Department of Health, 2000). A recent survey conducted by the Health Foundation (2004) in the UK estimated that as many as 40,000 deaths a year were due to medical error.

Smith (2004) estimated that 10–20% of adverse medical events are due to medication errors. In a study of 550,000 prescriptions written by GPs in Britain, pharmacists identified and averted 54 potentially harmful cases (0.01%) (Greene, 1995). However, a large proportion of errors go undetected or unreported. For this reason, Smith proposed a medication error iceberg to describe the situation. At the tip of the iceberg were those errors that cause actual damage and are reported. But then there are the unreported errors that include errors identified with potential to cause harm (near-misses), errors identified but considered insignificant, potential errors and unnoticed actual errors. Together, this indicates that the extent of the problem is much greater than appears from the initial figures.

Explanations for Medical Error

Explanations of medical error frequently distinguish between the person and systems approaches (Reason, 2000). The person approach focuses on the individual and leads to the so-called 'name, blame and shame' approach to error management. The alternative systems approach considers the broader context with which errors occur. It emphasizes the importance of organizational change in order to reduce the risk of error. A summary of the person and systems explanations of medical error is provided in Figure 17.4.

In hospitals it is junior physicians who do most of the prescribing. They are the ones with least knowledge and also the ones who make the most prescribing errors (Lesar et al., 1996). Wu et al. (1991) surveyed junior hospital physicians in internal medicine training programmes. They found that 45% reported making at least one error, 31% of which resulted in a patient's death.

Weingrad et al. (2000) in their review of medical error identified a series of potential risk factors. These included:

- age of patient – older patients are more at risk;
- type of intervention – certain types of surgery are particularly risky;
- emergency room usage;
- lengthy medical care;
- intensive medical care.

They concluded: 'Unless we make substantial changes to the organization and delivery of medical care, all patients – particularly the most vulnerable – will continue to bear the burden of medical error' (p. 776).

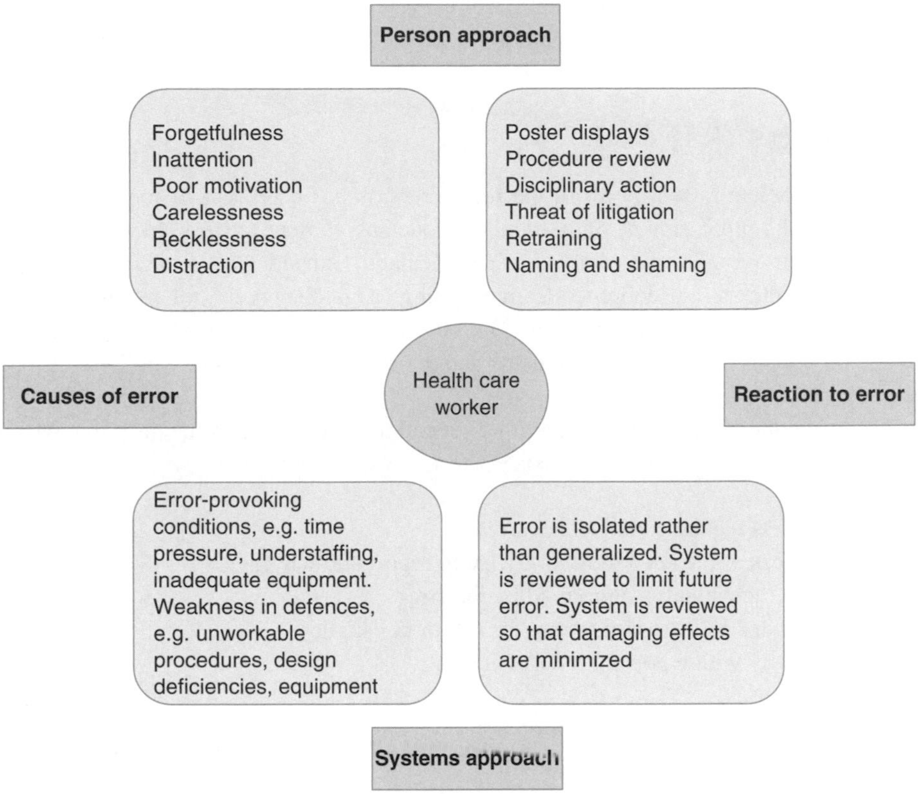

Figure 17.4 Person and systems approaches to medication error

Source: Smith, 2004

An important factor overall is the character of the physician–patient relationship. A survey of American physicians and members of the general public (Blendon et al., 2002) found that they agreed on two possible causes of medical error: shortage of nurses (53% physicians vs. 65% of the public) and overwork, stress and fatigue of health providers (50% vs. 70%). In addition, 72% of the public referred to too little time with their physician and 67% referred to health care professionals not working as a team or not communicating.

In a national survey of residents (junior hospital doctors) in the Netherlands (sample of over 2,000 with 41% response rate) it was found that 94% reported that they had made one or more mistakes that did not have negative consequences for the patient. However, more than half (56%) reported that they had made at least one mistake that had a negative consequence for the patient (Prins et al., 2009). The strongest predictors of self-reported errors were emotional exhaustion and depersonalization. In addition, burnout was more predictive of perceived errors due to lack of time than errors due to judgement/inexperience. They concluded that there was a need for greater supervision and emotional support for junior doctors.

MEDICAL SILENCE

One common problem raised by all of the recent reports has been that of medical silence: the reluctance of health professionals, in particular physicians, to report errors. In a survey of physicians conducted in five countries (Australia, New Zealand, Canada, USA and UK) a large proportion reported that they felt discouraged from reporting or that they were not encouraged to report (Blendon et al., 2001). The proportion was over 60% in Australia and about 30% in the UK. This contrasts with the large proportion of patients and the general public who would prefer reporting of medical errors (Gallagher et al., 2003).

The Department of Health (2000) identified several reasons for this reluctance to report on the part of medical personnel. These included:

- lack of awareness that an error has occurred;
- lack of awareness of the need to report, what to report and why;
- perception that the patient is unharmed by the error;
- fear of disciplinary action or litigation, for self or colleagues;
- lack of familiarity with reporting mechanisms;
- loss of self-esteem;
- staff feeling they are too busy to report;
- lack of feedback when errors are reported.

The Insititute of Medicine (1999) report expressed alarm that despite the high rate of error, 'silence surrounds this issue. For the most part, consumers believe they are protected' (p. 3). It continued:

> The goal of this report is to break this cycle of inaction. The status quo is not acceptable and cannot be tolerated any longer. Despite the cost pressures, liability constraints, resistance to change and other seemingly insurmountable barriers, it is simply not acceptable for patients to be harmed by the same health care system that is supposed to offer healing and comfort. (p. 3)

This reluctance on the part of physicians to report has led to the establishment of mandatory reporting systems in many countries.

However, the reluctance of the physician to report also reflects their power and status in society and the reticence of the public and the patient to question medical authority. Whistle-blowers have often suffered stigma and discrimination, and sometimes unemployment, as a consequence of speaking out. Thus implicit within any model to reduce medical error and to improve patient safety is the challenge of increasing public and patient involvement in the quality control of health care.

PATIENT EMPOWERMENT

Rather than attempting to control the patient – an approach that is implicit within models of compliance – empowerment attempts to increase patient autonomy and self-control. The empowerment approach is derived from the work of community educators and psychologists and is defined as the process whereby 'people gain mastery over their lives' (Rappoport, 1987). Instead of imposing the views of the expert health professional, empowerment seeks to enhance the patients' self-understanding and the potential of self-care (Feste and Anderson, 1995).

The focus of this approach is the enhancement of the strengths and potential of the patient. Through dialogue the health professional seeks to understand the needs of the patient. Skelton (1997) suggests that the aim of patient education within this model is to 'blur' the boundaries between professional-as-teacher and patient-as-learner. Instead of the professional's health knowledge being considered paramount, the patient's lay health beliefs and knowledge are considered of equal or greater value. A central component of this understanding is the opportunity for patients to tell their stories. In describing this process, Hunter (1991) notes that 'medicine has the power not only to rewrite the patient's story of illness but also to replot its course' (p. 139). Dependent upon the story that is handed back the patient will assess its relevance to their lives. As Hunter (1991) continues: 'If the two are widely disparate and the physician fails to recognize the distance between them, the interaction founders. The medicine will go untaken, the consultation unsought, the prescription unfilled' (p. 142).

Desire for Control

Patient empowerment can aim to involve the patient more in health care through attention to patient needs or it can increase the patients' awareness of the broader social and political factors that adversely affect their health status. Admittedly, as Lupton (1997) found, not all patients wish to be actively involved in their personal health care or in taking broader collective action.

Desire for control can be conceptualized along three dimensions (Auerbach, 2001):

- *Cognitive/informational control* is concerned with processing relevant information and thereby reducing ambiguity and leading to an enhanced sense of control over the particular situation. In the case of health care this involves obtaining and reviewing information about the health problem and the proposed treatment.
- *Decisional control* refers to the opportunity for reviewing and selecting preferences for treatment.
- *Behavioural control* involves direct action whereby the individual is involved in changing the situation. It implies that the patient has the opportunity to select and guide the actual treatment.

There is substantial evidence that patients desire information about their health (Auerbach and Pegg, 2002). Younger, more educated patients having a greater desire for such information. In the case of decisional control, the evidence is more equivocal with many patients indicating that they would prefer physician control or at best some form of joint or collaborative control. A variety of factors influence this preference: (1) less desire for control when the disease is serious, (2) less desire for control among older patients, and (3) less desire for control among patients with lower education. In concluding his review, Auerbach (2001) concluded: 'If there is a predisposition on the part of patients to want to assume control, it is strongly influenced by their appraisal of whether they think involvement on their part will positively influence the outcome of their situation' (p. 197).

Critical Approach To Empowerment

Many health care providers have enthusiastically endorsed the idea of empowerment. However, there is a need for some caution as regards why this idea has become so popular and its implications for patient care. Although most physicians prefer to adopt the dominant role in patient care (Beisecker et al., 1996) there is increasing evidence that many are promoting greater control by the patient (e.g. Coulter, 1999). Indeed, this orientation connects with the identification of the patient as responsible in some way for both their illness and their treatment. This is particularly the case in those illnesses associated with lifestyle practices such as smoking, diet and exercise, but also with chronic diseases.

This critical approach to patient empowerment considers it part of the extended biopsychosocial model (Salmon and Hall, 2003). This model extends the traditional dualistic approach to the body by identifying psychosocial factors as aetological agents of disease. This in turn leads to concern with promoting increased control and various coping strategies as ways of patient empowerment. Implicit in this discourse is the transformation of the patient from a passive sufferer to an active manager of their own suffering 'from which it is a small step to locating with the patient the moral responsibility to become well' (Salmon and Hall, 2003: 1,973). This provides the physician with the opportunity to evade responsibility for treatment of those problems for which they have limited insight (e.g. chronic illness and mental illness). Thus the language of empowerment can serve the physician's interests rather than those of the patient. It can also absolve the physician of responsibility for certain medical errors.

A graphic illustration of the negative impact of empowerment is the enthusiasm of many physicians to promote the so-called 'fighting spirit' attitude among cancer patients. Initial research by Greer et al. (1979) had suggested that patients with this attitude had better survival prospects. Many patients report that their clinicians encourage them to be positive and to fight (e.g. Byrne et al., 2002). Unfortunately, such encouragement can be disempowering as the patient feels depressed because she/he cannot control the disease. In our review of the evidence, there is no empirical support for the hypothesis that personality or coping strategies improve the prospects of survival (see Chapters 16 and 19).

Another example of this disempowering advice is the case of 'patient-controlled analgesia' (PCA), which is a strategy designed to provide post-operative patients with control over their analgesia. However, in interviews with the patients it was found that PCA did not give them control over their pain. Rather, they liked PCA because it freed them of the need to exercise control by 'bothering' nurses with requests for analgesia (Taylor et al., 1996). In a comparison study that involved teaching post-operative patients to feel in control of their recovery it was found that patients interpreted the programme as a request not to annoy the staff. Together these studies question the practice of strategies designed to empower patients.

Kugelman (1997) develops a similar critique in his review of the growth of the gate control theory of pain. He notes that an important component of this and other biopsychosocial models is the insistence on personal responsibility for pain management. The alternative to assuming responsibility is learned helplessness and passivity. While the patient is expected to assume responsibility 'they should not expect, however, that the professionals should relinquish their salaries or expertise' (p. 61). Kugelman also connects his critique with the ignorance of social problems: 'If pain is truly epidemic today, then something is terribly wrong, not only with patients, or "inadequate pain technologies, but with the social matrix that produces suffering. To tempt people to be co-managers in such a social world only deepens our true helplessness' (p. 62).

Other researchers have questioned the whole movement towards promoting empowerment. As Lord and McKillop Farlow (1990) noted: 'People mistakenly talk about "empowering families" or "empowering professionals" as if empowerment is something one person does to another' (p. 2). Powers (2003) argues that rather than challenging the traditional medical paternalism, 'empowerment equals paternalism' (p. 229). Within a capitalist state, the promotion of empowerment has a hidden agenda:

- It allows health care disciplines to reframe questions regarding oppression to questions regarding free individual choices among predetermined alternatives in the context of a belief in natural rights.
- It allows the health care provider to assign blame when the strategy fails, i.e. when the patient chooses the 'wrong' option.
- It makes health education a technology of the self, a way to manipulate people to think they are taking charge of their own health and exercising their rights instead of being dependent.

The move towards empowerment is especially directed at those people who do not conform to mainstream values and practices rather than attempting to promote broader changes in social structures. The physician and other health professionals can now continue to disparage the most deprived and marginalized, not now for their non-compliance but rather for their refusal to accept responsibility for self-management.

These criticisms highlight the need for health psychologists to adopt a broad critical perspective so that they do not simply continue to be another agent of health care oppression under the 'empowerment' umbrella.

FUTURE RESEARCH

1. New medical procedures and drugs are constantly being developed. There is an ongoing need to assess the problems involved in their adoption in the community.
2. Large-scale prospective studies are needed to investigate the association between psychological factors and non-adherence.

3. Not everyone will accept certain procedures. Further research is needed to explore the meaning of different treatments to different populations.
4. Research needs to address how best to involve people more directly in all aspects of their health care.

SUMMARY

1 Adherence refers to the extent to which the patient follows the prescribed treatment regimen.

2 A wide range of social and psychological factors have been found to be associated with non-adherence. These factors are associated with the characteristics of the patients, the disorders they have, the treatments they are given, and the relationships they have with their physicians and organizational factors.

3 It is difficult to compare the results from different studies because of the complex nature of non-adherence and the variety of methods and criteria that are employed.

4 An alternative approach is to consider the impact on patient behaviour of the socio-political role of the physician and the meaning of the health problem and of the prescribed medication for the patient.

5 Medical silence has traditionally concealed the extent of medical error.

6 Medical error leads to a wide range of health problems. Explanations of medical error include both person and system factors.

7 Patient empowerment aims to involve patients in health care through listening to their needs, not as recipients but as active partners in health care.

8 Patient empowerment conversely can place responsibility for illness management on the patient and, to some degree, absolve physicians and other health care professionals from responsibilities.

9 A broad, critical perspective suggests the need for health psychologists to not simply reinforce oppressive forms of health care by positioning themselves under the umbrella of 'empowerment'.

18 PAIN AND PAIN CONTROL

[M]edicine has overlooked the fact that the activity of this (pain) apparatus is subject to a constantly changing influence of the mind.

(Bonica, 1990: 12.)

OUTLINE

In this chapter we discuss the complex and multifactorial nature of pain, starting with the direct line of transmission, pattern and multidimensional gate control theories. Psychological and social processes that mediate and moderate pain behaviour and experience are considered. We summarize the pros and cons of different pain assessment methods. The fear-avoidance model and relevant empirical evidence are reviewed. Finally, we explore psychological techniques used in pain management and the evidence for their effectiveness.

WHAT IS PAIN?

Pain is a highly adaptive but complex and multifaceted phenomenon that is poorly understood by many health care practitioners, especially physicians. As a consequence, many of those afflicted suffer prolonged periods without sufficient understanding, care and support.

It has been wisely asserted that 'pain is not a monolithic entity. Pain is, rather, a concept used to focus and label a group of behaviours, thoughts and emotions. Pain has many dimensions, including sensory and affective components, location, intensity, time course, and the memories, meaning, and anticipated consequences that it elicits … no isomorphic relationship exists among tissue damage, nociception, and pain report' (Turk and Wilson, 2013: 314).

A GP or physician is unlikely to be able to allocate the time necessary to analyse all of the variables that influence the waxing and waning of chronic pain reported by an individual sufferer. An account of the initiation, exacerbation and maintenance of pain, however, remains a compelling and engaging task for the patient and their carers. If they are lucky, they will have access to a health psychologist with training in the area of chronic pain management. However, there is a dearth of expertise, and millions of patients globally receive inadequate care and are left to their own devices.

Pain evidently evolved as a biological safety alarm to warn us when something is physically wrong, allowing action to alleviate the problem. Its importance can be seen when cases of congenital universal insensitivity to pain (CUIP) are considered. Most cases of CUIP involve premature death. A different concept, 'psychological pain', is used to refer to mental anguish or suffering. Pain is a performance of affliction of a person in a social situation suggesting that pain can affect any aspect of existence, not only the physical body. However, in this chapter, we discuss physical pain.

Pain is a uniquely personal experience, which has been defined in many ways, including:

- An aversive, personal, subjective experience, influenced by cultural learning, the meaning of the situation, attention and other psychological variables, which disrupts ongoing behaviour and motivates the individual to attempt to stop the pain (Melzack and Wall, 1982/1988).
- Whatever the person experiencing it says it is, existing whenever the experiencing person says it does (McCaffery and Thorpe, 1988).
- An unpleasant sensory and emotional experience associated with actual or potential tissue damage, or described in terms of such damage (Merskey, 1996).

Such definitions highlight the subjective, emotional and multidimensional nature of pain experience. Pain is further classified as either acute or chronic, differentiated only by duration (acute being under six months and chronic over six months). The six-month cut-off is arbitrary; other suggested cut-off points are 30 days, 3 months or 12 months.

The International Association for the Study of Pain (IASP) published pain terminology in 1994 and in slightly revised form in 2007 (IASP, 2010). Changes were made to definitions of central pain: 'pain initiated or caused by a primary lesion or dysfunction in the central nervous system'; and hyperpathia: 'a painful syndrome characterized by an abnormally painful reaction to a stimulus, especially a repetitive stimulus, as well as an increased threshold' (IASP, 2010).

Acute pain is a useful biological response provoked by injury or disease (e.g. broken leg, appendicitis), which is of limited duration (IASP, 2010). It tends to be amenable to pharmacological treatment. **Chronic** pain is described as pain persisting for six months or more and tends not to respond to pharmacological treatment. The time continuum is imperfect because there are many cases of acute recurrent pain, e.g. migraine headaches, and also pain from progressive illnesses such as metastatic cancer.

Further useful distinctions include:

- malignant (associated with progressive illness, e.g. cancer);
- benign (not associated with progressive illness, e.g. lower back pain, LBP);

- progressive (becomes worse over time, e.g. arthritis);
- intractable (resistant to treatment, e.g. LBP);
- intermittent (pain that fluctuates over time and in intensity, e.g. fibromyalgia);
- recurrent (acute pain occurring periodically, e.g. migraine);
- organic (involving observable tissue damage, e.g. arthritis);
- psychogenic (absence of demonstrable pathology, e.g. fibromyalgia);
- referred (pain originating in one body area which is perceived as originating from another, e.g. perceiving an 'earache' that originates from a bad tooth).

As noted, pain can affect anyone at any time, can be highly disabling, often involving all aspects of a person's life including physical, psychological and emotional states, disrupting daily activities, work, finances, social, marital and family life and relationships (e.g. Marcus, 2000). In addition to the association between many chronic illnesses and pain (e.g. cancer, HIV/AIDS, sickle-cell anaemia), particular groups appear more likely to experience chronic pain, especially the elderly and many disabled people even in the absence of illness (e.g. pain from braces or harnesses).

Pain is an extremely interesting phenomenon to physicians, physiologists and psychologists alike: *pain is perceived in the body, produced by the central nervous system, and processed by the mind*. To the sufferer, however, pain can be the primary determining influence on a person's quality of life and well-being. Talking about pain in simple terms or using tired clichés must always be avoided. It is lamentable to 'psychologize' pain; little else can be more infuriating to a pain sufferer.

One response to pain is to misinterpret it as a catastrophe, a sign of serious injury or pathology over which one has little or no control. This can lead to an excessive fear of pain that gradually extends to a fear of physical movements such that people will avoid physical activities that they presume will worsen their problem, and as their inactivity is reinforced, their disablement worsens as a consequence. We review in a later section the fear-avoidance model (FAM) (Asmundson et al., 1999; Vlaeyen and Linton, 2000; Crombez et al., 2012).

PAIN COSTS

Pain inflicts significant costs on individuals, their families, the health services and society in general. The 2010 Global Burden of Disease study reported that musculo-skeletal disorders, with chronic pain as the primary symptom, ranked as the second leading cause of disability worldwide (Lim et al., 2012). It is the most commonly cited reason for patients seeking medical help. It is estimated that 80% of all doctor consultations in the USA and around 40% in the UK relate to pain. Pain is associated with extended hospital stays, lost working days and increased take-up of benefits. The resultant economic costs are very high. Back pain is the most common chronic pain condition. Estimates of the prevalence of chronic pain vary, but a recent estimate is that 7.8 million people in the UK suffer moderate to severe pain that has lasted for more than six months. It appears that prevalence of chronic pain is rising, with more cases now compared with 40 years ago. Studies suggest that it is more commonly reported by women and those from socially or financially disadvantaged groups (Bridges, 2012).

Health economists estimated that the annual cost of chronic pain is in the range of $560–$635 billion a year, which is more than the yearly costs for cancer, heart disease and diabetes (Gaskin and Richard, 2012). This analysis did not consider the costs of pain for institutionalized and non-civilian populations, for persons under 18 and for caregivers.

The cost of pain in human suffering is inestimably high. Pain statistics are likely to under-represent the problem as many people endure significant levels of pain without seeking help. Pain is often the most distressing and debilitating aspect of chronic illness. Its effects on quality of life can be devastating to the individual and their significant others, including distress, loss of function, relationship problems, social, financial and employment difficulties and stigma. Chronic pain is often the major contributor to the burden of a disorder. The emotional toll of severe chronic pain should not be underestimated. It is estimated that around 50% of severe chronic pain patients consider suicide. This association is mediated by depression. Similarly, the experience of unremitting pain in cancer patients has been reported as the most common reason underlying requests for physician-assisted dying.

PAIN ASSESSMENT

Pain **assessment** is by no means a simple process. The inherent difficulty is trying to interpret a uniquely individual experience related by another person. Assessment is crucial to the understanding and treatment of pain including its underlying mechanisms and mediating factors, as well as the development of effective treatment programmes.

Assessments are mostly undertaken for medical, research or compensation claim purposes and the purpose will influence the type of assessment used. Assessment measures may include intensity, psychological and functional effects and pain behaviours. Assessment methods can generally be grouped under one of four categories: physiological measures, pain questionnaires, mood assessment questionnaires and observations (direct observations or self-observations) (Table 18.1).

Pain questionnaires typically present commonly used descriptive words (for aspects of pain or mood) that the individual uses to rate their current experience. The words may be presented in rating scales or descriptive lists. The McGill Pain Questionnaire (MPQ; Melzack, 1975; Melzack and Katz, 2013) is the best known and most frequently used questionnaire. In the McGill Pain Questionnaire, descriptive pain terms are clustered in groups of two to five words. Participants are asked to circle the words that describe their pain, with one word from each group. Then they must go back and circle the three words in groups 1–10 that most convey their pain response, two words in groups 11–15 that do the same thing, and one word in group 16. Finally, they are asked to pick one word in groups 17–20. At the end they should have seven words that they can take to their doctor that will help describe the quality and intensity of the pain. Examples are as follows: Group 1 – Flickering, Pulsing, Quivering, Throbbing, Beating, Pounding; Group 2 – Jumping, Flashing, Shooting; Group 3 – Pricking, Boring, Drilling, Stabbing; Group 19 – Cool, Cold, Freezing; Group 20 – Nagging, Nauseating, Agonizing, Dreadful, Torturing (Melzack, 1975).

Table 18.1 summarizes some of the common measures that have been described in the literature. Medical examinations form the backbone of clinical pain assessments and include joint mobility and heart rate. Physiological measures attempt to objectively measure responses to pain. Psychological measures assess pain using psychometric instruments of different kinds.

Table 18.1 Summary of common pain assessment measures

Physiological measures	Questionnaires assessing pain	Questionnaires assessing mood and pain-related attitudes	Observations – direct or self
Medical examination including pain sites, joint mobility, history, etc.	McGill Pain Questionnaire (MPQ) (Melzack, 1975)	Beck's Depression Inventory (Beck, 1977)	Activity levels
Muscle tension – electromyography (EMG)	Multidimensional pain inventory (MPI) (Kearns, Turk and Rudy, 1985)	Hospital Anxiety and Depression Scale (Zigmond and Snaith, 1983)	Standing and sitting time (uptime and downtime)
Heart rate	Sickness Impact Profile (SIP) (Follick et al., 1985)	Pain Anxiety Symptoms Scale (McCracken, Zayfert and Gross, 1992)	Sleep patterns
Hyperventilation	Survey of Pain Attitudes (Jensen et al., 1987)	Well-being Questionnaire (Pincus et al., 1997)	Sexual activity
Galvanic skin response (GSR)	Pain Information and Beliefs Questionnaire (Shutty et al., 1990)	Chronic Pain Acceptance Questionnaire (McCracken et al., 2004)	Medication requests and usage
Electroencephalograph (EEG)	Pain diagram (Chan et al., 1993)		Normal household activities Appetite and eating
Pedometer	Bio-behavioural Pain Profile (Dalton et al., 1994)		Leisure activities

Fear of pain has been implicated in the development and maintenance of chronic pain behaviour. McCracken et al. (1992) developed an instrument to measure fear of pain across cognitive, behavioural and physiological domains – the Pain Anxiety Symptoms Scale (PASS). Related to the fear of pain is the concept of acceptance of chronic pain, which occurs when an individual reduces attempts to avoid or control pain and tries to focus instead on carrying out valued activities in the pursuit of personal goals. McCracken et al. (2004) investigated the psychometric properties of the Chronic Pain Acceptance Questionnaire (CPAQ). They found that factors assessing

(a) the degree to which one engaged in life activities regardless of the pain and (b) willingness to experience pain both were significantly related to the other measures of patient functioning.

Other methods include verbal rating scales, visual analogue scales and a pain diagram that shows front and back outlines of a body on which patients mark areas that correspond to the distribution of pain. However, Walker et al. (2014) found that the area of the pain diagram that was shaded in was not associated with any psychosocial factors.

Visual analogue scales may be the most appropriate for use with diverse cultural groups, children, the elderly and people with communication difficulties. They are easy to use and therefore frequent ratings can be made then averaged, or peak times and triggers identified. Most pain questionnaires attempt to assess sensory, affective and evaluative dimensions of pain. They can be completed by the individual or as part of an interview. Specific types of pain seem to be described using similar words, and questionnaires have been found to discriminate between different pain populations.

Observations of individual pain behaviours and functional levels are also used in assessments, either direct observations by another person (e.g. a nurse on a hospital ward), or self-observations (e.g. in diaries or logs). However, direct and self-observations have drawbacks. Direct observations can never elicit unbiased data, being influenced by the setting in which they occur (e.g. clinical setting, home), the purpose of the assessment (e.g. benefit claim vs. treatment assessment) and assessor characteristics (e.g. gender, ethnicity). Similarly, self-observations (e.g. pain diaries) may be inaccurate or overly subjective. Scales exist for patients and carers to rate their ability, on a 0–10 scale, to carry out everyday tasks such as sitting, car riding, dressing, sleeping, having sex, walking, house work, getting up from a chair or bed, shopping and carrying out light work, e.g. the Activities of Daily Living Scale (Linton, 1990).

An alternate approach is to use interviews in an attempt to assess all aspects of the pain experience including a full pain history, assessing emotional adjustment and pre- and post-pain lifestyle. However, interviews need to be as structured as possible or they will tend to tail off in different directions as sufferers need to talk about their pain(s) and disrupted life experience at length, often feeling unlistened to by doctors.

Issues in Pain Assessment

Many assessment instruments are insensitive to age, disability and culture. For groups who have communication difficulties, due to age, language problems, or sensory or cognitive deficits, assessment may require extended assessment time to enable rapport building. Herr et al. (2006) found that there is no standardized tool based on non-verbal/behavioural pain indicators in English that can be recommended for clinical practice. It is therefore necessary to rely on the reports of significant others (e.g. carer, interpreter), which has additional challenges of perception, interpretation and motivation. More work is required to address issues around the impact of situational context and assessor characteristics on the assessment process. Further investigation is needed of the influence of assessment, including the impact of compensation claim assessments, and of the need to prove the existence of pain and how it restricts the sufferer's daily activities.

MECHANISMS, MEDIATORS AND MODERATORS OF PAIN

A useful framework for conceptualizing pain includes attention, expectations, beliefs, knowledge, emotions, coping strategies, along with cultural and family influences, which all can play a role in mediating and moderating pain experience (Linton and Shaw, 2011). The diagram in Figure 18.1 is self-explanatory. All of the processes are familiar ones. Moving from a framework to a model and then to a theory are massive steps, however, that have yet to be convincingly taken. A few faltering steps have been made but there is thin ice afoot for the unwary. We are not even going to discuss here the philosophical complexities, but they are substantial.

The **biopsychosocial model** (see Chapter 1) summarizes the contemporary view that chronic pain and disability have multiple causes. Psychosocial factors are important predictors of chronic pain and disability early in acute and sub-acute stages of pain (Boersma et al., 2014). The transition from acute to chronic pain and to disability is moderated by depression, anxiety, pain beliefs,

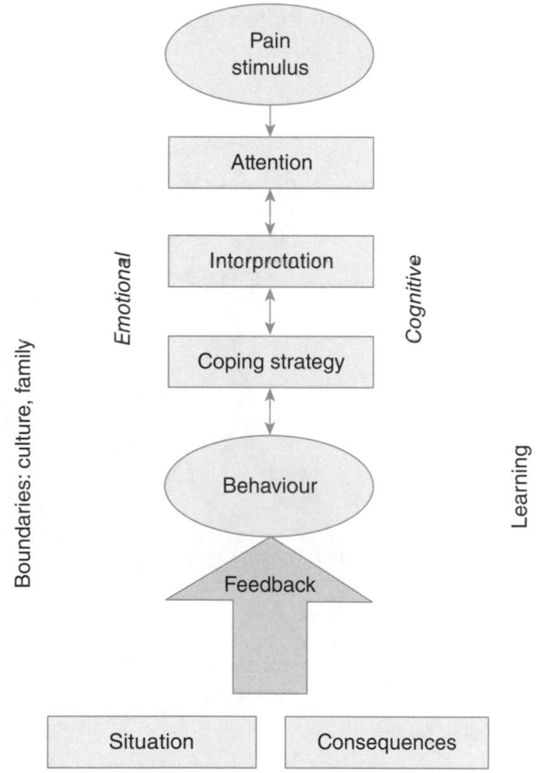

Figure 18.1 Psychosocial mechanisms involved in the perception and performance of pain

Source: Linton and Shaw (2011)

catastrophizing, and coping behaviours. All of the factors shown in Figure 18.1 are instantiated in a single nervous system to produce the pain experience. An external observer can only surmise what the resulting experience feels like from the subject's verbal and non-verbal behaviour.

Specificity Theory

Theories about pain production are few in number, and none to date has been able to explain all of the known facts. The specific mechanisms for the transmission and perception of pain are not well understood, although knowledge in the form of empirical data is expanding. Three main theories have been proposed: specificity theory, pattern theory and gate control theory.

Specificity theory was suggested by René Descartes in 1664 (Figure 18.2) and taken up by von Frey in 1894. This describes a direct causal relationship between pain stimulus and pain experience. Stimulation of specific pain receptors (nociceptors) throughout the body sends impulses along specific pain pathways (A-delta fibres and C-fibres) through the spinal cord to specific areas of the sensory cortex of the brain. Stimulus intensity correlates with pain intensity, with higher stimulus intensity and pain pathway activation resulting in a more intense pain experience. Failure to identify a specific cortical location for pain, realization that pain fibres do not respond

Figure 18.2 The pain pathway in René Descartes' *Traité de l'homme* (1664). The specificity view of pain has been replaced with more complex theories

exclusively to pain but also to pressure and temperature, and the disproportional relationship between stimulus intensity and reported pain intensity (e.g. injured soldiers reporting little pain while similarly injured civilians requiring substantial medication) led to specificity theory losing favour. The theory was simply wrong.

Pattern Theory

Pattern theorists proposed that stimulation of nociceptors produces a pattern of impulses that are summated in the dorsal horn of the spinal cord. Only if the level of the summated output exceeds a certain threshold is pain information transmitted onwards to the cortex resulting in pain perception. Evidence of deferred pain perception (e.g. soldiers not perceiving pain until the battle is over), intact pain transmission systems where pain is perceived without injury (e.g. phantom limb) and injury without pain perception (e.g. CUIP) raised questions about pattern theories. In addition, there was growing evidence for a mediating role for psychosocial factors in the experience of pain, including cross-cultural differences in pain perception and expression. The theory was inadequate.

Gate Control Theory

Conscious experience, whether pain or otherwise, is derived from a multiplexed array of afferent information arriving via sensory transducers allied with cognitive and emotional information about the context, history and future implications of the stimulus environment. The growing body of evidence contradicting direct line of transmission and pattern theories culminated in the development of the **gate control theory** by Melzack and Wall (1982/1988). In the gate control theory pain is viewed as a multidimensional, subjective experience in which ascending physiological inputs and descending psychological inputs are equally involved. The gate control theory posits that there is a gating mechanism in the dorsal horn of the spinal cord that permits or inhibits the transmission of pain impulses (see Figure 18.3).

The dorsal horn receives inputs from nociceptors that it projects to the brain via a neural gate. The dorsal horn also receives information from the brain about the psychological and emotional state of the individual. This information can act as an inhibitory control that closes the neural gate preventing the transmission of the nociceptive impulses and thus modifying the perception of pain. The mechanism operates based on the relative activity of the peripheral nociceptor fibres and the descending cortical fibres. Pain impulses must reach conscious awareness before pain is experienced. If awareness can be prevented, the experience of pain is decreased, eliminated or deferred.

The gate control theory has been an influential theory that continues to inform theoretical and empirical work. Gate control theory offered substantial explanatory power by acknowledging a role for descending control and psychological, social and behavioural factors. However, the absence of any direct evidence of a 'gate' in the spinal cord is a problem. Also, gate control theory is unable to explain several chronic pain problems, such as phantom limb pain.

Melzack (1999; see also Melzack and Katz, 2014) updated gate control theory by describing a 'body-self neuromatrix', in place of the gate. The body-self neuromatrix is a proposal that pain

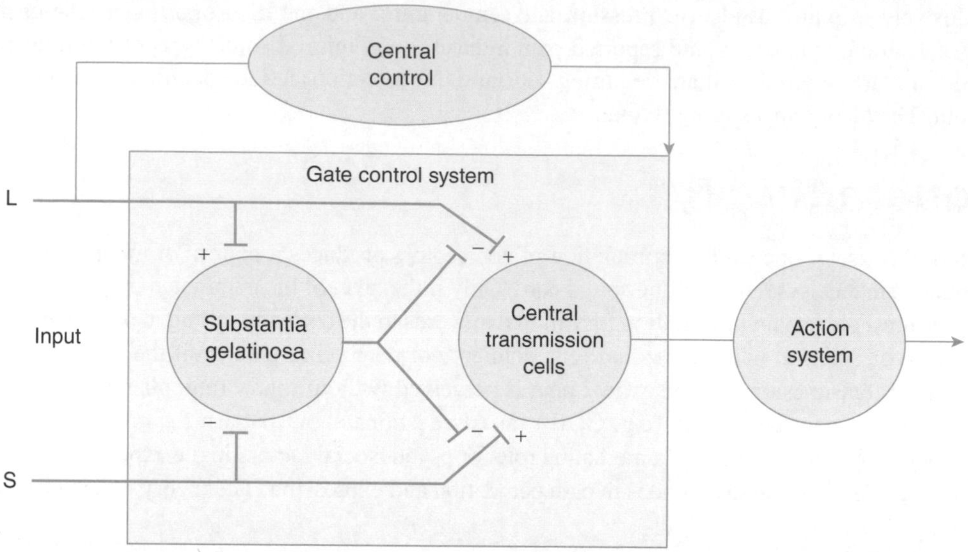

Figure 18.3 The Melzack–Wall gate control theory of pain

Source: Melzack and Wall (1965: 975), Figure 4

is a multidimensional experience produced by characteristic 'neurosignature' patterns of nerve impulses generated by a widely distributed neural network in the brain. These neurosignatures may be triggered by sensory inputs or generated independently of them. Pain is produced by a 'widely distributed neural network in the brain rather than directly by sensory input evoked by injury, inflammation or other pathology' (Melzack, 1999: 880).

Pain is the output of this neural network determined by sensory, cognitive, affective, experiential and genetic influences, as indicated in Figure 18.1. Melzack (1999) claims that the new 'theory' of a 'neuromatrix' provides an explanation for phantom limb pain and pain experience more generally. However, the 'theory' consists of the familiar black box type model of overlapping circles with some arrows pointing at them, which seems incredibly vague, and one might ask, what exactly is the 'theory' saying and which predictions does it make? It is a truism that pain experience must be coded in the nervous system. Using the definitions and terminology of Chapter 1, the 'neuromatrix' is not a theory but a framework summarizing one knowledgeable scientist's ideas about pain. A 'work in progress' is a phrase that springs to mind. There appear to be no definite predictions that can be based upon it, which means that the search for the neural networks of pain will go on but without any specific guidance from this particular approach.

NEURAL CORRELATES OF PAIN

What kind of neural networks exist in the brain that may help to explain how pain is coded? Are differences in self-reported pain associated with measurable neural differences? Coghill et al. (2003)

used psychophysical ratings to define pain sensitivity, and functional magnetic resonance imaging (fMRI) to assess brain activity. They found positive evidence that individuals who were more sensitive to pain stimuli exhibited more frequent and more robust pain-induced activation of the primary somatosensory cortex, anterior cingulate cortex, and prefrontal cortex than did insensitive individuals. Coghill et al. identified objective neural correlates of subjective differences, validating the use of self-reported pain from introspection as a method of communicating a first-person experience.

BOX 18.1
KEY STUDY: HOW CAN WE KNOW WHEN ANOTHER PERSON REALLY EXPERIENCES PAIN?

First-person introspection is necessary for communicating pain experience to a third-person observer. Therefore can we ever be sure they are not fabricating? This study by Coghill et al. (2003) identified the neural correlates of an individual's subjective experience of pain. Seventeen healthy volunteers (eight women and nine men of mean age 26) participated in a psychophysical and fMRI study of individual differences in pain sensitivity. Thermal stimuli were delivered and assessed with a ten-unit mechanical VAS for pain intensity. Thirty-two stimuli (35°C, 43–49°C, 5-s duration) were applied to their non-dominant ventral forearm. Each participant underwent functional imaging during thermal stimulation of the skin of the right lower leg. For painful stimulation, five 30-s duration epochs of 49°C stimulation were interleaved with six 30-s duration epochs of 35°C stimulation. At the end of each 330-s series, participants provided a rating of pain intensity. Participants were assigned to a high- (mean VAS rating = 7.43), moderate- (mean VAS rating = 4.44), or low-sensitivity (mean VAS rating = 2.43) sub-group. To identify brain regions that were activated more frequently in the high-sensitivity individuals, the frequency map of the low-sensitivity group was subtracted from that of the high-sensitivity group.

Cortical regions involved in sensation, attention and affect were activated more frequently in pain sensitive individuals than in those who were insensitive. The most robust difference between high-sensitivity and low-sensitivity sub-groups was located within a portion of the anterior cingulate cortex, where 6/6 of the highly sensitive volunteers, but none of the insensitive volunteers, displayed statistically significant activation. This study shows that individuals with similar subjective reports of pain evoke similar patterns of activation magnitude, suggesting that people can accurately represent their conscious experience via introspection.

Source: Coghill et al. (2003)

On the other hand, Mouraux et al. (2011) found that the largest part of the fMRI responses elicited by phasic nociceptive stimuli reflected non nociceptive-specific cognitive processes, i.e. nociceptive and non-nociceptive stimuli triggered overlapping sets of brain activity. The search for nociceptive-specific brain activities continues. Meanwhile, millions of chronic pain patients deserve better health care and support. Enter the health psychologists.

PSYCHOLOGICAL FACTORS IN CLINICAL PRACTICE

Many psychosocial factors have been investigated in relation to pain and these appear to exert independent effects on the experience of pain. The most significant determinant of pain chronicity appears to be the level of impact on activities of daily living, the functional disability associated with the pain. While the role of psychological factors in the experience of pain is now generally accepted, discussion of psychological inputs to pain is likely to provoke passionate responses and/or denials from sufferers, who fear invalidation of their very real experiences as 'all in the mind'. Health professionals need to be sensitive to this fear and present psychological issues skilfully, in ways that cannot be interpreted as invalidating the experience of the individual. Eccleston (2001) provided a helpful set of guidelines for the clinical care of a patient with pain (Table 18.2).

Table 18.2 Using psychological factors in clinical practice

Vigilance to pain	Patients are distracted by the pain and are urged to react. Pain patients will have impaired concentration as they are being interrupted constantly by an aversive stimulus. Keep all communications clear and brief. Repeat key points often. Expect patients to talk about the pain often, as it is being brought repeatedly into attentional focus for them. This is not a sign of a somatization disorder or hypochondria
Avoidance	Patients will naturally avoid pain and painful procedures. Be aware that this will occur and plan for it. Painful treatments will be avoided and patients will compensate for any disability caused by avoidance (e.g. shifted body weight distribution). If a habitual pattern of avoidance develops, this may lead to chronic pain. Patients must be given an understanding that pain does not necessarily equal damage. A credible medical authority must deliver this message
Anger	Patients with pain may shout at you, abuse you and generally be hostile to you. If they are hostile to you they have probably been hostile to everyone. Most often this will have nothing to do with you, and you will need to understand that anger normally means extreme frustration, distress and possibly depression. Anger functions to push people away and isolate a person. The angry pain patient is therefore less likely to have received or heard any information about their problems and be more confused than the non-angry patient

Involve the patient	First, assess the patient's normal way of coping with pain by simply asking how he or she has coped with predictable pain, such as a visit to the dentist. Second, match your strategy to the patient's preference. If the patient needs information, inform them how much pain they may expect to feel, what it may feel like and, critically, for how long (if this information is known). Always slightly overestimate the time rather than underestimate it. Finally, if possible, involve the patient in the delivery of any pain management strategy
Make sense of the pain	Always ask the patient what they know and fear about the cause of the pain, the meaning of the pain and the time course of the pain. Expect the unexpected. What makes sense to one person is nonsense to another. What matters is that it is their understanding, not yours, that will inform their behaviour. Uncertain diagnoses or unknown diagnoses will lead to increased vigilance to pain and increased symptom reporting
Consistency	Develop a consistent approach to clinical information, patient instruction and patient involvement within pain management. Practice should be consistent over time for each patient and from each member of the pain team

Source: Eccleston (2001). Reproduced by permission

COGNITIONS AND EMOTIONS

Cognitions influence and interact with our **emotions** to produce pain-related behaviour. An individual's cognitions influence the experience of pain, particularly the appraisal of situations for their significance and meaning (e.g. association of pain and sexual pleasure for masochists). Three aspects of cognition that have received attention in relation to pain are attention, interpretation with or without dysfunctional thinking, and coping style.

Increased attention to pain has been associated with increased pain perception. Pain may demand attention, reducing the ability to focus on other competing activities and therefore increasing pain perception. This may explain why distraction techniques are useful in combating pain. However, the role of attention may differ for acute and chronic pain. In acute pain, taking attention away from pain (e.g. via distraction) appears to be associated with reduced anxiety and depression whereas it has an opposite effect for chronic pain patients, for whom attending to rather than avoiding the pain may be more adaptive.

Dysfunctional thoughts, attitudes and beliefs about pain are automatic patterns of thinking that block the attainment of an individual's goals (e.g. participating in work or social activity). A major form of dysfunctional thinking that influences the pain experience is **catastrophizing** (e.g. 'It's hopeless, pain has ruined my life, I can't cope, it will never get better'). Catastrophic thinking has been found to increase likelihood of chronicity, level of perceived intensity and disability, and even to have a small association with pain onset (e.g. Crombez et al., 2003). Other dysfunctional thoughts include negative mental bias, discounting the positive, fortune telling and magnification.

Cognitive coping styles are strategies an individual uses to attempt to deal with their pain. They can be divided into active and passive coping. Both can be functional or dysfunctional.

Active coping might include keeping oneself busy or taking recreational drugs, which could easily become dysfunctional. Passive coping might include resting, which would be useful in the early stages of pain but could become dysfunctional if continued for too long. In general, active coping styles have been found to be associated with improved coping, reduced pain intensity and improved recovery rates. However, McCracken and Eccleston (2003) suggest that acceptance of pain and its incorporation into one's sense of self appears to be an adaptive cognitive technique for chronic pain. Specific coping techniques are detailed below under pain management.

LEARNING: PREVIOUS EXPERIENCE AND CONDITIONING

Previous experience of pain is a significant factor in current pain experience. Both **classical** and **operant conditioning** have been implicated in the aetiology of chronic pain via the association of behaviour and pain. In classical conditioning theory a particular situation or environment may become associated with pain (e.g. the dentist) and therefore provoke increased anxiety and pain perception. Jamner and Tursky (1987) reported that even the words used by migraine sufferers to describe their pain appear to reinforce the experience by provoking stronger physiological responses than non-pain words. In operant conditioning theory, pain stimuli are perceived as a sensation and an unpleasant affect that generally evokes responses like grimacing or limping, demonstrating that the person is in pain. Pain behaviours become conditioned responses through positive (e.g. attention, medication, time off work) and negative reinforcements (e.g. disapproval of others, loss of earnings). Pain behaviours may be functional and appropriate (e.g. removing hand from a burning source of heat), or they may be less functional and therefore pain maintaining (e.g. avoidance, alcohol).

SECONDARY GAINS

The role of secondary gains in the development and maintenance of pain and illness behaviours has been described. Secondary gain relates to social rewards accruing from the demonstration of pain behaviours (e.g. receiving attention, financial benefits, time off work). These secondary gains are thought to reinforce pain behaviours and thus maintain the condition. For example, receipt of financial disability compensations has been associated with slower return to work and increased pain. However, this may actually reflect that those in receipt of compensation can allow themselves appropriate time to recover and says nothing about the quality of life of those who returned to work earlier. For many individuals, pain results in the loss of jobs, social contact, leisure activities, valued identities, reduced incomes and concomitant reduced standard of living. Such losses are very real and distressing and are often associated with substantial hardships, lowered mood and loss of self-esteem, unlikely to be outweighed by incidental benefits.

MOOD

The most common moods that have been associated with pain are anxiety and depression. Where these moods are present, pain appears to be increased. It has been reported that acute pain increases anxiety but once pain is decreased through treatment the anxiety also decreases, which can cause further decreases in the pain – a cycle of pain reduction. Alternatively, chronic pain remains unalleviated by treatment and therefore anxiety increases, which can further increase the pain, creating a cycle of pain increase. Research has shown that anxiety increases pain perception in children with migraine and people with back pain and pelvic pain (McGowan et al., 1998).

Anxiety is normally a result of fear. Pain-related fear can be specific or general (e.g. 'The pain is going to get worse' or 'What will the future be like?'). The FAM of pain suggests that fear of pain amplifies perception and leads to pain avoidance behaviours in some people, especially those with a propensity to catastrophic thinking (Vlaeyen and Linton, 2000). This cycle results in pain experience and behaviours becoming separated from pain sensation through exaggerated pain perception. A prospective study by Klenerman et al. (1995) found fear-avoidance variables correctly predicted future outcome in 66% of patients. A more recent prospective study (Linton et al., 2000) also found that higher baseline scores for fear-avoidance in a non-pain population were associated with double the likelihood of reporting back pain in the following year and a significantly increased risk of reduced physical functioning.

While correlations between mood states and pain have been found, the causal direction and the nature of the relationships remain unclear. Most recent work appears to indicate that negative mood states are an outcome of chronic pain rather than a cause.

FEAR-AVOIDANCE MODEL

The fear-avoidance model (FAM) explains how individuals develop chronic musculo-skeletal pain as a result of avoidance of activities based on their fear of pain (Lethem et al. in 1983). This model helps to explain how individuals experience pain *despite the absence of pathology*. If an individual experiences acute pain and manages the situation by using avoidant behaviour, a lack of pain increase reinforces this behaviour. However, this avoidant behaviour causes the individual to decrease exercise, which may in turn lead to increased disability (Figure 18.4).

Vlaeyen and Linton (2000) explained how and why some individuals with musculo-skeletal pain develop a chronic pain syndrome using the FAM of exaggerated pain perceptions. 'Confrontation' and 'avoidance' are postulated as the two extreme responses to the fear of pain. While the former leads to the reduction of fear over time, avoidance leads to the maintenance or even exacerbation of fear. Possible precursors of pain-related fear include negative appraisal of internal and external stimuli, negative affectivity, and anxiety sensitivity. Subsequently, a number of fear-related processes including escape and avoidance behaviours resulting in poor behavioural performance, hypervigilance to internal and external illness information, muscular

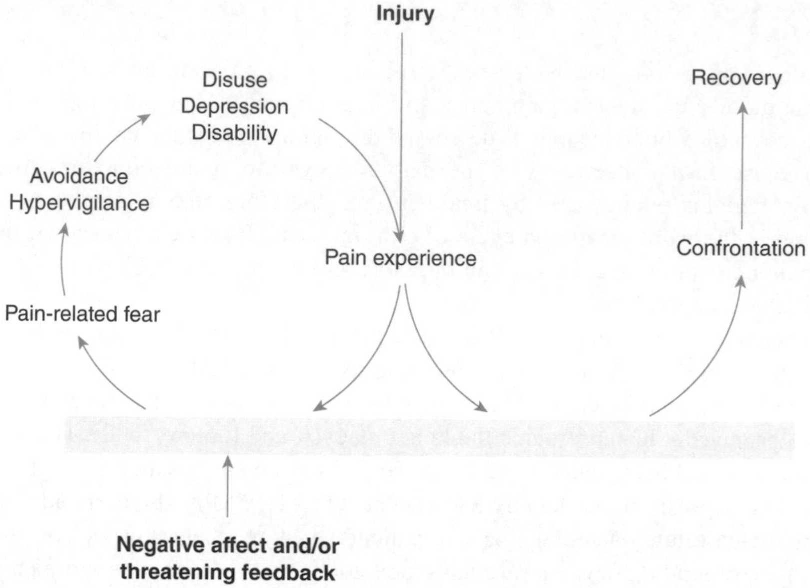

Figure 18.4 The FAM. If pain, from an injury or other cause, is interpreted as threatening (pain catastrophizing), fear evolves – which leads to avoidance behaviours and hypervigilance to bodily sensations. This may lead to disability, disuse and depression. The latter will maintain the pain experience, fuelling a vicious circle of increasing fear and avoidance. In non-catastrophizing patients, no pain-related fear and rapid confrontation with daily activities is likely to occur, leading to fast recovery. Pain catastrophizing is assumed also to be influenced by negative affectivity and threatening illness information

Source: Vlaeyen and Linton (2000)

reactivity, and physical disuse in terms of deconditioning and guarded movement. Vlaeyen and Linton (2000) concluded that: 'Pain-related fear and avoidance appear to be an essential feature of the development of a chronic problem for a substantial number of patients with musculo-skeletal pain.' A substantial body of evidence to date supports the FAM of chronic pain. Waddell et al. (1993) developed the 'Fear-Avoidance Beliefs Questionnaire' (FABQ) to investigate the role of fear-avoidance beliefs in chronic LBP and disability.

Chronic musculo-skeletal pain relates to impaired health related quality of life, disability indices and health risk behaviours. Patients with chronic pain report lower scores on several factors related to quality of life compared to controls and other patient groups. In a study of over 1,000 participants, patients with back pain and patients with multiple pain localizations reported the lowest quality of life, pain catastrophizing showing the strongest association with decreased quality of life, even stronger than pain intensity (Lamé et al., 2005). Beliefs about pain – pain catastrophizing – were the biggest single factor in the quality of life scores. Across all eight domains, from physical to mental, those who catastrophized pain more (i.e. those who tended to have exaggerated negative reactions) scored significantly lower. This effect was even stronger than the actual intensity of pain itself. These results emphasize the important role that a person's psychological reaction to pain can play. How people respond to pain is an important factor in the transition from an acute painful episode to a chronic experience.

Wertli et al. (2014) carried out a systematic review of RCTs that suggested that fear-avoidance beliefs are associated with poor treatment outcome in patients with LBP of less than six months. Patients with strong fear-avoidance beliefs are more likely to improve when fear-avoidance beliefs are addressed in treatments than when these beliefs are ignored, and treatment strategies should be modified if fear-avoidance beliefs are present. The findings of Wertli et al. (2014) support the FAM in suggesting that early treatment, including interventions to reduce fear-avoidance beliefs, may avoid delayed recovery and chronicity.

Social interaction has critical influence in experience and expression of pain, particularly during early development. Children's and adolescents' cognitions and beliefs about pain, including fear-avoidance beliefs, develop within the family context. Asmundson et al. (2011) amended the FAM for paediatric populations. The paediatric model recognizes distinct fear/escape and anxiety/avoidance pathways and increases the possible influences of predispositional and current psychological factors. The paediatric FAM emphasizes the two-way relationship between parental pain management behaviour (e.g. protectiveness, solicitousness), parent psychological responses (e.g. parent catastrophizing, anxiety sensitivity, general distress) and child/adolescent psychological responses (e.g. catastrophizing, acceptance, anxiety sensitivity) in influencing child/adolescent escape and avoidance behaviours. In this paediatric model, both child/adolescent and parent psychological responses encompass the individual's overt expression of pain and/or fear. The child/adolescent escape and avoidance behaviours can directly impact parent psychological responses and, indirectly, through parent psychological responses, impact parent pain management behaviours. Furthermore, the model includes the likely effect that parent pain management behaviours (e.g. removing children and adolescents from pain-inducing activities) would have on child/adolescent escape and avoidance behaviours.

Crombez et al. (2012) argue that the FAM needs to be extended by adopting a motivational perspective on chronic pain and disability. They propose that the next generation of the FAM needs to adopt an explicit motivational perspective built around goals and self-regulatory processes. This might yield a better understanding of how the disruptiveness of pain to an individual's life goals can be overcome in successful problem solving, moving away from efforts to remove pain to fostering acceptance and palliation.

BOX 18.2
CLINICAL CASE STUDY: CHRONIC PAIN RESPONSE AND REDUCED QUALITY OF LIFE FOLLOWING AN ACCIDENTAL INJURY

A woman, Miss D, aged 75, was a spectator at a yacht race where she was struck at close quarters with a piece of fast-moving shrapnel from a starting cannon. Fortunately, the physical injury itself was slight, leaving a small red mark in close proximity to a scar from a cancer operation on her right breast. However, the trauma would bring profound changes to Miss D's quality of life.

A health psychologist at a multidisciplinary pain clinic diagnosed Miss D as suffering from a **chronic pain** syndrome as a direct consequence of the accident. This syndrome was triggered initially by an intense fear that she would suffer a recurrence of breast cancer. While this fear may seem irrational, for Miss D it was a very palpable consequence of being struck with some force.

The mechanism for the development of the chronic pain syndrome can be explained by the FAM. Since the accident, Miss D progressively decreased her activity levels to avoid the pain that was mysteriously appearing in different parts of her body. This complex of unexplained pain led to a vicious circle of pain–fear–avoidance of activity–more pain.

Miss D gave up many of her normal daily physical activities, which included walking, cycling, yoga and dancing. Starting with the trauma, triggering her fear of cancer recurrence, her consequent avoidance of activity to prevent pain, hyper-vigilance to internal and external illness information, sleeplessness, disuse of her body, depression and finally progressive disability. The quality of life for Miss D had been significantly lowered by the incident and her suffering seemed likely to continue until a suitable treatment could be identified. Cognitive behavioural therapy and graded exercise were offered and these led to a partial recovery. However, following legal compensation and treatment, Miss D believes that she will never make a full recovery from what was an unlucky 'wrong place at the wrong time' chance event.

INTERVENTIONS

Before the complex and multidimensional nature of pain had been accepted, pain was treated through the administration of analgesic drugs, surgery and rest. Today pain management programmes seek to address the pain experience utilizing psychological and physical interventions, with considerable emphasis on psychology, and weaning patients off opiates. The historical aim of pain management was to eliminate pain. More recently the aims have shifted towards acceptance of pain, reducing pain perception, improving coping ability, increasing functional ability, and decreasing drug reliance and distress. Many commonly used pain management strategies are listed in Table 18.3.

Table 18.3 Common pain management strategies

Behavioural	Cognitive	Pharmacological	Physical	Other
Operant conditioning	Cognitive restructuring	Non-opioid analgesics	Surgical	Hypnosis
Contingency management	Cognitive coping skills training, e.g. distraction	Paracetamol, NSAIDs, e.g. ibuprofen, aspirin	Transcutaneous electrical nerve stimulation (TENS)	Other alternative therapies, e.g. Reiki, Chinese medicine, music therapy
Graded exercise	Acceptance	Opioid analgesics: morphine and derivatives, e.g. codeine	Acupuncture, physiotherapy, heat and cold	Support groups
Biofeedback	Imagery	Local anaesthetics	Vibration, massage, aromatherapy	Internet advice
Autogenic training	Meditation and prayer	Indirect action drugs, e.g. sedatives, anti-depressants, tranquillizers	Spinal cord stimulation	Self-help books
Relaxation	Information	Placebos	Reflexology	Spiritual, including prayer
Progressive muscle relaxation	Stress management	Self-medications, e.g. cannabis, alcohol, heroin	Mobility-enhancing exercise	

Whether prescribed by health professionals or independently adopted by the individual, any pain management strategy has the potential to improve the situation (e.g. numbing pain sensations with drugs or improving mood with aromatherapy). Equally any strategy can worsen the situation, as with medication side effects or lowered mood induced by substance abuse. It is important that an individual's own attempts at self-management are respected and that health professionals work in partnership with the individual to identify the optimum programme for that individual.

Behavioural Strategies

Most behavioural strategies are based upon operant learning processes, like using operant conditioning in which pain behaviours are ignored (negative reinforcement) and improved activity is praised (positive reinforcement). Conditioning is integral to contingency management. Typically this is a 2–6-week inpatient programme during which nursing staff would ignore medication requests, reinforce targeted 'well' behaviours, introduce increasing exercise quotas, and employ a fixed-schedule 'pain cocktail'. The pain cocktail delivers medication within a strong tasting masking fluid that allows medication dosages to be reduced without the patient noticing. While such programmes have had good (even dramatic) short-term results, they have been less successful in maintaining such gains, possibly due to non-generalization outside the hospital environment. It is rare for programmes today to focus solely on conditioning methods.

Graded exercise strategies involve setting a starting level of activity that the person can manage and then developing a schedule to gradually increase the length of time and intensity of the exercise. The schedule allows the person to gain the confidence to handle each new level before the next increment.

Cognitive Strategies

Cognitive strategies work on the principle that our cognitions (thoughts, beliefs, etc.) are responsible for the consequences of events, not the event itself, and if these cognitions can be changed, the consequence(s) will also change. In relation to pain management, cognitive strategies aim to help the individual identify and understand their cognitions and their connection with their experience of pain and then change negative cognitions to improve it. This includes teaching individuals to identify and challenge distorted thinking (e.g. catastrophizing) – a process known as cognitive restructuring, an active coping technique that promotes the internal attribution of positive changes.

While coping strategies can be helpful, there is growing evidence that pain control efforts directed at uncontrollable pain can come to dominate an individual's life and distance them from important and valued aspects of their lives like family, friends and work. McCracken et al. (2004) described acceptance as an acknowledgement of reality (i.e. pain is present, persistent and not easily controlled) and a willingness to persist in valued activities in spite of pain-related sensations, thoughts and related feelings. They found pain acceptance was associated with better work status, lower reports of pain and lower pain-related anxiety, avoidance behaviour, depression and disability, independent of pain intensity.

Morley et al. (1999) carried out a meta-analysis of 25 randomized controlled trials of CBT and behaviour therapy for chronic pain in adults, excluding headache. CBT showed significant and fairly large effect sizes on pain measures greater than alternative active treatments for pain experience, cognitive coping and appraisal (positive coping measures), and reduced behavioural expression of pain. Tatrow and Montgomery (2006) reviewed cognitive behavioural therapy techniques for distress and pain in a meta-analysis of CBT techniques with breast cancer patients.

The results showed that CBT techniques have significant impact on distress and pain, with 62% and 69% of breast cancer patients in the CBT groups reporting less distress and less pain respectively, relative to the control groups.

Imagery

Imagery involves forming and maintaining pleasant, calming or coping image in the mind. In guided imagery attention is guided away from an undesirable sensation or mood (e.g. pain) by another person who verbally describes the image while the patient relaxes. Most imagery involves relaxation and employs images of a peaceful, safe, pain-free place, which the individual focuses upon while relaxing. The person may also be guided to visualize energy flowing into their body and pain flowing out. The benefits derived from this type of imagery are probably due to relaxation and distraction effects. Alternatively, confrontational imagery may be employed, for example visualizing white blood cells as an army attacking the source of pain (e.g. a tumour). Imagery has been found to be effective for the treatment of pain. The benefits of imagery may relate to relaxation, distraction effects and an active stance increasing feelings of self-efficacy. As imagery generally involves elements of relaxation it is unclear what unique and independent effects it has. Syrjala et al. (1995) compared relaxation and imagery with cognitive behavioural training to reduce pain during cancer treatment in a controlled clinical trial. Results confirmed that patients who received either relaxation and imagery alone or patients who received the package of cognitive behavioural coping skills reported less pain than patients. Adding cognitive behavioural skills to the relaxation with imagery did not further improve pain relief.

Meditation also frequently forms part of relaxation training and involves the individual focusing their attention on a simple stimulus, such as a meaningless monosyllable or disyllabic sound repeated slowly and continuously (aloud or in their head), to the exclusion of all other stimuli. Prayer is another common coping strategy patients have reported to be helpful in response to pain, including headaches, neck pain and back pain (McCaffery et al., 2004). Both meditation and prayer inherently involve some distraction and possibly aspects of relaxation, although this is far from consistent.

Information provision has been shown to reduce pain reports and intensity, possibly by alleviating the fear and anxiety of not knowing what to expect for acute and post-operative pain (Williams et al., 2004). The widespread interest in self-help literature, Internet information and support groups may be indicative of the desire of people in pain to understand their experience, what to expect and potential treatment options.

Cognitive Behavioural Therapy and Mindfulness-Based Methods

Cognitive behavioural therapy (CBT) utilizes the full range of cognitive and behavioural techniques already described in individualized programmes that emphasize relapse prevention strategies. The literature on CBT and pain suggests considerable promise as an effective treatment for pain in adults (Eccleston et al., 2002). It forms the major component of most current pain management programmes. Improved mood, affect, function and coping have been associated with CBT in up to 85% of pain patients. While there is some support for the efficacy of CBT for the control of headache pain in children, there is a paucity of research relating to other pain conditions in children, as well as CBT for pain in the elderly and people with intellectual or communication difficulties, probably as it may be assumed not to be an appropriate treatment option for these groups. acceptance and commitment therapy (ACT) and mindfulness-based approaches, which can be seen as sub-types of CBT, may hold more potential for future progress (McCracken and Vowles, 2014).

Another approach is based on **mindfulness**. The concept follows the Buddhist tradition of living in the present. Mindfulness is the practice of 'observing' physical symptoms, emotions or thoughts. The goal is to change how pain is experienced and the influences it exerts on behaviour. Brown and Ryan (2003) developed a Mindful Attention Awareness Scale (MAAS) containing items such as: 'I find it difficult to stay focused on what is happening in the present', 'I rush through activities without being really attentive to them', 'I find myself preoccupied with the future or the past'. In a study of chronic pain, McCracken et al. (2007) found that mindfulness was associated with measures of depression, pain-related anxiety, physical, psychosocial and 'other' disability. In each instance greater mindfulness was associated with better functioning.

The results from systematic reviews are mixed. Rajguru et al. (2014) found that mindfulness meditation has minimal effects on chronic pain. Better trials with better controls and larger samples are necessary before strong conclusions can be drawn

Pharmacological Strategies

Various analgesics and anaesthetics are prescribed for the treatment of pain. Anaesthetics (local or central) are used to numb the sensation of pain. The identification of endogenous opioid mechanisms have confirmed the status of opioid analgesics as an effective pain treatment. However, the associated perceived high risk of addiction has resulted in their use being restricted to severe pain cases like cancer, a perception challenged by the findings from studies of patient-controlled analgesia and low dose opioid treatment that suggest the risk of addiction may not be very high (e.g. Urban et al., 1986). Non-opioid analgesics, NSAIDs (non-steroidal anti-inflammatory drugs) and drugs that control pain indirectly (e.g. antidepressants, sedatives) are commonly used. Drugs with indirect effects may be beneficial due to their action on higher brain regions, modulating the downward transmission of pain, or due to their modulating effects on negative mood states.

Another aspect relating to drugs is the placebo effect. It has been shown that substantial pain relief occurs in about 50% of patients when they are treated with an inert compound rather than the drug they are expecting, often equalling the relief felt by those receiving the actual medication (Melzack and Wall, 1982/1988). The effect is strongest with high doses, when it is injected, and depends upon the individual believing they are receiving a pain-relieving substance. Unsurprisingly, the effect rapidly declines with repeated use: you cannot fool all of the people all of the time!

In addition to prescribed drug treatments many individuals self-medicate with recreational drugs like alcohol and cannabis to alleviate their pain. However, there is considerable anecdotal evidence for cannabis as an effective pain control treatment, and an endogenous cannabinoid pain control system has now been identified. This system functions as a parallel but distinct mechanism from the opioid system in modulating pain (Notcutt, 2004). Cannabinoids have been authorized for the treatment of pain and other conditions in a number of countries and states, including the Netherlands, many states in the USA and the UK. While current research may result in new cannabinoid-based NSAID-like treatments in the future, problems with the restricted range of dosages that allow pain control before producing psychotropic effects, and concerns about the incidental condoning of recreational cannabis use, mean this is far from being certain. The informal use of cannabis for pain control and its interaction with other pain control strategies warrants further investigation (Eisenberg, Ogintz and Almog, 2014).

Physical Strategies

Surgical control of pain mainly involved cutting the pain fibres to stop pain signal transmission. However, it provided only short-term results and the risks associated with surgery mean it is no longer viewed as a viable treatment option (Melzack and Wall, 1982/1988).

Physiotherapy may be used to increase mobility and correct maladjusted posture, encourage exercise and movement (often despite pain), and education. In addition individuals may be taught safe ways to function (e.g. stand up, sit down, lift objects). Physiotherapy is about maintaining mobility, increasing function and helping the individual manage their lives (e.g. Eccleston and Eccleston, 2004).

An additional strategy is the promotion of mobility-enhancing exercise to help retain and improve physical function and prevent lack of mobility from exacerbating pain problems. General practitioners can refer pain patients to specialist rehabilitation classes at local fitness centres, which has shown some success for older people with musculo-skeletal disorders (Avlund et al., 2000).

Other Strategies and Approaches

There are many other strategies and alternative therapies that individuals use in their efforts to deal with their pain. Acupuncture has been around for centuries and while the mechanisms by which it produces beneficial effects are not well understood it does appear to exert substantial analgesic effects (World Health Organization, 2003). This may derive from the incidental involvement of counter-stimulation, placebo effects, distraction and relaxation, as well as the release of natural pain-relieving endorphins.

There is evidence that hypnosis has beneficial effects for the treatment of acute (e.g. childbirth) and chronic pain (e.g. cancer-related) conditions. Hypnosis involves relaxation, assurances of pain reduction, distraction, and cognitive restructuring (via guided imagery), and may include an altered state of consciousness (Marks et al., 1988). However, it is still uncertain whether hypnosis works over and above placebo. Jensen and Patterson (2006) systematically reviewed controlled trials of hypnotic treatment of chronic pain. The findings indicated that hypnotic analgesia is capable of producing significantly greater decreases in pain relative to no-treatment and non-hypnotic interventions. However, tthe effects of self-hypnosis training on chronic pain are similar to those from progressive muscle relaxation and autogenic training. No published study had, by the time of Jensen and Patterson's review, compared hypnosis to an equally believable placebo or minimally effective pain treatment. This gap in methodology means that definite conclusions, concerning whether hypnotic analgesia treatment is specifically effective beyond its effects on patient expectancy, are lacking.

Crawford et al. (1993) studied the effects of hypnosis on regional cerebral blood flow during ischaemic pain with and without hypnotic analgesia. Using Xe-133 regional cerebral blood flow (CBF) imaging, two male groups with high and low hypnotic susceptibility were compared in waking and after hypnotic induction. During hypnotic analgesia, highly hypnotizable persons showed CBF increases over the somatosensory cortex, while low-hypnotizable persons showed decreases.

Individuals frequently use complementary or alternative therapies (e.g. aromatherapy, Chinese medicine) to combat pain and there is growing support for the belief that they help chronic pain control (e.g. National Institutes of Health, 1997). Again the mechanisms are not well understood and may derive from placebo effects, relaxation, distraction or improved self-efficacy from active coping. Bardia et al. (2006) reviewed complementary and alternative medicine therapies for the relief of cancer pain. The authors reported that: 'Hypnosis, imagery, support groups, acupuncture, and healing touch seem promising, particularly in the short term, but none can be recommended because of a paucity of rigorous trials' (Bardia et al., 2006: 5457).

The widespread use of alternative strategies may reflect dissatisfaction with mainstream approaches. It is important that such strategies are evaluated in independent clinical trials using control groups in conjunction with traditional approaches.

INTERDISCIPLINARY PAIN REHABILITATION PROGRAMME

Originally run as inpatient programmes, today pain management programmes tend to be run in specialist pain management or rehabilitation centres. Interdisciplinary teams may include doctors, nurses, physiotherapists, psychologists, psychiatrists, occupational therapists and counsellors, and provide a range of management techniques usually underpinned by CBT. An interdisciplinary chronic pain rehabilitation programme (IPRP) is a partial-hospitalization programme in which patients with chronic non-cancer pain who are resistant to opiate management, steroid injections, and surgery receive a tailored combination of interventions. Programmes are developed that aim to improve the individual's quality of life by reducing pain as far as possible, increasing activity and coping, restoring function, and promoting self-efficacy and self-management.

The patient receives a full history-taking assessment, education, skills training, exercise schedules, relapse prevention and family work. Multidisciplinary rehabilitation programmes represent the most comprehensive approach to date, by targeting the individual's specific pain experience and tailoring appropriate treatment combinations.

Flor et al. (1992) evaluated the efficacy of 65 studies of multidisciplinary pain treatments for chronic back pain. Multidisciplinary treatments for chronic pain were found to be superior to no treatment, waiting list controls, as well as single-discipline treatments such as medical treatment or physical therapy. The beneficial effects included improvements in pain, mood and behavioural variables such as return to work or use of the health care system. However, the quality of the study designs and study descriptions was marginal and so caution is necessary in interpreting these findings.

Bosy et al. (2010) described a private, intensive eight-week IPRP with a CBT emphasis and the results obtained with a cohort of 338 consecutive patients who completed the programme over a three-year period. Improvements in vocational status occurred in 75% of patients with chronic pain; pain levels reduced by 16%; levels of anxiety and depression were reduced by 13% and 17% respectively; and 61% of patients were able to reduce or eliminate their pain medications.

Vowles et al. (2014) studied acceptance and commitment therapy in 117 completers of an interdisciplinary programme of rehabilitation for chronic pain. A significant change in at least one measure of functioning (depression, pain anxiety, and disability) was achieved by 46.2% of patients. Changes in psychological flexibility were found to mediate changes in disability, depression, pain-related anxiety, number of medical visits, and the number of classes of prescribed analgesics.

A note of caution must be struck about whether such programmes are economically affordable on a mass scale; probably not, according to a health economist, who noted that 'there is still a long way to go to understand the economic implications of interdisciplinary rehabilitation from the perspectives of society, the health insurers, and the patients' (Becker, 2012: 127).

Treatment Issues

Pain management can be a particularly controversial issue. Evidence suggests that in many circumstances pain is under-treated. Some of the reasons for this include inadequate assessment, focus on underlying pathologies, negative stereotypes and erroneous assumptions about certain population groups, addiction fears, the inappropriateness of non-pharmacological treatments and patients' inability to verbalize pain information or requests for medication (e.g. Greenwald et al., 1999). Many medical professionals have their own benchmarks concerning acceptable pain behaviour and medication levels for different conditions. It has also been shown that many prejudices and misconceptions operate in the treatment of pain patients, with various populations (e.g. children, people with communication difficulties and the elderly) being under-treated for pain (Todd et al., 2000). For example, sickle-cell patients are often assumed to be drug addicts and their pain outcries to be drug-seeking behaviour, resulting in inadequate medication being administered. Similarly, pain has only recently been recognized as part of the symptom repertoire of people with HIV infection or AIDS and therefore up to 85% of people with HIV infection or AIDS receive inadequate pain management (Marcus et al., 2000).

Karus et al. (2005) investigated patients' reports of symptoms and their treatment at three palliative care projects servicing individuals with HIV infection or AIDS in Alabama, Baltimore and New York City. Pain, lack of energy, and worry were reported by a majority of patients at all sites, often with a high level of associated distress. However, only four symptoms (pain, nausea, difficulty swallowing and mouth sores) were being treated in half or more of patients at all sites.

Pain is sometimes deemed to be psychogenic, resulting from emotional, motivational or personality problems. However, the distinction between organic and psychogenic pain may have little practical value. A number of diseases where historically pain was not thought to be a valid symptom have subsequently had a physiological basis for pain identified, including multiple sclerosis and HIV and AIDS (e.g. Marcus et al., 2000), so some pain designated as psychogenic may relate to as-yet-undetected or unidentified organic pathology. Health psychologists must endeavour to promote the sensitive and respectful treatment of individuals reporting pain in terms of research, intervention development, and treatment.

FUTURE RESEARCH

1. A testable theory of the neural coding of pain needs to be developed.
2. Long-term, prospective studies are required to further elucidate the relationships between various psychosocial factors and pain, particularly the relative weights of their influence and the identification of relatively homogeneous sub-groups within the chronic pain patient population.
3. Additional research is needed regarding the pain experience of under-represented groups, especially those who are verbally challenged (e.g. babies, older people, people with disabilities, people with a diagnosis of dementia), including development of improved measurement instruments and assessing the efficacy of CBT in these groups.
4. The FAM requires refinement and extension with in-depth investigation of the special needs of children and adolescents and to provide a better understanding of non-psychopathological pain.

SUMMARY

1 Early pain theories proposed that pain was a sensation that involved a direct line of transmission from the pain stimulus to the brain.

2 The growing body of evidence for the psychological mediation of pain saw the development of the gate control theory, and this acknowledged psychosocial influences.

3 The body of research suggests that pain is a complex and multidimensional phenomenon that includes biological, psychological and behavioural components.
4 Recent neuropsychological studies have demonstrated cortical correlates of experienced pain.
5 Many psychological variables that influence the pain experience have been examined, including cognitions, prior experience, conditioning, secondary gains, personality and mood.
6 Particular groups appear to be under-represented in the pain literature, including ethnic minorities, children, the elderly, some disabled people and people with certain medical conditions (e.g. dementia, HIV and CFS).
7 Assessment of pain is difficult and various techniques are used singly or in combination, such as medical examinations, observations, questionnaires, diaries and logs, and interviews.
8 A wide variety of pain management strategies exist. Currently, the most successful approach appears to be tailored programmes that use cognitive behavioural therapies fostering acceptance and the reduction of fear.
9 The assessment and treatment of pain, particularly chronic pain, can be influenced by misconceptions about specific patient groups including ethnic minorities, children, the elderly, some disabled people, and people with rare medical conditions.
10 Health psychologists can make a significant contribution in promoting sensitive and respectful research and treatment for people experiencing long-standing painful conditions.

19 CANCER AND CHRONIC DISEASES

Chronic diseases – such as heart disease, cancer, and diabetes – are the leading causes of death and disability. Adopting healthy behaviors such as eating nutritious foods, being physically active, and avoiding tobacco use can prevent or control the devastating effects of these diseases.

(US Centers for Disease Control and Prevention, 2005)

OUTLINE

In this chapter we consider three life-threatening and disabling diseases: cancer, coronary heart disease and HIV infection and AIDS. In each case we consider five issues: 'What is xx?'; 'Interventions for xx'; 'Living with xx'; 'Adaptation to xx'; and 'Caring for someone with xx'. The contribution of psychosocial interventions for patients suffering from these conditions has been evaluated in systematic reviews. The evidence suggests that psychosocial interventions have not yet demonstrated their full potential. The quality of evaluation research with psychosocial interventions has generally been rather poor and the findings inconclusive. We discuss the importance of end-of-life care and research on the quality of death and dying. Finally, we suggest ways to strengthen the psychological understanding of treatment and care and for improving the quality of death and dying.

GENERAL ISSUES

Chronic illnesses have replaced acute illnesses as the predominant disease pattern over the past 50 years. Greatly improved longevity and higher cancer survival rates have meant an increased

burden of disease caused by conditions such as heart disease, stroke, AIDS, cancer, back pain, diabetes and dementia. As life expectancy of the human population increases, so does the prevalence of diseases of older age. A large proportion of the global burden of disease is caused by a **toxic environment** that encourages health-aversive behaviours and choices. As we saw in Chapter 1, the major risks of underweight (developing countries), overweight and obesity (developed countries), unsafe sex, high blood pressure, alcohol and tobacco (everywhere) account for 30% of the global disease burden. All are consequences of the toxic environment, which is creating a significant proportion of ill health and suffering in the world.

Over 60% of people in developed countries live to at least 70 years of age, compared with only about 30% in developing countries. Of the 45 million deaths among adults worldwide in 2002, 32 million were caused by non-communicable diseases. HIV infection and AIDS has become the leading cause of mortality among adults aged 15–59 years. Unipolar depressive disorders are the leading cause of disability for females.

Chronic illnesses most often strike in middle and older age and, while they can be fatal, most people with a chronic illness live for many years with the condition. As a consequence cardiovascular and coronary heart disease and HIV infection and AIDS are significant causes of disability (see Chapter 1 for figures).

The evidence suggests that personality is a poor predictor of the development of disease (Chapter 12). Health-aversive behaviours, and genetic factors, are the primary determinants of many chronic illnesses. The focus of this chapter will be on the psychological aspects of disease management. Management of fatal or chronic diseases is a principal feature in the lives of 10–15% of the population. This informal care occurs almost invisibly with little recognition or financial support from society at large.

People with serious chronic illnesses have similar concerns and needs (World Health Organization, 2004b). Chronic illness typically involves restrictions on activities of daily living, increases in pain, fatigue, depression and anxiety. Patients must cope with ongoing symptoms, their ambiguity, the life threat involved, and the requirements of treatment. Maintaining effective relationships with health-service personnel and family and friends requires many adaptations (Stanton and Revenson, 2005) and adjustments in lifestyle. Uncertainties over prognosis can cause a great deal of worry and fear. In cancer, prognosis can often be predicted, as there is a short period of evident decline, but in CHD people tend to live with greater disability for longer time, but die suddenly with little warning after a rapid deterioration (World Health Organization, 2004b). In all life-threatening conditions, family members can experience significan emotional, economic and social challenges.

Cancer survival rates are increasing and cancer can be both an acute and a chronic condition. Fear is being reduced. Early detection is the key to improved survival. Over the past 30 years, there has been a 34% reduction in breast cancer mortality (Pearlman, 2014). Breast cancer awareness and awareness of the risk factor of excessive alcohol consumption are increasing.

In the next three sections we review health psychology research and psychosocial interventions relevant to people diagnosed with cancer, CHD, and HIV infection or AIDS. In Table 19.1 key features of the three conditions are compared.

Table 19.1 Comparison of three life-threatening conditions

Feature	Cancer	CHD	HIV infection and AIDS
Preventable	In part	In part	100%
Behavioural risk factors	Smoking, diet, drinking	Diet, smoking, drinking	Unprotected sex
Stigma	Strong	Some	Severe
Onset	Mixed	Slow	Slow
Treatable	Mixed	Mixed	HAART expensive
Prognosis	Mixed	Good	With HAART, good, but not otherwise

CANCER

The study of the psychosocial aspects of cancer care and treatment is referred to as '**psycho-oncology**'. Psycho-oncology is concerned with (1) the psychological responses of patients, families and caregivers to cancer at all stages of the disease, and (2) the psychosocial factors that may influence the disease process. Unfortunately many cancer patients remain untreated owing to **stigmatization** and lack of resources to diagnose, treat and support. Cancer causes anxiety and depression in more than one-third of patients and often affects the sufferer's family emotionally, socially and economically. Inequalities in cancer treatment and care occur across different regions and social groups. In spite of increased publicity, and reduced incidence of breast cancer, breast self-examination has not been proven to prevent cancer (Gøtzsche, 2013).

What is Cancer?

'Cancer' is an umbrella term for more than 100 different but related diseases. Cancer occurs when cells become abnormal and keep dividing and forming more cells without any internal control or order. Normally, cells divide to produce more when the body needs them to remain healthy. However, if cells keep dividing when new cells are not needed, a mass of extra tissue known as a **tumour** or neoplasm forms, which can be benign or malignant. Benign tumours are not cancerous and usually can be removed, and when removed, in most cases, do not re-form. Cells from benign tumours also do not spread to other parts of the body and so benign tumours are rarely life-threatening. In the case of malignant tumours, cancer cells can invade and damage nearby tissues and organs. They can also break away from a malignant tumour and enter the bloodstream or the lymphatic system, forming new tumours in other parts of the body (**metastasis**). This process is described in more detail in Figure 19.1.

Risk factors for cancer are:

- growing older;
- tobacco;
- sunlight, sunlamps and tanning machines, i.e. ultraviolet (UV) radiation;

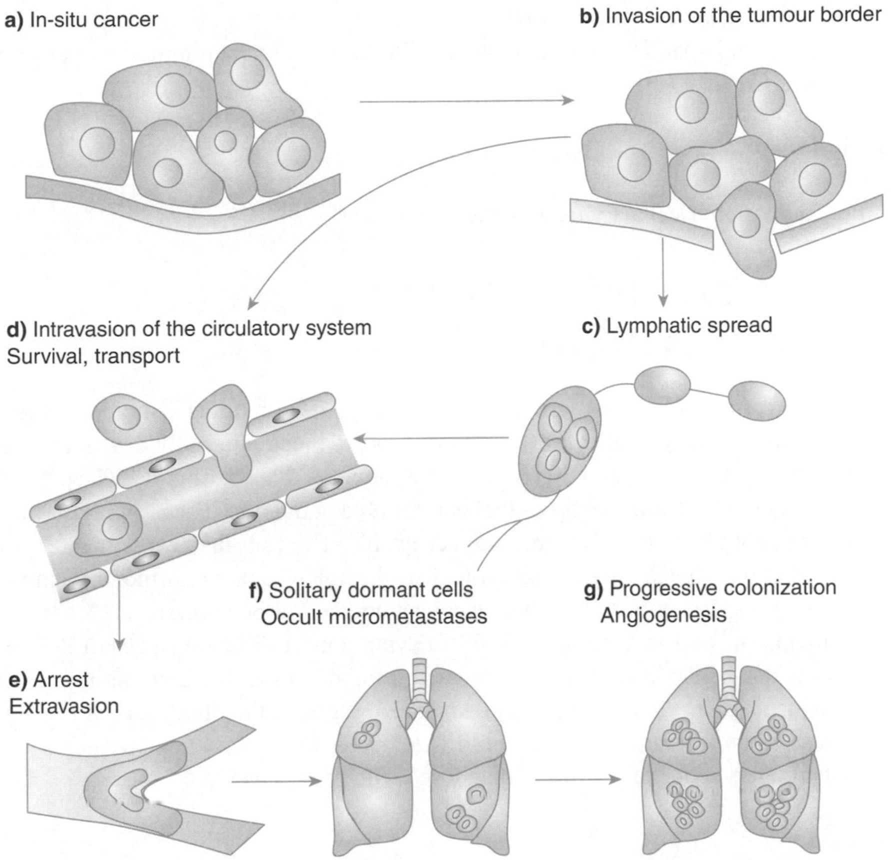

Figure 19.1 A schematic of cancer and the metastatic process: (a) An in-situ cancer surrounded by an intact basement membrane. (b) Invasion requires reversible changes in cell–cell and cell–extracellular-matrix adherence. Metastasizing cells can (c) enter via the lymphatics, or (d) directly enter the circulation. (e) Survival and arrest of tumour cells, and extravasion of the circulatory system. (f) Metastatic colonization of the distant site progresses through single cells and (g) progressively growing, angiogenic metastases

Source: Steeg (2003). Reproduced with permission

- ionizing radiation, e.g. radioactive fallout, radon gas, X-rays;
- certain chemicals and other substances, e.g. asbestos, benzene, benzidine, cadmium, nickel, or vinyl chloride;

- some bacteria (e.g. *helicobacter pylori*);
- some viruses (e.g. hepatitis B virus, human papillomavirus, human immunodeficiency virus, *helicobacter pylori*, and others);
- certain hormones;
- family history of cancer;
- alcohol;
- poor diet, lack of physical activity, or being overweight.

Psychosocial Interventions for Cancer Patients

The purpose of treatment can be to cure the cancer, control it, or treat its symptoms. The type of treatment depends on the type of cancer, the stage of the cancer, and individual factors such as age, health status and the personal preferences of the patient and his/her family. The patient needs to be helped and informed sufficiently to feel comfortable enough to discuss with the care team which treatment choices are most suitable and acceptable. The four major treatments for cancer are surgery, radiation, chemotherapy and biological therapies such as hormone therapies (e.g. tamoxifen), and transplant options (e.g. with stem cell therapy or bone marrow).

Cancer patients suffer from a complex range of symptoms at different stages of their disease. Of these, pain is one of the most distressing symptoms and is often the dominating symptom at time of diagnosis, and also in relapse, and in advanced stages of the disease. Pain is often associated with depression and impaired quality of life (Chapter 18).

Psychosocial interventions for patients diagnosed with cancer include:

counselling;

psychotherapy;

behaviour therapy (e.g. systematic desensitization);

cognitive behavioural therapy;

pain control techniques (see Chapter 18);

biofeedback;

relaxation;

hypnosis;

guided imagery;

music therapy;

art therapy;

group support;

complementary therapies;

yoga and meditation.

Objective evidence of efficacy is mixed, and, overall, not strong. Reviews focus on the four main categories of psychosocial intervention: behavioural therapy (including relaxation, biofeedback and hypnosis); educational therapy (including training in coping skills and providing information to enhance a patient's sense of control); psychotherapy (including counselling); and support groups (which help patients to express their emotions) indicated some limited evidence of efficacy.

Some researchers even extravagantly claimed that their interventions extended their patients' survival but, apart from one highly publicized report, the evidence is non-existent. Spiegel et al. (1989) reported a positive effect of psychosocial treatment on survival of patients with metastatic breast cancer, claiming an increased survival time of about 18 months. Although the findings of this study have never been replicated, it raised many false hopes among cancer sufferers, a false hope that became reinforced by practitioners offering glamorous-sounding but ineffective therapies. Edwards et al. (2004) and Chow et al. (2004) both reported systematic reviews of psychosocial interventions in which effects on survival proved statistically non-significant.

A more justifiable aim has been to use psychosocial interventions to facilitate improved quality of life (QoL). Meyer and Mark's (1995) meta-analysis of 62 studies of different kinds of psychosocial interventions showed significant beneficial effect sizes ranging from 0.19 to 0.28. A meta-analysis by Duijts et al. (2011) of the effects of behavioural and exercise interventions in breast cancer patients and survivors found that physical exercise is an effective intervention to improve fatigue, depression, body-image and QoL.

Henderson et al. (2012) investigated the effects of mindfulness-based stress reduction (MBSR) on psychosocial outcomes and QoL in early-stage breast cancer patients in a randomized trial, in which 172 women, aged 20–65 with stage 1 or 2 breast cancer, were randomly alloted to an eight-week MBSR or a nutrition education programme (NEP) or usual supportive care (UC). MBSR produced a significant improvement in QoL and coping outcomes compared to the NEP, UC, or both, including spirituality at four months, but the differences waned at 12 and 24 months.

Unfortunately, the quality of evaluation research has generally been poor with small samples, poor designs and weak effects that are generally disappointing. Larger-scale evaluations with longer-term follow-up times are needed.

Living with Cancer

There are several aspects of cancer experience that psychological expertise can help to understand, especially pain, fatigue, depression and anxiety. Treatments with chemotherapy (CT) and radiotherapy (RT) tend to be aggressive, and psychosocial function decline before during and after treatment is quite common. In a review of 97 studies, Hess and Chen (2014) reported that approximately one-third of RT patients experienced some form of psychosocial function decline. Their review indicated that anxiety may dissipate after initiation of RT, whereas depression tends to persist throughout and after RT. They reported that severe physical symptoms and time-related factors predicted psychosocial function decline, which can be improved by psychotherapy and interventions aimed to improve patient education. Lack of consistency across studies, however, suggests measurement, conceptual and methodological issues remain unsolved. Hess and Chen (2014) reported that no less than 86 different assessment tools were being used to monitor RT-related psychosocial function decline, with the Hospital Anxiety and Depression Scale (HADS; 25.8%) and the psychiatric interview (22.6%) being most utilized.

Miovic and Block (2007) reviewed evidence that around 50% of patients with advanced cancer met the criteria for a psychiatric disorder, the most common being adjustment disorders (11–35%) and major depression (5–26%). Most clinical assessments of pain, depression and fatigue rely on self-report. A variety of assessment tools is available. The HADS and the EORTC OLQ-C30 have both shown promise for screening treatable unmet needs in patients attending for radiotherapy. However, few instruments exist for children and adolescents, older adults, individuals with cognitive impairments, and individuals from different ethnic and cultural groups. There is also relatively little research on the role played by informal caregivers in the management of symptoms. The most commonly described strategy for improving symptom management involves regular assessment using visual analogue or numerical scales, followed by QoL improvement interventions. Studies on efficacy of interventions on QoL have found positive results.

Eysenbach (2003) explored the impact of the Internet on cancer outcomes. Eysenbach distinguished four areas of Internet use: communication (electronic mail), community (virtual support groups), content (health information on the World Wide Web) and e-commerce. Eysenbach estimated that, in the developed world, 39% of cancer patients were using the Internet, and approximately 2.3 million persons living with cancer worldwide were online. Recent systematic reviews of online support have yielded mixed outcomes (Hong et al., 2012; Kuijpers et al., 2013). A trial by Bantum et al. (2014) reported significantly greater reductions in insomnia and greater increases in vigorous exercise and stretching compared to controls (based on self-reports).

Adaptation to Cancer

A variety of factors have been associated with adaptation to cancer patients, partners and families, and the interactions between the patients and their families. A large amount of research has studied coping styles such as fighting spirit, helplessness/hopelessness, denial and avoidance. This topic has also led to inconsistent findings. Watson et al. (1999) studied the influence of psychological responses on survival in women with early-stage breast cancer. Psychological response was measured by the Mental Adjustment to Cancer (MAC) Scale, the Courtauld Emotional Control (CEC) scale, and the HADS 4–12 weeks and 12 months after diagnosis. The women were followed up for at least five years. There was a significantly increased risk of death from all causes by five years in women with high scores on depression, helplessness and hopelessness. No significant results were found for 'fighting spirit'.

The MAC Scale has been used to measure adaptive coping under the label of 'fighting spirit'. Goodwin et al. (2014) explored adaptation in 275 patients with advanced cancer receiving palliative care by examining the factor structure of the MAC Scale. They found that patients with a desire for hastened death had lower acceptance and positivity while social support was positively associated with acceptance and positivity. Higher scores on acceptance and positivity were associated with reduced odds of a desire for hastened death. The results suggested that adaptation to advanced cancer differs from adaptation to early stage cancer, comprising a general acceptance of the illness and trying to make the most of the time that is left. Individuals with low social support were less likely to evidence appropriate adaptation to their illness.

The recent growth of 'positive psychology' has been perceived as offering scientific confirmation of strongly held cultural beliefs and values. Coyne and Tennen (2010) examined four widely accepted claims in the positive psychology literature regarding adaptational outcomes among individuals living with cancer:

> the role of positive factors, such as a 'fighting spirit' in extending the life of persons with cancer;
>
> effects of interventions cultivating positive psychological states on immune functioning and cancer progression and mortality;
>
> and evidence concerning:
>
> benefit finding;
>
> post-traumatic growth following serious illness such as cancer and other highly threatening experiences.

These claims from positive psychology were all found to be wanting. In particular they noted the:

> incoherence of claims about the adaptational value of benefit finding and post-traumatic growth among cancer patients, and the implausibility of claims that interventions that enhance benefit finding improve the prognosis of cancer patients by strengthening the immune system . . . We urge positive psychologists to rededicate themselves to a positive psychology based on scientific evidence rather than wishful thinking.
>
> (Coyne and Tennen, 2010: 16).

Well said! Much harm can be done by raising false hopes among patients, families and the lay public. Pseudoscience has no place in health care.

Caring for Someone with Cancer

The stress experienced by family members of cancer sufferers can often be high. The condition fosters emotional turmoil, with fear, anxiety, stigma, depression, hopelessness, fatigue, pain, burn-out and insomnia all entering the arena at various stages. The social support provided by immediate family and friends can be a key factor in promoting the patient's adaptation and QoL. The so-called 'caregiver burden' can be high, and interventions are available to support the informal caregiver.

Kroenke et al. (2006) prospectively investigated the role of social networks, social support, and survival after breast cancer diagnosis. Participants were 2,835 women who had been diagnosed with stages 1 to 4 breast cancer between 1992 and 2002. Of these women, 224 deaths (107 of these related to breast cancer) had occurred by the year 2004. Women who were socially isolated before diagnosis had a subsequent 66% increased risk of all-cause mortality and a two-fold increased risk of breast cancer mortality compared with women who were socially integrated. The authors concluded this effect is likely to be caused by their lack of beneficial caregiving from friends, relatives, and adult children.

The US Institute of Medicine (IOM) (2007a) report, *Cancer Care for the Whole Patient: Meeting Psychosocial Health Needs*, concluded that, despite the evidence for the effectiveness of services, cancer care often fails to meet patients' psychosocial needs. One possible reason for this failure is the tendency of cancer care providers to underestimate patients' distress (Fallowfield and Jenkins, 2015) and to not link patients to appropriate services when their needs are identified (Institute of Medicine, 2007b). The IOM report recommends a model for elective delivery of psychosocial services with a five-step sequence of processes:

1. Identify each patient's psychosocial needs.
2. Link patients and families to needed psychosocial services.
3. Support patients and families in managing the illness.
4. Coordinate psychosocial and biomedical care.
5. Follow up on care delivery to monitor the effectiveness of services and make modifications if needed.

Jacobsen (2009) discussed reasons why evidence-based psychosocial care for cancer patients is not more widely promoted and adopted by clinicians. First, there are inconsistent findings attributable, at least in part, to differences in demographic, disease and treatment characteristics of the samples, and the type of outcome assessments employed. Considerable variation also exists across studies in the number and content of sessions for interventions that share the same name, e.g. relaxation training. Inadequate reporting of study methodology and lack of transparency in reports of trials is a problem for anybody wishing to replicate an intervention in their practice (Marks, 2009). Newell et al. (2002) found that only 3% of trials provided sufficient information to permit evaluation of ten indicators of study quality. Methodological issues are common; e.g. the majority of studies fail to account for patients lost to follow-up in the outcome analyses. This means that it is impossible to calculate with accuracy the odds ratio for a treatment compared to the control condition.

Seitz et al. (2009) systematically reviewed psychosocial interventions for adolescent cancer patients. The authors concluded that:

> Taken together, the findings point out that there is a lack of intervention research in psycho-oncology with adolescents. So far, there is only limited evidence for the effectiveness of psychosocial interventions to improve coping with cancer-associated problems in adolescent patients . . . In order to establish more conclusive results, larger samples and interventions particularly designed for adolescent patients ought to be studied.
>
> (Seitz et al., 2009: 683)

CORONARY HEART DISEASE

What is Coronary Heart Disease?

Coronary heart disease (CHD) or coronary artery disease (CAD) occurs when the walls of the coronary arteries become narrowed by a gradual build-up of fatty material called atheroma. **Myocardial infarction (MI)** occurs when one of the coronary arteries becomes blocked by a blood clot and part of the heart is starved of oxygen. It usually causes severe chest pain. A person having a heart attack may also experience sweating, light-headedness, nausea or shortness of breath. A heart attack may be the first sign of CHD in many people. Over time, CHD can weaken the heart muscle and cause heart failure and arrhythmias.

Angina pectoris is the most common form of CHD with 9.8 million people in the USA and 1.98 million in the UK suffering from it. It is characterized by a heavy or tight pain in the centre of the chest that may spread to the arms, necks, jaw, face, back or stomach. Angina symptoms occur when the arteries become so narrow from the atheroma that insufficient oxygen-containing blood can be supplied to the heart muscle when its demands are high, such as during exercise. There are two categories of angina: stable or unstable angina. Stable angina is characterized by chest pain relieved by rest, resulting from the partial obstruction of a coronary artery by atheroma. Unstable angina occurs with lesser degrees of exertion or while at rest. This type increases in frequency and duration and worsens in severity. Unstable angina is an acute coronary syndrome requiring immediate medical attention. This is usually caused by the formation of a blood clot at the site of a ruptured plaque in a coronary artery. If left untreated, it can result in heart attack and irreversible damage to the heart.

Risk factors for CHD include:

- increasing age;
- male sex;
- heredity;
- tobacco smoking;
- high blood cholesterol;

- high blood pressure;
- physical inactivity;
- obesity and overweight;
- diabetes mellitus;
- high alcohol consumption;
- possibly stress/distressed personality;
- possibly depression.

Another alleged risk factor is type D or 'distressed' personality (Denollet et al., 1996). The jury is still out with regard to type D. The size of the effect of type D on prognosis appears to have been overestimated and has decreased as more studies have been conducted (Grande, 2012).

Similarly, depression has yet to be proven as a risk factor for CHD. Nicholson et al. (2006) carried out a meta-analysis of depression among 146,538 participants in 54 observational studies of coronary heart disease. Results need to be adjusted for left ventricular function, a risk factor for CHD, but such results were available in only eight studies. It was concluded that depression has yet to be established as an independent risk factor for CHD because of incomplete adjustment for conventional risk factors and severity of coronary disease.

Interventions for CHD

People with suspected CHD usually undergo several different tests for absolute diagnosis and to determine the best treatment to relieve symptoms. These include stress **exercise tolerance test (ETT)**, **electrocardiogram (ECG)** and **coronary angiogram**. Seeking a diagnosis can be a stressful time for people with suspected CHD and their family and friends. Patients commonly feel apprehension about the procedure and find some parts of the procedure unexpected with doctors' technical language being an obstacle to understanding.

Many people with CHD have to make lifestyle changes and take a regime of medication such as ACE inhibitors, statins, anticoagulant drugs and beta-blockers. Clinical guidelines are not always implemented because of a lack of time for physicians, who only have an average of about 15 minutes to discuss risk factors, lifestyle changes or treatment. This may not be an appropriate time to discuss such issues with a patient who may well feel shocked by the diagnosis of being at risk of CHD and show low levels of compliance with physician advice.

Riesen et al. (2004) acknowledged that, although high rates of compliance with lifestyle changes and lipid-lowering agents are reported in clinical trials, rarely are the findings reproduced in regular practice. They recommended the use of educational materials as well as regular telephone contact to improve compliance. However, further research is needed into the causes of poor compliance and methods of improving adherence with lipid-lowering agents.

People living with angina have increased risk of anxiety and depression. Lewin et al. (2002) evaluated the efficacy of a CBT disease management programme, the **Angina Plan** (AP; Box 19.1), to aid the psychological adjustment of patients with newly diagnosed angina. At six-month follow-up, AP patients showed a significantly greater reduction in anxiety, depression, frequency of angina, use of glyceryl trinitrate and physical limitations. They were also more likely to report a change in diet and they increased their daily walking.

BOX 19.1
THE ANGINA PLAN: A PSYCHOLOGICAL DISEASE MANAGEMENT PROGRAMME FOR PEOPLE WITH ANGINA

The Angina Plan (AP) consists of a patient-held booklet and audio-taped relaxation programme. Before commencing the 30–40-minute AP session, the patient is sent a questionnaire designed to establish if she/he holds any of the common misconceptions about angina (e.g. each episode is a mini-heart attack or angina is caused because your heart is worn out). The patient's partner or a friend is invited to the session.

After blood pressure has been taken and body mass index has been recorded, the AP facilitator discusses any misconceptions that were revealed in the questionnaire with the patient, and if possible his or her partner, in an effort to correct their understanding. Personal risk factors are identified, and personal goals to reduce the risk factors are then set. They are provided with a relaxation tape and encouraged to use it. The Plan also contains written information such as the role of frightening thoughts and misconceptions in triggering adrenaline (epinephrine) release and anxiety and how this can result in poor coping strategies.

The patient is contacted by the facilitator at the end of weeks 1, 4, 8 and 12. During these phone calls, the patient is praised for any success. They are also asked if they want to extend successful goals. Unsuccessful goals can be revisited. Adding procedures that encourage specific implementation intentions to this programme could well improve the success of the AP.

Zetta et al. (2011) carried out a trial to evaluate the AP against standard care (SC) with 218 hospitalized angina patients assessed pre-discharge and six months later. A

(Continued)

(Continued)

structured interview, self-report and physiological measurement were used to assess between-group changes in mood, knowledge and misconceptions, cardiovascular risk, symptoms, QoL and health service utilization. The intention-to-treat analysis found no reliable effects on anxiety and depression at six months. However, Zetta et al. found that AP participants reported increased knowledge, less misconceptions, reduced body mass index (BMI), increased self-reported exercise, less functional limitation, and improvements in general health perceptions and social and leisure activities compared to those receiving SC.

Source: Lewin et al. (2002)

Other forms of invasive treatment may be necessary when medication alone does not relieve angina. Referral to a cardiologist or a heart surgeon may be required for further treatment to gain effective control of angina symptoms and for some people to prolong life. Invasive **revascularization** treatment may include either a **percutaneous coronary intervention (PCI)** or **coronary artery bypass graft (CABG)** surgery.

Living with CHD

Waiting for invasive treatment to improve or prolong life can be very stressful and have deleterious effects on the quality of daily life. Pre-surgical depression predicts cardiac hospitalization, continued surgical pain, failure to return to previous activity and depression at six months (Burg et al., 2003). Arthur et al. (2000) conducted a trial of a multidimensional pre-operative intervention on pre-surgery and post-surgery outcomes in low-risk patients awaiting elective CABG. The intervention consisted of individualized, prescribed exercise training twice per week in a supervised environment, education and reinforcement, and monthly nurse-initiated telephone calls to answer questions and provide reassurance. Patients who received the intervention spent one day less in the hospital and less time in the intensive care unit. Patients in the intervention group reported a better QoL during the waiting period than the control group. The improved QoL continued up to six months after surgery. Using outcome measures such as length of hospital stay as well as QoL measures provides evidence of cost-effectiveness, helpful information for budget holders wondering whether to invest in such interventions.

Rutledge et al. (2006) carried out a meta-analytic review of prevalence, intervention effects, and associations with clinical outcomes of depression in heart failure. Clinically significant depression was present in at least one in five patients with heart failure but rates can be higher among patients screened with questionnaires. The authors concluded that the relationship between depression and poorer heart failure outcomes is consistent and strong across multiple end points.

Unsurprisingly then, depression is a common response to heart disease. A special committee of the American Heart Association published recommendations for the screening, referral and treatment of depression in heart patients (Lichtman et al., 2008). The committee recommended:

1. Routine screening for depression in patients with CHD in settings, including the hospital, physician's office, clinic, and cardiac rehabilitation centre.
2. Patients with positive screening results should be evaluated by a qualified mental health professional.
3. Patients with cardiac disease who are under treatment for depression should be carefully monitored for adherence to their medical care, drug efficacy, and safety with respect to their cardiovascular as well as mental health.
4. Monitoring mental health may include, but is not limited to, the assessment of patients receiving antidepressants for possible worsening of depression or suicidality, especially during initial treatment when doses may be adjusted, changed, or discontinued.
5. Coordination of care between health care providers is necessary in patients with combined medical and mental health diagnoses.

Social support is of key importance. Mookadam and Arthur (2004) systematically reviewed social support and its relationship to morbidity and mortality after acute myocardial infarction. Having low social support networks was a predictor of one-year mortality following acute myocardial infarction. Low social support is equivalent to many 'classic' risk factors, such as elevated cholesterol level, tobacco use and hypertension. Another review found that low functional social support is associated with prevalence of CHD and all cause mortality but concluded that it remained uncertain whether low structural social support causally increases mortality in patients with CHD (Barth et al., 2010).

Adaptation to CHD

Cognitive adaptation has been shown to predict psychological adjustment to diseases such as arthritis, cancer, AIDS and heart disease. According to the cognitive adaptation theory, some people who are faced with a chronic illness maintain or develop an optimistic outlook, attempt to regain control or mastery over the event and find ways to restore or enhance their self-esteem (Taylor, 1983). Helgeson and Fritz (1999) tested whether people with high cognitive adaptation scores would be less vulnerable to a new coronary event due to **restenosis** within six months of initial PCI. Three components of cognitive adaptation were measured: self-esteem, optimism and control. Patients with a low cognitive adaptation score were more likely to have a new cardiac event even when demographic variables and medical variables thought to predict restenosis were statistically controlled.

A large number of MI patients do not return to work or regain normal functioning despite being physically well. There is evidence that cardiac rehabilitation programmes can reduce distress and disability, increase confidence and improve modifiable risk factors. However, many patients do not attend rehabilitation programmes after their MI. Patients' beliefs and perception about their illness are key determinants of recovery after an MI. Petrie et al. (2002) evaluated a brief hospital intervention designed to alter patients' perceptions about their MI. The content of the intervention was individualized according to the patients' responses on the Illness Perception Questionnaire (Weinman et al., 1996). The intervention caused significant positive changes in patients' views of their MI. The intervention group reported being better prepared for leaving hospital and subsequently returned to work at a significantly faster rate than the control group. At the three-month follow-up, the intervention group reported a significantly lower rate of angina symptoms.

Cooper et al. (1999) investigated whether the illness beliefs held during their hospital stay by patients who had an MI or who had undergone CABG could predict cardiac rehabilitation attendance. As well as being older, less aware of their cholesterol values and less likely to be employed, non-attenders were less likely to believe their condition was controllable and that their lifestyle may have contributed to their illness. Stewart et al. (2004) found a difference in the health information needs between men and women recovering from an acute coronary event. Men that had received significantly more information reported a greater satisfaction with health care professionals meeting their information needs. Women reported wanting more information than men concerning angina and hypertension. Men wanted more information about sexual function. Patients who reported receiving more information reported less depressive symptomatology. Most patients of both sexes preferred a shared decision-making role with their doctor. The majority felt their doctor had made the main decisions. Cardiac rehabilitation that is individualized to patients' needs may be more attractive and effective than current practice of thinking of cardiac rehabilitation as a place to do exercise and be informed about lifestyle changes.

Caring for Someone With CHD

Concordance occurs between men with CHD and their spouses for body mass index, history of smoking, current smoking status, frequency of exercise, miles per exercise session and the amount of fat and fibre in the diet. Behavioural risk factors are correlated among marital partners. Involving partners in lifestyle interventions may be more efficacious than individual patient education strategies.

Moser and Dracup (2004) compared the emotional responses and perception of control of MI and revascularization patients and their spouses, and examined the relationship between spouses' emotional distress and patients' emotional distress and psychosocial adjustment to their cardiac event. They found that spouses had higher levels of anxiety and depression than the patients. There were no differences in level of hostility. The patients also had a higher level of perceived control than did the spouses. Spouse anxiety, depression and perceived control were correlated with patient psychosocial adjustment to illness even when patient anxiety and depression were kept constant. The patients' psychosocial adjustment to illness was worse when spouses were more anxious or depressed than patients. Attention should be given to the psychological needs of spouses of patients who have suffered a cardiac event. Moser and Dracup also found that patients' psychosocial adjustment was best when patients were more anxious or depressed than spouses. This finding suggests that interventions that address the psychological distress of spouses may well improve patient outcomes.

Johnston et al. (1999) evaluated the effectiveness of a cardiac counselling rehabilitation programme for MI patients and their partners. They found that the programme resulted in more knowledge, less anxiety, less depression and greater satisfaction with care for both patients and their partners and less disability in patients. This study was published five years earlier than the Moser and Dracup (2004) study in the same journal, thus highlighting that it can take a long time for research findings to be disseminated, synthesized and put into practice. Conducting research to influence practice is very time consuming and there are usually many barriers to overcome. In order for research to have an impact, health psychologists must have an awareness of promotional techniques, the politics of the context in which they practise and the power of economical factors.

One problem for evaluation of cardiac patients' experience of QoL is identifying an instrument that is not only reliable and valid but also responsive to change. Instruments that are not very responsive will tend to under-represent the benefits of programme attendance. Research indicates that the most responsive instruments are: Beck Depression Inventory, Global Mood Scale, Health Complaints Checklist, Heart Patients' Psychological Questionnaire and Speilberger State–Trait Anxiety Inventory.

Rees et al. (2004) reviewed psychological interventions for coronary heart disease, typically stress management interventions. They included RCTs, either single modality interventions or a part of cardiac rehabilitation with a minimum follow-up of six months. Stress management (SM) trials were identified and reported in combination with other psychological interventions and separately. The quality of many trials was poor, making the findings unreliable. The authors concluded that psychological interventions showed no evidence of effect on total or cardiac mortality, but small reductions in anxiety and depression in patients with CHD. Similar results were seen for SM interventions when considered separately.

In 2007, the American Heart Association's Exercise, Cardiac Rehabilitation, and Prevention Committee and the American Association of Cardiovascular and Pulmonary Rehabilitation reported on the core components of cardiac rehabilitation/secondary prevention programmes (Balady et al., 2007). The associations recommended that all cardiac rehabilitation/secondary prevention programmes should contain baseline patient assessment, nutritional counselling, risk factor management (lipids, blood pressure, weight, diabetes mellitus and smoking), psychosocial interventions, and physical activity counselling and exercise training. Cardiac rehabilitation services are now routinely offered to patients but many invited patients fail to attend the sessions. Cooper et al. (2002) reviewed the literature. The results showed that non-attenders are more likely to be older, to have lower income/greater deprivation, to deny the severity of their illness, are less likely to believe they can influence its outcome.

HIV INFECTION AND AIDS

What Are HIV Infection and AIDS?

HIV infection and AIDS are a worldwide pandemic that has infected around 60 million people, and become the fourth largest killer in the world. There are estimated to be around 3 million new cases each year and about 2 million deaths from **AIDS (acquired immune deficiency syndrome)** with around 34 million people living with HIV infection or AIDS in 2011. The number of deaths peaked around 2004, and has since declined slightly. **HIV (human immunodeficiency virus)** is a retrovirus that infects and colonizes cells in the immune system and the central nervous system (T-helper and monocyte macrophage cells). Initial flu-like symptoms are followed by a quiescent, asymptomatic period (lasting years) during which the immune system battles the virus. Eventually the virus compromises the immune system and the individual becomes symptomatic. Finally the immune system is overwhelmed and the individual becomes vulnerable to opportunistic diseases, signifying development of AIDS and eventually likely resulting in death.

An HIV particle is around 100–150 billionths of a metre in diameter, one-seventieth the size of a human CD4+ white blood cell. HIV particles are coated with fatty material known as the viral envelope or membrane; 72 spikes, formed from the proteins gp120 and gp41, project out of the membrane. Below the viral envelope is the matrix layer, made from protein p17. The core is usually bullet-shaped and made from the protein p24. Inside the core there are three enzymes, called reverse transcriptase, integrase and protease, together with HIV's genetic material, consisting of two identical strands of RNA.

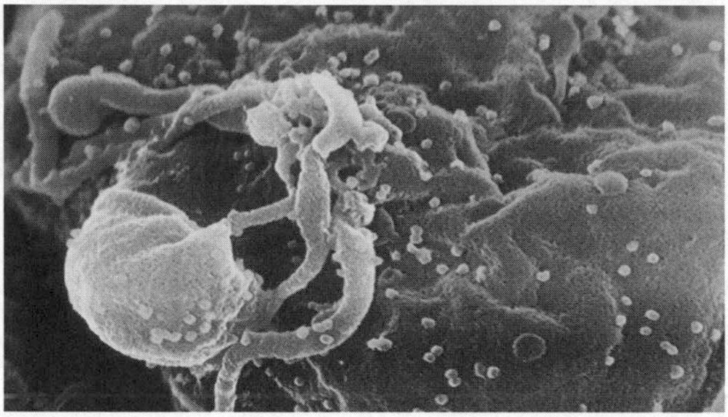

Figure 19.2 The human immunodeficiency virus. Scanning electron micrograph of HIV-1 (in light grey) budding from cultured lymphocyte. Multiple round bumps on cell surface represent sites of assembly and budding of virions

Source: US Centers for Disease Control and Prevention (2010)

HIV has nine genes (compared to around 20,000–25,000 in a human). Three HIV genes, gag, pol and env, make proteins for new virus particles. The other six genes, tat, rev, nef, vif, vpr and vpu, govern HIV's ability to infect a cell, produce new copies of the virus, or cause disease.

In 1996, the introduction of highly active antiretroviral therapy (HAART) redefined the illness and improved the outlook for infected individuals. HAART is the treatment of choice for HIV or AIDS, and has to be taken every day for the rest of a person's life. The aim of antiretroviral treatment is to keep the amount of HIV in the body at a low level. This stops weakening of the immune system and allows it to recover from any damage that HIV might have caused. However, antiretrovirals do not eliminate the virus, but only suppress it and, currently, only one in ten who need the treatment actually receive it. HIV persistence eventually causes disease in all infected persons (Sleasman and Goodenow, 2003). Denial has been a factor in reducing access to HAART in South Africa, and access to HAART in African countries, India and China is still way below optimum levels.

Risk factors for HIV infection are: unprotected intercourse, injection drug use, STIs, blood exposure, mother–infant transmission, breastfeeding transmission, mother–fetus transmission, and mother–infant childbirth transmission.

Men who have sex with men (MSM) may attempt to reduce HIV risk by adapting condom use, partner selection, or sexual position to the partner's HIV serostatus. This practice is known as 'serosorting'. Vallabhaneni et al. (2012) assessed the association of serosorting practices with HIV acquisition in 12,277 US participants, with 663 HIV positive conversions. No unprotected anal intercourse (UAI) was reported in 47.4% of intervals; UAI with some seroadaptive practices in 31.8%; and UAI with no seroadaptive practices in 20.4%. Vallabhaneni et al. found that serosorting appeared to be protective when compared with UAI without serosorting, but serosorting appeared to be twice as risky as no UAI. Condom use and limiting number of partners should remain the first-line prevention strategy, but serosorting reduces risk of harm for men at greatest risk.

Interventions for HIV Infection and AIDS

In the USA, women are one of the fastest growing groups of people with AIDS, among whom women of colour are disproportionately affected (US Centers for Disease Control and Prevention, 1999). Mize et al. (2002) carried out a meta-analysis of the effectiveness of HIV prevention interventions for women. The authors evaluated five ethnic groupings (all ethnicities combined, African-American, White, Hispanic and a mixed ethnicity group) over four time periods (post-test, less than 2 months after the intervention, 2–3 months after the intervention and 6–24 months after the intervention) on three HIV-related sexuality outcome variables (HIV infection and AIDS knowledge, self-efficacy and sexual risk reduction behaviour). The HIV interventions appeared effective at improving knowledge about HIV infection and AIDS and increasing sexual risk reduction behaviours for all ethnicities except that the findings for self-efficacy are less consistent. The interventions were less consistently effective for African-American women, for whom significant improvements in feelings of self-efficacy were only seen six months or longer after the intervention.

The HIV virus has a short half-life allowing rapid replication and mutation, which makes vaccine development problematic and increases the likelihood of drug resistance. Absence of a workable vaccine means antiviral medications are the primary treatment for HIV. HAART decreases an individual's HIV viral load to undetectable levels, reducing associated morbidity and mortality. However, 95–100% adherence is required to produce and maintain successful virologic suppression, with even 80–90% adherence rates showing no viral suppression in some patients. Non-adherence promotes viral drug resistance and cross-resistance, and drug resistant strains can be transmitted to uninfected patients leaving them without effective treatment options. HIV combination drug therapies involve complex, disrupting and challenging medication regimens involving numerous drugs taken several times a day with specific food instructions. In addition, treatment often commences during the asymptomatic phase; drug toxicity commonly results in severe, unpleasant side effects (e.g. vomiting, lipodystrophy); and treatment must continue for the rest of the person's life. Moreover, the long-term treatment stability and maintenance of viral suppression are not certain.

Adherence rates for HAART tend to be sub-optimal. Fogarty et al.'s (2002) review yielded 200 variables associated with adherence to HIV medication regimens falling into four broad categories: regimen characteristics, psychosocial factors, institutional resources, and personal attributes. Of the psychosocial factors reported, positive disease and treatment attitudes, good mental health and adjustment to HIV were positively associated with adherence while perceived negative social climate was negatively associated. Lack of access to institutional resources (financial, institutional, medical) was negatively associated with adherence. Finally, non-adherence was linked to personal attributes of younger age, minority status and history of substance use. Patients' active involvement in their medical care and treatment decision making also promotes adherence while low health literacy is associated with poor adherence.

Many studies have reported that stress accelerates disease processes in a variety of diseases including HIV. The chronic status of HIV infection and AIDS and the limited accessibility to HAART for many people living with HIV infection or AIDS (PLWHA) means that psychosocial support interventions are increasingly important. Programmes of pain management, stress management, coping effectiveness training, sleep disorders and exercise promotion have been found to enhance immune system function, medication adherence and adaptive coping, and to decrease anxiety, stress and depression (Chesney et al., 2003). Supportive interventions, especially those that improve function and self-management and maximize independence, represent an essential part of treatment for people living with HIV infection or AIDS.

In antiretroviral therapy (ART) for the management of HIV infection, stress may increase viral replication, suppress immune response, and impede adherence to ART (Riley and Kalichman, 2014). Stressful living conditions caused by poverty and dealing with a chronic life-threatening illness and stigma all can exacerbate chronic stress in HIV-affected populations. Interventions to reduce stress among PLWHA have been explored as an adjunct to pharmacotherapy. Scott-Sheldon et al. (2008) reviewed stress management interventions for HIV+ adults as evaluated in trials from 1989 to 2006. The authors were interested in measuring the impact of stress-management interventions designed to enhance the psychological, immunological and hormonal outcomes among HIV+ adults. The findings indicated that, in comparison to controls, stress-management interventions reduced anxiety, depression, distress and fatigue, and improved QoL. However, stress-management interventions did not appear to affect immunological or hormonal processes compared with controls.

Men who have sex with men (MSM) are increasingly using smartphone apps, such as Grindr, to meet sex partners (Holloway et al., 2014). Casual sex with hook-ups is often associated with alcohol and drug use. Scott-Sheldon et al. (2013) observed that perceived stress in PLWHA was associated with an increase in the frequency of alcohol use (drinking days, intoxication, and drinking in shebeens/taverns). They found that stress mediated the association between HIV status and alcohol use.

In a systematic review, Riley and Kalichman (2014) identified 11 studies that have examined mindfulness-based stress reduction (MBSR) as an intervention for HIV-positive populations. The preliminary outcomes supported MBSR to decrease emotional distress with mixed evidence for impact on disease progression. However, effect sizes were generally small to moderate in magnitude. The number of PLWHA who are likely to access such interventions, even if shown to be effective, is likely to be only a tiny proportion of the total number who are at risk.

Living with HIV Infection or AIDS

People living with HIV infection or AIDS face the general stressors of the chronically ill and may face additional stresses unique to HIV infection and AIDS, e.g. additional uncertainty and decision making due to rapidly changing treatment developments/outlook, infectivity persistence, the imperative for major behaviour change (e.g. sexual behaviour), anticipatory grief and the excessive stigma associated with the condition. The QoL of PLWHA is severely compromised, particularly in the later stages of the disease, due to pain (experienced by 30–90% PLWHA), discomfort, and mobility difficulties (e.g. Hughes et al., 2004).

The major stressors encountered by PLWHA are summarized in Box 19.2. Different stressors may be experienced at different stages of the illness, with stress peaks at initial diagnosis, onset of symptomology, sudden immune system cell (CD4) count decline, onset of opportunistic infections and diagnosis of AIDS.

BOX 19.2
STRESSORS RELATED TO HIV INFECTION AND AIDS

Disease-related stressors

- Being tested and receiving test results
- Diagnoses – seropositivity, symptomatic phase and AIDS
- Treatment commencement
- Intermittent symptoms and opportunistic disease
- Emergence of new symptoms
- For children, neurocognitive and emotional developmental problems
- Developing drug resistance and treatment failures

(Continued)

(Continued)

- Co-infections (e.g. hepatitis)
- Further exposure to the virus
- Medication side effects
- Pain, discomfort, sexual difficulties, mobility restrictions and progressive physical deterioration
- Complications from ongoing substance use
- Drug trials and drug holidays

External life-stressors

- Enacted stigma (e.g. ostracism and discrimination)
- Disclosure reactions
- Bereavement
- Substance use
- Employment changes
- Reduced income
- Loss/lack of health insurance
- Access to treatment
- Rejection and loss of social support
- Uncertainty

Emotional/psychological stressors

- Felt stigma (internalization, fear, shame, guilt)
- Disclosure decisions
- Reproductive decision making
- Grief
- Risk behaviour and decision making
- Anger
- Rejection and isolation
- Changing expectations
- Preparing for death
- Guilt

Few conditions have provoked such unprecedented levels of stigma, fear and uncertainty as HIV infection and AIDS, even in the well-informed. These fears are layered on top of pre-existing stigmas and moral judgements associated with particular groups, including gay men, sex workers, drug users and people with mental illnesses, reinforcing existing social inequalities. PLWHA have been treated as pariahs, discriminated against, abandoned and ostracized. HIV infection and

AIDS has even evoked appeals for mandatory testing and elimination of infected individuals. Stigma can intensify all the stressors and problems of living with the disease and is an obstacle to PLWHA fulfilling their human rights and to slowing the progression of HIV infection to AIDS.

The decision to disclose HIV-positive status is a daunting and multifaceted issue that recurs throughout the course of the disease. Non-disclosure increases the likelihood of infecting others and denies knowledge to previous sexual partners, so represents a major barrier to controlling the pandemic. Non-disclosure also decreases social support and access to services. Disclosure decisions are often conflated with simultaneous disclosure of lifestyle choices (e.g. sexuality, drug use) to family and friends. Disclosure decisions may revert to someone other than the PLWHA, particularly regarding children, when family members make decisions, including whether to tell the child their own serostatus (DeMatteo et al., 2002).

AIDS-related deaths may generate atypical bereavement complicated by a host of factors including survivor guilt, the effects of stigma and inadequate social support. AIDS-related deaths tend to be among relatively younger people. Many people who are affected by HIV infection and AIDS experience multiple bereavements, increasing distress and psychological problems (e.g. guilt, depression, suicidality, disenfranchised grief, numbing).

Ironson et al. (2002) investigated the relationship between spirituality and religiousness and health outcomes for people living with HIV. Four factors of the Ironson–Woods Spirituality/Religiousness Index were identified: sense of peace, faith in god, religious behaviour and compassionate view of others. Each of the four sub-scales was related to long survival with AIDS. Also, the Ironson–Woods Index was significantly correlated with lower distress, more hope, social support, health behaviours, helping others, and lower cortisol levels. In a related study, Ironson et al. (2006) found an increase in religiousness/spirituality in 45% of a sample after HIV diagnosis, which predicted slower disease progression over four years in people with HIV. The mechanism remains unclear, but it could be that those following a religious practice have higher adherence to medication.

Adaptation to HIV Infection and AIDS

Post-HAART, AIDS has been defined as an incurable, chronic and life-threatening illness. Coping with HIV infection and AIDS is a complex, multidimensional phenomenon that is influenced by personality, contextual and cultural factors. It involves a process of continual adjustment in response to stress, challenging life events, and personal and interpersonal issues. Multiple stressors and negative psychological outcomes are deterrents to successful adjustment. Adaptation is also influenced by health behaviours, which have a bi-directional influence on mood states (e.g. depressed people drink more, which increases depression, resulting in increased alcohol consumption as well as increased risky sex behaviours). An increased number of symptoms and onset of the symptomatic stage are key predictors of adjustment. Factors associated with good psychosocial adjustment to HIV infection and AIDS include healthy self-care behaviours (medical care, healthy lifestyle, awareness and ability to take action to meet personal needs); a sense of connectedness (one close confidante, openness, disclosure); a sense of meaning and purpose (cognitive appraisal that there is something to live for, optimistic attitude); and maintaining perspective (realistic acceptance, e.g. not viewing the condition as imminently fatal). Adaptive coping skills have consistently been associated with increased self-esteem, increased self-efficacy and perceived control. They include active behavioural (planning, help and information seeking, relaxation exercises) and cognitive strategies (cognitive reframing, finding meaning, emotion work, problem solving). Problem-focused coping appears more appropriate for situations that cannot be changed, whereas emotion-focused coping is more suitable where change is not possible (Park et al., 2001).

Adaptive coping strategies along with good social support can mediate the negative effects of stress. Adaptive coping strategies have also been associated with health-related benefits. Finding meaning in the experience of HIV infection and AIDS has been associated with maintaining immune system cell (CD4) levels, optimism with higher CD4 counts, medication adherence and lower distress, and perceived control, problem-focused coping and social support associated with longer survival. Adaptive and maladaptive coping strategies are not mutually exclusive, co-occuring or changing depending on context. Maladaptive coping strategies have been associated with poor adjustment including lower fighting spirit, higher hopelessness, anxious preoccupation and a fatalistic attitude. Passive and avoidant coping, psychological inhibition and withdrawal have been associated with increased risk behaviours, distress and more rapid disease progression (Stein and Rotheram-Borus, 2004).

Another factor associated with successful adaptation is social support. Zuckerman and Antoni (1995) reported that seven social support criteria were especially related to optimal adjustment to HIV infection and AIDS: feeling supported, satisfaction with support received, perceived helpfulness of peers, total perceived availability and individual dimensions of support, absence of social conflict, greater involvement of AIDS-related community activities and greater number of close friends. These criteria were related to adaptive coping strategies, increased self-esteem and sense of well-being, and decreased depression, hopelessness, anxiety, mood disturbances, dysphoria and risk behaviour. Parental adaptation and support may be the most important influences on the adaptation of children and adolescent PLWHA.

The Internet has had a massive influence on public perception and awareness of HIV infection and AIDS, not all entirely positive. Kalichman et al. (2003) surveyed 147 HIV-positive persons to examine factors associated with Internet use. The authors found that Internet use was associated with HIV disease knowledge, active coping, information-seeking coping, and social support among persons who were using the Internet. These preliminary findings suggest an association between using the Internet for health-related information and health benefits among people living with HIV infection and AIDS, supporting the development of interventions to close the digital divide in the care of people with HIV infection and AIDS.

Caring for Someone with HIV Infection or AIDS

The burden of care for people with HIV infection or AIDS, both formal and informal, is being borne primarily by lay caregivers within the family or the community, the majority of whom are women and girls (UNAIDS, 2004). There is some evidence, especially in Africa and Asia, that the least acknowledged caregivers are children (caring for a lone or surviving parent) and that older women, already vulnerable through higher levels of chronic poverty, lack of resources and their own substantial health problems, are disproportionately affected.

Caring involves a broad spectrum of psychological, spiritual, emotional and practical work throughout the course of the illness. It can be a rewarding undertaking from which caregivers derive a sense of purpose and self-esteem, and close bonds can become even stronger. However, the caring literature consistently reports the inherently stressful nature of caring for someone with a chronic illness (e.g. Chesler and Parry, 2001). Many of the stressors and negative psychological outcomes experienced by PLWHA equally affect their caregivers. Caring is associated with anxiety, depression, overwork, fatigue, fear of death, decreased libido, helplessness, frustration and grief. While other care domains may be similar (e.g. cancer), the greater dependence of PLWHA, and involvement and identification with them, result in increased patient contact and higher intensity of emotional work increasing the negative consequences. Neurological and/or cognitive symptoms associated with AIDS (from direct effects, opportunistic diseases or other causes) can make the burden of care especially arduous. The effects of multiple bereavements and the caregivers' own health problems (including own HIV-positive status) also increase mental health problems. The circumscribing effects of stigma create barriers to accessing social support and resources for caregivers.

The needs of caregivers are rarely prioritized and 'burnout' is common. Burnout is defined as emotional exhaustion, depersonalization and a damaged sense of personal accomplishment (e.g. Maslach and Jackson, 1981). Emotional support and stress management can prevent stress, depression and burnout in caregivers if they are lucky enough to access it.

QUALITY OF DYING AND DEATH, AND END-OF-LIFE CARE

Improvements in public health and survivorship of potentially fatal conditions has led to increased life expectancy. Increased prolongation of life often means that many people are living with varying degrees of illness, suffering and disablement for longer periods of time. As a consequence, family members are exposed to long periods of caring and may face a daunting array of life-and-death decisions. Palliative or end-of-life (EOL) care and the hospice movement currently are evolving into a major part of the health care industry. This has led to a significant line of research on the quality of dying and death (QoDD).

Based on the earlier ideas of Bowlby (1961) and Parkes (1965), Elisabeth Kübler-Ross (1997) constructed an influential five-stage theory of death and dying. She viewed death as 'the final stage of growth'. Psychological and medical thinking about death and dying drew inspiration from Kübler-Ross's (1969) landmark work. She defined five stages experienced when terminally ill patients face their own deaths: denial–dissociation–isolation, anger, bargaining, depression and acceptance (DABDA). Kübler-Ross made her own personal observations of the often appalling circumstances of patients dying in hospital. Although widely cited, the five-stage model has received little empirical support.

Numerous studies have highlighted the poor quality of end-of-life care, with many patients dying in pain and distress while receiving life-sustaining treatments they did not actually ask for, and grieving families carrying great emotional and financial burdens. There are basic preferences and needs that should be met if an individual's QoDD is to be maximized. Yet, in many instances, these basic needs are unlikely to be met in any modern technology-based, efficiency-driven hospital. As far as possible, decisions about health and social care must always remain with the individual person. However, the control over an individual's care inevitably may be passed to an increasing extent to medical and nursing staff and to the patient's family. This prospect is especially likely when the person's cognitive abilities suffer deterioration because of illnesses such as stroke, heart failure, dementia or neurological conditions. Troubling ethical issues are raised on an everyday basis and family and relatives are thrown into sensitive, emotionally charged, life-changing scenarios for which they may be ill-prepared. Important practical decisions that have to be made on behalf of an incapacitated patient may include:

- diet, hydration, and personal hygiene;
- treatment including pain relief;
- visits by family members;
- transfer to a care or nursing home;
- transfer to a hospital;
- transfer to a hospice;
- do-not-resuscitate (DNR) decisions;
- physician-aided dying.

The complexity of these end-of-life scenarios and the resulting outcomes can obviously play a decisive role in any patient's QoL and QoDD. To the young, fit and able-bodied, these aspects of health care may seem remote and abstract issues yet, one day, they could have an impact on each and every one of us.

It has been apparent for many decades that end-of-life care is not best left in the hands of staff in care homes and hospitals. These environments are not compatible with high-quality end-of-life care; this requires quiet, unpressured, sensitive care that is especially tailored to each individual and his/her family. A quarter of a century ago, Wallston et al. (1988) compared the quality of death (QoD) for hospice and non-hospice patients and found that the QoD scores were higher for terminally ill patients in hospices, either at home or hospital-based, than similar patients who received conventional care. Hospices are increasingly recognized as institutions which specialize in end-of life care. The hospice movement is growing in momentum internationally and the numbers of people who spend their last months of life in nursing homes and hospices are increasing rapidly (Najafi et al., 2014). The percentage of older people in the USA who received hospice care in the last 30 days of life increased from 19% in 1999 to 43% in 2009. The percentage that died at home increased from 15% in 1999 to 24% in 2009. A survey of 57 health care providers found that the most common attributes associated with a 'good death' were being pain free, having family present, and sudden or peaceful death. Severe pain or discomfort were the most commonly reported attributes of a 'bad death' (Najafi et al., 2014).

With globalization, cultural differences are becoming increasingly important in relation to end-of-life (EOL) care. Gysels et al. (2014) explored cultural issues that shape EOL care in seven European countries. They reviewed 868 papers using the following themes: setting, caregivers, communication, medical EOL decisions, minority ethnic groups, and knowledge, attitudes and values of death and care. They inferred evidence of clearly distinguishable national cultures of EOL care, with differences in meaning, priorities, and expertise in each country. The diverse ways that EOL care is understood and practised form a necessary part of what constitutes best evidence for the improvement of EOL care in the future.

High-quality EOL care should ideally reflect each patient's individual values and wishes, promote compassionate communication and provide family-oriented care. It should also lead to a reduction of non-beneficial, unnecessary care and avoid prolongation of dying, prevent patient suffering and allow less wastage of precious intensive care unit (ICU) resources.

A 'Study to Understand Prognoses and Preferences for Outcomes and Risks of Treatments' (SUPPORT) investigated how to improve EOL care and reduce the frequency of a 'mechanically supported, painful, and prolonged process of dying' (Conners et al., 1995: 1591). In this highly cited, large-scale study in five US teaching hospitals, Conners et al. made a two-year prospective observational study (phase I) with 4,301 patients followed by a two-year controlled clinical trial (phase II) with 4,804 patients and their physicians randomized to the intervention group ($n = 2{,}652$) or control group ($n = 2{,}152$). The patients were hospitalized with one or more of nine life-threatening diagnoses having a six-month mortality rate of 47%.

A specially trained nurse had multiple contacts with the patient, family, physician and hospital staff to elicit preferences, improve understanding of outcomes, encourage attention to pain control, and facilitate advance care planning and patient–physician communication. Physicians in the intervention group received estimates of the likelihood of six-month survival for every day up to six months, outcomes of cardiopulmonary resuscitation (CPR), and functional disability at two months. The phase I observations found many concerning issues in communication, the frequency of aggressive treatment, and the characteristics of hospital deaths. Less than half (47%) of physicians knew when their patients preferred to avoid CPR; 46% of do-not-resuscitate (DNR) orders were written within two days of death; 38% of patients who died spent at least ten days in an ICU; and for 50% of conscious patients who died in the hospital, family members reported moderate to severe pain at least half the time.

During the phase II intervention, patients experienced no improvement in patient–physician communication (e.g. 37% of control patients and 40% of intervention patients discussed CPR preferences) or in the five targeted outcomes. Thus, SUPPORT suggested that enhanced opportunities for more patient–physician communication may be inadequate to change established practices. The study authors concluded: 'To improve the experience of seriously ill and dying patients, greater individual and societal commitment and more proactive and forceful measures may be needed' (Conners et al., 1995: 1591).

Two decades later, is there any solid evidence that the low QoDD in hospitalized patients is changing? Or that hospital physicians are more 'teachable' about practices conducive to raising QoDD? Sadly, the evidence suggests they may not be. Curtis et al. (2011) evaluated an intervention to ICU EOL care in 12 community hospitals in Washington State, USA. The intervention was based on self-efficacy theory: changes in clinician performance were facilitated by increasing knowledge, enhancing attitudes and modelling appropriate behaviours. Unfortunately, the primary outcome, family-QoDD, showed no change with the intervention. Also, no change occurred in family satisfaction or nurse-QoDD.

A French study has shown a positive effect on QoDD by improving communication. Providing relatives of patients who are dying with a proactive EOL conference and a brochure may lessen the burden of bereavement (Lautrette et al., 2007). Lautrette et al. randomly assigned family members of 126 patients dying in 22 ICUs in France to the intervention format or to the customary EOL conference. Symptoms of anxiety and depression were less common in the intervention group compared to a control group.

Assessment of QoDD is a complex problem for the obvious reason that the real experts died before they could tell us their opinions! Neverthless, there are ways and means in which the nature of a good death can be deciphered (Curtis et al., 2002). The views of loved ones, family members, nurses and other professionals can all go into the 'mix' to generate some working assumptions.

Care of the dying and support for family members losing a loved one is a role requiring specialist knowledge, experience and training. EOL care appears to be another 'weak link' in medical training along with communication skills and psychosocial issues more generally. Specialist palliative care has two main client groups: the majority with a diagnosis of cancer, and a minority with other critical illnesses. In order to provide better patient care, it is helpful to go back to first principles and work with direct knowledge of people's beliefs about what makes a 'good death'. Steinhauser et al. (2000) researched descriptions of what makes a good death from patients, families and providers, using focus group discussions and interviews. The participants identified six components of a good death:

- pain and symptom management;
- clear decision making;
- preparation for death;
- completion;
- contributing to others;
- affirmation of the whole person.

Steinhauser et al. found, unsurprisingly, that physicians held a more biomedical perspective than other people, while patients and families felt that psychosocial and spiritual issues are as important as physiological concerns.

Bingley et al. (2006) reviewed narratives by people facing death from cancer and other diseases. The search identified 148 narratives since 1950 from which a sub-sample of 63 narratives could be reviewed. Bingley and colleagues found that the therapeutic benefits of writing were generally viewed as: *a way of making sense of dying, together with a strong sense of purpose in sharing the story*. Common themes were: changes in body image, an awareness of social needs when dying, communication with medical staff, symptom control, realities of suffering, and spiritual aspects of dying. Writing about cancer in comparison to other illnesses showed differences in content and style. The authors suggested that: 'The narrative acts as companion and witness to the encroaching disability and debility, as well as charting the changes in relationships with loved ones, oneself and one's body image' (Bingley et al., 2006: 194).

It is understandable that most patients want to die at home. Informal caregivers are vital to the support of patients at home but often have unmet needs. Anxiety, depression and feelings of isolation are common, particularly after the patient's death. In some cases, the death of a loved one may be described as a 'blessed relief'. Ramirez et al. (1998) report that approximately one-third of cancer patients in the UK receive care from one close relative only, while about half are cared for by two or three relatives, typically a spouse and an adult child. Approximately two-thirds of cancer patients and a third of non-cancer patients typically receive some kind of formal home nursing.

Harding and Higginson (2003) reviewed interventions to support caregivers in cancer and palliative care. Poor designs and methodology, a lack of outcome evaluation, small sample sizes and a reliance on intervention descriptions and formative evaluations characterized the literature. They suggested that alternatives to 'pure' RCTs would need to be considered in carrying out evaluation research in this domain. As was the case in reviewing interventions for obesity, smoking and drinking (Chapters 7–9) it is apparent that larger-scale studies of high quality are needed.

Lorenz et al. (2008) published a systematic review with clinical guidelines on evidence for improving end-of-life care. To assess interventions to improve palliative care, Lorenz et al. selected systematic reviews that addressed 'end of life', including terminal illness (e.g. advanced cancer) and chronic, eventually fatal illness with ambiguous prognosis (e.g. advanced dementia), and intervention studies that addressed pain, dyspnoea, depression, advance care planning, continuity and caregiving. Lorenz et al. (2008) screened 24,423 titles to identify 33 high-quality systematic reviews and 89 relevant intervention studies. Strong evidence existed for treating cancer pain with opioids, non-steroidals, radionuclides and radiotherapy; dyspnoea (shortness of breath) from chronic lung disease with short-term opioids; cancer-associated depression with psychotherapy, tricyclics and selective serotonin reuptake inhibitors; and multi-component interventions to improve continuity in heart failure.

Spiritual aspects are often missing in studies of EOL care. Williams (2006) summarized the qualitative literature on spirituality at the end of life. The majority of participants in 11 relevant studies had a diagnosis of cancer, but those with AIDS, cardiovascular disease and amyotrophic lateral sclerosis were also represented. The studies suggested three main themes within spiritual perspectives at the end of life:

spiritual despair – alienation, loss of self, dissonance;

spiritual work – forgiveness, self-exploration, search for balance;

spiritual well-being – connection, self-actualization, consonance.

Qualitative studies have explored the quality of care from a patient perspective. Singer et al. (1999) used in-depth, open-ended, face-to-face interviews and content analysis in Toronto, Ontario, with 48 dialysis patients, 40 people with HIV infection and 38 residents of a long-term care facility. They identified five domains of quality EOL care: receiving adequate pain and symptom management, avoiding inappropriate prolongation of dying, achieving a sense of control, relieving burden, and strengthening relationships with loved ones.

Death with Dignity – Physician-Assisted Death

Increasing interest in physician-assisted death (PAD) has occurred since its legalization in 1997 by Oregon's Death with Dignity Act (ODDA). Three other states, Washington, Montana and Vermont, recently passed similar laws. The Netherlands and Belgium also permit euthanasia and, as this book went to press, a new assisted dying law was being hotly debated in the UK parliament. Since 1988 in Zurich, Switzerland, an organization called 'Dignitas' has helped people with terminal illnesses and severe physical and mental conditions to die assisted by qualified doctors and nurses. Dignitas has helped over 1,000 people die in suicide clinics in Zurich. Additionally, Dignitas provides assisted suicide for people that are deemed to be of sound judgement and submit to an in-depth medical report prepared by a psychiatrist that establishes the patient's condition. In Oregon, until 2012, 1,050 people have received prescriptions for lethal medication and 673 died after making the choice to take the drugs (Oregon Public Health Division, 2014).

To determine whether there is a difference in the quality of the dying experience, from the perspective of family members, Smith et al. (2011) surveyed 52 Oregonians who received lethal prescriptions, 34 who requested but did not receive lethal prescriptions, and 63 who did not pursue PAD. Family members retrospectively rated the dying experience of their loved one with the 33-item QoDD (Curtis et al., 2002). Differences were reported in 9 of the 33 items but few significant differences were noted in items that measured domains of connectedness, transcendence, and overall quality of death. Those who had received PAD prescriptions had higher quality ratings on items measuring symptom control (e.g. control over surroundings and control of bowels/bladder) and better preparedness for death scores (saying goodbye to loved ones, and possession of a means to end life if desired) than those who did not pursue PAD or, in some cases, those who requested but did not receive a lethal prescription. The authors concluded that the quality of death experienced by those who received lethal prescriptions is no worse than those not pursuing PAD, and in some areas it is rated by family members as better.

The Royal College of General Practitioners (RCGP) in the UK rejected the newly proposed Assisted Dying Bill. Consultation with RCGP members (n = 1,700) showed that 77% were in favor of supporting the group's opposition to change the law (Baker, 2014). On the other hand, the *British Medical Journal* (*BMJ*) supported the bill, stating that 'people should be able to exercise choice over their lives, which should include how and when they die, when death is imminent' (Delamothe et al., 2014: 4349). While the right to exercise choice is one of the main arguments presented by those who support the bill, choice may not be an option for all. As McCartney (2014) argued:

> ... our death is always potentially imminent, and we clearly do not enjoy omnipotent choice over our lives; otherwise, people in poorer areas would live just as long, with as much money and power as those more comfortably off. Indeed, 'choice' in healthcare is often proffered as a consumer interest, pandering to the profit motive in our dissolving NHS. The choices that affect our lives most – income, status, employment – have more to do with the luck of the environment we grow up in than with personal volition. Why should 'choice' over death remain uninfluenced by the bad luck of our environment? And if such choice is paramount, why doesn't the *BMJ* argue for assisted suicide at any other point in life, not just in terminal illness? Also, we can't be sure that the law will be properly followed . . . The care of dying people is already difficult. It makes me uncomfortable when articulate, middle-class people want more so-called choice, when they may hardly know of the stresses and vulnerabilities of others. (p. 4502)

Issues were also raised concerning the conceptualization of 'mental capacity' upon which the proposed bill relies. Price et al. (2014) explored how the experts presenting evidence to the Commission on Assisted Dying conceptualized the 'mental capacity' of patients requesting assistance for their death. Findings from this qualitative study suggest that 'mental capacity' was considered as a central safeguard in the proposed bill. However, its conceptualization remained inconsistent. While 'mental capacity' could be defined within the legal 'cognitive' definition of capacity (i.e. a person will be considered mentally capable unless significantly cognitively impaired), it can also be defined within the grounds of autonomy, rationality, voluntariness and motivation. The authors argued that more work is needed to establish consensus as to what constitutes 'mental capacity'. Furthermore, frameworks need to be in place to support professionals in determining 'mental capacity' in practice.

In a systematic review examining the attitudes of health professionals, patients, carers and the public on assisted dying in dementia, Tomlinson and Stott (2014) found that health professionals held more restrictive views towards assisted dying than the public, patients and carers. However, these opinions varied depending on the severity of a patient's condition and capacity. Age, ethnicity, gender and religion also appeared to influence people's attitudes towards assisted dying. Similarly, a systematic review by Vezina-Im et al. (2014) compared physicians' and nurses' motivations to participate in assisted dying. A total of 27 studies were included in the review. Findings suggest that physicians and nurses showed motivation to practise voluntary euthanasia when they are already familiar with this process. However, motivation may vary according to medical speciality. This can also be influenced by patients' prognosis and depressive symptoms.

In a qualitative study in New Zealand, Malpas et al. (2014) presented reasons as to why some older adults would oppose physician-assisted dying. Findings suggest that participants' personal experiences of good death strengthened their views that speeding the dying process is unnecessary. Religious reasoning and beliefs also contributed to their attitudes. 'Slippery slope' worries too were raised that reflected concerns about the potential risk of making this practice the norm in the future. Additionally there were concerns about potential abuses if this process was legalized. As a participant recalled a conversation with a family member: 'She thought that I should be euthanized. If I was overseas, Holland, or somewhere they would put me out of my misery. And she actually said to me, "If you were my dog, I would shoot you to put you out of your misery"' (p. 356).

The taken-for-granted assumption that underlies arguments for assisted dying is the belief that the quality of life for such individuals is so severely reduced that it makes it unendurable and is bound up with a rhetoric of the moral imperative to relieve suffering. The entrenched disablement prejudices held by health care professionals result in unsupported assumptions that the quality of life of people with disabilities is diminished in such a way that it makes it more unendurable, more hopeless and more limited than that of people for whom other factors have diminished their quality of life (e.g. someone whose family have been killed and finds life unbearable without them). However, as suggested in a study by Terrill et al. (2014), resilience can mitigate the impact of secondary symptoms (e.g. pain and fatigue) on the quality of life of people with long-term physical disablement.

In addition, assisting certain disabled people to die would not be countenanced. For example, it is unlikely that assisting the survivors of genocide to die would be countenanced, despite them enduring extreme suffering, pain, disablement and distress. There are a number of forms of 'assisted-dying', including a person ending their own life by their choice using a tool supplied by someone else; someone else ending a person's life with their consent; someone else ending a person's life without their consent; and withholding life-sustaining treatment (with or without that person's consent). All of these forms of 'assisted-dying' have been applied to disabled people. That 'assisted-dying' can refer to the act without the consent of the person who dies is particularly worrying. It has been suggested that many disabled people fear that episodes of illness may be viewed as an opportunity to 'allow' them 'merciful' release (Marks, 1999), and there may be some basis for this. In states and countries where assisted suicide has been legalized, people with physical and psychiatric disabilities have been helped to die both with and without their consent. One cannot doubt that physician-assisted dying happens unofficially on a daily basis in hospitals and homes everywhere.

Brain Death and Organs for Transplant

Brain death is irreversible brain damage causing the end of independent respiration and is regarded as indicative of death. Discussion about death, especially one's own, is a delicate, almost 'taboo' subject. Viable organs for transplant often are obtained from someone who is brain dead (Bresnahan, 2015). However, brain death is a controversial and sensitive issue, yet ideally families should discuss their personal wishes about organ donation in advance in case brain death should be an issue for them in the future. Unsurprisingly, family members dealing with a brain-dead loved one who is supported on a ventilator often are not able to carry out the person's expressed wishes to donate organs. To facilitate clear communications about brain death, Bresnahan and Zhuang (2015) published the Communicating with Family about Brain Death Scale, which assesses the willingness of individuals to communicate about brain-dead organ donation with their family members. This scale is a step towards facilitating such discussions in a more open basis and its use could help save many more lives of people waiting for transplants.

FUTURE RESEARCH

1. Adherence – research into the optimum time to give information about treatment and how to tailor the content of information for different patients.
2. Research designed to understand the experience of waiting for PCI and other procedures, and how interventions can improve outcomes.
3. We need a better understanding about why some people do not attend cardiac rehabilitation. The focus of the research should be on the content of the programme and how to make it more appealing.
4. More research is needed into the psychological impact of being told a spouse or family member has a serious illness, in order to cater for the needs of family members.
5. More longitiudinal studies are needed with HAART. The literature spans a short timeframe, and is based on specific populations (e.g. MSM) from developed countries, unrepresentative of the developing world, where the AIDS pandemic is at its highest.
6. A variety of psychosocial interventions have been developed for patients with cancer and other life-threatening conditions. Although these studies have shown short-term benefits, in regard to long-term QoL and survival, the evidence to date is disappointing. Large-scale, better-designed evaluation studies are required.
7. Many issues concerning EOL care lack high-quality evidence. Future research should address psychosocial support and interventions across different conditions and settings focused on the last part of life.

SUMMARY

General points

1 Chronic illnesses can strike at any age but more often in middle and older age groups and, while they can be fatal, most people diagnosed with a chronic illness live for many years with the condition.

2 Management of fatal or chronic diseases is a principal feature in the lives of 10–15% of the population. This huge amount of informal care occurs almost invisibly to outsiders with little recognition or financial support from society at large.

3 Chronic illness involves restrictions on activities of daily living, and increases in pain and fatigue. 'Juggling' relationships with health professionals, family and friends requires many adaptations and adjustments. Patients may have views about their care and treatment that differ from those of the professionals.

(Continued)

(Continued)

4 Life-threatening diseases are associated with a great variety of metaphors and meanings. Metaphor can be a useful way of coping but may lead to guilt, self-blame and feelings of hopelessness.

5 Stigmatization adheres to people with cancer and chronic diseases. This can be a heavy extra burden for victims to carry.

6 It is important to consider the needs of the family members of people with cancer and chronic diseases.

Cancer

1 Approximately one out of every two men and one out of every three women have cancer during their lifetime. Because of higher survival rates, cancer is being considered alongside other serious chronic conditions.

2 Cancer occurs when cells keep dividing and forming more cells without internal control or order. This cell growth is known as a tumour or neoplasm and can be benign or malignant.

3 Treatment can aim to cure the cancer, control it, or treat its symptoms. The type of treatment depends on the type of cancer, the stage of the cancer, and individual factors such as age, health status, and the personal preferences of the patient and his/her family. The patient ideally is empowered to discuss with the professionals the treatment choices.

4 The four major treatments for cancer are surgery, radiation, chemotherapy, and biological therapies such as hormone therapies (e.g. tamoxifen) and transplant options (e.g. with bone marrow or stem cell therapy).

5 Interview and diary studies suggest common themes among long-term survivors: 'authenticity', 'autonomy' and 'acceptance'.

Coronary heart disease

1 CHD is a leading cause of death.

2 The two main forms of CHD are myocardial infarction and angina.

3 Decreases in the CHD death rates are mainly due to a reduction in major risk factors, principally smoking. Spending on primary prevention does not reflect this finding.

4 Seeking treatment for CHD can be stressful for both people with CHD and their family members. It is important to tailor the information about CHD to the needs of individual patients.

5 Psychological disease management can help angina patients to adjust but psychological services are currently patchy and inadequate.

HIV infection and AIDS

1 HIV infection and AIDS are a worldwide pandemic that has infected around 60 million people, and become the fourth largest killer in the world. There are around 3 million new cases each year.

2 HIV (human immunodeficiency virus) is a retrovirus that infects and colonizes cells in the immune system and the central nervous system (T-helper and monocyte macrophage cells). Initial flu-like symptoms are followed by a quiescent, asymptomatic period (lasting years) during which the immune system battles the virus.

3 The most effective treatment consists of combination therapies (HAART) that decrease an individual's HIV viral load to undetectable levels, reducing associated morbidity and mortality.

4 Adaptive coping strategies along with good social support can moderate the negative effects of stress. Finding meaning in the experience of living with HIV infection or AIDS has been associated with medication adherence, lower distress and perceived control.

5 Interventions that target adaptive coping skills, emotion work and increasing social support appear to be most effective in helping patients to adapt to living with their illness.

Glossary

ACE (angiotensin converting enzyme) inhibitor a drug that is important in the regulation of blood pressure.

Acquisition the process of learning a response or taking up a specific behaviour through association or conditioning.

Action research a type of research concerned with the process of change and what else happens when change occurs. Action research is particularly suitable for organizations or systems requiring improvement or change.

Action stage one of the stages proposed by the *transtheoretical model of change (TMC)* in which a person takes specific actions with the aim of changing unwanted behaviour, bringing positive benefits to well-being.

Acute the early stages of a condition; normally defined as a condition that lasts for less than six months.

Acute pain pain that lasts for less than six months.

Addiction a term used to describe a person's physical and psychological dependency on an activity, drink or drug, seemingly beyond conscious control. Addiction is said to occur when there is: a strong desire to engage in the particular behaviour (especially when the opportunity to engage in such behaviour is not available); an impaired capacity to control the behaviour; discomfort and/or distress when the behaviour is prevented or ceased; persistence of the behaviour despite clear evidence that it is leading to problems.

Addiction theories theories based on the construct of addiction used to explain alcoholism and other excessive behaviours (e.g. gambling, shopping, drug use, over-eating).

Adipose tissue tissue in the body in which fat is stored as an energy reserve and which in excess leads to obesity.

Affluenza the combination of affluence and influenza and referring to the negative psychological consequences of the restless pursuit of more in the consumerist era.

Agency the capacity to take action in pursuit of intentions and goals.

AIDS (acquired immune deficiency syndrome) an advanced HIV infection which generally occurs when the CD4 count is below 200/ml. It is characterized by the appearance of opportunistic infections which take advantage of the weakened immune system and include: pneumocystis carinii pneumonia; toxoplasmosis; tuberculosis; extreme weight loss and wasting; exacerbated by diarrhoea; meningitis and other brain infections; fungal infections; syphilis; and malignancies such as lymphoma, cervical cancer and Kaposi's sarcoma.

Alcohol dependence syndrome a psychophysiological disorder characterized by increased tolerance of alcohol, withdrawal symptoms following reduced consumption, a persistent desire, or unsuccessful efforts to reduce or control drinking.

Anchoring the process whereby unfamiliar concepts are given meaning by connecting them with more familiar concepts.

Angina pectoris the most common form of coronary heart disease. It is characterized by a heavy or tight pain in the centre of the chest that may spread to the arms, necks, jaw, face, back or stomach. Angina symptoms occur when the arteries become so narrow from the *atheroma* that insufficient oxygen-containing blood can be supplied to the heart muscle when its demands are high, such as during exercise.

Angina Plan a psychological intervention for angina patients; it consists of a patient-held booklet and audio-taped relaxation programme.

Anti-essentialist view of human sexuality the view of human sexuality as a set of potentialities which may or may not be realized within differing social, cultural and historical contexts.

Anticipated regret the anxiety about the outcome of making a decision.

Anticoagulant drugs drugs that prevent the clotting of blood.

Aromatherapy is a type of complementary medicine that involves the use of essential oils from plant extracts for therapeutic purposes.

Artefact an uncontrolled and possibly unknown variable or factor causing a misleading, spurious finding in a study.

Assessment a procedure through which a patient, client, participant or situation can be evaluated against a benchmark or criterion enabling further actions or interventions to be administered, interpreted or understood.

Atheroma furring-up of an artery by deposits, mainly of cholesterol, within its walls. Associated with atherosclerosis, atheroma has the effect of narrowing the lumen (channel) of the artery, thus restricting blood flow. This predisposes a person to a number of conditions, including thrombosis, angina, and stroke.

Attachment the bond that forms between parent and child, which can have lifelong consequences.

Attitudes the sum of beliefs about a particular behaviour weighted by evaluations of these beliefs.

Attribution bias the tendency to attribute positive things to oneself and negative things to others.

Attribution theory theory of lay causal explanations of events and behaviours.

Attributions perceived or reported causes of actions, feelings or events.

Authoritarian doctor a personality type or leadership style favouring obedience rather than freedom of expression.

Autonomy the ability to act without reference to others.

Behaviour change approach an approach to health promotion that targets behaviour change in individual members of the population.

Benign tumour a growth that is not cancerous.

Beta-blockers drugs that block the actions of the hormone adrenaline (epinephrine) that makes the heart beat faster and more vigorously.

Between groups design a research design involving two or more matched groups of participants that receive different conditions, for example, an intervention versus a control condition.

Biological reductionism the assumption that all human experience can be directly traced to and explained with reference to its biological basis.

Biomedicine a health system that identifies the cause of agreed diseases and symptoms as lying in certain physiological processes.

Biopsychosocial model the view that health and illness are produced by a combination of physical, psychological and cultural factors (Engel, 1977).

Black Report a report on health inequalities published in the UK in 1980 named after the chairman of the committee who produced the report, Sir Douglas Black.

Body image a person's perception of the physical character of their body.

Body mass index (BMI) the body weight in kilograms divided by the square of the height in metres; has a normal range of 20 to 25.

Bottom-up listening to people about what they perceive their needs to be and acting upon that information together in an attempt to meet those needs.

Buddhist a person who practices the religion of Buddhism; living in the present.

Built environment the physical human-made objects in the everyday world.

Bupropion otherwise known as Zyban, initially employed as an antidepressant, used in smoking cessation.

Burden of disease a concept referring to the overall costs associated with a disease measured by the economic, social and psychological resources that are expended during care, treatment and rehabilitation.

Calorie the energy needed to increase the temperature of 1 kg of water by 1°C, which is about 4.184 kJ. Fat contributes 9 calories per gram, alcohol 7 calories per gram and carbohydrates 4 calories per gram.

Carcinogens substances, radionuclides and radiation that act directly or indirectly in causing cancer.

Case studies retrospective written reports on individuals, groups or systems.

Case-control study an epidemiological study in which exposure of patients to factors that may cause their disease (cases) is compared to the exposure to the same factors of participants who do not have the disease (controls).

Catastrophizing the tendency to become emotional and pessimistic about symptoms, illness or difficulties.

Causal ontologies of suffering causal frameworks for explaining illness and suffering.

Cessation the process of stopping (ceasing) a specific behaviour, habit or activity; one possible outcome of the *action stage* in the *transtheoretical model of change* (*TMC*).

Chlamydia a common sexually transmitted infection (STI) caused by the bacterium, *Chlamydia trachomatis*, which can damage a woman's reproductive organs. Even though symptoms of chlamydia are usually mild or absent, serious complications that cause irreversible damage, including infertility, can occur 'silently' before a woman ever recognizes a problem. Chlamydia also can cause discharge from the penis of an infected man.

Cholesterol a lipid produced in the body from acetyl-CoA and present in the diet.

Chronic any condition that continues for at least six months.

Chronic fatigue syndrome (CFS) a syndrome identified in Nevada, USA, in 1984, characterized by severe fatigue and other symptoms suggesting a viral infection and persisting over long periods of time. There is much current controversy as to whether it is a *psychosomatic disorder* or caused by an as-yet-unidentified virus. CFS is thought to be identical to *myalgic encephalomyelitis* (*ME*).

Chronic pain pain that lasts longer than six months; whether mild or excruciating, episodic or continuous, merely inconvenient or totally incapacitating, it takes a physical and emotional toll on a person.

Classical conditioning a learning process whereby a previously neutral stimulus (*conditioned stimulus, CS*) comes to evoke a certain response (unconditioned response, UCR) as a result of repeated previous pairings with a stimulus (*unconditioned stimulus, UCS*) that naturally evokes the response.

Clinical health psychology the application of psychological theory and research to the prevention and treatment of illness and the identification of aetiologic and diagnostic correlates of health and illness and related dysfunctions.

Cognitions thoughts, beliefs and images forming the elements of a person's knowledge concerning the physical and psychosocial environment.

Cognitive behavioural therapy (CBT) modification of thoughts, images, feelings and behaviour using the principles of *classical* and *operant conditioning* combined with cognitive techniques concerned with the control of mental states.

Communication styles different approaches to verbal interaction which are characterized by particular linguistic and rhetorical techniques and strategies such as listening or question asking.

Communicative event a joint achievement that is the product of participants' strategic deployment of culturally available discursive resources.

Communitarian an approach that focuses on the whole community rather than individuals, working towards social justice and reducing inequities.

Community development approach an approach to health promotion that recognizes the close relationship between individual health and socio-economic factors. It aims to remove the socio-economic and environmental causes of ill health through the collective organization of members of the community.

Community health psychology advancing theory, research and social action to promote positive well-being, increase empowerment, and prevent the development of problems of communities, groups and individuals.

Compensatory conditioned response model influential model put forward by Siegel (1975) to account for the phenomena of addiction, such as tolerance, dependence and withdrawal, using the principles of *classical conditioning.*

Complementary and Alternative Medicine (CAM) forms of health care that are not controlled by professional medicine and are based on non-orthodox systems of healing.

Compliance (or adherence) the extent to which a person's behaviour changes as a direct consequence of specific social influence, e.g. a measure of the extent to which patients (or doctors) follow a prescribed treatment plan.

Concordance model of physician–patient relationship based upon mutual respect and involvement in treatment.

Conditioned stimulus (CS) a stimulus that, because of pairing with another stimulus (*unconditioned stimulus, UCS*) which naturally evokes a reflex response, is eventually able to evoke that response (see *classical conditioning*). The acquisition is believed to occur when there is a positive contingency between two events such that event A is more likely in the presence of event B than in the absence of B.

Conditioning processes of associating stimuli and responses (see *classical conditioning* and *operant conditioning*) producing learning and experience.

Confidence interval an interval around the mean of a sample that one can state with a known probability contains the mean of the population.

Confucianism A Chinese philosophy which views human suffering as a result of destiny or *ming.*

Conscientiousness one of the five factors of personality proposed by McCrae and Costa in their influential theory which was originally developed in 1985. The other four factors are openness to experience, extraversion, agreeableness and neuroticism.

Consumerist style of health care that emphasizes opportunities for patient choice.

Contemplation stage the stage of intending to change at some as yet unspecified time in the future; one of the stages of the *transtheoretical model of change.*

Control group a group of participants assigned to a condition that does not include the specific treatment being evaluated; used for comparative purposes.

COPE questionnaire devised by Carver et al. (1989) to assess the individual's predominant coping strategies in response to stress.

Coronary angiogram an X-ray of the arteries to help to see if any of the arteries are blocked by atheroma.

Coronary artery bypass graft (CABG) an operation that enables a blocked area of the coronary artery to be bypassed so that blood flow can be restored to heart tissue that has been deprived of blood because of coronary heart disease (CHD). During CABG, a healthy artery or vein is taken from the leg, arm or chest and transferred to the outside of the heart. The new healthy artery or vein then carries the oxygenated blood around the blockage in the coronary artery.

Coronary heart disease (CHD) restriction of the blood flow to the coronary arteries often evidenced by chest pains (angina) and which may result in a heart attack.

Cost effectiveness method of economic analysis that takes account of both the effectiveness and the cost of an intervention.

Critical consciousness (*conscientizacao*) a concept developed by Paulo Freire referring to the ability to perceive social, political and economic oppression and to take action against oppressive elements of society.

Critical health psychology analyses how power and macro-social processes influence health, health care and social issues, and studies the implications for the theory and practice of health psychology.

Cross-cultural psychology compares and contrasts samples of populations said to be from different cultures in terms of attitudes, beliefs, values and behaviours that are viewed as stable and essential characteristics of particular cultures.

Cross-over or within-participants design a research design in which participants are placed in two or more conditions; in theory, participants 'act as their own controls'. However, there are sequence effects, practice effects and other issues that make this design more complicated.

Cross-sectional design involve obtaining responses from a sample of respondents on one occasion only. With appropriate randomized sampling methods, the sample can be assumed to be a representative cross-section of the population(s) under study and it will be possible to make comparisons between different sub-groups, e.g. males vs. females, older vs. younger, etc.

Cues to action reminders or prompts to take action consistent with an intention; cues may be internal (e.g. feeling fatigued can trigger actions to take time out or relax) or external (e.g. seeing health promotion leaflets or posters).

Cultural competence A set of competencies that involve cultural sensitivity and appropriateness of staff and health systems.

Cultural psychology the study of human conduct as a form of meaning-making; according to the approach of Valsiner (2013) and others.

Culture a system of meanings and symbols that defines a worldview that frames the way people locate themselves within the world, perceive the world, and find meaning within it.

Death gradient the variation in mortality that occurs across a population when the population is segmented according to socio-economic status such that the mortality rate is higher among those groups which have lower socio-economic status.

Decisional balance weighing the pros and cons of behaviour change.

Deficit mode the absence of something which is valued.

Deficit model an explanation used by health care professionals to account for low compliance, e.g. women who do not use a screening service may be characterized as lacking in knowledge and concern about their health.

Deviant patient a perspective on doctor–patient communication focusing on the characteristics of the patient as creating problems for the doctor.

Diary techniques any data collection method in which the data are linked to the passage of time. They often involve self-report but may also contain information about observations of others.

Direct observation directly observing behaviour in a relevant setting, e.g. patients waiting for treatment in a doctor's surgery or clinic. The observation may be accompanied by recordings in written, oral, auditory or visual form. Includes casual observation, formal observation and participant observation.

Disability (1) 'A physical or mental impairment that substantially limits one or more major life activities, a record of such impairment, or a perception of such impairment.' (2) 'Any physical and/or mental impairment that substantially limits one or more of the major life activities (caring for one's self, walking, seeing, hearing, and the like)' (The Americans with Disabilities Act, 1990).

Disability-adjusted life year (DALY) the total amount of healthy life lost, to all causes, whether from premature mortality or from some degree of disability during a period of time. The DALY is the sum of years of life lost from premature mortality plus years of life with disability, adjusted for severity of disability from all causes, both physical and mental (Murray and Lopez, 1997).

Disability culture a group identity, a common history of oppression and a common bond of resilience held with pride and consisting of art, music, literature, and other expressions of the experience of disability.

Discourse talk or text embedded in social interaction presenting an account of the constitution of subjects and objects; an opinion or position concerning a particular subject.

Discourse analysis a set of procedures for analysing language as used in speech or texts. It has links with ethnomethodology, conversation analysis and the study of meaning (semiology).

Discourse of risk ways of talking and practices that attribute ill health to personal characteristics, and construct an 'at-risk' status as a state in between health and illness.

Disease prototype cognitive construct or model of a representative case of a specific disease.

Disease theories the idea that the loss of control of behaviour such as alcohol consumption or eating is a disease based on personal or inherited characteristics that predispose particular individuals to the condition (e.g. alcoholism or obesity).

Doctor-centred communication style a communication style which primarily makes use of the doctor's expertise by keeping control of the interview agenda.

Dopamine a neurotransmitter in the brain thought to be responsible for sensations of pleasure triggered by events or by the intake of substances such as tobacco or alcohol.

Double-blind control a procedure used in randomized controlled trials to prevent bias in which neither the participant not the investigator knows the condition or group that a participant has been allocated to.

Dual energy X-ray absorptiometry (DXA) originally used to measure bone density and total body composition; can also be used to determine abdominal fat mass.

Dual processing model the idea that cognitive representations of danger (e.g. illness threat) are processed independently of the emotional processing.

E-health the application of information and communication technology to health or health care.

Ecological approach a model or theory about health and behaviour that emphasizes environmental influences.

Ecological validity the extent to which the environment within which behaviour or experience is studied captures the relevant features of the real-world environment.

Effect size the size of an observed effect measured in standard deviation units.

Effort–reward balance the balance between the workload of a job and the pay received.

Electrocardiogram (ECG) a physiological measure used to examine the electrical activity of the heart.

Emotional liability a personal characteristic referring to an unstable, variable pattern in a person's responses to events.

Emotions feelings associated with facial, bodily and verbal expressive behaviour, and internal, visceral activity and thoughts, when affected by interpersonal and environmental events; examples include love, joy, pleasure, ecstasy, pride, lust, greed, envy, jealousy, sadness, fear, worry, anger, disgust, distress or hate; also referred to as positive or negative 'affect'.

Empowerment any process by which people, groups or communities exercise increased control or sense of control over aspects of their everyday lives, including their physical and social environments.

Energy balance equation (EBE) an equation relating energy intake to internal heat produced by food, external work and energy storage as follows: energy intake = internal heat produced + external work + energy stored.

Energy expenditure use by the body of chemical energy from food and drink or body stores during the processes of metabolism that is dissipated as heat, including heat generated by muscular activity; the day's total energy expenditure is measured in calories of heat lost.

Energy intake the chemical energy in food and drink that can be metabolized to produce energy in the body; the day's total energy intake is measured in calories supplied by all food and drink consumed.

Environmental foundations key elements of the working environment relevant to the occupational health and well-being of employees.

Epidemiological transition in middle- and low-income countries, the time at which non-communicable disease prevalence equals and overtakes the prevalence of communicable diseases.

Epidemiology the study of associations between patterns of disease in populations and environmental, lifestyle and genetic factors.

Equity theory the tendency of individuals to balance the effort invested in a role with the rewards obtained from the role in return.

Ethical approval the requirement of any research project to present before a panel of experts on ethical issues, and have the panel's explicit approval of the aims, design, the sample size and power analysis, the participants, how they will be chosen, the information provided to the participants, the method of consent used, methods of data analysis, nature and timing of debriefing of participants, and methods of dissemination.

Ethnicity pertaining to ethnic group or race.

Ethnocentrism a bias in perception, thinking or principles stemming from membership of a particular ethnic or cultural group.

Ethnographic methods seek to build a systematic understanding of a culture from the viewpoint of the insider. Ethnographic methods are multiple attempts to describe the shared beliefs, practices, artefacts, knowledge and behaviours of an intact cultural group. They attempt to represent the totality of a phenomenon in its complete context and naturalistic setting. The methods include autoethnography, combining autobiography with ethnography.

Eudaimonic referring to self-realization; defining well-being in terms of the degree to which a person's life activities mesh with deeply held values and are fully engaged in authentic personal expression.

Evaluation the assessment of the efficacy or effectiveness of an intervention, project or programme in terms of processes and/or outcomes.

Evidence-based practice (EBP) a policy of using only techniques and procedures that have a solid empirical foundation, i.e. the procedures have been demonstrated to benefit the service user.

Exercise tolerance test (ETT) the recording of the heart's electrical activity while it is under the stress of increased physical demand.

Extrinsic motives motives based on external factors such as appearance, conformity or norms.

False positive a result of a medical test that incorrectly identifies the person as having a certain condition.

Fat *triglycerides* that are either solid (e.g. butter, lard) or liquid (e.g. vegetable or fish oil) at room temperature.

Fat balance equation states that the rate of change of fat stores equals the rate of fat intake minus the rate of fat oxidation.

Fetal alcohol syndrome abnormality found in children whose mothers drink heavily during pregnancy, characterized by facial abnormalities, mental impairment and stunted growth.

Flowchart model a diagrammatic representation of the relationships between processes and/or variables which are believed to be related to each other.

Focus groups one or more group discussions in which participants focus collectively upon a topic or issue usually presented to them as a group of questions (or other stimuli) leading to the generation of interactive data.

Food reward theory the theory that suggests overconsumption of food, which may lead to overweight and obesity, is a consequence of activation of pleasure centres in the brain and the reinforcement of eating as a learned behaviour.

Framework a general representation for conceptualizing a research field or question.

Gain-framed messages information about a health behaviour that emphasizes the benefits of taking action.

Galenic medicine health system derived from Greek and Arabic health beliefs.

Gate control theory a theory that views pain as a perceptual experience, in which ascending physiological inputs and descending psychological inputs are equally involved. It posits a gating mechanism in the dorsal horn of the spinal cord that permits or inhibits the transmission of pain impulses to the brain.

General adaptation syndrome (GAS) influential three-stage model of the physiological response to stress put forward by Hans Selye but no longer thought to be valid.

Germ theory theory of disease that focuses on identifying specific germs or pathogens as the primary cause of disease.

Global burden of disease (GBD) the universal totality of economic, social and psychological costs of a disease attributable to both morbidity and mortality over a fixed interval of time.

Globalization the process by which businesses or other organizations develop international influence or start operating on an international scale.

Glycaemic index a measure of the rise in the blood glucose/sugar level produced by a food.

Gonorrhoea a sexually transmitted disease (STI) caused by *Neisseria gonorrhoeae*, a bacterium that can grow and multiply easily in the warm, moist areas of the reproductive tract, including the cervix (opening to the womb), uterus (womb), and fallopian tubes (egg canals) in women, and in the urethra (urine canal) in women and men. The bacterium can also grow in the mouth, throat, eyes and anus.

Gradient of reinforcement principle applied mainly to *operant conditioning* whereby the acquisition of a learned response occurs more quickly, the more rapidly reward follows the occurrence of the response.

Grass roots a movement founded in groups of local people working cooperatively to achieve greater well-being.

Gross domestic product (GDP) the value of the goods and services produced by all sectors of the economy: agriculture, manufacturing, energy, construction, the service sector and government.

Gross national income (GNI) the total net value of all goods and services produced within a nation over a specified period of time, representing the sum of wages, profits, rents, interest and pension payments to residents of the nation.

Grounded theory analysis an analysis of transcripts involving coding followed by the generation of categories, using constant comparative analysis within and between interview transcripts. This is followed by memo-writing, which requires the researcher to expand upon the meaning of the broader conceptual categories. This, in turn, can lead to further data generation through theoretical sampling.

Hardiness personality trait first proposed by Kobasa and consisting of a high level of commitment, sense of control and willingness to confront challenges. Hardiness may protect the individual against the effects of stress.

Hassles scale life events stress scale designed by Kanner and associates and focusing on everyday events that cause annoyance or frustration. See also *uplifts scale* and *social readjustment rating scale* (*SRRS*).

Health a state of well-being with satisfaction of physical, cultural, psychosocial, economic and spiritual needs, not simply the absence of illness.

Health belief model (HBM) psychological model which posits that health behaviour is a function of a combination of factors including the perceived benefits of and barriers to treatment and the perceived susceptibility to and seriousness of the health problem.

Health belief system ways of thinking about the causes of health and illness.

Health communication the field of study concerned with the ways in which communication can contribute to the promotion of health.

Health education the process by which individuals' knowledge about the causes of health and illness is increased.

Health gradient the relationship between *socio-economic status* (*SES*) and mortality or morbidity that normally shows a monotonic increase as SES changes from low to high.

Health habits routine behaviours acquired by learning or conditioning that protect health or put health at risk.

Health literacy the ability to read and understand about health and healthcare enabling an individual to take decisions about treatment and prevention.

Health promotion any event, process or activity which facilitates the protection or improvement of the health of individuals, groups, communities or populations.

Health psychology an interdisciplinary field concerned with the application of psychological knowledge and techniques to health, illness and health care.

Healthism an ideology that situates health and disease as the personal responsibility of the individual; can lead to the 'medicalization' of everyday life. Healthist ideas can be used as a form of social control.

Healthy living centres local organizations designed to promote health and reduce health inequalities.

Herbal medicine is a type of complementary medicine that involves the use of plants and plant extracts to treat illnesses or to promote well-being.

Hermeneutic phenomenology study of personal meanings underpinning everyday reality.

Hierarchy of needs a concept developed by Abraham Maslow in his 1943 theory of motivation in which human needs are alleged to be in a fixed order starting with physiological need satisfaction and ending with self-actualization.

Historical analysis the use of data produced from memory, historical sources or artefacts.

HIV (human immunodeficiency virus) the virus that causes acquired immune deficiency syndrome (AIDS); it replicates in and kills the helper T cells. The virus is passed from one person to another through blood-to-blood and sexual contact. In addition, infected pregnant women can pass HIV infection to their baby during pregnancy or delivery, as well as through breast-feeding.

Homeopathy is a form of CAM which involves the use of highly diluted substances to trigger the body's natural healing system.

Human sexual response cycle a sequence of stages of sexual arousal taking the individual from initial excitement to a plateau phase, through orgasm, to resolution of sexual tension.

Humours (doctrine of the four humours) dating back to the physicians of ancient Greece, the belief that the body is essentially composed of four constituents or humours (blood, phlegm, and black and yellow bile), and that diseases and psychological characteristics are attributable to an excess or shortage of one or more of the four.

Hysteria (conversion hysteria) physical symptoms that appear to indicate organic disease but where there is no clinical evidence of disease. Nowadays this term is often replaced by *psychosomatic (or somatoform) disorder*.

Iatrogenesis health problems caused by medical or health care interventions including accidents, inappropriate treatments, incorrect diagnoses, drug side effects and other problems.

Identity control term used to describe the process by which a person deliberately attempts to control the image they present to others.

Illness perceptions beliefs about illness.

Illness representations organized mental model of character of illness.

Immunization medical procedure designed to protect susceptible individuals from communicable diseases by the administration of a vaccine. This procedure is aimed at both immediate protection of individuals and also immunity across the whole community where the uptake rate is high.

Implementation intentions specific plans about how intentions to change a piece of behaviour will actually be successfully implemented.

Incidence the rate at which new cases of a disease occur in a population during a specified period. In the simplest terms, for example, 'The incidence of STIs in 2008 was 200 cases per 10,000 people per year in Newtown compared with 150 cases per 10,000 people per year in Oldtown'.

Income distribution the distribution of income across the population. It can be measured in terms of the percentage share of national income earned by the best-off or worst-off proportions of the population; e.g. in the USA in 1991 the highest 20% of the population received 41.9% of the total national income while the worst-off 20% received 4.7%.

Indigenous belonging to a particular culture, race or tribal group.

Individualism a cultural value that enshrines the personal control and responsibility of the individual.

Inequalities a difference in life opportunities that is correlated with social position or status, ethnicity, gender, age or any other way of grouping people (see also *social inequality*).

Inequities a lack of fairness or justice between different social groups.

Insulin theory the theory that obesity is caused by a chronic elevation in insulin in a diet that contains too much carbohydrate (Taubes, 2007, 2009).

Interaction analysis system (IAS) an observation instrument that identifies, categorizes and quantifies features of the doctor–patient encounter.

Interactive dyad focusing on communication between two people.

Internal validity the degree to which the results of a study can be attributed to the manipulations of the researchers and are likely to be free of bias.

Interpretative phenomenological analysis (IPA) a technique for analysing qualitative data which seeks the meaning of experience.

Interpretative repertoire linguistic devices that people draw upon in constructing their accounts of events.

Intervention the intentional and systematic manipulation of variables with the aim of improving health outcomes.

Interviews (structured or semi-structured) a structured interview schedule is a prepared standard set of questions which are asked in person, or perhaps by telephone, of a person or group of persons concerning a particular research issue or question. A semi-structured interview is much more open ended and allows the interviewee scope to address the issues which he/she feels to be relevant to the topics being raised by the investigator.

Intrinsic motives motives based on feelings of pleasure, pride or enjoyment brought about by participating in an activity.

Inverse care law the observation that the highest access to care is available to those who need it least (e.g. the more educated, articulate, affluent members of society) while the lowest access to care is available to those who need it most.

Job satisfaction a positive emotional state resulting from work experience.

Job security holding an employed position which has a high probability of long-term continuation.

Job strain or demand control model the idea that employee well-being depends upon the interaction of role demand and control as proposed by Karasek.

Latent benefits the less tangible benefits of employment, e.g. satisfaction of psychological needs.

(To) Legitimate to justify one's position in the face of stigma, illness or invalidity.

Liberation psychology draws inspiration from the liberation theology developed by the worker-priest movement in Latin America during the 1950s and 1960s. This movement argues that it is the duty of Catholics to fight against social injustice and to adopt a *preferential option for the poor*. These ideas were practised by Salvadorian Jesuit psychologist Ignacio Martín-Baró.

Life events and difficulties schedule (LEDS) a psychological measurement of the stressfulness of life events, created by Brown and Harris in 1978. The schedule is based upon an interview which discusses the contextual information around the event.

Lifestyle sports sports associated with a particular lifestyle, e.g. snowboarding, surfing.

Literature search 'combing through' or 'mining' the literature relevant to a review or a new study.

Liver cirrhosis frequently fatal form of liver damage usually found among long-term heavy drinkers. Initially fat accumulates on the liver, enlarging it; this restricts blood flow, causing damage to cells, and scar tissue develops, preventing the liver from functioning normally.

Locus of control personality traits first proposed by social psychologists and then adapted by health psychologists to distinguish between those who attribute their state of health to themselves, powerful others or chance.

Longitudinal designs involves measuring responses of a single sample on more than one occasion. These measurements may be prospective or retrospective, but prospective longitudinal designs allow greater control over the sample, the variables measured and the times when the measurements take place.

Loss-framed messages information about a health behaviour that emphasizes the costs of failing to take action.

Machismo strong and exaggerated sense of masculinity emphasizing physical attributes.

Macronutrient environmental substance used for energy, growth, and bodily functions needed in large amounts by humans: carbohydrates (sugar), lipids (fats), and proteins.

Macro-social large-scale social, economic, political and cultural forces that influence the life course of masses of people simultaneously.

Maintenance stage the continued practice of or adherence to a specific health-promoting behaviour, e.g. abstinence from smoking; one of the stages in the *transtheoretical model of change.*

Mammography a method for imaging breast tissue of women using radiography for detecting early signs of breast cancer.

Manifest benefits the concrete benefits of employment, e.g. income.

Meaning having purpose or value.

Medical error errors in medical diagnosis and treatment.

Medical model a way of thinking about health and illness that assumes all health and illness phenomena are physiological in nature. According to this model, health, illness and treatments have a purely biological or biochemical basis.

Medical silence reluctance of the medical profession to publicly acknowledge or report errors.

Medicalization the process by which experiences and practices which do not match those defined as 'natural' and 'healthy' are pathologized and treated as dysfunctional.

Meta-analysis a quantitative literature review that combines the evidence from relevant previous studies, taking account of criteria for quality and allowing high statistical power.

Metastasis the spread of cancer cells to secondary sites in the body.

Mindfulness a Buddhist concept, developed from 1979 and popularized in many publications by Jon Kabat-Zinn; paying attention to one's thoughts, feelings and actions; an acute awareness of the conscious flow of experience.

Mindfulness-based relapse prevention (MBRP) application of the methods of *mindfulness-based stress reduction* (*MBSR*) to the treatment of alcohol and substance use disorders, first proposed by Witkiewitz et al. (2005).

Mindfulness-based stress reduction (MBSR) a method of stress management based on the concept of mindfulness.

Model an abstract representation of relationships between processes believed to influence each other.

Moral discourses of suffering language derived from moral principles used to describe and explain health and illness.

Motivation enhancement therapy brief intervention developed by W.R. Miller for the treatment of alcohol and drug problems, which aims to boost the clients' self-esteem and motivation to change, in contrast to traditional, more confrontational approaches.

Motivational interviewing brief intervention developed by W.R. Miller for the treatment of alcohol and drug problems, which aims to boost the clients' self-esteem and motivation to change, in contrast to traditional confrontational approaches.

Multidimensional Health Locus of Control (MHLC) scale a popular scale for assessing a person's attributions of experience as internally/externally controlled, controlled by powerful others, or by chance.

Multiple regression a statistical technique based on correlations between variables enabling predictions to be made about dependent variables using a combination of two or more independent variables.

Myalgic encephalomyelitis (ME) syndrome first observed in an epidemic at the Royal Free Hospital, London, in 1955, now usually thought to be identical to *chronic fatigue syndrome* and controversial for the same reasons.

Myocardial infarction (MI) a form of *coronary heart disease* (CHD) or 'heart attack' that occurs when one of the coronary arteries becomes blocked by a blood clot and part of the heart is starved of oxygen. It usually causes severe chest pain. MI is often the first sign of CHD in many people.

Narrative structured discourse which connects agents and events over time in the form of a story.

Narrative approaches seek insight and meaning through the acquisition of data in the form of stories concerning personal experiences (Murray, 1997a). These approaches assume that human beings are natural storytellers and that the principal task of the psychologist is to explore the different stories being told.

Need satisfaction necessary for health and well-being; the attainment of physical health, agency, and autonomy; the satisfaction of all physical, cultural, psychosocial, economic and spiritual needs.

Nicotine a chemical found in tobacco that acts as a stimulant, can be fatal in large amounts, and is largely responsible for the addictive properties of tobacco; also used as an insecticide.

Nicotine paradox nicotine is a stimulant yet smokers experience relaxation when they smoke.

Nicotine replacement therapy (NRT) a medical treatment for smoking cessation that has obtained marginally superior results to a placebo in trials sponsored and hyped by the pharmaceutical industry and its consultants. The method definitely should be avoided in pregnancy and adolescence. Real-world studies in the general population show lack of effectiveness.

Obesity an excessive accumulation of body fat, usually defined as a body mass index (BMI) greater than 30.

Obesogenic referring to an environment that exposes the population to a large number of foods and drinks that have a high percentage of fats and sugars.

Objectification the process whereby a more abstract concept acquires meaning through association with everyday phenomena. The process transforms an abstract concept into a concrete image.

Observational studies studies that are designed to evaluate the effectiveness of interventions that, for whatever reason, cannot or do not use a randomized controlled design.

Obstructive sleep apnoea (OSA) temporary cessation of breathing during sleep caused by a physical block to airflow despite respiratory effort; can be worsened by overweight and obesity; associated with snoring.

Occupational stress psychological, emotional or physical strain resulting from workplace demands and environment.

Operant conditioning a learning process whereby a normally voluntary form of behaviour comes to occur with increasing frequency in a particular situation, or in the presence of a particular stimulus, as a result of previously and repeatedly having been rewarded in similar circumstances.

Operationism the use of rules or a method of measurement to define an object or quality.

Opportunistic intervention an attempt to modify health hazardous behaviour, such as smoking or heavy drinking, by a health professional, frequently a doctor, who has been consulted for other reasons.

Outcome evaluation an assessment of an intervention that examines the objective outcome in a controlled investigation of the effects or impact of the intervention.

Outreach programme an intervention which aims to achieve sub-cultural change among hard-to-reach target constituencies in order to improve health outcomes.

Pap test a medical procedure for conducting cervical screening examinations.

Participatory action research (PAR) a form of action research that deliberately seeks to provoke some form of social or community change in which the instigator/investigator works collaboratively with stakeholders by taking actions to bring about desired change in a step-by-step process.

Participatory learning the full participation of people in the processes of learning about their needs and opportunities, and in the action required to address them.

Patient-centred communication style a doctor's communication style which mobilizes the patient's knowledge, experience and involvement through techniques such as silence, listening and reflection.

Patient informatics a programme that aims to enable patients to make better use of information and communication technology for health and health care.

Patient safety prevention of avoidable errors and adverse effects to patients associated with health care.

Patient satisfaction a measure of the extent to which patients' expectations of what a medical encounter ought to provide have been met (as judged by the patients).

Perceived behavioural control the feeling of having control over one's actions in response to others and the environment.

Percutaneous coronary intervention (PCI) a procedure that unblocks narrowed coronary arteries without performing surgery. This may be done with either a balloon catheter to push the atheroma to the side of the artery or a stent inserted to keep the artery open.

Pessimistic explanatory style tendency of some individuals to blame themselves for everything that goes wrong in their lives, believed to be associated with poor physical health.

Phenomenology study of the participant's perspective of the world.

Physical activity bodily movement produced by skeletal muscles that requires energy expenditure.

Physical dependency evidenced when a person experiences unpleasant physical symptoms when he/she stops using or reduces consumption of a drug, tobacco or alcohol.

Physical education systematic instruction in sports and physical activity given as part of school or college education

Physical side effects unwanted physiological effects that accompany medication.

Placebo an inert substance or treatment that lacks any specific effect but which may induce the perception of benefit.

Placebo control a control condition that appears similar to a treatment when in fact it is completely general.

Placebo effect an effect from a placebo drug or treatment, which cannot be attributed to the properties of the placebo itself.

Population pyramid a graphical method of representing the age distribution of populations at different time points showing number of people in each, differently coloured, age band indicated by the width of the band, with younger age groups at the base and older age groups at the top, with males on one side, females on the other.

Positivism the epistemological position which places scientific method as the sole source of reliable knowledge.

Post-traumatic stress disorder (PTSD) long-term psychological and physiological effects of exposure to traumatic stress, including insomnia, nightmares, flashbacks, problems of memory and concentration, acting or feeling as if the event is recurring and a greatly increased sensitivity to new stressful events.

Poverty the level of income below which people cannot afford a minimum, nutritionally adequate diet and essential non-food requirements.

Power analysis a method for deciding how large a sample is needed to enable a statistical judgement that is accurate and reliable and how likely it is that the particular statistical test to be used will be able to detect effects of a given size in a particular situation, e.g. how big a sample is necessary to have a .8 probability of detecting a difference at the .05 level of significance.

Pre-contemplation stage the stage of knowing that a habit or behaviour is hazardous but without any intention to change it in the foreseeable future; one of the stages in the *transtheoretical model of change.*

Preparation stage intending to take action in the immediate future, having developed a specific plan of action; one of the stages in the *transtheoretical model of change.*

Prevalence the number of people with a disease or behaviour as a proportion of the population or sub-population at any point in time.

Preventive health behaviours behaviours people choose to engage in with the aim of protecting and/or improving their health status.

Process evaluation an assessment of how well an intervention is implemented in terms of the activities that occur, who is conducting the activities, who is being reached, what inputs or resources have been allocated, and what the strengths, weaknesses, and areas that need improvement are.

Prospect theory the theory that influenced message framing in health promotion; it proposes that people consider their ‘prospects’ (i.e. potential gains and losses) when making a decision.

Protein leverage hypothesis the hypothesis that humans prioritize protein when regulating food intake (Simpson and Raubenheimer, 2005).

Psycho-oncology the psychological aspects of cancer care and treatment.

Psychological dependency a state associated with repeated activity or consumption of a drug or drink which leads to negative affect following reduced consumption or abstinence and a persistent desire or unsuccessful efforts to cut down or control the activity.

Psychoneuroimmunology (PNI) the study of the effects of psychological variables and especially stress on the immune system.

Psychosocial explanations accounts of events and experiences based on theories and research from psychology and the social sciences.

Psychosomatic (or somatoform) disorders physical ailments believed to be psychologically caused including *hysteria* and some conditions which have organic features such as ulcers and asthma.

Psychosomatic medicine a precursor of modern health psychology which flourished from the 1930s to the 1950s; its proponents, including Alexander and Dunbar, believed that psychoanalytic theories about unconscious conflicts could be extended to explain susceptibility to various organic diseases.

Public health psychology the application of psychological theory, research and technologies towards the improvement of the health of the population.

Qualitative research methods methods that are intended to provide improved understanding of the meanings, purposes and intentions of behaviour, not its amount or quantity.

Quality of life (QoL) the general well-being of a person or society, defined in terms of physical health and mental well-being, including happiness and autonomy, not necessarily wealth.

Quasi-experimental design comparison of two or more treatments in as controlled a manner as possible but without the possibility of manipulating an independent variable or randomly allocating participants.

Questionnaires many constructs in health psychology are measured using questionnaires consisting of a standard set of items with accompanying instructions. Ideally a questionnare will have been demonstrated to be both a reliable and valid measure of the construct(s) it purports to measure.

Quit For Life (QFL) Programme a psychological therapy using cognitive behavioural principles enabling smokers to quit (Marks, 1993, 2005).

Racism discrimination on the basis of race or skin colour.

Randomized controlled trials (RCTs) these involve the systematic comparison of interventions employing a fully controlled application of one or more interventions or 'treatments' using a random allocation of participants to the different treatment groups.

Reactance theory a theory concerning the tendency to resist attempts by others to control one's behaviour.

Reflexology is a type of complementary medicine that involves the application of pressure and massage to specific reflex areas in the body.

Relapse going back to consumption of tobacco, alcohol or a drug after a period of voluntary abstinence.

Relapse prevention therapy strategies and procedures for reducing the likelihood of *relapse*.

Replication the attempt by an investigator to repeat a study to determine whether the original findings can be repeated.

Responsible consumer a consumer who takes a measured, rational, evidence-based approach to his or her consumption of foods, beverages, and other potentially hazardous products such as tobacco.

Restenosis coronary artery blockage that occurs following *percutaneous coronary intervention* (*PCI*).

Revascularization a term that describes surgical and catheter procedures that are used to restore blood flow to the heart.

Role ambiguity lack of information necessary to conduct the role and information deficiency regarding expected role behaviours, role objectives and responsibilities.

Role conflict incompatible role demands placed upon an individual.

Role demand the expectations placed upon a person within a role.

Safer sex practices those sexual practices that do not involve the exchange of bodily fluids which may contain the human immunodeficiency virus. Such bodily fluids are blood, semen and vaginal fluids.

Screening procedure for the identification of the presence of certain diseases, conditions or behaviours in a community. Those sections of the population who are most at risk of developing a particular disease are examined to see whether they have any early indications. The rationale behind this strategy is that the earlier the disease is identified and treated, the less likely it is to develop into a fatal condition.

Second-hand smoke smoke exhaled by smokers polluting the environment of others, whether 'smokers' or 'non-smokers', which they are forced to inhale.

Sedentary referring to the absence of physical activity.

Self-concept a sense of who you are.

Self-determination engaging in activities for their enjoyment or intrinsic motivation.

Self-efficacy belief that one will be able to carry out one's plans successfully; a term proposed by Bandura (1977) and thought to be associated with positive health behaviours.

Self-esteem a personality trait consisting of positive self-regard, originally proposed by Rosenberg (1965).

Self-regulation process by which individuals monitor and adjust their medication on an ongoing basis.

Self-regulatory model this model suggests that health-related practices or coping responses are influenced by patients' beliefs or representations of the illness. These illness representations have a certain structure.

Sensation seeking a personality trait or type that is characterized by a strong desire for new sensations.

Sense of coherence a personality trait originally proposed by Antonovsky (1979) to characterize people who see their world as essentially meaningful and manageable; associated with coping with stress.

Sense of community a feeling that one belongs to a group located in space and time with a common identity, history and culture.

Sex survey a large-scale, questionnaire-based instrument which aims to provide quantifiable, descriptive data about a population's sexual habits.

Sexology the scientific study of human sexual behaviour.

Sexual behaviour any activity that arouses sexual arousal for pleasure or procreation.

Sexual meanings the significance which is attributed to sexual practices as a result of the application of socio-historically and culturally variable and changing interpretative frames.

Sexuality those aspects of human experience which are influenced by and/or expressive of sexual desire and/or practice.

Sexually transmitted infections (STIs) infections that can be transferred from one person to another through sexual contact through vaginal or anal intercourse, kissing, oral–genital contact, and the use of sexual 'toys' such as vibrators.

Single case experimental design investigation of a series of experimental manipulations on a single research participant.

Skin fold thickness a method of determining body composition and body fat percentage using calipers at different positions on a persons's body.

Social capital the institutions, relationships, and norms that shape the quality and quantity of a society's social interactions. Social capital is not just the sum of the institutions which underpin a society – it is the glue that holds them together.

Social cognition a cognitive model of social knowledge.

Social cognition models (SCMs) theories about the relationship between social cognitions, such as beliefs and attitudes, and behaviour, which aim accurately to predict behaviour or behavioural intentions.

Social constructionism (1) the philosophical belief that there is no single, fixed 'reality' but a multiplicity of descriptions, each with its own unique pattern of meanings; (2) 'many potential worlds of meaning that can be imaginatively entered and celebrated, in ways which are constantly changing to give richness and value to human experience' (Mulkay, 1991: 27–8).

Social Darwinism the concept that competition drives social evolution.

Social inequality being treated differently as a consequence of age, race, gender, disability, sexual preference or other attribute (see also *inequality*).

Social justice the process of treating a person, group or community fairly and equally.

Social marketing the application of consumer-oriented marketing techniques in the design, implementation and evaluation of programmes aimed towards influencing behaviour change. Social marketing draws upon concepts from behavioural theory, persuasion psychology, and marketing science.

Social Readjustment Rating Scale (SRRS) measurement scale for life events stress developed by Holmes and Rahe and widely used in research on life events stress and illness (see also *hassles scale* and *uplifts scale*).

Social representation theory (SRs) system of ideas, values and practices specific to a particular community which enables individuals to orient themselves in the world and communicate with each other.

Social support informal and formal supportive relationships.

Socio-economic status (SES) position or class based on occupation, education or income.

Spirituality the quality or state of being spiritual, with or without religious beliefs.

Sudden infant death syndrome (SIDS) unexplained death of infants while lying in a crib or cot.

Stages of change the stages of pre-contemplation, contemplation, preparation, action, maintenance, and termination in the *transtheoretical model of change.*

Statins drugs used to reduce cholesterol levels.

Stigma the process of marginalizing a group or class of people by labelling them as different and understanding them in terms of stereotypes; results in a loss of social status and discrimination, affecting many areas of life.

Stigmatization being treated as an object of derision and shame purely as a consequence of others' ignorance and prejudice.

Stress ambiguous term, sometimes used to refer to environmental pressure and sometimes to a particular type of response to pressure. Currently it is often used to describe an inner state that can occur when either real or perceived demands exceed either the real or the perceived capacity to cope with them.

Stress innoculation training (SIS) a *cognitive behavioural* method for stress management devised by Meichenbaum (1985), focusing on changing the way in which participants appraise situations as stressful and cope with stressful events.

Stress management workshop a training programme in stress management usually delivered to groups, frequently lasting for a whole day or a weekend, and focusing on changing the way in which participants appraise situations as stressful and cope with stressful events.

Subjective norms the beliefs of other people about the importance of carrying out a behaviour.

Subjective well-being (SWB) a concept that, in plain English, would be called 'happiness'. The adjective 'subjective' is necessary because well-being cannot be inferred from outward appearances or objective characteristics of the person.

Surveys systematic methods for determining how a defined sample of participants respond to a set of standard questions attempting to assess their feelings, attitudes, beliefs or knowledge at one or more particular times.

Symmetry rule a tendency to search for a label for bodily symptoms and to expect symptoms if we have an illness label.

Syphilis a chronic infectious disease caused by a spirochete (*Treponema pallidum*), transmitted by direct contact, usually in sexual intercourse, or passed from mother to child in utero, and progressing through three stages characterized respectively by local formation of chancres, ulcerous skin eruptions, and systemic infection leading to general paresis.

Systematic review a review of the empirical literature concerning the efficacy or effectiveness of an intervention that considers all of the relevant studies taking account of quality criteria.

Systems theory approach a theory concerned with the contextual structures, processes or relationships within communities, groups or families.

Taoism A Chinese philosophy which views the universe as being governed by the two basic powers of yin and yang.

Tautological an empty statement consisting of simpler statements that make it logically true whether the simpler statements are true or false, e.g. the statement: *Either I will wear a condom the next time I have sexual intercourse or I will not.*

Taxonomy a system for the description, identification, nomenclature, and classification of objects, organisms or interventions.

Teleworking working outside of the traditional workplace and using information technology and telecommunication systems.

Temperance societies originating in the USA in the nineteenth century, these societies, of which Alcoholics Anonymous is an example, are dedicated to counteracting the harmful effects of drinking, usually advocating teetotalism.

Tension reduction hypothesis the hypothesis that people enjoy alcohol primarily because it reduces tension (anxiety, stress), rather than as a drug which directly produces positive moods.

Theory a general account of relationships between processes believed to influence, cause changes in, or control a phenomenon.

Theory of planned behaviour (TPB) theoretical model which argues that behavioural intention is controlled by attitudes, subjective norms and perceived control.

Theory of reasoned action (TRA) theoretical model which argues that behavioural intention is controlled by attitudes and subjective norms.

Therapeutic alliance is a term used to describe the relationship between mental health practitioners and their clients.

Top-down controlled, directed, or organized from the top using a preconceived theory or model about the processes that are expected to occur.

Toxic environment a term referring to environmental and social conditions that promote disease, disorder and death.

Transparency a description of a method or procedure that is detailed and explicit; enabling replication by another investigator.

Transtheoretical model of change (TTM) a model of behaviour change developed by DiClementi, Prochaska and others which attempts to identify universal processes or stages of change specified as *pre-contemplation*, *contemplation*, *preparation*, *action*, *maintenance* and termination.

Triangulation collecting evidence using different methods to provide complementary perspectives.

Triglyceride the main component of dietary fats and oils and the principal form in which fat is stored in the body; it is composed of three fatty acids attached to a glycerol molecule which are saturated, mono-unsaturated and polyunsaturated.

Tumour (benign or malignant) an abnormal new mass of tissue that serves no purpose; a tumour may be malignant or non-malignant depending on whether it is life-threatening or not.

Twelve-step facilitation programme a theraputic regime which attempts to change thinking and behaviour in a series of 12 steps, as advocated by Alcoholics Anonymous.

Type A/B personality the Type A personality, in contrast to the Type B personality, is characterized by intense achievement motivation, time urgency and hostility.

Unconditioned stimulus (UCS) stimulus that evokes a response or reflex without training, e.g. a loud sound will naturally evoke a startle response.

Uncontrolled variable a background variable that remains uncontrolled by the investigator and which may affect or bias the results of a study.

Uplifts scale life events scale designed by Kanner and associates (1981) to assess desirable events, in contrast to their *hassles scale.*

Varenicline (also known as Champix) used in smoking cessation to prevent craving and withdrawal symptoms.

Vegan a plant-based diet that excludes all animal-based foods.

Vegetarian a diet that includes eggs and/or dairy but no other foods derived from animal sources.

Viral challenge studies method of studying the relationship between stress and susceptibility to infectious disease in which volunteers are deliberately exposed to minor viruses, usually colds or flu, to determine whether those who have experienced higher levels of stress prior to exposure are more likely to contract the infection.

Visceral fat fat that accumulates in organs such as the liver that causes insulin resistance and MS.

Waist circumference a measure of central adiposity or body fat.

Well-being the state of 'wellness'; the general state of health of an individual.

Wernicke–Korsakoff syndrome a form of irreversible brain damage sometimes found among long-term heavy drinkers, its symptoms include extremely impaired short-term memory, confusion and visual disorders.

Withdrawal symptoms unpleasant symptoms and craving accompanying cessation of tobacco or other drug use, e.g. uncontrolled sweating, palpitations, depression, fear or anxiety.

World Health Organization (WHO) the directing and coordinating authority for health within the United Nations. The Director-General of the WHO is Dr Margaret Chan, from the People's Republic of China.

References

Aaron, L.A. and Buchwald, D. (2001). A review of the evidence for overlap among unexplained clinical conditions. *Annals of Internal Medicine*, 131: 868–81.

Aboumatar, H., Carson, K., Beach, M., Roter, D. and Cooper, L. (2013). The impact of health literacy on desire for participation in health care, medical visit communication, and patient reported outcomes among patients with hypertension. *Journal of General Internal Medicine*, 28: 1469–76.

Abraham, C. and Michie, S. (2008). A taxonomy of behaviour change techniques used in interventions. *Health Psychology*, 27: 379–87.

Abraham, C. and Sheeran, P. (1994). Modelling and modifying young heterosexuals' HIV-preventive behaviour: a review of theories, findings and educational implications. *Patient Education and Counselling*, 23: 173–86.

Abraham, C. and Sheeran, P. (2004). Deciding to exercise: the role of anticipated regret. *British Journal of Health Psychology*, 9: 269–78.

Academy of Medical Sciences (2004). *Calling Time: The Nation's Drinking as a Major Health Issue.* London: Academy of Medical Sciences.

Acheson, D. (1998). Inequalities in health report on inequalities in health did give priority for steps to be tackled. *British Medical Journal* (Clinical Research Edition), 317 (7173): 1659.

Ackerson, K. and Preston, S.D. (2009). A decision theory perspective on why women do or do not decide to have cancer screening: systematic review. *Journal of Advanced Nursing*, 65: 1130–40.

Action on Smoking and Health (2010). *Tobacco Explained: The Truth About the Tobacco Industry ... in its Own Words.* Available: http://ash.org.uk/files/documents/ASH_599.pdf [accessed 5 December 2014].

Action on Smoking and Health (2014). Smoking statistics. Available: http://ash.org.uk/files/documents/ASH_106.pdf [accessed 5 December 2014].

Adams, G. and Salter, P.S. (2007). Health psychology in African settings: a cultural-psychological analysis. *Journal of Health Psychology*, 12: 539–51.

Adams, S., Pill, R. and Jones, A. (1997). Medication, chronic illness and identity: the perspective of people with asthma. *Social Science & Medicine*, 45: 189–201.

Adler, N.E. and Matthews K.A. (1994). Health psychology: why do some people get sick and some stay well? *Annual Review of Psychology*, 45: 229–59.

Agostinelli, G. and Grube, J.W. (2002). Alcohol counter-advertising and the media. *Alcohol Research and Health*, 26: 15–21.

Ahern, A.L., Bennett, K.M., Kelly, M. and Hetherington, M.M. (2011). A qualitative exploration of young women's attitudes towards the Thin Ideal. *Journal of Health Psychology*, 16: 70–9.

Ahnquist, J., Wamala, S.P. and Lindstrom, M. (2012). Social determinants of health: a question of social or economic capital? Interaction effects of socioeconomic factors on health outcomes. *Social Science & Medicine*, 74 (6): 930–9.

AIESEC International (2009). 50% of young people admit they don't know enough about HIV and AIDS. Available: www.aiesec.org/cms/aiesec/AI/press.ht [accessed 1 Janaury 2010].

Ainsworth, M.D.S., Blehar, M.C., Waters, E. and Wall, S. (1978). *Patterns of Attachment: A Psychological Study of the Strange Situation*. Hillsdale, NJ: Erlbaum.

Ajzen, I. (1985). From intention to actions: a theory of planned behavior. In J. Kuhl and J. Beckmann (eds.), *Action-Control: From Cognition to Behavior*. Heidelberg: Springer. pp. 11–39.

Ajzen, I. (2002). The theory of planned behaviour. Available: www.people.umass.edu/aizen.

Ajzen, I. (2014). The theory of planned behaviour is alive and well, and not ready to retire: a commentary on Sniehotta, Presseau, and Araújo-Soares. *Health Psychology Review*, (ahead-of-print), 1–7.

Ajzen, I. and Fishbein, M. (1980). *Understanding Attitudes and Predicting Social Behavior*. Englewood Cliffs, NJ: Prentice-Hall.

Albarracín, D., Gillette, J.C., Earl, A.N., Glasman, L.R., Durantini, M.R. and Ho, M.H. (2005). A test of major assumptions about behavior change: a comprehensive look at the effects of passive and active HIV-prevention interventions since the beginning of the epidemic. *Psychological Bulletin*, 131: 856–97.

Albarracín, D., Johnson, B.T., Fishbein, M. and Muellerleile, P.A. (2001). Theories of reasoned action and planned behavior as models of condom use: a meta-analysis. *Psychological Bulletin*, 127: 142–61.

Alderman, K., Turner, L.R. and Tong, S. (2012). Floods and human health: a systematic review. *Environment International*, 47: 37–47.

Aldwin, C.M. and Park, C.L. (2004). Coping and physical health outcomes: an overview. *Psychology & Health*, 19: 277–81.

Alexander, F. (1950). *Psychosomatic Medicine*. New York: Norton.

Amadi-Obi, A., Gilligan, P., Owens, N. and O'Donnell, C. (2014). Telemedicine in pre-hospital care: a review of telemedicine applications in pre-hospital environment. *International Journal of Emergency Medicine*, 7: 29.

Amelang, M. and Schmidt-Rathjens, C. (1996). Personality, cancer and coronary heart disease: further evidence on a controversial issue. *British Journal of Health Psychology*, 1: 191–205.

American Cancer Society (2003). *Cancer Facts & Figures*. Atlanta: Georgia.

American Cancer Society (2009). *Cancer Facts & Figures*. Atlanta: Georgia.

American College Health Association (2005). *American College Health Association – National College Health Assessment (ACHA-NCHA) Web Summary*. Available: www.acha-ncha.org/data_highlights.html.

Anand, S. and Sen, A. (2000). Human development and economic sustainability. *World development*, 28: 2029–49.

Andersen A.M.N., Andersen, P.K., Olsen, J., Gronbaek, M. and Strandberg-Larsen, K. (2012). Moderate alcohol intake during pregnancy and risk of fetal death. *International Journal of Epidemiology*, 41: 405–13.

Anderson, I., Crengle, S., Kamaka, M.L., Chen, T., Palafox, N. and Jackson-Pulver, L. (2006). Indigenous health in Australia, New Zealand, and the Pacific. *The Lancet*, 367: 1775–85.

Anderson, K.F. (2013). Diagnosing discrimination: stress from perceived racism and the mental and physical health effects. *Sociological Inquiry*, 83: 55–81.

Anderson, L.M., Scrimshaw, S.C., Fullilove, M.T., Fielding, J.E., Normand, J. and the Taskforce on Community Preventive Services (2003). Culturally competent healthcare systems: a systematic review. *American Journal of Preventive Medicine*, 24: 68–79.

Anderson, P. and Baumberg, B. (2006). *Alcohol in Europe: A Public Health Perspective – A Report for the European Commission*. London: Institute of Alcohol Studies.

Andreouli, E., Howarth, C. and Sonn, C. (2014). The role of schools in promoting inclusive communities in contexts of diversity. *Journal of Health Psychology*, 19: 16–21.

Anjana, R.M., Ali, M.K., Pradeepa, R., Deepa, M., Datta, M., Unnikrishnan, R., et al. (2011). The need for obtaining accurate nationwide estimates of diabetes prevalence in India – rationale for a national study on diabetes. *Indian Journal of Medical Research* [online] 133: 369–80. Available: www.ijmr.org.in/text.asp?2011/133/4/369/80127 [accessed 10 August 2014].

Ansell, N. (2014). Challenging empowerment: AIDS-affected southern African children and the need for a multi-level relational approach. *Journal of Health Psychology*, 19: 22–33.

Anthony, J.C. and Echeagaray-Wagner, F. (2013). Epidemiologic analysis of alcohol and tobacco use – patterns of co-occurring consumption and dependence in the United States. *Alcohol Research & Health*, 24: 201–8.

Antonovsky, A. (1979). *Health, Stress, and Coping*. San Francisco, CA: Jossey-Bass.

Antonovsky, A. (1979). Health, stress and coping: new perspectives on mental and physical well-being. *Aufl., San Francisco*.

Argyris, C. (1975) Dangers in applying results from experimental social psychology. *American Psychologist*, 30: 469–85.

Armitage, C.J. (2009). Is there utility in the transtheoretical model? *British Journal of Health Psychology*, 14: 195–210.

Armstrong, N. (2007). Discourse and the individual in cervical cancer screening. *Health (London)*, 11: 69–85.

Arrow, K. (1963). *Social Choice and Individual Values* (2nd edn). New York: Wiley.

Arthur, H.M., Daniels, C., McKelvie, R., Hirsh, J. and Rush, B. (2000). Effect of a preoperative intervention on preoperative and postoperative outcomes in low-risk patients awaiting elective coronary artery bypass graft surgery: a randomized, controlled trial. *Annals of Internal Medicine*, 133: 253–62.

Asmundson G.J.G., Norton, P.J. and Norton, G.R. (1999). Beyond pain: the role of fear and avoidance in chronicity. *Clinical Psychological Review*, 19: 97–119.

Astin, J.A. (1998). Why patients use alternative medicine: results of a national study. *JAMA*, 279: 1548–53.

Auerbach, S.M. (2001). Do patients want control over their own health care? A review of measures, findings, and research issues. *Journal of Health Psychology*, 6: 191–204.

Auerbach, S.M. and Pegg, P.O. (2002). Appraisal of desire for control over healthcare: structure, stability, and relation to health locus of control and to the 'Big Five' personality traits. *Journal of Health Psychology*, 7: 39–408.

Austin, R.M. and McLendon, W.W. (1997). The Papanicolaou smear: medicine's most successful cancer screening procedure is threatened. *Journal of the American Medical Association*, 277: 754–5.

Australian Bureau of Statistics (2014). *Australian Aboriginal and Torres Strait Islander Health Survey: First Results, Australia, 2012–13*. Canberra: Australian Bureau of Statistics. Available: www.abs.gov.au/ausstats/abs@.nsf/Lookup/3D7CEBB5503A110ECA257C2F00145AB4?opendocument.

Aveling, E. and Jovchelovitch, S. (2014). Partnerships as knowledge encounters: a psychosocial theory of partnerships for health and community development. *Journal of Health Psychology*, 19 (1): 34–45.

Avert Organisation (2004). *History of AIDS*. Available: www.avert.org/historyi.htm.

Avlund, K., Osler, M., Damsgaard, M.T., Christensen, U. and Schroll, M. (2000). The relations between musculoskeletal diseases and mobility among old people: are they influenced by socio-economic, psychosocial and behavioural factors? *International Journal of Behavioural Medicine*, 7: 322–39.

Ayo, N. (2012). Understanding health promotion in a neoliberal climate and the making of health conscious citizens. *Critical Public Health*, 22: 99–105.

Babor, T.F. and Winstanley, E.L. (2008). The world of drinking: national alcohol control experiences in 18 countries. *Addiction*, 103: 721–5.

Babor, T.F., Caetano, R., Casswell, S., Edwards, G. et al. (Alcohol & Public Policy Group) (2003). *Alcohol: No Ordinary Commodity – Research and Public Policy.* Oxford and London: Oxford University Press.

Bachen, E., Cohen, S. and Marsland, A.L. (2007). Psychoimmunology. In S. Ayers, A. Baum, C. McManus, S. Newman, K. Wallston, J. Weinman and R.West (eds.), *Cambridge Handbook of Psychology, Health and Medicine* (2nd edn). Cambridge: Cambridge University Press. pp.167–72.

Baerger, D.R. and McAdams, D.P. (1999). Life story coherence and its relation to psychological well-being. *Narrative Inquiry*, 9: 69–96.

Bailey, J.A., Fleming, C.B., Henson, J.N., Catalano, R.F. and Haggerty, K.P. (2008). Sexual risk behavior 6 months post-high school: associations with college attendance, living with a parent, and prior risk behavior. *Journal of Adolescent Health*, 42: 573–9.

Baker, D.W., Parker, R.M., Williams, M.V., Pitkin, K., Parikh, N.S., Coates, W. and Imara, M. (1996). The health care experience of patients with low literacy. *Archive of Family Medicine*, 5: 329–34.

Baker, M. (2014). RCGP consultation on assisted dying was comprehensive and conclusively in favour of no change to the law. *British Medical Journal* (Clinical Research Edition), 349: g4003.

Baker, S. (2002). Bardot, Britney, bodies and breasts. *Perfect Beat*, 6: 18–32.

Balady, G.J., Williams, M.A., Ades, P.A., Bittner, V., Comoss, P., Foody, J.M. et al. (2007). *Circulation*, 115: 2675–82.

Balarajan, R. and Soni Raleigh, V. (1993). *Ethnicity and Health: A Guide for the NHS*. London: Department of Health.

Balbach, E.D., Smith, E.A. and Malone, R.E. (2006). How the health belief model helps the tobacco industry: individuals, choice, and 'information'. *Tobacco Control*, 15: 37–43.

Bancroft, A., Wiltshire, S., Parry, O. and Amos, A. (2003). 'It's like an addiction first thing … afterwards it's like a habit': daily smoking behaviour among people living in areas of deprivation. *Social Science & Medicine*, 56: 1261–7.

Bandura, A. (1977). Self-efficacy: towards a unifying theory of behavioural change. *Psychological Review*, 84: 191–215.

Bandura, A. (1986). *Social Foundations of Thought and Action: A Social Cognitive Theory*. Englewood Cliffs, NJ: Prentice-Hall.

Bandura, A. (1994). Self-efficacy. In V.S. Ramachaudran (ed.), *Encyclopedia of Human Behavior* (Vol. 4). New York: Academic Press. pp. 71–81.

Bandura, A. (ed.). (1995). *Self-efficacy in Changing Societies*. Cambridge: Cambridge University Press.

Bandura, A. (1997). The anatomy (2001). Social cognitive theory: an agentic perspective. *Annual Review of Psychology*, 52: 1–26

Bantum, E.O.C., Albright, C.L., White, K.K., Berenberg, J.L., Layi, G., Ritter, P.L. and Lorig, K. (2014). Surviving and thriving with cancer using a web-based health behavior change intervention: randomized controlled trial. *Journal of Medical Internet Research*, 16 (2): e54.

Barak, A. and Fisher, W.A. (2001). Toward an Internet-driven, theoretically-based innovative approach to sex education. *Journal of Sex Research*, 38: 324–32.

Bardia, A., Barton, D.L., Prokop, L.J., Bauer, B.A. and Moynihan, T.J. (2006). Efficacy of complementary and alternative medicine therapies in relieving cancer pain: a systematic review. *Journal of Clinical Oncology*, 24: 5457–64.

Barker-Ruchti, N., Barker, D., Sattler, S., Gerber, M. and Pühse, U. (2013). Sport – 'it's just healthy': locating healthism within discourses of social integration. *Journal of Ethnic & Migration Studies*, 39 (5): 759–72.

Barraclough, J., Pinder, P., Cruddas, M., Osmand, C., Taylor, I. and Perry, M. (1992). Life events and breast cancer prognosis. *British Medical Journal*, 304: 1078–81.

Barrett, A.E. (2003). Socioeconomic status and age identity: the role of dimensions of health in the subjective construction of age. *Journal of Gerontology, Series B: Psychological Sciences and Social Sciences*, 58: S101–9.

Barry, M.J. and Edgman-Levitan, S. (2012). Shared decision making – the pinnacle of patient-centered care. *New England Journal of Medicine*, 366: 780–1.

Barth, J. and Lannen, P. (2011). Efficacy of communication skills training courses in oncology: a systematic review and meta-analysis. *Annals of Oncology: Official Journal of the European Society for Medical Oncology/ESMO*, 22: 1030–40.

Barth, J., Schneider, S. and von Känel, R. (2010). Lack of social support in the etiology and the prognosis of coronary heart disease: a systematic review and meta-analysis. *Psychosomatic Medicine*, 72 (3): 229–38.

Bartlett, D. (1998). *Stress: Perspectives and Processes.* London: Open University Press.

Bass, C. (2007). Psychosomatics. In S. Ayers, A. Baum, C. McManus, S. Newman, K. Wallston, J. Weinman and R. West (eds.), *Cambridge Handbook of Psychology, Health and Medicine* (2nd edn). Cambridge: Cambridge University Press. pp 173–7.

Bassett, R.A., Osterhoudt, K. and Brabazon, T. (2014). Nicotine poisoning in an infant. *New England Journal of Medicine*, 7 May.

Bassett-Gunter, R., Martin Ginis, K.A. and Latimer-Cheung, A. (2013). Do you want the good news or the bad news? Gain- versus loss-framed messages following health risk information: the effects on leisure time physical activity beliefs and cognitions. *Health Psychology*, 32: 1188–98.

Bauld, L., Bell, K., McCullough, L., Richardson, L. and Greaves, L. (2009). The effectiveness of NHS smoking cessation services: a systematic review. *Journal of Public Health*, 31: 1–12.

Baum, F. (2000). Social capital, economic capital and power: further issues for a public health agenda. *Journal of Epidemiology & Community Health*, 54: 409–10.

BBC (2013). London cyclist deaths: officers at dangerous junctions. *BBC News*, 25 November 2013 [online] [accessed 30 December 2013].

Beacom, A.M. and Newman, S.J. (2010). Communicating health information to disadvantaged populations. *Family & Community Health*, 33 (2): 152–62.

Beals, J., Spicer, P., Mitchell, C.M., Novins, D.K., Manson, S.M., the AI-SUPERPFP Team et al. (2003). Racial disparities in alcohol use: comparison of 2 American Indian reservation populations with national data. *American Journal of Public Health*, 93: 1683–5.

Beccuti, G. and Pannain, S. (2011). Sleep and obesity. *Current Opinion in Clinical Nutrition & Metabolic Care*, 14: 402–12.

Beck, A.M. and Meyers, N.M. (1996). Health enhancement and companion animal ownership. *Annual Review of Public Health*, 17: 247–57.

Beck, N.C., Parker, J.C., Frank, R.G., Geden, E.A., Kay, D.R. and Gamache, M. (1988). Patients with rheumatoid arthritis at high risk for noncompliance with salicylate treatment regimens. *Journal of Rheumatology*, 15: 1081–84.

Beck, U. (1992). *Risk Society: Towards a New Modernity*. London: Sage.

Becker, A. (2012). Health economics of interdisciplinary rehabilitation for chronic pain: does it support or invalidate the outcomes research of these programs? *Current Pain & Headache Reports*, 16: 127–32.

Becker, M.H. (ed.) (1974). The health belief model and personal health behavior. *Health Education Monographs*, 2: 324–508.

Becker, M.H. and Mainman, L.A. (1975). Sociobehavioral determinants of compliance with health and medical care recommendations, *Medical Care*, 13: 10–14.

Beisecker, A.E. (1990) Patient power in doctor–patient communication: what do we know? *Health Communication*, 2: 105–27.

Benegal, V. (2005). India: alcohol and public health. *Addiction*, 100: 1051–6.

Bennett, P., Murphy, S., Carroll, D. and Ground, I. (1995). Psychology, health promotion and aesthemiology. *Health Care Analysis*, 3: 15–26.

Benoist, J. and Cathebras, P. (1993). The body: from immateriality to another. *Social Science & Medicine*, 36: 857–65.

Bent, S. (2008). Herbal medicine in the United States: review of efficacy, safety, and regulation. *Journal of General Internal Medicine*, 23: 854–9.

Bent, S. and Ko, R. (2004). Commonly used herbal medicines in the United States: a review. *American Journal of Medicine*, 116: 478–85.

Benveniste, J., Lecouteur, A. and Hepworth, J. (1999) Lay theories of anorexia nervosa: a discourse analytic study. *Journal of Health Psychology*, 4: 59–69.

Benyamini, Y., Leventhal, E.A. and Leventhal, H. (2009). Self-assessments of health: what do people know that predicts their mortality? *Research on Aging*, 21: 477–500.

Berghom, I., Svensson, C., Berggren, E. and Kamsula, M. (1999). Patients' and relatives' opinions and feelings about diaries kept by nurses in an intensive care unit: a pilot study. *Intensive & Critical Care Nursing*, 15: 185–91.

Berkhof, M., van Rijssen, H.J., Schellart, A.J., Anema, J.R. and van der Beek, A.J. (2011). Effective training strategies for teaching communication skills to physicians: an overview of systematic reviews. *Patient Education and Counseling*, 84: 152–62.

Berkman, L.F., Blumenthal, J., Burg, M., Carney, R.M., Catellier, D., Cowan, M.J. et al. (2003). Effects of treating depression and low perceived social support on clinical events after myocardial infarction: the Enhancing Recovery in Coronary Heart Disease Patients (ENRICHD) randomized trial. *Journal of the American Medical Association*, 289: 3106–16.

Berkman, N.D., Sheridan, S.L., Donahue, K.E., Halpern, D.J. and Crotty, K. (2011). Low health literacy and health outcomes: an updated systematic review. *Annals of Internal Medicine*, 155: 97–107.

Bermejo, I., Kriston, L. and Muthny, F.A. (2012). Lay theories toward cancer and myocardial infarction: a trans-cultural comparison of Germans and Spaniards. *Journal of Health Psychology*, 17: 77–86.

Berners-Lee, M., Hoolohan, C., Cammack, H. and Hewitt, C.N. (2012). The relative greenhouse gas impacts of realistic dietary choices. *Energy Policy*, 43: 184–90.

Bernstein Hyman, R., Baker, Ephraim, R., Moadal,and Philip, J. (1994). Health belief model variables as predictors of screening mammography utilization. *Journal of Behavioral Medicine*, 17: 391–406.

Bero, L. (2013). Industry sponsorship and research outcome: a Cochrane Review. *Journal of the American Medical Association Internal Medicine*, 173: 580–1.

Berry, T.R. and Carson, V. (2010). Ease of imagination, message framing, and physical activity messages. *British Journal of Health Psychology*, 15: 197–211.

Bertakis, K.D. (2009). The influence of gender on the doctor–patient interaction. *Patient Education and Counseling*, 76: 356–60.

Bertakis, K.D., Roter, D. and Putnam, S.M. (1991). The relationship of physician medical interview style to patient satisfaction. *Journal of Family Practice*, 32: 175–81.

Bertholet, N., Daeppen, J.B., Wietlisbach, V., Fleming, M. and Burnard, B. (2005) Reduction of alcohol consumption by brief alcohol intervention in primary care: systematic review and meta-analysis. *Archives of Internal Medicine*, 165: 986–95.

Betsche, C. and Sachse, K. (2013). Debunking vaccination myths: strong risk negations can increase perceived vaccination risks. *Health Psychology*, 32: 146–55.

Bigelow, G.E. (2001). An operant behavioural perspective on alcohol abuse and dependence. In N. Heather, T.J. Peters, and T. Stockwell (eds.), *International Handbook of Alcohol Dependence and Problems*. London: Wiley. pp. 299–315.

Bingley, A.F., McDermott, E., Thomas, C., Payne, S. and Seymour, J.E. and Clark, D. (2006). Making sense of dying: a review of narratives written since 1950 by people facing death from cancer and other diseases. *Palliative Medicine*, 20: 183–95.

Birch, L.L., McPhee, L., Shoba, B.C., Pirok, E. and Steinberg, L. (1987). What kind of exposure reduces children's food neophobia? Looking vs. tasting. *Appetite*, 9: 171–8.

Birks J. and Grimley Evans, J. (2009). Ginkgo biloba for cognitive impairment and dementia. *Cochrane Database of Systematic Reviews*, 1 (CD003120).

Bishop, F., Yardley, L. and Lewith, G.T. (2008). Treatment appraisals and beliefs predict adherence to complementary therapies: a prospective study using a dynamic extended self-regulation model. *British Journal of Health Psychology*, 13: 701–18.

Bjørnskov, C. and Sønderskov, K.M. (2013). Is social capital a good concept? *Social Indicators Research*, 114 (3): 1225–42.

Blaschke, T.F., Osterberg, L., Vrijens, B. and Urquhart, J. (2012). Adherence to medications: insights arising from studies on the unreliable link between prescribed and actual drug dosing histories. *Annual Review of Pharmacology and Toxicology*, 52: 275–301.

Blaxter, M. (1983). The causes of disease: women talking. *Social Science & Medicine*, 17: 59–69.

Blaxter, M. (1990) *Health and Lifestyles*. London: Routledge.

Blaxter, M. (1997). Whose fault is it? Peoples' own conceptions of the reasons for health inequalities. *Social Science & Medicine*, 44: 747–56.

Blendon, R.J., DesRoches, C.M., Brodie, M., Benson, J.M., Rosen, A.B., Schneider, E. et al. (2002). Views of practicing physicians and the public on medical errors. *NEJM*, 347: 1933–40.

Blendon, R.J., Schoen, C., Donelan, K., Osborn, R., DesRoches, C.M., Scoles, K. et al. (2001). Physicians' views on quality of care: a five-country comparison. *Health Affairs*, 20: 233–43.

Blume S. (2006). Anti-vaccination movements and their interpretations. *Social Science and Medicine*, 62: 628–42.

Blumhagen, D. (1980). Hyper-tension: a folk illness with a medical name. *Culture, Medicine & Psychiatry*, 4: 197–227.

Boehm, J.K. and Kubzansky, L.D. (2012). The heart's content: the association between positive psychological wellbeing and cardiovascular health. *Psychological Bulletin*, 138: 655–91.

Boeing, H. (2013). Obesity and cancer – the update 2013: best practice and research. *Clinical Endocrinology & Metabolism*, 27: 219–27.

Boersma, K., Carstens-Söderstrand, J. and Linton, S.J. (2014). From acute pain to chronic disability: psychosocial processes in the development of chronic musculoskeletal pain and disability. In *Handbook of Musculoskeletal Pain and Disability Disorders in the Workplace*. New York: Springer. pp. 205–17.

Bogart, K.R. (2014). 'People are all about appearances': A focus group of teenagers with Moebius Syndrome. *Journal of Health Psychology*, in press.

Bogart, L.M., Collins, R.L., Ellickson, P. and Klein, D.J. (2006a). Adolescent predictors of generalized health risk in young adulthood: a 10-year longitudinal assessment. *Journal of Drug Issues*, 36: 571–95.

Bogart, L.M., Collins, R.L., Ellickson, P.L. and Klein, D.J. (2006b). Adolescent predictors of college students' spontaneous and anonymous sexual experiences. *Journal of Sex Research*, 37: 76–88.

Bogg, T. & Roberts, B.W. (2004). Conscientiousness and health-related behaviors: a meta-analysis of the leading behavioral contributors to mortality. *Psychological Bulletin*, 130: 887–919.

Bogg, T. and Roberts, B.W. (2013). The case for conscientiousness: evidence and implications for a personality trait marker of health and longevity. *Annals of Behavioural Medicine*, 45: 278–88.

Boisvert, J. and Harrell, W.A. (2014). Dog walking: a leisurely solution to pediatric and adult obesity? *World Leisure Journal*, 56: 168–71.

Bojorquez, I., Unikel, C., Mendoza, M.E. and de Lachica, F. (2013) Another body project: the thin ideal, motherhood and body dissatisfaction among Mexican women. *Journal of Health Psychology*, 19: 1120–31.

Bon, S.R., Hittner, J.B. and Lawandales, J.P. (2001). Normative perceptions in relation to substance use and HIV-risky sexual behaviors of college students. *Journal of Psychology*, 135: 165–78.

Bond, C.A. and Monson, R. (1984). Sustained improvement in drug documentation, compliance, and disease control: a four-year analysis of an ambulatory care model. *Archives of Internal Medicine*, 144: 1159–62.

Bonica, J.J. (1990). *The Management of Pain* (2nd edn). Philadelphia, PA: Lea and Febiger.

Borg, T. (2013). Commissioner Borg addresses the European Parliament's Interest Group on Complementary and Alternative Medicine. Available: http://ec.europa.eu/commission_2010-2014/borg/docs/speech_cancer_27062013_en.pdf.

Borges, G., Cherpitel, C.J., Orozco, R., Bond, J., Ye, Y., Macdonald, S. et al. (2006). Acute alcohol use and the risk of non-fatal injury in sixteen countries. *Addiction*, 101: 993–1002.

Bosy, D., Etlin, D., Corey, D. and Lee, J.W. (2010). An interdisciplinary pain rehabilitation programme: description and evaluation of outcomes. *Physiotherapy Canada*, 62: 316–26.

Bourdieu, P. (1984). *Distinction: A Social Critique of the Judgement of Taste*. London: Routledge & Kegan Paul.

Boureaudhuij, I.D. (1997). Family food rules and healthy eating in adolescents. *Journal of Health Psychology*, 2: 45–56.

Bowen, S., Witkiewitz, K., Clifasefi, S.L., Grow, J., Chawla, N., Hsu, S.H. et al. (2014). Relative efficacy of mindfulness-based relapse prevention, standard relapse prevention, and treatment as usual for substance use disorders: a randomized clinical trial. *Journal of the American Medical Association – Psychiatry*, 71: 547–56.

Bowlby J. (1961). Processes of mourning. *International Journal of Psychoanalysis*, 42: 317–39.

Bowlby, J. (1969). *Attachment and Loss: Attachment*. New York: Basic Books.

Bowlby, J. (1973). *Attachment and Loss: Separation, Anxiety and Anger*. New York: Basic Books.

Bowlby, J. (1980). *Attachment and Loss: Sadness and Depression*. New York: Basic Books.

Boylan, S., Louie, J.C.Y. and Gill, T.P. (2013). Consumer response to healthy eating, physical activity and weight-related recommendations: a systematic review. *Obesity Reviews*, 13: 606–17.

Bradley, B.S., Deighton, J. and Selby, J. (2004). The 'Voices' project: capacity-building in community development for youth at risk. *Journal of Health Psychology*, 9: 197–212.

Brady, J.E. and Li, G. (2014). Trends in alcohol and other drugs detected in fatally injured drivers in the United States, 1999–2010. *American Journal of Epidemiology*, 179: 692–9.

Brainard, D., Hyslop, N.E., Mera, R. and Churchill, J. (1997). Long-term outcome of inpatients with tuberculosis assigned to outpatient therapy at a local clinic in New Orleans. *Journal of Investigative Medicine*, 45: 381–7.

Brawley, L.R., Martin, K.and Gyurcsik, N.C. (1998). Problems in assessing perceived barriers to exercise: confusing obstacles with attributions and excuses. In J.L. Duda (ed.), *Advances in Sport and Exercise Psychology Measurement*. Morgantown, WV: Fitness Information Technology. pp. 337–50.

Bray, G.A. (2003a). Obesity is a chronic, relapsing neurochemical disease. *International Journal of Obesity*, 28: 34–8.

Bray, S.R., Gyurcsik, N.C., Culos-Reed, S.N., Dawson, K.A. and Martin, K.A. (2001). An exploratory investigation of the relationship between proxy efficacy, self-efficacy and exercise attendance. *Journal of Health Psychology*, 6: 425–34.

Brehm, J.W. (1966). *A Theory of Psychological Reactance*. New York: Academic Press.

Brehm, S.S. and Brehm, J.W. (1981). *Psychological Reactance: A Theory of Freedom and Control*. New York: Academic Press.

Brennan, T.A., Leape, L.L., Laird, N.M. et al. (1991). Incidence of adverse events and negligence in hospitalized patients: results of the Harvard Medical Practice Study. *New England Journal of Medicine*, 324: 370–6.

Bresnahan, M. and Zhuang, J. (2015). Development and validation of the Communicating with Family about Brain Death Scale. *Journal of Health Psychology*, in press.

Brett, J. and Austoker, J. (2001). Women who are recalled for further investigation for breast screening: psychological consequences 3 years after recall and factors affecting re-attendance. *Journal of Public Health Medicine*, 23: 292–300.

Brewer, N.T., Chapman, G.B., Gibbons, F.X., Gerrard, M., McCaul, D. and Weinstein, N. (2007). Meta-analysis of the relationship between risk perception and health behavior: the example of vaccination. *Health Psychology*, 26: 136–45.

Brewin, C.R., Dalgleish, T. and Joseph, S. (1996). A dual representation theory of posttraumatic stress disorder. *Psychological Review*, 103: 670–86.

Brien, S.E., Ronksley, P.E., Turner, B.J., Mukamal, K.J. and Ghali, W.A. (2011). Effect of alcohol consumption on biological markers associated with risk of coronary heart disease: systematic review and meta-analysis of interventional studies. *British Medical Journal*, 342: d636.

Britten. N. (1994). Patients' ideas about medicines: a qualitative study in a general practice population. *British Journal of General Practice,* 44: 465–8.

Broadbent, E., Petrie, K.J., Main, J. and Weinman, J. (2006). The Brief Illness Perception Questionnaire. *Journal of Psychosomatic Research*, 60: 631–7.

Broadstock, M., Michie, S. and Marteau, T. (2000). Psychological consequences of predictive genetic testing: a systematic literature review. *European Journal of Human Genetics*, 8: 731–8.

Brochu, P.M. and Esses, V.M. (2011). What's in a name? The effects of the labels 'fat' and 'overweight' on weight bias. *Journal of Applied Social Psychology*, 41: 1981–2008.

Brocki, J.M. and Wearden, A.J. (2006). A critical evaluation of the use of interpretative phenomenological analysis (IPA) in health psychology. *Psychology & Health*, 21: 87–108.

Brodersen, J. and Siersma, V.D. (2013). Long-term psychosocial consequences of false-positive screening mammography. *Annals of Family Medicine*, 11: 106–15.

Brodie, M., Weltzien, E., Altman, D., Blendon, R.J. and Benson, J.M. (2006). Experiences of Hurricane Katrina evacuees in Houston shelters: implications for future planning. *American Journal of Public Health*, 96: 1402–8.

Bronfenbrenner, U. (1979). *The Ecology of Human Development*. Cambridge, MA: Harvard University Press.

Brown, D. (2007). Herbal medicine. In A.D. Cumming, K.R. Simpson and D. Brown (eds.), *Complementary and Alternative Medicine: An Illustrated Color Text*. Edinburgh: Elsevier. pp. 52–6.

Brown, J.A.C. (1964). *Freud and the post-Freudians*. London: Penguin.

Brown, J.B., Stewart, M., Weston, W.W. and Freeman, T.R. (2003). Introduction. In M. Stewart, J.B. Brown, W.W. Weston, I.R. McWhinney, C.L. McWilliam and T.R. Freeman (eds.), *Patient-Centred Medicine: Transforming the Clinical Method*. Oxford: Radcliffe Medical Press. pp. 1–15.

Brown, J.E., Luo, W., Isabelle, L. and Pankow, J.F. (2014). Candy flavorings in tobacco. *New England Journal of Medicine*, 7 May.

Brown, K.W. and Ryan, R.M. (2003). The benefits of being present: mindfulness and its role in psychological well-being. *Journal of Personality & Social Psychology*, 84: 822.

Brown, R.J. (2004). Psychological mechanisms of medically unexplained symptoms: an integrative conceptual model. *Psychological Bulletin*, 130: 793–812.

Brown, S.D. (1996). The textuality of stress: drawing between scientific and everyday accounting. *Journal of Health Psychology*, 1: 173–93.

Brown, S.G. and Rhodes, R.E. (2006). Relationships among dog ownership and leisure-time walking in Western Canadian adults. *American Journal of Preventive Medicine*, 30: 131–6.

Brown, S.L. and Whiting, D. (2014). The ethics of distress: toward a framework for determining the ethical acceptability of distressing health promotion advertising. *International Journal of Psychology*, 49: 89–97.

Brownell, K.D. (1992). Dieting and the search for the perfect body: where physiology and culture collide. *Behavior Therapy*, 22: 1–12.

Brownell, K.D. (1994). Get slim with higher taxes. *New York Times*, 15, A29.

Brownell, K.D. and Fairburn. C.G. (1995). *Eating Disorders and Obesity: A Comprehensive Handbook.* New York: Guilford Press.

Brydon-Miller, M. (2004). Using partipatory action research to address community health issues. In M. Murray (ed.), *Critical Health Psychology*. London: Palgrave. pp. 187–202.

Bueno, N.B., de Melo, I.S., de Oliveira, S.L. and da Rocha Ataide, T. (2013). Very-low-carbohydrate ketogenic diet v. low-fat diet for long-term weight loss: a meta-analysis of randomised controlled trials. *British Journal of Nutrition*, 110: 1178–87.

Buller, M.K. and Buller, D.B. (1987). Physicians' communication style and patient satisfaction. *Journal of Health & Social Behavior*, 28: 375–89.

Bunke, S., Apitzsch, E. and Backstrom, M. (2013). The impact of social influence on physical activity among adolescents – a longitudinal study. *European Journal of Sport Science*, 13: 86–95.

Burg, M.M., Benedetto, M.C., Rosenberg, R. and Soufer, R. (2003). Presurgical depression predicts medical morbidity 6 months after coronary artery bypass graft surgery. *Psychosomatic Medicine*, 65: 111–18.

Burnham, B.E. (1995). Garlic as a possible risk for postoperative bleeding. *Plastic and Reconstructive Surgery*, 95: 213.

Burns, M. and Gavey, N. (2004). 'Healthy weight' at what cost? 'Bulimia' and a discourse of weight control. *Journal of Health Psychology*, 9: 549–66.

Butland, B., Jebb, S., Kopelman, P., McPherson, K., Thomas, S., Mardell, J. and Parry, V. (2007). *Foresight. Tackling Obesities: Future Choices – Project Report*. Government Office for Science.

Butler, L. and Pilkington, K. (2013). Chinese herbal medicine and depression: the research evidence. *Evidence-Based Complementary & Alternative Medicine (eCAM)*, Article ID 739716: 1–14.

Byrne, A., Ellershaw, J., Holcombe, C. and Salmon, P. (2002). Patients' experience of cancer: evidence of the role of 'fighting' in collusive clinical communication. *Patient Education and Counseling*, 48: 15–21.

Byrne, D.G. and Espnes, G.A. (2008). Occupational stress and cardiovascular disease. *Stress & Health*, 24: 231–8.

Byrne, P.S. and Long, B.E.L. (1976) *Doctors Talking to Patients*. London: HMSO.

Cahill, K., Stevens, S., Perera, R. and Lancaster, T. (2013). Pharmacological interventions for smoking cessation: an overview and network meta-analysis. *Cochrane Database of Systematic Reviews*, 5: 5.

Calnan, M. (1987). *Health and Illness: The Lay Perspective*. London: Tavistock.

Calnan, M. and Williams, S. (1991). Style of life and the salience of health: an exploratory study of health related practices in households from differing socio-economic circumstances. *Sociology of Health & Illness*, 13: 506–29.

Cameron L.D. and Reeve J. (2006). Risk perceptions, worry, and attitudes about genetic testing for breast cancer susceptibility. *Psychology and Health*, 21: 211–30.

Campbell, A. and Hausenblas, H.A. (2009). Effects of exercise interventions on body image: a meta-analysis. *Journal of Health Psychology*, 9, 14: 780–93.

Campbell, C. (2004). Health psychology and community action. In M. Murray (ed.), *Critical Health Psychology*. London: Palgrave. pp. 203–21.

Campbell, C. (2006) *Creating Social Environments that Support the Possibility of Health.* Commonwealth Health Ministers' Reference Report. London: Commonwealth Secretariat.

Campbell, C. (2014). Community mobilisation in the 21st century: updating our theory of social change? *Journal of Health Psychology*, 19: 46–59.

Campbell, C. and Cornish, F. (2014). Reimagining community health psychology: maps, journeys and new terrains. *Journal of Health Psychology*, 19: 3–15.

Campbell, C. and McLean, C. (2002). Representations of ethnicity in people's accounts of local community participation in a multi-ethnic community in England. *Journal of Community & Applied Social Psychology*, 12: 13–29.

Campbell, C. and McLean, C. (2003). Social capital, local community participation and the construction of Pakistani identities in England: implications for health inequalities policies. *Journal of Health Psychology*, 8: 247–62.

Campbell, C. and Murray, M. (2004). Community health psychology: promoting analysis and action for social change. *Journal of Health Psychology*, 9: 187–95.

Campbell, C. and Scott, K. (2011). Mediated health campaigns: from information to social change. In D. Hook, B. Franks and M. Bauer (eds.), *The Social Psychology of Communication*. Basingstoke: Palgrave Macmillan. pp. 266–83.

Campbell, C., Cornish, F., Gibbs, A. and Scott, K. (2010). Heeding the push from below: how do social movements persuade the rich to listen to the poor? *Journal of Health Psychology*, 15 (7): 962–71.

Campbell, C., Nair, Y., Maimane, S. and Nicholson, J. (2007). 'Dying twice': a multi-level model of the roots of AIDS stigma in two South African communities. *Journal of Health Psychology*, 12: 403–16.

Campbell, C., Scott, K., Nhamo, M. et al. (2013). Social capital and HIV competent communities: the role of community groups in managing HIV/AIDS in rural zimbabwe. *AIDS Care*, 25 (suppl. 1): S114–22.

Cancer Research UK (2013) Breast cancer statistics. Available: www.cancerresearchuk.org/cancer-info/cancerstats/types/breast/.

Capaldi, E. (1996). Conditioned food preferences. In E.D. Capaldi (ed.), *Why We Eat What We Eat: The Psychology of Eating*. Washington, DC: American Psychological Association. pp. 53–80.

Carey, M.P., Braaten, L.S., Maisto, S.A., Gleason, J.R., Forsyth, A.D., Durant, L.E. and Jaworski, B.C. (2000). Using information, motivational enhancement, and skills training to reduce the risk of HIV infection for low-income urban women: a second randomized clinical trial. *Health Psychology*, 19: 3–11.

Carlson, J.A., Sallis, J.F., Conway, T.L., Saelens, B.E., Frank, L.D. et al. (2012). Interactions between psychosocial and built environment factors in explaining older adults' physical activity. *Preventive Medicine*, 54: 68–73.

Carnegie, D. (1913). *How to Win Friends and Influence People*. New York: The World's Work.

Carter, S.M., Rychetnik, L., Lloyd, B. et al. (2011). Evidence, ethics, and values: a framework for health promotion. *American Journal of Public Health*, 101: 465–72.

Carver, C.S., Scheier, M.F. and Weintraub, J.K. (1989). Assessing coping strategies: a theoretically based approach. *Journal of Personality & Social Psychology*, 56: 267–83.

Casey, M.M., Eime, R.M., Payne, W.R. and Harvey, J.T. (2009). Using a socioecological approach to examine participation in sport and physical activity among rural adolescent girls. *Qualitative Health Research*, 19: 881–93.

Cassidy, B., Braxter, B., Charron-Prochownik, D. and Schlenk, E.A. (2014). *A Quality Improvement Initiative to Increase HPV Vaccine Rates Using an Educational and Reminder Strategy with Parents of Preteen Girls*. United States: Mosby.

Cassim, S., Stolte, O. and Hodgetts, D. (2014). Metonymic objects, cultural practices and narrative repair: Sri Lankan responses to the Indian Ocean tsunami. *Journal of Health Psychology*, in press.

Casswell, S. and Marks, D. (1973). Cannabis induced impairment of performance of a divided attention task. *Nature*, 24: 60–1.

Cavanagh, K., Vartanian, L.R., Herman, C.P. and Polivy, J. (2014). The effect of portion size on food intake is robust to brief education and mindfulness exercises. *Journal of Health Psychology*, 19: 730–9.

Chacko, M.R., Wiemann, C.M., Kozinetz, C.A., von Sternberg, K., Velasquez, M.M., Smith, P.B. and DiClemente, R. (2009). Efficacy of a motivational behavioral intervention to promote chlamydia and gonorrhea screening in young women: a randomized controlled trial. *Journal of Adolescent Health*, 46: 152–61.

Chaiton, M., Sabiston, C., O'loughlin, J., McGrath, J.J., Maximova, K. and Lambert, M. (2009). A structural equation model relating adiposity, psychosocial indicators of body image and depressive symptoms among adolescents. *International Journal of Obesity*, 33: 588–96.

Chalmers, B. (1996). Western and African conceptualizations of health. *Psychology & Health*, 12: 1–10.

Chamberlain, K. and Zika, S. (1990). The minor events approach to stress: support for the use of daily hassles. *British Journal of Psychology*, 81: 469–81.

Chan, C.W., Goldman, S., Ilstrup, D.M., Kunselman, A.R., O'Neill, P.I. (1993). The pain drawing and Waddell's nonorganic physical signs in chronic low-back pain. *Spine*, 18: 1717–22.

Chan M. (2013). Re: doctors and the alcohol industry: an unhealthy mix? *British Medical Journal*, 346: f1889.

Chapin, J. (2001). It won't happen to me: the role of optimistic bias in African American teens' risky sexual practices. *Howard Journal of Communication*, 12 (1): 49–59.

Chapman, G.B. and Coups, E.J. (2006). Emotions and preventive health ehaviour: worry, regret, and influenza vaccination. *Health Psychology*, 25: 82–90.

Chapman, S. and MacKenzie, R. (2010). The global research neglect of unassisted smoking cessation: causes and consequences. *PLoS Medicine*, 7 (2): e1000216.

Charmaz, K. (2003). Grounded theory. In J.A. Smith (ed.), *Qualitative Psychology: A Practical Guide to Research Methods*. London: Sage. pp. 81–110.

Chen, J., Choi, Y.C., Mori, K., Sawada, Y. and Sugano, S. (2012). Recession, unemployment, and suicide in Japan. *Japan Labor Review*, 9: 75–92.

Chen, W.C., Rosner, B., Hankinson, S.E., Colditz, G.A. and Willett, W.C. (2011). Moderate alcohol consumption during adult life, drinking patterns, and breast cancer risk. *Journal of the American Medical Association*, 306: 1884–90.

Cheng, Y.H. (1997). Explaining disablement in modern times: hand-injured workers accounts of their injuries in Hong Kong. *Social Science & Medicine*, 45: 739–50.

Chen, Y.-H., Tsai, S.-Y. and Lin, H.-C. (2009). Increased risk of acute myocardial infarction for patients with panic disorder: a nationwide population-based study. *Psychosomatic Medicine*, 71: 798–804.

Chervin, C., Clift, J., Woods, L., Krause, E. and Lee, K. (2012). Health literacy in adult education: a natural partnership for health equity. *Health Promotion Practice*, 13: 738–46.

Chesler, M.A. and Parry, C. (2001). Gender roles and/or styles in crisis: an integrative analysis of the experiences of fathers of children with cancer. *Qualitative Health Research*, 11: 363–84.

Chesney, M.A., Chambers, D.B., Taylor, J.M. Johnson, L.M. and Folkman, S. (2003). Coping effectiveness training for men living with HIV: results from a randomised clinical trial testing a group-based intervention. *Psychosomatic Medicine*, 65: 1038–46.

Chigwedere, P., Seage III, G.R., Gruskin, S., Lee, T.H. and Essex, M. (2008). Estimating the lost benefits of antiretroviral drug use in South Africa. *Journal of Acquired Immune Deficiency Syndromes*, 49: 410–15.

Chiu, Y. and Hsieh, Y. (2013). Communication online with fellow cancer patients: writing to be remembered, gain strength, and find survivors. *Journal of Health Psychology*, 18 (12): 1572–81.

Choi, J. (2012). Development and pilot test of pictograph-enhanced breast health-care instructions for community-residing immigrant women. *International Journal of Nursing Practice*, 18: 373–8.

Chow, E., Tsao, M.N. and Harth, T. (2004). Does psychosocial intervention improve survival in cancer? A meta-analysis. *Palliative Medicine*, 18: 25–31.

Christakis, N.A. and Fowler, J.H. (2007). The spread of obesity in a large social network over 32 years. *New England Journal of Medicine*, 357: 370–9.

Christiannse, M.E., Lavigne, J.V. and Lerner, C.V. (1989) Psychosocial aspects of compliance in children and adolescents with asthma. *Developmental and Behavioral Pediatrics*, 10: 75–80.

Christopher, S., Saha, R., Lachapelle, P. et al. (2011). Applying indigenous community-based participatory research principles to partnership development in health disparities research. *Family & Community Health*, 34: 246–55.

Chu, Y.L., Farmer, A., Fung, C., Kuhle, S., Storey, K.E. and Veugelers, P.J. (2013). Involvement in home meal preparation is associated with food preference and self-efficacy among Canadian children. *Public Health Nutrition*, 16: 108–12.

Chung, J.E. (2013). Patient-provider discussion of online health information: results from the 2007 Health Information National Trends Survey (HINTS). *Journal of Health Communication*, 18: 627–48.

Churchill, S. and Pavey, L. (2013). Promoting fruit and vegetable consumption: the role of message framing and autonomy. *British Journal of Health Psychology*, 18: 610–22.

Ciccone, D.S., Weissman, L. and Natelson, B.H. (2008). Chronic fatigue syndrome in male Gulf War Veterans and civilians: a further test of the single syndrome hypothesis. *Journal of Health Psychology*, 13: 529–36.

Clark, H.R., Goyder, E., Bissell, P., Blank, L. and Peters, J. (2007). How do parents' child feeding behaviours influence child weight? Implications for childhood obesity policy. *Public Health*, 29: 132–41.

Clark, S., Farrington, K. and Chilcot, J. (2014). Nonadherence in dialysis patients: prevalence, measurement, outcome, and psychological determinants. *Seminars in Dialysis*, 27 (1): 42–9.

Clark, W. (2008). Treatment of substance abuse disorders among Latinos. Invited address presented at the 14th Annual Latino Behavioral Health Institute Conference, Los Angeles, CA.

Clark-Carter, D. (1997). *Doing Quantitative Psychological Research: From Design to Report*. Hove: Psychology Press.

Clark-Carter, D. and Marks, D.F. (2004). Intervention studies: design and analysis. In D.F. Marks and L. Yardley (eds.), *Research Methods for Clinical and Health Psychology*. London: Sage. pp. 166–84.

Clarke, P. and Eves, F. (1997). Applying the transtheoretical model to the study of exercise on prescription. *Journal of Health Psychology*, 2: 195–207.

Coakley, J. and White, A. (1992). Making decisions: gender and sport participation among British adolescents. *Sociology of Sport Journal*, 9: 20–35.

Coalter, F. (2007). *A Wider Social Role for Sport: Who's Keeping the Score?* London: Routledge.

Coburn, D. (2004). Beyond the income inequality hypothesis: class, neo-liberalism and health inequalities. *Social Science & Medicine*, 58: 41–56.

Cochrane, T., Davey, R.C., Gidlow, C., Smith, G.R., Fairburn, J., Armitage, C.J. et al. (2009). Small area and individual level predictors of physical activity in urban communities: a multi-level study in Stoke-on-Trent, England. *International Journal of Environmental Research & Public Health*, 6: 654–77.

Cockburn, C. and Clarke, G. (2002). 'Everybodys looking at you!': girls negotiating the 'femininity deficit' they incur in physical education. *Women's Studies International Forum*, 25: 651–65.

Coghill, R.C., McHaffie, J.G. and Yen, Y.-F. (2003). Neural correlates of interindividual differences in the subjective experience of pain. *Proceedings of the National Academy of Science*, 100: 8538–42.

Coen Structured Advertising Expenditure Dataset (2011). Retrieved from http:// purplemotes.net/2008/09/14/usadvertisingexpendituredata/

Cohen, A. (1974). *Two-dimensional Man: An Essay on the Anthropology of Power & Symbolism in Complex Society.* Berkeley, CA: University of California Press.

Cohen, J. (1994). The earth is round (p<.05). *American Psychologist*, 49: 997.

Cohen, S. (2004). Social relationships and health. *American Psychologist*, 59 (special issue): 676–84.

Cohen, S., Janicki-Deverts, D. and Miller, G.E. (2007). Psychological stress and disease. *Journal of the American Medical Association*, 298: 1685–7.

Cohen, S. and Miller, G.E. (2001). Stress, immunity and susceptibility to upper respiratory infection. In R. Ader, D. Felten and N. Cohen (eds.), *Psychoneuroimmunology* (3rd edn). London: Academic Press. pp. 499–509.

Cohen, S. and Williamson, G.M. (1991). Stress and infectious disease in humans. *Psychological Bulletin*, 109: 5–24.

Coleman, L., Cox, L. and Roker, D. (2008). Girls and young women's participation in physical activity: psychological and social influences. *Health Education Research*, 23: 633–47.

Collins, R.L. and Bradizza, C.M. (2001). Social and cognitive learning processes. In N. Heather, T.J. Peters, and T. Stockwell (eds.), *International Handbook of Alcohol Dependence and Problems.* London: Wiley. pp. 317–37.

Compton, W.C., Smith, M.L., Cornish, K.A. and Qualls, D.L. (1996). Factor structure of mental health measures. *Journal of Personality and Social Psychology*, 71: 406.

Connell, R. (2005). *Masculinities* (2nd edn). Cambridge: Polity.

Conner, M. and Armitage, C. (1998). Extending the theory of planned behavior: a review and avenues for further research. *Journal of Applied Social Psychology*, 28: 1429–64.

Connors, A.F., Dawson, N.V., Desbiens, N.A., Fulkerson, W.J., Goldman, L., Knaus, W.A. et al. (1995). A controlled trial to improve care for seriously ill hospitalized patients: the study to understand prognoses and preferences for outcomes and risks of treatments (SUPPORT). *Journal of the American Medical Association*, 274: 1591–8.

Conrad, K.M., Flay, B.R. and Hill, D. (1992). Why children start smoking: predictors of onset, *British Journal of Addiction*, 87: 1711–24.

Conrad, P. (1985). The meaning of medications: another look at compliance. *Social Science & Medicine*, 20: 29–37.

Conroy, D. and de Visser, R. (2013). 'Man up!': discursive constructions of non-drinkers among UK undergraduates. *Journal of Health Psychology*, 18: 1432–44.

Conroy, D. and de Visser, R. (2014). The importance of authenticity for student non-drinkers: an interpretative phenomenological analysis. *Journal of Health Psychology*, in press.

Consedine, N.S., Horton, D., Magai, C. and Kukafka, R. (2007). Breast screening in response to gain, loss, and empowerment framed messages among diverse, low-income women. *Journal of Health Care for the Poor and Underserved*, 18: 550–66.

Cook, C.C.H. and Gurling, H.M.D. (2001). Genetic predisposition to alcohol dependence and problems. In N. Heather, T.J. Peters and T. Stockwell (eds.), *International Handbook of Alcohol Dependence and Problems.* London: Wiley. pp. 257–80.

Cookson, C. (2002). Benefit and risk of vaccination as seen by the general public and the media. *Vaccine*, 20: S85–8.

Cooper A., Lloyd G., Weinman J. and Jackson G. (1999). Why patients do not attend cardiac rehabilitation: role of intentions and illness beliefs. *Heart*, 82: 234–6.

Cooper, A.F., Jackson, G., Weinman, J. and Horne, R. (2002). Factors associated with cardiac rehabilitation attendance: a systematic review of the literature. *Clinical Rehabilitation*, 16: 541–52.

Cordain, L., Miller, J.B., Eaton, S.B., Mann, N., Holt, S.H. and Speth, J.D. (2000). Plant–animal subsistence ratios and macronutrient energy estimations in worldwide hunter-gatherer diets. *American Journal of Clinical Nutrition*, 71: 682–92.

Corin, E. (1995). The cultural frame: context and meaning in the construction of health. In B.C. Amick III, S. Levine, A.R. Tarlov and D. Chapman Walsh (eds.), *Society and Health*. New York: Oxford University Press. pp. 272–304.

Cornish, F. (2009). Let's get real (with a small 'r'): for a health psychology that prioritizes the concrete. *Journal of Health Psychology*, 14: 638–42.

Cornish, F., Montenegro, C., van Reisen, K., Zaka, F. and Sevitt, J. (2014). Trust the process: community health psychology after Occupy. *Journal of Health Psychology*, 19 (1): 60–71.

Cornwell, J. (1984). *Hard-Earned Lives*. London: Tavistock.

Costanza, M.E. (1992). Breast cancer screening in older women: synopsis of a forum. *Cancer* (Supplement) 69: 1925–31.

Coulter, A. (1999). Paternalism or partnership? Patients have grown up – and there's no going back. *British Medical Journal*, 319: 719–20.

Courtenay, W.H. (2000). Constructions of masculinity and their influence on men's well-being: a theory of gender and health. *Social Science & Medicine*, 50: 1385–401.

Covey, J. (2014). The role of dispositional factors in moderating message framing effects. *Health Psychology*, 33: 52–65.

Cox, T. (1978). *Stress*. London: Macmillan.

Coyne, J.C. and Tennen, H. (2010). Positive psychology in cancer care: bad science, exaggerated claims, and unproven medicine. *Annals of Behavioural Medicine*, 39: 16–26.

Craig, P., Dieppe, P., Macintyre, S., Michie, S., Nazareth, I. and Petticrew, M. (2013). Developing and evaluating complex interventions: the new Medical Research Council guidance. *International Journal of Nursing Studies*, 50 (5): 587–92. doi:10.1016/j.ijnurstu.2012.09.009

Cramm, J.M., Møller, V. and Nieboer, A.P. (2010). Improving subjective well-being of the poor in the Eastern Cape. *Journal of Health Psychology*, 15 (7): 1012–19.

Cranmer, H.H. and Biddinger, P.D. (2014). Typhoon Haiyan and the professionalization of disaster response. *New England Journal of Medicine*, 370: 1185–7.

Crawford, H.J., Gur, R.C., Skolnick, B., Gur, R.E. and Benson, D.M. (1993). Effects of hypnosis on regional cerebral blood-flow during ischemic pain with and without suggested hypnotic analgesia. *International Journal of Psychophysiology*, 15: 181–95.

Crawford, R. (1980). Healthism and the medicalization of everyday life. *International Journal of Health Services*, 10 (3): 365–88.

Crombez, G., Bijttebier, P., Eccleston, C., Mascagni, T., Mertens, G., Goubert, L. and Verstraeten, K. (2003). The child version of the Pain Catastrophizing Scale (PCS-C): a preliminary validation. *Pain*, 104: 639–46.

Crombez, G., Eccleston, C., Van Damme, S., Vlaeyen, J.W. and Karoly, P. (2012). Fear-avoidance model of chronic pain: the next generation. *Clinical Journal of Pain*, 28: 475–83.

Cromby, J. (2012). Beyond belief. *Journal of Health Psychology*,17: 943–57.

Cropley, M., Ayers, S. and Nokes, L. (2003). People don't exercise because they can't think of reasons to exercise: an examination of causal reasoning with the Transtheoretical Model. *Psychology, Health & Medicine*, 8: 409–14.

Crossley, M.L. (1999). Making sense of HIV infection: discourse and adaptation to life with HIV positive diagnosis. *Health*, 3: 95–119.

Crossley, M.L. (2003). 'Would you consider yourself a healthy person?' Using focus groups to explore health as a moral phenomenon. *Journal of Health Psychology*, 8: 501–14.

Crowe, F.L., Appleby, P.N., Allen, N.E. and Key, T.J. (2011). Diet and risk of diverticular disease in Oxford cohort of European Prospective Investigation into Cancer and Nutrition (EPIC): prospective study of British vegetarians and non-vegetarians. *British Medical Journal*, 343: d4131.

Crowe, F.L., Appleby, P.N., Travis, R.C. and Key, T.J. (2013). Risk of hospitalization or death from ischemic heart disease among British vegetarians and nonvegetarians: results from the EPIC-Oxford cohort study. *American Journal of Clinical Nutrition*, 97: 597–603.

Csikszentmihalyi, M. (1997). *Finding Flow: The Psychology of Engagement with Everyday Life.* New York: Basic Books.

Cuffee, Y.L., Hargraves, J.L. and Allison, J. (2012). Exploring the association between reported discrimination and hypertension among African Americans: a systematic review. *Ethnicity & Disease*, 22: 422–31.

Cunningham, M. (2009). Health in the United Nations. *State of the World's Indigenous Peoples*. New York: United Nations. pp. 156–87.

Curtis, J. and White, P. (1992). Toward a better understanding of the sport practices of Francophone and Anglophone Canadians. *Sociology of Sport Journal*, 9: 403–22.

Curtis, J.R., Nielsen, E.L., Treece, P.D. et al. (2011). Effect of a quality-improvement intervention on end-of-life care in the intensive care unit: a randomized trial. *American Journal of Respiratory Critical Care Medicine*, 183: 348–55.

Curtis, J.R., Patrick, D.L., Engelberg, R.A. et al. (2002) A measure of the quality of dying and death: initial validation using after-death interviews with family members. *Journal of Pain Symptoms Management*, 24: 17–31.

Dahlgren, G. and Whitehead, M. (1991). *Policies and Strategies to Promote Equity and Health*. Stockholm: Institute for Future Studies.

Daley, A.J., Copeland, R.J., Wright, N.P. and Wales, J.K.H. (2008). 'I can actually exercise if I want to. It isn't as hard as I thought': a qualitative study of the experiences and views of obese adolescents participating in an exercise therapy intervention. *Journal of Health Psychology*, 13: 810–19.

Daniels, N., Kennedy, B. and Kawachi, I. (2000). Justice is good for our health: how greater economic equality would promote public health. *Boston Review*, February/March: 25.

Dante, G., Pedrielli, G., Annessi, E. and Facchinetti, F. (2013). Herb remedies during pregnancy: a systematic review of controlled clinical trials. *Journal of Maternal-Fetal & Neonatal Medicine*, 26: 306–12.

Dar, R., Stronguin, F. and Etter, J.F. (2005). Assigned versus perceived placebo effects in nicotine replacement therapy for smoking reduction in Swiss smokers. *Journal of Consulting & Clinical Psychology*, 73: 350–3.

Dasen, P.R., Berry, J.W. and Sartorius, N. (eds.). (1988). *Health and Cross-cultural Psychology: Towards Applications*. Newbury Park, CA: Sage.

Datta, J. and Petticrew, M. (2013). Challenges to evaluating complex interventions: a content analysis of published papers. *BMC Public Health*, 13: 568–82.

Datz, T. (2011). Harvard serves up its own 'Plate'. *Harvard Gazette*, September 14.

Davidson, K.W., Goldstein, M., Kaplan, R.M., Kaufmann, P.G., Knatterund, G.L., Orleans, C.T. et al. (2003). Evidence-based behavioral medicine: what is it and how do we achieve it? *Annals of Behavioral Medicine*, 26: 161–71.

Davis, C. and Abraham, J. (2013). Is there a cure for corporate crime in the drug industry? *British Medical Journal*, 346: 755.

Davis, O.I. (2011). (Re)framing health literacy: transforming the culture of health in the black barbershop. *Western Journal of Black Studies*, 35: 176–86.

Davison, C., Macintyre, S. and Davey Smith, G. (1994). The potential social impact of predictive genetic testing for susceptibility to common chronic diseases: a review and proposed research agenda. *Sociology of Health & Illness*, 16: 340–71.

De Gruchy, J. and Coppel, D. (2008). 'Listening to reason': a social marketing stop-smoking campaign in Nottingham. *Social Marketing Quarterly*, 14: 5–17.

De Jong, K. and Kleber, R.J. (2007). Emergency conflict-related psychosocial interventions in Sierra Leone and Uganda: lessons from Médecins Sans Frontières. *Journal of Health Psychology*, 12: 485–97.

De Ridder, D., De Vet, E., Stok, M., Adriaanse, M. and De Wit, J. (2013). Obesity, overconsumption and self-regulation failure: the unsung role of eating appropriateness standards. *Health Psychology Review*, 7: 146–65.

De Vadder, F., Kovatcheva-Datchary, P. et al. (2014). Microbiota-generated metabolites promote metabolic benefits via gut-brain neural circuits. *Cell*, 156: 84–96.

De Visser, R. and Smith, J.A. (1999). Mister in-between: a case study of masculine identity and health-related behaviour. *Journal of Health Psychology*, 11: 685–95.

Deci, E.L. and Ryan, R.M. (1985). *Intrinsic Motivation and Self-determination in Human Behavior.* New York: Plenum Press.

Dedert, E.A., Calhoun, P.S., Watkins, L.L., Sherwood, A. and Beckham, J.C. (2010). Posttraumatic stress disorder, cardiovascular and metabolic disease: a review of the evidence. *Annals of Behavioural Medicine*, 39: 61–78.

Delamothe, T., Snow, R. and Godlee, F. (2014). Why the assisted dying bill should become law in England and Wales: it's the right thing to do, and most people want it. *British Medical Journal*, 348 (7965): g4349-2.

DeLilly, C.R. and Flaskerud, J.H. (2012). Discrimination and health outcomes. *Issues in Mental Health Nursing*, 33: 801–4.

DeMatteo, D., Harrison, C., Arneson, C., Salter Goldie, R., Lefebvre, A., Read, S.E. and King, S.M. (2002). Disclosing HIV/AIDS to children: the paths families take to truthtelling. *Psychology, Health & Medicine*, 7: 339–56.

Dempsey, J.A., Veasey, S.C., Morgan, B.J. and O'Donnell, C.P. (2010). Pathophysiology of sleep apnea. *Physiological Review*, 90: 47–112

Denison, J., Varcoe, C. and Browne, A.J. (2014). Aboriginal women's experiences of accessing health care when state apprehension of children is being threatened. *Journal of Advanced Nursing*, 70: 1105–16.

Denollet, J., Sys, S.U., Stroobant, N., Rombouts, H., Gillebert, T.C. and Brutsaert, D.L. (1996). Personality as independent predictor of long-term mortality in patients with coronary heart disease. *The Lancet*, 347: 417–21

Department of Health (1999). *Saving Lives: Our Healthier Nation.* London: The Stationery Office.

Department of Health (2000). *An Organization with a Memory: Report of an Expert Group on Learning from Adverse Events in the NHS, Chaired by the Chief Medical Officer*. London: The Stationery Office.

Department of Health *Building a Safer NHS for Patients – Implementing an Organisation with a Memory*. London: The Stationery Office.

Department of Health (2000). *Health Survey for England 1998*. London: The Stationery Office.

Department of Health (2008). *Ambitions for Health: A Strategic Framework for Maximising the Potential of Social Marketing and Health-related Behaviour*. London: NHS. Available at www.dh.gov.uk/prod_consum_dh/groups/dh_digitalassets/documents/digitalasset/dh_086289.pdf [accessed 16 January 2010].

Department of Health (2011) *Start Active, Stay Active: A Report on Physical Activity from the Four Home Countries' Chief Medical Officers*. London: Department of Health.

Des Jarlais, D.C., Lyles, C. and Crepaz, N. (2004). Improving the reporting quality of nonrandomized evaluations of behavioral and public health interventions: the TREND statement. *American Journal of Public Health*, 94: 361–6.

Devcich, D., Ellis, C.J., Gamble, G. and Petrie, K.J. (2008). Psychological responses to cardiac diagnosis: changes in illness representations immediately following coronary angiography. *Journal of Psychosomatic Research*, 65: 553–6.

Dew, K. (1999). Epidemics, panic and power: representations of measles and measles vaccine. *Health*, 3: 379–98.

DeWalt, D.A. (2007). Low health literacy: epidemiology and interventions. *North Carolina Medical Journal*, 68: 327–30.

Dickens, C., Lambert, B.L., Cromwell, T. and Piano, M.R. (2013). Nurse overestimation of patients' health literacy. *Journal of Health Communication*, 18: 62–9.

Dickerson, S.S. and Kemeny, M.E. (2004). Acute stressors and cortisol responses: a theoretical integration and synthesis of laboratory research. *Psychological Bulletin*, 130: 355–91.

Diener, E. and Chan, M.Y. (2011). Happy people live longer: subjective well-being contributes to health and longevity. *Applied Psychology: Health and Well-Being*, 3: 1–43.

Diener, E.D., Emmons, R.A., Larsen, R.J. and Griffin, S. (1985). The Satisfaction With Life Scale. *Journal of Personality Assessment*, 49: 71–5.

Dietary Guidelines Advisory Committee (2010). *Report of the Dietary Guidelines Advisory Committee on the Dietary Guidelines for Americans, 2010, to the Secretary of Agriculture and the Secretary of Health and Human Services*. Agricultural Research Service.

DiMatteo, M.R. (2004). Social support and patient adherence to medical treatment: a meta-analysis. *Health Psychology*, 23: 207–18.

DiMillo, J., Samson, A., Thériault, A., Lowry, S., Corsini, L., Verma, S. and Tomiak, E. (2014). Genetic testing: when prediction generates stigmatization. *Journal of Health Psychology*, in press.

Ding, C. and Xia, L. (2014). Posttraumatic reactions to an earthquake: multidimensional scaling profile analysis of adolescent survivors. *Journal of Health Psychology*, in press.

Dishman, R.K. (1986). Exercise compliance: a new view for public health. *Physician & Sports Medicine*, 14: 127–45.

Dixon-Woods, M., Bonas, S., Booth, A., Jones, D.R., Miller, T., Sutton, A. J. et al. (2006). How can systematic reviews incorporate qualitative research? A critical perspective. *Qualitative Research*, 6: 27–44.

Doise, W. (1986). *Levels of Explanation in Social Psychology*. Cambridge: Cambridge University Press.

Dolezsar, C.M., McGrath, J.J., Herzig, A.J.M. and Miller, S.B. (2014). Perceived racial discrimination and hypertension: a comprehensive systematic review. *Health Psychology*, 33: 20–34.

Dolgin, M.J., Katz, R., Doctors, S.R. and Siegel, S.E. (1986). Caregivers' perceptions of medical compliance in adolescents with cancer. *Journal of Adolescent Health Care*, 7: 22–7

Doll, R. and Hill, A.B. (1952). A study of the aetiology of carcinoma of the lung. *British Medical Journal*, 2: 1271–86.

Dombrowski, S.U., Sniehotta, F.F., Avenell, A., Johnston, M., MacLennan, G. et al. (2012). Identifying active ingredients in complex behavioural interventions for obese adults with obesity-related co-morbidities or additional risk factors for co-morbidities: a systematic review. *Health Psychology Review*, 6: 7–32

Donovan, J.L. and Blake, D.R. (1992). Patient non-compliance: deviance or reasoned decision-making? *Social Science & Medicine*, 34: 507–13.

Doran, C.M., Valenti, L., Robinson, M., Britt. H. and Mattick, R.P. (2006). Smoking status of Australian general practice patients and their attempts to quit. *Addictive Behavior*, 31: 758–66.

Douglas, M. and Nicod, M. (1974). Taking the biscuit: the structure of British meals. *New Society*, 19 December.

Doyal, L. and Gough, I. (1991). *A Theory of Need.* London: Macmillan.

Downing-Matibag, T.M. and Geisinger, B. (2009). Hooking up and sexual risk taking among college students: a health belief model perspective. *Qualitative Health Research* 19: 1196–209.

Downward, P., Hallmans, K. and Pawlowski, T. (2014). Assessing parental impact on the sports participation of children: a socio-economic analysis of the UK. *European Journal of Sport Science*, 14: 84–90.

Drobes, D.J., Saladin, M.E. and Tiffany, S.T. (2001). Classical conditioning mechanisms. In N. Heather, T.J. Peters and T. Stockwell (eds.), *International Handbook of Alcohol Dependence and Problems.* London: Wiley. pp. 281–97.

Druet, C., Stettler, N., Sharp, S., Simmons, R.K., Cooper, C., Davey Smith, G. et al. (2012). Prediction of childhood obesity by infancy weight gain: an individual-level meta-analysis. *Paediatric & Perinatal Epidemiology*, 26: 19–26.

Drummond, D.C., Tiffany, S.T., Glautier, S. and Remington, B. (eds.) (1995). *Addictive Behaviour: Cue Exposure Theory and Practice*. London: Wiley.

DuCharme, K.A. and Brawley, L.R. (1995). Predicting the intentions and behavior of exercise initiates using two forms of self-efficacy. *Journal of Behavioral Medicine*, 18: 479–97.

Duijts, S.F., Faber, M.M., Oldenburg, H.S., van Beurden, M. and Aaronson, N.K. (2011). Effectiveness of behavioral techniques and physical exercise on psychosocial functioning and health-related quality of life in breast cancer patients and survivors: a meta-analysis. *Psycho-oncology*, 20: 115–26.

Duijts, S.F., Zeegers, M.P. and Borne, B.V. (2003). The association between stressful life events and breast cancer risk: a meta-analysis. *International Journal of Cancer*, 107: 1023–9.

Duncan, N., Bowman, B., Naidoo, A., Pillay, J. and Roos, V. (2007). *Community Psychology: Analysis, Context and Action.* Cape Town: UCT Press.

Dwyer, J.J.M., Allison, K.R., Goldberg, E.R., Fein, A.J., Yoshida, K.K. and Boutilier, M.A. (2006). Adolescent girls' perceived barriers to participation in physical activity. *Adolescence*, 41: 75–89.

Eaker, E.D., Sullivan, L.M., Kelly-Hayes, M., D'Agostino, R.B., Sr. and Benjamin, E.J. (2004). Does job strain increase the risk for coronary heart disease or death in men and women? *American Journal of Epidemiology*, 159: 950–8.

Eardley, A. and Elkind, A. (1990). A pilot study of attendance for breast cancer screening. *Social Science & Medicine*, 30: 693–9.

Easton, P., Entwistle, V.A. and Williams, B. (2013). How the stigma of low literacy can impair patient-professional spoken interactions and affect health: insights from a qualitative investigation. *BMC Health Services Research*, 13: 1–12.

Eaton, S.B. and Eaton, S.B. (2003). An evolutionary perspective on human physical activity: implications for health. *Comparative Biochemistry and Physiology – Part A: Molecular and Integrative Physiology*, 136: 153–9.

Ebbeling, C.B., Pawlak, D.B. and Ludwig, D.S. (2002). Childhood obesity: public-health crisis, common sense cure. *The Lancet*, 360: 473–82.

Eccleston, C. (2001). Role of psychology in pain management. *British Journal of Anaesthesia*, 87: 144–52.

Eccleston, C., Morley, S., Williams, A., Yorke, L. and Mastroyannopoulou, K. (2002). Systematic review of randomised controlled trials of psychological therapy for chronic pain in children and adolescents, with a subset meta-analysis of pain relief. *Pain*, 99: 157–65.

Eccleston, Z. and Eccleston, C. (2004). Interdisciplinary management of adolescent chronic pain: developing the role of physiotherapy. *Physiotherapy*, 90: 77–81.

Edwards, A.G., Hailey, S. and Maxwell, M. (2004). Psychological interventions for women with metastatic breast cancer. *Cochrane Database of Systematic Reviews*, 2 (CD004253).

Eisenberg, E., Ognitz, M. and Almog, S. (2014) The pharmacokinetics, efficiency, safety, and ease of use of a novel portable metered-dose cannabis inhaler in patients with chronic neuropathic pain: a phase Ia study. *Journal of Pain and Palliative Care Pharmacotherapy*, 28: 216–25.

Eissa, M.A., Poffenbarger, T. and Portman, R.J. (2001). Comparison of the actigraph versus patients diary information in defining circadian time periods for analysing ambulatory blood pressure monitoring data. *Blood Pressure Monitoring*, 6: 21–5.

Elmore, J.G., Barton, M.B., Moceri, V.M., Polk, S., Arena, P.J. and Fletcher, S.W. (1998). Ten year risk of false positive screening mammograms and clinical breast examination. *New England Journal of Medicine*, 338: 1089–96.

Engel, G.L. (1977). The need for a new medical model: a challenge for biomedicine, *Science*, 196: 129–36.

Engel, G.L. (1980). The clinical application of the biopsychosocial model. *American Journal of Psychiatry*, 137: 535–44.

Engels, F. (1845/1958). *The Condition of the Working Class in England in 1844*. London: Lawrence & Wishart.

Enriquez, V.G. (1993). Developing a Filipino psychology. In K. Uichol and J.W. Berry (eds.), *Indigenous Psychologies: Research and Experience in Cultural Context*. London: Sage. pp. 152–69.

Epstein, L. and Ogden, J. (2005). A qualitative study of GPs' views of treating obesity. *British Journal of General Practice*, 55: 750–4.

Epstein, R.M., Franks, P., Fiscella, K., Shields, C.G., Meldrum, S.C., Kravitz, R.L. and Duberstein, P.R. (2005). Measuring patient-centered communication in patient–physician consultations: theoretical and practical issues. *Social Science & Medicine*, 61: 1516–28.

Eriksson, M. and Lindström, B. (2006). Antonovsky's Sense of Coherence Scale and the relation with health: a systematic review. *Journal of Epidemiology and Community Health*, 60: 376–81.

Ernst, E. (2012). Homeopathy for eczema: a systematic review of controlled clinical trials. *British Journal of Dermatology*, 166: 1170–2.

Ernst, E. and Pittler, M.H. (2000). Efficacy of ginger for nausea and vomiting: a systematic review of randomized clinical trials. *British Journal of Anaesthesia*, 84: 367–71.

Erwin, H., Fedewa, A., Beighle, A. and Ahn, S. (2012). A quantitative review of physical activity, health, and learning outcomes associated with classroom-based physical activity interventions. *Journal of Applied School Psychology*, 28: 14–36.

Escalante, Y., Backx, K. and Saavedra, J.M., García-Hermoso, A. and Domínguez, A.M. (2013). Play area and physical activity in recess in primary schools. *Kinesiology 44,* 123–129

Estacio, E.V. (2009). Media exploitation, racism and health. *Journal of Health Psychology*, 14: 155–7.

Estacio, E.V. (2013). Health literacy and community empowerment: it is more than just reading, writing and counting. *Journal of Health Psychology*, 18 (8): 1056–68.

Estacio, E.V. and Marks, D.F. (2010). Critical reflections on social injustice and participatory action research: the case of the indigenous Ayta community in the Philippines. *Procedia – Social and Behavioral Sciences*, 5: 548–52.

Estacio, E.V. and Marks, D.F. (2012). Liberation of the social consciousness through alternative learning and action research: a work in progress with the Aytas in the Philippines. In C. Walker, K. Johnson and L. Cunningham (eds), *Community Psychology and the Economics of Mental Health: Global Perspectives* London: Palgrave Macmillan, pp. 238–52.

Euripides (1954/414 BC). *The Bacchae*, trans. P. Vellacott. London: Penguin.

European Commission (2014). *Eurobarometer on Sport and Physical Activity*. MEMO/14/207. Available: http://europa.eu/rapid/press-release_MEMO-14-207_en.htm.

Evans, P., Hucklebridge, F. and Clow, A. (2000). *Mind, Immunity and Health: The Science of Psychoneuroimmunology.* London: Free Association Books.

Evans, R.I. (1988). Health promotion – science or ideology? *Health Psychology*, 7: 203–19.

Evans, W.D. (2006). How social marketing works in health care. *British Medical Journal*, 332: 1207–10.

Everitt, A. and Hardiker, P. (1997) Towards a critical approach to evaluation. In M. Sidell, L. Jones, J. Katz and A. Peberdy (eds.), *Debates and Dilemmas in Promoting Health: A Reader*. Basingstoke: Open University Press.

Eysenbach, G. (2003). The impact of the Internet on cancer outcomes. *CA: A Cancer Journal for Clinicians*, 53: 356–71.

Eysenck, H.J. (1965/1970). *Fact and Fiction in Psychology*. London: Penguin.

Eysenck, H.J. (1988). Personality, stress and cancer: prediction and prophylaxis. *British Journal of Medical Psychology*, 61: 57–75.

Eysenck, H.J. and Grossarth-Maticek, R. (1991). Creative novation behaviour therapy as a prophylactic treatment for cancer and coronary heart disease. Part II: effects of treatment. *Behaviour Research & Therapy*, 29: 17–31.

Eysenck, H.J., Tarrant, M. and Woolf, M. (1960). Smoking and personality. *British Medical Journal*, 280: 1456–60.

Ezzati, M., Lopez, A.D., Rodgers, A., Hoorn, S.V., Murray, C.J.L. and the Comparative Risk Assessment Collaborating Group (2002). Selected major risk factors and global and regional burden of disease. *The Lancet*, 360: 1347–60.

Ezzy, D. (2000). Illness narratives: time, hope and HIV. *Social Science & Medicine*, 50: 605–17.

Faber, A. and Dubé, L. (2015). Parental attachment insecurity predicts child and adult high caloric food consumption. *Journal of Health Psychology*, 20: in press.

Fallowfield, L. and Jenkins, V. (2015). Falomir-Pichastor, J.M., Toscani, L. and Despointes, S.H. (2009). Determinants of flu vaccination among nurses: the effects of group identification and professional responsibility. *Applied Psychology*, 58: 42–58.

Feinman, R.J. and Fine, E.J. (2004). 'A calorie is a calorie' violates the second law of thermodynamics, *Nutrition Journal*, 3: 9.

Fekjær, H.O. (2013). Alcohol – a universal preventive agent? A critical analysis. *Addiction*, 108: 2051–7.

Fensham, R. and Gardner, S. (2005). Dance classes, youth cultures and public health. *Youth Studies Australia*, 24: 14–20.

Ferguson, J., Bauld, L., Chesterman, J. and Judge, K. (2005). The English smoking treatment services: one-year outcomes. *Addiction*, Supplement 2: 59–69.

Ferrie, J.E. (2004). Work, stress and health: the Whitehall II study. London: Cabinet Office. Accessed on 2 December 2014 at: http://www.ucl.ac.uk/whitehallII/pdf/Whitehallbooklet_1_.pdf

Ferriman, A. (2007). BMJ readers choose the 'sanitary revolution' as greatest medical advance since 1840. *British Medical Journal*, 334: 111.

Ferron, C., Narring F., Couderey, M. and Michael, P.-A. (1999). Sport activity therefore adolescence Associations with health perceptions are experimental behaviour. *Health Education Research*, 14: 225–33.

Feste, C. and Anderson, R.M. (1995). Empowerment: from philosophy to practice. *Patient Education & Counseling*, 26: 139–44.

Fieldhouse, P. (1996). *Food and Nutrition: Customs and Culture* (2nd edn). Cheltenham: Stanley Thornes.

Fillmore, K.M., Stockwell, T., Chikritzhs, T., Bostrom, A. and Kerr, W. (2007). Moderate alcohol use and reduced mortality risk: systematic error in prospective studies and new hypotheses. *Annals of Epidemiology*, 17 (suppl. 5): S16–23.

Fincham, J.E. and Wertheimer, A.I. (1985). Using the Health Belief Model to predict initial drug therapy defaulting. *Social Science & Medicine*, 20: 101–5.

Fine, E.J. and Feinman, R.D. (2004). Thermodynamics of weight loss diets. *Nutrition & Metabolism*, 1: 15.

Fine, M. and Asch, A. (1982). The question of disability: no easy answers for the women's movement. *Reproductive Rights National Network Newsletter*, 4: 19–20.

Fiore, M. (2008). *Treating Tobacco Use and Dependence: 2008 Update: Clinical Practice Guideline.* DIANE Publishing.

Fisher, J.D. and Fisher, W.A. (1992). Changing AIDS risk behavior. *Psychological Bulletin*, 111: 455–74.

Fisher, J.D. and Fisher, W.A. (2000). Individual level theories of HIV risk behavior change. In J. Peterson and R. DiClemente (eds.), *Handbook of HIV Prevention.* New York: Plenum. pp. 3–56.

Fitzpatrick, M. (2001). *The Tyranny of Health.* London: Routledge.

Flanagan, J.C. (1978). A research approach to improving our quality of life. *American Psychologist*, 33: 138–47.

Flick, U. (1998). The social construction of individual and public health: contributions of social representations theory to a social science of health. *Social Science Information*, 37: 639–62.

Flor, H., Fydrich, T. and Turk, D.C. (1992). Efficacy of multidisciplinary pain treatment centers – a meta-analytic review. *Pain*, 49: 221–30.

Flowers, P., Hart, G. and Marriott, C. (1999). Constructing sexual health. *Journal of Health Psychology*, 4: 483–95.

Flowers, P., Langdridge, D., Gough, B. and Holliday, R. (2013). On the biomedicalisation of the penis: the commodification of function and aesthetics. *International Journal of Men's Health*, 12 (2): 121–37.

Floyd, D.L., Prentice-Dunn, S. and Rogers, R.W. (2000). A meta-analysis of research on protection motivation theory. *Journal of Applied Social Psychology*, 30: 407–29.

Fogarty, J.S. (1997). Reactance theory and patient non-compliance. *Social Science & Medicine*, 45: 1277–88.

Fogarty, L., Roter, D., Larson, S., Burke, J.G., Gillespie, J. and Levy, B. (2002). Patient adherence to HIV medication regimens: a review of published and abstract reports. *Patient Education & Counseling*, 46: 93–108.

Fogel, R. (2004) *The Escape from Premature Hunger and Death, 1700–2100: Europe, America and the Third World.* Cambridge University Press.

Fogelholm, M., Anderssen, S., Gunnarsdottir, I. and Lahti-Koski, M. (2012). Dietary macronutrients and food consumption as determinants of long-term weight change in adult populations: a systematic literature review. *Food & Nutrition Research*, 56.

Foley, J.A., Ramankutty, N., Brauman, K.A. et al. (2011). Solutions for a cultivated planet. *Nature*, 478: 337–42.

Folkman, S. and Moskowitz, J.T. (2004). Coping: pitfalls and promise. *Annual Review of Psychology*, 55: 745–74.

Follick, M.J., Smith, T.W. and Ahern, D.K. (1985). The Sickness Impact Profile: a global measure of disability in chronic low back pain. *Pain*, 21: 67–76.

Food and Agriculture Organization (2006). *World Agriculture: Towards 2030/2050*. Rome.

Foresight Report (2007). *Tackling Obesities: Future Choices*. Government Office for Science and Department of Health. Available: https://www.gov.uk/government/collections/tackling-obesities-future-choices.

Foucault, M. (1976). *The Birth of the Clinic*. London: Routledge.

Foucault, M. (1979). *The History of Sexuality, Vol. 3: The Care of the Self.* London: Allen Lane.

Foucault, M. (1980). *Power/Knowledge: Selected Interviews and Other Writings.* New York: Parthenon.

Fox, B.H. (1988). Psychogenic factors in cancer, especially its incidence. In S. Maes, D. Spielberger, P.B. Defares and I.G. Sarason (eds.), *Topics in Health Psychology.* New York: Wiley. pp. 37–55.

Foxcroft, D.R., Ireland, D., Lister-Sharp, D.J., Lowe, G. and Breen, R. (2003). Longer term primary prevention for alcohol misuse in young people: a systematic review. *Addiction*, 98: 397–411.

Frank, A.W. (1993). The rhetoric of self-change: illness experience as narrative. *Sociological Quarterly*, 34: 39–52.

Frank, A.W. (1995). *The Wounded Storyteller: Body, Illness and Ethics.* Chicago, IL: University of Chicago Press.

Frankenberg, R. (1982). *Time, Health and Medicine*. London: Sage.

Fraser-Thomas, J., Côté, J. and Deakin, J. (2008). Examining adolescent sport dropout and prolonged engagement from a developmental perspective. *Journal of Applied Sport Psychology*, 20: 318–33

Frattaroli, J. (2006). Experimental disclosure and its moderator: a meta-analysis. *Journal of Abnormal Psychology*, 96: 3–13.

Frazier, E.L., Jiles, R.B. and Mayberry, R. (1996). Use of screening mammography and clinical breast examination among Black, Hispanic and White women. *Preventive Medicine*, 25: 118–25.

Fredericks, B., Maynor, P., White, N., English, F.W. and Ehrich, L.C. (2014). Living with the legacy of conquest and culture: social justice leadership in education and the Indigenous peoples of Australia and America. In *International Handbook of Educational Leadership and Social (In)Justice*. Amsterdam: Springer Netherlands. pp. 751–80.

Fredrickson et al. (2015) Weight perception in overweight adolescents. *JHP*, under review.

Freire, P. (1973). *Education for Political Consciousness*. New York: Continuum.

French, D.P., Cooke, R., Mclean, N., Williams, M. and Sutton, S. (2007). What do people think about when they answer Theory of Planned Behaviour questionnaires? *Journal of Health Psychology*, 12: 672–87.

French, D.P., Cooper, A. and Weinman, J. (2006). Illness perceptions predict attendance at cardiac rehabilitation following acute myocardial infarction: a systematic review with meta-analysis. *Journal of Psychosomatic Research*, 61: 757–67.

French, J. and Adams, L. (1986) From analysis to synthesis: theories of health education. *Health Education Journal*, 45: 71–4.

Frew, P.M., Saint-Victor, D., Owens, L.E. and Omer, S.B. (2014). Socioecological and message framing factors influencing maternal influenza immunization among minority women. *Vaccine*, 32: 1736–44.

Friedman, A.L., Brookmeyer, K.A., Kachur, R.E., Ford, J., Hogben, M., Habel, M.A. et al. (2014). An assessment of the GYT: Get Yourself Tested campaign: an integrated approach to sexually transmitted disease prevention communication. *Sexually Transmitted Diseases*, 41: 151–57.

Friedman, H.S. and Kern, M.L. (2014). Personality, well-being and health. *Annual Review of Psychology*, 65: 719–42.

Friedman, H.S., Martin, L.R., Tucker, J.S., Criqui, M., Kern, M.L. and Reynolds, C. (2008). Stability of physical activity across the life-span. *Journal of Health Psychology*, 13: 966–78.

Friedson, E. (1970). *Profession of Medicine*. New York: Harper & Row.

Frostholm, L., Oernboel, E., Christensen, K.S., Toft, T., Olesen, F., Weinman, J. and Fink, P. (2007). Do illness perceptions predict health outcomes in primary care patients? A 2-year follow-up study. *Journal of Psychosomatic Research*, 62: 129–38.

Fugh-Berman, A. (2003). *The 5-minute Herb & Dietary Supplement Consult.* Philadelphia, PA: Lippincott Williams & Wilkins.

Gable, S., Chang, Y. and Krull, J.L. (2007). Television watching and frequency of family meals are predictive of overweight onset and persistence in a national sample of school-aged children. *Journal of the American Dietetic Association*, 107: 53–61.

Galindo, R.W. (2004). Fighting hunger in Brazil. [La lucha contra el hambre en Brasil]. *Perspectives in Health*, 9: 26–9.

Gagnon, M., Jacob, J.D. and Holmes, D. (2010). Governing through (in)security: a critical analysis of a fear-based public health campaign. *Critical Public Health*, 20 (2): 245–56.

Gainforth, H.L. and Latimer, A.E. (2012). Risky business: risk information and the moderating effect of message frame and past behaviour on women's perceptions of the human papillomavirus vaccine. *Journal of Health Psychology*, 17 (6): 896–906.

Gallagher, K. and Updegraff, J. (2012). Health message framing effects on attitudes, intentions, and behavior: a meta-analytic review. *Annals of Behavioral Medicine*, 43: 101–16.

Gallagher, T.H., Waterman, A.D., Ebers, A.G., Fraser, V.J. and Levinson, W. (2003). Patients' and physicians' attitudes regarding the disclosure of medical errors. *Journal of the American Medical Association*, 289 (8): 1001–7.

Gallant, S.J., Keita, G.P. and Royak-Schaler, R. (eds.) (1997). *Health Care for Women: Psychological, Social and Behavioral Influences*. Washington, DC: American Psychological Association.

Galvin, R. (2002). Disturbing notions of chronic illness and individual responsibility: towards a geneaology of morals. *Health (London)*, 6: 107–37.

Gan, Y., Xie, X., Wang, T., Rodriguez, M.A. and Tang, C.T. (2013). Thriving in the shadow of the 2008 Sichuan Earthquake: two studies on resilience in adolescents. *Journal of Health Psychology*, 18: 1232–41.

Garcia, J., Ervin, R.R. and Koelling, R.A. (1966). Learning with prolonged delay of reinforcement. *Psychonomic Science*, 5: 121–2.

Garcia-Retamero, R. and Cokely, E.T. (2011). Effective communication of risks to young adults: using message framing and visual aids to increase condom use and STD screening. *Journal of Experimental Psychology – Applied*, 17: 270–87.

Garrison, M.M., Christakis, D.A., Ebel, B.E., Wiehe, S.E. and Rivara, F.P. (2003). Smoking cessation interventions for adolescents: a systematic review. *American Journal of Preventive Medicine*, 25: 363–7.

Gee, G.C., Spencer, M.S., Chen, J. and Takeuchi, D. (2007). A nationwide study of discrimination and chronic health conditions among Asian Americans. *American Journal of Public Health*, 97: 1275–82.

Geertz, C. (1973). *The Interpretation of Culture*. New York: Basic Books.

Gerend, M.A. and Shepherd, M.A. (2013). Message framing, it does a body good: effects of message framing and motivational orientation on young women's calcium consumption. *Journal of Health Psychology*, 18 (10): 1296–306.

Gergen, K. and Gergen, M. (1986). Narrative and the construction of psychological science. In T. Sarbin (ed.), *Narrative Psychology: The Storied Nature of Human Conduct*. New York: Praeger. pp. 22–44.

Getrich, C.M., Sussman, A.L., Helitzer, D.Hoffman, R.M., Warner, T.D., Sánchez, V. et al. (2012). Clinicians. expressions of machismo in colorectal cancer screening among New Mexico Hispanic subpopulations. *Qualitative Health Research*, 22: 546–59.

Gifford, S. (1986). The meaning of lumps: a case study of the ambiguities of risk. In C.R. Janes, R. Stall and S.M. Gifford (eds.), *Anthropology and Epidemiology: Interdisciplinary Approaches to the Study of Health and Disease*. Dordrecht: Reidel. pp. 213–46.

Gilbert, K.L., Quinn, S.C., Goodman, R.M., Butler, J. and Wallace, J. (2013). A meta-analysis of social capital and health: a case for needed research. *Journal of Health Psychology*, 18 (11): 1385–99.

Giles, M., McClenahan, C., Armour, C., Millar, S., Rae, G., Mallett, J. and Stewart-Knox, B. (2014). Evaluation of a theory of planned behaviour-based breastfeeding intervention in Northern Irish schools using a randomized cluster design. *British Journal of Health Psychology*, 19: 16–35.

Giles-Corti, B. and Donovan, R.J. (2003). The relative influence of individual, social and physical environmental determinants of physical activity. *Social Science & Medicine*, 54: 1793–812.

Gillies, V. and Willig, C. (1997). 'You get the nicotine and that in your blood': constructions of addiction and control in women's accounts of cigarette smoking. *Journal of Community & Applied Social Psychology*, 7: 285–301.

Gilmartin, J., Long, A. and Soldin, M. (2014). Body-contouring surgery: an exploratory study Identity transformation and a changed lifestyle following dramatic weight loss and body-contouring surgery: an exploratory study. *Journal of Health Psychology*, in press.

Ginzel, K.H., Maritz, G.S., Marks, D.F., Neuberger, M., Pauly, J.R., Polito, J.R. et al. (2007). Critical review: nicotine for the fetus, the infant and the adolescent? *Journal of Health Psychology*, 12: 215–24.

Girginov, V. and Hills, L. (2008). A sustainable sports legacy: creating a link between the London Olympics and sports participation. *International Journal of Sports History*, 25: 2091–116.

Glaser, B.G. (1992). *Basics of Grounded Theory Analysis: Emergence Versus Forcing*. Mill Valley, CA: Sociology Press.

Glaser, B.G. and Strauss, A. (1967). *The Discovery of Grounded Theory: Strategies for Qualitative Research*. Chicago, IL: Aldine.

Glasgow, R.E., Hampson, S.E., Strycker, L.A. and Ruggiero, L. (1997). Personal-model beliefs and social-environmental barriers related to diabetes self-management. *Diabetes Care*, 20: 556–61.

Gleeson, K. and Frith, H. (2006). (De)constructing body image. *Journal of Health Psychology*, 11: 79–90.

Glynn, T.J. (2014). E-cigarettes and the future of tobacco control. *CA: A Cancer Journal for Clinicians*, 64: 164–8.

Goffman, E. (1963). *Stigma: Notes on the Management of Spoiled Identity*. London: Penguin.

Goins, R.T., Spencer, S.M. and Williams, K. (2011). Lay meanings of health among rural older adults in Appalachia. *Journal of Rural Health*, 27: 13–20.

Goldacre, M.J. and Roberts, S.E. (2004). Hospital admission for acute pancreatitis in an English population, 1963–98: database study of incidence and mortality. *British Medical Journal*, 328: 1466–9.

Goldfield, G.S., Moore, C., Henderson, K., Buchholz, A., Obeid, N. and Flament, M.F. (2010). Body dissatisfaction, dietary restraint, depression, and weight status in adolescents. *Journal of School Health*, 80: 186–92.

Gone, J.P. (2013). Redressing First Nations' historical trauma: theorizing mechanisms for indigenous culture as mental health treatment. *Transcultural Psychiatry*, 50 (5): 683–706.

Gonzalez, J.S., Peyrot, M., McCarl, L.A., Collins, E.M., Serpa, L., Mimiaga, M.J. and Safren, S.A. (2008). Depression and diabetes treatment nonadherence: a meta-analysis. *Diabetes Care*, 31: 2398–403.

Goodman, M.J., Ogdie, A., Kanamori, M.J., Cañar, J. and O'Malley, A.S. (2006). Barriers and facilitators of colorectal cancer screening among Mid-Atlantic Latinos: focus group findings. *Ethnicity and Disease*, 16: 255–61.

Goodwin, P.J., Bruera, E. and Stockler, M. (2014). Pain in patients with cancer. *Journal of Clinical Oncology*, 32 (16): 1637–9.

Goossens, L., Braet, C., Van Durme, K., Decaluwé, V. and Bosmans, G. (2012). The parent–child relationship as predictor of eating pathology and weight gain in preadolescents. *Journal of Clinical Child & Adolescent Psychology*, 41: 445–57.

Gore-Felton, C. and Koopman, C. (2008). Behavioral mediation of the relationship between psychosocial factors and HIV disease progression. *Psychosomatic Medicine*, 70: 569–74.

Gostin, L.O. and Friedman, E.A. (2013). Towards a framework convention on global health: a transformative agenda for global health justice. *Yale Journal of Health Policy, Law, and Ethics*, 13 (1): 1–75.

Gotay, C.C., Shimizu, H., Muraoka, M., Ishihara, Y., Tsuboi, K. and Ogawa, H. (2004). Health attitudes and behaviors: comparison of Japanese and Americans of Japanese and European ancestry. *Health & Place*, 10: 153–61.

Gøtzsche, P. (2013). *Deadly Medicines and Organised Crime: How Big Pharma has Corrupted Healthcare*. London: Radcliffe.

Gøtzsche, P.C. (2013). Regular self-examination or clinical examination for early detection of breast cancer. *Cochrane Database of Systematic Reviews*, 2: 1–14.

Gøtzsche, P.C. and Nielsen, M. (2009). Screening for breast cancer with mammography. *Cochrane Database Systematic Review, 4*.

Goyal, M., Singh, S., Sibinga, E.M.S., Gould, N.F., Rowland-Seymour, A., Sharma, R. et al. (2014). Meditation programs for psychological stress and well-being: a systematic review and meta-analysis. *JAMA Internal Medicine*, 174: 357–68.

Gracey, M. and King, M. (2009). Indigenous health part 1: Determinants and disease patterns. *The Lancet*, 374: 65–75.

Grafstrom, M. (1994). The experience of burden in the care of elderly persons with dementia. Unpublished doctoral dissertation, Karolinska Institute, Stockholm, Sweden.

Graham, H. (1976). Smoking in pregnancy: the attitudes of expectant mothers. *Social Science & Medicine*, 10: 399–405.

Graham, H. (1987). Women's smoking and family health. *Social Science & Medicine*, 25: 47–56.

Graham, R., Kremer, J. and Wheeler, G. (2008). Physical activity and psychological well-being among people with chronic illness and disability. *Journal of Health Psychology*, 13: 447–58.

Grande, G., Romppel, M. and Barth, J. (2012). Association between type D personality and prognosis in patients with cardiovascular diseases: a systematic review and meta-analysis. *Annals of Behavioral Medicine*, 43: 299–310.

Grant, B.C. (2001). 'You're never too old': beliefs about physical activity and playing sport in later life. *Ageing & Society*, 21, 777–98.

Gray, R. and Henderson, J. (2006) *Report to the Department of Health: Review of the Fetal Effects of Prenatal Alcohol Exposure.* Oxford: University of Oxford, National Perinatal Epidemiology Unit.

Gray, R. and Sinding, C. (2002) *Standing Ovation: Performing Social Science Research About Cancer.* Walnut Creek, CA: Altamira Press.

Gray, R.E., Fergus, K.D. and Fitch, M.I. (2005). Two Black men with prostate cancer: a narrative approach. *British Journal of Health Psychology*, 10: 71–84.

Gray, R.E., Ivonoffski, V. and Sinding, C. (2001). Making a mess and spreading it around: articulation of an approach to research-based theatre. In A. Bochner and C. Ellis (eds.), *Ethnographically Speaking*. Walnut Creek, CA: Altamira Press. pp. 57–75.

Green, L.W. (2014). Closing the chasm between research and practice: evidence of and for change. *Health Promotion Journal of Australia*, 25: 25–9.

Greene, R. (1995). Survey of prescription anomalies in community pharmacies: (1) prescription monitoring. *Pharmacy Journal*, 254: 476–81.

Greenwald, B.D., Narcessian, E.J. and Pomeranz, B.A. (1999). Assessment of psychiatrists' knowledge and perspectives on the use of opioids: review of basic concepts for managing chronic pain. *American Journal of Physical Medicine & Rehabilitation*, 78: 408–15.

Greenwood, M.L. and de Leeuw, S.N. (2012). Social determinants of health and the future well-being of Aboriginal children in Canada. *Paediatrics & Child Health*, 17 (7): 381.

Greer, S., Morris, T. and Pettingale, K.W. (1979). Psychological response to breast cancer: effect on outcome. *The Lancet*, 2: 785–7.

Gregg, J. and Curry, R.H. (1994). Explanatory models for cancer among African-American women at two Atlanta neighborhood health centers: the implications for a cancer screening program. *Social Science & Medicine*, 39: 519–26.

Gregory, S. and McKie, Griffiths, C., Panteli, N., Brunton, D., Marder, B. and Williamson, H. (2014). Designing and evaluating the acceptability of Realshare: An online support community for teenagers and young adults with cancer. *Journal of Health Psychology*, in press.

Grimshaw, J.M., Eccles, M.P., Lavis, J.N., Hill, S.J. and Squires, J.E. (2012). Knowledge translation of research findings. *Implementation Science*, 7: 50–66.

Grogan, S. (2006). Body image and health: contemporary perspectives. *Journal of Health Psychology*, 11: 523–30.

Grogan, S. and Richards, H. (2002). Body image: focus groups with boys and men. *Men & Masculinities*, 4: 219–32.

Grollman, E.A. (2012). Multiple forms of perceived discrimination and health among adolescents and young adults. *Journal of Health and Social Behavior*, 53: 199–214.

Grossardt, B.R., Bower, J.H., Geda, Y.E., Colligan, R.C. and Rocca, W.A. (2009). Pessimistic, anxious, and depressive personality traits predict all-cause mortality: the Mayo Clinic cohort study of personality and aging. *Psychosomatic Medicine*, 71: 491–500.

Grossarth-Maticek, R. and Eysenck, H.J. (1991). Creative novation behaviour therapy as a prophylactic treatment for cancer and coronary heart disease: part I – description of treatment. *Behaviour Research and Therapy*, 29: 1–16.

Gurrieri, L., Previte, J. and Brace-Govan, J. (2013). Women's bodies as sites of control: inadvertent stigma and exclusion in social marketing. *Journal of Macromarketing*, 33: 128–43. doi:10.1177/0276146712469971

Guse, K., Levine, D., Martins, S., Lira, A., Gaarde, J., Westmorland, W. and Gilliam, M. (2012). Interventions using new digital media to improve adolescent sexual health: a systematic review. *Journal of Adolescent Health*, 51 (6): 535–43.

Gutierrez, N., Kindratt, T.B., Pagels, P., Foster, B. and Gimpel, N.E. (2014). Health literacy, health information seeking behaviors and internet use among patients attending a private and public clinic in the same geographic area. *Journal of Community Health*, 39: 83–9.

Guyenet, S. (2012). The Carbohydrate Hypothesis of obesity: a critical examination. Available: http://wholehealthsource.blogspot.co.uk/.

Gysels, M., Evans, N., Meñaca, A. et al. (2012). Culture and end of life care: a scoping exercise in seven European countries. *PLOS ONE*, 7: e34188.

Haaken, J.K. and O'Neill, M. (2014). Moving images: psychoanalytically informed visual methods in documenting the lives of women migrants and asylum seekers. *Journal of Health Psychology*, 19: 79–89.

Hadjez-Berrios, E. (2014). A socio-psychological perspective on community participation in health during the Unidad Popular Government: Santiago de Chile, from 1970 to 1973. *Journal of Health Psychology*, 19 (1): 90–6.

Hafekost, K., Lawrence, D., Mitrou, F., O'Sullivan, T.A. and Zubrick, S.R. (2013). Tackling overweight and obesity: does the public health message match the science? *BMC Medicine*, 11: 41.

Hagger, M.S. and Orbell, S. (2003). A meta-analytic review of the common-sense model of illness representations. *Psychology & Health*, 18: 141–84.

Hagger, M.S., Chatzisarantis, N.L.D. and Biddle, S.J.H. (2002). A meta-analytic review of the theories of reasoned action and planned behaviour in physical activity: predictive validity and the contribution of additional variables. *Journal of Sport & Exercise Psychology*, 24: 3–32.

Hagger, M.S., Chatzisarantis, N.L.D., Culverhouse, T. and Biddle, S.J.H. (2003). The processes by which perceived autonomy support in physical education promotes leisure-time physical activity intentions and behavior: a trans-contextual model. *Journal of Educational Psychology*, 95: 784–95.

Hagger-Johnson, G., Sabia, S., Nabi, H., Brunner, E., Kivimaki, M., Shipley, M. and Singh-Manoux, A. (2012). Low conscientiousness and risk of all-cause, cardiovascular and cancer mortality over 17 years: Whitehall II cohort study. *Journal of Psychosomatic Research*, 73: 98–103.

Haines, A.P., Imeson, J.D. and Meade, T.W. (1987). Phobic anxiety and ischaemic heart disease. *British Medical Journal* (Clinical Research Edition), 295: 297–99.

Halkitis, P.N., Kutnick, A. and Slater, S. (2005). The social realities of adherence to protease inhibitor regimens: substance use, health care, and psychological states. *Journal of Health Psychology*, 10: 545–58.

Hall, A. (2008). Brazil's Bolsa Família: a double-edged sword? *Development and Change*, 39(5): 799–822.

Hall, A. (2012). The last shall be first: political dimensions of conditional cash transfers in Brazil. *Journal of Policy Practice*, 11: 25–41.

Hall, A.M., Ferreira, P.H., Maher, C.G., Latimer, J. and Ferreira, M.L. (2010). The influence of the therapist-patient relationship on treatment outcome in physical rehabilitation: a systematic review. *Physical Therapy*, 90: 1099–10.

Hall, J.A., Roter, D.L. and Katz, N.R. (1988). Meta-analysis of correlates of provider behavior in medical encounters. *Medical Care*, 26: 1–19.

Hamajima, N., Hirose, K., Rohan, T., Calle, E.E. et al. (Collaborative Group on Hormonal Factors in Breast Cancer) (2002). Alcohol, tobacco and breast cancer – collaborative reanalysis of individual data from 53 epidemiological studies: including 58,515 women with breast cancer and 95,067 women without the disease. *British Journal of Cancer*, 87: 1234–45.

Hamilton, C. and Denniss, R. (2010). *Affluenza: When Too Much is Never Enough*. London: Allen & Unwin.

Hamilton, K. and White, K. (2010). Understanding parental physical activity: meanings, habits, and social role influence. *Psychology of Sport and Exercise*, 11: 275–85

Hammerness, P., Basch, E., Ulbricht, C. et al. (2003). St. John's wort: a systematic review of adverse effects and drug interactions for the consultation psychiatrist. *Psychosomatics*, 44: 271–82.

Hans, M.B. and Koeppen, A.H. (1989). Huntington's chorea: its impact on the spouse. *Journal of Nervous & Mental Disease*, 168: 209–14.

Harding, R. and Higginson, I.J. (2003). What is the best way to help caregivers in cancer and palliative care? A systematic literature review of interventions and their effectiveness. *Palliative Medicine*, 17: 63–74.

Hardy, S. and Grogan, S. (2009). Preventing disability through exercise: investigating older adults' influences and motivations to engage in physical activity. *Journal of Health Psychology*, 14: 1036–106.

Hargreaves, D.A. and Tiggemann, M. (2006). Body image is for girls: a qualitative study of boys' body image. *Journal of Health Psychology*, 11: 567–76

Hariri, A.A., Oliver, N.S., Johnston, D.G., Stevenson, J.C. and Godsland, I.F. (2013). Adiposity measurements by BMI, skinfolds and dual energy x-ray absorptiometry in relation to risk markers for cardiovascular disease and diabetes in adult males. *Disease Markers*, 35: 753–64.

Harlan, L.C., Bernstein, A.M. and Kessler, L.G. (1991). Cervical cancer screening: who is not screened and why? *American Journal of Public Health*, 81: 885–90.

Harrington, M. and Fullagar, S. (2013). Challenges for active living provision in an era of healthism. *Journal of Policy Research in Tourism, Leisure & Events*, 5: 139–57.

Harris, P., Cooper, K., Relton, C. and Thomas, K. (2012). Prevalence of complementary and alternative medicine (CAM) use by the general population: a systematic review and update. *International Journal of Clinical Practice*, 66: 924–39.

Harris, T.O. (1997). Life events and health. In A. Baum, S. Newman, J. Weminan, R. West and C. McManus (eds.), *Cambridge Handbook of Psychology, Health and Medicine*. Cambridge: Cambridge University Press. pp. 136–8.

Harvey, A.G. and Bryant, R.A. (2002). Acute stress disorder: a synthesis and critique. *Psychological Bulletin*, 128: 886–902.

Harvey, H., Good, J., Mason, J. and Reissland, N. (2013). A Q-methodology study of parental understandings of infant immunisation: implications for health-care advice. *Journal of Health Psychology*, 12 December.

Hastings, G. and MacFadyen, L. (2000). *Keep Smiling, No One's Going to Die: An Analysis of Internal Documents From the Tobacco Industry's Main UK Advertising Agencies*. Centre for Tobacco Control Research. (Examples of the documents can be viewed at: www.tobaccopapers.com.)

Haug, M. and Lavin, B. (1983). *Consumerism in Medicine: Challenging Physician Authority*. Beverly Hills, CA: Sage.

Hausenblas, H.A. and Fallon, E.A. (2006). Exercise and body image: a meta-analysis. *Psychology & Health*, 21: 33–47.

Hausenblas, H.A., Carron, A.V. and Mack, D.E. (1997). An application of the theories of reasoned action and planned behavior to exercise behavior. *Journal of Sport & Exercise Behavior*, 199: 36–51.

Healey, J. (ed.) (2006). *Body Image and Self Esteem*. Thirroul, Australia: Spinney Press.

Health and Social Care Information Centre, Lifestyles Statistics (2008). *Statistics on NHS Stop Smoking Services: England, April 2007 to March 2008*. Available: www.ic.nhs.uk/webfiles/publications/Stop%20 smoking%20ANNUAL%20bulletins/SSS0708/SSS%202007-08%20final%20format%20v2.pdf.

Health and Social Care Information Centre (2014). *Health Survey for England – 2013*. Leeds: Health and Social Care Information Centre.

Heath, A.C. and Madden, P.A.F. (1995). Genetic influences on smoking behavior. In J.R. Turner, L.R. Carden and J.K. Hewitt (eds.), *Behavior Genetic Approaches in Behavioral Medicine*. New York: Plenum Press. pp. 45–66.

Heather, N. and Robertson, I. (1997). *Problem Drinking*. Oxford: Oxford University Press.

Heider, F. (1958). *The Psychology of Interpersonal Relations*. New York: Wiley.

Heidigger, M. (1962). *Being and Time*. New York: Harper & Row.

Heikkilä, K., Nyberg, S.T., Theorell, T. et. al. (2013). Work stress and risk of cancer: meta-analysis of 5700 incident cancer events in 116,000 European men and women. *British Medical Journal*, 346, doi: http://dx.doi.org/10.1136/bmj.f165.

Helgeson, V.S. and Fritz, H.L. (1999). Cognitive adaptation as a predictor of new coronary events after percutaneous transluminal coronary angioplasty. *Psychosomatic Medicine*, 61: 488–95.

Hemingway, H. and Marmot, M. (1999). Psychosocial factors and the aetiology and prognosis of coronary heart disease: systematic review of prospective cohort studies. *British Medical Journal*, 1318: 1460–7.

Henderson, K.A. and Ainsworth, B.E. (2003). A synthesis of perceptions about physical activity among older African American and American Indian women. *American Journal of Public Health*, 93: 313–17.

Henderson, V.P., Clemow, L., Massion, A.O., Hurley, T.G., Druker, S. and Hébert, J.R. (2012). The effects of mindfulness-based stress reduction on psychosocial outcomes and quality of life in early-stage breast cancer patients: a randomized trial. *Breast Cancer Research and Treatment*, 131: 99–109.

Herman, C.P., Roth, D.A. and Polivy, J. (2003). Effects of the presence of others on food intake: a normative interpretation. *Psychological Bulletin*, 129: 873–86.

Herndon, J.B., Chaney, M. and Carden, D. (2011). Health literacy and emergency department outcomes: A systematic review. *Annals of Emergency Medicine*, 57: 334–45.

Herr, K., Bjoro, K. and Decker, S. (2006). Tools for assessment of pain in nonverbal older adults with dementia: a state-of-the-science review. *Journal of Pain and Symptom Management*, 31: 170–92.

Hersch, J., Jansen, J., Barratt, A., Irwig, L., Houssami, N., Howard, K., Dhillon, H. and McCaffery K (2013). Women's views on overdiagnosis in breast cancer screening: a qualitative study. *BMJ*, 346: f158

Herzlich, C. (1973). *Health and Illness: A Social Psychological Approach*. London: Academic Press.

Herzlich, C. and Pierret, J. (1987). *Illness and Self in Society*. Baltimore, MD: Johns Hopkins University Press.

Herzog, T.A. (2008). Analyzing the Transtheoretical Model using the framework of Weinstein, Rothman, and Sutton (1998): the example of smoking cessation. *Health Psychology*, 27: 548–56.

Hesketh, T. and Xing, Z.W. (2006). Abnormal sex ratios in human populations: causes and consequences. *Proceedings of the National Academy of Sciences*, 103: 13271–5.

Hess, C.B. and Chen, A.M. (2014). Measuring psychosocial functioning in the radiation oncology clinic: a systematic review. *Psycho-oncology*, in press.

Hevey, D. and Dolan, M. (2013). Approach/avoidance motivation, message framing and skin cancer prevention: a test of the congruency hypothesis. *Journal of Health Psychology*, doi:10.1177/1359105313483154.

Heyman-Monnikes, I., Arnold, R., Florin, I., Herda, A., Melfsen, S. and Monnikes, H. (2000). The combination of medical treatment plus multicomponent behavioural therapy is superior to medical treatment alone in the therapy of irritable bowel syndrome. *American Journal of Gastroenterology*, 95: 981–94.

Hilbert, A., Martin, A., Zech, T., Rauh, E. and Rief, W. (2010). Patients with medically unexplained symptoms and their significant others: illness attributions and behaviors as predictors of patient functioning over time. *Journal of Psychosomatic Research*, 68: 253–62.

Hingle, M., Nichter, M., Medeiros, M. and Grace, S. (2013). Texting for health: the use of participatory methods to develop healthy lifestyle messages for teens. *Journal of Nutrition Education & Behavior*, 45: 12–19.

Hirani, S.P., Pugsley, W.B. and Newman, S.P. (2006). Illness representations of coronary artery disease: an empirical examination of the Illness Perceptions Questionnaire (IPQ) in patients undergoing surgery, angioplasty and medication. *British Journal of Health Psychology*, 11: 199–220.

Hittner, J.B. and Kennington, L.E. (2008). Normative perceptions, substance use, age of substance use initiation, and gender as predictors of HIV-risky sexual behavior in a college student sample. *Journal of Applied Biobehavioral Research*, 13: 86–101.

Hittner, J.B. and Kryzanowski, J.J. (2010). Residential status moderates the association between gender and risky sexual behavior. *Journal of Health Psychology*, 15: 634–40.

HLS-EU Consortium (2012). *Comparative Report of Health Literacy in Eight EU Member States: The European Health Literacy Survey (HLS-EU).*

HMSO (2009). *Chief Medical Officer's Annual Report for* 2008. London: Her Majesty's Stationery Office.

Hodgetts, D. and Chamberlain, K. (2006). Media and health: a continuum concern for health psychology. *Journal of Health Psychology*, 11: 171–4.

Hodgetts, D. and Stolte, O. (2009). Questioning 'black humour': racial exploitation, media and health. *Journal of Health Psychology*, 14: 643–6.

Hodgetts, D., Chamberlain, K., Tankel, Y. and Groot, S. (2014). Looking within and beyond the community: lessons learned by researching, theorising and acting to address urban poverty and health. *Journal of Health Psychology*, 19: 97–102.

Hofstede, G. and Bond, M.H. (1988). The Confucius connection: from cultural roots to economic growth. *Organizational Dynamics*, 16 (4): 5–21.

Hollis, J.F., Connett, J.E., Stevens, V.J. and Greenlick, M.R. (1990). Stressful life events, Type A behaviour, and the prediction of cardiovascular and total mortality over six years. *Journal of Behavioural Medicine*, 13: 263–81.

Holloway, I.W., Rice, E., Gibbs, J., Winetrobe, H., Dunlap, S. and Rhoades, H. (2014). Acceptability of smartphone application-based HIV prevention among young men who have sex with men. *AIDS and Behavior*, 18: 285–96.

Hollywood, A. and Ogden, J. (2014). Gaining weight after taking orlistat: a qualitative study of patients at 18 months. *Journal of Health Psychology*.

Holmes, T.H. and Rahe, R.H. (1967). The social readjustment rating scale. *Journal of Psychosomatic Research*, 11: 213–18.

Holroyd, K.A. and Coyne, J. (1987). Personality and health in the 1980s: psychosomatic medicine revisited? *Journal of Personality*, 55: 359–76.

Holt, N.L., McHugh, T.-L.F., Tink, L.N., Kingsley, B.C., Coppola, A.M., Neely, K.C. and McDonald, R. (2013). Developing sport-based after-school programmes using a participatory action research approach. *Qualitative Research in Sport, Exercise and Health*, 5: 332–55.

Homans, H. and Aggleton, P. (1988). Health education, HIV infection and AIDS. In P. Aggleton and H. Homans (eds.), *Social Aspects of AIDS*. London: Falmer Press. pp. 154–76.

Hong, Y., Peña-Purcell, N.C. and Ory, M.G. (2012). Outcomes of online support and resources for cancer survivors: a systematic literature review. *Patient Education & Counseling*, 86: 288–96.

Horne, R. (1997). Representations of medication and treatment: advances in theory and measurement. In K.J. Petrie and J.A. Weinman (eds.), *Perceptions of Health and Illness*. Amsterdam: Harwood Academic. pp. 155–88.

Horne, R. and Weinman, J. (1999). Patients' beliefs about prescribed medicines and their role in adherence to treatment in chronic physical illness. *Journal of Psychosomatic Research*, 47: 555–67.

Horne, R. and Weinman, J. (2002). Self-regulation and self-management in asthma: exploring the role of illness perceptions and treatment beliefs in explaining non-adherence to preventive medication. *Psychology & Health*, 17: 17–32.

Horne, R. et al (2005). *Concordance, Adherence and Compliance in Medicine Taking.* Report for the National Co-ordinating Centre for NHS Service Delivery and Organisation (R&D).

Horton, R. (2006). Indigenous peoples: time to act now for equity and health. *The Lancet*, 367: 1705–7.

Hossenbaccus, Z. and White, P.D. (2013). Views on the nature of chronic fatigue syndrome: content analysis. *Journal of the Royal Society of Medicine Short Reports*, 4 (1): 4.

Howard, T., Jacobson, K.L. and Kripalani, S. (2013). Doctor talk: physicians' use of clear verbal communication. *Journal of Health Communication*, 18: 991–1001.

Huang, T., Yang, B., Zheng, J., Li, G., Wahlqvist, M.L. and Li, D. (2012). Cardiovascular disease mortality and cancer incidence in vegetarians: a meta-analysis and systematic review. *Annals of Nutrition & Metabolism*, 60: 233–40.

Hughes, J., Jelsma, J., Maclean, E., Darder, M. and Tinise, X. (2004). The health-related quality of life of people living with HIV/AIDS. *Disability & Rehabilitation*, 26: 371–6.

Hulka, B.S. (1979). Patient–clinician interactions and compliance. In R.B. Haynes, D.W. Taylor and D.L. Sackett (eds.), *Compliance in Health Care*. Baltimore, MD: Johns Hopkins University Press. pp. 63–77.

Hulka, B.S., Cassel, J.C. and Kupper, L.L. (1976). Disparities between medications prescribed and consumed among chronic disease patients. In L. Lasagna (ed.), *Patient Compliance*. Mount Kisco, NY: Futura Publishing. pp. 123–52.

Human Development Report (2000). *Human Rights and Human Development*. New York: Oxford University Press.

Humpel, N., Owen, N. and Leslie, E. (2002). Environmental factors associated with adults' participation in physical activity: a review. *American Journal of Preventive Medicine*, 22: 188–99.

Hunter, K.M. (1991). *Doctors' Stories: The Narrative Structure of Medical Knowledge*. Princeton, NJ: Princeton University Press.

Hunter, M.S., O'Dea, I. and Britten, N. (1997). Decision-making and hormone replacement therapy: a qualitative analysis. *Social Science & Medicine*, 45: 1541–8.

Hur, M., Lee, M.S., Kim, C. and Ernst, E. (2012). Aromatherapy for treatment of hypertension: a systematic review. *Journal of Evaluation in Clinical Practice*, 18: 37–41.

Hursti, U.K.K. and Sjödén, P.O. (1997). Food and general neophobia and their relationship with self-reported food choice: familial resemblance in Swedish families with children of ages 7–17 years. *Appetite*, 29: 89–103.

Husted, M. and Ogden, J. (2014). Emphasising personal investment effects weight loss and hedonic thoughts about food after obesity surgery. *Journal of Obesity*, in press.

Hutchison, A.J., Jonhston, L.H. and Breckon, J.D. (2013). A grounded theory of successful long-term physical activity behaviour change. *Qualitative Research in Sport, Exercise and Health*, 5: 109–26.

Huynh, H.P. and Sweeny, K. (2013). Clinician styles of care: transforming patient care at the intersection of leadership and medicine. *Journal of Health Psychology*, doi:10.1177/1359105313493650.

Hwang, Y., Cho, H., Sands, L. and Jeong, S. (2012). Effects of gain- and loss-framed messages on the sun safety behavior of adolescents: the moderating role of risk perceptions. *Journal of Health Psychology*, 17: 929–40.

Ikard, F.F., Green, D. and Horn, D. (1969). A scale to differentiate between types of smoking as related to management of affect. *International Journal of the Addictions*, 4: 649–59.

Illich, I. (1976). *Limits to Medicine*. London: Calder & Boyars.

Independent UK Panel on Breast Cancer Screening (2012). The benefits and harms of breast cancer screening: an independent review. *The Lancet*, 380: 1778–86.

Ingledew, D.K., Markland, D. and Medley, A.R. (1998). Exercise motives and stages of change. *Journal of Health Psychology*, 3: 477–89.

Insel, K.C., Meek, P.M. and Leventhal, H. (2005). Differences in illness representation among pulmonary patients and their providers. *Journal of Health Psychology*, 10: 147–62

Institute of Alcohol Studies (2003). *Crime and Disorder, Binge Drinking and the Licensing Bill.* London: Institute of Alcohol Studies.

Institute of Medicine (2000). *To Err is Human: Building a Safer Health System.* Washington, DC: Institute of Medicine, National Academy of Science.

Institute of Medicine (2001). *Crossing the Quality Chasm: A New Health System for the 21st Century.* Washington, DC: National Academies Press.

Institute of Medicine (2007a). *Cancer Care for the Whole Patient: Meeting Psychosocial Health Needs.* Washington, DC: National Academies Press.

Institute of Medicine (2007b). *Implementing Cancer Survivorship Care Planning.* Washington, DC: National Academies Press.

International Association for the Study of Pain (1992). *Management of Acute Pain: A Practical Guide.* Seattle, WA: IASP Press.

Internet World Stats (2014). Available: www.internetworldstats.com/stats.htm.

Ironson, G., Solomon, G.F., Balbin, E.G., O'Cleirigh, C., George, A., Kumar, M. et al. (2002). The Ironson–Woods spirituality/religiousness index is associated with long survival, health behaviors, less distress, and low cortisol in people with HIV/AIDS. *Annals of Behavioral Medicine*, 24: 34–48.

Ironson, G., Stuetzle, R. and Fletcher, M.A. (2006). An increase in religiousness/spirituality occurs after HIV diagnosis and predicts slower disease progression over 4 years in people with HIV. *Journal of General Internal Medicine*, 21: S62–8.

Jacobsen, P.B. (2009). Promoting evidence-based psychosocial care for cancer patients. *Psycho-oncology*, 18: 6–13.

Jalilian, F., Motlagh, F.Z., Solhi, M. and Gharibnavaz, H. (2014). Effectiveness of self-management promotion educational program among diabetic patients based on health belief model. *Journal of Education and Health Promotion*, 3: 14.

James, D. (2007). *Affluenza: How to be Successful and Stay Sane.* London: Vermillion.

Jamner, L.D. and Tursky, B. (1987). Syndrome specific descriptor profiling: a psychophysiological and psychophysical approach. *Health Psychology*, 6: 417–30.

Jarvis, M.J. (2004). Why people smoke. *British Medical Journal*, 328: 277–9.

Jason, L.A., Sunnquist, M., Brown, A., Evans, M. and Newton, J.L. (2014). Are myalgic encephalomyelitis and chronic fatigue syndrome different illnesses? A preliminary analysis. *Journal of Health Psychology*, doi:1359105313520335.

Jefferson, G. (2004). Glossary of transcription symbols with an introduction. In G.H. Lerner (ed.), *Conversation Analysis: Studies from the First Generation*. Amsterdam: John Benjamins. pp. 13–31.

Jensen, M. and Patterson, D.R. (2006). Hypnotic treatment of chronic pain. *Journal of Behavioral Medicine*, 29: 95–124.

Jensen, M.P., Karoly, P. and Huger, R. (1987). The development and preliminary validation of an instrument to assess patients' attitudes toward pain. *Journal of Psychosomatic Research*, 31: 393–400.

Jernigan, D.H. (2012). Global alcohol producers, science, and policy: the case of the International Center for Alcohol Policies. *American Journal of Public Health*, 102: 80–9.

Jha, P., Jacob, B., Gajalakshmi, V., Gupta, P.C., Dhingra, N., Kumar, R. et al. for the RGI–CGHR Investigators (2008). A nationally representative case–control study of smoking and death in India. *New England Journal of Medicine*, 358: 1137–47.

Jin, M., Cai, S., Guo, J., Zhu, Y., Li, M., Yu, Y. et al. (2013). Alcohol drinking and all cancer mortality: a meta-analysis. *Annals of Oncology*, 24: 807–16.

Joffe, H. (1996). AIDS research and prevention: a social representational approach. *British Journal of Medical Psychology*, 69: 169–91.

Joffe, H. (2003). Social representations and health psychology. *Social Science Information*, 41: 559–80.

Joffe, H. and Bettega, N. (2003). Social representations of AIDS among Zambian adolescents. *Journal of Health Psychology*, 8: 616–31.

Joffe, H. and Haarhoff, G. (2002). Representations of far-flung illnesses: the case of Ebola in Britain. *Social Science & Medicine*, 54: 955–69.

Joffress, M., Reed, D.M. and Nomura, A.M.Y. (1985). Psychosocial processes and cancer incidence among Japanese men in Hawaii. *American Journal of Epidemiology*, 121: 488–500.

Johnson, A.M. and Wellings, K. (1994). Studying sexual lifestyles. In A.M. Johnson, J. Wadsworth, K. Wellings and J. Field (eds.), *Sexual Attitudes and Lifestyles*. Oxford: Blackwell. pp. 1–18.

Johnson, F. and Wardle, J. (2005). Dietary restraint, body dissatisfaction, and psychological distress: a prospective analysis. *Journal of Abnormal Psychology*, 114: 119–25.

Johnston, M., Foulkes, J., Johnston, D.W., Pollard, B. and Gudmundsdottir, H. (1999). Impact on patients and partners of inpatient and extended cardiac counseling and rehabilitation: a controlled trial. *Psychosomatic Medicine*, 61: 225–33.

Joint Committee on Terminology (2001). Report of the 2000 Joint Committee on Health Education and Promotion Terminology. *American Journal of Health Education*, 32: 89–103.

Jones, D.R., Goldblatt, P.O. and Leon, D.A. (1984). Bereavement and cancer: some data on deaths of spouses from the longitudinal study of Office of Population Censuses and Surveys. *British Medical Journal*, 289: 461–4.

Jones, F. and Bright, J. (eds.) (2001). *Stress: Myth, Theory and Research*. Englewood Cliffs, NJ: Prentice Hall.

Jones, L., Crabb, S., Turnbull, D. and Oxlad, M. (2014). Barriers and facilitators to effective type 2 diabetes management in a rural context: a qualitative study with diabetic patients and health professionals. *Journal of Health Psychology*, 19: 441–53.

Jong, M.C., van de Vijver, L., Busch, M., Fritsma, J. and Seldenrijk, R. (2012). Integration of complementary and alternative medicine in primary care: what do patients want? *Patient Education & Counseling*, 89: 417–22.

Jorenby, D.E., Hays, J.T., Rigotti, N.A., Azoulay, S., Watsky, E.J., Williams, K.E. et al. (2006). Efficacy of varenicline, an alpha4beta2 nicotinic acetylcholine receptor partial agonist, vs placebo or sustained-release bupropion for smoking cessation: a randomized controlled trial. *Journal of the American Medical Association*, 296: 56–63.

Jovchelovitch, S. & Grevais, M.C. (1999). Social representations of health and illness: the case of the Chinese community in England. *Journal of Community and Applied Social Psychology*, 9: 247–260.

Jylhä, M. (2009). What is self-rated health and why does it predict mortality? Towards a unified conceptual model. *Social Science and Medicine*, 69: 307–16.

Kabat-Zinn, J. (1990). *Full Catastrophe Living: How to Cope with Stress, Pain and Illness Using Mindfulness Meditation.* New York: NY: Bantam Dell.

Kadianaki, I. (2014). The transformative effects of stigma: coping strategies as meaning-making efforts for immigrants living in Greece. *Journal of Community & Applied Social Psychology*, 24 (2): 125–38.

Kagee, A. and Delport, T. (2010). Barriers to adherence to antiretroviral treatment: the perspectives of patient advocates. *Journal of Health Psychology*, 15: 1001–11.

Kagee, A., Swartz, A. and Swartz, L. (2014). Theorising beyond the individual: adherence to antiretroviral therapy in resource-constrained societies. *Journal of Health Psychology*, 19: 103–9.

Kalichman, S.C. (2009). *Denying AIDS*. New York: Springer.

Kalichman, S.C., Ramachandran, B. and Catz, S. (1999). Adherence to combination antiretroviral therapies in HIV patients of low health literacy. *Journal of General Internal Medicine*, 14: 267–73.

Kamin, L.J. (1977). *The Science and Politics of IQ*. London: Penguin.

Kammann, R. and Flett, R. (1983). Affectometer 2: a scale to measure current level of general happiness. *Australian Journal of Psychology*, 35: 259–65.

Kanner, A.D., Coyne, J.C., Schaefer, C. and Lazarus, R.S. (1981). Comparison of two modes of stress measurement: daily hassles and uplifts versus major life events. *Journal of Behavioral Medicine*, 4: 1–39.

Karademas, E.C., Bati, A., Karkania, V., Georgiou, V. and Sofokleous, S. (2013). The association between Pandemic Influenza A (H1N1) public perceptions and reactions: a prospective study. *Journal of Health Psychology*, 18: 419–28.

Karasek, R. and Theorell, T. (1990). *Healthy Work: Stress, Productivity, and the Reconstruction of Working Life*. New York: Basic Books.

Karlson, S., Nazroo, J.Y., McKenzie, K., Bhui, K. and Weich, S. (2005). Racism, psychosis and common mental disorder among ethnic minorities in England. *Psychological Medicine*, 35: 1795–1803.

Kart, C.S., Kinney, J.M., Subedi, J., Basnyat, K.B. and Vadakkan, M.F. (2007). Lay explanations and self-management of diabetes in Kathmandu. *Nepal Journal of Aging & Health*, 19: 683–704.

Karus, D., Raveis, V.H., Alexander, C., Hanna, B., Selwyn, P., Marconi, K. and Higginson, I. (2005). Patient reports of symptoms and their treatment at three palliative care projects servicing individuals with HIV/AIDS. *Journal of Pain and Symptom Management*, 30: 408–17.

Kassavou, A., French, D.P. and Chamberlain, K. (2014). How do environmental factors influence walking in groups? A walk-along study. *Journal of Health Psychology.*

Kaufman, M. (1987). The construction of masculinity and the triad of men's violence. In *Beyond Patriarchy: Essays an Pleasure, Power, and Change*. Toronto: Oxford University Press.

Kawachi, I., Colditz, G.A., Ascherio, A., Rimm, E.B., Giovannucci, E., Stampfer, M.J. and Willett, W.C. (1994). Prospective study of phobic anxiety and risk of coronary heart disease in men. *Circulation*, 89: 1992–7.

Kay, C., Davies, J., Gamsu, D. and Jarman, M. (2009). An exploration of the experiences of young women living with type 1 diabetes. *Journal of Health Psychology*, 14: 242–50.

Kearney, A. (2006). Increasing our understanding of breast self-examination: women talk about cancer, the health care system, and being women. *Qualitative Health Research*, 16: 802–20.

Kearney, A. and Murray, M. (2009). Breast cancer screening recommendations: Is mammography the only answer? *Journal of Midwifery and Women's Health,* 54: 393–400.

Kearns, R.D., Turk, D.C. and Rudy, T.E. (1985). The West Haven–Yale Multidimensional Pain Inventory. *Pain*, 23: 345–56.

Keefe, R.J., Hauck, E.R., Egert, J., Rimer, B. and Kornguth, P. (1994). Mammography pain and discomfort: a cognitive behavioural perspective. *Pain*, 56: 247–60.

Keegan, A., Liao, L.-M. and Boyle, M. (2003). Hirsutism: a psychological analysis. *Journal of Health Psychology*, 8: 327–46.

Keehn, R.J. (1980). Follow-up studies of World War II and Korean conflict prisoners. III: Mortality to January 1, 1976. *American Journal of Epidemiology*, 111: 194–211.

Kelder, S.H., Perry, C.L. and Klepp, K.I. (1994). Longitudinal tracing of adolescent smoking, physical activity and food choice behaviours. *American Journal of Public Health*, 84: 1121–6.

Kelly, J.A., St Lawrence, J.S., Diaz, Y.E. et al. (1991). HIV risk behavior reduction following intervention with key opinion leaders of population: an experimental analysis. *American Journal of Public Health*, 81: 168–71.

Kelly, J., Saggers, S., Taylor, K. et al. (2012). 'Makes you proud to be black eh?': reflections on meaningful indigenous research participation. *International Journal for Equity in Health*, 11: 40.

Kelly, Y., Iacovou, M., Quigley, M., Gray, R., Wolke, D., Kelly, J. and Sacker, A. (2013). Light drinking versus abstinence in pregnancy – behavioural and cognitive outcomes in 7-year-old children: a longitudinal cohort study.

Kemeny, M.L. (2011). Psychoneuroimmunology. In H.S. Friedman (ed), *The Oxford Handbook of Health Psychology*. Oxford: Oxford University Press

Kendall, E., Marshall, C.A. and Barlow, L. (2013). Stories rather than surveys: a journey of discovery and emancipation. *International Journal of Qualitative Methods*, 12: 258–71.

Keng, S.L., Smoski, M.J. and Robins, C.J. (2011). Effects of mindfulness on psychological health: a review of empirical studies. *Clinical Psychology Review*, 31: 1041–56.

Kennedy, A., Rogers, A., Blickem, C., Daker-White, G. and Bowen, R. (2014). Developing cartoons for long-term condition self-management information. *BMC Health Services Research*, 14: 1–20.

Kenny, D.A., Veldhuijzen, W., Weijden, T. v.d., LeBlanc, A., Lockyer, J., Légaré, F. and Campbell, C. (2010). Interpersonal perception in the context of doctor–patient relationships: a dyadic analysis of doctor–patient communication. *Social Science & Medicine*, 70 (5): 763–8.

Kern, M.L. and Friedman, H.S. (2008). Do conscientious individuals live longer? A quantitative review. *Health Psychology*, 27: 505–12.

Kerr, J., Eves, F.F. and Carroll, D. (2001). Getting more people on the stairs: the impact of a new message format. *Journal of Health Psychology*, 6: 495–500.

Key, T.J., Appleby, P.N., Spencer, E.A. et al. (2009). Cancer incidence in British vegetarians. *British Journal of Cancer*, 101: 192–7.

Key, T.J., Fraser, G.E., Thorogood, M., Appleby, P.N., Beral, V., Reeves, G. et al. (1998). Mortality in vegetarians and non-vegetarians: a collaborative analysis of 8,300 deaths among 76,000 men and women in five prospective studies. *Public Health Nutrition*, 1: 33–41.

Khoury, B., Lecomte, T., Fortin, G., Masse, M., Therien, P., Bouchard, V. et al. (2013). Mindfulness-based therapy: a comprehensive meta-analysis. *Clinical Psychology Review*, 33: 763–71.

Kickbusch, I., Wait, S. and Maag, D. (2005). *Navigating Health: The Role of Health Literacy.* Available: www.ilonakickbusch.com/health-literacy/NavigatingHealth.pdf [accessed 29 December 2009].

Kimmel, M.S. (2004). Masculinity as homophobia: fear, shame, and silence in the construction of gender identity. In P.S. Rothenberg (ed.), *Race, Class, and Gender in the United States: An Integrated Study.* New York: Worth. pp. 81–93.

King, A.C. (1994). Community and public health approaches to the promotion of physical activity. *Medicine & Science in Sports & Exercise*, 26: 1405–12.

King, L.A., Hicks, J.A., Krull, J.L. and Del Gaiso, A.K. (2006). Positive affect and the experience of meaning in life. *Journal of Personality and Social Psychology*, 90: 179–96.

Kirsch, I., Jungleblut, A., Jenkins, L. and Kolstad, A. (1993). *Adult Literacy in America: A First Look at the Results of the National Adult Literacy Survey.* Washington, DC: National Center for Education Statistics, US Department of Education.

Kivimäki, M., Leino-Arjas, P., Luukkonen, R., Riihimäki, H., Vahtera, J. and Kirjonen, J. (2002). Work stress and risk of cardiovascular mortality: prospective cohort study of industrial employees. *British Medical Journal*, 325: 857–60.

Kivimäki, M., Nyberg, S.T., Batty, G.D. et al. (2012). Job strain as a risk factor for coronary heart disease: a collaborative meta-analysis of individual participant data. *The Lancet*, 380: 1491–7.

Kivits, J. (2006). Informed patients and the internet: a mediated context for consultations with health professionals. *Journal of Health Psychology*, 11: 269–82.

Kleinman, A. (1980). *Patients and Healers in the Context of Culture*. Berkeley, CA: University of California Press.

Klenerman, L., Slade, P.D., Stanley, I.M., Pennie, B., Reilly, J.P., Atchinson, L.E. et al. (1995). The prediction of chronicity in patients with an acute attack of low back pain in a general practice setting. *Spine*, 20: 478–84.

Klinner, C., Carter, S.M., Rychetnik, L., Li, V., Daley, M., Zask, A. and Lloyd, B. (2014). Integrating relationship- and research-based approaches in Australian health promotion practice. *Health Promotion International*, doi:10.1093/heapro/dau026.

Knibb, R.C. and Horton, S.L. (2008). Can illness perceptions and coping predict psychological distress amongst allergy sufferers? *British Journal of Health Psychology*, 13: 103–19.

Koch-Weser, S., Bradshaw, Y.S., Gualtieri, L. and Gallagher, S.S. (2010). The internet as a health information source: findings from the 2007 Health Information National Trends Survey and implications for health communication. *Journal of Health Communication*,15: 279–93.

Koniak-Griffin, D. and Stein, J.A. (2006). Predictors of sexual risk behaviors among adolescent mothers in a human immunodeficiency virus prevention program. *Journal of Adolescent Health*, 38: 297.e1–11.

Konttinen, H., Haukkala, A. and Uutela, A. (2008). Comparing sense of coherence, depressive symptoms and anxiety, and their relationships with health in a population-based study. *Social Science and Medicine*, 66: 2401–12.

Krantz, D.S. and McCeney, M.K. (2002). Effects of psychological and social factors on organic disease: a critical assessment of research on coronary heart disease. *Annual Review of Psychology*, 53: 341–69.

Krause E.D. (2003). The transformation of social representations of chronic disease in a self-help group. *Journal of Health Psychology*, 8: 599–615.

Krieger, N. (1987). Shades of difference: theoretical underpinnings of the medical controversy on black/white differences in the United States, 1830–1970. *International Journal of Health Services*, 17: 259–78.

Krieger, N. and Davey Smith, G. (2004). 'Bodies count', and body counts: social epidemiology and embodying inequality. *Epidemiologic Reviews*, 26: 92–103.

Kroenke, C.H., Kubzansky, L.D., Schernhammer, E.S., Holmes, M.D. and Kawachi, I. (2006). Social networks, social support, and survival after breast cancer diagnosis. *Journal of Clinical Oncology*, 24: 1105–11.

Kruger, A.K., Reither, E.N., Peppard, P.E., Krueger, P.K. and Hale, L. (2014). Do sleep-deprived adolescents make less-healthy food choices? *British Journal of Nutrition*, 111: 1898–904.

Kübler-Ross, E. (1969). *On Death and Dying*. New York, NY: Macmillan.

Kübler-Ross, E. (ed.) (1997). *Death*. New York: Simon and Schuster.

Kuehn, B.M. (2013). More than one-third of US individuals use the internet to self-diagnose. *Journal of the American Medical Association*, 309 (8): 756–7.

Kugelmann, R. (1997). The psychology and management of pain: gate control as theory and symbol. *Theory & Psychology*, 7: 43–66.

Kuhlmann, A.K.S., Kraft, J.M., Galavotti, C., Creek, T.L., Mooki, M. and Ntumy, R. (2008). Radio role models for the prevention of mother-to-child transmission of HIV and HIV testing among pregnant women in Botswana. *Health Promotion International*, 23: 260–8.

Kuhn, T.S. (1970). *The Structure of Scientific Revolutions*. Chicago, IL: University of Chicago Press.

Kuijpers, W., Groen, W.G., Aaronson, N.K. and van Harten, W.H. (2013). A systematic review of web-based interventions for patient empowerment and physical activity in chronic diseases: relevance for cancer survivors. *Journal of Medical Internet Research*, 15 (2).

Kunesh, M.A., Hasbrook, C.A. and Lewthwaite, R. (1992). Physical activity socialization: peer interactions and affective responses among a sample of sixth grade girls. *Sociology of Sport Journal*, 9: 385–96.

Kuper, H. and Marmot, M. (2003). Job strain, job demands, decision latitude, and risk of coronary heart disease within the Whitehall II study. *Journal of Epidemiology & Community Health*, 57: 147–53.

Kvikstad, A. and Vatten, L. (1996). Risk and prognosis of cancer in middle-aged women who have experienced the death of a child. *International Journal of Cancer*, 67: 165–9.

Kvikstad, A., Vatten, L. and Tretli, S. (1995). Widowhood and divorce in relation to overall survival among middle-aged Norwegian women with cancer. *British Journal of Cancer*, 71: 1343–7.

Lai, D.W.L. & Surood, S. (2009). Chinese beliefs of older Chinese in Canada. *Journal of Aging and Health*, 21: 38–62.

Lamé, I.E., Peters, M.L., Vlaeyen, J.W., Kleef, M.V. and Patijn, J. (2005). Quality of life in chronic pain is more associated with beliefs about pain, than with pain intensity. *European Journal of Pain*, 9: 15–24.

Landrine, H. (1997). From the back of the bus. *Journal of Health Psychology*, 2: 428–30.

Landrine, H. and Corral, I. (2014). Sociocultural correlates of cigarette smoking among African-American men versus women: implications for culturally specific cessation interventions. *Journal of Health Psychology*, 1359105314542821.

Lanigan, J.D. (2012). The relationship between practices and child care providers' beliefs related to child feeding and obesity prevention. *Journal of Nutrition Education & Behaviour*, 44: 521–9.

Latner, J.D. and Ciao, A.C. (2014). Weight-loss history as a predictor of obesity treatment outcome: prospective, long-term results from behavioral, group self-help treatment. *Journal of Health Psychology*, 19: 253–61.

Lau, R.R. and Hartman, K.A. (1983). Common sense representations of common illnesses. *Health Psychology*, 2: 167–86.

Lautrette, A., Darmon, M., Megarbane, B. et al. (2007). A communication strategy and brochure for relatives of patients dying in the ICU. *New England Journal of Medicine*, 356: 469–78.

Law, M.R., Frost, C.D. and Wald, N.J. (1991). By how much does dietary salt lower blood pressure? I – Analysis of observational data among populations. *British Medical Journal*, 302: 811–15.

Lawson, J., Reynolds, F., Bryant, W. and Wilson, L. (2014). 'It's like having a day of freedom, a day off from being ill': exploring the experiences of people living with mental health problems who attend a community-based arts project, using interpretative phenomenological analysis. *Journal of Health Psychology*, 19: 765–77.

Lawson, K, Wiggins, S., Green, T., Adam, S., Bloch, M. and Hayden, M.R. (1996). Adverse psychological events occurring in the first year after predictive testing for Huntington's disease. *Journal of Medical Genetics*, 33: 856–62.

Lazarus, R.S. and Folkman, S. (1984). *Stress, Appraisal and Coping*. New York: Springer.

Lee, H., Pollock, G., Lubek, I. et al. (2010). Creating new career pathways to reduce poverty, illiteracy and health risks, while transforming and empowering Cambodian women's lives. *Journal of Health Psychology*, 15: 982–92.

Lee, J. and Macdonald, D. (2010). 'Are they just checking our obesity or what?' – the healthism discourse and rural young women. *Sport, Education & Society*, 15: 203–19.

Lee, M.S., Choi, J., Posadzki, P. and Ernst, E. (2012). Aromatherapy for health care: an overview of systematic reviews. *Maturitas*, 71: 257–60.

Leichter, H.M. (1997). Lifestyle correctness and the new secular morality. In A. Brandt and P. Rozin (eds.), *Morality & Health*. New York: Routledge. pp. 359–78.

Leitch, A.M. (1995). Controversies in breast cancer screening. *Cancer*, 76 (S10): 2064–9.

Leitzmann, C. (2014). Vegetarian nutrition: past, present, future. *American Journal of Clinical Nutrition*, ajcn-071365.

Lemle, R. and Mishkind, M.E. (1989). Alcohol and masculinity. *Journal of Substance Abuse Treatment*, 6: 213–22.

Leone, T., Pliner, P. and Herman, C.P. (2007). Influence of clear versus ambiguous normative information on food intake. *Appetite*, 49: 58–65.

Lepe, M., Bacardi Gascon, M. and Jimenez Cruz, A. (2011). Long-term efficacy of high-protein diets: a systematic review. *Nutrition in Hospitals*, 26: 1256–9.

Lerman, C. (1997). Psychological aspects of genetic testing: introduction to the special issue. *Health Psychology*, 16: 3–7.

Lerman, C.E. and Rimer, B.K. (1993). Psychosocial impact of cancer screening. *Oncology*, 7: 67–72

Lerner, W.D. and Fallon, H.J. (1985). The alcohol withdrawal syndrome. *New England Journal of Medicine*, 313: 951–2.

Lesar, T.S., Lomaestro, B.M. and Pohl, H. (1997). Medication-prescribing errors in a teaching hospital: a 9-year experience. *Archives of Internal Medicine*, 157: 1569–76

Leserman, J. (2008). Role of depression, stress, and trauma in HIV disease progression. *Psychosomatic Medicine*, 70: 539–45.

Leshan, L.L. and Worthington, R.E. (1956). Personality as a factor in the pathogenesis of cancer: a review of the literature. *British Journal of Medical Psychology*, 29: 49–56.

Leslie, C. (1976). *Asian Medical Systems: A Comparative Study*. Los Angeles, CA: University of California Press.

Lethaby, A., Brown, J., Marjoribanks, J., Kronenberg, F., Roberts, H. and Eden, J. (2007). Phytoestrogens for vasomotor menopausal symptoms. *Cochrane Database of Systematic Reviews*, 4 (7).

Lethem, J., Slade, P.D., Troup, J.D.G. and Bentley, G. (1983) Outline of fear-avoidance model of exaggerated pain perceptions. *Behavior Research & Therapy*, 21: 401–8.

Lett, H.S., Blumenthal, J.A., Babyak, M.A., Sherwood, A., Strauman, T., Robins, C. and Newman, M.F. (2004). Depression as a risk factor for coronary artery disease: evidence, mechanisms, and treatment. *Psychosomatic Medicine*, 66, 305–15.

Leventhal, H. (1986). Symptom reporting: a focus on process. In S. McHugh and T.M. Vallis (eds.), *Illness Behavior: A Multidisciplinary Model*. New York: Plenum Press.

Leventhal, H. and Cameron, L. (1987). Behavioral theories and the problem of compliance. *Patient Education & Counseling*, 10: 117–38.

Leventhal, H., Brissette, I. and Leventhal, E.A. (2003). The common-sense model of self-regulation of health and illness. In L.D. Cameron and H. Leventhal (eds.), *The Self-regulation of Health and Illness Behaviour.* London: Routledge. pp. 42–65.

Leventhal, H., Leventhal, E.A. and Schaefer, P. (1989). *Vigilant Coping and Health Behaviour: A Lifespan Problem*. New Brunswick, NJ: State University of New Jersey, Rutgers.

Leventhal, H., Meyer, D. and Nerenz, D. (1980). The commonsense representation of illness changes. In S. Rachman (ed.), *Contributions to Medical Psychology*, vol. 2. Oxford: Pergamon. pp. 17–30.

Lever, J., Frederick, D.A. and Peplau, L.A. (2006). Does size matter? Men's and women's views on penis size across the lifespan. *Psychology of Men & Masculinity*, 7: 129.

Levi, O., Liechtentritt, R. and Savaya, R. (2014). Binary phenomenon of hope: perceptions of traumatized veterans. *Journal of Health Psychology*, 18: 1153–65.

Levine, D., McCright, J., Dobkin, L., Woodruff, A.J. and Klausner, J.D. (2008). SEXINFO: a sexual health text messaging service for San Francisco youth. *American Journal of Public Health*, 98 (3): 393.

Levine, M.E., Suarez, J.A., Brandhorst, S. et al. (2014). Low protein intake is associated with a major reduction in IGF-1, cancer, and overall mortality in the 65 and younger but not older population. *Cell Metabolism*, 19: 407–17.

Lewin, K. (1936). Topological psychology. *McGraw-Hill*, *28*, 207.

Lewin, K. (1947). Frontiers in group dynamics: II. Channels of group life; social planning and action research. *Human Relations*, 1: 143–53.

Lewin, R.J., Furze, G., Robinson, J., Griffith, K., Wiseman, S., Pye, M. and Boyle, R. (2002). A randomised controlled trial of a self-management plan for patients with newly diagnosed angina. *British Journal of General Practice*, 52: 199–201.

Lewis, J.E., Miguez-Burbano, M.-J. and Malow, R.M. (2009). HIV risk behavior among college students in the United States. *College Student Journal*, 43: 475–91.

Lewis, S.P., and Michal, N.J. (2014). Start, stop, and continue: preliminary insight into the appeal of self-injury e-communities. *Journal of Health Psychology,* doi:10.1177/1359105314527140.

Lexchin, J., Bero, L.A., Djulbegovic, B. and Clark, O. (2003). Pharmaceutical industry sponsorship and research outcome and quality: systematic review. *British Medical Journal*, 326: 1167–70.

Ley, C. and Rato Barrio, M. (2013). Evaluation of a psychosocial health programme in the context of violence and conflict. *Journal of Health Psychology*, 18 (10): 1371–81.

Ley, P. (1979). Memory for medical information. *British Journal of Social & Clinical Psychology*, 18: 245–56.

Li, X., Han, M., Wang, Y. and Liu, J. (2013). Chinese herbal medicine for gout: a systematic review of randomized clinical trials. *Clinical Rheumatology*, 32: 943–59.

Li, Y., Ju, J., Yang, C., Jiang, H., Xu, J. and Zhang, S. (2014). Oral chinese herbal medicine for improvement of quality of life in patients with chronic heart failure: a systematic review and meta-analysis. *Quality of Life Research*, 23: 1177–92.

Lichtman, J.H., Bigger, J.T., Blumenthal, J.A., Frasure-Smith, N., Kaufmann, P.G., Lespérance, F. et al. (2008). Depression and coronary heart disease. *Circulation*, 118: 1768–75.

Lidbrin, E., Elfving, J., Frisell, J. and Jonsson, E. (1996). Neglected aspects of false positive findings of mammography in breast cancer screening: analysis of false positive cases from the Stockholm trial. *British Medical Journal*, 312: 273–6.

Lie, D., Carter-Pokras, O., Braun, B. and Coleman, C. (2012). What do health literacy and cultural competence have in common? Calling for a collaborative health professional pedagogy. *Journal of Health Communication*, 17: 13–22.

Lightfoot, N., Steggles, S., Wilkinson, D., Bissett, R., Bakker, D., Darlington, G. et al. (1994). The short-term psychological impact of organized breast cancer screening. *Current Oncology*, 1: 206–11.

Liimakka, S. (2014). Healthy appearances–distorted body images? Young adults negotiating body motives. *Journal of Health Psychology*, 19: 230–41.

Lim, J.S., Mietus-Snyder, M., Valente, A., Schwarz, J.-M. and Lustig, R.M. (2010). The role of fructose in the pathogenesis of naFlD and the metabolic syndrome. *Nature Reviews Gastroenterology & Hepatology*, 7: 251–64.

Lim, S., Warner, S., Dixon, M., Berg, B., Kim, C. and Newhouse-Bailey, M. (2011). Sport participation across national contexts: a multilevel investigation of individual and systemic influences on adult sport participation. *European Sport Management Quarterly*, 11: 197–224.

Linde, K., Barrett, B., Wolkart, K., Bauer, R. and Melchart, D. (2006). Echinacea for preventing and treating the common cold. *Cochrane Database of Systematic Reviews*, 1 (CD000530)

Lindor, K.D., Dickson, E.R., Baldus, W.P. et al. (1994). Ursodeoxycholic acid in the treatment of primary biliary cirrhosis. *Gastroenterology*, 106: 1284–90.

Link, B.G. and Phelan, J. (2014). Stigma power. *Social Science & Medicine*, 103: 24–32.

Linn, A.J., van Weert, J.C., van Dijk, L., Horne, R. and Smit, E.G. (2014). The value of nurses' tailored communication when discussing medicines: exploring the relationship between satisfaction, beliefs and adherence. *Journal of Health Psychology*, doi:10.1177/1359105314539529

Linton, S.J. (1990). Activities of daily living scale for patients with chronic pain. *Perceptual and Motor Skills*, 71: 722.

Linton, S.J., Buer, N., Vlaeyen, J. and Hellsing, A. (2000). Are fear-avoidance behaviours related to the inception of one episode of back pain? A prospective study. *Psychology & Health*, 14: 1051–9.

Litt, I.F. (1993). Health issues for women in the 1990s. In S. Matteo (ed.), *American Women in the Nineties: Today's Critical Issues*. Boston, MA: Northeastern University Press.

Liu, W.M. and Iwamoto, D.K. (2007). Conformity to masculine norms, Asian values, coping strategies, peer group influences and substance use among Asian American men. *Psychology of Men & Masculinity*, 8: 25.

Livingston, E.H. (2010). The incidence of bariatric surgery has plateaued in the US. *American Journal of Surgery*, 200: 378–85.

Llewellyn, C.D., McGurk, M. and Weinman, J. (2007). Illness and treatment beliefs in head and neck cancer: is Leventhal's common sense model a useful framework for determining changes in outcomes over time? *Journal of Psychosomatic Research*, 63: 17–26.

Lloyd, R. (2008). Embodying critical pedagogy: a movement towards vitality. Available: http://freire.mcgill.ca.

Locke, A. and Horton-Salway, M. (2010). 'Golden age' versus 'Bad old days': a discursive examination of advice giving in antenatal classes. *Journal of Health Psychology*, 15: 1214–24.

Lofters, A., Slater, M., Kirst, M., Shankardass, K. and Quiñonez, C. (2014). How do people attribute income-related inequalities in health? A cross-sectional study in Ontario, Canada. *PLOS ONE*, 9 (1): 1–8.

Lollis, C.M., Johnson, E.H. and Antoni, M.H. (1997). The efficacy of the Health Belief Model for predicting condom usage and risky sexual practices in university students. *AIDS Education & Prevention*, 9: 551–63.

Lord, J. and McKillop Farlow, D. (1990). A study of personal empowerment: implications for health promotion. *Health Promotion International*, 29: 2–8.

Lorenc, A., Leach, J. and Robinson, N. (2014). Clinical guidelines in the UK: do they mention complementary and alternative medicine (CAM) – are CAM professional bodies aware*? European Journal of Integrative Medicine*, 6: 164–75.

Lorenc, T., Petticrew, M., Welch, V. and Tugwell, P. (2013). What types of interventions generate inequalities? Evidence from systematic reviews. *Journal of Epidemiology & Community Health*, 67 (2): 190–3. doi:10.1136/jech-2012-201257.

Lorenz, K.A., Lynn, J., Dy, S.M., Shugarman, L.R., Wilkinson, A., Mularski, R.A. et al. (2008). Clinical guidelines. Evidence for improving palliative care at the end of life: a systematic review. *Annals of Internal Medicine*, 148: 147–59.

Lovell, S.A., Kearns, R.A. and Prince, R. (2014). Neoliberalism and the contract state: exploring innovation and resistance among New Zealand health promoters. *Critical Public Health*, 24 (3): 308–20. doi:10.1080/09581596.2013.808317.

Loveman, E., Frampton, G.K., Shepherd, J., Picot, J., Cooper, K., Bryant, J. et al. (2011). The clinical effectiveness and cost-effectiveness of long-term weight management schemes for adults: a systematic review. *Health Technology Assessment*, 15.

Lowe, D.J. and de Lange, W.P. (2000). Volcano-meteorological tsunamis, thec. AD 200 Taupo eruption (New Zealand) and the possibility of a global tsunami. *The Holocene*, 10: 401–7.

Lowe, M.R. and Fisher Jr, E.B. (1983). Emotional reactivity, emotional eating, and obesity: a naturalistic study. *Journal of Behavioral Medicine*, 6: 135–49.

Lowther, M., Mutrie, N. and Scott, E.M. (2007). Identifying key processes of exercise behaviour change associated with movement through the stages of exercise behaviour change. *Journal of Health Psychology*, 12: 261–72.

Lubek, I. (2005). Beer and women: excessive alcohol consumption and risk of HIV/AIDS among Cambodian beer promotion women ('beer girls'). Presentation at the Universiteit van Leiden, 26 January 2005. Available: www.fairtradebeer.com/reportfiles/sirchesi/siemreapnewsletter2008.pdf [accessed 10 December 2009].

Lubek, I., Lee, H., Kros, S., Wong, M.L., Van Merode, T., Liu, J. et al. (2014). HIV/AIDS, beersellers and critical community health psychology in Cambodia: a case study. *Journal of Health Psychology*, 19 (1): 110–16. doi:10.1177/1359105313500253.

Lubek, I., Wong, M.L., Dy, B.C., Kros, S., Pen, S., Chhit, M. et al. (2003). *Only 'Beer Girls', No 'Beer Boys' in Cambodia: Confronting Globalisation and Inequalities in Literacy, Poverty, Employment, and Risk for HIV/AIDS.* Chichester: Wiley-Blackwell.

Luborsky, L., Rosenthal, R., Diguer, L., Andrusyna, T.P., Berman, J.S., Levitt, J.T. et al. (2002). The Dodo bird verdict is alive and well – mostly. *Clinical Psychology: Science and Practice*, 9: 2–34.

Luborsky, L., Singer, B. and Luborsky, L. (1975). Comparative studies of psychotherapies: is it true that 'Everyone has won and all must have prizes'? *Archives of General Psychiatry*, 32: 995–1008.

Luhmann, M., Hofmann, W., Eid, M. and Lucas, R.E. (2012). Subjective well-being and adaptation to life events: a meta-analysis. *Journal of Personality & Social Psychology*, 102: 592.

Lundahl, B. and Burke, B.L. (2009). The effectiveness and applicability of motivational interviewing: a practice-friendly review of four meta-analyses. *Journal of Clinical Psychology*, 65: 1232–45.

Luppino, F.S., de Wit, L.M., Bouvy, P.F., Stijnen, T., Cuijpers, P., Penninx, B.W. and Zitman, F.G. (2010). Overweight, obesity, and depression: a systematic review and meta-analysis of longitudinal studies. *Archives of General Psychiatry*, 67: 220–9.

Lupton, D. (1995) *The Imperative of Health.* London: SAGE Publications.

Lupton, D. (1997). Consumerism, reflexivity and the medical encounter. *Social Science & Medicine*, 45: 373–81.

Lurie, N., Slater, J., McGovern, P., Ekstrum, J., Quam, L. and Margolis, K. (1993). Preventive care for women: does the sex of the physician matter? *New England Journal of Medicine*, 329: 478–82.

Luschen, G., Cockerham, W. and Kunz, G. (1996). The socio-cultural context of sport and health: problems of causal relations and structural interdependence. *Sociology of Sport Journal*, 13: 197–213.

Lustig, R.H. (2013). *Fat chance: the hidden truth about food, obesity, and disease*. London: Fourth Estate.

Lykes, M.B. (2001). Activist participatory research and the arts with rural Mayan women: interculturality and situated meaning making. In D. Tolman and M. Brydon-Miller (eds.), *From Subjects to Subjectivities: A Handbook of Interpretive and Participatory Methods*. New York: New York University Press. pp. 183–97.

Lynch, J.W. and Davey Smith, G. (2002). Commentary: income inequality and health: the end of the story? *Journal of Epidemiology & Community Health*, 31: 549–51.

Lynch, J., Davey Smith, G., Harper, S., Hillemeier, M., Ross, N., Kaplan, G.A. and Wolfson, M. (2004). Is income inequality a determinant of population health? Part 1. A systematic review. *Milbank Quarterly*, 82: 5–99.

Lynch, J.W., Davey Smith, G., Kaplan, G.A. and House, J. (2000). Income inequality and mortality: importance to health of individual income, psychosocial environment, or material conditions. *British Medical Journal*, 320: 1200–4.

Ma, Q., Ono-Kihara, M., Cong, L., Pan, X., Xu, G., Zamani, S. et al. (2009). Behavioral and psychosocial predictors of condom use among university students in Eastern China. *AIDS Care*, 21: 249–59.

MacArtney, J.I. and Wahlberg, A. (2014). The problem of complementary and alternative medicine use today: eyes half closed*? Qualitative Health Research*, 24: 114–23.

Macinko, J.A., Shi, L., Starfield, B. and Wulu, J.T. (2003). Income inequality and health: a critical review of the literature. *Medical Care Research & Reviews*, 60: 407–52.

Macintyre, S. and Hunt, K. (1997). Socio-economic position, gender and health. *Journal of Health Psychology*, 2: 315–34.

Mackay, S.J. and Parry, O. (2014). Two world views: perspectives on autistic behaviours. *Journal of Health Psychology*, in press.

MackSense Ltd (2014). Obesity in the UK. Available: http://MackSense.co.uk/en/research-reports/.

MacLachlan, M. (2000). Cultivating pluralism in health psychology. *Journal of Health Psychology*, 5: 373–82.

MacLachlan, M. (2009). Health in the Inter-land. *Journal of Health Psychology, 14*, 647–50.

Macleod, J. and Davey Smith, G. (2003). Psychosocial factors and public health: a suitable case for treatment? *Journal of Epidemiology & Community Health*, 57: 565–70.

Macleod, J., Davey Smith, G., Heslop, P., Metcalfe, C., Carroll, D. and Hart, C. (2002). Psychological stress and cardiovascular disease: empirical demonstration of bias in a prospective observational study of Scottish men. *British Medical Journal*, 324: 1247–51.

MacMillan, M. (1997). *Freud Evaluated: The Completed Arc.* Cambridge, MA: MIT Press.

Maguen, S., Lucenko, B.A., Reger, M.A. et al. (2010). The impact of reported direct and indirect killing on mental health symptoms in Iraq war veterans. *Journal of Traumatic Stress*, 23 (1): 86–90.

Maier, S.F. and Watkins, L.R. (1998). Cytokines for psychologists: implications of bi-directional immune-to-brain communication for understanding behaviour, mood and cognition. *Psychological Review*, 105: 83–107.

Malpas, P.J., Wilson, M.K.R., Rae, N. and Johnson, M. (2014). Why do older people oppose physician-assisted dying? A qualitative study. *Palliative Medicine*, 28 (4): 353–9.

Marcus, B.H., Banspach, S.W., Lefebvre, R.L., Rossi, J.S., Carleton, R.A. and Abrams, D.B. (1992). Using the stages of change model to increase the adoption of physical activity among community participants. *American Journal of Health Promotion*, 6: 424–9.

Marcus, B. Eaton, C.A., Rossi, J.S. and L. (1994). Self-efficacy, decision-making and stages of change: an integrative model of physical exercise. *Journal of Applied Social Psychology*, 24: 489–508.

Marcus, D.A. (2000). Treatment of non-malignant chronic pain. *American Family Physician*, 61: 1331–8.

Marcus, K.S., Kerns, R.D., Rosenfeld, B. and Breitbart, W. (2000). HIV/AIDS-related pain as a chronic pain condition: implications of a biopsychosocial model for comprehensive assessment and effective management. *Pain Medicine*, 1: 260–73.

Marcus, M.D., Wing, R.R. and Lamparski, D.M. (1985). Binge eating and dietary restraint in obese patients. *Addictive Behaviors*, 10: 163–8.

Marinker, M. (1997). Writing prescriptions is easy. *British Medical Journal*, 314: 747.

Markova, I. and Wilkie, P. (1987). Representations, concepts and social change: the phenomenon of AIDS. *Journal for the Theory of Social Behaviour*, 17: 389–409.

Marks, D. (1999a). Dimensions of oppression: theorising the embodied subject. *Disability & Society*, 14: 611–26.

Marks, D. (1999b). *Disability: Controversial Debates and Psychosocial Perspectives*. London: Routledge.

Marks, D.F. (1992). Smoking cessation as a testbed for psychological theory: a group cognitive therapy programme with high long-term abstinence rates. *Journal of Smoking-Related Disorders*, 3: 69–78.

Marks, D.F. (1993). *The QUIT FOR LIFE Programme: An Easier Way to Stop Smoking and Not Start Again.* Leicester, UK: The British Psychological Society.

Marks, D.F. (1996). Health psychology in context. *Journal of Health Psychology*, 1: 7–21.

Marks, D.F. (1998). Addiction, smoking and health: developing policy-based interventions. *Psychology, Health & Medicine*, 3: 97–111.

Marks, D.F. (1999). Health psychology as agent of change: reconstructing health psychology. *First International Conference on Critical and Qualitative Approaches to Health Psychology*. St John's, Newfoundland, Canada.

Marks, D.F. (2002a). Freedom, responsibility and power: contrasting approaches to health psychology. *Journal of Health Psychology*, 7: 5–19.

Marks, D.F. (2002b). *The Health Psychology Reader*. London: Sage.

Marks, D.F. (2002c). *Perspectives on Evidence*. London: National Institute for Health and ClinicalExcellence. Available: www.nice.org.uk/aboutnice/whoweare/aboutthehda/evidencebase/publichealthevidence steeringgroupproceedings/perspectives_on_evidence_based_practice.jsp.

Marks, D.F. (2004). Rights to health, freedom from illness: a life and death matter. In M. Murray (ed.), *Critical Health Psychology*. London: Palgrave. pp. 61–82.

Marks, D.F. (2005). *Overcoming Your Smoking Habit*. London: Robinson.

Marks, D.F. (2009). How should psychology interventions be reported? *Journal of Health Psychology*, 14: 475–89.

Marks, D.F. (2013). Health psychology: overview. *Handbook of Psychology, Vol. 9: Health Psychology*. New York: Wiley. pp. 3–25.

Marks, D.F. (2015). Homeostatic theory of obesity. *Health Psychology Open*, 1.

Marks, D.F. and MacAvoy, M.G. (1989). Divided attention performance in cannabis users and non-users following alcohol and cannabis separately and in combination. *Psychopharmacology*, 99: 397–401.

Marks, D.F. and Sykes, C.M. (2002a). A randomized controlled trial of cognitive behaviour therapy for smokers living in a deprived part of London. *Psychology, Health & Medicine*, 7: 17–24.

Marks, D.F. and Sykes, C.M. (2002b). Evaluation of the European Union Programme of Community Action on Health Promotion, Information, Education and Training 1996–2000. *Health Promotion International*, 17: 105–18.

Marks, D.F. and Sykes, C.M. (2000c). Randomized controlled trial of cognitive behavioural therapy for smokers living in a deprived area of London: outcome at one-year follow-up. *Psychology, Health & Medicine*, 7: 17–24.

Marks, D.F. and Yardley, L. (2004). *Research Methods for Clinical and Health Psychology*. London: Sage.

Marks, D.F., Baird, J.M. and McKellar, P. (1989). Replication of trance logic using a modified experimental design: highly hypnotizable subjects in both real and simulator groups. *International Journal of Clinical & Experimental Hypnosis*, 37: 232–48.

Marmot, M.G. (2002). *Redefining Public Health: Epidemiology and Social Stratification*. Berkeley, CA: University of California, Institute of International Studies.

Marmot, M. (2013). Fair society, healthy lives. *Inequalities in Health: Concepts, Measures, and Ethics*, 282.

Marsh, H.W., Papaioannou, A. and Theodorakis, Y. (2006). Causal ordering of physical self-concept and exercise behavior: reciprocal effects model and the influence of physical education teachers. *Health Psychology*, 25: 316–28.

Marteau, T. (1990). Reducing the psychological costs. *British Medical Journal*, 301: 26–8.

Martin, F., Russell, S. and Seeley, J. (2014). Adjustment as process and outcome: measuring adjustment to HIV in Uganda. *Journal of Health Psychology*, in press.

Martín-Baró, I. (1994). Writings for a liberation psychology. In A. Aron and S. Corne (ed.), *Writings for a Liberation Psychology*. Cambridge, MA: Harvard University Press.

Martinez, S.M., Arredondo, E.M. and Roesch, S. (2013). Physical activity promotion among churchgoing Latinas in San Diego, California: does neighborhood cohesion matter? *Journal of Health Psychology*, 18 (10): 1319–29.

Martinez Cobo, J. (1987). *Study of the Problem of Discrimination against Indigenous Populations*, Vol. 5. UNESCO.

Martinez-Cordero, C., Kuzawa, C.W., Sloboda, D.M., Stewart, J., Simpson, S.J. and Raubenheimer, D. (2012). Testing the protein leverage hypothesis in a free-living human population. *Appetite*, 59: 312–15.

Masek, B.J. (1982) Compliance and medicine. In D.M. Doleys, R.L. Meredith and A.R. Ciminero (eds.), *Behavioral Medicine: Assessment and Treatment Strategies*. New York: Plenum Press.

Maslach, C. and Jackson, S. (1981). The measurement of experienced burnout. *Journal of Occupational Behaviour*, 2: 99–113.

Maslow, A.H. (1943). A theory of human motivation. *Psychological review*, 50 (4): 370–96.

Mason, J.W. (1971). A re-evaluation of the concept of 'non-specificity' in stress theory. *Journal of Psychiatric Research*, 8: 323–33.

Mason, J.W. (1975). A historical view of the stress field: parts 1 and 2. *Journal of Human Stress*, 1: 6–12, 22–36.

Masunaga, R. (1972). *A Primer of Soto Zen: A Translation of Dogen's Shobogenzo Zuimonki*. London: Routledge.

Masur, H. (1981). Infection after kidney transplantation. *Archives of Internal Medicine*, 141: 1582–4.

Mathieson, C. and Stam, H. (1995). Renegotiating identity: cancer narratives. *Sociology of Health and Illness*, 17: 283–306.

Matsumoto, D., Pun, K.K., Nakatani, M., Kadowaki, D., Weissman, M., McCarter, L. et al. (1995). Cultural differences in attitudes, values, and beliefs about osteoporosis in first and second generation Japanese-American women. *Women and Health*, 23: 39–56.

Mauksch, L.B., Dugdale, D.C., Dodson, S. and Epstein, R. (2008). Relationship, communication, and efficiency in the medical encounter: creating a clinical model from a literature review. *Archives of Internal Medicine,* 168 (13): 1387–95.

Mazzoni, D., and Cicognani, E. (2014). Sharing experiences and social support requests in an internet forum for patients with systemic lupus erythematosus. *Journal of Health Psychology*, 19 (5): 689–96. doi:10.1177/1359105313477674

McAllister, M., Payne, K., MacLeod, R., Donnai, D. and Davies, L. (2008). Developing outcome measures for clinical genetics services: a triangulation approach. *Psychology & Health*, 23: 179–180.

McAuley, E. and Jacobson, L. (1991). Self-efficacy and exercise participation in adult sedentary females. *American Journal of Health Promotion*, 5: 185–191.

McCaffery, A.M., Eisenberg, D.M., Legedza, A.T.R., Davis, R.B. and Phillips, R.A. (2004). Prayer for health concerns: results of a national survey on prevalence and patterns of use. *Archives of Internal Medicine*, 164: 858–62.

McCaffery, K.J., Holmes-Rovner, M., Smith, S.K., Rovner, D., Nutbeam, D., Clayman, M.L. et al. (2013). Addressing health literacy in patient decision aids. *BMC Medical Informatics and Decision Making*, 13 (Suppl 2): S10–S10.

McCaffery, M. and Thorpe, D. (1988). Differences in perception of pain and development of adversarial relationships among health care providers. *Advances in Pain Research & Therapy*, 11: 113–22.

McCambridge, J., Kypri, K., Miller, P., Hawkins, B. and Hastings, G. (2014). Be aware of Drinkaware. *Addiction*, 109: 519–24.

McCartney, M. (2014). The BMJ is wrong: doctor assisted dying would overmedicalise death. *British Medical Journal* (Clinical Research Edition), 349: g4502.

McCaul, K.D., Dyche Branstetter, A., Schroeder, D.M. and Glasgow, R.M. (1996). What is the relationship between breast cancer risk and mammography screening? A meta-analytic review. *Health Psychology*, 15: 423–9.

McCormick, M., and Seta, J.J. (2012). Lateralized goal framing: how selective presentation impacts message effectiveness. *Journal of Health Psychology*, 17 (8): 1099–1109.

McCracken, L.M. and Vowles, K.E. (2014). Acceptance and commitment therapy and mindfulness for chronic pain: model, process, and progress. *American Psychologist*, 69: 178–87.

McCracken, L.M., Gauntlett-Gilbert, J. and Vowles, K.E. (2007). The role of mindfulness in a contextual cognitive-behavioral analysis of chronic pain-related suffering and disability. *Pain*, 131: 63–9.

McCracken, L.M. and Eccleston, C. (2003). Coping or acceptance: what to do about chronic pain? *Pain*, 105: 197–204.

McCracken, L.M., Carson, J.W., Eccleston, C. and Keefe, F.J. (2004). Acceptance and change in the context of chronic pain *Pain*, 109: 4–7.

McCracken, L.M., Vowles, K.E. and Eccleston, C. (2004). Acceptance of chronic pain: component analysis and a revised assessment method. *Pain*, 107: 159–66.

McCracken, L.M., Zayfert, C. and Gross, R.T. (1992). The Pain Anxiety Symptoms Scale: development and validation of a scale to measure fear of pain. *Pain*, 50: 67–73.

McCrae, R.R. and Costa, P.T. (1985). Updating Norman's 'adequate taxonomy': intelligence and personality dimensions in natural language and in questionnaires. *Journal of Personality & Social Psychology*, 49: 710–21.

McCrae, R.R. and Costa, P.T. (2003). *Personality in Adulthood: A Five-Factor Theory Perspective* (2nd edn). New York: Guilford.

McEachan, R.R.C., Conner, M., Taylor, N.J. and Lawton, R.J. (2011). Prospective prediction of health-related behaviours with the theory of planned behaviour: a meta-analysis. *Health Psychology Review*, 5: 97–144.

McEwan, J., King, E. and Bickler, F. (1989). Attendance and non-attendance for breast screening at the South East London breast screening service. *British Medical Journal*, 299: 104–6.

McGee, H.M., Hevey, D. and Horgan, J.H. (1999). Psychosocial outcome assessments for use in cardiac rehabilitation service evaluation: a 10-year systematic review. *Social Science & Medicine*, 48: 1373–93.

McGlynn, E.A. (1988). *Physician Job Satisfaction: Its Measurement and Use as an Indication of System Performance.* Unpublished doctoral dissertation, RAND Graduate School, Santa Monica, CA. (Cited in DiMatteo et al., 1993)

McGowan, L., Luker, K., Creed, F. and Chew, C.A. (2007). 'How do you explain a pain that can't be seen?': the narratives of women with chronic pelvic pain and their disengagement with the diagnostic cycle. *British Journal of Health Psychology*, 12: 261–74.

McInnes, N. and Haglund, B.J. (2011). Readability of online health information: implications for health literacy. *Informatics for Health & Social Care*, 36 (4): 173–189.

McKeown, T. (1979). *The Role of Medicine*. Princeton, NJ: Princeton University Press.

McKie, L. (1993). Women's views of the cervical smear test: implications for nursing practice – women who have not had a smear test. *Journal of Advanced Nursing*, 18: 972–9.

McKie, L. (1995). The art of surveillance or reasonable prevention? The case of cervical screening. *Sociology of Health & Illness*, 17: 441–57.

McKinlay, A. and McVittie, C. (2008). *Social Psychology and Discourse.* London: Wiley-Blackwell.

McLeroy, K.R., Norton, B.L., Kegler, M.C., Burdine, J.N. and Sumaya, C.V. (2003). Community-based interventions. *American Journal of Public Health*, 93: 529–33.

McMullan, M. (2006). Patients using the internet to obtain health information: how this affects patient-health professional relationship. *Patient Education and Counseling*, 63: 24–8.

McVittie, C. and Goodall, K. (2009). Harry, Paul and the Filipino maid: Racial and sexual abuse in local contexts. *Journal of Health Psychology*, 14: 651–4.

Meares, R. (2012). *A Dissociation Model of Borderline Personality Disorder* (Norton series on interpersonal neurobiology). New York: WW Norton & Company.

Medeiros, E. (2007). Integrating mental health into post-conflict rehabilitation: the case of Sierra Leonean and Liberian 'child soldiers'. *Journal of Health Psychology*, 12: 498–504.

Medical Research Council (2000). *A Framework for the Development and Evaluation of RCTs for Complex Interventions to Improve Health.* London: Medical Research Council.

Medical Research Council (2008). *Developing and Evaluating Complex Interventions: New Guidance.* London: Medical Research Council.

Meichenbaum, D. (1985). *Stress Inoculation Training*. New York: Pergamon.

Meichenbaum, D. (1996). Stress inoculation training for coping with stressors. *Clinical Psychologist*, 49: 4–7.

Meichenbaum, D. (2014). Ways to implement interventions in schools in order to make them safer, more inviting and pedagogically more effective. Available: www.melissainstitute.org/documents/Conf18-Meichenbaum-WaysToImplement.pdf.

Meichenbaum, D. and Turk, D.C. (1987). *Facilitating Treatment Adherence: A Practitioner's Guidebook.* New York: Plenum Press.

Melzack, R. (1975) The McGill Pain Questionnaire: major properties and scoring methods. *Pain*, 1: 277–99.

Melzack, R. (1999). From the gate to the neuromatrix: *Pain*, 82 (Supplement 1): S121–6.

Melzack, R. and Katz, J. (2013). McGill Pain Questionnaire. In *Encyclopedia of Pain*. Berlin/Heidelberg: Springer. pp. 1792–4.

Melzack, R. and Katz, J. (2014). The neuromatrix in behavioral medicine. *The Handbook of Behavioral Medicine*, 759–74.

Melzack, R. and Wall, P. (1982/1988). *The Challenge of Pain*. London: Penguin Books.

Mennella, J.A. and Beauchamp, G.K. (1996). The early development of human flavor preferences. In E.D. Capaldi (ed.), *Why We Eat What We Eat: The Psychology of Eating*. Washington, DC: American Psychological Association. pp. 83–112.

Merskey, J. (1996). Classification of chronic pain: descriptions of chronic pain syndromes and definitions of pain terms. *Pain*, 3 (suppl.): S1–225.

Meyer, T.J. and Mark, M.M. (1995). Effects of psychosocial interventions with adult cancer patients: a meta-analysis of randomized experiments. *Health Psychology*, 14: 101–8.

Meyerowitz, B.E., Richardson, J., Hudson, S. and Leedham, B. (1998). Ethnicity and cancer outcomes: behavioral and psychosocial considerations. *Psychological Bulletin*, 123: 47–70.

Mezey, G. and Robbins, I. (2001). Usefulness and validity of post-traumatic stress disorder as a psychiatric category. *British Medical Journal*, 323: 561–3.

Michell, J. (1999). *Measurement in Psychology: Critical History of a Methodological Concept*. Cambridge: Cambridge University Press.

Michell, J. (2002). Measurement: a beginner's guide. *Journal of Applied Measurement*, 4: 298–308.

Michell, J. (2012). 'The constantly recurring argument': inferring quantity from order. *Theory & Psychology*, 22: 255–71.

Michie, S., Axworthy, D., Weinman, J. and Marteau, T. (1996). Genetic counselling: predicting patient outcomes, *Psychology & Health*, 11: 797–809.

Michie, S., McDonald, V. and Marteau, T. (1996). Understanding responses to predictive genetic testing: a grounded theory approach. *Psychology & Health*, 11: 455–70.

Middleton, D. (1996). A discursive analysis of psychosocial issues: talk in a 'parent group' for families who have children with chronic renal failure. *Psychology & Health*, 11: 243–60.

Midford, R. and McBride, N. (2001). Alcohol education in schools, in N. Heather, T.J. Peters and T. Stockwell (eds.), *International Handbook of Alcohol Dependence and Problems*. London: Wiley. pp. 785–804.

Mielewczyk, M. and Willig, C. (2007). Old wine and an older look: the case for a radical makeover in health. *Theory & Psychology*, 17: 811–37.

Miles, A. (1981). *The Mentally Ill in Contemporary Society*. Oxford: Martin Robertson.

Miller, A.L., Kaciroti, N., LeBourgeois, M.K., Chen, Y.P., Sturza, J. and Lumeng, J.C.B. (2014). Sleep timing moderates the concurrent sleep duration–body mass index association in low-income preschool-age children. *Academic Pediatrics*, 14: 207–13.

Miller, G., Chen, E. and Cole, S.W. (2009). Health psychology: developing biologically plausible models linking the social world and physical health. *Annual Review of Psychology*, 60: 501–24.

Miller, G.E. and Cohen, S. (2001). Psychological interventions and the immune system: a meta-analytic review and critique. *Health Psychology*, 20: 47–63.

Miller, L.M.S., Zirnstein, M. and Chan, P.K. (2013). Knowledge differentially supports memory for nutrition information in later life. *Journal of Health Psychology*, 18 (9): 1141–52.

Miller, M.J., Abrams, M.A., McCLintock, B., Cantrell, M.A., Dossett, C.D., McCleeary, E.M. et al. (2008). Promoting health communication between the community-dwelling well-elderly and pharmacists: the Ask Me 3 program. *Journal of the American Pharmacists' Association*, 48: 784–92.

Miller, N.H. (1997). Compliance with treatment regimens in chronic asymptomatic diseases. *American Journal of Medicine*, 102: 43–9.

Miller, T.Q., Smith, T.W., Turner, C.W., Guijarro, M.L. and Hallet, A.J. (1996). A meta-analytic review of research on hostility and physical health. *Psychological Bulletin*, 119: 322–48.

Miller, V.A. and Drotar, D. (2007). Decision making competence and adherence to treatment in adolescents with diabetes. *Journal of Pediatric Psychology*, 37: 292–306.

Miller, V.A. and Jawad, A.F. (2014). Relationship of youth involvement in diabetes-related decisions to treatment adherence. *Journal of Clinical Psychology in Medical Settings*, 21: 183–9.

Miller, W.R. and Rollnick, S. (2013). *Motivational Interviewing: Helping People Change* (3rd edn). New York: Guilford Press.

Miller, W.R. and Wilbourne, P. (2002). Mesa Grande: a methodological analysis of clinical trials of treatments for alcohol use disorders. *Addiction*, 97: 265–77.

Miller, W.R., Walters, G.D. and Bennett, M.E. (2001). How effective is alcoholism treatment in the United States? *Journal of Studies on Alcohol & Drugs*, 62: 211–20.

Miovic, M. and Block, S. (2007). Psychiatric disorders in advanced cancer. *Cancer*, 110: 1665–76.

Mishler, E. (1994). The struggle between the voice of medicine and the voice of the lifeworld. In P. Conrad and R. Kern (eds.), *The Sociology of Health and Illness: Critical Perspectives*. New York: St Martin's Press.

Mize, S.J.S., Robinson, B.E., Bockting, W.O. and Scheltema, K.E. (2002). Meta-analysis of the effectiveness of HIV prevention interventions for women. *Aids Care*, 14: 163–80.

Mo, P.K. and Lau, J.T. (2014). Illness representation on H1N1 influenza and preventive behaviors in the Hong Kong general population. *Journal of Health Psychology*, in press.

Modi, A.C., Pai, A.L., Hommel, K. et al. (2012). Pediatric self-management: a framework for research, practice, and policy. *Pediatrics*, 129: e473–85.

Modi, N., Murgasova, D., Ruager-Martin, R. et al. (2011). The influence of maternal body mass index on infant adiposity and hepatic lipid content. *Pediatric Research*, 70: 287–91.

Modood, T., Berthoud, R., Lakey, J., Nazroo, J., Smith, P., Virdee, S. and Beishon, S. (1997). *Ethnic Minorities in Britain: Diversity and Disadvantage*. London: Policy Studies Institute.

Mohan, A.V., Riley, M.B., Boyington, D.R., and Kripalani, S. (2013). Illustrated medication instructions as a strategy to improve medication management among Latinos: a qualitative analysis. *Journal of Health Psychology*, 18 (2): 187–97.

Moher, D., Schultz, K.F., Altman, D.G. and the CONSORT Group (2001). The CONSORT statement: revised recommendations for improving the quality of reports of parallel-group randomized trials. *The Lancet*, 357: 1191–4.

Mohr, N. (2012). Average and total numbers of animals who died to feed Americans in 2010. Available: https://docs.google.com/file/d/0Bzm1dJXWcgufMjdiNDNmZTItOWMwMy00ZjhjLWE2NGUtN-WRkMDM1NmRlNjU3/edit.

Moloney, G. and Walker, I. (2002). Talking about transplants: social representations and the dialectical, dilemmatic nature of organ donation and transplantation. *British Journal of Social Psychology*, 41: 299–320.

Mongkuo, M.Y., Lucas, N. and Taylor, A. (2012). The effects of motivation and knowledge on HIV prevention behavior among historically black college students: an application of the information-motivation-behavioral skills model. *Greener Journal of Medical Sciences*, 2: 1–7.

Monroe, S.M. and Simons, A.D. (1991). Diathesis-stress theories in the context of life stress research: implications for the depressive disorders. *Psychological Bulletin*, 110: 406–25.

Montenegro, R.A. and Stephens, C. (2006). Indigenous health in Latin America and the Caribbean. *The Lancet*, 367: 1859–69.

Moodie, R., Stuckler, D., Monteiro, C. et al. (2013). Profits and pandemics: prevention of harmful effects of tobacco, alcohol, and ultra-processed food and drink industries. *The Lancet*, 381: 670–9.

Mookadam, F. and Arthur, H.M. (2004). Social support and its relationship to morbidity and mortality after acute myocardial infarction: systematic overview. *Archives of Internal Medicine*, 164: 1514–18.

Mooney, M., White, T. and Hatsukami, D. (2004). The blind spot in the nicotine replacement therapy literature: assessment of the double-blind in clinical trials. *Addictive Behavior*, 29: 673–84.

Moore, S., Barling, N. and Hood, B. (1998). Predicting testicular and breast self examination: a test of the Theory of Reasoned Action. *Behaviour Change*, 15, 41–9.

Moore, T., Norman, P., Harris, P.R. and Makris, M. (2008). An interpretative phenomenological analysis of adaptation to recurrent venous thrombosis and heritable thrombophilia: the importance of multi-causal models and perceptions of primary and secondary control. *Journal of Health Psychology*, 13: 776–84.

Moorhead, S.A., Hazlett, D.E., Harrison, L., Carroll, J.K., Irwin, A. and Hoving, C. (2013). A new dimension of health care: Systematic review of the uses, benefits, and limitations of social media for health communication. *Journal of Medical Internet Research*, 15 (4): e85. doi:10.2196/jmir.1933.

Morinis, C.A. and Brilliant, G.E. (1981). Smallpox in northern India: diversity and order in a regional medical culture. *Medical Anthropology*, 5: 341–64.

Morley, S., Eccleston, C. and Williams, A. (1999). Systematic review and meta-analysis of randomized controlled trials of cognitive behaviour therapy and behaviour therapy for chronic pain in adults, excluding headache. *Pain*, 80: 1–13.

Moscovici, S. (1973). Foreword. In C. Herzlich (ed.), *Health and Illness: A Social Psychological Analysis*. London: Academic Press.

Moscovici, S. (1984). The phenomenon of social representations. In R.M. Farr and S. Moscovici (eds.), *Social Representations*. Cambridge: Cambridge University Press. pp. 3–70.

Moser, D.K. and Dracup, K. (2004). Role of spousal anxiety and depression in patients' psychosocial recovery after a cardiac event. *Psychosomatic Medicine*, 66: 527–32.

Moser, K., Patnick, J. and Beral, V. (2009). Inequalities in reported use of breast and cervical screening in Great Britain: analysis of cross-sectional survey data. *British Medical Journal*, 338: b2025.

Moss-Morris, R., Weinman, J., Petrie, K.J., Horne, R., Cameron, L.D. and Buick, D. (2002). The Revised Illness Perception Questionnaire (IPQ-R). *Psychology & Health*, 17: 1–17.

Mouraux, A., Diukova, A., Lee, M.C., Wise, R.G. and Iannetti, G.D. (2011). A multisensory investigation of the functional significance of the 'pain matrix'. *Neuroimage*, 54: 2237–49.

Moynihan, P.J. and Kelly, S.A.M. (2014). Effect on caries of restricting sugars intake: systematic review to inform WHO guidelines. *Journal of Dental Research*, 93: 8–18.

Moynihan, R., Heath, I. and Henry, D. (2002). Selling sickness: the pharmaceutical industry and disease mongering. *BMJ*, 324: 886.

Mozaffarian, D., Hao, T., Rimm, E.B., Willett, W.C. and Hu, F.B. (2011). Changes in diet and lifestyle and long-term weight gain in women and men. *New England Journal of Medicine*, 364: 2392–404.

Mulatu, M.S. (1995). Lay beliefs about the causes of psychological and physical illness in Ethiopia. *Canadian Health Psychologist*, 3: 38–43.

Mulkay, M. (1991). *Sociology of Science: A Sociological Pilgrimage*. Milton Keynes: Open University Press.

Mulveen, R. and Hepworth, J. (2006). An interpretative phenomenological analysis of participation in a pro-anorexia internet site and its relationship with disordered eating. *Journal of Health Psychology*, 11: 283–96.

Munro, S., Lewin, S., Swart, T. and Volmink, J. (2007). A review of health behaviour theories: how useful are these for developing interventions to promote long-term medication adherence for TB and HIV/AIDS? *BMC Public Health*, 7: 104–19.

Murphy, D.J. and Hall, C.A. (2011). Energy return on investment, peak oil, and the end of economic growth. *Annals of the New York Academy of Sciences*, 1219 (1): 52–72.

Murray, C.J.L. and Lopez, A.D. (1997). Alternative projections of mortality and disability by cause 1990–2020: Global Burden of Disease Study. *The Lancet*, 349: 1498–504.

Murray, D. (2005). The social meanings of prosthesis use. *Journal of Health Psychology*, 10: 425–41.

Murray, M. (1993). Social and cognitive representations of health and illness. In H. Schroder, K. Reschke, M. Johnson and S. Maes (eds.), *Health Psychology: Potential in Diversity*. Regensburg: Roderer. pp. 124–31.

Murray, M. (1997a). A narrative approach to health psychology: background and potential. *Journal of Health Psychology*, 2: 9–20.

Murray, M. (1997b). *Narrative Health Psychology*. Palmerston North, NZ: Massey University.

Murray, M., Swan, A.V. and Mattar, N. (1983). The task of nursing and risk of smoking. *Journal of Advanced Nursing*, 8: 131–8.

Murray, M., Jarrett, L., Swan, A.V. and Rumun, R. (1988). *Smoking Among Young Adults*. Aldershot: Gower.

Murray, M. (1999). The storied nature of health and illness. In M. Murray and K. Chamberlain (eds.), *Qualitative Health Psychology: Theories and Methods*. London: Sage. pp. 47–63.

Murray, M. (2000). Levels of narrative analysis in health psychology. *Journal of Health Psychology*, 5: 337–48.

Murray, M. (2002). Connecting narrative and social representation theory in health research. *Social Science Information*, 41: 653–73.

Murray, M. (2003). Narrative psychology. In J.A. Smith (ed.), *Qualitative Psychology: A Practical Guide to Research Methods*. London: Sage.

Murray, M. (2007). 'It's in the blood and you're not going to change it': fish harvesters' narrative accounts of injuries and disability. *Work*, 28: 165–74.

Murray, M. (2009). Telling stories and making sense of cancer. *International Journal of Narrative Practice*, 1: 25–36.

Murray, M. (2012a). Social and political health psychology in action. In M. Forshaw and D. Sheffield (eds.), *Health psychology in action*. London: Wiley-Blackwell. pp. 128–37.

Murray, M. (2012b). Critical health psychology and the scholar-activist tradition. In C. Horrocks and S. Johnson (eds.), *Advances in Health Psychology: Critical Approaches*. London: Palgrave Macmillan. pp. 29–43.

Murray, M. (2014a). Social history of health psychology: context and textbooks. *Health Psychology Review*, 8: 215–237.

Murray, M. (2014b). *Critical Health Psychology* (2nd edn). London: Palgrave.

Murray, M. and Campbell, C. (2003). Living in a material world: reflecting on some assumptions of health psychology. *Journal of Health Psychology*, 8: 231–6.

Murray, M. and Chamberlain, K. (eds.) (2015) *New Directions in Health Psychology* (Volumes I–V). London: Sage.

Murray, M. and Crummett, A. (2010). 'I don't think they knew we could do these sorts of things': social representations of community and participation in community arts by older people. *Journal of Health Psychology*, 15: 777–85.

Murray, M. and McMillan, C. (1988). *Working Class Women's Views of Cancer*. Belfast: Ulster Cancer Foundation.

Murray, M. and McMillan, C. (1993a). Gender differences in perceptions of cancer. *Journal of Cancer Education*, 8: 53–62.

Murray, M. and McMillan, C. (1993b). Health beliefs, locus of control, emotional control and women's cancer screening behaviour. *British Journal of Clinical Psychology*, 32: 87–100.

Murray, M. and Tilley, N. (2004). Developing community health action and research through the arts. In R. Flowers (ed.), *Education and Social Action Conference 2004*. Sydney: University of Technology Sydney. pp. 150–6.

Murray, M., Pullman, D. and Heath Rodgers, T. (2003). Social representations of health and illness among 'baby-boomers' in Eastern Canada. *Journal of Health Psychology*, 8: 485–500.

Mykletun, A., Bjerkeset, O., Dewey, M., Prince, M., Overland, S. and Stewart, R. (2007). Anxiety, depression, and cause-specific mortality: the HUNT study. *Psychosomatic Medicine*, 69: 323–31.

Myrtek, M. (2001). Meta-analyses of prospective studies on coronary heart disease, type A personality and hostility. *International Journal of Cardiology*, 79: 245–51.

Nadimpalli, S.B. and Hutchinson, M.K. (2012). An integrative review of relationships between discrimination and Asian American health. *Journal of Nursing Scholarship*, 44: 127–35.

Nahon, S., Lahmek, P., Saas, C., Durance, C., Olympie, A., Lesgourgues, B. and Gendre, J.-P. (2011). Socioeconomic and psychological factors associated with nonadherence to treatment in inflammatory bowel disease patients: results of the ISSEO survey. *Inflammatory Bowel Diseases*, 17: 1270–6.

Nairn, R., Peaga, F., McCreanor, T., Rankine, J. and Barnes, A. (2006). Media, racism and public health psychology. *Journal of Health Psychology*, 11: 183–96.

Najafi, S., Lieto, J. and Johnson, L.A. (2014). Physicians' practices and end of life.

Nambiar, D., Ramakrishnan, V., Kumar, P., Varma, R., Balaji, N., Rajendran, J. et al. (2011). Knowledge, stigma, and behavioral outcomes among antiretroviral therapy patients exposed to Nalamdana's Radio and Theater Program in Tamil Nadu, India. *AIDS Education and Prevention*, 23: 351–66.

Nan, C., Guo, B., Warner, C. et al. (2012). Heritability of body mass index in pre-adolescence, young adulthood and late adulthood. *European Journal of Epidemiology*, 27: 247–53.

Nansel. T.R., Rovner, A., Haynie, D.L., Iannotti, R.J., Simons-Morton, B., Wysocki, T. et al (2009). Development and validation of the Collaborative Parent Involvement scale for youths with type 1 diabetes. *Journal of Pediatric Psychology*, 34: 30–40.

Nath, J. (2011). Gendered fare? A qualitative investigation of alternative food and masculinities. *Journal of Sociology*, 47: 261–78.

National AIDS Trust (2008). Over 90 percent of the British public do not fully understand how HIV is transmitted. Press release. Available: www.nat.org.uk/News-and-Media/Press-Releases/2008/January/over-90-percent-of-the-british-public.aspx [accessed 26 November 2009].

National Cancer Institute, Breast Cancer Screening Consortium (1990). Screening mammography: a missed clinical opportunity. *Journal of the American Medical Association*, 264: 54–8.

National Center for Health Statistics (1994). *Healthy People 2000 Review, 1993*. Hyattsville, MD: Public Health Service.

National Health Service (2010). Free local NHS stop smoking services. Available: http://smokefree.nhs.uk/what-suits-me/local-nhs-services/ [accessed 5 January 2010].

National Institutes of Health (1997). Acupuncture. *NIH Consensus Statement*, vol. 15 (5). Rockville, MD: US Department of HHS Public Health Services.

NCCAM (2013). Complementary, alternative, or integrative health: what's in a name? Available: http://nccam.nih.gov/health/whatiscam [accessed 7 May 2014].

NCHStats (2014). Adults' daily protein intake much more than recommended. Available: http://nchstats.com/2010/03/03/adults'-daily-protein-intake-much-more-than-recommended/.

Neuberg, S.L., Smith, D.M. and Asher, T. (2000). Why people stigmatize: toward a biocultural framework. In T.F. Heatherton, R.E. Kleck, M.R. Hebl and J.G. Hull (eds.), *The Social Psychology of Stigma*. New York: Guilford. pp. 31–61.

New, S.J. and Senior, M. (1991). 'I dont believe in needles': qualitative aspects of study into the update of infant immunisation in two English health authorities. *Social Science & Medicine*, 33: 509–18.

Newell, S.A., Sanson-Fisher, R.W. and Savolainen, N.J. (2002). Systematic review of psychological therapies for cancer patients: overview and recommendations for future research. *Journal of the National Cancer Institute*, 94: 558–84.

Ng, D.M. and Jeffery, R.W. (2003). Relationships between perceived stress and health behaviours in a sample of working adults. *Health Psychology*, 22: 638–42.

Ng, E.C.W. (2010). Community-building: a strategy to address inequality of health in Australia. *Journal of Health Psychology*, 15 (7): 1020–9.

Ng, S.C., Lam, Y.T., Tsoi, K.K.F., Chan, F.K.L., Sung, J.J.Y. and Wu, J.C.Y. (2013). Systematic review: the efficacy of herbal therapy in inflammatory bowel disease. *Alimentary Pharmacology & Therapeutics*, 38: 854–63.

Nguyen, V.K. (2004). Antiretroviral globalization, biopolitics, and therapeutic citizenship. In A. Ong and S. Collier (eds.), *Global Assemblages: Technology, Politics, and Ethics as Anthropological Problems*. London: Blackwell. pp. 124–44.

Nicholls, S. (2009). Beyond expressive writing: evolving models of developmental creative writing. *Journal of Health Psychology*, 14: 171–80.

Nicholson, A., Kuper, H. and Hemingway, H. (2006). Depression as an aetiologic and prognostic factor in coronary heart disease: a meta-analysis of 6362 events among 146 538 participants in 54 observational studies. *European Heart Journal*, 27: 2763–74.

Nickerson, R.S. (1998). Confirmation bias: a ubiquitous phenomenon in many guises. *Review of General Psychology*, 2 (2): 175.

Nielsen, G., Gronfeldt, V., Toftegaard-Stockel, J. and Andersen, L.B. (2012). Predisposed to participate? The influence of family socio-economic background on children's sports participation and daily amount of physical activity. *Sport in Society*, 15: 1–27.

Nielsen, N.R., Zhang, Z.-F., Kristensen, T.S., Netterstrøm, B., Schnohr, P. and Grønbæk, M. (2005). Self-reported stress and risk of breast cancer: prospective cohort study. *British Medical Journal*, 331: 548–53.

Nimnuan, C., Rabe-Hesketh, S. Wesseley, S. and Hotopf, M. (2001). How many functional somatic syndromes? *Journal of Psychosomatic Research*, 51: 549–57.

Nissen, N., Schunder-Tatzber, S., Weidenhammer, W. and Johannessen, H. (2012). What attitudes and needs do citizens in Europe have in relation to complementary and alternative medicine? *Forschende Komplementarmedizin*, 19: 9.

Noar, S.M., Black, H.G. and Pierce, L.B. (2009). Efficacy of computer technology-based HIV prevention interventions: a meta-analysis. *AIDS*, 23: 107–15.

Nolas, S. (2014). Towards a new theory of practice for community health psychology. *Journal of Health Psychology*, 19 (1): 126–36. doi:10.1177/1359105313500252.

Norman, P. and Brain, K. (2005). An application of an extended health belief model to the prediction of breast self-examination among women with a family history of breast cancer. *British Journal of Health Psychology*, 10: 1–16.

Notcutt, W. (2004). Cannabis in the treatment of chronic pain. In G.W. Guy (eds.), *The Medicinal Uses of Cannabis and Cannabinoids*. pp. 271–99.

Nutbeam, D. (1998). Health promotion glossary. *Health Promotion International*, 13: 349–64.

Nutbeam, D. (1999). Health promotion effectiveness: the questions to be answered. In International Union for Health Promotion and Education, *The Evidence of Health Promotion Effectiveness: Shaping Public Health in a New Europe*. Brussels–Luxembourg: ECSC-EC-EAEC.

Nutbeam, D. (2000). Health literacy as a public health goal: a challenge for contemporary health education and communication strategies into the 21st century. *Health Promotion International*, 15: 259–67.

Nykjaer, C., Alwan, N.A., Greenwood, D.C., Simpson, N.A.B., Hay, A.W.M., White, K.L.M. and Cade, J.E. (2014). Maternal alcohol intake prior to and during pregnancy and risk of adverse birth outcomes: evidence from a British cohort. *Journal of Epidemiology and Community Health*, 68: 542–9.

O'Brien Cousins, (2000). 'My heart couldn't take it': older women's beliefs about exercise benefits and risks. *Journals of Gerontology Series B: Psychological Sciences and Social Sciences*, 55: 283–94.

O'Keefe Jr, J.H. and Cordain, L. (2004). Cardiovascular disease resulting from a diet and lifestyle at odds with our Paleolithic genome: how to become a 21st-century hunter-gatherer. *Mayo Clinic Proceedings*, 79 (1): 101–8.

O'Leary, A. (1990). Stress, emotion and human immune function. *Psychological Bulletin*, 108: 363–82.

O'Leary, A. and Helgeson, V.S. (1997). Psychosocial factors and women's health: integrating mind, heart, and body. In S.J. Gallant, G.P. Keita and R. Royal-Schaler (eds.), *Health Care for Women: Psychological, Social and Behavioral Influences*. Washington, DC: American Psychological Association. pp. 25–40.

O'Malley, D.A., and Latimer-Cheung, A.E. (2013). Gaining perspective: the effects of message frame on viewer attention to and recall of osteoporosis prevention print advertisements. *Journal of Health Psychology*, 18 (11): 1400–10.

Oakley, A. (2001). Evaluating health promotion: methodological diversity. In S. Oliver and G. Peersman (eds.), *Using Research for Effective Health Promotion.* Buckingham: Open University Press. pp. 16–31.

Ochieng, B.M.N. (2013). Black families' perceptions of barriers to the practice of a healthy lifestyle: a qualitative study in the UK. *Critical Public Health*, 23: 6–16.

Oeppen, J. and Vaupel, J.W. (2002). Demography: broken limits to life expectancy. *Science*, 296: 1029–31.

Office for National Statistics (2009). Teen pregnancy rates go back up. Available: http://news.bbc.co.uk/1/hi/uk/7911684.stm [accessed 26 November 2009].

Office of National Statistics (2004). *The UK Time Use Survey.* London: ONS.

Ogden, J. (2003). Some problems with social cognition models: a pragmatic and conceptual analysis. *Health Psychology*, 22: 424–8.

Ogden, J., Bandara, I., Cohen, H. et al. (2001). General practitioners' and patients' models of obesity: whose problem is it? *Patient Education and Counseling*, 44: 227–33.

Ogden, J. and Flanagan, Z. (2008). Beliefs about the causes and solutions to obesity: a comparison of GPs and lay people. *Patient Education and Counseling*, 71: 72–8.

Ohenjo, N., Willis, R., Jackson, D., Nettleton, C., Good, K. and Mugarura, B. (2006). Health of Indigenous people in Africa. *The Lancet*, 367: 1937–76.

Oken, B.S., Storzbach, D.M. and Kaye, J.A. (1998). The efficacy of ginkgo biloba on cognitive function in Alzheimer disease. *Archives of Neurology*, 55: 1409–15.

Omran, A.R (1971). The epidemiological transition: a theory of the epidemiology of population change, *The Milbank Quarterly*, 83: 731–57.

Onyike, C.U., Crum, R.M., Lee, H.B., Lyketsos, C.G. and Eaton, W.W. (2003). Is obesity associated with major depression? Results from the Third National Health and Nutrition Examination Survey. *American Journal of Epidemiology*, 158: 1139–47.

Oregon Public Health Division (2014). Available: www.ocregister.com/articles/physician-524739-death-oregon.html.

Ormandy, P. (2011). Defining information need in health – assimilating complex theories derived from information science. *Health Expectations*, 14 (1): 92–104.

Oster, E. (2013). *Expecting Better.* London: Orion.

Osterberg, L. and Blaschke, T. (2005). Adherence to medication. *New England Journal of Medicine*, 353: 487–97.

Oulton, N. (2012). The wealth and poverty of nations: true PPPs for 141 countries. Centre for Economic Performance Discussion Paper No. 1080.

Owen, C.G., Nightingale, C.M., Rudnicka, A.R., Ekelund, U., McMinn, A.M., van Sluijs, E.M.F. et al. (2010). Family dog ownership and levels of physical activity in childhood: findings from the child heart and health study in England. *American Journal of Public Health*, 100: 1669–71.

Oygard, L. and Anderssen, N. (1998). Social influences and leisure-time physical activity levels in young people: a twelve-year follow-up study. *Journal of Health Psychology*, 3: 59–69.

Ozer, E.J., Best, S.R., Lipsey, T.L. and Weiss, D.S. (2003). Predictors of posttraumatic stress disorder and symptoms in adults: a meta-analysis. *Psychological Bulletin*, 129: 52–73.

Paasche-Orlow, M.K., Schillinger, D., Greene, S.M. and Wagner, E.H. (2006). How health care systems can begin to address the challenge of limited literacy. *Journal of General Internal Medicine*, 21: 884–7.

Pace, C.S., Velotti, P. and Zavattini, G.C. (2012). Representations of health and illness by Eastern European, South American and Italian care workers: a qualitative study. *Journal of Health Psychology*, 17: 490–9.

Pachankis, J.E., Westmaas, J.L. and Dougherty, L.R. (2011). The influence of sexual orientation and masculinity on young men's tobacco smoking. *Journal of Consulting & Clinical Psychology*, 79: 142–52.

Padez, C., Mourão, I., Moreira, P. and Rosado, V. (2009). Long sleep duration and childhood overweight/obesity and body fat. *American Journal of Human Biology*, 21: 371–6.

Paechter, C. (2003). Power, bodies and identity: how different forms of physical education construct varying masculinities and femininities in secondary schools. *Sex Education*, 3: 47–59.

Paljärvi, T., Mäkelä, P. and Poikolainen, K. (2005). Pattern of drinking and fatal injury: a population-based follow-up study of Finnish men. *Addiction*, 100: 1851–9.

Palmer, C.K., Thomas, M.C., von Wagner, C. and Raine, R. (2014). Reasons for non-uptake and subsequent participation in the NHS Bowel Cancer Screening Programme: a qualitative study. *British Journal of Cancer*, 110: 1705–11.

Palmer, R.H.C., McGeary, J.E., Francazio, S., Raphael, B.J., Lander, A.D., Heath, A.C. and Knopik, V.S. (2012). The genetics of alcohol dependence: advancing towards systems-based approaches. *Drug and Alcohol Dependence*, 125: 179–91.

Park, C.L., Folkman, S. and Bostrom, A. (2001). Appraisals of controllability and coping in caregivers and HIV men: testing the goodness-of-fit hypothesis. *Journal of Consulting & Clinical Psychology*, 69: 481–8.

Parker, I. (1997). Discursive psychology. In D. Fox and I. Prilleltensky (eds.), *Critical Psychology: An Introduction*. London: Sage.

Parkes, C.M. (1965). Bereavement and mental illness. 2. A classification of bereavement reactions. *British Journal of Medical Psychology*, 38: 13–26.

Parsons, J.T., Rosof, E. and Mustanski, N. (2007). Patient-related factors predicting HIV medication adherence among men and women with alcohol problems. *Journal of Health Psychology*, 12: 357–70.

Patterson, L., Kee, F., Hughes, C. and O'Reilly, D. (2014). The relationship between BMI and the prescription of anti-obesity medication according to social factors: a population cross-sectional study. *BMC Public Health*, 14: 87.

Patterson, T.L., Semple, S.J., Fraga, M., Bucardo, J., Davila-Fraga, W. and Strathdee, S.A. (2005). An HIV-prevention intervention for sex workers in Tijuana, Mexico: a pilot study. *Hispanic Journal of Behavioral Sciences*, 27: 82–100.

Paul, E.L., McManus, B. and Hayes, A. (2000). 'Hookups': characteristics and correlates of college students' spontaneous and anonymous sexual experiences. *Journal of Sex Research*, 37: 76–88.

Paulson, S. (2005). The social benefits of belonging to a dance exercise group for older people. *Generations Review*, 15: 37–41.

Paulson, S. (2011). The use of ethnography and narrative interviews in a study of 'cultures of dance'. *Journal of Health Psychology*, 16: 148–57.

Pavalko, E.K. and Caputo, J. (2013). Social inequality and health across the life course. *American Behavioral Scientist*, 57 (8): 1040–56.

Pavlov, I.P. (1927). *Conditioned Reflexes*. Oxford: Oxford University Press.

Paxton, S.J., Neumark-Sztainer, D., Hannan, P.J. and Eisenberg, M.E. (2006). Body dissatisfaction prospectively predicts depressive mood and low self-esteem in adolescent girls and boys. *Journal of Clinical Child and Adolescent Psychology*, 35: 539–49.

Pearce, P.F. (2009). Physical activity: not just for quantitative researchers. *Qualitative Health Research*, 19: 879–80.

Pearl, R.L., Puhl, R.M. and Dovidio, J.F. (2014). Differential effects of weight bias experiences and internalization on exercise among women with overweight and obesity. *Journal of Health Psychology*, 19: in press.

Pearlman, M.D. (2014). Separating the baby from the bath water: breast self-awareness and breast self-examination. *Obstetrics & Gynecology*, 123: 731–3.

Peckham, C., Bedford, H., Senturia, Y. and Ades, A. (1989). *National Immunization Study: Factors Influencing Immunization Uptake in Childhood*. Horsham: Action Research for the Crippled Child.

Peckham, E.J., Nelson, E.A., Greenhalgh, J., Cooper, K., Roberts, E.R. and Agrawal, A. (2013). Homeopathy for treatment of irritable bowel syndrome. *Cochrane Database of Systematic Reviews*, 11 (CD009710).

Pellowski, J.A., Kalichman, S.C., Matthews, K.A. and Adler, N. (2013). A pandemic of the poor: social disadvantage and the US HIV epidemic. *American Psychologist*, 68: 197–209.

Pelosi, A.J. and Appleby, L. (1992). Psychological influences on cancer and ischaemic heart disease. *British Medical Journal*, 304: 1295–8.

Pelosi, A.J. and Appleby, L. (1993). Personality and fatal diseases. *British Medical Journal*, 306: 1666–7.

Pennebaker, J.W. (1995). *Emotion, Disclosure, and Health*. Washington, DC: American Psychological Association.

Pennebaker, J.W. and Beall, S.K. (1986). Confronting a traumatic event: toward an understanding of inhibition and disease. *Journal of Abnormal Psychology*, 95: 274–81.

Penninx, B.W., Guralnik, J.M., Pahor, M., Ferrucci, L., Cerhan, J.R., Wallace, R.B. and Havlik, R.J. (1998). Chronically depressed mood and cancer risk in older persons. *Journal of the National Cancer Institute*, 90: 1888–93.

Pe-Pua, R. (2006). From decolonizing psychology to the development of a cross-indigenous perspective in methodology: the Philippine experience. In U. Kim, K.S. Yang and K.K. Hwang (eds.), *Indigenous and Cultural Psychology: Understanding People in Context*. New York: Springer. pp. 109–37.

Perri, M.G. and Foreyt, J.P. (2004). Preventing weight regain after weight loss. In G.A. Bray and C. Bouchard (eds.), *Handbook of Obesity* (2nd edn.). New York: Marcel Dekker, Inc.

Peter, J. and Valkenburg, P.M. (2014). Does exposure to sexually explicit Internet material increase body dissatisfaction? A longitudinal study. *Computers in Human Behavior*, 36: 297–307.

Peters, G.Y., Ruiter, R.A.C. and Kok, G. (2014). Threatening communication: a qualitative study of fear appeal effectiveness beliefs among intervention developers, policymakers, politicians, scientists, and advertising professionals. *International Journal of Psychology*, 49 (2): 71–9.

Petrie, K.J., Cameron, L.D., Ellis, C.J., Buick, D. and Weinman, J. (2002). Changing illness perceptions after myocardial infarction: an early intervention randomized controlled trial. *Psychosomatic Medicine*, 64: 580–6.

Petrie, K.J., Weinman, J., Sharpe, N. and Buckley, J. (1996). Role of patients' view of their illness in predicting return to work and functioning after myocardial infarction: longitudinal study. *British Medical Journal*, 312: 1191–4.

Pettersen, B.J., Anousheh, R., Fan, J. et al. (2012).Vegetarian diets and blood pressure among white subjects: results from the Adventist Health Study-2 (AHS-2). *Public Health Nutrition*, 15: 1909–16.

Petticrew, M., Bell, R. and Hunter, D. (2002). Influence of psychological coping on survival and recurrence in people with cancer: systematic review. *British Medical Journal*, 325: 1066–9.

Petticrew, M., Fraser, J.M. and Regan, M.F. (1999). Adverse life events and risk of breast cancer: a meta-analysis, *British Journal of Health Psychology*, 4: 1–17.

Petticrew, M.P., Lee, K. and McKee, M. (2012). Type A behavior pattern and coronary heart disease: Philip Morris's 'Crown Jewel'. *American Journal of Public Health*, 102: 2018–25.

Pfeiffer, D.A. (2013). *Eating Fossil Fuels: Oil, Food and the Coming Crisis in Agriculture*. New Society Publishers.

Pierce, J.P. and Gilpin, E.A. (2002). Impact of over-the-counter sales on effectiveness of pharmaceutical aids for smoking cessation. *Journal of the American Medical Association*, 288: 1260–4.

Pincus, T., Griffith, J., Isenberg, D. and Pearce, S. (1997). The Well-Being Questionnaire: testing the structure in groups with rheumatoid arthritis. *British Journal of Health Psychology*, 2: 167–74.

Pinhas, L., Toner, B.B., Ali, A., Garfinkel, G.E. and Stuckless, N. (1998). The effects of the ideal of female beauty on mood and body satisfaction. *International Journal of Eating Disorders*, 25: 223–6.

Pinto, R.Z., Ferreira, M.L., Oliveira, V.C., Franco, M.R., Adams, R., Maher, C.G. and Ferreira, P.H. (2012). Patient-centred communication is associated with positive therapeutic alliance: a systematic review. *Journal of Physiotherapy*, 58 (2): 77–87.

Pittler, M.H. and Ernst, E. (2000). Ginkgo biloba extract for the treatment of intermittent claudication: a meta-analysis of randomized trials. *American Journal of Medicine*, 108: 276–81.

Pittler, M.H. and Ernst, E. (2003). Kava extract versus placebo for treating anxiety. *Cochrane Database of Systematic Reviews*, 1 (CD003383).

Plant, M. (2004). Editorial: The alcohol harm reduction strategy for England. *British Medical Journal*, 328: 905–6.

Plant, M. and Plant, M. (2006). *Binge Britain: Alcohol and the National Response.* Oxford: Oxford University Press.

Pliner, P. and Hobden, K. (1992). Development of a scale to measure the trait of food neophobia in humans. *Appetite*, 19 (2): 105–20.

Poag-DuCharme, K.A. and Brawley, L.R. (1993). Self-efficacy theory: use in the prediction of exercise behavior in the community setting. *Journal of Applied Sport Psychology*, 5: 178–94.

Polito, J.R. (2008). Smoking cessation trials. *Canadian Medical Association Journal*, 179: 10.

Polivy, J., Herman, C.P. and Warsh, S. (1978). Internal and external components of emotionality in restrained and unrestrained eaters. *Journal of Abnormal Psychology*, 87: 497–504.

Pollock, K. (1988). On the nature of social stress: production of a modern mythology. *Social Science & Medicine*, 26: 381–92.

Porter, R. (1997). *The Greatest Benefit to Mankind: A Medical History of Humanity*. New York: Norton.

Porto, A. (2007). Social representations of tuberculosis: stigma and prejudice. *Revista de Saude Publica*, 41 (S1): 1–7.

Posadzki, P., Alotaibi, A. and Ernst, E. (2012). Adverse effects of homeopathy: a systematic review of published case reports and case series. *International Journal of Clinical Practice*, 66: 1178–88.

Posadzki, P., Watson, L.K., Alotaibi, A. and Ernst, E. (2013a). Prevalence of use of complementary and alternative medicine (CAM) by patients/consumers in the UK: systematic review of surveys. *Clinical Medicine*, 13: 126–31.

Posadzki, P., Watson, L.K., Alotaibi, A. and Ernst, E. (2013b). Prevalence of herbal medicine use by UK patients/consumers: a systematic review of surveys. *Focus on Alternative & Complementary Therapies*, 18: 19–26.

Posluszny, D., Spencer, S. and Baum, A. (2007). Post-traumatic stress disorder. In S. Ayers, A. Baum, C. McManus, S. Newman, K. Wallston, J. Weinman and R.West (eds.), *Cambridge Handbook of Psychology, Health and Medicine* (2nd edn). Cambridge: Cambridge University Press. pp. 814–20.

Potter, J. and Wetherell, M. (1987). *Discourse and Social Psychology*. London: Sage.

Potter, J. and Wetherell, M. (1995). Discourse analysis. In J. Smith, R. Harré, and R. van Langenhove (Eds), *Rethinking methods in psychology*. London: Sage

Potvin, L., Camirand, J. and Beland, F. (1995). Patterns of health services utilization and mammography use among women aged 50–59 in the Québec Medicare system. *Medical Care*, 33: 515–30.

Pound, P., Britten, N., Morgan, M., Yardley, L., Pope, C., Daker-White, G. and Campbell, R. (2005). Resisting medicines: a synthesis of qualitative studies of medicine taking. *Social Science and Medicine*, 61: 133–55.

Pourhabib, S., Chessex, C., Murray, J. and Grace, S.L. (2014). Elements of patient–health-care provider communication related to cardiovascular rehabilitation referral. *Journal of Health Psychology*, doi:10.1177/1359105314529319.

Powers, P. (2003). Empowerment as treatment and the role of health professionals. *Advances in Nursing Science*, 26: 227–37.

Prabhu, A., Obi, K.O. and Rubenstein, J.H. (2014). The synergistic effects of alcohol and tobacco consumption on the risk of esophageal squamous cell carcinoma: a meta-analysis. *American Journal of Gastroenterology*, in press.

Prescott-Clarke, P. and Primatesta, P. (eds.) (1998). *Health Survey for England 95–97*. London: The Stationery Office.

Prestwich, A., Sniehotta, F.F., Whittington, C., Dombrowski, S.U., Rogers, L. and Michie, S. (2014). Does theory influence the effectiveness of health behaviour interventions? Meta analysis. *Health Psychology*, 33: 465–74.

Price, A., Goodwin, L., Reyner, L., Hansford, P., Sykes, N., Monrow, B. et al. (2012). Illness perceptions, adjustment to illness, and depression in a palliative care population. *Journal of Pain & Symptom Management*, 43: 819–32.

Price, A., McCormack, R., Wiseman, T. and Hotopf, M. (2014). Concepts of mental capacity for patients requesting assisted suicide: a qualitative analysis of expert evidence presented to the commission on assisted dying. *BMC Medical Ethics*, 15: 32.

Priest, J. (2007) The healing balm effect: using a walking group to feel better. *Journal of Health Psychology*, 12: 36–52.

Priest, N., Paradies, Y., Trenerry, B., Truong, M., Karlsen, S. and Kelly, Y. (2013). A systematic review of studies examining the relationship between reported racism and health and wellbeing for children and young people. *Social Science & Medicine*, 95: 115–27.

Pringle, P. (1996). Eysenck took £800,000 tobacco funds. *The Independent*, 31 October. Available: www.independent.co.uk/news/eysenck-took-pounds-800000-tobacco-funds-1361007.html.

Prins, J.T., van der Heijden, F.M., Hoekstra-Weebers, J.E., Bakker, A.B., van de Wiel, H.B., Jacobs, B. and Gazendam-Donofrio, S.M. (2009). Burnout, engagement and resident physicians' self-reported errors. *Psychology, Health and Medicine*, 14: 654–66.

Prochaska, J.O. and DiClemente, C.C. (1983). Stages and processes of self-change of smoking: toward an integrative model of change. *Journal of Consulting & Clinical Psychol*ogy, 51: 390–5.

Prochaska, J.O. and DiClemente, C.C. (1992). *The Transtheoretical Approach: Crossing the Traditional Boundaries of Therapy*. Homewood, IL: Dow Jones/Irwin.

Prohaska, A. and Gailey, J.A. (2010). Achieving masculinity through sexual predation: the case of hogging. *Journal of Gender Studies*, 19: 13–25.

Project MATCH Research Group (1997). Matching alcoholism treatments to client heterogeneity: project MATCH post-treatment drinking outcomes. *Journal of Studies on Alcohol*, 58: 7–29.

Prospective Studies Collaboration (2009). Body-mass index and cause-specific mortality in 900 000 adults: collaborative analyses of 57 prospective studies. *The Lancet*, 373: 1083–96.

Protheroe, J. and Rowlands, G. (2013). Matching clinical information with levels of patient health literacy. *Nursing Management – UK*, 20 (3): 20–21.

Protheroe, J., Brooks, H., Chew-Graham, C., Gardner, C. and Rogers, A. (2013). 'Permission to participate?' A qualitative study of participation in patients from differing socio-economic backgrounds. *Journal of Health Psychology*, 18 (8): 1046–55.

Puhl, R.M. and Heuer, C.A. (2009). The stigma of obesity: a review and update. *Obesity*, 17: 941–64.

Putnam, R. (2000). *Bowling Alone: The Collapse and Revival of American Community.* New York: Simon & Schuster.

Putnam, R.D., Leonarchi, R. and Nanetti, R.Y. (1993). *Making Democracy Work: Civic Traditions in Modern Italy*. Princeton, NJ: Princeton University Press.

Qureshi, S.U., Pyne, J.M., Magruder, K.M., Schulz, P.E. and Kunik, M.E. (2009). The link between post-traumatic stress disorder and physical comorbidities: a systematic review. *Psychiatric Quarterly*, 80: 87–97.

Radley, A. and Billig, M. (1996). Accounts of health and illness: dilemmas and representations. *Sociology of Health & Illness*, 18: 220–40.

Radtke, H.R. and Van Mens-Verhulst, J. (2001). Being a mother and living with asthma: an exploratory analysis of discourse. *Journal of Health Psychology*, 6: 379–91.

Ragland, D.R. and Brand, R.J. (1988). Type A behaviour and mortality from coronary heart disease. *New England Journal of Medicine*, 318: 65–9.

Raistrick, D. (2005). The United Kingdom: alcohol today. *Addiction*, 100: 1212–14.

Rajguru, P., Kolber, M.J., Garcia, A.N., Smith, M.T., Patel, C.K. and Hanney, W.J. (2014). Use of mindfulness meditation in the management of chronic pain: a systematic review of randomized controlled trials. *American Journal of Lifestyle Medicine*, in press.

Ramirez, A., Addington-Hall, J. and Richards M. (1998). ABC of palliative care: the carers. *British Medical Journal*, 316: 208–11.

Randolph, M.E., Pinkerton, S.D., Somlai, A.M., Kelly, J.A., McAuliffe, T.L., Gibson, R.H. and Hackl, K. (2009). Seriously mentally ill women's safer sex behaviors and the theory of reasoned action. *Health Education & Behavior*, 36: 948–58.

Randrianasolo, B., Swezey, T., Van Damme, K., Khan, M.R., Ravelomanana, N., Rabenja, N.L. et al. (2008). Barriers to the use of modern contraceptives and implications for woman-controlled prevention of sexually transmitted infections in Madagascar. *Journal of Biosocial Science*, 40: 879–93.

Ranjbar, V., McKinlay, A. and McVittie, C. (2014). The micro and the macro: how discourse of control maintains HIV-related stigma. *Journal of Health Psychology*, in press.

Ranney, L., Melvin, C., Lux, L., McClain, E. and Lohr, K.N. (2006). Systematic review: smoking cessation intervention strategies for adults and adults in special populations. *Annals of Internal Medicine*, 145: 845–56.

Ranzijn, R. (2010). Active ageing – another way to oppress marginalized and disadvantaged elders? Aboriginal elders as a case study. *Journal of Health Psychology*, 15: 716–23.

Rappaport, J. (1987). Terms of empowerment/examples of prevention: towards a theory for community psychology. *American Journal of Counseling Psychology*, 15: 121–49.

Rathert, C., Wyrwich, M.D. and Boren, S.A. (2013). Patient-centered care and outcomes: a systematic review of the literature. *Medical Care Research & Review*, 70 (4): 351–79. doi:10.1177/1077558712465774

Rawls, J. (1999). *A Theory of Justice*. Cambridge, MA: Belknap Press.

Reason, J. (2000). Human error: models and management. *BMJ*, 320: 768–70.

Reddy, C.V. (1989). Parents' beliefs about vaccination. *British Medical Journal*, 299: 739.

Reed, D.M., LaCroix, A.Z., Karasek, R.A., Miller, D. and MacLean, C.A. (1989). Occupational strain and the incidence of coronary heart disease. *American Journal of Epidemiology*, 129: 495–502.

Rees, K., Bennett, P., West, R., Davey, S.G. and Ebrahim, S. (2004). Psychological interventions for coronary heart disease. *Cochrane Database of Systematic Reviews*, 2 (CD002902).

Rehm, J., Mathers, C., Popova, S., Thavorncharoensap, M., Teerawattananon, Y. and Patra J. (2009). Global burden of disease and injury and economic cost attributable to alcohol use and alcohol-use disorders. *The Lancet*, 373: 2223–33.

Reiss, I.L. (1991). Sexual pluralism: ending America's sexual crisis. *SIECUS Report*, February–March.

Renzaho, A.M.N., Romios, P., Crock, C. and Sønderlund, A.L. (2013). The effectiveness of cultural competence programs in ethnic minority patient centered health care – a systematic review of the literature. *International Journal for Quality in Health Care*, 25: 261–9.

Rhodes, R.E., Courneya, K.S., Blanchard, C.M. and Plotnikoff, R.C. (2007). Prediction of leisure-time walking: an integration of social cognitive, perceived environmental, and personality factors. *International Journal of Behavioral Nutrition and Physical Activity*, 4: 51.

Richardson, S., Shaffer, J.A., Falzon, L., Krupka, D., Davidson, K.W. and Edmondson, D. (2012). Meta-analysis of perceived stress and its association with incident coronary heart disease. *American Journal of Cardiology*, 110: 1711–16.

Ridd, M., Shaw, A., Lewis, G. and Salisbury, C. (2009). The patient–doctor relationship: a synthesis of the qualitative literature on patients' perspectives. *British Journal of General Practice*, 59 (561): e116–33.

Rief, W., Nanke, A., Emmerich, J., Bender, A. and Zech, T. (2004). Causal illness attributions in somatoform disorders: associations with comorbidity and illness behavior. *Journal of Psychosomatic Research*, 57: 367–71.

Riesen, W.F., Darioli, R. and Noll, G. (2004). Lipid-lowering therapy: strategies for improving compliance. *Current Medical Research & Opinion*, 20: 165–73.

Riley, B.D., Culver, J.O., Skrzynia, C. et al. (2012). Essential elements of genetic cancer risk assessment, counseling, and testing: updated recommendations of the National Society of Genetic Counselors. *Journal of Genetic Counseling*, 21 (2): 151–61.

Riley, K.E. and Kalichman, S. (2014). Mindfulness-based stress reduction for people living with HIV/AIDS: preliminary review of intervention trial methodologies and findings. *Health Psychology Review*, (preprint): 1–20.

Rimal, R.N. (2001). Longitudinal influences of knowledge and self-efficacy on exercise behavior: tests of a mutual reinforcement model. *Journal of Health Psychology*, 6: 31–46.

Rimer, B.K. (1990). Perspectives on intrapersonal theories in health education and health behavior. In K. Glanz, F.M. Lewis and B.K. Rimer (eds.), *Health Behavior and Health Education.* San Francisco, CA: Jossey-Bass.

Rimer, B.K., Keintz, M.K., Kessler, H.B., Engstrom, P.F. and Rosan, J.R. (1989). Why women resist screening mammography: Patient-related barriers. *Radiology*, 74: 2034–41.

Riska, E. (2000). The rise and fall of Type A man. *Social Science & Medicine*, 51: 1665–74.

Rizzo, N.S., Sabate, J., Jaceldo-Siegl, K. et al. (2011). Vegetarian dietary patterns are associated with a lower risk of the metabolic syndrome. *Diabetes Care*, 34: 1225–7.

Robinson, J.I. and Rogers, M.A. (1994). Adherence to exercise programmes: recommendations. *Sports Medicine*, 17: 39–52.

Robinson, M., Oddy, W., McLean, N., Jacoby, P., Pennell, C.E., de Klerk, N. et al. (2010). Low–moderate prenatal alcohol exposure and risk to child behavioural development: a prospective cohort study. *British Journal of Obstetrics and Gynaecology*, 117: 1139–52.

Roche, A.M. and Freeman, T. (2004). Brief interventions: good in theory but weak in practice. *Drug & Alcohol Review*, 23: 11–18.

Rochelle, T.L. and Marks, D.F. (2010). Medical pluralism of the Chinese in London: an exploratory study. *British Journal of Health Psychology*, 15: 715–28.

Rodgers, R.F., Salès, P. and Chabrol, H. (2010). Psychological functioning, media pressure and body dissatisfaction among college women. *Revue Européenne de Psychologie Appliquée/European Review of Applied Psychology*, 60: 89–95.

Rodin, J. (1973). Effects of distraction on performance of obese and normal subjects. *Journal of Comparative and Physiological Psychology*, 83: 68–75.

Roerecke, M. and Rehm, J. (2012). The cardioprotective association of average alcohol consumption and ischaemic heart disease: a systematic review and meta-analysis. *Addiction*, 107: 1246–60.

Rogers, R.W. (1975). A protection motivation theory of fear appeals and attitude change. *Journal of Psychology*, 91 (1): 93–114.

Rohrmann, S., Overvad, K., Bueno-de-Mesquita, H.B. et al. (2013). Meat consumption and mortality – results from the European Prospective Investigation into Cancer and Nutrition. *BMC Medicine*, 11: 63.

Ronksley, P.E., Brien, S.E., Turner, B.J., Mukamal, K.J. and Ghali, W.A. (2011). Association of alcohol consumption with selected cardiovascular disease outcomes: a systematic review and meta-analysis. *British Medical Journal*, 342: d671.

Room, R., Babor, T. and Rehm, J. (2005). Alcohol and public health. *The Lancet*, 365: 519–29.

Rootman, I. and Gordon-El-Bihbety, D. (2008). *A Vision for a Health Literate Canada*. Ottawa: CPHA.

Roseman, M., Milette, K., Bero, L.A., Coyne, J.C., Lexchin, J., Turner, E.H. and Thombs, B.D. (2011). Reporting of conflicts of interest in meta-analyses of trials of pharmacological treatments. *JAMA*, 305: 1008–17.

Rosenberg, M. (1965). *Society and the Adolescent Self-image*. Princeton, NJ: Princeton University Press.

Rosengren, A., Tibblin, G. and Wilhelmsen, L. (1991). Self-perceived psychological stress and incidence of coronary artery disease in middle-aged men. *American Journal of Cardiology*, 68: 1171–5.

Rosenstock, I.M., Strecher, V.J. and Becker, M.H. (1994). The health belief model and HIV risk behavior change. In *Preventing AIDS* (pp. 5–24). Springer US.

Rosenthal, L., Earnshaw, V.A., Carroll-Scott, A., Henderson, K.E., Peters, S.M., McCaslin, C. and Ickovics, J.R. (2013). Weight- and race-based bullying: health associations among urban adolescents. *Journal of Health Psychology*.

Rosenzweig, S. (1936). Some implicit common factors in diverse methods of psychotherapy: 'At last the Dodo said, "Everybody has won and all must have prizes."' *American Journal of Orthopsychiatry*, 6: 412–15.

Ross, (2000). Walking, exercising, and smoking: does neighborhood matter? *Social Science & Medicine*, 51: 265–74.

Rossow, I. and Norström, T. (2013) The use of epidemiology in alcohol research *Addiction*, 108: 20–5.

Rotblatt, M. and Ziment, I. (2002). *Evidence-based Herbal Medicine*. Philadelphia, PA: Hanley and Belfus.

Rothman, A.J. and Salovey, P. (1997). Shaping perceptions to motivate healthy behaviour: the role of message framing. *Psychological Bulletin*. 121: 3–19.

Rothman, A.J., Bartels, R.D., Wlachin, J. and Salovey, P. (2006). The strategic use of gain- and loss-framed messages to promote healthy behaviour: how theory can inform practice. *Journal of Communication*, 56: S202–20.

Rothman, K. and Keller, A. (1972). The effect of joint exposure to alcohol and tobacco on risk of cancer of the mouth and pharynx. *Journal of Chronic Diseases*, 25: 711–16.

Royal College of Physicians (1962). *Smoking and Health*. London: RCP.

Royal Pharmaceutical Society of Great Britain (1997). *From Compliance to Concordance: Toward Shared Goals in Medicine Taking*. London: RPS.

Rozin, E. (1982). The structure of cuisine. In L.M. Barker (ed.), *The Psychobiology of Human Food Selection*. Westport, CT: AVI. pp. 192–202.

Rozin, P. (1996). Sociocultural influences on human food selection. In E.D. Capaldi (ed.), *Why We Eat What We Eat: The Psychology of Eating*. Washington, DC: American Psychological Association. pp. 233–63.

Rudd, R.E. (2013). Needed action in health literacy. *Journal of Health Psychology*, 18 (8): 1004–10.

Ruiter, R.A.C., Kessels, L.T.E., Peters, G.Y. and Kok, G. (2014). Sixty years of fear appeal research: current state of the evidence. *International Journal of Psychology*, 49 (2): 63–70.

Ruiz, P. and Ruiz, P.P. (1983). Treatment compliance among Hispanics. *Journal of Operational Psychiatry*, 14: 112–114.

Rutledge, T., Reis, V.A., Linke, S.E., Greenberg, B.H. and Mills, P.J. (2006). Depression in heart failure – a meta-analytic review of prevalence, intervention effects, and associations with clinical outcomes. *Journal of the American College of Cardiology*, 48: 1527–37.

Ryan, R.M. and Deci, E.L. (2000). Self-determination theory and the facilitation of intrinsic motivation, social development, and well-being. *American Psychologist*, 55: 68–78.

Ryan, R.M. and Deci, E.L. (2001). On happiness and human potentials: a review of research on hedonic and eudaimonic well-being. *Annual Review of Psychology*, 52 (1): 141–66.

Ryerson, W.N. (2010). The effectiveness of entertainment mass media in changing behavior. Available: www.populationmedia.org/wp-content/uploads/2008/02/effectiveness-of-entertainment-education-112706.pdf [accessed 1 January 2010].

Rytwinski, N.K., Avena, J.S., Echiverri-Cohen, A.M., Zoellner, L.A. and Feeny, N.C. (2014). The relationship between posttraumatic stress disorder severity, depression severity and physical health. *Journal of Health Psychology*, 19: 509–20.

Sabido, M. (1981). Towards the social use of commercial television: Mexico's experience with the reinforcement of social values through TV soap operas. Paper presented at the annual conference of the International Institute of Communications (Strasbourg, France). Institute for Communications Research, AC (Mexico City, Mexico).

Sackett, D.L. and Snow, J.C. (1979) The magnitude of compliance and non-compliance. In R.B. Haynes, D.L. Sackett and D.W. Taylor (eds.), *Compliance in Health Care*. Baltimore, MD: Johns Hopkins University Press.

Sadeghi, S., Brooks, D. and Goldstein, R.S. (2013). Patients' and providers' perceptions of the impact of health literacy on communication in pulmonary rehabilitation. *Chronic Respiratory Disease*, 10 (2): 65–76.

Saffer, H. and Dave, D. (2002). Alcohol consumption and alcohol advertising bans. *Applied Economics*, 34: 1325–34.

Saha, S., Mundle, M., Ghosh, S., Koley, M. and Sheikh, I.H. (2013). Qualitative systematic review of homeopathic outcome studies in patients with HIV/AIDS. *International Journal of High Dilution Research*, 12: 2–12.

Sallis, J.F., Bauman, A. and Pratt, M. (1998). Environmental and policy interventions to promote physical activity. *American Journal of Preventive Medicine*, 15: 379–97.

Sallis, J.F., King, A.C., Sirard, J.R. and Albright, C.L. (2007). Perceived environmental predictors of physical activity over 6 months in adults: activity counseling trial. *Health Psychology*, 26: 701–9.

Salmon, J. and Timperio, A. (2011). Childhood obesity and human animal interaction. In P. McCardle, S. McCune, J.A. Griffin and V. Maholmes (eds.), *How Animals Affect Us: Examining the Influences of Human–Animal Interaction on Child Development and Human Health*. Washington, DC: American Psychological Association. pp. 183–92.

Salmon, J., Owen, N., Crawford, D., Bauman, A. and Sallis, J.F. (2003). Physical activity and sedentary behavior: a population-based study of barriers, enjoyment, and preference. *Health Psychology*, 22: 178–188.

Salmon, P. and Hall, G.M. (2003). Patient empowerment and control: a psychological discourse in the service of medicine. *Social Science & Medicine*, 57: 1969–80.

Sandberg, S., Paton, J., Ahola, S., McCann, D., McGuinness, D, Hillary, C.R. and Oja, H. (2000). The role of acute and chronic stress in asthma attacks in children. *The Lancet*, 356: 982–7.

Sandhu, H., Adams, A., Singleton, L., Clark-Carter, D. and Kidd, J. (2009). The impact of gender dyads on doctor–patient communication: a systematic review. *Patient Education and Counseling*, 76 (3): 348–55.

Santana, S., Lausen, B., Bujnowska-Fedak, M., Chronaki, C.E., Prokosch, H. and Wynn, R. (2011). Informed citizen and empowered citizen in health: results from a European survey. *BMC Family Practice*, 12 (1): 20–34.

Santesso, N., Akl, E.A., Bianchi, M., Mente, A., Mustafa, R., Heels-Ansdell, D. and Schunemann, H.J. (2012). Effects of higher- versus lower-protein diets on health outcomes: a systematic review and meta-analysis. *European Journal of Clinical Nutrition*, 66: 780–8.

Santos, F.L., Esteves, S.S., da Costa Pereira, A., Yancy Jr, W.S. and Nunes, J.P.L. (2012). Systematic review and meta-analysis of clinical trials of the effects of low carbohydrate diets on cardiovascular risk factors. *Obesity Reviews*, 13: 1048–66.

Sarbin, T. (ed.) (1986) *Narrative Psychology: The Storied Nature of Human Conduct*. New York: Praeger.

Savitz, D.A. (2012). Re: Moderate alcohol intake during pregnancy and risk of fetal death. *International Journal of Epidemiology*, 41: 1847.

Sayette, M.A. (2007). Alcohol abuse. In S. Ayers, A. Baum, C. McManus, S. Newman, K. Wallston, J. Weinman and R.West (eds.), *Cambridge Handbook of Psychology, Health and Medicine* (2nd edn). Cambridge: Cambridge University Press. pp. 534–7.

Schaal, B. and Orgeur, P. (1992). Olfaction in utero: can the rodent model be generalized? *Quarterly Journal of Experimental Psychology*, 44: 245–78.

Schachter, S. and Rodin, J. (1974). *Obese Humans and Rats*. Lawrence Erlbaum.

Scheib, H.A. and Lykes, M.B. (2013). African American and Latina community health workers engage PhotoPAR as a resource in a post-disaster context: Katrina at 5 years. *Journal of Health Psychology*, 18: 1069–84.

Schellong, K., Schulz, S., Harder, T. and Plagemann, A. (2012). Birth weight and long-term overweight risk: systematic review and a meta-analysis including 643,902 persons from 66 studies and 26 countries globally. *PLOS ONE*, 7 (10).

Schober, R. (1997). Complementary and conventional medicines working together. *Canadian Health Psychologist*, 5: 14–18.

Schroeder, D.H. and Costa, P.T., Jr. (1984). Influence of life event stress on physical illness: substantive effects or methodological flaws? *Journal of Personality & Social Psychology*, 46: 853–63.

Schulz, A., Gravlee, C.C., Williams, D., Israel, B.A., Mentz, G. and Rowe, Z. (2006). Discrimination, symptoms of depression, and self-rated health among African American women in Detroit: results from a longitudinal analysis. *American Journal of Public Health*, 96: 1265–70.

Schulz, P.J., and Nakamoto, K. (2013). Health literacy and patient empowerment in health communication: the importance of separating conjoined twins. *Patient Education and Counseling*, 90 (1): 4–11.

Schumacher, J.R., Hall, A.G., Davis, T.C., Arnold, C.L., Bennett, R.D., Wolf, M.S. and Carden, D.L. (2013). Potentially preventable use of emergency services: the role of low health literacy. *Medical Care*, 51 (8): 654–8.

Schuster, J. et al. (2006). Aids, alcohol and violence against women: strategies for reducing workplace health risks to Cambodian beer-selling women. Paper presented at the XVI International Aids Conference, Toronto, Canada, 13–18 August 2006.

Schütze, M., Boeing, H., Pischon, P., Rehm, J., et al. (2011). Alcohol attributable burden of incidence of cancer in eight European countries based on results from prospective cohort study. *British Medical Journal*, 342/bmj.d1584.

Schwartz, M., Savage, W., George, J. and Emohare, L. (1989). Women's knowledge and experience of cervical screening: a failure of health education and medical organization. *Community Medicine*, 11: 279–89.

Schwingshackl, L. and Hoffmann, G. (2013). Long-term effects of low-fat diets either low or high in protein on cardiovascular and metabolic risk factors: a systematic review and meta-analysis. *Nutrition Journal*, 12: 48–58.

Science Media Centre (2014). Expert reaction to early pregnancy alcohol intake and birth outcomes. Available at: http://www.sciencemediacentre.org/expert-reaction-to-early-pregnancy-alcohol-intake-and-birth-outcomes/.

Scott, S.D., Hartling, L., O'Leary, K.A., Archibald, M. and Klassen, T.P. (2012). Stories – a novel approach to transfer complex health information to parents: a qualitative study. *Arts & Health: International Journal for Research, Policy & Practice*, 4 (2): 162–73. doi:10.1080/17533015.2012.656203

Scottish Government (2008). *Equally Well*. Report of the Ministerial Task Force on Health Inequalities. Available: www.scotland.gov.uk/Resource/Doc/229649/0062206.pdf [accessed 6 August 2014].

Scott-Sheldon, L.A., Carey, M.P., Carey, K.B. et al. (2013). Does perceived life stress mediate the association between HIV status and alcohol use? Evidence from adults living in Cape Town, South Africa. *AIDS Care*, 25: 1026–32.

Scott-Sheldon, L.A.J., Carey, M.P., Vanable, P.A., Senn, T.E., Coury-Doniger, P. and Urban, M.A. (2010). Predicting condom use among STD clinic patients using the Information-Motivation-Behavioral Skills (IMB) model. *Journal of Health Psychology*, 15: 1093–102.

Scott-Sheldon, L.A.J., Kalichman, S.C., Carey, M.P. and Fielder, R.L. (2008). Stress management interventions for HIV+ adults: a meta-analysis of randomized controlled trials, 1989 to 2006. *Health Psychology*, 27: 129–39.

Seacat, J.D., Dougal, S.C. and Roy, D. (2014). A daily diary assessment of female weight stigmatization. *Journal of Health Psychology*, 19: in press.

Searle, A., Haase, A.M., Chalder, M., Fox, K.R., Taylor, A.H., Lewis, G. and Turner, K.M. (2014). Participants' experiences of facilitated physical activity for the management of depression in primary care. *Journal of Health Psychology*, in press.

Searle, A., Norman, P., Thompson, R. and Vedhara, K. (2007). A prospective examination of illness beliefs and coping in patients with type 2 diabetes. *British Journal of Health Psychology*, 12: 621–38.

Segar, J. (2012). Complementary and alternative medicine: exploring the gap between evidence and usage. *Health*, 16 (4): 366–81.

Segerstrom, S.C. and Miller, G.E. (2004). Psychological stress and the human immune system: a meta-analytic study of 30 years of enquiry. *Psychological Bulletin*, 130: 601–30.

Seitz, D.C.M., Besier, T. and Goldbeck, L. (2009). Psychosocial interventions for adolescent cancer patients: a systematic review of the literature. *Psycho-oncology*, 18: 683–90.

Seligman, M.E. and Csikszentmihalyi, M. (2000). *Positive Psychology: An Introduction.* Washington, DC: American Psychological Association.

Seligman, M.E., Steen, T.A., Park, N. and Peterson, C. (2005). Positive psychology progress: empirical validation of interventions. *American Psychologist*, 60 (5): 410.

Selye, H. (1976). *Stress in Health and Disease*. Reading, MA: Butterworth.

Sen, A. (1999). *Development as Freedom*. Oxford: Oxford University Press.

Serpell, J. (1991). Beneficial effects of pet ownership on some aspects of human health and behavior. *Journal for the Royal Society of Medicine*, 84: 717–20

Shah, N.R. and Braverman, E.R. (2012). Measuring adiposity in patients: the utility of body mass index (BMI), percent body fat, and leptin. *PLOS ONE*, 10: 1371.

Shahab, L. and McEwen, A. (2009). Online support for smoking cessation: a systematic review of the literature. *Addiction*, 104: 1792–804.

Shakespeare, T. (1998). Choices and rights: eugenics, genetics and disability equality. *Disability & Society*, 13: 665–81.

Shannon, C. (2004). Public health programmes will have to prove they are cost effective. *British Medical Journal*, 328: 1: 222.

Shannon, C.E. and Weaver, W. (1949). *The Mathematical Theory of Communication*. Urbana, IL: University of Illinois.

Shaper, A.G., Wannamethee, G. and Walker, M. (1988). Alcohol and mortality in British men: explaining the U-shaped curve. *The Lancet*, 2: 1267–83.

Sharp, D.J., Peter, T.J., Bartholomew, J. and Shaw, A. (1996). Breast screening: a randomised controlled trial in UK general practice of three generations designed to increase uptake. *Journal of Epidemiology and Community Health*, 50: 72–5.

Sharpe, K. and Earle, S. (2002). Feminism, abortion and disability: irreconcilable differences? *Disability & Society*, 17: 137–45.

Shaw, S. (1979). A critique of the concept of the alcohol dependence syndrome. *British Journal of Addiction*, 74: 339–48.

Shields, C.A. and Brawley, L.R. (2007). Limiting exercise options: depending on a proxy may inhibit exercise self-management. *Journal of Health Psychology*, 12: 663–71.

Shinya, K., Ebina, M., Yamada, S., Ono, M., Kasai, N. and Kawaoka, Y. (2006). Avian flu: influenza virus receptors in the human airway. *Nature*, 440: 435–6.

Shorter, E. (1992). *From Paralysis to Fatigue: A History of Psychosomatic Illness in the Modern Era*. New York: Free Press.

Showalter, E. (1997). *Hystories: Hysterical Epidemics and Modern Culture*. London: Picador.

Siegel, S. (1975). Conditioned insulin effects. *Journal of Comparative Physiology & Psychology*, 89: 189–99.

Sieverding, M., Matterne, U. and Ciccarello, L. (2010). What role do social norms play in the context of men's cancer screening intention and behavior? Application of an extended theory of planned behavior. *Health Psychology*, 29: 72–81.

Sijtsma, K. (2012). Psychological measurement between physics and statistics. *Theory & Psychology*, 22: 786–809.

Silva, S.A., Pires, A.P., Guerreiro, C. and Cardoso, A. (2013). Balancing motherhood and drug addiction: the transition to parenthood of addicted mothers. *Journal of Health Psychology*, 18: 359–67.

Simmel, G. (1903/1964). *Conflict and the Web of Group Affiliations.* New York: Free Press.

Simpson, S.J. and Raubenheimer, D. (2012). *The Nature of Nutrition: A Unifying Framework.* Princeton, NJ: Princeton University Press.

Singer, P. (1993). *Practical Ethics*. Cambridge: Cambridge University Press.

Singer, P.A., Martin, D.K. and Kelner, M. (1999). Quality end-of-life care: patients' perspectives. *Journal of the American Medical Association*, 281: 163–8.

Sinha, S., Curtis, K., Jayakody, A., Viner, R. and Roberts, H. (2007). 'People make assumptions about our communities': sexual health amongst teenagers from Black and Minority Ethnic backgrounds in East London. *Ethnicity & Health*, 12: 423–41

Skelton, A.M. (1997). Patient education for the millennium: beyond control and emancipation? *Patient Education and Counseling*, 31: 151–8.

Skinner, C.S., Champion, V.L., Gonin, R. and Hanna, M. (1997). Do perceived barriers and benefits vary by mammography stage? *Psychology, Health & Medicine*, 2: 65–75.

Skinner, J. (2007). Reflexology. In A.D. Cumming, K.R. Simpson and D. Brown (eds.), *Complementary and Alternative Medicine: An Illustrated Color Text*. Edinburgh: Elsevier. pp. 72–4.

Skogerbø, Å., Kesmodel, U., Wimberley, T., Støvring, H., Bertrand, J., Landrø, N. and Mortensen, E. (2012). The effects of low to moderate alcohol consumption and binge drinking in early pregnancy on executive function in 5-year-old children. *British Journal of Obstetrics and Gynaecology*, 119: 1201–10.

Slater, A. and Tiggemann, M. (2006). The contribution of physical activity and media UK during childhood and adolescence to adult women's body image. *Journal of Health Psychology*, 11: 553–65.

Sleasman, J.W. and Goodenow, M.M. (2003). HIV-1 infection. *Journal of Allergy & Clinical Immunology*, 111: S582–92.

Slenker, S. and Grant, M. (1989). Attitudes, beliefs and knowledge about mammography among women over forty years of age. *Journal of Cancer Education*, 4: 61–5.

Slenker, S.E. and Spreitzer, E.A. (1988). Public perceptions and behaviors regarding cancer control. *Journal of Cancer Education*, 3: 171–80.

Sloan, R.P. (2011). Virtue and vice in health and illness: the idea that wouldn't die. *The Lancet*, 377: 896–7.

Smedslund, G. (2000). A pragmatic basis for judging models and theories in health psychology: the axiomatic method. *Journal of Health Psychology*, 5: 133–49.

Smee, C., Parsonage, M., Anderson, R. and Duckworth, S. (1992). Effect of tobacco advertising on tobacco consumption: a discussion document reviewing the evidence. London: Economics and Operational Research Division, Department of Health.

Smith, H.E. and Herbert, C.P. (1993). Preventive practice among primary care physicians in British Columbia: relation to recommendations of the Canadian Task Force on the Periodic Health Examination. *Canadian Medical Association Journal*, 149: 1795–1800.

Smith, J. (2004). *Building a Safer NHS for Patients: Improving Medication Safety. A Report by the Chief Pharmaceutical Officer*. London: The Stationery Office.

Smith, J.A. (1996). Beyond the divide between cognition and discourse: using interpretative phenomenological analysis in health psychology. *Psychology & Health*, 11: 261–71.

Smith, J.A. (2011a). Evaluating the contribution of interpretative phenomenological analysis. *Health Psychology Review*, 5: 9–27.

Smith, J.A. (2011b). Evaluating the contribution of interpretative phenomenological analysis: a reply to the commentaries and further development of criteria. *Health Psychology Review*, 5: 55–61.

Smith, J.A. and Osborn, M. (2003). Interpretative phenomenological analysis. In J.A. Smith (ed.), *Qualitative Psychology: A Practical Guide to Research Methods*. London: Sage. pp. 51–80.

Smith, J.A. and Osborn, M. (2007). Pain as an assault on the self: an interpretative phenomenological analysis of the psychological impact of chronic benign back pain. *Psychology & Health*, 22: 517–34.

Smith, J.A., Flowers, P. and Larkin, M. (2009). *Interpretative Phenomenological Analysis: Theory, Method and Research*. London: Sage.

Smith, J.A., Jarman, M. and Osborn, M. (1999). Doing interpretative phenomenological analysis. In M. Murray and K. Chamberlain (eds.), *Qualitative Health Psychology: Theories and Methods*. London: Sage.

Smith, K.A., Goy, E.R., Harvath, T.A. and Ganzini, L. (2011). Quality of death and dying in patients who request physician-assisted death. *Journal of Palliative Medicine*, 14: 445–50.

Smith, P., Haberl, H., Popp, A. et al. (2013). How much land-based greenhouse gas mitigation can be achieved without compromising food security and environmental goals? *Global Change Biology*, 19: 2285–302.

Smith, R. (2013). Is the pharmaceutical industry like the mafia? *The BMJ blog*, Available at: http://blogs.bmj.com/bmj/2013/09/10/ [Accessed 15 December 2014].

Smyth, J.M., Stone, A.A., Hurewitz, A. and Kaell, A. (1999). Effects of writing about stressful experiences on symptom reduction in patients with asthma and rheumatoid arthritis. *Journal of the American Medical Association*, 281: 722–33.

Sniehotta, F.F., Presseau, J. and Araujo-Soanes, V. (2014). Time to retire the theory of planned behaviour. *Health Psychology Review*, 8 (1): 1–7.

Sointu, E. (2013). Complementary and alternative medicines, embodied subjectivity and experiences of healing. *Health*, 17: 530–45.

Somerfield, M.R. (1997). The utility of systems models of stress and coping for applied research: the case of cancer adaptation. *Journal of Health Psychology*, 2: 133–83.

Sonneville, K.R., Calzo, J.P., Horton, N.J., Haines, J., Austin, S.B. and Field, A.E. (2012). Body satisfaction, weight gain and binge eating among overweight adolescent girls. *International Journal of Obesity*, 36: 944–9.

Sontag, S. ([1978, 1988] 2002). *Illness as Metaphor*. London: Penguin.

Sontag, S. (1988). *AIDS and its Metaphors*. London: Penguin.

Sorensen, K., Van den Broucke, S., Fullam, J., Doyle, G., Pelikan, J., Slonska, Z. et al. (HLS-EU) Consortium Health Literacy Project European. (2012). Health literacy and public health: a systematic review and integration of definitions and models. *BMC Public Health,* 12: 80-2458-12-80.

Speer, P.W., Tesdahl, E.A. and Ayers, J.F. (2014). Community organizing practices in a globalizing era: building power for health equity at the community level. *Journal of Health Psychology*, 19 (1): 159–69.

Spiegel, D., Kraemer, H., Bloom, J. and Gottheil, E. (1989). Effect of psychosocial treatment on survival of patients with metastatic breast cancer. *The Lancet*, 334: 888–91.

Stam, H.J. (2014). A sound body in a sound mind: a critical historical analysis of health psychology. In M. Murray (ed.), *Critical Health Psychology* (2nd edn). London: Palgrave.

Stansfeld, S., Head, J. and Marmot, M. (2000). *Work Related Factors and Ill Health: The Whitehall II Study*. London: HSE Books.

Stanton, A. and Revenson, T.A. (2005). Progress and promise in research on adaptation to chronic illness. In H.S. Friedman and R.C. Silver (eds.), *The Oxford Handbook of Health Psychology*. New York: Oxford University Press.

Starkes, J.M. and Baydala, L.T. (2014). Health research involving First Nations, Inuit and Métis children and their communities. *Paediatrics & Child Health*, 19: 99–102.

St Claire, L., Watkins, C.J. and Billinghurst, B. (1996). Differences in meanings of health: an exploratory study of general practitioners and their patients. *Family Practice*, 13: 511–16

Steeg, P.S. (2003). Metastasis suppressors alter the signal transduction of cancer cells. *Nature Reviews Cancer*, 3: 55–63.

Steger, M.F., Frazier, P., Oishi, S. and Kaler, M. (2006). The Meaning in Life Questionnaire: assessing the presence of and search for meaning in life. *Journal of Counseling Psychology*, 53: 80–93.

Stein, J. and Rotheram-Borus, M. (2004). Cross-sectional and longitudinal associations in coping strategies and physical health outcomes among HIV-positive youth. *Psychology & Health*, 19: 321–36.

Stein, J.A., Fox, S.A., Murata, P.J. and Morisky, D.E. (1992). Mammography usage and the Health Belief Model. *Health Education Quarterly*, 19: 447–62.

Steinhauser, K.E., Clipp, E.C., McNeilly, M., Christakis, N.A., McIntyre, L.M. and Tulsky, J.A. (2000). In search of a good death: observations of patients, families, and providers. *Annals of Internal Medicine*, 132: 825–32.

Stensland, P. and Malterud, K. (1999). Approaching the locked dialogues of the body: communicating illness through diaries. *Journal of Primary Health Care*, 17: 75–80.

Stephens, C. (2008). *Health Promotion: A Psychosocial Approach.* New York: McGraw-Hill International.

Stephens, C. (2009). Racism and inequalities in health: notes towards an agenda for critical health psychology. *Journal of Health Pscychology*, 14: 655–9.

Stephens, C. (2010). Privilege and status in an unequal society: shifting the focus of health promotion research to include the maintenance of advantage. *Journal of Health Psychology*, 15 (7): 993–1000. doi:10.1177/1359105310371554.

Stephens, C. (2014). Beyond the barricades: social movements as participatory practice in health promotion. *Journal of Health Psychology*, 19 (1): 170–5. doi:10.1177/1359105313500245.

Stephens, C., Nettleton, C., Porter, J., Willis, R. and Clark, S. (2005). Indigenous peoples' health – why are they behind everyone, everywhere? *The Lancet*, 366: 10–13.

Stevens, G.A., Singh, G.M., Lu, Y. et al. (2012). National, regional, and global trends in adult overweight and obesity prevalences. *Population Health Metrics*, 10: 22.

Stevens, S.S. (1951). Mathematics, measurement, and psychophysics. In S.S. Stevens (ed.), *Handbook of Experimental Psychology*. Oxford: Wiley. pp. 1–49.

Stevinson, C., Pittler, M.H. and Ernst, E. (2000). Garlic for treating hypercholesterolemia: a meta-analysis of randomized clinical trials. *Annals of Internal Medicine*, 133: 420–9.

Stewart, D.E., Abbey, S.E., Shnek, Z.M., Irvine, J. and Grace, S.L. (2004). Gender differences in health information needs and decisional preferences in patients recovering from an acute ischemic coronary event. *Psychosomatic Medicine*, 66: 42–8.

Stewart, S., Riecken, T., Scott, T., Tanaka, M. and Riecken, J. (2008). Expanding health literacy: indigenous youth creating videos. *Journal of Health Psychology*, 13: 180–9.

Stewart, W.F., Lipton, R.B., Simon, D., Liberman, J. and Von Korff, M. (1999). Validity of an illness severity measure for headache in a population sample of migraine sufferers. *Pain*, 79: 291–301.

Stice, E., Shaw, H. and Marti, C.N. (2006). A meta-analytic review of obesity prevention programs for children and adolescents: the skinny on interventions that work. *Psychological Bulletin*, 132: 667–9.

Stiles, W.B., Shapiro, D.A. and Elliott, R. (1986). Are all psychotherapies equivalent? *American Psychologist*, 41: 165–80.

Stilley, C.S., Sereika, S., Muldoon, M.F., Ryan, C.M. and Dunbar-Jacob, J. (2004). Psychological and cognitive function: predictors of adherence with cholesterol lowering treatment. *Annals of Behavioral Medicine*, 27: 117–24.

Stokols, D. (1992). Establishing and maintaining healthy environments: toward a social ecology of health promotion. *American Psychologist*, 47: 6–22.

Stolerman, I.P. and Jarvis, M.J. (1995). The scientific case that nicotine is addictive. *Psychopharmacology*, 117: 2–10.

Stolte, O. and Hodgetts, D. (2014). Being healthy in unhealthy places: health tactics in a homeless lifeworld. *Journal of Health Psychology*, in press.

Stone, D.H. and Stewart, S. (1996). Screening and the new genetics: a public health perspective and the ethical debate. *Journal of Public Health Medicine*, 18: 3–5.

Stone, G.C., Weiss, S.M., Matarazzo, J.D., Miller, N.E. and Rodin, J. (eds.) (1987). *Health Psychology: A Discipline and a Profession*. Chicago, IL: University of Chicago Press.

Stone, S.V. and Costa, P.T. (1990). Disease-prone personality or distress-prone personality? The role of neuroticism in coronary heart disease. In H.S. Friedman (ed.), *Personality and Disease*. London: Wiley. pp. 178–200.

Stone, S.V. and McCrea, R.R. (2007). Personality and health. In S. Ayers, A. Baum, C. McManus, S. Newman, K. Wallston, J. Weinman and R. West (eds.), *Cambridge Handbook of Psychology, Health and Medicine* (2nd edn.). Cambridge: Cambridge University Press. pp 151–5.

Strauss, A.L. (1987). *Qualitative Analysis for Social Scientists*. New York: Cambridge University Press.

Street, R.L. (1991). Information-giving in medical consultations: the influence of patients' communicative styles and personal characteristics. *Social Science & Medicine*, 32: 541–8.

Street, R.L. (1992). Communicative styles and adaptations in physician-parent consultations. *Social Science & Medicine*, 34 (10): 1155–63.

Street, R.L., Gordon, H. and Haidet, P. (2007). Physicians' communication and perceptions of patients: is it how they look, how they talk, or is it just the doctor? *Social Science & Medicine*, 65 (3): 586–98.

Street, R.J., Gordon, H.S., Ward, M.M., Krupat, E. and Kravitz, R.L. (2005). Patient participation in medical consultations: why some patients are more involved than others. *Medical Care*, 43 (10): 960–9.

Street, R.L., Makoul, G., Arora, N.K. and Epstein, R.M. (2009). How does communication heal? Pathways linking clinician–patient communication to health outcomes. *Patient Education and Counseling*, 74 (3): 295–301.

Stroebe, W. and Stroebe, M.S. (1995). *Social Psychology and Health*. Buckingham: Open University Press.

Stuckler, D., McKee, M., Ebrahim, S. and Basu, S. (2012). Manufacturing epidemics: the role of global producers in increased consumption of unhealthy commodities including processed foods, alcohol, and tobacco. *PLoS medicine*, 9 (6): e1001235.

Sullivan, J., Petronella, S., Brooks, E., Murillo, M., Primeau, L. and Ward, J. (2008). Theatre of the oppressed and environmental justice communities: a transformational therapy for the body. *Journal of Health Psychology*, 13: 166–79.

Sulloway, F.J. (1980). *Freud, Biologist of the Mind*. London: Fontana.

Suls, J. and Bunde, J. (2005). Anger, anxiety and depression as risk factors for cardiovascular disease: the problems and implications of overlapping affective dispositions. *Psychological Bulletin*, 131: 260–300.

Suls, J. and Rittenhouse, J.D. (1990). Models of linkages between personality and disease. In H.S. Friedman (ed.), *Personality & Disease*. London: Wiley. pp. 38–64.

Sulzberger, P. and Marks, D.F. (1977). *The ISIS smoking cessation programme.* Dunedin, NZ: ISIS Research centre.

Summerfield, D. (2001). The intervention of post-traumatic stress disorder and the social usefulness of a psychiatric category. *British Medical Journal*, 322: 95–8.

Surtees, P., Wainwright, N., Luben, R., Khaw, K.-T. and Day, N. (2008). Sense of coherence and mortality in men and women in the EPIC-Norfolk United Kingdom prospective cohort study. *American Journal of Epidemiology*, 158: 1202–9.

Surtees, P.G., Wainwright, N.W.J., Luben, R.N., Wareham, N.J., Bingham, S.A. and Khaw, K.-T. (2008). Depression and ischemic heart disease mortality: evidence from the EPIC-Norfolk United Kingdom prospective cohort study. *American Journal of Psychiatry*, 165: 515–23.

Sutin, A.R., Ferrucci, L., Zonderman, A.B. and Terracciano, A. (2011). Personality and obesity across the adult life span. *Journal of Personality and Social Psychology*, 101: 579–92.

Sutton, S. (2000a). A critical review of the Transtheoretical Model applied to smoking cessation. In P. Norman, C. Abraham and M. Conner (eds.), *Understanding and Changing Health Behaviour: From Health Beliefs to Self-regulation*. Amsterdam: Harwood Academic Publishers. pp. 207–25.

Sutton, S. (2000b). Interpreting cross-sectional data on stages of change. *Psychology & Health*, 15: 163–71.

Sutton, S., Bickler, G., Aldridge, J. and Saidi, G. (1994). Prospective study of predictors of attendance for breast screening in inner London. *Journal of Epidemiology & Community Health*, 48: 65–73.

Suziedelyte, A. (2012). How does searching for health information on the internet affect individuals' demand for health care services? *Social Science & Medicine*, 75 (10): 1828–35.

Swartzman, L.C. and Lees, M.C. (1996). Causal dimensions of college students' perceptions of physical symptoms. *Journal of Behavioral Medicine*, 19: 95–110.

Swedish Council on Health Technology Assessment (2013). *Dietary Treatment for Obesity*. Stockholm: SBU.

Swinburn, B., Egger, G. and Raza, F. (1999). Dissecting obesogenic environments: the development and application of a framework for identifying and prioritizing environmental interventions for obesity. *Preventive Medicine*, 29: 563–70.

Sykes, C.M. and Marks, D.F. (2001). Effectiveness of cognitive behaviour therapy self-help programme for smokers in London, UK. *Health Promotion International*, 16: 255–60.

Sykes, C.M., Willig, C. and Marks, D.F. (2004). Discourses in the European Commission's 1996–2000 Health Promotion Programme. *Journal of Health Psychology*, 9: 131–41.

Syrjala, K.L., Donaldson, G.W., Davis, M.W., Kippes, M.E., Taira, D.A., Safran, D.G. et al. (1997). The relationship between patient income and physician discussion of health risk behaviors. *Journal of the American Medical Association*, 278: 1412–17.

Syrjala, K.L., Donaldson, G.W., Davis, M.W., Kippes, M.E. and Carr, J. E. (1995). Relaxation and imagery and cognitive-behavioral training reduce pain during cancer treatment: a controlled clinical trial. *Pain*, 63: 189–98.

Swales, J. (2000). Population advice on salt restriction: the social issues. *American Journal of Hypertension*, 13: 2–7.

Taku, K., Umegaki, K., Sato, Y., Taki, Y., Endoh, K. and Watanabe, S. (2007). Soy isoflavones lower serum total and LDL cholesterol in humans: a meta-analysis of 11 randomized controlled trials. *American Journal of Clinical Nutrition*, 85: 1148–56.

Tan, J., Ward, L. and Ziaian, T. (2010). Experiences of Chinese immigrants and Anglo-Australians ageing in Australia: a cross-cultural perspective on successful ageing. *Journal of Health Psychology*, 15 (5): 697–706.

Tang, M.Y., Shahab, L., Robb, K.A. and Gardner, B. (2014). Are parents more willing to vaccinate their children than themselves? *Journal of Health Psychology*.

Tatrow, K. and Montgomery, G.H. (2006). Cognitive behavioral therapy techniques for distress and pain in breast cancer patients: a meta-analysis. *Journal of Behavioral Medicine*, 29: 17–27.

Tatzer, E., Schubert, M.T., Timischi, W. and Simbruner, G. (1985). Discrimination of taste and preference for sweet in premature babies. *Early Human Development*, 12: 23–30.

Taubes, G. (2007). *Good Calories, Bad calories*. New York: Knopf.

Taubes, G. (2009). *The Diet Delusion*. New York: Random House.

Taubes, G. (2012). Treat obesity as physiology, not physics. *Nature*, 492: 155.

Taylor, C., Carlos Poston, W.S., Jones, L. and Kraft, M.K. (2006). Environmental justice: obesity, physical activity, and health eating. *Journal of Physical Activity & Health*, (suppl. 1): S30–54.

Taylor, K. (2009). Paternalism, participation and partnership – the evolution of patient centeredness in the consultation. *Patient Education and Counseling*, 74 (2): 150–5.

Taylor, K.P. and Thompson, S.C. (2011). Closing the (service) gap: exploring partnerships between Aboriginal and mainstream health services. *Australian Health Review*, 35 (3): 297–308.

Taylor, S.E. (1983). Adjustment to threatening events: a theory of cognitive adaption. *American Psychologist*, 38: 1161–73.

Taylor, S.E., Repetti, R.L. and Seeman, T. (1997). Health psychology: what is an unhealthy environment and how does it get under the skin? *Annual Review of Psychology*, 48: 411–47.

Te Morenga, L., Mallard, S. and Mann, J. (2013). Dietary sugars and body weight: systematic review and meta-analyses of randomised controlled trials and cohort studies. *British Medical Journal*, 346: e7492.

Terrill, A.L., Molton, I.R., Ehde, D.M., Amtmann, D., Bombardier, C.H., Smith, A.E. and Jensen, M.P. (2014). Resilience, age, and perceived symptoms in persons with long-term physical disabilities. *Journal of Health Psychology*, 1359105314532973.

Thaler, J.P., Yi, C.X., Schur, E.A. et al. (2012). Obesity is associated with hypothalamic injury in rodents and humans. *Journal of Clinical Investigation*, 122: 153–62.

Thom, B. (2001). A social and political history of alcohol. In N. Heather, T.J. Peters and T. Stockwell (eds.), *International Handbook of Alcohol Dependence and Problems.* London: Wiley. pp. 281–97.

Thomas, E.L., Parkinson, J.R., Frost, G.S. et al. (2012). The missing risk: MRI and MRS phenotyping of abdominal adiposity and ectopic fat. *Obesity*, 20: 76–87.

Thomas, I. (1979). *The Medusa and the Snail*. New York: Bantam.

Thompson, J.K. and Stice, E. (2001). Thin-ideal internalization: mounting evidence for a new risk factor for body-image disturbance and eating pathology. *Current Directions in Psychological Science*, 10: 181–3.

Thompson, S.L., Chenhall, R.D. and Brimblecombe, J.K. (2013). Indigenous perspectives on active living in remote Australia: a qualitative exploration of the socio-cultural link between health, the environment and economics. *BMC Public Health*, 13: 1–11.

Tibben, A., Frets, P.G., van de Kamp, J.J., Niermeijer, M.F., Vegter-van der Vlis, M., Roos, R.A. et al. (1993). Presymptomatic DNA testing for Huntington disease: pre-test attitudes and expectations of applicants and their partners in the Dutch program. *American Journal of Medical Genetics*, 48: 10–16.

Tibben, A., Timman, R., Banninck, E.C. and Duinvoorden, H.J. (1997). Three year follow-up after presymptomatic testing for Huntington's disease in tested individuals and partners. *Health Psychology*, 16: 20–35.

Tiggemann, M., Martins, Y. and Churchett, L. (2008). Beyond muscles: unexplored parts of men's body image. *Journal of Health Psychology*, 13: 1163–72.

Tillotson, L.M. and Smith, M.S. (1996) Locus of control, social support, and adherence to the diabetes regimen. *Diabetes Educator*, 22: 133–9.

Timperio, A., Salmon, J., Chu, B. and Andrianopoulos, N. (2008). Is dog ownership or dog walking associated with weight status in children and their parents? *Health Promotion Journal Australia*, 19: 60–3.

Titmuss, R.M. (1968). *Commitment to Welfare*. London: George Allen & Unwin.

Tobias, J.K., Richmond, C.A.M. and Luginaah, I. (2013). Community-based participatory research (CBPR) with indigenous communities: producing respectful and reciprocal research. *Journal of Empirical Research on Human Research Ethics: JERHRE*, 8: 129–40.

Todd, K.H., Deaton, C., D'Adamo, A.P. and Goe, L. (2000). Ethnicity and analgesic practice. *Annals of Emergency Medicine*, 35: 11–16.

Tollefson, D., Bloss, E., Fanning, A., Redd, J.T., Barker, K. and McCray, E. (2013). Burden of tuberculosis in indigenous peoples globally: a systematic review. *The International Journal of Tuberculosis and Lung Disease: The Official Journal of the International Union Against Tuberculosis and Lung Disease*, 17: 1139–50.

Tomlinson, A., Ravenscroft, N., Wheaton, B. and Gilchrist, P. (2005). *Lifestyle Sports and National Sport Policy: An Agenda for Research*. Eastbourne: University of Brighton.

Tomlinson, E. and Stott, J. (2014). Assisted dying in dementia: a systematic review of the international literature on the attitudes of health professionals, patients, carers and the public, and the factors associated with these. *International Journal of Geriatric Psychiatry*, in press.

Tong, E.K., England, L. and Glantz, S.A. (2005). Changing conclusions on secondhand smoke in a sudden infant death syndrome review funded by the tobacco industry. *Pediatrics*, 115: 356–66.

Tonstad, S., Butler, T., Yan, R. and Fraser, G.E. (2009). Type of vegetarian diet, bodyweight, and prevalence of type 2 diabetes. *Diabetes Care*, 32: 791–6.

Tonstad, S., Stewart, K., Oda, K. et al. (2013). Vegetarian diets and incidence of diabetes in the Adventist Health Study-2. *Nutrition, Metabolism & Cardiovascular Diseases*, 23: 292–9.

Torre, R., and Myrskylä, M. (2014). Income inequality and population health: an analysis of panel data for 21 developed countries, 1975–2006. *Population Studies*, 68 (1): 1–13.

Townsend, P. and Davidson, N. (1982). *Inequalities in Health: the Black Report*. London: Penguin.

Townsend, P., Davidson, N. and Whitehead, M. (1992). *Inequalities in Health: The Black Report and the Health Divide*. London: Penguin Books.

Trafimow, D. (2009). The theory of reasoned action: a case study of falsification in psychology. *Theory & Psychology*, 19: 501–18.

Trafimow, D., Sheeran, P., Conner, M. and Finlay, K.A. (2002). Evidence that perceived behavioural control is a multidimensional construct: perceived control and perceived difficulty. *British Journal of Social Psychology*, 41: 101–21.

Treharne, G.J., Lyons, A.C. and Kitas, G.D. (2004). Medication adherence in rheumatoid arthritis: effects of psychosocial factors. *Psychology, Health & Medicine*, 9: 337–49.

Triandis, H.C. (1995). *Individualism & Collectivism*. Westview Press.

True, W.R., Heath, A.C., Scherrer, J.F., Waterman, B., Goldberg, J., Lin, N. et al. (1997). Genetic and environmental contributions to smoking. *Addiction*, 92: 1277–87.

Trumbull, R. and Appley, M.H. (1986). A conceptual model for the understanding of stress dynamics in M.H. Appley and R. Trumbull (eds.), *Dynamics of Stress: Physiological, Psychological and Social Perspectives*. New York: Plenum. pp. 21–45.

Truong, M., Paradies, Y. and Priest, N. (2014). Interventions to improve cultural competency in healthcare: a systematic review of reviews. *BMC Health Services Research*, 14 (1): 1–31.

Truong, V.D. (2014). Social marketing: a systematic review of research 1998–2012. *Social Marketing Quarterly*, 20 (1): 15–34.

Tucker, I. and Smith, L.A. (2014). Topology and mental distress: self-care in the life spaces of home. *Journal of Health Psychology*, 19: 176–83.

Tudor Hart, J. (1971). The Inverse Care Law. *The Lancet*, 297: 405–12.

Turati, F., Edefonti, V., Bravi, F., Ferraroni, M., Talamini, R., Giacosa, A. et al. (2012). Adherence to the European Food Safety Authority's dietary recommendations and colorectal cancer risk. *European Journal of Clinical Nutrition*, 66: 517–22.

Turk, D.C. and Wilson, H.D. (2013). Chronic pain. In A.M. Nezu (ed.), *Handbook of Psychology*, vol. 9. Chichester: John Wiley.

Turner, B. (1984). *The Body and Society: Explorations in Social Theory*. Oxford: Blackwell.

Tversky, A. and Kahneman, D. (1981). The framing of decisions and the rationality of choice. *Science*, 221: 453–8.

Tyler, R.E. and Williams, S. (2014). Masculinity in young men's health: exploring health, help-seeking and health service use in an online environment. *Journal of Health Psychology*, 19: 457–70.

UNAIDS (2004). *Report on the Global AIDS Epidemic: 4th Global Report*. Geneva: Joint United Nations Programme on HIV/AIDS.

UNAIDS (2011). *UNAIDS Data Tables 2011*. Geneva: Joint United Nations Programme on HIV/AIDS (UNAIDS). Available from: http://bit.ly/118Tsuo [accessed 16 March 2012].

Union of Concerned Scientists (2012). *Grade A Choice? Solutions for Deforestation – Free Meat*. Cambridge, MA: UCS Publications.

United Nations (2008). World leaders pledge to reinvigorate 'global partnership of equals' to end poverty, hunger, underdevelopment in Africa. Available at: http://www.un.org/press/en/2008/ga10748.doc.htm [accessed 2 December 2014].

United Nations (2009). *State of the World's Indigenous Peoples*. New York: United Nations.

United Nations Development Programme (1995). *Human Development Report*. New York: Oxford University Press.

United Nations General Assembly (1948). *Universal Declaration of Human Rights*. Available online at: http://www.un.org/Overview/rights.html. Retrieved 1 April 2005.

Updegraff, J.A. and Rothman, A.J. (2013). Health message framing: moderators, mediators, and mysteries. *Social and Personality Psychology Compass*, 7 (9): 668–79. doi:10.1111/spc3.12056.

Uphoff, E.P., Pickett, K.E., Cabieses, B., Small, N. and Wright, J. (2013). A systematic review of the relationships between social capital and socioeconomic inequalities in health: a contribution to understanding the psychosocial pathway of health inequalities. *International Journal for Equity in Health*, 12 (1): 54–65. doi:10.1186/1475-9276-12-54.

Urban, B.J., France, R.D., Steinberger, E.K., Scott, D.L. and Maltbre, A.A. (1986). Long-term use of narcotic/antidepressant medication in the management of phantom limb pain. *Pain*, 24: 1991–6.

US Census Bureau (2014). Available at: www.census.gov/cgi-bin/ipc/popclockw [accessed 3 December 2014].

US Census Bureau (2014). International data base. Available: www.census.gov/ipc/www/idb/country.php [accessed 10 January 2009].

US Centers for Disease Control and Prevention (CDC) (1999). *HIV/AIDS Surveillance Report*, 11 (2): 14, 16, 20, 22, 38.

US Centers for Disease Control and Prevention (CDC) (2005). Available: www.cdc.gov/nccdphp/ [accessed 7 January 2005].

US Centers for Disease Control and Prevention (CDC) (2012). *National Healthcare Disparities Report.* Available: www.ahrq.gov/research/findings/nhqrdr/nhdr12/chap2.html.

U.S. Centers for Disease Control and Prevention (CDC) (2012). Colerectal cancer screening rates. *MMWR, 61,* 41–45.

US Centers for Disease Control and Prevention (CDC) (2013). *Make a Difference at Your School.* Chronic Disease. Paper 31.

US Centers for Disease Control (CDC) (2009). Teen birth rates up slightly in 2007 for second consecutive year. Press release. Available: www.cdc.gov/media/pressrel/2009/r090318.htm [accessed 26 November 2009].

US Department of Health, Education and Welfare (1964). *Smoking and Health: Report of the Advisory Committee to the Surgeon General of the Public Health Service*. Washington, DC. PHS Pub. No. 1103.

US Department of Health and Human Services (2004). *The Health Consequences of Smoking: A Report of the Surgeon General*. Atlanta, GA: US Department of Health and Human Services, Centers for Disease Control and Prevention, National Center for Chronic Disease Prevention and Health Promotion, Office on Smoking and Health, 62.

US Surgeon General (1989). *Reducing the Health Consequences of Smoking: 25 Years of Progress: A Report of the Surgeon General*. Bethesda, MD: Center for Chronic Disease Prevention and Health Promotion.

US Surgeon General (2010). *The Surgeon General's Vision for a Healthy and Fit Nation*. US Department of Health and Human Services. Public Health Service.

Valery, P.C., Coory, M., Stirling, J. and Green, A.C. (2006). Cancer diagnosis, treatment, and survival in Indigenous and non-Indigenous Australians: a matched cohort study. *Lancet*, 367: 1842–8.

Vallabhaneni, S., Li, X., Vittinghoff, E., Donnell, D., Pilcher, C.D. et al. (2012) Seroadaptive practices: association with HIV acquisition among HIV-negative men who have sex with men. *PLOS ONE*, 7 (10): e45718.

Valsiner, J. (2013). *An Invitation to Cultural Psychology*. New Delhi, India: Sage.

Van Dyck, D., Cerin, E., Conway, T.L., De Bourdeaudhuij, I., Owen, N., Kerr, J. et al. (2014). Interacting psychosocial and environmental correlates of leisure-time physical activity: a three-country study. *Health Psychology*, 33: 699–709.

van Melle, J.P., de Jonge, P., Honig, A., Schene, A.H., Kuyper, A.M., Crijns, H.J. et al. (2007). Effects of antidepressant treatment following myocardial infarction. *British Journal of Psychiatry*, 190: 460–66.

van Riet, J., Ruiter, R.A.C., Smerecnik, C. and de Vries, H. (2010). Examining the influence of self-efficacy on message-framing effects: reducing salt consumption in the general population. *Basic & Applied Social Psychology*, 32 (2): 165–72. doi:10.1080/01973531003738338

van't Riet, J., Ruiter, R. and De Vries, H. (2012). Preaching to the choir? The influence of personal relevance on the effects of gain- and loss-framed health-promoting messages. *Journal of Health Psychology*, 17 (5): 712–23.

Van Uden-Kraan, C.F., Drossaert, C.H.C., Taal, E., Shaw, B.R., Seydel, E.R. and van de Laar, M.A.F.J. (2008). Empowering processes and outcomes of participation in online support groups for patients with breast cancer, arthritis, or fibromyalgia. *Qualitative Health Research*, 18: 405–17.

Vandewalle, J., Moens, E. and Braet, C. (2014). Comprehending emotional eating in obese youngsters: the role of parental rejection and emotion regulation. *International Journal of Obesity*, 38: 525–30.

Vaughan, C. (2014). Participatory research with youth: idealising safe social spaces or building transformative links in difficult environments? *Journal of Health Psychology*, 19 (1): 184–92.

Velasquez, M.M., von Sternberg, K., Johnson, D.H., Green, C., Carbonari, J.P. and Parsons, J.T. (2009). Reducing sexual risk behaviors and alcohol use among HIV-positive men who have sex with men: a randomized clinical trial. *Journal of Consulting and Clinical Psychology*, 77: 657–67.

Verhoef Vézina-Im, L.A., Lavoie, M.J., Love, E.J., Krol, P. and Rose Olivier-D, M.S. (1992). Women's social roles (2014). Motivations of physicians and their exercise participation. *Women's Health*, 19: 14–29.

Verlinde, E., De Laender, N., De Maesschalck, S., Deveugele, M. and Willems, S. (2012). The social gradient in doctor–patient communication. *International Journal for Equity in Health*, 11 (12): 1–14.

Vermeire, E., Hearnshaw, H., Van Royen, P. and Denekens, J.W. (2001). Patient adherence treatment: three decades of research. A comprehensive review. *Journal of Clinical Pharmacy and Therapeutics*, 26, 331–42; *BMC Palliative Care*, 13: 20.

Vincent, C., Neale, G. and Woloshynowych, M. (2001). Adverse events in British hospitals: preliminary retrospective record review. *BMJ*, 322: 517–19.

Virtanen, M., Ferrie, J.E., Batty, G.D. et al. (2014). Socioeconomic and psychosocial adversity in midlife and depressive symptoms post retirement: a 21-year follow-up of the Whitehall II Study. *American Journal of Geriatric Psychiatry*, in press.

Vlaeyen, J.W.S. and Linton, S.J. (2000). Fear-avoidance and its consequences in chronic musculoskeletal pain: a state of the art. *Pain*, 85: 317–32.

Vogler, B., Pittler, M. and Ernst, E. (1999). The efficacy of ginseng: a systematic review of randomised clinical trials. *European Journal of Clinical Pharmacology*, 55: 567–75.

Volkow, N.D., Wang, G.J. and Baler, R.D. (2011). Reward, dopamine and the control of food intake: implications for obesity. *Trends in Cognitive Science*, 15: 37–46.

Von Lengerke, T., Vinck, J., Rutten, A., Reitmeir, P., Abel, T., Kannas, L. et al. (2004). Health policy perception and health behaviours: a multilevel analysis and implications for public health psychology. *Journal of Health Psychology*, 9: 157–75.

Vowles, K.E., Witkiewitz, K., Sowden, G. and Ashworth, J. (2014). acceptance and commitment therapy for chronic pain: evidence of mediation and clinically significant change following an abbreviated interdisciplinary program of rehabilitation. *Journal of Pain*, 15: 101–13.

Waddell, G., Newton, M., Henderson, I., Somerville, D. and Main, C.J. (1993). A Fear-Avoidance Beliefs Questionnaire (FABQ) and the role of fear-avoidance beliefs in chronic low back pain and disability. *Pain*, 52: 157–68.

Waitzkin, H. (1989). A critical theory of medical discourse: ideology, social control, and the processing of social context in medical encounters. *Journal of Health and Social Behavior*, 30: 220–39.

Wald, N., Kiryluk, S., Darby, S., Doll, R., Pike, M. and Peto, R. (1988). *UK Smoking Statistics*. Oxford: Oxford University Press.

Walker, B.F., Losco, C.D., Armson, A., Meyer, A. and Stomski, N.J. (2014). The association between pain diagram area, fear-avoidance beliefs, and pain catastrophising. *Chiropractic & Manual Therapies*, 22: 1–5.

Wallston, K.A., Burger, C., Smith, R.A. and Baugher, R.J. (1988). Comparing the quality of death for hospice and non-hospice cancer patients. *Medical Care*, 26: 177–82.

Wallston, K.A., Maides, S. and Wallston, B.S. (1976). Health-related information seeking as a function of health-related locus of control and health value. *Journal of Research in Personality*, 10 (2): 215–22.

Walters, G.D. (2002). The heritability of alcohol abuse and dependence: a meta-analysis of behaviour genetic research. *American Journal of Drug & Alcohol Abuse*, 28: 557–84.

Wang, C., Burris, M. and Xiang, Y.P. (1996). Chinese village women as visual anthropologists: a participatory approach to reaching policymakers. *Social Science & Medicine*, 42: 1391–400.

Wardle J. (2007). Eating behaviour and obesity. *Obesity Review*, 8: 73–5.

Wardle, J., McCaffery, K., Nadel, M. and Atkin, W. (2004). Socioeconomic differences in cancer screening participation: comparing cognitive and psychosocial explanations. *Social Science & Medicine*, 59: 249–61.

Wardle, J., Waller, J. and Rapoport, L. (2001). Body dissatisfaction and binge eating in obese women: the role of restraint and depression. *Obesity Research*, 9: 778–87.

Ware Jr, J.E. and Sherbourne, C.D. (1992). The MOS 36-item Short-Form Health Survey (SF-36): I. Conceptual framework and item selection. *Medical Care*, 30 (6): 473–83.

Ware, K., Davies, J., Rowse, G. and Whittaker, S. (2014). The experience of hepatitis C treatment for people with a history of mental health problems: an interpretative phenomenological analysis. *Journal of Health Psychology*, in press.

Warr, P., Jackson, P. and Banks, M. (1988). Unemployment and mental health: some British studies. *Journal of Social Issues*, 44: 47–68.

Wassertheil-Smoller, S., Shumaker, S., Ockene, J., Talavera, G.A., Greeland, P., Cochrane, B. et al. (2004). Depression and cardiovascular sequelae in postmenopausal women. *Archives of Internal Medicine*, 164: 289–98.

Waterman, A.S. (1993). Two conceptions of happiness: contrasts of personal expressiveness (eudaimonia) and hedonic enjoyment. *Journal of Personality and Social Psychology*, 64: 678–91.

Watson, M., Haviland, J.S., Greer, S., Davidson, J. and Bliss, J.M. (1999). Influence of psychological response on survival in breast cancer: a population-based cohort study. *The Lancet*, 354: 1331–6.

Wear, A. (1985). Puritan perceptions of illness in seventeenth century England. In R. Porter (ed.), *Patients and Practitioners: Lay Perceptions of Medicine in Preindustrial Society*. Cambridge: Cambridge University Press. pp. 55–100.

Weinman, J. and Petrie, K.J. (1997). Illness perceptions: a new paradigm for psychosomatics? *Journal of Psychosomatic Medicine*, 42: 113–16.

Weinman, J., Petrie, K.J., Moss-Morris, R. and Horne, R. (1996). The Illness Perception Questionnaire: a new method for assessing the cognitive representation of illness. *Psychology & Health*, 11: 431–46.

Weinman, J., Petrie, K.J., Sharpe, N. and Walker, S. (2000). Causal attributions in patients and spouses following first-time myocardial infarction and subsequent lifestyle changes. *British Journal of Health Psychology*, 5: 263–73.

Weiss, B.D. (2007). *Health Literacy and Patient Safety: Helping Patients Understand. Manual for Clinicians* (2nd edn). Chicago, IL: AMA Foundation.

Weiss, K.B., Gergen, P.J. and Hodgson, T.A. (1992). An economic evaluation of asthma in the United States. *New England Journal of Medicine*, 326: 862–6.

Weiss, M.R. and Williams, L. (2004). The why of youth sport involvement: a developmental perspective on motivational processes. In M.R. Weiss (ed.), *Developmental Sport and Exercise Psychology: A Lifespan Perspective*. Morgantown, WV: Fitness Information Technology. pp. 223–68.

Wertheimer, A.I. and Santella, T.M. (2003). Medication compliance research: still so far to go. *Journal of Applied Research in Clinical & Experimental Therapeutics*, 3: 1–11.

Wertli, M.M., Rasmussen-Barr, E., Held, U., Weiser, S., Bachmann, L.M. and Brunner, F. (2014). Fear avoidance beliefs: a moderator of treatment efficacy in patients with low back pain: A systematic review. *The Spine Journal*, in press.

West, C. (1984) *Routine Complications*. Bloomington, IN: Indiana University Press.

West, D.M. and Miller, E.A. (2009). *Digital Medicine: Health Care in the Internet Era*. Washington, DC: Brookings Institution Press. p. 4.

West, R. (2005). Time for a change: putting the Transtheoretical (Stages of Change) Model to rest. *Addiction*, 100: 1036–9.

Whaley, A.L., Smith, M. and Hancock, A. (2011). Ethnic/racial differences in the self-reported physical and mental health correlates of adolescent obesity. *Journal of Health Psychology*, 16: 1048–57.

Wheeler, S. (2012). The significance of family culture for sports participation. *International Review for the Sociology of Sport*, 47: 235–52.

White, J. and Halliwell, E. (2010). Alcohol and tobacco use during adolescence: the importance of the family mealtime environment. *Journal of Health Psychology*, 15: 526–32.

White, P.D., Goldsmith, K.A., Johnson, A.L., Potts, L., Walwyn, R., DeCesare, J.C. et al. (2011). Comparison of adaptive pacing therapy, cognitive behaviour therapy, graded exercise therapy, and specialist medical care for chronic fatigue syndrome (PACE): a randomised trial. *The Lancet*, 377: 823–36.

Whiteman, M.C., Fowkes, F.G.R., Deary, I.J. and Lee, A.J. (1997). Hostility, cigarette smoking and alcohol consumption in the general population. *Social Science and Medicine*, 44: 1089–96.

Whitlock, E.P., Polen, M.R., Green, C.A., Orleans, T. and Klein, J. (2004). Behavioural counseling interventions in primary care to reduce risky/harmful alcohol use by adults: a summary of the evidence for the U.S. Preventive Services Task Force. *Annals of Internal Medicine*, 140: 557–68.

Whitmarsh, T.E. (2007). Homeopathy. In A.D. Cumming, K.R. Simpson and D. Brown (eds.), *Complementary and Alternative Medicine: An Illustrated Color Text*. Edinburgh: Elsevier. pp. 67–70.

Whittaker, R., Borland, R., Bullen, C., Lin, R.B., McRobbie, H. and Rodgers, A. (2009). Mobile phone-based interventions for smoking cessation. *Cochrane Database of Systematic Reviews*, 4 (CD006611).

Whooley, M.A. and Browner, W.S. (1998). Association between depressive symptoms and mortality in older women. *Archives of Internal Medicine*, 158: 2129–35.

WHOQoL Group (1995). The World Health Organization quality of life assessment (WHOQOL): position paper from the World Health Organization. *Social science and medicine*, 41 (10): 1403–9.

Wiggers, L.C., De Wit, J.B., Gras, M.J., Coutinho, R.A. and Van Den Hoek, A. (2003). Risk behavior and social-cognitive determinants of condom use among ethnic minority communities in Amsterdam. *AIDS Education & Prevention*, 15: 430–47.

Wiggins, S., Potter, J. and Wildsmith, A. (2001). Eating your words: discursive psychology and the reconstruction of eating practices. *Journal of Health Psychology*, 6: 5–15.

Wilkinson, J.M., and Stevens, M.J. (2014). Use of complementary and alternative medical therapies (CAM) by patients attending a regional comprehensive cancer care centre. *Journal of Complementary and Integrative Medicine*, 11 (2): 139–45.

Wilkinson, R. (1996). *Unhealthy Societies*. London: Routledge.

Wilkinson, S. (1998). Focus groups in health research: exploring the meaning of health and illness. *Journal of Health Psychology*, 3: 329–48.

Williams, A. (2006). Perspectives on spirituality at the end of life: a meta-summary. *Palliative & Supportive Care*, 4: 407–17.

Williams, D.C., Golding, J., Phillips, K. and Towell, A. (2004). Perceived control, locus of control and preparatory information: effects on the perception of an acute pain stimulus. *Personality & Individual Differences*, 36: 1681–91.

Williams, D.M., Anderson, E.S. and Winett, R.A. (2005). A review of the outcome expectancy construct in physical activity research. *Annals of Behavioral Medicine*, 29: 70–9.

Williams, D.M. (2010). Outcome expectancy and self-efficacy: theoretical implications of an unresolved contradiction. *Personality and Social Psychology Review*, 14: 417–25.

Williams, D.R. and Collins, C. (1995). US socioeconomic and racial differences in health: patterns and explanations. *Annual Review of Sociology*, 21: 349–86.

Williams, D.R., Yu, Y., Jackson, J.S. and Anderson, N.B. (1997). Racial differences in physical and mental health: socio-economic status, stress and discrimination. *Journal of Health Psychology*, 2: 335–51.

Williams, G. (1984). The genesis of chronic illness: narrative reconstruction. *Sociology of Health & Illness*, 6: 175–200.

Williams, S.J. and Calnan, M. (1996). The 'limits' of medicalization? Modern medicine and the lay populace in 'late' modernity. *Social Science & Medicine*, 42: 1609–20.

Willig, C. (2001). *Qualitative Research in Psychology: A Practical Guide to Theory and Method*. Buckingham: OUP.

Willig, C. (2004). Discourse analysis and health psychology. In M. Murray (ed.), *Critical Health Psychology*. London: Palgrave.

Willig, C. (2008). A phenomenological investigation of the experience of taking part in extreme sports. *Journal of Health Psychology*, 13: 690–702.

Willig, C. (2009). 'Unlike a rock, a tree, a horse or an angel ...': reflections on the struggle for meaning through writing during the process of cancer diagnosis. *Journal of Health Psychology*, 14: 181–9.

Willig, C. and Paulson, S. (2008). Older women and everyday talk about the ageing body. *Journal of Health Psychology*, 13: 106–20.

Wilson, D.K., Ainsworth, B.E. and Bowles, H. (2007). Body mass index and environmental supports for physical inactivity among active and inactive. *Health Psychology*, 26: 710–17.

Wilson, J. and Junger, G. (1968). Principles and practice of screening for disease. World Health Organization Public Health Paper 34. Geneva: WHO.

Wilson, R.H., Wisely, J.A., Wearden, A.J., Dunn, D., Edwards, J. and Tarrier, N. (2011) Do illness perceptions and mood predict healing time for burn wounds? A prospective, preliminary study. *Journal of Psychosomatic Research*, 71: 364–66.

Windlin, B. and Kuntsche, E. (2012). Differences in the impact of the frequency and enjoyment of joint family activities on adolescent substance use and violence. *Journal of Health Psychology*, 17: 509–19.

Wing, R.W. (2004). Behavioural approaches to the treatment of obesity. In G.A. Bray and C. Bouchard (eds.), *Handbook of Obesity* (2nd edn). New York: Marcel Dekker, Inc..

Wire, T. (2009). *Fewer Emitters, Lower Emissions, Less Cost*. London: London School of Economics.

Wisner, B. (ed.) (2004). *At Risk: Natural Hazards, People's Vulnerability and Disasters*. Psychology Press.

Witkiewitz, K., Marlatt, G.A,. and Walker, D. (2005). Mindfulness-based relapse prevention for alcohol and substance use disorders. *Journal of Cognitive Psychotherapy*, 19: 211–28.

Wolf, M.S., Davis, T.C., Osborn, C.Y., Skripkauskas, S., Bennett, C.L. and Makoul, G. (2007). Literacy, self-efficacy, and HIV medication adherence. *Patient Education and Counseling*, 65 (2): 253–60.

Wong, D., Sullivan, K. and Heap, G. (2012). The pharmaceutical market for obesity therapies. *Nature Reviews Drug Discovery*, 11: 669–70.

Woodgate, J. and Brawley, L.R. (2008). Self-efficacy for exercise in cardiac rehabilitation: review and recommendations. *Journal of Health Psychology*, 13: 366–87.

Wooley, S.C. and Garner, D.M. (1991). Obesity treatment: the high cost of false hope. *Journal of the American Dietetic Association*, 91: 1248–51.

World Bank (2002). Available: www.worldbank.org/poverty/health/data/index.htm.

World Health Organization (1946). Constitution of the World Health Organization as adopted by the International Health Conference, New York 19–22 June, 1946; signed on 22 July 1946 by the representatives of 61 States (Official Records of the World Health).

World Health Organization (1989). *World Health Statistics Annual*. Geneva: WHO.

World Health Organization (2002). *Investing in Health: A Summary of Findings of the Commission on Macroeconomics and Health*. Geneva: WHO. Available:http://apps.who.int/iris/bitstream/10665/42709/1/9241562412_eng.pdf [accessed 5 December 2014].

World Health Organization (2003). *Global Action Against Cancer – Now!* Geneva: WHO. Available: http://www.who.int/cancer/publications/action_against_cancer/en/ [accessed 5 December 2014].

World Health Organization (2004a). *Global Strategy on Diet, Physical Activity and Health*. Available: www.who.int/dietphysicalactivity/strategy/eb11344/strategy_english_web.pdf. [accessed 5 December 2014].

World Health Organization (2004b). *Palliative Care: The Solid Facts*. Copenhagen: WHO.

World Health Organization (2007). *World Health Organization Expert Committee Second Report on Problems Related to Alcohol Consumption*. Geneva: WHO. Available: http://www.who.int/substance_abuse/expert_committee_alcohol/en/ [accessed 5 December 2014].

World Health Organization (2013). Tobacco control economics. Available: http://www.who.int/tobacco/economics/en/ [accessed 5 December 2014].

World Health Organization (2014). *10 Facts on Noncommunicable Diseases*. Available: www.who.int/features/factfiles/noncommunicable_diseases/en/ [accessed 5 December 2014].

Wright, E.C. (1993). Non-compliance – or how many aunts has Matilda? *The Lancet*, 342: 909–13.

Wright, J., MacDonald, D. and Groom, L. (2003). Physical activity and young people: beyond participation. *Sport, Education & Society*, 8: 17–33.

Wu, A.W., Folkman, S., McPhee, S.J. and Lo, B. (1991). Do house officers learn from their mistakes? *Journal of the American Medical Association*, 265: 2089–94.

Wu, P., Wilson, K., Dimoulas, P. and Mills E.J. (2006). Effectiveness of smoking cessation therapies: a systematic review and meta-analysis. *BMC Public Health*, 6: 300–15.

Wulsin, L.R. and Singal, B.M. (2003). Do depressive symptoms increase the risk for the onset of coronary disease? A systematic quantitative review. *Psychosomatic Medicine*, 65: 201–10.

Yamazaki, Y. and Omori, M. (2014). The relationship between mothers' thin-ideal and children's drive for thinness: a survey of Japanese early adolescents and their mothers. *Journal of Health Psychology*, in press.

Yang, Q., Zhang, Z., Gregg, E.W., Flanders, W.D., Merritt, R. and Hu, F.B. (2014). Added sugar intake and cardiovascular diseases mortality among US adults. *JAMA Internal Medicine*, 174: 516–24.

Yardley, L. (ed.) (1997). *Material Discourses of Health and Illness*. London: Routledge.

Yardley, L., Sharples, K., Beech, S. and Lewith, G. (2001). Developing a dynamic model of treatment perceptions. *Journal of Health Psychology*, 6: 269–82.

Yaskowich, K.M. and Stam, H.J. (2003). Cancer narratives and the cancer support group. *Journal of Health Psychology*, 8: 720–37.

Yeich, S. (1996). Grassroots organizing with homeless people: a participatory research approach. *Journal of Social Issues*, 52: 111–21.

Yeung, W., Chung, K., Poon, M.M., Ho, F.Y., Zhang, S., Zhang, Z. et al. (2012). Acupressure, reflexology, and auricular acupressure for insomnia: a systematic review of randomized controlled trials. *Sleep Medicine*, 13: 971–84.

Yiengprugsawan, V., Khamman, S., Seubsman, S., Lim, L.L. and Sleigh, A.C. (2011). Social capital and health in a national cohort of 82,482 Open University adults in Thailand. *Journal of Health Psychology*, 16 (4): 632–642.

Yokoyama, Y., Nishimura, K., Barnard, N.D. et al. (2014). Vegetarian diets and blood pressure: a meta-analysis. *JAMA Internal Medicine*, 10.1001.

Yong, E. (2012). In the wake of high profile controversies, pyschologists are facing up to problems with replication. *Nature*, 483: 298–300.

Young, A. (1995). *The Harmony of Illusions: Inventing Post-Traumatic Stress Disorder*. Princeton, NJ: Princeton University Press.

Zarcadoolas, C., Pleasant, A. and Greer, D.S. (2005). Understanding health literacy: an expanded model. *Health Promotion International*, 20: 195–203.

Zaridze, D., Lewington, S., Boroda, A., Scélo, G., Karpov, R., Lazarev, A. et al. (2014). Alcohol and mortality in Russia: prospective observational study of 151,000 adults. *The Lancet*, 363: 1465–73.

Zerach, G., Greene, T. and Solomon, Z. (2013). Secondary traumatization and self-rated health among ex-POWs' wives: the moderating role of marital adjustment. *Journal of Health Psychology*, in press.

Zetta, S., Smith, K., Jones, M., Allcoat, P. and Sullivan, F. (2011). Evaluating the Angina Plan in patients admitted to hospital with angina: a randomized controlled trial. *Cardiovascular Therapeutics*, 29 (2): 112–24.

Zigmond, A.S. and Snaith, R.P. (1983). The Hospital Anxiety and Depression Scale. *Acta Psychiatrica Scandinavica*, 67: 361–70.

Zika, S. and Chamberlain, K. (1992). On the relation between meaning in life and psychological well-being. *British Journal of Psychology,* 83: 133–45.

Zlatevska, N.S., Dubelaar, C. and Holden, S.S. (2014). Sizing up the effect of portion size on consumption: a meta-analytic review. *Journal of Marketing*, in press.

Zuckerman, M. (1979). *Sensation Seeking: Beyond the Optimal Level of Arousal*. Hillsdale, NJ: Lawrence Erlbaum.

Zuckerman, M. and Antoni, M.H. (1995). Social support and its relationship to psychological, physical and immune variables in HIV infection. *Clinical Psychology & Psychotherapy*, 2: 210–19.

Name Index

Subject Index